C000149525

The Telegraph

Complete History of

BRITISH FOOTBALL

THIS IS A CARLTON BOOK

First edition published in 1993

This edition published in 2013

A CIP catalogue record for this book is available from the British Library

ISBN 978-1-78097-392-0

Editors – Martin Corteel and Conor Kilgallon
Art direction – Paul Messam
Production – Sarah Corteel and Janette Burgin
Picture Research – Debora Fioravanti and Paul Langan

Printed and bound in Dubai
by Oriental Press

ACKNOWLEDGEMENTS

The author would like to acknowledge the use of extracts from reports and articles that have appeared in *The Daily Telegraph* and *The Sunday Telegraph* by the following correspondents: Michael Calvin, Christopher Davies, Robert Dick, Roddy Forsyth, Charles Freeland, Colin Gibson, Edward Giles, Paul Haywood, William Johnson, John Ley, Denis Lowe, Colin Malam, Roger Malone, Bill Meredith, John Moynihan, Robert Oxby, Patrick Barclay, Ian Peebles, Donald Saunders, Alan Smith and Henry Winter.

Opposite: The Manchester United squad, with the retiring Sir Alex Ferguson, pose on an open-top bus at the start of their Premier League victory parade outside Old Trafford in May 2013.
Pages 6-7: Bayern Munich players celebrate winning the 2013 Champions League, overcoming Borussia Dortmund in the all-German final.

The Telegraph

Complete History of

BRITISH FOOTBALL

150 years of season-by-season action

NORMAN BARRETT WITH MARTIN SMITH

CONTENTS

Introduction 5
Early Years 8
1880s 10
1890s 12
Rise of professionalism 14
1899–1900 16
1900–01 17
1901–02 18
1902–03 19
1903–04 20
1904–05 21
1905–06 22
1906–07 23
1907–08 24
1908–09 25
The First Heroes 26
1909–10 28
1910–11 29
1911–12 30
1912–13 31
1913–14 32
1914–15 33
The Great War (1914–18) 34
1919–20 36
1920–21 37
1921–22 38
1922–23 39
1923–24 40
1924–25 41
Development of the Laws 42
1925–26 44
1926–27 45
1927–28 46
1928–29 47
Heroes of the Twenties 48
1929–30 49
World Cup Special 1930 50
1930–31 52
1931–32 53
1932–33 54
1933–34 55
World Cup Special 1934 56
1934–35 58
1935–36 59
1936–37 60
1937–38 61
World Cup Special 1938 62
1938–39 64
Heroes of the Thirties 65
World War II (1939–45) 66
1946–47 68
1947–48 70
1948–49 72
1949–50 74
World Cup Special 1950 76
1950–51 78
1951–52 80
1952–53 82
1953–54 84
World Cup Special 1954 86
1954–55 88
1955–56 90
1956–57 92
1957–58 94
World Cup Special 1958 96
1958–59 98
Post-War Heroes 100
1959–60 102
1960–61 104
1961–62 106
World Cup Special 1962 108
1962–63 110
1963–64 112
1964–65 114
1965–66 116
World Cup Special 1966 118
1966–67 120
Heroes of the 1960s 122
1967–68 124
1968–69 128
1969–70 132
World Cup Special 1970 136
1970–71 138
1971–72 142
1972–73 146
1973–74 150
World Cup Special 1974 154
1974–75 156
1975–76 160
Heroes of the Seventies 164
1976–77 166
1977–78 170
World Cup Special 1978 174
1978–79 176
1979–80 180
1980–81 184
1981–82 188
World Cup Special 1982 192
1982–83 194
1983–84 198
Heroes of the Eighties 202
1984–85 204
1985–86 210
World Cup Special 1986 216
1986–87 218
1987–88 224
1988–89 230
1989–90 236
World Cup Special 1990 242
1990–91 244
1991–92 250
1992–93 256
1993–94 262
World Cup Special 1994 268
1994–95 270
Impact of foreign players 276
1995–96 278
Euro 96 Special 284
1996–97 288
Cult of the Manager 294
1997–98 296
World Cup Special 1998 302
1998–99 306
Heroes of the Nineties 312
1999–2000 314
Euro 2000 320
2000–2001 322
The Impact of Foreign Coaches 328
2001–2002 330
World Cup Special 2002 336
2002–2003 338
2003–2004 344
Heroes of the New Millennium 350
Euro 2004 Special 352
2004–2005 354
2005–2006 358
World Cup Special 2006 364
2006–2007 368
2007–2008 374
Euro 2008 Special 380
2008–2009 382
2009–2010 388
World Cup Special 2010 394
2010–2011 398
2011–2012 404
Euro 2012 Special 410
2012–2013 414
Index 420

INTRODUCTION

In compiling this celebration of 150 years of football, choices have had to be made all down the line. While a large proportion of the entries have been automatically included – the major milestones, important finals, great achievements, tragedies and triumphs – other factors have been taken into consideration. In order to provide a greater breadth of coverage, not every Cup final between Celtic and Rangers, or League triumph by Liverpool or Manchester United, has been featured. Rarer, if not worthier, achievements by lesser clubs have been given priority. The Football Focus feature of every year has proved useful in highlighting aspects of the game, to give a comprehensive overview of a century and a half of football history.

The match reports and other stories are not taken verbatim from the newspaper. In fact, for earlier years, when The Daily Telegraph did not give the unrivalled coverage to football that it now boasts, the pieces have been compiled from my extensive library of histories, reference books and biographies. Admittedly, they are written with hindsight, but I hope I have retained topicality and avoided anachronisms altogether. It is only from the 1970s, when more space was available per year, that any substantial extracts from Telegraph reports have been used, and the writers of these have been duly acknowledged elsewhere in this book.

There is an intentional bias within these covers towards British football, particularly in the early years. As international competition has grown, so has its coverage in the UK, and this is reflected both in the stories and in the statistics. Each World Cup has been featured from the start, even though it is almost impossible to find much about the pre-War tournaments in any British newspaper.

The special features have been designed to give regular summaries of trends in the game, as well as provide comparative assessments of its stars. "Years" have been based on British seasons, and there have been no strict rules as to where events in the "close season" are included. In the Final Score statistical boxes, the European Footballer of the Year – chosen always at the end of a calendar year – has been placed in the season covering the end of that year. Results of that benighted competition, the World Club Championship, are given in the season when the European clubs concerned won the European Cup, even though the match is regularly played well into the next season. This may not initially seem logical, but I hope it will make it easier for the reader to follow.

The journey through the seasons has been a fascinating one. Every period threw up its headlines, its triumphs and its tragedies, its heroes and its occasional villains. The changes over the years appear to be astonishing, yet David Jack's transfer for £10,000 in 1928 made no less a stir than the mind-boggling, multi-million pound deals of today. Indeed, while the fees have gone up, the goals have gone down, and it has been intriguing to chart some of the scatterbrained law changes made in recent times in an effort to reverse the trend.

Working through the years, reliving the highlights of this great game in words and pictures, has been sheer joy, and I hope that the spirit and flavour of each era have been conveyed to the reader. Much has happened in football in the two decades since the first edition. On the debit side have been bribery, "bung" and drug scandals, plus on-field controversies, some unfortunately involving racist abuse; events of a more positive nature have included two Manchester United Premiership trebles during 27 years of unprecedented success under their recently-retired manager, Sir Alex Ferguson; English clubs re-merging as major forces in European competition; Rangers' nine successive Scottish titles, before their financial fall from grace; and Spain's meteoric rise to dominate world football after years of flattering to deceive. The Premier League goes from strength to strength, at least in terms of media coverage, even if no more than three or four of the teams have any conceivable chance of winning it. The arrival of an increasing number of foreign players and managers has improved the quality of football on display in Britain. Of continuing significance to the broad picture of the game have been the European Court rulings on transfers and players' contracts, the increasing amount of money being poured into the game by TV, sponsors and foreign billionaires, the gradual improvement in the laws of the game and the imminent introduction of goal-line technology.

Norman Barrett (with Martin Smith), 2013

WEMBLEY
adidas

WEMBLEY 2013
FINAL WEMBLEY 2013
CHAMPIONS LEAGUE
FINAL WEMBLEY 2013

Birth of Association Football

ON MONDAY, 26 October 1863, a meeting was convened of representatives from a dozen of the leading London and suburban football clubs to form an association and to establish an agreed set of rules for the game. The meeting, which took place at the Freemasons' Tavern in Great Queen Street, formed the Football Association, with 11 of the 12 clubs present enrolling as founder members. But it has taken another six meetings to formulate the rules of football.

The problem has been co-ordinating the disparate codes of football played around the country. There was a strong body of opinion in favour of banning some of the practices allowed by the Rugby (School) code, already outlawed by the Sheffield Rules of 1857 and the Cambridge Rules of 1862 and 1863. But representatives of the Blackheath club, strong advocates of the Rugby game, were unyielding. They insisted on the inclusion of two clauses in the rules: first, that "A player may be entitled to run with the ball towards his adversaries' goal if he makes a fair catch" and, second, "If any player shall run with the ball towards his adversaries' goal, any player on the opposite side shall be at liberty to charge, hold, trip or hack him, or wrest the ball from him..."

Finally, at a meeting held on 8 December, the dispute came to a head. The proposal by the Blackheath group to adjourn the meeting was defeated by 13 votes to 4, and as a consequence they withdrew from the Association. The Laws of the Game, evolved from the Cambridge Rules and now agreed by the Association, were formally accepted, heralding the birth of Association Football.

Wanderers win the Cup

THE WANDERERS FC beat the Royal Engineers by a goal to nil at Kennington Oval on 16 March 1872 to win the newly inaugurated Football Association Challenge Cup competition. A crowd of some 2,000 spectators saw C.W.Alcock, captain of the victorious team, presented with the trophy, a silver cup scarcely 18 inches high.

It was highly appropriate that Mr Alcock should be the recipient of the trophy for, as secretary of the Football Association, he was the moving spirit in the inception of the competition, which was born on 16 October 1871. There were 15 entrants, eight of them from London, but no northern clubs, their fixture cards for the season having already been completed. Donington School from Lincolnshire entered and so did Queen's Park of Glasgow, the first Scottish football club.

Both of these clubs were given byes in the first round, and then Queen's Park had a walk-over in the second when Donington scratched. With five clubs left in the third round, Queen's Park received another bye, so were in the semi-finals without having played a match. They were drawn against the Wanderers, and travelled to London from Glasgow with the help of public subscription. After a hard-fought goalless draw, Queen's Park, whose accurate passing style was a complete revelation in the South, could not afford to stay in London for a replay and had to scratch. So Wanderers were in the final.

The Royal Engineers were favourites to win the final at odds of 7–4 on, but the Wanderers were a strong side composed of the best players to have graduated from the public schools and universities. Their star player, the Rev. R.W.S.Vidal, was famed as the "Prince of Dribblers", and it was he who broke away and passed to M.P.Betts who proceeded to score the only goal of the game.

There was a bad-luck story for the gallant losers, for Lieutenant Cresswell broke a collar-bone 10 minutes after the start, but bravely played on to the end of the game. For the victors, there was not only the glory of winning the Challenge Cup, but also the privilege of exemption next year until the final, when they would also have choice of venue.

The Royal Engineers, who appeared in three of the first four FA Cup finals, losing two and winning the third.

No goals in history-making Scotland-England encounter

THE GAME WAS a long time in coming, Scotland versus England on 30 November 1872 at the West of Scotland Cricket Ground, Partick. For some time, the idea of a Scotland-England match had been brewing in men's minds. On 5 March 1870, England took on a Scottish representative side in the first of five matches played over two years at the Oval, in London. The result was a 1–1 draw, and in all England won three and drew two of these unofficial internationals with what was a "London Scottish" side.

It was the Scots who first suggested the match, seeking help in spreading the game north of the border, where no more than 10 football clubs had been established. The FA accepted the invitation, and on 24 October wrote to all the member clubs requesting assistance in paying the railway expenses of England's 11 chosen representatives and officials. The prime mover for the FA was C.W.Alcock, their first secretary. He was due to captain the team, but had to withdraw because of injury, and travelled as England's umpire.

More than 2,000 spectators turned out to watch the match in Partick, paying £109 at the gate, and they were not disappointed with the action despite the absence of goals. The Scots, six of them from Queen's Park, were smaller and lighter than their adversaries, giving away an estimated two stone per man, and it called for an outstanding performance from their two backs, J.J.Thomson and R.W.Ker, to save the day. For England, the magnificent dribbling of the captain, C.J.Ottaway, A.S.Kirke-Smith and J.Brockbank was greatly admired by the crowd, who kept the utmost order.

Scotland 0 England 0 — a selection of sketches from the match.

Playing the game by electric light

TWO TEAMS drawn from the Sheffield area and captained respectively by the brothers W.E. and J.C.Clegg, both England internationals, played an historic match at Bramall Lane, Sheffield, on 14 October 1878 under electric lights. There were four lamps standing on 30-foot wooden towers erected in each corner of the ground, and powered by portable generators. Nearly 20,000 people saw this novelty on a crisp moonlit night.

Other clubs have repeated this experiment, including Birmingham and Accrington, although the first night match to be played in London, at the Oval on 4 November, was not such a success, owing to uneven illumination and high winds.

Football by floodlight — an impression of the Sheffield scene.

FOOTBALL FOCUS

● A return England-Scotland match was played at the Oval on 8 March 1873 and England won 4–2. Alexander Bonsor (Old Etonians and The Wanderers) went into the record books as the scorer of England's first-ever international goal. Thereafter the match became an annual fixture, alternating between the two countries. The Scots pulled off a hat-trick of victories towards the end of the decade, culminating in their remarkable 7–2 triumph at Queen's Park in 1878.

● In March 1873, the Scots instituted their own Cup competition and founded the Scottish Football Association. With a credit balance of only £1.11s.4d in its first year, the Scottish FA had to seek donations from its member clubs to pay for the trophy and badges, which cost £56.12s.11d.

● The Royal Engineers, from Chatham, appeared in three of the first four FA Cup finals, losing twice before beating Old Etonians 2–0 in 1875. During that period, they lost only three out of 86 matches, mostly played against leading clubs, and boasted an extraordinary goalscoring record of 244 scored and a mere 21 conceded.

● Wales entered the international scene for the first time, losing 4–0 to Scotland in Glasgow in 1876 and 2–1 to England at London's Kennington Oval in 1879.

FINAL SCORE

FA Cup Finals

1872	Wanderers	1	Royal Engineers	0
1873	Wanderers	2	Oxford University	0
1874	Oxford Uty.	2	Royal Engineers	0
1875	Royal Eng.	1	Old Etonians	1
Replay:	Royal Eng.	2	Old Etonians	0
1876	Wanderers	1	Old Etonians	1
Replay:	Wanderers	3	Old Etonians	0
1877	Wanderers (after extra time)	2	Oxford University	1
1878	Wanderers	3	Royal Engineers	1
1879	Old Ets.	1	Clapham Rovers	0

Scottish FA Cup Finals

1874	Queen's Pk.	2	Clydesdale	0
1875	Queen's Pk.	3	Renton	0
1876	Queen's Pk.	1	Third Lanark	1
Replay:	Queen's Pk.	2	Third Lanark	0
1877	Vale of Leven	0	Rangers	0
Replay:	Vale of Leven	1	Rangers	1
Replay:	Vale of Leven	3	Rangers	2
1878	Vale of Leven	1	Third Lanark	0
1879	Vale of Leven (Vale of Leven won replay by default)	1	Rangers	1

Artisans beat the aristocrats

THE PLUMBERS and weavers of Blackburn Olympic beat the gentlemen of the Old Etonians to take "t'Coop" up North for the first time in its 11-year history.

Blackburn, in existence for only five years, needed extra time to win the 1883 final 2–1 after reaching it with 6–3, 9–1, 8–0, 2–0, 4–0 and 4–0 victories in the earlier rounds. They had been moulded into an imposing force by half-back and trainer Jack Hunter, who before the final took his team away to Blackpool to prepare them for the great day, the first time such systematic training had been implemented.

Sketches from the 1883 Cup final between Blackburn Olympic and Old Etonians.

Old Etonians, the Cup-holders, fielded six internationals, including the Hon. A.F.Kinnaird, a veteran of the competition who was playing in his ninth final. There was little to choose between the two sides in the first half, although the Etonians took the lead through Goodhart.

Blackburn began to press in the second half, but Kinnaird, who was playing magnificently, hit a place-kick through the posts only to have it disallowed because the ball did not touch an opponent. This was the turning point of the game. Matthew dribbled down the right and hit an angled shot to equalize, and then Dunn went off injured, a severe handicap for the Etonians, who were tiring fast.

The 10 men managed to contain the Olympians for the remainder of the 90 minutes. But they were no match for their fitter opponents in extra time, and Crossley converted a pass from Dewhurst soon after the change-over for the winner.

England's new formation Scotched

ENGLAND, having lost seven of their last eight annual internationals to the Scots, and conceded 36 goals in the process, appeared for the 1884 game at Cathkin Park, Glasgow, with a revolutionary defensive formation. Instead of the customary two half-backs and six forwards, they turned out with three half-backs and only five forwards. This might have had the effect of restricting the Scots to a single goal, but Scotland still triumphed 1–0 for their fifth win in a row.

As always, despite the individual brilliance of the Englishmen, it was the smaller Scots' greater cohesion and understanding that won the day. And an historic day it is, for with this victory Scotland have won the first International Championship, having already roundly beaten Wales (4–1 in Glasgow) and Ireland (5–0 in Belfast).

'Offside' storm as Villa beat the favourites

IN THE FIRST all-Midlands Cup final in 1887, Aston Villa beat West Bromwich Albion 2–0 after a hotly disputed goal gave them the lead on the hour. West Bromwich, confident after their unexpected but comprehensive 3–1 semi-final win over Preston, dominated the game in the first 20 minutes. Only the brave goalkeeping of Warner kept their hungry forwards at bay. On more than one occasion, he scooped the ball up and over his own cross-bar to avoid being bundled into the goal.

It was a different story in the second half. Villa, 3–1 conquerors of Glasgow Rangers in the semi-finals, began to take charge. With the wind now at their backs, they proceeded to demoralize their opponents. But when they did score, it caused a furore. West Bromwich keeper Roberts, assuming Hodgetts was offside, made no attempt to stop the Villa winger's shot. The umpires on both sides, however, ruled in favour of Villa, much to the distress of the Albion side and the wrath of their supporters.

Two minutes from the end, the game was appropriately wrapped up by Villa's captain and inspiration, Archie Hunter. Intercepting a back-pass, the centre-forward defied Roberts's effort to block him, and slid the ball into the net for a 2–0 victory.

West Bromwich centre-forward Bayliss heads towards Villa's goal.

Blackburn Rovers, a 'hat-trick' of Cup wins with victories over Queen's Park (twice) and West Brom.

Joy for the Rovers

BLACKBURN ROVERS celebrated their third successive Cup triumph, equalling the Wanderers' feat of the 1870s, when they beat West Bromwich Albion 2–0 at the Racecourse Ground, Derby, in the replayed 1886 final after the goalless draw at the Oval. They received a silver shield for their achievement.

The Rovers' record in the eighties has been one of remarkable accomplishment. When they reached their first Cup final in 1882, they had gone 35 games without defeat against some of the best sides in the land, including a 16–0 trouncing of Preston in North End's first professional fixture. Old Etonians beat them in the final, but Rovers came back in 1884 to take over the Cup mantle of their neighbours Blackburn Olympic, beating Queen's Park to take the trophy. They repeated their victory over the Scottish challengers the following year, and now they have "scored a hat-trick", with seven of their players appearing in all three of the finals.

FOOTBALL FOCUS

- The Scotland-Ireland fixture in 1884 completed the six-match cycle amongst the four home countries, and the International Championship was born. Scotland won four of the eighties Championships outright and shared the title with England in 1886.
- Professionalism was recognized in England in 1885. Blackburn Rovers left-half James Forrest, at 19, became the first professional to play for England against Scotland, despite Scottish protestations that both teams should be strictly amateur.
- England won the International Championship for the first time in 1888 with a thumping 5–0 victory in Scotland, after beating both Wales and Ireland 5–1.
- In 1887–88, Preston scored 51 goals in six FA Cup ties, including a Cup record 26–0 defeat of Hyde, before losing 2–1 to West Bromwich in the final.
- Scottish Cup-winners Renton beat FA Cup-winners West Bromwich in 1888 in a match for the "Championship of the World".
- The Football League was inaugurated on 17 April 1888 at the Royal Hotel, Manchester. It was the brainchild of a Scot, William McGregor, a director of the Aston Villa club. The 12 clubs forming the League, all from the Midlands or the North, were Accrington, Aston Villa, Blackburn Rovers, Bolton Wanderers, Burnley, Derby County, Everton, Notts County, Preston North End, Stoke, West Bromwich Albion and Wolverhampton Wanderers.

Bon Accord lambs to the slaughter

ON 5 SEPTEMBER 1885, in the first round of the Scottish FA Cup, Arbroath beat Bon Accord 36–0, a record for any British first-class match. The visitors, playing in their working clothes and without a proper pair of football boots between them, had replaced their unfit keeper with a half-back who had never played in goal before.

The Arbroath goalkeeper was not called upon to touch the ball once, and winger John Petrie scored 13 goals — a record for an individual player. On the same day, Dundee Harp beat Aberdeen Rovers 35–0.

Invincible Preston's twin triumphs

PRESTON NORTH END have gone through the first League season, 1888–89, without losing a match and have become the first League champions. In addition, they have won the FA Cup without conceding a goal. They are indeed "double" champions.

With the emphasis on attack, Preston scored 74 goals in their 22 matches, and only at Accrington were they denied scoring. They finished 11 points ahead of runners-up Aston Villa, with 40 points out of the maximum 44. And they conceded only 15 goals.

Centre-forward John Goodall was the brains of the side, with inside-right Jimmy Ross a prolific goalscorer. They were well supported by the Scottish half-back trio of Sandy Robertson, David Russell and John Graham. The keeper, Jimmy Trainer, known as the "Prince of Goalkeepers", is a Welshman. He joined Preston from Bolton only a few months after Preston had knocked 12 goals past him in one match!

Preston eased their way through to the semi-finals of the FA Cup, where they met West Bromwich, who had beaten them in last year's final. This time Preston won 1–0. In the final they easily beat Wolves 3–0 in front of a record 22,000 crowd. They truly earned their nickname "The Invincibles".

FINAL SCORE

Football League Champions

1888-89 Preston North End

FA Cup Finals

Year	Winner		Runner-up	
1880	Clapham R.	1	Oxford University	0
1881	Old Carthusians	3	Old Etonians	0
1882	Old Etonians	1	Blackburn Rovers	0
1883	Blackburn Olyp (after extra time)	2	Old Etonians	1
1884	Blackburn R.	2	Queen's Park	1
1885	Blackburn R.	2	Queen's Park	0
1886	Blackburn R.	0	WBA	0
Replay:	Blackburn R.	2	WBA	0
1887	Aston Villa	2	WBA	0
1888	WBA	2	Preston N. E.	1
1889	Preston N. E.	3	Wolves	0

Scottish FA Cup Finals

Year	Winner		Runner-up	
1880	Queen's Park	3	Thornlibank	0
1881	Queen's Park (after 2–1 cancelled)	3	Dumbarton	1
1882	Queen's Park	2	Dumbarton	2
Replay:	Queen's Park	4	Dumbarton	1
1883	Dumbarton	2	Vale of Leven	2
Replay:	Dumbarton	2	Vale of Leven	1
1884	Queen's Park beat Vale of Leven on default			
1885	Renton	0	Vale of Leven	0
Replay:	Renton	3	Vale of Leven	1
1886	Queen's Park	3	Renton	1
1887	Hibernian	2	Dumbarton	1
1888	Renton	6	Cambuslang	1
1889	Third Lanark (after 3–0 cancelled)	2	Celtic	1

International Firsts

1882 Wales v Ireland (at Wrexham, 7–1)
1882 Ireland v England (at Belfast, 0–13)
1884 Ireland v Scotland (at Belfast, 0–5)
1884 International Champ. (Scotland, 6 pts)

Townley goes to town

WILLIAM TOWNLEY, playing on the left wing for Blackburn Rovers, hit three goals in the 1890 FA Cup final as Rovers beat Sheffield Wednesday 6–1. He is the first player to score a hat-trick in the final.

Rovers, who themselves scored a hat-trick of Cup wins in the mid-eighties, were favourites to beat their Yorkshire rivals in this first ever "War of the Roses" final, at Kennington Oval. They included only Forrest, Lofthouse and Walton from those earlier triumphs, but boasted nine internationals among their ranks.

Wednesday fielded all local products, but were not dismayed at the prospect of playing the mighty Rovers. They had, indeed, accounted for three Football League sides on their progress to the final — Accrington, Notts County and, in the semi-finals, Bolton Wanderers, conquerors of "Proud" Preston in the previous round. Bolton were certainly a prize scalp, having humiliated Belfast Distillery 10–1 and Sheffield United 13–0 before overcoming Preston.

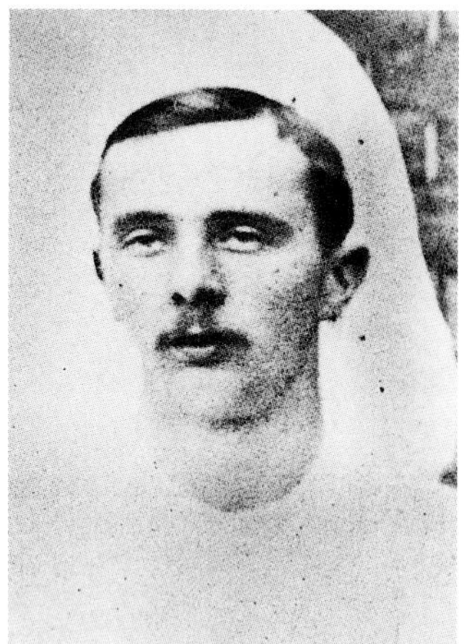

William Townley, Rovers' hat-trick hero in the 1890 final.

In the final, however, Wednesday were outplayed, but to their credit they never gave up. They were disadvantaged by some "primitive" keeping by their custodian Smith, while his counterpart in the Rovers goal, Horne, had little work to do. At the end, the crowd sportingly carried off the little Wednesday right-back Hadyn Morley for a gallant display against the odds.

Descent of Darwen

DARWEN FINISHED BOTTOM of the Second Division in 1899 and were not re-elected to the League. This is not surprising in view of their record, only nine points from 34 games. Their away record was extraordinary, one point from 17 games, with six goals for and an unprecedented 109 against. They were beaten 10–0 on three occasions: by Manchester City, the Second Division champions, by Walsall and, incredibly, by Loughborough, who finished second from bottom but were re-elected. Other crushing defeats for Darwen included 9–0 by Newton Heath, 9–2 by Grimsby, 8–0 by Small Heath, 8–1 by Luton and 7–0 by New Brighton.

No game for ladies!

THE BRITISH LADIES' Football Club was formed in 1895, and played their first match at Crouch End. Some 10,000 spectators turned out to watch this novelty, regarded by the football authorities as a "farce". The ladies turned out in nightcaps and heavy, cumbersome skirts, and wore shinguards.

Bassett hounds Villa

WILLIAM BASSETT, who as an 18-year-old inspired West Bromwich Albion to their shock Cup final victory over Preston in 1888, has done it again. Albion once more started as underdogs, this time to their neighbours Aston Villa. But Albion had knocked out Blackburn Rovers, depriving them of a chance to notch another hat-trick of Cups.

Only four minutes had passed when the diminutive right-winger raced down the line and crossed for Geddes to shoot home. Bassett repeated the performance, this time for 20-year-old centre-forward Nicholls to send Albion in with a 2–0 interval lead. Right-half Reynolds completed the scoring in the second half, with a long shot into the net — the first time nets and crossbars have been used in the final.

The British Ladies play their first match at Crouch End, North London.

Scots get their own League

A SCOTTISH LEAGUE, first mooted 10 years earlier, was formed in 1890. Eleven clubs joined the League: Abercorn, Celtic, Cowlair, Cambuslang, Dumbarton, Hearts, Rangers, St Mirren, Renton, Third Lanark and Vale of Leven. Renton, however, were kicked out after five games, having been found guilty of professionalism. There were plenty of goals in this first season, 409 in 90 matches, without a single goalless draw. Dumbarton and Rangers shared the inaugural Championship, each finishing with 29 points from their 18 games and drawing a play-off decider 2–2.

Jimmy Logan, who scored three goals in the Cup final.

Cup-winners stay in Division Two

NOTTS COUNTY of the Second Division beat Bolton Wanderers 4–1 in the 1894 Cup final, but failed to win promotion to Division One when, after finishing third in their division, they were beaten 4–0 by Preston in a "test match".

James Logan was County's hero in the final, played at Everton's Goodison Park, scoring a hat-trick to equal Townley's record for Blackburn of four years ago. But the Second Division side outplayed the beleaguered Bolton side, who unwisely fielded four or five men in various states of injury or unfitness. Indeed, were it not for an heroic performance in their goal by John Sutcliffe, who knows what the score might have been!

FOOTBALL FOCUS

- On 15 March 1890, England fielded two international sides on the same day, beating Wales 3–1 at Wrexham and Ireland 9–1 at Belfast.

- There was some heavy scoring in the first round of the 1890–91 FA Cup. Darwen, whose 3–1 win over Kidderminster was cancelled after a protest, won the replay 13–0. Aston Villa beat Casuals 13–1, and Sheffield Wednesday beat Halliwell 12–0. The other Sheffield side, United, lost 9–1 at home to eventual finalists Notts County. But pride of place must go to their neighbours Nottingham Forest, who chalked up a record away win, 14–0 at Clapton.

- James Forrest equalled the record of five Cup winners' medals when he helped Blackburn Rovers win their fifth Cup final in 1891, 3–1 over Notts County. Remarkably, only a week earlier, County had won 7–1 at Blackburn.

- The Scottish FA recognized professionalism in 1893, and a 10-club Second Division was introduced.

- The English Second Division came into being in 1892 with 12 clubs. At the end of the season, "test matches" took place in which the bottom three of Division One played the top three in Division Two (in reverse order), to determine promotion or relegation.

- There was a new venue for the FA Cup final in 1895, Crystal Palace, in London, and over 42,000 saw Aston Villa beat West Bromwich 1–0 with a goal scored in just 40 seconds by John Devey.

Sheffield on the razor's edge

SHEFFIELD UNITED, last season's League champions, eventually won their first FA Cup, beating Derby County in the 1899 final, but what a time they had to get there! In the semi-finals, it took them a record four games to account for Liverpool. The first was a 2–2 draw. In the second, at Bolton, they were 4–2 down with eight minutes to play before Fred Priest scored twice to earn a second replay. This was played at Fallowfield, and abandoned when the crowd encroached on to the field with Liverpool leading 1–0. Sheffield finally settled the tie with a 1–0 win at Wolverhampton.

A record 73,833 crowd for the final saw Sheffield's right-back Harry Thickett turn out with two broken ribs, protected by some 50 yards of bandages. The match turned on the duel between United's captain and left-half, Ernest "Nudger" Needham, and Derby's prolific goalscoring inside-right, Steve Bloomer. Needham won the encounter, although Bloomer uncharacteristically missed several chances. Sheffield were a goal down at half-time, after Boag shot past goalkeeper Foulke, but with four goals in the second half, scored by Bennett, Beers, Almond and Priest, they ran out easy winners. At the end of the match, the brave Thickett passed out with the pain.

FINAL SCORE

Football League Champions

1889–90	Preston North End
1890–91	Everton
1891–92	Sunderland
1892–93	Sunderland
1893–94	Aston Villa
1894–95	Sunderland
1895–96	Aston Villa
1896–97	Aston Villa
1897–98	Sheffield United
1898–99	Aston Villa

FA Cup Finals

1890	Blackburn R.	6	Sheffield Wed.	1
1891	Blackburn R.	3	Notts County	1
1892	WBA	3	Aston Villa	0
1893	Wolves	1	Everton	0
1894	Notts Co.	4	Bolton W.	1
1895	Aston Villa	1	WBA	0
1896	Sheff Wed.	2	Wolves	1
1897	Aston Villa	3	Everton	2
1898	Nottm For.	3	Derby County	1
1899	Sheffield Utd	4	Derby County	1

Scottish League Champions

1890–91	Dumbarton and Rangers (joint)
1891–92	Dumbarton
1892–93	Celtic
1893–94	Celtic
1894–95	Heart
1895–96	Celtic
1896–97	Hearts
1897–98	Celtic
1898–99	Rangers

Scottish FA Cup Finals

1890	Queen's Pk.	1	Vale of Leven	1
Replay:	Queen's Pk.	2	Vale of Leven	1
1891	Hearts	1	Dumbarton	0
1892	Celtic	5	Queen's Park	1
	(after 1–0 cancelled)			
1893	Queen's Pk.	2	Celtic	1
1894	Rangers	3	Celtic	1
1895	St Bernard's	2	Renton	1
1896	Hearts	3	Hibernian	1
1897	Rangers	5	Dumbarton	1
1898	Rangers	2	Kilmarnock	0
1899	Celtic	2	Rangers	0

International Champions

England 1890 (joint), 1891, 1892, 1893, 1895, 1898, 1899

Scotland 1890 (joint), 1894, 1896, 1897

The rise of professionalism

ORGANIZED FOOTBALL began as an amateur sport, played purely for fun and for exercise, with no commercial reward. The Football Association was founded by amateurs in 1863, and the FA Cup, inaugurated in 1872, was contested by all amateur clubs. The "amateur era" was dominated by sides such as the Wanderers, Old Etonians and Oxford University.

England's Vivian Woodward beats the Scottish defence to the ball at Bramall Lane in 1903. A dedicated amateur, he scored 29 goals in 23 full internationals, over 50 in amateur internationals, and won two gold medals with the UK Olympic football team.

Opposing the Cup

In the early days, there was no thought of players being paid. It was against all the ideals of sport and sportsmanship. Things began to change with the advent of competition in the shape of the FA Cup. For the Cup had its opponents when it was first mooted, whose chief objection was that the rivalry generated would lead to the destruction of the true spirit of the game. In some respects they were right. A direct outcome of the enthusiasm to win the "little tin idol" was the subversive growth of professionalism.

Bob McColl, the Scotland and Queen's Park centre-forward, who turned professional to play for Newcastle in 1901, returned to Glasgow in 1904 with Rangers, and went back to Queen's Park in 1907 as a reinstated amateur.

The first obvious signs of a chink in the amateur code came in the FA Cup of 1879. Lancashire club Darwen reached the last six, but were not expected to trouble Old Etonians. Nor did they look likely to when they trailed 5–1 at the Oval with 15 minutes to go. But they shocked the old boys with four goals in that time. Old Etonians declined to play extra time, as was their right, so Darwen had to return for a replay. They drew this, too, causing quite a stir. How could a virtually unknown provincial club hold one of the best teams in the land twice? They lost the second replay 6–2, but they had made their mark. Among their side were two Scots, Fergus Suter and James Love, arguably their star players. Now what were two Scotsmen doing playing for an English club?

The answer was that they had played against Darwen when their Scottish club Partick Thistle were on tour, and had been persuaded to stay on. Rumours soon became rife that they would find money in their boots on returning from their after-match baths.

Darwen, of course, were not the only northern club in this situation. Football had become extremely popular in the North, especially in Lancashire, where it was soon appreciated that a successful football club could help bring prosperity to its town. There was a desire to challenge the superiority of the southern masters. Under-the-counter payments to players became rife; "shamateurism" began to rot the very soul of football.

Scottish clubs, for their part, were producing fine players, well versed in the passing game and other tactical skills found only north of the border. They were attracted by the greater opportunities to be found in the industrial North of England. And so, gradually, the flow of Scots across the border developed from a trickle to a torrent.

FA members split

The surreptitious infiltration of professionalism caused a rift in the FA. There were those who felt it was degrading for "respectable men to play with professionals" — this view mainly from the North and Midlands. On the other side, paradoxically, were the greatest advocates of amateurism, from the South. These more enlightened members of the old guard included FA secretary C.W.Alcock, who pioneered both the FA Cup and the first internationals. While no supporter of professionalism himself, he defended the right of players to embrace it and regarded it as a necessity for the growth of the game.

He objected to the idea that professionals were the "utter outcasts some people represent them to be". He realized, too, that the deadlock would continue until professionalism was legalized and could be controlled.

The struggle continued, however. The so-called "importation" of players by amateur clubs, who paid them, was banned, and protests began to be lodged by one club against the other for playing these "importations" in Cup ties. The FA brought in a rule in 1882 prohibiting any payments to players other than strict expenses or compensation for wages lost through taking part. Any player breaking this rule would be barred from Cup games and internationals, and guilty clubs would lose their FA membership.

But the rising tide of professionalism could not be stemmed. People were getting fed up with all the bickering and endless meetings and commissions. Preston were disqualified from the Cup when their opponents alleged they had used professionals, and the club openly admitted it. Everyone was doing it, they said, so why pick on them? Bolton managed to fool an investigative commission, but later owned up to having paid their players. Such confessions brought the situation to a head and suddenly opposition to professionalism began to melt away. On 20 July 1885, a Special General Meeting of the FA in a Fleet

Prolific amateur goalscoring centre-forward G.O.Smith of the Corinthians.

Street hotel, with the necessary two-thirds majority (35-15), voted to legalize professionalism.

Bringing professionalism into the open did not end all the arguments immediately. Strict regulations were laid down, and indiscriminate "importation" banned. But the game could now grow, unfettered by subversion and by regulations constantly broken. The most dramatic effect of the change was to pave the way for the formation of the Football League in 1888.

Scottish resistance

In Scotland, the persecution of professionalism was even greater than in England. Thus when it arrived south of the border, the difference in status led to the breaking-up of relationships between clubs that had been on good terms and enjoyed regular fixtures. When Rangers — who as FA members regularly entered the FA Cup — found in 1885 that they were drawn against professionals, they withdrew (the FA fined them 10 shillings). Two years later the Scottish FA banned their clubs from entering the English competition.

Open professionalism in England was attracting even more Scottish players south. The top northern clubs began to send their scouts in disguise, to save them from being beaten up. But English clubs did not always find it possible to lure a player with the promise of "gold", as Accrington once found to their embarrassment when they offered international Frank Shaw £120 per annum to join them. Football in Scotland had always been promoted as a middle-class sport, and Shaw's reply began: "Dear Sir, On return from a fortnight's cruise among the Western Islands on my yacht, I found your letter... "

Attempts to prevent the poaching of Scotland's best players by legalizing payment in Scotland were repeatedly destroyed by the more powerful upholders of pure amateurism. Thus the only way to counter the temptations of England was to make illegal payments. This went on openly, and the Scottish FA turned a blind eye. The champions of amateurism were powerless.

But to be able to make these payments, regular fixtures between the top teams became essential. The success of the Football League in England persuaded the Scottish clubs that this was the solution. Several clubs met in semi-secrecy to found the Scottish League in 1890. When the rules were made public, there was an outcry in the Press, *Scottish Sport* going so far as to declare: "The entire rules stink of... moneymaking and money grabbing." Nevertheless, the League was an immediate success, and sure enough the expected gate money came rolling in.

The League grew in membership, with all the leading clubs clamouring for admission — except for Queen's Park, that last bastion of amateurism, who resented the idea of linking themselves with a body of clubs who were swaying towards professionalism. But the prime mover of the Scottish League, J.H.McLaughlin, had no doubts: "You might as well try to stop the flow of Niagara with a kitchen chair as endeavour to stem the tide of professionalism." In 1893, the Scottish FA finally succumbed to popular demand and opened its doors to the paid player.

A slow transition

The professional clubs of the North and Midlands soon began to dominate the Football League and FA Cup. But this is not to say that the amateur clubs disappeared. The South remained amateur for some years (Royal Arsenal were the first to embrace professionalism, in 1891), and one amateur club the professionals continued to fear was Corinthians. In 1884, the year before professionalism came in, they beat Cup-winners Blackburn Rovers 8–1. In 1886 they supplied nine players to the England side (the other two came from Blackburn Rovers), and in 1904 they beat the Cup-winners Bury (6–0 conquerors of Derby in the final) by 10 goals to three! The Corinthians, who had been founded in 1882 from old boy and university players, did not enter the Cup — it was against their rules to play in competitions. Had they done so, they most certainly would have won it, but they carried the torch of amateurism well into the 20th century.

FA secretary C.W.Alcock, who defended the right of players to embrace professionalism.

The Preston side of 1889, with chairman Major William Sudell (standing, third from right) who openly admitted to paying players.

Villa supreme

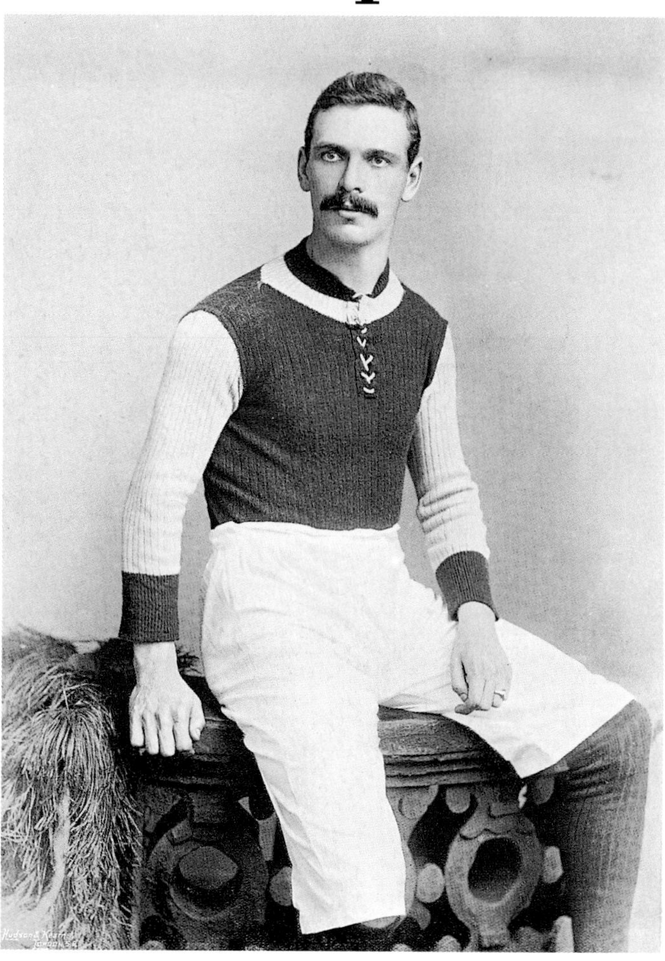

John Devey, highly-successful captain of Aston Villa.

SHEFFIELD UNITED, not surprisingly, failed to beat Burnley by eight goals at Turf Moor, so Aston Villa pip them by two points for the Championship. This is Villa's fifth title in seven seasons, during which they have also won the Cup twice. At the beginning of a new century they reign supreme.

Three players shared in all seven of these successes. Captain and inside- or centre-forward John Devey played in 143 out of a possible 158 matches in the five Championship seasons, centre-half Jimmy Cowan one fewer, and outside-right Charlie Athersmith in 137.

The 1900 League triumph was hard fought. With two-thirds of the season gone, Sheffield United were unbeaten, two points ahead of Villa and with two games in hand. But Villa were the stronger finishers, suffering only one defeat in their last 13 matches and dropping only one point in their last six games. They finished their programme on 16 April, leaving Sheffield needing to win their remaining two matches — both away — by at least eight goals in aggregate. They beat Wolves 2–1, but they failed at the last to do the impossible at Burnley.

Loughborough lurch out of League

LOUGHBOROUGH TOWN, who have been clinging to League membership ever since they were elected to the Second Division in 1895, finally had to let go. Their position has steadily deteriorated — 12th in 1896, 13th, 16th (bottom), 17th, and finally 18th and bottom in 1900.

With only eight points from 34 matches, one fewer than Darwen's dismal record last season, it is hardly surprising that they failed to gain re-election this time. They achieved but a single victory, 2–1 over Burton United in January, but lost all 17 of their away games. They gave away 100 goals, 74 of them in away matches, in which they scored only six — not as bad as Darwen's record, though. They also suffered some heavy defeats, the greatest being a 12–0 massacre by Woolwich Arsenal.

Non-Leaguers 'Buryed'

SOUTHAMPTON came to Crystal Palace with high hopes of becoming the first "outsiders" to win the FA Cup since the inception of the Football League. But Bury proved too much for them and ran out easy 4–0 winners.

Perhaps it was the occasion that got to the non-Leaguers, although they had played on the ground in the semi-finals. They had also disposed of three First Division sides on their way to the final — Everton 3–0, Newcastle 4–1 and West Bromwich 2–1 — all at the Dell. Only fellow Southern Leaguers Millwall gave them any trouble, drawing their semi-final 0–0 before going down 3–0 in the replay at Reading.

Nearly 69,000 turned out on a blazing hot April day to watch the final. Southampton kicked off with the sun in their eyes, and found themselves three goals down within 23 minutes, two of them from centre-forward McLuckie. They came back into the game for spells in the second half, but never seriously challenged Bury's lead, and a fourth goal for the northerners 10 minutes from time was the final nail in their coffin.

A rare Southampton attack in the final against Bury.

FOOTBALL FOCUS

- With 77 goals, Aston Villa are the leading scorers in Division One for the sixth season running.
- Racehorse owner Lord Rosebery attended the Scotland-England match at Parkhead and somehow persuaded the Scottish FA to allow the team to play in his racing colours of primrose and pink. Whether this Derby-winning combination had any galvanizing effect on the players is a moot point, but the Scots won 4–1, aided by a hat-trick from centre-forward R.S.McColl, the last remaining amateur in the side and the only representative from Queen's Park.
- Celtic retained the Scottish Cup, beating Queen's Park 4–3 in the final after losing a 3–1 half-time lead. They scored 25 goals in their six Cup matches, including a 4–0 win over Rangers in a semi-final replay.
- Rangers ran away with the Scottish League Championship again, although this season they lost four points — three of them to Celtic.

FINAL SCORE

Football League
Division 1: Aston Villa
Top scorer: Bill Garratt (Aston Villa) 27
Division 2: Sheffield Wednesday

FA Cup Final
Bury 4 Southampton 0

Scottish League
Division 1: Rangers
Division 2: Partick Thistle

Scottish FA Cup Final
Celtic 4 Queen's Park 3

International Championship
Scotland, 6 pts

Spurs win their first Cup

THE 1901 CUP FINAL drew a record crowd of 110,820 to the Crystal Palace and produced the first draw for 15 years. In the replay Tottenham Hotspur beat Sheffield United 3–1 to become the first club from outside the League to win the Cup since the League started. Their hero was centre-forward Alex "Sandy" Brown, the first player to score in every round of the Cup. He got both of their goals in the first final, and scored again in the replay for a record 15 goals in one tournament.

Tottenham, who won the Southern League last season, are the first team to break the dominance in the Cup of the great northern and Midlands clubs. They were unlucky not to win the final at the first attempt, for the Sheffield equalizer was a dubious affair. The linesman gave a corner, but the referee, who was hardly in a position to see, decided the ball had crossed the line before being cleared, and awarded a goal.

Sheffield, with the 20-stone Willie Foulke in goal, took the lead after 40 minutes in the replay at Burnden Park, Bolton, when Needham put Priest through. But the Spurs, in front of a much smaller crowd of 20,470, came back strongly in the second half for a thoroughly deserved victory with goals by Cameron, Smith and — inevitably — the remarkable Brown.

United repel a Spurs attack in the replay.

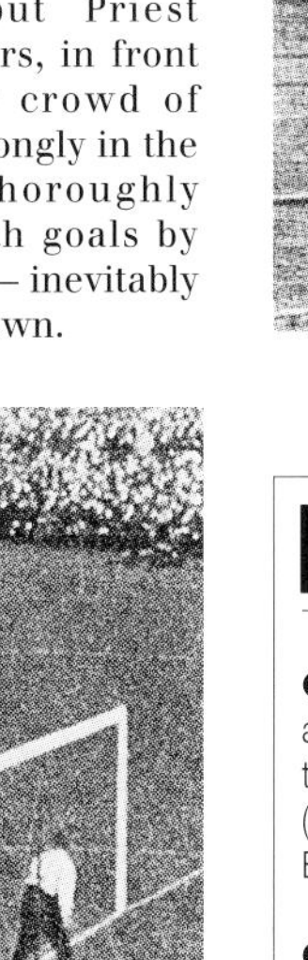

Brown scores for Spurs in the first match.

FOOTBALL FOCUS

● The scorer of England's first goal against Scotland in the drawn international at Crystal Palace was Blackburn (Blackburn) — Fred Blackburn of Blackburn Rovers, that is.

● Celtic beat Rangers in the Scottish Cup for the third successive season, this time in the first round. But they failed to bring off a hat-trick of Cups, losing 4–3 in the final to Hearts. Like their opponents Queen's Park last year, they fought back to equalize after being 3–1 down, but Hearts scored a late winner. Rangers won their third League title running.

● The bottom of Division One at the end of the 1900-01 season had a curious look to it — four of the last five clubs had formerly won either the Championship or the Cup or both. Sheffield United and the lately supreme Aston Villa stayed up. But both "Proud" Preston and West Bromwich were relegated to Division Two.

● On 23 February, Scotland beat Ireland 11–0, their highest international score, but they drew their other two games and England won the Championship.

● The Sheffield United keeper Billy "Fatty" Foulke, who lined up against Tottenham Hotspur in the 1901 Cup final, stood 6ft 2$\frac{1}{2}$in and weighed an amazing 20 stone.

Liverpool at last

AFTER NEARLY A DECADE of ups and downs between the divisions, Liverpool have finally won the League title. Their 1–0 victory over relegation-doomed West Bromwich at the Hawthorns was enough to put them two points clear of Sunderland and clinch the Championship.

Liverpool made a bright start to the season, winning their first three games. But in-and-out form left them well adrift of Sunderland, and when they suffered their third defeat in four games, at Bolton in mid-February, there was no thought of the Championship. Then came the turning point. They went to Roker Park and beat Sunderland 1–0, the start of a 12-match unbeaten run that took them through the field to the title.

Even so, it was a close-run thing. Sunderland finished their programme with a 2–0 victory at Newcastle, to take them two points clear. Liverpool beat Nottingham Forest 2–0 to draw level, but with a far inferior goal average. They needed just a draw in their last game, and West Bromwich bravely held them scoreless until Liverpool got a late goal to settle the issue.

With only 59 goals, Liverpool have nevertheless broken the First Division scoring dominance of Aston Villa, who finished well down the table with only 45. But their real strength has been in defence, with Scottish international centre-half Alec Raisbeck outstanding in the middle.

Alec Raisbeck, outstanding for Liverpool and Scotland.

FINAL SCORE

Football League
Division 1: Liverpool
Top scorer: Steve Bloomer (Derby County) 24
Division 2: Grimsby Town

FA Cup Final

Tottenham Hotspur 2		Sheffield United	2
Replay: Tottenham H. 3		Sheffield United	1

Scottish League
Division 1: Rangers
Division 2: St Bernard's

Scottish FA Cup Final

Hearts	4	Celtic	3

International Championship
England, 5 pts

Terrible disaster at Ibrox Park

A COLLAPSE in the new stand at Ibrox Park, Glasgow, during an international match has caused 25 deaths, with hundreds more injured, many of them seriously. Most of the crowd were oblivious to the horrific scenes under the stand. The match was stopped, but first reports were of just a few injuries, and the authorities decided to continue the game to prevent panic. Only after the match was the full scale of this catastrophe revealed.

Three Scottish clubs vied to stage the lucrative Scotland-England international: Celtic, Rangers and Queen's Park. Most recent internationals have been played at Celtic Park or Hampden Park, but Rangers "won" this time, largely because of the new West Stand constructed at a cost of £20,000. It was a fatal decision.

The Ibrox Park stadium is said to hold 80,000, but there were more likely nearly 100,000 crammed in, such is the fanaticism of the Scots for the game. As the eastern terrace became full, latecomers made a dash for the new stand, constructed of wooden planking set on steel pylons. The game was only six minutes old when there was a sudden rending of timber as a vast hole appeared in one section of the terracing. The unfortunate spectators there just fell through the gap, 40 feet to the ground below and on top of each other. Seven rows of wooden planking had collapsed, leaving a gap 30 yards wide.

The result of the match, which was played without passion and more as an exhibition, was a 1–1 draw, but this will not count in the records. It has been determined to replay the fixture next month in England, when the proceeds will go to a fund set up for the bereaved and injured.

The dead and dying are brought out from the collapsed Ibrox stand.

The gaping hole through which the unfortunate people fell.

Sunderland's Scots do it again

WHILE NOT AS commanding as their "Team of All the Talents" of the mid-nineties, Sunderland have won their first League title for six years. And again they have done it by packing their side with Scots, regularly fielding a team with at least nine men from across the border.

Two players remained from their last title-winning team, Scottish internationals Ted Doig, their goalkeeper, and centre-forward Jimmy Millar. For both it was their fourth Championship medal. But Millar, who spent four seasons with Glasgow Rangers before returning to Sunderland in 1900, also has two League and two Cup medals from Scotland.

Only Everton have provided any kind of challenge to the new champions. But, with games in hand, Sunderland have kept their noses comfortably in front, and their 3–0 victory over Bury has clinched the title with 10 days of the season remaining.

Sunderland finished with 44 points to Everton's 41, with Newcastle United in third place on 37. West Bromwich topped Division Two with 55 points, a record.

FINAL SCORE

Football League
Division 1: Sunderland
Top scorers: James Settle (Everton), Fred Priest (Sheffield United) 18
Division 2: West Bromwich Albion

FA Cup Final

Sheffield United	1	Southampton	1
Replay: Sheffield Utd	2	Southampton	1

Scottish League
Division 1: Rangers
Division 2: Port Glasgow

Scottish FA Cup Final

Hibernian	1	Celtic	0

International Championship
Scotland, 5 pts

FOOTBALL FOCUS

- A maximum wage of £4 per week was introduced in England.

- The result of the Scotland-England game, scene of the Ibrox disaster, did not count towards the International Championship. The replay a month later at Villa Park ended in a 2–2 draw. These were the first matches in which both sides fielded all-professional teams.

- The Cup final was contested by the previous two years' beaten finalists, Southampton and Sheffield United, but the Southern League club lost again. It was a second consecutive replayed Cup final running for Sheffield. This time they won 2–1, after a 1–1 draw. The celebrated amateur, C.B.Fry, played right-back for Southampton. The Crystal Palace provided seated accommodation for 12,000, with "crowds of almost any size" watching from the slopes. The gate for the 1902 final was 76,914, although only 33,068 turned up for the replay, also at Crystal Palace, a week later.

- Scoring in Division One of the Football League reached a new low, averaging 2.75 goals per game.

Sunderland fail to sabotage Scots

ENGLAND were favourites to beat Scotland in 1903 and clinch the International Championship. They had beaten the other two countries, whereas Scotland had suffered their first defeat at the hands of Ireland, and that at home, in Glasgow, too.

Scotland had six Anglo-Scots in the side, and three of these — the keeper and the two backs — were from Sunderland. It was learnt from official quarters that Sunderland tried to prevent their players, Doig, McCombie and Watson, from taking part, threatening them with the loss of their wages. The three men played, and Scotland won 2–1. It was much easier than the score suggests, for the English keeper Baddeley made save after save from the marauding Scots, who were brilliant on the day.

The win gave Scotland a share in the Championship with England and Ireland, who were the first country other than the "big two" to win such an honour. The three Sunderland players did not suffer, as after the game the Scottish treasurer received instructions to "commemorate the game in a generous manner"! And Sunderland won their League match without them.

'Threatened' Doig repels a rare English attack in the internationl match played at Sheffield.

Newcastle sabotage Sunderland's Championship hopes

CHAMPIONS Sunderland went to St James's Park on 25 April for their last game of the season knowing that a win would ensure that they retained their Championship title. Their League record at Newcastle was four wins in four seasons, although they had lost there in the Cup last year. Sadly for them, they lost again, 1–0, and Sheffield Wednesday, having finished their programme a week ago with a 3–1 win over West Bromwich, are the new League champions.

Sunderland did not even finish second, being beaten to that position, on goal average, by Aston Villa.

It has been the tightest title race so far, with Sunderland favourites to win again. But they lost a vital match at home to Wednesday on 21 March, and their form has been in and out since then. It is ironic, considering Sunderland's strong Scottish connections, that it should be a Scot — Newcastle's goalscorer Bob McColl — who finally ended their chances.

This is Wednesday's first League title. They won it despite 11 defeats, more than any other previous champions. They owe their success largely to their home record, where they lost only twice and conceded just seven goals, equalling Preston's record in the first League season, when there were 11 home matches as opposed to 17 now. Their outstanding players this season have been Scottish centre-forward Andy Wilson, who scored 12 goals and made many more with his accurate passing, and stalwart centre-half Tom Crawshaw, a local lad and a great favourite with the fans.

Bury break Cup records

BURY'S 6–0 DEFEAT of Derby County at Crystal Palace is a record margin of victory in an FA Cup final. That's 10 goals without reply for the "Shakers" in two finals over four years. And this time, they did not concede a goal in the Cup at all, only the second side to accomplish this feat (Preston did it in 1889).

The match as a contest was over soon after the interval, when Bury scored four goals in 12 minutes to add to their half-time lead of 1–0. Derby disappointed. They just did not put up any kind of showing. True, they were without the injured Steve Bloomer, their ace goalscorer, but there can be no excuses. Their keeper was hurt trying to save a goal and left the field when they were 5–0 down, but by then they were well beaten.

So Derby's record of "failure" in the FA Cup continues. In eight seasons from 1896, they have lost three times in the semi-finals and now three times in the final.

FOOTBALL FOCUS

- A change in pitch markings for the 1902-03 season — the goal area is now a rectangle measuring 6 x 20 yards, and there is a penalty spot (at 12 yards) and a penalty area (at 18 yards).
- A crowd of 22,000 paid to see a junior Scotland-England match at Celtic Park, a tribute to the Scottish enthusiasm for international football. The full international, played at Bramall Lane, Sheffield, drew 33,000, and some 6,000 of those were Scots.
- When Sunderland lost a crucial Championship match 1–0 at home to Sheffield Wednesday, displeased fans stoned the referee's carriage as he left the ground, as a result of which Roker Park was ordered to be closed for a week.
- A storming Championship finish by Aston Villa, who won their last five games (four of them at home) in 15 days, with a goal record of 15-3, was just too late, as they finished a point behind winners Wednesday.

FINAL SCORE

Football League
Division 1: Sheffield Wednesday
Top scorer: Alec Raybould (Liverpool) 31
Division 2: Manchester City

FA Cup Final

Bury	6	Derby County	0

Scottish League
Division 1: Hibernian
Division 2: Airdrieonians

Scottish FA Cup Final

Rangers	1	Hearts	1
Replay: Rangers	0	Hearts	0
Replay: Rangers	2	Hearts	0

International Championship
England, Ireland, Scotland, 4pts

The mighty Quinn

CELTIC'S young centre-forward Jimmy Quinn plundered a hat-trick in the Scottish Cup final against deadly rivals Rangers to give his side a dramatic 3–2 victory after the Cup-holders had built up a 2–0 lead. The new Hampden Park, opened on 31 October and staging its first Cup final, could not have had a better introduction. With solid earth terracing for the spectators, rather than the wooden steps and scaffolding that caused the Ibrox disaster, and much reduced admission prices, 65,000 turned up to see the "show".

Quinn's success was a triumph for manager Willie Maley, who has patiently built up this exciting Celtic side despite the doubters and the criticism. His courageous policy of removing the old guard and, instead of buying established players, finding and rearing junior talent, has paid off. Even the directors, however, were beginning to doubt his wisdom in persevering with Quinn, a shy, unassuming lad whom he had nurtured from the juniors, mainly on the left wing. The breakthrough came in 1902, when Celtic beat Rangers 3–2 for the Glasgow Exhibition Trophy, Quinn scoring all three from the centre-forward position. Since then, he has gone from strength to strength, but the directors were still dubious when Maley put him in for the regular centre-forward Alec Bennett for the Cup final.

Celtic were in for an early shock at Hampden, when Speedie twice penetrated their defence to put Rangers two up. But they fought back furiously, and Quinn burst through to pull one back and then hit an unstoppable shot for the equalizer before half-time.

The younger Celts continued to press in the second half without being able to find the net. Then, with 10 minutes to go, the mighty Quinn — all 5ft 8in of him — broke away again. He scythed his way through the Rangers defence, brushing aside tackles from those redoubtable backs Smith and Drummond, to fire the ball past Watson for the clincher. It had been a wonderful match, and this was a goal worthy of winning any Cup final.

The 1904 Scottish Cup final at the new Hampden Park.

'Welsh Wizard' clinches it for City

OUTSIDE-RIGHT and captain of Manchester City, Billy Meredith, scored the only goal of the game against Bolton Wanderers in the first all-Lancashire Cup final. There was just a suspicion of offside as Meredith received the ball from his right-wing partner Livingstone, but the referee had no doubts. Meredith went on to round Bolton left-back Struthers before netting in the 23rd minute.

Manchester City, challenging leaders Wednesday for the League Championship, were only slight favourites against Second Division Bolton, who are renowned Cup fighters. They deserved their half-time lead, but Bolton pressed strongly for most of the second half, and would have improved their chances of victory had they shot more frequently and more effectively. On the other hand, Meredith, apart from scoring, did not live up to his glowing reputation as the finest winger in the land. Had he played to his usual brilliant form, City's win would surely have been more convincing.

Billy Meredith scores the winning goal in the FA Cup final at Crystal Palace.

FOOTBALL FOCUS

- Relegated Liverpool scored 49 goals in Division One, one more than Wednesday, champions for the second year in succession. Wednesday scored only 14 away goals to Liverpool's 25.
- Woolwich Arsenal won promotion from Division Two and will be the first southern side to play in the top division.
- Sheffield FC, founded in 1857 and the oldest club in existence, won their first major honour, the FA Amateur Cup, which itself was founded in 1893.
- The Scottish First Division was extended to 14 clubs, and Third Lanark won the title for the first time.
- The managers of the winners of the FA Cup and Scottish Cup are brothers, Tom Maley of Manchester City and Willie Maley of Celtic.
- A "world governing body" for football was formed on 21 May in Paris by representatives of Belgium, Denmark, France, Holland, Spain, Sweden and Switzerland. It is to be called the Fédération Internationale de Football Association.

FINAL SCORE

Football League
Division 1: Sheffield Wednesday
Top scorer: Steve Bloomer (Derby County) 20
Division 2: Preston North End

FA Cup Final
Manchester City 1 Bolton Wanderers 0

Scottish League
Division 1: Third Lanark
Division 2: Hamilton Academical

Scottish FA Cup Final
Celtic 3 Rangers 2

International Championship
England, 5 pts

Villa spoil Newcastle's 'double' dreams

NEWCASTLE'S visions of bringing off the Cup and League "double" were shattered by Aston Villa in the FA Cup final. The Villa, without a trophy to their name for five years, are nevertheless still a powerful side, as they soon demonstrated to Newcastle's discomfort at Crystal Palace. Spencer, Leake and Bache all played for England a fortnight ago, and in centre-forward Harry Hampton, six days from his 20th birthday, they have a brave, no-nonsense spearhead who has already built up a reputation for himself back in Birmingham, where he is more popular than local politician Joseph Chamberlain.

The Villa's brand new style of attacking football, in which the dynamic Hampton swings long balls out to the wings and then does the damage when they are returned, was soon in evidence. After only three minutes he gave them the lead, latching on to a loose ball after Newcastle failed to clear a cross from left-winger Hall, and rifling it inside the right-hand post. Villa dominated for most of the match, and Hampton clinched it when he pounced after Lawrence had dropped another cross from Hall. It was their fourth FA Cup win, only one short of the record held jointly by Backburn and Wanderers.

Harry Hampton (white shorts, centre) fires in Villa's first goal in the Cup final.

Newcastle make up for Cup defeat

NEWCASTLE'S victory at Middlesbrough on the last day of the season has earned them the Championship, their first major trophy. Overcoming the disappointment of losing to Aston Villa in the Cup final, they produced a powerful finish and have beaten Everton by a point.

Packed with Scottish talent, the "Geordies" have succeeded with the type of close-passing game favoured north of the border, built on triangular movements involving inside-forward, winger and wing-half. Their all-Scottish half-back line of Alex Gardner, Andy Aitken and Peter McWilliam has been the backbone of the side, while up front their centre-forward, bustling Bill Appleyard, and right-wing Jack Rutherford, already capped against Scotland at 20, have provided the punch.

A series of seven wins in eight games — their only defeat coming at Blackburn on 1 April, when they sportingly released five of their players for the England-Scotland international (four of them played, all Scots) — set them up for their exciting finish. But as they were losing to Villa in the Cup, Everton were winning their League match and going three points ahead of them and Manchester City. Newcastle had a game in hand, however; although they lost at home 3–1 to Sunderland, they ended up needing to win their last two matches, both away, to take the title.

The first match was at the Wednesday, the outgoing champions whom they had thrashed 6–2 earlier in the season. And despite finding themselves a goal down with only 10 minutes left, they bravely fought back, and goals from Orr, Howie and McWilliam gave them a precious 3–1 victory. Then came the 3–0 defeat of Middlesbrough at Ayresome Park — the match that earned Newcastle the title in style.

FOOTBALL FOCUS

- On 5 December, Woolwich Arsenal beat a visiting side of French "Internationals" 26–1.
- Wales's 3–1 victory at Wrexham was their first ever over the Scots. It was the 30th match between the two countries and Wales had conceded 120 goals.
- The first £1,000 transfer fee was paid by Middlesbrough to Sunderland for England international inside-right Alf Common in February.
- Everton were unlucky to finish as runners-up in the League. They lost at Arsenal 2–1 in their penultimate match, a replay of a game abandoned earlier in the season through fog, with just a few minutes to go. At the time they were leading 3–1.
- Rangers made a gallant effort to bring off the first ever Scottish Cup and League "double". They lost the Cup final after a replay, and then lost the League title in a play-off, after finishing level with Celtic on points. On the English system of goal average, Rangers would have been champions, with a goal record of 83-28 to Celtic's 68-31.

Alf Common — the subject of a record transfer.

FINAL SCORE

Football League
Division 1: Newcastle United
Top scorer: Arthur Brown (Sheffield United) 23
Division 2: Liverpool

FA Cup Final

Aston Villa	2	Newcastle United	0

Scottish League
Division 1: Celtic
Division 2: Clyde

Scottish FA Cup Final

Third Lanark	0	Rangers	0
Replay: Third Lanark	3	Rangers	1

International Championship
England, 5 pts

Promoted Liverpool win title

LIVERPOOL have won the League Championship for the second time, although it needed a season in Division Two to sharpen up their goalscoring. After their relegation in 1904, they set the Second Division alight last season with 93 goals, 60 of them at home, where they were unbeaten.

It is the first time that a promoted side have won the League title in the following year. Yet they made a poor start to their campaign, losing the first three games. Indeed, in their very first match, away to Arsenal, they not only went down 3–1, but they lost their speedy centre-forward Jack Parkinson with a broken wrist that kept him out of the game for several weeks. Although he did come back to score six goals in nine games, his injury enabled Liverpool to bring in Joe Hewitt, whose 22 League goals were an invaluable contribution.

Another success was goalkeeper Sam Hardy, bought from Chesterfield for £500, who replaced veteran Ted Doig early in the season. Still there from Liverpool's 1901 Championship team were left-back Billy Dunlop, centre-half Alec Raisbeck, outside-right Jack Cox and prolific centre-forward Alec Raybould.

It was not until late October that Liverpool asserted their authority, putting together nine wins and a draw in 10 matches. The only dropped point was at home to Preston, who in the end ran them closest for the title. But they won 2–1 at Deepdale at the end of March to give them some breathing space, and finished four points clear.

Liverpool's Parkinson breaks a wrist and sees his effort go wide of the Arsenal goal.

FINAL SCORE

Football League
Division 1: Liverpool
Top scorers: Bullet Jones (Birmingham City), Albert Shepherd (Bolton Wanderers) 26
Division 2: Bristol City

FA Cup Final
Everton 1 Newcastle United 0

Scottish League
Division 1: Celtic
Division 2: Leith Athletic

Scottish FA Cup Final
Hearts 1 Third Lanark 0

International Championship
England, Scotland, 4 pts

Raisbeck is the rock on which England's forwards founder

THE ENGLISH forwards found the commanding figure of centre-half Alec Raisbeck of Division One leaders Liverpool too much for them at Hampden Park, where they lost the international 2–1. Raisbeck, arguably the best centre-half in Britain, and his fellow "Anglo-Scots" Andy Aitken and Peter McWilliam, both of Newcastle, were dominant in the air. Scotland surely have never had such a fine half-back line.

Crowds began converging on Hampden Park for hours before the start, on foot, in cabs and trolleys and from scores of special trains from all around the country. It was the first official 100,000 gate for an international, and although the match was not a classic, the Scots were delighted to see their team dominate the "Saxon invaders" until a late England goal produced a misleading scoreline.

Scotland failed to press home their superiority until five minutes before the interval, when Jim Howie, another Newcastle exile, crashed a fierce shot at James Ashcroft. The Arsenal keeper held the ball, but the force of it spun him round, and the referee judged it to have crossed the line. Howie added another, in the second half, after a fine run by outside-left Alec Smith. England's consolation was scored with a low free-kick by centre-forward Albert Shepherd, the only time he escaped Raisbeck's attentions all afternoon.

The win produced only a share in the International Championship for Scotland, who had lost to Wales, but it deprived England of the outright title.

FOOTBALL FOCUS

- Last season Liverpool put six goals past Chesterfield keeper Sam Hardy in one match. Yet they bought him, and he won a Championship medal with them.

- Bristol City set two records when they won the Second Division title. Their 66 points is the highest total yet in either Division and they ran up 14 consecutive League wins.

- England joined the Fédération Internationale de Football Association (FIFA) in 1905, and the FIFA Congress of 1906 in Berne elected Daniel Burley Woolfall of the Football Association as their new president.

- The first international in South America took place, for the Lipton Cup, between Argentina and Uruguay, and was drawn.

Everton make it a Merseyside double

EVERTON BEAT Newcastle United in the FA Cup final to make sure that both of this season's major trophies go back to Liverpool. This is Everton's first Cup triumph, and they inflicted a second consecutive defeat in the final on poor Newcastle, this one by a single goal after 75 minutes scored by Sandy Young from a right-wing centre by Jack Sharp.

The Cup has been a harder grind this year, with the competition proper increased from five rounds to six (including the final). Everton won all their ties at the first attempt, including an exciting 4–3 win over Sheffield Wednesday in the quarter-finals and — the one that pleased their fans most — a 2–0 victory over neighbours and champions-elect Liverpool in the semi-finals.

The final itself was disappointing as a spectacle. Newcastle never played up to their known standards, with their much-vaunted half-back line of Gardner, Aitken and McWilliam having an off day. Everton deserved their win, but it was the case of the poorer side losing.

Arsenal go top

WOOLWICH Arsenal beat champions Liverpool 2–1 at Plumstead on 6 October to become the first southern club ever to top the First Division table. They were a goal down at half-time, but after the interval outside-left David Neave, who established his first-team place last season with seven goals in 18 games, opened his account for this term, scoring both of Arsenal's goals. Beaten only once so far this season, Arsenal now have 11 points out of a possible 14.

Twenty-two thousand fans and a dog see Arsenal beat Liverpool and go top of Division One.

Wales win the Championship

THE ENGLAND-SCOTLAND dominance of the International Championship has been ended at last. When Scotland held England to a 1–1 draw at St James's Park, Newcastle, on 6 April, it meant that Wales had won the Championship outright, for the first time, with five points to England's four.

The international season began on 16 February, when England beat Ireland 1–0 at Goodison Park. A week later Wales also beat Ireland, 3–2 in Belfast. Then, for the third season running, Wales beat Scotland, 1–0 at Wrexham on 4 March.

Two weeks later they held England to a 1–1 draw at Craven Cottage, Fulham, thanks to a goal by inside-forward William "Lot" Jones of Manchester City, who also had scored against the Irish, and were assured of at least a share in the Championship. But they had to wait until the England-Scotland match on 4 April before they knew that they were outright winners.

The inspiration of Wales has, as usual, been right-winger Billy Meredith, now with Manchester United after moving across town from City last May. In the England match, he was making his 25th appearance in the red shirt of Wales.

The International Championship has now been contested 24 times, with England winning it outright on 10 occasions to Scotland's nine and now one by the Welsh. There have been three titles shared by England and Scotland, and in 1902–03 there was a triple tie between the "Big Two" and Ireland.

FOOTBALL FOCUS

● The Football League season opened, on 1 September, in searing heat, over 90°F in most of the country. This did not appear to bother Chelsea, who beat Glossop 9–2, with George Hilsdon scoring five goals on his debut. Chelsea went on to win 18 of their 19 home games, losing only to Nottingham Forest and earning promotion to Division One for the first time.

● It hardly seemed worth the fare when Crystal Palace, languishing near the bottom of the Southern League, were drawn to play mighty Newcastle at St James's Park in the first round of the Cup. But they went up there and beat them 1–0.

● In winning the League title for the second time in three years, Newcastle dropped only one point at home. This was in their last home match, but the point they earned from their goalless draw with Sheffield United was enough to clinch the title.

● Celtic became the first club to do the Scottish League and Cup "double". They ran away with the Championship, their third consecutive title, finishing up seven points ahead of Dundee. They lost only twice and scored 80 goals in their 34 matches. They beat Rangers 3–0 at Ibrox in the quarter-finals of the Cup, but needed two replays in the semi-finals to get past Hibs, before beating Hearts in the final.

● Arsenal faded after their brief spell at the top of the League, finishing seventh, but only one point behind third-placed Everton. They toured Europe in May, playing eight games in 16 days and winning seven of them — including 9–1 in Berlin and 9–0 in Budapest.

FINAL SCORE

Football League
Division 1: Newcastle United
Top scorer: Alec Young (Everton) 30
Division 2: Nottingham Forest

FA Cup Final
Sheffield Wed 2 Everton 1

Scottish League
Division 1: Celtic
Division 2: St Bernard's

Scottish FA Cup Final
Celtic 3 Hearts 0

International Championship
Wales, 5 pts

Bristol's small wonder

ARSENAL MIGHT have topped the League briefly early on, but newly promoted Bristol City came with a late run in Division One, winning their last four games to finish up in second place, three points behind Newcastle and three in front of Everton. This is the highest position yet achieved by a southern club.

Bristol's remarkable progress in their first season in the top echelon has in no small part been due to their centre-half Billy "Fatty" Wedlock. Standing only 5ft 4½in, he nevertheless dominates the middle of the field with his skills, and his lack of inches does not seem to affect his heading prowess. He has boundless energy, roaming the pitch in support of his forwards, yet his powers of recovery enable him to get back to his defensive duties whenever necessary. The Bristol-born pivot fully deserved to win his first cap this season, and played in all three of England's internationals.

Bristol City were founded as recently as 1894, and joined the Football League only six years ago. Progress indeed!

Billy Wedlock, Bristol City.

Newcastle's Cup 'jinx' strikes again

THERE MUST BE a jinx on Newcastle in the FA Cup, beaten in the 1908 final for the third time in four years. It was almost gift-wrapped for them — four home draws and then a semi-final against Second Division Fulham, which they won 6–0. But they lost to Wolverhampton Wanderers, who finished only ninth in Division Two, in the final.

The Newcastle side was packed with internationals, from England, Scotland and Ireland. Wolves, on the other hand, were a team made up largely of unknowns. But somehow Wolves were able to impose their style of play — based on speed and strength — on their more illustrious opponents. Yet there was never any suggestion of "strong-arm" tactics. It might have been a different story had Newcastle taken their early chances. But Wolves delivered a double blow just before the interval, and never looked like losing after that. The first goal came from amateur international the Rev. Kenneth Hunt on 40 minutes, followed three minutes later by one from centre-forward George Hedley, twice a Cup-winner with Sheffield United and who played once for England in 1901.

Newcastle could not get their famous short-passing game going, although Scottish cap Jim Howie gave them a glimmer of hope when he scored with 17 minutes left. But Billy Harrison settled it for Wolves 12 minutes later, and six of the Newcastle side sadly went to collect their third runners-up medal. It must seem as though they will never win the Cup.

FOOTBALL FOCUS

- The British attendance record, 110,000 for the 1901 Cup final, was beaten when between 120,000 and 130,000 crammed into Hampden Park on 4 April to see the Scotland-England international. The result was a 1–1 draw.
- Manchester United continued to dominate Division One, running up 10 consecutive wins, making it 13 in the first 14 games, in which they scored 48 goals. They faltered in the second half of the season, but such was their lead that they won the title by nine points.
- All-conquering Celtic were outdone in just one department — goalscoring. Their 86 League goals were bettered by one club, Falkirk, whose 103 is the highest ever total in the Scottish League, and the first ever hundred.
- England played their first full international on foreign soil on 6 June 1908, beating Austria 6–1 in Vienna. Within a week, they repeated the dose — 11–1 this time — and beat Hungary 7–0 and Bohemia 4–0.

Wolves, shock Cup-winners when beating Newcastle at Crystal Palace.

FINAL SCORE

Football League
Division 1: Manchester United
Top scorer: Enoch West (Nottm Forest) 27
Division 2: Bradford City

FA Cup Final

Wolves	3	Newcastle United	1

Scottish League
Division 1: Celtic
Division 2: Raith Rovers

Scottish FA Cup Final

Celtic	5	St Mirren	1

International Championship
England, Scotland, 5 pts

Who can stop United now?

United captain Charlie Roberts.

MANCHESTER UNITED, in only their second season back in the top flight, have taken Division One by storm. Their extraordinary 6–1 win over champions Newcastle at St James's Park is their seventh in the eight games they have played, and they have already built up a commanding lead.

Credit for the 27 goals they have scored so far must go not only to the forwards, fired by wingmen Billy Meredith and George Wall, but also to the masterly half-back line of Dick Duckworth, Charlie Roberts and Alec Bell. Roberts, the captain, has been the inspiration of the side. Will he lead them to the title? It's early days yet, but it's difficult to see who will stop them.

Another double Scotch!

CELTIC, who brought off the first ever Scottish League and Cup "double" last year, have done it again. They clinched it at Ibrox Park, too, beating Rangers 1–0 to confirm the mastery they have exerted over their Glasgow rivals and, indeed, over the rest of Scotland. They still have two games to play, but no other club can catch them now.

Pity poor Rangers, beaten twice in the League by Celtic as well as in the second round of the Cup and in the final of the Glasgow Cup. Celtic, who also beat Queen's Park 3–0 in the final of the Charity Cup, won every tournament they entered. Their only defeats were at Aberdeen and Dundee in the League. In last week's Cup final, they romped to a 5–1 victory over an overawed St Mirren, who offered little resistance. Such is Celtic's form and consistency that it is difficult to see anyone mounting a challenge to their supremacy.

In the past five seasons they have won the Championship four times and the Scottish Cup three times.

Newcastle 1 Sunderland 9

YES, THE SCORELINE is correct. Believe it or not, England's top team — twice League champions and three times Cup-finalists in the last four years, and now challenging for the League title once more — have been beaten 9–1 at home by their neighbours.

There was no inkling that such a shock was in store at half-time, with the score at 1–1. But in the space of 28 second-half minutes, Sunderland hammered eight goals past the hapless Magpies, the last five coming in eight minutes. Newcastle were just stunned by the onslaught.

Sunderland have an excellent recent record at St James's Park, having won seven of their last 10 League games there. But nothing could have prepared even their wildest fans for the goal glut to come after the interval. Newcastle-born Billy Hogg added another three to his first-half goal, and George Holley also helped himself to three.

With Everton beating champions Manchester United to go further ahead in the table, it remains to be seen whether Newcastle can recover from this extraordinary setback and keep up their challenge for the League title.

George Holley, who scored a hat-trick for Sunderland.

FOOTBALL FOCUS

- The 1908 League champions Manchester United played Southern League winners Queen's Park Rangers for a new trophy in September, the Charity Shield, winning 4–0 after a 1–1 draw.

- Leicester Fosse, already doomed to relegation, lost 12–0 at Nottingham Forest on 21 April, a record score for Division One.

- Newcastle won the League despite their 9-1 home defeat by Sunderland. They won 10 out of their next 11 matches, and won at Roker Park, 3–0 in the fourth round of the Cup, after a 2–2 draw at St James's Park.

- After the trauma of the Cup final riots, Celtic found themselves needing six points from four games in five days to win the League. Thanks to a couple of hat-tricks from Jimmy Quinn, they achieved their fifth Championship on the trot, a Scottish record.

The United Kingdom team, with Hunt top left and Woodward seated centre.

England win Olympic soccer tournament

BEATING DENMARK 2–0 in the final at the White City Stadium, the United Kingdom, represented by an England side chosen by the Football Association, won the gold medals in the London Olympic Games. All the competitors in the tournament were, of course, amateurs, England's best-known players being their captain, the Tottenham and England inside-forward Vivian Woodward, and the Rev. Kenneth Hunt, who won an FA Cup medal with Wolves last season.

The six entrants to the competition included two teams from France. In the semi-finals, however, the French "A" side let in 17 goals, 10 of them scored by Sophus Nielsen. England, meanwhile, had accounted for Sweden 12–1, C.H.Purnell of Clapton scoring four, and Holland 4–0, all scored by Harry Stapley of Glossop. The final was a hard-fought match, with the Danes a little unlucky to lose to goals from centre-half F.W.Chapman (South Notts) and Woodward.

FINAL SCORE

Football League
Division 1: Newcastle United
Top scorer: Bert Freeman (Everton) 38
Division 2: Bolton Wanderers

FA Cup Final

Manchester United	1	Bristol City	0

Scottish League
Division 1: Celtic
Division 2: Abercorn

Scottish FA Cup Final

Rangers	2	Celtic	2
Replay: Rangers	1	Celtic	1

(Cup withheld)

International Championship
England, 6 pts

Whisky fuels fire of Hampden riot and rules out Celtic 'double'

THE 1909 SCOTTISH CUP has been withdrawn following the riot at Hampden Park after the replayed final between Celtic and Rangers. The action by the Scottish FA, readily agreed to by the clubs concerned, confirms the seriousness in which they regard the events, and puts paid to Celtic's chances of completing the Cup and League "double" for the third season running.

The trouble started when the replay was drawn after 90 minutes. Many of the players and most of the crowd expected extra time. But the rules had been laid down beforehand and could not be changed, extra time being possible only for a second replay.

Some of the crowd became unsettled and spilled on to the pitch. The police moved in, and the violence escalated into a full-blown riot, with fires started and an attempt to burn down the pay boxes using whisky as fuel. When the fire brigade arrived, they were attacked and their hoses cut. Hundreds of people were injured. Both clubs have shamefacedly agreed to help compensate Queen's Park for the extensive damage done to the ground.

The First Heroes

FOOTBALL is a team game, but right from the start it has produced its heroes, the men the crowd love to watch. There has always been more glamour attached to certain positions. The wingers and the goalscorers, as well as the tricky providers, are purveyors of the more spectacular skills. But the crowds appreciate the great defenders, too, the brave and the skilful, the men who get their side out of trouble when the going gets tough.

Amateur days

In the early days, there were the great amateurs. There was the Hon. A.F.Kinnaird, later an earl and president of the FA,

Lord Kinnaird, the "W.G.Grace" of football.

unmistakable with his red beard and long white trousers. He played in nine FA Cup finals, for the Wanderers and the Old Etonians, and earned five winners' medals. In those days when hacking was legal, he was a fearsome opponent. It is said that when Captain Marindin of Royal Engineers fame called on Kinnaird's mother, she expressed her fear that her son would come back one day from that horrid rough game with a broken leg. The reply was: "Don't worry, ma'am, it won't be his own."

Centre-forwards

John Goodall, perhaps the most brilliant of the Preston "Invincibles", played inside-right or centre-forward for England, and was one of the pioneers of scientific football in the country. Another outstanding centre-forward in the 1890s was G.O.Smith of Oxford University, Old Carthusians and the Corinthians. With a frail physique and gentle disposition, he did not look a footballer. But he had courage, a fine tactical brain, and was a lethal finisher. He gained 20 caps for England. Emulating Smith in the early 1900s was Vivian Woodward, also an amateur, with Spurs and Chelsea, who played for England in 23 full and 43 amateur internationals, winning two Olympic gold medals. Renowned for his sportsmanship, he was fast off the mark and scored 29 goals for England, 53 in amateur internationals.

The most prolific scorer of all was Steve Bloomer, an inside-forward famed for his quick thinking and first-time shooting. His career with Derby, Middlesbrough and Derby again lasted from 1892 to 1914, when he was 40. He scored 353 goals in 598 League appearances, and 28 in 23 matches for England. In many of those nineties internationals, he had G.O.Smith on one side of him and either William Bassett or Charlie Athersmith on the other.

John Goodall of Preston's "double"-winning side.

Wingmen

Bassett was the outside-right supreme, a little man (5ft 5½in) for the big occasion, whether playing for England or West Bromwich Albion. He sprang to fame as a young lad when West Brom beat Preston in the 1888 Cup final, and won an England cap on his showing. For a decade he was in a class of his own. He inspired West Brom to another Cup success in 1892, against Villa, after his legendary display in the third semi-final with Forest. That day, in a blinding snowstorm, Bassett was magnificent. All Albion's goals in their 6–2 victory came as a result of his crosses.

Yet there was another outside-right who would challenge

Billy Bassett, a little man for the big occasion.

Bassett in those days, another Billy, Meredith of Wales, whose career with the two Manchester clubs ran from 1894 to 1923. He played a record 48 times for Wales, his international career spanning 25 years. Patrolling the touchline and chewing the inevitable toothpick, he could score goals as well as make them, and helped both his clubs to major honours.

Scottish idol

Contemporary with Meredith, but a left-winger, was Scottish idol Alec Smith of Rangers, who won 20 international caps between 1898 and 1911. Taking the ball straight up to an opponent and then slipping round him at the last moment, he electrified the crowds with his dashes up the wing, and was a model of consistency. With Rangers, he won six Championship and four Cup-winners' medals, and was one of five Rangers men in Scotland's side that beat England 4–1 at Celtic Park in 1900.

Half-backs

Two half-backs also stand out from that match. Scotland's centre-half Alec Raisbeck was so often a thorn in England's side, a tower of strength for Liverpool as well as his country. He played the pivotal role to perfection, always thinking, moving around the field in defence and attack, perpetual motion personified.

Ernest "Nudger" Needham, England's left-half, was a polished performer, the "Prince of Half-backs". Never known to shirk a tackle, he was a key figure in Sheffield United's side from 1891 for 22 years, inspiring them to two Cup wins and a League title.

Villa men

The most successful English side of the 1890s and early 1900s were Aston Villa, with six League titles and five Cup wins before the Great War. Archie Hunter, captain and centre-forward who led them to the first of their Cup victories in 1887, was idolized by the Villa crowd. John Devey, another inside- or centre-forward, took over as skipper from Hunter and was a key figure in Villa's success. So was Scottish international Jimmy Cowan, their attacking centre-half who was fast enough to win the Powderhall Handicap. Even faster, though, was outside-right Charlie Athersmith, whose combination with inside partner Devey was devastating. The versatile Jimmy Crabtree played in every defensive position, but Villa rated him their best ever wing-half. Later, before the Great War, Joe Bache and Harry Hampton shot them to further honours. Centre-forward Hampton, lethal in front of goal, scored a club record 213 in the League, while Bache, a scheming inside-forward, was always among the goals.

Sunderland talents

When Villa weren't winning the League in the 1890s, it was usually Sunderland, the "Team of All the Talents", packed with Scottish footballers. They were much feared, and famed for their goals — from that powerhouse of a centre-forward John Campbell and tricky inside-right James Miller. But the dominant personality of their side was right-half Hugh Wilson. His anticipation in defence was legendary, his throw from the touchline unsurpassed, and his shot as deadly as any forward's.

Custodians

Prominent between the posts were those literally "great" keepers Billy "Fatty" Foulke and Albert Iremonger. Foulke, an enormous man, was 15 stone when he joined Sheffield United in 1894, and five more when he played for Chelsea and Bradford City over 10 years later. Yet despite his bulk, he was remarkably agile and one of the finest keepers of his era, winning major honours with Sheffield and playing once for England. Iremonger, capped for England in the early 1900s and a stalwart of Notts County, stood 6ft 6in, but had difficulty getting down to low balls. The safest of all was Sam Hardy, of Liverpool and Villa, capped 21 times for England over 14 years.

Hugh Wilson led Sunderland's "Team of All the Talents".

Combinations

With full-backs Bob Crompton and Jesse Pennington, Hardy formed a matchless defensive combination for England in the pre-war years. Crompton, of Blackburn Rovers, amassed 41 caps and was an influential skipper, a man of great presence and the accepted leader of English football from 1902 to the outbreak of war. Pennington, of West Bromwich, was the perfect complement, always covering, relying on skill rather than brawn.

Many players, like these, are remembered for their partnerships or combinations. Perhaps the most famous pre-war half-back combination was Duckworth-Roberts-Bell of the Manchester United League- and Cup-winning sides. The power of Dick Duckworth, thighs like tree-trunks, allied to the more delicate skills of Alec Bell on the left, flanked the commanding figure of the constructive Charlie Roberts in the middle. A dominating six-footer, Roberts was the most complete centre-half of his day, mixing power with perfect touch. His pioneering work with the Players' Union and his rebellious nature — his penchant for short shorts prompted the FA to rule in 1904 that "footballers' knickers must cover the knee" — did not perhaps endear him to the England selectors and he won only three caps.

Celtic stars

One of the outstanding attacking combinations was the Celtic inside-forward trio of Jimmy McMenemy, Jimmy Quinn and Peter Somers. Quinn, a charismatic character, the archetypal centre-forward, robust, courageous and a goalscorer supreme, was the idol of the Celtic crowd for years as he terrorized opposing defences, always, it seems, saving his best performances for the clashes with Rangers. McMenemy and Somers were perfect foils, subtle schemers, the former the "Napoleon" of the side, the latter a nimble conjurer. That whole Celtic side were stars, with six pre-war League wins on the trot and averaging a Cup win every other year.

"Fatty" Foulke towards the end of his career, flanked by Chelsea team-mates.

'Dirty' jibes as Newcastle break their Cup jinx

NEWCASTLE FINALLY buried their Cup jinx, beating Second Division Barnsley 2–0 in the replayed final at Goodison Park. But the manner of their victory left much to be desired, and there were unprecedented cries of "Dirty Newcastle" heard around the ground before the end of the match.

It seemed that certain Newcastle players came out on to the pitch determined to win at all costs. Early on, Alex Higgins floored the Barnsley keeper Mearns, who, when he recovered, had to be restrained by the referee and a team-mate as he chased after the culprit. Barnsley right-back Downs, limping from a foul in the first half, was laid out after the interval by a kick in the stomach and had to be carried off for treatment. The punishment was a mere free-kick, but even his Newcastle teammates showed their disapproval with the offender.

There is no denying that Newcastle had the better of the play, with their captain and right-half Colin Veitch outstanding in a goalless first half. They adapted better to the muddy, churned-up pitch than their lighter opponents, and went one up through centre-forward Albert Shepherd, who ploughed through the middle to finish off a move started by Veitch seven minutes after the interval. Barnsley missed a glorious chance to equalize and then gave away a penalty for a trip on Higgins. It was Shepherd's privilege to score from the first penalty ever conceded in an FA Cup final.

So Newcastle — albeit having sullied their hitherto fine reputation for fair play — have finally added the Cup to their three League titles.

Albert Shepherd, scorer of both Newcastle goals

FOOTBALL FOCUS

- Vivian Woodward became the first player to score double hat-tricks in two games, when he hit six goals for England in the amateur international against Holland at Stamford Bridge on 11 December. The famous Tottenham Hotspur centre-forward and Olympic gold-medallist had scored a phenomonal eight times against France three years earlier, also in an amateur international.
- Aston Villa won their sixth League title, their first for 10 years, finishing with a record-equalling 53 points, five points ahead of runners-up Liverpool.
- Ireland drew with England and then beat Scotland, but, with the Championship at their mercy for the first time, they went down 4–1 to Wales, giving Scotland their first outright win for eight years.

Vivian Woodward – goalscorer supreme.

West Auckland win World Cup

AMATEUR CLUB West Auckland Town from County Durham went to Italy and won the World Cup, a trophy put up by British tea merchant and famous yachtsman Sir Thomas Lipton.

Sir Thomas organized the tournament as a gesture of gratitude after being made a Knight of the Grand Order of Italy. The FA were not interested in sending an English team to compete, so Sir Thomas invited West Auckland, third from bottom of the Northern Amateur League, to represent England in Turin.

This rugged, gritty team of miners have done England proud. And what personal sacrifices they made to finance their trip! With little money in the club's coffers, they were forced to sell furniture and other personal belongings, as well as losing wages in the pit.

But it was all worthwhile in the end. They beat the best that Europe could produce, including Red Star Zurich and Stuttgart, before conquering the hosts, Juventus, 2–0 in the final.

The next season, this gallant team of part-timers went back to Italy and successfully defended their title. They again beat Juventus in the final to win the magnificent silver trophy outright.

A new name on the Scottish Cup

DUNDEE HAVE WON the Scottish Cup for the first time, beating Clyde 2–1 at Ibrox Park in the second replay of the final.

What a remarkable Cup campaign Dundee have fought. After two goalless draws in their semi-final against Hibs, they won the second replay 1–0 to reach their first final. And they looked dead and buried 11 days ago against Clyde, when they were 2–0 down with only seven minutes to go. But goals by John Hunter and Johnny Langland earned them a replay, which ended in another goalless draw.

FINAL SCORE

Football League
Division 1: Aston Villa
Top scorer: John Parkinson (Liverpool) 29
Division 2: Manchester City

FA Cup Final

Newcastle United	1	Barnsley	1
Replay: Newcastle United	2	Barnsley	0

Scottish League
Division 1: Celtic
Division 2: Leith Athletic

Scottish FA Cup Final

Dundee	2	Clyde	2
Replay: Dundee	0	Clyde	0
Replay: Dundee	2	Clyde	1

International Championship
Scotland, 4 pts

New Cup stays in Bradford

THE NEW TROPHY for the FA Cup was made in Bradford, and after the replayed Cup final at Old Trafford it is staying there. Bradford City beat Newcastle 1–0 to win their first major honour.

For Newcastle United it is the same old story. They reached the Cup final for the fifth time in seven years, a truly remarkable feat in itself. They were again unable to win at Crystal Palace, and after a poor match there, in which they sorely missed last year's scoring hero Albert Shepherd, it was expected that their scientific play and individual skills would prevail against the rugged Bradford defence in the replay.

In the event, however, it was the resolute Bradford rearguard that prevailed. Bolstered at centre-half by the outstanding Torrance, who had missed the first match, Bradford enjoyed another fine performance from full-backs Campbell and Taylor. A bad goalkeeping error by Lawrence, who had played in all his club's five finals, allowed Scottish international inside-forward Jimmy Speirs the chance to score a simple goal after 15 minutes, and Newcastle could find no answer.

Speirs scores the winning goal for Bradford City.

FOOTBALL FOCUS

● Newcastle did not hold on to the FA Cup for long last year. The FA presented the trophy to Lord Kinnaird to mark his 21st year as president, and commissioned a new design for this season because the old one had been pirated for a minor competition in Manchester.

● Twelve Scots played in this year's FA Cup final, eight of them for the winners, Bradford City. The attendance for the replay at Old Trafford was a midweek record 66,646.

FINAL SCORE

Football League
Division 1: Manchester United
Top scorer: Albert Shepherd (Newcastle United) 25
Division 2: West Bromwich Albion

FA Cup Final

Bradford City	0	Newcastle United	0
Replay: Bradford City	1	Newcastle United	0

Scottish League
Division 1: Rangers
Division 2: Dumbarton

Scottish FA Cup Final

Celtic	0	Hamilton Acad	0
Replay: Celtic	2	Hamilton Acad	0

International Championship
England, 5 pts

Dramatic finish to title race

THREE DAYS after Bradford City won the Cup at Manchester United's new home, Old Trafford, the ground was the scene of a great United victory, 5–1 over Sunderland, which gave them their second League title in four years. Again they won with 52 points, and again it was Aston Villa who were runners-up, but this time by only one point instead of nine.

Manchester made a wonderful start to the season, with seven wins in their first eight matches. But it looked all over for them when Villa edged in front on goal average last Saturday by beating the Reds 4–2 at Villa Park in a bad-tempered match in which a player from each side was sent off in the closing minutes. Villa had a game in hand, but could only draw at Blackburn on Monday, setting up the last day for a dramatic finish. They crashed 3–1 to Liverpool at Anfield, and Manchester's resounding defeat of third-placed Sunderland won the day.

United have triumphed with largely the same team that won the League in 1908 and the Cup a year later. New signing Enoch West led the scorers with 19 goals, although Alec Turnbull still made a valuable contribution with 18. Charlie Roberts was again an inspiring captain, and the incomparable Billy Meredith was still chewing his toothpick and teasing full-backs on the right wing.

Manchester United with the League Championship trophy, won for the second time in four years.

New order over the border

CELTIC'S SUPREME reign in Scotland has finally come to a close. Admittedly they won the Cup — after a stuttering campaign — but fifth place in the League after winning it six times on the trot is evidence of a dramatic decline. Their defence has not been the problem — 18 goals conceded is better than in any of those six Championship years. But their goalscoring has fallen from a peak of 86 in 1907–08 to a dismal 48 this season.

Despite home draws in every round, Celtic struggled to reach the semi-finals of the Cup, particularly in the second round, when they scraped past non-League Galston 1–0. They beat Aberdeen by the same score in the semi-finals, and they needed a replay before they beat lowly Hamilton 2–1 in the final.

Rangers have taken full advantage of their rivals' fall from grace in the League, emerging four points clear of Aberdeen in the title race.

Battling Barnsley show Yorkshire grit

BARNSLEY played six goalless games in an extraordinary Cup campaign that saw them reach the final for the second time in three years, a record for a Second Division club. This time they emerged victorious, beating West Bromwich 1–0 after extra time in the Cup final replay.

Their saga is a story of attrition rather than glamour, their triumph down to stamina and heroic defending. They played 12 matches, of which three went to extra time, and conceded only four goals. The first final was a dull affair for the spectators, with brilliant defence dominating. The speed and tackling of Barnsley's, with right-back Dicky Downs in his element, smothered Albion's attacks before they got too near goal. And despite Barnsley's poor attack, it was the Albion's goal that had the luckier escapes.

Both sides performed better in the replay, with Barnsley's wing-halves Glendinning and Utley to the fore. But the match seemed to be heading the same way, when Barnsley suddenly broke away with two minutes of extra time to go. Utley broke up an Albion attack on the left before hitting a cross-field pass to inside-right Harry Tufnell, standing on the half-way line. Showing remarkable stamina after two hours of solid effort, the Barnsley forward made for the Albion goal, swerving past the formidable challenge of England left-back Jesse Pennington and taking the ball on another 30 yards before shooting past the advancing keeper. It was a glorious goal to win the match and, for Barnsley, a fitting climax to an epic Cup journey.

Harry Tufnell — scored a solo winner for Barnsley.

FOOTBALL FOCUS

- In the first round of the FA Cup, Wolves were held to a 0–0 draw at Watford and won the replay 10–0.
- After a third drawn Cup final in a row, the FA determined that extra time would in future be played in the first match if level after 90 minutes.
- Rangers retained the Scottish League title, finishing six points clear of Celtic, who retained the Cup.
- Blackburn Rovers, five times Cup-winners, won their first League title, beating runners-up Everton by three points. Their total of 49 points is the lowest since Division One was increased to 20 teams in 1905.
- In a consolation tournament staged for teams eliminated in the first two rounds of the Olympic football tournament, Germany beat Russia 16–0.

FINAL SCORE

Football League
Division 1: Blackburn Rovers
Top scorers: Harry Hampton (Aston Villa), George Holley (Sunderland), Dave McLean (Sheffield Wednesday) 25
Division 2: Derby County

FA Cup Final

Barnsley	0	WBA	0
Replay: Barnsley	1	WBA	0

(after extra time)

Scottish League
Division 1: Rangers
Division 2: Ayr United

Scottish FA Cup Final

Celtic	2	Clyde	0

International Championship
England, Scotland 5 pts

Danish keeper Hansen in action against England in Stockholm.

Another Olympic triumph for England

ENGLAND represented the United Kingdom again and retained their Olympic title in Stockholm. And again it was Denmark who provided the strongest opposition, but England beat them more convincingly in the final this time, by four goals to two. The tournament took place between 29 June and 5 July, and it was so hot that buckets of water were placed by the touchlines so that players could refresh themselves during the game.

Out of 14 original entrants, all from Europe, France and Belgium were late withdrawals and Bohemia could not be accepted because they were not members of FIFA. Six of the 11 teams had to play a preliminary round, and then in the first round proper both England and Denmark enjoyed 7–0 victories, Harold Walden scoring five of England's goals against the Hungarians.

England coasted through their semi-final against Finland, winning 4–0 and ostentatiously hitting a penalty over the cross-bar when they considered the award too harsh. Denmark also scored four in their semi-final, while conceding a single goal to Holland, who gave them a good match.

England gained a well-deserved win in the final, although Denmark were unlucky to lose Buchwald owing to a sprained wrist with the score 2–1. England went in at half-time with a 4–1 lead. The Danes, with Nils Middleboe moving from defence to centre-forward, pressed hard in the second half, scoring again, but never managed a serious threat to England's supremacy.

Battle of the giants ends level

THE BATTLE of the giants has ended with honours even. Sunderland, a week after losing to Aston Villa in the Cup final, have beaten Bolton 3–1 to clinch the League Championship. Three days ago they went to Villa Park and earned a brave draw that put paid to Villa's title hopes. The Wednesday were still in with a chance, but now they have lost 3–1 at Everton the title is Sunderland's, whatever happens in the last games next week.

What a battle it has been, with two teams both going for the League and Cup "double". Sunderland's League campaign has been quite extraordinary. They failed to win any of their first seven matches, managing only two draws and conceding 18 goals. A dip into the transfer market in October to bolster their defence transformed their season. Joe Butler, a reliable keeper from Glossop, and Charlie Gladwin, an inspirational right-back from Blackpool, shored up the holes at the back and enabled the right-wing "triangle" of Frank Cuggy (right-half), Charlie Buchan (inside-right) and Jackie Mordue (outside-right) to weave their intricate attacking patterns.

Sunderland stormed up the table with five straight wins. They lost a couple of away games, but they beat Villa 3–1 and Liverpool 7–0, with Buchan scoring five times. In 17 matches from 28 December, they have lost on only one occasion.

In the Cup, meanwhile, Villa charged through to the semi-finals with three 5–0 victories. Sunderland's progress was hardly less impressive, although they needed two replays to dispose of Newcastle in the quarter-finals. They also needed a replay in the semi-finals before beating Burnley 3–2, while Villa reached the final with a 1-0 victory over Oldham.

The final drew a record crowd of 120,081 to see a battle royal between the two Championship challengers. It was a thrilling, if bruising, match. A series of clashes between Villa centre-forward Harry Hampton and Sunderland centre-half Charlie Thomson could have had them both sent off. (Indeed, they and referee A. Adams were all suspended for a month by the FA, the players for their behaviour and the official for his leniency.)

Early on Villa were awarded a penalty — only the second in the history of the Cup final — but Charlie Wallace shot wide. Defences got on top, but when Villa keeper Sam Hardy had to go off for 20 minutes in the second half with an injury, Sunderland failed to capitalize on their chances. With Villa centre-half Jim Harrop wearing the keeper's jersey, Sunderland peppered away at goal and twice hit the upright. Hardy returned, and with 15 minutes to go, Wallace sent a corner-kick to the edge of the penalty box. Right-half Tom Barber met it with his head, and the Sunderland defence watched spellbound as the ball rolled into the corner of the net.

That was the only score, so Villa won the Cup for the fifth time, equalling the record of the Wanderers and Blackburn Rovers. But they could not emulate their own feat of League and Cup "double", achieved back in 1896-97, as the other "giants" Sunderland have gone on to win the battle for the League.

Butler (Sunderland) foils Villa's Hampton in the Cup final.

FOOTBALL FOCUS

- Despite England's disastrous start, losing to Ireland, they beat Wales and Scotland to win the International Championship.
- Sunderland won the League Championship with a record number of points, 54, after gleaning only two from their first seven games.
- Rangers completed a hat-trick of League titles in Scotland, but there was a new name on the Scottish Cup, Falkirk. Neither they nor runners-up Raith Rovers had reached the final before.
- Morton of the Scottish Division One created a curious record — every player who appeared for them in the League scored, even the keeper, who converted a penalty kick.

Ten Irish heroes

ENGLAND LOST to Ireland for the first time in an international, going down 2–1 in Belfast. The England side, described as "the greatest ever sent across the Irish Sea", was full of stars. Sunderland's Charlie Buchan, making his England debut, headed them in front after 10 minutes. And when, shortly afterwards, Ireland lost inside-left James McAuley of Huddersfield with a knee injury, only one result seemed possible.

But the 10 Irish heroes fought like tigers, and Sheffield United centre-forward Billy Gillespie scored twice with shots deflected by English defenders.

About three minutes from time, the referee blew for a free-kick to Ireland. The crowd, thinking it was the final whistle, surged on to the field and carried their heroes off shoulder-high. There was no way that the referee was going to get the game restarted in those circumstances, and the amazing result stood.

FINAL SCORE

Football League
Division 1: Sunderland
Top scorer: David McLean (Sheffield Wednesday) 30
Division 2: Preston North End

FA Cup Final

Aston Villa	1	Sunderland	0

Scottish League
Division 1: Rangers
Division 2: Ayr United

Scottish FA Cup Final

Falkirk	2	Raith Rovers	0

International Championship
England, 4 pts

A great day for the Irish

IRELAND have won the International Championship outright for the first time in their history. A draw with Scotland in Belfast was enough to secure them the title with five points. When before has the Championship been decided by mid-March?

But you have to go back a couple of months, to Wrexham in January, for the start of this epic story. Before a goal was scored, Ireland lost Everton's Harris with a torn ligament, but they took charge of the game and beat Wales 2–1.

In February, Ireland confounded the critics again and won for the first time on English soil, 3–0 at Middlesbrough. They outplayed England, and a magnificent goal from Gillespie, sandwiched between two from Lacey, did not exaggerate their superiority.

The stage was set for the showdown with Scotland on 14 March. A record Irish crowd of 26,000 turned out in appalling weather to watch their heroes. Yet again the Irish side, without the forceful Gillespie, were soon affected by injury, and once more they showed the greatest fighting spirit in the face of desperate odds. First, centre-half O'Connell had to leave the field with an arm injury. Then right-back McConnell was carried off. Worse was to follow. Goalkeeper McKee, hurt in a collision, carried on until just after the interval, when he could no longer continue. So into goal went the injured McConnell!

With O'Connell back in the fray, the nine-and-a-half Irish warriors held out against the rampaging Scots until 20 minutes from time, when makeshift keeper McConnell inadvisedly left his charge and Donnachie found the unguarded net. That should have been the end, but you cannot write off these remarkable Irishmen. Centre-forward Young grabbed an equalizer eight minutes from time and, with the crowd swarming on the touchlines, they held out for the draw that gave them a richly-deserved Championship.

Celtic back with a 'double'

THEY LAUGHED at the little waif when he first took the field at Parkhead. But the jeers changed to cheers as soon as small, fragile-looking Patsy Gallagher touched the ball. The control, intelligence, skills and toughness of this seven-stone "mighty atom" made him an instant hero. And now, in his third season with Celtic, he has revitalized the forward line and finished as top scorer, with 21 goals in the League.

It needed a replay before Hibs were convincingly conquered in the Cup final. Celtic then finished their League programme six points ahead of Rangers, with 81 goals scored and only 14 conceded in their 38 matches. It is their third League and Cup "double", and they are still the only Scottish side to have achieved the feat.

FOOTBALL FOCUS

- Preston have changed divisions again — relegated from Division One in 1912, promoted in 1913, they have now gone straight down again to Division Two.
- Playing for Stockport against Fulham on 4 October, Norman Wood headed an own goal, gave away a penalty for hands from which the visitors scored, and then missed a penalty. Stockport lost 3–1.

King at Palace for Cup final

KING GEORGE V became the first reigning monarch to see the Cup final, when he presented the trophy at the Crystal Palace to the winning captain, Burnley's centre-half Tommy Boyle. It was a great occasion for football, if not a great match. For the fourth consecutive season, the result was 1–0, although the last two finals have not needed a replay.

Neither Burnley nor Liverpool had enjoyed a particularly distinguished season in the League, and the first half bore witness to their lowly positions in the table. The goal, a fierce shot by England international centre-forward Freeman after 58 minutes, changed the mood of the game, however, and the King, along with the 72,000 spectators at this last final at the Crystal Palace, was treated to a lively last half-hour in which Liverpool strove vainly for an equalizer.

Burnley goalkeeper Sewell, deputizing for injured regular Dawson, made some vital saves — one, when the ball hit him in the face, completely by accident.

The captains are presented to the King.

FINAL SCORE

Football League
Division 1: Blackburn Rovers
Top scorer: George Elliott (Middlesbrough) 31
Division 2: Notts County

FA Cup Final

Burnley	1	Liverpool	0

Scottish League
Division 1: Celtic
Division 2: Cowdenbeath

Scottish FA Cup Final

Celtic	0	Hibernian	0
Replay: Celtic	4	Hibernian	1

International Championship
Ireland, 5 pts

Freeman's shot beats Liverpool keeper Campbell for the only goal of the game.

A change of uniform

Buchan in Sunderland strip and (right) Grenadier Guards uniform.

THE DECISION to continue with the League and Cup programme while the country was engaged in war had been a controversial one. Both the English and Scottish authorities were motivated by the desire to provide "an antidote to the war", and in August, when Britain declared war on Germany, few people expected hostilities to last more than a few months, anyway.

But as the war dragged on, and news came back of terrible casualties at the front, the football authorities began to view the situation with growing concern. The season was allowed to finish, although the fixtures played out with little enthusiasm. It was understandably difficult for the players to concentrate on football when their fellow men were fighting — and dying — in the trenches. As soon as the season was over, there was a rush to change their football strip for uniforms of the armed forces.

FOOTBALL FOCUS

● The result of Oldham's game at Middlesbrough, abandoned by the referee with the score 4–1 against them, was allowed to stand. Billy Cook, the player who refused to leave the field when sent off, was suspended for a year. Oldham, severely reprimanded and fined £350, finished runners-up to champions Everton, just a point behind. The title had been theirs for the taking, but they lost their last two matches, both at home.

● A debate in Parliament about shells failing to explode in battle — the implication being that munitions workers had possibly not been concentrating on their work — led to an FA decree that no games were to be played near munitions factories during working hours. As a result, the second-round Cup replay at Lincoln between Bradford City and Norwich was played behind closed doors.

● There was a three-way tie in Scotland's Division Two, necessitating three play-off matches. Cowdenbeath won both theirs to finish top, with Leith second and St Bernard's third. But none of them won promotion, as only the top division played during the war.

● League champions Everton owed their success largely to their results away from home, where they won 11 times and conceded just 18 goals in 19 games. Only bottom club Spurs won fewer than Everton's eight at home. Everton's winning total, 46 points, was the lowest since the First Division was increased to 20 clubs, and only six points separated them from West Bromwich Albion in 11th place.

The man who wouldn't go

IN AN UNPRECEDENTED incident at Middlesbrough on Easter Monday, Oldham's left-back Billy Cook refused to go when ordered off by the referee. So the referee himself left the field, and the match ended half an hour early.

Oldham had arrived at Ayresome Park full of confidence. They were challenging for the First Division title, in fourth position but only two points behind leaders Manchester City. But as the game progressed, their frustration built up. Not only did they find themselves three down in 20 minutes, but they felt aggrieved at some of the decisions that were going against them, including a penalty appeal that had been turned down.

Then, 10 minutes after the interval, the referee gave Middlesbrough a penalty for a Cook foul on Carr. Tinsley scored from the spot to complete his hat-trick. Shortly afterwards, Cook again fouled Carr and the referee stopped the game and sent him off — or at least he tried to. The Oldham left-back seemed reluctant to go, and his team-mates crowded round the referee. The harassed official, Mr H.Smith of Nottingham, then gave Cook a minute to leave the field. When he still stood his ground, Mr Smith, after looking at his watch, walked off, with the players of both sides following. The spectators could hardly believe their eyes.

The Khaki Cup final

WITH THE WAR in progress since August, the Cup final was a very low-key affair. It was held at Old Trafford in wet, gloomy conditions, with thousands of servicemen in uniform among the near 50,000 crowd, many of them bearing signs of injuries sustained at the front.

The outcome was an easy 3–0 win for Sheffield United over a Chelsea side whose forwards never managed to reproduce the form that got them to the final. Chelsea's defence, on the other hand, had nothing to reproach themselves for, and held their opponents to a single goal until seven minutes from the end. For Sheffield, their captain and left-half George Utley was outstanding, just as he was for Barnsley three years ago.

In a poignant speech to the crowd after presenting the trophy and medals to the players, Lord Derby said that the clubs and their supporters had "seen the Cup played for, and it was now the duty of everyone to join with each other and play a sterner game for England".

FINAL SCORE

Football League
Division 1: Everton
Top scorer: Bobby Parker (Everton) 35
Division 2: Derby County

FA Cup Final
Sheffield United 3 Chelsea 0

Scottish League
Division 1: Celtic
Division 2: Cowdenbeath

Scottish FA Cup
No competition

International Championship
No competition

The Great War (1914–18)

BRITAIN entered what has become known as the Great War on 4 August 1914, when Germany invaded Belgium. Britain sent forces to help stop the German advance across France, and few thought that they would not return before Christmas. But by 1915 the opposing sides had dug themselves into a system of trenches that zigzagged along the Western Front, a battlefield extending some 450 miles across Belgium and North-eastern France to the border of Switzerland. They remained deadlocked in this trench warfare until 1918.

Aiding the war effort

At the beginning of the war, there was no conscription. But the continuation of the football programme caused a great deal of controversy. Criticism was vociferous and widespread. Clubs were accused of helping the enemy, and the Dean of Lincoln wrote to the FA of "onlookers who, while so many of their fellow men are giving themselves in their country's peril, still go gazing at football".

But the FA had consulted the War Office before taking its decision to stage the 1914–15 Cup. And while many players quit their clubs to volunteer for the armed forces, the League, too, decided to carry on with their programme. The football authorities contributed to war charities, and more importantly assisted in the recruitment of volunteers — some half a million, it was claimed, by early 1915.

As the war took a grip in 1915, more players began to enlist, and gates dwindled. In July, it was decided to cancel the regular League and Cup programmes, and replace them with regional leagues. The players would not be paid, and nor would there be any medals or trophies. No internationals would be played, either. Matches were to be scheduled only for Saturdays and holidays, so there would be no midweek games to interfere with work in the munitions factories. In Scotland, although the Cup was cancelled, the First Division of the League continued. But players were not allowed to make a full-time living from the game, being paid a maximum of £2 a week. And players not in the forces were required to work in a war-related industry.

Sam Hardy kept for Forest during the war.

'Match-fixing'

Allegations of "match-fixing" that first surfaced in the Manchester area near the end of the 1914–15 season, and had been published in the *Sporting Chronicle* on 24 April, developed into a full-blown scandal during the year. The accusations, first printed on a handbill issued by a firm of bookmakers, were that a Manchester match at Easter had been squared for the home club to win by a particular score. There were only two matches this could apply to, and the *Sporting Chronicle* demanded a Football League inquiry.

The Football League did indeed set up a committee to look into these serious allegations, but it was Christmas before they delivered their final report. The verdict caused a sensation. Manchester United's match against Liverpool at Easter turned out to be the fixture under investigation, and it transpired that considerable wagers had been struck in the area at odds of 7–1 that United would win 2–0. Eight players, four from each side, were found guilty of conspiring to fix the match and were suspended from football for life. But, perhaps because there were more important things going on in the world, the result was allowed to stand.

The Liverpool players involved were Tom Fairfoul, Tommy Miller, Bob Purcell and Jackie Sheldon, a former Manchester United player who acted as the go-between. Of the four United players, three — Laurence Cook, Sandy Turnbull and Arthur Whalley — did not play in the match in question. The fourth was Enoch "Knocker" West, who was the only player not to have the ban lifted after the war.

FOOTBALL FOCUS

- Steve Bloomer, England's most prolific pre-war goalscorer, retired in 1914 and took up a job coaching in Germany, where he was interned for the whole of the war. With other British footballers at the Ruhleben camp, he set up an "association" and they played league matches every day on a nearby racecourse for the duration of the war.

- With midweek matches banned, clubs in Scotland were occasionally called upon to play two matches in one day. On 15 April 1915, Celtic beat Raith 6–0 at home in the afternoon, while Motherwell lost 3–0 to Ayr, also at home. Then, in the evening, Celtic went to Motherwell and beat them 3–1.

- In unofficial "Victory" internationals at the end of the 1918–19 season, England and Scotland drew 2–2 at Goodison Park and England won 4–3 at Hampden Park.

Celtic supreme

Glasgow Celtic's remarkable unbeaten run that stretched over 17 months and 62 matches finally came to an end on 21 April 1917 when they lost 2–0 at home to Kilmarnock in the last game of the 1916–17 season. For their last defeat — also 2–0 — you have to go back to 13 November 1915, when they lost at Hearts.

Celtic's almost complete domination of Scottish football during the war led to rumours and suggestions that the club's war effort was not all it should be. But the club and players made their contributions in many and various ways, just like other clubs. Players served in the forces, worked in the factories and shipyards, and down the mines. The club made half-time appeals for more volunteers to the forces, made their ground available for recruiting rallies and fund-raising events, sent footballs to recruits in training and to the soldiers at the front, and did whatever they could to help wounded soldiers back in hospital and prisoners-of-war in Germany.

In the 1917–18 season, Rangers controversially broke Celtic's supremacy, winning the League title by a single point in a struggle that went to the last day

Steve Bloomer was interned in Germany throughout the war.

of the season. But they were heavily criticized for the manner in which they went about doing it. During the war, "temporary transfers" were permitted in which players were allowed to turn out for other clubs at short notice as they found themselves in different locations on account of their war service. Rangers, it seemed, took undue advantage of this to gather in star players stationed in Scotland to replace their own missing men. The *Glasgow Observer* in particular was scathing in its reference to the "conglomeration of Queen's Park, Oldham Athletic, Hearts, Hibernian, Clyde, Dumbarton, Raith Rovers, Dundee, Morton and Sheffield Wednesday" players that masqueraded in Rangers' colours during this title-winning season.

The great rivalry between the two Glasgow clubs was becoming even more intense, and in the 1918–19 season, which began before the end of the war, Celtic sprang back to the top in what was another two-horse race. Five points behind at the turn of the year, they gradually eroded Rangers' lead and finished with a run of 20 matches unbeaten to pip them by a point.

The 'Championship'

In both 1918 and 1919 there were two-legged play-offs between the Lancashire and Midland Regional winners for the "League Championship", with gate receipts going to the National Footballers' War Fund. Leeds City (Midlands winners) won the 1917–18 Championship cup, beating "Lancashire" winners Stoke 2–0 at home and holding them to a single goal in the return.

In the following year's play-offs, Nottingham Forest were held at home by Everton to a goalless draw, but went to Goodison and beat the Lancashire champions 1–0 in the return. In goal for Forest was England and Aston Villa keeper Sam Hardy, who guested for them during the war.

FINAL SCORE

Scottish League Champions

1915–16	Celtic
1916–17	Celtic
1917–18	Rangers
1918–19	Celtic

Wartime League Championship

1917–18	Leeds City
1918–19	Nottingham Forest

Lancashire Regional Tournament

1915–16	Manchester City
1916–17	Liverpool
1917–18	Stoke City
1918–19	Everton

Midland Regional Tournament

1915–16	Nottingham Forest
1916–17	Leeds City
1917–18	Leeds City
1918–19	Nottingham Forest

London Combination

1915–16	Chelsea
1916–17	West Ham United
1917–18	Chelsea
1918–19	Brentford

Aftermaths

Football took a time to find its feet again when hostilities were finally over in November 1918. Many clubs needed reorganization, and grounds needed repair.

There was a move by the clubs of the Football League to renew the FA Challenge Cup for the 1918–19 season on a modified scale. Their suggestion was to dispense with the qualifying competition, in which hundreds of clubs usually took part, and restrict entry to just 64 clubs — the 40 in Divisions One and Two together with 20 members of the Southern League and another four selected clubs. But the FA decided against it, on the grounds that it would be unfair to the vast body of their membership.

"Knocker" West, banned for match-fixing.

'We wuz robbed'

SPURS felt they had cause for grievance when they found themselves in the Second Division at the restart of the Football League after the war. Admittedly, they had finished bottom of the First Division in 1914–15, the last season before hostilities stopped play. But the League has been augmented by two extra teams in each division. The last time that happened, in 1905, no teams were relegated. But this time there was a certain amount of activity behind the scenes.

The result was that Derby and Preston, first and second in Division Two, were promoted as expected, and Chelsea, second from bottom in Division One, were re-elected (the match-fixing scandal in which Manchester United players were involved saw to that). But Spurs were replaced by their new North London neighbours Arsenal, who had finished only fifth in Division Two. Arsenal chairman Sir Henry Norris might have used his influence to ensure an election for the remaining Division One place, for which seven clubs put their names forward, but the voting went Arsenal 18, Spurs eight, with the other five clubs sharing the remaining 15 votes.

England hand it to Wales

ENGLAND came back from 4–2 down at half-time to beat Scotland 5–4 at Hillsborough, but in doing so they handed the International Championship to Wales, who beat them 2–1 at Highbury last month. Nevertheless, this remarkable victory over Scotland was reward in itself, gained as it was in one of the finest and most thrilling matches in this long series of internationals.

The match was played at hectic pace in driving rain. The England heroes were two new caps who scored the second-half goals, Bob Kelly (Burnley) two and Fred Morris (West Brom) one, all in the space of seven minutes midway through the half.

FOOTBALL FOCUS

- With 42 matches instead of 38, it was not surprising that the points records for both divisions were broken this season, West Bromwich winning the League title with 60 and Spurs the Second Division with a massive 70. Both scored over 100 goals, and West Brom's 104 is a record for the top division.
- In the newly expanded Scottish League, Rangers accumulated a record 71 points from their 42 games, and scored 106 goals. Celtic had to take a back seat this time with "only" 68 points. There was no Division Two.
- There was a new name on the Scottish Cup, Kilmarnock. The runners-up were even more surprising — Albion Rovers, who finished bottom of the League but had the audacity to beat Rangers in the semi-finals after two replays.
- Semi-final winners Shelbourne won the Irish Cup by default. In the other semi-final, both teams were disqualified, Belfast Celtic being blamed for the disruption when shots were fired in the crowd, and Glentoran for fielding an ineligible player.

FINAL SCORE

Football League
Division 1: West Bromwich Albion
Top scorer: Fred Morris (WBA) 37
Division 2: Tottenham Hotspur

FA Cup Final
Aston Villa 1 Huddersfield Town 0
(after extra time)

Scottish League
Division 1: Rangers
Top scorer: Hugh Ferguson (Motherwell) 33

Scottish FA Cup Final
Kilmarnock 3 Albion Rovers 2

International Championship
Wales, 4 pts

Bargain buy hits Cup-winner in extra time

THE ROMANCE of the Cup is back with us. At its new venue, Stamford Bridge, the final went to extra time before Aston Villa beat Huddersfield 1–0 with a goal scored by inside-right Bill Kirton, a converted full-back whom Villa had picked up for £250 when the Leeds City players were auctioned earlier in the season.

So Villa win the Cup for a record sixth time. In the final they had much the better of the play. But when the goal came after 10 minutes of the first period of extra time, there was a touch of luck about it. As the heads went up for a corner from outside-left Dorrell, the ball flew into the net. The referee later said it had come off a defender, but the goal has been credited to Kirton, who as Villa's best forward deserves the honour.

Villa captain Andy Ducat clears in the new setting of Stamford Bridge.

Sale of the century

PLAYERS OF DISGRACED Leeds City were auctioned at the Hotel Metropole in a most bizarre sale in October, a week after the club were expelled from the League for irregularities in payments to players during the war. Meanwhile Port Vale have taken over their fixtures in the Second Division, as well as the 10 points already won from the eight games Leeds had played.

After allegations made by a player earlier in the year, the FA and Football League set up a joint commission to investigate Leeds's affairs. During the war years, no fewer than 35 "guest" players had turned out for Leeds, including seven internationals. When the club refused to produce their accounts for the last two seasons, the League had no choice but to expel them.

Although the League regretted the decision, recognizing that Leeds were a new club with bright prospects, they regarded the charges of breaking wartime regulations by paying players more than the permitted rates as extremely serious. So much so that they also banned four Leeds directors and two previous managers, Herbert Chapman and George Cripps, from taking any further part in football management or even attending football matches.

The players fetched a total of little more than £10,000, going at bargain prices, ranging from £250 to £1,250, to managers who flocked to Leeds from clubs in various parts of the country. Some of those managers must have had mixed feelings, for it was no secret that Leeds were not the only club to have stretched the wartime regulations by paying "generous" expenses.

Spurs beat Wolves on quagmire of pitch

NEWLY PROMOTED Tottenham beat Second Division Wolves 1–0 in the FA Cup final at Stamford Bridge in the most terrible conditions. Despite continuous rain and an increase in admission prices to keep the numbers down, a crowd of nearly 73,000 began streaming into the ground over four hours before the kick-off and spilled on to the pitch surrounds.

They paid record gate money of £13,400, but because of the conditions the match turned out to be a poor spectacle.The pitch was a quagmire, enveloping the football skills of the Spurs stars — their captain and left-half Arthur Grimsdell, inside-right Jimmy Seed, and the left-wing pair of Bert Bliss and Jimmy Dimmock. It was the dogged persistence of Dimmock that won them the game eight minutes into the second half, rather than the artistry they have become known for.

Stopped in his tracks by Woodward, the opposing full-back, Dimmock regained the ball, dragged it through the mud into the penalty area, and hit a shot that skidded across the keeper into the far corner. It was not the most elegant of goals, but Spurs were worthy winners and have brought the Cup back south for the first time since they first won it 20 years ago.

Peter McWilliam, their manager, is the first man to play in and then manage a cup-winning team. He was in the Newcastle side in 1910.

Dimmock of Tottenham defies mud and defenders to score the winning goal.

Third division for League

THE NEW LEAGUE season starts with 66 clubs, made up of three divisions of 22. An *en bloc* application from the Southern League's First Division to join the League was accepted, and the new Third Division is composed of those clubs with the exception of Cardiff. The Welsh club go straight into Division Two at the expense of Grimsby Town, who were demoted to the new Third Division. There will be automatic promotion and relegation of one club between Divisions Two and Three.

Lincoln City, who finished second from bottom of Division Two last season, were not re-elected. Their place in Division Two has been taken by Leeds United, the club that sprang up like a phoenix from the ashes of the disgraced Leeds City and who will operate from the same Elland Road ground.

FINAL SCORE

Football League
Division 1: Burnley
Top scorer: Joe Smith (Bolton Wanderers) 38
Division 2: Birmingham City
Division 3: Crystal Palace

FA Cup Final
Tottenham Hotspur 1 Wolveerhampton W 0

Scottish League
Division 1: Rangers
Top scorer: Hugh Ferguson (Motherwell) 43

Scottish FA Cup Final
Partick Thistle 1 Rangers 0

International Championship
Scotland, 6 pts

Burnley defeated at last

BURNLEY'S RECORD League run without defeat has finally been broken. Last beaten way back on 4 September, 2–0 by Bradford City, they went 30 matches in the League without losing, 21 wins and nine draws. Now, on 26 March, they have lost 3–0 at Maine Road to their challengers for the Championship, Manchester City.

What an extraordinary season this has been so far for Burnley, who started off with three straight defeats. Then on 6 September they beat Huddersfield 3–0, the start of the run that has given them 51 points and put them in a commanding position at the head of the First Division table. The only blemish in their season so far has been their 3–0 defeat at Second Division Hull in the third round of the Cup, a big shock in view of their 7–3 win at Leicester in the first round.

They have been particularly strong at home, where they have lost only their first match of the season, 4–1 to Bradford City. Their home triumphs have included 7–1 victories over Oldham and Aston Villa and 6–0 over Sheffield United. Centre-forward Joe Anderson and inside-right Bob Kelly have scored most of the goals, while Jerry Dawson has been as safe as always in goal, and centre-half Tom Boyle an inspirational skipper.

FOOTBALL FOCUS

- The Third Division got off to a good start with gates of 25,000 at Millwall and 20,000 at Portsmouth and Queen's Park Rangers on the first Saturday, while Swindon beat Luton 9–1. Crystal Palace, who lost 2–1 at Merthyr Town, eventually finished top.
- After their record run was broken, Burnley won their next two games, including revenge over Manchester City by 2–1, and although they failed to win any of their last six matches, they ran out easy League winners by five points from Manchester City.
- Cardiff, promoted at the first attempt, will play in the First Division next year — the first Welsh club to do so.
- The biggest non-event of the season was Stockport's home game with Leicester on 7 May, the last day. Already relegated, and with their own ground under suspension, they had to play at Old Trafford, where a record low "crowd" of 13 on the vast terraces were entertained to a goalless draw.
- The pendulum continues to swing Rangers' way in Scotland, where they amassed a record 76 points, with only one defeat (at home to Celtic), and won the title by 10 points from Celtic. Their Cup "hoodoo" continues, however. They lost 1–0 to Partick in the final, despite being odds-on favourites.

Liverpool wrap title up at Easter

Keeper Elisha Scott, solid at the back.

LIVERPOOL are the new kings of English football. They beat last year's champions Burnley 2–1 on 17 April to complete their Easter programme. With three games to go, Burnley can no longer catch them, and nor can Spurs, in second place, who lost their last chance when they went down 1–0 at Oldham.

Liverpool's third Championship has not been a spectacular one, but has been earned by good defence — they have kept a clean sheet in 17 of the 39 matches played so far — and a consistency that saw them, after losing their first match, go through 30 more with but one further defeat. Irish international Elisha Scott has established himself in goal in the best tradition of Liverpool keepers, and with four international full-backs to call on, it is not surprising that they have had no problems in defence.

Preston's Cup of woe

WHILE HUDDERSFIELD were popular winners of the Cup, the final itself was a depressing affair and it is perhaps appropriate that the result should have turned on a disputed penalty. There can be no doubt that a deliberate foul brought England outside-left Billy Smith down. But there can be little doubt either that the offence was committed outside the penalty area. However, the referee saw fit to award the spot-kick, Smith picked himself up to score, and few neutrals at the match felt it was an unjust result.

Preston right-back Hamilton, who fouled Smith from behind when the winger was making for goal, should have been sent off for such a disgraceful offence, and shame on once "Proud" Preston for protesting, even if the referee failed to follow the letter of the law. Perhaps the best entertainment of the match came when their bespectacled amateur keeper J.F.Mitchell tried to put Smith off by dancing around on his line.

Ignoring the match, but looking back on Huddersfield's progress to the final, they are to be congratulated for their spirited play in earlier rounds and overall for their revival since the dark days of their financial crisis just after the war. Then, but for the generosity of their fans, the club would have been transplanted to the ground at Elland Road vacated by the disbanded Leeds City.

Their new manager, Mr Herbert Chapman, is to be congratulated, too. The first thing he did on his appointment last year was to pay Aston Villa £4,000 for the veteran inside-forward Clem Stephenson. And it is Stephenson's leadership on the field that has knitted the young players of Huddersfield into such a formidable side

Clem Stephenson, inspired Chapman buy.

FOOTBALL FOCUS

- Dumbarton goalkeeper James Williamson died after the game with Rangers on 12 November.
- Stockport, relegated from Division Two last season, have gone straight back up again as the first winners of the new Division Three (North).
- The reorganized Scottish League, with a new 20-club Division Two, saw Alloa promoted by right as champions, but three Division One clubs relegated, including Queen's Park for the first time.
- Southend, who finished bottom of the Third Division (S), scored only 34 goals. Their top scorer was a full-back, Jimmy Evans, whose 10 goals were all penalties.
- Celtic are back in business as the "Auld Firm" struggle continues in Scotland, beating Rangers by a point for the title, while Rangers are again beaten in the Cup final.

Another Third Division

WITH THE ADVENT of the new Third Division North, the League has virtually doubled in just two years. Clubs from the North were invited to apply for membership, and 20 clubs were accepted into what is now officially called the Northern Section of the Third Division. Last year's Third Division, still 22 clubs, is the Southern Section. The top club from each section will be promoted in place of the bottom two clubs of the Second Division. The last two clubs of each section will have to apply for re-election.

FINAL SCORE

Football League
Division 1: Liverpool
Top scorer: Andy Wilson (Middlesbrough) 31
Division 2: Nottingham Forest
Division 3S: Southampton
Division 3N: Stockport County

FA Cup Final

Huddersfield Town	1	Preston North End	0

Scottish League
Division 1: Celtic
Top scorer: Duncan Walker (St Mirren) 45
Division 2: Alloa

Scottish FA Cup Final

Morton	1	Rangers	0

International Championship
Scotland, 4 pts

Crowd chaos at Cup final: 'mounties to the rescue!'

IT IS A MIRACLE the game was played at all, incredible that no one was killed in the crush. The first Cup final to be staged at Wembley Stadium took place in spite of the greatest crowd chaos ever witnessed. The official attendance has been given as 126,047, but there must have been close to a quarter of a million packed inside the ground, overflowing right up to the boundaries of the pitch itself.

At one stage, before the start, the crowd almost completely covered the pitch, and there seemed little hope that the match could possibly take place. Thousands upon thousands of fans had scaled Wembley's outer walls and broken down the flimsy barriers. A few mounted police on the pitch managed to clear portions of it at a time, one officer in particular, Constable Scorey, on a white horse, earning the cheers of the "gallery" as again and again he resourcefully coaxed the crowd back.

At last the reinforcements arrived, hundreds more police on foot and on horseback, and gradually they herded the crowd back over the lines and behind the goals. The match started 40 minutes late and, within two minutes, Bolton were in front with a goal from David Jack, scored while a West Ham player was still struggling to get back on to the pitch after retrieving the ball for a throw-in. Eight minutes into the second half, Bolton scored a second, a thunderbolt shot from Jack Smith that rebounded from the wall of spectators pressed against the net and almost hit him on the way back. That was the end of the scoring. Bolton deserved their win, although West Ham, a Second Division side pressing for promotion, never showed their true ability.

Immediate reactions to the crowd fiasco have been for an official inquiry to be set up. The size of the crowd was drastically — almost fatally — underestimated by the British Empire Exhibition authorities, who handled the match arrangements, and by the police.

The great stadium, completed only four days earlier, will have its barriers strengthened, and there have been calls for future Cup finals to have ticket-only admission.

The crowd overflows on to Wembley's pitch. PC Scorey is circled.

David Jack (white shirt) scores the first goal.

FOOTBALL FOCUS

- During the 1922 close season, the players' maximum wage was cut from £9 to £8 a week. A strike was threatened, but, as usual, nothing came of it.
- A player in a preliminary round FA Cup tie scored seven goals and finished up on the losing side! He was Billy Minter, whose team, St Alban's City, lost 8–7 to Dulwich Hamlet on 22 November.
- Liverpool smoothed their way to a second consecutive League title, leading virtually from start to finish. Again, though, they scored only 20 goals away from home.

FINAL SCORE

Football League
Division 1: Liverpool
Top scorer: Charlie Buchan (Sunderland) 30
Division 2: Notts County
Division 3S: Bristol City
Division 3N: Nelson

FA Cup Final

Bolton Wanderers	2	West Ham United	0

Scottish League
Division 1: Rangers
Top scorer: John White (Hearts) 30
Division 2: Queen's Park

Scottish FA Cup Final

Celtic	1	Hibernian	0

International Championship
Scotland, 5 pts

West Ham go up

WEST HAM, beaten at home by Notts County, still win promotion on what has been the most dramatic last day of the season in Division Two. And what a week it's been for the East London club, striving to get into the top division for the first time. After their depressing, and exhausting, experience at Wembley last Saturday, they had to pick themselves up for an away game at Sheffield Wednesday on Monday. They did, and won 2–0, to go back on top of the table on goal average from both Leicester and Notts County.

The scene was set for a last day of many possibilities, with West Ham entertaining Notts County and Leicester away to disinterested Bury. A shock for West Ham — County beat them 1–0. But all was not lost, because Bury beat Leicester, and West Ham are promoted in second place on goal average behind Notts County.

West Ham earned their success by dint of their excellent away record — 42 goals scored (twice as many as at home!) and 11 games won, including, in hindsight, the crucial 6–0 victory at Leicester back in February. Their promotion gives London four teams in Division One for the first time.

West Ham's Vic Watson was a fine centre-forward, well worth his first England cap, which he celebrated with a goal against Wales. Ted Hufton (goal) and winger Jimmy Ruffell also shone.

Long division settles First Division

AFTER THE CLOSEST battle for the League title yet, Huddersfield have beaten Cardiff on goal average by 0.024. It does not seem much after a long, hard season, but the mathematicians had their slide-rules out on the last day, working out the possibilities. Basically, all Cardiff had to do was win. Huddersfield, who seemed to have it all sewn up, dropped some vital points in the later stages, leaving themselves a point behind Cardiff with one match to play.

Huddersfield were playing at home to Nottingham Forest, but the drama was all at Birmingham for Cardiff's last game. Cardiff were awarded a penalty when an opponent handled the ball on the goal-line. None of the senior players would accept the responsibility of taking it, so Len Davies stepped up for his first ever spot-kick. The keeper saved it, and the match finished 0–0. Meanwhile, Huddersfield won 3–0. It was just enough. Huddersfield's 60–33 beats Cardiff's 61–34. Those are the rules.

The Championship is another triumph for manager Herbert Chapman, who not only transformed the side by signing the inside-forward Clem Stephenson, but has made further inspired signings and initiated improvements at the club for the benefit of both the playing staff and the fans.

Huddersfield: Football League champions — just.

FINAL SCORE

Football League
Division 1: Huddersfield Town
Top scorer: Bill Chadwick (Everton) 28
Division 2: Leeds United
Division 3S: Portsmouth
Division 3N: Wolverhampton Wanderers

FA Cup Final
Newcastle United 2 Aston Villa 0

Scottish League
Division 1: Rangers
Top scorer: Dave Halliday (Dundee) 38
Division 2: St Johnstone
Division 3: Arthurlie

Scottish FA Cup Final
Airdrieonians 2 Hibernian 0

International Championship
Wales, 6 pts

Wales win Triple Crown

THE "TRIPLE CROWN", victory over each of the other nations in the International Championship, has gone to Wales for the first time. England have accomplished the feat seven times and Scotland four.

Wales clinched it in Belfast, the first time they have won there since 1913. All they needed was a draw to make sure of the Championship, but they won 1–0 thanks to a penalty goal scored by veteran Plymouth right-back Moses Russell.

Wales started the season with a 2–0 victory over Scotland at Cardiff on 16 February. This was a particularly proud day for Cardiff, as their club provided both captains — centre-half Fred Keenor of Wales and left-back Jimmy Blair of Scotland. This left the Championship table in a decidedly unusual state — Wales and Ireland top with two points, Scotland and England bottom without a point, as Ireland had beaten England 2–1 at Everton in October. Then came the Welsh victory over England, 2–1 at Blackburn earlier this month.

The only other time Wales have won the Championship, 13 years ago, they needed England to draw with Scotland. They won't need any help this time when the two clash at Wembley in April.

FOOTBALL FOCUS

- The Scottish League increased its membership again by the introduction of a 16-club Third Division with promotion for two clubs.
- England played their first match at Wembley, drawing 1–1 with Scotland for their only point in the Championship.
- In a Division Two match against Manchester United on 6 October, Oldham full-back Sam Wynne scored twice for each side, a free-kick and a penalty for his own team and two own goals for the visitors. Oldham won 3–2.
- Newcastle right-back Walter Hampson was 41 years 8 months when he played in the Cup final, and is believed to be the oldest player to do so, at least since the 1870s.

The Welsh team, Triple Crown winners for the first time.

Airdrie a third force in Scotland

AIRDRIEONIANS have established themselves in just two seasons as real rivals to Rangers and Celtic in Scotland. Not only have they now won the Cup, beating Hibernian 2–0 in the final, but they have again finished second in the League to Rangers, relegating Celtic to third place.

A young team with tremendous forward power, they have matched Rangers goal for goal this season, with their small but highly effective centre-forward Hughie Gallacher to the fore.

Drastic change in offside law

ONE WORD has been changed in football's offside law — one word that could have untold effects on how the game is played. Football, since it restarted after the Great War, has lost much of its entertainment value, bogged down as it is in defensive tactics, particularly the "offside-trap" as perpetrated so successfully by Newcastle United.

After 15 years of argument, the FA arranged a trial at Highbury between sides of Amateurs and Professionals. One 45-minute period was played under an offside law that stipulated a player needed only two rather than three (the one-word change) opponents behind him to remain onside. The other period was played under the present offside law but with the onside area extended. On the flimsy evidence of this highly inadequate experiment, the FA decided on the former solution at their meeting in London on 15 June. It was the Scottish FA who put the proposal to the International Football Association Board, by whom it has now been ratified. The change becomes effective next season.

The following Proposals by the Scottish Football Association were adopted :—

PRESENT LAW.	PROPOSED ALTERATION.
6.—When a player plays the ball, any player of the same side who at such moment of playing is nearer to his opponents' goal-line is out of play and may not touch the ball himself nor in any way whatever interfere with an opponent, or with the play, until the ball has been again played, unless there are at such moment of playing at least three of his opponents nearer their own goal-line. A player is not out of play when the ball is kicked off from goal, when a corner-kick or a throw in is taken, when the ball has been last played by an opponent, or when he himself is within his own half of the field of play at the moment the ball is played by any player of the same side.	From the first sentence of Law 6 delete the word "three" and substitute the word "two."
7.—When the ball is played behind the goal-line by a player of the opposite side, it shall be kicked off by any one of the players behind whose goal-line it went, within that half of the goal area nearest the point where the ball left the field of play; but, if played behind by any one of the side whose goal-line it is, a player of the opposite side shall kick it from within 1 yard of the nearest corner flagstaff (*a*). In either case an opponent shall not be allowed within 10 yards of the ball until it is kicked off.	Add— "and the kicker shall not again play the ball until it has been played by another player."

Changes in the offside and corner-kick laws.

The 'mighty atom' strikes

LITTLE Patsy Gallagher scored a goal of extraordinary audacity in the Scottish Cup final, never to be forgotten by the fans who saw it, because they are not likely to see its equal again. And what a time to score it, with Dundee leading 1–0 and holding everything that Celtic could throw at them in the closing stages.

With 15 minutes remaining, Gallagher, the "mighty atom", picked up a flighted free-kick from Paddy Connolly and, surrounded by blue shirts, began to wriggle his way towards goal, squeezing past and through defenders until he was held up a few feet short of the posts. Tackled heavily, he stumbled to the ground, but, with amazing presence of mind, kept the ball lodged between his feet and somersaulted into the net with it.

Hampden Park, chock-full of Celtic fans, went wild, and Dundee wilted visibly. Minutes from the end, Jimmy McGrory, Celtic's leading scorer, snatched the winner with a diving header. So Celtic chalk up their 11th Scottish Cup win to overtake Queen's Park's record. It is consolation for another season's trailing in the wake of Rangers and Airdrieonians in the League.

Patsy Gallagher, acrobatic scorer for Celtic.

FOOTBALL FOCUS

- The law allowing players to score directly from corner-kicks came into operation this season, and Huddersfield's Billy Smith scored the first such goal in the League, against Arsenal on 11 October. The law was so vaguely worded, however, that many people in the footballing community were under the impression that players could dribble the ball from the flag. The law has now been clarified, and a player may not touch the ball more than once when taking a corner.

- Huddersfield, winning their second successive League title, were undefeated in their first 10 and last 17 matches, and collected more points away than at home. The club's reserves won the Central Lague, too.

- After Cardiff's near misses, Welsh success came in the Third Division (S), when Swansea, unbeaten at home, won promotion this season.

Wake goes to sleep

After last season's heart-stopping anti-climax to the League season, Cardiff fans were put through the mangle again, this time in the Cup. In the first round, they were twice held to goalless draws by Third Division Darlington before beating them 2–0 at Anfield. In the fourth round they needed a history-making goal from Willie Davies, who scored with the last kick of the game against Leicester direct from a corner, the first Cup goal under the new law.

But now, at Wembley, after a good 3–1 semi-final win over Blackburn, their luck ran out. In front of hordes of Welshmen who flooded into London for what was an "international" Cup final, Cardiff right-half Harry Wake belied his name and went to sleep, allowing Sheffield United's Fred Tunstall to rob him of the ball and run in to score the only goal of the game after half an hour. It was one of the few scoring chances allowed to either side's attack by two strong defences.

FINAL SCORE

Football League
Division 1: Huddersfield Town
Top scorer: Fred Roberts (Manchester City) 31
Division 2: Leicester City
Division 3S: Swansea Town
Division 3N: Darlington

FA Cup Final
Sheffield United 1 Cardiff City 0

Scottish League
Division 1: Rangers
Top scorer: Willie Devlin (Cowdenbeath) 33
Division 2: Dundee United
Division 3: Nithsdale Wanderers

Scottish FA Cup Final
Celtic 2 Dundee 1

International Championship
Scotland, 6 pts

Development of the laws

FOOTBALL was a part of Shrovetide festivities in England at least from the 1100s. Early football was a free-for-all, with perhaps hundreds taking part, in which the objective might be to carry a ball to one end or other of the town or village. But there were no rules as to how this should be accomplished, and most of the kicking was directed at the person. Over the centuries, football was banned by royal decree in England, Scotland and France, either because it had become an excuse for violence or because it interfered with archery practice.

But in some places, football began to be accepted on a higher plane. A game called *calcio* took root in 15th-century Florence, where teams known as the Red and the Green were led by young cavaliers of the Florentine aristocracy, the first instance of special colours being worn by opposing sides. In 1581, the headmaster of St Paul's School, in London, a Richard Mulcaster, claimed in a treatise that football had positive educational values, and could be used to promote health and strength. And it is in the English public schools that the laws of football first began to be codified.

By the early 19th century, various schools in England played their own form of football. An 11-a-side game was introduced at Eton in 1841, and the office of "referee" four years later. In 1846, the rules at Rugby School were finally codified, having been in a state of flux since William Webb Ellis is said to have caught the ball and run with it in 1825.

Before 1891, the referee stayed outside the field of play.

Cambridge Rules

The most important breakthrough came in 1848, when 14 men, representing Eton, Harrow, Winchester, Rugby and the non-public schools, met at Trinity College Cambridge to hammer out the "Cambridge Rules". These rules included provisions for the kick-off and for restarting the game when the ball went out of play (that is, beyond an area bounded only by four corner flags), such as the straight throw-in. A goal was scored when the ball went "through the flag-posts and under the string". Players could use their hands only to stop the ball or to catch a kick, in which case they could kick it from hand but were not allowed to run with it. A player was offside unless there were three opponents "before" him. Holding, pushing or tripping an adversary was prohibited.

These rules were the basis for other sets drawn up over the next 15 years, notably the Sheffield Rules (by the first ever football club) in 1857, J.C. Thring's *The Simplest Game* (for Charterhouse School) in 1862, and a further set promulgated at Cambridge the following year. All of these outlawed the Rugby School practice of running with the ball after a "fair catch" and devices such as holding and tripping. The 1865 Cambridge Rules, with some modifications leaning towards earlier versions, were adopted by the new Football Association in 1865, when a breakaway group who advocated the Rugby rules went off to play their own game.

The FA continued to govern the rules in England until they joined with the associations of Scotland, Wales and Ireland in the creation of the International Football Association Board in 1888 for that sole purpose. Gradually, as football became more organized, with cups, leagues, internationals and professionalism, the laws of the game were refined.

In the 1870s, a tape joined the goal-posts at the top.

First FA laws

In the first FA laws, the pitch (maximum 200 by 100 yards) was marked off by flags, and the goal was defined by two uprights, eight yards apart, without any tape or bar, although a tape was introduced in 1865. In these early days, the laws delineated what was fair play, but made no provisions for penalizing breaches of the laws. The only free-kicks were kick-offs and goal-kicks. There was no mention of a referee, and it was left to the captains to ensure fair play.

Another early influence on the laws was the Sheffield Association, and certain of their laws differed from those of the FA and were to have an effect on later changes. Their members played on a 120- by 80-yard ground, with a bar connecting nine-foot goal-posts, wore distinguishable jerseys and used a "no. 5 ball". They had a kick-in from touch with the opposite team putting the ball back into play, and corner kicks for both attacking and defending sides (goal-kicks were used only when the ball went out of play over the bar). They used the term "off-side" for the first time, and designated a goalkeeper (the defender nearest his own goal). Most important, free-kicks were awarded for breaches of the rules, with an umpire from each side appointed to enforce them.

Spurs score in the 1901 Cup final, when the 12-yard line stretched across the pitch.

Special Cup rules

The FA applied special roles for Cup competitions and internationals in the early 1870s, notably the duration of a match (90 minutes), the appointment of two neutral umpires and a referee, and the restoration of a "custodian's" right to use his hands in defense of his goal. They also adopted the free-kick from the Sheffield Rules, and stipulated the ball size (27-28 inches circumference).

In 1874, with the increasing importance of Cup games, the FA empowered officials to "rule out of the game any player who persistently infringed the Laws". They introduced the cross-bar in 1875, along with half-time. In 1877, the FA and the Sheffield Association agreed on a unified code (the only concession necessary being that a throw-in could be taken in any direction), and the rest of the country followed suit.

Although appearing in Cup rules in 1871, the referee was not mentioned in the laws until 1880, when his duties included adjudicating in disputes between the umpires, time-keeping, and cautioning or, for "violent conduct", sending players off. An experimental law in 1881 empowered the referee to award a goal in cases where, in his opinion, a score had been prevented by the wilful handling of the ball by one of the defending side. This rule proved unacceptable to the clubs and was thrown out after a year.

International Board

There were still differences of opinion between associations, particularly between the FA and their Scottish counterpart. A meeting at Manchester in 1882 between the four home associations settled the differences. Cross-bars were made obligatory, touchlines to be clearly marked, charging from behind permitted only if a player was impeding an opponent, and the two-handed throw-in introduced. This conference led to the establishment of the International Board in 1886.

A penalty-kick was first introduced in 1891, for intentional tripping or holding an opponent or handling the ball within 12 yards of the goal-line. It could be taken from any point 12 yards from the goal-line, the opposing keeper cold not advance more than six yards from his line, and all other players had to be behind the ball and at least six yards from it. At the same time, it was decided to abolish dual control of the field by the two umpires, and invest it in one man, the referee, assisted by two linesmen, whose chief duty was to signal, with a flag, when the ball had gone out of play over the touchline.

The FA approved goal-nets in 1891, but did hot make them compulsory. Pitch markings underwent several changes as the laws progressed, especially after the introduction of the penalty kick. This required a 12-yard line, and marks six yards behind it for the rest of the players to retreat behind when a kick was taken. The goal area was delineated by arcs of six-yard radius from each goal-post (for the taking of goal-kicks).

The International Board made a thorough revision of the laws in 1897, when the outside dimensions of the pitch still in use today were laid on. But it was not until 1902 that the marking for today's penalty area, goal area and penalty spot were introduced.

Direct free-kicks came in during 1903, for intentional tripping, pushing, holding and kicking an opponent, or for jumping at or charging him from behind, and for handball. The referee was also empowered to refrain from giving a free-kick if by doing so it would give the offending side an advantage. Charging an opponent was made permissible in 1905, provided it was neither violent nor dangerous. Striking an opponent was subsequently added to the list of offences in 1914.

A Corner-Kick in the 1904 Cup final between Bolton and Manchester City — only the penalty area "D" is now missing.

£100-a-goal Buchan fails to score

Buchan gets in a header against Spurs on his debut for his new club.

ARSENAL CHAIRMAN Sir Henry Norris watched with mixed feelings as controversial new signing Charlie Buchan made his debut in the opening match at Highbury on Saturday. Under the terms of his transfer, Arsenal will pay Sunderland an extra £100 this season for every goal the veteran inside-forward scores. He didn't add to his price against Spurs, but none of his colleagues could find the net either, and Arsenal lost 1–0.

When new manager Herbert Chapman said he wanted the 34-year-old former England star to bolster his flagging forward line, Sir Henry had to swallow his aversion to high transfer fees and make the money available. He was certainly taken aback by Sunderland's asking price, £4,000, but when their manager Bob Kyle justified it for the 20 goals Buchan was "bound to score" in his first season with the Gunners, Sir Henry turned this to his own advantage by offering £2,000 plus £100 a goal.

The flood-gates opened

WITH THE CHANGE in the off-side law, the expected goal glut arrived. The total number of goals scored in the Football League rose from last season's 4,700 to 6,373 this season. The rise was most spectacular in the First Division, where Manchester City conceded 100 goals and were relegated, and Burnley conceded 108 and stayed up. Four Third Division clubs scored 100 goals or more, and none of them was promoted.

The initial reaction of the clubs had been to play full-backs squarer and closer to their goal. But this enabled forwards to move unchallenged into shooting range. The free-scoring abated noticeably in the second half of the season, as defences realized they were allowing attackers too much space and tightened up.

Hat-trick for Huddersfield

LEAGUE CHAMPIONS again, Huddersfield have become the first club to win the title three seasons running. Their achievement is a monument to Herbert Chapman, who left them to manage Arsenal before the start of the season. He built up the side and he made the club famous. And before he left he made one of his typical swoops in the transfer market, snatching Alex Jackson from under the noses of Liverpool.

The 19-year-old Scottish international Jackson proved a valuable buy, at £2,500, from Aberdeen. A roaming, goalscoring outside-right, he contributed 16 goals to Huddersfield's 92 in his first season with them, and made many more for others, particularly centre-forward George Brown, who set a club goalscoring record in the First Division with 35.

Alex Jackson, a coup for Chapman.

FOOTBALL FOCUS

- With a number of clubs in the Scottish Division Three getting into financial difficulties, the whole League was suspended before the programme was completed.
- Charlie Buchan cost Arsenal an extra £2,000, with 19 League goals and one in the Cup, so Sunderland's manager was spot-on with his forecast.
- Bobby Skinner of Dunfermline set a British record with 53 goals in the Scottish Division Two.

Goals but no glory

MANCHESTER CITY have become the first Football League club to reach the Cup final and be relegated in the same season. They went down in most unfortunate circumstances only eight days after losing 1–0 to Bolton at Wembley.

What an extraordinary season it has been for City. They scored 89 goals, more than any relegated club in the history of the League. And they stormed into the Cup final after an orgy of goalscoring in earlier rounds. Then they couldn't score a single goal at Wembley. But it was a thrilling final.

On the last day of the season, with Notts County already condemned to the drop, Leeds United and Burnley were a point behind Manchester. So City, with a superior goal average, needed only to draw their game at Newcastle even if the other two won. City lost 3–2 after missing a penalty, the other two both won 4–1... and City were down.

FINAL SCORE

Football League
Division 1: Huddersfield Town
Top scorer: Ted Harper (Blackburn Rovers) 43
Division 2: Sheffield Wednesday
Division 3S: Reading
Division 3N: Grimsby Town

FA Cup Final
Bolton Wanderers 1 Manchester City 0

Scottish League
Division 1: Celtic
Top scorer: Willie Devlin (Cowdenbeath) 40
Division 2: Dunfermline Athletic

Scottish FA Cup Final
St Mirren 2 Celtic 0

International Championship
Scotland, 6 pts

English Cup goes to Wales

CARDIFF CITY beat Arsenal 1–0 at Wembley to take the FA Cup out of England for the first time, with a remarkable goal scored by centre-forward Hughie Ferguson in the 75th minute. It was a personal tragedy for Arsenal's Welsh international keeper Dan Lewis, who seemed to have the shot under control, but allowed the ball to squirt out of his hands and over the line.

The key to Cardiff's victory was the play of veteran left-half Billy Hardy, the only Englishman in the side, who managed to keep Charlie Buchan quiet for most of the time. When Buchan did manage to break free, the chances he laid on for his colleagues were not taken. The powerful tackling of Cardiff captain Fred Keenor was another major factor. But Arsenal's half-back line of Baker, Butler and John were also splendid, and the two sides were restricted to a handful of shots on target over the 90 minutes.

When the goal did come, it was totally unexpected. Ferguson shot hard, and Lewis caught and held the ball while on one knee. But in turning to avoid a challenge from Len Davies, he swung round and spilled the ball, which spun away from him and over the line. It was the difference between winning and losing.

The ball slips away from the unfortunate Lewis.

Scot is new Tyneside idol

HUGHIE GALLACHER has sparked a revival on Tyneside in his first full season with Newcastle, leading them to the League Championship for the first time since 1909. The little Scottish international centre-forward, bought from Airdrie last season for £5,500, has set a club record with 36 League goals in his 38 games.

Newcastle virtually acquired the title in front of their own fans, winning a record 19 home matches and dropping only three points at St James's Park. Their derby with Sunderland in March drew a record 67,211 attendance, and they have rewarded their supporters with goals galore, averaging over three per home game. It did not matter that they lost 10 away matches. They still won the title with ease, five points ahead of Huddersfield.

Hughie Gallacher, Tyneside hero in his first season.

More goal records tumble

MIDDLESBROUGH have won promotion to Division One largely through centre-forward George Camsell. His League record of 59 goals makes up nearly half their total, 122, also a League record. Camsell hit nine hat-tricks, and that's never been done before either. Middlesbrough's first four games produced only one goal and one point.

While Middlesbrough were coasting into the First Division, there was an almighty struggle going on behind them for the other promotion place. Portsmouth and Manchester City were level on points on the last day, but Portsmouth had the better goal average. Manchester had already scored 92 goals, and proceeded to thrash bottom club Bradford City 8–0. Portsmouth, whose match against Preston had kicked off 15 minutes later, were 4–1 up when the news filtered through that, unless they scored another, City would beat them. They did, in the last few minutes, and were promoted with a goal average of 1.77551 to City's 1.77049.

George Camsell — 59 goals in Division Two.

FOOTBALL FOCUS

- The first football match broadcast on radio was the Arsenal-Sheffield United League game on 22 January. An "announcer" gave a running commentary while a colleague called out numbers referring to sections of the pitch, to help listeners follow the play on a simple chart.
- Jimmy McGrory set a Scottish First Division record with 49 goals for Celtic despite missing the last five matches through injury. Celtic scored 101 goals but could still finish only third to Rangers. They won the Cup, but McGrory missed the final.
- England beat Scotland 2–1 at Hampden Park for the first time since 1904, thanks to two goals from Everton's Bill Dean, their new centre-forward, who has scored 12 goals in five games for his country, including hat-tricks against Belgium and Luxembourg.

FINAL SCORE

Football League
Division 1: Newcastle United
Top scorer: Jimmy Trotter (Sheffield Wednesday) 37
Division 2: Middlesbrough
Division 3S: Bristol City
Division 3N: Stoke City

FA Cup Final
Cardiff City 1 Arsenal 0

Scottish League
Division 1: Rangers
Top scorer: Jimmy McGrory (Celtic) 49
Division 2: Bo'ness

Scottish FA Cup Final
Celtic 3 East Fife 1

International Championship
England, Scotland, 4 pts

Scottish masters give England a lesson: wizard show at Wembley

SCOTLAND came to Wembley at the end of March and, in the pouring rain and in front of 80,000 people, proceeded to give England a lesson in how football should be played. The "Wee Blue Devils" — hat-trick hero Alex Jackson was the tallest of the forwards at 5ft 7in — turned on an exhibition of ball skill and artistry that left their opponents breathless, bewildered and thoroughly beaten.

Scotland took the lead in three minutes. Left-half Jimmy McMullan set up a string of passes with Jimmy Gibson and the mercurial Alex James, who put Alan Morton away on the left. Over came the cross, and there was Alex Jackson on the other wing steaming in to head the ball home. James put them two up, shrugging off a challenge as only he can do and volleying the ball past the hapless Hufton from 25 yards.

In the second half the Scots really turned it on. Morton came into his own on the left and made two more for Jackson. In between, James scored the fourth, smashing in a loose ball after Gallacher had been tackled. The rout was complete. A late goal by Kelly made it 5–1, but the skill and science of the Scots had triumphed over the more direct English style.

McMullan leads the Scots out at Wembley, followed by Jackson and Gallacher.

FINAL SCORE

Football League
Division 1: Everton
Top scorer: Billy Dean (Everton) 60
Division 2: Manchester City
Division 3S: Millwall
Division 3N: Bradford Park Avenue

FA Cup Final

Blackburn Rovers	3	Huddersfield Town	1

Scottish League
Division 1: Rangers
Top scorer: Jimmy McGrory (Celtic) 47
Division 2: Ayr United

Scottish FA Cup Final

Rangers	4	Celtic	0

International Championship
Wales, 5 pts

Dixie Dean does it! Hat-trick to reach 60

THE SCENE is Goodison Park, the date 5 May 1928. Everton already have the League title sewn up, but a crowd of over 48,000 turn up for the last game of the season, against Arsenal, to see what they hope will be the climax of the greatest feat of individual goalscoring in the history of the League. Billy "Dixie" Dean has 57 League goals to his credit and needs another three to beat the record set last season by Middlesbrough's George Camsell in the Second Division.

Arsenal scored within two minutes of the kick-off. But less than a minute later Dean converted a Critchley corner, and when, after only a few more minutes, Dean was brought down in the box and netted the resultant penalty, the crowd went wild. They had to wait with bated breath, however, until the 82nd minute before Alec Troup, provider of so many of Dean's goals, placed a perfect corner for Dean to rise above the Arsenal defence at the far post and power a typical header into the net. The resulting roar from the crowd could be heard all over Merseyside.

FOOTBALL FOCUS

- Jimmy McGrory scored eight goals, a Scottish Division One record, when Celtic beat Dunfermline 9–0 on 14 January.
- A week after their Cup triumph, Rangers made sure of the League, too, for their first ever "double".
- Jim Smith of Ayr United scored a British record 66 goals in the Scottish Division Two.
- Millwall scored a League record 127 goals in Division Three (S) and were promoted.

Dean (left) heads his 60th goal of the season.

Rangers beat Cup hoodoo

THE HOODOO — a very real hoodoo to their fans — was finally laid to rest at Hampden Park when Rangers beat Celtic 4–0 to win the Scottish Cup for the first time since 1903. A crowd of 118,000, divided into blue and green, turned out to see this fifth "Old Firm" final.

It was mostly Celtic in the first half, when only the brilliance of Tom Hamilton in the Rangers goal kept them from taking advantage of a strong wind. The match turned on a penalty in the second half, given away when Celtic captain Willie McStay handled the ball on the goal-line with his keeper beaten. Rangers captain David Meiklejohn courageously took the responsibility for the kick himself, and converted it to an explosion of relief and joy among the fans in blue. Bob McPhail then scored a second and right-winger Sandy Archibald made certain with two spectacular goals hit from near the touchline.

Jack's the lad for £10,000

LIKE THE Canadian Mounties, Arsenal manager Herbert Chapman always gets his man – even if the asking price is twice the transfer record. When Charlie Buchan decided to retire last season, Mr Chapman knew he had to find a replacement quickly. As always he set his sights on the best, and there is none better than David Jack of the celebrated body-swerve, whose goals have helped Bolton to two Cup triumphs at Wembley.

The first problem was getting Bolton to agree to sell. Whatever Mr Chapman did to persuade the Bolton board, they finally gave him a price — £13,000. It took another week and two more meetings between the clubs before the final figure was agreed — £10,890, which knocks the previous record out of sight.

The FA president, Sir Charles Clegg, has stated that no player in the world is worth £10,000. Arsenal feel they have got themselves a bargain in the England inside-right, at 29 one of the most cultured footballers in the country. And Mr Chapman's record in getting his money's worth from players speaks for itself.

David Jack, subject of a transfer record.

First defeat — England slip in Spain

ENGLAND LOST for the first time to a foreign side when they went down 4–3 to Spain in Madrid on 15 May. Coming as it did at the end of an arduous tour in which this was their third match in a week, it is perhaps not so surprising that they were found wanting. But it is still a shock to discover that the Continentals are catching up.

Even without Dean, England won easily in France (4–1) and Belgium (5–1), with Camsell scoring two and four goals respectively. They should have been warned, however, that Spain had just accounted for Portugal 5–0 and France 8–1, and were not the Continental pushovers England were accustomed to facing. And Spain's crafty coach Fred Pentland, the 46-year-old former Middlesbrough and England winger, had made sure that the match would be played when the sun was at its height.

Unfortunately Camsell had to miss the game through injury, but without him England still gained a half-time lead. The torrid heat, however, was beginning to take its toll. After the interval, with 30,000 excited fans urging them on and the ball bouncing shoulder-high on the bone-hard pitch, the Spaniards' fine dribbling and passing skills began to bear fruit. England led 2–0 and 3–2, but finally wilted and Spain gained a famous 4–3 victory, truly a milestone in the history of the game.

The combination of the conditions, the strange atmosphere and skilful opponents had proved too much for an inexperienced England side who relied too much on full-backs Cooper and Blenkinsop.

FOOTBALL FOCUS

- Numbered shirts were worn in the League for the first time on 25 August, by Arsenal at Hillsborough and Chelsea against Swansea at Stamford Bridge.
- Hughie Gallacher scored a record five goals for Scotland in their 7-3 win over Ireland in Belfast on 23 February.
- Scotland beat England 1–0 at Hampden Park when Alex Cheyne scored in the dying minutes direct from a corner, the first such goal in an international.
- Bradford City won Division 3N with a League record 128 goals, 82 of them at home. They opened the season with an 11–1 win over Rotherham and hit eight goals three times, including once away.
- Bolton won their third Wembley final, and keeper Dick Pym kept his third clean sheet.
- After last year's triumphant "double", Rangers' Cup hoodoo paid them a return visit, when Jock Buchanan became the first player to be sent off in a final. Rangers, who lost only once in the League and won the title by a record 16 points from Celtic, lost 2–0 at Hampden to unfancied Kilmarnock.
- Despite Sheffield Wednesday's fine home record, they were outscored at home by six other clubs, including Leicester and Sheffield United, who both enjoyed 10–0 victories, over Portsmouth and Burnley respectively, neither of whom were relegated. Cardiff, the only side in Division One to concede fewer than 60 goals and who conceded fewest goals away, were relegated.

Seed sprouts League title

WHEN WEDNESDAY manager Bob Brown made veteran Jimmy Seed captain last season, he inspired the Sheffield club to rise from the bottom of the table to 14th, with 17 points in their last 10 games. The transformation has continued this season, and although the 33-year-old former Spurs inside-right is not as sprightly as he was, his influence on the team has been paramount in their annexation of the League Championship. Wednesday's success has been achieved despite an away record that would not look out of place at the bottom of the table. They were, however, unbeaten at Hillsborough. In early October they started a run of 16 matches with only one defeat that took them into the lead at the start of December, and they remained there until the finish, to claim their third League title.

Jimmy Seed, influence behind Wednesday's success.

FINAL SCORE

Football League
Division 1: Sheffield Wednesday
Top scorer: Dave Halliday (Sunderland) 43
Division 2: Middlesbrough
Division 3S: Charlton Athletic
Division 3N: Bradford City

FA Cup Final
Bolton Wanderers 2 Portsmouth 0

Scottish League
Division 1: Rangers
Top scorer: Evelyn Morrison (Falkirk) 43
Division 2: Dundee United

Scottish FA Cup Final
Kilmarnock 2 Rangers 0

International Championship
Scotland, 6 pts

Heroes of the Twenties

THE GAME in the 1920s was blessed with two of the most prolific goalscorers in the history of British football, Dixie Dean and Jimmy McGrory. Admittedly, with the change of the offside law in the mid-twenties, there was a sudden explosion of goals. But these two stars, Dean of Everton and McGrory of Celtic, continued to find the net regularly long after defences had got to grips with the new law.

Heading for success

Dean began to hit the headlines in the first season after the change, 1925–26, when as an 18-year-old he scored 32 goals in 38 matches. Two seasons later, he was never out of the headlines, as the whole country followed his successful pursuit of the League record. Tremendously strong and with two good feet, he was famed for his heading ability, and he scored 17 goals in 13 games for England in the twenties.

At Celtic, McGrory had a hard act to follow — Jimmy Quinn. But he became the greatest goalscorer in British football, and was perhaps Celtic's best-loved player. He was not particularly tall, but he was fast and powerful, with a deadly knack for converting the half-chance. He scored perhaps a third of his goals with his head, many by diving full length to meet low crosses.

Scottish masters

McGrory's international career was limited because he happened to be the contemporary of Hughie Gallacher, rated by many as the best centre-forward of them all. The little Scot stood barely 5ft 6in,

Alan Morton, the "Wee Blue Devil".

but he was a giant among footballers, and idolized in Scotland, where he played for Airdrie, and on Tyneside, where he starred for Newcastle. He had all the gifts — powerful shooting, the ability to poke the ball in with little backlift, a flair for the unexpected, speed off the mark, a deceptive body-swerve, ball control and, despite his lack of inches, remarkable heading ability. He scored 22 goals in 17 internationals before he went to Chelsea in 1930.

For Scotland, Gallacher played between two of the finest wingers they have ever had, Alan Morton and Alex Jackson. Left-winger Morton helped Rangers to seven League titles in the twenties (and two more afterwards), and won 31 Scottish caps, tormenting every right-back England tried. Only 5ft 4in, he possessed fabulous dribbling skills, speed and close control. The goalscoring Jackson, on the right, had gazelle-like speed and style, and for Scotland was adept at getting on the end of Morton's floated crosses. He played for Scotland in his first League season, with Aberdeen, and became the idol of the fans at Huddersfield and known as the "Laughing Cavalier" to crowds everywhere, but retired surprisingly early.

Forward for England

In addition to Dean, the English stars who were playing up front in this period included Middlesbrough's equally prolific George Camsell, a man who never let England down, and a

Dean climbs above the Arsenal defence at Highbury.

quartet of inside-forwards — Charlie Buchan, Joe Smith, Billy Walker and David Jack. Smith and Buchan, who both came to prominence before the Great War, were inspiring captains, Smith leading Bolton to two Cup wins, while Buchan became the brains of Arsenal after an outstanding career with Sunderland. The elegant,

Hughie Gallacher (left) and Alex Jackson.

thoughtful Jack also starred for Bolton before, like Buchan, signing for Arsenal in a record transfer. Billy Walker was a long-time inspiration for Aston Villa and scored nine goals in 17 games for England during the twenties.

The 'Old Firm'

Even in their lean years, when Rangers reigned supreme, Celtic had their heroes. Patsy Gallagher was still with them till the mid-twenties, rivalling McGrory in their affections before joining Falkirk. Rangers' stronger all-round squad of players, apart from Morton, included their impressive and authoritative skipper David Meiklejohn at centre-half, forceful winger Sandy Archibald, and Andy Cunningham, a powerhouse of an inside-forward with an explosive shot.

Wales and Ireland

Wales won three International Championships in the twenties, and both their success and Cardiff's rise to fame was in no small measure due to Fred Keenor, an outstanding captain and centre-half. Ireland, for their part, were unable to repeat their triumph of 1914. But Sheffield United captain Billy Gillespie, a star of that era, guided them throughout the twenties, and with Celtic's Patsy Gallagher often in the other inside-forward berth Ireland managed to achieve a degree of respectability in the international arena.

Charlie Buchan leads Arsenal out.

Quick-thinking James schemes Arsenal victory

A SLICK PIECE of thinking by Alex James from a free-kick after 16 minutes set Arsenal on their way to victory over Huddersfield in the Cup final at Wembley. James, fouled by Goodall, placed the ball on the ground and knocked it out to Cliff Bastin without even straightening up, having paused just long enough to get the nod from the referee. The young winger beat his man on the left before slipping the ball inside again to James, who took it in his stride and slammed it past Turner. And it was from James's pass out of defence that Lambert scored late on to clinch the game 2–0 for Arsenal.

When the two teams came out in pairs — a new idea — it must have been a very proud moment for Arsenal manager Herbert Chapman, who built the Huddersfield club into such a footballing force in the 1920s. James and Bastin, both signed by Mr Chapman last summer, were the Arsenal stars. But the score-line does not do justice to Huddersfield's second-half rally. Preedy in Arsenal's goal brought off some fine saves, but he also made some appalling blunders which remarkably went unpunished. For Huddersfield, left-winger Billy Smith was most dangerous, but the chances he made went begging.

This is Arsenal's first major honour. Mr Chapman has tried various forward permutations, but finally seems to have got it right at the expense of his old club. Huddersfield's half-back line were outstanding, and they contributed to one of the best finals seen for some years.

An uninvited visitor to the Cup final, the German airship Graf Zeppelin over Wembley.

FOOTBALL FOCUS

- Jim Dyet scored eight goals on his first-class debut, in King's Park's 12–2 win over Forfar in the Scottish Division Two on 2 January.
- Five days before the Cup final, Arsenal drew 6–6at Leicester, the highest-scoring draw in British first-class football.
- Plymouth finally made it into the Second Division, winning Division Three (S) by seven points, after finishing second for six of the last eight years. They were unbeaten at home again, and in the last nine years have lost only nine League games at the well-named Home Park.
- The first World Cup took place in Uruguay in July, and the hosts beat deadly rivals Argentina 4–2 in the final. Thirteen countries took part. There were no British entries, the home countries having left FIFA.

Tactical talk key to England success

FOR THE first time, the England players met on Friday evening to discuss their match the next day against Scotland at Wembley. If the result is anything to go by, the tactical talk worked wonders, as England won 5–2. It won them the International Championship outright for the first time since before the war, and it was their best victory over Scotland since the 1890s, going some way towards wiping out memories of the 5–1 defeat by the "Wembley Wizards" two years ago.

England were one up in 11 minutes, and scored another three in a five-minute spell midway through the first half. All four goals were made by Derby outside-right Sammy Crooks, who had a brilliant match on his international debut. The other winger, Ellis Rimmer of Sheffield Wednesday, also playing his first game for his country, scored twice.

Skipper David Jack, doubtful up to the day of the match, limped through most of the last hour, otherwise the score might have been greater.

Scotland never stopped trying, however, and made a fine match of it in the second half.

Slip it to Joe

"SLIP IT TO JOE" was the cry at Celtic Park, as Northern Ireland ran up their biggest ever win, 7–0 over Wales in the International Championship. And nearly every time the big centre-forward Joe Bambrick got the ball, he seemed to put it in the net — six goals, the highest individual tally for any British player in an international. The last time the lads in green scored seven — the only time — was back in February 1891, when Ireland beat Wales 7–2, also at Belfast.

Bambrick, from Linfield, was up against doughty centre-half Fred Keenor, the Welsh captain, who could not have had a more embarrassing match. In the Welsh defence, however, apart from Keenor, only left-back T. Jones, with three caps, had experienced international football before.

Joe Bambrick, six goals for Northern Ireland.

FINAL SCORE

Football League
Division 1: Sheffield Wednesday
Top scorer: Vic Watson (West Ham United) 41
Division 2: Blackpool
Division 3S: Plymouth Argyle
Division 3N: Port Vale

FA Cup Final

Arsenal	2	Huddersfield Town	0

Scottish League
Division 1: Rangers
Top scorer: Benny Yorston (Aberdeen) 38
Division 2: Leith Athletic

Scottish FA Cup Final

Rangers	0	Partick Thistle	0
Replay: Rangers	2	Partick Thistle	1

International Championship
England, 6 pts

The World Cup kicks off

When FIFA were founded in 1904, they included in their statutes a clause giving them the sole right to organize a World Championship. It was another 26 years before such a competition came about, and by that time the four British associations, who had been in and out of FIFA twice, were no longer members.

THE MAN who pioneered the World Cup was Jules Rimet, a French lawyer who became president of FIFA in 1921. Uruguay won the Olympic football competition in 1924, but in 1926 FIFA decided that, because of the difference in standards between amateur and professional football, the Olympics were no longer representative of the top level of the game. At the FIFA meeting during the 1928 Olympics at Amsterdam, it was decided to stage a World Championship every four years from 1930.

There were six contenders to stage the first World Cup — Holland, Hungary, Italy, Spain, Sweden, who had originally opposed the idea, and Uruguay. The South Americans were the obvious choice. Not only had they won the last two Olympic football tournaments, but they were due to celebrate their independence centenary in 1930, they undertook to build a special 100,000-capacity stadium for the World Cup and, an important consideration, they promised to pay the full expenses of every participating country.

Even so, the response from Europe was disappointing. The problem was the time that players would have to be away — with travel to and from Uruguay by boat, at least two months. The major Continental soccer powers, including Germany, Italy and Spain, all declined. With eight weeks to go, there was not a single entry from Europe. It required the intervention of M.Rimet to persuade France to go, and likewise the Belgian FIFA representative Rudolphe Seeldrayers secured his country's entry. King Carol of Romania selected a side himself and arranged their release from work. Yugoslavia were a late entry, making Europe's contingent up to four. They joined seven South American countries, Mexico and the United States.

WORLD CUP FOCUS

- Hector Castro, the centre-forward who played in one group match and the final for Uruguay and scored in both, had the lower part of one arm missing.
- Argentina's captain and centre-forward Manuel Ferreyra missed the game against Mexico to take his university exams. His replacement Guillermo Stabile scored a hat-trick, stayed in the team with Ferreyra at inside-left, and finished as the tournament's top scorer.
- When the referee gave a foul against the United States in the semi-final, their medical attendant rushed on to the pitch to protest, threw down his bag, smashing a bottle of chloroform, was overcome by fumes and had to be helped off.
- The two halves of the final were played with different balls after an argument between the two sides.

Nasazzi (Uruguay), left, and Ferreyra (Argentina) toss up before the final.

Qualifying groups

The original idea to stage a knock-out tournament was dropped because of the low number of entrants, and the 13 countries were divided into four groups, the winners of each to qualify for the semi-finals. The Uruguayan hosts provided armed guards — soldiers with fixed bayonets — for all the teams. Although the four European teams were given a huge welcome when they arrived in Montevideo, they were by no means the cream of European football, and none of them was seeded. The four seeds were Argentina, Brazil, Uruguay and, surprisingly, the United States.

There were no drawn matches in the qualifying groups, each semi-finalist coming through with a 100 per cent record. The first ever World Cup match took

Soldiers with fixed bayonets guarded all the teams . . . boatloads of Argentinians crossed the River Plate and were searched for arms

place on 13 July, France beating Mexico 4–1 despite losing their keeper after 10 minutes with a kick on the jaw. This was the group of four countries, and the organization was such that France had to appear again two days later to play Argentina.

In the meantime, Belgium had gone down 3–0 to the United States, a team, nicknamed the "shot-putters" by the French, that included five former Scottish professionals, and also an Englishman. But the other European entries, Yugoslavia and Romania, had victories over South American teams.

Stabile, arm in air, puts Argentina 2-1 up in the final.

Argentinian anger

The first signs of trouble came in Group One, when the Brazilian referee blew for time some six minutes too soon, with Argentina one up on France. The Argentine fans in the crowd invaded the pitch, while the French players harangued the referee. After consulting his linesmen, he managed to restart the match, which finished with no further score. The Argentine players, angry that the Uruguayan crowd had supported France throughout, were further incensed when they carried two Frenchmen off shoulder-high at the finish. There were complaints to the organizing committee, and Argentina threatened to go home.

They completed their matches, however, though not without incident. In their game with Mexico, the Bolivian referee awarded five penalties, each side scoring from two, and against Chile, "hatchet-man" centre-half Luisito Monti started a brawl that needed the police to quell. Nevertheless, Argentina qualified for the semi-finals, where they joined Yugoslavia and the United States, who both went through comfortably.

Uruguay, the hosts, who had to wait for the late completion of the Centenary Stadium before they could start their matches, struggled to beat Peru, but found their form in the group decider against Romania.

Semi-final slaughter

The two great rivals, Uruguay and Argentina, Olympic finalists two years earlier, emerged from their semi-finals with comprehensive victories, both 6–1. Uruguay, with the nucleus of their Olympic side, went a goal down, but proved far too strong in the end for the Yugoslavs. Argentina, too, proved too strong — literally — even for the fit and fast American "shot-putters", who found themselves only one down at half-time but with one player missing (broken leg after 10 minutes), another suffering from a kick on the jaw, and their keeper also badly injured. It was not surprising that Argentina put five goals past them in the second half.

Argentine keeper Botasso is helpless to stop Uruguay's third goal.

Trouble-free final

The final took place in the Centenary Stadium, Montevideo, on 30 July. Boatloads of Argentinians crossed the River Plate for this "local derby" and were searched for arms. The rivalry between the opposing sets of fans was intense, bitter even. The referee, the Belgian John Langenus, in his customary plus-fours, agreed to officiate only hours before the start, having secured a guarantee of his and his fellow officials' safety. Yet the game itself, expected to be a cauldron of emotion, went off without any trouble.

Uruguay scored first through Dorado after 12 minutes. But Peucelle equalized for Argentina, and centre-forward Guillermo Stabile, who had been brought in for their second match and already scored seven goals, put them ahead 10 minutes before the interval with a disputed goal. Thankfully, the Uruguayan fans accepted the referee's courageous decision.

In the second half, Uruguay's renowned half-back line — the "Iron Curtain", as it was known — of Andrade, Fernandez and Gestido began to take charge, and Uruguay exerted their technical superiority. The goals came though Cea, Iriate and Castro, and they ran out deserved 4–2 winners.

The trophy was presented by Jules Rimet to the winning captain, José Nasazzi. Montevideo went wild, and the authorities proclaimed the next day a national holiday. Sadly, in Buenos Aires, the Uruguayan consulate was stoned, such is the uncontrollable nationalism that so often surfaces in the name of sport.

FINAL SCORE

Group 1

France	4	Mexico	1
Argentina	1	France	0
Chile	3	Mexico	0
Chile	1	France	0
Argentina	6	Mexico	3
Argentina	3	Chile	1

	P	W	D	L	F	A	P
Argentina	3	3	0	0	10	4	6
Chile	3	2	0	1	5	3	4
France	3	1	0	2	4	3	2
Mexico	3	0	0	3	4	13	0

Group 2

Yugoslavia	2	Brazil	1
Yugoslavia	4	Bolivia	0
Brazil	4	Bolivia	0

	P	W	D	L	F	A	P
Yugoslavia	2	2	0	0	6	1	4
Brazil	2	1	0	1	5	2	2
Bolivia	2	0	0	2	0	8	0

Group 3

Romania	3	Peru	1
Uruguay	1	Peru	0
Uruguay	4	Romania	0

	P	W	D	L	F	A	P
Uruguay	2	2	0	0	5	0	4
Romania	2	1	0	1	3	5	2
Peru	2	0	0	2	1	4	0

Group 4

United States	3	Belgium	0
United States	3	Paraguay	0
Paraguay	1	Belgium	0

	P	W	D	L	F	A	P
USA	2	2	0	0	6	0	4
Paraguay	2	1	0	1	1	3	2
Belgium	2	0	0	2	0	4	0

SEMI-FINALS

Argentina	6	United States	1
Uruguay	6	Yugoslavia	1

FINAL

Uruguay	4	Argentina	2

Montevideo, 30 July 1930. Attendance 90,000

Uruguay: Ballesteros, Nasazzi, Mascheroni, Andrade, Fernandez, Gestido, Dorado, Scarone, Castro, Cea, Iriarte
(Scorers: Dorado, Cea, Iriate, Castro)

Argentina: Botasso, Della Torre, Paternoster, Evaristo J, Monti, Suarez, Peucelle, Varallo, Stabile, Ferreyra, Evaristo M
(Scorers: Peucelle, Stabile)

Leading scorers: 8 Stabile (Argentina) 5 Cea (Uruguay) 4 Subiabre (Chile)

Division One record for Arsenal

ARSENAL, the first southern club to win the League Championship, have done so with a record 66 points. Their goal tally was only one fewer than the new record of 128, set by runners-up Villa, seven points behind Arsenal. Arsenal's remarkable away record — won 14, drawn five, lost two, identical to their performance at home — sets new First Division figures for matches won and points scored away from home. And their 60 away goals is a new League record — no club in the four divisions has reached 50 before.

The shining star of this Arsenal triumph has been little Alex James, revelling in his new role of making goals rather than scoring them. Those to benefit have been his left-wing partner Cliff "Boy" Bastin (28 goals), bustling centre-forward Jack Lambert (38, a new club record), peerless inside-right David Jack (31) and right-winger Joe Hulme, the "Highbury Express", who provided a splendid service for the central attackers as well as scoring 14 goals.

Arsenal started the season with five straight wins and never looked back. They suffered their first loss on 11 October, 4–2 at Derby, their only defeat in the first 18 games. They failed to score in only one match, a goalless draw at home to Huddersfield on 7 March, which, oddly enough, was the first time they kept a clean sheet themselves. Their only lapse was a 5–1 reverse at Villa Park in mid-March, revenge for Villa who had lost 5–2 at Highbury and were knocked out of the Cup by Arsenal in the third round. But that was Arsenal's last defeat.

Bastin – goals from Arsenal's left wing.

Giant-killers slain

GALLANT SOUTHPORT from the Third Division North, Cup conquerors of three sides from higher divisions, were finally put in their place by Second Division leaders Everton. There were no half-measures at Goodison Park, where Dixie Dean and company, still smarting from last season's relegation, thrashed the upstarts 9–1, a record win for the sixth round.

After wins over Millwall, Blackpool and Bradford PA, Southport's hopes of reaching the semi-finals were shattered. Dean, who scored four goals when Everton won 6–0 at Crystal Palace in the fourth round, collected four more.

Dean heads one of his four against Southport.

Throstles singing in the rain

THE MIDLANDS came into their own at Wembley in the wettest Cup final seen for years, when Second Division West Bromwich Albion beat their First Division neighbours Birmingham 2–1. With centre-forward W.G.Richardson, scorer of their two goals, in splendid form, the Throstles really were on song. Such was their team spirit and their superior teamwork that, were it not for the brilliance of England's Harry Hibbs in the Birmingham goal, they would have won by a cricket score.

Despite the dreadful conditions, the football was of a high standard. The 21-year-old Billy Richardson — the phantom "G" is for "Ginger" to distinguish him from the Albion centre-half of the same name — opened the scoring after 26 minutes. England leader Joe Bradford equalized for Birmingham 12 minutes into the second half, but Richardson restored Albion's lead straight from the kick-off, and after that there was only one team in it.

FOOTBALL FOCUS

- Celtic were 2–0 down in the Scottish Cup final against Motherwell with eight minutes left, but a goal from McGrory and an own goal in the last seconds earned them a replay, which they won 4–2. Over 200,000 saw the two games at Hampden Park.
- West Bromwich became the first club to win the Cup and promotion in the same season, finishing seven points behind Everton, whom they beat in the semi-finals.
- On a disastrous tour in May, Scotland suffered their first foreign defeats, losing 5–0 to Austria and 3–0 to Italy, before beating Switzerland 3–2.

FINAL SCORE

Football League
Division 1: Arsenal
Top scorer: Pongo Waring (Aston Villa) 49
Division 2: Everton
Division 3S: Notts County
Division 3N: Chesterfield

FA Cup Final
West Bromwich Albion 2 Birmingham City 1

Scottish League
Division 1: Rangers
Top scorer: Barney Battles (Hearts) 44
Division 2: Third Lanark

Scottish FA Cup Final

Celtic	2	Motherwell	2
Replay: Celtic	4	Motherwell	2

International Championship
England, Scotland, 4 pts

Pongo Waring, leading League scorer.

Tragedy of Celtic keeper

WHEN 23-YEAR-OLD Celtic keeper John Thomson died, there were 30,000 mourners at Glasgow's Queen Street Station to see his coffin off, and 3,000 attended his funeral. He was a much-loved hero at Parkhead, and had already established himself in the Scotland side.

Thomson was renowned for his dashes off the line and his daring saves at the feet of onrushing forwards. So it was no surprise when he left his goal to thwart a Rangers attack when the two great Glasgow clubs met at Ibrox Park on 5 September. As Rangers' Sam English collected a long through-ball and ran it into the penalty area, Thomson threw himself at the attacker's feet to deflect the ball wide of goal. But this time he didn't get up. His skull was fractured in the collision, and he died five hours later in the nearby Victoria Infirmary.

Thomson joined Celtic as a 17-year-old, having been spotted in a junior game in his native Fife. He was at first reluctant to sign for the big club and make soccer his career, because his mother had dreamt that he would be seriously injured keeping goal. He won two Cup-winners' medals with Celtic, and was set to keep goal for Scotland for the next decade before his tragic death.

John Thomson goes down to make his fatal save.

'New' England outclass Scots

ENGLAND wrapped up the International Championship with a 3–0 victory over Scotland at Wembley, finishing with maximum points and a 12–3 goal record.

With an experimental eleven that included five new caps, England outclassed a poor Scottish side, although they needed two goals in the last 10 minutes to confirm their superiority. The outstanding player of the match was a newcomer, left-half Sam Weaver of Newcastle, whose 30-yard throw-ins have brought a new dimension to wing-half play.

Sam Weaver, throw-in expert.

FOOTBALL FOCUS

- Wigan Borough of Division Three (N) became the first League club to resign during a season. They had played only six games, and their record was expunged.
- Motherwell won their first ever Scottish title, beating Rangers by five points and scoring a record 119 goals. Centre-forward Bill McFadyen, who played in 34 of their 38 games, scored 52 goals, a Scottish Division One record. Motherwell were the first club outside the Glasgow "Old Firm" to triumph since Third Lanark 28 years earlier.
- Everton won the League title in their first season back, with a Division One home record of 84 goals, including nine against Leicester and third-placed Wednesday, eight against Cup-winners Newcastle, and seven against Chelsea, with Dean twice notching five.
- England gained revenge over Spain for their 1929 defeat, winning 7–1 at Highbury in December.

FINAL SCORE

Football League
Division 1: Everton
Top scorer: Dixie Dean (Everton) 44
Division 2: Wolverhampton Wanderers
Division 3S: Fulham
Division 3N: Lincoln City

FA Cup Final

Newcastle United	2	Arsenal	1

Scottish League
Division 1: Motherwell
Top scorer: Bill McFadyen (Motherwell) 52
Division 2: East Stirlingshire

Scottish FA Cup Final

Rangers	1	Kilmarnock	1
Replay: Rangers	3	Kilmarnock	0

International Championship
England, 6 pts

Cup final controversy ends Arsenal's 'double' dream

A frame from the news film shows the ball clearly over the line.

ARSENAL, striving to become the first club this century to achieve the elusive League and Cup "double", had their hopes dashed when Newcastle beat them 2–1 at Wembley after the Gunners had taken an early lead through Bob John.

It was not a great Cup final, but the game will go down in history as one of the most controversial because of Newcastle's hotly disputed equalizer. When Jimmy Richardson chased the ball to the byline, it seemed to have gone out of play before he crossed it for Jack Allen to shoot in from close range. The Arsenal defence certainly thought so; they made no attempt to stop Allen. But the referee was unrepentant: "It was a goal... As God is my judge, the man was in play. I was eight yards away." But if British Movietone News were judge, the ball was clearly over the line and the referee was 20 yards away!

Arsenal had come to the final as favourites, despite missing their injured midfield genius Alex James. But they just weren't the same without the little Scot to weave his magic. Allen scored a second after 71 minutes, and Newcastle held on to run out worthy winners.

England beat Austria's 'Wunderteam'

ENGLAND WON the long-awaited showdown at Stamford Bridge on 7 December with the much-vaunted "Wunderteam", but were given a fright by the skilful Austrians before they emerged 4–3 victors.

Austria, coached by former Bolton player Jimmy Hogan, arrived with an imposing reputation, earned by such victories as their 5–0 shaming of Scotland (admittedly without any Rangers or Celtic players) in Vienna in May 1931. They had compiled an 18-match unbeaten run, including 15 wins, before they met England.

England, however, expected to win. Their own reputation on the Continent was formidable, the only real blemishes being their 1929 defeat in Madrid and a 5–2 reverse in Paris last year. At home, where Austria were only the third team to be invited, they could look back on a 6–1 defeat of Belgium in 1923 and their 7–1 humiliation of the overawed Spaniards a year ago.

Austria, too, seemed overawed, despite their standing as the "unofficial champions of the Continent". Before they could settle down, England scored through Blackpool centre-forward Jimmy Hampson, who added another after 27 minutes.

It is a great tribute to the Austrians that they did not fall apart at this stage. Calmed down during the interval by their manager Hugo Meisl, the architect of Austrian football, they began to play with their accustomed confidence, and some of their moves brought the sporting English crowd to their feet in admiration. They soon put England under greater pressure, with their elusive centre-forward Matthias Sindelar, the "Man of Paper", continually pulling the English defence out of position. Nevertheless, England always managed to keep in front.

England score through Hampson before Austria settle down.

FOOTBALL FOCUS

- Wales, who won the International Championship, scored their best ever win against Scotland and their first on Scottish soil since 1906, when they won 5–2 at Tynecastle despite playing with 10 men for 80 minutes.
- Numbered shirts were worn for the first time in the FA Cup final, winners Everton being numbered from 1 (the keeper) to 11 and Manchester City from 12 to 22 (keeper).
- Motherwell (114 goals) outscored Rangers by one goal again, but Rangers regained their League title from them by three points, and they were also pipped for the Cup by Celtic.

Numbered shirts were used in the Cup final.

Mighty Arsenal are humbled by Walsall

LOWLY Third Division Walsall pulled off perhaps the biggest shock in the history of the FA Cup when they beat League-leaders Arsenal 2–0 in the third round. True, Arsenal had just hit a bad patch with three defeats in five games, and a flu epidemic going round the country had robbed them of Eddie Hapgood, Jack Lambert and Bob John. But this should not have mattered. Nor should the fact that Walsall were unbeaten at home in the League. Perhaps manager Herbert Chapman made a rare mistake by replacing his stars with three players who had never appeared in the first team before and by dropping the off-form Joe Hulme.

The tiny ground was unfamiliar, and if Walsall's over-vigorous game took undue advantage of a lenient referee, they cannot be blamed for playing in the only way that would upset the First Division giants.

Arsenal were, indeed, thrown out of their stride. Alex James took a severe battering. And the new players proved a disaster. Charlie Walsh, who thought he was the best centre-forward on Arsenal's books, was a bag of nerves. He missed chance after chance and completely disrupted their attack. Outside-right Billy Warnes was too fragile for such a baptism of fire, and left-back Tommy Black allowed himself to get rattled.

When centre-forward Gilbert Alsop headed in a corner on the hour to put Walsall in front, the roar of the crowd could be heard two miles away. Five minutes later, Bill Sheppard completed the job, converting a penalty after Black had badly and gratuitously fouled Alsop — something so alien to Arsenal tradition that Black was immediately put on the transfer list.

FINAL SCORE

Football League
Division 1: Arsenal
Top scorer: Jack Bowers (Derby County) 35
Division 2: Stoke City
Division 3S: Brentford
Division 3N: Hull City

FA Cup Final

Everton	3	Manchester City	0

Scottish League
Division 1: Rangers
Top scorer: Bill McFadyen (Motherwell) 45
Division 2: Hibernian

Scottish FA Cup Final

Celtic	1	Motherwell	0

International Championship
Wales, 5 pts

Death of a sporting colossus

ARSENAL manager Herbert Chapman is dead. The shock news came out on the morning of Arsenal's home match with Sheffield Wednesday, and players and fans learned of it from the newspaper billboards on their way to the ground. He died at three o'clock on Saturday morning, 6 January, having bestrode the football world like a colossus, not only as a club manager, but as a tactician and an innovator. He brought success to every club he managed, and he was adored by both spectators and players, whose welfare was always uppermost in his mind.

Mr Chapman died in the course of his duty. He caught a chill watching a game at Bury on New Year's Day, but still decided to go to Sheffield the following day to watch Wednesday, Arsenal's next opponents. Despite a high temperature, he ignored doctor's advice and went to Guildford to see Arsenal's reserves. When he finally took to his bed, it was too late, for pneumonia had set in.

Born in Sheffield, Herbert Chapman was an enthusiastic wing-half or inside-forward with a number of clubs — he was Spurs' leading scorer in 1905–06 with 11 goals in the Southern League — before joining Northampton as player-manager in 1907. He transformed them from nonentities to Southern League champions in 1909. He joined struggling Second Division club Leeds City as secretary-manager in 1912, building them up to wartime champions before transferring his efforts to managing an arms factory.

He was lost to football after the war, when Leeds were expelled from the League and club officials banned for irregular payments to players during the hostilities. But he cleared his name of any involvement in the scandal before taking over at Huddersfield in 1921. His successes since then are legion: the Cup and the first two of Huddersfield's record three successive Championships, followed at Arsenal by the Cup and two League titles in the last four years as he transformed them into the most famous club side in the world. He leaves Arsenal on top of the League again as they begin the New Year without him.

Herbert Chapman (bottom right) with one of his early Arsenal teams.

FOOTBALL FOCUS

- Scottish League and Cup champions Rangers beat Blairgowrie 14–2 in the first round of the Cup, and Jim Fleming scored nine.
- Broadcaster and Arsenal managing director George Allison took over as secretary-manager at Highbury on the death of Herbert Chapman. His first buy, centre-forward Ted Drake from Southampton, scored seven goals in 10 games to help Arsenal retain the Championship.
- A crowd of 84,569, a record for any English club game other than the Cup final, saw eventual Cup-winners Manchester City beat Stoke 1–0 at Maine Road in the sixth round on 3 March.
- Stanley Rous, a Hertfordshire schoolteacher, refereed the Cup final and was then appointedsecretary of the Football Association.

Teenage keeper faints after Cup victory

FRANK SWIFT, Manchester City's 19-year-old goalkeeper, was so overcome at the end of the Cup final that he collapsed under his cross-bar and had to be helped to the Royal Box to collect his winners' medal. It was a close game, and Swift blamed himself for the goal that gave Portsmouth a half-time lead. In the dressing-room during the interval, centre-forward Freddy Tilson, trying to console the youngster, told him not to worry because he would score a couple in the second half. He was true to his words!

Swift, who joined City as a 17-year-old, has played only half a season in the first team. So it is not surprising that the nervous tension got to him in the end, especially with photographers behind his goal counting away the last minutes.

The tall keeper with the huge hands felt he should have done more than just touch Rutherford's cross-shot on its way to the net after 27 minutes of the first half. But City became only the second team to recover from a goal deficit at Wembley when Tilson took advantage of Portsmouth centre-half Allen's temporary absence to equalize, and then scored the winner four minutes from time.

Frank Swift, Manchester City's young keeper.

FINAL SCORE

Football League
Division 1: Arsenal
Top scorer: Jack Bowers (Derby County) 35
Division 2: Grimsby Town
Division 3S: Norwich City
Division 3N: Barnsley

FA Cup Final
Manchester City 2 Portsmouth 1

Scottish League
Division 1: Rangers
Top scorer: Jimmy Smith (Rangers) 41
Division 2: Albion Rovers

Scottish FA Cup Final
Rangers 5 St Mirren 0

International Championship
Wales, 5 pts

Italy win — by a fluke!

WORLD CUP QUOTES

"It was a brawl, not an exhibition of football."

HUGO MEISL,
Austria's supremo, after his team's 2–1 victory over Hungary in the quarter-finals.

"I was off balance and late to react when Orsi scored from eight yards."

FRANTISEK PLANICKA,
Czechoslovakia's perfectionist goalkeeper, blaming himself for Italy's late equalizer in the final from Orsi's freak shot. Next day, Orsi — watched by photographers — tried 20 times to reproduce the shot, but without success.

"Every one of our guests felt the pulsating of the masculine energies of a bursting vitality, in this our Mussolini's Italy."

GIOVANNI MAURO,
Italian delegate to FIFA and one of the tournament's organizers.

"In the majority of countries, the World Championship was called a sporting fiasco, because, beside the desire to win, all other sporting considerations were non-existent."

JOHN LANGENUS,
Belgian referee who had taken the 1930 final and one of the first-round matches in 1934.

In this second World Cup, Europe showed that South America had not cornered the market in violent play and fanatical nationalism, while the standard of refereeing still left much to be desired. There were again no British teams, and the South American contingent was weak, so Austria and Italy were the favourites.

THE 1934 WORLD CUP was the first international football competition exploited for propaganda purposes. Italy, with a Fascist government, won the right to stage Europe's first World Cup only after eight meetings of FIFA. They had the resources, the stadiums and sufficient big cities to handle what had now become a prestigious event, with political capital an extra prize for the victors. There were originally 32 entrants, but the holders, Uruguay, were missing, piqued at the poor response from Europe when they staged the first World Cup and beset with domestic troubles. The countries were divided into 12 geographical groups to produce 16 finalists. Even Italy had to qualify by playing Greece. Brazil and Argentina qualified without playing when their scheduled opponents withdrew, and the United States beat Mexico 4–2 in an extra qualifier in Rome before the start of the tournament proper.

The finals were organized as a straight knock-out event, with eight of the 16 teams seeded in the first round. Both Brazil and 1930 runners-up Argentina, who, having already lost some of their players to Italian football, had left more of their stars at home, were beaten and found themselves making the long return trip after only one game.

Italy, who had selected three Argentinians of Italian extraction, including the ruthless centre-half Monti of Montevideo notoriety, beat the other long-distance travellers, the United States, by 7–1. Egypt, the African representatives, put up a spirited fight against Hungary in Naples before succumbing 4–2. Every team scored in the first round, which, apart from the football, was relatively free from incident. Hattricks were scored by Schiavio for Italy and Conen for Germany, 5–2 winners over Belgium.

Austrian keeper Platzer thwarts Italy's Schiavio in the semi-final.

European mayhem

The last eight now represented what was virtually a European Championship. And that's when the trouble started. Spain took the lead against Italy in Florence, but what had been a rough game went into an even more brutal extra time. The Italian ruthlessness went unpunished by the referee, and only a brilliant display by captain and keeper Ricardo Zamora enabled the crippled Spaniards to hold on for a replay. This took place the next day, and seven Spaniards, including the influential Zamora, as well as four Italians, were unfit to play.

If the Belgian referee for the first game had failed to control the mayhem, the Swiss official

Home advantage tells again in a 'sporting fiasco' where 'beside the desire to win, all other sporting considerations were non-existent' — JOHN LANGENUS, one of the 'intimidated' referees.

Combi dives too late to stop Puc's goal in the final, but Italy recovered to win in extra time.

for the replay was so poor that he was later suspended by his national association, adding fuel to the accusations of intimidation that abounded during the finals. It was a tough game for both sides, but the fitter Italians — manager Vittorio Pozzo had instilled discipline and prepared his squad physically and mentally in a secluded resort for six weeks before the finals — outlasted the Spaniards despite a fine display from the young replacement keeper Noguet.

The clash between neighbours and rivals Austria and Hungary promised to be a classic but developed instead into a brawl, with players arguing and Markos, the Hungarian right-winger, sent off. Austria played some good football, however, and deserved their win.

The Austrians should have been fresher for their semi-final than the Italians, who were playing their third match in four days. But they weren't, and the heavy rain in Milan before the kick-off produced a muddy pitch and the sort of conditions detested by the skilful passers and dribblers of the Viennese school. The Italians were also skilful, and they had been better prepared. A goal after 18 minutes by one of their Argentinian wingers, Guaita, settled the match.

In the other semi-final, played in Rome, Germany, conquerors of Sweden in the quarter-finals, met Czechoslovakia, who, in Frantisek Planicka, had perhaps the best goalkeeper of the tournament. The Czechs had improved as the finals progressed, and they outplayed the unimaginative Germans. They served up inventive, entertaining football, and their finishing proved better than that of their otherwise methodical opponents. The manner of their 3–1 victory, with Oldrich Nejedly scoring twice, promised a combative final with Italy.

A freak equalizer

The final provided a curiosity – both captains were goalkeepers. In a goalless first half, the Czechs looked the more dangerous side, with Antonin Puc proving a handful on the left for the Italian defence. At the other end, Planicka safely thwarted the Italian forwards. It was Puc, returning after going off with cramp, who stunned the crowd 20 minutes from time with a goal from a long shot for which Giampiero Combi dived too late. The Czechs could then have clinched the match. Centre-forward Sobotka should have done, but missed an open goal. Then inside-right Svoboda hit a post.

The Italians, watched by dictator Benito Mussolini, desperately piled on the pressure, but it took a freak goal by their Argentinian left-winger Raimondo Orsi to beat Planicka eight minutes from the end of normal time. Orsi, lured out of South America by Juventus in 1929, was noted for his speed, skill and powerful shot. He used the first two of these attributes as he took a ball from Guaita and hared through the Czech defence. He feinted with his left foot and then, eschewing the third of his qualities, somehow struck a right-foot shot-cum-lob that swerved and dipped crazily over Planicka and into the net.

In extra time, the Italians lasted the pace better, despite having inside-right Guiseppe Meazza limping on the wing. The Czechs had tended to ignore him, but he was no passenger, as he proved seven minutes into the first period. Receiving the ball on the right, he crossed it to Guaita, who in turn found Schiavio. The centre-forward neatly sidestepped a defender and shot past Planicka for what proved to be the winning goal. Tired as they were, the two sides continued to battle it out, with both keepers kept busy right to the end.

At the final whistle, the Italian players still had enough strength to hoist Pozzo on to their shoulders in triumph, and Combi was presented with the trophy by a jubilant Mussolini, gratified that the team's success had enhanced the prestige of his Fascist regime.

FINAL SCORE

FIRST ROUND

Italy	7	United States	1
Czechoslovakia	2	Romania	1
Germany	5	Belgium	2
Austria	3	France	2
Spain	3	Brazil	1
Switzerland	3	Holland	2
Sweden	3	Argentina	2
Hungary	4	Egypt	2

QUARTER-FINALS

Germany	2	Sweden	1
Austria	2	Hungary	1
Italy	1	Spain	1
Czechoslovakia	3	Switzerland	2

Replay

Italy	1	Spain	0

SEMI-FINALS

Czechoslovakia	3	Germany	1
Italy	1	Austria	0

THIRD-PLACE MATCH

Germany	3	Austria	2

FINAL

Italy (after extra time)	2	Czechoslovakia	1

Rome, 10 June 1934. Attendance 55,000

Italy: Combi, Monzeglio, Allemandi, Ferraris IV, Monti, Bertolini, Guaita, Meazza, Schiavio, Ferrari, Orsi
(Scorers: Orsi, Schiavio)
Czechoslovakia: Planicka, Zenizek, Ctyroky, Kostalek, Cambal, Krcil, Junek, Svoboda, Sobotka, Nejedly, Puc
(Scorer: Puc)

Leading scorers
4 Conen (Germany) Nejedly (Czechoslovakia) Schiavio (Italy)

Vittorio Pozzo (left) encourages his team before extra time.

Battle of Highbury

IT WASN'T SO much a football match, more a pitched battle, when England beat world champions Italy 3–2 at Highbury. Battered but unbowed, the eleven English heroes were queuing up for treatment after the match in the dressing-room, which looked more like a casualty clearing station.

When, after two minutes, Luisito Monti, Italy's ruthless Argentinian centre-half, broke a foot in a clash with Ted Drake and had to go off, the rest of the side went berserk. Pushing, elbowing, kicking, even jumping on players in their efforts to "retaliate" for what the crippled Monti had claimed was a deliberate foul, the Italians forgot about the football.

Italy's Ceresoli saves, with England's Drake (right) in close attendance.

England, with seven Arsenal players, a record for one club, were three up in 15 minutes despite missing a penalty. The culprit, outside-left Eric Brook, soon made amends, heading in a cross from 19-year-old right-winger Stanley Matthews and then whacking in a free-kick. England's new captain Eddie Hapgood received an elbow in his face and was off the field having the resultant broken nose treated when Drake hooked in a Matthews cross.

To the fore for England was rugged left-half Wilf Copping, whose famous shoulder-charge and tackle were never put to better use. It is a mystery, however, why the Swedish referee did not take a firmer hand. His reluctance to send anyone off might have been due to fear of causing a riot, as the Italian contingent in the 50,000 crowd was considerable.

After the interval — and spurred on by a pep-talk from Vittorio Pozzo — the Italians began to play football at last, and their skilful and stylish centre-forward Guiseppe Meazza scored twice in a four-minute spell and later hit the cross-bar. England, bruised and limping, managed to hold out, with keeper Frank Moss outstanding. Their unbeaten home record against foreign teams was still intact, even if the same could not be said of their players.

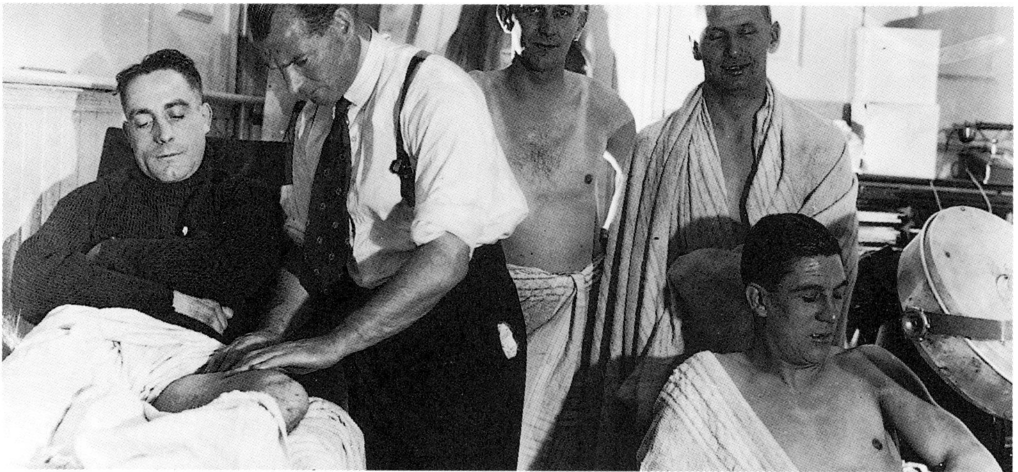

Tom Whittaker treats Copping, while Moss, Bastin and Drake wait their turn.

Arsenal complete a hat-trick

ARSENAL built another monument to the late Herbert Chapman when they tied up their third consecutive League title, emulating Huddersfield's feat in the twenties — which was also inspired by the great man. Carrying on the Chapman policies and the style that has become the hallmark of Arsenal, manager George Allison has steered the Gunners to another comfortable win, by four points from Sunderland. His two early-season signings, half-backs Crayston and Copping — both players Chapman had sought — have fitted in perfectly to the Arsenal machine. And Ted Drake, signed near the end of last season, has electrified the attack with his lion-hearted play. He topped the League scorers with 42 goals, and so did Arsenal with 115.

FINAL SCORE

Football League
Division 1: Arsenal
Top scorer: Ted Drake (Arsenal) 42
Division 2: Brentford
Division 3S: Charlton Athletic
Division 3N: Doncaster Rovers

FA Cup Final

Sheffield Wed	4	WBA	2

Scottish League
Division 1: Rangers
Top scorer: Dave McCulloch (Hearts) 38
Division 2: Third Lanark

Scottish FA Cup Final

Rangers	2	Hamilton A	1

International Championship
England, Scotland, 4 pts

FOOTBALL FOCUS

- Carlisle, who finished bottom of Division Three (N), were earlier humiliated 6–1 at home in the Cup by non-League Wigan Athletic.
- Rangers brought off their second successive League and Cup "double", their fourth in all, to beat Celtic's record of three. It was their third Championship on the trot, their eighth in nine seasons.

Rimmer the winner in Wembley thriller

IN ONE OF the most exciting finals seen for years, Ellis Rimmer scored twice in the last three minutes to give Sheffield Wednesday their first Cup victory since 1907. West Bromwich, with nine of their winning side of four years ago, were looking for a repeat performance, but were never in front.

Wednesday opened the scoring through Palethorpe after only two minutes, but Albion left-winger Boyes equalized with a spectacular drive after racing half the length of the field. When Sandford equalized again for Albion soon after Hooper's 67th-minute goal, it began to look like extra time would be needed. But outside-left Rimmer kept up his record of scoring in every round when he beat the Albion keeper to a bouncing through-ball and headed in, and he clinched the match with another goal a minute from time.

Wounded-knee Drake scores seven

RAMPAGING centre-forward Ted Drake equalled the League goalscoring record at Villa Park on 14 December when he scored all Arsenal's goals in their 7–1 win. With the triple champions struggling to remain in the title race, this burst of scoring came out of the blue. The schemer-in-chief of Arsenal's goal machine, Alex James, was missing, and Drake himself played despite the handicap of an injured knee, which had troubled him for some time and was strapped up.

Villa, struggling to stave off relegation, begin brightly enough, and there is no hint of the devastation to come. Early on, Drake skids off the pitch and falls flat on his face, to the great amusement of the Villa fans. This is the last time they laugh all afternoon.

It starts for Arsenal, and Drake, after 15 minutes. Moving out to the left to collect a pass from Pat Beasley, he pushes the ball through the legs of Tommy Griffiths, Villa's recently acquired Welsh international centre-half, and runs on to shoot past keeper Harry Morton. The next goal, after 28 minutes, rounds off a typical solo run after Bastin puts him clear 10 yards inside the Villa half. Shouldering off challenges from Griffiths and left-back George Cummings, he slams the ball past the helpless Morton. He notches his hat-trick after 34 minutes, presented with an open goal after a Beasley shot rebounds from a defender.

When Drake puts another two in the net within five minutes of the interval, the Villa crowd begin to sense a record is on. First, he chases a ball that Griffiths thinks is going out, catches it just in time and flicks it past the bemused keeper. Then good work by Bowden and Bastin sets him up for a first-time shot for his fifth goal.

Another first-time shot from just outside the box, after a poor Villa clearance — 58 minutes, six shots, six goals! The whole Villa half-back line is now making a concerted effort to shackle the Arsenal centre-forward, and Drake's next shot crashes down from the underside of the bar and is cleared by a defender. Then Villa score their only goal, a header by centre-forward Jack Palethorpe. Drake has to wait until the 89th minute for his seventh. He finds space for himself to take another Bastin pass and joyfully blasts the ball home.

The Villa players sportingly applaud Drake's history-making performance, and all sign the match ball before it is presented to the seven-goal hero, who has matched James Ross's seven for Preston against Stoke in 1888.

Ted Drake, Arsenal's seven-goal hero.

FOOTBALL FOCUS

- Chelsea's game against Arsenal at Stamford Bridge on 12 October drew 82,905, a League record. Result: 1–1.
- Ted Drake's knee lasted another six matches after his seven-goal spree before it needed an operation. In his comeback match, a try-out at Highbury for the Cup final, he scored the only goal of the game — against Aston Villa — and proceeded to do the same to win the final against Sheffield United..
- Aston Villa and Blackburn Rovers, original members of the League, were both relegated from the First Division for the first time.

FINAL SCORE

Football League
Division 1: Sunderland
Top scorer: W. "Ginger" Richardson (West Bromwich Albion) 39
Division 2: Manchester United
Division 3S: Coventry City
Division 3N: Chesterfield

FA Cup Final
Arsenal 1 Sheffield United 0

Scottish League
Division 1: Celtic
Top scorer: Jimmy McGrory (Celtic) 50
Division 2: Falkirk

Scottish FA Cup Final
Rangers 1 Third Lanark 0

International Championship
Scotland, 4 pts

Third-choice centre-forward Payne hits 10

JOE PAYNE, a reserve wing-half with Luton Town in the Third Division South, was given the job as makeshift centre-forward on 13 April when Luton's regular No. 9 and his deputy were injured, and he proceeded to rewrite the record books with 10 goals in the 12–0 thrashing of poor Bristol Rovers.

It took the 22-year-old Payne 20 minutes or so to settle into his new role, but once he got the hang of it he couldn't stop scoring. Four goals up at half-time, with three of the goals having been scored by the newcomer, Luton took Rovers apart in the second half. Every time Payne got the ball, the cry went up, "Come on, Joe, let's have another one". And nearly every time, Joe obliged.

Ten-goal Joe Payne, Luton's makeshift record-breaker.

Everything went right for him. For his last goal, after 86 minutes, he was lying on the ground outside the penalty box with his back to goal. As the ball came to him, he swivelled and swung his boot to send it unerringly into the net.

Derbyshire-born Payne originally joined the club as a centre-forward, but failed to make the grade in their reserves. It is safe to say he has now returned to his rightful position.

Payne's record surpasses the nine goals scored by Robert "Bunny" Bell for Tranmere only four months earlier, in the 13–4 win over Oldham on Boxing Day. Tranmere, beaten 4–1 at Oldham on the previous day, responded by equalling the League record score by a club in a single match and — with Oldham's help — set an aggregate record as well.

Sunderland's Cup at last

SUNDERLAND HAVE WON the FA Cup for the first time in their long and illustrious history. At long last, after a difficult campaign, they reached the final, and now, coming back typically from a half-time deficit, they have beaten Preston 3–1 at Wembley.

They needed a replay to beat Luton in the fourth round and two before they slammed Wolves 4–0 in the sixth. And they were a goal down against Third Division Millwall in the semi-finals before emerging 2–1 winners.

In what was by no means a great final, Preston's Scottish international centre-forward Frank O'Donnell put them ahead after 38 minutes. Sunderland, under the astute generalship of their captain and inside-right Raich Carter, took charge in the second half, and Bobby Gurney equalized after seven minutes with a header following a corner. Carter put them ahead 20 minutes later from a Gurney pass, and shortly afterwards, Eddie Burbanks shot home from a narrow angle to clinch the match and the Cup for this talented, and delighted, Roker side.

Carter (striped shirt, behind goalkeeper Burns) puts Sunderland in front.

World record crowd at Hampden Park

IT DIDN'T SEEM to matter that Scotland were playing England for second place in the International Championship, Wales having already sewn up the title and the Triple Crown, as 149,547 fans passed through the Hampden Park turnstiles, a world record attendance. It is estimated that at least another 10,000 broke in and saw the game without paying. This huge mass of spectators were not disappointed. They saw what they came for — defeat of the "auld enemy" by 3–1. But they had a fright in the first half, when England went into a goal lead that should have been three.

Playing in numbered shirts for the first time, they gave a superb exhibition of football, with right-winger Stanley Matthews outstanding, but all they had to show for it was a goal by Matthews's Stoke team-mate Freddie Steele.

It was a different story in the second half, when Scotland, inspired by Hearts inside-right Tommy Walker, equalized after just two minutes through Frank O'Donnell of Preston. In a classic match, England were then floored by two goals from Bob McPhail of Rangers in the last 10 minutes.

Tommy Walker, inspired Scotland.

Freddie Steele, goal for England.

FINAL SCORE

Football League
Division 1: Manchester City
Top scorer: Freddie Steele (Stoke City) 33
Division 2: Leicester City
Division 3S: Luton Town
Division 3N: Stockport County

FA Cup Final
Sunderland 3 Preston North End 1

Scottish League
Division 1: Rangers
Top scorer: David Wilson (Hamilton Academical) 34
Division 2: Ayr United

Scottish FA Cup Final
Celtic 2 Aberdeen 1

International Championship
Wales, 6 pts

FOOTBALL FOCUS

- A Scottish Cup record attendance of 144,433 watched the final at Hampden Park.
- Everton's Dixie Dean passed Steve Bloomer's record of 352 League goals, and finished the season with 375.
- Both Division Three (N) and Three (S) goalscoring records were broken with 55 goals, by Ted Harston (Mansfield) and Joe "10-goal" Payne (Luton) respectively.
- England, who beat Hungary 6–2 at Highbury in December, with Ted Drake scoring three, hit 18 goals without reply on their three-match Scandinavian tour in May. Joe Payne scored two in his only appearance, an 8-0 defeat of Finland.

Millwall make history

LITTLE MILLWALL made football history when they beat First Division giants Manchester City 2–0 at the Den to become the first Division Three side to reach the semi-finals of the FA Cup. The giant-killer had to be a David, of course — player-manager Dave Mangnall, who scored both Millwall's goals. But all eleven Millwall players were heroes to the 42,000 crowd as they swept the Championship challengers aside — Peter Doherty, Eric Brook and all.

Millwall's only excursion away from the Den was in the first round, when they thrashed lowly Aldershot 6–1. This was followed by a 7–0 trouncing of Third Division North strugglers Gateshead, and then further home victories over Second Division Fulham (2–0), First Division Chelsea (3–0) and Derby County (2–1) in front of a ground record 48,672 crowd.

The London club have reached the semi-finals twice before, in 1900 and 1903, when they were a Southern League side. Their next hurdle is another formidable First Division outfit, Sunderland, at Leeds Road.

In addition to Millwall's historic effort, the cup produced one remarkable result — when Second Division Tottenham Hotspur beat First Division Everton 4–3 in a fifth-round replay, after being two down with only four minutes left.

Penalty drama at Wembley

AFTER 119 minutes of dull, featureless football, the Cup final between Huddersfield and Preston suddenly came to life when the referee blew for a penalty. It was the first to be awarded in a Wembley Cup final, and the first time extra time had been necessary.

The fans had already begun to depart, referee Jimmy Jewell was consulting his watch, and BBC radio commentator Commander Tom Woodroofe had promised his listeners: "If they score now, I'll eat my hat." Suddenly George Mutch, Preston's Scottish international inside-right, was making a determined run on goal. There seemed little danger, however, as England centre-half Alf Young, a rock for Huddersfield all afternoon, was about to challenge. But his tackle was mistimed, and over went Mutch. Was it a foul? Was it in the penalty area? The referee had no doubt and pointed to the spot.

A still dazed Mutch picked himself up and slammed the ball into the net off the cross-bar. It was the last kick of the match.

Goalkeeper Hesford dives, but Mutch's penalty is straight.

England give Nazi salute, then humble Germany 6–3

THE ENGLAND players did not want to do it, but the British ambassador felt it would be a serious snub not to give the Nazi salute, so the team reluctantly complied. The scene was the impressive Olympic Stadium in Berlin, where two years ago Herr Hitler had used the Olympics in an attempt to whitewash his evil regime.

Fortunately for the German team, including some Austrian players who had been absorbed into the side with the recent annexation of their country, Hitler was not among the 110,000 present to see them turned over, although his henchmen were — Goering, Goebbels and company. The swastikas came out briefly when Germany equalized an early Bastin goal, but the crowd were stunned into silence as England built up a 4–2 half-time lead. The Germans, carefully selected after months of trials and fresh from 10 days' special training in the Black Forest, were no match for the determined English. The game was capped with a dream goal, as Stanley Matthews, who had run the German defence ragged all afternoon, mesmerized them once again before sending over one of his flighted crosses to West Ham's Len Goulden, who struck a 25-yard left-foot volley screaming into the net. The final score was thus a triumph for sport over politics: Germany 3 England 6.

A reluctant England team, in the traditional white shirts, give the Nazi salute.

FOOTBALL FOCUS

- East Fife became the first Division Two side to win the Scottish Cup.
- Raith Rovers won the Scottish Division Two with a British record 142 goals in only 34 games. They scored 74 away goals, including eight three times.

Champions relegated — top scorers City go down

IN AN UNUSUALLY close First Division campaign, only 16 points separated winners Arsenal (52) from the relegated pair Manchester City and West Bromwich. Wolves, top by a point as the season went into its last day, lost 1–0 at Sunderland, while Arsenal beat Bolton 5–0 to take their fifth title in eight years.

But the biggest drama was unfolding at the other end of the table. On Cup final day, a week before the end of the season, any of the bottom 11 teams could have been relegated, including Cup-finalists Huddersfield.

The last day saw six teams joint bottom with 36 points. Birmingham got out of trouble with a 4–1 win at Leicester, while Grimsby, Portsmouth and Stoke all had home wins. The crucial match was Huddersfield v Manchester City. Huddersfield won it 1–0 to stay up and doom City, First Division top scorers (80 goals) and champions a year ago.

FINAL SCORE

Football League
Division 1: Arsenal
Top scorer: Tommy Lawton (Everton) 28
Division 2: Aston Villa
Division 3S: Millwall
Division 3N: Tranmere Rovers

FA Cup Final

Preston North End	1	Huddersfield Town	0

(after extra time)

Scottish League
Division 1: Celtic
Top scorer: Andy Black (Hearts) 40
Division 2: Raith Rovers

Scottish FA Cup Final

East Fife	1	Kilmarnock	1
Replay: East Fife	4	Kilmarnock	2

International Championship
England, Scotland, 4 pts

Goals galore as Italy retain World Cup

WITH FIFA membership up to 57 countries, there were a record 36 entries for the 1938 World Cup. Of these, for the first time, the holders, Italy, and the host country, France, did not have to qualify. The rest had to be whittled down to 16 for the finals.

Uruguay, the first World Cup-winners, were still suffering a professionalism crisis and did not enter. Argentina, upset at being overlooked as hosts, prevaricated before finally withdrawing. This left Brazil as the only South American representatives. They qualified automatically along with Cuba from their group, as Mexico, the United States and others also withdrew.

In Europe, war-torn Spain also pulled out before being allocated qualifying fixtures. But the Austrians, who had qualified in October 1937 when they eliminated Latvia, found their nation swallowed up by Germany in the 1938 Anschluss, and their best players were greedily incorporated within the German team. This left the way open for England, but the FA spurned FIFA's overtures.

In other qualifying groups, Norway eliminated the Republic of Ireland and Hungary beat Greece by a record 11–1. In the Far East, Japan's withdrawal let the Dutch East Indies through to the finals.

Again, England stayed aloof from the World Cup, even though they were offered a late entry to take part in France. A competition without the home countries, and with Argentina and Uruguay also missing, would again be a World Championship in name only. But the Axis powers Germany and Italy were out to milk it for all the propaganda they could get. Italy indeed retained the trophy after a severe fright in the first round, but the Germans came an early cropper.

Swiss repel Germans

Of the seven first-round matches (Sweden had a bye), five went to extra time, and two of these required a replay. And the replays provided the two shock results of the round, Germany and Romania going out to Switzerland and Cuba respectively.

The Germans, although demoralized by their 6–3 defeat at the hands of England a few weeks earlier, were among the tournament's favourites. They had a new manager, Sepp Herberger, and an injection of Austrian talent. But Switzerland had beaten the touring England side 2–1, and had little respect for the Germans — to the extent of refusing to give the Nazi salute during the playing of the national anthem. Germany had to hang on for a draw after having Pesser, one of their four Austrians, sent off. In the replay, the Swiss won a remarkable 4–2 victory, recovering from a two-goal deficit despite playing most of the game with 10 men or with the injured Aebi a passenger.

The biggest surprise of the first round, however, was Cuba. They held the experienced and tactically superior Romanians to a 3–3 draw, and then dropped their widely praised keeper Carvajeles for the replay. His replacement, Ayra, performed even better, and limited Romania to a solitary first-half goal before his team-mates scored two in the second.

Goal feast

The tie of the round turned out to be Brazil's clash with Poland, a goal feast that stood at 4–4 after 90 minutes before Brazil edged it 6–5. Their acrobatic little centre-forward Leonidas da Silva became the first player to score four goals in a World Cup match — followed a few minutes later by his opposite number Ernst Willimowski for Poland.

The only first-round matches that did not go to extra time were Hungary's predictable rout of the Dutch East Indies and France's smooth victory over Belgium. Italy, however, were stopped in their tracks by the Norwegian team of amateurs, who had beaten Germany in the 1936 Olympics and run eventual gold-medallists Italy close. They did so again, after Italy had taken the lead in the second minute. Norway hit the woodwork three times before equalizing, and a goal in extra time by Piola saw a relieved Italian side through.

The goals continued to flow in the quarter-finals, at least for Sweden, playing their first game. The tired Cubans were no match for the fresh Swedes, who swamped them 8–0, with outside-right Gustav Wetterstroem hitting four to the dismay of recalled keeper Carvajeles. Switzerland, also suffering replay fatigue and without skipper Minelli, were no match for Hungary. And Italy, producing a much better display against the hosts, went through 3–1, their brilliant

Piola scores Italy's fourth to clinch the World Cup final victory over Hungary.

A Jekyll and Hyde performance from Brazil hints at South American magic, while a spate of goals sees attacks come out on top

Vittorio Pozzo, four years older, with the trophy again and another jubilant team.

FINAL SCORE

FIRST ROUND			
Switzerland	1	Germany	1
Hungary	6	Dutch East Indies	0
France	3	Belgium	1
Brazil	6	Poland	5
Czechoslovakia	3	Holland	0
Italy	2	Norway	1
Cuba	3	Romania	3
Replays			
Switzerland	4	Germany	2
Cuba	2	Romania	1
QUARTER-FINALS			
Sweden	8	Cuba	0
Hungary	2	Switzerland	0
Italy	3	France	1
Brazil	1	Czechoslovakia	1
Replay			
Brazil	2	Czechoslovakia	1
SEMI-FINALS			
Italy	2	Brazil	1
Hungary	5	Sweden	1
THIRD-PLACE MATCH			
Brazil	4	Sweden	2
FINAL			
Italy	4	Hungary	2

Paris, 19 June 1938. Attendance 55,000

Italy: Olivieri, Foni, Rava, Serantoni, Andreolo, Locatelli, Biavati, Meazza, Piola, Ferrari, Colaussi
(Scorers: Colaussi 2, Piola 2)
Hungary: Szabo, Polgar, Biro, Szalay, Lazar, Sas, Vincze, Sarosi, Zsengeller, Titkos
(Scorers: Titkos, Sarosi)

Leading scorers
8 Leonidas (Brazil)
7 Zsengeller (Hungary)
5 Piola (Italy)

centre-forward Silvio Piola ominously scoring twice.

After Brazil's first-round goal-fest and Czechoslovakia's cool extra-time execution of the Dutch, this seemed an appropriate pairing for the opening of Bordeaux's new stadium. But the match set record lows in World Cup thuggery. Brazil's Zeze started the carnage with a gratuitous kick at Nejedly, one of the leading scorers from the last World Cup. The Brazilian was sent off, but Leonidas put the South Americans ahead. The game then degenerated into a brawl, and just before half-time Machado and Riha became involved in their own private scrap and both received their marching orders. Brazil conceded a penalty for handball, and Nejedly equalized before he too went off, with a broken leg. The game finished at one each — and nine men each — with the Czech keeper Planicka having bravely played on with a broken arm.

The replay, with 15 new players, turned out to be a mild affair, and the crowd were treated to some good football. The Czechs badly missed the influential Planicka and Nejedly, and their left-winger Puc, but they took a first-half lead through Kopecky, who soon went off with an injury. Brazil, with a far stronger squad, had retained only their keeper Walter and the prolific Leonidas, the latter equalizing and the former recovering a ball thought by many to be well over his goal-line. Right-winger Roberto finally broke the magnificent Czech defence once more with a rasping hook shot, and Brazil marched confidently into the semi-finals.

Brazilian blunder

Perhaps the Brazilians were over-confident. Their coach Ademar Pimenta made wholesale changes again for their clash with Italy. Only three players kept their places and — to the utter disbelief of everyone following the World Cup — Leonidas, the "Black Diamond", the jewel in Brazil's crown, was omitted. According to Pimenta, Leonidas and his inside partner, the ball-juggling expert Tim, were being saved for the final.

It was a gamble that did not come off. Colaussi put Italy ahead after 55 minutes, and shortly afterwards Domingos, Brazil's hitherto immaculate right-back, conceded a penalty. Admittedly, Piola made a meal of the foul, and this antagonized the Brazilians. After Meazza converted the spot-kick, they allowed their tempers to interfere with their acknowledged artistry. They pulled a late goal back, but the Italians in the end earned an impressive victory.

Sweden made a sensational start in the other semi-final, left-winger Arne Nyberg scoring with only 35 seconds gone. But the Hungarians appeared not in the least perturbed by this setback and soon took complete control. Inside-right Gyula Zsengeller contributed a hat-trick to a classy 5–1 victory.

In the third-place match three days later, Sweden were 2–1 up at half-time. But Brazil, with Leonidas restored as captain, put on a brilliant exhibition and ran out 4–2 winners, with another two from the "Black Diamond" to take him to the top of the scoring list.

Win or die!

It was rumoured, after the final, that the Italian players had received a telegram warning them "Win or die!" Whether or not there was any truth in this, the Italians won, and won well, without any hint of undue pressure. It was an exciting final with plenty of fine play and movement. Outside-left Colaussi put Italy in front, finishing off a quick break in which right-winger Biavati raced almost the length of the field. The neat Hungarians replied two minutes later, when Titkos rifled the ball in from a narrow angle.

Italy soon exerted their control over midfield, however, and began to take advantage of the weak right flank of the Hungarian defence. Piola put them ahead again, and Colaussi gave them a 3–1 half-time lead. An opportunist goal from Sarosi unexpectedly put Hungary back into the game after 65 minutes. But the Italians re-exerted their superiority, and with 10 minutes left finished off their opponents with a flourish — a back-heel from Biavati arrowed home by the triumphant Piola.

No one could deny that Italy were worthy winners. They were better than the 1934 champions, of whom only Meazza and Ferrari remained. More organized and more direct, they were a credit to Vittorio Pozzo, who had rebuilt the side in the intervening years. Of the others, the Brazilians had shown some quite remarkable ball skills, but poor organization and a brittle temperament let them down. It was a great shame there were no British representatives in this increasingly exciting tournament. And with war clouds threatening over Europe, it would be a long time before the fathers of soccer would test themselves against the new rising powers of the game.

Lambs devour Wolves

IT WAS LIKE lambs to the slaughter, Pompey taking on the Wolves at Wembley in the FA Cup final — or so the pundits would have it. Wolves, second in the League, had stormed through to the final with a 19–3 goal record. They had beaten the new League champions Everton 2–0 in the quarter-finals and thrashed them 7–0 in a League match. At 5–1 on, they were the biggest favourites in years.

But Portsmouth, having just fought clear of the First Division relegation zone, had other ideas, and they had their secret weapon — manager Jack Tinn's lucky spats. Whether or not the ritual that veteran outside-right Freddie Worrall went through of buckling the famous white spats on his manager's feet (left one first!) before the game had anything to do with boosting their confidence, Portsmouth came out at Wembley and caned the Wolves 4–1. Once inside-left Bert Barlow — a Wolves player only two months ago — had given them the lead on the half-hour, there was only one team in it.

FOOTBALL FOCUS

- Aided and abetted by an unplayable Stanley Matthews and an unselfish Tommy Lawton, inside-right Willie Hall of Spurs equalled England's scoring record with five goals against Northern Ireland on 16 November at Maine Road.
- The Rangers-Celtic match at Ibrox on 2 January drew a record League crowd of 118,567.

FINAL SCORE

Football League
Division 1: Everton
Top scorer: Tommy Lawton (Everton) 35
Division 2: Blackburn Rovers
Division 3S: Newport County
Division 3N: Barnsley

FA Cup Final

Portsmouth	4	Wolves	1

Scottish League
Division 1: Rangers
Top scorer: Alec Venters (Rangers) 34
Division 2: Cowdenbeath

Scottish FA Cup Final

Clyde	4	Motherwell	0

International Championship
England, Scotland, Wales, 4 pts

England hold world champs despite fisted goal

THE MATCH was billed as "The Masters of Association Football versus the World Cup-holders", and it lived up to its advance publicity. England took on Italy in Milan on 14 May, and although any misgivings that England might have had that this would be another Battle of Highbury were soon dispelled, the fists of the Italians featured prominently in the drama.

The incident that will be remembered above all else was Italy's second goal. Young Lawton had headed England into a first-half lead, which the speedy winger Biavati cancelled out soon after the interval. Centre-forward Piola then took centre-stage, fisting the ball into England's goal from five yards out as he fell. Everyone in the 70,000 crowd saw it, and most of them were laughing. The players saw it. The Italian Crown Prince and FA secretary Stanley Rous saw it from the Royal Box. But German referee Dr Bauwens apparently did not see it. After consulting his linesman when England protested, he still awarded a goal. Even the "scorer" looked suitably embarrassed, and Mr Rous diplomatically refused the Crown Prince's request that they go down and jointly explain to the referee that the goal was illegal!

The England players got on with the game. Joe Mercer was magnificent in midfield. The forwards threw everything at Italy's goal, and the Italians brought everyone back to protect it. England rained in shot after shot. One goalbound effort was certainly fisted out by the left-back, others were handled, too, and the ball crossed the line more than once. Dr Bauwens finally had to give a goal when Willie Hall crashed the ball into the net.

The England players had arrived prepared for the worst, but came away at the end proud to have taken part in what had been a sporting and hard-fought draw — despite the curious decisions of an idiosyncratic referee.

Willie Hall, five-goal hero against Ireland, equalized in Milan.

Bryn Jones, Arsenal's record-breaking buy.

'Moneybags' splashes out again to sign Bryn Jones

ARSENAL MANAGER George Allison unscrewed his fountain pen on 4 August and signed a cheque for £14,000 to secure Welsh international inside-forward Bryn Jones from Wolves. When Arsenal want something, they usually get it. But "Moneybags" Allison had to smash the transfer record to obtain what he hopes will be a replacement for schemer-in-chief Alex James.

It is 10 years since Allison witnessed his predecessor as Highbury manager, Herbert Chapman, break the old record by paying Bolton nearly £11,000 for David Jack, and he later acquired James from Preston for £9,000. If Jones achieves half the success of either of those two marvellous inside-forwards, it will again be money well spent.

Jones, who is 25, is not much taller than James, but a clever player and a strong character, something of a late developer. He had trials with Southend and Swansea, and played in Ireland, for Glenavon, before joining Aberaman, where Wolves discovered him.

Heroes of the Thirties

THE THIRTIES were a glamorous decade for football — high attendances, high-scoring teams and, outside the United Kingdom, three World Cups.

On either side of the border, Dixie Dean of Everton and Jimmy McGrory of Celtic were still operating at the highest level. Dean's international career was almost over at the start of the thirties (18 goals in 16 games), McGrory's short one (six in seven) just beginning. But they both accumulated huge aggregates in domestic football. Dean broke Bloomer's all-time Football League record (352) in 1936 and went on to total 379 in 437 matches. McGrory amassed 410 goals in 408 matches, the only British goalscorer to average more than a goal a game.

Spoilt for choice

It might appear strange that the international careers of these thirties idols were comparatively short. But there were so many wonderful centre-forwards around, especially in England. Middlesbrough's George Camsell played only nine internationals, scoring in every one — 18 goals in all. Other fine leaders enjoyed even fewer appearances: long-striding opportunist Pongo Waring of Aston Villa (five caps/four goals); Freddy Tilson (four/six) of Manchester City, quick thinker with an elusive body-swerve; fearless, swashbuckling Ted Drake (five/six) of Arsenal; Fred Steele (six/eight), who set several scoring records for Stoke. "Ten goal" Joe Payne of Luton scored twice in his sole international, against Finland. Joe Bambrick of Linfield and Chelsea scored 12 goals in 11 games for Northern Ireland, six of them in one match.

The careers of those fine inside-forwards of the twenties, David Jack and Billy Walker, spilled well into the thirties. Later, Spurs' Willie Hall, considered to be one of the most complete inside-forwards in the game, scored nine in 10 games for England, including five in a memorable match against Ireland. Tommy Walker (Hearts) was a fixture at inside-right for Scotland from the mid-thirties, and scored some important goals.

Arsenal's Alex James is away, leaving three of Manchester City's defenders gasping at his wizardry.

Young England and Stoke right-winger Stanley Matthews.

The supreme artist

But perhaps the most famous player of the thirties was another Scottish inside-forward, who made but a handful of appearances for his country — Alex James of the baggy pants and shuffling gait. Herbert Chapman transformed him from the goalscorer of Preston and "Wembley Wizards" fame into arguably the greatest scheming inside-forward of all time, the maestro who made Arsenal tick. Not only was he the supreme artist, but he had the gift to spark the genius in others. Whenever he got the ball, a thrill of expectation surged through the crowd, waiting in awe to see how this Chaplinesque figure would accomplish his next piece of magic.

On England's right wing for much of the thirties was another goalscorer, the fast and direct Sammy Crooks of Derby, until he could no longer keep out Stoke City's young Stanley Matthews, an entirely different kind of winger, with unsurpassed ball control and crossing ability that centre-forwards dream about. Derby had another fast-raiding man on the left, Dally Duncan, who took over for Scotland when Alan Morton's record international career finally ended.

Rangers were to Scotland in the thirties what Arsenal were to England, only more so. They had many heroes as well as Morton, notably Bob McPhail, a prolific goalscoring inside-left, Jimmy Simpson, Scotland's first stopper centre-half, and the cultured George Brown at left-half. On the other side for Scotland was Alex Massie of Hearts and Aston Villa, converted from a moderate forward into a scintillating right-half.

Alf Strange of Sheffield Wednesday took a similar route, blossoming from centre-forward to a fine wing-half for England in the early thirties. Behind him was a solid England defence, with Harry Hibbs (Birmingham) in goal, Tom Cooper (Derby) or Roy Goodall (Huddersfield) at right-back paired with Wednesday's Ernie Blenkinsop on the left, before Arsenal's Male and Hapgood took over.

Long live the King

In the latter thirties were players whose careers were to be curtailed or at best interrupted by the war, notably two wonderful ball-playing inside-forwards who could also score goals, Peter Doherty of Blackpool, Manchester City and Northern Ireland, and Raich Carter of Sunderland and England. Still in his teens, but already twice the League's leading scorer, Tommy Lawton looked like doing the impossible — filling the shoes of the legendary Dixie Dean for Everton and England. The King is dead; long live the King.

World War II (1939–45)

IT WAS 2 SEPTEMBER 1939. With German armies marching all over Europe and now the sudden Nazi invasion of Poland, Britain was teetering on the edge of war. Nevertheless, the football season had started, and in England the teams had just completed the third round of League matches. The Sunday papers next day printed the first set of League tables.

Blackpool were sitting on top of Division One, the only side with maximum points. Just below them were Arsenal, 5–2 victors over Sunderland at Highbury, with Ted Drake scoring four. Tommy Lawton scored two for champions Everton in their draw at Blackburn. It looked like being another exciting season. But there would be no more League football for seven years. Hardly had the Sunday papers hit the door-mat than Britain declared war on Germany. All sport came to a temporary halt. But it was not long before regional football leagues and cups were organized in both England and Scotland and, as in the First World War, clubs were permitted to field "guest" players who were stationed locally. This ruling kept the game going during the hostilities, although it was often abused.

One club who gained particular benefit from guest players was Third Division Aldershot. As the traditional home of the British Army, they enjoyed the services at various times of most of the leading internationals.

The England half-back line — Britton, Cullis, Mercer — often turned out for Aldershot.

FOOTBALL FOCUS

● On Christmas morning 1940, Brighton travelled to Norwich with only five players, hoping to recruit more on the way — not so unusual in wartime. They made up their team with some Norwich reserves and soldiers from the crowd of 1,419, but were beaten 18–0.

● Arsenal's pre-war reserve back Leslie Compton played two seasons at centre-forward during the war, scoring 76 goals in 70 regional league and cup games, including 10 against Clapton Orient on 8 February 1941, when his brother Denis also scored two in Arsenal's 15–2 win.

● England agreed to let Stan Mortensen, their 12th man, go on as substitute for Wales in the second half of their match at Wembley on 25 September 1943 for the injured Ivor Powell, as Wales had no spare players. It made little difference — England won 8–3.

● The 1946 FA Cup was played on a two-legged home-and-away basis before the semi-final stage. Bradford PA lost their fourth-round home leg 3–1 to Manchester City and then proceeded to win 8–2 at Maine Road.

● Aberdeen beat Rangers 3–2 on 11 April 1946 in the final of the Scottish Southern League Cup, the forerunner of the League Cup.

Maine Road massacre

ENGLAND thrashed Scotland 8–0 at Maine Road, Manchester, on 16 October 1943, emphasizing their wartime superiority over the Scots. This was their sixth win against Scotland's two in the 10 unofficial internationals played so far.

England were irresistible. With a forward line that read Matthews, Carter, Lawton, Hagan, Denis Compton, backed up by a half-back line of Britton, Cullis and Mercer, they tore the unfortunate Scottish defence to shreds. Tommy Lawton scored four, including a first-half hat-trick in 10 minutes. One of his goals was hooked in while sitting on the ground with his back to the net.

Stanley Matthews tormented Scotland's left flank throughout the match, laying on goal after goal. He capped a wonderful display and brought the house down — a capacity 60,000 — when near the end he dribbled in and out of the bemused Scottish defence on a run from the half-way line and rounded the keeper to score the last goal. Even the Scottish fans generously joined in the applause.

England's Tommy Lawton climbs above the Scottish defence.

Barriers collapse at Burnden Park — 33 crushed to death, hundreds more hurt

A TERRIBLE TRAGEDY occurred at Burnden Park on 9 March 1946, as the sixth-round FA Cup tie between Bolton and Stoke got under way. It was the second leg, the ties of this first post-war Cup being played on a home-and-away basis, and Bolton had won the first leg 2–0.

A huge crowd passed through the turnstiles to see, among others, Stoke's Stanley Matthews. The gates were closed, with some 65,000 having paid, but another 20,000 were milling around outside and many managed to force their way in. Suddenly, two crash-barriers collapsed under sheer weight of numbers. The result was horrific. Spectators piled on top of each other, and many were trodden underfoot.

The match kicked off as casualties were being attended to, but as soon as it was known that there were fatalities, the referee called the players off the pitch. The police recommended the resumption of play to avoid panic, as most of the crowd were unaware of the disaster. The match continued, without an interval or any score. The death list totalled 33, and more than 500 spectators were injured.

The Moscow mysteries leave British soccer agog

IN AND OUT in just over two weeks, those marvellous men from Moscow took Britain by storm. With names like Stankevitch, Blinkov, Archangelski and Bobrov, Moscow Dynamo arrived in Britain in mid-November 1945 for a four-match tour. Nobody knew anything about them before they came, and we know little more now that they've gone — except that they certainly can play football.

Before they agreed to the tour, Moscow presented the FA with a dozen or more conditions, including the use of substitutes and that their own referee would be allowed to take at least one match. They also expressed the desire to play Arsenal. While the Dynamo and embassy officials of our recent wartime allies seemed intent on making propaganda out of the tour, the players proceeded to give spectacular demonstrations of teamwork.

Their first match, against Chelsea, was a lock-out. Nearly 85,000 people crammed into Stamford Bridge, overflowing on to the dog track. The Dynamo team, all in blue, came out 15 minutes before the start to practise, and when they later emerged with Chelsea, each man carried a bouquet of flowers for his opposite number. Despite this embarrassment, Chelsea, playing in red, took a 2–0 half-time lead. But the Dynamos, fast and physically fit, showed what they were capable of after the interval and held their hosts to a 3–3 draw.

The Dynamo players come out at Stamford Bridge with flowers for their opponents.

The next match was at Ninian Park, against a Cardiff City team composed mainly of working men who came straight from their jobs — some in the pits — to play. They were no match for the rampant Russians, who trounced them 10–1.

Next came a controversial match with Arsenal, who were still playing at White Hart Lane because Highbury had been converted into an Air Raid Patrol Centre during the war. A reluctant Arsenal, with most of their leading players still abroad, needed to draft in six guests, including Matthews and Mortensen, and the Russians objected strongly. However, they had their own referee, the match was played in dense fog, and they somehow managed to convert a 3–1 deficit into a 4–3 victory. The game ended in complete farce — the referee disallowed a goal by Ronnie Rooke (a guest from Fulham), tried to send Arsenal's George Drury off, and allowed Dynamo to play for a time with 12 men!

Even so, the Arsenal team, among the few who could see what was going on, were impressed with Dynamo's first-time passing and the way they all ran into position. The goalkeeper, "Tiger" Khomich, made some remarkable saves to inspire his team's recovery. And the Russians gave a last exhibition of their skills at Ibrox Park, where 90,000 saw them hold Rangers to a 2–2 draw. Then they went home — to be made "Heroes of the Soviet Union".

A close thing at Ibrox in Dynamo's last match.

FINAL SCORE

League Cup

1939–40	West Ham United
1940–41	Preston North End
1941–42	Wolverhampton Wanderers
1942–43	Blackpool (North)
	Arsenal (South)
1943–44	Aston Villa (North)
	Charlton Athletic (South)
1944–45	Bolton Wanderers (North)
	Chelsea (South)

Regional Leagues

1941–42	Blackpool (North)
	Arsenal (London)
1942–43	Blackpool (North)
	Arsenal (South)
1943–44	Blackpool (North)
	Tottenham Hotspur (South)
1944–45	Huddersfield Town (North)
	Tottenham Hotspur (South)
1945–46	Sheffield United (North)
	Birmingham City (South)

FA Cup Final 1946

Derby County 4 Charlton Athletic 1
(after extra time)

Scottish Regional Leagues

1939–40 Rangers (S/W) 2 Falkirk (N/E) 1
Southern: 1940–45 Rangers
Southern League "A": 1945–46 Rangers

Scottish Southern League Cup

1940–43,1945	Rangers
1944	Hibernian
1946	Aberdeen

Two for Stamps' collection after ball bursts

WITH THEIR RECENTLY purchased inside-forwards, Peter Doherty and Raich Carter, two of the finest in the United Kingdom, it is perhaps surprising that Derby needed extra time to beat Charlton in the first FA Cup final since the war. In a thrilling match of end-to-end football, the talking points will be Bert Turner's own goal to put Derby ahead near the end, and then his equalizer in the next minute from a free-kick that was deflected into the net. Jack Stamps might have won it for Derby, but the ball burst as he shot, and Bartram held it easily.

In a whirlwind extra-time finish, however, Derby's class told, and they hammered three goals without reply. It was a triumph for Stamps, who had been injured in the war at Dunkirk and told that he would never play again. He broke away from the restart, and sent over a perfect cross for Doherty to restore Derby's lead. The centre-forward then scored two more to make sure of Derby's first major honour after 58 years of effort.

Debut boy hits six in record Newcastle win

OCTOBER the 3rd was a special day for inside-forward Len Shackleton. He was making his debut for Newcastle United, having just been transferred from Bradford PA for £13,000, a record sum for a Second Division club. If he was nervous, he didn't show it, and by the end of the game he had put six goals past the unfortunate Charlie Turner in Newport's goal. And what a day it was for Newcastle, too. They amassed 13 goals, a Second Division record and equalling the League best.

It did not start out like being Newcastle's day. There were 52,000 fans at St James's Park, and they groaned when Charlie Wayman missed a penalty after just two minutes. But the centre-forward soon made amends and opened the scoring three minutes later. Shackleton opened his account in the seventh minute, and the pair of them proceeded to run Newport ragged. Wayman scored four, Jackie Milburn chipped in with a couple from the right wing, and inside-right Roy Bentley got into the act with one. But for a fine performance by Turner and several near misses, the score could have been in the region of 20.

Len Shackleton (right), a scorer six times on his record debut for Newcastle.

FOOTBALL FOCUS

- Newport conceded 133 goals in Division Two and were relegated, but they had their revenge on Newcastle, who finished fifth, beating them 4–2 in the return game in June.
- In winning Division Three (N), Doncaster Rovers set four League records: most points 72, wins 33, away points 37, away wins 18. They equalled the fewest defeats (three) for the division, and had the League top scorer, Clarrie Jordan (42).
- At the end of a long, protracted season, Stoke went to Bramall Lane on 14 June and lost 2–1 to Sheffield United, handing the League title to Liverpool and finishing fourth themselves to equal their best ever position.

SOCCER SOUNDBITES

"What if I was off form? What if my colleagues did not fit in with me or I with them? What if I muffed chances and things went wrong?"

LEN SHACKLETON'S
thoughts before he scored six of Newcastle's 13 on his debut.

"It seemed as though we could see into each other's minds."

TOM FINNEY,
on England's 10–0 defeat of Portugal.

Duffy breaks deadlock and Charlton win the Cup

THE 1947 FA Cup final at Wembley will be remembered for the winning goal, six minutes from the end of extra time, if for nothing else. The dreadful prospect of a replay was beginning to look a certainty when Chris Duffy's spectacular volley hit the back of Burnley's net to break a boring deadlock such as Wembley had probably never witnessed before.

The final was representative of this first post-war League campaign — long, dominated by defence, and short on goalmouth action. But what a contrast this sweltering day was to the big freeze-up responsible for extending the League season until June, and playing such havoc with the earlier rounds of the Cup.

The only incident of note in the first half was when the ball burst — for the second final running, a million to one chance. Midway through the second half, Harry Potts hit the Charlton bar in a rare Burnley attack. But the game went into extra time in a strange atmosphere, the players wilting in the heat and the crowd subdued.

With the first Cup final replay since 1912 now very much on the cards, Charlton suddenly struck. Centre-forward Bill Robinson picked up a pass on the right and pulled the ball back into the centre. Don Welsh went up for the ball, but it merely grazed off the top of his balding head, dropping on to Duffy's boot. The scorer's reaction was an equally spectacular gallop down the field, pursued by his colleagues, before they caught him in a mass embrace.

Duffy, arms upraised, sees his volley win the cup for the first time in Charlton's history.

England run wild in Portugal

ENGLAND finished their two-match end-of-season tour on a high note in Lisbon, thrashing Portugal 10–0. The Portuguese, encouraged by England's 1–0 defeat in Switzerland, felt they had a chance. They did everything they could to put England out of their stride. They changed the ball, they changed their captain and they changed their goalkeeper. But nothing short of changing the England forward line would have made any difference.

Last-minute injuries had forced England to reshuffle their side, and Blackpool's Stan Mortensen won his first full cap, partnering his new club-mate, Stanley Matthews, recently transferred for £11,500, on the right. With left-winger Bobby Langton out, the selectors decided to try Tom Finney there, to partner Mannion, thus, at a stroke, solving the long Matthews-Finney debate of which one to play.

The start was held up because of a dispute about the ball, Portugal wanting to use their smaller one. England team manager Walter Winterbottom won the argument, but England's ball lasted only 20 seconds, the time taken for Lawton to head it into the Portuguese net. After that, the smaller one mysteriously appeared.

It made not the slightest bit of difference. England ran riot. Finney was fantastic; there is no other word for it. He turned Portugal's captain and right-back Cardoza inside-out, to the extent that Cardoza's manager persuaded him to feign injury so that he could be substituted. And after the hapless Azevedo, jeered by his own crowd, had fished the ball out of the net for the fifth time — including an oblique shot from Finney after an electrifying run from half-way that brought the house down — he, too, was replaced, without even bothering to simulate damage.

Again it failed to stem the tide of England's attack. Lawton and Mortensen scored four each, and Matthews, not wishing to be left out, allowed himself the luxury of a solo goal to round off the bloodless massacre.

Tom Finney, torturer-in-chief of the Portuguese.

Britain trounce Rest of Europe 6–1

Mannion (second left) scores Britain's first goal as keeper Da Rui dives in vain.

A COMBINED Great Britain side celebrated the post-war return of the four home countries to FIFA by giving a Rest of Europe XI a lesson in football at Hampden Park. Despite a long, hard season, which is set to continue for another month in England because of the winter freeze-up, the British side outplayed the cream of Europe to the tune of six goals to one.

Wilf Mannion, aided and abetted by his England wing partner Stanley Matthews, was outstanding for Britain, and scored three goals. Tommy Lawton scored two, and Billy Steel — who had played only 10 Scottish League games at the time of his selection — cracked in a raking drive from 35 yards. The 135,000 crowd were treated to an exhibition match, hard-fought but without a single intentional foul. It lived up to its billing as the "Match of the Century", although allowances had to be made for the European team, drawn from nine countries and comprising players with little knowledge of their colleagues. Captain Johnny Carey of Manchester United was the only one with English as his native language. Teams:

Great Britain: Swift, Hardwick (E), Hughes (W), Macaulay (S), Vernon (NI), Burgess (W), Matthews, Mannion, Lawton (E), Steel, Liddell (S)

Rest of Europe: Da Rui (Fr), Peterson (Den), Steffen (Switz), Carey (Eire), Parola (It), Ludl (Cz), Lambrechts (Bel), Gren, Nordahl (Swed), Wilkes (Neth), Praest (Den)

FINAL SCORE

Football League
Division 1: Liverpool
Top scorer: Dennis Westcott (Wolves) 37
Division 2: Manchester City
Division 3S: Cardiff City
Division 3N: Doncaster Rovers

FA Cup Final
Charlton Athletic 1 Burnley 0
(after extra time)

Scottish League
Division A: Rangers
Top scorer: Bobby Mitchell (Third Lanark) 22
Division B: Dundee

Scottish FA Cup Final
Aberdeen 2 Hibernian 1

Scottish League Cup Final
Rangers 4 Aberdeen 0

International Championship
England, 5 pts

Victory at Wolves — now Liverpool must wait

IN A STORMING finish to their League programme, Liverpool have beaten Division One leaders Wolves 2–1 at sunbaked Molineux to take over at the top, and now they must wait to see how Stoke fare in their last match. Because of the fixture pile-up due to the winter freeze-up, Liverpool found themselves playing their last four games away. They dropped only one point. Indeed, they have won seven and drawn one of their last eight matches to make a marvellous bid for the Championship.

Jack Balmer, who has been with Liverpool since 1935, opened the scoring in the match at Molineux, and Albert Stubbins, their £13,000 early season buy from Newcastle who scored 244 goals in wartime football, put them two up before half-time, joining Balmer as the Anfielf outfit's joint leading scorer on 24 League goals for the season.

Wolves managed to pull one back after the interval, but Liverpool held out to take the two points that put them on top with 57. Stoke City are currently situated two points behind Liverpool in the table with a better goal average. They must beat Sheffield United at Bramall Lane on 14 June if they are to win their first League Championship. It is a long, nerve-wracking time for Liverpool to wait.

Lawton in shock record transfer to Third Division Notts County

AFTER ONLY ONE full season at Chelsea, Tommy Lawton has been the subject of a sensational transfer to Notts County. The Third Division side paid £20,000 for the unsettled England leader, £5,000 more than the previous record, and they had to throw in wing-half Bill Dickson for good measure. Lawton, with 20 goals in 19 games for England (as well as 25 in 23 wartime internationals), leaves after a protracted dispute with Chelsea. A part-time job goes with his new contract, but at 28 years old, it is a tragedy that Lawton's supreme talents are now lost to first-class League football, and his international career must surely be in some considerable jeopardy.

Tommy Lawton makes his debut for Notts County.

Classic Cup final goes United's way

IF EVER A team deserved to win the Cup it was Manchester United. Their epic 6–4 victory at Villa Park in the third round set the ball rolling. All five of their opponents on the way to Wembley were First Division sides, United scoring 18 goals to six. But Blackpool were no slouches, 18 goals and only one conceded, and that in their heart-stopping semi-final at Villa Park with Spurs, when Mortensen equalized with four minutes to go and completed his hat-trick in extra time.

When two great attacking sides play to their form to a man, and some above it, you have a classic. The Manchester forward line — Delaney, Morris, Rowley, Pearson, Mitten — were brilliant. For Blackpool, Matthews, the first Footballer of the Year, was his scintillating self until United cut off his supply of passes in the second half. Mortensen was ever-dangerous with his electric speed, while right-half and captain Johnston worked furiously in defence.

The first drama occurred with 12 minutes gone, when Mortensen went racing through on goal and was brought down from behind by Chilton. Was it a penalty? It looked outside the box. But if the referee's decision was not right, it was certainly just, and Shimwell scored from the spot. It took United 16 minutes to equalize, when Rowley made the most of a mix-up in the Blackpool defence. But Mortensen restored their lead just before half-time with a typically opportunist goal.

Manchester began to take charge after the interval, but there were only 21 minutes left when Rowley equalized again with a spectacular diving header. The turning point came 10 minutes later. Mortensen broke through again and smashed a shot at goal which Crompton brilliantly held. He cleared the ball to right-half Anderson, who transferred it to Pearson, and the inside-left ran on to crack a low 25-yarder in off a post. Three minutes later, Anderson hit a speculative shot from way out, which curled into the net off a Blackpool defender. That was the end of a great Cup final.

Rowley (dark shirt, on ground) heads Manchester United's second equalizer.

FOOTBALL FOCUS

- A Football League record crowd on 17 January of 83,260 saw Manchester United draw 1–1 with Arsenal at Maine Road (United's temporary post-war home).
- On 27 March, a British record gate for a non-final club game of 143,570 saw Rangers beat Hibs 1–0 in a Cup semi-final at Hampden Park. A record midweek gate of 133,570 saw the replayed final on 21 April, when Ragers defeated Morton 1–0.
- Stan Mortensen scored in every round of the Cup for Blackpool, 10 goals in all.
- Arsenal led the First Division from start to finish, winning their sixth title in 11 seasons to equal the total of Aston Villa and Sunderland. They conceded only 32 goals, a record for Division One, and over two million people saw their games.
- Newcastle sold Len Shackleton to Sunderland for a record £20,050 in February, but still won promotion without him.

Aston Villa just fail in a thriller

HERE WAS a match worthy of a final, this third-round tie in front of 65,000 half-drenched spectators at a muddy Villa Park. In 14 seconds, the crowd were on their feet as keeper Crompton became the first United player to touch the ball when he picked it out of the net. It had been put there by right-winger Edwards — what a start for Villa. Who'd have thought they would be 5–1 down by half-time!

Inspired by their captain Johnny Carey, United's forwards proceeded to play some of the most breathtaking football ever seen at Villa Park. Within six minutes they were level, through Rowley, and Morris (two), Pearson and Delaney also scored before the interval.

Unbowed, Villa came back out better equipped than United in the strength-sapping mud. Gradually they clawed their way back to 4–5 with nine minutes to go. The menacing Ford hit the bar for Villa. Could United hold out? They did so in the only way they know — by attacking. They won a corner. Mitten took it and Pearson shot the ball home — 6–4. What a game!

Magnificent Matthews

STANLEY MATTHEWS played possibly his greatest game as England continued where they left off last season with an impressive win on the Continent. This time it was in Brussels, and their 5–2 victory over Belgium was down to the Blackpool wing wizard.

Matthews made every goal. England were ahead in 15 seconds as he put a cross right on Tommy Lawton's head. Another pinpoint centre, a Lawton deflection, and Mortensen was through. Then Matthews was fouled, took the kick himself, and this time Finney headed in to put England 3–0 up in 20 minutes.

Belgium came back strongly with two goals, and with the 70,000 crowd behind them, they looked like completing their revival — until Matthews took charge again. Picking the ball up at half-way, he beat tackle after tackle as he made his way to the byline, and then chipped the ball over the keeper for Finney to walk it into the empty net.

He wasn't quite finished. The only way to stop him was to foul him. But then he put another free-kick on Lawton's head for the last goal. It was sheer, unadulterated magic.

England draw shroud over Turin

MANY HAVE been England's famous victories down the years, over the Scots and against increasingly stronger Continental opposition. But they reached new heights on 15 May 1948, when they beat the rampant, arrogant Italians 4–0 in Turin.

It needed one of the most memorable goals in England's history to set them on their way and silence the frenzy of the 85,000 Latin crowd in the sweltering heat of the Comunale Stadium. The Italians, fresh from special training in a mountain retreat and wins against Czechoslovakia and France, made a confident start. Then, after four minutes, Matthews, dropping back, collected the ball from Wright. A feint and a jink wrong-footed two defenders, but instead of taking his usual route up the touchline he hit a left-footed pass inside the back for his Blackpool team-mate Mortensen to run on to. Taking the ball in his stride, Mortensen accelerated through the Italian defence towards the byline. Just outside the penalty box and only a few feet from the line, with an opponent moving in to tackle, he swivelled at speed and lanced in a shot that flashed past the startled keeper at the near post.

It was like a shot in the arm for the England side. But they needed all the brilliance of Frank Swift, the first keeper to captain England this century — as well as the fearless honesty of the Spanish referee Escartin, who disallowed two Italian efforts for offside — to stay ahead as Mazzola and company brought all their dazzling skills to bear. Then came another breakaway, the same as before, Matthews sending Mortensen away on the right. This time he pulled the ball back for Lawton to drive home. Half-time, and England were 2–0 ahead.

Both teams were wilting in the humidity, but the Italians came back strongly. Then Swift threw the ball out to Scott, who switched it to Wright, then on to Mannion and Lawton, for Finney to waltz it round the keeper. What a beautiful move, and it knocked the stuffing out of the Italians. Finally, Mortensen streaked away again and made another for Finney. That left them with a scoreline of Italy 0 England 4 — Turin was like a morgue that night.

FINAL SCORE

Football League
Division 1: Arsenal
Top scorer: Ronnie Rooke (Arsenal) 33
Division 2: Birmingham City
Division 3S: Queen's Park Rangers
Division 3N: Lincoln City
Footballer of the Year: Stanley Matthews (Blackpool)

FA Cup Final

Manchester United	4	Blackpool	2

Scottish League
Division A: Hibernian
Top scorer: Archie Aikman (Falkirk) 20
Division B: East Fife

Scottish FA Cup Final

Rangers	1	Morton	1
Replay: Rangers	1	Morton	0

Scottish League Cup Final

East Fife	0	Falkirk	0
Replay: East Fife	4	Falkirk	1

International Championship
England, 5 pts

Ronnie Rooke (Arsenal), League leading scorer.

Mortensen (on ground, left) scores from a seemingly impossible impossible angle.

Sunderland slope off after Yeovil defeat

GIANT-KILLERS Yeovil from the Southern League have done it again. Mighty Sunderland came down from the North-East to play on their infamous slope in Somerset, and went back home again with their tails between their legs. It was Second Division Bury in the third round, and now they have a First Division scalp.

Nobody really gave the non-Leaguers a chance. When Yeovil's keeper was hurt in training, and had to be replaced by 23-year-old solicitor's clerk Dickie Dyke, with only one senior outing under his belt, it became a question of how many Shackleton and company would score. The odds lengthened further against Yeovil when winger Hargreaves pulled a muscle after 10 minutes and became a passenger.

The only Yeovil player with any League experience was their captain and player-manager Alec Stock, 30, who had played for Charlton and QPR before the war. And it was he who put the skids under Sunderland after 26 minutes, cracking in a flick-on from the edge of the box — his first goal of the season.

Robinson equalized for Sunderland after an hour, after Dyke, who had an heroic game, made his only mistake of the match and dropped the ball at the forward's feet.

As fog began to swirl around, the game went to extra time, with the fighters of Yeovil still on top. The 17,000 spectators packed into the ground, hundreds of them on beer crates set up as extra seating, and hundreds more outside listening on police car radios, could feel in the atmosphere that something momentous was about to happen. Sure enough, Yeovil took the lead again just before the turnround. Eric Bryant finished off a slick four-man move and sent a low shot past the Sunderland keeper from 15 yards.

Now Sunderland were stung into attack. The Yeovil defenders hacked the ball away, anywhere they could. The referee blew for a free-kick just outside their box, and the crowd invaded the pitch, thinking it was over. They had to be cleared before Sunderland could take the kick. They made a mess of it. Now it was all over, and the party could begin.

Stand-in keeper Dyke clears once again on the greatest day in Yeovil's history.

SOCCER SOUNDBITES

"Player–managership is violent exercise on top of a pile of worries."

ALEC STOCK,
player-manager of giant-killers Yeovil.

'No-star' Portsmouth's championship at last

UNFASHIONABLE Portsmouth, never before better than fourth in Division One and without a single international in their side, won the League title in their jubilee year. It has been a fine team performance, and they proved unbeatable at Fratton Park, where they won 18 games and drew the other three.

They led the table for most of the season, and a remarkable 5-0 victory at St James's Park over nearest rivals Newcastle in early April put them well clear. They looked on course for the "double" before suffering a shock defeat in the Cup semi-finals by lowly Second Division side Leicester, who won 3–1 at Highbury. But they clinched the title with three games to spare, and finished on 58 points, five ahead of Manchester United, second for the third season in a row, and Derby.

Reg Flewin, Portsmouth captain.

Treble chance comes off for Rangers

THERE WASN'T much left for Glasgow Rangers to do, and now they've done it. They have completed the Scottish "treble" — League, Cup and League Cup. Their 4–1 defeat of Clyde last Saturday in the Cup final was merely the end of a veritable stroll through the tournament. Their League Cup success did not come so readily, especially in the group stage, when they recovered from a bad start to qualify for the last eight at the expense of Celtic. And Division B champions Raith gave them a run for their money in the final in March, before going down 2–0.

The League proved their toughest hurdle, and in the end it was out of their hands. Two days after the Cup final they won 1–0 at Morton to lead Dundee by a point. But on Wednesday Dundee leapfrogged back to the top with their game in hand, and it was all down to the last Saturday. Rangers went to Coatbridge and beat Albion Rovers 4–1, Willie Thornton scoring a hat-trick. They could do no more. Poor Dundee, however, lost 4–1 at Falkirk, and the Championship — and the "treble" — went to Rangers.

FOOTBALL FOCUS

- Giant-killers Yeovil, without home advantage, crashed to Manchester United 8–0 (Jack Rowley 5) at Maine Road in the fifth round of the Cup, and were cheered to the echo by the 81,565 crowd.
- Derby paid a record £25,000 for Manchester United inside-forward Johnny Morris in March.
- Cup-finalists Leicester needed three points from their last three games to stay in Division Two, and then one point from their last match, at Cardiff: they drew 1–1, condemning Nottingham Forest to the drop.

England fall to Scottish Steel at Wembley

ENGLAND, with only one defeat in 18 post-war internationals, were shocked at Wembley by a Scottish side given little hope after the 3–0 defeat the Scottish League suffered at Ibrox last month at the hands of the Football League. England, on paper, looked stronger, while the Scots chose only two players from the Inter-League game.

Two of the Scottish heroes were keeper Jimmy Cowan and forward Billy Steel. Cowan, of Morton, recently recovered from a broken arm that threatened to end his career, kept England at bay with some marvellous saves in the first 20 minutes, when England were on top. Then Jim Mason (Third Lanark) broke away to score with a shot that went in off the foot of a post.

Steel (Derby), Scotland's fireball of an inside-left and the only "Anglo" in the side, put Scotland two up on 50 minutes after a fine move, and the cultured Hibernian Lawrie Reilly clinched it before Newcastle's new cap, Jackie Milburn, scored a consolation goal for England.

Steel (left) scores the second goal for Scotland with goalkeeper Swift helpless.

FINAL SCORE

Football League
Division 1: Portsmouth
Top scorer: Willie Moir (Bolton Wanderers) 25
Division 2: Fulham
Division 3S: Swansea Town
Division 3N: Hull
Footballer of the Year: Johnny Carey (Manchester United)

FA Cup Final

Wolves	3	Leicester City	1

Scottish League
Division A: Rangers
Top scorer: Alec Stott (Dundee) 30
Division B: Raith Rovers

Scottish FA Cup Final

Rangers	4	Clyde	1

Scottish League Cup Final

Rangers	2	Raith Rovers	0

International Championship
Scotland, 6 pts

Easy as Pye for Wolves in the end

LEICESTER CITY put up a brave show at Wembley, but in the end were no match for Wolves. The lowly Second Division side sorely missed the inspiration of the sick Don Revie, their 21-year-old inside-right. But they gave Wolves a fright in the second half, halving their 2–0 lead and being desperately unlucky to have an equalizer disallowed for offside.

Wolves had appeared to be coasting to victory after Jesse Pye's two first-half goals, the first a header from a fine Johnny Hancocks cross, the second an opportunist prod-in. But two minutes after the interval, Leicester struck. Bert Williams parried a scorcher from Ken Chisholm, only for Mal Griffiths to hook the ball into the net.

Now Leicester were giving as good as they got, and it needed all of England captain Billy Wright's experience to keep them at bay. With 67 minutes gone, Chisholm put the ball in the net, but the referee gave him offside, a close call. A minute later, Sammy Smyth picked up the ball in midfield and carried it forward for 30 yards or more against the retreating Leicester defenders, evading their tackles before planting the ball past the advancing keeper. That knocked the stuffing out of Leicester, and Wright was soon collecting the Cup from Princess Elizabeth.

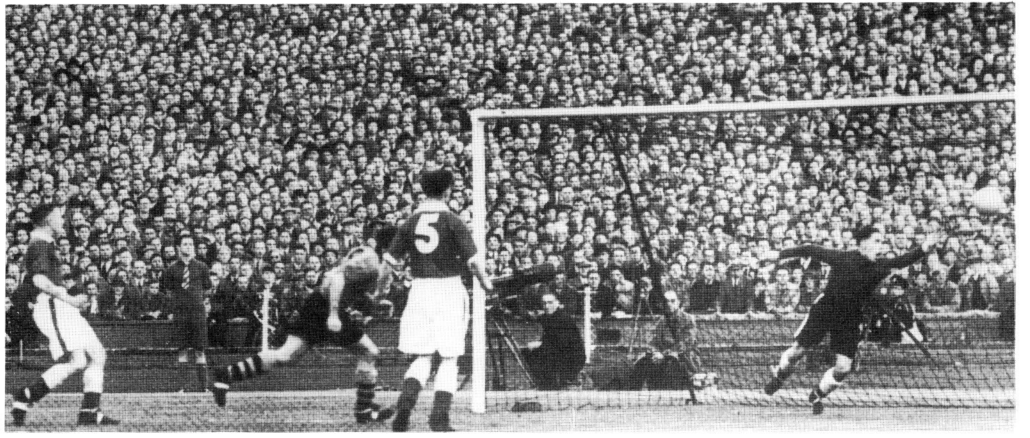

Pye heads the ball past Bradley, Leicester's keeper, for the first goal.

Champions killed in air crash

THE CREAM of Italian football died in an air crash on 4 May, when the plane carrying the Torino team back from a game in Portugal hit a hillside at Superga, just outside Turin. The tragedy claimed the lives of 18 players, including the bulk of the Italian national side. Among the stars who died was Italy's captain Valentino Mazzola. In all, 31 people perished, including journalists, club officials and their English manager Leslie Lievesley.

The finest club team in the history of Italian football, Torino had won four consecutive League titles and were four points clear on the day of the crash. Their youth team completed their last four fixtures against the youth teams of their opponents, winning them all to earn a sad consolation for the grief-stricken club.

England Rio-bound, but Scotland won't go to World Cup as losers

THE SCOTLAND-ENGLAND match in April had more than national pride and the Home International Championship riding on it. An extra prize this time was qualification for the World Cup finals in the summer. In fact, with the British countries now eligible for their first World Cup, FIFA had generously offered them two places for the tournament, to be held in Brazil. But the stubborn, insular Scottish FA had announced that they would go only as champions.

With Wales and Northern Ireland already well beaten by both sides, the Hampden match was the decider. And Scotland, as holders, needed only a draw. The England experiment of playing Chelsea leader Roy Bentley as inside-left to Mortensen's centre-forward, creating a twin spearhead, paid off when an interchange between the two allowed Bentley to score midway through the second half. It turned out to be the winner, although a shot from Willie Bauld hit the underside of the bar and bounced down on England's line.

After the match, England captain Billy Wright begged his opposite number George Young to appeal to the Scottish FA, as the whole England side wanted Scotland to join them in Rio. But Young's pleas fell on deaf ears.

Bentley's goal puts England on the road to Rio.

Championship thriller as Pompey pip Wolves

THE FIRST Division Championship went down to the last day, with three teams still in the race. Last season's champions Portsmouth led with 51 points, on goal average from Wolves, who had started the season with six straight wins, and Sunderland were just a point behind.

In reality, Portsmouth needed only to win, so superior was their goal average. In the event, they beat Aston Villa 5–1. Wolves hammered bottom club Birmingham 6–1 to become only the second side to miss the title on goal average, and Sunderland beat Chelsea 4–1, but had to be content with third place. In the end, only six points separated the first nine clubs.

Big 'ead to the rescue

WITH ARSENAL a goal down in their pulsating Cup semi-final with Chelsea at White Hart Lane, and only five minutes to go, centre-half Leslie Compton ignored his captain's instructions and went up for a corner. Compton, known affectionately by the Highbury fans as "Big 'ead" for his dominance in the air as a stopper, arrived in the Chelsea goalmouth at the same time as his brother Denis's inswinger, and he headed it powerfully into the net.

That completed a dramatic comeback for Arsenal from two down, and earned them a replay.

Chelsea had surprised Arsenal in the first half with two beautifully taken goals from centre-forward Roy Bentley. Arsenal clawed one back somewhat luckily with the last kick of the half, when a corner from right-winger Freddie Cox, no stranger to White Hart Lane, swerved into goal at the near post. Time had then looked like running out for Arsenal until Compton took a hand. Captain Joe Mercer will have forgiven him for disobeying orders.

Leslie Compton is mobbed after his semi-final equalizer.

England in Carey Street

THE REPUBLIC of Ireland scored a shock win over England at Goodison Park on 21 September. Inspired and orchestrated by their captain Johnny Carey in their first ever international on English soil, they grew in confidence as the match progressed. Tommy Godwin played the game of his life in goal, Con Martin gave them a shock lead when he converted a penalty after 36 minutes, and as England began to fade they scored a second five minutes from time. It was England's first home defeat by a team outside the four home countries, although with nine of the Irish playing for English club sides, Carey and company could hardly be described as foreigners.

England, as usual, had started as strong favourites. Taking the opposition too lightly, perhaps, the selectors brought in three new caps: Derby's Bert Mozley at right-back and, in place of Matthews and Mortensen, Portsmouth's pacy winger Peter Harris and Jesse Pye of Wolves.

England attacked from the start, but Pye missed two easy chances before Mozley, making his debut on his 26th birthday, gave away the penalty. Bert Williams got a hand to Martin's fierce shot but could not prevent it from crossing his line.

With Carey containing Finney, Eire began to see more of the ball. As much as Billy Wright pushed England forward in the second half, Godwin, a carpenter and a part-timer with Shamrock Rovers, continued to foil England's forwards, and when England were caught square, Peter Farrell of Everton, playing for the away team on his home ground, lobbed the second goal.

Arsenal's 'capital' victory in Cup

ARSENAL have won the FA Cup without having to leave London. Drawn at home in the first four rounds, they progressed each time at the first attempt. The only replay they needed was in the semi-final against Chelsea, and both ties were played at White Hart Lane. Now they've beaten Liverpool 2–0 at Wembley.

Liverpool also had a local derby in their semi-final, beating Everton 2–0. Both Cup-finalists were high in the League, and indeed both had tilts at the title. Liverpool went unbeaten at the start for a record 19 games, but fell off the pace later. Arsenal, after a poor start, came within three points of leaders Liverpool before Christmas, but a 2–0 defeat at Anfield on New Year's Eve left them with just too much to do.

Nevertheless, at Wembley, Arsenal always had the edge. Their half-back line of the fiery dynamo Alex Forbes, the rock-like Leslie Compton and the inspirational Joe Mercer, Footballer of the Year, was outstanding. In inside-right Jimmy Logie they had the man of the match, and young centre-forward Peter Goring proved a handful for the Liverpool defence. It was Logie who produced the perfect through-pass for Reg Lewis to score after 18 minutes. Lewis, an ice-cool finisher, got a second on 63 minutes after a Denis Compton cross had been touched on by Cox.

With the rain pouring down, Liverpool made gallant efforts to come back, none more so than their star outside-left Billy Liddell. But they were denied even the goal they deserved by an excellent Arsenal defence, none of whom would see the right side of 30 again!

Joe Mercer (6) shows his delight as Reg Lewis (10) glides through for his first goal.

FINAL SCORE

Football League
Division 1: Portsmouth
Top scorer: Dickie Davis (Sunderland) 25
Division 2: Tottenham Hotspur
Division 3S: Notts County
Division 3N: Doncaster Rovers
Footballer of the Year: Joe Mercer (Arsenal)

FA Cup Final
Arsenal 2 Liverpool 0

Scottish League
Division A: Rangers
Top scorer: Willie Bauld (Hearts) 30
Division B: Morton

Scottish FA Cup Final
Rangers 3 East Fife 0

Scottish League Cup Final
East Fife 3 Dunfermline Ath 0

International Championship
England, 6 pts

Arsenal's captain Joe Mercer, Footballer of the Year.

FOOTBALL FOCUS

- Centre-half John Charles (Leeds United) became Wales's youngest international, at 18 years 71 days, when he played in the 0–0 draw against Northern Ireland at Wrexham on 8 March.

- Northern Ireland suffered two massive defeats in the Home International Championship, 8–2 by Scotland at Belfast in October, and 9–2 by England at Maine Road in November.

- Rangers completed their second hat-trick of Cup wins and won the championship, but did not manage another "treble", losing to East Fife in the semi-finals of the League Cup.

Fabulous Finney, but this England team won't do for Rio

MEMORIES OF their 10-goal triumph must have come flooding back to Wright, Finney, Mannion and Mortensen when the England team returned to Lisbon after three years. They won again, but this time their victory was not so convincing and does not bode well for the coming World Cup. Finney, with the help of two penalties, scored four of their five goals, but a leaky defence let in three. But for the impressive Williams in goal, it would have been more.

Finney put England ahead from the penalty spot after he had been brought down when right through, and Mortensen and Finney again put England 3–0 up at half-time. Any thoughts of another double-figure massacre were soon dispelled after the interval, when centre-forward Ben David pulled one back with a fine header. Finney restored England's three-goal margin with a gem of a goal, beating man after man before slamming the ball into the net for his hat-trick.

Portugal would not lie down, however, and pulled the score back to 3–4 as they dominated the game for 20 minutes. Thankfully, right-back Alf Ramsey kept calm and saw England out of further trouble. Finally, Finney cut through the Portuguese defence once more, was brought down, and scored from the spot again to clinch the game for England.

England humiliated

Brazil, the hosts, and England, who were newcomers to the World Cup, were joint favourites to win the 1950 tournament. Brazil fell at the last hurdle, and the whole nation mourned. England, the traditional home of football and feared for so long by the rest of the world, did not make the final pool. They met with an accident on the way, and the headlines read: England 0 United States 1.

THERE WERE only 31 original entries for this first post-war World Cup, and a number of withdrawals left an unwieldy 13 finalists. Italy qualified automatically as holders, but West Germany were not yet members of FIFA. The home countries were allotted two places in the finas, with the International Championship as their qualifying group, but Scotland incomprehensibly refused to go as mere runners-up, and withdrew. Portugal, who had been eliminated by Spain, declined to replace them. Yugoslavia qualified at the expense of France, who were given a reprieve when Turkey withdrew, but backed out when they heard their travel programme. Sweden eliminated the Republic of Ireland.

The four South American places were decided without a match being played, because of withdrawals, including Argentina, from the qualifying groups. Mexico beat the United States 6–0 and 6–2, but they both qualified above Cuba. Late withdrawals by Turkey and India, after both had qualified, left a lop-sided tournament.

No World Cup final

A new system was used in the finals. The countries were divided into four groups of four, with the winners of each group to go into a final pool, where they would play each other. The winners of this pool would be the world champions. Brazil, England, Italy and Uruguay were seeded, but because of the lateness of the withdrawals, the groups could not be rearranged, so there was one group of three countries and one of two. In the latter, Uruguay beat Bolivia 8–0, so they were in the final pool without having to play any qualifying games and having had only one match in the finals.

Gaetjens glances the ball past Williams to the horror of all England.

A freak result

The group that made the headlines was England's. With Chile and the United States as virtual "makeweights", England did not anticipate any problems until their last match, against Spain. England's World Cup debut, against Chile in the massive, unfinished Maracana Stadium in Rio, was ponderous, but they came through with goals from Mortensen and Mannion.

Meanwhile, the United States were giving Spain the fright of their lives, holding on to a 1–0 half-time lead until Spain hit three face-saving goals in the last 10 minutes.

Forewarned, England should still have thrashed this team of part-timers, captained by one Eddie McIlvenny, a Glasgow-born right-half who had played seven games for Wrexham in 1947 and had then been given a free transfer. But even with an unchanged line-up that included Billy Wright, Alf Ramsey and Tom Finney, and a post-war record of 23 wins and only four defeats in 30 internationals, the expected flood of goals did not materialize.

On a bumpy pitch at Belo Horizonte, in front of barely 10,000 spectators, England struck the woodwork four times, a Mullen header was cleared from a position seemingly a yard behind the line, and two plausible penalty appeals were turned down.

Instead, the Americans defen-ded valiantly, grew in confidence, and scored in the 37th minute when Haitian-born Larry Gaetjens beat Bert Williams to a cross, deflecting it with his head past the astonished keeper. The impossible, the unthinkable had happened.

The four finalists

England still had a chance to qualify for the final pool — if they beat Spain, they would earn a play-off. They drafted the out-of-favour Stanley Matthews into the side on the right, switching Finney to the left, and brought Milburn and Baily in for Bentley and Mannion — to no avail. They lost 1–0.

So Spain joined Uruguay, Olympic champions Sweden and Brazil in the final pool. Sweden's 3–2 victory over Italy had been the deciding factor in the group of

WORLD CUP FOCUS

- Brazil might not have got through their first-round group but for an accident to Yugoslavia's inside-right, Rajko Mitic, who cut his head on a girder outside their dressing-room. By the time he made it on to the pitch, Ademir had scored Brazil's first goal.
- After their elimination by Spain, the England squad, instead of staying to be educated, left for home — together with all the English journalists.

England's humiliating defeat by the part-timers of the United States was the main talking point back home, tending to obscure what was an awesome triumph for South American football.

Uruguay's keeper Maspoli goes up for the last Brazilian corner as English referee George Reader (far right) turns round to whistle for time.

three. Although the holders had been seriously weakened by the loss of eight internationals in the 1949 Superga air crash, their defeat at the hands of the Swedish amateurs was still a shock.

Brazil qualified through Group One, but not without a certain amount of anxiety. They easily took care of Mexico at the Maracana in the opening match of the tournament, but were held to a draw by the Swiss, whose second equalizer came two minutes from time. Brazil now had to beat Yugoslavia. They made several changes, stumbling on the effective inside-forward trio of Zizinho-Ademir-Jair, and ran out winners by 2–0.

Sensational Brazil

Having overcome their first-round nerves and settled on their best side, Brazil came out against Sweden and entertained the near-140,000 crowd to a sensational display of football. Sweden, whose performance in reaching the final pool was a wonderful tribute to their English coach George Raynor, were swamped 7–1 by the dazzling Brazilians, for whom the unstoppable Ademir scored four.

There was more joy for Brazil with the result from São Paulo, where Spain held Uruguay, now their biggest obstacle to success. And when Brazil put on another scintillating exhibition of attacking football for over 150,000 at the Maracana, beating Spain 6–1, there seemed to be no stopping them. Uruguay, meanwhile, managed to edge past the Swedes 3–2 in the last five minutes after twice being a goal down. But they would have to beat Brazil in the deciding match — in effect, the final of a competition designed not to have one.

Triumph for tactics

For Brazil to lose was unthinkable. Their overwhelming displays against Sweden and Spain had given them an aura of invincibility in the eyes of their millions of followers, who felt sure they would engulf Uruguay. Brazil's team manager Flavio Costa was wary, however, knowing Uruguay's propensity over the years for upsetting Brazil. He feared that his team would be overconfident, that the flamboyance they had shown against the European teams — as when Zizinho beat the Spanish keeper and then waited for him to get up so that he could beat him again — would be dangerous against Uruguay, who knew them too well.

A world record crowd of some 200,000 squeezed into the still unfinished Maracana on the big day, and the atmosphere was electric. From the start, Brazil's inside trio carved their way through the Uruguayan defence, but there was always someone there to frustrate them. The Uruguayan captain, Varela, once an inside-left and now a roaming centre-half of the old school, eschewed his attacking tendencies to bind his defence, while Roque Maspoli performed superbly in goal.

They kept the Brazilians at bay for 45 minutes, but two minutes after the break their defence was finally breached. Drawn out to cover danger on Brazil's left flank, they were caught out when the ball was suddenly switched, and right-winger Friaca came flying in to crack the ball first time into the net.

Now, surely, the floodgates would open, thought the fans. But Uruguay had already shown signs of aggression, having weathered the first-half storm, and Varela was beginning to move menacingly upfield. Brazil sensed danger, but their instinct was to attack, not to pull back and protect their lead — after all, Uruguay needed two goals.

They got the first midway through the second half. Appropriately it was Varela who started the move, sending Ghiggia away on the right. He then found Schiaffino, who had scored four against Bolivia, and he gave Barbosa no chance.

The Brazilians were demoralized. But worse was to follow. Perez made a resolute incursion upfield, and laid on a chance that Ghiggia took with relish. Uruguay held out for the remaining 10 minutes. It was a triumph for tactics and determination. And no one deserved more to receive the newly named Jules Rimet Trophy than Obdulio Varela, a hero among heroes.

FINAL SCORE

Group 1

Brazil	4	Mexico	0
Yugoslavia	3	Switzerland	0
Brazil	2	Switzerland	2
Yugoslavia	4	Mexico	1
Brazil	2	Yugoslavia	0
Switzerland	2	Mexico	1

	P	W	D	L	F	A	P
Brazil	3	2	1	0	8	2	5
Yugoslavia	3	2	0	1	7	3	4
Switzerland	3	1	1	1	4	6	3
Mexico	3	0	0	3	2	10	0

Group 2

England	2	Chile	0
Spain	3	United States	1
United States	1	England	0
Spain	2	Chile	0
Spain	1	England	0
Chile	5	United States	2

	P	W	D	L	F	A	P
Spain	3	3	0	0	6	1	6
England	3	1	0	2	2	2	2
Chile	3	1	0	2	5	6	2
USA	3	1	0	2	4	8	2

Group 3

Sweden	3	Italy	2
Sweden	2	Paraguay	2
Italy	2	Paraguay	0

	P	W	D	L	F	A	P
Sweden	2	1	1	0	5	4	3
Italy	2	1	0	1	4	3	2
Paraguay	2	0	1	1	2	4	1

Group 4

Uruguay	8	Bolivia	0

Final Pool

Brazil	7	Sweden	1
Uruguay	2	Spain	2
Brazil	6	Spain	1
Uruguay	3	Sweden	2
Sweden	3	Spain	1
Uruguay	2	Brazil	1

Deciding match: Maracana Stadium, Rio, 16 July 1950. Attendance 199,854

Uruguay: Maspoli, Gonzales M, Tejera, Gambetta, Varela, Andrade, Ghiggia, Perez, Miguez, Schiaffino, Moran
(Scorers: Schiaffino, Ghiggia)
Brazil: Barbosa, Augusto, Juvenal, Bauer, Danilo, Bogode, Friaca, Zizinho, Ademir, Jair, Chico
(Scorer: Friaca)

Leading scorers
9 Ademir (Brazil)
5 Schiaffino (Uruguay)
Basora (Spain)

Pegasus leave fans hoarse

THE WHOLE COUNTRY cheered when Pegasus beat Bishop Auckland 2–1 in the Amateur Cup final at Wembley. This was no disrespect to the mighty Bishops, playing in their 14th final. It was sheer admiration for the "new Corinthians", whose dramatic and romantic rise has captured the public imagination.

Formed in 1948 from graduates of Oxford and Cambridge Universities, Pegasus do not play in a league or have a ground of their own. To reach the final, they played seven away fixtures and came from behind to win five of them, sometimes perilously close to the end. At Wembley, in front of a record 100,000 crowd for an amateur game, they absorbed Bishop's pressure in the first half, and took the lead through Potts six minutes after the interval. Ten minutes from time they made sure with a goal from Tanner, although Bishop Auckland pulled one back before the end.

Never has there been a more popular victory in the competition's 57-year history. Pegasus embody all the traditions of true amateurism, good sportsmanship and fine team spirit, and their success has brought back to the game something of the romance and the glory of the early days of soccer.

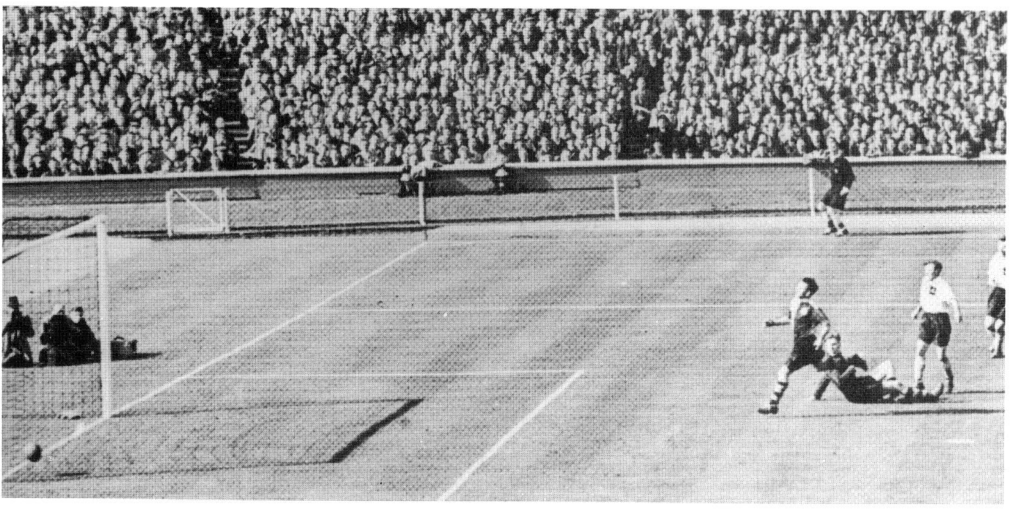

Tanner (second from the right) puts Pegasus two up.

Push-and-run Spurs win first Championship

WHILE NEWCASTLE were winning the Cup at Wembley, just a few miles down the road Spurs were clinching the League title by beating Sheffield Wednesday 1–0. It was a nervy match, and Sheffield battled hard in their efforts to stave off relegation. But a goal from Channel Islander Len Duquemin just before the interval was enough to give Spurs the two points they needed to beat off Manchester United's challenge.

Playing the same push-and-run game that earned them promotion last season — ironically together with Wednesday — Spurs have hit the top echelon like a breath of fresh air. Their second successive title win is a tribute to manager Arthur Rowe. The goals have been shared around, with much of the inspiration coming from left-half Ron Burgess, right-back Alf Ramsey and inside-left Eddie Baily. But all the side have worked hard, none more so than right-half Billy Nicholson, who covered acres of ground every match in both defence and attack, and thoroughly earned an England cap, against Portugal.

Heroic 10-man England finally succumb to Scots

ENGLAND fought an heroic rearguard action for most of the game at Wembley after losing Wilf Mannion, and even took the lead. But in the end they could not resist the Scottish pressure any longer and lost a thrilling match 3–2.

England were struggling to hold the rampant Scots from the start. Billy Liddell on the left was dangerous every time he got the ball, but his crosses were being wasted. Then came the cruel blow for England. In the 13th minute, Mannion, dropping back to help his overworked defence, went up for the ball with Liddell and their heads cracked together. The Scot was able to play on, but Mannion was carried off on a stretcher.

It looked bad for England, but against the run of play they scored first through a breakaway. Finney, now at inside-right, and Mortensen carved out the opening, and Harold Hassall, on his international debut, cracked a tremendous shot past Cowan, high into the Scottish net. Scotland continued to press, however, and Lawrie Reilly set up an easy equalizer for Bobby Johnstone.

Scotland took the lead early in the second half, Johnstone returning the compliment for Reilly to score. Then Bert Williams, the player most responsible for keeping the score down, made his one mistake. He fumbled an apparently harmless cross, and Liddell swept the ball into the net.

That should have been the end for the 10 brave men, but they would not lie down. Matthews and especially Finney made some dangerous runs. And when Finney brought down a defence-splitting chip from Mortensen, ran on and coolly flicked the ball over the keeper, England were back in the game. A Mortensen drive flashed just wide of the post. But in the end Scotland were worthy winners.

Mannion is carried off with a fractured cheek-bone.

Milburn and Mortensen rescue England

ELEVEN DAYS after spearheading opposing teams in the Cup final, Jackie Milburn and Stan Mortensen returned to Wembley and dramatically snatched victory out of Argentina's grasp.

In the first international between the two countries, played as part of the Festival of Britain, Argentina took an 18th-minute lead. From then on, it was all England, but they just could not penetrate Argentina's well-organized defensive screen. Milburn twice hit a post, but time began to run out, and England were in danger of losing at home for the first time to a team from outside the British Isles.

Then, with the Wembley roar spurring them on, England finally cracked it. Mortensen, who often claims to be a poor header of the ball, nodded a Finney corner home with 11 minutes to go, and then got above the defence to head a Ramsey free-kick down on to Milburn's foot for the winner.

Mortensen heads England's equalizer past Argentine keeper Rugilo.

Scotland lose home record

SCOTLAND lost their proud home record against foreign sides when Austria beat them 1–0 on a bone-hard ground at Hampden Park on 13 December. There can be no excuses for the Scots, who never seem to be able to produce the passion against Continental teams that they show against the "auld enemy" England. Scotland exhibited a marked lack of shooting power against the far from impressive Austrians — no "Wunderteam", this — and a goal from outside-right Ernst Melchior was enough to make history.

This was the first match between the two countries since the war. Austria humbled the Scots 5–0 in Vienna in 1931, and there have been two draws since. Scotland's withdrawal from the World Cup last year was narrow-minded and inexcusable. Perhaps this defeat will drive home the need to broaden their international outlook.

FOOTBALL FOCUS

- The two Divisions Three were increased to 24 clubs each.
- Arsenal centre-half Leslie Compton became the oldest British player to make his international debut when, at 38 years 2 months, he represented England against Wales on 15 November.
- Rangers took a back seat for a change in Scotland. They were runners-up in the League to Hibs, who lost in the League Cup final to Motherwell, who lost in the Cup final to Celtic — a chain of events that must have gone down well at Parkhead.
- Scotland, having lost their home record to Austria, were beaten 4-0 in Vienna in May, when Billy Steel became the first Scottish player to be sent off in an international.
- Alec Herd, 39,and his son David, just 17, played together in Stockport's last game of the season, a 2–0 win over Hartlepool.

FINAL SCORE

Football League
Division 1: Tottenham Hotspur
Top scorer: Stan Mortensen (Blackpool) 30
Division 2: Preston North End
Division 3S: Nottingham Forest
Division 3N: Rotherham United
Footballer of the Year: Harry Johnston (Blackpool)

FA Cup Final

Newcastle United	2	Blackpool	0

Scottish League
Division A: Hibernian
Top scorer: Lawrie Reilly (Hibernian) 22
Division B: Queen of the South

Scottish FA Cup Final

Celtic	1	Motherwell	0

Scottish League Cup Final

Motherwell	3	Hibernian	0

International Championship
Scotland, 6 pts

Stanley is magic, but it's Jackie's match

STANLEY MATTHEWS played his heart out for Blackpool and at times seemed to be taking on the whole Newcastle defence by himself. But the FA Cup final belongs to Jackie Milburn, whose two goals will be recalled for decades to come.

All in all, Newcastle were the better side. Blackpool's attack relied too much on Mortensen in the middle, the "maestro" on the right wing, and the driving force behind them, Harry Johnston, captain and Footballer of the Year. Milburn, England inside colleague and sometime rival of Mortensen, was the obvious Newcastle danger man, well supported by the explosive Bobby Mitchell on the left wing and at inside-right by the diminutive Ernie Taylor, a crafty box of tricks.

The first half was even, although Blackpool had the better chances. But they were playing a dangerous game at the back, and when Milburn beat their offside trap, only a fine save from Farm kept his shot out. The warning went unheeded, and five minutes into the second half, Milburn was put away again, by Chilean George Robledo. Racing through from half-way, he slotted the ball right-footed past the advancing Farm to keep up his record of scoring in every round.

Four minutes later, Newcastle were two up. Walker pushed the ball inside to Taylor on the edge of the box. The little schemer casually caressed the ball underfoot and then, without looking around, rolled it back to Milburn, who cracked it, left-footed this time, high into the net from an angle and some 25 yards out. The speed, simplicity and execution of the goal were breathtaking.

Blackpool came back strongly, and Matthews, who hasn't scored for over two years, uncharacteristically cut inside several times to shoot, despairing of the efforts of his colleagues. It was to no avail, however, and Newcastle defended well enough to survive the onslaught.

Milburn wheels away after pushing the ball past Farm to score his first goal.

To Newcastle the Cup – to Arsenal the glory

THE CRIES of "Lucky Arsenal", familiar since their triumphs in the thirties, were absent at Wembley on Saturday, when their gallant 10 men finally succumbed to the persistence of the Newcastle attack. The bad luck that had destroyed their Championship hopes followed Arsenal to Wembley, when right-back Walley Barnes badly injured a knee in the first half. Typical of Arsenal's spirit, he twice came back with his knee strapped up, but finally had to leave the field after 27 minutes.

Arsenal had been on top until then, with Doug Lishman giving the Newcastle defence a fright when his elegant overhead kick scraped a post. But as the game wore on, it seemed inevitable that Newcastle would score. Arsenal's walking wounded — Ray Daniel with his broken wrist in a cast, Lishman with a septic cut and Jimmy Logie with an internal haemorrhage — had to fight a desperate rearguard action.

Lishman's overhead effort just fails after two minutes at Wembley.

Skipper Joe Mercer played his greatest game, an unforgettable display of courage and captaincy. Daniel, a highly skilful centre-half, subdued last year's Wembley hero, Jackie Milburn. And Don Roper, a makeshift right-back, did a marvellous job on the elusive Bobby Mitchell. Indeed, Roper was lying on the ground injured when Mitchell finally broke through to put over the cross from which George Robledo headed the winner — off a post with only five minutes to go.

Newcastle are the first team this century to retain the Cup. Perhaps it was merciful that Arsenal were spared extra time. They won more friends in defeat than with all their triumphs of the past.

SOCCER SOUNDBITES

"We have won the Cup, but the glory is yours."

STAN SEYMOUR,
Newcastle director-manager to Arsenal after their brave display in the Cup final.

"Joe Mercer is the greatest player I have ever met in this game."

JOE HARVEY,
of his opposing Cup final captain (also his former wartime sergeant-major).

"Boys, I have never been so proud of you in victory as I am in defeat."

TOM WHITTAKER,
Arsenal manager.

Mission impossible

THAT ARSENAL failed in the first leg of their Herculean attempt to bring off the League and Cup "double" was not surprising. They needed to beat champions elect Manchester United by seven goals at Old Trafford, so it was a chance in fantasy only. In the event, an Arsenal side already disjointed by injuries and reduced to 10 men after only 24 minutes — they finished with nine — were beaten 6–1, with Jack Rowley scoring a hat-trick.

The League triumph is no more than United deserve, after finishing runners-up in four of the five seasons since the war. Johnny Carey, as ever, has been an inspirational leader, and with Allenby Chilton and Henry Cockburn provided a powerful springboard for United's supremacy. Rowley spearheaded the goals department with 30, while Stan Pearson chipped in with an invaluable 22. It is United's third League title, but their first for 41 years.

Gunners throw light on night football

The sight of things to come: floodlit football at Highbury.

THE FIRST official match under floodlighting since 1878 took place at Highbury on 19 September, when Arsenal entertained the Hapoel club of Tel Aviv in a friendly. A crowd of 44,000 saw the Gunners cruise to a 6–1 victory, but the important thing was that they saw it — very clearly, indeed.

It was Arsenal manager the late Herbert Chapman, back in the thirties, who advocated the use of floodlights. Impressed with what he had seen on the Continent, he had them built into the West Stand. But the FA banned them for use in official matches, because they feared that, if the idea caught on, "clubs would be drawn into spending too much money". Chapman's protégé Tom Whittaker, the current Arsenal manager, put on a literally brilliant show for Press and public at Highbury, and the verdict from each was a unanimous thumbs-up.

Lofthouse, the Lion of Vienna

NAT LOFTHOUSE'S two goals for England at the Prater Stadium, particularly his brave winner, earned him the nick-name "Lion of Vienna". It was an important match, against Austria, with reputations at stake.

Austria had been slamming goals past European defences — eight against Belgium, seven Yugoslavia, six Eire — and had beaten Scotland home and away. Earlier in the season they had held England to a draw at Wembley. England, unbeaten in their last eight games, had just played out a most unconvincing 1-1 draw in Italy and looked a tired side. They were there for the taking. The match was billed in Vienna as the "Championship of Europe", and the city, still under post-war Allied occupation, was tense with expectation. There were some 2,000 British troops in the 60,000 crowd.

After 20 minutes of canny defence, England struck, with Lofthouse volleying home a Sewell cross. Seconds later, however, Froggatt brought Dienst down and Huber scored from the spot. England hit back immediately, and Sewell, with a feint and a shot, restored their lead. Nevertheless, Dienst managed to get away from Wright and put Austria level again just before the interval.

In the second half, Austria stepped up the pressure, and it became a physical game. The England defence worked over-time, with Merrick having an inspired game in goal. Austria were determined to win, but they left themselves wide open for a counter-attack, and this is what happened. Merrick leapt high to pluck a corner out of the air, and threw the ball out to Tom Finney. The England winger drew the only defender and put Lofthouse away on a lone 50-yard run. It was a duel between Lofthouse and the keeper, who came out to meet him. Lofthouse shot as they collided, and was out cold when the ball hit the net. There were only eight minutes left when he was carried off the field on a stretcher, but he returned to help England protect their lead. Although hobbling on the wing, he still managed to crash a shot against the post. A mass of khaki-clad servicemen invaded the field to carry off the England players at the end.

Nat Lofthouse, Lion of Vienna.

'Clockwork' Ocwirk makes Austrians tick

THE IMPRESSIVE Austrians earned a 2–2 draw with England at Wembley at the end of November in the long-awaited clash. Having beaten Scotland at Hampden last season — the first foreign side to win on Scottish soil — and then routed them 4–0 in Vienna, Austria seemed to be returning to their pre-war eminence, and were expected to challenge England's proud home record.

The match was not a disappointment. The head-on collision between the two soccer schools provided a fascinating comparison. Austria, their slow, close-passing style revolving around "centre-half" Ernst Ocwirk, rely on precision and positioning. England's traditional "third-back" game, with speed and close marking the basic virtues, was put to the test.

The tall Ocwirk, quickly dubbed "Clockwork" by the England fans, was a revelation. He is a centre-half of the old school, the hub of all his side's build-ups, a supremely gifted player with impeccable ball control and passing skills.

Because of injuries, England had been forced to chop and change their side, and they fielded a completely new right wing, Ivor Broadis of Manchester City inside and Arthur Milton of Arsenal on the flank. Broadis, nearly 29, was an experienced schemer, creative, fast and with a powerful shot. Milton, at 23, had rocketed into contention with no more than a dozen first-team appearances. Unfortunately the Wembley crowd did not see what he could do because Broadis starved him out of the game.

Austria scored first, from a superb long ball by Ocwirk to Melchior. Alf Ramsey equalized from the spot, and seven minutes from time placed an indirect free-kick, which the Austrians were still disputing, on to the head of the unmarked Nat Lofthouse to give England the lead. But Stojaspal scored a deserved equalizer two minutes later from a penalty for hands.

Ramsey equalizes from the penalty spot against the impressive Austrians.

FOOTBALL FOCUS

- Wales, who shared the Home International Championship with England (both got five points), beat a Rest of the UK selection 3–2 at Cardiff on 5 December in a match to celebrate the Welsh FA's centenary.
- Derek Dooley scored 46 goals in 30 League games for Division Two champions Sheffield Wednesday.
- Billy Wright won his 42nd cap against Austria in Vienna to beat Bob Crompton's long-standing record for England.

FINAL SCORE

Football League
Division 1: Manchester United
Top scorer: George Robledo (Newcastle United) 33
Division 2: Sheffield Wednesday
Division 3S: Plymouth Argyle
Division 3N: Lincoln City
Footballer of the Year: Billy Wright (Wolverhampton Wanderers)

FA Cup Final

Newcastle United	1	Arsenal	0

Scottish League
Division A: Hibernian
Top scorer: Lawrie Reilly (Hibernian) 27
Division B: Clyde

Scottish FA Cup Final

Motherwell	4	Dundee	0

Scottish League Cup Final

Dundee	3	Rangers	2

International Championship
England, Wales, 5 pts

Matthews gets his medal at last

The "Wizard of the Dribble" gets his FA Cup-winners' medal at last.

WEMBLEY was the stage as the world's most famous footballer, Stanley Matthews, at last won the FA Cup medal that had eluded him for 20 years. After a dramatic finish in which he made Blackpool's winner for Bill Perry, Matthews went up to receive his medal from the newly crowned Queen Elizabeth II, who was only six when Stan first turned out for Stoke City.

Twice in three years (1948 and 1951) Matthews was on the losing side in classic finals, and for years the whole country has been behind the "Wizard of the Dribble" in his season-by-season quest for a winners' medal. When Bolton were 3–1 up after 55 minutes, it seemed Matthews would again be denied. But Bolton had played much of the game with left-half Eric Bell a passenger on the wing, and in the last quarter of the match, inspired by Matthews's irresistible runs along the wing, Blackpool began to overrun the Bolton defence.

With 22 minutes left, Stan Mortensen, who had scored in the first half, added a second, poking the ball in when keeper Stan Hanson fumbled a Matthews cross. The gallant Bolton defence then held out until the last minute of normal time before the equalizer came. Jackie Mudie was brought down outside the box as he fastened on to another Matthews centre, and Morty crashed the free-kick past the defensive wall.

The fans now knew the Cup was Blackpool's as extra time loomed. But it wasn't needed. In injury time, Matthews again jinked past his man and towards the touchline, cut in and laid the ball back invitingly into the path of left-winger Perry, and the South African swept it into the net from 10 yards.

Stan had his medal in a fairy-tale ending, but there were other heroes on the day, not least his England colleague Mortensen, who became the first man to score a hat-trick in a Wembley final. There was Bell, who tore a muscle after 20 minutes, yet courageously rose to head Bolton's third goal. And one can only feel sympathy for left-back Ralph Banks, who was increasingly lame and had to suffer being turned inside-out by the 38-year-old maestro. One wonders just how long the ageless wonder can continue to turn it on — days like this could keep him going for ever.

Nail-biting finish as Arsenal win record seventh title

ARSENAL clinched the League Championship on Friday evening in a nerve-tingling match that they had to win in order to overtake Preston, who had already finished their programme. Pity poor Preston. When they beat Arsenal at Deepdale last Saturday, they gave themselves a chance of their first Championship since they won the first two inaugral League titles at the end of the 1880s. Burnley were Arsenal's opponents, and they gave the anxious 51,000 fans at Highbury a fright when they took the lead after only three minutes.

Jimmy Logie (8) scores Arsenal's crucial third goal in the title decider against Burnley.

Fortunately for Arsenal, Alex Forbes, who played a blinder, chose the occasion to score his only goal of the season and put them on level terms. Lishman and Logie added further goals, and the crowd began to relax. Burnley pulled one back after the interval, however, and Arsenal's nerves began to show. But with Joe Mercer as calm as ever at the helm — what an Indian summer the old man's having! — Arsenal held out for a 3–2 win and the title, a record seventh, on goal average.

The Gunners and Preston had identical results — 21 wins, 12 draws and nine defeats — but Arsenal's goal average was 1.51 to North End's 1.41.

Old-timer Sagar leaves his post after 24 years

LONG-STANDING Goodison Park fans found they had to acquire a new habit during the 1952–53 season. They had to look at the programme to see who was in goal for the Toffeemen. Ted Sagar retired in May after only one appearance in the season, bringing to an end the longest continuous spell any player has served with one club as a professional. Sagar joined Everton on 26 March 1929, so has completed 24 years' service and has just had his 43rd birthday.

As a youngster, Sagar had a trial with Hull City, who were so slow to offer him a contract that Everton nipped in. Sagar won a regular place in the first team in 1931, and has played in every season since, winning two League Championship and one Cup-winners' medal, a Second Division title medal, and four England caps. Not a big man, Sagar relied on skill and positioning, and was utterly fearless in diving at the feet of forwards. Despite losing a great part of his career to the war, he accumulated an Everton record of 465 League appearances.

Goalkeeper Ted Sagar hangs up his boots after his record spell of 24 years with Everton.

FOOTBALL FOCUS

- On Boxing Day at Hillsborough, three Wednesday players, Vince Kenny, Norman Curtis and Eddie Gannon, scored own goals. Their opponents West Bromwich gratefully accepted the Christmas presents and went home with a 5–4 win.
- In Huddersfield's 8–2 defeat of Everton in Division Two, Jimmy Glazzard scored five goals — all headers from crosses by winger Vic Metcalfe.
- Nat Lofthouse scored six goals for the Football League against the League of Ireland at Molineux on 24 September, a record for an Inter-League match.
- Irish international Charlie Tully scored direct from a corner for Celtic at Falkirk in the Cup on 28 February, but the goal was disallowed because some of the crowd had spilled on to the pitch. So Tully retook the corner and promptly scored again.
- Leicester City's Arthur Rowley, signed from Fulham two seasons earlier, scored a hat-trick in both League games against his former team.
- Amateur club Walthamstow Avenue beat two League clubs in the FA Cup before remarkably holding Manchester United to a 1–1 draw at Old Trafford in the fourth round. But they lost the replay 5–2 at Highbury.

Derek Dooley loses leg

DEREK DOOLEY, Sheffield Wednesday's exciting young centre-forward, on the brink of a great career, has had to have his right leg amputated. He broke it against Preston on 14 February, challenging the keeper for a fifty-fifty ball. A couple of days later, in Preston Royal Infirmary, with Dooley about to be discharged and getting used to the idea of missing the rest of the season, it was discovered that gangrene had set in. There was no alternative but to amputate.

Big and strong, but looking cumbersome and unpolished when he was establishing a place in the team last season, he cracked 46 goals in 30 games to lead Wednesday to promotion. With a fast-growing reputation for scoring goals from impossible situations, the 23-year-old had accrued 16 in 29 First Division games this season and was already in the running for an England cap. The whole football world now mourns the loss of a rising young star.

Dooley: a tragic end to a meteoric career.

FINAL SCORE

Football League
Division 1: Arsenal
Top scorer: Charlie Wayman (Preston North End) 24
Division 2: Sheffield United
Division 3S: Bristol Rovers
Division 3N: Oldham Athletic
Footballer of the Year: Nat Lofthouse (Bolton Wanderers)

FA Cup Final

Blackpool	4	Bolton Wanderers	3

Scottish League
Division A: Rangers
Top scorers: Charlie Fleming (East Fife), Lawrie Reilly (Hibernian) 30
Division B: Stirling Albion

Scottish FA Cup Final

Rangers	1	Aberdeen	1
Replay: Rangers	1	Aberdeen	0

Scottish League Cup Final

Dundee	2	Kilmarnock	0

International Championship
England, Scotland, 4 pts

Struth! Another 'double' for Rangers

RANGERS brought off the League and Cup "double" again, although it was a close call in both competitions. Centre-half George Young had to go in goal for 18 minutes of the Cup final when keeper George Niven was off injured. He played well enough for Rangers to draw 1–1 with Aberdeen, and they went on to win the replay 1–0.

They now needed three points from their remaining two fixtures to pip Hibs for the League title. A 3–1 win over Dundee three days after the replayed Cup final left them requiring a draw with Queen of the South at Dumfries. Thanks to a dramatic Willie Waddell equalizer in the 75th minute, they did it, just edging past Hibs on goal average.

What a catalogue of success manager Willie Struth, now in his 75th year, has compiled with the Gers since he took over as manager in 1920 — 18 Championships, 10 Cups and three League Cups. That is a record without equal in first-class football. Yet Struth had had little experience as a player. He was a stonemason and a professional runner before getting a job as trainer at Ibrox Park, becoming manager when the previous boss died in an accident. An inspired choice by the board!

Ramsey saves England from banquet blues

ENGLAND took on the Rest of Europe as part of the FA's 90th birthday celebrations. The Rest, an untried combination of stars from Austria, Germany, Italy, Spain, Sweden and Yugoslavia — the Hungarians, who come to Wembley next month, ominously withdrew their players — felt they had no chance. But it was England who played as if they'd never met before, and who were lucky in the end to escape with a draw.

When the teams came out on to the pitch, the biggest cheer was for Stanley Matthews, recalled to the side at 38. But Matthews apart, there was little to cheer the 97,000 fans. Inside-forwards Kubala of Spain and Vukas of Yugoslavia soon showed they were streets ahead of the labouring Englishmen in technique and tactics.

Eckersley finds the only way to stop Vukas is to bring him down, after just five minutes, and Kubala scores from the spot. But England are fighters, and Mortensen equalizes two minutes later. Boniperti of Italy scores twice — England 1 The Rest 3. Some Matthews magic gives England heart. Mullen takes advantage of a defensive lapse and pulls one back — half-time 2–3. Another Matthews dribble brings the crowd to its feet and he sets Mullen up for the equalizer. But still the Europeans control the game, and they take the lead when Kubala fires the ball in, with the England defence spread-eagled. England's hopes are waning, but Mortensen is brought down in the box. Up steps ice-cool Alf Ramsey to send substitute keeper Beara the wrong way for a last-minute equalizer — it's 4–4, England's home record is still intact, and the FA notaries can enjoy the celebratory banquet.

England's bastion breached by the magicians — Hungary win 6-3

IT HAD TO HAPPEN — England's proud undefeated home record against Continental invaders had to go sometime. All the signs were there. But it didn't just slip away, it was shattered. Those "Magic Magyars", unbeaten since May 1950, produced a truly wonderful display of football, the like of which has not been seen at Wembley since that legendary one-off performance by the Scots in 1928.

England did not play badly. But the Hungarians were in another class. Speedy, fluent, and with the confidence that comes with 20 wins in 23 games since their last defeat, they were superior in every aspect of the game. Indeed, led by the remarkable Ferenc Puskas — what a superb left foot he has — they seemed to be playing a different game altogether.

Puskas and the other inside-forward, the tall, elegant Sandor Kocsis, a brilliant header of the ball, spearheaded the attack, while Nandor Hidegkuti, the No. 9, foraged behind them. In the past, England have survived against cleverer Continental opposition because of their inability to shoot. Not this time, though. Hidegkuti dispelled any such delusions in the very first minute, slashing a 20-yarder past the bewildered Merrick. Bewilderment is perhaps the best word to describe the reactions of the England defence throughout the match. Time and again they were left gaping as Puskas and company ran rings round them.

Puskas (10) acclaims his exquisitely executed first goal.

Yet England equalized after 13 minutes, when Mortensen put Sewell through to score a classic goal. The hopes of 100,000 fans rose — only to be dashed a short time later in a seven-minute spell that surely marked the end of an era. First Hidegkuti scored from close in, then Puskas left Wright tackling thin air as he dragged the ball back with his studs and rifled it in from a narrow angle. The unstoppable Puskas then deflected a Bozsik free-kick into the net to put his side 4–1 up, before Mortensen pulled one back. The Hungarians continued to dominate after the interval. Bozsik — has there ever been a finer wing-half? — scored with a tremendous drive and Hidegkuti volleyed his third. It could have been more had these footballers from another planet not slackened in the last half-hour, and a Ramsey penalty was little consolation.

The English players knew they'd been given a lesson, and Billy Wright, their captain, summed it up when he said ruefully: "The Hungarians produced some of the finest, most brilliantly applied football it has ever been my privilege to see. The ball did precisely what they wanted . . . They were relentless. They were superb."

Billy Wright exchanges pennants with the deceptively podgy Puskas.

FINAL SCORE

Football League
Division 1: Wolverhampton Wanderers
Top scorer: Jimmy Glazzard (Huddersfield T) 29
Division 2: Leicester City
Division 3S: Ipswich Town
Division 3N: Port Vale
Footballer of the Year: Tom Finney (Preston NE)

FA Cup Final

West Brom	3	Preston North End	2

Scottish League
Division A: Celtic
Top scorer: Jimmy Wardhaugh (Hearts) 27
Division B: Motherwell

Scottish FA Cup Final

Celtic	2	Aberdeen	1

Scottish League Cup Final

East Fife	3	Partick Thistle	2

International Championship
England, 6 pts

Port Vale pull welcome mat from under Matthews's feet

WHEN CUP-HOLDERS Blackpool were drawn away to Port Vale in the fifth round, Stanley Matthews looked forward to a welcome return to the Potteries. They gave him a welcome all right — they cleverly forced him away from the drier areas on the wing into the middle, where he met mud as well as a massed defence. The tactics worked, and Vale won 2–0 to pull off a giant-killing act to rival Norwich's in the last round — a tribute to manager Freddie Steele, a long-time Stoke team-mate of Matthews in the thirties!

Vale, who won 2–0 at First Division Cardiff in the last round, are set to visit a fellow Division Three side, Leyton Orient, in the last eight, so there will be a Third Division club in the semi-finals for only the second time (Millwall did it in 1937).

The Port Vale defence block a Matthews effort from close in.

Magyars dish out lesson No. 2

THE RETURN came too quickly for England to have absorbed the lesson they received at Wembley. Six months ago they were shown to be years behind the Hungarians in the very basics of football — control, technique, accuracy and movement. Now, at the People's Stadium in Budapest, they were given a second lesson in the arts of the game they introduced to the world.

This time, those "Magnificent Magyars" showed no mercy. Puskas, who scored twice, once again dictated their play and was the architect of their victory — 7–1, the heaviest defeat ever suffered by an English side. Only Merrick, Wright, Dickinson and Sewell kept their places from Wembley, while Hungary made just one change. It would not have mattered what combination was chosen to represent England; the result would have been the same. Perhaps England will finally learn from this defeat, and take note of the advances in the game that have been made outside the hidebound home countries.

On this form, Hungary are clear favourites for the next World Cup

Kocsis, completely unchallenged, about to hit Hungary's fourth goal.

Norwich do a 'Walsall' on Arsenal

LEAGUE CHAMPIONS Arsenal suffered their most humiliating Cup defeat since Walsall ruffled the pride of the great Herbert Chapman team in 1933, when Third Division Norwich City beat them at Highbury in the fourth round. At least Walsall had the decency to do the dirty on their own ground!

Nearly 55,000 turned up to see what they hoped would be a comfortable victory, especially after the 5–1 defeat of Villa in the third round. They were in for a rude awakening when Arsenal conceded a penalty in the second minute, but Jack Kelsey saved from Bobby Brennan. And although Arsenal took a second-half lead through Jimmy Logie, Norwich's reserve centre-forward Tom Johnston stunned the Arsenal faithful by scoring twice. The Gunners fired everything bar the kitchen sink at Norwich in the last 10 minutes without any luck. That's Cup football for you, as the old adage goes. "David" wins again!

Johnston (left) heads Norwich's winner past Dodgin, Wills and Kelsey.

FOOTBALL FOCUS

- Port Vale beat Orient 1–0 in the sixth round of the Cup, but lost 2–1 in the semi-finals to eventual winners WBA. However, in the League, they topped Division Three (N) by 11 points and set records for the fewest goals conceded (21) and the most games with a clean sheet (30), and a Division Three (N) record for fewest defeats (three).
- Former Scottish international winger Jimmy Delaney pulled off a unique treble when he won a Cup-winners' medal with Derry City in Northern Ireland, having already won a Scottish Cup medal with Celtic in 1937 and an FA Cup medal with Manchester United in 1948.
- Sam Bartram made his 500th League appearance for Charlton on 6 March in their Division One game with Portsmouth at the Valley, a record for any League club.

The world weeps for Hungary

The all-conquering 'Magic Magyars' were the popular favourites to win the 1954 World Cup in Switzerland. They had thrilled the world with their speedy, breathtakingly fluent football, and on the way to the final they scored 25 goals in four matches, including four each against Brazil and Uruguay. But they fell, controversially, at the last hurdle. And it is sad for the winners, a fine West German side, that the 1954 tournament will always be remembered as Hungary's World Cup.

THERE WERE 38 original entries, England and Scotland were again allowed to qualify from the Home Championship, and there were nine other groups. Brazil emerged without trouble from South America and, with holders Uruguay automatic finalists, Argentina again declined to enter.

A curious format

Yet again the format was changed. The 16 finalists were divided into four groups of four, but two seeded countries in each group would not play each other. Extra time would be played in group matches level at 90 minutes, and there would be play-offs if the second and third teams in a group finished level on points. The only sane decision was to revert to the knock-out system from the last eight onwards.

Hungary gave immediate confirmation of their strong favouritism by beating South Korea 9–0 and then West Germany 8–3. Sepp Herberger's gamble in playing a weakened side was derided by the 30,000 German fans who travelled to Basle to see the match. The German coach, however, was confident they could win a play-off, as indeed they did, 7–2 against Turkey, to earn a quarter-final against Yugoslavia rather than Brazil.

Stanley Matthews (left) was in fine form for England against Belgium.

Mixed British luck

Scotland, who condescended this time to play in their first World Cup as runners-up in the Home Championship, found themselves having to play Austria and Uruguay. They were a little unlucky to lose 1–0 to Austria, but their team manager Andy Beattie resigned and they were hammered out of the competition 7–0 by Uruguay, showing form worthy of world champions.

Meanwhile, England progressed through to the quarter-finals without setting the tournament alight. They took a 3–1 lead against Belgium, but lost it in the last 15 minutes, and were held 4–4. It did not matter, because they qualified by beating Switzerland 2–0 and heading their group. In Group One, Brazil and Yugoslavia both went through after playing out a 1–1 draw.

The Battle of Berne

It was unfortunate that arguably the two top teams of the competition, Hungary and Brazil, met so early. But what was expected to be a classic quarter-final between the best from Europe and South America turned out to be a most violent match and ended in a riot, with the fighting on the field carried on into the dressing-rooms and hundreds of spectators also involved.

Only three minutes after the start, Hidegkuti scored for Hungary despite having half his shorts ripped off. Five minutes later he crossed for Kocsis to head his eighth goal of the tournament. The Brazilians, instead of trying to play themselves back into the game, resorted to violence. The Hungarians began to retaliate, and the match degenerated into a battle, finishing at 4–2 to Hungary, and only nine players on either side, two Brazilians having been sent off along with the Hungarian captain Bozsik (Puskas did not play), and with Toth a virtual passenger on the wing.

Meanwhile, the West Germans were qualifying for the semi-finals with a 2–0 win over Yugoslavia. The previous day, the hosts Switzerland had lost a 3–0 lead in a record 12-goal classic, Austria emerging 7–5 victors, having been 5–3 up only 10 minutes after being three down!

England found themselves up against formidable opponents in the world champions. They were outplayed in the end, even though Uruguay had three players injured, and lost 4–2, Merrick's goalkeeping errors proving costly.

The goals flow

The "Battle of Berne" apart, the tournament so far had been a

How is it possible to lose a group match in the World Cup finals by eight goals to three and then beat the same nation in the final? Germany did it — and the Hungarians, so desperately unlucky, were the fall-guys.

Czibor opens the scoring for Hungary in the classic semi-final against Uruguay.

wonderful advertisement for exciting soccer, with plenty of goals. And they continued unabated in the semi-finals. The Austrian defence, so shaky in the Swiss match, proved no better against the Germans, who won a convincing and ominous 6–1 passage to the final.

If there were misgivings about the other semi-final, another clash between Europe and South America, they were soon dispelled, as Hungary and Uruguay put on one of the finest exhibitions of football ever seen. With 15 minutes to go, Hungary were two up through goals by Czibor and Hidegkuti, but Uruguay pulled them back, Schiaffino twice putting Hohberg in to score, the second with only three minutes to go. In extra time, the Hungarians, still without Puskas, called on all their resources, and Kocsis produced two more towering headers to put them in the final, and inflict on Uruguay their first ever defeat in the World Cup.

Sad end for Hungary

Puskas insisted on playing in the final, even though he was not 100 per cent fit. And it looked like his gamble had paid off when he followed up a blocked shot from Kocsis to put Hungary ahead after six minutes. Two minutes later, Czibor nipped in to take advantage of a defensive mistake and put them two up.

But the Germans did not crack. They came back immediately. Their captain and inside-left Fritz Walter hit a fast cross which Morlock, stretching out, converted at the near post. In the 18th minute, Rahn scored after a corner, and Germany were level. Hungary returned to the attack and some of their moves were breathtaking, but when German keeper Turek was beaten, Kohlmeyer popped up to save on the line.

The Germans began to come back into the game with a quarter of an hour to go, gaining strength from Hungary's inability to score. Bozsik made a rare mistake and Schaefer put Fritz Walter away. His cross was only half-cleared, and there was Rahn on hand to shoot home from 15 yards. With just five minutes to go, Puskas, who had almost faded from the game, suddenly latched on to a pass from Toth and cracked the ball past Turek. But the linesman's flag was up for offside. It was all over for the magnificent Magyars. West Germany were the new world champions.

Rahn (20) hits the winner for West Germany in the final.

WORLD CUP FOCUS

- Turkey enjoyed a curious qualification for the finals, drawn in a group of two with Spain. They lost 4–1 in Madrid, but won the return 1–0 in Istanbul. The two teams then met in Rome for a play-off. On receipt of a mysterious telegram, Spain left out their star player, Kubala, and could only draw 2–2. Lots were drawn out of a hat by a blind Italian boy, and Turkey were through to Switzerland.
- Inquiries into the so-called "Battle of Berne" took place, but, apart from reprimanding the guilty players, the international disciplinary committee left any punitive action to the respective national bodies. When Bozsik was asked later by the referee Arthur Ellis how he had been dealt with, he replied: "We don't punish Members of Parliament in Hungary."

FINAL SCORE

Group 1

Yugoslavia	1	France	0
Brazil	5	Mexico	0
France	3	Mexico	2
Brazil	1	Yugoslavia	1

	P	W	D	L	F	A	P
Brazil	2	1	1	0	6	1	3
Yugoslavia	2	1	1	0	2	1	3
France	2	1	0	1	3	3	2
Mexico	2	0	0	2	2	8	0

Group 2

Hungary	9	South Korea	0
West Germany	4	Turkey	1
Hungary	8	West Germany	3
Turkey	7	South Korea	0

	P	W	D	L	F	A	P
Hungary	2	2	0	0	17	3	4
Turkey	2	1	0	1	8	4	2
W Germany	2	1	0	1	7	9	2
South Korea	2	0	0	2	0	16	0

Play-off

West Germany	7	Turkey	2

Group 3

Austria	1	Scotland	0
Uruguay	2	Czechoslovakia	0
Austria	5	Czechoslovakia	0
Uruguay	7	Scotland	0

	P	W	D	L	F	A	P
Uruguay	2	2	0	0	9	0	4
Austria	2	2	0	0	6	0	4
Czech	2	0	0	2	0	7	0
Scotland	2	0	0	2	0	8	0

Group 4

England	4	Belgium	4
Switzerland	2	Italy	1
England	2	Switzerland	0
Italy	4	Belgium	1

	P	W	D	L	F	A	P
England	2	1	1	0	6	4	3
Italy	2	1	0	1	5	3	2
Switzerland	2	1	0	1	2	3	2
Belgium	2	0	1	1	5	8	1

Play-off

Switzerland	4	Italy	1

QUARTER-FINALS

Austria	7	Switzerland	5
Uruguay	4	England	2
West Germany	2	Yugoslavia	0
Hungary	4	Brazil	2

SEMI-FINALS

Hungary	4	Uruguay	2
West Germany	6	Austria	1

THIRD-PLACE MATCH

Austria	3	Uruguay	1

FINAL

West Germany	3	Hungary	2

Wankdorf Stadium, Berne, 4 July 1954. Attendance 60,000

West Germany: Turek, Posipal, Kohlmeyer, Eckel, Liebrich, Mai, Rahn, Morlock, Walter O, Walter F, Schaefer
(Scorers: Morlock, Rahn 2)

Hungary: Grosics, Buzansky, Lantos, Bozsik, Lorant, Zakarias, Czibor, Kocsis, Hidegkuti, Puskas, Toth
(Scorers: Puskas, Czibor)

Leading scorers

11 Kocsis (Hungary)
6 Hugi (Switzerland)
Morlock (West Germany)

Wolves restore English pride — Puskas and Co. beaten

WOLVES have done it again. Last month it was Moscow Spartak, beaten 4–0 under the Molineux floodlights with an unforgettable three-goal burst in the last three minutes. Now it's Honved, arguably the best club side in the world, studded with internationals and fielding five of the Hungarian side that so humiliated England 7–1 in May. The Hungarian Army club looked like emulating the national side when they went two up inside 15 minutes. But the Football League champions came storming back in the second half for a famous 3–2 victory to restore some of the lost English pride.

It was a case of déjà vu for home fans when Sandor "Golden Head" Kocsis gave Honved the lead after just 10 minutes with one of his inimitable headers. The inside-forward trio of Kocsis, Puskas and Machos were causing the Wolves defence all kinds of trouble, and when Machos scored a second after 14 minutes, it really did look as if another rout was on the cards. But Billy Wright was magnificent at the heart of the Wolves defence, inspiring his side by example. In the last year, the England captain has seen enough of Puskas and Co. to last him a lifetime. But he's not the sort of man to capitulate, and the Wolves side went in at half-time without conceding any further goals.

Roy Swinbourne celebrates his winning goal for Wolves.

Whatever manager Stan Cullis said to his men during the interval, it had a galvanizing effect. They stormed into the attack, and little Johnny Hancocks was brought down in the box. He took the kick himself and scored. Spurred on by the goal and by the roar of the 55,000 fans, Wolves began to take command, but it was 14 minutes from time before they got a deserved equalizer, Swinbourne heading in a Wilshaw cross.

The shouting had not died down when, two minutes later, Leslie Smith left two defenders in his wake as he cut the ball inside for Swinbourne again to lash it into the net on the run — a fitting winner for a fabulous game.

Newcastle take advantage as Cup jinx strikes again

Milburn opens the scoring with less than a minute gone. Not even Trautmann could stop his header.

MANCHESTER CITY right-back Jimmy Meadows injured knee ligaments and had to go off after just 20 minutes of the Cup final, leaving City to battle with 10 men for the rest of the match before Newcastle finally broke them down. If you think you've heard the story before, you're right. Look back three years to when Newcastle last won the Cup, and you will find that Arsenal's right-back Walley Barnes suffered the same injury at about the same time, no more than a few yards from the spot where Meadows fell. And the man whom both were trying to tackle was the same Bobby Mitchell, Newcastle's elusive outside-left.

It was a tragedy for Meadows, but the accident should not be allowed to detract from Newcastle's fine win, their third in five years. They were in front after only 50 seconds, through Milburn, and only brilliant goalkeeping by Bert Trautmann prevented them from increasing their lead. But Manchester City, despite their handicap, still managed some dangerous attacks, and drew level with a Johnstone header a minute before half-time.

After the interval, it was plain to see that both Milburn and White, Newcastle's right wing, were struggling with injuries, so this evened up matters. Their captain and right-half Jimmy Scoular was majestic in midfield, and Bob Stokoe ably looked after things at the back. But the Newcastle star was Mitchell, who really put makeshift right-back Spurdle through the mangle. Even the magnificent Trautmann had to give him best. Twice Scoular put Mitchell away with raking cross-field passes. Twice he shot, the first, from the narrowest of angles, surprising Trautmann at the near post. The second was parried, only for Hannah to lash in the rebound.

FOOTBALL FOCUS

- Tommy Briggs set a Second Division scoring record with seven goals in Blackburn's 8–3 win over Bristol Rovers on 5 February.
- Two pairs of brothers played for Wales against N.Ireland on 20 April at Belfast, John and Mel Charles and Len and Ivor Allchurch, John Charles scoring all their goals in a 3–2 win.
- Birmingham won a three-way tie for the Division Two title on goal average from Luton and Rotherham, helped by a record 16 goals in consecutive home games (7–2 against Port Vale and 9–1 against Liverpool) in mid-season.
- After their Wembley débâcle, Scotland beat Portugal and Austria, but lost 3–1 in Hungary, while England had a disastrous tour, losing in France and Portugal.
- Chelsea, who won their first League title, were scheduled to play Djurgarden of Sweden in the new European Cup next season, but withdrew on the advice of the Football League.

York battle in vain

Bottom (8) scores against Notts County to put York in the semi-finals.

WITH THE scalps of Blackpool and Spurs already under their belts, York City so very nearly became the first Third Division side to reach the FA Cup final when they took giants Newcastle to a semi-final replay. In the first match, at Hillsborough, they went ahead through Arthur Bottom, scorer of the goal that put Notts County out in the sixth round. And they kept Newcastle out with sterling defence until Keeble finally squeezed an equalizer. In the replay, at Roker Park, they were soon a goal down, scored by White, and, with centre-half Stewart going to the wing with a cut head, they looked down and out. But they still came at Newcastle until Keeble, again, finished them off in the last minute.

The extraordinary thing is that York did all this without a manager. When Jimmy McCormick resigned in September, he had built up a side around a nucleus of players signed from the proceeds of the sale of centre-forward David Dunmore to McCormick's former former club, Spurs. And when York beat Spurs 3–1 in the fifth round, Dunmore had sat and watched the upset as twelfth man!

FINAL SCORE

Football League
Division 1: Chelsea
Top scorer: Ronnie Allen (West Bromwich Albion) 27
Division 2: Birmingham City
Division 3S: Bristol City
Division 3N: Barnsley
Footballer of the Year: Don Revie (Manchester City)

FA Cup Final

Newcastle United	3	Manchester City	1

Scottish League
Division A: Aberdeen
Top scorer: Willie Bauld (Hearts) 21
Division B: Airdrieonians

Scottish FA Cup Final

Clyde	1	Celtic	1
Replay: Clyde	1	Celtic	0

Scottish League Cup Final

Hearts	4	Motherwell	2

International Championship
England, 6 pts

Matthews still magic at 40 — Scots downed 7–2!

SCOTLAND reached a new low at Wembley, annihilated 7–2 by the "auld enemy", their biggest defeat in the Home Championship and equalling their own record victory against England way back in 1878. They retained 10 of the team that lost 4–2 to Hungary at Hampden in December — regarded by some of the Scottish media as a "moral victory" because it was by a smaller margin than England's defeats by the "Magic Magyars"! With such thinking, it's sackcloth and ashes time for Scottish football. This side was outgunned in every department.

Without a win against Scotland at Wembley since 1934, England scored twice in the first eight minutes, after which no other result looked possible. Stanley Matthews, so often the scourge of the Scots, is still tormenting them at 40. He was unplayable, and created so many openings that England could have scored twice as many. Dennis Wilshaw scored four, Nat Lofthouse two (it should have been more). The other was notched by inside-right Don Revie, playing as a midfield schemer and aiding and abetting Matthews in the destruction of the Scots. Duncan Edwards of Manchester United, just 18 years 183 days old, made an impressive debut at left-half, while Jimmy Meadows and Ken Armstrong were also winning their first England caps.

But it was "old man" Matthews who won the honours again, and the Wembley crowd rose to applaud him off the field at the end of the game.

Dennis Wilshaw (10) jumps above Willie Cunningham and heads England's fifth goal against Scotland.

Manchester United win 11-goal thriller at Stamford Bridge

THE STAMFORD BRIDGE crowd went home with mixed feelings after watching an 11-goal thriller in which their side went desperately close to making the comeback of the season. Leading 3–2 at half-time, Manchester United were soon 5–2 up, and although Chelsea managed to pull one back, United restored their three-goal lead.

But Chelsea continued to pile on the pressure. Two more goals, and they were only one down with 12 minutes to go. But United held out for a 6–5 victory.

One Chelsea player will remember the match with particular pride. Seamus O'Connell, an amateur inside-left making his debut, scored a hat-trick.

Trautmann the hero: latest Cup final casualty plays on in spite of his broken neck

MANCHESTER CITY keeper Bert Trautmann played the last 15 minutes of the Cup final in great pain, not realizing his neck was broken. With his side two up, this latest victim of the "Wembley hoodoo" could have been excused for going off after a dive to save at the feet of Birmingham's Peter Murphy left him dazed and reeling. When the highly popular ex-German POW, newly elected Footballer of the Year, staggered to his feet, the fans burst out into a refrain of "For he's a jolly good fellow". He went up with his team-mates to collect his medal after their 3–1 victory, and it was only later that X-rays showed the fracture which could easily have been fatal.

This was a Cup final that had everything. Birmingham started as firm favourites after a dazzling Cup run that saw them reach Wembley without a single home tie, scoring 18 goals against two. Manchester City, by contrast, scraped through with single-goal victories in every round. And injuries forced a last-minute reshuffle of their team for the final. The out-of-favour Don Revie, dropped by both England and his club earlier in the season, was brought back from reserve-team football to play his deep-lying centre-forward role, and Bobby Johnstone was moved out to the right wing.

These controversial moves by manager Les McDowall proved to be match-winners. If Trautmann's heroics stole some of the headlines, Revie was the man of the match. He set up the first goal with a long cross-field ball to Roy Clarke from near half-way, was in the box for the return pass, and back-heeled the ball for Joe Hayes to score — this after only three minutes.

Birmingham equalized against the run of play after 15 minutes through Noel Kinsey. It was another 50 minutes before Jack Dyson restored Manchester's lead. And five minutes later the same player headed a long Trautmann clearance into the path of Johnstone, who beat the advancing Gil Merrick with ease to become the first man to score goals in successive Wembley finals.

The save that left Bert Trautmann with a broken neck... and a place in football folklore.

'Boom-Boom' Edwards stars as England beat world champions

NOT YET 20, Duncan Edwards, one of the "Busby Babes" who ran away with the Championship this season, turned the game around for England against West Germany in Berlin at the end of their summer tour. England were being overrun by the world champions when Edwards brought the ball out of defence, powered his way through the middle of the field, swerving past defender after defender, and unleashed an unstoppable shot from 25 yards.

This giant of a man, immediately nicknamed "Boom-Boom" by the spectators, has established his place as a tower of strength in the England side. After his 27th-minute wonder goal, England took control, and further goals by Grainger and Haynes midway through the second half wrapped it up before Fritz Walter scored a consolation five minutes before the end.

England powerhouse Duncan Edwards scored a great goal.

South American 'Real' king of the first European final

ARGENTINE-BORN Alfredo di Stefano orchestrated Real Madrid's thrilling victory over French club Reims in Paris in the first ever European Cup final. The No.9, a prolific goalscorer but not a centre-forward in the accepted sense, likes to dominate a game from one penalty area to another. With Reims two goals up, he illustrated this in the best possible fashion.

Beating two men in midfield, he put Marsal away, lost his markers by stopping, and then accelerated into the box to lash the return pass into the net. Di Stefano continued to be the driving force as Real equalized, fell behind again and then snatched two more goals for a brilliant 4–3 victory.

This first European Cup has been a marked success. With Chelsea refused entry by the short-sighted Football League, who did not look kindly on additions to the fixture list, Hibs of Scotland were Britain's only representatives, and they were beaten by Reims in the semi-finals.

Alfredo di Stefano led Real Madrid to victory.

Boston pitch Rams out at Baseball Ground

WHEN DERBY, the first post-war Cup-winners, dropped down to Division Three (North) last season for the first time in their history, they did not think they could sink any lower. But they have reached a new nadir — beaten in the second round of the FA Cup, beaten at home by a non-League side, and not just beaten, but thrashed 6–1.

There are a couple of instances of non-League giant-killers beating League opposition by similar scores before, but never away from home, and certainly not so illustrious a team as Derby, who are challenging for promotion. Boston United's feat must go down as one of the most sensational results in the Cup's long history.

The part-timers from the Midland League went ahead after 26 minutes, and were 3–1 up by half-time, Derby's only reply coming from a penalty scored by former Wolves and England star Jesse Pye. Any thoughts of a Derby comeback were snuffed out midway through the second half, when Boston hit three more in a 10-minute spell. Geoff Hazledine completed his hat-trick, and Ray Wilkins scored two. Both players were formerly with Derby, among seven in the side.

Derb's player-manager Ray Middleton, their goalkeeper, had picked up a "job lot" of five players at the end of last season when Derby had a relegation clear-out. They certainly came back to haunt the Rams.

England beat ball-juggling Brazilians at Wembley: Matthews stars again

AGELESS Stanley Matthews had a hand in three of England's goals as they beat the touring Brazilians 4–2 at Wembley in an extraordinary match packed with incident. Atyeo and Byrne both missed penalties. After French referee Marcel Guigue awarded one of these, a Brazilian player grabbed the ball and walked away with it, followed in single file by the referee, half the Brazilian team, and England captain Billy Wright — much to the crowd's amusement.

This was one of England's best victories. The Brazilians gave a wonderful display of ball-juggling skills, but they did not appear to have any kind of tactical plan. England were two up in five minutes. The first was begun and finished by players from the impressive young Manchester United side, the new League champions. Left-half Duncan Edwards found Matthews on the right. A square cross was touched forward by Johnny Haynes, and Tommy Taylor was at the far post to hit the ball home first time.

When outside-left Colin Grainger, making his England debut, scored the second, it looked as if Brazil were in for a thrashing. But they came back well, and drew level soon after the interval with goals by Paulinho and Didi. England, however, took control again, the halves Clayton, Wright and Edwards tackling hard and providing the springboard for their attacks. Taylor, proving a fine leader of the forward line, restored England's lead from close in, and Matthews, still delighting the crowd and bamboozling left-backs with his footwork under the new Wembley floodlights, put the ball on Grainger's head for England's fourth.

Both penalties were awarded for hands by Zozimo, and both were saved by Gilmar.

Sheffield United winger Colin Grainger (11) heads England's fourth on a memorable debut.

FOOTBALL FOCUS

● Tranmere centre-half Harold Bell finally missed a match in September after completing a record 401 consecutive League appearances from the start of the 1946–47 season.

● Wolves equalled the Division One away goalscoring record (set by Sunderland at Newcastle in December 1908) when they won 9–1 at Cardiff on 3 September.

● A last-minute equalizer by Johnny Haynes at Hampden gave England a 1–1 draw and ensured the first ever four-way tie for the Home International Championship.

● The first floodlit matches between League teams in first-class competitions were played, in a second-round Cup replay at Newcastle between Carlisle and Darlington on 28 November, and in the League between Portsmouth and Newcastle at Fratton Park on 22 February.

● Manchester United equalled the record margin of victory in Division One, finishing on 60 points, 11 ahead of Blackpool and Wolves.

● Arsenal were leading Blackpool 4–0 in a First Division match at Highbury on 17 December, when someone in the crowd blew a whistle. Dennis Evans, Arsenal's left-back, thought it was the referee blowing for time, and whacked the ball into his own net. Result: 4–1.

FINAL SCORE

Football League
Division 1: Manchester United
Top scorer: Nat Lofthouse (Bolton W) 32
Division 2: Sheffield Wednesday
Division 3S: Leyton Orient
Division 3N: Grimsby Town
Footballer of the Year: Bert Trautmann (Manchester City)

FA Cup Final
Manchester City 3 Birmingham City 1

Scottish League
Division A: Rangers
Top scorer: Jimmy Wardhaugh (Hearts)
Division B: Queen's Park

Scottish FA Cup Final
Hearts 3 Celtic 1

Scottish League Cup Final
Aberdeen 2 St Mirren 1

International Championship
Four-way tie on 3 pts

European Cup Final
Real Madrid 4 Reims 3

United still clear after classic with Spurs

A TREMENDOUS top-of-the-table clash at White Hart Lane between leaders Manchester United and nearest rivals Spurs finished even. Just three days after their second-leg European Cup match in Dortmund, where their magnificent rearguard action earned them a 0–0 draw to put them through to the quarter-finals, the "Busby Babes" travelled to North London to protect their two-point First Division lead.

United soon found themselves struggling and were two down in eight minutes. But their defence gradually stifled the Spurs threat, and they then took up the attack. Just before half-time, left-back Roger Byrne produced one of his long-distance dribbles, finishing with a shot that rattled the cross-bar, and Duncan Edwards smashed the rebound against a post. Immediately after the interval, outside-right Johnny Berry pulled one back for United, and they continued to pile on the pressure. Danny Blanchflower had a magnificent game for Spurs, and it looked like they were going to draw level with United at the top when, three minutes from the end, little Eddie Colman popped up to bang the ball into the net.

What an advertisement for football this match was, and who is going to stop the almost frighteningly mature "Busby Babes" from taking the title again?

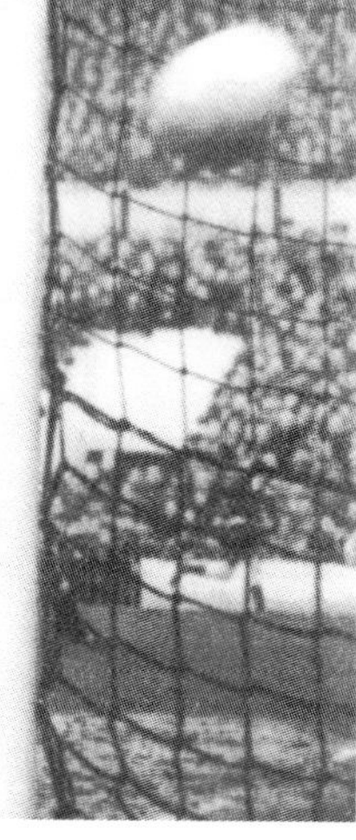

United's Tommy Taylor fails to connect with goalkeeper Ted Ditchburn beaten.

Busby's boys take Europe by storm

THE Football League tried to stop them and failed. Poor Anderlecht tried to stop them, but it was like trying to stand up in the face of a tornado. Manchester United have made an immediate mark on the European Cup competition, and will go into the next round as feared and respected on the Continent as they are at home.

With the Old Trafford floodlights not yet ready, United played their preliminary-round, second-leg tie at Maine Road, starting with a two-goal lead from their match in Belgium. That had not been an easy game: Anderlecht missed a penalty just before Dennis Viollet scored the first, and Tommy Taylor gave United a somewhat flattering 2–0 scoreline. So no-one was prepared for the avalanche of goals in the return.

Viollet scored four, Taylor three, Whelan two and Berry one. It was a superb, flawless exhibition of football, and United did not let up for a moment. Man of the match David Pegg, the only forward not on the score-sheet, made more than half their goals. What price the Football League's advice now?

'Babes' meet their match in Madrid, but will be chasing again next season

MANCHESTER UNITED have been knocked out of the European Cup by Real Madrid, but they retained their League title and will be back next year for another tilt at the Champions' Cup.

What a fortnight this has been for the English champions. On 11 April, they held out for an hour in Madrid against the champions of Europe in the first leg of the semi-finals before succumbing 3–1 to Di Stefano and company. Then came four League matches in 10 days: on the 13th, a 2–0 win at Luton; the 19th (Good Friday), a 3–1 win at Burnley; and the 20th, the 4–0 victory over Sunderland at Old Trafford that clinched the League Championship for the second season running, before fielding seven reserves against Burnley on Easter Monday and still winning 2–0!

But now they have finally been eliminated from the European Cup, by surely the greatest club side in the world. Although United had come back from two down in the quarter-finals to beat Spanish champions Athletic Bilbao, Real Madrid were a different proposition. They took a 2–0 lead under the new Old Trafford floodlights, before United hit back through Taylor and young Bobby Charlton to make the aggregate score respectable. They were beaten by experience and a genius called Di Stefano, but their turn will surely come. Now their thoughts turn to the Cup and that elusive "double".

League champions Manchester United: back row, Bill Foulkes, Eddie Colman, Liam "Billy" Whelan, Ray Wood, Mark Jones, Duncan Edwards; front, Johnny Berry, Dennis Viollet, Roger Byrne (capt.), Tommy Taylor, David Pegg; insets, Bobby Charlton, Jackie Blanchflower.

Cutler wins argument with post before knocking out Wolves

BOURNEMOUTH brought off the shock of the fourth round of the Cup when they went to Molineux and beat mighty Wolves 1–0. Billy Wright and his men have conquered the best in Europe in a series of thrilling floodlit friendlies that gave impetus to the inception of the European Cup. So they were not expected to have any trouble with a Third Division side. But that's the romance of the Cup, as we hear it said year after year. The man who did the damage — in more ways than one — was left-winger Reg Cutler. First he collided with a goal-post, and the game had to be stopped for repairs — to the post! Then he scored the winning goal.

Under manager Freddie Cox, no stranger to Wembley, Bournemouth can cause one or two more surprises.

Play stops while post receives treatment at Molineux.

Villa rob United of 'double' as Wembley jinx strikes again

YET AGAIN we have had to witness the sight of a team struggling through most of a Cup final with only 10 men. This time it was no accident, but a foul charge by Aston Villa's Peter McParland on Ray Wood that left the Manchester United keeper concussed and with a broken cheek bone. This, after only six minutes, completely disrupted a United side who were bidding to become the first club to bring off the League and Cup "double" since Villa did it 60 years ago.

But for Wood's injury, United would almost certainly have achieved it. Centre-half Jackie Blanchflower went in goal — and played a blinder! Edwards went to centre-half, where he is perfectly at home, and was another United hero. But Whelan's dropping back to left-half left the forward line unbalanced and lacking his goalscoring power (he was United's leading League scorer with 26 goals). A groggy Wood returned for 10 minutes half an hour later, but only as nuisance value on the wing.

The reorganized Manchester side held out until midway through the second half, when two goals from outside-left McParland virtually killed their chances. With seven minutes to go, however, Taylor headed in an Edwards corner, and United brought Wood back into goal for a last desperate effort. But Villa's defence, admirably marshalled by Dugdale at centre-half, held out against all their opponents could do, and the Midlanders had won their record seventh FA Cup.

Villa captain and inside-left Johnny Dixon had an outstanding match, but their star was Irish international McParland, always the danger man, although his second goal was arguably offside. His performance, however, should not be allowed to whitewash the unforgivable foul that laid out the United keeper. Wood had already caught the ball from McParland's header and was standing still, some four yards from his goal-line, when the oncoming winger, who could easily have avoided him, crashed into him. At best, it was reckless and irresponsible. Yet the referee did not even caution McParland. Sadly, it left a nasty taste in the mouth.

Villa "villain" McParland crashes into United keeper Wood.

SOCCER SOUNDBITES

"I can still see young Colman running to collect the ball for a throw-in with only two or three minutes left."

MANCHESTER UNITED MANAGER MATT BUSBY,
on his side's keenness even when 10 goals up.

"Why don't they pick the whole side for England? The best teams from Hungary have never beaten us like this."

JEF MERMANS, ANDERLECHT CAPTAIN,
after their 10–0 defeat by Manchester United.

FINAL SCORE

Football League
Division 1: Manchester United
Top scorer: John Charles (Leeds United) 38
Division 2: Leicester City
Division 3S: Ipswich Town
Division 3N: Derby County
Footballer of the Year: Tom Finney (Preston North End)

FA Cup Final

Aston Villa	2	Manchester United	1

Scottish League
Division 1: Rangers
Top scorer: Hugh Baird (Airdrieonians) 33
Division 2: Clyde

Scottish FA Cup Final

Falkirk	1	Kilmarnock	1
Replay: Falkirk	2	Kilmarnock	1

Scottish League Cup Final

Celtic	0	Partick	0
Replay: Celtic	3	Partick Thistle	0

International Championship
England, 5 pts

European Cup Final

Real Madrid	2	Fiorentina	0

European Footballer of the Year 1956
Stanley Matthews (Blackpool & England)

FOOTBALL FOCUS

● Non-League Bedford Town drew 2–2 at Arsenal in the third round of the Cup and were leading 1–0 in the replay with seconds left, when Arsenal equalized and beat them 2–1 in extra time.

● Stoke outside-right Neville Coleman scored seven goals in their 8–0 win over Lincoln on 23 February, a League record for a winger and equalling the Division Two goalscoring record.

● All four Football League divisional champions scored more than 100 goals, for the first time since 1931–32.

● After their triumph at Molineux, Cup giant-killers Bournemouth beat Spurs 3–1 and were leading a 10-man Manchester United (Mark Jones had gone off injured) by 1–0 at Dean Court in the quarter-finals before two goals from Berry ended their adventures.

United bring out the best in Arsenal but remain supreme

Bobby Charlton (left) scores United's second goal.

IN PERHAPS the finest match seen at Highbury since the thirties, Manchester United emerged as winners by the odd goal in nine to stay in second place in the League, four points behind Wolves. The capacity 64,000 crowd gasped at the breathtaking football of the visitors as they took a first-half 3–0 lead. Edwards and Colman, in their different ways, dominated the midfield, and their wingers were running Arsenal ragged — no, not Berry and Pegg, but Morgans and Scanlon. There seems no end to the talent Mr Busby has nurtured at Old Trafford.

Edwards, Charlton and Taylor all scored to give United a seemingly impregnable lead. The ground was abuzz at half-time, marvelling at the magic conjured up by the "Busby Babes", looking to dominate English football for years to come. Even the Arsenal fans sat back, resigned to another exhibition in the second half, and possibly a thrashing.

But perhaps some of the magic rubbed off after the interval on what is frankly a mediocre Arsenal side. Galvanized into action by their captain Dave Bowen, they scored three goals in as many minutes. But the "Babes" brushed aside their challenge almost imperiously, as Viollet and Taylor made the score 5–3. Still Arsenal were not finished: Tapscott pulled a goal back, Groves nearly equalized — but United held out. The crowd rose to the masters and a team of artisans who, for one glorious afternoon, almost matched their magic.

FOOTBALL FOCUS

- Northern Ireland had their first win at Wembley (3–2) on 6 November, and on 15 January they beat Italy 2–1 in Belfast to qualify for the World Cup finals. All four home countries made it to Sweden.
- Hereford United equalled the record score for non-League clubs against League opposition in the FA Cup when they beat QPR (Division Three (South) 6–1 in the second round. First Division Newcastle lost 3–1 at home to Third Division Scunthorpe.
- Cardiff City (Division Two) won at Leeds (Division One) for the third season running in the FA Cup — in the same round (third) and by the same score (2–1) — the only difference being that they have swapped divisions since 1956!
- Hearts scored a record 132 goals in Scottish Division One, with a record goal difference (103).
- Sunderland were relegated for the first time, after an unbroken run in Division One since their election in 1890.
- While all the attention was focused on Manchester United, Wolves quietly won the League, and became the first club other than United to win the FA Youth Challenge Cup, coming back from a 5–1 first-leg deficit in the final to beat Chelsea 7–6 on aggregate.
- In his first season in Italy, John Charles led Juventus to the title and was the championship's leading goalscorer with 28 in 34 games.

'Busby Babes' in plane crash: the football world mourns

THE AIRCRAFT carrying the Manchester United football team, officials and journalists crashed on take-off at Munich Airport on 6 February. Over half the 40 aboard were killed, while many others are fighting for their lives in a Munich hospital.

The Elizabethan airliner had stopped to refuel on the way back from Belgrade, where United had drawn 3–3 with Red Star to earn a place in the European Cup semi-finals. Snow was falling as it prepared to take off for the third time, after two aborted attempts. It reached the point of no return, but failed to get off the ground and ploughed through the perimeter fence. It split in half, the port wing and part of the tail section hitting a house.

The dead include left-back and captain Roger Byrne, reserve left-back Geoff Bent, right-half Eddie Colman, centre-half Mark Jones, outside-left David Pegg, centre-forward Tommy Taylor and inside-right Liam "Billy" Whelan. Club secretary Walter Crickmer also was killed, along with team coach Bert Whalley and trainer Tom Curry. Several journalists also died, including former England goalkeeper Frank Swift.

Among the seriously injured are United manager Matt Busby, who is in a critical condition with a crushed chest, and England international Duncan Edwards, who is in a coma. Survivors with no more than minor injuries include Bobby Charlton, who was thrown from the plane still strapped to his seat, Dennis Viollet, Ken Morgans, Billy Foulkes and Harry Gregg. Johnny Berry and Jackie Blanchflower also survived but are thought unlikely to play again.

The whole country is in deep shock, and the football world mourns the tragic loss of so many young lives.

The wreck of the Elizabethan airliner lies on the Munich snow.

Bolton win the Cup: United's triumph was getting there

BOLTON were in a "no-win" situation from the start. Manchester United, shattered three months earlier by the Munich plane crash, had reached the Cup final on a wave of public sympathy and thanks largely to the inspirational play of Bobby Charlton, on to whose young shoulders all United's hopes have now been transferred. Five years ago, Bolton were in a similar position, when the weight of "neutral" support was behind Stanley Matthews and Blackpool. They lost that one, but this time they won — and they won well.

But United were also winners. Their remarkable resurgence after the tragedy, and their determination to succeed have won the hearts of the footballing world. Of the immediate survivors of the crash, Duncan Edwards hung on for two more weeks before he also died. Matt Busby miraculously clung to life, and was passed fit enough to attend the final. His assistant Jimmy Murphy, who missed the Belgrade trip only because he was managing the Welsh international side, had taken charge of the club and hastily drafted some experienced players into his team of reserves and the few Munich survivors. Berry and Blanchflower would never play again. But Charlton and Viollet had recovered from their injuries and, with Gregg and Foulkes, played in the final — the only four of the "Babes" to make it.

Nat Lofthouse scored for Bolton after three minutes. Then, early in the second half, a Charlton shot hit a post and bounced into goalkeeper Hopkinson's hands, Bolton raced away, and Lofthouse scored again, controversially charging Gregg into the net with the ball as he parried a shot.

In the end, perhaps, the result was not important. A Manchester win would not have brought the lost "Babes" back. What matters is that the club is alive, and that the spirit is still there.

Lofthouse, both feet off the ground, illegally charges Gregg over the line, but the referee awarded a goal.

Seven-goal Celtic crush rivals Rangers in major final

THE SCORELINE was sensational, Rangers 1 Celtic 7, in the Scottish League Cup final — the highest score in any major British final. It was a day when Celtic suddenly clicked. They led only 2–0 at half-time but had already struck the woodwork three times. Rangers, though, were completely demoralized, and Bobby Evans broke up their few attacks with ease. Neil Mochan, restored on the left wing, scored twice and was a permanent thorn in Rangers' right side. Billy McPhail, who hit a second-half hat-trick, had the beating of Valentine in the air and on the ground. And, it was highly appropriate that right-half Willie Fernie, the chief architect of Celtic's victory, should score their last goal, albeit from a penalty.

No praise is too much for Fernie. On this day, he was unplayable, a master craftsman who shrugged off all crude attempts to unsettle him without ever resorting to the physical himself. In front of him, he had the superb right-wing pair of Charlie Tully and inside-right Bobby Collins.

Inside-left Sammy Wilson opened the scoring after 23 minutes, and a brilliant solo effort from Mochan put Celtic in command before the second-half floodgates opened.

One could only feel sorry for Rangers' centre-half Johnny Valentine, who came from Queen's Park at the start of the season and has tried desparately to fill the gap left by the incomparable George Young. But he was out of his depth, and it will be a long time before he forgets the humiliation he suffered against the highly skilled McPhail. It will be even longer before the inconsolable Rangers fans are allowed to forget this quite extraordinary Old Firm thrashing.

SOCCER SOUNDBITES

"No team should be able to beat Rangers 7–1. It just should not be possible."

RANGERS FAN,
in utter disbelief as he left Hampden Park.

Cliff-hanger at Valley as Charlton climb back from the depths

CHARLTON BROUGHT OFF the most extraordinary comeback in League history when they beat Huddersfield 7–6 at the Valley in a Division Two match on 21 December. They were reduced to 10 men after 15 minutes when centre-half Derek Ufton broke a collar-bone, and were 2–0 down at half-time. Ten minutes later, the score was 1–5! But from this hopeless position they proceeded to score five goals in a sensational spell, as left-winger Johnny Summers ran riot. Five of their six goals at that stage had come from the right boot of the naturally left-footed Summers, and the other was made by him for centre-forward Johnny Ryan. Charlton allowed Huddersfield to draw level two minutes from time, but Summers wasn't finished yet: he made one final surge and put Ryan through for the winner with the last kick of the game.

FINAL SCORE

Football League
Division 1: Wolverhampton Wanderers
Top scorer: Bobby Smith (Tottenham H) 36
Division 2: West Ham United
Division 3S: Brighton & Hove Albion
Division 3N: Scunthorpe United
Footballer of the Year: Danny Blanchflower (Tottenham Hotspur)

FA Cup Final
Bolton Wanderers 2 Manchester United 0

Scottish League
Division 1: Hearts
Top scorer: Jimmy Wardhaugh, Jimmy Murray (both Hearts) 28
Division 2: Stirling Albion

Scottish FA Cup Final
Clyde 1 Hibernian 0

Scottish League Cup Final
Celtic 7 Rangers 1

International Championship
England, N.Ireland, 4 pts

European Cup Final
Real Madrid 3 AC Milan 2
(after extra time)

Inter-Cities Fairs Cup (1955–58)
Final: Barcelona beat London 2-2, 6-0

European Footballer of the Year
1957 Alfredo di Stefano (Real Madrid & Spain)

Brazil conquer Europe

Brazil, when they finally settled down, gave Europe a lesson in tactics as well as in football. All their players displayed a complete mastery of the ball, and their stars entertained with outstanding skills, from Didi's midfield genius to Pele's precocious finishing. The home countries were pedestrian by comparison, light-years behind in technique, although Wales and Northern Ireland came out of their first World Cups covered in glory.

IN THE qualifying competition, England and Scotland did no more than was expected of them, but Northern Ireland, orchestrated by Danny Blanchflower, dramatically beat Italy 2–1 in Belfast to get through. Wales were at first eliminated in Czechoslovakia's group, but qualified by the back door. As country after country in the Asia/Africa region withdrew rather than face political outcasts Israel, someone had to play them for the place. Wales won the ballot of the second-placed teams and beat them twice.

In the finals, teams level on points for second place in their group were to replay two days before the quarter-finals, a "fate" that befell three of the home countries. Scotland did not even get that far, however, finishing bottom of their group with a single point.

Busby Babes missed

England, not really recovered from the loss of Edwards, Byrne and Taylor in the Munich air crash four months earlier, were in arguably the toughest group. They drew with the USSR after being two down. But Finney, who equalized from a penalty, was injured and took no further part. Against Brazil, their forward line was ineffective, but they drew 0–0 thanks to an excellent, well-organized defence in which Billy Wright and keeper Colin McDonald were outstanding.

England fielded an unchanged side against Austria, and struggled to earn a point after a colourless performance. Meanwhile, Brazil had found the right blend and their form, with the explosive Garrincha coming in at outside-right, Vava replacing Mazzola at centre-forward, and the 17-year-old Pele, recovered from injury, at inside-left. Didi, as usual, dictated the play from midfield, and the Soviets were lucky to keep the score to 2–0.

This left England and the USSR to play off. England made some changes, but not the one the Press and public were demanding — Bobby Charlton for Kevan in the middle. With Haynes still sadly out of sorts, England failed to score, and a single goal was enough for a somewhat fortunate Soviet victory.

Pele (third left) volleys Brazil's third goal in the final to complete a breathtaking solo effort.

British pride saved

Northern Ireland and Wales, for so long regarded as the "minnows" of British international football, excelled themselves in their first World Cup finals and restored some of Britain's lost pride. They both had world-class players in Danny Blanchflower and John Charles, who were huge influences on their respective teams, and there were no better goalkeepers than Jack Kelsey and, on his day, Ireland's Harry Gregg.

Ireland, astutely managed by former inside-forward Peter Doherty, had the skilful, scheming Jimmy McIlroy to link up with Blanchflower, and two dangerous wingers in Billy Bingham and Peter McParland, complemented by a group of players guaranteed to rise to the occasion in the green shirts. Two players who did so in their first match, against Czechoslovakia, were 5ft 5in Wilbur Cush, who headed the winner, and Gregg, who performed heroics in goal. But Ireland were outplayed by the otherwise disappointing Argentina side, and needed all Gregg's brilliance — and two McParland goals — to earn a draw with West Germany. This put them in a play-off, where they again had to beat the Czechs, sensational 6–1 victors over Argentina. With Gregg injured, the Irish were given no

WORLD CUP QUOTES

"Our tactics are to equalize before the other side scores."

DANNY BLANCHFLOWER,
Northern Ireland captain.

Ungainly but effective, Just Fontaine (France) digs another one in against West Germany.

'Here indeed was a match to remember — a clean, sporting struggle between two great teams, one worthy of the World Championships.'
ARTHUR DREWRY, PRESIDENT OF FIFA, of the World Cup final.

Peter McParland (centre) scores one of his two equalizers for Northern Ireland in their draw with West Germany.

chance of a repeat performance; yet they came back from a goal down, and two more goals from McParland, the second in extra time, saw them through to the quarter-finals, a magnificent achievement.

Wales, meanwhile, had been taking the same route, but with three draws. They held Hungary — a shadow of the great pre-Uprising side — with John Charles equalizing an early Bozsik strike with a towering header. They, in turn, were surprisingly held by the Mexicans. Sweden, still coached by Yorkshireman George Raynor and now professionals, had two wins in the bag, so fielded several reserves against Wales. But Kelsey had to be at his imperturbable best to earn a 0–0 draw.

Tichy gave Hungary a half-time lead in the play-off, but Wales, urged on by their captain and left-half Dave Bowen, produced one of the finest performances in their history. Shamefully, the Soviet referee ignored the brutal treatment being dished out to John Charles. But he returned limping after one particularly bad assault and crossed for Ivor Allchurch to equalize with a cracking 35-yard volley on the run. Terry Medwin then scored the winner after stealing the ball from a careless Grosics clearance-kick.

Pele scored his first World Cup goal against Wales in the quarter-finals. It was not one of his greatest, but it was enough to beat the Welsh, always struggling after their play-off, from which the battered John Charles did not recover in time. Only the brilliant Kelsey held the rampant Brazilians at bay, somehow keeping out all that Garrincha, Didi, Mazzola, Pele and Zagalo threw at him — until Pele's shot was deflected past him.

Northern Ireland, also exhausted from their play-off exertions, and with the injured Gregg back in goal because his replacement Norman Uprichard was in even poorer shape, were no match for the French. Raymond Kopa tormented them, and Just Fontaine added two more goals to what was already an impressive tally.

Numbers tell in semis

In both semi-finals, one side played much of the match with only 10 men, and the handicap proved too much for them. Against Brazil, France lost Jonquet, the hub of their defence, injured after 37 minutes. Fontaine — who else? — had equalized a Vava goal in the first 10 minutes, but no sooner had Jonquet gone than Didi put Brazil ahead with a 30-yard "banana" shot, and the precocious Pele scored a hat-trick in the second half.

Kurt Hamrin was both hero and villain in the other semi-final. He played the game of his life, and beat several defenders before scoring Sweden's third and clinching goal. But he had Juskowiak sent off for retaliation, and a subsequent foul by Parling left Fritz Walter a virtual passenger. Thus depleted, West Germany succumbed late on.

Four days later, in the match for third place, the Germans were destroyed by the wizardry of Kopa and the immaculate finishing of Fontaine, who scored four goals to bring his total for the finals to a record 13.

A joy to watch

It was a tribute to Raynor that his unfancied Sweden side reached the final at all. But any hopes that an early Liedholm goal stirred in the home fans were soon stifled as Brazil unleashed all their brilliance, to give the breathtaking display of football they had promised from the start of the tournament but never quite yet achieved. Vava scored twice, from identical Garrincha low crosses after dazzling right-wing runs, to give them a half-time lead. The third goal, scored by Pele, was sheer poetry, and not only confirmed Brazil as worthy winners, but was a celebration of their joyous football, their willingness to improvise and their supreme ball skills. The young inside-left — first capped a year earlier when not yet 17 — was closely marked in the box and standing with his back to goal, when he took a pass on his thigh, flicked the ball over his head with his foot, and turned past his marker to smash it on the volley into goal.

Brazil proceeded to stroll through the rest of the match. Zagalo scored a fourth, Simonsson snatched one for Sweden and then, right at the end, it was Pele appropriately who headed Brazil's fifth. They had triumphed in Europe, the first country to win the World Cup outside their own continent.

FINAL SCORE

Group 1

West Germany	3	Argentina	1
N.Ireland	1	Czechoslovakia	0
West Germany	2	Czechoslovakia	2
Argentina	3	N.Ireland	1
West Germany	2	N.Ireland	2
Czechoslovakia	6	Argentina	1

	P	W	D	L	F	A	P
W.Germany	3	1	2	0	7	5	4
Czech	3	1	1	1	8	4	3
N.Ireland	3	1	1	1	4	5	3
Argentina	3	1	0	2	5	10	2

Play-off
N.Ireland 2 Czechoslovakia 1

Group 2

Yugoslavia	1	Scotland	1
France	7	Paraguay	3
Paraguay	3	Scotland	2
Yugoslavia	3	France	2
France	2	Scotland	1
Paraguay	3	Yugoslavia	3

	P	W	D	L	F	A	P
France	3	2	0	1	11	7	4
Yugoslavia	3	1	2	0	7	6	4
Paraguay	3	1	1	1	9	12	3
Scotland	3	0	1	2	4	6	1

Group 3

Sweden	3	Mexico	0
Hungary	1	Wales	1
Mexico	1	Wales	1
Sweden	2	Hungary	1
Sweden	0	Wales	0
Hungary	4	Mexico	0

	P	W	D	L	F	A	P
Sweden	3	2	1	0	5	1	5
Wales	3	0	3	0	2	2	3
Hungary	3	1	1	1	6	3	3
Mexico	3	0	1	2	1	8	1

Play-off
Wales 2 Hungary 1

Group 4

USSR	2	England	2
Brazil	3	Austria	0
Brazil	0	England	0
USSR	2	Austria	0
Brazil	2	USSR	0
England	2	Austria	2

	P	W	D	L	F	A	P
Brazil	3	2	1	0	5	0	5
England	3	0	3	0	4	4	3
USSR	3	1	1	1	4	4	3
Austria	3	0	1	2	2	7	1

Play-off
USSR 1 England 0

QUARTER-FINALS

France	4	N.Ireland	0
West Germany	1	Yugoslavia	0
Sweden	2	USSR	0
Brazil	1	Wales	0

SEMI-FINALS

Brazil	5	France	2
Sweden	3	West Germany	1

THIRD-PLACE MATCH
France 6 West Germany 3

FINAL
Brazil 5 Sweden 2
Rasunda Stadium, Solna, Stockholm, 29 June 1958. Attendance 49,737

Brazil: Gylmar, Santos D, Santos N, Zito, Bellini, Orlando, Garrincha, Didi, Vava, Pele, Zagalo (Scorers: Vava (2), Pele (2), Zagalo)
Sweden: Svensson, Bergmark, Axbom, Borjesson, Gustavsson, Parling, Hamrin, Gren, Simonsson, Liedholm, Skoglund (Scorers: Liedholm, Simonsson)

LEADING SCORERS
13 Fontaine (France) 6 Pele (Brazil)
6 Rahn (West Germany)

Wright is the first football 'centurion'

BILLY WRIGHT, the England and Wolves captain and centre-half, became the world's first footballer to win 100 caps when he led England to victory over Scotland at Wembley on 11 April. It was his 85th game as skipper, and of the 100 matches, England have won 59 and drawn 22. He has made a record 65 consecutive appearances for England, and has missed only three of their 103 post-war matches.

A one-club man, and originally a right-half, Wright led Wolves to their second League title in five years last season, and is poised to make it three before the month is out. He won a Cup-winners' medal in 1949 and was voted Footballer of the Year in 1952.

He has been a wonderful ambassador for football, and it was highly appropriate that he should reach this soccer milestone at Wembley and with a win over Scotland (Bobby Charlton scored the only goal of the game).

Wright is chaired off the field by Ron Clayton (left) and Don Howe.

It's 10–4 and out for Everton as Spurs welcome new manager

THE SPURS players heard of the appointment of Bill Nicholson as manager in the dressing-room before the game. It was no surprise: he had been with Spurs since before the war, as player and latterly as coach. So it was nothing he said, no new tactical plan, that turned a potentially gritty battle between two sides in the relegation zone into the highest scoring match in the First Division this century.

Spurs had brought back little Tommy Harmer, dropped four matches earlier. Light as a feather, but on his day the trickiest schemer in the land, Harmer was behind nearly every Spurs move, and nearly every move seemed to lead to a goal. All Spurs' forwards scored: centre-forward and captain Bobby Smith (four), Alf Stokes (two), Terry Medwin, George Robb and Harmer, and centre-half Ryden, a passenger on the wing for the last 15 minutes, chipped in with the final goal to make the score 10–4. Jimmy Harris hit a hat-trick for Everton, and Bobby Collins scored the other. Stand-in Everton keeper Albert Dunlop is going to find it hard to hold his place, just as new Spurs manager Nicholson is going to be hard put to maintain his sensational start.

Hatters cage Canaries in a replay

LUTON FINALLY put a stop to Third Division Norwich's remarkable FA Cup run when they beat them 1–0 in the replayed semi-final at St Andrews, Birmingham. This season, managed by former Scottish international Archie Macaulay and skippered by Ron Ashman, the Canaries surpassed their giant-killing exploits of 1954, when they beat Arsenal at Highbury in the fourth round. They first hit the headlines in the third round, when they beat Manchester United 3–0 at Carrow Road. Another home tie saw them defeat Second Division Cardiff 3–2, and then they held Spurs 1–1 in the fifth round and won the home replay 1–0.

But their bravest performance came in their sixth-round tie at Bramall Lane, when keeper Ken Nethercott played the last half-hour with a dislocated shoulder. They were already a goal down, but they managed to keep Sheffield at a distance, equalized, and then won the replay 3–2. Norwich played well in the semi-final, but were out of luck, and Billy Bingham put an end to their dreams with the only goal.

Billy Bingham (far right) scores in the semi-final replay to put Norwich out of the Cup.

FOOTBALL FOCUS

- Denis Law, Huddersfield's inside-left, became Scotland's youngest international when he won his first cap at the age of 18 years 236 days against Wales in October, and he scored in their 3–0 win.

- Centre-forward Brian Clough is emulating his 1920s predecessor at Middlesbrough, George Camsell, leading the Division Two goalscorers (with 42 goals) for the second year running. It is the third season he has averaged a goal a game, and he has reached 100 League goals in quicker time than any player previously.

- Aston Villa, needing to win at West Brom on the last day of the season to be sure of staying in Division One, conceded a goal a minute from time when leading 1–0. Rivals Manchester City won their game, so Villa were relegated.

Tired England flop in New World, but Wright finishes his career on a high note

THE FA have been strongly criticized in many quarters for planning a 20,000 mile summer tour for England on top of a heavy League season. It was no surprise when they lost their first match 2–0 to world champions Brazil in Rio; under the circumstances, this was a creditable performance against Didi, Pele and company in front of 151,000 partisan fans in the great Maracana Stadium. But the rest of the Latin American trip was a disappointment. England lost 4–1 against Peru, whose players were individually more skilful — how England missed the injured Tom Finney on this tour! Jimmy Greaves, however, could be pleased with his performance and a goal in his first international.

There followed a frustrating 2–1 defeat in the sweltering heat and thin air of Mexico City to a Mexican side who did not possess the sophistication of the South Americans. But the tour ended on a high note, especially for Billy Wright, who retired from international football with 105 caps after this last match. It was in Los Angeles against the United States, who nine years earlier had humbled England in the World Cup finals. Wright, the only survivor from that débâcle, must have taken particular satisfaction in England's 8–1 victory.

Henrique stretches a leg to score Brazil's second goal against England.

FINAL SCORE

Football League
Division 1: Wolverhampton Wanderers
Top scorer: Jimmy Greaves (Chelsea) 32
Division 2: Sheffield Wednesday
Division 3: Plymouth Argyle
Division 4: Port Vale
Footballer of the Year: Syd Owen (Luton Town)

FA Cup Final

Nottingham Forest	2	Luton Town	1

Scottish League
Division 1: Rangers
Top scorer: Joe Baker (Hibernian) 25
Division 2: Ayr United

Scottish FA Cup Final

St Mirren	3	Aberdeen	1

Scottish League Cup Final

Hearts	5	Partick Thistle	1

International Championship
England, N.Ireland, 4 pts

European Cup Final

Real Madrid	2	Reims	0

European Footballer of the Year 1958
Raymond Kopa (Real Madrid & France)

Forest overcome Wembley 'hoodoo' to win Cup with 10 men

THAT WEMBLEY CUP final jinx struck again. Nottingham Forest right-winger Roy Dwight was carried off with a broken leg after 32 minutes, but Forest, two up at the time, defended stoutly and held out for a 2–1 victory over Luton.

Any other result would have been a travesty. For half an hour, Forest outplayed Luton with a display of confident, fast-moving football, the like of which we have not seen in a Cup final since the Manchester United-Blackpool game in 1948.

Luton, with experienced big-match players such as Billy Bingham, Allan Brown and Syd Owen in their side, started as favourites. Only three weeks ago they beat Forest 5–1 in the League. But they were two down in 14 minutes as Forest's fluent passing tore them apart. Dwight was the star of that brilliant early attack, slamming the ball in to put his side one up after great work from Stewart Imlach on the left. Four minutes later, Tom Wilson finished off another glorious move with a header. Forest were two up, and their keeper had not touched the ball.

Only Luton keeper Ron Baynham kept the score down, but it must surely have been a rout had not Dwight had a shinbone cracked in what seemed a harmless challenge with Brendan McNally. Now the sides were even. Forest continued to play the better football — the only football — but were gradually forced on the defensive as the spongy turf took its toll on their 10 men. David Pacey pulled one back after a corner, but Luton could not score again.

Luton are helpless as Dwight's shot finds the net.

Busby saves Quixall from Division Two and breaks British transfer record

MANCHESTER UNITED bought unsettled Sheffield Wednesday star Albert Quixall for a British record fee of £45,000 on 18 September. After a poor start to the season, Matt Busby stepped into the transfer market again when it became clear that his side, tragically depleted in the Munich air crash, still needed strengthening.

The fair-haired inside-forward won the first of his five England caps five years ago while still on National Service, but has not been picked since May 1955. Last season he played against United in their first match after Munich, when Wednesday lost 3–0. He later became captain, but Wednesday were relegated at the end of the season, and he made it clear that he did not relish playing in Division Two.

Quixall is the third player to figure in a record deal involving Wednesday in the last nine years. Eddie Quigley was sold to Preston for £26,000, and Jackie Sewell was bought from Notts County for £34,000.

Post-War heroes

THE POST-WAR period is often referred to as the "Golden Age of Football", with grounds up and down the country bursting at the seams every Saturday to see their sporting heroes perform. It was a time, still, of attacking football, and the fans went along to see goals and goalmouth incident, wingers who could beat their man and send in wicked crosses, centre-forwards who could put the ball in the net. If a Matthews or a Lawton were on the visitors' teamsheet, the gates were sure to be closed with thousands more locked out.

The goalscorers

Tommy Lawton stands out from the immediate post-war period in Britain as the complete centre-forward. It is remarkable that Everton should have found such a player to replace the "irreplaceable" Dixie Dean, although his best years, his early 20s, were consumed by the war, as were those of many contemporary heroes. After the war, with Chelsea and later with Third Division Notts County, Lawton continued to spearhead the England side, but he played as many wartime games as he did in peace, and his total haul was 47 goals in 46 internationals. He was fast, smooth, packed a powerful shot in both feet, and was supreme in the air.

After Lawton came Jackie Milburn, a converted winger, with a winger's speed and silky skills, an idol in the North-East, where he played for Newcastle and won Cup glory. Nat Lofthouse of Bolton made the position his own in the early fifties (30 goals in 33 games to set an England record), a brave battering ram of a leader, more in the Ted Drake mould. Often playing alongside one or other of these centre-forwards, or in place of them, was Blackpool's Stan Mortensen, and he also knew how to score — 23 in 25 England games, and the only man to score a Cup final hat-trick this century.

At international level, Scotland's football had declined, their ambitions still anachronistically rooted to beating the "auld enemy". Lawrie Reilly became their most capped centre-forward, with 38 appearances, and scored 22 goals. Only 5ft 7in, he was an all-round player with fast reflexes, and starred in the high-scoring Hibs forward line that dominated Scottish football for a while in the early fifties.

John Charles: equally effective at centre-half or centre-forward.

At the same time, the powerful Trevor Ford was scoring a Welsh record 23 goals in his 38 internationals. But directly behind him, on the field, was the man who became the biggest of all Welsh stars, John Charles, the "Gentle Giant", a master of aerial combat. There was no better centre-half in the game, but Leeds transformed him into a centre-forward, and when he took his powerful skills to Juventus in the mid-fifties he became the idol of Italian football.

In the early fifties, when it became increasingly obvious that the rest of the world had caught up with British football and were in the process of overtaking it, foreign stars suddenly became household names. Ferenc Puskas, the plumpish "Galloping Major" of the 1953 Hungarians, stamped his personality and his class on the Wembley turf, rifling the ball in from all angles with that remarkable left foot of his and demonstrating that his goalscoring feats — eventually 83 goals in 84 internationals for Hungary — could be reproduced at the highest level. The Magyars' other inside-forward, Sandor Kocsis, scored many of his 75 international goals (in 68 games) with elegant headers. "Golden Head", as he was known, ranked with Dean, Lawton and Charles in the air.

Wing wonders

A feature of post-war football was wing-play, as epitomized, above all, by Matthews and Finney. It was the classic duel, the winger and his opposing full-back. Stanley Matthews was over-simplified as the "one-trick wizard", because the back knew what he was going to do 90 per cent of the time — go past him on the outside — but somehow Matthews always seemed to be behind him before he could make his tackle. Tom Finney could play on either wing and, like Matthews, was beautifully balanced with a superb body swerve. Matthews spanned the war and was to play on into a fourth decade, and all the time he was the greatest draw in English football. Finney had a fine shot with either foot, and was a complete forward who scored 30 goals for England. Both, above all, had a wonderful temperament, and there were no finer sportsmen in the whole of football.

Scotland's wing heroes were Billy Liddell on the left and Willie Waddell on the right. Liddell of Liverpool was hard, fast and fair, with a ferocious shot, and his inspiration of both team and fans justified the name "Liddellpool" applied to the club in his day. He later moved to centre-forward and took his League tally to a club record 216 goals. Waddell of Rangers was in the same mould, and the pair first played for Scotland together

Ferenc Puskas of Hungary.

in 1942 at Hampden in a rare 5–4 wartime victory over England.

When Wolves developed their long-ball game in the early fifties, they had the wingers to play it in Hancocks and Mullen, always remembered as a pair. The tiny Johnny Hancocks on the right, with dynamite in his boots, perfectly complemented left-winger Jimmy Mullen, also a consistent scorer.

Schemers

The midfield general of post-war days was still called a schemer. He was the inside-forward who made the team tick, linking defence and attack with astute passes. Wilf Mannion of Middlesbrough took over the role for England from Raich Carter, and he too could score goals as well as make them. Blond and compactly built, he used his pace and ball control to go past defenders. He was an exciting player to watch, as was his contemporary, Len Shackleton, who won only five caps to Mannion's 26. "Shack", a footballing maverick forever at odds with authority, was considered "too good for the rest of the team" by the England selectors. He was a marvellous showman with a portfolio of tricks, and he entertained the crowds royally at Newcastle, where he scored six goals on his debut in 1946, and at Sunderland, where he spent most of his career.

Alfredo di Stefano: the master.

Danny Blanchflower: the "thinking man's footballer".

Other schemers overlooked by the selectors were those diminutive North London heroes Jimmy Logie of Arsenal, who won a solitary Scottish cap, and Tommy Harmer of Spurs, who played once for England "B" in 1952.

In the mid-fifties, Johnny Haynes made the England schemer position his own, despite playing for Second Division Fulham. Famed for his passing ability, he won 56 caps, latterly as captain, and scored 18 goals, too. But when it came to passing skills, Brazil's Didi had no equal, and keepers never got to grips with his famous "dry leaf" free-kick.

Of the scheming wing-halves, two were conspicuous by their talents in post-war football: Danny Blanchflower of Spurs and Northern Ireland, and Joszef Bozsik of Hungary and Honved. Blanchflower, known as the "thinking man's footballer", was a master tactician, never afraid to try something new, and a perfect distributor of the ball. His captaincy was an inspiration to both club and country. Bozsik was the general of the "Magic Magyars" and won a record 100 caps.

Unsung heroes

The men who perform the heroics at the back often do not get their fair share of the limelight, although wing-halves Joe Mercer (Arsenal) and Billy Wright (Wolves) were idolized by the fans, and Wright broke all records as captain of England, converting to centre-half in 1954. Perhaps the greatest centre-half of the period was John Charles — when he wasn't playing up front. All three were renowned for their sportsmanship and fair play.

Scotland, hitherto known for attacking football, could call on some of the finest defenders in their history in the post-war years. They began to turn defence into a fine art in the late 1940s, with the introduction of the so-called "Iron Curtains". George Young and Sammy Cox of Rangers were probably Scotland's best ever full-back pairing, with club-mate Willie Woodburn an outstanding centre-half. Young eventually took over as centre-half, and was a tower of strength for Rangers and Scotland.

Among the many fine post-war goalkeepers, Frank Swift of the huge hands continued his popular and spectacular wartime guardianship of the England goal until he retired in 1949. Jack Kelsey kept Wales and Arsenal in many a match when they were being outplayed — unflappable, courageous, making the difficult look easy. The German Bert Trautmann, who took over from Swift in the Manchester City goal, soon won the hearts of the fans, played over 500 League games and represented the Football League.

The masters

Two players stand out from this period as "total footballers" before the term was coined, not so much players who could play anywhere, but players whose territory was the whole pitch. Duncan Edwards was one of those rare masters of the game, already a legend at the age of 21 when he died in the Munich air crash. Nominally a left-half, he was back in defence or up in attack when he wasn't spraying passes to his team-mates, he had a sensational shot, and he was a model professional.

The other "master" was Alfredo di Stefano, the Argentinian who was nominally a centre-forward in Spain for Real Madrid in their five successive European Cup final victories. But he was more than that: he controlled the game, endlessly moving up and down the pitch from box to box, starting moves, finishing them, directing the pattern of the play. And he was a goalscoring genius who amassed 428 for Real in 510 games, including 49 in the European Cup. He was the undisputed "King of Football".

Stanley Matthews: the wizard.

England all wrong without Wright

WITH THE SAME SIDE that drew in Cardiff 11 days earlier, England lost 3–2 to Sweden, their first defeat by foreign opposition at Wembley since the Hungarians beat them there seven years ago. The World Cup finalists, even without those players who are with Italian clubs, were too good for an England side ably led by Ronnie Clayton, yet still unable to get used to the absence of the retired Billy Wright.

Centre-forward Brian Clough and left-winger Eddie Holliday of Second Division Middlesbrough were together in their second international outing, but the potentially lethal partnership of Clough and Jimmy Greaves again failed to click, and England's goals were scored by John Connelly and Bobby Charlton. Even so, the same side might still have won had keeper Eddie Hopkinson played up to anything like his normal form

Clough fires a great chance straight at the Swedish keeper.

FOOTBALL FOCUS

- Brian Clough scored all the Football League's goals in their 5–0 defeat of the Irish League in Belfast on 23 September and scored 39 League goals for Second Division Middlesbrough, but was dropped after just two appearances for England.
- St Mirren's Gerry Baker, brother of England centre-forward Joe, scored 10 goals in their 15–0 thrashing of Glasgow University on 30 January in the first round of the Scottish Cup.
- Former Arsenal star Cliff Holton, the League's leading scorer with 42 goals for Fourth Division Watford, became the first player ever to score hat-tricks on successive days, on 15 and 16 April in Easter wins over Chester (4–2) and Gateshead (5–0).
- Motherwell's Ian St John notched a hat-trick in two-and-a-half minutes on 15 August in a League Cup tie at Hibs.
- After being held 2–2 at Fourth Division Crewe in a fourth-round Cup tie, Spurs won the replay 13–2 at White Hart Lane.
- Wolves became the first Division One club to score 100 goals in three consecutive seasons.
- European champions Real Madrid won the first World Club Championship, beating the South American champions Penarol in a two-legged home-and-away tie.

Wembley final spoilt by injury again, and by boorish behaviour of some fans

THE 1960 FA CUP final will be remembered for the pre-match rows, for the disgraceful behaviour of the Blackburn fans, and for yet another serious injury that left one side struggling against impossible odds.

Poor Wolves — they won the Cup, but had to run the gauntlet of angry Blackburn fans when they attempted to parade it. The fans were upset for a number of reasons. Discontent at the club had been building up over the weeks before the final and, an hour before the kick-off, Derek Dougan, their popular but maverick Irish centre-forward, had put in a transfer request. The final had been a poor advertisement for football, and was made even worse by the accident to Blackburn left-back Dave Whelan, who broke a leg trying to tackle an opponent. Ironically Whelan had been in hospital on Cup final day the previous year, with knee trouble.

The accident occurred shortly before half-time, and just after Wolves had gone ahead with an own goal by Mick McGrath. Wolves played their usual long-ball game, and typically it was a winger, little Norman Deeley, who scored the two goals that wrapped the match up 3–0 in the last quarter. The booing and jeering they had to face from the Blackburn supporters, not to mention the rubbish thrown at the referee, was shameful. If anything good is to come out of this game, then surely it is time for substitutes to be allowed.

Wolves go one up as Blackburn's McGrath (right) puts through his own goal

Real Madrid are kings of Europe again as di Stefano and Puskas share seven goals in Hampden feast

THIS WAS SURELY the greatest club match ever played. A crowd of 127,621 packed into Hampden Park to see Eintracht Frankfurt take on the undisputed "Kings of Europe", Real Madrid, in the final of the European Cup.

Real, four times champions, have dominated the competition since its inception in 1955–56. The club have been transformed into a formidable force by the president and former player Santiago Bernabeu. After building a magnificent new stadium, he set about recruiting the best players in the world to fill it. First came the Argentinian Alfredo di Stefano, the virtuoso around whom the whole side revolves. Others who followed included the brilliant fleet-footed left-winger Francisco Gento, a Spaniard from Real Santander, the scheming Reims star Raymond Kopa, who had faced them in the first final, the Uruguayan Jose Santamaria, who became the kingpin of their defence; and the overweight Hungarian exile Ferenc Puskas.

Puskas played a part in last year's campaign, but this was his first final. He has struck up a magical partnership with di Stefano, and the two "generals" have blended perfectly. Against the unfortunate Germans, these two ageing stars rolled back the years and produced as breathtaking a display of attacking football and clinical finishing as has been seen in Britain since the Hungarians gave England a lesson in 1953 — when, remarkably, Puskas was also a central figure.

It cannot be said, either, that Eintracht were pushovers. They had put six goals past Rangers in both legs of their semi-final, so their reputation in Glasgow was sky-high. They, too, had a redoubtable duo of veterans in schemer Alfred Pfaff and right-winger Richard Kress. And it was Kress who burst through to put them ahead after 18 minutes.

This was not the first time Real had been down in a final, and typically it was di Stefano who replied, lashing home a cross from Brazilian outside-right Canario eight minutes later and then putting Real ahead after a mistake by the German defence. At this stage, the South American maestro was orchestrating the match, bestriding the pitch from box to box. Then Puskas took over the baton, rifling the ball in from the byline, and after the interval converting a penalty. He then completed his hat-trick with a header from a Gento cross after the flying winger had sprinted 50 yards with the ball, and scored his fourth with a delightful pivot from just inside the box.

The Frankfurt side emphasized their worth by scoring twice more, through Erwin Stein, but in between di Stefano again stamped his majesty on the game with an interpassing move out of defence that he finished off sublimely for his third and Real's seventh goal. At the end, the normally partisan Scottish crowd gave the Spanish side an ovation usually reserved for the victories of their own national team.

FINAL SCORE

Football League
Division 1: Burnley
Top scorer: Dennis Viollet (Manchester U) 32
Division 2: Aston Villa
Division 3: Southampton
Division 4: Walsall
Footballer of the Year: Bill Slater (Wolverhampton Wanderers)

FA Cup Final
Wolves 3 Blackburn Rovers 0

Scottish League
Division 1: Hearts
Top scorer: Joe Baker (Hibernian) 42
Division 2: St Johnstone

Scottish FA Cup Final
Rangers 2 Kilmarnock 0

Scottish League Cup Final
Hearts 2 Third Lanark 1

International Championship
England, Scotland, Wales, 4 pts

European Nations Cup Final
USSR 2 Yugoslavia 1
(after extra time)

European Cup Final
Real Madrid 7 Eintracht Frankfurt 3

Inter-Cities Fairs Cup Final
Barcelona beat Birmingham City 0–0, 4–1

European Footballer of the Year 1959
Alfredo di Stefano (Real Madrid & Spain)

World Club Championship
Real Madrid (Spain) beat Penarol (Uruguay) 0–0, 5–1

Di Stefano scores the first of his three goals against Eintracht at Hampden Park.

Dennis Viollet, Division One leading scorer.

USSR first European champions

A TOURNAMENT that started in 1958 ended with victory for the USSR. They won the first European Nations Cup when they beat Yugoslavia 2–1 in the final on 10 July in Paris. Once again the four home countries absented themselves from a major international competition, West Germany and Italy did not take part, and Spain withdrew for political reasons when drawn against the USSR in the second round.

The contest was played on a home-and-away basis until the semi-finals, played in France. The final was settled in extra time by a goal from Ponedelnik.

Burnley's title a triumph for football

AFTER A UNIQUE campaign in which they did not lead the table until their last game, Burnley found themselves needing to beat Manchester City to take the League title. They thrillingly won 2–1 at Maine Road, thus depriving leaders Wolves, who beat them 6–1 only five weeks ago, of a hat-trick of League titles.

If Burnley had drawn, Wolves would have been champions on goal average. Spurs were third, missing their chance when beaten 1–0 at home in two successive matches late on.

Burnley deserved their first Championship triumph since 1921 for playing pure football with the accent on attack. Their success stems from midfield, where captain and right-half Jimmy Adamson and inside-forward Jimmy McIlroy have been outstanding, setting up the chances for England right-winger John Connelly (20 goals), centre-forward Ray Pointer (19) and inside-forward Jim Robson (18). Left-back Alex Elder, not 19 until April, made a remarkable impression. Manager Harry Potts always sent the team out to "Play football and enjoy your game". They did so, and thousands of fans all over the country have enjoyed watching them.

'Slavery' abolished: players' strike off

SATURDAY'S threatened football strike has been called off as the Football League gave in to the demands of the Professional Footballers Association on Wednesday 18 January. In a meeting between the League and the PFA at the Ministry of Labour, the League agreed to scrap the contract binding players to their clubs for life — the so-called "slavery" contract. They abolished the £20 maximum wage a week ago, so this is another great victory for the PFA, led by their outspoken chairman, Jimmy Hill of Fulham.

It is also good news for George Eastham, who has been playing for Arsenal since November, but is taking former club Newcastle United to court on a "restraint of trade" charge for refusing him a transfer.

Arsenal's George Eastham, no longer a "slave".

Spurs' record run halted, but who will catch them now?

AT LAST SPURS have shown signs of mortality, losing their first point of the season after 11 straight victories. Nobody could have predicted that Manchester City would be the team to spoil their 100 per cent record by holding them to a 1-1 draw, and at White Hart Lane, too, especially after their last two victories, 6-2 over Aston Villa and 4-0 over Wolves at Molineux.

Sheffield Wednesday are also still unbeaten, and are four points behind with a game in hand: not an unbridgeable gap. But the way Spurs have been playing and scoring — with 37 goals, almost twice as many as Wednesday — it is difficult to see them slipping.

Scots staggered by England's one over the eight

Spread-eagled Haffey dives in vain as another England goal hits the net.

SCOTLAND SUFFERED the most humiliating defeat in their history on Saturday when England, the "auld enemy", crushed them 9–3 at Wembley.

Celtic's Frank Haffey, called in because of injuries to two other keepers, had a nightmare match, but this should take nothing away from England's brilliant attacking performance, which is yet another vindication of team manager Walter Winterbottom's policy of keeping to a settled team. They have now won their last five games, scoring 32 goals, with 11 of them coming from Chelsea's prolific inside-right Jimmy Greaves, whose transfer to AC Milan has just been agreed. He had another outstanding game against Scotland, hitting three, while inside-left Johnny Haynes (Fulham) tore the defence to shreds with his devastating passing and scored twice. The other goals were scored by Bobby Smith (two), Bobby Robson and Bryan Douglas.

FOOTBALL FOCUS

- As if there weren't enough fixtures in an already overcrowded programme, a new competition, the Football League Cup, was launched in 1960. Played on a knock-out basis, with two-legged ties from the semi-finals, it was somewhat devalued when five top clubs — Arsenal, Sheffield Wednesday, Spurs, WBA and Wolves — declined to take part.

- Not quite emulating his brother Gerry's 10-goal feat last season, Joe Baker scored nine for Hibs in their 15–1 win over Peebles Rovers in the second round of the Scottish Cup.

- Denis Law scored all six of Manchester City's goals in a fourth-round Cup tie at Luton, but they didn't count because the game was abandoned. He scored again when City lost the replay 3–1.

- The marvellous Real Madrid were finally beaten in the European Cup, by their great domestic rivals, Barcelona, in the first round. But the Spanish champions, with Hungarian exiles Kocsis and Czibor, lost to Portuguese side Benfica in the final. Burnley reached the quarter-finals, but lost 4–1 in Hamburg after taking the first leg 3–1.

- Spurs' outright Championship records included most wins (31) and most away wins (16).

- Peterborough United, elected to the League in 1960 after 12 times having the "old pals' act" slammed in their face, made a sensational debut, winning the Fourth Division and scoring a League record 134 goals, with centre-forward Terry Bly hitting a post-war record 52.

- The "lure of the lira" led some of Britain's leading players to Italy: Joe Baker (£73,000) and Denis Law (£100,000) to Turin, Jimmy Greaves (£80,000) to AC Milan, and Gerry Hitchens (£80,000) to Inter-Milan. Johnny Haynes stayed with Fulham and was rewarded by becoming England's first £100-a-week footballer.

Rangers restore Scots pride but fail in new Euro final

JUST FOUR DAYS after three of their stars shared the ignominy of Scotland's 9–3 Wembley defeat, Rangers went to Molineux where a draw with Wolves was sufficient to see them through to the final of the European Cup-Winners' Cup. There were 10 entries for this new competition, and Rangers, who last season reached the semi-finals of the European Cup, soon avenged their crushing defeat by a West German side — Eintracht Frankfurt — in the senior competition by thrashing Borussia Moenchengladbach 3–0 and 8–0 in the quarter-finals.

Rangers, whose close-season signing of the classy Jim Baxter from Raith Rovers has transformed them from a workman-like defensive team into a flair side committed to attack, won the League Cup and then, despite a crippling injury list, the Championship. The first British club to reach a European final, they could not, however, break down the Fiorentina defence at Ibrox, and the Italian side had no trouble protecting a two-goal lead in the return in Florence.

FINAL SCORE

Football League
Division 1: Tottenham Hotspur
Top scorer: Jimmy Greaves (Chelsea) 41
Division 2: Ipswich Town
Division 3: Bury
Division 4: Peterborough United
Footballer of the Year: Danny Blanchflower (Tottenham Hotspur)

FA Cup Final
Tottenham Hotspur 2 Leicester City 0

League Cup Final
Aston Villa beat Rotherham United 0–2, 3–0

Scottish League
Division 1: Rangers
Top scorer: Alex Harley (Third Lanark) 42
Division 2: Stirling Albion

Scottish FA Cup Final
Dunfermline Athletic 0 Celtic 0
Replay: Dunfermline Athletic 2 Celtic 0

Scottish League Cup Final
Rangers 2 Kilmarnock 0

International Championship
England, 6 pts

European Cup Final
Benfica 3 Barcelona 2

Cup-Winners' Cup Final
Fiorentina beat Rangers 2–0, 2–1

Inter-Cities Fairs Cup Final
AS Roma beat Birmingham City 2–2, 2–0

European Footballer of the Year 1960
Luis Suarez (Barcelona & Spain)

World Club Championship
Penarol (Uruguay) beat Benfica (Portugal) 0–1, 5–0, 2–1

Terry Bly scored 52 goals for Fourth Division champions Peterborough.

Team of the century Spurs complete the 'impossible double'

Leicester's defence is finally beaten by Smith (centre) as Jones (7) celebrates.

THEY SAID it couldn't be done again, the League and Cup "double". Many clubs have tried to emulate a feat previously accomplished by Preston and Aston Villa in the 1800s, when the fixtures were fewer and the competition not so intense. Some have been a whisker away from success when their luck ran out, as happened with Manchester United in 1957, when only an injury to their goalkeeper at Wembley deprived them of the honour. But it was Spurs' opponents Leicester City who suffered the Wembley "hoodoo", losing right-back Len Chalmers after only 18 minutes. It still took off-colour Spurs another 48 minutes to score, and in the end they ran out 2–0 winners.

Spurs made sure of the League Championship nearly three weeks ago, setting various records as they did so. When they beat Sheffield Wednesday 2–1 at White Hart Lane on 17 April, after going a goal down, the title was theirs. In a magnificent campaign, Spurs were never headed. They dropped only one point in their first 16 matches, before their first defeat — 2–1 to Wednesday. They finished up with 115 goals, the highest First Division total for 27 years, with Bobby Smith (28) and Les Allen (23) their leading scorers. And they equalled the points record of 66, set by Arsenal in 1931.

At Wembley, the mental strain on Tottenham showed. Manager Billy Nicholson's great team looked and played like jaded men, and Leicester were on top until Chalmers's unfortunate injury, incurred in a clash with Allen. Leicester were superb in defence, with young Gordon Banks outstanding in goal. But there was nothing he could do about the goals when they did eventually come. First Smith took a Dyson through-ball and for once beat the formidable Ian King to crash an unstoppable shot into the net. A few minutes later, Smith returned the compliment for Dyson to head Spurs' second and clinching goal.

Spurs will be remembered, however, not for their tense Cup final performance, but for the scintillating football they played week after week, a thrilling, attacking game in which every man played his part. The Cup final team — Brown, Baker, Henry, Blanchflower, Norman, Mackay, Jones, White, Smith, Allen and Dyson — were the eleven that had turned out regularly in the League, eight of them playing 40 or more games (of the others, only right-winger Terry Medwin played enough League games to win a medal). This mix — the great and the good — blended into arguably one of the finest English club sides of the century, and few of the record two-and-a-half million people who watched Spurs throughout the season would disagree.

'Ramsey's Rustics' are new League champions

IPSWICH MANAGER Alf Ramsey has worked a minor miracle in a corner of East Anglia, guiding his unfancied club to the League title in their first season in Division One. The pundits laughed when the former England right-back "strengthened" his collection of unknowns and discards after they won promotion — signing one new player. He paid a club record £12,000 for schemer Doug "Dixie" Moran from Falkirk. They would have to do more than that if they were to stay in the top echelon. Nobody dreamt they would win it.

But Ramsey has proved a remarkable motivator and strategist. Getting his players to believe in themselves and fulfil their potential as individuals, he also designed tactics to blend them into a formidable team. Ray Crawford (33 goals) and Ted Phillips (28) have been outstanding. And 33-year-old Jimmy Leadbetter, ostensibly a left-winger, has confused defences with his unorthodox positioning.

Ipswich made a poor start to the season, with only one point from their first three matches. But when they beat Burnley 6–2, people began to take notice. Burnley and Spurs proved to be their chief rivals, although both were involved in other competitions and suffered a pile-up of fixtures at the end of the season. When Ipswich lost 5–0 at Old Trafford on 7 April, however, they appeared to have shot their bolt. With five games left, they were a point behind Burnley, who had two games in hand and a far superior goal average. But Burnley, going for the "double", blew up and won only one of their last seven games. Ipswich continued to play fresh, fluent football, and took the title by three points.

League champions Ipswich, average age nearly 28, won the title at the first attempt.

Spurs provide a 'passport to paradise' for Greaves: £99,999 brings him back from Italy

BILL NICHOLSON, manager of Spurs, has brought off the coup of the season, bringing back homesick Jimmy Greaves from Italy, where England's prolific young goalscorer has not been able to settle down.

Greaves scored nine goals in 14 matches for AC Milan and made a hit with the fans, but the extremely strict discipline within the club and the defensive style of Italian football have been anathema to him. He was extremely unhappy about being prevented from playing for England as a disciplinary measure. Needless to say, he is delighted to be back home again.

Nicholson broke the British transfer record to get his man, but paid £99,999 to avoid saddling him with the title of Britain's first £100,000 footballer. With a third of the season gone, Spurs are chasing the European Cup as well as domestic honours, and Greaves, who last season became the youngest player to reach 100 League goals in England, while still only 21 years of age, will be an invaluable asset in their challenge on all fronts.

Night of the long shots

FERENC PUSKAS, the Hungarian star of Real Madrid's wonderful 1960 European Cup-winners, hit a first-half hat-trick in the final against holders Benfica in Amsterdam. But the Portuguese side staged a splendid comeback and emerged 5–3 winners in a match notable for goals scored from a distance.

The evergreen Puskas is tubbier now but still was recognisable as the "Galloping Major", at least in the first period, when he ran half the length of the pitch after being put away by di Stefano to score one of his goals. He hit a typical long-range piledriver for another, then Aguas and Cavem, with another power-drive, put Benfica level before Puskas completed his hat-trick. During the interval, Bela Guttmann, Benfica's wily Hungarian coach, produced the tactics to negate the ageing di Stefano and isolate Puskas. Coluna equalized with another long shot, a 30-yarder.

Then the 20-year-old prodigy Eusebio took charge, scoring from the penalty spot after being pulled down, and thundering a tapped free-kick from Coluna into the net via a hapless defender.

FOOTBALL FOCUS

● Prolific scorer Brian Clough — 197 goals in 213 League games — left Middlesbrough for Sunderland in a £45,000 transfer at the start of the season, and scored 29 goals in 34 matches for the club, who missed promotion by a point.

● A record crowd for a friendly match, 104,493, saw Eintracht Frankfurt beat Glasgow Rangers 3–2 at Hampden Park on 17 October.

● Stanley Matthews, at 46, left Blackpool in October. But he did not retire. He went back to Stoke for a nominal £2,500 fee and trebled their gates in Division Two.

● The Italian League beat the Scottish League 2–0 at Hampden on 1 November — with the help of Denis Law (Scotland), John Charles (Wales) and Gerry Hitchens (England).

● Three players scored hat-tricks for Wrexham in their 10–1 Fourth Division defeat of Hartlepool on 3 March — Ron Barnes, Roy Ambler and Wyn Davies.

● Accrington Stanley resigned from the League on 6 March, because of financial difficulties, and their Division Four results were expunged.

● Former England captain Billy Wright took over from George Swindin as manager of Arsenal in March.

● England suffered their first defeat at Hampden Park for 25 years when Scotland won 2–0, a fine comeback after their Wembley débâcle last season.

Stanley Matthews, 46, back in the Potteries.

Spurs retain Cup at Wembley: not a stretcher in sight

TOTTENHAM HOTSPUR beat Burnley 3–1 at Wembley to retain the FA Cup in a match for once not marred by the sight of an injured player being carried off or hobbling helplessly on the wing. Spurs, who blew their chances of another League and Cup "double" at Easter, and Burnley, who let the Championship slip out of their grasp in the closing stages, put on a show befitting teams finishing third and second respectively in the table. But it was not a memorable match in that Spurs never really seemed to be in danger of losing it.

Burnley, after their disappointing form of late in the League, played well, but without that spark, that belief in themselves that might have turned the game. And their confidence was jarred after only three minutes, when Spurs took the lead. Jimmy Greaves, so glad to be back on English soil after his early-season misery in Milan, came out bursting with enthusiasm. He latched on to a Smith flick-on, overran the ball, but as the Burnley defence were putting on the brakes, cleverly slotted it past them inside the far post.

Oozing confidence now, Spurs put together some fine, flowing moves. But Burnley, with the classy Adamson and McIlroy — Footballer of the Year and runner-up, respectively — in midfield, managed to come back into the game. They equalized five minutes after half-time, when Jimmy Robson converted a near-post cross for the 100th Cup final goal in Wembley history. But Spurs hit back immediately through a thumping Smith shot, and Blanchflower sealed it with a late penalty after Cummings had handled with goalkeeper Blacklaw beaten.

Tottenham beat Euro champs but lose semi

Spurs go a goal down and effectively give Benfica a three-goal start.

AFTER A NIGHT full of drama and passion at White Hart Lane, Spurs just failed to pull back their 3–1 first-leg deficit in the European Cup semi-final against holders Benfica. In Lisbon, they paid the price of fielding an uncharacteristically defensive formation, and gave away two early goals.

The atmosphere at White Hart Lane was electric, and the roar of the 65,000 crowd would have done Hampden or Wembley proud. But Benfica, strengthened since last season by the addition of Simoes and the amazing Eusebio up front, began like true champions and Aguas scored after 15 minutes to put them 4–1 up overall. Undaunted, Spurs came roaring back, and the dynamic Mackay hit a post. Then they had what looked like a perfectly good goal disallowed when the speed of Greaves beat that of the linesman's eye.

The pace did not slacken thereafter. First Smith scored for Spurs, then Aguas hit their bar, on the stroke of half-time. Four minutes after the interval, Cruz brought down White, and Blanchflower coolly sent Costa Pereira the wrong way from the penalty spot — 3–4 now, and Mackay was driving Spurs on, seemingly at the heart of their every move.

Did Germano handle Medwin's header? The referee waved play on. Mackay made one last surge through the binding mud and smashed a shot past the keeper... and against the crossbar. It just was not Spurs' night.

FINAL SCORE

Football League
Division 1: Ipswich Town
Top scorer: Ray Crawford (Ipswich Town) 33
Division 2: Liverpool
Division 3: Portsmouth
Division 4: Millwall
Footballer of the Year: Jimmy Adamson (Burnley)

FA Cup Final

Tottenham Hotspur	3	Burnley	1

League Cup Final
Norwich City beat Rochdale 3–0, 1–0

Scottish League
Division 1: Dundee
Top scorer: Alan Gilzean (Dundee) 24
Division 2: Clyde

Scottish FA Cup Final

Rangers	2	St Mirren	0

Scottish League Cup Final

Rangers	1	Hearts	1
Replay: Rangers	3	Hearts	1

International Championship
Scotland, 6 pts

European Cup Final

Benfica	5	Real Madrid	3

Cup-Winners' Cup Final

Atletico Madrid	1	Fiorentina	1
Replay: Atletico	3	Fiorentina	0

Inter-Cities Fairs Cup Final
Valencia beat Barcelona 6–2, 1–1

European Footballer of the Year 1961
Omar Sivori (Juventus & Italy)

World Club Championship
Santos (Brazil) beat Benfica (Portugal) 3–2, 5–2

SOCCER SOUNDBITES

"The men who got us into the First Division will prove themselves good enough to keep us there."

Understatement of the season by Ipswich manager
ALF RAMSEY.

A World Cup to forget

What was expected to be a soccer feast, a showpiece for football artistry, turned out to be a defence-ridden scrap where the fear of failure dominated and onfield violence was the norm. The pressure on teams in the early stages has become too great, and some of the scenes transmitted by television to millions of viewers around the world warranted an "X" rating. Brazil deservedly retained the trophy, but rarely reached the heights of 1958, and it was sad that injury deprived the fans of Pele for all but their first two matches. That other master of the game, Spain's Alfredo di Stefano, was unable to play at all.

UNLIKE LAST TIME, only England of the home countries qualified for Chile. The choice of host country had lain between Argentina and Chile. The former looked set to get the vote until, paradoxically, Chile was hit by a series of devastating earthquakes in mid-1960. FIFA awarded them the 1962 finals after a plea from Carlos Dittborn, president of their FA: "We have nothing: that is why we must have the World Cup."

Chile, an impoverished nation, nevertheless built a magnificent National Stadium in Santiago, but there were only three other venues. The organization was competent, but high admission prices resulted in poor gates at all venues except the capital. In the group matches, goal difference was to count, obviating the need for play-offs.

Early casualties

After just two days of matches, with each team having played once, the World Cup image was severely blemished. After another full round, it had become tarnished beyond repair. With teams desperate not to make an early exit, the "casualty count" had mounted to nearly 50, including four players in hospital with fractures. In addition, Bulgaria had lost their centre-forward and outside-right, Spain their two full-backs, and four players had been sent off.

In an attempt to check the savagery, the World Cup organizing committee called the 16 team managers together to warn them and to impress upon the players that such violence would not be tolerated. But they let the guilty players off lightly.

Greaves scores from close in against Argentina, and Charlton (11) joins in the celebration.

Chile-Italy débâcle

Chile had made a good start in Group 2, beating Switzerland 3–1. But the match that really hit the headlines — for all the wrong reasons — was their second game, against Italy. Two Italian journalists in Chile had written insulting, patronizing articles about the country and, by the time the two teams met, the atmosphere between them was hostile and potentially violent. Italy were soon riled by the spitting Chileans. Chile's outside-left Leonel Sanchez, who had scored a glorious solo goal against the Swiss, was involved in a private kicking match with Italy's Giorgio Ferrini behind the back of English referee Ken Aston. Then Landa kicked Ferrini, who was seen kicking back and ordered off. It took eight minutes, several Italian officials and a squad of policemen to persuade him to leave the field!

Italy, notoriously defensive anyway with their catenaccio system, retreated even more. Players of both sides were to be seen rolling around in feigned agony after nearly every tackle. Sanchez broke Maschio's nose with a left hook clearly seen on television but missed by a linesman almost on top of the incident. A few minutes before half-time, Sanchez was fouled by Mario David and knocked him down, too, but amid scenes of furore involving police, photographers and officials the referee took no action. Just before half-time David aimed a kick at Sanchez and was sent off. Even so, Chile needed another half-hour to score against nine man; they eventually won 2–0.

The immediate result of this most disgraceful episode in the history of the World Cup was the suspension of Ferrini for one game and the "severe admonishment" of David and Sanchez. These so-called punishments arguably left FIFA as guilty as the teams who perpetrated the incidents and the officials who failed to control them.

Ken Aston sends off Italy's Ferrini in the infamous game with Chile.

Back to the football

Football had largely been forgotten. But there was little of it to stir the blood, anyway. In Group 3, at the charming coastal resort of Vina del Mar, Pele treated the meagre crowds to some of his magic before hobbling out of the tournament. Against Mexico, he made Brazil's first for Zagalo, then went on a spectacular dribble half the length of the pitch before scoring with a cracking shot. He pulled a muscle early on against Czechoslovakia, and was replaced against Spain by Amarildo, the "White Pele".

The Spain-Brazil match was one of the highlights of the finals. The Spanish team manager Helenio Herrera dropped inside-forwards Luis del Sol and Luis

There were some moments of Chile's World Cup that we should all like to forget, but at least the best team won, and there were some signs of sportsmanship if you looked hard enough.

Zito (19) heads Brazil's second goal in the World Cup final in Santiago.

Suarez, the captain, both of whom had been signed by Italian clubs in world record transfers. Ageing Hungarian exile Puskas was still playing well and Gento was on the wing, but the other Real star, di Stefano, had been ruled out by injury before the start. Puskas made a first-half goal for Adelardo, but two fine goals late on from the 22-year-old Amarildo gave Brazil victory and eliminated Spain.

England's 'progress'

England never settled down in Chile, but they managed to struggle through to the quarter-finals, despite losing the first match, against Hungary. No longer the "Magic Magyars" of the early fifties, Hungary were nevertheless a workmanlike side and won 2–1, a Flowers penalty being the only consolation for an uninspired England.

With Inter-Milan's Gerry Hitchens struggling to get to grips with England's football, he was replaced against Argentina by the untried Alan Peacock of Middlesbrough, and it was Peacock's header, handled as it was crossing the line, that gave Flowers the opportunity for another successful spot-kick. Charlton and Greaves also scored in a fine, and surprising, victory. A deadly dull goalless draw with Bulgaria was then enough to see them through.

Brazil proved too good for England at Vina del Mar in a game that restored some of the World Cup's lost reputation for open, attacking football. Knocks to inside-forwards Didi and Amarildo limited their efficiency, but right-winger Garrincha was Brazil's star. Time and again he sent the England defence the wrong way with his swerve, explosive acceleration and ball control. But it was with a header that he opened the scoring after half an hour, popping up to convert Zagalo's corner.

England were in danger of cracking, but suddenly they were back on terms. Greaves headed a Haynes free-kick against a post, and Hitchens, back for the injured Peacock, knocked the ball in. Soon after the interval, however, Springett failed to hold a vicious Garrincha free-kick, and Vava nodded the ball home. On the hour, Garrincha made sure with a dipping, swinging, curling 25-yarder that left Springett gasping.

Chile inspired

The shock of the quarter-finals was the USSR's 2–1 defeat by Chile, who were inspired by the fanatical support of the whole country. It was a sad day for the normally impeccable Lev Yashin in the Soviet goal, who perhaps should have stopped both Chile's long-range efforts.

The biggest crowd of the finals — 76,594 at the National Stadium — saw Chile's progress halted at last by Brazil, in particular by Garrincha, who scored twice and made one of Vava's two in a 4–2 victory. He was then sent off for a retaliatory push after being sworn at, spat upon and pushed. In the other semi-final, only 6,000 turned up to watch Czechoslovakia emerge 3–1 victors over Yugoslavia.

Brazil retain the cup

FIFA allowed Garrincha to compete in the final, a welcome decision after some of their earlier judgements. But Brazil found themselves a goal down for the second final running, when Masopust, Czechoslovakia's attacking left-half, ran on to a defence-splitting Scherer pass and left-footed the ball past Gylmar. Their lead was short-lived, however, as Amarildo scored a stunning equalizer, taking the ball to the left byline, drawing the keeper to the near post, and then hitting a swerving shot round him just inside the far post.

The counter-attacking Czechs held their own against the still-adventurous Brazilians until the 69th minute, when again it was Amarildo who pierced their defence with Pele-like skills on the left and crossed for Zito to head in. Another eight minutes, and it was all over — the hapless Schroif, blinded by the sun, fumbled a speculative Djalma Santos lob, and Vava pounced to put the loose ball away. Brazil were now level with Italy and Uruguay with two World Cups to their credit.

FINAL SCORE

Group 1

Uruguay	2	Colombia	1
USSR	2	Yugoslavia	0
Yugoslavia	3	Uruguay	1
USSR	4	Colombia	4
USSR	2	Uruguay	1
Yugoslavia	5	Colombia	0

	P	W	D	L	F	A	P
USSR	3	2	1	0	8	5	5
Yugoslavia	3	2	0	1	8	3	4
Uruguay	3	1	0	2	4	6	2
Colombia	3	0	1	2	5	11	1

Group 2

Chile	3	Switzerland	1
West Germany	0	Italy	0
Chile	2	Italy	0
West Germany	2	Switzerland	1
West Germany	2	Chile	0
Italy	3	Switzerland	0

	P	W	D	L	F	A	P
W.Germany	3	2	1	0	4	1	5
Chile	3	2	0	1	5	3	4
Italy	3	1	1	1	3	2	3
Switzerland	3	0	0	3	2	8	0

Group 3

Brazil	2	Mexico	0
Czechoslovakia	1	Spain	0
Brazil	0	Czechoslovakia	0
Spain	1	Mexico	0
Brazil	2	Spain	1
Mexico	3	Czechoslovakia	1

	P	W	D	L	F	A	P
Brazil	3	2	1	0	4	1	5
Czech	3	1	1	1	2	3	3
Mexico	3	1	0	2	3	4	2
Spain	3	1	0	2	2	3	2

Group 4

Argentina	1	Bulgaria	0
Hungary	2	England	1
England	3	Argentina	1
Hungary	6	Bulgaria	1
Hungary	0	Argentina	0
England	0	Bulgaria	0

	P	W	D	L	F	A	P
Hungary	3	2	1	0	8	2	5
England	3	1	1	1	4	3	3
Argentina	3	1	1	1	2	3	3
Bulgaria	3	0	1	2	1	7	1

QUARTER-FINALS

Yugoslavia	1	West Germany	0
Chile	2	USSR	1
Brazil	3	England	1
Czechoslovakia	1	Hungary	0

SEMI-FINALS

Czechoslovakia	3	Yugoslavia	1
Brazil	4	Chile	2

THIRD-PLACE MATCH

Chile	1	Yugoslavia	0

FINAL

Brazil	3	Czechoslovakia	1

National Stadium, Santiago, 17 June 1962. Attendance 68,679

Brazil: Gylmar, Santos D, Santos N, Zito, Mauro, Zozimo, Garrincha, Didi, Vava, Amarildo, Zagalo (Scorers: Amarildo, Zito, Vava)
Czechoslovakia: Schroif, Tichy, Novak, Pluskal, Popluhar, Masopust, Pospichal, Scherer, Kadraba, Kvasnak, Jelinek (Scorer: Masopust)

Leading scorers
4 Albert (Hungary) Garrincha (Brazil) Ivanov (USSR) Jerkovic (Yugoslavia) Sanchez (Chile) Vava (Brazil)

End of the big freeze: soccer back to normal at last

AT LAST, on 16 March, it has been possible to play a complete programme of League football. The "big freeze" started on 22 December, and has played havoc with League and Cup competitions throughout the country. This has been the worst winter in football history, even worse than 1946–1947.

Only three third-round FA Cup ties out of 32 were played on the day they were scheduled for, 5 January. Fourteen of them were postponed 10 or more times, the Lincoln-Coventry game 15 times! The replayed Blackburn-Middlesbrough tie was not completed until 11 March. Only four Football League fixtures were completed on 5 January, and five on 2 February. The following week there were seven League fixtures but the whole Scottish League programme was frozen off. Bolton Wanderers went the longest period without a match in League history, from their 1–0 win over Spurs at Burnden Park on 8 December to their 3–2 defeat at Arsenal on 16 February.

The Football Pools were affected, of course, and for three consecutive Saturdays in January the coupons were declared void. Then the companies came up with the idea of a special panel of "experts" — four former players and a referee — to determine the likely "results" of matches not played. The panel sat for four Saturdays, some of the decisions causing much controversy.

All manner of ideas and devices were tried to beat the freeze — flame-throwers at Bloomfield Road, a tar-burner at Stamford Bridge, a hot-air tent at Filbert Street, a Danish snow-shifting tractor at St Andrews, and 80 tons of sand at Wrexham's Racecourse Ground — but the clubs were fighting a losing battle, and the season will now have to be extended to almost the end of May.

Birmingham use a snow-shifting tractor at St Andrews.

'Cheque-book champions': Everton clinch League title

EVERTON CLINCHED their sixth League title in front of 60,000 delirious fans at Goodison Park on Saturday 11 May when they beat Fulham 4–1. Of the leading clubs in Division One, Everton are the only one to have finished their programme, but no other team can catch them now. Spurs lost their last slender chance when they went down 1–0 at Manchester City.

Already Everton are being called "cheque-book champions", but it has been money well spent. After forking out some £175,000 on five players last season, new manager Harry Catterick completed the "jigsaw" during this season's big freeze, with left-half Tony Kay (£60,000 from Sheffield Wednesday) and right-winger Alex Scott (£40,000 from Rangers).

Although they lost their pre-freeze lead, Everton went back to the top of the table when they beat Spurs 1–0 on 20 April, and have stayed there to the end. Against Fulham, inside-left and captain Roy Vernon scored a hat-trick to make him leading scorer with 24 goals, above centre-forward Alex Young (22). Although it is invidious to pick out names from this side of stars, the brilliantly creative Young and centre-half Brian Labone have been outstanding.

Manager Harry Catterick with his Championship-winning Everton team.

A 5–2 rout in France emphasizes magnitude of Ramsey's task

IF ENGLAND'S new manager Alf Ramsey thought life was going to be easier with England than with Ipswich, he suffered a rude awakening in Paris. England, in his charge for the first time, lost 5–2 to France and go out of the European Nations Cup in the first round.

When Walter Winterbottom resigned after the 1962 World Cup, it was decided to appoint a full-time team manager for the first time. Ramsey, who worked a minor miracle at Ipswich, accepted the post on the understanding that he would have sole responsibility for team selection. He was charged with building a team capable of winning the World Cup when England host the finals in three years' time.

Ramsey introduced only one new cap, Ron Henry of Spurs, in his first team selection, and made few changes. But England's performance was disjointed, and Springett had a poor game in goal. They pulled back from a 3-0 half-time deficit with headers from Bobby Smith and Bobby Tambling, but their revival was short-lived. Defeat in France is a setback. But at least Ramsey knows the magnitude of the task that lies ahead.

FOOTBALL FOCUS

- Before the start of the season, Denis Law returned to Manchester — United this time — for a British record £115,000 from Torino, who also sold Joe Baker to Arsenal for £70,000. Law starred for United in their Cup final triumph, although they went close to relegation.
- Fulham's Johnny Haynes was badly hurt in a car crash on 23 August and was out of action for most of the season.
- Chelsea achieved the win they needed against Portsmouth to take them into Division One, and at 7–0 it was their biggest since the 1910–11 season. At the other end of the table, Charlton won 2–1 at Walsall to go ahead of them on goal average and stay up.
- In a momentous High Court decision on 4 July 1963, in George Eastham v Newcastle United FC and others, Mr Justice Wilberforce declared that the regulations of the Football League in relation to the retention and transfer of professional footballers were in "unreasonable restraint of trade".

Glory, glory night as Spurs win Cup-Winners' Cup

SPURS BECAME the first British side to win a European trophy when they whipped Atletico Madrid 5–1 in Rotterdam on 15 May in the final of the Cup-Winners Cup. What another "glory, glory" night this was for their fans, out in force in Holland to see them take on the holders. Spurs suffered a blow before the game, when the dynamic Dave Mackay failed a fitness test. But inspired by their captain, Danny Blanchflower, and with Cliff Jones unstoppable on the right wing, they took a two-goal half-time lead through Greaves and White. The match, however, was to belong to left-winger Terry Dyson. Content usually to play a supporting role to his more illustrious team-mates, the little Yorkshireman has never served Spurs better.

Match-winner Terry Dyson shows the trophy to the fans.

Two minutes after the interval, Henry fisted out a goalbound shot, and Collar scored from the spot. For 20 minutes, Spurs needed all their fight and resolve to prevent the revitalized Spaniards from forcing an equalizer. Then Dyson, already proving a handful on the wing, took the match by the scruff of the neck. First he curled in a shot that the keeper could not prevent crossing the line. Then he centred for Greaves to score. And finally he burst 25 yards down the middle and hammered the ball into the net, a glorious climax to a glorious victory.

Stoke up! Maestro's first goal of the season clinches promotion

STOKE CITY beat Luton Town 2–0 at the Victoria Ground on 18 May to clinch promotion and the Second Division title, while sending Luton down to Division Three. With a great sense of occasion, Stanley Matthews chose to score his first goal of the season, Stoke's second. What an inspiration the ageing maestro has been to his old club, in his first full season since rejoining them. Those 48-year-old legs have seen him through more than 30 League games, and were prominent again last week when Stoke won 1–0 at Chelsea to set up this climax.

But Chelsea, after their stirring 1–0 victory at Roker Park, are favourites to join Stoke in Division One next year. That was Sunderland's last game, and they finished a point behind Stoke. Chelsea, a further two points behind, but with a superior goal average, now need to beat Portsmouth in their last game on Tuesday to go up.

Matthews's 48-year-old legs elude those of Chelsea's Eddie McCreadie, 23, at Stamford Bridge.

FINAL SCORE

Football League
Division 1: Everton
Top scorer: Jimmy Greaves (Tottenham Hotspur) 37
Division 2: Stoke City
Division 3: Northampton Town
Division 4: Brentford
Footballer of the Year: Stanley Matthews (Stoke City)

FA Cup Final
Manchester United 3 Leicester City 1

League Cup Final
Birmingham City beat Aston Villa 3–1, 0–0

Scottish League
Division 1: Rangers
Top scorer: Jimmy Millar (Rangers) 27
Division 2: St Johnstone

Scottish FA Cup Final
Rangers 1 Celtic 1
Replay: Rangers 3 Celtic 0

Scottish League Cup Final
Hearts 1 Kilmarnock 0

International Championship
Scotland, 6 pts

European Cup Final
AC Milan 2 Benfica 1

Cup-Winners' Cup Final
Tottenham Hotspur 5 Atletico Madrid 1

Inter-Cities Fairs Cup Final
Valencia beat Dynamo Zagreb 2–1, 2–0

European Footballer of the Year 1962
Josef Masopust (Dukla Prague & Czechoslovakia)

World Club Championship
Santos (Brazil) beat AC Milan (Italy) 2–4, 4–2, 1–0

England on top of the world after 100 years

Law beats Banks to score for the World XI.

ENGLAND BEAT a Rest of the World XI 2–1 at Wembley on 23 October in a match to celebrate the centenary of the Football Association. A crowd of 100,000 turned up to see world stars such as di Stefano, Puskas, Gento, Raymond Kopa, Lev Yashin, Djalma Santos and Eusebio — the World XI were allowed to use 16 players in all — and they were not disappointed. They were treated to a feast of football from both sides.

For England, Greaves was in exceptional form, and the two Scots in the World XI, Law and Baxter, were thoroughly at home in such illustrious company. All the goals came in the last 20 minutes. Terry Paine shot England ahead after a Greaves effort was blocked. Then Law combined with Puskas and di Stefano to put the Rest level.

England went close when Bobby Charlton thundered a shot against the base of the post and Greaves scraped the bar, then finally produced the winner with seven minutes remaining. Goalkeeper Soskic, who had replaced Yashin for the second half, could not hold another Charlton thunderbolt, and Greaves, as ever, was at hand to crack the ball home.

Danny Boy bows out

DANNY BLANCHFLOWER, 38, announced that he will be retiring from football at the end of the season when his contract with Spurs expires. He was dropped from the first team in November and later aggravated a knee injury playing for the reserves. Last month Bill Nicholson paid Fulham £72,500 for Alan Mullery, a British record for a half-back, to take over from Blanchflower.

Blanchflower, who made his League debut for Barnsley in 1949, cost Spurs a then club record of £30,000 when they bought him from Aston Villa in 1954, arguably the best money they ever spent. A constructive right-half, he led them to this century's first League and Cup "double" in 1961 and to the first British success in Europe last season, when they won the Cup-Winners' Cup. He also played the last of his record 56 Irish internationals last season.

A cultured footballer with a cultured mind (which he has never been afraid to speak!), he has not always seen eye to eye with management. But he has been a supreme leader for both club and country, a master tactician, respected and revered by those he has played with.

Rangers reign supreme in Scotland: Cup gives them the 'treble'

A CROWD OF nearly 121,000 at Hampden Park saw Rangers climax another record season with two goals in the last minute to beat Dundee 3–1 in the Cup and clinch the domestic "treble". In a hugely entertaining match played to the almost continuous roar of the crowd, Rangers took the lead in 66 minutes through Millar, but Cameron hooked in a spectacular equalizer within a minute. Millar, again, and Brand took advantage of Henderson's nippiness on either wing to provide the dramatic climax.

Having already won the League Cup, with Jim Forrest scoring four goals in the final, and the League Championship, Rangers emulated their own "treble" feat of 15 years ago, the only other time it has been done. They will carry Scotland's colours again next season in the European Cup, the only competition they entered and failed to win, having suffered a 6–0 thrashing by Real in Madrid.

Greaves (right) pounces to hit England's winner past Eyzaguirre and Soskic.

Top stars in betting scandal: England internationals accused of match fixing

DISCLOSURES IN *The People* newspaper have revealed a widespread bribery scandal in English football, with money paid to players for "fixing" matches for betting purposes.

Among the footballers so far named are three Sheffield Wednesday players: England internationals Peter Swan and Tony Kay (now with Everton) and David "Bronco" Layne. It is alleged that they took part in arranging the outcome of a Sheffield Wednesday First Division game, one which they lost 2–0 at Ipswich in December 1962. Further revelations are expected to be made.

Mackay breaks leg as United knock Spurs out of Europe

SPURS SUFFERED a double blow at Old Trafford on 10 December. Not only did Manchester United beat them 4–1 to win their European Cup-Winners' Cup tie 4–3, but Dave Mackay was carried off to hospital with a broken leg after only eight minutes. The Cup-holders battled bravely with 10 men, and remained ahead on aggregate until the last 13 minutes.

It was a night of high emotion, a game of tremendous action, played sportingly throughout. Spurs, with a 2–0 lead from White Hart Lane, almost made it three when Smith put his point-blank header straight at Gaskell from Mackay's early cross. This was, in retrospect, the turning point of the tie. For, only a minute later, David Herd pulled the all-important early goal back for United. David Sadler beat Spurs keeper Brown to a loose ball, crossed it from the bye-line, and there was Herd flying in with a diving header.

So when Mackay was carried off, Spurs' lead had been reduced to just one goal and, soon after the interval, Herd scored again to level the scores.

This should have spelt the end for Spurs. But they immediately went onto the attack. They broke through on the left with John White, who floated a perfect cross for Jimmy Greaves to score with a rare header. So they were in front again.

They held out until Charlton latched on to a floated Crerand pass and smashed a volley home, and then, with only two minutes remaining, the same player lashed in the winner from another Crerand pass to provide the game with a dramatic climax — but you had to feel sorry for Spurs.

FOOTBALL FOCUS

● England beat Northern Ireland 8–3 on 20 November in the first international at Wembley played entirely under lights.

● There was a First Division goal glut on Boxing Day, when 66 goals were scored in 10 games. Fulham beat Ipswich Town by 10–1, and leaders Blackburn won 8–2 at West Ham.

● Oxford United, in only their second season since being elected to the League, beat Blackburn 3–1 to become the first Fourth Division side to reach the quarter-finals of the FA Cup. Earlier, non-League Bedford Town won 2-1 at Second Division Newcastle in the third round.

● Jim Fryatt of Bradford PA scored the fastest goal on record on 25 April against Tranmere Rovers, timed by the referee's watch at four seconds.

● England beat USA 10–0 in New York on 27 May, but lost 5–1 to Brazil three days later in Rio.

● On 25 May, the blackest day in football history, more than 300 died in Lima during riots after a Peruvian goal against Argentina was disallowed.

Rioting at Lima leads to 300 deaths.

Bold Boyce hits West Ham's Cup-winner in injury time

The ball is tantalizingly over the line for Hurst's goal.

IN THE MOST exciting FA Cup final since the "Matthews match" 11 years ago, West Ham twice came from behind to beat Second Division Preston 3–2, with Ron Boyce scoring the winner in the second minute of time added on for stoppages.

It became clear from the start that this was not going to be a walk-over for the First Division side. Preston matched them in skills, and scored first, after 10 minutes. Howard Kendall, at 17 years 345 days the youngest ever FA Cup-finalist, started the move, Dawson's shot was only parried, and Holden forced the ball in. West Ham, despite looking nervous, equalized immediately. Skipper Bobby Moore stole the ball and moved upfield before finding Byrne, who put 18-year-old John Sissons away on a fine run, finishing with a shot past Kelly.

Undaunted, Preston continued to have the better of the game in the first half, controlling the midfield in which young Kendall was prominent. They deservedly regained the lead five minutes before half-time when Dawson headed in from a corner.

Manager Ron Greenwood changed West Ham's tactics at the interval, and they began to erode Preston's midfield superiority. Eventually a Hurst header hit the bar, rebounded against Kelly, and rolled slowly over the line. So the Hammers were level with 38 minutes left.

Both teams were tiring, but not Hurst, who went on one last powerful run through the middle before slipping the ball out to Brabrook on the right. The former England winger cut in before floating a centre to the far post for Boyce to head the ball back into the opposite corner for the dramatic winner.

FINAL SCORE

Football League
Division 1: Liverpool
Top scorer: Jimmy Greaves (Tottenham Hotspur) 35
Division 2: Leeds United
Division 3: Coventry City
Division 4: Gillingham
Footballer of the Year: Bobby Moore (West Ham United)

FA Cup Final
West Ham United 3 Preston North End 2

League Cup Final
Leicester City beat Stoke City 1–1, 3–2

Scottish League
Division 1: Rangers
Top scorer: Alan Gilzean (Dundee) 32
Division 2: Morton

Scottish FA Cup Final
Rangers 3 Dundee 1

Scottish League Cup Final
Rangers 5 Morton 0

International Championship
England, N. Ireland, Scotland, 4 pts

European Cup Final
Inter-Milan 3 Real Madrid 1

Cup-Winners' Cup Final
Sporting Lisbon 3 MTK Budapest 3
Replay: Lisbon 1 MTK Budapest 0

Inter-Cities Fairs Cup Final
Real Zaragoza 2 Valencia 1

European Footballer of the Year 1963
Lev Yashin (Moscow Dynamo & USSR)

World Club Championship
Inter-Milan (Italy) beat Independiente (Argentina) 0–1, 2–0, 1–0

Farewell Sir Stan: England maestro retires at 50

INTERNATIONAL footballers past and present paid tribute to Sir Stanley Matthews at Stoke on Wednesday night, 28 April, in a special benefit match to celebrate his retirement. The ageless maestro was knighted in the New Year, the first footballer to be so honoured. He played his last first-class match on 6 February, five days after his 50th birthday, when he helped Stoke beat Fulham 3–1.

It is incredible to think that Matthews made his League debut for Stoke in March 1932 at the age of 17 — 33 years ago. The remarkable career of the "Wizard of the Dribble" for Stoke, Blackpool and England (54 caps) is now part of football folklore. He showed all his familiar tricks on the right wing in his farewell match against an International XI that included Alfredo di Stefano, Ferenc Puskas, Lev Yashin and Josef Masopust, and he was carried off shoulder-high in triumph at the end.

Sir Stan on the shoulders of Yashin (left) and Puskas.

John White killed by lightning

JOHN WHITE, the Spurs and Scotland inside-forward, was struck by lightning and killed while playing golf on 21 July. His wife had dropped him at the Crews Hill club, Enfield, and he had just driven off the first tee when it started raining. He took shelter under a line of oak trees, and was seen sitting under one by golfers running for the clubhouse. There was a single flash of lightning, and White's body was found later by two groundsmen.

White's tragic death at 27 is a terrible blow to his family, to Spurs and to football as a whole. His frail physique belied the strength in his legs, and although he was known best for his defence-splitting passes, he also had a fierce shot. He earned the nickname the "Ghost of White Hart Lane" for his uncanny ability to drift unseen into dangerous positions. His midfield partnership with Danny Blanchflower was at the heart of Spurs' "double" triumph in 1961 and their later successes in domestic and European cups. He won 22 international caps, and will be sorely missed by both club and country.

Footballers jailed for match-fixing: internationals Kay and Swan among those found guilty

TEN PROFESSIONAL footballers were found guilty at Nottingham Assizes on 26 January of "fixing" match results. They were all sent to prison. Aberdeen-born Jimmy Gauld, an inside-forward who played for Charlton, Everton, Plymouth, Swindon and Mansfield between 1955 and 1960, was sentenced to four years with £5,000 costs, while the others received terms of between four and 15 months.

After years of rumours, Gauld, who was found to be at the centre of the conspiracy, decided last April to "tell all" to a Sunday paper, for which he received £7,000. The evidence for these articles was later handed to the Director of Public Prosecutions. Among those jailed are former England players, centre-half Peter Swan (Sheffield Wednesday) and left-half Tony Kay (Everton, formerly with Wednesday), along with David Layne (Wednesday) and former Celtic and Scottish Under-23 keeper Dick Beattie, who also played for Portsmouth and Peterborough. The Football Association are to obtain transcripts of the court proceedings before deciding what action they will take.

Agony of Dave Mackay: breaks leg again in comeback match

SPURS AND SCOTLAND left-half Dave Mackay has broken his leg again in his comeback match after nine gritty months spent regaining fitness. Playing for the reserves against Shrewsbury Reserves at White Hart Lane on 14 September, he suddenly spun agonizingly to the ground just outside the opposition penalty area, clutching the same left leg that he broke against Manchester United in the European Cup-Winners' Cup.

There are no stouter hearts in football than the fearless midfield dynamo, inspiration of all his colleagues. But he will need all his courage, only two months from his 30th birthday, to come back again from such a devastating blow.

Mackay goes down in agony, clutching his broken leg.

Hammers triumphant in Wembley classic

BOBBY MOORE climbed the Wembley stairs to collect another trophy, little more than a year after leading West Ham to FA Cup victory, when the Hammers beat Munich 1860 by 2–0 in the final of the European Cup-Winners' Cup. With both sides going out from the start to play attacking football, the 100,000 crowd enjoyed one of the finest matches ever seen at Wembley Stadium. And it was played in a highly sporting manner throughout.

West Ham's triumph is the perfect tribute to manager Ron Greenwood's belief in positive, stylish football, and Wembley was the ideal setting for it. With the inexperienced Alan Sealey and Brian Dear replacing injured England international forwards Brabrook and Byrne, the Hammers fans could be excused for feeling apprehensive. But both newcomers blended in seamlessly from the start, and it was Sealey who scored both goals, in the 69th and 71st minutes, to bring the trophy to England for the second time.

Sealey (right) celebrates his second goal with Martin Peters.

Extra-time drama as Liverpool lift Cup: Leeds suffer second let-down in a week

LIVERPOOL BEAT Leeds 2–1 at Wembley in the FA Cup final, all the goals coming in extra time. For Leeds, still in with a chance of the "double" only a week ago, it was their second disappointment in six days. On Monday, while they drew 3–3 at Birmingham, Manchester United beat Arsenal 3–1 to pip them for the League title on goal average.

Liverpool thoroughly deserved their first Cup win. The football, although not in itself remarkable, was played in a highly-charged emotional atmosphere, and the passionate singing of the Liverpool fans, before, during and after the match, will be the abiding memory of the occasion. Leeds, in their first final, started as favourites, but could not get their attack going, although they defended superbly. There was, fortunately, none of the unpleasantness too frequently associated with Leeds teams this season.

For Liverpool, Stevenson was outstanding in the middle, and Tommy Smith, playing as an extra centre-half, helped them win midfield control. After three minutes of extra time, Liverpool finally found a way through when Hunt stooped low to head in a cross from Byrne, later found to have played 115 minutes with a broken collar-bone. This setback would have finished most sides, especially in the heavy rain and on the energy-sapping Wembley turf, but not Don Revie's men. Charlton, stealing up into attack, nodded down a Hunter lob, and there was the dynamic Bremner, still full of fire, to hit an unstoppable volley.

Liverpool were stunned, but they too are fighters, and with nine minutes left St John met a Callaghan cross with his head to flash it past Sprake. The refrains of "Ee-ay-addio, we won the Cup" seemed to go on for ever.

St John powers a header into the Leeds goal for the winner.

FOOTBALL FOCUS

- Portsmouth and England wing-half Jimmy Dickinson retired with a record 764 League appearances for his only club. He made his League debut in 1946, won two Championship medals and played 48 times for England.
- Shrewsbury player-manager Arthur Rowley hung up his boots in February with a British record of 434 League goals to his name. He made his debut in 1946 and scored his goals with West Brom (four), Fulham (27), Leicester (251) and Shrewsbury (152) in a total of 619 matches.
- The players found guilty in the courts of match-fixing were suspended for life by the FA in April.
- Kilmarnock needed to win by two clear goals at Hearts in the last match of the season to pip them on goal average for the title. They did just that, and claimed their first Scottish Championship.

FINAL SCORE

Football League
Division 1: Manchester United
Top scorer: Jimmy Greaves (Tottenham Hotspur), Andy McEvoy (Blackburn) 29
Division 2: Newcastle United
Division 3: Carlisle United
Division 4: Brighton & Hove Albion
Footballer of the Year: Bobby Collins (Leeds U)

FA Cup Final
Liverpool 2 Leeds United 1
(after extra time)

League Cup Final
Chelsea beat Leicester City 3–2, 0–0

Scottish League
Division 1: Kilmarnock
Top scorer: Jim Forrest (Rangers) 30
Division 2: Stirling Albion
Footballer of the Year: Billy McNeill (Celtic)

Scottish FA Cup Final
Celtic 3 Dunfermline Ath 2

Scottish League Cup Final
Rangers 2 Celtic 1

International Championship
England, 5 pts

European Cup Final
Inter-Milan 1 Benfica 0

Cup-Winners' Cup Final
West Ham United 2 Munich 1860 0

Inter-Cities Fairs Cup Final
Ferencvaros 1 Juventus 0

European Footballer of the Year 1964
Denis Law (Manchester United & Scotland)

World Club Championship
Inter-Milan (Italy) beat Independiente (Argentina) 3–0, 0–0

'El Beatle' gives Benfica a hard day's night

MANCHESTER UNITED went to Lisbon with a slender one-goal lead for the second leg of their quarter-final European Cup tie against Benfica, twice winners of the trophy and twice runners-up in the last five years. The Portuguese champions had a formidable home record in Europe and had been quite happy to come away from Old Trafford with a 3–2 defeat. United, up against the likes of Eusebio, Coluna and Germano, would have their work cut out to gain the draw they needed to take them through to the semi-finals in this, their first year back in the competition since the Munich air crash in 1958.

Manager Matt Busby told his side to play a holding game for the first 20 minutes, but George Best, as Busby joked after the game, "must have had cotton wool in his ears". The young Irishman with the Beatle hairstyle proceeded to take Benfica's defence apart, and put United two up in only 12 minutes. Best, not yet 20 but already capped 12 times by Northern Ireland, and a major force in United's title-winning side last year, has just about every skill in the game. His first goal was a perfectly timed header from a Dunne free-kick. It stunned the crowd to silence. The second, a swerving, jinking run right through the Benfica defence to slide the ball past Costa Pereira in goal, had them gasping in astonishment.

Hardly had the crowd recovered their breath from this onslaught than left-winger John Connelly scored a third to put United 6–2 up on aggregate. Benfica tried to salvage some of their self-respect in the second half, but their main striking force Eusebio was being well held by the ungainly Stiles, and their only consolation was a Brennan back-pass that beat his own keeper. Then, in the last few minutes, Law put wing-half Crerand through for the fourth, and Bobby Charlton went on one of his majestic solo runs from his own half before slamming the ball wide of the keeper. The final tally was 5–1 — what a scoreline! In Benfica's own Stadium of Light! This was one of the finest team performances by a side away from home in European competition. But the Portuguese have already singled out one hero — brilliant George Best or, as they now call him in Portugal, "El Beatle".

George Best, "El Beatle", with United fans.

Liverpool clinch League: Arsenal's record equalled

LIVERPOOL WON the League easing up, finishing their programme with a draw at Nottingham Forest on 10 May after clinching the title 10 days earlier, when they beat Chelsea 2–1 at Anfield. In between, however, they lost in the European Cup-Winners' Cup final to Borussia Dortmund.

Under Bill Shankly's shrewd guidance, Liverpool have emerged as arguably England's leading side, and certainly the most consistent, with their third major honour in three years. They finished on 61 points, six ahead of runners-up Leeds, and have equalled Arsenal's record of seven League titles. They have also set a record by winning the Championship using the remarkable total of only 14 players — virtually 12, as two players made only four appearances between them, one of them in the last match.

A well-balanced side with a strong defence, in which Tommy Smith and skipper Ron Yeats serve as twin stoppers, Liverpool conceded only 34 goals. Roger Hunt was their top scorer for the fifth season running, with 30 League goals, and he and Ian St John have enjoyed excellent service from wingers Peter Thompson and Ian Callaghan, the latter ever-present, as he was in the title-winning side of two years ago. Liverpool took over at the top on 27 November, and were never headed after that.

Liverpool, the FA Cup-holders, went out at home to Chelsea in the third round this time, but atoned for that lapse in champion style.

A jubilant Liverpool acclaim Roger Hunt's second goal against Chelsea, knowing the title is theirs.

FOOTBALL FOCUS

- On the first day of the season, 21 August, Charlton's Keith Peacock became the first player to come on as substitute, against Bolton at Burnden Park in Division Two, under the new rule allowing one substitute for an injured player.

- When Frank Saul was sent off against Burnley at Turf Moor on 4 December, it marked the end of a proud and probably unique record for Spurs, who had not had a player dismissed in a League match since 27 October 1928.

- The Italian FA, satisfied that Roma had actively encouraged the crowd disorder in the Fairs Cup tie against Chelsea, fined them a derisory £500, although the Fairs Cup committee banned them from participation for three years. Chelsea and Leeds were both knocked out in semi-final play-offs.

- Billy Wright has been unable to repeat his onfield success in the managerial chair, and parted company with Arsenal at the end of the season to take up a career in television.

More violence in the 'Not Fairs' Cup

THE VIOLENT Leeds-Valencia clash in the third round of the Inter-Cities Fairs Cup on 2 February at Elland Road provided yet another reason for branding this season's competition the "Not Fairs" Cup. At the unedifying sight of Jack Charlton furiously chasing an opponent round the pitch, the police went on to intervene and the referee ordered both sides to their dressing-rooms for a 10-minute cooling-off period. Charlton stayed off, and two Valencia players were also dismissed from a scandalous game that finished 1–1.

This season's tournament has been marked by a series of violent incidents. Leeds suffered a terrible blow in the first round, in Italy against Torino, when a tackle from Poletti broke captain Bobby Collins's thigh. But the most scandalous tie was the Chelsea-Roma first-round clash, in which Eddie McCreadie was sent off in the Stamford Bridge brawl (won 4–1 by Chelsea) for retaliating, and in the return, won 1–0 by Roma, the crowd, fired up by the Italian Press, pelted Chelsea with an avalanche of rubble and rubbish and stoned their coach as it left the stadium.

World Cup found: unearthed by dog in a London front garden

A WEEK AFTER it was stolen when on show at a stamp exhibition in Westminster, the World Cup has been found by a dog out for a walk with his owner. The little black and white mongrel, called Pickles, has saved the embarrassment not only of the Football Association but of the whole country.

Londoner David Corbett was walking Pickles in Norwood, a South London suburb, when the dog disappeared into a front garden. Mr Corbett found him digging up a brown paper parcel, and was astonished to find it contained the Jules Rimet Trophy. Mr Corbett stands to gain a considerable reward, and no doubt there will also be some juicy bones for the four-legged hero.

Hero Pickles, World Cup saviour.

Double by Trebilcock sparks Everton Cup comeback

OUTSIDERS Sheffield Wednesday almost had the Cup in their grasp at Wembley, but defensive errors in the last half-hour allowed Everton to complete a thrilling comeback. The Everton hero, with two goals, was 21-year-old Mike Trebilcock, a surprise replacement up front for their experienced and expensive top scorer, Fred Pickering.

Everton, who reached Wembley without conceding a goal in seven matches, found themselves one down in four minutes to Wednesday, who had reached the final without a single home draw. Centre-forward Jim McCalliog, a Chelsea discard and the brains behind the constantly switching Wednesday attack, fired in a shot that was deflected past the helpless Gordon West. Wednesday went further ahead after 57 minutes through Dave Ford. But Trebilcock flashed a half-volley past Springett in the next minute to make it 2–1.

The first of the errors came five minutes later, when a poor headed clearance by Wednesday's inexperienced centre-half Sam Ellis, a stand-in for the injured Vic Mobley, let Trebilcock in for another chance which he gladly accepted. Everton's third goal was a personal tragedy for another defender, Gerry Young, who failed to control a harmless-looking punt, and left-winger Temple, with a clear run on goal, slipped the ball past Springett for a dramatic winner.

FINAL SCORE

Football League
Division 1: Liverpool
Top scorer: Roger Hunt (Liverpool) 30
Division 2: Manchester City
Division 3: Hull City
Division 4: Doncaster Rovers
Footballer of the Year: Bobby Charlton (Manchester United)

FA Cup Final
Everton 3 Sheffield Wed 2

League Cup Final
WBA beat West Ham United 1–2, 4–1

Scottish League
Division 1: Celtic
Top scorer: Joe McBride (Celtic), Alex Ferguson (Dunfermline Athletic) 31
Division 2: Ayr United
Footballer of the Year: John Greig (Rangers)

Scottish FA Cup Final
Rangers 0 Celtic 0
Replay: Rangers 1 Celtic 0

Scottish League Cup Final
Celtic 2 Rangers 1

International Championship
England, 5 pts

European Cup Final
Real Madrid 2 Partizan Belgrade 1

Cup-Winners' Cup Final
Borussia Dortmund 2 Liverpool 1
(after extra time)

Inter-Cities Fairs Cup Final
Barcelona beat Real Zaragoza 0–1, 4–2

European Footballer of the Year 1965
Eusebio (Benfica & Portugal)

World Club Championship
Penarol (Uruguay) beat Real Madrid (Spain) 2–0, 2–0

Trebilcock (8) wheels away after beating Springett for Everton's equaliser.

The Boys of '66

When Alf Ramsey took over as manager of the England team on 1 May 1963, he gave an interview to a local reporter in Ipswich, where he was ending a successful eight-year spell with Ipswich Town. "England will win the World Cup in 1966," said Ramsey. This remark came to haunt him over the next three years as he tried to mould an England team that would have at least a sporting chance.

RAMSEY SOON sorted out his defence, giving caps to George Cohen, Jack Charlton and Nobby Stiles. With Gordon Banks, Ray Wilson and skipper Bobby Moore, he had a firm base. Bobby Charlton and Jimmy Greaves were established up front. The rest was to come very late, with Martin Peters who, Ramsey said, was "ten years ahead of his time", and Alan Ball staking a midfield claim. However, it was among the wingers that the manager had his big problems. Among those tried were Peter Thompson, Bobby Tambling, Gordon Harris, Alan Hinton, Terry Paine, Ian Callaghan and John Connelly, the last three all playing in early World Cup matches. But by the quarter-finals Ramsey had dispensed with wingers altogether, and Geoff Hurst finally came into his own as a replacement for the injured Greaves. Ramsey's team of "wingless wonders" was complete.

The demise of Brazil

Brazil, the holders, were the firm favourites when the finals began on 11 July. Their group, played in the north-west, was the strongest, including also Hungary and Portugal. Pele scored the first goal of the tournament as Brazil beat Bulgaria 2–0 at Goodison Park, but vicious tackling virtually put him out of the competition. He was unable to play against Hungary, who won a marvellous match 3–1, Brazil's first World Cup defeat since Hungary, again, beat them in the "Battle of Berne" in 1954. Brazil then needed to beat Portugal, but the returning Pele was literally and disgracefully kicked out of it again, Eusebio was inspired, and Brazil went down, and out, 3–1.

England's matches were all at Wembley. The opener was a dreadful goalless stalemate with Uruguay. But England got under way in their second match, a great individual effort by Bobby Charlton, climaxed with a 20-yard drive, setting them on their way to a 2–0 win over Mexico. The game with France, also won 2–0, with both goals by Roger Hunt on his 28th birthday, brought trouble when Stiles perpetrated such a bad foul (ignored by the referee) that FA Council members suggested he should be left out of the team thereafter. Ramsey threatened to resign if he could not pick the players he wanted, and the FA Council backed down. England qualified with Uruguay.

The greatest shock came in Group 4 at Middlesbrough. The defensive Italians, needing only a draw with the mysterious North Koreans to be virtually certain of going through, contrived to lose 1–0, and were eliminated. Pak Doo Ik was the unlikely name on the scoresheet. The efficient West Germans and talented Argentinians were too good for Spain and Switzerland in Group 2 and also went through.

The Rattin incident

England's quarter-final with Argentina proved explosive. For the first time, England played without wingers, using a 4–4–2 combination in which the front men were Hunt, with three goals already to his credit, and Hurst. Despite a penchant for petty fouling, for which many were booked, the Argentinians played well and looked the more likely winners until their outstanding skipper Antonio Rattin intervened when the referee was booking yet another of his teammates. He appeared to be abusing the referee and, already booked once, was sent off. But he refused to go, and it took 10 minutes and the deployment of several officials before he went.

Thirteen minutes from the end, England finally scored — a glancing header from Hurst. The referee was escorted off the pitch with a heavy police guard. Ramsey physically prevented Cohen swapping shirts with an opponent and, after more disgraceful behaviour from the Argentinians in the dressing-rooms, likened them to "animals", a justifiable but perhaps imprudent remark.

There was a sensation of a different kind at Goodison, and nobody could believe the intermediate scoreline flashed around the country, "North Korea 3 Portugal 0". Eusebio finally pulled his team together and scored four (two penalties) as Portugal recovered to win 5–3.

The Uruguayans, a goal down to West Germany and smarting after having a penalty appeal for handball turned down, proceeded to lose their heads. They had two men sent off, and three late goals gave the Germans a 4–0 victory when, in the first half, Uruguay had been the better side. The USSR caught Hungary on an off day and won the fourth semi-final place.

A classic semi-final

England's semi-final with Portugal was a classic match of good, clean, sporting football. Nearly an hour had gone by before the referee blew for the first foul. Stiles managed to keep Eusebio reasonably quiet, while Bobby Charlton was finding more space for his forays from midfield to the Portuguese penalty area. In the 31st minute, Pereira, the Portuguese keeper, dashed to the edge of the box to beat Hunt to a through-ball, but it ricocheted to Charlton, following up, and he side-footed it in from outside the area.

Ten minutes from time, Charlton scored a great second, running on to a ball pulled back by Hurst to hammer it into the far corner. It is an indication of the sportsmanship of this match that the Portuguese players congratulated Charlton — one shook his hand — as he trotted back to the centre circle. Shortly afterwards, Jack Charlton fisted the ball out from under the bar, and Eusebio scored from the spot — the first goal Banks had conceded in the tournament. Portugal pressed for the remaining seven minutes, to no avail.

West Germany beat the USSR in the other semi-final, in a match that turned on an incident just before half-time. The Soviets' Chislenko seemed to be badly fouled, but the referee did not

'And there are some people on the pitch. They think it's all over... IT IS NOW!'
KENNETH WOLSTENHOLME — the famous lines of his World Cup final commentary as Geoff Hurst scored in the 120th minute.

England skipper Bobby Moore holds the Jules Rimet Trophy aloft after a pulsating final.

blow, and West Germany carried on to open the scoring. On the resumption, the incensed Chislenko kicked the first German he came across, and was sent off. West Germany won 2–1.

A late equalizer

The final opened badly for England when, after 13 minutes, Haller scored from an attempted Wilson clearance. Six minutes later, however, the West Ham connection registered an equalizer as Moore's free-kick was headed in by Hurst. With 12 minutes left in the game, a Hurst shot was blocked and the third West Ham finalist, Martin Peters, slammed the ball in. England seemed to be home.

But the Germans scored an equalizer in the dying seconds. A disputed free-kick against Jack Charlton found its way across the England goal — arguably via a German hand — and Weber netted from close in. Thirty gruelling minutes of extra time were now necessary.

The disputed goal

Of all World Cup controversies, England's goal after 10 minutes of extra time remains one of the biggest. Ball, with typical energy, chased a forlorn long ball towards the right-hand corner flag, caught it and pulled it back to the ever-available Hurst near the angle of the six-yard box. Hurst turned and hooked the ball past Tilkowski on to the underside of the bar. The ball bounced down almost straight, but then bounced up and out of goal. The inrushing Hunt, instead of trying to put it in, wheeled round with his arm aloft, convinced that the ball had crossed the line. Charlton thought that it had, too. Weber headed it away behind the goal.

There was a heart-stopping delay while Swiss referee Gottfried Dienst consulted his Soviet linesman, Tofik Bakhramov, who signalled towards the centre spot. England led 3–2. The goal is still argued about today, and film evidence, while inconclusive, veers towards the German view that the ball did not cross the line. But in the last minute, Moore, cool as ever under pressure, floated a long clearance to Hurst, who ran on and hit a fabulous fourth for his hat-trick. England had won 4–2. Ramsey's prophecy was fulfilled. And the country that gave football to the world had finally won the World Cup.

FINAL SCORE

Group 1

England	0	Uruguay	0
France	1	Mexico	1
Uruguay	2	France	1
England	2	Mexico	0
Uruguay	0	Mexico	0
England	2	France	0

	P	W	D	L	F	A	P
England	3	2	1	0	4	0	5
Uruguay	3	1	2	0	2	1	4
Mexico	3	0	2	1	1	3	2
France	3	0	1	2	2	5	1

Group 2

West Germany	5	Switzerland	0
Argentina	2	Spain	1
Spain	2	Switzerland	1
Argentina	0	West Germany	0
Argentina	2	Switzerland	0
West Germany	2	Spain	1

	P	W	D	L	F	A	P
W.Germany	3	2	1	0	7	1	5
Argentina	3	2	1	0	4	1	5
Spain	3	1	0	2	4	5	2
Switzerland	3	0	0	3	1	9	0

Group 3

Brazil	2	Bulgaria	0
Portugal	3	Hungary	1
Hungary	3	Brazil	1
Portugal	3	Bulgaria	0
Portugal	3	Brazil	1
Hungary	3	Bulgaria	1

	P	W	D	L	F	A	P
Portugal	3	3	0	0	9	2	6
Hungary	3	2	0	1	7	5	4
Brazil	3	1	0	2	4	6	2
Bulgaria	3	0	0	3	1	8	0

Group 4

USSR	3	North Korea	0
Italy	2	Chile	0
Chile	1	North Korea	1
USSR	1	Italy	0
North Korea	1	Italy	0
USSR	2	Chile	1

	P	W	D	L	F	A	P
USSR	3	3	0	0	6	1	6
North Korea	3	1	1	1	2	4	3
Italy	3	1	0	2	2	2	2
Chile	3	0	1	2	2	5	1

QUARTER-FINALS

England	1	Argentina	0
West Germany	4	Uruguay	0
Portugal	5	North Korea	3
USSR	2	Hungary	1

SEMI-FINALS

West Germany	2	USSR	1
England	2	Portugal	1

THIRD-PLACE MATCH

Portugal	2	USSR	1

FINAL

England	4	West Germany	2

(after extra time)
Wembley, 30 July 1966. Attendance 93,000
England: Banks, Cohen, Wilson, Stiles, Charlton J, Moore, Ball, Hurst, Hunt, Charlton R, Peters (Scorers: Hurst (3), Peters)
West Germany: Tilkowski, Hottges, Schnellinger, Beckenbauer, Schulz, Weber, Held, Haller, Seeler, Overath, Emmerich (Scorers: Haller, Weber)

Leading scorers 9 Eusebio (Portugal) 5 Haller (West Germany) 4 Beckenbauer (West Germany) Hurst (England) Porkujan (USSR)

League Cup comes to Wembley: QPR win thriller

THE FOOTBALL League Cup has come alive. The first Wembley final of this unpopular and largely unwanted competition could not have made a better impact, as Third Division Queen's Park Rangers came back in the last half-hour from two down to beat the holders West Bromwich 3–2.

Known as "Hardaker's Horror" after Alan Hardaker, the Football League secretary whose brainchild it was in 1960, the League Cup has only recently been contested, somewhat reluctantly, by all the League's leading teams. The glamour of Wembley — and a 30,000 allocation of tickets to each of the competing clubs — drew a crowd of 97,952, which was some 28,000 more than the aggregate attendance of any of the previous finals.

It was no surprise when West Bromwich went into an early lead, and it was thanks largely to QPR's veteran left-back Jim Langley that they were only two up at the break, both goals being scored by former Rangers left-winger Clive Clark. But a half-time pep-talk from wily manager Alec Stock sent QPR out a new team. After 18 minutes, Roger Morgan headed them back into the game. Twelve minutes later, the inspirational Rodney Marsh picked the ball up on the half-way line, jinked his way through the defence and struck a low shot in off a post.

Now Rangers were on top, and they piled on the pressure, although the winner was a controversial goal scored by winger Mark Lazarus after West Brom keeper Dick Sheppard had lost the ball in a collision with QPR centre-half Ron Hunt. Sadly, QPR will not be able to take advantage of the new League Cup "carrot" of qualification for the Fairs Cup — which is open only to First Division clubs — but they will be more concerned with their bid for promotion.

Rodney Marsh, the King of Sheperd's Bush, entertains the QPR fans.

Scottish shock of the century: Berwick beat Rangers in Cup!

IT WAS A CASE OF "Jock the Giant-killer" at Shielfield Park, where a jubilant, if incredulous, record 13,365 crowd saw Berwick Rangers knock mighty Glasgow Rangers out of the Scottish FA Cup in the first round. The Berwick hero was Jock Wallace, their goalkeeper-manager, who kept the marauding Rangers forwards at bay with a string of spectacular saves after Sammy Reid had put Berwick ahead in the 32nd minute.

Berwick, the only club in the Scottish League whose ground is in England, have never finished higher than eighth in Division Two. But they have enjoyed previous giant-killing fame in the Cup. In 1953–54, two years before they were elected to the League, they beat Ayr 5–1 and First Division Dundee 3–0 before losing to Rangers 4–0 in the quarter-finals. And three years ago they reached the semi-finals of the League Cup before Rangers, again, beat them 3–1.

This time they got their revenge over the Cup-holders, the team that have won the trophy four times in the last five years. It is arguably the most sensational result in the history of Scottish soccer.

Rangers keeper Martin cannot believe that Berwick have scored.

Celtic 'Kings of Europe': grand slam for Jock Stein's men

CELTIC'S stirring victory in Lisbon over Inter-Milan in the final of the European Cup is a triumph for attacking football over the ultra-defensive Italian style that has been threatening to suffocate the game on the Continent. Former captain Jock Stein has worked wonders since he took charge at Parkhead two years ago. First he transformed the ailing club into the best team in Scotland, and now they have proved themselves truly "Kings of Europe".

No British side had even reached the final before, but Celtic went into the match brimful of confidence, having cleaned up at home in League, Cup and League Cup — their first domestic "treble". Now they were going for the "grand slam". But the 12,000 fans who travelled to Portugal to lend their vociferous support to the "Bhoys" were briefly silenced after only eight minutes when Mazzola converted a penalty.

This was the signal for Inter to retreat into their shell, and for the rest of the game it was Celtic's attack against the formidable Italian defence. Tricky right-winger Jimmy Johnstone proceeded to give Burgnich a trying time, and Bobby Murdoch put himself majestically in control of the midfield. But Celtic's greatest threat was their overlapping backs, Jim Craig and particularly Tommy Gemmell on the left.

With Sarti performing heroics in goal, and Auld and Gemmell both hitting the bar, it was well into the second half before Celtic broke the Italians down. Gemmell fed Murdoch, who switched play to the right. Craig cut the ball back across field for the advancing Gemmell to take it in his stride and hammer it past Sarti from 25 yards. Six minutes from time, the heroic Gemmell moved up again on the left and squared the ball to Murdoch, who drove the ball low into the crowded penalty area. As Sarti moved to cover it, Steve Chalmers deflected it past him for the winner.

What a climax! That was Celtic's 200th goal of the season, in 64 games, and they had won everything they entered. But above all, they had won the battle for the attacking game.

Ronnie Simpson gathers a cross in Lisbon.

FINAL SCORE

Football League
Division 1: Manchester United
Top scorer: Ron Davies (Southampton) 37
Division 2: Coventry City
Division 3: Queen's Park Rangers
Division 4: Stockport County
Footballer of the Year: Jack Charlton (Leeds United)

FA Cup Final
Tottenham Hotspur 2 Chelsea 1

League Cup Final
QPR 3 WBA 2

Scottish League
Division 1: Celtic
Top scorer: Steve Chalmers (Celtic) 21
Division 2: Morton
Footballer of the Year: Ronnie Simpson (Celtic)

Scottish FA Cup Final
Celtic 2 Aberdeen 0

Scottish League Cup Final
Celtic 1 Rangers 0

International Championship
Scotland, 5 pts

European Cup Final
Celtic 2 Inter-Milan 1

Cup-Winners' Cup Final
Bayern Munich 1 Rangers 0
(after extra time)

Inter-Cities Fairs Cup Final
Dynamo Zagreb beat Leeds United 2–0, 0–0

European Footballer of the Year 1966
Bobby Charlton (Manchester United & England)

World Club Championship
Racing Club (Argentina) beat Celtic 0–1, 2–1, 1–0

FOOTBALL FOCUS

- England's Alan Ball moved from Blackpool to Everton for £110,000 in August, the first £100,000 transfer between British clubs.
- Billy Ferguson (Linfield) became the first Irish footballer to be sent off in an international, and the first ever player in the Home International Championship, when N.Ireland lost 2–0 to England in Belfast on 22 October.
- England manager Alf Ramsey was knighted in the New Year's honours list.
- Blackpool beat Newcastle 6–0 on 22 October in a Division One match, not an unusual result except that it was their only home win. Needless to say, they finished bottom of the table.
- England lost their first game since winning the World Cup, on 15 April at Wembley, 3–2 to Scotland, whose delirious fans regarded it as their own World Championship and proceeded to invade the pitch at the end and cut out pieces of turf.
- Rangers just failed to make it a Scottish double in Europe when they lost the Cup-Winners' Cup final 1–0 to Bayern Munich in extra time.

Cockerels coast through Cockney final

IN THE FIRST all-London FA Cup final this century, Spurs enjoyed a much easier victory over Chelsea than the final 2–1 scoreline suggests. It was their third Cup win in the sixties, but only two men remained from their previous success in 1962 — Dave Mackay and Jimmy Greaves. Bill Nicholson has built another fine footballing side after the break-up of the "double" team, the heart of which was wrenched out with the retirement of Blanchflower, the tragic death of White and the serious injuries to Mackay. But Mackay's undoubted courage has never been better demonstrated than by his double comeback, and it was entirely appropriate that he should lead the new Spurs to their latest triumph.

Spurs seemed to stroll through the match, always in control, individually and collectively superior to a Chelsea side they never allowed into the game. Up front, Greaves and Gilzean were always dangerous; at the back England was dominant. Chelsea's few threats came from Charlie Cooke's exciting but erratic dribbling.

Spurs went ahead on the stroke of half-time when Mullery broke down the middle and his shot was blocked to Robertson, who swept it in past Bonetti. Saul put them two up midway through the second half with a spectacular hook shot on the turn. Tambling's goal for Chelsea four minutes from time never threatened to disturb the result of the match.

Heroes of the Sixties

By David Miller

The sixties were significant in three respects. It was the last decade in which there still existed in Britain a profusion of individually talented players — a few of them such as John Charles and Stanley Matthews, Danny Blanchflower and Jimmy McIlroy survivors from the Fifties — and simultaneously there was the remorseless advance of defensive strategies, stretching the laws to the limit and designed to stifle the stars. Defensiveness was aided by a dramatic rise in fitness, players covering twice the ground, eliminating space.

It was a philosophy perfected by Helenio Herrera and others abroad and emulated in Britain by Bill Shankly with Liverpool, Harry Catterick at Everton, Don Revie with Leeds, and to a reluctant degree by both Alf Ramsey as manager of England and Matt Busby with Manchester United. Ramsey was the absolute pragmatist, demonstrated first with his team-without-stars, Ipswich, and eventually, hastening his own demise, with England.

Busby, together will Bill Nicholson at Tottenham, clung to the conviction that the game was above all intended to be entertaining, that great players should be liberated, not chained. Yet long before 1969, Busby lamented that the game was becoming destructive. "Every team now has an acknowledged hard man," he said. "And some of them have two or more." At the same time, Nicholson was observing: "It is becoming more and more difficult to find skilful players. They are no longer there."

Danny Blanchflower, Irish jewel.

Seven of the best

It is no coincidence that the juxtaposition of many great players and highly developed tactical intelligence produced seven of the finest club teams this century: Burnley, Tottenham, Everton, Manchester United, Liverpool, Leeds and Manchester City. It did not matter which way you looked, there were exceptional players. In November 1960, an England Under-23 team had Mullery (Fulham), Labone (Everton) and Moore (West Ham) at half-back, Connelly (Burnley), Dobing (Blackburn), Baker (Hibernian), Fantham (Sheffield Wednesday) and Charlton (Manchester United) in attack. The contrast with today is sharp, when the one true master of the ball is the fading Paul Gascoigne and, in the absence of others, exaggeration is made of the ability of David Beckham and Ryan Giggs — who cross a lightweight ball no better than a dozen or more players did 30 years ago — and of Michael Owen.

The spread of Charles's 38 Welsh caps started in 1950, aged 18, up to 1964. Physically and metaphorically he was a colossus, a Corinthian in modesty and sportsmanship, equally adept at centre-half or centre-forward, a massive header of the ball yet perhaps the best tall dribbler there has been. With Juventus, he was adored, and helped win three League titles. Even more monumental was Matthews, returning to the Potteries from Blackpool in 1961, and winning a second Division Two title with Stoke 30 years after the first, in 1963 when, aged 48, he was again Footballer of the Year after a 15-year interval. At this age, his mesmerising footwork was still

Sir Stanley Matthews, football knight.

making seasoned full-backs such as Eddie McCreadie and Ray Wilson fall over in attempting to hold him.

The decade began with Wolves winning the FA Cup and narrowly losing the League to Burnley. Peter Broadbent was Wolves' guiding light, a refined passer who was never quite able to fulfil the same function for England. Stan Cullis, expressionless in the directors' box, watched McIlroy clinch the League for Burnley at Maine Road, seemingly dribbling in an endless figure of eight by the corner flag for the last quarter of an hour to play out time. For three seasons, together with Jimmy Anderson and others, McIlroy wove a tapestry of witchcraft under manager Harry Potts that was one of the finest sights in England. Brilliant in the 1958 World Cup when Northern Ireland charmed their way to the quarter-final, McIlroy was masterful in the FA Cup final of 1962 when Burnley had to concede to majestic Tottenham.

International action

What a wonderful year was 1961. Matching the sixth-sense vision of McIlroy was either Allchurch, who during a lengthy career with Swansea, Newcastle and Cardiff gained the then record of 68 Welsh caps. His passing was as lyrical as the voice of Charlotte Church, yet his shooting — 251 goals in 692 League matches — could be ferocious. In a World Cup qualifier against Spain in Madrid, outshining Del Sol and Di Stefano and scoring in a 1–1 draw, insufficient to take Wales to the finals in Chile, he had his finest hour.

Scotland were also unlucky not to reach those finals. In spite of failing in three qualifying competitions in the Sixties, this was perhaps the greatest era of Scottish football. In November 1961 they lost a play-off in Brussels against eventual runners-up Czechoslovakia. Behind an attack including Denis Law and Ian St John was the legendary Jim Baxter, one of the romantic Scottish figures ultimately undermined by his weakness for a bevy. It is debatable whether Baxter was the equal in talent of George Best. His touch, tactical perception and shooting were as acute. The difference, perhaps, was that while Best visibly took pleasure in destroying the opposition, Baxter at times seemed not to care.

Simply knowing that he was different from other men was enough for him. With Rangers he won 10 Scottish titles, lost the Cup-Winners' Cup final of 1961 to Fiorentina, and played for the Rest of the World against

West Ham's three England heroes (left to right): hat-trick hero Geoff Hurst, captain Bobby Moore and second goal scorer Martin Peters.

England in 1963. In the European Cup the next year he gave the greatest 90-minute performance by any British player I have ever seen, Best not excluded, when playing Rapid almost single-handedly in Vienna. Half-a-minute from the end he broke his ankle, following which he was never the same again.

Super Spurs

The English season 1960–61 had been dominated by Tottenham's historic double, masterminded by Blanchflower. Tottenham appeared to control matches almost at will. Before the Cup final against Leicester, a match which turned out to be somewhat of an anti-climax, Blanchflower gave me one of his obscure Irish aphorisms — "It appears that we appear to control." The most engaging football conversationalist, he was probably the outstanding captain in British history, the leader of Northern Ireland in the 1958 World Cup, and then, having just recovered from a cartilage operation aged 36, of Tottenham's Cup-Winners' Cup victory in 1963. Looking little more athletic than Eric Morecambe, Blanchflower could do with a ball what Ballesteros could with 14 golf clubs. Put simply, his craft was a joy to watch.

Tottenham's European semi-final at home to Benfica in 1962 was as tumultuous as any foreign cup tie ever played, at the heart of which was Dave Mackay, a passionate Scot with a will of iron. Twice recovering from a broken leg, Mackay was the James Bond to Blanchflower's Smiley. A heroic performance against Benfica proved to be in vain: few players in the Sixties left such an imprint.

Internationals

The 1962 World Cup in Chile saw the effective end of the international career of Johnny Haynes, one of the most astute long passers of all time. Often a one-man band at Fulham, he was the first to receive £100 a week when wages were freed, though as captain of club and country he tended to be too moody and intolerant of lesser men. Chile was the mid-point in the phenomenal career of Bobby Charlton, voted the best outside left of the tournament. It was Alf Ramsey who later guided Charlton towards the role of free-range midfield creator. His speed and shooting were an exhilarating sight during my own youth. His partnership at Old Trafford with Paddy Crerand, Denis Law and George Best produced unforgettable pinnacles. If Law's dazzling finishing and Best's voluptuous trickery drew awed admiration from all who saw them in action, there was an affection for Charlton that endures to this day. Best's meteoric, relatively brief peak reached its climax in the 1968 European Cup victory over Benfica. It is argued by some that Best was selfish, yet the magic and enjoyment that he brought to millions exceeded anything he took from the game.

Young guns

Great players tend to be both the personality and the soul of their team. Two such men were Alec Young and Ian St John: stealthy and deft, Young with the more imagination and St John with the greater physical resilience and exceptional heading, such as his fantastic winner in the FA Cup final of 1965. Through the mid-Sixties they gave Merseyside, Everton and Liverpool respectively, five titles between them. They brought ballet to the war-game.

Simultaneously, a formidable trio were emerging at West Ham, the nucleus of the team that would go on to win the World Cup: Bobby Moore, Geoff Hurst and Martin Peters. Here, concurrently were the best defensive mind, the best "target" centre-forward and the best attacking midfielder that England had ever possessed. Of Moore, Jock Stein, the Celtic manager, once said: "There should be a law against him. He sees things 20 minutes before anyone else." Ramsey said of Peters: "He is 10 years ahead of his time." So true. Only Bryan Robson and David Platt were to emulate him in later years. Missing from England's greatest moment, however, was the incomparable Jimmy Greaves, on his day untouchable. His genius was to make goalscoring look so easy, it was achieved almost before anyone noticed, as an example, witness his opening goal of the 1962 FA Cup final against Burnley.

European success

Scotland continued to under-perform nationally, but Jimmy Johnstone was weaving a sorcerers spell on the wing for Celtic, in front of Bertie Auld, a midfield brain and another non-athlete. Johnstone could catch moonbeams, as could Willie Henderson on the wing for Rangers. In the same spring, their respective clubs won the European Cup — the first British club to do so — and were runners-up in the Cup-Winners' Cup, while their compatriot Charlie Cooke was narrowly failing, for Chelsea, against Spurs at Wembley.

All this time, Leeds were being driven onwards by the demonic Billy Bremner, another Scot, his club somehow managing to lose four titles they should have won besides the one they did during the decade. And emerging from the Second Division were Manchester City, about to win three major titles under the inspired midfield guidance of Colin Bell, a throwback to unassuming attitudes in the days of the £20 maximum wage. Bell and colleagues such as Francis Lee brought to a climax the Sixties — a decade in which I have not found room to mention stars such as Joe Baker, Gordon Banks, Johnny Byrne, Billy Bingham, Bryan Douglas, Eddie Gray, Harry Gregg, Roger Hunt, Pat Jennings, Cliff Jones, Jack Kelsey, Billy McNeil, Paul Madeley, John White and others who would today be regarded as priceless.

Six sent off in World Club brawl

IN A MATCH that should never have been played, four men from Celtic and two from Racing Club (Argentina) were sent off in a play-off for the so-called World Club Championship. This abomination of a competition reached its nadir in Montevideo as Celtic clearly decided to get their retaliation in first. There is no excuse for Celtic's behaviour, tried though they must have been after their experience in Buenos Aires three days earlier.

For a start, the format of the competition between the respective champions of Europe and South America is flawed, the winner being decided not by aggregate goals but by games won. This is the fourth time in the eight years since its inception that a third match has been necessary. Celtic won the first leg, at Hampden Park on 18 October, with a header from their captain, Billy McNeill. Then in Buenos Aires on 1 November, they came up against the same bitter atmosphere of intimidation that faced Inter-Milan both inside and outside the stadium two years ago. Keeper Ronnie Simpson was struck by a missile from the crowd before the game began and had to be replaced by Fallon. Celtic led by a Gemmell penalty but, with their little right-winger Jimmy Johnstone bearing the brunt of persistently savage treatment, they succumbed to two goals from Racing, and the tie went into a decider.

The play-off was sheer carnage, with each side perpetrating atrocious acts. At times, police had to go on to the pitch to break up the fighting. The referee warned the captains that if the savagery continued, he would start sending players off. Johnstone, who had to wash the spittle out of his hair during the interval, was one of the Celtic players expelled, although Auld refused to go. A Cardenas goal after 57 minutes won the game for Racing. Celtic have fined their players £250 each. The Racing players each received a new car.

Police intervene as Celtic and Estudiantes players fight at the World Club Cup playoff.

Luck of the Irish: Jennings scores

NOT TOO MANY FA Charity Shield matches are memorable games. But Spurs' Irish international keeper Pat Jennings will remember the one against Manchester United at Old Trafford on 12 August. Moving to the edge of his area, he sent a mighty punt upfield, well into the United half. The ball sailed over the Spurs forwards and United defenders, and swirled in the high wind. United keeper Alex Stepney was back-pedalling furiously, but there was nothing he could do as the ball bounced over his head and into the goal.

Jennings was not sure if it counted at first, but it did (it's the goal-kick that cannot be scored from), and it helped Spurs to a 3–3 draw. Another memorable moment in the match was a magnificent overhead kick by Denis Law that sent the ball flashing past Jennings into the Spurs net. It brought the 63,000 crowd to its feet, but they gasped again when the referee disallowed the goal, for some obscure reason. Jennings is an outstanding keeper, but he had more than his share of luck in this game.

SOCCER SOUNDBITES

"I couldn't believe it. I wasn't even sure it counted in the laws of the game."

PAT JENNINGS
on his goal in the FA Charity Shield game.

England make their point in needle match with Scotland

THE SCOTLAND-ENGLAND clash at Hampden on 24 February was a real needle match. England needed only to draw to earn qualification for the Nations Cup — now called the European Football Championships — which was based this time on the aggregate of this and last season's Home Championship. Scotland desperately wanted to win, not only for European qualification, but to confirm last season's victory over the world champions, which had been devalued by injuries to the England team.

Fortunately, the bitterness built up between the two camps did not spill over on to the field. England controlled the match, despite the brilliant runs of Chelsea's Charlie Cooke for Scotland, who badly missed the unfit Law and Baxter. England, without Stiles, Cohen and Jack Charlton, went ahead through Peters. And although Hughes equalized in the 39th minute, Scotland finished relieved that England's overall superiority was not translated into an avalanche of goals. The 1–1 draw takes England through to the quarter-finals of the European Championships, and a two-legged tie with Spain.

John Hughes (right) heads past Banks to put Scotland level.

Sad Rangers booed off after first defeat

THE FANS of Glasgow Rangers are certainly hard to please. The scene is Ibrox, on 27 April, where Rangers complete their League programme. They go to the game unbeaten, with 61 points out of a possible 66. But they lose 3–2 as Aberdeen score a last-minute goal, and their own supporters jeer and whistle them off the pitch.

This might sound incomprehensible, but Rangers have just handed deadly rivals Celtic the title on a plate. It has been a strange season for Rangers, who went ahead in the League when they beat Celtic 1–0 on 16 September (Celtic's only defeat) and promptly sacked their manager Scot Symon, who had brought them 15 major honours in 13 years. Knocked out of the League Cup, the Scottish Cup and the Fairs Cup, Rangers just had to succeed in the League. But the unthinkable has happened. Celtic, who would have had to fight for a result in three days' time at Dunfermline, recent winners of the Cup, are currently level on points with a far superior goal average. Only a 16–0 defeat will hand the title to Rangers now!

FOOTBALL FOCUS

- The International Board introduced a rule limiting keepers to four steps while in possession of the ball before releasing it into play.
- Martin Chivers moved from Southampton to Spurs in January for a British record fee of £125,000, exceeded in June by Allan Clarke's £150,000 move from Fulham to Leicester.
- Bobby Charlton scored his 45th goal for England in the 3–1 win over Sweden at Wembley on 22 May, to go ahead of Jimmy Greaves as England's all-time leading scorer.
- Cardiff's valiant effort in the Cup-Winners' Cup continued in the semi-finals, where they drew 1–1 in Hamburg before going down 3–2 at home — and they avoided relegation to Division Three!
- With a few minutes to go on the last day of the season, Keith Bradley turned a cross past his own keeper at Villa Park, giving QPR the win they needed to beat Blackpool on goal average for the second promotion place to Division One.

Mercer's men pride of Manchester after last-day drama

MANCHESTER CITY have pipped rivals United at the post and are the new League champions. A stirring 4–3 victory at Newcastle while United lost 2–1 at home to Stoke has put them two points clear, with Liverpool, who beat Forest 6–1 and still have a game to play, a further point behind.

United were five points ahead at one time, but have found the strain of the European Cup too much. With two games left, City were ahead on goal average, and Leeds were a point behind with a game in hand. Leeds blew their chances, however, losing their unbeaten home record in their last home match, 2–1 to Liverpool.

When City persuaded old pro Joe Mercer to come out of semi-retirement to take the helm in 1965, they were at their lowest ebb, having finished 11th in Division Two. In his first week, Mercer signed Malcolm Allison as coach and assistant manager, and in their first season together they took City back to Division One. Mercer's shrewd buys have included Francis Lee (£60,000), Colin Bell (£45,000) and Mike Summerbee (£35,000), but it was local product Neil Young who led the scoring with 19 goals. Veteran Tony Book, a bargain at £13,500, has made an inspirational captain. Full-back Book was wellknown to Allison, who managed him at Bath and Plymouth, his previous clubs, and he was City's only ever-present in the League.

United can still go on to win the European Cup, but for now City are the toast of Manchester.

Joe Mercer, with the Championship trophy, and Allison (left).

Russian revenge for Cardiff, 23 years after

WELSH CLUBS, who have a relatively easy qualification for the European Cup-Winners' Cup, are looked down upon by the teams from England and Scotland. But this season, Cardiff, languishing in the lower regions of the English Second Division, excelled themselves in Europe and put their more illustrious neighbours to shame.

While Spurs and Aberdeen were being knocked out in the second round, Cardiff beat Dutch side NAC Breda to progress to the quarter-finals, in which they have now accounted for Moscow Torpedo. Not that this should come as such a surprise, for Cardiff previously showed their fighting qualities when they knocked out holders Sporting Lisbon in the 1964-65 tournament.

Cardiff won their home leg against Moscow 1–0 through a Barrie Jones goal. Manager Jimmy Scoular, a redoubtable Cup fighter himself with Newcastle in the fifties, prepared the side well for their long trip to Tashkent, where the second leg was being played because of the severe Muscovite winter. They received a warm welcome from their Uzbek hosts, and held Torpedo to a single goal. It was an astounding performance in such a foreign environment. But thanks to Scoular's experience and attention to detail, the team were completely relaxed and not in the least overawed.

Now, remarkably, with five reserves in the side, including centre-half Ritchie Morgan making his first-team debut, they have won the play-off, which took place at Augsburg, West Germany on 3 April. Again there was only one goal in it, scored three minutes before half-time by reserve centre-forward Norman Dean after 19-year-old John Toshack had brilliantly nodded the ball down.

Victory against a Moscow side is all the sweeter for Cardiff, whose older fans remember their 10–1 thrashing at the hands of Dynamo just after the war. But now they must get back to the more mundane task of avoiding relegation before taking on Hamburg and Uwe Seeler in the semi-finals.

Magic in Madrid takes United through to Euro final

MANCHESTER UNITED took their slender 1–0 lead to Spain for the second leg of the European Cup semi-final with Real Madrid and found themselves trailing 3–2 on aggregate at half-time. But they staged a courageous recovery against the six-times champions and won the tie 4–3.

Pirri put Real level overall after 32 minutes, and then, just before half-time, Gento scored a second. Zoco put one in his own net for United, but Amancio restored Real's aggregate lead. United went in at the break thoroughly shaken: Real were rampant and bursting for more, the crowd's noise intimidating. But Matt Busby gently encouraged his players in the interval, and told David Sadler to move up into attack. United went out and held their own, and it was Sadler who scored with some 15 minutes left to even up the tie.

Then came a typical piece of magic from George Best, who had scored United's home goal. He left the Real defence floundering as he took the ball to the right-hand byline and pulled it back for centre-back Bill Foulkes, of all people, to turn one of his rare goals into the net for the winner. The crowd were stunned, and United are in the final at last.

The vital goal in the first leg, scored by Best (centre).

Errant Husband's miss is the turning point in Cup final

Jeff Astle (9) fires in Albion's extra time winner.

WEST BROMWICH, equalling Newcastle's record of appearing in 10 finals, won the Cup in the third minute of extra time with a goal by Jeff Astle. But the additional period would not have been necessary had Jim Husband taken an easy chance five minutes from the end of normal time.

It was not an adventurous final, with the first half dominated by spoiling tactics. Ball was his usual industrious self for Everton, and Hope a live wire for Albion. Everton had the edge of the goalless 90 minutes, and should have won when a cross from Morrissey found Husband unmarked six yards out. But he somehow contrived to head the ball over the bar.

Astle's winner was spectacular. Kendall's foul tackle disturbed his momentum as he advanced towards the box, but when his right-foot drive cannoned back off Harvey, he smashed the rebound with his weaker left foot 20 yards into the far corner of the net. Astle, who had scored in every round so far, had done little else in the final, thanks to Everton stopper Brian Labone, but Albion could not have asked for more.

Sadler (10) scores and has an hypnotic effect on the Real defence.

FINAL SCORE

EUROPEAN CHAMPIONSHIPS 1968

QUARTER-FINALS
England v Spain 1–0, 2–1
Bulgaria v Italy 3–2, 0–2
France v Yugoslavia 1–1, 1–5
Hungary v USSR 2–0, 0–3

Last four in Italy:

SEMI-FINALS

Yugoslavia	1	England	0
Italy	0	USSR	0

(Italy won toss)

THIRD-PLACE MATCH

England	2	USSR	0

FINAL

Italy	1	Yugoslavia	1

(after extra time)
Rome, 8 June 1968. Attendance 75,000

Italy: Zoff, Burgnich, Facchetti, Ferrini, Guarneri, Castano, Domenghini, Juliano, Anastasi, Lodetti, Prati
(Scorer: Domenghini)
Yugoslavia: Pantelic, Fazlagic, Damjanovic, Pavlovic, Paunovic, Holcer, Petkovic, Acimovic, Musemic, Trivic, Dzajic
(Scorer: Dzajic)

FINAL REPLAY

Italy	2	Yugoslavia	0

Rome, 10 June 1968. Attendance 60,000

Italy: Zoff, Burgnich, Facchetti, Rosato, Guarneri, Salvadore, Domenghini, Mazzola, Anastasi, De Sisti, Riva
(Scorers: Riva, Anastasi)
Yugoslavia: Pantelic, Fazlagic, Damjanovic, Pavlovic, Paunovic, Holcer, Hosic, Acimovic, Musemic, Trivic, Dzajic

Busby: from tragedy to triumph as United win European glory

WHEN MATT BUSBY lay fighting for his life in a Munich hospital 10 years ago, his magnificent young team decimated, his dreams of European glory smashed, who would have thought he would have the physical strength and mental fortitude not only to recover from these great personal blows, but to start all over again. But at Wembley, on 29 May, in a night charged with emotion, his third great Manchester United side beat Benfica 4–1 after extra time to win the European Cup, the first English club to do so.

The win was also a personal triumph for Bobby Charlton, a survivor of the Munich air crash who has become a national hero. He captained United and scored two goals. His first, a rare headed effort, put United ahead eight minutes into the second half. Continued United pressure failed to extend their lead, however, as the chances made on the left by John Aston, playing a blinder, went begging. With nine minutes left, Graca scored, and Benfica were transformed. Eusebio came bursting through in the last minute, but Stepney was there heroically to block his fearsome shot.

Three minutes into extra time, Kidd flicked on a Stepney punt and Best pounced. Steering the ball skilfully away from a couple of tackles, he made for goal with a panicking defence in hot pursuit. He was the coolest man in the stadium as he drew the keeper and slid the ball into the net. There could only be one result now. Kidd, on his 19th birthday, headed a third and then made the fourth for Charlton. Yes, United had won the European Cup: Busby's dream was fulfilled. Nothing could make up for Munich, but here at last was a tribute to those who perished there.

Busby, with — at last — a dream fulfilled.

Kidd leaps in celebration of his goal, along with Best (centre).

FINAL SCORE

Football League
Division 1: Manchester City
Top scorer: George Best (Manchester United), Ron Davies (Southampton) 28
Division 2: Ipswich Town
Division 3: Oxford United
Division 4: Luton Town
Footballer of the Year: George Best (Man U)

FA Cup Final

WBA	1	Everton	0

(after extra time)

League Cup Final

Leeds United	1	Arsenal	0

Scottish League
Division 1: Celtic
Top scorer: Bobby Lennox (Celtic) 32
Division 2: St Mirren
Footballer of the Year: Gordon Wallace (Raith R)

Scottish FA Cup Final

Dunfermline Athletic	3	Hearts	1

Scottish League Cup Final

Celtic	5	Dundee	3

International Championship
England, 5 pts

European Cup Final

Manchester United	4	Benfica	1

(after extra time)

Cup-Winners' Cup Final

AC Milan	2	SV Hamburg	0

Inter-Cities Fairs Cup Final
Leeds United beat Ferencvaros 1–0, 0–0

European Footballer of the Year 1967
Florian Albert (Ferencvaros & Hungary)

Leading European Scorer (Golden Boot)
Eusebio (Benfica) 43

World Club Championship
Estudiantes (Argentina) beat Manchester United (England) 1–0, 1–1

Mullery the first England player to be sent off

IT WAS A black day for the world champions in Florence on 5 June, when a ruthless Yugoslavia beat them 1–0. Not only did this end England's hopes of winning their first European Football Championships, but it is the first time an England player has been sent off in a full international.

Alan Mullery was the culprit, kicking at an opponent who had just hit him with a late tackle, and who leapt up from his display of horizontal theatricals as soon as the Spurs wing-half left. Mullery, perhaps, was paying for Norman Hunter's crippling tackle that put Osim out of what was a vicious game. A beautifully volleyed late goal by star outside-left Dragan Dzajic settled the issue.

Argentinians win world clubbing championship

MANCHESTER UNITED were again victims of South American violence in the return leg of the so-called World Club Championship at Old Trafford on 16 October. In the first leg last month in Buenos Aires, which they lost 1–0, they bit the bullet and allowed the wild men of Estudiantes to trample all over them. Charlton needed three stitches after being hacked down, while Stiles, a marked man from the start, was back-headed in the face, and was later sent off for dissent.

Estudiantes went ahead after only five minutes in the return. Law had to be substituted after getting the "stud treatment" from the keeper. And Best, hit, kicked, fouled and spat upon, was sent off along with Medina for fighting. Morgan equalized, but United failed to score again, which is perhaps a blessing in disguise.

Medina of Estudiantes departs in tears after he and Best are sent off.

Sir Matt to hand over the reins

SIR MATT BUSBY of Manchester United announced on 14 January that he is to relinquish his job as team manager and will become general manager of the club that he has served for 23 years. Knighted after United's European Cup triumph last season, Sir Matt is the League's longest-serving manager. He was a wing-half with Manchester City, playing in the FA Cup finals of 1933 and 1934, later joined Liverpool, won one full cap, and captained Scotland later in wartime.

Busby took over at United straight after the war and built three great sides, all renowned for playing an attacking, entertaining brand of football that has had the crowds flocking to Old Trafford in droves. Busby has always moulded the outstanding products of his vast scouting network and excellent youth policy with astute buys, and has never been afraid to allow individual flair its full rein.

When his first side, post-war winners of League and Cup under the captaincy of Johnny Carey, got too old, he built another. These, with an average age of 22 and nicknamed the "Busby Babes", were twice League champions and potentially the greatest English club side of all before they were tragically broken up in the Munich air disaster, which took the lives of Duncan Edwards and several other outstanding young footballers. Almost at death's door himself, Busby fought back, took up the reins again and began rebuilding his beloved United. With Munich survivor Bobby Charlton, the young genius George Best, and the irrepressible Denis Law, brought back from Italian football, they won the League again, and then last year fulfilled Busby's dream by winning the European Cup.

Now Sir Matt can relax and look back on a quarter-century of achievement during which he has remained a modest, compassionate man loved and admired throughout the game.

Sir Matt Busby, a father figure of football.

Six of the best for Hurst — well, five anyway

WEST HAM thrashed Sunderland 8–0 at Upton Park on 19 October, and World Cup hero Geoff Hurst scored six of them, so equalling Vic Watson's club record for a League game, set in 1929. The last individual six in a League match was scored by Bert Lister for Oldham against Southport in Division Four six years ago.

Hurst, who hit a hat-trick in each half, completed the scoring in 75 minutes. Perhaps it's just as well he failed to equal Ted Drake's First Division record of seven, scored for Arsenal at Villa Park in 1935, as he later admitted putting the first of his goals in with a hand as he dived on the blindside of the referee.

Hurst dives to put the first past Sunderland's Montgomery — with his hand, as he was later to admit.

Derby's Dave in back four is the real Mackay

THEY SAID Dave Mackay was finished, that age and injury had slowed him down and that he would never recapture the barnstorming form of his halcyon days as a wing-half with Tottenham and Scotland. But, relishing his new role in the back four, he has used his head to save his legs, and has led Derby to promotion from Division Two, clinched with their 5–1 win over Bolton on 5 April in front of 30,000 delighted fans at the Baseball Ground.

Mackay, joint Footballer of the Year with Manchester City's equally inspirational veteran captain Tony Book, has been the key factor in a side shaped by manager Brian Clough that should be a credit to the First Division next season.

With a sound defence and a free-scoring attack, Derby had seven points to spare over their nearest rivals at the finish.

'Treble' in three weeks for rampant Bhoys

CELTIC COMPLETED their second domestic "treble" in three years when they thrashed Rangers 4–0 in the Scottish Cup final at Hampden on 26 April. It was their second thumping Cup win, having beaten Hibs 6–2 in the League Cup three weeks earlier. They had already clinched the League on 21 April, when a late goal by Tommy Gemmell earned them a 2–2 draw at Kilmarnock.

A fire at Hampden Park that damaged a stand put the League Cup final back, but 74,000 saw the demolition of Hibs, in which Lennox hit a hat-trick. In the quarter-finals, Celtic had enjoyed 10–0 and 4–2 wins over Hamilton, and had twice beaten Rangers in the qualifying group. But neither Glasgow club could match last season's record in the League; despite beating Celtic twice, which might have been decisive in any other season, Rangers dropped points all over the place and allowed their rivals a smooth passage in the end.

The "grand slam" eluded the Bhoys this season, although they held AC Milan to a goalless draw at the San Siro in the quarter-finals of the European Cup. But they were without the injured Lennox in the return and never recovered from an early Prati goal. Still, some say this is a better Celtic side than the so-called "Lisbon Lions" of two years ago. They are a more mature side now, and Jock Stein has further strengthened his squad. If their performance in the Cup final against a Rangers side who had beaten Aberdeen 6–1 in the semis is anything to go by, they will certainly continue to reign supreme in Scotland for the foreseeable future.

Chalmers (hoops) scores Celtic's fourth goal in the Cup final.

Piracy at Wembley as jolly Rogers plunders Arsenal

THIRD DIVISION Swindon shocked Arsenal at Wembley in the final of the League Cup, and winger Don Rogers was their hero. His two buccaneering goals in extra time finished off the flu-stricken Gunners, who were all at sea in the heavy mud.

Arsenal, who lost narrowly to Leeds in last year's final, have been enjoying a good season and giving away few goals. But several of their players were suffering from the after-effects of the flu epidemic. Swindon went to Wembley unfancied but confident: they had accounted for two First and two Second Division sides to get there.

For most of the first half, Arsenal were in control, and only the fine form of Peter Downsborough in goal kept Swindon in the game. But 10 minutes before the interval, Ian Ure made a hash of a back-pass to keeper Bob Wilson, and Roger Smart was left with a simple tap-in. In the second half, Arsenal put Downsborough under real pressure with nine corners in a 10-minute spell. They finally equalized with four minutes left, when the persistent Bobby Gould forced Downsborough into his only error.

If anyone thought this was the signal for Arsenal to take charge in extra time, they were mistaken. The mud and the flu had taken their toll, and Arsenal had given their all. From the restart, Swindon looked and played like the stronger team, and began to tear huge gaps in the Arsenal defence. The inevitable goal came seconds before the break, Rogers cracking the ball in after a corner. He finished it off with a flourish in the last minute, racing over the half-way line on to a pass from Smart and waltzing round Wilson to plant the ball into the unguarded net. As a Third Division side, Swindon don't qualify for Europe, but they are in a good position to emulate QPR's feat of two seasons ago, and win promotion to go with the unexpected silverware they collected at Wembley.

The Arsenal defence is beaten as Swindon's second goal finds the net.

Leeds set new League marks

A GOAL by Johnny Giles five minutes from the end of their last League match on 30 April against Nottingham Forest gave Leeds a 1–0 win and the two points they needed to set a new First Division record. Leeds's first League title has been a long time in coming, but they did it in no uncertain manner, with only two defeats — another League record for 22-club divisions.

Their 67 points beats by one the long-standing mark, set first by Arsenal in 1931, when the Gunners scored 127 goals — almost twice Leeds's tally of 66. Leeds, indeed, become only the fifth club to win the Championship with more points than goals; they have scored fewer than any title-winning team since before the off-side law change in 1925.

Don Revie has assembled an enormously powerful side, strong in every department and with a team spirit that borders at times on the fanatical. But they were building up a reputation as the "nearly men" — beaten Cup-finalists in 1965 and Fairs Cup-finalists in 1966, and League runners-up in those years, too — until last season's double success of League Cup and Fairs Cup.

When Revie took charge at Elland Road eight years ago, Leeds were an unfashionable, struggling Second Division side. With very little recourse to the transfer market, he developed the considerable raw talent available, knitted it into a team and made the players believe in themselves. They won promotion in 1964 and were beaten only on goal average for the League title the following year.

Only three players in the title-winning side cost money — Johnny Giles (£35,000) from Manchester United, England outside-left Mike O'Grady (£30,000) from Huddersfield, and striker Mick Jones (£100,000) from Sheffield United — a tribute to Revie's scouting system and youth policy, which unearthed and brought on the Scottish wingers Peter Lorimer and Eddie Gray. Other products of the youth scheme include Welsh international keeper Gary Sprake and the versatile Paul Madeley.

Giles, who moved in from the wing when Bobby Collins broke a thigh, has been a key figure as a midfield schemer, striking up a formidable partnership with the dynamic Billy Bremner. Revie also transformed Jack Charlton from a solid club centre-half to a World Cup-winner, and the fierce-tackling Norman Hunter into another England international. With Paul Reaney and Terry Cooper behind them, Leeds conceded only 26 goals, fewer than any previous champions in a 42-match season, although runners-up Liverpool beat that by two.

Mick Jones was top scorer with only 14 League goals. Critics of Leeds label them as destructive and defensive, but only two clubs in the First Division scored more goals this season. Leeds's finest accolade came in their penultimate match, at Anfield, where a 0–0 draw put them out of Liverpool's reach and clinched the League title for them. At the end of the game, they did a lap of honour and were cheered generously by the fans on the Kop.

Giles (centre) and Bremner (above), the midfield heart of Leeds United's title-winning side.

FOOTBALL FOCUS

- Scottish club Dunfermline beat West Bromwich in the quarter-finals of the European Cup-Winners' Cup, and only narrowly lost to eventual winners Slovan Bratislava in the semis.
- Rangers broke the transfer record between Scottish clubs by a massive £40,000 when they signed striker Colin Stein from Hibs for £100,000 at the end of October.
- Tommy Docherty managed three clubs in six weeks: he resigned from Rotherham on 6 November to take over at QPR, but walked out on them a month later after a row with the chairman, and he became Aston Villa's manager on 18 December.
- League Cup-winners Swindon and FA Cup-finalists Leicester will meet next season in the Second Division, after Swindon duly won promotion and Leicester were unable to stave off relegation.
- Northampton have completed a remarkable cycle of promotion and relegation in the 1960s, going from Division Four in 1960 to Division One in 1965, and now back again to Division Four in 1969.
- After years of struggling to stay in Division One, Fulham have gone straight down to Division Three in two seasons.
- Champions Leeds broke the British transfer record in June when they signed striker Allan Clarke from Leicester for £165,000.

Magpies steal a march on Hungarians

A delighted Bobby Moncur breaks the ice in the Fairs Cup.

NEWCASTLE UNITED, the club who got into the Fairs Cup although finishing only 10th in the First Division last season, have confounded everyone and won it. They went to Budapest with a 3–0 lead from the first leg of the final and proceeded to beat Ujpest Dozsa again, this time by 3–2.

Newcastle's "back-door" qualification came about because of the "one city, one team" rule in the Fairs Cup (which precluded Everton, Spurs and Arsenal); the increase in England's entry to four clubs; and the participation of Manchester United and West Bromwich, respectively, in the Champions' Cup and the Cup-Winners' Cup. While Liverpool and Chelsea went out of the competition on the toss of a coin, and Leeds lost both quarter-final legs to Ujpest, Newcastle were accounting for Feyenoord, Sporting Lisbon, Real Zaragoza, Vitoria Setubal and, in the semis, Glasgow Rangers.

Skipper Bobby Moncur was their hero in the first leg of the final, at St James's Park. A defensive wing-half, he went up to help his forwards, who had been battering vainly at the Ujpest defence, and scored after 63 minutes — his first goal in seven years at the club. No doubt flushed with success, he scored again nine minutes later, and Scott made it 3–0 six minutes from the end.

The return was no foregone conclusion. Newcastle did not have a good away record, and the Hungarian side were a different proposition on their own pitch, with the great Ferenc Bene in their side. And it was Bene who pulled a goal back after 20 minutes; Gorocs scored a second before half-time, and Ujpest looked as if they were going to run away with it. But again Moncur intervened, scoring his third goal of the final a minute after the interval with a volley from Sinclair's cross. Danish international Ben Arentoft soon scored a second, and teenage substitute Alan Foggon made it 3–2 after 67 minutes. It was an extraordinary result, 6–2 on aggregate, and a performance to rank with United's FA Cup feats of the fifties.

Tired England fade in Rio

ENGLAND'S June tour included a trip to Mexico for a taste of the conditions they will experience in next year's World Cup. They found the heat and altitude of Mexico City a little too much of a handicap in the end, and could only draw 0–0 with Mexico in the Aztec Stadium, where the World Cup final will be played.

Two days later, and 2,000 feet lower, an England XI cruised to a 4–0 victory over a Mexican XI in Guadalajara, where England will play their group matches. England then moved on to Montevideo and beat Uruguay 2–1.

The big test was reserved for their last match, against Brazil and Pele in Rio. England went ahead in the first half through Colin Bell, who was first to the ball when a Peters cross hit a defender. Tommy Wright tripped Gerson in the box, but Gordon Banks managed to save Carlos Alberto's spot-kick.

England continued to play well until they began to tire late in the second half. Tostao equalized for Brazil 10 minutes from time and, two minutes later, laid one on a plate for Jairzinho to score the winner. Nevertheless, it was by no means an unsuccessful tour, and both Sir Alf Ramsey and the England team will have learnt a lot to hold them in good stead for the World Cup in a year's time.

FINAL SCORE

Football League
Division 1: Leeds United
Top scorer: Jimmy Greaves (Tottenham H) 27
Division 2: Derby County
Division 3: Watford
Division 4: Doncaster Rovers
Footballers of the Year: Tony Book (Manchester City) and Dave Mackay (Derby County)

FA Cup Final
Manchester City 1 Leicester City 0

League Cup Final
Swindon Town 3 Arsenal 1
(after extra time)

Scottish League
Division 1: Celtic
Top scorer: Kenny Cameron (Dundee United) 26
Division 2: Motherwell
Footballer of the Year: Bobby Murdoch (Celtic)

Scottish FA Cup Final
Celtic 4 Rangers 0

Scottish League Cup Final
Celtic 6 Hibernian 2

International Championship
England, 6 pts

European Cup Final
AC Milan 4 Ajax Amsterdam 1

Cup-Winners' Cup Final
Slovan Bratislava 3 Barcelona 2

Inter-Cities Fairs Cup Final
Newcastle United beat Ujpest Dozsa 3–0, 3–2

European Footballer of the Year 1968
George Best (Manchester United & N Ireland)

World Club Championship
AC Milan (Italy) beat Estudiantes (Argentina) 3–0, 1–2

Leading European Scorer (Golden Boot)
Petar, Jekov (CSKA Sofia) 36

Joint Footballers of the Year, Dave Mackay (left) and Tony Book.

Six of the Best on bad boy's return

GEORGE BEST, the man you just can't keep out of the news, equalled the FA Cup scoring record on 7 February with six goals in Manchester United's 8–2 fifth-round victory at Northampton. Coming back from a month's suspension, controversially imposed as punishment for a petulant incident, he treated the 22,000 fans at the County Ground to a rare exhibition of all the skills in the game. He scored with his head, with flashing shots, and by dribbling round the keeper, sending the hapless Book the wrong way with the merest shrug of his shoulder.

Northampton, who were in the First Division only four years ago, have a reputation as Cup fighters. But this time Goliath gave David a rare thrashing. Kidd scored the other United goals, while McNeil and Large were on target for the Cobblers. It is not the first time a United player has scored six in the Cup: Denis Law did so at Luton in 1961, but the match was abandoned and the records expunged... and United lost in the replay.

Bad boy Best heads the first of his six goals against Northampton.

Leeds go down fighting: great run comes to an end at Goodison

LEEDS'S RECORD unbeaten run in the First Division finally came to an end on 30 August when League leaders Everton beat them 3–2 at Goodison. Three goals down soon after the interval, Leeds threw everything at Everton and clawed two back. But it was not quite enough.

Leeds's last defeat was 5–1 at Burnley on 19 October 1968, after which they went 28 games unbeaten to take the League title with a record number of points and, with another six games this season, they took their unbeaten League run to 34 matches.

In the first half, Leeds looked anything but champions as Everton ran them ragged, with left-winger John Morrissey in particular giving the normally solid Paul Reaney a roasting. They deserved more than goals from Jimmy Husband and Joe Royle to show for their dominance at half-time. Royle was giving Jack Charlton the run-around, superior both in the air and on the ground. Only Billy Bremner and Norman Hunter prevented a Leeds thrashing.

And it was the never-say-die Bremner who brought Leeds back into the game after Royle had given Everton a 3–0 lead four minutes after half-time. He chested in a Johnny Giles corner after 62 minutes, and wrested the initiative from the home side. An Allan Clarke goal then gave Leeds 15 minutes in which to equalize. But Everton held out. They have dropped only one point in seven matches this season, but Leeds demonstrated that they will not be giving up their title without a struggle.

Sucks to Leeds as Toffeemen take title

EVERTON MADE sure of the League title on 1 April when they beat West Bromwich 2–0 at Goodison for their third win of the Easter holidays, while their only challengers, Leeds, were losing the first leg of their European Cup semi-final to Celtic at Elland Road. Leeds, last season's champions with a record total of 67 points, also lost at home to struggling Southampton on Saturday, their first home defeat in the League, and were thrashed 4–1 at Derby on Monday. They can no longer catch Everton.

The pile-up of fixtures caused by their marathon Cup semi-final with Manchester United and their involvement in the European Cup has proved too much for Leeds. They took over the League leadership from Everton in mid-January, but the Toffeemen regained it two months later, and now need to win their two remaining matches away from home to equal Leeds's points record.

More history for Celtic

CELTIC WROTE another page of Scottish football history at Hampden on 25 October when they won their fifth successive League Cup. But all credit must go to their opponents, lowly St Johnstone, not only for holding the Bhoys to a single goal, but for reaching the final in the first place. With Ayr United forcing Celtic to a replay in the semi-finals, this has been quite a tournament for the provincial clubs.

Manager Jock Stein dropped Tommy Gemmell for the final, after he had been sent off playing for Scotland against Germany, and Celtic were also without the injured Bobby Lennox and suspended Willie Wallace. But when they took an early lead through Bertie Auld, another huge Celtic score in the League Cup final looked on the cards. In the end, however, they had to settle for 1–0.

Celtic's Auld hits the only goal.

The happy Highbury days are here again

IN AN EMOTION-PACKED night at Highbury on 28 April, Arsenal came back from a 3–1 first-leg deficit to win the European Fairs Cup, their first major honour for 17 years. Goals by Kelly, Radford and Sammels gave them a 3–0 victory over Belgian club Anderlecht on the night, but the all-important goal was scored last week by young substitute Ray Kennedy, with a header five minutes from the end that gave Arsenal a lifeline when they looked down and out.

It was right-half Eddie Kelly, another 18-year-old, who ignited Arsenal at Highbury, flicking the ball up with his left foot and blasting it in with his right from the edge of the box to give them a 26th-minute lead. Arsenal, playing their 18th cup-tie of a gruelling season, now needed one goal to put them ahead on the "away goals" rule, and John Radford got it with a soaring header from Bob McNab's cross with 18 minutes left. A minute later, John Sammels swept a long Charlie George pass in with a crisp cross-shot to seal a glorious evening for the Gunners.

Radford climbs high to head Arsenal's second goal.

Dons dash Celtic's hopes of another grand slam

CELTIC'S HOPES of another grand slam of domestic and European titles were ended abruptly at Hampden when Aberdeen brought off a shock 3–1 Cup final victory. Celtic, League Cup winners, runaway champions again and going into the home leg of their European Cup semi-final with Leeds on Wednesday with a 1–0 lead, were the hottest favourites in years to retain the Cup. But, perhaps like Leeds in England, involvement in so many competitions has proved too much for them this season, and their heads went down after a couple of early setbacks in the final.

Aberdeen's hero was young outside-right Derek McKay, virtually unknown until an influenza epidemic forced a drastic reshuffle in the Dons' side. They brought the 20-year-old Dundee reject into the side for the quarter-final against Falkirk, he scored the winner and has not looked back since. Aberdeen's first goal in the final resulted from a McKay cross that hit a defender's hand. The referee awarded a hotly disputed penalty, and Joe Harper scored from the spot. When Bobby Lennox had a goal ruled out a few minutes later, Celtic seemed to lose heart. But with almost an hour left, it was still anybody's game — until the last hectic seven minutes. First McKay smashed the ball in after a fine run by Jim Forrest. Then Lennox scored for Celtic with only two minutes to go. But McKay then raced upfield again for a spectacular clincher, and the Dons had won their first Cup triumph for 23 years.

Leeds beaten by own success as Celtic reach Euro final

LEEDS UNITED, held to a draw by Chelsea in Saturday's strength-sapping Cup final on the heavily sanded Wembley pitch, went out of the European Cup to Celtic 3–1 on aggregate. Celtic had a 1–0 cushion from the first leg of the semi-final, at Elland Road, the goal scored after 90 seconds by George Connelly. The return was played at Hampden in front of 134,000 impassioned fans, most of whom were knocked back after 13 minutes when Billy Bremner scored with a thundering shot from outside the box.

Both teams had suffered from a congestion of fixtures because of their involvement in three competitions — Leeds had played seven Cup ties in 32 days, and fielded a reserve side in the League after they finally gave up chasing Everton. It was Celtic who proved the stronger at Hampden, with Murdoch and Auld wresting the vital midfield control from Bremner and Giles. Two minutes after the interval, John Hughes, who had come in for the injured Wallace, headed an Auld cross past Sprake to put Celtic ahead again on aggregate.

Shortly afterwards, Sprake was injured and had to be replaced by David Harvey, whose first chore was to pick the ball out of the net. Jimmy Johnstone, who had given Cooper such a torrid time in the first leg, was at it again. He beat man after man on the left before laying the ball into Murdoch's path for the big man to crack it into goal. The best of Scotland had beaten the best of England.

Gary Sprake (nearest ball) moves too late to stop George Connelly's early goal in the first leg.

Webb the unlikely hero as Chelsea finally conquer Leeds

DAVID WEBB put the humiliation of Wembley behind him to score Chelsea's extra-time winner in the Cup final replay and leave poor Leeds with nothing to show for a magnificent season's effort. Webb was turned inside-out by Leeds winger Eddie Gray in the 2–2 draw at Wembley 18 days ago that necessitated the first replayed Cup final since 1912. Switching places with Ron Harris for the Old Trafford return, he was less vulnerable in the centre of defence and finished up as Chelsea's hero.

It is perhaps hard to feel sorry for Leeds, whose superb play has earned them universal admiration, but whose gamesmanship and "win at all costs" attitude has won them few friends. In Chelsea they found a team that gave as good as they got, and this resulted in two bitterly fought games, especially the replay, where a repeat of Mr Jennings's weak refereeing allowed players from both sides to get away with a series of unpleasant fouls.

For Chelsea, it has been an uphill battle all the way. At Wembley, on that terrible surface, Peter Houseman equalized Jack Charlton's headed goal in the first half, but they looked finished when Mick Jones scored a second for Leeds six minutes from time. However, only two minutes later, Ian Hutchinson headed them level again from a John Hollins cross.

In the first half at Old Trafford, Chelsea keeper Peter Bonetti needed prolonged treatment after being laid out by a late charge from Jones, and had not fully recovered when the Leeds striker scored a brilliant goal after racing through the Chelsea defence. Chelsea equalized — for the third time in the tie — with a spectacular goal 12 minutes from time. Charlie Cooke sent the ball through the Leeds defence for Peter Osgood, coming up fast on the blind side, to score with a diving header. The climax came a minute before the extra-time break. Hutchinson took a mighty throw on the left, it was deflected to the far post as the heads went up, and there was Webb to bundle it into goal with head and shoulder.

Mick Jones' shot eludes John Hollins (right) and Peter Bonetti.

Webb heads Chelsea's winner in the replay.

Second Cup for Manchester City

WHILE CHELSEA were winning the FA Cup at Old Trafford, the other half of Manchester was celebrating victory in another knockout competition — Manchester City 2 Gornik Zabrze 1 in the European Cup-Winners' Cup final in Vienna. This climaxes another fine season for City, who won the Football League Cup only last month. In that competition, they enjoyed three home ties, beating Liverpool, Everton and QPR, before accounting for rivals United in the semis and WBA in the final. And it was at Maine Road where they laid the foundations for the European triumph.

They won all four of their home legs, the last with an impressive display of attacking football to beat West German side Schalke 04 by 5–1 after losing the away leg 1–0. They continued to play fluent football in the final, and Neil Young gave them an early lead after a shot from the elusive Francis Lee hit a post. Two minutes before the interval, Lee scored from a penalty after the Polish keeper, Kostka, had brought Young down when he was clean through. Gornik scored 20 minutes from time, through Ozlizlo, but City held out for a well-merited victory, to follow Spurs and West Ham, the previous English winners of the trophy.

Neil Young (right) moves in to score City's first.

Bobby Moore is freed: theft charges dropped

THE AFFAIR of the emerald bracelet is over. The accusations of theft against England captain Bobby Moore have been withdrawn and he has been freed from house arrest in Colombia. He is now on his way to join the rest of the international squad in Mexico.

The incident was said to have taken place after England beat Colombia 4–0 in the first match of their World Cup acclimatization tour, when Moore and Bobby Charlton visited the Green Fire jewellery shop in their hotel. The team went on to Ecuador, winning 2–0, but en route for Mexico City they stopped again in Bogota, where Moore was arrested.

Salesgirl Clara Padilla, who made the allegations, claimed that she had only just recognized the England captain. Now, four days from England's opening World Cup match with Romania, she has retracted them, claiming she was confused. The Colombian Press denounced the accusations from the start as a national scandal, citing several recent attempts at framing foreign celebrities for the purpose of extortion. But Moore, who had denied even seeing the bracelet in question, was ordered to remain in Bogota pending further investigations.

Not surprisingly, the whole squalid affair has unsettled the England squad and disrupted their captain's training. Moore will need all his unshakeable temperament to put this behind him.

Favourites Celtic fall to Feyenoord

CELTIC FAILED to repeat their European Cup triumph of three years ago when they surprisingly went down 2–1 to Dutch team Feyenoord after extra time in the final in Milan. Celtic, perhaps overconfident after their semi-final victory against Leeds, were not the same side, and the Rotterdam team deserved to win.

Feyenoord, who beat holders AC Milan in the second round, employed a sweeper, the skilful Rinus Israël, in a form of catenaccio that was not, like the Italian method, purely defensive. But most critically, they marked the dangerous Jimmy Johnstone out of the game.

Celtic scored first, after 30 minutes, when left-back Tommy Gemmell provided a repeat of his piledriver in the 1967 final, after Bobby Murdoch had back-heeled a free-kick. But Israël moved up from defence to head an equalizer only two minutes later. As the game progressed it got faster and better, with the Dutch side taking charge. It went into extra time and, four minutes from the end, Billy McNeill handled a lob. The referee waved play on and the Swede Ove Kindvall beat Celtic keeper Evan Williams with ease. So Celtic failed to make it a grand slam for British clubs in Europe.

The Celtic defence is aghast as Israël (third from right) equalizes.

FOOTBALL FOCUS

- The great Pele scored his 1,000th first-class goal from a penalty in Santos's 2–1 win over Vasco da Gama at the Maracana Stadium on 20 November. The goal, which had been eagerly awaited for some weeks, sparked wild scenes of rejoicing throughout Rio de Janeiro.

- Martin Peters cost Tottenham Hotspur an estimated £200,000 (including, sadly, a makeweight Jimmy Greaves in part exchange) when Spurs signed him from West Ham United in March, a British record.

- Bobby Charlton made his 100th appearance for England at Wembley on 21 April against Northern Ireland, the World Cup holders last home game before defending their title. Charlton, team captain for the match, scored England's third goal in a 3–1 win. Charlton later passed Billy Wright's record of 105 caps in the World Cup quarter-final match against West Germany.

- The goalless draw between Scotland and England at Hampden on 25 April was the first in the series since the very first match, also at Hampden, in 1872.

- How are the mighty fallen! Last century's League and Cup "double" winners, Aston Villa and Preston, both suffered the ignominy of being relegated to Division Three for the first time in their history. Sunderland and Sheffield Wednesday went down to Division Two, and Bradford Park Avenue were voted out of the League to make way for Cambridge United.

Pele (right) scores from the spot — his 1,000th career goal.

FINAL SCORE

Football League
Division 1: Everton
Top scorer: Jeff Astle (West Bromwich Albion) 25
Division 2: Huddersfield Town
Division 3: Leyton Orient
Division 4: Chesterfield
Footballer of the Year: Billy Bremner (Leeds United)

FA Cup Final

Chelsea	2	Leeds United	2
(after extra time)			
Replay: Chelsea	2	Leeds United	1
(after extra time)			

League Cup Final

Manchester City	2	WBA	1

Scottish League
Division 1: Celtic
Top scorer: Colin Stein (Rangers) 24
Division 2: Falkirk
Footballer of the Year: Pat Stanton (Hibernian)

Scottish FA Cup Final

Aberdeen	3	Celtic	1

Scottish League Cup Final

Celtic	1	St Johnstone	0

International Championship
England, Scotland, Wales, 4 pts

European Cup Final

Feyenoord	2	Celtic	1
(after extra time)			

Cup-Winners' Cup Final

Manchester City	2	Gornik Zabrze	1

Inter-Cities Fairs Cup Final
Arsenal beat Anderlecht 1-3, 3–0

European Footaller of the Year 1969
Gianni Rivera (AC Milan & Italy)

Leading European Scorer (Golden Boot)
Gerd Muller (Bayern Munich) 38

World Club Championship
Feyenoord (Holland) beat Estudiantes (Argentina) 2-2, 1–0

Brilliant Brazilians

Mexico was a controversial choice to host the 1970 World Cup, and the distressed condition of some of the athletes in the Olympic Games held there two years earlier did nothing to help the Mexican cause. But in the event the finals not only provided thrilling competition and splendid entertainment, but there was little of the negativity and thuggery that blighted football in the sixties. Brazil, with the incomparable Pele, raised the game to new heights and were universally popular winners. And England, who did not give up their hold on the trophy without a fight, took part in two unforgettable matches.

A RECORD 71 countries entered the 1970 World Cup, but none had a more eventful passage to Mexico than El Salvador from the Concacaf zone. They played 10 games before qualifying, and one win over the neighbouring Honduras sparked off a two-week war between the mutually antagonistic countries. By contrast, Brazil qualified effortlessly from South America, winning all six matches and scoring 23 goals (Tostao nine, Pele six, Jairzinho four) to two. With England exempt as holders, West Germany were the most impressive European qualifiers, dropping only one point. Gerd Muller scored 10 of their 20 goals, and they mauled Cyprus 12–0 in one game. The Germans conceded only three, all to Scotland, who were eliminated.

Banks's save

England and Brazil were drawn in the same group, played out in Guadalajara — without the severe altitude problem of Mexico City, but with an appalling 98 degrees of torrid heat. Nevertheless, the clash of the two favourites, after they had both won their opening matches, produced a classic encounter, won 1–0 by the South Americans but remembered for evermore for one Banks save from Pele.

Tostao (left) and Pele celebrate a Brazil goal in the Final.

England were on top early on, and both Peters and Lee missed chances. Then Jairzinho powered past Cooper to the byline and crossed the ball from the corner of the penalty box to the far post, where the leaping Pele unleashed a perfect downward header towards the empty net. The crowd's roar to acclaim a goal was stifled as Banks appeared, seemingly from nowhere, but from the other side of his goal, to paw the ball up and over the bar. England took heart from this reprieve, but in the end it was to no avail, as Brazil got on top in the second half and Tostao and Pele made a goal for Jairzinho. Nevertheless, England had done enough — with Moore, despite his recent problems in Colombia, outstanding — to hope that the two might meet again in the final.

West Germany were impressive qualifiers in Leon, apart from an initial hiccup against Morocco, with Muller hitting two hat-tricks. The Soviet Union looked dangerous in Group One, coping well with the problems of Mexico City and going through with the host country. Italy scored just one goal in Group Two, but typically conceded none and finished top.

It could be said that England lost their quarter-final with West Germany because Banks, arguably the best keeper in the world, couldn't hold his drink — the bottle of Mexican beer, that is, that left him weak and groggy. This attack of "Montezuma's revenge" crucially kept him out of the game in Leon. It was another epic encounter between the teams who contested the 1966 final. England, playing their best football so far, deservedly went two up in 50 minutes with goals from Mullery and Peters, both from crosses by right-back Newton. But early in the second half they started back-pedalling and lost the initiative. Beckenbauer cleverly broke through and pulled one back for the Germans. Ramsey — now Sir Alf — put Bell on for Bobby Charlton, and Hunter for Peters, but Seeler equalized with a freakish back-header.

England went into extra time looking tired, but the excellent Hurst soon had the ball in the net from Lee's pull-back — yet had it disallowed for no apparent reason. Inevitably it was Muller who scored the winner, volleying in from close range. Pity poor Bonetti, without a competitive match for more than a month.

The goals flow

It was in the quarter-finals that the goals began to flow — 17 in four matches. Only in the Uruguay-USSR game was there a paucity, Uruguay's winner coming in extra time, just three minutes away from the iniquitous drawing of lots. Brazil and Peru — the surprise of the tournament — put on a dazzling show at Guadalajara, with Brazil's shaky keeper Felix almost letting the Peruvians back into the game before Brazil won 4–2. In Toluca, against Mexico, Italy conceded their first goal of the finals, but after a lucky, deflected equalizer, their attack was seen at last, and they won 4–1 with second-half goals from Riva (two) and substitute Rivera.

The two semi-finals had more goals, thrills aplenty and exhibition stuff from Pele, 12 years after he first exploded on to the World Cup scene as a 17-year-old in Sweden. Intent, as always, not only on winning but

Against all the odds and most of the predictions, the heat and altitude of Mexico produced the most memorable World Cup of all — thanks largely to those brilliant ball-playing Brazilians, who restored faith in international competition.

on entertaining with his efforts to score the unique goal, Pele had already had one remarkable near miss against Czechoslovakia, with a shot from the centre circle. In the 3–1 win over Uruguay, he will always be remembered for the dummy that transfixed keeper Mazurkiewicz to the spot before he hooked the ball just wide.

The other semi became a thriller in extra time, not because of any pretensions of open football, rather for sheer fatigue. Boninsegna had given Italy the lead in the ninth minute, and his team-mates closed up shop in the second half, unwisely allowing West Germany to take control of midfield. But, after battering away incessantly at the Italian goal, it was not until injury time that they equalized, when left-back Schnellinger suddenly arrived to convert Grabowski's cross. The Germans began extra time with a distinct disadvantage, Beckenbauer having been cynically hacked down and playing with an arm strapped to his side as they had used their substitutes. Both sides scored twice more before Rivera, on as substitute for the third match running, gave the Italians a 4–3 victory.

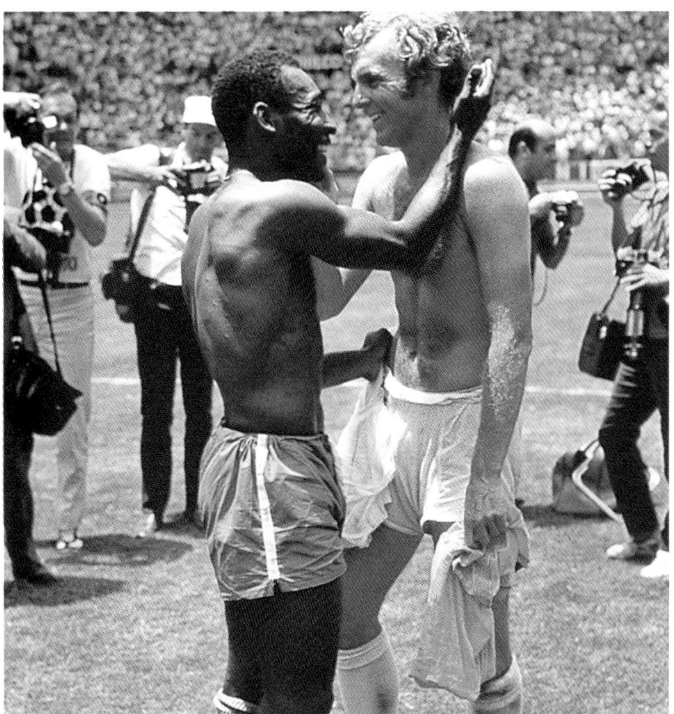

Pele and Bobby Moore after the England-Brazil match.

A beautiful finale

Brazil did not disappoint the hundreds of millions of television fans around the world who were glued to their sets in the expectation of seeing a triumph for adventurous football. With arguably the most inventive and deadly attacking force seen in modern times, Brazil knew no other way to play, although they dared not fall back on defence with Felix as their last line. Indeed, it was a bad defensive error that allowed Italy back into the game after Pele had put his side ahead with one of his power-headers, his fourth goal of the finals. A casual back-heel from Clodoaldo put Brazil in trouble, and a mad rush from Felix allowed Boninsegna to find the unguarded net.

In the second half, with Clodoaldo and particularly Gerson taking control of the midfield, Brazil mounted attack after attack. Rivelino had a swerving shot parried by Albertosi and then crashed a drive on to the bar with his rarely employed right foot. After 65 minutes, Gerson unleashed a left-foot drive from outside the box to put them ahead, and then lifted a 50-yard pass which Pele nodded down for Jairzinho to run in and maintain his record of scoring in every game.

The last 20 minutes were sheer magic, a celebration of the beautiful Brazilian game, climaxed with an exhibition goal. It was started by Clodoaldo in his own half, who beat five men as he sambaed upfield, carried on by Rivelino, Jairzinho and Pele, before it was finished off in spectacular fashion by right-back and captain Carlos Alberto. It was Brazil's World Cup and, appropriately, as the first three-time winners, they kept the Jules Rimet Trophy.

Pele's arms are raised, but Banks has somehow denied him.

FINAL SCORE

Group 1

Mexico	0	USSR	0
Belgium	3	El Salvador	0
USSR	4	Belgium	1
Mexico	4	El Salvador	0
USSR	2	El Salvador	0
Mexico	1	Belgium	0

	P	W	D	L	F	A	P
USSR	3	2	1	0	6	1	5
Mexico	3	2	1	0	5	0	5
Belgium	3	1	0	2	4	5	2
El Salvador	3	0	0	3	0	9	0

Group 2

Uruguay	2	Israel	0
Italy	1	Sweden	0
Italy	0	Uruguay	0
Israel	1	Sweden	1
Sweden	1	Uruguay	0
Israel	0	Italy	0

	P	W	D	L	F	A	P
Italy	3	1	2	0	1	0	4
Uruguay	3	1	1	1	2	1	3
Sweden	3	1	1	1	2	2	3
Israel	3	0	2	1	1	3	2

Group 3

England	1	Romania	0
Brazil	4	Czechoslovakia	1
Romania	2	Czechoslovakia	1
Brazil	1	England	0
Brazil	3	Romania	2
England	1	Czechoslovakia	0

	P	W	D	L	F	A	P
Brazil	3	3	0	0	8	3	6
England	3	2	0	1	2	1	4
Romania	3	1	0	2	4	5	2
Czech	3	0	0	3	2	7	0

Group 4

Peru	3	Bulgaria	2
West Germany	2	Morocco	1
Peru	3	Morocco	0
West Germany	5	Bulgaria	2
West Germany	3	Peru	1
Bulgaria	1	Morocco	1

	P	W	D	L	F	A	P
W. Germany	3	3	0	0	10	4	6
Peru	3	2	0	1	7	5	4
Bulgaria	3	0	1	2	5	9	1
Morocco	3	0	1	2	2	6	1

QUARTER-FINALS

Uruguay	1	USSR	0
Italy	4	Mexico	1
Brazil	4	Peru	2
West Germany	3	England	2

SEMI-FINALS

Italy (after extra time)	4	West Germany	3
Brazil	3	Uruguay	1

THIRD-PLACE MATCH

West Germany 1 Uruguay 0

FINAL

Brazil 4 Italy 1

Aztec Stadium, Mexico City, 21 June 1970. Attendance 107,000

Brazil: Felix, Carlos Alberto, Brito, Piazza, Everaldo, Clodoaldo, Gerson, Jairzinho, Tostao, Pele, Rivelino (Scorers: Pele, Gerson, Jairzinho, Carlos Alberto)

Italy: Albertosi, Burgnich, Facchetti, Cera, Rosato, Bertini (Juliano), Riva, Domenghini, Mazzola, De Sisti, Boninsegna (Rivera) (Scorer: Boninsegna)

Leading scorers

10 Muller (West Germany) 7 Jairzinho (Brazil) 5 Cubillas (Peru)

Mighty Leeds crash in Cup to 'Grandad's Army' from Colchester

FOURTH DIVISION Colchester 3 First Division leaders Leeds 2! There has been plenty of giant-killing in the FA Cup before, but this remarkable result from the fifth round at little Layer Road beggars belief. Mighty Leeds, the most talented, resolute, battle-hardened, ruthlessly efficient outfit in the land, would surely not succumb to a collection of veterans and rejects labelled "Grandad's Army"? But they did.

Colchester's "trump card" was centre-forward Ray Crawford, who led the First Division scorers 10 years ago with Ipswich and played twice for England. Manager Dick Graham had rescued him from non-League football. Five of his team-mates were also over 30, but instead of being overawed, Colchester gambled on all-out attack. They ruffled Leeds, and Crawford put them in front with a header after 18 minutes. Before Leeds could recover, Crawford scored again, hooking the ball in while on the ground. Gasps of disbelief were heard at grounds around the country as the half-time score was flashed up.

Without any thought of sitting on their lead, Colchester came out after the interval playing inspired football, and Dave Simmons swept through to head past goalkeeper Gary Sprake and put them 3–0 up. But with 35 minutes left, they began to tire, and Leeds at last began to play the cultured football they are famous for. Norman Hunter and Johnny Giles pulled goals back. There was 15 minutes left, but the "no-hopers" found another hero in keeper Graham Smith. Time and again Leeds broke through, but the brilliant Smith was always there to frustrate them. By the end of the match, "Grandad's Army" were panting and creaking. But they were in the sixth round of the Cup.

SOCCER SOUNDBITES

"I always play well against Leeds. I always score goals against Jack Charlton."

The prophetic **RAY CRAWFORD** (speaking from a long memory), before Colchester shocked Leeds in the Cup.

Ray Crawford (facing) is about to swivel and score Colchester's second goal.

From spoiler to scorer: it's another Storey

PETER STOREY'S reputation has been built up as a midfield spoiler, a ruthless destroyer, the "iron man" of Arsenal's defence. But every dog has his day, and Storey's came at Hillsborough in the FA Cup semi-final against Stoke. It did not start out that way, as Denis Smith blocked an attempted Storey clearance for the ball to sail into Arsenal's net. John Ritchie then took advantage of a poor Charlie George back-pass to put Stoke deservedly two up at half-time. Soon after the interval, though, Storey struck back with probably the finest goal he will ever score. He is not known for his shooting, but when the ball came out to him on the edge of the box, he took off and hit the sweetest of right-foot volleys past Gordon Banks.

Stoke, however, held out, and with the match going into injury time, Arsenal's hopes of the "double" appeared to be shattered. Then, with one last attack, they won a disputed corner — Banks claimed he was pushed. Frank McLintock's header was bound for the net when John Mahoney dived full length to push it aside — no dispute about the penalty. George had gone off injured, so Storey — the other penalty-taker, not because of any dead-ball ability, but for his ice-cool temperament — strode up to take the spot-kick against the world's best keeper. It was not a particularly good kick, but he sent Banks the wrong way, and had kept Arsenal in the Cup.

Mahoney (left) handles and referee Partridge awards a last-gasp penalty — for Storey to take.

Offside rumpus leads to riot at Leeds: chairman and Revie condone pitch invasion

A CONTROVERSIAL referee's decision at Elland Road on 17 April sparked some of the most deplorable scenes witnessed on any football ground in Britain. They were started by a mass protest of the Leeds players, who jostled the referee after West Bromwich Albion's second goal. Some 30 or 40 angry fans raced on to the field, and the players found themselves obliged to protect the referee, Ray Tinkler, while a linesman was hit on the head with a stone. It took the police five minutes and 32 arrests to clear the pitch.

The dispute occurred 20 minutes into the second half, with Albion already a goal up. Albion's Tony Brown blocked a Hunter pass, and followed the ball as it rebounded into the Leeds half. The linesman flagged because Colin Suggett was in an offside position near the centre circle. But the referee decided he was not interfering with play and allowed Brown to continue. Brown took the ball on, then released it to Jeff Astle, who scored with ease. Many referees would have blown for offside, but it was by no means a clear-cut decision. It certainly did not warrant the continued protests of the Leeds players or the comments of the disappointed Leeds chairman and manager Don Revie after the match, condoning the pitch invasion.

Leeds scored just before the end, and Albion won 2–1, their first away victory for 16 months. On the day, they were the better team, but Leeds appear to believe they have a divine right to win, and they have an appalling habit of whingeing, on and off the field, whenever a decision goes against them. They were at one time seven points clear in Division One, but Arsenal's win over Newcastle takes them above Leeds on goal average, with two games in hand.

As Billy Bremner (in white, left) remonstrates with the referee, police and fans grapple on the Elland Road pitch.

SOCCER SOUNDBITES

"I don't blame them at all. The referee's decision in allowing West Bromwich's second goal was diabolical."

Leeds manager **DON REVIE** on the reaction of his team's fans.

"I am not blaming the spectators. There was every justification for it."

ALDERMAN PERCY WOODWARD, Leeds chairman.

"You have cost us a lot of money."

UNNAMED LEEDS PLAYER to referee Tinkler as the injured linesman was being treated.

Arsenal beat Spurs for first leg of 'double'

THE CULMINATION of a remarkable League campaign saw Arsenal get the result they needed at White Hart Lane to snatch the title from Leeds by a single point. Arsenal went into the match needing a win or a goalless draw to clinch their eighth Championship. Defeat or a scoring draw would give Leeds the title, so tight was the situation at the top. And Spurs, well behind in third place, were out to stop their North London rivals emulating their "double" season of 10 years ago.

The match, played before a capacity crowd with another 20,000 locked out, provided a nail-biting night for Arsenal fans. They did not go on the defensive, and had marginally the better of a fast, exciting struggle, but it was two minutes from time before Ray Kennedy headed them into the lead. This could have been Arsenal's undoing, because a Spurs goal at this stage would still have deprived them of the title. And it needed all Bob Wilson's courage and sharpness in the dying seconds to dive into a forest of legs and grab the ball as Spurs threatened to score.

Arsenal's triumph has been a team effort, with the occasional injection of flair from the mercurial Charlie George just when it was needed. Frank McLintock's conversion to centre-half has been a major factor in Arsenal's season, his class and his unflappable leadership knitting the side together and providing an example for the youngsters. Kennedy, in his first full season, has forged a fine twin spearhead with John Radford and finished top scorer with 20 League goals. One more match, against Liverpool on Saturday, now stands between Arsenal and the "double".

Bob Wilson jumps for joy at the final whistle: Arsenal are champions.

Another Ibrox disaster: worst day in British football

SIXTY-SIX PEOPLE were killed in a terrible crush at Ibrox Park, as the New Year's fixture between Rangers and Celtic was coming to a close. About another 200 were injured. The disaster occurred when crush-barriers collapsed on a staircase leading out of the ground. With Celtic leading 1–0 and only a minute or two left, thousands of spectators began to make their way out from the terraces. Suddenly, there was a tremendous roar as Colin Stein snatched a last-gasp equalizer for Rangers. Hundreds of fans on the wide staircase turned to try to get back into the ground. As they met others still streaming out, the tubular steel barriers buckled, and hundreds of people began to fall. Most of the victims died through suffocation as they were swept down and piled on top of each other.

Ibrox was the scene of a similar tragedy in April 1902, when part of a new stand collapsed at the Scotland-England international. And 10 years ago, two people were killed and several injured when crush barriers collapsed during a Rangers-Celtic match.

'Double' joy for Arsenal, as they come from behind again

ARSENAL COMPLETED the "double" in dramatic fashion at Wembley, coming from behind, as they have all season, to beat Liverpool 2–1. They made enough chances to have won comfortably, but the game had gone into extra time when Heighway broke away on the left and put Liverpool into the lead within two minutes.

Against a Liverpool defence that had given away a record low 24 League goals and only one in the Cup, it looked all up for Arsenal now. But they refused to panic, and Kelly, who had gone on in the second half for Storey, took advantage of a rare defensive lapse to push the ball goalwards and Graham, the man of the match, might just have touched it in. Whoever scored, it was Arsenal's equalizer, just before the change-around. And it was George who stole the headlines again with a scorching winner from Radford's pass eight minutes from time.

For Arsenal's captain McLintock, Footballer of the Year, it was a first Cup-winner's medal after four fruitless trips to Wembley. Wilson and all-purpose winger Armstrong played in all 64 of Arsenal's competitive matches this term, McLintock, Kennedy and Rice all but one. England internationals McNab, Radford and newly capped Storey missed only two. Arsenal's feat is the result of a tremendous team performance, with a great deal of credit going to manager Bertie Mee, their former physiotherapist, and coach Don Howe.

They survived away draws in every round, and came from behind in the semi-final and final. At times they played brilliant, powerful football, but often had to rely on sheer professionalism and team spirit to survive. Above all, they have finally laid to rest the ghost of the great Arsenal sides of the past.

Charlie George hits the winner from the edge of the box.

Best penalized for robbing Banks of England

George Best is about to knock the loose ball away from Gordon Banks.

AN ORIGINAL scoring attempt by George Best in Northern Ireland's match against England at Belfast was disallowed by a referee who was almost as embarrassed as the England keeper. As the visitors' No.1, Gordon Banks, released the ball to punt it upfield, Best, with the perfect timing that characterizes all his play, flicked the ball up and over Banks's head and headed it into goal. The referee disallowed the score, presumably for "foot up", but Best had not even touched the keeper. England were outplayed in the first half, and their late winner by Allan Clarke was an injustice to an Irish side for whom Best, Derek Dougan and a solid defence were outstanding.

FOOTBALL FOCUS

● Barnet became the fifth non-League club to beat League opposition 6–1 in the Cup when they thrashed Newport County of Division Four by that score.

● The Scottish League have introduced "goal difference" instead of "goal average" to determine League positions when clubs are equal on points.

● Rangers ended the most barren period in their history, four years without a major trophy, when they beat Celtic 1–0 in the final of the Scottish League Cup, the goal scored by Derek Johnstone, at 16 the youngest player ever to appear in a final.

● Leeds's 64 points in Division One was the highest ever obtained by the runners-up. The FA fined them £750 and ordered their ground to be closed for the first four matches of next season as a result of the pitch invasion in April.

● Celtic brought off the Cup and League "double" for the third time in five seasons, and equalled their own early-1900s record of six League titles in a row.

● Bolton and Blackburn, founder members of the League, were both relegated to Division Three for the first time.

● Jimmy Greaves (44 goals, 57 caps) and Jimmy Armfield (43 caps, 15 times England captain) retired at the end of the season.

Chelsea beat the old masters in Athens

Chelsea captain Ron Harris with the trophy.

CHELSEA BEAT mighty Real Madrid in Athens to take the European Cup-Winners' Cup in the replayed final, the fourth English side to do so. Real Madrid may not be the force of old, but this was their ninth European final and they are still formidable Cup fighters. Chelsea owe their success largely to the motivation of Charlie Cooke in midfield, the brilliance of Peter Bonetti in goal, and the determination that won them the FA Cup last season despite being outplayed. They also had to overcome injury problems.

In the semi-final, without strikers Hutchinson and Osgood, they beat holders Manchester City, themselves severely depleted by injuries, 1–0 in each leg to avenge an earlier defeat by City in the FA Cup. They looked to have won the final at the first attempt, with an Osgood goal before he went off injured, but Zoco equalized for Real in the dying moments when Dempsey mis-kicked, and it was Chelsea who had to hold out in extra time.

Dempsey made amends in the replay, slamming the ball in when his first headed attempt had been saved, and Osgood put Chelsea two up before again having to go off. Cooke, in at right-half for the injured Hollins, had another fine game and, although Fleitas scored for Real with 15 minutes to go, they could not get past Bonetti again. Chelsea's triumph climaxed a remarkable season for London clubs, after Tottenham's League Cup and Arsenal's "double".

Consolation for Leeds at the last

LEEDS HAD TO wait until 3 June before they finally won a trophy at the end of a gruelling season in which they had again played the bridesmaid. They held Juventus to a 1–1 draw at Elland Road, which was enough to give them the Fairs Cup on the away goals rule, having drawn 2–2 in Turin five days earlier. It was somewhat of an anti-climax after the stirring semi-final with Liverpool, in which a single goal at Anfield by Bremner, returning after a long spell off through injury, decided the tie. This put Leeds into their third Fairs Cup final, although they must have been relieved that holders Arsenal had been knocked out by Cologne in the quarter-finals.

Eddie Gray dislocated a shoulder in the first leg of the final, before it was abandoned in torrential rain. Leeds twice had to come back in the replay, with goals from Madeley and, 13 minutes from time, substitute Bates. An early goal from Clarke in the return was equalized by the expensive Anastasi, but Leeds's disciplined defence denied Juventus any more, and the Italians, who had not been beaten in any of their 12 games in the competition, had lost on the technicality.

The Fairs Cup, now won for the fourth year running by an English club, will be succeeded next season by the UEFA Cup.

Mick Bates (left) scores a vital equalizer in Turin.

FINAL SCORE

Football League
Division 1: Arsenal
Top scorer: Tony Brown (WBA) 28
Division 2: Leicester City
Division 3: Preston North End
Division 4: Notts County
Footballer of the Year: Frank McLintock (Arsenal)

FA Cup Final

Arsenal	2	Liverpool	1
(after extra time)			

League Cup Final

Tottenham Hotspur	2	Aston Villa	0

Scottish League
Division 1: Celtic
Top scorer: Harry Hood (Celtic) 22
Division 2: Partick Thistle
Footballer of the Year: Martin Buchan (Aberdeen)

Scottish FA Cup Final

Celtic	1	Rangers	1
Replay: Celtic	2	Rangers	1

Scottish League Cup Final

Rangers	1	Celtic	0

International Championship
England, 5 pts

European Cup Final

Ajax Amsterdam	2	Panathinaikos	0

Cup-Winners' Cup Final

Chelsea	1	Real Madrid	1
(after extra time)			
Replay: Chelsea	2	Real Madrid	1
(after extra time)			

Inter-Cities Fairs Cup Final
Leeds United beat Juventus 2–2, 1–1 (on away goals)

European Footballer of the Year 1970
Gerd Muller (Bayern Munich & West Germany)

Leading European Scorer (Golden Boot)
Josip Skoblar (Marseille) 44

World Club Championship
Nacional (Uruguay) beat Panathinaikos (Greece) 1–1, 2–1

Radford and George in classic giant-killing act

IT WAS NOT the Arsenal pair, but non-League Hereford's Ron Radford and substitute Ricky George who made the headlines, completing the giant-killing of First Division Newcastle in the third-round FA Cup replay.

The drama started in early January, at St James's Park, where the Southern League side held Newcastle to a 2–2 draw. A month and half a dozen postponements later, 15,000 fans packed into the little Edgar Street ground for the return. Newcastle did everything but score; Malcolm Macdonald should have done, at least twice. But Fred Potter in the Hereford goal made some breathtaking saves and, when he was beaten, the woodwork came to the rescue.

As Newcastle's confidence began to wane, Hereford took charge, and it was against the run of play that Macdonald put the Magpies ahead with 10 minutes left. But three minutes later, Radford won a tackle in midfield, strode on through the mud and hit a blinding 30-yarder past the startled Iam McFaul in Newcastle's goal. In extra time, Radford pushed the ball through for George to score the winner amid a tumult of sound.

Whatever happens now when they entertain First Division West Ham United in the fourth round on Wednesday, Hereford have made their point, and it would be a travesty of justice if they are not playing League football next season.

Newcastle keeper McFaul is too late to stop George's winner for Hereford.

Celtic stung by Thistle

CELTIC, IN THEIR eighth consecutive League Cup final, lost 4–1 to unfancied Partick Thistle in the biggest upset for years in Scottish football. It may seem out of place to talk about giant-killing when a mid-table First Division side win a Cup final, but this really was a sensational result. Celtic, admittedly without their influential captain Billy McNeill, have been riding high in domestic and European football for several years now, while Partick have to go back more than 50 years for their only previous honour, the Cup in 1921.

A friendly, popular Glasgow club with a reputation for entertaining play and unpredictability, Partick demonstrated both when they went into a 4–0 lead in just 37 minutes. They attacked Celtic from the start, with strikers Frank Coulston and Jimmy Bone to the fore and Denis McQuade and Bobby Lawrie creating problems on the flanks. But even when skipper Alex Rae scored after nine minutes and Lawrie put Partick two up after 15, the Celtic fans were not unduly worried. Then Celtic winger Jimmy Johnstone had to go off injured and was substituted by full-back Jim Craig. Thistle continued to play glorious stuff, and further goals by McQuade and Bone to one by Dalglish produced a scoreline greeted with utter disbelief around the country.

Brave Moore in goal, but Stoke win marathon

STOKE FINALLY settled this epic tie in the second play-off at Old Trafford, beating West Ham 3–2 to go through to the League Cup final at Wembley. The Hammers can consider themselves desperately unlucky to go out, and it is a pity, after four fine games, that there had to be a loser.

West Ham won the first leg 2–1 at Stoke, but Stoke equalized at Upton Park and took the tie into extra time. With three minutes left, Banks made a brilliant penalty save from World Cup colleague Geoff Hurst, who had scored from the spot in the first tie. The first play-off at Hillsborough was full of all good things except goals. So seven weeks after the first game, the fourth and, ultimately, deciding fixture took place on 26 January.

There was early drama as West Ham keeper Bobby Ferguson had to go off. When he returned 20 minutes later, the saga had taken some more dramatic turns. Bobby Moore had gone in goal and saved a penalty from Bernard, who followed up to score. Then 10-man West Ham (they had gambled on Ferguson's return) carried the game to Stoke and took the lead, with goals by Bonds and Brooking. Stoke seemed to play better against the full West Ham side. Dobing equalized and, shortly after the interval, Conroy put them in front again. The Hammers came storming back, but finally had to admit defeat, after 420 minutes.

Moore parries Bernard's penalty, only to be beaten by a second shot from the rebound.

England need to rebuild from the rubble of humiliation

ENGLAND WERE outclassed by West Germany at Wembley in the first leg of their European Championship quarter-final, although it was late in the game before the Germans translated their superiority into a 3–1 victory.

Nothing could symbolize more poignantly England's decline since their 1966 World Cup triumph than the withdrawal of Geoff Hurst in the 58th minute. As the hat-trick hero of England's 4–2 victory six years ago walked sadly to the bench, we were witnessing the end of an era.

West Germany have blossomed since then, and they humbled England with a side still in the early stages of preparation for the 1974 World Cup. Beckenbauer has brought a new meaning to the term "sweeper", commanding the middle of the pitch in front of his defenders as well as behind them. The fleet-footed Günter Netzer was a revelation as a midfield general. With the eager Hoeness and the powerful Wimmer also outstanding, England's midfield of Ball, Bell and Peters were rendered ineffective.

Agony for Banks as Netzer (out of picture) converts a penalty.

Hoeness put the Germans ahead after 27 minutes. But England kept plugging away, and Lee popped home a flattering equalizer with 13 minutes to go. In the last six minutes, however, Banks could not stop a Netzer penalty, given away by Moore, and Muller scored a third.

Boosting England's morale for the return in two weeks' time is manager Ramsey's immediate task, but it pales into insignificance when compared with the long hard grind of rebuilding English soccer.

Triumphant Leeds set for 'double'

LEEDS DESERVEDLY beat Arsenal 1–0 at Wembley in the 100th FA Cup final, although the match was not the best advertisement for English soccer. The two sides knew each other too well and, with the emphasis on stopping the other team playing, there was a surfeit of fouls. Four players were booked, McNab and George for Arsenal, Bremner and Hunter for Leeds. But the only serious injury was when Leeds striker Mick Jones dislocated an elbow in a last-minute collision with Arsenal keeper Geoff Barnett. He will be missed when Leeds go for the second leg of the "double" at Molineux, in a match senselessly scheduled by the Football League for two days after the Cup final.

Allan Clarke scored the winner after 54 minutes with a fine lunging header from a Jones cross. Hunter and Charlton completely subdued the threat of Radford and George, although the latter did provide one moment of magic when he hooked the ball fiercely on to the bar. And, in the first half Alan Ball hit a perfect volley that Reaney instinctively cleared off the line. Apart from those two efforts, however, it was mostly Leeds.

Banks and Eastham inspire Stoke to first major trophy

ON THEIR FIRST ever visit to Wembley, Stoke beat Chelsea 2–1 in the League Cup Final to win their first major honour in 109 years. Two players who are familiar with the Wembley turf, however, had a big say in Stoke's triumph: their senior citizens George Eastham and Gordon Banks. Eastham, 35, scored the winner, his first goal in 18 months. And Banks, 34, made two late saves that demonstrated why he is still one of the world's greatest keepers.

Credit must also go to Terry Conroy, whose brave one-man raids kept Stoke in the game when Chelsea were threatening to crush them. He also scored the first goal, a header after five minutes, and made the cross that led to their winner.

But Chelsea must be wondering how they lost a match they had controlled for so long, with Hudson and Hollins dominating the midfield. The answer lies in the iron grip of the unflappable Smith and Bloor over Chelsea's front line. Osgood had a mixed match, cautioned and lucky not to be sent off after a couple of bad fouls, and then scoring an extraordinary equalizer just before half-time, when he hooked the ball in while on the ground.

After 73 minutes, Ritchie headed down a cross from Conroy, and although Bonetti parried Greenhoff's shot, he could do nothing about Eastham's follow-up. Chelsea rallied, but Banks had an answer to everything.

Eastham (right) hits Stoke's winning goal.

Derby win League in Majorca as Leeds and Liverpool slip

IN A MOST extraordinary finish to the title race, Derby County have won their first Championship thanks to Leeds's defeat at Wolves and Liverpool's failure to beat Arsenal at Highbury. Having seen Derby complete their programme with a 1–0 win over Liverpool, which took them to the top of the table on 58 points, Brian Clough took his team on holiday. He had brought them from near bottom of the Second Division in just five years, but had not expected success so soon.

Even allowing for their Cup exertions two days earlier, Leeds were expected to get the point they needed at Wolves. That they did not was down largely to bad luck. First, Wolves played their best football of the season, and their keeper Phil Parkes made some world-class saves. Second, Leeds had two penalty appeals turned down after blatant handling offences by defenders. Third, they had to play a heavily strapped Eddie Gray and Allan Clarke dosed up with pain-killing injections. And finally, when they got back into the game in the last minutes, a Lorimer header hit the bar.

Munro scored for Wolves three minutes before half-time when Giles muffed a clearance, and Dougan added a second after 67 minutes. Leeds drew on all their resources to pull one back — typically through Bremner — before Clarke had to be substituted by Yorath. But Parkes, and the cross-bar, kept their last efforts out, and Leeds had to be content with finishing League runners-up for the fifth time in eight seasons.

At Highbury, meanwhile, the night was just as electric, the drama as poignant, although Liverpool could only snatch the title if Leeds lost. A young Liverpool side with only one defeat in their last 16 matches had not played for a week and were fresh. Arsenal, of course, had been at Wembley two days earlier, which was hard to believe given the effort put in by such as McLintock, Ball, Rice and Storey.

Again, it was a marvellous match, one of the best seen at Highbury all season. Hughes struck the Arsenal bar after 17 minutes with a 30-yard volley, and Keegan, having a brilliant game on the right, put the rebound inches wide with an overhead kick. But Liverpool's unluckiest moment came two minutes from time when, with their fans chanting "Leeds are losing", they had a goal from Toshack disallowed for a marginal offside.

By such narrow decisions are Championships won and lost. But Derby are worthy champions. It is perhaps unfair to pick out individuals, but McFarland and Todd at the back, Gemmill in midfield, and Hector, O'Hare and Hinton up front were all major contributors to their success.

Derek Dougan and John Richards celebrate Frank Munro's opening goal.

FOOTBALL FOCUS

● Chelsea broke all records in the Cup-Winners' Cup with a first-round massacre of Luxembourg's Jeunesse Hautcharage 13–0 at Stamford Bridge for a 21–0 aggregate score. Peter Osgood scored eight goals in the tie.

● Ted MacDougall set a scoring record for the FA Cup proper on 20 November when he hit nine against non-League Margate, three more than the previous best, in Bournemouth's 11–0 first-round win.

● Giant-killers Hereford continued their Cup progress in the fourth round, holding West Ham to a 0–0 draw before going down 3–1 at Upton Park, and were duly elected to the League in place of Barrow, albeit by only one vote.

● Arsenal reached the Cup final for the second season running without a single home draw.

● Leeds cancelled the proposed transfer of Asa Hartford from West Brom when a medical uncovered a "hole-in-the-heart" condition, although this did not stop the player from winning his first caps for Scotland.

● Rangers were banned from European competition for a year as a result of their fans' behaviour in Barcelona.

Dixie Deans's hat-trick atones for penalty miss

DIXIE DEANS, the Scot with the famous football name — well, nearly — scored a Cup-final hat-trick in Celtic's 6–1 demolition of Hibs, and so made up for the penalty miss that sealed the Bhoys' elimination from the European Cup last month. Deans, signed from Motherwell as part of Celtic's rebuilding programme, was the unfortunate individual whose effort in the ridiculous penalty shoot-out at Parkhead, after two goalless semi-final draws, was the only one of the 10 not converted.

Hibs were overwhelmed at Hampden, and Deans took his goals brilliantly. Skipper McNeill and Lou Macari (two) scored the others. With a transitional side this season, Jock Stein has guided Celtic to their second consecutive League and Cup "double", and he has high hopes of further success in Europe next season.

Dixie Deans heads past Hibernian goalkeeper Jim Herriot to score Celtic's second goal.

Spurs win first UEFA Cup in all-England final

SPURS, PIONEERS of English success on the Continent, became the first English club to win two different European competitions when they held off a brave rally by Wolves and carried off the UEFA Cup at White Hart Lane. With a 2–1 lead from the first leg at Molineux a fortnight ago, the 1–1 draw was enough to win them the new trophy.

So England's domination of the Fairs/UEFA competition continues, despite holders Leeds's shock defeat in the first round. They had a 2–0 lead over Lierse from the first leg in Belgium, but, because of fixture congestion at home, fielded a virtual reserve side at Elland Road and lost 4–0.

Chivers scored two breakaway goals for Spurs at Molineux, sandwiching McCalliog's effort for Wolves. Skipper Mullery, the man Spurs called in from the cold last month — he was on loan with Fulham — scored with a spectacular header from Peters's free-kick to increase Spurs' lead in the return and, with Perryman, ensured his team's grip on midfield. But, five minutes from the interval, Wolves pulled a goal back when Wagstaffe hit a fierce 20-yarder in off a post. Wolves staged a late rally, but they could not get past Jennings.

Spurs players celebrate with Wolves looking on in despair

FINAL SCORE

Football League
Division 1: Derby County
Top scorer: Francis Lee (Manchester City) 33
Division 2: Norwich City
Division 3: Aston Villa
Division 4: Grimsby Town
Footballer of the Year: Gordon Banks (Stoke City)

FA Cup Final
Leeds United 1 Arsenal 0

League Cup Final
Stoke City 2 Chelsea 1

Scottish League
Division 1: Celtic
Top scorer: Joe Harper (Aberdeen) 33
Division 2: Dumbarton
Footballer of the Year: Dave Smith (Rangers)

Scottish FA Cup Final
Celtic 6 Hibernian 1

Scottish League Cup Final
Partick Thistle 4 Celtic 1

International Championship
England, Scotland, 4 pts

European Cup Final
Ajax Amsterdam 2 Inter-Milan 0

Cup-Winners' Cup Final
Rangers 3 Moscow Dynamo 2

UEFA Cup Final
Tottenham Hotspur beat Wolverhampton Wanderers 2–1, 1–1

European Footballer of the Year 1971
Johan Cruyff (Ajax Amsterdam & Holland)

Leading European Footballer of the Year (Golden Boot)
Gerd Muller (Bayern Munich)

World Club Championship
Ajax Amsterdam (Holland) beat Independiente (Argentina) 1–1, 3–0

Best quits at 26; flies off to Spain

GEORGE BEST, who failed to turn up to play for Northern Ireland at Hampden last week, has announced that he is quitting soccer. At 26, the wayward genius, arguably the most talented British footballer of all time, spoke to a Sunday newspaper of his premature retirement from the game before flying off to Spain. Best, who was Manchester United's leading scorer again this season with 18 goals in 40 League games, described himself as a mental and physical wreck and confessed to having done nothing but drink for the last year.

No other footballer has had to live with the off-field pressures that Best, with his pop-star lifestyle, has faced. If this is the end of his career, rather than just another escapade, it will be a sad loss to the game he has enriched with his unique skills.

Rangers fans out of control as they win Cup-Winners' Cup

Johnston celebrates Rangers' third goal — or is he trying to hold the crowd back?

RANGERS' FINE 3–2 victory over Moscow Dynamo in the final of the European Cup-Winners' Cup in Barcelona was marred by the disgraceful, puerile behaviour of their fans, who invaded the pitch at every opportunity.

Some 20,000 Rangers fans had flown from Glasgow to support their heroes and, as they overflowed on to the pitch, the players had to leave the field three times before the game could start. Each Rangers goal — from Colin Stein in 24 minutes, Willie Johnston in 40 and 49 minutes — was the signal for a pitch invasion.

John Greig was outstanding for Rangers: he seemed to be everywhere at once. But they appeared to relax when 3–0 up, and Dynamo scored on the hour and then three minutes from the end, through Estrekov and Makovikov. Scottish supporters were grateful to Peter McCloy for some brave saves that ensured victory.

The final pitch invasion at the end developed into a riot, as club-wielding police battled with Glasgow fans throwing broken seats and bottles. Many fans and police were injured, and there were several arrests. As the crowd finally streamed out, they continued their behaviour, bringing further violence to the streets of Barcelona.

FINAL SCORE

EUROPEAN CHAMPIONSHIP 1972

QUARTER-FINALS
England v West Germany 1–3, 0–0
Italy v Belgium 0–0, 1–2
Hungary v Romania 1–1, 2–2, 2–1
Yugoslavia v USSR 0–0, 0–3

Last four in Belgium:

SEMI-FINALS
USSR 1 Hungary 0
West Germany 2 Belgium 1

THIRD-PLACE MATCH
Belgium 2 Hungary 1

FINAL
West Germany 3 USSR 0
Brussels, 18 June 1972. Attendance 43,437

West Germany: Maier, Hottges, Schwarzenbeck, Beckenbauer, Breitner, Hoeness, Wimmer, Netzer, Heynckes, Muller, Kremers (Scorers: Muller 2, Wimmer)
USSR: Rudakov, Dzodzuashvili, Khurtsilava, Kaplichny, Istomin, Troshkin, Kolotov, Baidachni, Konkov (Dolmatov), Banishevski (Kozinkievits), Onishenko

Clough outbursts upset League: Derby warned

LEAGUE CHAMPIONS Derby County could face severe disciplinary action from the Football League if they cannot persuade their manager, the outspoken Brian Clough, to modify his criticisms of the football establishment. Club chairman Sam Longson reluctantly revealed as much on the return flight from Sarajevo, after Derby had withstood substantial provocation in beating Zeljeznicar in the European Cup with a display that was a credit to British football. Longson was apparently sent for and told that Clough is not entitled to make comments about matters not concerning Derby!

Clough has, of course, been a major critic of England manager Sir Alf Ramsey. He has also made caustic remarks about the two-year ban from international football imposed on Colin Todd, the Derby defender.

This is merely the background to the failure of the Derby board and their manager to reach an amicable agreement over his new contract. Clough, who won't be gagged, reckons they are still "a million miles apart". One cannot blame him. He is totally involved in football, and perfectly entitled to speak about it, even if he does ruffle a few feathers. Clough's abrasive personality might irritate a lot of people, but the other side of the coin was demonstrated after the Zeljeznicar game, when he insisted his players meet the tiny knot of County fans who had travelled to the match.

Clough: a man who refuses to be gagged.

SOCCER SOUNDBITES

"These people have come 2,000 miles to see you. Go and shake their hands and thank them."

BRIAN CLOUGH
to his players, referring to the Derby fans staying in the same hotel in Yugoslavia.

"Are your players aware of the rules?"

FIFA OBSERVER,
before the Derby-Zeljeznicar match.

"Are you?"

BRIAN CLOUGH,
in reply.

Jennings thwarts League leaders with two penalty saves

SPURS WON A rare point at Anfield on 31 March, thanks largely to a brilliant display from keeper Pat Jennings, who saved two penalties. Jennings played a blinder: apart from the penalty saves — from Keegan (38 minutes) and Smith (85) — he also stopped a six-yard shot from Cormack and a point-blank header from Hall. Even the 70th-minute goal that beat him was a mishit by Keegan into the ground, the ball sailing over Jennings's head.

Spurs had gone in front with a fine goal by Gilzean after 21 minutes. Neither penalty was well struck, although Jennings's huge presence in goal must have been daunting to the taker. But the loss of a point was not as serious to the League leaders as was first thought after this pre-lunch game. By tea-time, Arsenal and Leeds had both lost, and Liverpool remain strong favourites for the title. They also are in the UEFA Cup semi-final... and face Spurs again.

Pat Jennings defies leaders Liverpool once again.

Banks hurt in crash: may lose sight of eye

ENGLAND KEEPER Gordon Banks was involved in a road accident on 22 October, when his car and a van met in a head-on collision. Surgeons are fighting to save the sight of his right eye, damaged by pieces of glass from his shattered windscreen. Although nearly 35, he recently signed a six-year contract with Stoke and still figures in Sir Alf Ramsey's plans for the 1974 World Cup. His uncanny anticipation and lightning reflexes have made him arguably the greatest goalkeeper in the history of soccer, and if his career is cut short now it will be a sad loss to the game.

Hibs' revenge as Celtic lose again

CELTIC LOST in the League Cup final for the third season running, as Hibs extracted their revenge for the 6–1 drubbing in last season's Scottish Cup final. Hibs won 2–1, with all the goals coming in the second half. Skipper Pat Stanton put Hibs ahead in the 60th minute and then laid on their second six minutes later for Jim O'Rourke, the "overnight success" who has been with Hibs for 10 years. Celtic's sole reply came from Kenny Dalglish after 71 minutes.

Bill Shankly holds the Championship trophy aloft.

All over bar the shouting: eighth title for Liverpool

WITH THEIR FINE 2–0 victory over Leeds at Anfield on Easter Monday, 23 April, and Arsenal's failure to win at Southampton, Liverpool have, to all intents and purposes, won the Championship. Leeds are no longer in a position to catch them, while Arsenal would have to win their last two matches (at West Ham and Leeds), and Liverpool lose their home game with Leicester — all by substantial margins — for the London side to overtake them. Full celebrations must wait until Saturday, however, but they were already partying on the Kop when Kevin Keegan clinched the match five minutes from time, after Cormack had put Liverpool in front on 47 minutes. Don Revie, manager of Cup-finalists Leeds, who have again failed to achieve the cherished "double", conceded that Liverpool were the better side on the day. Liverpool manager Bill Shankly, in turn, was overjoyed at his team's display. He built up a great side in the mid-sixties, and this one looks even better. He has had particular success in his dealings in the transfer market: Ray Clemence, Alex Lindsay, Larry Lloyd, Emlyn Hughes and Kevin Keegan were all virtually unknown when he plucked them from the obscurity of the lower divisions. Hughes has been outstanding this season, a dynamic midfielder for Liverpool, and now an established left-back for England, while Keegan and Clemence have both won their first England caps.

Liverpool's success is based above all on a blend of skill, power and sheer determination Every member of the side shows a tremendous work-rate, constantly running and challenging. They took over the League leadership from Everton on 23 September and, apart from one brief period in February, stayed there.

Bobby Charlton retires: end of an era at Old Trafford

WHEN Bobby Charlton played his last game for Manchester United at Stamford Bridge on 28 April, it marked the end of a great era. With Denis Law and Tony Dunne moving on, and the defection again of George Best (although he has had talks with manager Docherty and is contemplating yet another comeback), United's great side of the sixties has all but disappeared.

It has been a traumatic season for the Red Devils, who seem to have lost the "devil" altogether. That Charlton finished top scorer with six goals speaks volumes. But he had the consolation of helping the club avoid relegation, for they failed to win any of their first nine games and did not finally climb out of the bottom two until March. Tommy Docherty, who took over as manager from Frank O'Farrell in December, will have a monumental job next season to revive United's fading fortunes.

Charlton, of course, is a last link with the "Busby Babes". He carried the mantle of that long-lamented side, and won just about every honour in the game. Above all, he won universal respect and admiration, as a sportsman as well as a footballer.

While Bobby was being saluted by the Chelsea crowd, his brother Jack of Leeds limped off the Southampton pitch with a hamstring injury in what could be his last competitive match before moving on to management.

Bobby Charlton: retiring from football.

England celebrate Moore's century and shatter Scotland's centenary

SCOTLAND'S CENTENARY celebrations became an icy nightmare on the evening of 14 February, as England humiliated them 5–0 at Hampden, their biggest victory there since 1888. The result was a fitting tribute to England skipper Bobby Moore, making his 100th international appearance, and must have cheered up Alf Ramsey, who was criticized after England's dismal goalless draw with Wales last month. But it was a dreadful baptism for Willie Ormond, Scotland's new team manager.

Scotland, as if bent on demonstrating the type of game that became a tradition in their great years, started out with some beautiful football, stroking the ball around between themselves for the first five minutes. Yet 10 minutes later they were 3–0 down! Channon hit a 20-yarder that Lorimer deflected into goal. Channon then sent Clarke away for the second, and scored the third with a half-volley from a Chivers throw.

Scotland's defence could not cope with either the frosty surface or the lively England attack. They were frequently torn apart by the nimble running of Clarke, Chivers and Channon, the outstanding forward of the match. There was positive intent in midfield, too, dominated by Ball, Peters and Bell. The 48,000 crowd jeered Scotland throughout the second half, and further goals from Chivers and Clarke did not improve their mood.

Double save of the season: 'Monty' the hero as Sunderland win the Cup

SUNDERLAND BECAME the first Division Two side to win the FA Cup for 42 years when they beat Leeds 1–0 at Wembley, and at the end manager Bob Stokoe ran on to the field straight into the arms of keeper Jim Montgomery. For "Monty" had made a double save midway through the second half that denied Leeds when an equalizer seemed inevitable, with one of the most remarkable pieces of goalkeeping ever seen.

Before the match, Sunderland were given no chance. Leeds were the Cup-holders, had finished third in the League and were in the final of the European Cup-Winners' Cup. They were a mean side and had seen it all before. Sunderland, though, had a tremendous Wearside following and, as their Cup run progressed, they became infected by the fanaticism of a wonderful crowd. And the manner in which they had beaten Arsenal in the semi-final should have been a warning.

At Wembley, they matched Leeds in spirit and showed no little skill. But it was still a shock when they took the lead through Ian Porterfield in the 32nd minute from their first corner. Leeds proceeded to grind away at Sunderland, yet the individual flair that might have made the breakthrough appears to have been sacrificed in this side for the sake of "professionalism".

It seemed, however, that they had finally cracked the Sunderland defence after 65 minutes. Right-back Reaney crossed a long ball to the far post where his partner Cherry had stolen up on the blind side. It looked a certain score as Cherry launched himself at the ball, met it perfectly with his head, and sent it hurtling towards the opposite corner of the goal. Montgomery, whose handling of the ball hitherto had been far from perfect, twisted in mid-air to parry the ball, but only on to the lethal right foot of Peter Lorimer. From six yards out, the Leeds winger lashed the ball towards the invitingly unguarded net, but somehow "Monty" managed to lift himself up and deflect the ball on to the bar and eventual safety.

This miracle reprieve gave his team-mates fresh heart, and planted the seeds of doubt in their opponents. With Horswill, a talented and impudent slip of a lad, and the intelligent Porterfield continuing to subdue Bremner and Giles, Sunderland firmly retained midfield control. So although the tremendous effort of Hughes, Halom and Tueart in the first hour began to take its toll of stamina in the closing stages, Sunderland never really looked like surrendering the initiative. And as Leeds desperately overreached themselves in the tense final minutes, Sunderland counter-attacked and very nearly scored again, with Harvey making a splendid save from Halom.

Sunderland's victory was the most popular at Wembley since the "Matthews final" 20 years ago, not so much because they were the underdogs, but because they emphasized, by beating Leeds, the apostles of cold efficiency, that there is no substitute, even in the commercial world of modern soccer, for flair, imagination and spirit.

Montgomery (by post) clambers to his feet after saving from Cherry.

Superb Rangers end seven-year itch

Alfie Conn (on ground) scores Rangers' second goal.

GLASGOW RANGERS brought their centenary celebrations to a perfect climax by beating Celtic 3–2 in one of the most exciting Cup finals seen at Hampden for years. Dalglish put Celtic ahead after 24 minutes with a fine shot from a Deans pass, and 10 minutes later Parlane equalized, heading in a MacDonald cross. Conn put Rangers ahead only seconds after the interval, but Celtic fought back and, six minutes later, after Greig handled in the box, Footballer of the Year George Connelly equalized from the spot.

It was Rangers, however, who continued to attack with more panache, and Forsyth forced in the winner after a Derek Johnstone header had struck a post and run along the line.

FOOTBALL FOCUS

- Derby paid Leicester a record British fee of £225,000 for full-back David Nish in August, and he won his first England cap in May.
- Johnny Giles made a record-equalling fifth Cup final appearance at Wembley (one for Man Utd, four for Leeds).
- Huddersfield were relegated for the second year running, and will play in Division Three for the first time.
- The first official women's international in Britain took place at Cappielow Park (Morton), England beating Scotland 3–2.
- Ajax Amsterdam won the European Cup for the third consecutive season.

Lesson for Liverpool, but they bravely take trophy

LIVERPOOL WERE ominously outplayed in Moenchengladbach but, although Borussia pulled back two of the three-goal deficit from the first leg, Bill Shankly's team staged a fine rearguard action to take the UEFA Cup final 3–2 on aggregate. The Reds certainly needed those three Anfield goals — from Keegan (two) and Lloyd — as they were given a first-half football lesson by a brilliant Borussia side, who flowed as beautifully as West Germany at Wembley last year. The Liverpool defence and midfield were rent constantly as Netzer, Danner and Wimmer swept with geometric precision towards their goal.

Twice Rupp, a stocky nuisance of a centre-forward, made goals for Heynckes, after 30 and 40 minutes, and Liverpool's terrible anxiety was revealed when Hughes was booked for a crude foul on Vogts and Lawler pulled down Netzer.

Yet Liverpool, in the second half, with defeat staring them in the face, drew on all their resources of character as Smith, their indomitable captain, drove them forward. They seldom looked like scoring, but at least they kept the now tiring Germans away from their penalty area, and brought their first European trophy back to Anfield. But the performance of the Germans gave a salutary message, not only for Liverpool but for English soccer at large. Last night was no cause for celebration.

Larry Lloyd (left) heads just wide, but would score later.

FINAL SCORE

Football League
Division 1: Liverpool
Top scorer: Bryan Robson (West Ham) 28
Division 2: Burnley
Division 3: Bolton Wanderers
Division 4: Southport
Footballer of the Year: Pat Jennings (Tottenham Hotspur)

FA Cup Final
Sunderland 1 Leeds United 0

League Cup Final
Tottenham Hotspur 1 Norwich City 0

Scottish League
Division 1: Celtic
Top scorer: Alan Gordon (Hibernian) 27
Division 2: Clyde
Footballer of the Year: George Connelly (Celtic)

Scottish FA Cup Final
Rangers 3 Celtic 2

Scottish League Cup Final
Hibernian 2 Celtic 1

International Championship
England, 6 pts

European Cup Final
Ajax Amsterdam 1 Juventus 0

Cup-Winners' Cup Final
AC Milan 1 Leeds United 0

UEFA Cup Final
Liverpool beat B Moenchengladbach 3–0, 0–2

European Footballer of the Year 1972
Franz Beckenbauer (Bayern Munich & West Germany)

Leading European Scorer (Golden Boot)
Eusebio (Benfica) 40

World Club Championship
Independiente (Argentina) 1 Juventus (Italy) 0

Heart-break again for Leeds as Milan steal Cup

IT WAS FLOODLIGHT robbery in Salonika as Leeds lost the Cup-Winners' Cup final to a team they outplayed. Usually cast as the villains of calculated efficiency and gamesmanship, Leeds went down to an early Milan goal of dubious origin and a string of baffling refereeing decisions that negated their all-out efforts to score.

As a heavy thunderstorm rolled around the stadium, Leeds were caught cold by Milan — and the first dubious decision — after only four minutes. Greek referee Christos Michas ruled that Madeley had impeded Bigon 20 yards out, and Chiarugi's free-kick was deflected off the Leeds wall past Harvey. Thereafter Leeds, without Bremner, Giles, Clarke and Eddie Gray because of injury or suspension, managed something like 30 goal attempts, while Harvey was barely troubled. Vecchi, in Milan's goal, superbly kept out a series of shots and headers, particularly from Jordan, Jones, the tenacious Lorimer, and those hard-working midfield operators Madeley and Bates.

But if Vecchi was the Milan hero, referee Michas ran him close. After 25 minutes he ignored Anquilletti's blatant trip on Jones in the box, which occurred right under his nose. Twice more, in the second half, he took no action over penalty offences, first when Zignoli handled Lorimer's cross, and then when Jones was pushed by Sabadini. The Greeks in the 45,000 crowd clearly showed their disapproval of the home-based referee, and began chanting for Leeds.

The game blew up in the closing stages when Rivera, pretty anonymous until now, chopped Hunter down as he attempted to break through on the left. Hunter retaliated, and scuffles broke out between two groups of players near the touchline, as a result of which Hunter and Sogliano were sent off.

At the end, the crowd left no doubts as to where their sympathy lay, shouting "Shame, shame" at the victorious Italians and singing the praises of the English side from outside the main stand: "Ole, ole, Leeds, ole" — some small consolation for Don Revie's men after they had lost their third trophy at the end of a heart-breaking season.

The free-kick goal by Chiarugi that gave AC Milan the Cup-Winners' Cup.

Polish 'clown' denies England World Cup chance

ON A NIGHT of missed chances and extraordinary saves from Jan Tomaszewski, the Polish keeper labelled a "clown" on TV by Brian Clough, England saw their World Cup hopes disappear at Wembley last night. They stumbled exhausted and heartbroken out of the competition after a 90-minute all-out assault had failed to break down Poland's grim determination.

On the pitch where, some seven years ago, they had won the trophy, Sir Alf Ramsey's men played with a spirit that deserved a better fate. But no one can deny that Poland's overall performances in the competition, after a disastrous defeat in their opening match against Wales, make them worthy of qualification. And at Wembley they fought a magnificent rearguard action before the most partisan crowd gathered there since the 1966 World Cup final.

The plain and unpalatable fact is that England moved boldly on to the offensive in this tournament when it was too late. Had they produced just a little of this attacking zeal against Wales at Wembley last March and Poland at Chorzow in June, they might not now have found themselves out in the cold. It can be fairly argued that Ramsey's overcaution in selection and tactics in recent years has been the major cause of this failure. Indeed, it became clear last night that England have become so used to playing with predominantly defensive efficiency that they could not switch smoothly enough into forward gear to overcome such stubborn opponents.

With Peters, Bell and Currie dominating the midfield from the early stages, and Channon leading the front line with dash, they launched and sustained an almighty assault on the Polish barrier, creating chance after chance. But it was Poland who scored first, after 58 minutes, when Hunter was uncharacteristically caught in possession by the flying winger Gadocha, who raced away and crossed for Domarski to shoot under Shilton's dive.

England equalized six minutes later, Clarke converting a borderline penalty. But they could not beat Tomaszewski again.

SOCCER SOUNDBITES

"I have never seen a better performance at Wembley by a visiting goalkeeper."

SIR ALF RAMSEY,
on Jan Tomaszewski, the architect of England's failure.

A diving Tomaszewski is glad to see Clarke's shot go wide.

Sub Jordan books Scotland's final place

SCOTLAND, SKILLED and tenacious on a night of fierce tension, reached the finals of the World Cup for the third time when they beat Czechoslovakia 2–1 at Hampden on 26 September. Leeds striker Joe Jordan became the hero of the 100,000 crowd when, six minutes after replacing Kenny Dalglish, he headed the 70th-minute winner from Willie Morgan's centre. Scotland, having beaten Denmark twice, cannot now be overhauled, no matter what happens in their final game, the return against the Czechs.

A goal behind after 33 minutes, when Nehoda took advantage of a right-wing breakaway, Scotland maintained their formidable pressure with neat, skilful football. They were rewarded when Jim Holton, the Manchester United centre-half, headed the equalizer in the 40th minute from a corner by Tommy Hutchison. Only a series of notable saves by the agile Viktor and rugged defensive work denied the Scots further goals.

David Hay, one of five Celtic men in the reshaped team, worked splendidly in midfield alongside Billy Bremner, while up front Denis Law, recalled after a 15-month absence for his 51st cap, and Coventry's Hutchison caused the Czechs continual problems. Morgan, Dalglish and even full-back Danny McGrain used the spaces on the flanks well. The first of many free-kicks was awarded after only 45 seconds, and the referee eventually booked two Czechs for scything fouls on the lively Bremner.

Jordan's header is Scotland's passport to the World Cup.

Clough: outspoken... outrageous... and out!

AFTER AN ORGY of allegations between himself and the board, Brian Clough, together with his partner Peter Taylor, have resigned from Derby County. The chief bone of contention has been Clough's outspoken comments on TV and in newspaper articles, and the club feared expulsion from the League. The last straw came when in his ghosted newspaper column he accused some of his England players of "cheating" by not giving 100 per cent because of their preoccupation with tonight's World Cup match against Poland.

From the moment Clough began to receive payment for his opinions, some public sympathy was lost, and unforgiving critics have accused him of being deliberately controversial. But in Derby, the club's supporters began demonstrating in Clough's favour and are seeking a showdown with the club.

Late strike ends Wolves' famine

JOHN RICHARDS'S goal in the 84th minute of an ultimately exciting League Cup final earned Wolves their first major success for 14 years. A solid, down-to-earth performance was just good enough to overcome the brittle skills of their more purposeful opponents from Manchester City.

The sensible and direct Midlanders dominated the first half and should have had more to show for their efforts at the interval than the 43rd-minute goal Ken Hibbitt scored with a mishit shot from Geoff Palmer's cross. But City improved immensely in the second half, wrested midfield control from Mike Bailey, and deservedly equalized on the hour with a powerful shot from Colin Bell.

Then, shortly after Bell had hammered the ball against the bar, Richards stepped in with his match-winner at the other end. Inexperienced reserve keeper Gary Pierce, who was told only on Thursday that he would be playing, contributed substantially to Wolves' victory with a series of agile saves when City threatened to take control after the break.

The one sour note was the churlish behaviour of Rodney Marsh, who left the arena without accompanying his team-mates to collect his loser's tankard or join in the applause for the winners. In contrast, team-mate Denis Law gave his shirt to Francis Munro, a fellow Scot who had beaten him all afternoon.

(left to right) Kenny Hibbitt, Geoff Palmer and John Richards celebrate the winning goal by Derek Parkin (3).

Bristol City put Leeds out of Cup

BRISTOL CITY, seventh from bottom of the Second Division, succeeded where the First Division elite have failed on 29 occasions this season. They defeated hitherto unbeaten Leeds, the League leaders and Cup favourites, in this hard-fought fifth-round FA Cup replay at Elland Road by 1–0, and richly deserved to do so.

Full of confidence and effort, and showing no little skill, Bristol were full value for a victory that earns them their first quarter-final place for 53 years and a home tie with League champions Liverpool. The decisive, splendidly taken goal came in the 23rd minute from Don Gillies, 22, their Scottish striker.

A well-conceived move, it began, as much did, with Gerry Gow in midfield, and Keith Fear then held off Bremner before feeding Gillies just inside the box. Gillies evaded a challenge from Hunter and shot past the unsighted Harvey.

SOCCER SOUNDBITES

"I'm not even thinking about what changes Leeds may make... Imagine a side that can bring in three internationals."

ALAN DICKS,
Bristol City manager, on Leeds's injury "problems" for the replay.

Leeds land League at Liverpool — without playing!

LEEDS FIND themselves in the improbable position of having long-time rivals Arsenal to thank for finally clinching them the League Championship, as Ray Kennedy's goal at Anfield inflicted Liverpool's only home defeat of the season and meant they could no longer catch Leeds.

It is ironic that Leeds should win their second title in six years by sitting on their backsides, after missing so many honours when their fate was in their own hands. But no one can deny their right to be called champions. They have led the table from the start, winning their first seven matches. They beat Sheffield United's all-time record of 23 opening games without defeat, and just failed to equal Burnley's undefeated run when they were beaten 3–2 at Stoke in their 30th match, on 23 February.

Before this defeat, they were nine points ahead of second-placed Liverpool. But the Leeds nerves began to jangle as Liverpool's refusal to give up saw their lead gradually eroded when they hit a run of three defeats in March: 1–0 at Anfield, amazingly 4–1 at home to Burnley, and 3–1 at West Ham. This left Liverpool only four points behind with three games in hand; but their involvement in the Cup, with a semi-final replay, proved too much and, as Leeds recovered, so Liverpool began to falter.

Leeds have been at the top of English soccer, or thereabouts, for the past decade, although they have not won the rewards they felt they deserved — five times League runners-up in those 10 years. Most of the side who won the League for the first time in 1969 are still there, although Harvey has replaced Sprake in goal, Cherry has come in for Cooper and McQueen for Charlton. Clarke and Jordan have reinforced the front line, although Mick Jones leads their League scorers with 14.

Above all, Billy Bremner has been the driving force behind their success, a tremendous all-round footballer and an inspiring captain. If he would only cut out the gamesmanship and stop whining at the referee, he would be the perfect player.

Manager Don Revie, too, deserves considerable praise for his astute buying and blending.

Shabby dismissal Ramsey's 'reward' after 11 years

THE FA'S DECISION to sack Sir Alf Ramsey apparently came out of the blue to the England manager who, according to associates, was badly shaken. It was obvious that there was considerable disenchantment about England's failure to reach the World Cup finals, and speculation has been rife concerning a possible successor. But even if the FA were in a desperate hurry to get rid of a faithful servant, they might at least have allowed him the opportunity to resign.

Coventry general manager Joe Mercer has been appointed caretaker-manager, but has made it clear that, at 60, he does not want the job permanently. Whoever succeeds Ramsey will still be obliged to accept that international matches are rarely granted priority over club fixtures, and will be frequently deprived of players for spurious reasons. It is a tribute to Ramsey's ability that he overcame such obstacles often enough to guide England to 69 victories and 27 draws in 113 matches.

Perhaps the satisfaction of leading England to their only World Cup triumph, a knighthood and an assured place in soccer history, as both player and manager, will be some compensation for the disappointments and, now, the bitterness of summary dismissal.

Sir Alf Ramsey in happier days.

Black day at Old Trafford: United go down as fans shame club

HUNDREDS OF young Manchester United fans shamed the great club's reputation as they invaded the pitch four minutes before full time, and in the end the referee had to abandon the game against Manchester City. United needed to win this match if they were to stand any chance of First Division survival.

The trouble started when Denis Law, not long ago an idol of Old Trafford, cheekily backheeled the ball into their net after 82 minutes, virtually condemning them to the Second Division. Some 400 hooligans invaded the pitch and, although it was cleared this time, a few minutes later a much larger and more determined invasion was launched from the Stretford End, and on police advice the referee abandoned the game.

The first thing the League have to decide is whether to allow the result to stand. United are relegated anyway, as both Birmingham and West Ham won the necessary points to stay up. More important, a disciplinary commission will have to determine what penalty if any to impose on United. A recent precedent is the similarly frightening episode at St James's Park during Newcastle's FA Cup quarter-final against Forest. Following an FA investigation, Newcastle were last week ordered to play any home FA Cup ties next season on opponents' grounds.

At the time, the commission emphasized that Newcastle could have done little to prevent the riot. The same conclusion may be reached about the Old Trafford pitch invasions. But the fact remains that British soccer fans are now among the most violent, unsporting partisans in Europe.

SOCCER SOUNDBITES

"The way things are going, the FA and the League will have to be thinking in terms of fences."

SIR MATT BUSBY.

Liverpool's red army take Wembley by storm

LIVERPOOL'S HANDSOME 3–0 victory over Newcastle at Wembley in the FA Cup final has established them as entertainers of the highest class. Since Bill Shankly became manager in December 1959, Liverpool have won the Second Division title, three League Championships, the UEFA Cup, and now their second FA Cup. Yet beyond Merseyside they have been regarded, without warmth, as a ruthlessly efficient machine.

The third team that Shankly has patiently built at Anfield do not deserve to be damned with such faint praise. Their virtuoso performance during the second half at Wembley was sweet music indeed to those who had begun to despair of the future of English soccer. They played so well that the much-vaunted Newcastle side simply could not live with them. Kevin Keegan emerged as the popular hero with two beautifully taken goals, but they were a triumph of superb teamwork. Smith made the first goal, in the 57th minute, with a cross that Keegan chested down and then drove with a flourish into the net.

With Hall, Callaghan and Cormack denying their opponents midfield possession, Liverpool boldly mounted wave after wave of attacks and moved further ahead in the 74th minute, when Toshack headed on a long pass and Heighway, bringing the ball under control, changed direction and placed it wide of McFaul. The third goal, two minutes from time and scored by Keegan, was the culmination of nearly a dozen passes and left Newcastle gaping.

Steve Heighway scores Liverpool's second goal.

Baton charge clears fans as Spurs lose UEFA Cup final

TOTTENHAM, FACING an uphill battle after their 2–2 draw at White Hart Lane in the first leg, lost for the first time in a Cup final when Dutch champions Feyenoord took the UEFA Cup with goals by Rijsbergen and Ressel before a 67,000 crowd in Rotterdam.

The team failed with dignity, but the occasion was made deplorable by the hooligan element among their supporters, who wrecked part of one end of the ground and flung chair backs at Dutch fans. They ignored public address appeals by Spurs chairman Sidney Wale and manager Bill Nicholson, who called them a disgrace to Britain. The trouble subsided only when a force of baton-wielding police finally charged among the rioters and appeared to clear all the Spurs supporters from the stadium.

On the pitch, Spurs found the strength and skill of Feyenoord totally daunting, and with England striker Chivers rarely a threat they never looked likely to score the crucial away goals that might have continued England's six-year run of success in this competition. The first Dutch goal, in the 41st minute, was the result of a collector's piece — an error by keeper Jennings. The second, six minutes from time, was made by a dazzling run and pass by substitute Boskamp. So Spurs, on the pitch where they earned glory in 1963 by becoming the first British club to win a European trophy, trailed sadly away, shamed utterly by their so-called admirers.

On another night of shame for British clubs in Europe, Dutch police break up the rioting Spurs rabble.

FOOTBALL FOCUS

- Three up/three down promotion and relegation was introduced between Divisions One and Two and between Two and Three.
- Johan Cruyff of Ajax signed for Barcelona in August for a world record £922,300, about £400,000 of which he pocketed himself.
- Three Notts County players missed the same penalty at Portsmouth on 22 September (two had to be retaken because of encroachment), but County won 2–1.
- Trevor Hockey (Aston Villa) became the first Welsh player to be sent off in an international, on 26 September in Poland.
- Sunday soccer was launched in England on 6 January with four FA Cup ties, the first being Cambridge v Oldham (2–2) at 11 am, and the gates were all high.
- Beaten Cup-finalists Newcastle enjoyed an extraordinary passage to Wembley. They needed replays in the third and fourth rounds after being held at home by amateurs Hendon and Fourth Division Scunthorpe. At home to Forest in the sixth round, the crowd invaded the pitch after United went 3–1 down when Lyall scored from the spot, and the referee took the players off. When they returned, with 10 men (Pat Howard had been dismissed for protesting at the penalty decision), Newcastle proceeded to win 4–3. The FA ordered the match to be played again, at Goodison Park: they drew 0–0 and then won the replay (also at Goodison) 1–0.
- Exeter, with nine players unfit, risked expulsion from the League by refusing to turn up for their fixture at Scunthorpe on 2 April. For this unprecedented action, the League fined them £5,000 and awarded Scunthorpe both points.
- Third Division Plymouth beat three Division One sides away in the League Cup — Burnley, QPR and Birmingham — before losing to Manchester City in the semi-finals.
- Jack Charlton guided Middlesbrough to the Division Two title in his first season as manager, and with 65 points they had a 15-point margin over the next club, a League record.
- Celtic won their ninth consecutive League title in Scotland, and achieved another League and Cup "double".
- Crystal Palace went down to Division Three, relegated for the second season running.
- Sir Stanley Rous was succeeded as president of FIFA by Brazil's Joao Havelange before the start of the 1974 World Cup.

Johan Cruyff, £400,000 signing-on fee from Barcelona.

FINAL SCORE

Football League
Division 1: Leeds United
Top scorer: Mick Channon (Southampton) 21
Division 2: Middlesbrough
Division 3: Oldham Athletic
Division 4: Peterborough United
Footballer of the Year: Ian Callaghan (Liverpool)

FA Cup Final
Liverpool 3 Newcastle United 0

League Cup Final
Wolves 2 Manchester City 1

Scottish League
Division 1: Celtic
Top scorer: Dixie Deans (Celtic) 24
Division 2: Airdrieonians
Footballers of the Year: Scottish World Cup Squad

Scottish FA Cup Final
Celtic 3 Dundee United 0

Scottish League Cup Final
Dundee 1 Celtic 0

International Championship
England, Scotland, 4 pts

European Cup Final
Bayern Munich 1 Atletico Madrid 1
Replay: B. Munich 4 Atletico Madrid 0

Cup-Winners' Cup Final
FC Magdeburg 2 AC Milan 0

UEFA Cup Final
Feyenoord beat Tottenham Hotspur 2–2, 2–0

European Footballer of the Year 1973
Johan Cruyff (Ajax, Barcelona & Holland)

Leading European Scorer (Golden Boot)
Hector Yazalde (Sporting Lisbon) 46

World Club Championship
Atletico Madrid (Spain) beat Independiente (Argentina) 0–1, 2–0

Total football

Holland won the hearts of the footballing world in West Germany, even if they did not win the World Cup. Playing an attacking brand of soccer dubbed "total football", they replaced Brazil as the "people's favourites" and excitingly stormed their way to the final, where they lost to the talented but less charismatic home nation.

GOAL DIFFERENCE was brought into play in the qualifying competition, cutting down on play-offs, although Sweden and Yugoslavia both needed one before eliminating Austria and Spain respectively. Belgium were the unluckiest non-qualifier, going out undefeated and without conceding a goal. They held Holland to two goalless draws, but massive Dutch victories over Norway and Iceland — they scored 24 goals in those four games — saw them through. The Soviet Union had to play off with Chile for a finals place but after drawing 0–0 in Moscow, they refused to play in Santiago for political reasons and were eliminated. Australia, East Germany, Haiti and Zaïre all qualified for the first time.

Scotland (near) line-up before their 2–0 victory over Zaire.

Behind the scenes

Before the World Cup got underway, it was almost overwhelmed by commercialism and greed, politics and power struggles, all of which provided a tense background as the teams prepared to do battle. With tight security necessary after the tragic terrorist activities at the Munich Olympics in 1972, the atmosphere was grim and unfriendly — and it rained throughout most of the tournament.

There was considerable unrest in both the Dutch and the West German camps, with players threatening to go on strike in rows over pay and bonuses. Everywhere, players seemed to have their hands out — for interviews, for having their pictures taken, or for wearing a certain manufacturer's product. The Scots fell out with their football boot company and erased its symbols with black boot polish.

Three days before the tournament began, Sir Stanley Rous was "ousted" as president of FIFA by the Brazilian millionaire Joao Havelange, who was said to have spent a fortune on canvassing support, and there were rumours of a possible European breakaway from the world governing body.

The format of the competition had been changed again, with the top two teams of the four groups in Round One going through to Groups A and B, the winners of these to play the final.

Scotland, managed by Willie Ormond, who had taken over when Tommy Docherty went to Manchester United half-way through the qualifying competition, and captained by Billy Bremner, put their internal squabbles behind them and went out with their colours flying. It was unfortunate that their first match was with Zaïre, as caution kept their win down to two goals. Yugoslavia proceeded to thrash the Africans 9–0, so for Scotland to be certain of going through, they had to beat Yugoslavia. A draw would let Brazil in, provided they beat Zaïre by more than two.

Yugoslavia took the lead against Scotland in Frankfurt with only eight minutes left. But Hutchison, who had replaced the ineffective Dalglish midway through the second half, made the equalizer for Jordan just before the end. All eyes turned to the electronic scoreboard to see how Brazil were faring in Gelsenkirchen. Alas for Scotland, Brazil scored their crucial third goal 10 minutes from time, and so avoided the toss of a coin. It was a shoddy performance from Brazil, which must have saddened the watching Pele.

Neeskens scores from the spot in the sensational opening to the final.

WORLD CUP QUOTES

"The World Cup is on a disaster course. The players have become money-mad."

JOAO SALDANHA,
former Brazilian manager.

"Great game!? You know what that was? Two Third Division teams trying to kick each other to death, that's what it was."

Liverpool manager
BILL SHANKLY,
on the Scotland-Brazil goalless draw.

Cruyff was in the German box in a flash, brought down, and Neeskens's spot-kick into the back of the net put Holland one up in the final before a West German player had touched the ball.

East Germany caused a stir in Round One when they beat West Germany 1–0, but the favourites were already sure of going through, and there was a feeling that they wanted to avoid Holland in the second round. The Dutch were very impressive, with the two Johans, Cruyff and Neeskens, outstanding. Cruyff had taken over from Pele as the world's acknowledged No.1, and he soon stamped his authority on this tournament.

Poland were a revelation in Group Four, with Lato and Szarmach up front capitalizing on the midfield mastery of Deyna. They toppled first Argentina and then Italy, who were eliminated.

The big two emerge

The results of the second round groups were clear-cut — both Holland and West Germany won all their matches, beating Brazil and Poland, respectively, in last-match "deciders". Holland's "total football" was wonderful to watch, with all their outfield players capable of switching into attack or defence. West Germany, the European champions, found their true form at last: while not as versatile as the Dutch, they had, under Helmut Schoen, thrown off the defensive shackles that for so long blighted the European game.

With wingers — the flying Hoeness on the right and the tricky Grabowski on the left — to feed the master goal-poacher Muller in the centre, Overath and Bonhof controlling midfield, and skipper Beckenbauer majestically leading them in his "attacking sweeper" role, the Germans opened up in Group B. But it was the all-purpose Breitner, nominally a left-back, who ignited them with the opening goal against Yugoslavia. Then, in appalling conditions, they produced a superb display against Sweden, before being brought down to earth again by the splendid Poles, on an even more atrocious pitch. Only keeper Maier redeemed them before Muller scored the late winner, although Tomaszewski did save a penalty from Hoeness.

Meanwhile, Cruyff and Co. were sweeping aside Argentina, East Germany and World Cup-holders Brazil, scoring eight goals without conceding one, and setting up a mouth-watering final.

A tale of two penalties

While not the classic of optimistic expectations, the 1974 World Cup final had the most dramatic opening, with a penalty for Holland before a German had touched the ball. Cruyff picked the ball up in his own half and was racing into the West German box before they knew it. Only the fleet-footed Hoeness had any chance of catching him, and that's exactly what he did — unfairly inside the area. Neeskens scored from the spot-kick.

There was no doubt about the foul, although not every referee would have had the courage of Jack Taylor to give such an early penalty against the Germans in Munich's Olympic Stadium. Whether this had a subconscious effect on his later decision is hard to say, but he awarded a borderline penalty against the Dutch after 25 minutes, when Holzenbein went down, also after a fine run into the box. Breitner equalized from the spot.

Vogts was booked for persistent fouling after only four minutes, and Neeskens was lucky to get away unpunished for two crude tackles on Hoeness. But Van Hanegem was shown the yellow card for an off-the-ball push on Muller, spotted by a linesman, and Neeskens, too, was finally cautioned. Soon after, two minutes before half-time, Bonhof got through the Dutch defence and squared a short pass to Muller, who cleverly swivelled and scored a typical, opportunist goal.

Cruyff, obviously unhappy with the way the decisions were going, and mindful no doubt of West Germany's notorious propensity for "conning" referees, had words with Jack Taylor as they walked off at the interval, was booked and, indeed, lucky not to be sent off. The second half was nearly all Holland, and West Germany had to withstand tremendous pressure. And although there is the feeling that the better team lost, the Germans — especially Vogts, who did a wonderful job in minimizing the effectiveness of Cruyff — must be applauded for their spirited and intelligent performance.

Muller (13) hits West Germany's winner in the final.

FINAL SCORE

First round

Group 1

West Germany	1	Chile	0
East Germany	2	Australia	0
West Germany	3	Australia	0
East Germany	1	Chile	1
Chile	0	Australia	0
East Germany	1	West Germany	0

	P	W	D	L	F	A	P
E. Germany	3	2	1	0	4	1	5
W. Germany	3	2	0	1	4	1	4
Chile	3	0	2	1	1	2	2
Australia	3	0	1	2	0	5	1

Group 2

Brazil	0	Yugoslavia	0
Scotland	2	Zaïre	0
Brazil	0	Scotland	0
Yugoslavia	9	Zaïre	0
Scotland	1	Yugoslavia	1
Brazil	3	Zaïre	0

	P	W	D	L	F	A	P
Yugoslavia	3	1	2	0	10	1	4
Brazil	3	1	2	0	3	0	4
Scotland	3	1	2	0	3	1	4
Zaïre	3	0	0	3	0	14	0

Group 3

Holland	2	Uruguay	0
Sweden	0	Bulgaria	0
Holland	0	Sweden	0
Uruguay	1	Bulgaria	1
Holland	4	Bulgaria	1
Sweden	3	Uruguay	0

	P	W	D	L	F	A	P
Holland	3	2	1	0	6	1	5
Sweden	3	1	2	0	3	0	4
Bulgaria	3	0	2	1	2	5	2
Uruguay	3	0	1	2	1	6	1

Group 4

Poland	3	Argentina	2
Italy	3	Haiti	1
Italy	1	Argentina	1
Poland	7	Haiti	0
Poland	2	Italy	1
Argentina	4	Haiti	1

	P	W	D	L	F	A	P
Poland	3	3	0	0	12	3	6
Argentina	3	1	1	1	7	5	3
Italy	3	1	1	1	5	4	3
Haiti	3	0	0	3	2	14	0

Second round

Group A

Holland	4	Argentina	0
Brazil	1	East Germany	0
Holland	2	East Germany	0
Brazil	2	Argentina	1
Holland	2	Brazil	0
East Germany	1	Argentina	1

	P	W	D	L	F	A	P
Holland	3	3	0	0	8	0	6
Brazil	3	2	0	1	3	3	4
E. Germany	3	0	1	2	1	4	1
Argentina	3	0	1	2	2	7	1

Group B

West Germany	2	Yugoslavia	0
Poland	1	Sweden	0
Poland	2	Yugoslavia	1
West Germany	4	Sweden	2
West Germany	1	Poland	0
Sweden	2	Yugoslavia	1

	P	W	D	L	F	A	P
W. Germany	3	3	0	0	7	2	6
Poland	3	2	0	1	3	2	4
Sweden	3	1	0	2	4	6	2
Yugoslavia	3	0	0	3	2	6	0

THIRD-PLACE MATCH

Poland	1	Brazil	0

FINAL

West Germany	2	Holland	1

Olympic Stadium, Munich, 7 July 1974. Attendance 77,833

West Germany: Maier, Vogts, Schwarzenbeck, Beckenbauer, Breitner, Hoeness, Bonhof, Overath, Grabowski, Muller, Holzenbein (Scorers: Breitner pen, Muller)

Holland: Jongbloed, Suurbier, Rijsbergen (De Jong), Haan, Krol, Jansen, Neeskens, Van Hanegem, Rep, Cruyff, Rensenbrink (Van der Kerkhof R (Scorer: Neeskens pen)

Leading scorers

7 Lato (Poland)

5 Szarmach (Poland)

Neeskens (Holland)

Shankly drops a bombshell: to retire as Liverpool chief

BILL SHANKLY, 58, probably the most popular figure in League soccer, caused the first major surprise of the close season by deciding to retire after 15 years in command at Anfield. His standing down comes barely a week after Don Revie's departure from Elland Road to become manager of England. So now Leeds, the champions, and Liverpool, the runners-up and Cup-winners, both face the prospect of starting the season with a new man in charge.

The club directors reluctantly accepted Mr Shankly's decision to end his illustrious career. He wants some relief from the strain of managing a club that has rarely been out of the limelight during his association with them. He took over at Anfield in December 1959, and two-and-a-half years later guided them to promotion. Since then, they have won the League three times, the Cup twice and the UEFA Cup once — with three outstanding teams.

He achieved all this with a blend of toughness, knowledge and a sharp wit that made him the most quotable and quoted manager in British soccer. He developed those qualities as the son of a Lanarkshire miner in the bleak late twenties, as a top-class wing-half with Carlisle and Preston (capped five times for Scotland), and as the industrious manager of Carlisle, Grimsby, Workington and Huddersfield. How many future managers will serve so long, hard and sound an apprenticeship, or achieve success so consistently, while remaining so human a character?

Bill Shankly: Tactically astute and a great organizer.

Disgrace of Bremner and Keegan: sent off in Wembley showpiece

THE JOINT DISGRACE of Billy Bremner and Kevin Keegan in becoming the first British players to be sent off at Wembley was only a part of the ugliness of a shabby Charity Shield match. If the season's traditional opener, between the country's two leading teams, held at Wembley and televised live for the first time, is an example of what's to come, then we might just as well forget about it. The match had everything — sly, niggling fouls, outrageous tackles, unseemly off-the-ball scuffles, and a major flare-up. Why the two players, dismissed after an hour by a too-patient referee for fighting, felt they were hard done by and compounded their ignominy by flinging their shirts on to the Wembley track, is a mystery. Mr Matthewson had no alternative but to issue marching orders.

For the record, Boersma scored for Liverpool in the 20th minute, and Cherry headed Leeds's equalizer in the 70th. They each scored from their first five penalties, and keeper Harvey, inexplicably asked by Leeds to take their sixth, hit it over the bar. Callaghan then gleefully thumped home the winning penalty for Liverpool. But no one was the winner in this travesty of a match, and "charity" was nowhere to be seen.

Keegan and Bremner: shameful performance.

Revie confirmed as new England manager

DON REVIE WAS confirmed as Sir Alf Ramsey's successor on 4 July on a five-year contract, and his first job as England supremo was to fly out to Munich to watch the World Cup final between West Germany and Holland. His main task, of course, will be to build an England squad capable of coping with the likes of those two countries in the European Championships, and eventually challenging for the 1978 World Cup.

Success in Europe could well depend on the outcome of England's first qualifying tie, against Czechoslovakia at Wembley in October. And unless arrangements are made for an earlier get-together, he will meet his players for the first time only four days before that game. In other words, he has inherited all Ramsey's old problems; for he knows only too well the reluctance of clubs to release players for England duty except when it is absolutely essential: nobody was less co-operative than he.

Revie's qualifications for the job are excellent. A gifted inside-forward who won six England caps while with Manchester City, he lifted Leeds from Division Two to being the most feared side in the land, with major successes at home and in Europe. But the FA must have given serious thought to some aspects of Leeds's "tactics".

SOCCER SOUNDBITES

"I made the first move. They did not contact me. I fancied being England manager."

DON REVIE,
after his appointment.

Clough's reign at Leeds ends after 43 days

BRIAN CLOUGH'S short, uneasy association with Leeds ended abruptly on 12 September following a four-hour meeting at the club between him, his solicitor, and chairman Manny Cussins. A terse statement gave no indication as to why he was leaving.

His departure from Elland Road, however, only 43 days after he was appointed manager of the League champions in succession to Don Revie, further emphasizes the increasing power now wielded in League soccer by First Division players. One has to conclude that the main reason for his leaving is that the players didn't want him. At all events, yesterday's meeting came less than 24 hours after the senior squad were reported to have passed a vote of no confidence in their new boss shortly before the midweek League Cup tie at Huddersfield.

Mr Clough can scarcely have expected the players to love him, since he had been highly critical of Leeds as a team, and had singled out several individuals for attack, in print and on television, during his days as manager of Derby. Moreover, his recent purchase of John McGovern and John O'Hare, from Derby, while no reflection on the players personally, is unlikely to have improved dressing-room harmony.

According to Leeds, Mr Clough will receive a "reasonably substantial" golden handshake. He will need it, as Brighton, apparently, have no intention of withdrawing their writ against him for breach of contract.

SOCCER SOUNDBITES

"The Leeds United club and the happiness of the Leeds United players must come first."

MANNY CUSSINS,
Leeds chairman, commenting on the sudden departure of manager Brian Clough.

Nicholson resigns: players getting too difficult

SPURS CHIEF Bill Nicholson, 54, has resigned after 38 years with the club as player and manager. Although this has come as a shock to the outside world, apparently his disenchantment with the modern game — the modern player, in particular — has been building up. He stressed that his resignation had nothing to do with Spurs' poor start to the season — their worst for 62 years — and that, if Spurs had won the UEFA Cup last season, he would have gone then. He and the board, who tried to dissuade him, emphasized that he would not be retiring, but would stay on to help a new manager in some capacity if required.

As a player, Nicholson made over 300 League appearances for Spurs, and was a key member of the Championship-winning team of 1951, as well as winning one England cap and scoring with his first kick. He then guided them to the first League and Cup "double" this century, in 1961; two more FA Cups, the Cup-Winners' Cup in 1963, when Spurs were the first British club to win a European trophy; and the UEFA Cup in 1972.

Contractual problems and transfer requests have perhaps precipitated Mr Nicholson's decision, but it is his disaffection with the attitude of players that is the root cause, particularly the illegal demands that had become the norm from players who might have joined the club. He complained that the club were defeated over two transfers because they refused to break the regulations, and that the problem of under-the-counter payments had affected all of his negotiations in the past two seasons. Spurs chairman Sidney Wale claimed that the "going rate" for joining a London club was a demand for seven to 10 thousand pounds tax-free.

The thought is surely bound to strike someone that, if Mr Nicholson is no longer to be Spurs manager, there should be a place for him in the administration of the game, which has a desperate need for his unique brand of honesty.

SOCCER SOUNDBITES

"Players have become impossible. They talk all the time about security, but are not prepared to work for it. I am abused by players when they come to see me. There is no longer respect."

BILL NICHOLSON.

Nicholson: 38 years with Spurs.

Leeds beat Guy at last: non-Leaguers out

WIMBLEDON'S CUP exploits have come to an end at last, in the replayed fourth round tie with Leeds at Selhurst Park. Keeper Dickie Guy, who played a blinder at Burnley in the third round, when Wimbledon became the first post-war non-League side to beat a First Division club away, and saved a Peter Lorimer penalty eight minutes from time at Elland Road to take this tie to a replay, was finally beaten — but not by a Leeds player. Mighty Leeds needed an own goal by Dave Bassett to take them through in the end.

Wimbledon's Dickie Guy saves Peter Lorimer's penalty at Elland Road.

West Ham's Taylor-made win in Cockney final

IT WAS NOT A fairy-tale ending for Fulham at Wembley, as they went down 2–0 to West Ham in this Cockney Cup final. While most neutrals were behind the Second Division side, eager to pay homage to the grand old masters Bobby Moore and Alan Mullery, and manager Alec Stock, it was young Alan Taylor who won the glory with two goals after an hour of an otherwise unmemorable match.

It was more a case of Fulham losing the Cup, as Peter Mellor, the brave, agile giant of a keeper who had done so much to put them into the final, failed to hold shots from Jennings and Paddon, and the quicksilver Taylor was there to pounce. This was Taylor's third consecutive Cup double, after scoring all West Ham's goals in the sixth round at Arsenal and the semi-final replay with Ipswich — in his first season with the club.

After another Wembley anti-climax, it was a poignant moment when Moore and Mullery, in the twilight of their careers, slowly walked off the pitch they have graced for so many years, one arm around the other's shoulders, the other hand clutching a losers' medal. Sadder, though, was the sight of the young West Ham supporters' manic invasion of the pitch, ending in a crude attempt to taunt the disappointed Fulham fans and stripping the last vestiges of the old standards from the Cup final, which had already dispensed with "Abide with Me", the traditional Wembley hymn.

Bobby Moore (centre) is consoled by his former West Ham colleagues.

Second 'non-playing' title for Derby

DERBY HAVE WON their second League title in four seasons — again without having to kick a ball. In 1972, under Brian Clough, they were in Spain when their challengers failed to catch them. They didn't leave the country this time, as they still had a match to play, but Ipswich's failure to win at Maine Road means that Dave Mackay's men have done it.

In a season during which the First Division lead changed hands a record 21 times, Derby took over for the first time only on 9 April, and have seen off the challenges of Liverpool, Ipswich and Everton. It was good to see centre-half Roy McFarland back for the last few matches after his long injury, although young Peter Daniel has been a splendid replacement. Despite the forward power of Kevin Hector, Roger Davies and Francis Lee, midfielder Bruce Rioch is leading scorer with 15. Colin Todd was the players' choice as Footballer of the Year, and skipper Archie Gemmill also had a fine season. Above all, their success is a wonderful tribute to Mackay, who had the unenviable task of following in the footsteps of Brian Clough — and did so.

Derby County: 1975 League Champions.

Wembley scoring record for five-goal Macdonald

MALCOLM MACDONALD, the Newcastle marksman who thought his brief international career had ended when he was twice passed over by Don Revie, put his name firmly in the record books on 16 April by becoming the first player to score five goals in a Wembley international. His feat equals the England goalscoring record, and only Willie Hall in 1938 has also hit five for England this century.

Cyprus, admittedly, were weak opponents. Yet if Macdonald and the equally industrious Keegan had not gone foraging for themselves, England's goal difference in Group One of the European Championships might not now look so healthy — and this could be an important factor in deciding whether England reach the quarter-finals next year.

It all looked too easy when Macdonald headed Hudson's free-kick in after only two minutes. And although Keegan made a second for him after 35 minutes, frustration began to set in. We did not see the midfield smoothness that Hudson, Ball and Bell demonstrated in the Wembley win over West Germany last month. But another three headers in the second half gave England a comfortable 5–0 victory and Macdonald an indisputable claim on the match ball.

Macdonald, five-goal hero.

Leeds deprived of Euro glory again as fans compound misery

Riot squad in action, Parisian style, as Leeds fans turn ugly.

LEEDS'S VERY real hopes of European Cup glory, as they outplayed Bayern Munich for most of the final in Paris, turned into a nightmare as two late strikes by the Cup-holders plunged them to defeat and their so-called fans again disgraced themselves on the Continent.

Leeds forced the Germans on to the defensive when Swedish World Cup star Andersson was carried off after a clash with Yorath early on, and Bayern had to make another first-half substitution when Uli Hoeness limped off. Beckenbauer was twice lucky not to be penalized in the box, for handball and then a trip on Clarke, and Giles, Bremner, Lorimer and Jordan continued to keep Leeds on top in the second half. But the turning point came after 66 minutes, when Lorimer smashed the ball past Maier, only to have his effort disallowed for offside against his team-mates. The Leeds fans erupted violently at this decision, and the rioting became worse six minutes later, when Roth scored from a Bayern breakaway. Gerd Muller, who had spent much of his time helping out a beleaguered defence, then sealed Leeds's fate nine minutes from the end.

The hooligans continued their deplorable and menacing behaviour after the final whistle, as a result of which Leeds have been banned from Europe for three years.

Keegan back after England walk-out

AS DAVID JOHNSON of Ipswich was making a dream debut for England, scoring both goals and salvaging a draw with Wales at Wembley, Kevin Keegan, the Liverpool striker, was disappearing from the national team's Hertfordshire headquarters, the third player to take French leave from England in the last year. Manager Don Revie had left Keegan out of the Home International Championship match after the goalless draw in Northern Ireland.

This follows a pattern set by QPR forward Stan Bowles, who walked out on the England squad a year ago as they prepared for the match against Scotland, and continued by Ipswich defender Kevin Beattie, who went to his parents' home in Carlisle last December instead of reporting to an England Under-23 squad meeting in Manchester.

However, Keegan returned to the fold the next day and, after a heart-to-heart talk with Revie, was back in the side to face Scotland at Wembley. The Scots, badly missing their Leeds contingent, were well and truly thrashed 5–1, so England, after two unconvincing performances, have won the Home Championship.

FOOTBALL FOCUS

- Keegan and Bremner received unprecedented punishments for "bringing the game into disrepute" in the Charity Shield — a fine of £500 and suspension for what amounted to 11 matches.
- Bobby Charlton, as Preston player-manager, returned to football, albeit in Division Three, and scored 10 times in League and Cup, taking his League goals above the 200 mark.
- It was third time lucky for manager Ron Saunders, reaching his third League Cup final running, with different clubs — Norwich, Manchester City, and now Aston Villa, who gave him his first success.
- Wales went top of their European Championship qualifying group with the aid of a double over Hungary, following a 2–0 home victory on 30 October by sensationally winning 2–1 in Budapest on 16 April, Hungary's first post-war home defeat in a competitive match.
- Celtic's League supremacy in Scotland (nine wins in a row) came to an end, and skipper Billy McNeill retired after leading them to victory in the Cup (their seventh successive final). In a reorganization of Scottish football next season, there will be a Premier League of 10 clubs and a First and a Second Division of 14 clubs each.

FINAL SCORE

Football League
Division 1: Derby County
Top scorer: Malcolm Macdonald (Newcastle United) 21
Division 2: Manchester United
Division 3: Blackburn Rovers
Division 4: Mansfield Town
Footballer of the Year: Alan Mullery (Fulham)

FA Cup Final
West Ham United 2 Fulham 0

League Cup Final
Aston Villa 1 Norwich City 0

Scottish League
Division 1: Rangers
Top scorer: Andy Gray (Dundee United), Willie Pettigrew (Motherwell) 20
Division 2: Falkirk
Footballer of the Year: Sandy Jardine (Rangers)

Scottish FA Cup Final
Celtic 3 Airdrieonians 1

Scottish League Cup Final
Celtic 6 Hibernian 3

International Championship
England, 4 pts

European Cup Final
Bayern Munich 2 Leeds United 0

Cup-Winners' Cup Final
Dynamo Kiev 3 Ferencvaros 0

UEFA Cup Final
Borussia Moenchengladbach beat Twente Enschede 0–0, 5–1

European Footballer of the Year 1974
Johan Cruyff (Barcelona & Holland)

Leading European Scorer (Golden Boot)
Dudu Georgescu (Dinamo Bucharest) 33

World Club Championship
Competition not held

Doyle carts off another medal as he inspires City to Wembley win

WHEN MIKE DOYLE looks back on his fourth appearance at Wembley for Manchester City, he may well conclude that this was the afternoon on which he reached the peak of an illustrious one-club career that has brought him every major prize domestic soccer can offer. During City's 2–1 League Cup victory over Newcastle, Doyle scaled heights rarely attained by players even in more glamorous competitions. As marshal of defence, instigator of counter-attacks, crucial contributor to the all-important opening goal and, above all, as a calm, authoritative captain, this elegant footballer gave a superb performance — comparable with that of Franz Beckenbauer when West Germany beat England at Wembley four years ago. Even so, City did not control the game as firmly as they should have, after a carefully rehearsed move enabled Doyle to head down a free-kick for Peter Barnes to score in the 12th minute. As they sat back, somewhat complacently, Newcastle equalized in the 34th minute when Alan Gowling finished off one of the slickest moves of the match.

The winning goal came seconds after the interval, when Dennis Tueart scored with a spectacular bicycle-kick after Tommy Booth had headed a cross back into the middle. Newcastle staged a grandstand finish, but Doyle made sure City stayed ahead to the final whistle.

Tueart goes horizontal to hit City's winner.

Wreckers on the rampage again

WITH THE SEASON only two weeks old, hooligans have already plunged the game into an abyss of despond. In one of the blackest days for British football to date, behaviour at grounds in various parts of the country plumbed new depths. The Chelsea following in the Second Division match at Luton sparked off violent scenes when they swarmed on to the pitch after their team had gone three down in the second half. They attacked players, police and stewards — one steward was knifed, another had his nose broken — and play was suspended for five minutes. Luton keeper Barber, who was earlier pelted with coins, was punched on the back of the head. The violence continued after the match, in the Luton streets and on the trains back to London, as the rampaging hooligans left a trail of vandalized cars, shops and railway carriages in their wake.

More than 100 Chelsea fans were arrested, and other black spots included Ibrox (60 arrests) and Stoke, where 50 of Manchester United's thugs were apprehended. The so-called "English disease" is still spreading and getting more virulent. Implementation of the findings of the government working party on crowd behaviour published a month ago cannot come soon enough, but it will be a massive and expensive task.

Liverpool pip QPR for title after fright from Wolves

LIVERPOOL WON the League Championship for a record ninth time amid tumultuous scenes at Molineux, when they came back from a goal down at half-time to win 3–1 and consign Wolves at the same time to Second Division football next season. And QPR's 10-day wait, as they sat on top of the table with a one-point lead, ended in disappointment. They fought a brave fight all season, and took 27 points from their last 15 games, but Liverpool dropped only one point in their last nine, and their total of 60 points was good enough.

Wolves had to win to stand a chance of staying up, and took the lead through Kindon after 12 minutes. Keegan and Heighway began to open up the Wolves defence but, as the minutes continued to go by, one's mind went back to 1972 when Leeds were thwarted at Molineux in a similar situation. But Bob Paisley brought Fairclough on for Case in the 65th minute and, 12 minutes later, Keegan powered the ball in from Toshack's nod down. That would have been enough to give Liverpool the title, but in the last five minutes Toshack and Kennedy made sure.

SOCCER SOUNDBITES

"Bill Shankly set such a high standard. Liverpool have been geared to this sort of thing for 15 years. I have just helped things along."

BOB PAISLEY,
Liverpool's ever-modest manager.

Bradford rise from sick beds to give Canaries dose of own medicine

FIRST DIVISION NORWICH, so often the giant-killers of the past, went down 2–1 at home to Bradford City, who become the third Division Four side to reach the quarter-finals of the FA Cup. Barely back off their sick beds after influenza had twice been the cause of postponements, Bradford were about to sink to their knees from exhaustion when Billy McGinley blocked a clearance and scored the winner two minutes from time in what was their only attack of the second half.

Bradford defended magnificently throughout, rode their luck, and scored with their only two chances. They took a brief lead six minutes from half-time with a solo effort from diminutive left-winger Don Hutchins, which was soon equalized by Martin Peters's header. Near the end, Norwich hit the woodwork twice and had a goal disallowed, before Bradford got their shock winner.

Bremner is one of six given life ban by Scotland

THE LONG, COLOURFUL, often controversial international career of Billy Bremner, captain of Scotland and Leeds, came to a sad and ignominious, if not entirely unpredictable, end in Glasgow on 8 September, when the Scottish selectors decided that he and four others should never play for their country again. The others banned following an investigation of alleged misconduct after last week's European Championship qualifier in Copenhagen were Joe Harper (Hibs), Pat McCluskey (Celtic), and Willie Young and Arthur Graham (Aberdeen). Bremner, 32, has won 54 Scottish caps, one fewer than Denis Law's record.

All five players were said to be involved in incidents at a Copenhagen night club and in the squad's hotel later. Bremner vehemently denied the charges over the weekend, but the committee accepted detailed reports of officials without calling on the players concerned. It was obvious that the committee, conscious of the current concern over hooliganism, would take a hard line.

Stokes fires Saints to stun Red Devils

SECOND DIVISION Southampton stunned hot favourites Manchester United at Wembley with a late goal from Bobby Stokes to win the first major honour in their 91-year history. Not since 1939, when Portsmouth also ridiculed the odds by defeating Wolves, has the South of England had so much to shout about on Cup final day. And the last time Southampton reached the Cup final, in 1902, they were in the Southern League and had the immortal C.B.Fry in their team.

United, who 10 days earlier still had hopes of the "double", failed to play up to their high standards, with the exception of Martin Buchan, their elegant captain, and his partner in central defence, Brian Greenhoff. They also failed utterly to prove that the reintroduction of a pair of conventional wingers is the answer to English soccer's prayers, and Tommy Docherty ultimately abandoned the policy by pulling off Gordon Hill after 66 ineffective minutes and replacing him with David McCreery.

Southampton, whose confidence had been growing as McCalliog gradually took midfield control away from the quietly fading Macari and Daly, now sensed their opponents were seriously worried, and pushed forward even more purposefully, with the eager Stokes, the surprisingly industrious Osgood and the fleet-footed Channon frequently harassing United's defence and testing the watchful Stepney.

At last, seven minutes from time, Stokes raced on to a beautifully judged through-pass from McCalliog and calmly placed a low, firm, left-foot shot wide of the diving keeper, fulfilling a prediction last week by jubilant manager Lawrie McMenemy that he would score the winner at Wembley.

SOCCER SOUNDBITES

"This is the first time that the Cup final will be played at Hillsborough... The other semi-final is a bit of a joke, really."

TOMMY DOCHERTY,
Manchester United manager, after his side were drawn to play Derby in the semi-finals, with Southampton facing Third Division Crystal Palace.

Stepney is left down and out by Stokes's winner for Southampton.

Hearts broken as Rangers clinch 'treble'

FOR THE THIRD TIME in their history, Rangers completed the "treble" when they beat Hearts 3–1 in the Scottish Cup final at Hampden. With the inaugural Premier League title and the League Cup already won, they rammed home their superiority from the start. They took only 41 seconds to find the back of Hearts' net: Jim Jeffries fouled Derek Johnstone and, from Tommy McLean's free-kick, the tall Johnstone outjumped the Hearts defence to head strongly in.

After such a great start, Rangers' victory never looked in doubt. Chances were missed by both sides, however, before they increased their lead just before half-time through Alex MacDonald, who shot home through a ruck of players following a corner. Continuous Rangers pressure brought them their third goal — and Johnstone's second — in the 81st minute and, a couple of minutes later, Graham Shaw tapped in Hearts' consolation.

Hearts were at full stretch to keep Rangers out.

Revival raises Anfield hopes for return

A MAGNIFICENT second-half comeback enabled Liverpool to wipe out Bruges's early two-goal advantage and gain a narrow but richly deserved win in the first leg of the UEFA Cup final at Anfield on 28 April. Three goals in five hectic minutes accounted for the surprised Belgians and, after one of Liverpool's most remarkable performances in 12 successive years of European competition, they have high hopes of aggregate victory in the return in three weeks' time.

The 50,000 crowd, stunned to silence as Lambert and Cools scored after five and 12 minutes, almost raised the roof when Liverpool, ever resolute, hit back on the hour. The atmosphere was electric, reminiscent of Anfield's most memorable European nights, as Liverpool attacked their favourite Kop end in the second half. They drew level with a splendid 20-yarder from the busy Kennedy, after Keegan and Heighway had linked up on the left, and a simple tap-in from substitute Case after Kennedy, put through by Keegan, had driven the ball against the far post. They then rounded off the revival when Keegan scored from the spot after Heighway was brought down.

Keegan scores from the spot to give Liverpool a first-leg lead.

Dutch double and Holland trip contribute to Hammers' downfall in Belgium

Pat Holland (far right) gives West Ham the lead against Anderlecht in the Cup-Winners' Cup Final.

FINAL SCORE

EUROPEAN CHAMPIONSHIP 1976

QUARTER-FINALS
Spain v West Germany 1–1, 0–2
Holland v Belgium 5–0, 2–1
Czechoslovakia v USSR 2–0, 2–2
Yugoslavia v Wales 2–0, 1–1

Last four in Yugoslavia

SEMI-FINALS

Czechoslovakia (after extra time)	3	Holland	1
West Germany	4	Yugoslavia	2

THIRD-PLACE MATCH

Holland	3	Yugoslavia	2

FINAL

Czechoslovakia (after extra time)	2	West Germany	2

Czechoslovakia won 5–3 on penalties
Belgrade, 20 June 1976. Attendance 45,000

Czechoslovakia: Viktor, Dobias (Vesely F), Pivarnik, Ondrus, Capkovic, Gogh, Moder, Panenka, Svehlik (Jurkemik), Masny, Nehoda (Scorers: Svehlik, Dobias)
West Germany: Maier, Vogts, Beckenbauer, Schwarzenbeck, Dietz, Bonhof, Wimmer (Flohe), Muller D, Beer (Bongartz), Hoeness, Holzenbein (Scorers: Muller, Holzenbein)

WEST HAM FAILED to repeat their Cup-Winners' Cup triumph of 11 years ago at Wembley, as this time they were the "away" side, and Anderlecht beat them 4–2 in Brussels. Yet they might have defeated the Belgians, but for a defensive error just before the interval that lost them the initiative of a goal lead. Dutch World Cup star Robert Rensenbrink was outstanding for Anderlecht.

West Ham appeared in command after taking the lead with a goal by Pat Holland in the 29th minute. Then, three minutes before half-time, a misjudged back-pass from Frank Lampard left keeper Mervyn Day stranded, and Ressel pushed the ball inside for Rensenbrink to score easily.

Soon after the interval, Rensenbrink put Van der Elst through to give Anderlecht the lead, although the Hammers fought back with skill and courage and equalized in the 66th minute, when the tireless Trevor Brooking worked his way to the left byline and curled a centre into the goalmouth for "Pop" Robson to head in off a post. But West Ham never looked in charge in the second half, and Rensenbrink and fellow Dutchman Ari Haan began to launch quick counter-attacks. In one of these, Holland brought down Rensenbrink, who scored from the spot.

Anderlecht, now playing beautiful football, made sure of victory a few minutes from the end, when Rensenbrink, again, found Van der Elst with a long through-pass, and the little winger rounded John McDowell and Day before popping the ball into the net.

SOCCER SOUNDBITES

"I refuse to have players at the club that I don't want... If they [the directors] want to have somebody to carry out their decisions, they can get anyone to do that!"

BOBBY CHARLTON,
on resigning from Preston.

"I have become increasingly disillusioned with the way English football is heading. I am sad and frustrated by some of the trends in the game."

MALCOLM ALLISON,
on resigning from Crystal Palace.

FOOTBALL FOCUS

- Bobby Charlton resigned as Preston manager on 21 August over a dispute with the directors about transfers.
- Aston Villa defender Chris Nicholl scored all four goals in their 2–2 draw with Leicester on 20 March!
- Real Madrid achieved a remarkable comeback against Derby County (for whom Charlie George scored four goals in the two legs) in the second round of the European Cup, returning from 4–1 down in the first leg, to take the second 5–1 after extra time. But they lost in the semis to Bayern Munich, who went on to win their third successive trophy by beating St. Etienne 1–0 at Hampden Park.
- Two of England's top strikers signed for Belgian clubs, Duncan McKenzie (£250,000) went to Anderlecht from Leeds, and Roger Davies (£130,000) to Bruges from Derby.
- The Football League arrived in the 20th century on 4 June, when they decided to replace the antediluvian goal average system for determining League positions by goal difference from next season.
- Jimmy Hill, managing director of Coventry City, signed a long-term contract to be Saudi Arabia's London-based soccer supremo, appointing coaches, officials and administrators.

The goal that won Bayern their third European Cup

Liverpool's Cup as battered red wall stands firm

LIVERPOOL, England's newly confirmed champions, completed a magnificent double in the Olympia Stadium on 19 May, when their second-leg 1–1 draw against Bruges, who had also won their national championship, was enough to give them the UEFA Cup for the second time in four years. Their task in this hard-fought final was never easy but, after Kevin Keegan had equalized an early penalty, Liverpool's formidable defence stood firm.

After the two goals had been scored in a hectic opening 15 minutes, Liverpool set out to contain a series of Bruges attacks, absorb the pressure, and break quickly from the back when their rare chances came. It was such a break that enabled them to hit back after Raoul Lambert's penalty, conceded for a Smith handball. Neal was fouled on the edge of the Bruges box, Hughes tapped the free-kick to Keegan, and the newly elected Footballer of the Year lashed a right-foot shot into goal from 18 yards.

The defence performed valiantly, with heads, bodies and legs blocking a succession of shots and headers and, although Jensen in the Bruges goal had little to do, Keegan's control and pace kept their defence on the alert. Clemence was lucky to see a tremendous shot from Lambert hit a post soon after the interval, but he made a vital stop from Van Gool four minutes from time that saved Liverpool from defeat.

Jimmy Case and Emlyn Hughes run to congratulate goalscorer Kevin Keegan (arm raised).

Czechs annex European prize: Germans pay the penalty

IN A DRAMATIC European Championship final in Belgrade, Czechoslovakia won the trophy for the first time when they defeated the holders and World Cup champions West Germany on penalties. The Germans, those marvellous survivors, had fought back from a 2–0 deficit, their equalizer coming in the last seconds of normal time. There was no further scoring in extra time, and it was a travesty of a fine game — and a splendid tournament — that it should have to be settled by the iniquitous penalty shoot-out.

Czechoslovakia matched the Germans in every department, and bewildered them with a series of cross-field movements, with Masny their constant inspiration. Their attacking football paid dividends after only eight minutes, when Svehlik drove the ball into an open goal with Maier stranded. In the 26th minute, a Masny free-kick was blocked to Dobias, who scored from 25 yards.

The Germans, who had been two down in the semi-finals too, replied immediately, when Dieter Muller, the hat-trick hero against Yugoslavia, scored with an acrobatic volley. The football remained of the highest standard, in keeping with the rest of the matches in Yugoslavia, and it seemed that Czechoslovakia were home and dry, before Holzenbein stunned everyone by heading in a Bonhof corner to take the match into extra time. There were no more goals, and eventually the unfortunate Uli Hoeness drove his penalty high and wide, leaving Panenka to win the game for Czechoslovakia.

Antonin Panenka chips the vital penalty over Sepp Maier.

FINAL SCORE

Football League
Division 1: Liverpool
Top scorer: Ted MacDougall (Norwich City) 23
Division 2: Sunderland
Division 3: Hereford United
Division 4: Lincoln City
Footballer of the Year: Kevin Keegan (Liverpool)

FA Cup Final
Southampton 1 Manchester United 0

League Cup Final
Manchester City 2 Newcastle United 1

Scottish League
Premier Division: Rangers
Top scorer: Kenny Dalglish (Celtic) 24
Division 1: Partick Thistle
Division 2: Clydebank
Footballer of the Year: John Greig (Rangers)

Scottish FA Cup Final
Rangers 3 Hearts 1

Scottish League Cup Final
Rangers 1 Celtic 0

International Championship
Scotland, 6 pts

European Cup Final
Bayern Munich 1 St Etienne 0

Cup-Winners' Cup Final
Anderlecht 4 West Ham United 2

UEFA Cup Final
Liverpool beat FC Bruges 3–2, 1–1

European Footballer of the Year 1975
Oleg Blokhin (Dynamo Kiev & USSR)

Leading European Scorer (Golden Boot)
Sotiris Kaiafas (Omonia Nicosia) 39

World Club Championship
Bayern Munich (West Germany) beat Cruzeiro (Brazil) 2–0, 0–0

Heroes of the Seventies

By Sue Mott

It is hard to know which was worse, the morality or the haircuts. The depravity of some of the tackles circa 1970 would have made a Viking flinch. There again, so would Charlie George's perm and that is bearing in mind the Thor-worshippers' fondness for helmets with curly horns.

Charlie George.

You wonder how we stood for it (no-one who was anyone sat). Peter Storey of Arsenal would go into tackles peculiarly sideways, crablike, inflicting maximum damage on the mortal bone and gristle in his way. Ron Harris of Chelsea was known as "Chopper", like a gangland executioner. Leeds United had a team full of enforcers, of which Norman Hunter was merely the most notorious.

To a man, though, they were short-back-and-sides. It was as though some helpful FA official had devised a failsafe coding system for novice spectactors. The shorter the follicle, the more advanced the murderous impulse. This really worked. For the long-haired lovers of trickery on the ball were united in their aversion to the barbers.

Hair and flare

Georgie Best, Rodney Marsh, Stanley Bowles, the aforementioned Charlie (pre-perm) had a Samsonite passion for long flowing, wispy, greasy hair which accurately mirrored their flouting of convention in other fields. Best, for instance, regularly went AWOL in this decade. Bowles, we now know, was down the betting shop. George was nurturing the great weight of his witlessness that would eventually deprive him of a finger in his lawnmower. "I wondered what was wrong with it, so I just put my hand in..."

But the beauty, while not perhaps apparent in the headgear nor even the bit between the sideburns, was miraculously present on the ball. When Charlie George capered through the glutinous mud of Maine Road in the fifth round of the FA Cup on Arsenal's way to the 1971 Double, it was a feat of balance and audacity that few others would have contemplated. George, partly because the powers of contemplation were beyond him, just did it. And scored, as he later would in the FA Cup final itself.

George Best, meanwhile, entangled by his genius and blondes, began his long painful disassociation from Manchester United. In 1971 he was sent off against Chelsea in only the club's second game of the season, returned to score a hat-trick against West Ham, including a goal where he beat three bemused defenders in succession before turning the pillar that was Bobby Moore inside out and fluidly ladelling the ball into the net. Yet, by the end of that season Best had fled to Spain and was threatening retirement at 26.

These were the rock stars of football. The Marc Bolans and David Bowies of their time. The flare of their brilliance was matched by the flares at the hems of George Graham's trousers. But the Rodneys, Charlies, Stanleys, rarely did they make it into the international team. Peter Osgood's short shorts, tight as clingfilm, may have given him a hernia but not the necessary apperance of studiousness.

Making music

Under the three R's of English football, ramrod Ramsey and Revie, there was emphasis on sweat and organisation. The players of the Seventies reminded you of its music. Mud and Sweet and Slade, one-syllable wonders. Fairly basic and derivative with a limited set of boom-bang-a-bang lyrics.

Alan Ball was contemptuous of Don Revie's regime. "Some of the players picked are donkeys," he said. "Give them a lump of sugar and they run all day and play bingo all night."

The magnificent hatching of Liverpool apart, the decade was loaded with ordinariness. Not once did England qualify for the World Cup finals after their West Germany-doused 1970 appearance in Mexico, and it was teamwork bordering on donkey-work that often won the domestic honours.

Fear and loathing

David Webb's bundled goal in the 226th minute of Chelsea's on-and-on-going FA Cup final against Leeds United in 1970 had the force of an oracle. It presaged the future in which Brian Clough's teams (Derby and Nottingham Forest) would take a set of basic ingredients and stir them with fear and inspiration into winners — or at least too terrified to be losers.

And Webb's face-splitting grin in a bobble-hat is the image that presides over the scene. There he was, so twisted and beguiled by the Leeds winger Eddie Gray in the Cup final draw at Wembley that his intestines had probably unravelled in the process, suddenly the no-nonsense hero of the replay.

George Best had the world at his feet, but he blew it.

Allan Clarke gets the better of Dick Malone, but Sunderland, thanks to goalkeeper Jim Montgomery, kept Leeds out.

Persistence and guts were to be the rewarded virtues.

Arsenal proved it the very next year. For while George was their crowning glory, their toy boy, their firework maker, George Armstrong, the veteran winger for whom Peter Marinello had been employed as a replacement, was the solid foundation of victory. His crosses, met with endless patience and unfussiness by John Radford and Ray Kennedy (who even Arsenal fans called a "carthorse"), may have been the difference to winning the Double or winning nothing. That and togetherness. They even went together on holiday when it was all over. To Torremolinos and it rained every day.

Going to the underdogs

This was the decade when underdogs won Cup finals. Sunderland (1973) over Leeds, Southampton (1976) over Manchester United, Ipswich Town (1978) over Arsenal. Second Division Sunderland's was perhaps the most unlikely, overturning the fortune of the most clinical, cynical yet successful side in the land and leading to one of the greatest pitch embraces of the post-War years, the Cathy-Heathcliffe collision of Sunderland goalkeeper, Jim Montgomery, and manager, Bob Stokoe, at the final whistle.

A season later, the FA's match committee suggested that players caught "kissing and cuddling" after a goal should be charged with bringing the game into disrepute. It was dismissed eventually as impracticable. It was a marvellous example of the bone-headed, backward-looking, tradition-clinging environment in which British football was still steeped. There was Billy Bremner, the captain of Leeds and Scotland, still going on nightclub benders in 1976 which brought the iron curtain down on his international career. The Scots wrecked Wembley, taking home bits of splintered goalpost as souvenirs. Tommy Docherty was sacked by Manchester United for adultery. A players strike was threatened. Sammy Nelson of Arsenal was fined £750 for dropping his shorts in front of spectators at Coventry.

Dumb and dumber

It was an almost endearingly non-cerebral time, all the more remarkable for its deliberate non-alignment with Europe. The Tories weren't the first Eurosceptics after all. Across the English Channel, Johann Cruyff existed. So did Franz Beckenbauer. Holland were playing total football in vivid tangerine. Good old England were playing badly in sepia.

But just as cogniscent man emerged from the primordial swamp, so did the thinking footballer arise from the hackneyed marshes. Kevin Keegan, Kenny Dalglish, Liam Brady and Trevor Francis, who broke the million-pound transfer barrier in 1979 moving from Birmingham to Nottingham Forest, were all players with wisdom and variety.

The era of the clogger was fading. Peter Storey was moving into his second career involving brothels and counterfeiting and, subsequently, gaol. Tottenham Hotspur, in a move of dazzling premonition, brought Ricky Villa and Ossie Ardilles of Argentina to White Hart Lane for, believe it or not, £700,000 inclusive.

So after all the stifling of talent and flair that had gone before, the decade closed to the syncopated sound of the Latin American tango. Which was a hell of a lot better than Mud.

Tough act: Ron "Chopper" Harris.

England World Cup hopes crash in Rome

ENGLAND FLEW HOME from Rome beaten for the first time in the current World Cup qualifying tournament and with their hopes of reaching the finals in Argentina in 1978 flickering only faintly. The sad fact is that England played as well as they were able, but could never match the liquid skills of the Italian master craftsmen. That is even more depressing than the 2–0 scoreline.

To prevent Italy lining up in the last 16, Don Revie's men almost certainly will have to win the return match, preferably by three clear goals, because the other nations in the group, Finland and Luxembourg, are merely making up the numbers.

Italy's first goal came after 36 minutes, following a foul on Causio just outside England's penalty box. Causio tapped the ball to Antognoni, who drove it at the England wall and got a crucial deflection off Keegan's body. A rout seemed on, but Italy allowed England back into the game — at least until 12 minutes from time, when they sealed victory with a brilliant second goal. Causio found Benetti on the left and, as his low cross came over, Bettega launched himself at it to head past Clemence in goal.

Bettega's spectacular header clinches the game for Italy.

Dutch masters put shaky England on canvas

IT WAS ONLY a friendly, but England's hopes of lifting their sagging morale following last autumn's World Cup defeat by Italy were soon shattered at Wembley on 9 February, when Holland, playing smooth, attacking football, moved into a two-goal lead before half-time and stayed in control throughout.

The Dutch masters quickly took charge in midfield, where Greenhoff alone, before he was injured and replaced by Todd after 34 minutes, offered England much prospect of success, and soon Revie's defenders were under heavy pressure. This was turned into goals by Jan Peters, who scored in the 30th and 39th minute, the first set up by Cruyff and Neeskens, the second by new cap Hovencamp.

Cruyff, indeed, seemed to be everywhere, and Madeley ultimately gave up trying to mark him. England tried to get back into the game, with Bowles and Francis spearheading one or two purposeful looking raids, although Keegan was having a quiet time for him. The attack received little help from midfield, however, and Holland soon reassumed complete control. Their performance was "the best at Wembley since the Hungarians in 1953", according to England manager Don Revie.

Record for super Bowles as QPR spill Cologne

QUEEN'S PARK RANGERS, at their scintillating best, took another impressive stride towards a major trophy in their first European season with the demolition of Cologne in the UEFA Cup third round, first leg at Loftus Road. Goals by Don Givens, David Webb and Stan Bowles took their tally to 22 in five UEFA matches so far, and Bowles, who has now collected 10 of them, broke the British joint record of Dennis Viollet, Denis Law and Derek Dougan for European goals in one season.

For the first time, QPR met worthy opposition, and they will not underestimate the Germans in the return leg, for they played attractive football throughout, and Parkes had to make three outstanding saves from Mueller in the second half. But with Rangers playing their exciting brand of attacking football, and Bowles at his most impudent, Rangers forced Cologne on to the defensive and struck with two goals just before the interval, both set up by Thomas and McLintock. Bowles crowned a splendid QPR performance with a superb goal 15 minutes from the end. Picking up the ball just outside the box, he dribbled round three defenders, walked up to the keeper Schumacher and coolly rounded him before slipping the ball into the net.

Little goals mean a lot as Villa end marathon

AFTER AN EPIC 5½-hour battle, Aston Villa finally won the League Cup when Brian Little scored the second of his goals in the last minutes of extra time to beat Everton 3–2 in this second replay at Old Trafford. Compared with the somewhat tame afternoon at Wembley in the first match in March, and the replay at Hillsborough, the atmosphere was electric. Both teams also played with much more endeavour, but, alas, the football was no better.

Everton seemed to be moving towards victory with a 38th-minute goal by Latchford, when there was suddenly a flurry of goals. First Nicholl equalized 10 minutes from time with a ferocious 35-yard left-foot drive, and then Little ran at the Everton defence and lashed the ball home a minute later to give Villa the lead. Everton, stunned as they were, came back and drew level again through Lyons, who headed in after a corner.

So the match went into extra time again and, just as a penalty decider looked ominously certain, Little burst through the tired Everton defence to convert a centre and produce a fitting climax to a thrilling match.

John Gidman (left) and Alex Cropley show off the League Cup.

Jack Charlton joins the exodus of managers

JACK CHARLTON'S resignation from Middlesbrough on 21 April completes a flurry of managerial drop-outs in the Football League over the last couple of days. Like his erstwhile team-mate at Leeds, Johnny Giles, who resigned from West Bromwich Albion the day before, Charlton will leave at the end of the season. Two other managers, however, did not just go — they were pushed. Tony Waiters was sacked at Plymouth, while Stockport have decided to part company with Eddie Quigley for reasons of economy.

Charlton has become increasingly disenchanted at the lack of enthusiasm shown by local supporters after he guided the team to Division One in his first season, 1973–74. This season, Middlesbrough were top in October, but have since slumped to mid-table.

At West Bromwich, chairman Bert Millichip tried to make player-manager Giles change his mind. Giles, who also had taken his club into the First Division, has made no secret of the fact that the insecurity of football management disturbs him, but emphasized that he had no disagreement with anyone at the club. He will have done the game a service if his comments cause directors throughout the country to reflect: in the last 10 months, 33 League clubs have changed managers. "The job should come with a health warning," says Giles.

Jack Charlton: disenchanted.

SOCCER SOUNDBITES

"We are on the crest of a slump."

JACK CHARLTON,
a few days before resigning from Middlesbrough.

"Football, and management, are precarious professions. There is so much fear in the game, it spreads like the plague."

JOHNNY GILES,
on resigning from West Brom.

Old Firm double for Conn as Lynch hangs one on Rangers

CELTIC HAD TO FIGHT all the way to beat Rangers in the Scottish Cup final at Hampden — so completing their League and Cup "double" — with their goal coming from a penalty by Andy Lynch in the 20th minute, after Johnstone had handled a chip from Celtic skipper Dalglish. And ex-Spurs star Alfie Conn made history by becoming the first player to win Cup medals with both Old Firm clubs. He won his medal with Rangers when they beat Celtic 3–2 in the final in 1973. Now, after a spell with Spurs, he's done it for Celtic, too.

Rangers' finishing was poor, with their twin strikers Parlane and Johnstone out of touch. Celtic had more trouble from Robertson, the Rangers substitute, who twice went close to equalizing near the end.

In the rain, the game deteriorated into a succession of fouls. The poor attendance, 54,000, the lowest for more than 50 years, was due partly to the miserable weather, but mainly to live television.

Celtic's history-making Alfie Conn in the thick of the action.

Fans to be caged next season after increased rowdiness

THERE WAS A disturbing end to the League season on many grounds, and fans at Stamford Bridge at least will be fenced in behind iron railings next season. There was even trouble at Anfield, where Liverpool played safely for a goalless draw with West Ham to make sure of retaining their League title, but were prevented from celebrating by hordes of young fans.

Hooligans purporting to be fêting the success of Wolves and Chelsea in the Second Division and of Brighton in the Third, and lamenting Tottenham's departure from the First, staged much uglier demonstrations. Chelsea's chairman Brian Mears was so disturbed by the wild behaviour at Stamford Bridge that he has already given orders for iron fences to be erected all round the ground next season. One celebration not marred by fans was that of Nottingham Forest, who won the third promotion place to Division One when Bolton lost at home to Wolves. Champagne must have been flowing in Forest's Majorca hotel — the same one in which their boss Brian Clough celebrated five years ago when his Derby County team won the League, thanks that time also to a Wolves victory!

An all-too-typical scene of soccer in the Seventies — a pitch invasion at Stamford Bridge.

Liverpool's 'treble' chance dashed: United's bold football triumphs

MANCHESTER UNITED beat Liverpool 2–1 at Wembley in a Cup final that went some way towards restoring faith, not only in football but in the behaviour of the fans. Champions Liverpool, their "treble" dreams shattered, will have a difficult task picking themselves up for Wednesday's European Cup final in Rome.

Sanity and sportsmanship came back to soccer on Saturday, with "Abide with Me" rendered with soul-stirring passion at the start, and the much-maligned United fans chanting "Liverpool, Liverpool" to salute their beaten rivals at the end.

United manager Tommy Docherty deserves great credit for not abandoning their policy of bold football after last year's Wembley defeat and failure in Europe this season. His response to those setbacks was to buy another attacking player, Jimmy Greenhoff, elder brother of Brian. And it was Jimmy who played a crucial part in taking United to the final, with the opening goal in the semi-final against Leeds, his former club. Greenhoff also scored the winner at Wembley — a fluke, as he admitted later. Trying to get out of the way of a Lou Macari shot (which was going wide), he deflected the ball over keeper Clemence and into goal. All the goals were crammed into a flurry of activity between the 50th and 55th minutes. Stuart Pearson had opened the scoring for United, racing through to hammer the ball in after Jimmy Greenhoff, again, had flicked it over Emlyn Hughes.

Lou Macari and Gordon Hill (11) celebrate the winning goal.

Two minutes later, Liverpool responded like true champions. Case, the game's outstanding player, controlled a centre on his thigh, turned and then drove one of the best Cup final goals for years into the roof of the net.

Ray Kennedy came closest to equalizing when he hammered a shot against the bar late on, but Liverpool had spurned their best chances in the first half, and United went on to win the most sporting, skilful and exciting final seen at Wembley for many a year.

Night of triumph for Paisley and Co.

LIVERPOOL'S 13 consecutive seasons of campaigning in European competitions reached a memorable climax at the Olympic Stadium in Rome on 25 May, when they won the major trophy, the European Cup, with one of the most distinguished performances of their long history. The League champions swept Borussia Moenchengladbach to decisive defeat with the smoothly skilled, intelligent football we had come to believe was now a Continental monopoly.

Any doubts as to the effect of Saturday's disappointing Wembley visit on Bob Paisley's men were allayed in the first quarter of an hour. With Case, Kennedy, Callaghan and in particular McDermott using the ball proficiently and running alertly into space, Liverpool soon commanded midfield. And Liverpool's front line of Keegan and Heighway looked much sharper than at Wembley.

It was no surprise when they took the lead after 28 minutes. McDermott spotted a gap, raced through it on to Heighway's perfectly timed pass, and hit the ball hard and low into the far corner of the net. But Liverpool lapsed into carelessness six minutes into the second half, and Simonsen pounced on Case's misplaced pass, sped into the box and lashed a fierce shot past Clemence.

Phil Neal's penalty sends Kneib the wrong way as Liverpool clinch their 3–1 win.

For 10 minutes, Liverpool lost their composure as Borussia, sensing they could steal victory, pushed forward eagerly. Appropriately, however, it was Tommy Smith, making his farewell appearance for the club, who came to the rescue. Due to retire at the end of the season, he was brought back into the team only a couple of months ago when Phil Thompson was injured. As two defenders followed Keegan, Smith moved into the vacated space to head a corner from Heighway forcefully into the net. Then, seven minutes from time, Keegan, who was also playing his last match in Liverpool colours before leaving for Hamburg, and who had led Vogts a merry dance all evening, went on a determined run into the box. Vogts could only pull him down, and Neal scored emphatically from the spot. At last Liverpool had translated their undoubted domestic domination into supremacy in Europe.

Footballer of the Year Emlyn Hughes received the trophy, to spark a night of prolonged — but thankfully well-behaved — celebrations among the thousands of supporters who had travelled to cheer the team.

Fans take Wembley turf... and gloss off Scottish victory

WHATEVER PLEASURE Scotland got from winning a dreadful match was spoilt by the hordes of their puerile, drunken fans who invaded the Wembley pitch at the end to celebrate by breaking both sets of goal-posts, ripping out the nets, and cutting out pieces of turf to take home as trophies of their triumph.

At least the Scots had the consolation of retaining the Home Championship. But England will have gained nothing from this hard, ill-tempered, disagreeable match of low technical and tactical quality other than a severe dent in their morale prior to their upcoming tour of South America. Scotland gave a competent, spirited performance, and achieved a merited 2–1 victory thanks largely to McGrain's polished defensive and attacking football, the midfield industry of Hartford, Masson's precise placing of the dead ball, the persistence of Dalglish and Macari, and the commanding presence of McQueen. England lost chiefly because they were overwhelmed in midfield, even before the departure of the injured Brian Greenhoff.

Scotland took control in the 42nd minute when McQueen headed home Masson's free-kick. Despite the loss of Jordan immediately afterwards, they remained on top, and Dalglish popped in No.2 in the 63rd minute. Three minutes from the end, Channon scored England's belated goal from a penalty after Francis was brought down. Then came the invasion.

SOCCER SOUNDBITES

"Another afternoon of British rubbish."

Disenchanted voice in the WEMBLEY PRESS BOX.

Kenny Dalglish (arms raised) runs towards his adoring fans.

Scottish fans show off Wembley turf to spoil the Tartan celebrations.

FINAL SCORE

Football League
Division 1: Liverpool
Top scorer: Andy Gray (Aston Villa), Malcolm Macdonald (Arsenal) 25
Division 2: Wolverhampton Wanderers
Division 3: Mansfield Town
Division 4: Cambridge United
Footballer of the Year: Emlyn Hughes (Liverpool)

FA Cup Final
Manchester United 2 Liverpool 1

League Cup Final
Aston Villa 0 Everton 0
Replay: Aston Villa 1 Everton 1
(after extra time)
Replay: Aston Villa 3 Everton 2
(after extra time)

Scottish League
Premier Division: Celtic
Top scorer: Willie Pettigrew (Motherwell) 21
Division 1: St Mirren
Division 2: Stirling Albion
Footballer of the Year: Danny McGrain (Celtic)

Scottish FA Cup Final
Celtic 1 Rangers 0

Scottish League Cup Final
Aberdeen 2 Celtic 1
(after extra time)

International Championship
Scotland, 5 pts

European Cup Final
Liverpool 3 B Moenchengladbach 1

Cup-Winners' Cup Final
SV Hamburg 2 Anderlecht 0

UEFA Cup Final
Juventus beat Athletic Bilbao 1–0, 1–2 on away goals

European Footballer of the Year 1976
Franz Beckenbauer (Bayern Munich & West Germany)

Leading European Scorer (Golden Boot)
Dudu Georgescu (Dinamo Bucharest) 47

World Club Championship
Boca Juniors (Arg) beat Borussia Moenchengladbach (W.Ger) 2–2, 3–0

FOOTBALL FOCUS

- George Best scored within 71 seconds of his debut for Fulham on 9 September and, on 2 October, the day red and yellow cards were introduced in the Football League, became one of the first players to receive a red card, sent off at Southampton for foul and abusive language.
- Republic of Ireland manager Johnny Giles awarded himself a record 48th cap on 30 March, and his side beat France 1–0 in Dublin in a World Cup qualifier.
- Bobby Moore played his 1,000th and last first-class game in Fulham's match at Blackburn, on 14 May, before retiring.
- Ex-England winger Terry Paine retired at the end of the season with a record 824 Football League appearances to his name, 713 for Southampton and 111 for Hereford.
- Wales beat England 1–0 in the Home Championship on 31 May, their first ever win at Wembley.
- Liverpool's Kevin Keegan signed for Hamburg on 3 June for £500,000, a record for a British club.
- Renowned Cup fighters Wimbledon of the Southern League were elected to the League in place of Workington, who finished bottom of Division Four.

Terry Paine of Hereford acknowledges the applause of his former club-mates at the Dell as he embarks on his 806th League appearance in his last season.

Revie defects to Middle East: FA read about it in papers

NOT ONLY HAS Don Revie resigned as England manager, as announced on 12 July in a national newspaper, but he has agreed to work in the United Arab Emirates for the next four years at a tax-free £60,000 a year plus bonuses — a contract he presumably negotiated while still England manager.

Don Revie: deserts to desert.

Revie, formerly an outstanding club manager with Leeds, had a mediocre record as national supremo with only 14 wins in 29 internationals during his three years at the helm. He was expected to remain in the post at least until the last World Cup qualifying match against Italy in November, even though it would need something out of the ordinary — Luxembourg drawing in Italy — for England to reach Argentina. Meanwhile, there is inevitable speculation as to Revie's successor. But Revie's tenure of office has been a cautionary tale for current aspirants, as he has discovered a vast gulf between the day-to-day running of a League club and the management of the national team.

SOCCER SOUNDBITES

"Don Revie's decision doesn't surprise me in the slightest. Now I only hope he can quickly learn how to call out bingo numbers in Arabic."

ALAN HARDAKER,
Football League secretary.

"The committee unanimously deplores the action of Don Revie... and the FA is taking legal advice."

TED CROKER,
FA secretary.

Revie accused of match-fixing attempts

NEW ALLEGATIONS have emerged of an attempt to "fix" the Wolves-Leeds League match in 1972, a game Leeds needed only to draw to complete the "double". They were made in an article in the Daily Mirror on 6 September, which also dealt with the rise of Don Revie, the former Leeds and England manager, now based in Dubai. The article alleged that a former Wolves and Leeds player acted as middleman in an unsuccessful attempt to guarantee Leeds at least the point they needed. An earlier investigation by the League failed to substantiate similar claims, and League secretary Mr Alan Hardaker said the only thing new to him was the name of the supposed go-between.

Further accusations have been made in the Mirror and the Sunday People concerning other attempts on the part of Mr Revie — and Leeds captain Billy Bremner — to affect the results of matches, and the names of several witnesses have been published. Both Revie and Bremner have denied all allegations, but the FA have ordered a top-level inquiry.

That record-breaking style: Dalglish (8) in action for Celtic.

Dalglish to Anfield for record £400,000

LIVERPOOL HAVE kept faith with their supporters by spending a large proportion of the £500,000 they received for Kevin Keegan to purchase Kenny Dalglish, the pride of Celtic and Scotland, as his replacement. The League and European champions indicated, when reluctantly agreeing to release Keegan last May, that they would reinvest the largest sum ever received by a League club as soon as the right player became available. They kept their word on 10 August by paying a British record fee of £400,000 to persuade Celtic to allow Dalglish, 27, to move to Anfield.

Although expensive, this signing could be the shrewdest move Bob Paisley has made since becoming manager just over two years ago. Liverpool needed an outstanding footballer to replace a player of Keegan's ability and charisma. Like Keegan, the personable Scot can play up front or in midfield. Indeed, in Scotland, he is considered a better player than England's captain in the deeper position and at least his equal further forward.

Docherty sacked for breaking 'moral code'

TWENTY-FOUR HOURS after Manchester United chairman Louis Edwards declared that reports of the impending departure of their manager were "nonsense", Tommy Docherty has been sacked. Docherty, 49, has paid the penalty for having a love affair with the wife of club physiotherapist Laurie Brown. He has been held to have breached his contract, presumably on the grounds that he has brought the club's reputation into disrepute.

At a Press conference two weeks ago, after news of the liaison had broken, Docherty said he thought that he and Mr Brown could still work amicably together. The club obviously thought otherwise. Docherty, only six weeks after steering United to victory in the FA Cup, is understandably shattered at what he described as an "abrupt" dismissal. He brought post-Busby success to the club after Wilf McGuinness and Frank O'Farrell had tried and failed.

Caretaker Greenwood gets England supremo job

Ron Greenwood: new England supremo.

RON GREENWOOD, who has been managing the England side on a temporary basis since last August, has been made supremo, with a contract until July 1980, coinciding with the end of the European Championship. Depending, presumably, on how England fare in Europe, he is likely to be asked to stay on and see them through to the next World Cup.

Greenwood, 55, was chosen for the job above Brian Clough — the popular choice — Ipswich manager Bobby Robson, and Lawrie McMenemy of Southampton. West Ham have said they will not be seeking compensation for the loss of Mr Greenwood's services, and John Lyall will take over as manager of the club — only their fourth in 46 years.

As manager of the London club, Greenwood gained a reputation for producing teams that were always a delight to watch, playing attractive, attacking football.

SOCCER SOUNDBITES

"He has got people believing in themselves and talking to each other. The family atmosphere had gone, but he has brought it back."

EMLYN HUGHES,
England captain, on Ron Greenwood's appointment.

Manchester fans on rampage in France

MANCHESTER UNITED fans fought pitched battles with French police and spectators on the terraces of the Geoffroy-Guichard Stadium in St Etienne on 14 September. At least a dozen fans lay injured on the field as fists, boots and bottles flew before the start of United's European Cup-Winners' Cup first leg match with St Etienne.

The trouble began on the terraces behind one of the goals, where most of the visiting fans were packed among thousands of Frenchmen. Dozens of frightened spectators climbed over the 15ft fences on to the pitch, and a reserve match in progress had to be abandoned.

Riot police climbed in among the feuding fans and, using fists and batons, drove a wedge between them. When neither side showed any real signs of giving up, the police ran headlong at the United contingent, driving dozens of them out of the ground and others into a corner where they could be arrested and taken off for questioning. Some spectators said later that St Etienne supporters had started the trouble by throwing bread and bottles at United fans. Order was restored after 20 minutes of chaos. For the record, the match was drawn 1–1. But there followed a night of violence, as Manchester supporters went on a rampage through the streets of the town, smashing windows and ransacking shops, and threatening passers-by. Several further arrests were made.

United go down fighting — in the nicest sense

IT WAS MANCHESTER United who did the fighting at Old Trafford on 2 November in the return leg of their second-round Cup-Winners' Cup tie with Porto, instead of their notorious fans. But United, having been kicked out of the tournament after the appalling behaviour of their following at St Etienne, and then reinstated after being ordered to play the second leg at faraway Plymouth, are finally out of the competition. They put up a magnificent battle to try to claw their way back from a 4–0 deficit, but in the end it proved too much and they went down 6–5 on aggregate.

They went in at half-time 3–1 up, with goals from Coppell, Murca (og) and Nicholl, but Porto's away goal meant that United had to win by five. Coppell made it 4–1, but Porto's striker, Seninho, scored his second goal five minutes from time, and another Murca own goal was immaterial. However, United's display of bold, attacking football did much to repair the damage inflicted on their pride in Portugal two weeks ago.

Pele's farewell

A TEARFUL PELE bade farewell to competitive soccer on 1 October, ending his 22-year career in an exhibition match watched by 77,000 people in Giants' Stadium, New Jersey. Pele, 36, shared his talents between the two teams taking part. He played the first half — and scored, with a stunning free-kick — for the New York Cosmos, and finished the game in a final reunion with Santos of Brazil, for whom he had scored 1,090 goals in 1,114 games before retiring in 1974.

Pele, perhaps the greatest player of all time, came back in 1975, signing a lucrative contract with the American club, and helped them win the NASL title this year.

Late penalty is Scots' passport to Argentina

SCOTLAND'S 2–0 victory over Wales at neutral Anfield made sure of their qualification for next summer's World Cup in Argentina. The Welsh played the better football and created the better chances, but with a team half-composed of players from outside the First Division, they could not sustain the effort. It was 12 minutes from time, however, before Scotland broke the deadlock, skipper Don Masson (QPR) scoring from a penalty awarded for a handling offence — a decision that TV playbacks indicated was wrong. The Scots in the crowd were celebrating before Dalglish, on his home turf, made sure with a glancing header three minutes before the end.

Scotland skipper Don Masson scores the hotly disputed penalty.

Burns, Woods raise Forest: champions beaten in League Cup

CHAMPIONSHIP LEADERS Nottingham Forest won the League Cup for the first time when they beat Liverpool 1–0 in the replayed final at Old Trafford. After a goalless draw at Wembley, it took a second-half penalty to separate the teams. But whereas Forest fought a two-hour rearguard action on Saturday, they created more chances and gave Liverpool more trouble in the first 20 minutes here than in the whole game at Wembley, and Withe and Woodcock were both profligate early on.

But Liverpool came back, and it was Dalglish's turn to squander an opportunity. Forest began the second half by pushing forward again, and as O'Hare moved on to a fine through-pass from Woodcock, he was brought down from behind by Thompson. Liverpool claimed it was outside the box, but the referee awarded a penalty, and Robertson put his kick out of Clemence's reach.

Liverpool, like true champions, immediately forged upfield, and three minutes later McDermott, who had a goal disallowed on Saturday, broke through to put the ball in the net again, but was adjudged to have handled.

Forest held out, and 18-year-old Chris Woods played another blinder in goal. As Cup-tied Peter Shilton's deputy, he has still to make his League debut! Having lost his skipper, John McGovern, injured in the second half at Wembley, manager Brian Clough played a master card in making "wild man" Kenny Burns captain. He was an inspiration to his team, who scored 24 goals during the competition, and conceded only five.

(Left to right) John McGovern, John Robertson and Larry Lloyd show off Nottingham Forest's silverware.

FOOTBALL FOCUS

- York City, who slumped from Division Two to Division Four in successive seasons, finished third from bottom and had to seek re-election.
- Three spectacular debuts during the season: Tony Woodcock (Nottingham Forest) and Peter Ward (Brighton) both scored hat-tricks on their first appearances for England Under-21s, and Colin Lee scored four on his debut for Spurs, when they beat Bristol Rovers 9–0 in Division Two on 22 October. Forest, of course, won the League and League Cup, while Spurs edged Brighton out of promotion to Division One on goal difference.
- Manchester United signed Scottish international defender Gordon McQueen from Leeds on 9 February for £495,000, a record deal between two English clubs.
- England fielded six Liverpool players plus their former star Kevin Keegan against Switzerland at Wembley on 7 September, but could only draw 0–0. This was the highest number of players from one club in an English team since 1934, when seven Arsenal men played against Italy at Highbury.

Blyth spirit too much for Potters

BLYTH SPARTANS of the Northern League earned a place in the fifth round of the FA Cup with a shock victory over Second Division Stoke at the Victoria Ground. A goal down with 13 minutes to go, they equalized and then scored a winner less than two minutes from time.

An upset looked likely as early as the 10th minute, when Stoke keeper Jones fumbled a corner and Terry Johnson easily scored from close range. But Stoke came back early in the second half with two goals in two minutes, from Busby and Crooks, which should have done for the non-Leaguers. But now it was Blyth's turn to come storming back: Guthrie's free-kick was deflected on to a post, Shoulder headed on to the other post and Carney bundled the ball in. It was another free-kick from Guthrie that led to the winner. It rebounded to Johnson, and from 15 yards out the centre-forward coolly slotted the ball into goal. So Blyth are the first non-League club to reach the fifth round since Colchester and Yeovil in the late 1940s.

Forest clinch title with four games to play

ANOTHER FINE performance from Peter Shilton helped earn Nottingham Forest a goalless draw at Coventry, and the point they needed to clinch their first League Championship with four games still to play. Brian Clough's controversial £250,000 purchase in September from Stoke, a club record and also the highest fee ever paid for a goalkeeper, has been justified many times over this season, and against a dominant Coventry side Shilton emphasized just what an asset a great keeper is to a team. Clough also bought the tempestuous Kenny Burns, the player nobody wanted, from Birmingham for £150,000 — and transformed him into the newly elected Footballer of the Year.

Mr Clough and his assistant Peter Taylor have brought off the League and League Cup double in their first season after promotion. In doing so, they have denied mighty Liverpool a hat-trick of League titles, and Clough, who guided Derby to League success in 1972, joins the immortal Herbert Chapman, the only other manager to win the Championship with two clubs.

Happy Rangers do the 'treble'

RANGERS' DOMINATION of Scottish football is complete once again. Their 2–1 victory over Aberdeen in the Scottish Cup final at Hampden gave the Ibrox club a clean sweep of the three domestic honours for the second time in three seasons.

Aberdeen had very little to offer, and Rangers' total superiority was rewarded by goals from Alex MacDonald (33 minutes) and Derek Johnstone (58), who scored in every round. The Dons made a bold late attempt to salvage the game, but could not break through until Ritchie scored four minutes from time.

The sponsor's £100 cheque for the man of the match went, almost inevitably, to gifted midfielder Robert Russell who, in his first season as a senior, has been astonishingly successful, even by Rangers' standards. For veteran skipper John Greig, in his 18th season, it was his sixth Scottish Cup-winners' medal, to go with five Championship and four League Cup gongs.

Liverpool kings of Europe again

LIVERPOOL HAVE WON the European Cup in successive seasons, and although they did not attain the high standard of football that defeated Borussia in Rome last year, their 1–0 defeat of Bruges was a patient, soundly professional performance, capped by a coolly taken goal by Kenny Dalglish in the 66th minute.

The Belgians, without their key forwards Lambert and Courant, could have been forgiven for thinking they had gone to Anfield by mistake when they emerged from the Wembley tunnel to a seething mass of red and a wall of sound from what was one massive Kop. But it took Liverpool some time to get into their stride. Eventually, Kennedy, McDermott and Souness began to get a grip in midfield, and Jensen in the Bruges goal was kept much busier than Clemence. Just before the interval, Hansen for Liverpool and Ku for Bruges headed just over the bar.

Both managers made tactical substitutions in the second half, Paisley sending on Heighway for Case to boost Liverpool's attack. Within a minute, Heighway touched the ball back to McDermott, who found Dalglish; he then exchanged passes with fellow Scot Souness, splitting the Bruges defence wide open, before gently chipping the ball over Jensen's dive. The Belgians then threw everything into attack and, indeed, Thompson, Liverpool's outstanding defender, had to clear the ball off the line. But Bruges had left their offensive too late.

Goalscorer Dalglish (arms raised) is mobbed by, from left: Case, Kennedy, McDermott, Souness and Smith.

Wembley 'walk-over' for Ipswich

THE 1–0 SCORELINE hardly suggests a walk-over, but Ipswich's triumph over favourites Arsenal in the FA Cup final was comprehensive in all but goals. Indeed, after the first 10 minutes, when Arsenal's initial flourish petered out, it was all Ipswich. Mariner struck the bar, Wark twice hammered fierce shots against a post, and Jennings atoned for his otherwise uncertain performance with the save of the match, from a Burley header.

Arsenal's gamble of playing Sunderland, clearly not match fit, and Brady, obviously not recovered from an ankle injury and replaced by Rix in the 65th minute, did not come off. Wark, the epitome of power and determination, Talbot, as industrious as ever, and Osborne, rising nobly to the occasion, quickly established control in midfield, where Hudson failed miserably to take up the burden. So, with Woods and Geddis torturing Arsenal on the flanks, Mariner tore the centre of Arsenal's defence apart. Yet there were only 14 minutes left when Geddis crossed low and hard into Arsenal's goalmouth, Young could not clear properly, and Osborne shot in. Justice, there is no doubt, had been done.

Roger Osborne (7) turns after scoring the only goal, with what turned out to be his last touch.

FINAL SCORE

Football League
Division 1: Nottingham Forest
Top scorer: Bob Latchford (Everton) 30
Division 2: Bolton Wanderers
Division 3: Wrexham
Division 4: Watford
Footballer of the Year: Kenny Burns (Nottingham Forest)

FA Cup Final

Ipswich Town	1	Arsenal	0

League Cup Final

Nottingham Forest	0	Liverpool	0
(after extra time)			
Replay: N. Forest	1	Liverpool	0

Scottish League
Premier League: Rangers
Top scorer: Derek Johnstone (Rangers) 25
Division 1: Morton
Division 2: Clyde
Footballer of the Year: Derek Johnstone (Rangers)

Scottish FA Cup Final

Rangers	2	Aberdeen	1

Scottish League Cup Final

Rangers	2	Celtic	1

International Championship
England, 6 pts

European Cup Final

Liverpool	1	FC Bruges	0

Cup-Winners' Cup Final

Anderlecht	4	Austria/WAC	0

UEFA Cup Final
PSV Eindhoven beat Bastia 0–0, 3–0

European Footballer of the Year 1977
Allan Simonsen (Borussia Moenchengladbach & Denmark)

Leading European Scorer (Golden Boot)
Hans Krankl (Rapid Vienna) 41

World Club Championship
Competition not held

Argentina at last

Argentina was a controversial choice to host the World Cup in view of the military coup there in 1976 and the state of the country. Such was the football that, in the end, neutral observers did not really care who won or lost. They were just glad it was all over. There were very few heroes on the pitch, and the world game had degenerated sadly since the heady days of 1970. It is easy to blame the poor refereeing for not controlling the violence on the field, and the inadequate laws for failing to punish the "tactical" fouls that are part and parcel of the game today. It is almost impossible for truly skilful players to operate in such an environment and, for that, considerable blame must attach to the managers and coaches, too.

FOR THE FIRST time, the number of World Cup entries exceeded 100, although six of the 106 withdrew without taking part. Only Scotland of the home countries qualified for the finals, but such was their performance, on and off the field, that they could be excused for wishing they had not.

England's early 2–0 defeat in Italy was demoralizing, and their preparations were not helped by the resignation midway through the qualifying tournament of their manager, Don Revie. Even when they reversed the Italian result at Wembley, their other wins had not provided enough goals, and Italy needed only to beat Luxembourg in Rome.

Among the qualifiers, Iran and Tunisia were making their first appearances in the finals.

Scotland's own goals

Scotland's World Cup campaign was a catalogue of catastrophes. All kinds of stories emanated from their camp before they even took the field — tales of players living it up, wrangles, as usual, over bonuses, complaints by the Mexicans about noise. Manager Ally MacLeod had acquired an almost messianic reputation among the Scottish fans and media before the finals, but was hampered by his lack of knowledge of international football, his opponents and even his own players, and no team could have gone out less prepared for their first match, against Peru. Despite taking an early lead through Jordan, they were pegged back by half-time and, after Masson had a penalty saved, the veteran Cubillas hit two viciously swerving, long-range shots past Rough for a 3–1 win. To add insult to injury, Willie Johnston failed a drug test — he had been taking stimulants — and was sent home in disgrace.

Iran proceeded to humiliate Scotland further, holding them to a draw after giving them an own goal just before half-time. This left the Scots needing to beat Holland by three clear goals to survive — and, all credit to them, they very nearly did. With Souness belatedly coming into the side and giving it more bite, Scotland came back from a goal down to put three past the Dutch, the last, from Archie Gemmill, the best of the tournament, as he beat man after man in a confined space before chipping in. But Holland scored again four minutes later, and Scotland made a sad exit, all the more depressing for what might have been had they gone better prepared.

Archie Gemmell celebrates his wonder goal against Holland.

Weak refereeing

Argentina won their first two matches, against Hungary and France, 2–1, helped by favourable decisions from weak referees intimidated by the crowd. The Hungarians had two players sent off, albeit deservedly, in the last four minutes — but what provocation striker Andres Torocsik suffered before he finally blew up. With a strong referee, Mr Klein of Israel, Italy beat the hosts 1–0, but both teams had by then qualified for the second round.

Poland came through strongly in Group Two, after drawing 0–0 with world champions West Germany. The Germans demolished Mexico 6–0, but scraped through with a goalless draw against the splendid Tunisians, when a defeat would have sent them out.

The matches in Group Three were the closest, with never more than a goal in it, and Austria were quickly through after beating Spain and Sweden. Brazil toiled to two lack-lustre draws, in the first of which Welsh referee Clive Thomas blew for time a split-second before the ball entered the Swedish goal for what would have been the Brazilian winner. They then beat a lukewarm Austria to go through to Round Two.

Europe v S. America

As things turned out, Group A was bound to produce a European finalist, and the odds were on a South American finalist emerging from Group B, unless Poland could spring a surprise. But the biggest shock of the second round was the elimination of West Germany, who failed to win any of their three matches.

Without Beckenbauer, who had "retired" to play in the United States, and with rumours of unrest in their camp, the Germans failed to produce their usual spirited performances, and hard-fought draws with Italy and Holland virtually put paid to their chances of retaining the Cup. But it was still a bombshell when

Controversy and Argentina are never far apart at World Cup time, and 1978 was no exception. They played some of the best football in the finals, but would they have won the competition away from home?

A section of the excited Argentinian crowd at the final.

they lost to Austria, a side whom the rapidly improving Dutch had thrashed 5–1. Ruud Krol was the dominating figure for Holland in the absence of that other famous retiree, Cruyff, although they were aided by weak refereeing in their victory over Italy.

The contentious issue in Group B was the planning that allowed Argentina to start their last match after Brazil's had ended, so they knew exactly what they had to do. Brazil had emerged from the shambles of their early matches with good wins against Peru and Poland, although the goalless draw with Argentina was featureless apart from the fouling.

Eventually, Argentina kicked off knowing they needed to beat Peru by better than 4–1 to reach the final, and the Peruvian defence looked suspiciously vulnerable as they allowed their hosts to make raid after raid and run in six goals without reply.

A flawed final

Before the start of the final, Argentina were inexcusably allowed to get away with two pieces of gamesmanship. They kept Holland — and the rest of the world — waiting for five minutes before they came out, and they made a calculated, unwarranted fuss about the protection on Rene Van der Kerkhof's injured arm, which he had worn in previous rounds. Having allowed these pieces of nonsense, Sergio Gonella, the compromise selection as referee, proceeded to give as ineffectual a performance as had been seen in what was one of the worst refereed World Cups for some years. With an average of one free-kick every 90 seconds, the final was no worse than some of the earlier games, and the Dutch were penalized more than twice as much as the host country. While it is probably fair to say that Argentina would not have won this World Cup had it been held anywhere else, this does not excuse Holland's tacky display.

The chief reason, however, for the Dutch defeat was their failure to take the chances they made. Although they had world-class goalscoring wingers in Rep and Rensenbrink, they missed not having a true central striker against the best opposition. Argentina had the best player in the tournament — and he was voted so — in Mario Kempes, and his partnership with Luque up front was decisive. Little Ardiles was a revelation in midfield, at the heart of every move. And skipper Passarella, when he wasn't engaged in skulduggery, was a superb defender.

Kempes put Argentina in front after 38 minutes, and it looked to be enough until substitute Dirk Nanninga rose to head an equalizer from Rene Van der Kerkhof's cross eight minutes from time. The Dutch almost stole the Cup when Rensenbrink hit a post, but the game went into extra time. Before the break, Kempes broke through and just managed to keep control and stab the ball past Jongbloed. It was all Argentina now, and Bertoni clinched it five minutes from the end of extra time after a lovely one-two with Kempes.

So Argentina had won at last, 48 years after they reached the first World Cup final, in Uruguay. It was a particularly sweet triumph for manager Cesar Menotti, who kept faith with an attacking style alien to most club football in the country, despite constant criticism from all sides.

Bertoni (right) scores the World Cup clincher in extra time.

FINAL SCORE

FIRST ROUND

Group 1

Italy	2	France	1
Argentina	2	Hungary	1
Italy	3	Hungary	1
Argentina	2	France	1
Argentina	0	Italy	1
France	3	Hungary	1

	P	W	D	L	F	A	P
Italy	3	3	0	0	6	2	6
Argentina	3	2	0	1	4	3	4
France	3	1	0	2	5	5	2
Hungary	3	0	0	3	3	8	0

Group 2

Poland	0	West Germany	0
Tunisia	3	Mexico	1
West Germany	6	Mexico	0
Poland	1	Tunisia	0
Poland	3	Mexico	1
West Germany	0	Tunisia	0

	P	W	D	L	F	A	P
Poland	3	2	1	0	4	1	5
W. Germany	3	1	2	0	6	0	4
Tunisia	3	1	1	1	3	2	3
Mexico	3	0	0	3	2	12	0

Group 3

Sweden	1	Brazil	1
Austria	2	Spain	1
Austria	1	Sweden	0
Spain	0	Brazil	0
Brazil	1	Austria	0
Spain	1	Sweden	0

	P	W	D	L	F	A	P
Austria	3	2	0	1	3	2	4
Brazil	3	1	2	0	2	1	4
Spain	3	1	1	1	2	2	3
Sweden	3	0	1	2	1	3	1

Group 4

Peru	3	Scotland	1
Holland	3	Iran	0
Iran	1	Scotland	1
Holland	0	Peru	0
Peru	4	Iran	1
Scotland	3	Holland	2

	P	W	D	L	F	A	P
Peru	3	2	1	0	7	2	5
Holland	3	1	1	1	5	3	3
Scotland	3	1	1	1	5	6	3
Iran	3	0	1	2	2	8	1

SECOND ROUND

Group A

Holland	5	Austria	1
West Germany	0	Italy	0
Holland	2	West Germany	2
Italy	1	Austria	0
Holland	2	Italy	1
Austria	3	West Germany	2

	P	W	D	L	F	A	P
Holland	3	2	1	0	9	4	5
Italy	3	1	1	1	2	2	3
W. Germany	3	0	2	1	4	5	2
Austria	3	1	0	2	4	8	2

Group B

Brazil	3	Peru	0
Argentina	2	Poland	0
Argentina	0	Brazil	0
Poland	1	Peru	0
Brazil	3	Poland	1
Argentina	6	Peru	0

	P	W	D	L	F	A	P
Argentina	3	2	1	0	8	0	5
Brazil	3	2	1	0	6	1	5
Poland	3	1	0	2	2	5	2
Peru	3	0	0	3	0	10	0

THIRD-PLACE MATCH

Brazil 2 Italy 1

FINAL

Argentina 3 Holland 1
(after extra time)

River Plate Stadium, Buenos Aires, 25 June 1978. Attendance 77,260

Argentina: Fillol, Olguin, Galvan, Passarella, Tarantini, Ardiles (Larrosa), Gallego, Kempes, Bertoni, Luque, Ortiz (Houseman)
(Scorers: Kempes 2, Bertoni)
Holland: Jongbloed, Poortvliet, Krol, Brandts, Jansen (Suurbier), Neeskens, Haan, Van der Kerkhof W, Van der Kerkhof R, Rep (Nanninga), Rensenbrink (Scorer: Nanninga)

Leading scorers

6 Kempes (Argentina)
5 Cubillas (Peru)
Rensenbrink (Holland)

Tottenham's South American coup

ON 10 JULY, just 15 days after Argentina's triumph over Holland in the World Cup final, Spurs manager Keith Burkinshaw brought off a sensational coup by signing two of their squad. Osvaldo Ardiles, the small, wiry midfielder from Huracan, was for many the most influential of the Argentinian team. The powerful Ricardo Villa, a wide midfield player from Racing Club, made only two appearances in the finals as a substitute but has a growing reputation in his own country. It appears that the two players, both 25, came as a "package" and the cost was in the region of £750,000, including agents' fees, signing-on fees, and a small percentage to the Argentinian FA.

Mr Burkinshaw was alerted to the fact that several of the successful Argentina side were up for sale by Sheffield United manager Harry Haslam, who has an Argentinian coach and had established links with agents in the country. While Second Division Sheffield could not afford to buy players of such quality, Burkinshaw was eager to strengthen his newly promoted side, and wasted no time in boarding a plane to Buenos Aires.

Argentinian stars Ardiles (left) and Villa: in Spurs' starting line-up.

Spurs go down to record defeat at Anfield

LIVERPOOL'S SEVEN-GOAL demolition of Tottenham on 2 September — the biggest defeat in the Londoners' 70-year membership of the League — suggests that the European Cup-holders are poised to achieve new heights in their illustrious post-war history. Manager Bob Paisley described the humiliation of Spurs, who included their £1 million new signings Ardiles, Villa and John Lacy, as "almost frightening at times".

Spurs have not won at Anfield for 66 years, and on Saturday Liverpool's Clemence was stretched by only one shot, from Lacy, who at the other end was hard pressed to provide the solidity at centre-back for which Fulham were recently paid so handsomely. But few teams could have withstood this onslaught, and Spurs deserve honourable mention because the avalanche never provoked spoiling tactics.

Daines was powerless to prevent all but Liverpool's fifth goal, which passed through his legs, and he made several excellent saves. Certainly, Dalglish might have at least doubled the goals he collected in the 10th and 22nd minutes. After the retirement of his captain Hughes, with a knee injury, Dalglish moved back into midfield, and two of his thrusts from there provided goals for substitute Johnson. Ray Kennedy had scored a third goal before half-time, and Neal made it 6–0 from a penalty. The best was saved till last, a high-speed, five-man move finished off by a spectacular header from McDermott, after a run of 60 yards.

Liverpool top the table, having won their first four games, with a goal record of 16–2. They have reached awesome form in time for this season's first defence of the European Cup. They meet Nottingham Forest, who have drawn all four of their League matches so far this season, in the first-round, first-leg match at the City Ground.

Forest end Liverpool's European reign

IN A PULSATING match at Anfield on 27 September, Nottingham Forest resisted everything Liverpool threw at them and emerged into the second round of the European Cup. Protecting the 2–0 first-leg lead Birtles and Barrett had given them a fortnight earlier, Forest stood firm as the European champions and League leaders drove forward with tremendous determination, sometimes flinging nine men into attack in their efforts to reduce the gap. But McGovern, Gemmill and Bowyer did an excellent holding job in midfield to restrain McDermott and Souness, and Lloyd and Burns somehow held on in the back line. Behind them, Shilton was calmness personified.

In a last effort, manager Paisley put on strikers Fairclough and Johnson for McDermott and Case, but they failed to make any impact and the result was, for Forest, a glorious goalless draw.

Viv Anderson (left) and Liverpool's Ray Kennedy in action.

Clough makes Trevor Francis the first £1m player

BIRMINGHAM and England striker Trevor Francis became Britain's first £1 million footballer on 9 February, when Brian Clough signed him for Nottingham Forest. This doubles the transfer record between British clubs, set last December when West Brom paid Middlesbrough £500,000 for David Mills.

When VAT, the contribution to the Football League Provident Fund and Francis's five-per-cent cut are added, Forest have committed themselves to paying £1,180,000. No other club had shown any inclination to approach the unprecedented figure Birmingham were demanding for Francis, 24, who first burst on to the scene with them as a prodigy of 16. He developed into an England player, though not a regular member of the team, but has suffered from Birmingham's repeated struggles to avoid relegation.

The fact that Forest have been able to find such a vast amount is, according to Mr Clough, due to good management. He claimed they would be able to pay a similar sum again if the right player became available.

Million-pound man Francis.

FA won't turn blind eye to Nelson

SAMMY NELSON, Arsenal's Northern Ireland international left-back, has been suspended for two weeks by his club and fined two weeks' wages for lowering his shorts in front of the crowd after equalizing in the 1–1 draw against Coventry at Highbury on 3 April. He also seems certain to be charged by the FA with bringing the game into disrepute. Nelson's gesture came after he had been barracked by the crowd for putting the ball into his own goal in the first half. The player is extremely contrite about his behaviour, and the only charitable thing that can be said is that it appeared to be entirely out of character.

Nelson finds a new way of celebrating!

Forest regain touch and retain League Cup

NOTTINGHAM FOREST will line up against Grasshoppers in the second leg of their European Cup quarter-final in Zurich on Wednesday with the comforting knowledge that they have regained the elusive touch of true champions. Forest left Wembley after beating Southampton 3–2, with the League Cup securely in their grasp for the second season in succession, after a second-half performance of the highest quality had swept away the doubts and inhibitions accumulated during the long, cold, frustrating winter.

When searching for the hero of Forest's victory, look no further than their manager, Brian Clough, whose few well-chosen words during the interval transformed a witless, dissident team, seemingly tottering towards defeat, into aggressive, conquering heroes. The star who caught the eye on the field was young Garry Birtles, a £5,000 bargain from neighbouring Long Eaton, who is in his first season of senior football. He scored two goals and had two disallowed for offside, one of them a borderline decision.

Birtles pounced on an error by the hesitant Nicholl in the 50th minute to equalize Peach's 17th-minute goal and, in effect, provide the base for Forest's victory. The goal inspired Gemmill and McGovern to take command in midfield from the previously dominating Ball, Holmes and Williams, and produce some of the most devastating attacking soccer seen at Wembley for years. Southampton's defence, who had conceded only two goals in their last eight games, was torn apart. They were outrageously fortunate to survive until the 78th minute, but then Birtles shook off a challenge by Nicholl and planted the newly styled red and white ball firmly past the diving Gennoe. Woodcock, who had so ably supported Birtles, added a third in the 82nd minute. Holmes volleyed home a defiant 15-yarder just before the end, but Southampton never really looked like saving the game.

Birtles scores to put Forest ahead in the League Cup final.

Brady sets up Arsenal's amazing Cup climax

WITH A MINUTE to go at Wembley, and Manchester United still on a high after sensationally scoring twice in two minutes to pull back their half-time deficit, Arsenal's Liam Brady collected the ball in his own half. As the elusive Irishman began to run with it, euphoria turned to panic in the United ranks. It seemed half the Manchester side were crowding round, jockeying back, fearful of the educated left foot that had tormented them all afternoon. Just when it seemed he was running into a cul-de-sac, Brady released the ball without breaking stride, and there was Graham Rix clear on the left. Over came a long, outswinging centre, above the defence and out of the reach of young Bailey in goal, for Alan Sunderland at the far post to hit into the empty net.

Three goals in four minutes: never has there been such a climax to an FA Cup final, and there must have been thousands who missed it, streaming out before the end with Arsenal apparently coasting to a comfortable victory. The player inadvertently responsible for this late avalanche of action was Arsenal substitute Steve Walford. He was sent on by manager Terry Neill for David Price five minutes from time, a decision that seemed to destroy Arsenal's concentration, perhaps persuading them that their task was complete.

Alan Sunderland (right), celebrates after scoring the Cup Final winner, with Walford and Rice in attendance.

Whether or not Arsenal dropped their guard, Jordan swept Coppell's free-kick back into the middle for McQueen to score in the 86th minute, and two minutes later Sammy McIlroy took a pass from Coppell, wriggled past O'Leary and Walford, and struck the equalizer out of Jennings's reach. What had been a predictable match, after Arsenal gained in confidence and took control early on, was transformed into a thriller, a game that will be talked about for years to come.

Brady was the jewel in an otherwise moderate Arsenal side, striding away in the 12th minute to instigate the move that Talbot finished off and, two minutes from half-time, accelerating to beat Albiston and Buchan before crossing perfectly for Stapleton to head powerfully down and into goal. It was wholly appropriate that it was then Brady, head and shoulders the man of the match, who should pick Arsenal up again and make the decider.

FOOTBALL FOCUS

- The International Board abolished the "played-onside" clause from the offside law before the start of the season. A ball deflected by an opponent will no longer put a player onside.
- Viv Anderson, the 22-year-old Forest full-back, became the first black footballer to represent England in a full international when he played against Czechoslovakia at Wembley on 29 November.
- When Forest lost 2–0 at Liverpool on 9 December, it was their first League defeat for one year and 13 days — a run of 42 games.
- The FA imposed a 10-year ban on Don Revie, dating from his unscheduled departure from England in July 1977, for "bringing the game into disrepute". Apparently, after he signed a contract with the United Arab Emirates in secret, he offered to resign his England post and asked for £50,000 tax-free compensation.

Liverpool break Leeds and their record

WHEN LIVERPOOL went to Elland Road on 17 May for their last match of the League season, they had sewn up the title nine days before and had 66 points, one fewer than the First Division record set by Leeds 10 year earlier. If Leeds, in fifth place, harboured any ideas that they might preserve their record, they were dispelled pretty quickly as the Reds began to show their devastating finishing power.

Johnson drove home their first goal after 21 minutes, and Case hammered in number two four minutes before half-time. Liverpool gave Leeds little scope for attack and, 10 minutes after the interval, Johnson made it three with a powerful header. That was the end of the scoring.

Dalglish, who had a hand in all three goals, finished as the Reds' leading League scorer with 21. They conceded an all-time Football League low of 16 goals in 42 matches, an extraordinary achievement. In amassing their record 68 points, they lost only four matches, none at Anfield, where they dropped only two points and boasted a goal record of 51–4. They led the table from start to finish, dropping just one point in their first 11 games, and used only 15 players in winning their record 11th Championship.

Dalglish, ever present again, and leading scorer for Liverpool.

SOCCER SOUNDBITES

"Tonight we practised everything we ever preached in the game. There was no dissent from the players, no shady tackling. We worked tremendously hard and gave a performance that everyone connected with the club can be proud of."

BRIAN CLOUGH,
Forest manager, after their semi-final triumph in Cologne.

"No way would Francis have played if the others [Gemmill and O'Neill] had been fully fit."

CLOUGH,
after the final.

"I have been with him [Brian Clough] longer than any other player, but don't ask me to define his success. I can only say he makes you want to play for him."

JOHN MCGOVERN,
Forest's captain.

Million-pound Francis inspires fairy-tale Forest triumph

Francis (right) sneaks in at the far post ot head home the winner.

MILLION-POUND striker Trevor Francis, eligible to play for Forest in the European Cup for the first time, was drafted in to play on the right wing against Malmö in the final in Munich, and he scored the only goal. What's more, he scored it with his head, a part of his anatomy he normally uses purely for outwitting the opposition, rather than for making physical contact with the ball.

Forest came to the final as strong favourites. They had done all the hard work in getting there: going through a baptism of fire against Liverpool, winners for the last two years; comfortably beating Puskas's AEK Athens 7–2 on aggregate and Grasshoppers of Zurich 5–2; and magnificently coming through against Cologne in the semi-finals, where they recovered from two down to 3–3 at home and then won in Germany with a goal from play-anywhere Ian Bowyer.

Archie Gemmill was still unavailable for the final, as was Forest's other influential midfield player Martin O'Neill, but the Swedes, managed by Englishman Bob Houghton, also had two important players ruled out by injury. After a nervy start, Forest began to put together some inventive, exciting attacking moves, with Francis the main inspiration. And it was Francis who scored just before half-time with a beautifully worked goal. Robertson beat two men on the left, and curled a cross over Malmö's defence to the far post, where Francis, after a 30-yard sprint, headed in. With McGovern giving a real captain's performance in midfield, Francis continuing to dominate out on the right, and Robertson causing all sorts of problems on the other flank, Forest remained firmly in charge after the interval.

Forest's triumph is nothing short of a fairy-tale, a remarkable rise for a team just scraping out of England's Second Division only two years ago and now champions of Europe. Above all, it is a tribute to the astute management and motivation of Brian Clough and Peter Taylor.

Ten-man Celtic snatch League title from Rangers

IN A THRILLING, late finish to the Scottish Championship race, Rangers needed at least a draw with Celtic at Parkhead to have a chance of the title. But Celtic, who went a goal down and then had John Doyle sent off, staged a fighting recovery and won 4–2.

Rangers were still leading with McDonald's goal 23 minutes from time. But in a finish to rival that of the FA Cup final, Aitken equalized and McCluskey put Celtic ahead. Back came Rangers with a goal from Russell to draw level again. But in the last five minutes, Jackson put the ball into his own net and McLeod scored Celtic's fourth for a dramatic victory.

Five points behind now, Rangers' last two matches are academic as far as the title is concerned, and they can only hope for consolation in their second Cup final replay with Hibs in a week's time.

This is not a vintage Celtic team — they have scored only 61 goals in their 36 league games, divided between 17 players — but they have shown great spirit, inspired by Aitken and McGrain in defence and Burns in midfield. They won nine and drew one of their last 11 matches: Champion form indeed.

FINAL SCORE

Football League
Division 1: Liverpool
Top scorer: Frank Worthington (Bolton Wanderers) 24
Division 2: Crystal Palace
Division 3: Shrewsbury Town
Division 4: Reading
Footballer of the Year: Kenny Dalglish (Liverpool)

FA Cup Final

Arsenal	3	Manchester United	2

League Cup Final

Nottingham Forest	3	Southampton	2

Scottish League
Premier Division: Celtic
Top scorer: Andy Ritchie (Morton) 22
Division 1: Dundee
Division 2: Berwick Rangers
Footballer of the Year: Andy Ritchie (Morton)

Scottish FA Cup Final

Rangers	0	Hibernian	0
Replay: Rangers	0	Hibernian	0
Replay: Rangers	3	Hibernian	2

Scottish League Cup Final

Rangers	2	Aberdeen	1

International Championship
England, 5 pts

European Cup Final

Nottingham Forest	1	Malmö	0

Cup-Winners' Cup Final

Barcelona	4	Fortuna Düsseldorf	3

(after extra time)

UEFA Cup Final
Borussia Moenchengladbach beat Red Star Belgrade 1–1, 1–0

European Footballer of the Year 1978
Kevin Keegan (SV Hamburg & England)

Leading European Scorer (Golden Boot)
Kees Kist (AZ 67 Alkmaar) 34

World Club Championship
Olimpia (Paraguay) beat Malmö (Sweden) 1–0, 2–1

McMenemy lands Keegan coup for Southampton

LAWRIE MCMENEMY, the persuasive manager of modest Southampton, pulled off the first truly big European transfer coup of the eighties on 11 February by talking Kevin Keegan into an agreement that will take him to the Dell when he leaves Hamburg in the summer. Mr McMenemy, having invited the Press to a hotel near Romsey to meet "someone who will play a big part in Southampton's future", then produced the little man who has become the hottest property in European soccer since leaving Liverpool three years ago.

Once Keegan had announced that he would be quitting the Bundesliga at the end of the season, it was generally assumed that not even the richest English clubs would be able to compete with their Continental counterparts for Keegan's expensive services. But Mr McMenemy, alive to the fact that fees between clubs from EEC countries are restricted to £500,000, eventually persuaded Hamburg to accept £400,000, a fraction of the current British record for the man twice voted European Footballer of the Year.

Kevin Keegan: a bargain buy for Southampton from Hamburg.

Harlow add up Cup success

JOHN MACKENZIE, 25, a company accountant, was the toast of Isthmian League part-timers Harlow as his goal in the third-round replay with Leicester created the season's first major Cup giant-killing act. Amid amazing scenes of jubilation, the like of which the Sports Centre ground has never seen before, he shocked the 1,600 Leicester fans and sent the home crowd wild when he struck Micky Mann's free-kick through a ruck of players two minutes before half-time.

The Second Division promotion hopefuls will rue the chances they missed on Saturday before Harlow's Neil Prosser equalized in the last minute. Harlow were now familiar with Leicester's policy of pumping high balls into the heart of their defence, and it foundered on the height and strength of Vic Clarke and Tony Gough. Harlow's best ever attendance of 9,723 will savour the night for a long time.

Aberdeen are 'Terrorized'

DUNDEE UNITED, the "Terrors", won their first major honour on 12 December, when they beat Aberdeen 3–0 in the replayed final of the Scottish League Cup. The Dons, who beat both Celtic and Rangers twice on their way to the final, were hot favourites when the teams met at Hampden Park, but Dundee United held them to a goalless draw against the run of play. Four days later, in the replay at Dens Park, home of their neighbours Dundee, Jim McLean's young Terrors dominated the Dons, and Willie Pettigrew set them on the way to victory with a goal in 15 minutes. He headed another midway through the second half, and Paul Sturrock then made it three.

Rocketing transfers: Daley and Gray fetch £1.5m each

THE BRITISH TRANSFER record was shattered on 5 September when Manchester City manager Malcolm Allison paid Wolves £1,437,500 for England B midfielder Steve Daley — but the new figure did not last for long. While Daley was completing his transfer forms at Maine Road, Aston Villa's Scottish international striker Andy Gray was on his way to Molineux to finalize details of his £1,469,000 transfer with Wolves manager John Barnwell. This is almost 10 times the club's previous record fee.

Revie: criticised for outrageous disloyalty.

Hollow victory for Revie

THE FA, ORDERED by the High Court to lift their 10-year ban on Don Revie, are unlikely to take any further action against the former England manager, although Mr Justice Cantley found him guilty of bringing the game into disrepute. FA secretary Ted Croker, interpreting the judge's remarks as a total justification of the charge they had brought, felt that the door was still open for further disciplinary proceedings, but that the FA, rather than be accused of vindictiveness, would take no further action.

Mr Justice Cantley's decision to lift the ban was made "with regret", as statements by FA chairman Sir Harold Thompson, made before presiding over the commission, raised a "real likelihood of bias". Mr Revie can now take up a consultancy, worth £90,000 over nine years, with former club Leeds United, and there is naturally speculation that he might return there as manager when his tax-free £340,000 contract with the United Arab Emirates ends in 18 months' time. Whether there will be a rush for his services then is another matter.

SOCCER SOUNDBITES

"A sensational, outrageous example of disloyalty, breach of duty, discourtesy and selfishness."

MR JUSTICE CANTLEY,
on Don Revie's conduct.

Gray day for Shilton: blunder gives Wolves League Cup

A HORRENDOUS Peter Shilton blunder cost Nottingham Forest the chance to make it a hat-trick of League Cups at Wembley, and allowed Andy Gray of Wolves to stroll through for the easiest goal he'll ever score. When Peter Daniel floated a long, high pass to the edge of the Forest area and David Needham shaped to chest the ball clear, Shilton came out and ran straight into his centre-back. As they staggered apart, both Andy Gray and the ball went through the gap, and the £1.5 million striker walked it into the empty net.

Overall, Wolves just about deserved to win. The first half was one of stupefying boredom. But after the interval, the advantage started to creep Forest's way, until the fateful defensive misunderstanding in the 67th minute. Kenny Burns was splendid throughout for Forest, but Viv Anderson, who was cautioned for a dreadful foul on John Richards in the sixth minute, was subsequently lucky not to be sent off. Daniel was Wolves' best player, and it was appropriate that he should have had a hand in their goal. It also was consolation for Gray, injured when Villa won the trophy four years ago.

Gray (right) about to pounce, with Needham and Shilton stranded.

Arsenal make third final: Liverpool's 'double' hopes shattered

ARSENAL AT LAST ended the marathon FA Cup semi-final with Liverpool at Coventry on 1 May with a goal by Brian Talbot that earned them a record-breaking third consecutive Cup final appearance and shattered their opponents' hopes of completing the "double". The decisive goal came in the 12th minute following an uncharacteristic error by Ray Kennedy, himself a "double" champion with Arsenal nine years ago. He trod on the ball just outside his six-yard box, and it ran to Stapleton, who put it neatly into the centre for Talbot to head home.

What a cliff-hanger this saga has been! The two sides, however, must be thoroughly sick of each other by now. After a goalless draw at Hillsborough, Sunderland equalized Fairclough's goal in the first replay at Villa Park; Dalglish responded with an injury-time equalizer in the second replay after Sunderland had put Arsenal ahead in 15 seconds, and now Arsenal have settled the issue after four games and seven hours — plus a 1–1 League draw at Anfield in between.

Rix and Brady did an excellent job in midfield for Arsenal at Highfield Road, and the Gunners thoroughly earned the right to meet fellow Londoners, Second Division West Ham, at Wembley on Saturday week.

Cooper the penalty pooper

IPSWICH KEEPER Paul Cooper saved another two penalties on 29 March, in the 1–1 draw with Derby at Portman Road, making his season's tally eight in 10 penalty attempts. He attributes his success to 90 per cent luck and 10 per cent research into the habits of penalty takers. Barry Powell had a 14 out of 14 record before Cooper ended it, and it was only Gerry Daly's second miss in nine attempts. Derby needed a win — they are in grave danger of relegation.

Brian Talbot (arms raised) turns after scoring the decisive goal.

SOCCER SOUNDBITES

"I did call, but David didn't hear my shout. You can't hear anything at Wembley."

PETER SHILTON,
taking the blame for Wolves' goal.

Avi's strange afternoon out

AVI COHEN WAS obliged to wait until the last Saturday of the League season to play his first senior game in front of the Liverpool crowd, but enough was packed into it to last him for years. After all, it is not every day of the week that an Israeli international makes his home debut in the Football League on the afternoon that his club win the Championship. Nor have many footballers from any country opened their account with an own goal and then balanced the books by scoring for their own side, at the same end, 25 minutes later.

Cohen's first goal put Aston Villa level in the 25th minute, wiping out the lead Johnson had snatched in the fourth. But five minutes after half-time, the Israeli left-back drove a low cross from Dalglish into the far corner of Villa's net, to restore Liverpool's lead and put his wavering team-mates back on course for their fourth Championship in five years.

From that moment, Bob Paisley's men played the highly skilled, attacking football with which they had opened up the substantial mid-season points gap that, ultimately, proved a valuable insurance against Manchester United's late challenge. Further goals by Johnson and Ray Kennedy brought the game — and the season — to a rousing climax.

Hammers outsmart Gunners at Wembley

Stuart Pearson (second from right) knocks the ball towards Trevor Brooking (10) who will stoop to score the only goal with a rare header.

WEST HAM TOOK a leaf out of Arsenal's book at Wembley to win the FA Cup for the second time in six years, this time as an unfancied Second Division side. They stole an early goal, a Trevor Brooking header in the 13th minute, and then sat back to employ the contain-and-counter-attack policy that has been the hallmark of Arsenal's game in their long Cup campaign.

West Ham's shrewd manager John Lyall had had ample time to study Arsenal in combat during their marathon semi-final against Liverpool, which seemed to have left the Gunners mentally and physically drained. He pulled Stuart Pearson back into midfield, adding to the flair of the interceptions and counter-thrusts of Brooking, Devonshire, Allen and Pike.

The West Ham goal came when a misdirected Pearson shot from an angle found the rarely used head of Brooking, who reacted quickly to score from close in. The other talking point was Willie Young's trip on 17-year-old Paul Allen — the youngest player to appear in an FA Cup final — just outside the box, as he was clear and likely to double the margin.

FINAL SCORE

Football League
Division 1: Liverpool
Top scorer: Phil Boyer (Southampton) 23
Division 2: Leicester City
Division 3: Grimsby Town
Division 4: Huddersfield Town
Footballer of the Year: Terry McDermott (Liverpool)

FA Cup Final

West Ham United	1	Arsenal	0

League Cup Final

Wolves	1	Nottingham Forest	0

Scottish League
Premier Division: Aberdeen
Top scorer: Doug Somner (St Mirren) 25
Division 1: Hearts
Division 2: Falkirk
Footballer of the Year: Gordon Strachan (Aberdeen)

Scottish FA Cup Final

Celtic	1	Rangers	0

(after extra time)

Scottish League Cup Final

Dundee United	0	Aberdeen	0
Replay: Dundee U	3	Aberdeen	0

International Championship
Northern Ireland, 5 pts

European Cup Final

Nottingham Forest	1	SV Hamburg	0

Cup-Winners' Cup Final

Valencia	0	Arsenal	0

(after extra time)
Valencia won 5–4 on penalties

UEFA Cup Final
Eintracht Frankfurt beat Borussia Moenchengladbach 2–3, 1–0 on away goals

European Footballer of the Year 1979
Kevin Keegan (SV Hamburg & England)

Leading European Scorer (Golden Boot)
Erwin Van Den Bergh (Lierse) 39

World Club Championship

Nacional (Uruguay)	1	Nottingham Forest	0

Penalty choker for Arsenal in European shoot-out

Rix's penalty is saved, and Arsenal lose their second final in five days.

IN THE FIRST major Cup final to be decided on penalties, Arsenal lost the European Cup-Winners' Cup to Valencia without conceding a goal in regular play in the final. Defences were on top throughout the match, although Brady made several threatening runs for Arsenal. The Spaniards were disappointing, and more was expected of the Argentinian Mario Kempes and the German Rainer Bonhof.

With no goals scored in 120 minutes, Kempes missed the first penalty and then Brady, of all people, threw away Arsenal's advantage. It went into sudden death after the next eight successful kicks. Then Arias scored for Valencia, and their keeper Pereira saved from Rix. No match should be decided in this fashion, let alone a Cup final, and it's high time the authorities came up with a more acceptable method.

FOOTBALL FOCUS

- Non-League Harlow, the FA Cup giant-killers, bravely went out at Watford in the fourth round 4–3, after taking a half-time lead and then going behind 4–1.
- Arsenal played 70 first-class games in the season, in League, FA Cup, League Cup, European Cup-Winners' Cup and Charity Shield.
- Colin Garwood finished as leading scorer for both Portsmouth (17 goals in 24 games) and Aldershot (10 in 16) in Division Four.
- As the result of a bribery scandal in Italy, AC Milan were demoted to the Second Division, club president Felici Colombo banned for life, and international Paolo Rossi of Perugia suspended for three years.

Shilton the hero as Forest retain European Cup

PETER SHILTON put his League Cup final blunder a long way behind him with a masterful performance in Madrid to help Nottingham Forest proudly retain the European Cup. For the second consecutive season, a single goal — this time scored by John Robertson in the 21st minute against Hamburg — was enough to earn Forest the most coveted trophy in club football. But let no one imagine Brian Clough's men were allowed as comfortable a passage to victory as against Malmö last year. This time the boot was on the other foot, as they battled to prevent Kevin Keegan and his spirited colleagues taking home the Cup for the first time.

It was indeed a great tactical triumph for Mr Clough and his partner, Peter Taylor, and they were given an even warmer reception than the team when they were persuaded to take a bow on the pitch at the end. Burns was superb in central defence, and Lloyd a dependable partner. Skipper McGovern and O'Neill, brave, skilful and selfless, also deserve great credit for intercepting, tackling and generally scuffling to great effect in amongst the determined Hamburg forwards. The industrious Bowyer and 18-year-old Mills did a highly efficient job in midfield, too. And Birtles ran himself into the ground as a lone raider.

In the absence of Francis and Bowles, Forest were forced to employ a hyper-defensive policy, and rely on quick breaks to snatch a goal. The decisive, four-man move was started by Frankie Gray, breaking quickly out of defence, and finished by Robertson with a 20-yarder hammered in off the far post.

SOCCER SOUNDBITES

"The odds were stacked against us... It was one of the best 90 minutes we have ever had, absolutely marvellous."

An emotional
BRIAN CLOUGH,
after the match.

John Robertson (one from left) is congratulated by Trevor Francis after scoring Forest's winner.

Belgium fail — what a lot of Hrubesch!

WEST GERMANY re-established themselves as a leading soccer power when they beat Belgium 2–1 in Rome, their third consecutive European Championship final over eight years and their second success. Two goals by Horst Hrubesch, the big blond striker, who has been playing alongside Kevin Keegan for Hamburg, were just enough to earn this young German side the triumph they deserved.

After two weeks of rubbish — boring football and poor refereeing — the Championship at last produced a match with thrills, drama and no little skill. During the first half-hour, the Germans played the most inventive football seen in the competition. Newcomer Bernd Schuster was a revelation in the West German midfield, which was disrupted when the splendid Hans-Peter Briegel had to go off in the second half, following which there was a period when the West Germans looked uncertain and their 10th-minute lead vulnerable. After 70 minutes, Belgium equalized from a disputed penalty: Van der Elst looked a foot outside the box when Stielike brought him down, but he was clean through, so justice was done when Vandereycken scored from the spot. Then, with three minutes left, Hrubesch rose above the rest to head Muller's corner into the net.

The new group format for the finals was not a success. Belgium went through to the final at the expense of host country Italy because they scored more goals. Italy's only goal in their three matches — struck late on by Marco Tardelli when he took time off from shackling Keegan — was enough to beat England, who had a disappointing tournament. Ron Greenwood's boys will have to show more imagination if they are to stand a chance in the 1982 World Cup in Spain.

Oh Brotherston! Noel's vital goal

A BEAUTIFULLY TAKEN goal by Noel Brotherston after 23 minutes against Wales brought Northern Ireland their first outright British International Championship since 1914. With the Championship taking place over nine days, the Irish success in Cardiff can be measured against England's 4–1 defeat there six days earlier. It also renders the coming Scotland-England clash irrelevant as far as the title is concerned. The Irish drew 1–1 at Wembley.

If the Championship is to be taken seriously, however, one would expect more than 13,000 to turn up for the deciding match. There were 24,000 at Wrexham when England played there, and 92,000 at Wembley to see England beat Argentina 3–1 in a friendly four days earlier. So what price the Home Championship now?

FINAL SCORE

EUROPEAN CHAMPIONSHIP 1980

Group 1

West Germany	1	Czechoslovakia	0
Holland	1	Greece	0
West Germany	3	Holland	2
Czechoslovakia	3	Greece	1
West Germany	0	Greece	0
Holland	1	Czechoslovakia	1

	P	W	D	L	F	A	P
W. Germany	3	2	1	0	4	2	5
Czech.	3	1	1	1	4	3	3
Holland	3	1	1	1	4	4	3
Greece	3	0	1	2	1	4	1

Group 2

England	1	Belgium	1
Italy	0	Spain	0
Italy	1	England	0
Belgium	2	Spain	1
England	2	Spain	1
Belgium	0	Italy	0

	P	W	D	L	F	A	P
Belgium	3	1	2	0	3	2	4
Italy	3	1	2	0	1	0	4
England	3	1	1	1	3	3	3
Spain	3	0	1	2	2	4	1

THIRD-PLACE MATCH

Italy 1 Czechoslovakia 1
Italy won 9–8 on penalties

FINAL

West Germany 2 Belgium 1

Rome, 22 June 1980. Attendance 47,864

West Germany: Schumacher, Briegel (Cullmann), Forster K, Dietz, Schuster, Rummenigge K-H, Hrubesch, Muller H, Allofs, Stielike, Kaltz (Scorer: Hrubesch 2)
Belgium: Pfaff, Gerets, Millecamps, Meeuws, Renquin, Cools, Vandereycken, Van Moer, Mommens, Van der Elst, Ceulemans (Scorer: Vandereycken pen)

Eerie silence greets Hammers' super victory

WEST HAM'S SPLENDID 5–1 victory over Castilla of Spain on 1 October to come back from their 3–1 first-leg deficit in the Cup-Winners' Cup was greeted by an eerie silence from the Upton Park terraces. This was because the match was played behind closed doors — West Ham's punishment for their followers' disgraceful, drunken behaviour at the Bernabeu Stadium in Madrid two weeks earlier. UEFA also imposed a heavy fine on the club, although West Ham had done everything in their power to prevent trouble in Madrid.

They made tickets available only to registered supporters, who were photographed and their passport numbers noted. And skipper Billy Bonds wrote to each ticket-holder stressing the need for sensible behaviour. But there was nothing the club could do about the so-called fans who travelled independently and bought their tickets in Spain or from other sources.

At Upton Park, the Hammers treated the 300 or so officials present to a splendid display, taking an overall lead with three goals before half-time. Castilla scored after the interval, and took the game into extra time, but two more goals by David Cross to complete his hat-trick put West Ham through to the second round 6–4 on aggregate.

No crowd trouble at Upton Park as West Ham play Castilla behind closed doors.

Jack Charlton reduced to tears by rioting Wednesday fans

SOCCER'S REPUTATION was done further damage at Oldham on 6 September when the behaviour of Sheffield Wednesday followers brought a 29-minute stoppage and tears of frustration to the eyes of manager Jack Charlton, who pleaded unsuccessfully for restraint and was struck by a missile for his pains. The crowd rioted after Wednesday striker Terry Curran had been sent off following a clash with Simon Stainrod. In the ensuing uproar, 20 people, including police, were injured. Fans hurled concrete, bricks, coins — anything they could find. They scaled six-foot barriers and carried their fight on to the pitch. Nine people were arrested.

There was violence at another Second Division match, Chelsea v West Ham at Stamford Bridge, where fighting broke out on the terraces. Forty-two people were arrested and two policemen injured.

A distressed Jack Charlton at Oldham.

Three points for a win from next season

AT A SPECIAL meeting of the Football League at Solihull on 9 February, a number of resolutions were passed arising out of football's "blueprint for the future". From next season, there will be three points for a win (still one for a draw); six matches will be allowed each weekend on Fridays or Sundays; no official (director or secretary) may be involved in the management or administration of more than one club; there will be a transfer embargo on clubs which have payments outstanding from other deals; and — this only a "gentlemen's agreement" — no club is to hire another League club's manager during the season.

Proposals rejected include the reduction of the "majority vote" from three-quarters to two-thirds, and an extension of the half-time interval to 15 minutes.

The "blueprint" was originally drawn up as a charter, "Soccer — The Fight for Survival", by a study group of club secretaries and managers last August. There are still a number of proposals requiring further discussion.

Allen and Sansom in swap deal

ARSENAL AND CRYSTAL Palace did the biggest exchange deal in the history of British soccer on 13 August, when striker Clive Allen — only 62 days on Arsenal's books — and reserve goalkeeper Paul Barron moved to Selhurst Park, and England left-back Kenny Sansom went to Highbury. For the second time in two months, since he left QPR for Arsenal, the 19-year-old Allen has been valued at £1.2 million, and his personal signing-on fees for the two deals add up to an estimated £100,000, without his having kicked a ball in competition. Sansom is valued at £1 million, and Palace have paid £400,000 for Barron, kept out of the Arsenal first team by the evergreen Pat Jennings.

Spending in the transfer market has now reached a staggering £14 million in three months since Cup final day, covering 72 major deals and including two other £1 million transfers, Ian Wallace from Coventry to Forest and Paul Goddard from QPR to West Ham.

Villa transistor champions

ASTON VILLA FANS, with the news of Ipswich's demise at Middlesbrough coming through on their transistor radios, celebrated their Championship triumph at Highbury on 2 May with a benign pitch invasion and a 2–0 defeat! With their thoughts on Ayresome Park, where their only challengers Ipswich were vainly trying to stay in the title race, Villa's nerves were stretched too tightly. So instead of playing the skilful, highly efficient attacking football that has earned them the title, they meekly surrendered control to Arsenal, who looked more like Championship material and clinched their place in the UEFA Cup next season.

Nevertheless, Villa have done enough this season to earn their first League title since 1910. In Cowans, Mortimer and Des Bremner, they possess a formidable midfield unit of well-balanced skill, power and drive. Further forward, Withe, a target-man who scores, Shaw, a young striker of great potential, and Morley, a genuine winger, emphasize Villa's ability to wreck opposing defences. Villa have used only 14 players, with seven of them ever-present.

There was a festival atmosphere before the start, with Highbury guest Pele saluting all parts of the 57,000 crowd and helping release hundreds of balloons. There were also hundreds of police to keep the peace, and at the end form a barrier between the 16,000 Villa supporters and the Arsenal North Bank fans who were allowed to converge on the pitch. Thankfully, it turned out to be a friendly invasion.

Skipper Dennis Mortimer and manager Ron Saunders celebrate in Birmingham.

Anarchy at Luton as mob run Wylde

THANK GOODNESS Luton look like missing promotion to the First Division. Their players may be good enough: their supporters certainly are not. The disgraceful scenes at Kenilworth Road on Saturday, when young fans invaded the pitch three minutes from time in an obvious attempt to get the game called off, were sickening. Fortunately, the police stayed calm, the referee took the players off the pitch for 10 minutes, and Oldham were able to complete a creditable 2–1 victory.

The trouble started an hour earlier, with a reckless tackle by Oldham's Rodger Wylde on Luton back Kirk Stephens. Even Oldham's manager Jimmy Frizzell later admitted that he had seen players sent off for less. The situation wasn't helped when the Luton scoreboard flashed "Send him off". Wylde was the subject of continuing abuse from the crowd, who were incensed still further when he scored two goals. When the referee restarted the match after the pitch was cleared, he advised Mr Frizzell to leave Wylde in the dressing-room but, to his credit, the Oldham manager insisted on sending the player back on, albeit with the warning to stay near the tunnel. Once anarchy takes over from the referee's whistle, football is dead. It looked very sick at Luton.

First League Cup success for Liverpool

LIVERPOOL FINALLY WON the League Cup, the only domestic competition that had eluded them, in a highly entertaining replay at Villa Park. Smartly taken goals by Kenny Dalglish and Alan Hansen helped them recover from Paul Goddard's early blow and take control against West Ham. If the final at Wembley was a great disappointment, the replay made up for it, with Liverpool putting on one of the finest displays of the season.

Most of the thrills at Wembley were crammed into the last three minutes of extra time: a highly disputed goal, when Alan Kennedy hammered a poor clearance past Parkes as Sammy Lee was lying on the ground in an offside position; and West Ham's equalizer, a Ray Stewart penalty with the last kick of the match after McDermott had handled with goalkeeper Clemence beaten.

At Villa Park, West Ham, runaway leaders of the Second Division, scored in their first serious attack, after nine minutes, when Goddard headed in Neighbour's cross at the near post. But Liverpool maintained the control they had exerted before this setback, with Lee outstanding in midfield. The nippy Rush, brought into the attack for only his second full game, drove Lee's free-kick against the angle and Ray Kennedy headed on to the bar.

Then came the goals, after 25 and 28 minutes. First, Dalglish burst past a lunging Bonds from McDermott's shrewd pass and hooked the ball past Parkes with consummate skill. Then Hansen headed home Case's corner at the far post, the ball clipping Bonds on the way. West Ham improved in the second half, with Brooking and Devonshire coming more into the game. But it was a brave effort on the Hammers' part to keep their defeat down to a single goal, with Liverpool playing such commanding football.

Liverpool's disputed goal in the 1-1 draw at Wembley.

Villa the Spurs hero in Cup replay

RICARDO VILLA, who left the pitch in tears on Saturday after being substituted in the 100th FA Cup final, returned to Wembley to score twice and earn Tottenham victory in a hard, exciting replay. After the bearded Argentinian had given Spurs an early lead, Manchester City fought back to equalize, then move in front. But a goal from Crooks and a sensational winner from Villa maintained Spurs' record of never losing a domestic Cup final.

When Villa was substituted by young Garry Brooke midway through the second half in the first match, with Spurs a goal down, he must have thought his season was over. But Hutchison, who had scored City's goal, deflected a Hoddle chip into his own net to afford Spurs a replay. Manager Keith Burkinshaw showed great courage in keeping faith with Villa for the return, and the Argentinian repaid him by sweeping a loose ball into the net after only seven minutes. Young Steve MacKenzie equalized for City three minutes later with a spectacular volley from 22 yards out, and they went ahead after the interval when Reeves converted a penalty. Spurs were regretting their earlier misses now, but they continued to play good football and press forward, with the other Argentinian, Ardiles, and Hoddle running the midfield.

It was a typical piece of Hoddle flair that led to their equalizer after 70 minutes, as he flicked the ball up and over the advancing City defence for Archibald to lay on Crooks's goal. The dramatic winner came seven minutes later. Villa got the ball on the left and began to run powerfully at the City defence. They held off, but he beat one man after another before cutting inside and hammering the ball past Corrigan. It was a fitting climax for what had become a classic Cup final.

Villa (5) evades Caton's last-ditch tackle to score the dramatic winner.

FOOTBALL FOCUS

- John Trollope made his 765th League appearance for Swindon on 18 October, beating the record for one club set 15 years ago by Portsmouth's Jimmy Dickinson. Full-back Trollope, 37, had relinquished his first-team place two seasons earlier to take charge of the youth team. He finally retired in November after five more games.
- The FA ended the red and yellow card system for dismissals and cautions with effect from 19 January, a decision unpopular with most referees.
- Ipswich gained a 1-2-3 in the PFA's Player of the Year poll, with John Wark winning it from Frans Thijssen (the Football Writers' Footballer of the Year) and Paul Mariner — a Scotsman, a Dutchman and an Englishman!
- Exeter were the Cup giant-killers of the season, reaching the quarter-finals despite being drawn away in five of their six rounds. The mid-table Third Division side drew at First Division Leicester in the fourth round and beat them 3–1 in the replay, with a hat-trick by Tony Kellow, who scored 33 goals during the season. They then drew at St James's Park before thrashing Second Division Newcastle 4–0 at their own St James Park! But they finally fell 2–0 to Spurs at White Hart Lane.
- Leicester, who were later relegated, won 2–1 at Anfield on 31 January to inflict Liverpool's first home defeat for three years 10 days, covering 85 League, FA Cup, League Cup and European matches.
- Arbroath, in Scotland's Division Two, won fewer home matches (three) and more away matches (10) than any other club in the division. They finished ninth of 14.

Battling Ipswich win UEFA Cup

WHEN IPSWICH took a 3–0 lead over AZ 67 Alkmaar to Holland in the final of the UEFA Cup, their travelling fans could not be confident of the outcome, bearing in mind their team's tendency in previous campaigns to collapse in the away leg, a failing that had twice proved almost fatal earlier this season. But they had recently produced good away results, particularly in the quarter-finals, when they went to France and beat St Etienne 4–1 despite an early Johnny Rep goal that had taken the home side's tally in the competition to 23–0.

AZ were the new Dutch champions, but a cracking 20-yard volley in four minutes from one of Holland's own stars, Frans Thijssen, gave Ipswich a dream start and meant AZ had to score at least five. They did score two, before John Wark got a priceless goal back for Town. Not only did it virtually ensure victory for Ipswich, but it was Wark's record-equalling 14th European goal of the season. AZ refused to surrender and scored twice more, but Ipswich thoroughly deserved their overall 5–4 triumph.

John Wark (one from right) is congratulated after scoring the vital goal in the UEFA Cup Final.

Third European Cup for Liverpool

LIVERPOOL MADE SURE the European Cup will remain in England for the fifth successive year when they earned their third victory in the competition with a spectacular goal from left-back Alan Kennedy in the 81st minute at the Parc des Princes. This equals the record of Spain (1956-60), whose five wins were all recorded by Real Madrid, Liverpool's 1–0 victims in Paris. Another triumph for the club was the behaviour of their 12,000 travelling fans, who took the Paris police by surprise by giving them no trouble.

The match was a highly interesting, if not over-exciting, battle of wits between two teams searching for openings and intent on offering their opponents as few opportunities as possible. Both managers gambled by bringing back players following long lay-offs: Liverpool's Dalglish after a month with ankle ligament trouble, and Real's English international Laurie Cunningham after six months with a foot injury. Cunningham caused Liverpool most trouble, but the Reds did most of the pressing, even if their goal attempts were mostly from long range.

The breakthrough came from a Ray Kennedy throw-in on the left. There seemed little danger when his namesake Alan chested the ball down in Real's penalty area, but Cortes took a wild swing at it, and Kennedy brushed past him and from a narrow angle slammed the ball past Real's keeper.

Liverpool skipper Phil Thompson with the European Cup.

FINAL SCORE

Football League
Division 1: Aston Villa
Top scorer: Steve Archibald (Tottenham Hotspur), Peter Withe (Aston Villa) 20
Division 2: West Ham United
Division 3: Rotherham United
Division 4: Southend United
Footballer of the Year: Frans Thijssen (Ipswich Town)

FA Cup Final
Tottenham Hotspur 1 Manchester City 1
(after extra time)
Replay: Tottenham H. 3 Manchester City 2

League Cup Final
Liverpool 1 West Ham United 1
(after extra time)
Replay: Liverpool 2 West Ham United 1

Scottish League
Premier Division: Celtic
Top scorer: Francis McGarvey (Celtic) 23
Division 1: Hibernian
Division 2: Queen's Park
Footballer of the Year: Alan Rough (Partick Thistle)

Scottish FA Cup Final
Rangers 0 Dundee United 0
Replay: Rangers 4 Dundee United 1

Scottish League Cup Final
Dundee United 3 Dundee 0

International Championship
Not completed

European Cup Final
Liverpool 1 Real Madrid 0

Cup-Winners' Cup Final
Dynamo Tbilisi 2 Carl Zeiss Jena 1

UEFA Cup Final
Ipswich Town beat AZ 67 Alkmaar 3–0, 2–4

European Footballer of the Year 1981
Karl-Heinz Rummenigge (Bayern Munich & West Germany)

Leading European Scorer (Golden Boot)
Georgi Slavkov (Trakia Plovdiv) 31

World Club Championship
Flamengo (Brazil) 3 Liverpool (England) 0

England booked for Spain — and not as tourists

Brooking's second goal stays where he placed it.

AFTER THEIR STIRRING 3–1 victory in Hungary on 6 June, England will begin their holidays knowing that they now have excellent prospects of visiting Spain next summer, not in the widely predicted role of tourists, but as one of the 24 World Cup finalists. There is still hard work to do in Oslo in September and against Hungary two months later, when the qualifying competition will be completed at Wembley. But success in Budapest — those who saw it will remember it as a famous victory — has put England back on the course from which the defeats in Romania and Switzerland had blown them.

There is a long way to go yet but, having come so perilously close to disaster, they are unlikely to lose their way again. Victory in Hungary was a major achievement for England after their recent run of failures, especially the defeat in Basle a week ago, which saw strident calls for Ron Greenwood's resignation. Against the Magyars, Mr Greenwood opted for experience, and the "old guard" simply closed their ears to the awesome noise of the Nep Stadium and played with a maturity their opponents could not match.

Though it was predominantly an admirable all-round team effort, Thompson and Brooking emerged as the heroes. Thompson held the defence together with an assurance that even the gifted Torocsik and powerful Kiss could not shake. Brooking exploited the space allowed him to engineer the dismantling of Hungary's nervous defence — and scored two goals into the bargain.

The first came in the 19th minute, when he hooked the ball home after a delightful move with Neal, Coppell and McDermott. Hungary equalized on the stroke of half-time through Garaba, but Brooking put England firmly back on top on the hour with a spectacular left-foot shot that left the ball jammed between the net and back stanchion. And, as the Hungarian spirit sagged, Keegan made it 3–1, converting a penalty after being brought down by Garaba.

England now have seven points from six matches, with a goal difference of plus five. Romania have six points from five games, Hungary five from four.

Shankly: soccer's true folk hero

FORMER LIVERPOOL manager Bill Shankly died on 29 September, aged 67, following a heart attack. In the world of professional football, "Shanks" was unique, a folk hero to the core.

He will best be remembered as the driving force behind Liverpool FC. In 15 glorious years as manager at Anfield, he made them into one of the world's most famous and respected clubs. A Second Division title, three League Championships, two FA Cups and one UEFA Cup remain as monuments to Shankly's magnificent work at Liverpool, where he built two great sides before his retirement in July 1974. And he laid the foundations for Bob Paisley, his eager lieutenant, to go on to even greater success.

Bill Shankly, idol of the Kop.

But the admiration which football people have for Shankly goes far beyond the Merseyside boundaries. He was born in the Ayrshire mining village of Glenbuck into a footballing family. He made his mark at Preston as a tenacious, dedicated wing-half, helping the club to the FA Cup final in 1937 (lost) and 1938 (won), and would have won more than his five Scottish caps but for the war. He turned to management in the late forties, with Carlisle, Grimsby, Workington and Huddersfield, before the call from Liverpool came in 1959. After signing men such as Ian St John and Ron Yeats, he took the slumbering giant back into Division One and on the road to 18 successive seasons in European competition.

A tremendous motivator of men, Shankly filled his teams with inspiration, and helped turn promising players such as Kevin Keegan — recruited from lowly Scunthorpe — into great ones. One of Shankly's greatest attributes was his judgment in the trnsfer market: few of his signings turned out wrong. He also became the idol of the Kop, developing a closer relationship with supporters than probably any other manager in history.

"Shanks" had a sharp, dry and sometimes abrasive wit, but was a soft, warm-hearted man. Impulsive and loquacious words poured from him in a crisp Scottish accent, and his countless quips have become part of soccer folklore.

SOCCER SOUNDBITES

"I have only felt like this once before, and that was when my father died, because Bill was like a second father to me."

KEVIN KEEGAN.

"He was a great man. His motivation could move mountains."

RON YEATS.

"Football is not a matter of life and death — it's much more important."

BILL SHANKLY.

England and Northern Ireland book tickets to Spain

ENGLAND'S WORLD CUP qualification campaign, so often teetering on the brink of disaster during the past year, finally ended in triumph at Wembley on 18 November when Ron Greenwood's men beat Hungary 1–0 and were assured by the crowd that they would not be walking alone in Spain next summer. Indeed, with Northern Ireland beating Israel by the same score in Belfast, and Scotland already qualified, they will be joined there by two other home countries. Wales, however, who lost 3–0 to the USSR, will only make it to the finals if their conquerors win in Czechoslovakia in the remaining match in Group Three.

Long after the players had disappeared down the Wembley tunnel, following the narrow but clear victory over Hungary, the fans were singing, cheering and waving their flags to celebrate England's right to feature in the finals for the first time since Mexico in 1970.

Although Greenwood said that "there was no great euphoria in the dressing room after the match — just gratitude that we had managed to get through", England had produced their best performance of the competition to wipe out all memory of their failures against Romania, Switzerland and, latterly, their almost catastrophic defeat in Oslo. Fortunately for England, Switzerland had subsequently taken three points off Romania; otherwise, England might have been out of the running instead of needing just to draw with Hungary. Although there was only Mariner's 16th-minute goal to separate the teams at the end, England produced an exhilarating performance, with Martin doing well alongside Thompson at the centre of the defence, and Robson, Brooking and Keegan in scintillating form in midfield. This display must encourage the belief that their journey to Spain next summer will not be a waste of time.

Malcolm Macdonald: first paid director

MALCOLM MACDONALD, the Fulham manager and former England striker, became the first paid director of a Football League club on 19 November, within minutes of an FA decision to approve the innovation at an Extraordinary General Meeting. As soon as the members decided to permit one paid director per club, by 522 votes to 28, Ernie Clay, the Fulham chairman and chief shareholder, told Mr Macdonald that the job was his. He will have responsibility for controlling the football side of the club's activities.

Fulham manager, and new paid director, Malcolm Macdonald.

SOCCER SOUNDBITES

"Now the gate is open for the game to be run by people with the necessary football knowledge and experience."

ERNIE CLAY,
Fulham chairman, speaking after Malcolm Macdonald's appointment.

Liverpool home with the Milk

LIVERPOOL LEFT IT late in defence of the League Cup — now the Milk Cup, sponsored by the Milk Marketing Board. They were trailing Spurs at Wembley to an 11th-minute Archibald goal until the 87th minute, when Ronnie Whelan snatched a dramatic equalizer. Only two minutes earlier, Archibald had missed a chance to clinch the match for Spurs. Now, in extra time, they were visibly wilting, and in the second period Dalglish coolly set up a second for the 20-year-old Whelan, who has established himself in the side this season as a goalscoring midfielder in place of Ray Kennedy, and Rush scored a third in the last minute. So Tottenham's "grand slam" dreams of a clean sweep at home and a European trophy are now shattered. Both sides have important European matches on Wednesday, and both will be challenging strongly for the Championship if they can capitalize on all those games in hand.

Keeper Bruce Grobbelaar leads Liverpool in a victory song, with last season's League Cup and their newly won Milk Cup: Top (l-r) Dalglish, Lawrenson, Lee, Rush, Grobbelaar, Hansen, McDermott, Thompson; crouched (l-r) Whelan, Johnson, Souness, Alan Kennedy, Neal.

Roberts hat-trick knocks Southampton off the top

Keegan finds a way to stop Roberts scoring.

SPURS PAID Weymouth £30,000 for Graham Roberts and converted him from a non-League striker into a central defender last season. He showed he had not lost his striking ability when he was drafted into the side on 20 March to replace the injured Ardiles against Southampton, his home-town team, and one of the League clubs that had rejected him. He scored three goals, and was unlucky not to get two or three more, as Spurs knocked the leaders off their perch with a 3–2 win at White Hart Lane. Southampton, indeed, only woke up when they were two down, but the scoreline flattered them.

Spurs, who reached the semi-finals of the Cup-Winners' Cup on Wednesday and are in the FA Cup semis, too, are still in with a good shout for the League. They are seven points behind new leaders Swansea, but have five games in hand — worth three points a time now, if they can win them!

Brazil 5 Southampton 3

AT FIRST SIGHT, the scoreline does not look so bad for First Division leaders Southampton, but the five goals against them were scored by Alan Brazil of Ipswich, and not the country of the same name. They stay top, but their challengers have played fewer games, and Ipswich are among them, six points adrift with five games in hand.

A series of setbacks for Ipswich over the last two weeks, including exits from both domestic Cup competitions, saw Brazil dropped before the 4–0 League defeat at Anfield. But he wasn't out for long and, boosted by his recall to the Scottish squad, he has now produced the deadliest exhibition of finishing seen in Division One since Roger Davies scored five for Derby against Luton seven years ago. He hit a first-half hat-trick and scored his fifth four minutes from time. But it was not a one-man show, and Brazil was the first to acknowledge the debt he owed to co-striker Mich D'Avray, deputizing for the injured Mariner, who made four of the goals. On the other side, strikers Keegan and Channon could do little more than stand and admire.

Brazil celebrates another goal.

SOCCER SOUNDBITES

"I wish that man would go back to Brazil, or wherever it is he comes from."

IVAN KATALINIC,
Southampton's Yugoslav goalkeeper.

Classy extra-time win for Dons

ABERDEEN BEAT Rangers in the Scottish Cup final at Hampden 4–1 after extra time, breaking the hold that the "Old Firm" have had on the trophy since the Dons last won it in 1970. Indeed, Rangers had not lost a final to any club but Celtic since 1929 — and they have been in a few!

Rangers took the lead with a John MacDonald goal after 15 minutes, one of the best of their entire season's output. Aberdeen equalized 18 minutes later with a swerving shot from centre-back Alex McLeish, who shared the Aberdeen honours with fellow redhead and World Cup colleague Gordon Strachan, as they took control of the match in the second half. But they failed to translate their class and superiority into goals until extra time, when they ran Rangers ragged and McGhee, Strachan and Cooper all scored.

It was a fitting reward for Alex Ferguson's men, who so narrowly missed catching Celtic in the League after winning 15 of their last 16 matches.

Gordon Strachan (right) keeps a step ahead of Rangers' Jim Bett.

FOOTBALL FOCUS

● FIFA's technical committee have expressed concern about the "excessive demonstrative attitude of some players and teams when a goal is scored". They felt that "the scorer should be congratulated by the team captain or the player who made the pass, but the exultant outbursts of several players at once jumping on top of each other, kissing and embracing, should be banned from the football pitch", and recommended that national associations should curb such behaviour.

● Before the transfer market slumped, with the deepening financial crisis in football, several more huge transfers took place, including Justin Fashanu from Norwich to Nottingham Forest for £1 million and Trevor Francis from Forest to Man City for £1.2 million. But the "last of the big spenders" proved to be new Man Utd manager Ron Atkinson, who bought John Gidman and Remi Moses for nearly £0.5 million each; Frank Stapleton, a "steal" at the tribunal valuation of £1.1 million; and then broke the British record by paying £1.7 million for Bryan Robson from West Brom.

● The international referees' committee, in answer to a question from the Swiss FA regarding a goal-kick in which the ball touched the referee in the penalty area before passing out of the area, agreed by a majority of votes that the referee should be considered as "air" and that the ball was in play.

● Glenn Hoddle scored from the spot with only the sixth penalty awarded in an FA Cup final (all successful) to give Spurs a 1–0 win in the replay against Second Division QPR.

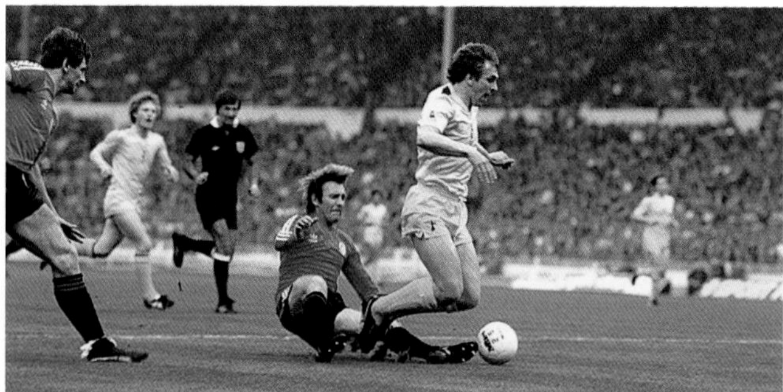

QPR captain Tony Currie brings Graham Roberts down in the box for Spurs' winning Cup final penalty.

Liverpool soar to majestic heights

ALL-CONQUERING Liverpool won their 13th League title, their fifth in seven seasons, when they beat Spurs 3–1 at Anfield on 15 May. Manager Bob Paisley, who has guided them to these successes, as well as three European Cups, a UEFA Cup win and two League Cups, rates this latest triumph as the greatest. Liverpool were languishing in mid-table at the turn of the year but, despite Paisley's rebuilding the side during the season, they came with a late run — 11 straight wins from 9 March to 1 May — and inexorably caught and passed all their rivals.

The turning point came shortly after the decision had been taken — in the famous Anfield Boot Room — to give Ray Kennedy's midfield job to young Irish international Ronnie Whelan and to confirm Ian Rush as Dalglish's front-line partner. The timing of the changes and, later, the employment of Australian Craig Johnston in place of McDermott, were crucial. Bruce Grobbelaar, too, settled in after a shaky start as Clemence's replacement in goal, and central defender Mark Lawrenson was another success story — although these two had an unfortunate match when Liverpool went out of the European Cup in the semi-finals to CSKA Sofia. It was a Grobbelaar error that conceded a late equalizer, and Lawrenson became the first Liverpool player to be sent off in 18 successive years of European competition.

But that was Liverpool's only real setback in another triumphant season, and they can't be expected to win everything — or can they?

Villa make it six in a row for England in European Cup

ASTON VILLA, WITH only two seasons of UEFA Cup experience in Europe, started as underdogs in the European Cup final against Bayern Munich in Rotterdam. But they pulled off a famous 1–0 victory over the three-times champions with a 67th-minute goal from Peter Withe, to ensure that Europe's premier trophy stayed in England for a record sixth successive season. Their triumph was even more remarkable in that it was achieved a mere 103 days after Tony Barton took over as manager from Ron Saunders, and 81 minutes after reserve keeper Nigel Spink had taken over in goal for only his second senior game for the club (the first was in December 1979!).

Spink, indeed, was Villa's hero. Going on for Jimmy Rimmer, who found a neck injury sustained in training too much of a handicap, he rose to the occasion magnificently, coming to Villa's rescue with a series of astonishingly confident saves when they were in danger of being overwhelmed. He was called into action soon after reaching the pitch to defy close-range efforts by Durnberger and Rummenigge. Then, when Bayern — the last Continental club to win the trophy before Liverpool ushered in the age of English supremacy — applied increasingly heavy pressure after the interval, his keen eyes, safe hands and instinctive agility stood between the Germans and victory.

This is not to belittle the performances of Spink's colleagues. Cowans and Mortimer, with commendably efficient displays in midfield, refused to allow Breitner to control the game. The combative Evans and calm McNaught, though sometimes outsmarted by Bayern's slick football, refused to bow the knee to the persistent Rummenigge and Hoeness. And, having spoilt many a promising move early on, Shaw, Morley and Withe ultimately produced the most telling strike of the night: Shaw conjured up a piece of skill on the left and fed left-winger Morley, who worked his own brand of magic, turning his man inside-out before sending a low centre across goal which Withe gleefully converted.

Withe scores the goal that won Villa the European Cup.

Nigel Spink: heroics as substitute keeper.

Sending-off proposed for 'professional foul'

AT AN Extraordinary General Meeting of the Football League, the clubs agreed in principle the proposals put forward in May by the Busby Advisory Committee. The committee, under the chairmanship of Sir Matt Busby and including Bobby Charlton and Jimmy Hill, had come up with a series of revolutionary and far-reaching suggestions, and the League recommended that the FA be asked to put those requiring law changes to the International Football Association board. Although there was no intent expressed to go it alone if FIFA refused permission to experiment, it was agreed that some of the proposals could be implemented by instructing referees on the interpretation of the laws.

Thus if the key proposal — that the so-called "professional" or "tactical" foul committed outside the penalty area be punishable by a penalty kick, if it prevented a likely goal — were rejected, referees could still be instructed to send the offender off, as provided for in the laws (presumably for "serious" foul play). In the same way, throwing in from the wrong place could be treated as a foul throw (i.e., a ball improperly thrown in).

FIFA's reactions will not be known until later on this summer, but the ruling body are unlikely to allow any unilateral experiments, having already warned that English football would be ostracized unless it "continued to abide by international rules".

FINAL SCORE

Football League
Division 1: Liverpool
Top scorer: Kevin Keegan (Southampton) 26
Division 2: Luton Town
Division 3: Burnley
Division 4: Sheffield United
Footballer of the Year: Steve Perryman (Tottenham Hotspur)

FA Cup Final

Spurs	1	QPR	1
(after extra time)			
Replay: Spurs	1	QPR	0

League Cup Final

Liverpool	3	Spurs	1
(after extra time)			

Scottish League
Premier Division: Celtic
Top scorer: George McCluskey (Celtic) 21
Division 1: Motherwell
Division 2: Clyde
Footballer of the Year: Paul Sturrock (Dundee United)

Scottish FA Cup Final

Aberdeen	4	Rangers	1
(after extra time)			

Scottish League Cup Final

Rangers	2	Dundee United	1

International Championship
England, 6 pts

European Cup Final

Aston Villa	1	Bayern Munich	0

Cup-Winners' Cup Final

Barcelona	2	Standard Liège	1

UEFA Cup Final
IFK Gothenburg beat SV Hamburg 1–0, 3–0

European Footballer of the Year 1981
Karl-Heinz Rummenigge (Bayern Munich & West Germany)

Leading European Scorer (Golden Boot)
Wim Kieft (Ajax Amsterdam) 32

World Club Championship

Penarol (Uruguay)	2	Aston Villa (England)	0

Restored Italian master

The increase from 16 to 24 entrants did not improve the World Cup, played in Spain, and the second-phase format was a failure. Italy were lucky to survive the first round, but suddenly came alive, as striker Paolo Rossi, recently restored to football after a two-year suspension for his part in a bribery scandal, rediscovered his scoring skills. England, after a bright start, and conceding only one goal, lost the art of scoring and went out like a damp squib.

Rossi, Italy's goalscoring hero.

THE HOME COUNTRIES took advantage of the extra qualifying places, and three got through to the finals, Scotland and Northern Ireland from the same group. England just muddled through. European champions West Germany qualified ominously well, with eight straight wins and 33 goals against three.

The first phase of the finals — six groups of four, with two going through from each — threw up a handful of surprises. Holders Argentina lost to Belgium in the opening match, and Algeria made a sensational World Cup debut, beating West Germany 2–1. They beat Chile, too, but were scandalously prevented from going through when West Germany and Austria contrived the result of their match, the last of the group.

England got a wonderful start, skipper Bryan Robson scoring against France in 27 seconds, a World Cup record, and they won their three matches. Brazil were the only other side to take six points, with displays of exciting, attacking football not seen since the days of Pele, Gerson, Tostao and company.

Scotland scored first against the Brazilians, a cracking goal from right-back David Narey. But, with Zico, Socrates, Cerezo and Falcao the elegant masters of midfield, knocking the ball about as if they were on a training session, Brazil crushed the brave Scots 4–1. This left Scotland needing to beat the Soviet Union to go through to the next phase. They could only draw, and went out on goal difference for the third World Cup running.

Viva Zapata

Although Honduras gave an excellent account of themselves in Group 5, with draws against Spain and Northern Ireland, the allocation of a second finals places to the Central and North American zone was looking a little sick when El Salvador went down to a record defeat, 10–1 against Hungary. Ramirez Zapata, their scorer, was El Salvador's hero.

Bryan Robson (right) celebrates his record-breaking goal.

New Zealand, making their World Cup debut, fared little better, although the two goals they scored against a criminally careless Scotland proved the Scots' downfall. Cameroon were expected to be the chopping-blocks of Group 1, but nobody could beat them. With their captain Thomas N'Kono an inspiration in goal and Roger Milla a dangerous striker, it was only inexperience that let them down. Had they taken their chances, Italy would have made a shock early exit.

The finest performance from an unfancied side in the first phase belonged to Northern Ireland. With a squad largely recruited from the lower reaches of the Football League, and a string of poor results behind them, they not only qualified from Group 5, they won it. They beat hosts Spain with a Gerry Armstrong goal just before the interval, and, despite having Mal Donaghy harshly sent off half an hour from the end, kept the Spaniards at bay.

Favourites depart

Both remaining South American countries, World Cup holders Argentina and favourites Brazil, were in the same group. Italy, despite their pitiful start to the competition, were not overawed, and set out against Argentina in typically cynical fashion, intent on stopping Maradona and company come what may. The first half was a disgrace to football, with the Italians the chief culprits along with the referee and the inappropriately named Gentile clobbering Maradona if he so much as thought of going for the ball. Having softened up the opposition, the Italians began to play the ball in the second half, and won 2–1.

Maradona took his frustration out on Brazil, and he was sent off for blatantly kicking Batista, but not before the Brazilians had scored three delightful goals. But Brazil lacked a competent central striker, and that is the department that finally gave Italy the edge when the two sides met in the decider, a wonderful match.

Paolo Rossi, hitherto struggling to find his form, was suddenly back to his old, sharp self. Twice he scored, typical opportunist goals, and twice the Brazilians came back, with magnificent efforts from Socrates and Falcao. But Rossi completed his hat-trick with 16 minutes to go, and the best side in the competition were out.

British exit

Northern Ireland's bubble was burst by France, who were beginning to play some lovely football and outclassed them 4–1. England were drawn with their old rivals West Germany in Madrid, but the game disappointed the 75,000 crowd in the magnificent Bernabeu Stadium. It was mostly tight and negative and, although England made the better chances, they were content with a 0–0 draw after Rummenigge erupted a 25-yarder onto the bar near the end.

When the Germans beat Spain, England needed a good win against the hosts (2–1 would have meant drawing lots). They were far superior to Spain, but just could

Brazil and France played the best football, England and Cameroon were undefeated, but Italy, thanks to the revival of Rossi, won their third World Cup.

not score. Ron Greenwood brought Keegan and Brooking — neither fully recovered from injury — off the bench after 63 minutes for their first taste of World Cup football in a desperate attempt to add penetration. But sadly they missed the easiest chances of the game, which at their sharpest they would probably have put away. The game ended goalless, and England — unbeaten — were out.

Italy had no trouble beating Poland — without the suspended Boniek, their star player — in the first semi-final. A goal in each half from Rossi saw to that. The every opportunity. Even the scandalous foul by German keeper Schumacher on substitute Battiston — for which he went unpunished and the Frenchman was carried off — did not stop their flow. But it was not until the first period of extra time that the French attack earned their reward, with brilliant goals from defender Tresor and from Giresse. But then they allowed the Germans back into the game. The half-fit Rummenigge, used only in spells, had not long been on the field, but scored an opportunist goal, and then Fischer

Platini remonstrates with the referee after Battiston is felled.

second semi, between France and West Germany, produced one of the most memorable matches in World Cup history. There could have been few neutral observers not willing the French to win, as they put on a dazzling performance that rivalled the Brazilians in inventiveness and sheer footballing artistry. Platini and Giresse were magically creative in midfield, where anchorman Tigana was the perfect foil. On the wing, Rocheteau — the "French George Best" — was always dangerous.

The first half was packed with incident and good football, and Platini equalized an early Littbarski goal with a penalty. It continued in the same vein in the second half, with the French on top, often leaving four or five men upfield, with backs Bossis and Amoros breaking forward at equalized with a spectacular overhead kick. Unfortunately this wonderful game went to penalties, where football is always the loser, and Hrubesch eventually put West Germany in the final.

Bearzot's triumph

The final, for the most part, was not a good advertisement for football, following the pattern of so many of the earlier matches — fouls, spoiling tactics, gamesmanship and incompetent refereeing. For almost an hour, it was a war of attrition. Italy's Cabrini shot wide from a first-half penalty, the first such miss in a World Cup final, and then Rossi put them ahead from close-in after 57 minutes. Only then did they show the skill and flair manager Enzo Bearzot had almost despaired of bringing out.

FINAL SCORE

FIRST ROUND

Group 1

Italy	0	Poland	0
Peru	0	Cameroon	0
Italy	1	Peru	1
Poland	0	Cameroon	0
Poland	5	Peru	1
Italy	1	Cameroon	1

	P	W	D	L	F	A	P
Poland	3	1	2	0	5	1	4
Italy	3	0	3	0	2	2	3
Cameroon	3	0	3	0	1	1	3
Peru	3	0	2	1	2	6	2

Group 2

Algeria	2	West Germany	1
Austria	1	Chile	0
West Germany	4	Chile	1
Austria	2	Algeria	0
Algeria	3	Chile	2
West Germany	1	Austria	0

	P	W	D	L	F	A	P
W. Germany	3	2	0	1	6	3	4
Austria	3	2	0	1	3	1	4
Algeria	3	2	0	1	5	5	4
Chile	3	0	0	3	3	8	0

Group 3

Belgium	1	Argentina	0
Hungary	10	El Salvador	1
Argentina	4	Hungary	1
Belgium	1	El Salvador	0
Belgium	1	Hungary	1
Argentina	2	El Salvador	0

	P	W	D	L	F	A	P
Belgium	3	2	1	0	3	1	5
Argentina	3	2	0	1	6	2	4
Hungary	3	1	1	1	12	6	3
El Salvador	3	0	0	3	1	13	0

Group 4

England	3	France	1
Czechoslovakia	1	Kuwait	1
England	2	Czechoslovakia	0
France	4	Kuwait	1
France	1	Czechoslovakia	1
England	1	Kuwait	0

	P	W	D	L	F	A	P
England	3	3	0	0	6	1	6
France	3	1	1	1	6	5	3
Czech.	3	0	2	1	2	4	2
Kuwait	3	0	1	2	2	6	1

Group 5

Spain	1	Honduras	1
Yugoslavia	0	Northern Ireland	0
Spain	2	Yugoslavia	1
Northern Ireland	1	Honduras	1
Yugoslavia	1	Honduras	0
Northern Ireland	1	Spain	0

	P	W	D	L	F	A	P
N. Ireland	3	1	2	0	2	1	4
Spain	3	1	1	1	3	3	3
Yugoslavia	3	1	1	1	2	2	3
Honduras	3	0	2	1	2	3	2

Group 6

Brazil	2	USSR	1
Scotland	5	New Zealand	2
Brazil	4	Scotland	1
USSR	3	New Zealand	0
USSR	2	Scotland	2
Brazil	4	New Zealand	0

	P	W	D	L	F	A	P
Brazil	3	3	0	0	10	2	6
USSR	3	1	1	1	6	4	3
Scotland	3	1	1	1	8	8	3
N. Zealand	3	0	0	3	2	12	0

SECOND ROUND

Group A

Poland	3	Belgium	0
USSR	1	Belgium	0
Poland	0	USSR	0

	P	W	D	L	F	A	P
Poland	2	1	1	0	3	0	3
USSR	2	1	1	0	1	0	3
Belgium	2	0	0	2	0	4	0

Group B

West Germany	0	England	0
West Germany	2	Spain	1
England	0	Spain	0

	P	W	D	L	F	A	P
W. Germany	2	1	1	0	2	1	3
England	2	0	2	0	0	0	2
Spain	2	0	1	1	1	2	1

Group C

Italy	2	Argentina	1
Brazil	3	Argentina	1
Italy	3	Brazil	2

	P	W	D	L	F	A	P
Italy	2	2	0	0	5	3	4
Brazil	2	1	0	1	5	4	2
Argentina	2	0	0	2	2	5	0

Group D

France	1	Austria	0
Northern Ireland	2	Austria	2
France	4	Northern Ireland	1

	P	W	D	L	F	A	P
France	2	2	0	0	5	1	4
Austria	2	0	1	1	2	3	1
N. Ireland	2	0	1	1	3	6	1

SEMI-FINALS

Italy	2	Poland	0
West Germany	3	France	3

(after extra time)
West Germany won 5–4 on penalties

THIRD-PLACE MATCH

Poland	3	France	2

FINAL

Italy	3	West Germany	1

Santiago Bernabeu Stadium, Madrid, 11 July 1982. Attendance 90,000

Italy: Zoff, Gentile, Collovati, Scirea, Cabrini, Conti, Oriali, Bergomi, Tardelli, Rossi, Graziani (Altobelli, Causio)
(Scorers: Rossi, Tardelli, Altobelli)
West Germany: Schumacher, Kaltz, Forster K-H, Stielike, Forster B, Briegel, Breitner, Dremmler (Hrubesch), Littbarski, Fischer, Rummenigge (Muller)
(Scorer: Breitner)

Leading scorers
6 Rossi (Italy)
5 Rummenigge (W.Germany)
4 Boniek (Poland)
Zico (Brazil)

Crucified over many months in the Italian Press for the team's poor results, he had long been frustrated in his attempts to harness their talent into adventurous attacking football, alien as that was to their negative domestic game. Tardelli and then Altobelli scored to make the game safe before Breitner scored a late goal for the by-now well-beaten Germans.

Bobby Robson is new England supremo

BOBBY ROBSON was appointed England team manager on 7 July for a five-year term, and is the second Ipswich manager in 19 years to take charge of the national team. Like Sir Alf Ramsey before him, he has brought considerable success to the East Anglian club and will leave somewhat reluctantly a job that he has relished.

As an inside-forward, Mr Robson made his debut for Fulham in 1950, clocked up 584 League appearances in two spells with the London club and one with West Bromwich, and played 20 times for England, including the 1958 and 1962 World Cups, scoring four goals. Now, at 49, he takes over from the retiring Ron Greenwood an England squad who promised more in the World Cup in Spain than they ultimately achieved. And, as no candidate for entry into the squad will have played more than three League games before England meet Denmark in Copenhagen in their opening European Championship fixture, he will be unlikely to make any startling changes as he begins his first task of building a team initially for Europe and, in the longer term, for the 1986 World Cup.

Robson, hoping to emulate Sir Alf Ramsey.

Fifty scored in First Division goal feast

Watford's hero Luther Blissett (8) scores one of his four goals.

IT IS A LONG TIME since the First Division enjoyed such a feast of goals, 50 in the 11 matches played on Saturday 25 September. Eight teams scored four or more. Ipswich, finally recovering it seems from the loss of manager Bobby Robson to the England team, took themselves off the bottom of the table with their first win of the season: 6–0 away to Notts County. But pride of place must go to newly promoted Watford, who went third in the table with their 8–0 thrashing of Sunderland, which equalled the club's record defeat, suffered at West Ham in 1968.

This was a majestic performance by any yardstick. They were so completely in control that they could have had at least 12; apart from a number of outstanding saves by Chris Turner, they struck the woodwork four times. Luther Blissett, the man of the match, scored four, with two each for Ross Jenkins and Nigel Callaghan.

There was another eight-goal match: Stoke 4 Luton 4. But this game was notable chiefly for the controversial sending-off of Stoke keeper Peter Fox, which highlighted the confusion and inconsistency surrounding the new FA ruling on "professional fouls". With Stoke leading 2–1, a free-kick by Watson rebounded off referee Mr G.J.Napthene, and ran loose. Fox raced out of his area to chest down an awkwardly bouncing ball, but it eluded him. He turned and tried to smother it on the edge of the box, but Paul Walsh rounded him and drove the ball home. The referee disallowed the goal and awarded Luton a free-kick just outside the area. Then, after consulting a linesman, he sent Fox off. Subsequent TV inquests confirmed that Fox, who left the field in a distraught state, had been harshly treated, since it was not clear what his offence had been. He did not appear to handle outside the area or, indeed, impede Walsh.

The sob story of the day came from the Third Division, where Reading's Kerry Dixon became one of the few players in history to score four goals and still finish on the losing side. Doncaster won 7–5!

International Board make yet another boob

THE INTERNATIONAL Football Association board have blocked the Football League's attempts to introduce a number of experimental rules for the 1982-83 season, because they feared that it could "confuse the rest of the world". The changes, proposed initially by the Busby Committee, and including the introduction of penalty-kicks for certain fouls outside the penalty area, the banning of passing to the keeper from outside the box, and a variation of the offside law, were rejected at the laws meeting in Madrid.

The board expressed interest in one of the proposals, that is, relaxing the offside rule from goalkeepers' clearances, and have promised to discuss it again next summer. They have introduced one new rule, to tighten up on time-wasting by goalkeepers. In future, a keeper may take no more than four steps, from the moment the ball comes under his control, before releasing it. Unfortunately, however, they have not felt the need to define the term "under his control", so confusion is guaranteed to reign as soon as the season starts. This is typical of the utterances spewed forth annually by the International Board, whose inability to write plain English is matched only by their complete ignorance of the game of football.

FA create handball chaos

THE HANDBALL controversy raged on in late October as the FA repeatedly threw the game into confusion. First they instructed referees that, contrary to edict they had handed down at the start of the season, deliberate handball should not now be considered "serious foul play" meriting dismissal, but should be dealt with by a caution under "ungentlemanly conduct".

That brought immediate protest from the referees, so the League obtained confirmation from the FA that the officials still had discretion to "treat handling as a sending-off offence, in appropriate situations". Now the FA have announced that they have deleted specific references to handball from their interpretation of foul play, and it is up to the referee to decide what is, in his opinion, serious foul play.

In other words, it is up to the referees to decide how the laws should be interpreted — which is what they appeared to be doing until they were told not to a week earlier! Let us hope that the FA now keep quiet and allow referees to get on with their campaign to combat the cheating that has turned so many former fans against the game.

Clubs reject Chester Report

THE SECOND REPORT compiled by Sir Norman Chester for the Football League was published on 28 March. The main proposals were: a reduction of the First Division to 20 clubs, with an increase in Division Two to 24 and the amalgamation of Divisions Two and Three, plus some newcomers, into four regional sections with 16 clubs in each; clubs most frequently seen on TV to receive a larger share of the money; the League's constitution to be changed so that only a three-fifths majority would be needed to approve changes instead of the present three-quarters.

A month later, however, the clubs rejected their last chance to come to terms with reality, and decided to take the long and painful road of natural wastage to restructure the League. The other proposals are to be put forward at the annual League meeting in June.

One proposal that is likely to meet with approval, certainly among the big clubs, is that all gate receipts should be retained by the home club, instead of being shared out with the visitors, as now.

Paisley leads final procession in triumph

BOB PAISLEY'S 12th and last visit to Wembley in charge of Liverpool ended wholly appropriately with his becoming the first manager to lead his men in triumph up the steps to the Royal Box after their 2–1 victory over Manchester United in the Milk Cup final. Even dyed-in-the-wool traditionalists will not fault the team's decision to accord their boss an honour no other manager has enjoyed since English soccer set up its playing headquarters at this stadium 60 years ago.

This was Liverpool's third League/Milk Cup win in a row, but all of the sympathy and most of the admiration went to Manchester United at the end of an eventful but undistinguished game. United found themselves without both central defenders with the score at 1–1 and 14 minutes of normal time left. They were desperately unlucky to lose Kevin Moran with a twisted ankle after 69 minutes and then, 10 minutes later, to see Gordon McQueen reduced by cramp and hamstring problems to a hobbling passenger. Yet, having established a 12th-minute lead through Norman Whiteside's beautifully struck goal, they let Liverpool off the hook. Six minutes after Moran's injury, Liverpool equalized when Alan Kennedy hit a swerving 25-yarder that Bailey saw too late to save.

Even so, it was a controversial "professional foul" by keeper Bruce Grobbelaar in the last minute of normal time that kept Liverpool in the game, but should have seen their keeper out of it. He deliberately body-checked the injured McQueen, who had broken away on the right, but was merely cautioned by referee George Courtney — an outrageous decision to those in the crowd who drew a parallel between Grobbelaar's action and the assault of West Germany's Schumacher on Battiston of France during last year's World Cup. According to Mr Courtney, he did not feel that McQueen had a scoring opportunity!

The burden of extra time was always going to be too much for United's heroic, beleaguered garrison, and they were finally forced to submit to Ronnie Whelan's spectacular dipping shot after nine minutes. Sadly, Liverpool lost more friends with their blatant and persistent time-wasting, which reached a ludicrous climax when Dalglish booted the ball towards the tunnel.

Bob Paisley (in cap) talks to Ronnie Whelan (who will score the winner) before the start of extra time.

Dons graduate in Europe

ABERDEEN BEAT Real Madrid 2–1 in Gothenburg in the final of the Cup-Winners' Cup, thanks to an extra-time goal by substitute John Hewitt, to win their first European trophy. Fierce and driving rain throughout the afternoon meant a soaking for Aberdeen's vast army of supporters, but they were soon cheering the opening goal. McLeish met Strachan's corner with a powerful downward header and, when the ball was deflected by a Madrid defender, Black pounced to score from close range. It was no more than Black deserved, for he had struck the cross-bar three minutes earlier with a fierce volley from another of Strachan's crosses.

Aberdeen, in their first European final compared with Real's 11th, looked happier in the difficult conditions until a defensive lapse led to Real's equalizer after 14 minutes. McLeish sent his back-pass well short of Leighton, who brought down Santillana in the box, and Juanito scored from the spot. Miller, an industrious captain, and McLeish nipped further danger in the bud, and Aberdeen got on top in the second half, with strong runs from Strachan and Simpson and some promising raids on the left from Weir.

Black took a painful kick and was replaced by Hewitt in the 87th minute, and it was the substitute who scored the winner with a spectacular goal midway through the second period of extra time. Weir won the ball with a timely tackle in his own half and jinked his way forward before sending McGhee away on the left with a perfectly weighted chip. McGhee then beat his man on the outside and crossed to the near post, where Hewitt met the ball at the end of a 70-yard run to place a conclusive header into the net.

The Dons, astutely managed by Alex Ferguson, won eight and drew two of their 11 games in the competition, scoring 25 goals and conceding only six. In effect, they have qualified for next year's tournament twice, for they won the Scottish Cup as well earlier this season.

John Hewitt scorer of Aberdeen's extra time winner.

Little Terrors win League glory

DUNDEE UNITED, the "Terrors", are at it again. Having won their first major honour, the Scottish League Cup, only three years ago, and retained it the following season, they have now won the Scottish League. Manager Jim McLean has nursed the club through a record-breaking season with a nucleus of only 12 players. In a dramatic run-in, they won their last six matches to overtake champions Celtic and, in a heart-stopping finale, held off the challenge of both Celtic and Aberdeen, fresh from their European triumph, who both finished a point behind. Celtic demonstrated on the last day that they would not relinquish their title readily by beating arch rivals Rangers 4–2 at Ibrox despite being 2–0 down at half-time, and Aberdeen could do no more than beat Hibs 5–0 at Pittodrie.

But United, who many thought might have faltered in their final Tayside derby match with Dundee at Dens Park, did nothing of the kind. They won 2–1, to earn themselves premier billing in Scottish soccer for the first time in their 74-year history. They equalled Celtic's Premier League record of 56 points, and both clubs scored a record 90 goals.

Dundee United players chair manager Jim McLean in triumph after clinching the Championship.

Camera company to sponsor League as TV talks fail

FROM NEXT SEASON, England's premier football competition will be known as the Canon Football League. The Japanese-owned Canon UK, manufacturers of cameras and business equipment, and the Football League have announced a £3 million sponsorship deal spread over three years. Each year £496,000 will be distributed to the clubs, with another £214,000 in prize money for the leading teams in each division and additional monthly and seasonal awards for the clubs scoring most goals.

This is the biggest sponsorship deal in British sport, but is contingent on TV coverage and could be thrown into confusion if the League fail to reach an agreement with the television companies for screening matches next season. The League have just rejected a package of £5.4 million for two seasons, which included limited shirt advertising and four live matches each weekend. Both the BBC and ITV have now withdrawn all previous offers in disgust.

SOCCER SOUNDBITES

"The Football League are strangling themselves to death. They have shown this with the Chester Report and the television negotiations. They are in chaos."

Joint **BBC-ITV** statement.

Brighton's leading man fluffs the punch line

IN THE MOST absorbing FA Cup final for years, Brighton threw off the depression of their recent relegation and the disappointment of skipper Steve Foster's suspension, to frighten the life out of Manchester United with a dramatic late equalizer, only for Gordon Smith to miss the chance of a lifetime to score the winner in the last seconds of extra time. Curiously, Smith had been on the losing side in the Scottish League Cup final earlier in the season, when on loan to Rangers.

With four goals, unremitting effort, no little subtlety, and constant changes of fortune, all of it on a soggy pitch that sucked at the players' legs, this was a game to remember. In the end, Brighton, the underdogs, proved every bit a match for the more talented and experienced team that had finished third in Division One. They took the lead as early as the 14th minute with a far-post header from Smith, and stayed in front without undue difficulty until half-time. The turning point came soon after the interval with the only blot on the match, a reckless, vicious tackle by young Norman Whiteside on Brighton's Chris Ramsey that crippled the right-back.

He played on briefly on one leg, but was unable to make an effective challenge when Duxbury's cross was headed on by Whiteside for Stapleton to plant in the net a minute later. Ramsey was replaced by substitute Gerry Ryan, but the end for Brighton seemed nigh in the 72nd minute when Muhren at last produced a long, defence-wrecking pass, and Wilkins sent a classic left-foot shot curling beyond Moseley's reach.

Then Gary Stevens, a Herculean figure who rose above even Bryan Robson in terms of achievement on the day, copied the attacking forays of the absent Foster to such good effect that he equalized with only three minutes of normal time remaining. He controlled a pass flicked on by Grealish from Case's corner, and directed it powerfully past Bailey from 10 yards.

The miss of the match came, understandably, in the last moments of extra time, an inhuman demand on this bog of a pitch. Mike Robinson rolled the ball carefully into the path of Smith in the box, when the two strikers were through and opposed by only one defender. But the tiring Scot delayed his shot and then struck it weakly at the grateful Bailey, who smothered it as he came out. It is a miss that will haunt Smith for ever if Brighton lose the replay.

Stevens (second right) hits Brighton's late equalizer.

SOCCER SOUNDBITES

"I wasn't expecting a pass from Robbo. Robbo never passes."

GORDON SMITH,
Brighton striker, on his crucial miss.

FOOTBALL FOCUS

- A Football League plan to allow two substitutes next season, as in international matches and Scottish and European club competitions, was rejected by the clubs, who felt they could not afford a "13th man".
- In their final League match of the season, Manchester City, second in the Division One table in November, were relegated when Luton substitute Raddy Antic scored in the 86th minute at Maine Road — a match Luton had to win to stay up themselves.
- Liverpool killed off their challengers for the title, their 14th Championship win, so early that, even though they took only two points from their last seven games, they still won by 11 points from nearest challengers Watford.
- Aberdeen became the first club apart from Celtic and Rangers to retain the Scottish FA Cup this century, with a goal from young striker Eric Black four minutes from the end of extra time. So Rangers had lost in both domestic Cup finals.

Black heads Aberdeen's Cup-winner against Rangers.

FINAL SCORE

Football League
Division 1: Liverpool
Top scorer: Luther Blissett (Watford) 27
Division 2: Queen's Park Rangers
Division 3: Portsmouth
Division 4: Wimbledon
Footballer of the Year: Kenny Dalglish (Liverpool)

FA Cup Final
Manchester United 2 Brighton & Hove A 2
(after extra time)
Replay: Man United 4 Brighton & Hove A 0

League Cup Final
Liverpool 2 Manchester United 1
(after extra time)

Scottish League
Premier Division: Dundee United
Top scorer: Charlie Nicholas (Celtic) 29
Division 1: St Johnstone
Division 2: Brechin City
Footballer of the Year: Charlie Nicholas (Celtic)

Scottish FA Cup Final
Aberdeen 1 Rangers 0
(after extra time)

Scottish League Cup Final
Celtic 2 Rangers 1

International Championship
England, 5 pts

European Cup Final
SV Hamburg 1 Juventus 0

Cup-Winners' Cup Final
Aberdeen 2 Real Madrid 1
(after extra time)

UEFA Cup Final
Anderlecht beat Benfica 1–0, 1–1

European Footballer of the Year 1982
Paolo Rossi (Juventus & Italy)

Leading European Scorer (Golden Boot)
Francisco Gomes (Porto) 36

World Club Championship
Gremio (Brazil) 2 SV Hamburg (W. Germany) 1
(after extra time)

England pay penalty as Denmark squeeze home at Wembley

ENGLAND'S PROSPECTS of reaching next year's European Championship finals took a nosedive at Wembley on 21 September, when Allan Simonsen earned Denmark their first victory in nine matches between the countries with a 38th-minute penalty. England gave their customary slovenly early-autumn performance, and were lucky not to be more than one goal down at half-time, the penalty having occurred when Neal handled the ball. In the second half, the Danes clung to their lead, and an England team sorely missing the injured Bryan Robson just could not break down a well-organized defence, so ably marshalled by Morten Olsen. Failure to beat Greece last March has now assumed disastrous proportions.

The decider: Simonsen scores from the penalty spot.

Historic Irish victory in Hamburg

NORTHERN IRELAND'S prestige in world football was raised to new heights on 16 November by their shock, but deserved, 1–0 victory over West Germany in a European Championship qualifier in Hamburg. It was one of their finest performances, and West Germany's first home defeat in nine years. Pat Jennings, aged 38, made three remarkable saves from Waas, Rummenigge and Matthaus, giving arguably his finest display in 102 appearances. Manager Billy Bingham achieved a tactical triumph, as the Irish back four stamped their authority on the game. Norman Whiteside scored their goal in the 50th minute, and they were unlucky not to score two more in quick breakaways near the finish.

Despite now having completed the double over West Germany, the Irish chances of qualifying for the finals are slim, as the Germans have only to win their final match with Albania to overtake them on goal difference.

Ireland have taken 11 points from their eight games, but the 1–0 defeat by Turkey in Ankara on October 16 has proved a vital blow. England's hopes have disappeared completely, even though they won 4–0 in Luxembourg, because Denmark won 2–0 in Greece.

Déjà vu for Arsenal, as Walsall humble them again

HUNDREDS OF ARSENAL supporters demanded manager Terry Neill's resignation after Arsenal's Milk Cup humiliation at the hands of Third Division Walsall at Highbury on 29 November. The fans laid siege to the ground's main entrance for almost 45 minutes after Walsall had swept aside a disgraceful Arsenal effort with some exhilarating attacking football.

Fifty years after the famous FA Cup giant-killing act at Fellows Park, when Walsall last toppled the Gunners, Ally Brown, 32, the former West Brom and Crystal Palace striker, helped them repeat the feat with a goal five minutes from time. Arsenal had gone ahead against the run of play in the 31st minute, when Nicholas put Robson through. But Walsall, riding high in Division Three with only one defeat in their last 15 matches, equalized in the 61st minute when Brown raced clear of the offside trap, hammered the ball against keeper Jennings, and pushed the rebound through for Ross to score. And Chris Whyte, who had a nightmare evening, then missed his kick completely to let Brown through for the winner.

Walsall manager Alan Buckley felt some of his side's football would have done justice to the First Division. Arsenal's, however, did not, and Neill can thank the seemingly ageless Jennings, who made some brilliant stops, for saving him from even greater embarrassment.

Holders make an early Cup exit at Bournemouth

MANCHESTER UNITED'S dismissal from both domestic Cup competitions by Third Division opponents in the space of 19 days indicates a serious flaw in the make-up of the men claiming to be the second best in the land, and this 2–0 defeat at Bournemouth must rank as one of the biggest surprises in the FA Cup's long history.

Failure at Oxford in a Milk Cup fourth-round second replay could be excused in a competition twice won at Wembley by Third Division challengers. But the collapse at Dean Court, in their first defence of the FA Cup they won last May, leaves a big question mark against United. The truth is that both Oxford and Bournemouth earned their victories by out-thinking and ultimately outplaying them, as well as outrunning and outgaming them.

Bournemouth went ahead on the hour, when Bailey misfielded a corner and Trevor Morgan nodded the ball back for Milton Graham to score. Then Robson failed to clear La Ronde's long free-kick, and Ian Thompson got number two. Admittedly, United were without McQueen and Moran, their central defence, and the loss of Albiston at half-time forced them to make further positional changes; but a team of their stature — 10 of the men on duty at Bournemouth are full internationals — should be able to take such setbacks in their stride.

Souness shot decides

LIVERPOOL WON THE Milk Cup for keeps when a solitary goal from Graeme Souness floored luckless Everton in a thrilling replay at Maine Road and earned them a record fourth consecutive triumph in the competition. It cannot be long, however, before Everton lose their label as second-class soccer citizens on Merseyside, for they were desperately unlucky not to win at Wembley, where they enjoyed the better of the play in the goalless draw, although they never quite managed to exploit the possession won by their skill and endeavour in the replay.

In both games, Everton had the outstanding midfielder in Peter Reid, despite the opposition of such accomplished footballers as Souness, Lee, Whelan and Johnston. Ably assisted by Richardson, he was in command for long periods, and gave Everton every chance to clinch the trophy. Yet they rarely created any clear-cut opportunities.

In contrast, Liverpool always looked dangerous when they broke out of defence. And it was a typical counter-attack, pressed home with speed and power, that brought them the crucial goal in the 21st minute of the return. Souness began the four-man move with a pass to Neal, and completed it himself by collecting a cross from the same player and shooting past Southall into the corner of the net.

As Everton tired towards the end, Liverpool took control, and would have won by more if Rush had not left his shooting boots in the dressing-room for once. But it would have been unjust had they won by more than a single goal.

Liverpool hat-trick down to continuity

LIVERPOOL BECAME only the third club in the history of the League, after Huddersfield in the twenties and Arsenal in the thirties, to achieve a hat-trick of Championships when they drew 0–0 at Notts County on 12 May. Their latest triumph emphasizes that careful planning and continuity of management are essential requirements for consistent success in modern League soccer. While other clubs have changed managers with distasteful and expensive frequency, Liverpool have quietly kept matters in the family, promoting Bob Paisley when Bill Shankly retired and, 12 months ago, appointing Joe Fagan to maintain that line of succession. And Mr Fagan has quietly gone about his job, too, with two major honours under his belt already and the European Cup final coming up at the end of the month.

Typical of the way the club works is the purchase of men such as John Wark, shrewdly signed from Ipswich a couple of months ago when the Anfield midfield unit was beginning to show occasional signs of faltering. Wark, who has missed only a handful of games through injury over the last 10 years and rarely turns in a bad performance, provided the extra touch needed during the tiring closing weeks. Players like him — and Lee, Hansen, Neal and Kennedy — provide essential support for the more gifted football of Souness, Lawrenson, Dalglish, Rush and Whelan. For anyone who has lost count, this was Liverpool's 15th Championship.

Sweet compensation for the spilt Milk

EVERTON RETURNED to Wembley to beat Watford 2–0 in the final of the FA Cup, their first trophy since 1970, and rich consolation for having lost to their Merseyside rivals Liverpool in the final of the Milk Cup two months earlier.

As always seemed likely, the redoubtable Everton defence proved strong enough — if only just at times — to hold Watford's rampant attack in check. At the other end, however, Watford were undone by the inexperience of their youthful back four and the fallibility of Steve Sherwood, although Everton's second goal, scored in the 41st minute when Andy Gray patently headed the ball out of his hands, would surely have been disallowed by nine out of ten referees. This virtually killed Watford off, for they had gone one down only four minutes earlier, when a bad clearance and poor marking allowed Sharp to shoot in unchallenged from 10 yards.

But Watford were not outplayed, and they gave the lie to their reputation for kick-and-rush, up-and-under football. Most of the progress they made in the first half was by subtle diagonal passing, intelligent use of set-pieces, and sheer individual brilliance. But for the brilliance of Southall in goal, Watford would have made much more of a game of it.

Andy Gray makes contact with Sherwood's hands for the controversial second goal.

Parks the Spurs hero in Euro shoot-out

TOTTENHAM spectacularly survived the emotional torture of a penalty shoot-out in the second leg of the UEFA Cup final against Anderlecht, when Keith Burkinshaw's fairy-tale farewell to White Hart Lane surpassed even the most extravagant expectations. And the two most important saves of Tony Parks's fledgling career ensured that the UEFA Cup will nestle in Spurs' trophy cabinet as a sparkling reminder of the nerve-shredding climax to Mr Burkinshaw's reign as manager.

After the 1–1 draw in Belgium, Cup-holders Anderlecht came to White Hart Lane determined not to give up the trophy without a fight. And they seemed capable of protecting their 60th-minute goal by Alex Czerniatinski before acting skipper Graham Roberts stormed through for a dramatic equalizer in the 83rd minute, after substitute Ardiles had hit the bar, to take the game into extra time and then to the penalty decider.

Parks, the understudy whose hopes at the start of the season went little further than the occasional first-team game, saved the first penalty from Olsen. But then, at 4–3, Danny Thomas missed Spurs' fifth spot-kick to give Anderlecht another chance. Parks, however, kept his nerve and beat out the penalty from Icelandic striker Gudjohnsen — before being swallowed up in the jubilant congratulations of his delirious team-mates.

Tony Parks smothers Anderlecht's fifth penalty to give Spurs the UEFA Cup.

Rome falls to all-conquering Reds

Alan Kennedy sends Roma's keeper the wrong way.

LIVERPOOL RETURNED home from Rome triumphantly as European Cup-winners for the fourth time, after becoming the second English club on consecutive Wednesdays to win a European final on penalties. And it was Alan Kennedy who, for the second time in successive finals, won the Cup for his team.

Liverpool, with the extreme disadvantage of playing in their opponents' back yard, took control of the game with a 14th-minute goal resulting from a double defensive error. The scorer, Phil Neal, was the only survivor of their first European Cup success on the same pitch seven years ago. But the Reds became uncharacteristically sloppy, and Pruzzo headed an equalizer just before half-time. With no further score at the end of 120 minutes, Nicol, who had come on for the tiring Johnston, hit the first kick way over the bar. Roma scored from their first penalty; Neal levelled the score; and then Conti, one of Italy's World Cup heroes, blasted his shot even higher than Nicol's. Roma's next miss, by Graziani, was at 3–2 down, leaving Kennedy to make history and settle the first penalty shoot-out in the 28-year history of the Champions' Cup.

Ireland win the last Home Championship

A GOAL OF STUNNING quality by England's Tony Woodcock against Scotland brought down the curtain on the final British International Championship at Hampden Park in May. But the 1–1 draw it produced provided Northern Ireland with only their third win in the Championship, which has been staged continuously, apart from the war years, since the 1883–84 season.

All four countries finished on three points for only the second time in history. In 1955–56, the title was shared; but this time goal difference counted, in Northern Ireland's favour, their 2–0 win over Scotland in Belfast last December being decisive. Wales finished second, completing an ironic twist to the story of how the oldest soccer competition in the world met its end. For it was England and Scotland who had decided to withdraw, because they felt the ailing Championship had outlived its usefulness and were deaf to all protests by the other FAs, who feared economic ruin as a result of losing their annual fixtures with the two major British nations.

Woodcock (9) celebrates his stunning goal – England's last in the Home Nations tournament.

FOOTBALL FOCUS

- A £10 million take-over bid for Manchester United by a consortium headed by millionaire publisher Robert Maxwell, chairman of Oxford United, fell through in mid-February after two weeks' negotiations.
- Aberdeen became only the second club this century, after Rangers, to win the Scottish FA Cup three times in a row, remarkably each one after extra time.
- England won the fourth European Under-21 Championship, beating Spain in the two-legged final in May, 1–0 in Seville and 2–0 at Bramall Lane.
- To qualify for the European Championship, Spain needed to beat Malta by 11 clear goals and, despite missing a penalty, they won 12–1 and so pipped Holland on goals scored — 24 to eight compared with 22 to six by the Dutch.
- Third Division sides reached the semi-finals of both the Milk Cup and FA Cup. Walsall held Liverpool to a 2–2 draw at Anfield in the Milk Cup before losing the second leg at home 2–0. Plymouth lost 1–0 to Watford in the FA Cup.
- Kenny Dalglish became only the third player to register a century of League goals in both Scotland and England, with Celtic and Liverpool.

Barnes goes native in Brazil

Barnes (11) wheels away after scoring his sensational goal in the Maracana Stadium.

AFTER A FAIRLY wretched second season under the management of Bobby Robson, England — who failed to qualify for the European Championship, lost miserably to Wales in the last Home International Championship and were beaten 2–0 at Wembley by the USSR — gained a measure of consolation by beating Brazil in Brazil for the first time ever. Although they subsequently lost to Uruguay and only drew with Chile in their South American tour, the game in Rio will be remembered for their second goal, scored by winger John Barnes. Taking the ball on a mazy run on the left in which he beat man after man, he cut in and waltzed right through Brazil's central defence before planting the ball in the net. The crowd of 56,000 rose as one to acknowledge a goal of such brilliance that even their own favourite Pele would have been proud of it.

French lesson good for the game

FRANCE SCORED A major triumph for the future of soccer at the Parc des Princes in Paris, overcoming fierce Spanish resistance to win the European Championship for the first time. Under the enlightened management of Michel Hidalgo, the French have remained in the forefront of the move away from the sterile, defensive school of soccer — despite cruel setbacks — and the manner of their victory should be a lesson to the rest of Europe.

Second-half goals from Platini — a free-kick that squirmed out of the otherwise reliable Arconada's arms — and a solo effort from Bellone in the last minute saw France through in a disappointing final. But they had done enough in the rest of the competition to demonstrate the skill and imagination that has made them Europe's leading team over the past two years. Michel Platini scored in every match, a record nine goals in all, including the only goal of the crucial game with the talented Danes and hat-tricks against Yugoslavia and Belgium.

The finals produced some of the most fluent and exciting football seen anywhere for years and, as well as France, Denmark and Portugal were outstanding. The French success will surely advance the cause of those trying to turn soccer back into a game which players and spectators can enjoy. World champions Italy failed miserably to qualify, winning only the last of their eight group matches (at home to Cyprus!), and West Germany's team manager Jupp Derwall resigned after his side's poor showing in the finals, with Franz Beckenbauer expected to take over the squad.

FINAL SCORE

Football League
Division 1: Liverpool
Top scorer: Ian Rush (Liverpool) 32
Division 2: Chelsea
Division 3: Oxford United
Division 4: York City
Footballer of the Year: Ian Rush (Liverpool)

FA Cup Final
Everton 2 Watford 0

League Cup Final
Liverpool 0 Everton 0
(after extra time)
Replay: Liverpool 1 Everton 0

Scottish League
Premier Division: Aberdeen
Top scorer: Brian McClair (Celtic) 23
Division 1: Morton
Division 2: Forfar Athletic
Footballer of the Year: Willie Miller (Aberdeen)

Scottish FA Cup Final
Aberdeen 2 Celtic 1
(after extra time)

Scottish League Cup Final
Rangers 3 Celtic 2
(after extra time)

International Championship
Northern Ireland, 3 pts

European Cup Final
Liverpool 1 AS Roma 1
(after extra time)
Liverpool won 4–2 on penalties

Cup-Winners' Cup Final
Juventus 2 Porto 1

UEFA Cup Final
Tottenham Hotspur beat Anderlecht 1–1, 1–1
4–3 on penalties

European Footballer of the Year 1983
Michel Platini (Juventus & France)

Leading European Scorer (Golden Boot)
Ian Rush (Liverpool) 32

World Club Championship
Independiente (Argentina) 1 Liverpool (England) 0

FINAL SCORE

EUROPEAN CHAMPIONSHIP 1984

Group 1

France	1	Denmark	0
Belgium	2	Yugoslavia	0
France	5	Belgium	0
Denmark	5	Yugoslavia	0
France	3	Yugoslavia	2
Denmark	3	Belgium	2

	P	W	D	L	F	A	P
France	3	3	0	0	9	2	6
Denmark	3	2	0	1	8	3	4
Belgium	3	1	0	2	4	8	2
Yugoslavia	3	0	0	3	2	10	0

Group 2

West Germany	0	Portugal	0
Spain	1	Romania	1
Spain	1	Portugal	1
West Germany	2	Romania	1
Spain	1	West Germany	0
Portugal	1	Romania	0

	P	W	D	L	F	A	P
Spain	3	1	2	0	3	2	4
Portugal	3	1	2	0	2	1	4
W. Germany	3	1	1	1	2	2	3
Romania	3	0	1	2	2	4	1

SEMI-FINALS

France	3	Portugal	2
Denmark	1	Spain	1

Spain won 5–4 on penalties

FINAL
France 2 Spain 0

Paris, 27 June 1984. Attendance 80,000.

France: Bats, Battiston (Amoros), Le Roux, Bossis, Domergue, Giresse, Platini, Tigana, Fernandez, Lacombe (Genghini), Bellone
(Scorers: Platini, Bellone)
Spain: Arconada, Urquiaga, Salva (Roberto), Gallego, Camacho, Francisco, Julio Alberto (Sarabia), Senor, Victor, Carrasco, Santillana

Heroes of the Eighties

By Paul Hayward

Many of football's most enlightened thinkers look back on the Eighties as the game's dark age. Off the pitch, the sport in these isles became synonymous with mayhem and death. The Bradford City, Heysel and Hillsborough disasters scarred a generation and heaped shame on our national game. In the Nineties, many coaches and tacticians traced the lack of success abroad at both club and national level to the dreaded doctrine of the long ball.

Peter Shilton was England's first choice for more than a decade, collecting 125 caps.

English football went aerial. Hoofed clearances and knock-downs became the common currency of the English game. Or did they? The paradox of the anti-Eighties backlash is that English clubs were hugely successful abroad. Brian Clough's Nottingham Forest won the second of their European Cups in 1980. Liverpool won two more in 1981 and 1984 and were beaten, not surprisingly, amid the hell of Heysel 12 months later. English clubs are still labouring to re-climb those peaks. In the Eighties it was assumed that the Liverpools and Nottingham Forests would go on winning European Cups forever. Fifteen years after Liverpool beat AS Roma on penalties, Manchester United ended England's embarrassing barren spell. For most of the Nineties, however, the financial enrichment of the Premiership seemed to be taking it no nearer to a conquest of the Champions League.

Gallery of stars

Another rich inheritance of the Eighties was the quality and range of individual star players. It could not be said of the decade which followed that British football managed to produce performers of the calibre of Peter Shilton, Graeme Souness, Bryan Robson, Ian Rush, Kenny Dalglish, Gary Lineker and, at the end of the period, Paul Gascoigne, whose combustible career rose and levelled out with the 1990 World Cup. These gifted players emerged across all nationalities and all positions. Few of us would back a team of the Nineties to defeat a side containing the luminaries listed above. Neville Southall, Ray Clemence and John Barnes – twice Footballer of the Year – could also make a strong case for inclusion.

Rush, Souness and Lineker were tempted abroad to huge European clubs. There was no comparable stampede to sign the best British players in the final 10 years before the Millennium (Paul Ince, Gascoigne and Steve McManaman were exceptions which prove the rule). The traffic travelled mostly the other way. In the Eighties our clubs relied almost exclusively on home-grown talent and raw native spirit. The long-ball theory did take hold. People theorized about how few passes could be involved in a move that covered the whole pitch and ended with an inelegant goal. At times it was medieval and instilled the worst possible habits in the young. But in Charles Hughes-ville there was considerable individual skill as well as the legacy of some of Britain's finest teams who rolled off the gilded conveyor belt of Anfield.

Super Souness

They had Dalglish and Rush and Alan Hansen and Mark Lawrenson. They had the fearsome Souness, too. This growling, industrious midfielder was arguably the most precious type of footballer. Like Emmanuel Petit and Patrick Vieira from a

Bryan Robson: Captain Marvel.

Gary Lineker: scored goals wherever he went.

later time, Souness could both attack and defend. His passing was excellent and his tackling immense. All players talk of the importance of having an enforcer who can also play. Liverpool never quite filled the gap left by Souness's departure. Other clubs have scoured the world since for a player from that mould.

In that British all-star team Souness would have enjoyed the security afforded by Shilton, Ray Clemence or Southall — goal-keeping fanatics, who maintained a tradition of excellence extended, in the Nineties, by David Seaman, but perhaps fewer world-class custodians than usual. The post-Sky gold rush pulled in an endless succession of talented foreigners — Peter Schmeichel, most obviously — with a commensurate drop in the number of top British 'keepers. Was it chicken or egg? Whatever, British goalies still ruled the world in the pre-Sky age. Shilton won an astonishing 125 caps, the last of them at Italia 90, and conceded only 80 goals. He was a manic trainer and perfectionist. Southall, who excelled in the lower-profile Welsh jersey, was Footballer of the Year in 1985 and finished the decade with two League titles, two FA Cups and a European Cup-Winners' Cup.

Robson reigns

Bryan Robson was the Manchester Souness. Despite enduring ceaseless injuries, he won 90 England caps and was the dominant midfielder of his age. How many caps would it have been had Robson's shoulder and knees and ankles stayed sound? Here again was a ferocious competitor who could play any number of ways: fancy triangles were fine, but so was a good machismo contest, a struggle of wills. Robson's record £1.5 million transfer from West Bromwich Albion to United in 1981 was the making of an exemplary career that conformed to the work-hard-play-hard ethic of the time. The age of the great cavorters was drawing to a close. Alex Ferguson, whose monarchical reign began in these times, ushered in a new, high-dedication era in which young bucks and not old-pros carried the Old Trafford flag.

Up ahead, Rush, Dalglish and Lineker would have provided one of the most lethal goalscoring triumvirates the English game has known. A Scotsman, a Welshman and an Englishman, all different but blessed with the same ruthless instincts when in sight of goal. Dalglish was a wondrously gifted player, probably the last truly world-class Scot of the century. He had touch and balance and agility. He could pirouette on a grain of sand and had that ineffable quality of being able to master the ball with his feet while his eyes were scanning every sector of the field. Players call it vision, for want of a better word. It is hell to defend against and not commonly seen on the local marsh. Dalglish won 26 major trophies and a record 102 caps for his country. His 30 international goals gave him a share of the Scottish record with Denis Law.

Gary's goals

Lineker, the mantra went, was a great goalscorer rather than a scorer of great goals. He knew where to be and when. He was a quiet but ever-present threat. He was not the sort of striker who would aim to hit scorchers from outside the penalty-area nor set off on destructive Ronaldoesque runs. But his record as a breaker of teams was exemplary. For England he finished one short of Bobby Charlton's record of 49 goals. He scored a hat-trick for Barcelona against Real Madrid — a guarantee of immortality in Catalonia. He struck 322 times in 631 senior appearances with Leicester, Everton, Barcelona and Spurs and won the Golden Boot at the 1986 World Cup with six goals. Lineker is a television celebrity and advertising icon now, so it is easy to forget what an exceptionally effective centre-forward he was.

Rush's in

Rush was Lineker's only serious rival for the title of pre-eminent striker of the Eighties. Ian James Rush's career took off when he moved from Chester City to Liverpool in 1980. He was a member of those superb Anfield sides who dominated the decade (in concert with Everton) before United and Arsenal laid siege to the silverware of the Nineties. Without Rush's finishing Liverpool's meticulous passing would have come to nought. He scored five goals in three winning FA Cup final appearances and was fluent in the Anfield dialect of pass-and-move. His year in Turin with Juventus was a flop but it never diminished his reputation in the English game. In 1984 he won the European Golden Boot with 32 goals. The memory has to guard against allowing the image of his steady decline at Leeds and Newcastle to distort his sterling achievements throughout the Eighties.

It would be criminally negligent, too, to forget the great managers of this time: Clough at Forest, Bobby Robson at Ipswich, Bob Paisley, Joe Fagan and Dalglish himself at Liverpool; Howard Kendall at Everton and George Graham at Highbury. Managers get the blame when things go wrong. We ought to give them some credit when they go so right.

Ian Rush: Liverpool's ace.

Turkey roasted by Robson's raiders

ENGLAND BEAT TURKEY 8–0 in Istanbul on 14 November, their biggest away victory in the World Cup since they won 9–0 in Luxembourg 24 years ago. They go top of Group 3 and establish themselves as firm favourites to qualify next autumn.

Turkey might not be a leading European soccer power, but they have never been so humiliated in front of their own fervent supporters. Bobby Robson's plan to start out tight and score in the first 20 minutes — to quell both the crowd and their opponents — worked to perfection. Indeed, England were two up in 17 minutes, as Bryan Robson scored the first of his three and Woodcock the first of his pair. Robson scored his second after Williams hit a post and England went in 3–0 up at half-time.

Bobby Robson, right-half in that rout of Luxembourg, geed his men up during the interval, and they put another five past the hapless Turks, Barnes contributing two and Anderson, Robson and Woodcock one each. Even allowing for the dreadful state of Turkey's game, England's football was a delight to watch and a much-needed confidence-booster after the trials of last season.

Odd spot: England used a "W" formation — Withe, Williams, Woodcock, Wright and Wilkins were all in the team.

Bryan Robson (right) heads his first in the rout of Turkey.

Hooligans compound Celtic's misery

CELTIC WENT DOWN 1–0 to Rapid Vienna at Old Trafford on 12 December, going out of the Cup-Winners' Cup and completing a miserable second round tie. They had already paid dearly for two bottles thrown on their Parkhead pitch last month, when they had their stirring 3–0 win — and overall 4–3 victory — annulled by UEFA and were ordered to replay the match at another, distant venue. Unfortunately, this did not stop the hooligan element from travelling, and just two among the 51,500 who followed them to Manchester have now put the club's long-term European future in jeopardy.

Midway through the second half, one of those two idiots raced onto the pitch and attacked Rapid's goalkeeper, Feurer. The other kicked Pacult, the Austrian goalscorer, as he was leaving the pitch at the final whistle.

On the pitch, Celtic never looked like repeating their Parkhead performance, and it was soon evident they were going out. UEFA have already fined them £4,000, and they may well decide now to suspend them from European competition for some time to come.

A crazed Celtic fan attacks Rapid keeper Herbert Feurer.

Bates loses faith after battle of Stamford Bridge

THE SECOND LEG of Chelsea's Milk Cup semi-final with Sunderland was a travesty of a match, with violence on the field, pitch invasions and even attacks on players. The result, a 3–2 win for Sunderland to give them a 5–2 aggregate score, seemed irrelevant on such a night of mayhem. When hooligans invaded the pitch after Sunderland's second goal, Chelsea chairman Ken Bates, his faith in the Chelsea fans shattered, offered to concede the tie.

Clive Walker, the winger who left Stamford Bridge to rebuild his career in the North-East, triggered the sadly predictable scenes when he returned to score the goals that put paid to Chelsea's chances. David Speedie, who was eventually sent off five minutes from time when he succumbed to the manic atmosphere in which seven players were booked, had brought the sense of excitement to fever pitch when he scored after only six minutes, reducing Chelsea's deficit to a single goal. But Walker scored for Sunderland before the interval, and killed the tie as a contest with his second after 71 minutes.

That proved the signal for a disgraceful demonstration by Chelsea's violent fringe. Referee Alan Gunn was forced to usher the teams into the centre circle while mounted police charged the invaders. The officers subsequently became targets for seats, staves, bottles and other missiles. And Walker's former team-mates had to come to his rescue when one hooligan tried to attack him.

The trouble started among supporters who were in the £6 seats, and Mr Bates has said that he will close that section of the East Stand for the rest of the season. But Chelsea must now brace themselves for a full-scale official enquiry.

SOCCER SOUNDBITES

"We need more action from the government to help curb these hooligans."

KEN BATES,
Chelsea chairman

Luton pitch a battleground as fans run amok

BRIAN STEIN'S 31st-minute goal decided a chaotic FA Cup quarter-final at Kenilworth Road on 13 March, which, during the last 10 minutes, was as close to being abandoned in disgrace as a match could be. There had already been a 25-minute hold-up soon after the start, caused by overcrowded Millwall supporters spilling onto the pitch. Then, during the last 10 minutes, several hundred so-called fans of the South London club, who had been marauding along the touchline, twice broke through police cordons and careered about on the pitch. Only the battling courage of the couple of dozen police who could be spared to move to that part of the ground prevented the situation getting completely out of hand. And only the determination to finish the match of referee David Hutchinson — a police inspector — enabled matters to be kept under control.

But after the referee and players bolted for the dressing-rooms at the final whistle, the pitch became a battleground. With the police no longer standing in their way, the trouble-makers went for the seated enclosure and ripped out dozens of seats. Incredible scenes ensued, with hooligans attacking police with ripped-out seats, and the police regrouping to win the battle with a series of baton charges and the use of dogs. Police and Millwall supporters from other parts of the ground joined in. There was complete chaos as police, stewards and innocent bystanders were led away for treatment. The rioting Millwall fans, who had caused damage in the town before the game, continued to do so when they finally left the ground.

FA chairman Mr Bert Millichip considered the events "probably the worst in the long catalogue that has blighted our game over the last 20 years". He was resigned to the fact that the Luton riots had now ruined the FA campaign to stage the 1988 European Championship finals in England.

Third time lucky for Canaries

SINCE WINNING the League's knock-out competition 23 years ago, when the two-legged final attracted as much attention as a local hospital tournament, Norwich have twice lost at Wembley. But they beat Sunderland 1–0 in the Milk Cup final on 24 March, and deserved their narrow win.

The match was decided in three crucial minutes at the start of the second half, when Norwich scored and Sunderland missed a penalty. Veteran ex-England striker Mick Channon mishit a shot which eventually fell to Asa Hartford, another old soldier, and his first-time effort was deflected past Turner in the Sunderland goal by the luckless Chisholm. Three minutes later, a determined Sunderland attack forced a handling offence from Van Wyk, but Walker's spot kick clipped the wrong side of a post. They never got a better chance.

Hartford (yellow, facing) about to strike the ball for the only goal.

Dons clinch Premier title

A 1–1 DRAW with Celtic at Pittodrie was enough for Aberdeen to retain their Premier League title in Scotland with two matches remaining. Despite the loss of Strachan, Rougvie and McGhee in transfer deals worth £1.13 million, the Dons have led from start to finish after dropping only one point in their first eight fixtures. They spent only £140,000, on Frank McDougall from St Mirren and Tommy McQueen from Clyde, and McDougall in particular, their top League scorer with 22 goals, has proved an excellent investment. This is now the third League title in six seasons for Alex Ferguson's men, who show no signs of relinquishing their new-found predominance north of the border.

Aberdeen skipper Willie Miller celebrates a rare goal, but one that clinched the Scottish League title.

Oxford graduate to First Division

OXFORD UNITED confirmed their promotion to Division One on 24 April with a nervous 1–0 victory over Shrewsbury at the Manor Ground. But while thousands of fans celebrated the historic achievement, their colourful chairman, Robert Maxwell, hurled another verbal volley at the local council on the subject of Oxford's cramped ground. He accused the Oxford City Council of cheating and lying for 30 years, and demanded financial help to bring the ground up to First Division standard or to find a new ground.

Formerly Headington United, Oxford were elected to the League only 23 years ago, and have now gone from Third to First Division in two seasons.

Wales take big step to Mexico

WITH THEIR comprehensive 3–0 victory over Spain at Wrexham on 30 April, Wales threw Group 7 of the European World Cup qualifying competition wide open, and took a big step nearer to the finals in Mexico next year. With just their home fixture with Scotland to come in September, they now lead by two points from the Scots and Spain, who both have two games left.

The match was a hard-fought, bruising clash with no quarter given. Although Wales dominated the first half territorially, they were well contained by the experienced Spanish defence and had to wait until just before the interval for their first goal. And then it was a gift for Ian Rush after a terrible mix-up between the keeper Arconada and two defenders. The strength of the lively Mark Hughes began to stretch the Spanish defence, and he produced a supreme piece of skill to put Wales two up after 54 minutes with a spectacular scissors kick. The striking pair combined four minutes from the end for the third Welsh goal, Hughes putting Rush through the middle for the sort of chance the Liverpool man relishes and rarely wastes.

Phillips (left) and Hughes congratulate Ian Rush after the first goal.

First leg of treble for Toffeemen

EVERTON REAPED the richly deserved reward for a magnificent season's work when a 2–0 victory over QPR in front of a season's best crowd of 50,514 at Goodison secured the Football League title for the eighth time, and with five games still to play. Though the season had once looked like producing the closest struggle for many years, Everton have settled the issue emphatically with five games to spare. Now they can concentrate on completing a unique treble, by taking the European Cup-Winners' Cup and retaining the FA Cup, with those finals coming up in the next 12 days.

Such an outstanding achievement would allow them to mingle once again, without embarrassment, with rivals Liverpool, who, since Everton last won the title in 1970, have amassed eight Championships and four European Cups. To accomplish their objective, the new champions will have to play with the commendable consistency that has taken them through their last 27 League games without defeat, outlasting Manchester United and Spurs and holding off Liverpool's late challenge.

Yet it would be wrong do describe Everton simply as an efficient team. Like Liverpool they have an abundance of individual talent, including Neville Southall, the Footballer of the Year, and Peter Reid, the PFA choice. Southall, whose keeping is now in the Shilton class, and Kevin Ratcliffe, one of Britain's most accomplished centre-backs, have formed, with Derek Mountfield, Gary Stevens and Pat Van Den Hauwe, the League's soundest defence. During the last eight months, Trevor Steven, Reid, Paul Bracewell and Kevin Sheedy have become as formidable a midfield unit as Liverpool possessed in the heyday of Graeme Souness. And despite the loss of Adrian Heath, potentially their most dangerous forward, through injury in December, Everton have scored more goals than any of their rivals, with substantial contributions from the Scottish pair Andy Gray and Graeme Sharp.

Goals, however, come from a wide range of positions, such is Everton's fluency and finishing power. They have scored in 35 of their 37 League games so far. The man responsible for bringing together these players and quietly and firmly building them into a team of true Championship quality is Howard Kendall, who, remarkably, has achieved this distinction while still in his thirties.

Big hand for Pat Jennings — and a handsome cheque, too

THE KEEPER WITH reputedly the largest hands in football — they have certainly appeared so to opposing strikers over the last 23 years — was given a big hand, and hand-out, when a crowd of 25,000 turned out for his testimonial at Highbury on 8 May. Jennings, 40 next month and no longer an Arsenal regular, earned around £100,000 from the match between his current club and North London rivals Spurs, for whom he played a record 472 League games. He went on to play another 237 for Arsenal, who paid Spurs a mere £40,000 for him in 1977.

In an unblemished career, the 110-cap Irish international keeper, who still figures in Northern Ireland's World Cup plans, has set a marvellous example for young players, and has been admired and respected by team-mates and opponents alike for his fine sportsmanship and healthy attitude to the game.

Deserved applause for goalkeeper Pat Jennings: a model professional.

Fifty dead in Bradford fire inferno

MORE THAN 50 soccer fans were feared killed when fire swept through the main stand at Bradford City's ground during the match with Lincoln City on 11 May. It was estimated that there were between 3,500 and 4,000 people in the stand when fire broke out and suddenly turned into a raging inferno. The number of injured may exceed 200 and the death toll is expected to rise.

The dramatic scenes were seen on the news by millions of television viewers, as the match, in which Bradford City were celebrating their newly won promotion to the Second Division, was being recorded. It was a terrifying sight, with fans — some with clothes and hair alight — scrambling over the barriers at the front of the stand, their escape fortunately unimpeded because the ground has no anti-vandal security fences. The fire horror was made worse because a strong breeze swept flames along the stand and the roof collapsed in a billowing cloud of smoke.

The charred remains of Bradford's stand: the tragedy was over in minutes.

The wooden structure, erected at the Valley Parade ground in 1909, was apparently underlaid with litter accumulated over the years, and this is thought to have acted as a tinder-box, ignited possibly by a carelessly discarded cigarette end or lit match. As with so many struggling clubs, it is inevitable that safety standards are lower in their old stands than would be considered adequate for a new stadium. Indeed, in recent years fire has destroyed or severely damaged stands at Bristol Rovers, Brighton, Brentford and Norwich, but until Bradford there had been no loss of life. Now there will almost certainly be a demand by fire chiefs for significant improvements in standards. And as FA chairman Bert Millichip has pointed out, that will probably mean the end for some clubs.

Teenager killed at Birmingham as Leeds fans go on rampage

VALLEY PARADE was not the only ground where tragedy struck on the last Saturday of the season. In violence at the Birmingham-Leeds clash at St Andrews, apparently initiated by hooligans from Leeds, a stretch of 12-foot high retaining wall collapsed, killing a teenage fan and injuring others.

Earlier in the day Leeds fans had wrecked a public house in the city centre, and the violence at the match started when Birmingham scored just before half-time. Angry Leeds fans tore up advertising hoardings, seats and cushions, and began hurling them at police. As mounted police and scores of officers in riot gear went in to restore order, about 200 City fans dashed onto the pitch, and for more than half an hour police struggled to break up violent clashes.

Police put the injury toll at over 150, including a police officer said to be in a serious condition. There were 125 arrests.

Rapid exit as Everton land second leg of treble

Andy Gray celebrates his goal in the Cup-Winners' Cup final.

EVERTON'S MAGNIFICENT season and their quest for a remarkable treble continued in style in Rotterdam on 15 May, when Howard Kendall's talented team became the seventh British winners of the Cup-Winners' Cup, beating Rapid Vienna in the final. Second-half goals by three men who have made outstanding contributions throughout the campaign — Andy Gray, Trevor Steven and Kevin Sheedy — brought a European trophy to Goodison for the first time.

Backed by a highly vocal travelling army of about 20,000 supporters in the Feyenoord Stadium, the League champions dominated throughout. But their failure to translate their complete control of the first half into goals gave their fans some cause for anxiety. They relaxed when Sharp intercepted a poor back pass in the 58th minute and laid on Gray's goal. And when Steven hooked the ball in after a corner 15 minutes later, they were jubilant. Krankl rounded the largely unemployed Southall to pull one back for the Austrians, but Everton struck back two minutes later when Sharp enabled Sheedy to clinch the match.

History created and crushed at Wembley

A TRULY HEROIC performance by Manchester United on a warm, oppressive afternoon at Wembley deprived Everton of their remarkable "treble" and redeemed an FA Cup final that had failed almost completely to realize its rich promise. What changed the whole character of the contest was the controversial sending-off of Kevin Moran, one of United's central defenders, 12 minutes from the end of normal time for committing what is known in the business as a "professional foul" on Everton's Peter Reid.

Moran having gained, in the 104th Cup final, the dubious distinction of being the first player to be sent off in any one of them, United were compelled to play with 10 men. But it was no backs-to-the-wall triumph. They responded by lifting their game to such a level of industry and inspiration that it came as no surprise when Norman Whiteside, their young Irish international, was able to score the winning goal.

The incident that paradoxically turned the match came when Reid intercepted a pass by McGrath and broke forward, with Gray and Sharp unmarked to his left and right. Moran swept his feet from under him — a foul, but no worse than one by Ratcliffe on Stapleton a little earlier, for which the Everton captain was not even cautioned. Under pressure from FIFA, the FA has long abandoned its campaign to eradicate the "professional foul" by sending off offenders, so it was a surprise to everyone when referee Peter Willis pointed to the dressing-rooms. Nevertheless, Moran's initial frenzied refusal to accept the decision was as outrageous a sight as seen at Wembley since the scandalous exhibition of Argentina's Rattin in the 1966 World Cup. And, however much sympathy one may have for the Manchester United player, this sort of behaviour must never be condoned.

The sending-off had a galvanizing effect on United, who twice went close in the remaining 12 minutes of normal time, and continued in the same vein for the extra 30 minutes. The winning goal came after five minutes of the second period. Hughes, who seemed to gain in strength as the game wore on, found Whiteside in the right. The youngster carried the ball forward, mesmerized Van Den Hauwe by feinting to shoot, and then did so, curling the ball past Southall and just inside the far post.

In the end, one's sympathy must be with Everton, because surely now it has been proved beyond doubt that a sending-off is no compensation for a lost opportunity. Only when FIFA appreciate this, perhaps by studying the report of the Busby Committee, instead of petulantly ignoring it, will the "professional foul" be eradicated from the game.

Neville Southall is beaten by Norman Whiteside's (outside picture) scorching winner.

FOOTBALL FOCUS

- The Scottish League Cup, now sponsored by Skol despite the ban on alcohol at Scottish grounds, was organized on a straight knock-out basis until the two-legged semi-finals this season.
- QPR had a chastening experience in the UEFA Cup, They took a 6–2 first-leg lead from their home tie (played at Highbury because of QPR's synthetic pitch) into the second round against Partizan Belgrade, were beaten 4–0 in Yugoslavia and lost on the away goals rule.
- The two Milk Cup finalists, Norwich and Sunderland, were both relegated to Division Two at the end of the season.
- England went down 1–0 to Scotland, their first defeat at Hampden Park since 1976, in the inaugural match for the Sir Stanley Rous Cup on 25 May.

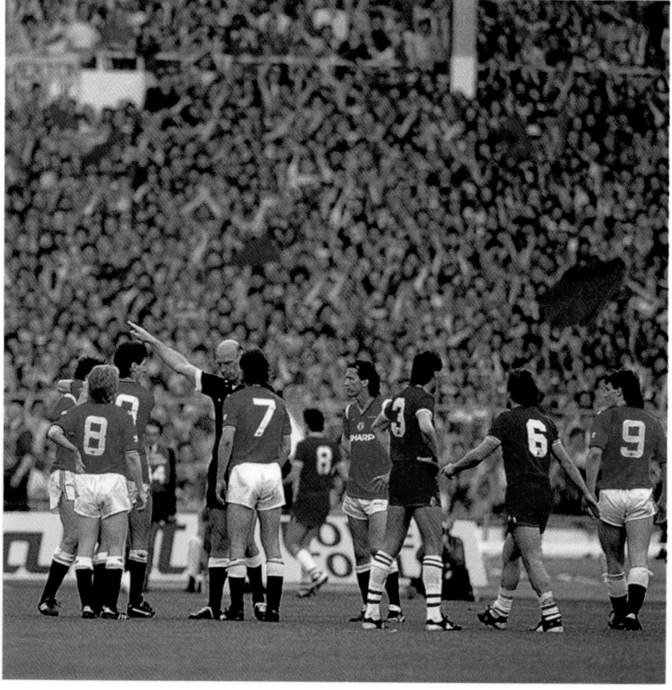

Moran has to be restrained by team-mates when he refuses to go.

Chinese fans on rampage after defeat

SQUADS OF baton-wielding police were drafted onto the streets of Peking to disperse thousands of rioting soccer fans after China lost their World Cup qualifier 2–1 to Hong Kong on 19 May. In scenes reminiscent of the Maoist Cultural Revolution, gangs of youths turned on foreigners as well as Chinese, attacking the cars of foreign correspondents and a diplomat. The 80,000 crowd at the Workers' Stadium had jeered the Hong Kong side throughout the match, and the visitors needed police protection when they left.

Forty killed in European Cup final riot

Liverpool fans confront Belgian riot police who needed protection despite the barricade.

ABOUT 40 PEOPLE were killed — many of them trampled to death — when a wall and a safety defence collapsed during rioting by Liverpool and Juventus fans before the European Cup final in Brussels on 29 May. More than 350 people were injured, and most of the casualties were Italians. Although Juventus fans throwing fireworks and other missiles at the police at one end were the first troublemakers, Liverpool fans charging into some Italians and causing the wall to collapse were apparently responsible for the disaster. Bodies were piled high in two tents outside the main gates of the stadium as helicopters and ambulances carried the injured people to hospitals. The match was eventually played to prevent escalation of the trouble, as police seemed helpless to control the problem.

The deaths were the hideous climax to a night of rioting during which fans, many of them drunk, had used flagpoles and metal torn from safety barriers as weapons, and had fireworks, bottles and cans and pieces of concrete. Events that led to the tragically fatal incident began when Liverpool supporters started to hurl cans and bottles at Juventus fans separated from them only by a wire fence. A few of the Liverpool mob encroached into a section of the terracing occupied by Italians, an action that the authorities of the antiquated Heysel Stadium had not anticipated despite previous football violence. As soon as the Belgian police charged forward in battle formation, hundreds of Liverpool fans swarmed out of their area to join in. According to witnesses, many Italians tried to climb over a wire perimeter fence and a wall, and dozens of them fell 40 feet from the back of the terracing when the wall collapsed under them.

In the dressing-rooms, the players were not officially told about the deaths, and, with the police still making pathetic and half-hearted attempts to restore order, the game began 85 minutes late. As professionals, the players went through the motions, but few people felt that the match — won 1–0 by Juventus with a Platini penalty — had any significance.

A scene more reminiscent of war than "the beautiful game".

SOCCER SOUNDBITES

"We were trying to pull people out, but idiots were still pushing. I've finished with Liverpool until those idiot supporters go away."

An innocent and distressed LIVERPOOL FAN caught up in the tragedy.

"There is no doubt that the Liverpool fans started the trouble. They are animals."

Another LIVERPOOL SUPPORTER.

"... like a sickening sight from the Middle Ages."

NEWS REPORTER on American TV.

FINAL SCORE

Football League
Division 1: Everton
Top scorer: Kerry Dixon (Chelsea), Gary Lineker (Leicester City) 24
Division 2: Oxford United
Division 3: Bradford City
Division 4: Chesterfield
Footballer of the Year: Neville Southall (Everton)

FA Cup Final
Manchester United 1 Everton 0
(after extra time)

League Cup Final
Norwich City 1 Sunderland 0

Scottish League
Premier Division: Aberdeen
Top scorer: Frank McDougall (Aberdeen) 22
Division 1: Motherwell
Division 2: Montrose
Footballer of the Year: Hamish McAlpine (Dundee United)

Scottish FA Cup Final
Celtic 2 Dundee United 1

Scottish League Cup Final
Rangers 1 Dundee United 0

European Cup Final
Juventus 1 Liverpool 0

Cup-Winners' Cup Final
Everton 3 Rapid Vienna 1

UEFA Cup Final
Real Madrid beat Videoton 3–0, 0–1

European Footballer of the Year 1984
Michel Platini (Juventus & France)

Leading European Scorer (Golden Boot)
Francisco Gomez (Porto) 39

World Club Championship
Juventus (Italy) 2 Argentinos Juniors (Argentina) 2
Juventus won 4–2 on penalties

POST-HEYSEL DIARY

30 May All British clubs banned from playing in Belgium.
31 May FA withdraws all English clubs from Europe for a year; 38 confirmed dead; Brussels fire officers disclose that Heysel Stadium had not been given full safety check since early 1930s and condemn it as inadequate for major international matches.
2 Jun UEFA place indefinite ban on all English clubs in Europe.
6 Jun FIFA ban all English clubs from playing clubs from other countries.
13 Jun FIFA ban on English clubs to include friendlies.
20 Jun UEFA ban Liverpool for three years.
21 Jun Liverpool to appeal against UEFA sentence, which is now understood to mean any three years in which they qualify for European competition after ban on other clubs is lifted.
6 Jul Belgian parliamentary investigation committee reports that politicians, police and soccer chiefs must all take part of blame.

French lesson for Bobby Robson

FRANCE BEAT URUGUAY 2–0 in the inaugural Intercontinental Cup match for the Artemio Franchi Trophy in Paris on 21 August, and in doing so offered England supremo Bobby Robson a memorable insight into the sumptuous standards required of credible World Cup candidates. A superb victory over the South American champions fuelled Gallic optimism that a romantic European Championship triumph will be surpassed in Mexico next summer. France's performance on a balmy evening embodied the qualities which make them Europe's most attractive side — instinctive skill, technical excellence and a gritty refusal to be intimidated.

The Uruguayans, whose team featured just four of the side that defeated England in Montevideo last summer, revealed little of their undoubted flair, and reverted to the darker principles of the South American game. But by a delicious irony, Toure — the target for the Uruguayans' most concerted assaults — sealed the victory with his first goal in international football.

The young forward stepped inside Diogo's lunge before continuing his run into the penalty box and hooking Giresse's delicate pass over the Uruguayan keeper to put France two up after 55 minutes.

Almost immediately, Platini hit a post with a typical curling shot. But for once, France's inspirational captain was not their most influential figure — an honour due to Giresse, his tiny lieutenant. It was the Bordeaux midfielder who signalled a performance of rare quality within three minutes of the start, when he picked out Platini, who put Rocheteau through for their first goal. From that moment on, envy and admiration must have been the major emotions felt by the watching Mr Robson, and virtually every other onlooker.

Gallic style: Platini (right) threads a pass through the Uruguay defence.

The lady is not amused

THE FOOTBALL LEAGUE has again disappointed the Prime Minister with its latest 10-point plan for curbing soccer violence. Mrs Thatcher may not be kicking the proposals into the stand, but she is known to be "deeply unimpressed" by what has been put forward.

Regarding the League's first proposal, individual club membership schemes for supporters — which rejects the national identity-card plan as unworkable — she believes that football organizations are showing a total lack of imagination. She says that she has been misrepresented, and that she has not argued for a national computerized membership scheme by the start of next season, but that membership cards introduced by individual clubs should be compatible, so that it could be developed gradually on a national scale — and this, in her view, could increase support for soccer.

The Prime Minister is opposed to the proposal that the executive boxes and viewing restaurants at grounds should be exempt from the alcohol ban, though she does favour more morning kick-offs, more all-ticket games, backing for the new Public Order Act giving police greater powers of arrest, and more closed-circuit television. But many of these items are already agreed.

Mrs Thatcher rejects the other major League proposals that the policing of grounds should be met by the government and that there should be a reduction in the pools Betting Duty by 2.5 per cent, equivalent to £20 million, and that this should go to improvements. What is seen as an attempt by the League to negotiate for more government funds — when high transfer fees are still being paid — is regarded as "totally unacceptable".

FIFA lift embargo on English clubs

BRITISH CLUBS may now play abroad, outside Europe, according to the latest FIFA edict of 11 July, amending their blanket ban of five weeks earlier. Their decision has been greeted by English clubs with a mixture of enthusiasm and chagrin, however.

While Spurs and Norwich, whose chairmen are getting together straight away, are amongst several clubs already interested in setting up a lucrative tournament in Saudi Arabia, others are frustrated that the timing of FIFA's ban, and now its removal, has not left sufficient time for foreign pre-season tours — originally planned and then cancelled — to be rearranged.

The six clubs denied their places in the European competitions — Everton, Liverpool, Spurs, Manchester United, Southampton and Norwich — are the ones most likely to make attempts to play abroad. Norwich chairman Sir Arthur South envisages not only the chance to make the money they are banned from making in Europe, but also the opportunity to show the European authorities that they can take supporters abroad who will behave themselves.

FIFA also spelt out that they would be keeping a watchful eye on English efforts to cure hooliganism, and they highlighted the current lack of agreement that appears to exist between the government and the clubs as to who is most responsible for spectator behaviour.

Death of Jock Stein

JOCK STEIN WAS truly a giant of British football, the most successful club manager in the history of the game. He became Scotland manager after the debacle of the 1978 World Cup, but will be remembered most for his remarkable reign at Celtic. He took over at Parkhead in 1965, and in 11 seasons (he missed 1975–76 after a near-fatal car crash), they won the League title 10 times, the Cup seven and the League Cup six. At the same time, in nine seasons of European Cup competition, Celtic became, in 1967, the first British club to win the trophy. Their 2–1 triumph over Inter Milan was a reward for Stein's philosophy of all-out attacking football.

Stein's rise from obscurity is like a fairy story. As a player, he was on the point of quitting the game and returning to the pits after an undistinguished career with Albion Rovers and non-League football when Celtic signed him as a reserve centre-half. Because of injury to the regular stopper, he found himself straight in the first team — and he never looked back.

In 1954, he captained Celtic to their first League and Cup double for 40 years. The next year, an ankle injury ended his playing career, and he coached Celtic for five years before becoming manager of Dunfermline, saving them from relegation and then taking them to their 1961 FA Cup victory over Celtic. After a brief spell with Hibs, he returned to Celtic and glory. Their "grand slam" in 1967 was unique, and he achieved it with a side that cost virtually nothing. Stein retired in 1977, but was persuaded to make a comeback with Leeds a year later. Then, after less than seven weeks, and before signing a contract, the call came from Scotland.

Jock Stein was a simple, straightforward man, completely dedicated to football. He possessed a vast knowledge of the game, and had an exceptional ability to bring out the best in his players. His death was a terrible loss to the Scots, but he will also be missed by all who love the game.

SOCCER SOUNDBITES

"The best place to defend is in the other side's penalty box."

JOCK STEIN

Jock Stein passes on some advice to his team, but he collapsed and died that night.

Manager's death mars Scots' late rescue

MOMENTS AFTER watching his side snatch a late equalizer at Ninian Park on 10 September to keep their hopes of qualification for the World Cup very much alive, Jock Stein, Scotland's supremo, collapsed and died of a heart attack.

Stein, who was 62, had survived a heart attack eight years ago. His death was a tragic end to a match that had virtually put paid to Welsh chances of going to Mexico but had paved the way for Scotland.

The draw puts the Scots above Wales on goal difference. But if Spain win the remaining match in Group 7 — which they should, at home to Iceland, having previously beaten them in Reykjavic — they will qualify as of right, leaving Scotland with the not too arduous task of playing off with the winner of the Oceania group for the last qualifying place. If Spain do not win, however, Scotland automatically qualify, and Wales play off.

With these simple permutations in their minds, the teams walked out to tumultuous applause from the 38,000 crowd, and the opening minutes brought intensely physical exchanges between the famed Welsh strikers Hughes and Rush and Scottish centre-back McLeish, with free-kicks going both ways — against Hughes and McLeish. Hughes soon stamped his class on the match, however, when he superbly struck in a low Nicholas cross, on the turn, after just 14 minutes.

Neville Southall (green) stares at the referee (white) in disbelief.

With so much at stake, the match continued to be physical. Following their defeat at Hampden by the Welsh last March, Scotland had made six changes, with Gough and McLeish attempting to close-mark Hughes and Rush and with Miller acting as sweeper. As the second half wore on, Scotland stepped up the pressure, but the award of a penalty against Phillips for hands with just 10 minutes left was perhaps a little harsh — especiaaly since a disputed penalty eight years ago also gave Scotland a World Cup finals place, and again at the expense of Wales.

Davie Cooper, who had come on as substitute for Strachan, converted it. So Scotland take a very large step towards Mexico — tragically, however, without Jock Stein.

Jennings the Great seals Mexico place

NORTHERN IRELAND clinched a place among the 24 World Cup finalists with a disciplined defensive performance against England that earned them the point sufficient to offset Romania's victory in Turkey and book their trip to Mexico. Thousands of delighted Irishmen at Wembley on 13 November will claim success was wholly merited. Rightly, they will point to the sensible football their team played to contain and frustrate England in this goalless draw — and to world-class goalkeeping by Pat Jennings in the closing minutes. If the Romanians take a look at the video of this match, they may well conclude that they are not going to Mexico because of the gross incompetence of an England side who had already booked their passage. The crowd began to chant "It's a fix", especially after one terrible Kerry Dixon miss, but England gave the lie to any such accusations when they swarmed round the penalty box in the closing stages and gave the Irish back four a hard time.

But Jennings, this great goalkeeper who has not played a senior club match for a year, was equal to their best efforts. Moving with the speed of a man half his 40 years, he blocked one shot from Dixon that had been deflected and then, a few minutes from the end, leapt across his area to tip over a close-range header from the same player. The sight of the venerable Jennings turning cartwheels on the Wembley turf at the final whistle confirmed that, once again, Northern Ireland had defied logic.

Jennings defies the England attack yet again.

Liverpool hooligans will not learn

A BRICK AND AEROSOL attack on Manchester United players before their game at Anfield on 9 February was the first serious outbreak of hooliganism at a football ground this season, although there have been incidents away from football stadiums. It is sickening, in view of their part in the Heysel tragedy, that Liverpool fans are again the ones involved. Predictably, in view of the bad blood between both clubs, it happened when it did.

Aerosol sprays were aimed at the United players as they disembarked from their coach, and a brick was thrown at a window. Although most of the players were affected by the spray, which left their eyes burning and throats spluttering, they soon recovered on getting treatment and it did not appear to affect their performance. The 1–1 draw was not enough to take them back on top above Everton, but they stay ahead of Liverpool, who are now without a home League victory over United in six League meetings.

SOCCER SOUNDBITES

"How could I take the job if I was told I could not sign a Catholic? I'm married to one."

GRAEME SOUNESS,
on signing for Rangers as player-manager.

Live soccer returns to TV

ON 20 DECEMBER, the long-running battle between the League and the television companies was finally settled — only two weeks after the announcement regretting that 15 months' negotiations had broken down irretrievably. As soon as the £1.3 million deal was done with the League, to cover the rest of the season, ITV and the BBC were then able to agree similar terms over the same period with the FA. Viewers can expect live telecasts of four League games, both Milk Cup semi-finals and the final, as well as four FA Cup ties plus semi-finals and final.

Rangers make catholic choice

GRAEME SOUNESS, Scotland's World Cup captain, signed as player-manager for Glasgow Rangers on 8 April and promised that sectarianism was out. The Sampdoria midfielder, who left Liverpool for the Italian club for £700,000 two seasons ago, will take over from the departing Jock Wallace, but will play out the rest of the season with Sampdoria, who are understood to be receiving a £300,000 fee.

Souness's brief, a daunting one for a man in his first managerial post, is to restore the club's prestige; Rangers have finished out of the top two places in the Premier Division for the last six seasons.

Souness, taking over at Rangers.

Distinction for Oxford

OXFORD UNITED achieved the distinction of winning the Milk Cup for the first time when they beat QPR 3–0 at Wembley for the most decisive victory in the final of this competition since it became a one-off match.

Though this was a commendable all-round team performance by the underdogs, 20th in the First Division, the key figure in a resounding triumph was Trevor Hebberd. This skilful, thoughtful former Southampton midfielder played a crucial part in the three goals that upset the odds in favour of a Rangers victory. After an exceptionally dull first half-hour, Oxford, with Hebberd, Phillips and Houghton working smoothly in midfield, began to undermine QPR's confidence. They deservedly took the lead five minutes before the break when Aldridge laid on a simple goal for Hebberd on the edge of the six-yard box.

Once in front, Oxford took complete control. Rangers simply did not show a glimpse of their usual form. Houghton played a defence-splitting one-two with Hebberd after 51 minutes and ran on to score the second goal. Aldridge, usually a lethal striker, missed a couple, before Hebberd put him through again with four minutes left. And, although his shot was beaten out, Charles followed up to score. Now Oxford must quickly return to earth and resume the grim business of trying to hang on to the First Division status they have enjoyed for less than a season.

Trevor Hebberd (left) shoots past Alan McDonald and Paul Barron for Oxford's first goal.

Broken Hearts 'Kidded' out of title

POOR, SAD HEARTS, they were so close to their first League title since 1960, when a Dundee substitute wrecked their dreams on the last day of the season. A week earlier, with only two teams still in the race, Celtic needed maximum points from their last three games and for Hearts to lose. Even then, they would have to make up the goal difference. But the unbelievable happened. Celtic won their two matches in hand, and it all hinged on the last day's action. They finished in magnificent style, winning 5–0 at St Mirren. At Dens Park, Hearts were not finding it easy against Dundee, but with eight minutes left the 0–0 scoreline would have been enough to give them the title. Then along came Dundee substitute Kidd to prise the title from their grasp with a goal in the 83rd minute, and kill them off completely with another in the 87th. Now Hearts must pick themselves up for the FA Cup final with Aberdeen in a week's time.

Albert Kidd (centre) celebrates his triumph and Hearts' misery.

Luton to ban away fans

LUTON ARE TO TAKE unilateral steps to keep visitors' supporters from Kenilworth Road. Understandably determined to avoid the disgraceful, costly riots suffered during Millwall's Cup visit last season, they announced their plans on 29 April. They will consider withdrawing from the FA Cup and the newly sponsored League Cup (by Littlewoods), or play on opponents' or neutral grounds, if the governing bodies insist on away supporters being allocated tickets.

All supporters attending Kenilworth Road will have to have bought a £1 membership card, with a magnetic code to be scanned in computer-controlled turnstiles costing £250,000. Card-holders must sign a good behaviour pledge, and the computer will reject stolen cards or those belonging to blacklisted members.

Luton chairman David Evans claims the club's novel scheme has the backing of the Prime Minister, the government, the police, local council and residents.

More power for big clubs

FIRST DIVISION CLUBS were granted a significant increase in power at a Football League Extraordinary Meeting on 28 April, making the threatened formation of a breakaway "super league" unlikely now. Resistance from the lower divisions to the 10-point plan sponsored by the leading clubs collapsed in less than 30 minutes, as compromise was reached over the crucial issue of voting. The majority required for constitutional changes was reduced from 75 per cent to 66, and First Division clubs will have one and a half votes each, Second Division clubs one each, with Third and Fourth sharing eight votes between them.

A major reform is the reduction in size of the First Division from 22 to 20 clubs (with the Second to be increased to 24), with end-of-season play-offs over the next two seasons for some promotion and relegation places in the League. Other proposals accepted give the First Division clubs larger shares in gate receipts and TV and sponsorship money.

It's Liverpool, d'ye Ken!

LIVERPOOL WON THE League Championship for the eighth time in 11 seasons when they beat Chelsea 1–0 at Stamford Bridge on 3 May, with a typically nerveless, smothering performance and a marvellous goal scored fittingly by player-manager Kenny Dalglish. In a game they had to win, Dalglish's single, first-half strike proved just enough to account for Chelsea, render meaningless the heroics elsewhere of West Ham and Everton, and take the title back to Anfield at the end of the scorer's first season in charge.

Dalglish would be the first to acknowledge that he owes much of his astonishing success to the strength of the squad he inherited from Bob Paisley and Joe Fagan. There was abundant proof of that at Stamford Bridge. The failure of Jan Molby, Liverpool's influential Danish international midfielder, to recover from a stomach ailment merely meant the reintroduction of Mark Lawrenson, the gifted Irish international who is regarded by many as the best defender in Europe!

Liverpool came up the finishing straight like the thoroughbreds they are, with 11 victories and one draw in their last 12 matches. Everton, who led for much of the season, fought all the way to retain their title before coming unstuck last Wednesday at Oxford. And West Ham, too, strung together six wins in 15 days, including the sensational 8–1 drubbing of Newcastle, but could not quite make up the leeway. Most extraordinary, however, was the slump of Manchester United, who won their first 10 matches, just failing to equal Spurs' long-standing record when they drew at Luton.

Liverpool were 10 points behind United at that time, and later 11 points behind leaders Everton. But, as so many teams have found to their dismay over the last dozen years or so, you discount Liverpool at your peril, and sure enough they snatched another League title. Kenny Dalglish is the first player-manager to accomplish such a remarkable feat, and history, with the FA Cup final coming up next Saturday, is still beckoning him vigorously.

Dalglish celebrates his title-winning goal.

Hero Hewitt the Heartbreaker

ABERDEEN, WITH AS clinical a performance as they've ever produced, beat Hearts 3–0 at Hampden in the 101st Scottish FA Cup final, and in doing so they completed the most depressing and shattering eight days in the history of Heart of Midlothian Football Club. It was, indeed, heartbreaking for the 40,000 fans of the Edinburgh club, nearly two-thirds of the attendance, having seen the League title snatched from their grasp only seven days earlier.

The player chiefly responsible this time was Man of the Match John Hewitt, who struck a severe body blow as early as the sixth minute, when he weaved his way beyond three defenders in the box before unleashing a low drive into the corner of the net. Hearts, who were never three goals inferior to the Dons, proceeded to miss two great chances to level the match before the second, killer goal came in the 49th minute. Hewitt, again, found himself on his own when MacDougall dummied Weir's cross, and tucked the ball away. With 15 minutes left substitute Stark stooped to head a third from another Weir cross. For Alex Ferguson's men, it was a second Cup of the season. For Hearts, it all ended in tears. They had three men booked, and their captain Walter Kidd, who had been cautioned in the first half, was sent off in the 77th minute for throwing the ball at an opponent in sheer frustration.

Stark (12) wraps it up for Aberdeen with number three.

FOOTBALL FOCUS

- "Double" winners Liverpool won the FA Cup final with only one player born in England — and he was Republic of Ireland international Mark Lawrenson, born in Preston!
- Reading, who won the Third Division title, created a League record by winning their first 13 games.
- Kenny Dalglish, not content with his club triumphs, became the first Scot to win 100 caps.
- Pat Jennings came out of partial retirement to rejoin Spurs as extra cover, and was signed on a non-contract basis for Everton, after the transfer deadline, as cover in the Cup when Neville Southall was injured. So he found himself in the unique position of being eligible for Spurs in the League and Everton in the Cup. In the event, he played for neither, but represented Northern Ireland in the 1986 World Cup, playing his 119th and last game (a world record) against Brazil on his 41st birthday.

Double-take: Rush job makes Dalglish's day

IN THE FIRST-EVER all-Merseyside FA Cup final, Liverpool beat Everton 3–1 at Wembley to become only the third club this century to complete the "double". It is an extraordinary achievement for Kenny Dalglish, in his first season as player-manager, to bring off what his illustrious predecessors had failed to do in all Liverpool's years of supremacy.

Yet in a thrilling match of curious shifts and changes, Liverpool at one time looked to be on the point of taking a heavy beating from their old rivals. But Rush came to the rescue with two typical pieces of finishing.

Rarely have Liverpool been so outplayed as they were for the best part of an hour. Grobbelaar was having one of his more eccentric games, and it was no surprise when Footballer of the Year Gary Lineker gave Everton the lead after 28 minutes, from an exquisite Reid through-pass.

What saved the day for Liverpool was a magnificent save by Grobbelaar from Sharp, and the determination of Jan Molby, their bulky Danish international, to stamp his influence on the game. Freeing himself from the dominance of Reid and Bracewell, no easy task in itself, he constructed Liverpool's first two goals and also contributed to their third. He provided an angled pass for Rush to score Liverpool's unexpected equalizer after 57 minutes, and six minutes later a low cross was missed by Dalglish but converted eagerly at the far post by the Australian Craig Johnston.

And it was Molby who, six minutes from the end, sent Liverpool forward with a searching pass from midfield for Whelan. The Irishman floated the ball across the penalty area to the unmarked Welshman Rush, who drove it firmly into the net — and beyond all hope for Everton.

Man of the Match Molby strides majestically through the Everton defence.

'El Tel' pays the penalty

WHEN TERRY VENABLES was chaired off the field by his players at the end of the dramatic European Cup semi-final second leg, in which Barcelona had overcome a 3–0 deficit to beat Gothenburg on penalties, it seemed as if the hard part had been accomplished. "El Tel's" men had beaten European champions Juventus in the quarter-finals, and before that had survived two close ties on the away goals rule. Now only the unheralded Steaua Bucharest stood between them and the title that had eluded them for a quarter of a century — and the final was being played in Spain.

But it was not to be. Steaua, a team of soldiers from the Romanian capital, beat the odds-on favourites in a bizarre shoot-out after a goalless draw in Seville, and so became the first Eastern Bloc holders of the European Cup.

In a close, exciting two-hour battle, the Romanians never really threatened Barcelona's goal. During the final stages, the Spaniards always looked likely to snatch victory — Steve Archibald missed a golden opportunity 10 minutes from normal time — and Steaua had to hang on grimly.

So for the second time in three years, this illustrious competition was reduced to a penalty decider. The crowd were ecstatic when Urruti saved the first spot-kick, but Steaua's Ducadam matched him, and they both saved the next one, too. Then Lacatus put the Romanians ahead, Ducadam saved his third penalty, Balint put Steaua two up, and the amazing Ducadam saved from Marcos — four out of four penalty stops, a unique feat in a major final. It was all over, and the desperately disappointed crowd sportingly applauded the victors off the field.

Helmut Ducadam makes his fourth and match-winning penalty save.

FINAL SCORE

Football League
Division 1: Liverpool
Top scorer: Gary Lineker (Everton) 30
Division 2: Norwich City
Division 3: Reading
Division 4: Swindon Town
Footballer of the Year: Gary Lineker (Everton)

FA Cup Final
Liverpool 3 Everton 1

League Cup Final
Oxford United 3 QPR 0

Scottish League
Premier Division: Celtic
Top scorer: Ally McCoist (Rangers) 24
Division 1: Hamilton Academical
Division 2: Dunfermline Athletic
Footballer of the Year: Sandy Jardine (Heart of Midlothian)

Scottish FA Cup Final
Aberdeen 3 Heart of Midlothian 0

Scottish League Cup Final
Aberdeen 3 Hibernian 0

European Cup Final
Steaua Bucharest 0 Barcelona 0
Steaua won 2–0 on penalties

Cup-Winners Cup Final
Dynamo Kiev 3 Atlético Madrid 0

UEFA Cup Final
Real Madrid beat Cologne 5–1, 0–2

European Footballer of the Year 1985
Michel Platini (Juventus & France)

Leading European Scorer (Golden Boot)
Marco Van Basten (Ajax Amsterdam) 37

World Club Championship
River Plate (Argentina) 1 Steaua Bucharest (Romania) 0

Maradona wins World Cup single-handed

THE ABIDING memories of the 1986 World Cup will be the magic of Diego Maradona (not to mention his sleight of hand), dazzling displays of fluent attacking football from France, Brazil, Denmark and the USSR, and a thrilling final in which the artistry of Argentina prevailed over the courage and discipline of West Germany.

It was arguably the best World Cup since the finals were last held in Mexico, in 1970 — remarkably so in view of the unwieldy format of the competition, the trying climatic conditions and the glaring inadequacy of the onfield officials. Football triumphed despite all these obstacles: a testimony to the game's enduring capacity to entertain.

Unpromising start

The 1986 World Cup was a juggernaut of a competition. There were 52 matches in all, played over a period of a month. It required two weeks and 36 matches to eliminate just eight of the 24 teams. Yet so tight was the timetable that three of the quarter-finals had to be decided on penalties, regarded by just about everyone as a terribly unsatisfactory way to determine a result. To accommodate television scheduling, matches were played in the hottest part of the day — in one centre, Monterrey, in appalling conditions of heat and humidity. Referees were drawn from many more countries than in previous competitions, which resulted in inconsistent and at times confusing decision-making by the officials.

Robson's choice

England played their first three matches in Monterrey, in Group F. The "Group of the Sleeping", the locals called it, because of the dearth of goals and the boring football served up in the first four matches. At that stage, England were in very great danger of going out of the competition. They had no goals and only one point. Against Morocco, they had lost their captain, Bryan Robson, injured, and their vice-captain, Ray Wilkins, sent off for throwing the ball at the referee.

To be sure of qualifying for the last 16, England needed to beat Poland in their last group match. They did so, arguably because manager Bobby Robson was now forced to make the changes that most of his critics had been advocating. Hitherto, he had persisted with his lion-hearted namesake Bryan, even though the England skipper had to play in a shoulder harness and could not possibly give anywhere near 100 per cent. And Wilkins had forgotten how to attack. Now supremo Robson had to replace them: he also dropped Waddle, and fielded a 4–4–2 line-up, with the splendid Beardsley replacing Hateley as Lineker's partner, and Reid and Hodge coming in to strengthen the midfield. The new formation clicked, Lineker scored a hat-trick inside 35 minutes, and England had survived.

In the knock-out stage, England again demonstrated how well they can play when they go into battle with the correct tactics. They chalked up another 3–0 win, against Paraguay, and Lineker scored another two. Morocco, for their remarkable achievement of heading the group, above three European nations, earned the dubious reward of another match in Monterrey, with West Germany for opponents. Courageously as they played, they were beaten by a fine free-kick from Matthaus two minutes from time.

Burruchaga (left) watches the World Cup winner on its way.

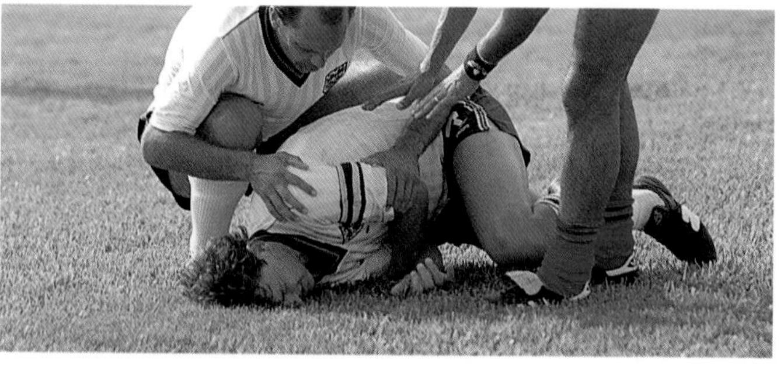

Ray Wilkins comforts Bryan Robson after he dislocated his shoulder.

Scotland lose bottle

Scotland were the underdogs in the toughest group, pitted against South American champions Uruguay and two of Europe's strongest teams, West Germany and Denmark. In their first two matches, against the latter two, they earned many friends and plenty of praise, but no luck and no points. Then, when suddenly an opportunity to progress was handed to Scotland on a plate, they, in the modern idiom, "lost their bottle". Playing against a Uruguayan side reduced to 10 men after a sending-off in the first minute, they disintegrated into amateurishness, failed to score, and were eliminated.

Argentina's progress

Argentina played football worthy of champions. They won their group, and then beat the talented but flawed Uruguayans. But their quarter-final win against England was devalued because of the nature of their first goal, propelled into the net by the hand of Maradona. He later made amends, however, taking the ball in a mazy, irresistible run before slotting it past Shilton.

It was Maradona, too, who masterminded his country's semi-final win over Belgium, the surprise packet of that half of the last 16. By that time, the main European threats, Denmark and the USSR, had been eliminated. The Soviets, the most sporting of all the teams on view, had opened up in their group with a comprehensive victory over Hungary. But against Belgium, a

Maradona, the world's greatest footballing talent in the 1980s, scored one of the greatest World Cup goals against England, but sadly will be remembered more for the one he fisted in.

Lineker scores his second against Paraguay.

combination of fine defending, at least one dubious decision, and the ability of the Belgians to surge out of defence in brilliant breakaways, led to their downfall after extra time.

Belgium proceeded to repeat their performance against Spain in the quarter-finals, prevailing this time on penalties. The Spaniards had knocked out Denmark 5–1 in the second round but, with due respect to Spain, the Danes were a great loss to the tournament and would have graced the later rounds. Against Spain, they were shaken by giving away a silly equalizer, and crumbled in the second half.

The finest match

In the other half of the knock-out stage, two of the best sides of the tournament, Brazil and France, clashed in the quarter-finals. Brazil, despite initial problems, were gradually justifying their rating as favourites, while European champions France had seen off reigning world champions Italy with an outstanding exhibition of mature football. The meeting of these most fancied teams from either side of the Atlantic produced a match of exquisite football, full of skill and imagination, worthy of a final. Many experts described it as the finest game they had ever seen, and it was a travesty that it had to be decided on penalties.

It was again a loss for the tournament as a whole when the victors of this classic, France, then came unstuck in the semi-finals against their bête noire, West Germany. For although the Germans outplayed them on the day, most neutral observers, having witnessed the heights France were capable of reaching, would rather have seen them in the final.

It was also sad to see in this tournament the last of some of the world's great footballers: Zico, Platini, Socrates, Karl-Heinz Rummenigge and, of course, Pat Jennings, who finished up with a world record 119 international caps. Happily, we were still able to enjoy the fabulous skills of Platini and Socrates, and Jennings went out in a blaze of sentimental glory against Brazil on his 41st birthday (although he didn't thank debutant right-back Josimar for the 25-yard "birthday present" that was Brazil's third goal). Injuries, however, prevented both Zico and Rummenigge from doing themselves justice.

The Maradona show

Above all others, individually, was Diego Maradona. It would not be fair to say he carried his team, but he made all the difference. He inspired them, he prompted, he directed their play, and he was always capable of turning a match with one brilliant thrust. He also scored five goals — four of them legal. Some of the treatment he had to endure was scandalous, but this time he kept his temper.

In the final, Argentina went two up from Maradona-inspired attacks: the excellent central defender José Luis Brown, of Irish ancestry, headed in from a free-kick after 22 minutes, and Valdano raced in from the left to score 11 minutes after the interval. The Germans then mounted one of their famous last-ditch comebacks, with 17 minutes left and Argentina seemingly cruising to victory. Rummenigge and Völler both scored after corners.

Argentina were devastated by this sudden turn-around. But in their moment of crisis, with six minutes to go and the Germans pressing hard for the winner, Maradona made his final contribution to a tournament he had dominated. Catching the Germans on the break, he set Jorge Burruchaga free with a beautifully timed pass, and the young Nantes midfielder ran through, calmly drew Schumacher, and then planted the most important goal of his life into the far corner — the goal that won the 1986 World Cup.

FINAL SCORE

FIRST ROUND

Group A

Bulgaria	1	Italy	1
Argentina	3	South Korea	1
Italy	1	Argentina	1
South Korea	1	Bulgaria	1
Argentina	2	Bulgaria	0
Italy	3	South Korea	2

	P	W	D	L	F	A	P
Argentina	3	2	1	0	6	2	5
Italy	3	1	2	0	5	4	4
Bulgaria	3	0	2	1	2	4	2
S. Korea	3	0	1	2	4	7	1

Group B

Mexico	2	Belgium	1
Paraguay	1	Iraq	0
Mexico	1	Paraguay	1
Belgium	2	Iraq	1
Mexico	1	Iraq	0
Paraguay	2	Belgium	2

	P	W	D	L	F	A	P
Mexico	3	2	1	0	4	2	5
Paraguay	3	1	2	0	4	3	4
Belgium	3	1	1	1	5	5	3
Iraq	3	0	0	3	1	4	0

Group C

France	1	Canada	0
USSR	6	Hungary	0
France	1	USSR	1
Hungary	2	Canada	0
France	3	Hungary	0
USSR	2	Canada	0

	P	W	D	L	F	A	P
USSR	3	2	1	0	9	1	5
France	3	2	1	0	5	1	5
Hungary	3	1	0	2	2	9	2
Canada	3	0	0	3	0	5	0

Group D

Brazil	1	Spain	0
Algeria	1	Northern Ireland	1
Brazil	1	Algeria	0
Spain	2	Northern Ireland	1
Spain	3	Algeria	0
Brazil	3	Northern Ireland	0

	P	W	D	L	F	A	P
Brazil	3	3	0	0	5	0	6
Spain	3	2	0	1	5	2	4
N. Ireland	3	0	1	2	2	6	1
Algeria	3	0	1	2	1	5	1

Group E

Denmark	1	Scotland	0
Uruguay	1	West Germany	1
Denmark	6	Uruguay	1
West Germany	2	Scotland	1
Denmark	2	West Germany	0
Scotland	0	Uruguay	0

	P	W	D	L	F	A	P
Denmark	3	3	0	0	9	1	6
W. Germany	3	1	1	1	3	4	3
Uruguay	3	0	2	1	2	7	2
Scotland	3	0	1	2	1	3	1

Group F

Morocco	0	Poland	0
Portugal	1	England	0
England	0	Morocco	0
Poland	1	Portugal	0
England	3	Poland	0
Morocco	3	Portugal	1

	P	W	D	L	F	A	P
Morocco	3	1	2	0	3	1	4
England	3	1	1	1	3	1	3
Poland	3	1	1	1	1	3	3
Portugal	3	1	0	2	2	4	2

SECOND ROUND

Belgium	4	USSR	3
Mexico	2	Bulgaria	0
Argentina	1	Uruguay	0
Brazil	4	Poland	0
France	2	Italy	0
West Germany	1	Morocco	0
Spain	5	Denmark	1
England	3	Paraguay	0

QUARTER-FINALS

Brazil	1	France	1
(aet) France won 4–3 on penalties			
West Germany	0	Mexico	0
(aet) West Germany won 4–1 on penalties			
Argentina	2	England	1
Belgium	1	Spain	1
(aet) Belgium won 5–4 on penalties			

SEMI-FINALS

Argentina	2	Belgium	0
West Germany	2	France	0

THIRD-PLACE MATCH

France	4	Belgium	2

FINAL

Argentina	3	West Germany	2

Aztec Stadium, Mexico City, 29 June 1986. Attendance 114,590

Argentina: Pumpido, Cuciuffo, Brown, Ruggeri, Olarticoechea, Giusti, Batista, Burruchaga (Trobbiani), Enrique, Maradona, Valdano (Scorers: Brown, Valdano, Burruchaga)

West Germany: Schumacher, Berthold, Briegel, Jakobs, Forster, Eder, Brehme, Matthaus, Allofs (Völler), Magath (Hoeness), Rummenigge (Scorers: Rummenigge, Völler)

Leading scorers
6 Lineker (England)
5 Butragueno (Spain), Maradona (Argentina), Careca (Brazil)

Divine intervention is the verdict

FIFA HAVE gone on record to defend what appeared to many to be the World Cup finals' most brazen piece of gamesmanship — Diego Maradona's "Hand of God" goal against England. In the July issue of *FIFA News*, the official publication of the world's governing body, an exonerating article exclaims that "Diego Maradona's football in Mexico was honest".

For the monthly publication to have stated that Maradona's strong, skilful and imaginative play throughout the 30 gripping days had proved him to be the world's most accomplished player, would have brooked no argument. But for there to be not an inkling of official disquiet over such a crucial and controversial goal – which shocked millions of TV viewers throughout the world – must come as a great surprise to many football supporters in England.

The crucial moment, as Maradona scores against England in Mexico.

New boss sent off in first match

THE HOMECOMING of Graeme Souness, the local boy who made good, ended in disgrace. Back in his native Edinburgh as new player-manager for Rangers, Souness was sent off in the 37th minute against Hibs, and not even a subsequent public apology could smooth things over.

Scotland's World Cup captain set the poorest of examples to his own players and fans alike with a lunging tackle on George McCluskey that put the Hibs striker out of the game. Coming after a caution for a late challenge on Kirkwood, there was only one punishment.

Shameful scenes then followed as the other players became involved in a punch-up before the game continued, with tempers flying high and nine bookings. So the dawning of a new age for Rangers got off to a nightmare start, culminating in a 2–1 defeat.

'English fans worse': UEFA chief

UEFA PRESIDENT Jacques George, speaking after an executive committee meeting in September, said that the behaviour of English fans had worsened. Although the meeting did not touch on the indefinite European ban on English clubs, he told the Press that he did not see how the ban could be lifted. The condition for doing so was improved behaviour of English fans, and this patently had not happened. He added that the ban would not be officially discussed until some time next year.

Ferry brawl a setback for English clubs

A FULL-SCALE battle between over 100 Manchester United and West Ham supporters on a ferry taking them to the Continent for pre-season friendlies has struck a critical blow to England's chances of returning to European club competition. Sealink Ferries admitted they made a grave error in relaxing their unwritten rule not to carry football supporters, against police advice, and that they did not realize they were rival fans.

During the trip, which had to turn round after 2.5 hours of the eight-hour journey between Harwich and the Hook of Holland, hooligans fought with knives, bottles and fire hoses. When the ship returned to Harwich, 14 arrests were made, and four people were taken to hospital with stab wounds, while others had injuries caused by broken glass, kicks and punches. Most accounts agreed that there were about 100 Manchester fans and 30 West Ham fans, described as well dressed and older. With no police on board, the Dutch crew members were unable to stop the brawling, and it was decided to turn around when some of the 2,000 passengers became alarmed.

Lineker bonanza

BARCELONA'S close-season signing of Everton and England striker Gary Lineker is reported to have cost Terry Venables's club £4,262,000, a new Spanish record. Lineker, the leading World Cup scorer in Mexico with six goals, will bank some £1.5 million over the six years of his contract — excluding wages and match bonuses!

He will receive this signing-on fee at the rate of £243,000 a year, or £4,672 a week. He will also collect a basic wage of £150 a week plus a match bonus that could bring in about £800 a week.

Lineker, born in November 1960, played for his local club, Leicester City, for several seasons before joining Everton for £800,000 in July 1985. He has since added 11 caps to the seven he gained with Leicester, and seems sure to be a key figure for years to come.

Gary Lineker, from riches to riches.

'Skolars', but no gentlemen

RANGERS BEAT CELTIC 2–1 in the Skol Cup on 26 October with a penalty eight minutes from time — their 14th success in this competition and their first trophy under Graeme Souness. But a crowd of almost 75,000 at Hampden saw an unsavoury end to a poor final, in which Celtic's Mo Johnston was sent off and nine other players booked.

Following a tame first half, the game was brought to life when Durrant put Rangers ahead in the 62nd minute and McClair equalized eight minutes later. Meanwhile the referee had booked five Celtic players and one from Rangers, all for bad tackles. He took two other Celtic names for protesting a penalty after 82 minutes, which was converted by Cooper. Two minutes from time, an off-the-ball incident between Munro and Johnston resulted in a booking for the Rangers player and the dismissal of Johnston, who had already been cautioned. In the ensuing chaos, it appeared that Celtic's Shepherd had also been sent off, but he remained on the field.

It can only be hoped that these scenes are not going to be repeated when the two sides meet again at Parkhead on Saturday in a League match.

Celtic's Maurice Johnston gets his marching orders.

FA back Luton in fight against hooligans

LUTON, FORCED TO withdraw from the Littlewoods Cup after refusing to compromise over their ban on visiting supporters, have received more than adequate compensation by being permitted to operate their membership scheme during FA Cup ties. The FA's admirably sensible decision came 48 hours after the League had told Luton they could be reinstated in the Littlewoods Cup only if they agreed to lift their restriction on fans of visiting clubs or play their home ties on their opponents' or neutral grounds.

Leeds fans cause new fire at Bradford

THERE SEEMS TO BE no depths to which the Leeds hooligan element won't stoop. Their latest, almost unthinkable act of vandalism has been to cause a mobile fish-and-chip shop at Valley Parade to turn over and catch fire, leading hundreds of spectators, mindful of last year's 56-death disaster, to take refuge on the pitch. The incident occurred on 20 September, after Bradford City had taken a 2–0 second-half lead. The match was held up for 20 minutes.

FA chairman Bert Millichip said that the club would not be punished for yet another instance of their supporters' hooliganism, but that he will press for serious consideration to reimpose the ban preventing Leeds supporters from being admitted to away matches.

FA gag Bobby Robson

ENGLAND MANAGER Bobby Robson has been banned by his employers, the FA, from writing his column in a national newspaper. Robson has been contributing his ghosted articles to the Sunday Mirror since he took over as England supremo four years ago. FA chairman Bert Millichip explained that he did not feel it appropriate that Robson should work exclusively for one newspaper, and that the England manager should be freely available to all the media, without payment for his views.

In a diary of the World Cup finals this summer, in his book *So Near and Yet So Far*, Mr Robson confesses he lied to the English Press about the extent of a leg injury sustained by England captain Bryan Robson, and disguised the fact that he had dislocated his suspect shoulder again. Although the FA embargo on Robson's newspaper articles has nothing to do with the publication of his book — indeed, the FA appear to be taking a surprisingly tolerant view of his revelations — other passages led one commentator to suggest that the FA might not have been quite so ready to extend his contract had they read his book first.

Clough pans Forest fans

NOTTINGHAM FOREST manager Brian Clough was furious with the club's fans for their treatment of Arsenal's Charlie Nicholas during the League match at the City Ground on 27 September, which Forest won 1–0. A few thousand in the crowd of 25,371 chanted abuse at the Arsenal striker throughout the match, and especially when he was carried off on a stretcher after an hour with a badly gashed knee. Mr Clough showed his disgust with gestures as he leapt out of his touchline dugout to remonstrate with the fans. And when the same section chanted Mr Clough's name in admiration, he refused to accept the tribute.

Mr Clough is clearly prepared to stand up and be counted — which is what everyone in and around the football world needs to do if the worst standards being displayed by the minority are not to hold sway and continue to damage the sport's image.

Brian Clough remonstrates with the Forest fans.

Atkinson latest victim of vain search for new Busby

RON ATKINSON, the most colourful showman in British football, has paid the traditional penalty for lack of success, and after five years as manager of Manchester United makes way for Alex Ferguson, the Aberdeen boss. The definition of "success" at Old Trafford is not the same as at most other clubs, as Mr Atkinson's predecessor Dave Sexton found when he was booted out after United were losing Cup finalists in 1979 and League runners-up in 1980.

Atkinson's "sin" was his failure to produce more than two FA Cup triumphs in his five years and a final League position that did not vary from third or fourth. This time last year, United were top of the League and unbeaten after 15 matches. Now they have only 13 points from 13 matches.

United and their customers understandably still hunger for the glory of Championship and European Cup, which they last enjoyed in the 1960s, when Matt Busby was in charge, and Charlton, Best and Law ruled on the pitch. Mr Atkinson didn't deliver the goods, so he had to go. It's a hard life, but a man of his energy, talents, knowledge and realistic attitude to league soccer is not likely to be out of work any longer than he chooses.

"Big Ron" Atkinson (right) with Everton's Howard Kendall.

Dutch catch 'English disease'

SOCCER HOOLIGANISM, justly described as the "English disease", has not vanished from Europe simply because English League clubs have been banished. Supporters of Dutch club Feyenoord ran amok in Moenchengladbach on 22 October, before, during and after their UEFA Cup tie with local side Borussia. Reporting "one of the worst outbreaks of soccer violence seen in West Germany", police said Dutch fans had fought with local citizens, plundered shops, started a fire in a bar, wrecked furniture in others and overturned cars. They made 71 arrests. Sounds all too depressingly familiar!

Rangers and Borussia face UEFA wrath over bruising clash

GLASGOW RANGERS went out in the third round of the UEFA Cup on 10 December on the away goals rule when they could only draw 0–0 with Borussia in Moenchengladbach. And both sides are to be reported to UEFA after their bruising clash, screened live across West Germany, in which six players were booked and two Rangers players were sent off.

Belgian referee Alexis Ponnet revealed that he almost sent off another Rangers player, Ally Dawson, but felt it was too early in the game. The two who received their marching orders were full-back Stuart Munro, for kicking an opponent after the ball had gone, and winger Davie Cooper, for a second bookable offence.

Dawson's early crude kick at Michael Frontzeck had set the tone for a game in which player-manager Graeme Souness was accused of a "brutal tackle" on Thomas Krisp. In a "counter action", Rangers are to report the referee, who explained that he showed Cooper the second yellow card for calling him a "dirty German", whereas the Scottish international claimed he had merely, and supposedly innocently, inquired if Mr Ponnet was allowed to book Germans.

Wolves at bottom of pack

THE DISMISSAL OF Wolves in the first round of the FA Cup by non-League Chorley marks a new low in the fortunes of this once-great club, and is a grim warning to others caught in soccer's vicious circle of escalating costs and declining income. "It was the most humiliating night in the history of the club," confessed Graham Turner, Wolves' 12th manager since Stan Cullis was sacked in the early 1960s.

Relegated three times in as many years after Derek Dougan's last-ditch rescue act in 1982, Wolves, once the scourge of Europe, not only suffered the indignity of inclusion in the first-round draw, but were held 1–1 by the non-Leaguers, playing their home tie at Bolton's ground, and then 1–1 again under the floodlights of Molineux — where, in their halcyon days of the mid-1950s, they saw off the likes of Honved and Spartak Moscow. Surely, with a third chance, again at Burnden Park, they would finish off those upstarts from the Multipart League? No, they were humiliated by three goals to nil, and clearly are in their greatest crisis.

A dismal Wolves go through the motions against non-League Chorley.

Charlie is my darling: part 2

SIXTEEN YEARS after Charlie George shattered Liverpool with an extra-time winner for Arsenal at Wembley in the FA Cup, another Charlie — Nicholas, this time — scored two to enable Arsenal to snatch the Littlewoods Cup from the Merseysiders, again after they had taken the lead. In doing so, Nicholas also ended one of football's most captivating legends — that Liverpool had never lost when Ian Rush scored. The Welsh star could point to 144 games that bore this out. But on the day that he wanted to leave British football with another memory before his much-publicized departure to Italy in return for the £3 million paid by Juventus, that particular myth was blown.

Arsenal's last Wembley appearance, in the 1980 FA Cup final, had coincided with Rush's £300,000 transfer to Anfield from Chester, and in the years between he has won virtually all there is to win in club competition. From the start it looked as if he was ready to deliver another trophy, as his terrific cunning and acceleration around the box began to unsettle the Arsenal defence.

Sure enough, when the breakthrough came in the 23rd minute, it was Rush who got the goal, clinically finishing a move put together by Molby and McMahon, who were looking ominously in control of the midfield, and giving goalkeeper Lukic no chance. At this stage, Arsenal looked like being torn apart. They had started very much as underdogs, having slipped from first in the League in January with a run of nine matches without a win and only one goal. But their gutsy comebacks against Spurs in the semi-finals must have given them a boost, and as Paul Davis began to assert himself in midfield, so the pattern of the game changed. And as soon as Nicholas scored in the 29th minute after a goalmouth scramble, it seemed that Wembley had decided that the inconsistent and unsettled Scot — a Highbury favourite who had not recaptured his Celtic goalscoring form of four years ago — was going to be the hero of the first Littlewoods Cup final, and not Rush.

Kenny Dalglish put himself on in the 72nd minute, but he could not upset the control that Davis, Rocastle and Williams were now exerting in midfield. Then Perry Groves went on for Quinn, and the first thing he did was leave Gillespie tackling thin air on the touchline, race into the box, and cross to the unmarked Nicholas. The Scot appeared to miscue his shot slightly, and Whelan diverted the ball beyond the fingertips of Grobbelaar. But the record books gave the goal to Nicholas, and that's how the fairy-tale should end.

Delighted Arsenal players do their celebratory lap of honour.

Charlie Nicholas (visible through the netting) turns away in triumph after equalizing for Arsenal.

England lose 8–3 in Berne: the message is 'keep away'

ENGLAND'S DREAMS of a rapid return to European club football after their two-year exile were quickly shattered in Berne on 10 March. The 11-man UEFA executive committee voted 8–3 in favour of retaining the ban, imposed after the horror of the Heysel Stadium disaster in May 1985. They issued a terse 12-line communique, which left League president Philip Carter "dreadfully disappointed", but in no doubt as to the message.

After a 90-minute plea to the committee by Mr Carter and FA chairman Bert Millichip, in which they outlined the improvements in crowd control in England, there were hopes, if not of a return, then of at least some criteria for clubs to fulfil. But the statement removed any glimmer of hope of a reprieve for clubs, players and genuine supporters, and concluded: "The situation will be reviewed during 1988."

In other words, "Don't call us, we'll call you".

League block QPR-Fulham merger

THE FOOTBALL LEAGUE management committee have called off the proposed merger between Queen's Park Rangers and Fulham and appealed for someone to buy the name of the Third Division club from Marler Estates, the owners of Craven Cottage.

The League refuse to accept that Fulham, who were bought by Marler from club chairman Ernie Clay for £9 million last year, need to go out of business despite attracting all-time low attendances. They will not allow the registrations of any Fulham players to be transferred to the new club, who were to be retained as Queen's Park Rangers, though the League do admit they have no power to prevent Fulham from going into liquidation.

The situation cannot help the club to succeed on the field, irrespective of what happens in boardrooms and banks.

Finally, a sky-blue heaven

COVENTRY CITY, upsetting all the odds, beat Tottenham 3–2 at Wembley to win the FA Cup in their first final, and earn their first major honour since their election to the League in 1919. They carried off the trophy with an extra-time own goal after an absorbing and thrilling a final as has been seen for some years. A goal down almost before they had time to take in the twin towers, the Sky Blues twice hit back to equalize. Their achievement in going on to win was a massive tribute to the transformation effected by the partnership of managing director George Curtis and chief coach John Sillett at Highfield Road.

Spurs, successful in all seven of their previous FA Cup finals, made the perfect start, taking the lead after only two minutes, almost inevitably through Clive Allen. But Bennett put Coventry level seven minutes later, spinning and scoring from close range.

With Hoddle's party tricks and Waddle's incisive running regularly threatening to tear Coventry apart, Spurs took a deserved lead again four minutes before the interval, when a flighted Hoddle free-kick was deflected by Kilcline past his own keeper. Houchen, however, put Coventry on terms again after 62 minutes, with a diving header from a pass that the increasingly influential Bennett curled beautifully behind the Spurs defence.

The winner came early in extra time when Mabbutt deflected a driven McGrath cross in a looping arc over Clemence's straining fingers into the goal — and the history books.

Keith Houchen heads a spectacular second equalizer for Coventry.

Big Mac indigestible on Wearside

LAWRIE MCMENEMY finally resigned his Sunderland job on 16 April after a season of recriminations and sniping, and a financial crisis at the club that forced him to take a huge cut in salary. The former Southampton manager, who brought great prosperity and success to the south coast club, never got off the ground on Wearside. He was hailed as a messiah when he arrived at Sunderland 22 months ago, but from the start was under the intense pressure of being expected to restore the club to their former glories in the top echelon.

After all, he appeared to be the perfect manager they had been seeking for 20 years, a man of the North-East, steeped in tradition, who could feel the footballing pulse of the area. Despite his charisma and his public appeal, however, Mr McMenemy, 50, could not find the magic formula on the field, and he leaves Roker Park with Sunderland closer to the Third Division than the First.

Lawrie McMenemy (left): failed to deliver.

Ten years for Chelsea soccer thugs

TWO RINGLEADERS of a gang of Chelsea football hooligans who plotted a six-year campaign of soccer violence at grounds across the country were each jailed for 10 years at Inner London Crown Court on 11 May. Three other members of the mob, known as the "Chelsea Headhunters", were sentenced to a total of 18 years for their part in the violent outbreaks that left many victims scarred for life.

Judge Shindler QC, whose hobbies listed in Who's Who include watching soccer, told the five they were "ruthless, violent and nasty" men who used football as an excuse or a platform for violence.

The five, who were trapped by "Operation Own Goal", in which six undercover officers infiltrated the gang, were convicted at the end of an 18-week trial costing £3 million. They had a total of 32 previous convictions, almost all for violence and threatening behaviour, several associated with soccer.

Violence in Italy is no surprise

SOCCER HOOLIGANISM, still referred to in much of Europe as the "English disease", is painfully rife elsewhere on the Continent, as the Italian police will bear out after serious disturbances sparked by results at the top and bottom of their First Division.

Supporters of leaders Napoli went on a rampage in historic Verona after their team's shock 3–0 defeat, and there were 38 arrests. And after Sampdoria's win at Ascoli that virtually condemned the home side to relegation, it was an hour before the visitors could leave their dressing-room. In battles outside the stadium, several police were injured, and a bus carrying Sampdoria fans was damaged by stones.

These events are most unlikely to come as any surprise, however, to anyone who witnessed the monstrous behaviour of the Juventus fans during the Heysel Stadium disaster in Brussels two years ago.

Vintage Porto are the pride of Portugal

PORTO REPAIRED the recently tarnished image of Portuguese football with a thrilling comeback against Bayern Munich in the European Cup final to win the country's first trophy for 25 years.

In the Prater Stadium, Vienna, packed with 60,000 enthralled fans, Porto wiped away the bitter memories of the financial wranglings and dissension that marred Portugal's World Cup campaign. They gave a display of tenacity and rare skill matched by exhilarating pace, epitomized by the talented Futre. And they clawed their way back into the match in three remarkable second-half minutes. With Bayern Munich, a goal up through a Kogl diving header in the 25th minute, seemingly cruising towards their fourth European Cup success, Porto conjured up an equalizer by their little-known Algerian winger Rabah Madjer, whose only claim to fame was a goal scored for his country in their 1982 World Cup triumph over West Germany. His goal against Bayern came in the 77th minute, when he took the German defence by surprise with a delightful back-heel into the net.

The celebrations were so boisterous that the Algerian limped away in need of treatment, and only just returned in time to play a part in Porto's winner. He sprinted past the tiring Winkelhofer, such an influence in the first half, before crossing a beautiful pass to the far post, where the unmarked substitute Juary volleyed home gleefully. The shocked West German champions never recovered.

Bayern keeper Pfaff can't prevent Juary from scoring Porto's winner.

FOOTBALL FOCUS

- The Rous Cup took the form of a three-cornered tournament this season, and was won by Brazil, who drew with England at Wembley and beat Scotland at Hampden Park.
- Scarborough, champions of the GM Vauxhall Conference, became the first club to win automatic promotion to the Football League.
- The Football League have agreed to allow two substitutes per team in the coming season.
- Because of two technical irregularities in the applications, 26 Liverpool fans won High Court orders in April blocking their extradition to Belgium to face manslaughter charges arising from the 1985 Heysel disaster.
- Promotion and relegation play-offs took place at the end of the season, in which Division One was reduced by one club to 21 and Division Two increased to 23. The last promotion place in each division was contested by the three clubs just below the automatic promotion spots and the club in the division above just above the automatic relegation spots. The four clubs played home-and-away semi-finals and finals.

Cup-tired Dundee United in vain fight-back

DUNDEE UNITED became the latest British team to be unable to overcome the difficulties of mounting a double cup campaign when they were beaten on aggregate goals by Gothenburg in the UEFA Cup final. Just four days after losing the Scottish FA Cup final against St Mirren, they found it impossible to defeat the highly efficient Swedish side at Tannadice Park. Rarely were they able to reproduce the passion and determination that had helped them overcome the formidable talents of Barcelona and Borussia Moenchengladbach in previous rounds.

United's hopes of crowning what had been an exciting and exhausting season by becoming the first Scottish club to win the UEFA Cup all but disappeared after 22 minutes. For that's how long it took Lennard Nilsson to score the crucial away goal to add to the Pettersson winner in the first leg a fortnight ago. Now United needed three goals. When they got one of them, on the hour, through Clark, they suddenly shook off the weariness of the 66 games they have played this season, and Clark's ability in the air gave Hysen an uncomfortable time. Indeed, he found Gallacher with a header just six yards out, but he could not keep his shot down. The ball flew over the bar, and with it went United's hopes.

Gothenburg's 'keeper Wernersson celebrates

FINAL SCORE

Football League
Division 1: Everton
Top scorer: Clive Allen (Tottenham Hotspur) 33
Division 2: Derby County
Division 3: Bournemouth
Division 4: Northampton Town
Footballer of the Year: Clive Allen (Tottenham Hotspur)

FA Cup Final
Coventry City 3 Tottenham H 2
(after extra time)

League Cup Final
Arsenal 2 Liverpool 1

Scottish League
Premier Division: Rangers
Top scorer: Brian McClair (Celtic) 35
Division 1: Morton
Division 2: Meadowbank Thistle
Footballer of the Year: Brian McClair (Celtic)

Scottish FA Cup Final
St Mirren 1 Dundee United 0
(after extra time)

Scottish League Cup Final
Rangers 2 Celtic 1

European Cup Final
Porto 2 Bayern Munich 1

Cup-Winners' Cup Final
Ajax Amsterdam 1 Lokomotiv Leipzig 0

UEFA Cup Final
IFK Gothenburg beat Dundee United 1–0, 1–1

European Footballer of the Year 1986
Igor Belanov (Dynamo Kiev & USSR)

Leading European Scorer (Golden Boot)
Rodion Camataru (Dinamo Bucharest) 44

World Club Championship
Porto (Portugal) 2 Penarol (Uruguay) 1
(after extra time)

England double scorer Robson challenges Maradona.

League win hands down

THE FOOTBALL League launched their centenary season in just about the best way possible before a crowd of 61,000 at Wembley on 8 August. Their representative side beat the impressive array of talent from around the world, assembled by Barcelona manager Terry Venables, by 3–0 in an interesting, if not wildly exciting, game. The goals were scored by Bryan Robson, who got the first and last, and Norman Whiteside, one of a horde of substitutes introduced in the second half, six by the League and seven by the Rest.

Before the start, the players were introduced to the crowd individually, American Super Bowl style, and predictably Diego Maradona emerged to a storm of booing, while the loudest cheers were reserved for another World star, Gary Lineker of Barcelona and England. The presentation of the players to the guest of honour was hardly routine, either. The celebrity in question, the legendary Pele, was genuinely moved by the experience, and stopped to embrace players in the line-ups.

The star of the show was not Maradona, the best player in the world at the moment and costing the League around £1,000 a minute for his appearance, but his predecessor in that role, the now retired Frenchman Michel Platini. While Maradona looked short of full match fitness, Platini stroked the ball around magnificently. Despite Robson's two goals, the pick of the League team was Neil Webb, the young Nottingham Forest midfield player. His adventurous, imaginative play did his prospects of winning his first full cap no harm at all.

Robson scored the first goal after 23 minutes, a far-post header from a long Sansom centre. The second goal, in 59 minutes, was an all-Irish affair, made by the Republic's Liam Brady for the North's Whiteside, while the third goal, which finished the contest two minutes from time, was an all-Manchester United production — made by Whiteside for Robson.

Barclays bank on fans in new deal

THE FOOTBALL League erased the nightmare of the ill-conceived Today newspaper sponsorship by unveiling, on 13 August, that £4.5 million backing for the next three years would be undertaken by Barclays Bank. Amid the delight at the speed with which they have managed to attract a major sponsor, League president Philip Carter warned of the threat to the deal posed by hooligans. Barclays chairman John Quinton confirmed that the Bank would have a get-out clause, as they would not wish to be associated with anything that "led to blood running in the streets".

Hopefully, much of the money will go to ensure that those smaller clubs in need of financial assistance will stay viable.

Silent Souness suspended

GLASGOW RANGERS player-manager Graeme Souness gave his impression of a petulant schoolboy when, with the inevitable "minder" in tow, he emerged from the Scottish FA headquarters on 24 September with his five-match suspension. All media questions were ignored as he thrust his hands into his pockets, whistled softly to himself and stared resolutely at the ground. No doubt his ghost-writer will soon be apprised of his views on the punishment, but he should consider himself lucky that the disciplinary committee took the easy option and dealt with him as a player rather than a manager.

His third dismissal in 14 months was for an offence committed in the impassioned environment of last month's "old firm" match against Celtic — a foul against opposing striker Billy Stark — and was compounded by his subsequent verbal abuse of the match referee.

Logic suggests that Souness should be basking in the glory of last season's League and Cup double. Instead, angered by insults — either real or imagined — he has adopted a hostile stance that overshadows the good things, such as regular capacity crowds, despite some erratic League results, and this week's arrival in the Skol Cup final.

Roast Turkey on England's menu again

HAVING ROASTED Turkey 8–0 in Istanbul three years ago, in a World Cup qualifier, England staged a repeat performance for the Wembley fans on 14 October. The unquenchable thirst of Gary Lineker for international goals, the rejuvenated talents of John Barnes and the youthful promise of Neil Webb emphatically atoned for the miserable performance in the goalless draw in Izmir last year. The goals, four in each half, came from Barnes (two), Lineker (three), Robson, Beardsley and Webb, entertaining the meagre 42,000 crowd. But they are irrelevant in the context of qualifying for West Germany, as Yugoslavia's 3–0 demolition of Northern Ireland in Sarajevo means England must earn at least a draw when they go to Belgrade next month if they are to be sure of reaching the European finals.

Lineker (left) and Barnes: five goals between them against Turkey.

Spurs in Vale of anguish

Ray Walker, scorer of Port Vale's first goal, runs into space.

PROUD PORT VALE capped Tottenham's miserable season with the first major FA Cup upset, producing a memorable 2–1 fourth-round victory that was surprisingly easier than the scoreline would suggest.

Everything went wrong for Spurs on an occasion Port Vale will never forget, as they took full advantage of the Londoners' apathy. Ray Walker, a £12,000 buy from Aston Villa, sparked off Vale's win with a superbly hit 25-yard drive in the 12th minute from Phil Sproson's defence-splitting pass, and 12 minutes later he returned the compliment for Sproson to add a second. As might be expected, Vale went onto the defensive in the second half, and Spurs pulled one back in the 64th minute when Neil Ruddock went up into the attack and atoned for earlier defensive gaffes by heading in from Waddle's free-kick, but it was to no avail.

Tottenham de-Pleated

DAVID PLEAT RESIGNED on 23 October after 17 months as Tottenham manager, following allegations in a national newspaper concerning his private life. It came on the day the newspaper published a second set of allegations that Mr Pleat had been questioned by the police about a kerb-crawling incident. The initial revelations in The Sun last June referred to incidents said to have occurred during his reign at Luton. At the time, Spurs chairman Irving Scholar stood by Mr Pleat. This time, however, the club presumably felt they had to protect their good name.

It is sad for Mr Pleat, who always appeared to have the ideal credentials for managing the fortunes of a club like Spurs or, ultimately, even his country. He joined Spurs on the dismissal of Peter Shreeves in the summer of 1986, and took them to the FA Cup final in his first season. Tottenham are expected to go for ex-Barcelona manager and their former star Terry Venables, at present on holiday in the United States, to take over from Mr Pleat.

England throw down gauntlet to Europe's best

ENGLAND FULFILLED the hopes not only of their much-criticized manager, Bobby Robson, but of the entire footballing nation with one of their finest performances, when they beat Yugoslavia 4–1 in Belgrade on 11 November to clinch their place in the European Championship finals. The systematic, skilful destruction of a highly-rated Yugoslav team will have sent shock waves through Europe, and already the bookmakers have made them second favourites, behind West Germany, the host country.

Needing a point to be sure of joining the seven other finalists, England achieved that and more in the space of 24 invigorating minutes. In that time, Peter Beardsley, John Barnes, Bryan Robson and Tony Adams scored the goals that stunned Yugoslavia and left 60,000 partisan fans howling derision at their own team. But for later generosity in front of goal and the bravery of substitute keeper Radaca, who replaced the unfortunate Ravnic, Yugoslavia might have been more embarrassed before they gained a consolation goal 10 minutes from time, by Katanec. It was the only goal England conceded in their six matches, having scored 19.

They will be joined in West Germany by the Republic of Ireland, who have to thank Scotland, out of it themselves, for winning in Bulgaria to secure their place. Wales, however, missed several chances before finally going down 2–0 in Czechoslovakia, so Denmark qualify from Group 6.

Tony Adams almost has his head taken off in scoring number four.

Sharp's the word for Toffeemen, with a Cup hat-trick

AFTER CALLING ON every ounce of courage, determination and experience merely to stay alive in the first three matches of their FA Cup third-round thriller with Sheffield Wednesday, Everton took an unbelievable and unbreakable grip on the third replay in 45 minutes of dominant football. There had rarely been anything to choose between the two in-form First Division teams in the previous encounters, which had all ended 1–1, so a packed Hillsborough watched in utter disbelief as, after seven hours, the rampant League champions secured another Goodison game — this time against Middlesbrough, on Saturday — with five well-taken goals, all scored in the first half.

Leading scorer Graeme Sharp was the chief assassin for the Toffeemen, with three goals past Hodge, a former Everton goalkeeper, and the others were scored by Heath and Snodin. Wednesday were left to reflect that it might have been so different had Colin West taken an outstanding chance after only 20 seconds.

Everton spoil 'pool party

WAYNE CLARKE, whose elder brother Allan helped to write Leeds's unbeaten 29-match run at the start of the 1973–74 season into the record books, guaranteed that it would not be obliterated by Liverpool at Goodison Park on Sunday, 20 March. Fuelled by local pride, and bolstered by an atmosphere resembling that of an FA Cup final, Everton, for the second time this season, demonstrated that, brilliant as Kenny Dalglish's side may be, they are not invincible. Clarke's 14th-minute goal, watched by Allan, ended a magnificent run that began on a sunlit afternoon at Highbury last August, and had by the dark days of this winter laid waste to the challenge offered by the rest of the First Division.

Everton knew this was the last chance they had of making any impact on a season in which they will almost certainly be called on to pack up the Championship trophy and send it across Stanley Park to Anfield. They went out for an early lead, they got it, and they defended it efficiently, if sometimes desperately, for the remainder of the game.

It will be a great consolation to Everton and their supporters, who milled onto the pitch to celebrate the final whistle, that, with this victory and October's win in the Littlewoods Cup at Anfield, they have inflicted the only two defeats thus far in Liverpool's all-conquering season.

Keeping it in the family: Wayne Clarke scores to end Liverpool's great run.

Court convictions follow on-field trouble: Woods and Butcher guilty

RANGERS AND ENGLAND soccer stars Chris Woods and Terry Butcher were found guilty on 15 April at a Glasgow Sheriff Court of disorderly conduct and breach of the peace on the field of play. The two players were fined, Woods £500 and Butcher £250. Another Rangers and England player, Graham Roberts, walked free on a not proven verdict, while Scottish striker Frank McAvennie, the only Celtic player to be charged as a result of the goalmouth fracas at a Rangers-Celtic game last October, was found not guilty.

The Glasgow police clearly detected a connection between trouble on the pitch and subsequent violence on the terraces; consequently, they had every right to prosecute. Shrewsbury magistrates had taken a similar view 24 hours earlier, when Swindon's Chris Kamara was fined £1,200, and ordered to pay £250 compensation, for causing grievous bodily harm to Shrewsbury striker Jim Melrose in a Second Division match last February.

The conviction of the two England footballers will further damage their country's reputation abroad, which has been badly tarnished by a list of previous incidents.

Ferguson claims refs are intimidated at Anfield

AFTER MANCHESTER United's epic recovery at Anfield to draw 3–3 with 10 men, manager Alex Ferguson launched a ferocious attack on the effect of referees of the "intimidating" Anfield atmosphere. His comments, while conducting an interview on local radio, sparked a harsh verbal exchange with Liverpool manager Kenny Dalglish. Mr Ferguson, clearly upset by the sending-off of defender Colin Gibson for a foul on Nicol, his second bookable offence, reckoned Steve McMahon was getting away with committing the same fouls all afternoon.

"I can now understand why clubs come away from here having to bite their tongues, knowing they have been done by referees," he said. "I am not getting at this referee. It is the whole intimidating atmosphere and the monopoly Liverpool have enjoyed here for years that gets to them eventually." At one stage, Mr Dalglish, who was carrying his six-week-old daughter, suggested the interviewer would get more sense if he spoke to the baby, to which Mr Ferguson responded with a couple of well-chosen words. All this should not detract, however, from an enthralling match in which Liverpool seemed to have restored normal service after losing only their second League match two days earlier at Forest. They shrugged off the effects of conceding a second-minute goal to Robson, and 45 minutes later were 3–1 up, with goals from Beardsley, Gillespie and McMahon.

Alex Ferguson tries to make his point.

When Gibson was sent off after an hour, there seemed very little chance that United would avert a thrashing, let alone preserve their eight-year run without defeat at Anfield. But they came storming back with a second goal from Robson after 65 minutes and a coolly taken equalizer from Strachan 12 minutes later. Liverpool, who would have sewn up their 17th title had they won their two Easter matches, will now have to wait a little longer.

Luton hit Littlewoods jackpot

BRIAN STEIN ADDED to Wembley's endless tradition of romance and high drama as Luton produced a most remarkable finish to the Littlewoods Cup final. Only 14 seconds separated Arsenal from extra time when Stein scored to write himself into the stadium's folklore and give Luton their first major trophy in their 98-year history. But if you're looking for a hero, then surely Luton's stand-in keeper Andy Dibble must be the prime candidate. Not only did he have a brilliant match, keeping Arsenal at bay when they were very much on top, but he saved Winterburn's penalty kick when Luton were 2–1 down with less than 10 minutes left.

That was the turning point of the game, or at least a critical one. For this was a game full of twists, of ifs and buts, and meaningful substitutions. Luton, complete underdogs — more so than Arsenal were last year when they shocked Liverpool — took the lead against a surprisingly hesitant Arsenal after only 13 minutes. And they nobly protected it until Hayes, going on after an hour for last year's galvanizing substitute Groves, soon scrambled Smith's cross in. Then Smith scored and Arsenal hit bar and post as they began to overpower tiring Luton. And when Rocastle escaped Johnson's clutches for once and was brought down by Donaghy in the box, Luton were looking dead and buried.

But Luton, who had gambled on the inexperience of Black and the rustiness of Hill and Preece, found new spirit and an untapped reservoir of stamina from Dibble's magnificent save. Caesar, like his Roman namesake, was caught unawares, in front of goal, and Wilson took advantage to equalize. The amazing Ricky Hill, in his first game since breaking a leg on Boxing Day, drove Luton forward. Ashley Grimes, who had gone on for Preece after 76 minutes, took the ball down the right and somehow contrived to cross it with the outside of his left foot, surprising Arsenal so that Stein could rifle the ball in.

It was a breathtaking finish, and left Luton nurturing a dream of possible European competition, while Arsenal are still searching for a route out of Liverpool's shadow.

Dibble makes his crucial penalty save from Winterburn.

Wimbledon's Cup in safe keeping

WIMBLEDON CAUSED the biggest FA Cup final upset since Sunderland beat Leeds 15 years ago when they gave an extraordinary display of defiance against League champions Liverpool and beat them 1–0. A Southern League club only 11 years ago, they were meant to be the whipping boys as the Merseysiders went looking for their second League and Cup "double" in three years. But they rarely allowed their opponents the space to play their fluent, attacking football, and when Liverpool did get through, brave Dave Beasant was there to thwart them, with some remarkable stops in the first half and a penalty save — the first ever in a Wembley FA Cup final — in the second. Oddly enough, 29-year-old Beasant lives within sight of the famous twin towers.

He played a true captain's part as the unpretentious South London club snatched a goal in the 36th minute — a Sanchez header from Wise's free-kick — and then denied Liverpool the space they needed to break down their stubborn defence. They frustrated Liverpool without resorting to much of the rough stuff that has become their stock in trade. True, Vinny Jones did clatter into Steve McMahon early in the game, but that was the only nasty tackle. There were no real excuses for Liverpool, although they could point to the incident in the first half when the referee blew for a foul on Beardsley before he recovered to chip the ball over Beasant into the net.

As in the Littlewoods Cup, the crisis for the underdogs was the penalty. Beasant, at 6ft 4in, is a daunting obstacle. But Aldridge, the League's leading scorer, had successfully converted 11 penalties this season. He stroked the ball low and firmly towards the inside of Beasant's left-hand post, but the keeper launched his huge frame sideways and clawed the ball away. This was after 61 minutes, and there was still much to do. Liverpool rang the changes, bringing on Johnston and Molby for Aldridge and Spackman in a desperate attempt to find a way through. But they could not raise their game enough to deprive Wimbledon of the most wonderful moment in their short history as a Football League club.

Beasant reaches out to paw Aldridge's penalty to safety.

Jubilant Irish leave England huge task

JACK CHARLTON, who helped England conquer the footballing world 22 years ago, has almost guaranteed that they will not this season be crowned champions of Europe. In Stuttgart, the team he created provided the Republic of Ireland with their most glorious, and unexpected, triumph and left England struggling to stay in the European Championship.

Ray Houghton, a Scot by birth and a footballer moulded by Liverpool, headed England towards defeat in the sixth minute of their opening match in Group 2. Houghton's goal, his first in 16 internationals and only the second headed goal of his career, was enough to beat England. Their failure to equalize, despite constant pressure, was due to a combination of Bonner's heroics in goal and Lineker's uncharacteristic failure to convert the chances that his nose for an opening made for him.

As Bonner made one more acrobatic save in the dying minutes from late substitute Hateley, the massive Irish contingent began to celebrate in and around the ground, and England were left to reflect on their afternoon of missed opportunity. They cannot feel confident about their prospects against Holland and the USSR.

Houghton heads the Republic's shock winner against England.

Chelsea go down fighting

A SINGLE GOAL at Stamford Bridge against Middlesbrough was not enough to keep Chelsea in the First Division as they lost the play-off final on aggregate. But more serious to English football as a whole is the damage their rioting fans might have done to the cause of England's return to European club competition. While English fans in Lausanne were passing the "Swiss test", in the knowledge that any misbehaviour at the friendly which England won 1–0 might result in their team being replaced in the European Championship by Yugoslavia, Chelsea's thugs were destroying all the goodwill built up over the past season.

The initial pitch invasion, according to Chelsea chairman Ken Bates, was of Middlesbrough fans wishing to congratulate their team. But the so-called Chelsea supporters needed no encouragement, and a rampaging mob swarmed onto the field. Innocent fans were beaten up, ambulancemen were attacked with stones and bottles, one policeman was knocked unconscious and another taken to hospital. In all, there were 102 arrests.

Sad scenes at Stamford Bridge.

FOOTBALL FOCUS

- New Huddersfield manager Malcolm Macdonald saw his team trounced 10–1 by Manchester City at Maine Road on 7 November, with three players scoring hat-tricks: Paul Stewart, Tony Adcock and David White. It was a record defeat for Huddersfield, who were relegated at the end of the season.
- The Scottish League (Skol) Cup final was settled on penalties for the first time on 25 October, when Rangers and Aberdeen finished level at 3–3 after extra time. Rangers won the shoot-out 5–3.
- Rangers signed 33-year-old Trevor Francis from Italian club Atalanta on 5 August to bring their complement of English players up to seven.
- Southampton's Alan Shearer, at 17 years 240 days, became the youngest player ever to score a First Division hat-trick, in their 4–2 defeat of Arsenal on 9 April.
- On 5 September, Third Division Chesterfield, the only side in the League not yet to have conceded a goal after five games, visited Gillingham and went down 10–0.

FINAL SCORE

Football League
Division 1: Liverpool
Top scorer: John Aldridge (Liverpool) 26
Division 2: Millwall
Division 3: Sunderland
Division 4: Wolverhampton Wanderers
Footballer of the Year: John Barnes (Liverpool)

FA Cup Final
Wimbledon 1 Liverpool 0

League Cup Final
Luton Town 3 Arsenal 2

Scottish League
Premier Division: Celtic
Top scorer: Tommy Coyne (Dundee) 33
Division 1: Hamilton Academical
Division 2: Ayr United
Footballer of the Year: Paul McStay (Celtic)

Scottish FA Cup Final
Celtic 2 Dundee United 1

Scottish League Cup Final
Rangers 3 Aberdeen 3
(after extra time)
Rangers won 5–3 on penalties

European Cup Final
PSV Eindhoven 0 Benfica 0
(after extra time)
PSV Eindhoven won 6–5 on penalties

Cup-Winners' Cup Final
Mechelen 1 Ajax Amsterdam 0

UEFA Cup Final
Bayer Leverkusen beat Espanol 0–3, 3–0
Bayer Leverkusen won 3–2 on penalties

European Footballer of the Year 1987
Ruud Gullit (AC Milan & Holland)

Leading European Scorer (Golden Boot)
Tanju Colak (Galatasaray) 39

World Club Championship
Nacional (Uruguay) 2 PSV Eindhoven 2
Nacional won 7–6 on penalties

Dutch are the masters of Europe

SOCCER SOUNDBITES

"Both teams played football of the future, and they deserved to be in the European Championship final."

RINUS MICHELS,
Holland's manager.

TWO SUPERB GOALS by Gullit and Van Basten, and a penalty save by Van Breukelen, gave Holland the 2–0 victory they so richly deserved in the European Championship final against the USSR. Holland's triumph, won by playing entertaining and exciting football, is a tribute to their retiring supremo Rinus Michels. Having avenged their 1974 World Cup final defeat by Germany, when Michels was also in charge, with their splendid win in the semi-final at Hamburg, Holland returned to the Olympic Stadium at Munich to exorcize that memory completely.

Marco van Basten, who travelled to Germany as a reluctant substitute and played only 33 minutes in the opening match when they lost to the Soviets, confirmed himself as player of the tournament. Having stunned England with a hat-trick and scored Holland's last-gasp winner against the Germans, he turned in another dazzling performance. After 33 minutes, he headed a cross back into the centre for his Milan team-mate Ruud Gullit to strike a perfect header past Soviet keeper Dassayev.

Then, eight minutes into the second half, he produced the crowning moment of the Championship, a masterpiece of a goal. Arnold Muhren, the former Ipswich and Manchester United midfield star giving a fine display to mark his international swan-song, swung over a long cross, beyond the far post, and there was Van Basten to strike the most perfect right-foot volley from the narrowest of angles past the startled Dassayev.

It could have developed into an exhibition, but the Soviets raised their game and threw themselves into the attack. Belanov flicked the ball onto a post in a goalmouth scramble, and then Van Breukelen recklessly and unnecessarily dived across an opponent to concede a penalty after 57 minutes. But the former Nottingham Forest keeper made amends by blocking Belanov's spot-kick. The crisis was over, and Holland, somewhat unlucky losers in the World Cup finals of both 1974 and 1978, marched on to their first major triumph in international football.

Gullit and Van Basten celebrate the latter's goal against England.

Van Basten's breath-taking volley clinches the Championship.

FINAL SCORE

EUROPEAN CHAMPIONSHIP 1988

Group 1

West Germany	1	Italy	1
Spain	3	Denmark	2
West Germany	2	Denmark	0
Italy	1	Spain	0
West Germany	2	Spain	0
Italy	2	Denmark	0

	P	W	D	L	F	A	P
W. Germany	3	2	1	0	5	1	5
Italy	3	2	1	0	4	1	5
Spain	3	1	0	2	3	5	2
Denmark	3	0	0	3	2	7	0

Group 2

Rep. Ireland	1	England	0
USSR	1	Holland	0
Holland	3	England	1
Rep. Ireland	1	USSR	1
Holland	1	Rep. Ireland	0
USSR	3	England	1

	P	W	D	L	F	A	P
USSR	3	2	1	0	5	2	5
Holland	3	2	0	1	4	2	4
Rep. Ireland	3	1	1	1	2	2	3
England	3	0	0	3	2	7	0

SEMI-FINALS

Holland	2	West Germany	1
USSR	2	Italy	0

FINAL

Holland	2	USSR	0

Munich, 25 June 1988. Attendance 72,308.

Holland: Van Breukelen, Van Aerle, Van Tiggelen, Wouters, Koeman R, Rijkaard, Vanenburg, Gullit, Van Basten, Muhren, Koeman E (Scorers: Gullit, Van Basten)
USSR: Dassayev, Khidiatulin, Aleinikov, Mikhailichenko, Litovchenko, Demianenko, Belanov, Gotsmanov (Baltacha), Protasov (Pasulko), Zavarov, Rats

England face total ban from foreign football

FOLLOWING VIOLENT clashes between German, Dutch and English fans on 15 June in Dusseldorf, where Holland beat England 3–1 to put them out of the European Championship, and further disturbances the next night in Frankfurt involving German and English mobs, the FA have withdrawn their request to UEFA for the return of English clubs to European competition. At the same time, after an emergency Downing Street "summit" on soccer hooliganism, Home Secretary Douglas Hurd announced a draconian five-point plan to crack down on soccer hooliganism, which incorporates a possible withdrawal of the England team from international matches, including the World Cup. Other proposed measures are powers for the courts to confiscate passports, a membership card scheme for all football supporters — Prime Minister Margaret Thatcher is a strong supporter of this idea — a review of the licensing laws and increased police intelligence gathering.

With over 200 English fans detained in Germany after the disgraceful scenes of violence, the FA decided to act quickly and pre-empt a possible worldwide ban. They felt, anyway, that there was little chance, in the current climate, of the three-year club ban being lifted, and they did not want to prejudice any further the very existence of the national side. They have also cancelled England's scheduled trip to Italy in September.

On the football front, England manager Bobby Robson is ignoring the hysterical demands from certain quarters for his resignation, and is even money with the bookmakers to remain in charge for start of the World Cup qualifying competition — that is, if England are not thrown out of it. Meanwhile, the Republic of Ireland's supremo, Jack Charlton, will return to a hero's welcome whether or not his team qualify for the European semi-finals in their last match, against Holland.

Spurs break transfer record for Gascoigne

PAUL GASCOIGNE, 21, became England's first £2 million footballer when he signed for Tottenham from Newcastle United on 7 July. The previous record fee paid by a British club was the £1.9 million Liverpool shelled out for Peter Beardsley last summer, also from Newcastle. But the fee pales in comparison with the world record £5.5 million AC Milan paid for Dutch star Ruud Gullit last year.

The signing of Gascoigne — who has yet to win a full cap — brings Terry Venables's spending since he took over at White Hart Lane in November to £6.5 million, including £1.7 million for Paul Stewart, signed earlier in the summer from Manchester City, and substantial sums for Paul Walsh, Terry Fenwick and Bobby Mimms. Gascoigne, the PFA Young Player of the Year, has deliberated over his future for months and, although Manchester United made a late attempt to sign him, he decided to join the new-look Tottenham.

Paul Gascoigne, first £2m British signing.

End of TV saga as clubs at last agree to a £44m deal

PFA SECRETARY Gordon Taylor emerged as peacemaker in the long-running television saga, which ended on 8 August when the Football League chairmen agreed to accept the £11 million a year deal from ITV. By dropping the PFA claim from 10 to 5 per cent, giving them £550,000 a year from the deal, still more than double their previous share, Mr Taylor has made it possible for the two sides to reach an agreement. Of the remaining £10,450,000, the First Division will get £7,837,500 and the Second Division £1,306,250, with the same amount being shared by the Third and Fourth.

SOCCER SOUNDBITES

"I'm disappointed that the priority today was football finance other than a solution to football hooliganism."

Sports Minister
COLIN MOYNIHAN,
who arrived at the League meeting to explain the proposals for a national membership scheme and was left waiting for an hour.

Butcher fined £500 for damaging door

ENGLAND CENTRE-BACK Terry Butcher was in trouble again in Scotland, fined £500 by the Scottish FA on 7 November for bringing the game into disrepute. The latest distasteful chapter in Butcher's two-year stint as captain of Rangers arises from an incident following Rangers' 2–1 defeat by Aberdeen last month. He was asked, at an hour-long appearance, how the referee's dressing-room door at Pittodrie came to be damaged. After the hearing, an SFA spokesman said that Butcher had caused the damage by kicking the door. Although the episode had been witnessed by officers of the Grampian Police, who later interviewed the former Ipswich defender, they decided not to take any further action. Butcher was angered in the Aberdeen game by Neal Simpson's tackle on Iain Durrant, which has ended the Scottish international's interest in the season.

Rush back to Anfield

KENNY DALGLISH pulled off the transfer coup of the decade on 18 August when he brought Ian Rush back from Italy, after allowing him to go to Juventus 12 months ago for £3.2 million. No details of the fee or the length of his new contract have been disclosed, but according to Italian sources Liverpool have paid £2.8 million for their 26-year-old Welsh striker, beating the British record fee of £2.5 million paid by Everton for West Ham's Tony Cottee last month.

Juventus decided to let Rush go because they have exceeded their permitted quota of three "imports", and Rush, who has never settled down with the Italian culture and language and has struggled in Italian football, needed no persuasion. So the deal was completed, quietly and without fuss, in five days. This was possible only because of the special relationship that has built up between the two clubs since the tragic events at the Heysel Stadium in 1985. Rush was at pains to praise Juventus for the way they treat non-Italian players, and insisted his spell in Turin, during which he scored 14 goals, had been much more enjoyable than some reports had indicated.

Ian Rush: struggled in Italian football.

European ban lifted... conditionally

THE RETURN OF English clubs to European competition for the 1990-91 season was announced by UEFA on 11 April, but with important conditions. Nearly four years after the Heysel Stadium tragedy that resulted in the ban, UEFA have agreed to end the exile provided that the British government supports a readmission. Their return will also depend on the behaviour of English fans in Italy should the national side qualify to play in the fnals of the 1990 World Cup.

Reaction within the game was muted. The authorities are in a dilemna: they are faced with a measure they desperately do not want — the Football Spectators Bill, which includes a membership card scheme, a condition demanded by the government if they are going to sanction the return — to gain something they desperately do want, European football.

Sealey blunder hands Cup to father and son

LES SEALEY, LUTON'S extrovert and erratic goalkeeper, will probably never be able to explain what possessed him in the 55th minute of the Littlewoods Cup final at Wembley. Whatever his excuse, there is no denying that his rash action in bringing down Steve Hodge and conceding a penalty tilted the balance of the match in favour of the Clough family. Suddenly, Nottingham Forest, running rapidly out of ideas, were handed the most comfortable route to winning the Cup, and so collecting their first domestic trophy of the decade.

Nigel Clough, calmness personified, took one pace and stroked the ball into the centre of the net — and the course of the game changed there and then. Luton, watched by Andy Dibble, the keeper whose penalty save turned the match in their favour last year, became the second successive holders to reach Wembley again but fail to retain their trophy. It was such a terrible waste, for until that moment Luton had outthought a Forest side who had spent the first half struggling to come to terms with Harford and Wegerle. Harford's height was unsettling for Terry Wilson and Walker, and Luton capitalized on it. After 36 minutes of inconclusive sparring, Danny Wilson sent over a perfect cross following a corner, and Harford barely needed to lift himself off the turf to head Luton in front.

Before the penalty. Luton squandered three chances to increase their lead. After it, two further Forest goals in the 70th and 76th minutes put the match out of their reach. First Clough robbed the disappointing Black to find Gaynor, from whose devastating long pass Webb put Forest in front. And it was Gaynor again, on the right, who cut past the Luton defence to cross for Clough's second.

Forest manager Brian Clough, restored to his touchline seat after the FA ban, was always destined to dominate this final. He was a model of good behaviour during the match, but in trying to avoid the spotlight he inevitably attracted even more publicity. Having accepted the cheers and applause of the adoring Forest fans, he promptly disappeared down the tunnel to become the first winning manager at Wembley to miss the presentation of the trophy to his team.

Neil Webb scores goal number two past Les Sealey.

Clough in trouble over clash with fans

Brian Clough: personal crusade against hooligans.

NOTTINGHAM FOREST manager Brian Clough could face police action after allegedly taking the law into his own hands to deal with fans who invaded the pitch after Forest's 5–2 defeat of QPR in the Littlewoods Cup on 18 January. Investigations may be carried further if any of the four home supporters allegedly manhandled makes an official complaint. The FA immediately ordered an inquiry, which could result in a lengthy touchline ban.

This latest incident in a career of controversy has almost certainly put paid to any ambitions Mr Clough might still have had of becoming England manager. Millions of television viewers watched in astonishment as he appeared to punch and grab fans running onto the City Ground to celebrate Forest's victory. He has led a personal crusade against hooligans in the past that has been warmly applauded. He made a citizen's arrest at a Forest game two years' ago, and has remonstrated with his club's fans when they have used obscene chants. In a statement afterwards, he said the the incident was "regrettable", but the action had been taken with the right motive.

Ninety-four fans killed in semi-final horror

NINETY-FOUR FOOTBALL fans, including several children, were killed and about 150 seriously injured at Sheffield on 15 April in Europe's worst soccer tragedy. A senior police officer had ordered a gate to be opened, allowing fans to surge into the Hillsborough ground, and thousands of supporters were crushed on an overcrowded terrace at the FA Cup semi-final between Liverpool and Nottingham Forest.

The dead and injured, who were crowded at the Liverpool end of the ground for the capacity all-ticket game, were buried under falling bodies when hundreds of fans poured into the ground as the game was kicking off. Several children died after being crushed against the security fence, where they had been sent to get a good view. Fans tore down advertising hoardings and perimeter boards and used them as makeshift stretchers until the arrival of the ambulance services.

Apparently, Liverpool fans, frustrated at the time it was taking to get into the Leppings Lane entrance to the ground, began to push towards the turnstiles about ten minutes before kick-off.

To ease the crush, the police opened a big metal gate and the fans surged in. They poured through the the narrow, dark 30-yard tunnel in the centre of the stand, which offered them their first glimpse of the pitch. They careered into the central pens, crushing those at the front, although there was room to accommodate the latecomers in pens to either side. Those unaware of people dying at the front of the terraces pushed forward for a better view of the action. As they did so, more were trampled underfoot and crushed into the perimeter fencing at the bottom of the terraces, which had been put there to prevent hooligans from invading the pitch. Because of the perimeter fencing, few of the spectators could get out, although some managed to climb over the fencing or get through a narrow escape gate onto the pitch. Their plight was not immediately realized by the police inside the ground, but as soon as it was, a policeman ran onto the pitch to get the match stopped, some six minutes after it kicked off. Ten minutes later, the first ambulance arrived.

So for the third time in four years — after the Bradford fire and the Heysel Stadium disaster — the football authorities are left with the onerous task of restoring confidence in the flagging fortunes of Britain's national sport. One thing is clear. In the next few years, football must change its priorities and break away from what Graham Kelly, the Football Association chief executive, describes as "the ritual of standing on the terraces". In simple terms, that means a move towards all-seater stadiums — and quickly.

Makeshift stretchers are used to carry the victims away.

Fans caught in the crush are helped to safety by those in the upper tier of the Leppings Lane Stand.

Liverpool fans jailed for Heysel manslaughter

THE VERDICTS of the long-drawn-out trial in Brussels relating to the Heysel Stadium disaster of 1985 were given on 28 April. Fourteen of the 24 Liverpool fans were found guilty of manslaughter and sentenced to three years' imprisonment, with half of each term suspended. They were also each fined £1,000, with a further three months' jail in default. The cases against the other 10 were dismissed because of insufficient evidence. The accused had spent up to eight months in prison in England and Belgium while awaiting trial, and this will have to be deducted from their sentences. After the verdicts, the guilty were given a fortnight to appeal and allowed to go home.

There did not appear to be any arrangements for the fans to return to serve what remained of their sentences after proceedings described by many involved as a farce, and there was even more confusion to follow when the judges tried to deal with compensation claims totalling up to £10 million lodged by families of those who died in the riot. The court approved a mixture of claims ranging from about £1,500 to £300,000, but it was unclear who would be required to pay compensation.

The judges cleared the Belgian state, Brussels city authorities and UEFA of negligence. UEFA president Jacques Georges, Mayor Herve Brouhon and various other officials also went without censure.

Liverpool's Cup triumph a final tribute

LIVERPOOL DID AT Wembley what they had made up their minds to do 35 days ago, and won the FA Cup as a final tribute to the fans who had died so tragically at Hillsborough following their team. Winning the Cup had become an obsession at Anfield, where the players had immersed themselves totally and selflessly in the mourning for the dead. And the sense of achievement that manager Kenny Dalglish felt at the final whistle was clear for all to see.

With all the earlier doubts as to whether the competition should have been abandoned, or perhaps the Cup presented to Liverpool, it turned out to be the most dramatic final since the Arsenal-Manchester United epic 10 years ago. In this second all-Merseyside clash in four years, Liverpool eventually beat Everton 3–2, but not without some heart-stopping moments and the dramatic intervention of Ian Rush in extra time.

Just when Liverpool appeared to be coasting to victory on the strength of John Aldridge's fourth-minute goal, Everton equalized through midfielder Stuart McCall, one of their substitutes, in the last minute. Rush, the striker who has been searching for his form ever since he returned from Juventus, had gone on for Aldridge, his lookalike, after 72 minutes. And after four minutes of extra time, he showed the doubters that he had lost none of his predatory skills, by controlling a centre from Nicol, turning Ratcliffe quite beautifully and driving the ball into the far corner of the goal.

McCall's second equalizer, eight minutes later, was just as thrilling. When Hansen headed out a Ratcliffe free-kick, McCall volleyed the ball straight back and into the Liverpool net from some 25 yards. But this time, Everton's elation lasted only two minutes. Barnes floated the ball into the centre, and with the subtlest of flicks Rush directed it with his head into the far corner for his second goal, and his fourth in two finals against his Merseyside neighbours.

It was a blow that crushed Everton, and Liverpool would have won handsomely but for Southall's extraordinary saves to deny Houghton, Rush, Barnes and Beardsley. But Liverpool had completed their mission and the first half of what could be a historic and emotional double.

Liverpool substitute Rush scores his second, and winning, goal against Everton.

'Exile' Lineker sets up Barcelona victory

BARCELONA OFFERED Gary Lineker one solitary, meaningful opportunity to remind Europe of his talents in Berne on 10 May, and with it he helped Barcelona win the Cup-Winners' Cup final, their first European trophy in seven barren years. The England goal-poacher has spent a frustrating season in the Catalan city, and once again he was exiled on the right wing by coach Johan Cruyff.

After four minutes on a wet Swiss evening, it was hard to argue with the decision, though, as Lineker left his Sampdoria marker Pari in a tangled, confused heap on the floor, raced clear and, with considerable poise, delivered the crucial pass. The ball travelled perfectly to Roberto, who redirected it to the head of Salinas to score the goal that really decided this contest of Latin styles.

But from then on, when it seemed that Lineker offered the simplest route to their third triumph in this competition, Barcelona ignored him. So they made hard work of a night which should have been a comfortable stroll against a side missing their most accomplished defenders. Eventually, Barcelona clinched the trophy with a second goal, scored in the 79th minute by their substitute full-back Rekarte.

Lineker will not be fooled, however, that this victory will provide him with another year at Barcelona. Mr Cruyff has made it quite clear that they intend to replace him this summer.

Stevens' slip denies Rangers treble

WHILE MERSEYSIDE was battling it out at Wembley, Hampden was hosting another Old Firm episode, with Celtic beating Rangers 1–0 to deny them another domestic treble. Graeme Souness has spent more than £10 million on imported talent — much of it from England — but at the end of the day it was home-grown skills in the shape of Joe Miller that returned the silverware to the East End of Glasgow.

Wee Joe swooped on a disastrous back-pass by England's Gary Stevens four minutes from half-time, and Peter Shilton's understudy Chris Woods was left virtually a spectator as he clipped the ball into the net. As it turned out, that was all that separated the teams, but without doubt Celtic deserved their victory. Even the presence as a second-half substitute of player-manager Souness failed to lift the Ibrox outfit. In the end, the defeat was too much to handle even for veterans such as Terry Butcher, who, like several of his colleagues, wept openly at the final whistle.

Rangers had won the League title by six points from Aberdeen, and beat the Dons 3–2 in a Skol Cup final that was far more exciting than the clash with Celtic. Even though Rangers slipped up at the last hurdle, their domination of the domestic game in Scotland is now so great, and their resources seemingly unlimited, that many people fear for the future of the game in Scotland.

Gunners break Anfield hearts in title decider

IN THE MOST DRAMATIC finish to a Championship race since the formation of the Football League 101 years ago, Arsenal went to Anfield for the last game of a traumatic season and scored the two-goal victory they needed to wrest the title from Liverpool. The game was played on 26 May, in a season extended because of the Hillsborough tragedy. And the crucial second goal, scored by 21-year-old midfielder Michael Thomas, came a minute into injury time.

Thomas broke the hearts of the Liverpool team and their fans when, fed by Alan Smith, he burst through, held off a double challenge and flicked the ball wide of the advancing Grobbelaar. In doing so, he brought to an end Liverpool's remarkable efforts to retain the title they had won nine times in the last 13 years and their hopes of a second League and Cup "double" in four years.

Liverpool had incurred a daunting backlog of fixtures after Hillsborough, and it says much for their courage and professionalism that they were able to put the events of that fateful day behind them, go on to win the Cup, and continue a charge up the First Division table that had seen them close from 19 points behind Arsenal at the end of February to three points in front. Arsenal, on the other hand, had faltered on the run-in, and from being hot favourites were now facing a formidable task. Not only were Liverpool unbeaten since early January, but Arsenal had not won at Anfield for nearly 15 years.

But George Graham's team were undaunted. They reverted to the sweeper system, which allowed them to push their full-backs further forward, and Dixon and Winterburn denied Barnes and Houghton space, driving them deeper into less dangerous positions. With the central back three of O'Leary, Bould and Adams performing tremendously against first Aldridge and Rush and then Aldridge and Beardsley, Arsenal seemed capable of containing Liverpool, who needed only to draw, or lose by one goal, to take the title. But it was not until the 52nd minute that they broke through, Smith heading in a Winterburn free-kick.

Thomas (right) scores the last, historic, goal of the season.

The crowd sensed they were witnessing a little slice of footballing history. Only once before in this century have the top two teams fought out a Championship decider in the last game, and that was in 1952, when Arsenal went to Old Trafford needing to win by seven goals — and lost 6–1. Now, however, they were in with a chance. The 40,000 fans and millions more watching on live television held their breath as Thomas raced through, agonizingly delaying his shot until he could see the whites of the keeper's eyes...

The quality and courage of Arsenal's performance was recognized by the sporting Liverpool fans even in their state of disappointment, as they gave George Graham and his men a standing ovation at the final whistle.

Dutch duo turn on style for Milan

RUUD GULLIT AND Marco van Basten, who last summer helped Holland to conquer Europe, repeated the feat at club level with AC Milan, who beat Steaua Bucharest 4–0 in Barcelona in one of the most spectacular performances seen in a European Cup final for years. Within 46 minutes, the superb skills of this pair of Dutch masters had guaranteed that Milan's 20-year wait for the return of Europe's biggest club prize was over. But it was the style in which they achieved their resounding victory that captivated the fans.

For Gullit, it was a marvellous personal triumph. Five weeks ago he seemed to have little chance of playing, when he was carried off in the 5–0 dismantling of Real Madrid in the semi-final second leg, with a knee injury that required cartilage surgery. He was only 60 per cent fit when he took the field in Barcelona, and had to go off after 59 minutes, but by then the damage was done, and the Dutch duo had shared four goals. The Romanian Army team, surprise winners of the trophy three years ago — when they beat Barcelona on penalties — never reproduced that form. They failed miserably to come to terms with Gullit, who not only scored twice but also hit a post and won everything in the air. Panic spread through the Bucharest defence whenever the ball approached the front pair. Van Basten's second goal, just after the interval, was his 10th of the competition, made for him by Frank Rijkaard, Milan's third great Dutchman.

Gullit (centre) opens the scoring for AC Milan.

Gullit went off to a standing ovation. Had he been fully fit, he and his Milan colleagues might have rivalled the Puskas-Di Stefano show for Real Madrid in the 1960 final.

Lineker puts England in Pole position

ENGLAND'S 3–0 VICTORY over Poland at Wembley in a World Cup qualifier edges them considerably closer to the finals in Italy next summer. It was a long time in coming, and all the while thoughts went back to the Polish visit that frustrated England's World Cup ambitions in 1973. The hero that night for Poland was giant keeper Jan Tomaszewski, but it was fortunate for England that his 6ft 5in protegé, Jaroslav Bako, never threatened to emulate the feats of his mentor. On the contrary, Bako displayed a notable lack of judgement throughout, and committed the crudest of body-checks on Gary Lineker early on, for which he was lucky to be only booked. Players have been dismissed — even at Wembley — for lesser offences.

Lineker, who made a name for himself by scoring all three of England's goals against Poland in the last World Cup, got the vital first-half opener at Wembley, following up to score when his first attempt was blocked. And he helped make the other two, late in the second half, starting the moves that led to Barnes's clean far-post volley and then Webb's clinching goal seven minutes from time.

A job well done: Neil Webb (4) scores England's third goal.

FINAL SCORE

Football League
Division 1: Arsenal
Top scorer: Alan Smith (Arsenal) 23
Division 2: Chelsea
Division 3: Wolverhampton Wanderers
Division 4: Rotherham United
Footballer of the Year: Steve Nicol (Liverpool)

FA Cup Final
Liverpool 3 Everton 2
(after extra time)

League Cup Final
Nottingham Forest 3 Luton Town 1

Scottish League
Premier Division: Rangers
Top scorer: Charlie Nicholas (Aberdeen), Mark McGhee (Celtic) 16
Division 1: Dunfermline Athletic
Division 2: Albion Rovers
Footballer of the Year: Richard Gough (Rangers)

Scottish FA Cup Final
Celtic 1 Rangers 0

Scottish League Cup Final
Rangers 3 Aberdeen 2

European Cup Final
AC Milan 4 Steaua Bucharest 0

Cup-Winners' Cup Final
Barcelona 2 Sampdoria 0

UEFA Cup Final
Napoli beat Stuttgart 2–1, 3–3

European Footballer of the Year 1988
Marco van Basten (AC Milan & Holland)

Leading European Scorer (Golden Boot)
Dorin Mateut (Dinamo Bucharest) 43

World Club Championship
AC Milan (Italy) 1 Atletico Nacional (Colombia) 0
(after extra time)

FOOTBALL FOCUS

- On 26 May, while Arsenal were celebrating their first League triumph for 18 years and Sir Matt Busby his 80th birthday, former Leeds and England manager Don Revie, 61, died after suffering for two years from the incurable motor neurone disease.

- After rejecting a more lucrative move to Monaco, Gary Lineker returned to England on 20 June to join Tottenham on a mere £5,000 a week. The £1.5 million deal with Barcelona included midfielder Nayim, who had been on loan to Spurs.

- Goalkeeper Peter Shilton set a new record for England when he won his 109th cap, against Denmark on 7 June, passing Bobby Moore's total.

- Three brothers — Danny, Rodney and Ray Wallace — appeared for Southampton at the Dell on 22 October, the first time that this has happened in the First Division since Middlesbrough's Carr brothers 68 years ago.

- The format of the end-of-season play-offs was changed this season, so that the ordeal was confined only to teams seeking promotion. In each of the lower divisions, the four clubs just below the automatic promotion places played off for the remaining one in two-legged, home-and-away semi-finals and finals.

- On 1 May Wolves earned promotion to the Second Division by beating Bristol City 2–0, with both goals coming from Steve Bull. Counting all competitions, Bull has now scored exactly 100 goals in two seasons, 48 this time to go with 52 in 1987–88, and despite playing in a lower division he seems likely to gain his first England cap before long.

Palace Wright for Division One

CRYSTAL PALACE strode triumphantly into Division One amid amazing scenes when Ian Wright scored a stunning winner three minutes from the end of time in the second leg of their promotion play-off at Selhurst Park. Wright's carefully placed header capped a magnificent performance from Steve Coppell's team as they clawed back Blackburn's two-goal advantage from the first leg.

In a contest that could not be bettered as a sporting spectacle, Palace remained true to their season-long philosophy and gambled on attack. It was daring, painfully exciting, but above all successful. In the frenzied atmosphere, Palace benefited from an early break, when the prolific Wright scrambled home his first goal after Pardew's cross had caused havoc. Only the heroics of central defender Hendry kept Blackburn from disintegrating, but they stayed ahead on aggregate until just after the interval. Atkins needlessly brought down McGoldrick, and Madden converted the penalty to set up the eventual dramatic finish.

Ian Wright (left) celebrates his promotion-winning goal.

Liverpool go one over the eight at Aldridge farewell party

ANFIELD HAS STAGED some extraordinary matches in its long and glittering history, but few could rival the "farewell party" laid on for departing striker John Aldridge against Crystal Palace on 12 September. Amid amazing scenes as Liverpool achieved their record First Division win of 9–0, Aldridge left the substitutes' bench in the 69th minute to collect his "present".

The prolific Republic of Ireland striker, who with some reluctance was due to complete his £1 million move to Spanish club Real Sociedad the next day, had dreamed of leaving Anfield with another goal to remember. Manager Kenny Dalglish, with a great sense of theatre, decided the moment for that dream to come true was when, with their lead at 5–0, Whelan had been fouled in the penalty area. He replaced Beardsley with Aldridge, who jogged straight to the penalty spot to a standing ovation, and promptly sent Suckling the wrong way with his kick. The Kop went wild. At the final whistle, Aldridge raced to the cheering Kop, pulled off his shirt and boots and threw them to the fans among whom he used to stand. His co-stars on the Liverpool scoresheet, the first time in Football League history that eight players had scored for one team in a single match, were Nicol (two), McMahon, Rush, Gillespie, Beardsley, Barnes and Hysen. It was an awesome performance by a side deprived of the title last season by dint of goals scored, and takes them to the top of the table, above Millwall. The First Division tends to shudder when Liverpool edge in front in the dark days of December. For them to go to the front in the light nights of September is extremely ominous.

John Aldridge: scoring from the spot in his emotional farewell.

SOCCER SOUNDBITES

"I have never been so nervous in my life as when I ran on to take that penalty."

JOHN ALDRIDGE,
on the goal that put Liverpool 6–0 up.

Waddle in surprise £4.5m move to France

OLYMPIQUE MARSEILLE made Spurs an offer they could not refuse — £4.5 million for Chris Waddle — which makes the England striker-cum-winger the third most expensive player in the world. Having rejected Marseille's original bid of £3 million for the Tottenham favourite, manager Terry Venables felt the new offer was too good to turn down for a player approaching his 29th birthday, while it would also be unfair to deny the former Newcastle forward the chance to become a millionaire.

Aware that losing Waddle would weaken Spurs, not to mention upsetting the fans, who had come to idolize a player many White Hart Lane supporters initially booed, Mr Venables promised that the windfall would be used to strengthen the team. However, while no one would doubt Waddle's value in the First Division, it is perhaps surprising that Marseille were willing to pay so much for a player who has never quite established himself at international level, despite his 44 England caps.

Mo Jo crosses the great divide

Maurice Johnston: Rangers' first big-name Catholic.

MAURICE JOHNSTON, who refused to join his former club Celtic in a £1.2 million transfer in June, surprised British football by signing for Glasgow Rangers from Nantes on 10 July in a £1.5 million deal. The fact that the 27-year-old Scottish international striker, who has 28 caps and once played for Watford, turned his back on Celtic to join their arch-rivals Rangers is enough to cause a stir. But inevitably the main talking point is his faith — he is the first high-profile Catholic player signed by the Ibrox club. When player-manager Graeme Souness took over at Rangers three years ago, he vowed that religion would be irrelevant if he thought a player was good enough, and he has kept his word as he takes his spending at Ibrox to £11 million.

The reaction of Rangers supporters to the signing of Johnston remains to be seen. One thing is certain, however: he will not be popular with the Celtic fans, who saw him paraded at Hampden at the Cup final before their deal with Nantes fell through. He will have to show great character, as well as skill, if he is to succeed.

Waddle: millionaire status.

Celtic hit five but still go out

Dziekanowski acclaims one of his four goals — but it was despair for Celtic at the finish.

FOUR GOALS BY their Polish international striker Dariusz Dziekanowski and one by his partner Andy Walker were still not enough to give Celtic victory in a remarkable European Cup-Winners' Cup tie against Partizan Belgrade on 27 September at Parkhead. Unfortunately, a leaky Celtic defence, not aided by the team's impatience to pull back from the 2–1 deficit incurred in the first leg, allowed the Yugoslavs four away goals. As a result, the final 6–6 aggregate score broke down in favour of Partizan.

Never can the 50,000 fans at Parkhead have been through such a night of roller-coaster emotions, as their hopes dipped and then soared with every goal that went in. A first-leg 2–1 away defeat is not a bad result in Europe, but Partizan snatched back that precious away goal after only eight minutes, and Celtic were two goals to the bad. But then Dziekanowski came into the picture, and levelled the overall scores with two opportunist goals, the second just after half-time. At three-all on aggregate and no advantage to either side, now was the time for Celtic to heed the words of manager Billy McNeill and be patient. Five minutes later, however, Partizan scored again, which meant Celtic had to win the match by two clear goals. They soon got one of them, with Dziekanowski's hat-trick, but let Partizan in again — 3–3 on the night. Now the irrepressible Dziekanowski made a goal for Walker, and, with the crowd at fever pitch, hit his fourth with nine minutes to go and made the score 5–3 to Celtic, 6–5 on aggregate.

Oh, the anticlimax, though, when, with the crowd baying for the final whistle, Celtic's defence was split wide open again, and Scepovic scored within 90 seconds of the finish. Sadly, the fans drooped off. The scriptwriter had written an unhappy ending to one of the most amazing games in Celtic's history.

United takeover collapses

PROPERTY DEALER Michael Knighton finally abandoned his dreams of owning Manchester United on 11 October, after long-drawn-out and at times acrimonious negotiations, by agreeing to cancel his £20 million takeover deal. He accused the Press of creating "a Frankenstein that has got out of control" in the image they projected of him, although it would be most unlikely for members of the fourth estate to confuse the good doctor with his creation in that way.

Admittedly, the Press did not treat the boyishly enthusiastic Mr Knighton too reverently when he appeared on the Old Trafford scene in an explosion of razzmatazz. Weeks of speculation about his ability to complete the deal soured his relationship with the Old Trafford board, and at one stage chairman Martin Edwards took out a temporary injunction preventing Mr Knighton from showing financial details of the club to his advisors.

The takeover appeared to be back on course, however, a few days earlier, until the sudden announcement that Mr Knighton had withdrawn his option to buy Mr Edwards's shares in return for a seat on the board as a non-executive director.

Michael Knighton does a turn at Old Trafford in August.

Proud Irish drink to Charlton

THE REPUBLIC of Ireland's 3–0 victory over Northern Ireland in Dublin on 11 October ensured their place in the World Cup finals for the first time — barring the extraordinary twin circumstances of defeat in Malta and a large Hungarian victory in Spain as their qualifying group ends. It is fairly safe to say, then, that the Free State will not wait another month before toasting manager Jack Charlton's outstanding achievement in bringing them such unprecedented success.

A sporting match was played in front of a benign crowd, who put the seedier world of English football to shame as they applauded the opposition from the start. Irish fans had been drinking in city-centre pubs since 7.30 am, but that did not turn them into crazed hooligans. After an anxious start in which the North could have taken the lead, Whelan settled the Republic down with a goal shortly before half-time. Goals from Cascarino and Houghton within 10 minutes of the interval put the result beyond doubt, and the celebrations began.

Taylor Report attacks 'squalid' state of soccer clubs

Hillsborough 1989: chaos and confusion as the dead and dying are laid on the pitch.

LORD JUSTICE TAYLOR'S final report on the Hillsborough disaster was published on 29 January, and featured an ultimatum to the clubs to improve the "squalid" conditions at their grounds and clean up their tarnished image. Acting immediately on the report's recommendations, the government announced that terracing would be banned from all First and Second Division stadiums by August 1994 and in all designated Football League grounds by 1999. The report said crowd behaviour could be linked to the low standard of accommodation at soccer grounds, and that the country's national sport was blighted by old grounds, poor facilities, hooliganism, poor leadership, and fans caged and penned, treated sometimes more like "prisoners of war" than people helping to support a multi-million-pound industry.

The government stressed that the football industry would be responsible for cleaning up its act, and that the bulk of the funds needed for the switch to all-seater stadiums would have to be raised by the clubs. The government would not step in to finance safety measures, despite warnings from MPs that many Third and Fourth Division clubs, and possibly others higher up the scale, would be bankrupted by the cost. The government accepted the rejection of the proposed National Membership Scheme on the grounds of safety and effectiveness.

In all, the 104-page report submitted 76 recommendations to "promote better and safer conditions" at sports grounds. These also included the removal of "prison-type" perimeter fences, the reduction in their height, and more clearly marked gates which should be left unlocked; a review of police operations at grounds, better communications between police and emergency services; the introduction of electronic tagging to keep offenders away from grounds; and the creation of new offences of throwing a missile, chanting obscene or racialist abuse, and invading the pitch without reasonable excuse. It should also be an offence to sell tickets on match day without the club's authority.

For all it should do to improve safety, however, Lord Justice Taylor's report is not entirely satisfactory. While he denies that seating is a panacea, the emphasis he places on it may convince some people otherwise, although hooligans in seats have been known to tear them out to use as weapons. The report criticizes police failure to control the crowd outside Hillsborough, but the behaviour of that crowd has escaped proper analysis. The evidence is that thousands of people, some the worse for drink, created the crush at the Leppings Lane end, provoked by the failure of the FA to administer this fixture properly. And the government must remember that improving safety and eradicating hooliganism inside grounds is only the start. They will need to devise a strategy to combat hooliganism if and when it is shifted away from football.

Lord Justice Taylor said that it is a "depressing and chastening" thought that his report is the ninth official report covering football ground safety and control. Previous investigations had followed deaths at the stadiums of Bradford, Bolton and Ibrox, and the first Cup final at Wembley, in 1923, when miraculously nobody was killed. It is "astounding" that after eight such reports, "95 people could die from overcrowding before the very eyes of those controlling the event".

SOCCER SOUNDBITES

"The years of patching up grounds, of having periodic disasters and narrowly avoiding many others by muddling through on a wing and a prayer, must be over."

LORD JUSTICE TAYLOR

McCoist puts Scotland through

A GOAL JUST BEFORE half-time by Ally McCoist against Norway on 15 November settled Scotland's nerves and took his country on a tidal wave of national fervour through to their fifth successive World Cup finals. With just a draw with Norway needed to put themselves out of reach of France, Scotland's policy of going for a win paid off, and McCoist sent the 64,000 Hampden crowd into raptures when he ran onto a perceptive Malpas through pass and flicked it delightfully over Thorstvedt to put them ahead. It was just as well, because it gave them the luxury of allowing Norway to score a minute from time, when Leighton misjudged a speculative Johnson drive from 45 yards. So Scotland join England and the Republic of Ireland in Italy for the 1990 World Cup.

Ally McCoist celebrates after scoring against Norway.

Palace find 10-goal improvement to beat Liverpool

THE FA CUP semi-final at Villa Park between Crystal Palace and Liverpool was a memorable match for several reasons, not least of which was the result — a 4–3 win for Palace over the team that had humiliated them 9–0 in the League earlier in the season. It was also the best, the most thrilling semi-final seen for years, and the highest scoring one since Manchester United beat Fulham 5–3 in a replay 32 years earlier. And it was played on a Sunday at noon, to accommodate the BBC, who were transmitting both semi-finals live.

Liverpool, the Cup-holders, were riding high again at the top of the First Division, and were the hottest of favourites to beat relegation-troubled Palace. Not that they were taking this game lightly after defeat by Wimbledon in the 1988 final. And they had the best of starts, as Ian Rush glided onto a McMahon pass and beat Nigel Martyn after 14 minutes. But Liverpool, without a replacement striker, had to reshuffle their side when Rush went off shortly afterwards with bruised ribs, and again when they lost centre-back Gary Gillespie at half-time with a groin strain.

Even so, with Palace missing their star striker Wright and Liverpool in firm control, there was no hint of the rush of goals to come after the interval. However, Palace came storming out in the second half and Mark Bright volleyed in a rebound to put them level after just 16 seconds. Now it was Palace's turn to get on top, and they took a deserved lead after 70 minutes when defender Gary O'Reilly scored from close in — his first goal of the season.

If any Palace fans thought this was enough to beat Liverpool, they were in for a rude awakening 11 minutes later, when McMahon equalized and then Barnes scored from the spot after Pemberton foolishly tripped Staunton in the area. Now, it certainly looked like a third final running for Liverpool. Yet Palace, remarkably, after such a crushing double blow, pulled themselves together and, with two minutes left, Andy Gray headed in, with the normally rock-like Liverpool defence in complete disarray. With Palace now rampant, only the cross-bar saved Liverpool before the whistle. The winner came four minutes into the second period, when Liverpool, not for the first time, were found wanting at a set-piece. Central defender Andy Thorn flicked on a near-post corner, and Alan Pardew came in to head Palace into their first final.

A bitter moment for Liverpool as Gray heads a late equalizer.

Souness banned for breaching ban!

THE GRAEME SOUNESS saga continued in Scotland when the Scottish FA imposed a record £5,000 fine on the voluble Rangers manager in May and extended his touchline ban to the end of the 1991–92 season.

Rangers immediately condemned these latest punishments as "draconian" and the use of TV evidence as "deplorable". However, they admitted that he was clearly caught shouting to his players on the pitch from the tunnel area in the League game against Hearts on 17 February. This was in breach of a previous ban, imposed by the Scottish FA along with a £2,000 fine a year ago, for failing to adhere to a previous ban during the Cup semi-final with St Johnstone at Parkhead in April 1989.

Oldham fantastic on plastic: West Ham hammered

UNFASHIONABLE Oldham moved to the brink of their first Wembley appearance with an irresistible display of attacking football to beat fellow Division Two club West Ham 6–0 in the first leg of their Littlewoods League Cup semi-final on the notorious Boundary Park plastic pitch. Oldham have put together an unbeaten run of 32 matches on their artificial surface, and this performance at least equalled their victories over Arsenal and Southampton on the way to what will surely be a place in the final on 29 April.

West Ham were turned into a shambles as Oldham moved the ball around at speed. Oldham's inspiration was Andy Ritchie, their bargain £50,000 buy from Leeds. He scored two to take his Littlewoods tally this season to 10, and has scored in every round.

Andy Ritchie: hot stuff on plastic.

Wright lights up final, but 'Sparky' earns United a replay

Manchester United's Lee Martin (3) scores the only goal in the replay.

A DRAMATIC LATE introduction of the partially fit Ian Wright into the game brought Crystal Palace within seven minutes of winning the FA Cup on their first appearance in the final, but Mark "Sparky" Hughes intervened to earn Manchester United a replay.

Wright has twice broken a leg this season, and his achievement in getting fit enough to claim a seat on the Palace substitutes bench was no small miracle in itself. Manager Steve Coppell gambled on leaving him there for 69 minutes, but when he unleashed the striker he lit up a hitherto undistinguished match.

Bryan Robson had equalized an early O'Reilly goal in the first half, and Hughes had put United ahead after 62 minutes. Wright's two goals were gems in a sea of mediocrity, the first coming with his first significant touch as he destroyed £3 million worth of reputations only three minutes after going on. Both Pallister and Phelan were left floundering as Wright came bursting through from the left and slashed the ball past Leighton in goal. Two minutes into extra time, he scored another superb goal, stealing in at the far post to volley Salako's fine centre into the roof of the net.

But Manchester were not to be denied by Wright's spring-heeled heroics. In the exhausting last period, class began to tell. Ince, Webb, Phelan, Wallace and Hughes, a large part of the £13 million it has cost to build this United team, all came into their own as men capable of deciding the issue. And no United player was more influential than their remarkable captain, Robson, who carried his team along with the sheer force of his intensely competitive nature. United might have scored three times before Webb and Wallace split Palace down the middle and Hughes beat Martyn to earn them a replay.

Wright (partially hidden, left) beats Leighton to put Palace 3–2 ahead in extra time in the first match.

League give police veto on high-risk fixtures

AFTER THE WEEKEND of violence in early May by Leeds supporters in Bournemouth, the Football League, who had insisted, against police advice, that the fixture went on as scheduled, were shamed into giving police the power to veto future fixtures likely to produce a repeat performance.

Leeds's 1–0 win at Dean Court, on the last day of the League season, clinched their promotion and the Second Division title, while at the same time condemned Bournemouth to relegation. More than 5,000 Leeds supporters made the trip, although fewer than half had been allocated tickets. There was violence in the town on the previous night, with nine injuries and 19 arrests. More than an hour before the kick-off, police in riot gear had to charge a huge crowd of Leeds fans, who began pelting them with cans and stones. Cars and shop windows were smashed, and two public houses near the seafront extensively damaged. Amid calls for Leeds to forfeit their place in Division One next season, Bournemouth chairman Jim Nolan demanded the Yorkshire club be made to pay for the orgy of violence that resulted in 104 arrests.

Home Secretary Mr David Waddington has delivered strong public and private rebukes to the Football League for ignoring police requests to reschedule the match from the Bank Holiday weekend. The initial requests were made as early as last June, when the fixtures were first published. Dorset police have accused the League of arrogance, naivety and high-handedness, and of ignoring the lessons of Hillsborough.

FOOTBALL FOCUS

- Sheffield Wednesday, bottom of Division One, won 8–0 at Aldershot on 3 October, a record League Cup away victory, after being held 0–0 at home in the first leg.
- FIFA decided, in the light of the Hillsborough disaster, that all World Cup spectators must be seated, starting with the qualifying competitions for the 1994 finals.
- Second Division Oldham enjoyed unprecedented success in both Cup competitions, reaching their first FA Cup semi-final since 1913 (losing 2–1 to Manchester United after a 3–3 draw) and their first League Cup final (losing 1–0 to Nottingham Forest).
- Frank Stapleton set an individual record for the Republic of Ireland when he scored his 20th goal in their 3–0 win in Malta on 2 June.
- UEFA decreed that only four foreigners will be allowed in any team in European club competitions next season, and that English, Scottish, Welsh and Irish players will be classed as foreigners if they play for a club not of their home country. Players signed before 3 May 1988 will be exempt for a transitional period.

Aberdeen win the Cup in sudden death shoot-out after goalless bore

WHILE MANCHESTER United manager Alex Ferguson was in the end happy to earn a replay in the English Cup final, he was astonished to learn after the match of the FA's decision to settle the replay if necessary by penalties. He also heard that his old club Aberdeen had won the Cup north of the border in a penalty shoot-out, so perhaps that was a good omen.

The Scottish FA had decreed last summer that, in the light of a busy pre-World Cup programme, their Cup, newly sponsored by Tennents, would not even have the luxury of a replay. Perhaps it was just as well, because the match between Aberdeen and Celtic, winners for the last two years, was mostly a shapeless, scrappy affair. And with the game goalless after 120 minutes, it then took 20 penalty kicks to produce a result.

Celtic missed their first, Aberdeen their fourth, so it went to sudden death. After four more successful conversions each, Aberdeen's Dutch keeper Theo Snelders leapt to his left to save Anton Rogan's kick, and Brian Irvine stepped up to settle the issue by making it 9–8 to Aberdeen — a memorable score for an otherwise eminently forgettable final.

Snelders makes the vital save.

SOCCER SOUNDBITES

"Penalty shoot-outs have nothing to do with football. It's like shooting poor wee ducks at a fairground."

ALEX SMITH,
Aberdeen manager, after his team's victory.

England manager Robson to go Dutch after World Cup

AT A HASTILY CALLED Press conference at Lancaster Gate on 24 May, England manager Bobby Robson announced he would be leaving his job after the World Cup to take over as manager of Dutch club PSV Eindhoven. A furious Mr Robson had planned to make the announcement in Sardinia the following Monday as England prepared for the World Cup finals, but a front-page story in a tabloid newspaper reporting that he was to quit because of an alleged affair with a woman 13 years ago brought matters to a head.

Mr Robson explained that he was leaving because he did not think there was still a job with the FA, having more or less been told by FA chairman Bert Millichip that it was unlikely his contract would be renewed unless England won the World Cup. That is why he accepted PSV's offer.

A puzzling aspect of the FA's stance, if they wanted to get rid of Mr Robson, is why they did not do so after England's disastrous showing in the 1988 European Championship — a logical time for him to go. Instead they chose to defy a vicious, counter-productive campaign carried out by certain tabloid newspapers demanding that he be removed from his post. He repaid them by steering England to the World Cup finals for the second time in his eight-year reign, and FA chief executive Graham Kelly paid due tribute to his achievements. One was left wondering why, if they rated him so highly, they were not prepared to renew his contract.

Bobby Robson (left): highly regarded but allowed to go.

Rise and fall of Swindon Town

ON 28 MAY, Swindon Town won promotion to Division One when they beat Sunderland 1–0 in the final of the play-offs, held at Wembley for the first time, in front of a 72,873 crowd. Ten days later, after the club admitted to 35 charges involving irregular payments to eight players going back to 1985, the Football League relegated them two divisions, to Division Three, as well as ordering them to pay as yet unspecified amounts in compensation to six clubs who suffered financially because of Swindon's dealings. After an appeal, the FA cut Swindon's punishment, allowing them to stay in the Second Division.

FINAL SCORE

Football League
Division 1: Liverpool
Top scorer: Gary Lineker (Tottenham Hotspur) 24
Division 2: Leeds United
Division 3: Bristol Rovers
Division 4: Exeter City
Footballer of the Year: John Barnes (Liverpool)

FA Cup Final

Manchester United	3	Crystal Palace	3
(after extra time)			
Replay: Man United	1	Crystal Palace	0

League Cup Final

Nottingham Forest	1	Oldham Athletic	0

Scottish League
Premier Division: Rangers
Top scorer: John Robertson (Heart of Midlothian) 17
Division 1: St Johnstone
Division 2: Brechin City
Footballer of the Year: Alex McLeish (Aberdeen)

Scottish FA Cup Final

Aberdeen	0	Celtic	0
(after extra time)			
Aberdeen won 9–8 on penalties			

Scottish League Cup Final

Aberdeen	2	Rangers	1
(after extra time)			

European Cup Final

AC Milan	1	Benfica	0

Cup-Winners' Cup Final

Sampdoria	2	Anderlecht	0
(after extra time)			

UEFA Cup Final
Juventus beat Fiorentina 3–1, 0–0

European Footballer of the Year 1989
Marco van Basten (AC Milan & Holland)

Leading European Scorer (Golden Boot)
Hugo Sanchez (Real Madrid),
Hristo Stoichkov (CSKA Sofia) 38

World Club Championship

AC Milan (Italy)	3	Olimpia (Paraguay)	0

Paying the penalty

The best thing about Italia '90 was Pavarotti. His singing of excerpts from Puccini, beamed out live on giant TV screens during the opening ceremony, will be remembered long after what football was served up by the 24 teams has been forgotten. This ailing competition, transmitted to countless millions around the world in a blaze of grandiose hype, was just about the worst imaginable advertisement for football. Fear and greed bedevilled the tournament, stifling adventure and squeezing the joy out of the occasion. Some would say, it was the referees' repeatedly flourished red and yellow cards that provided most of the colour.

"Gazza" injects a little light relief against Belgium.

THE ONLY RECORDS broken in Italy were unwanted ones. A total of 164 yellow and 16 red cards displayed by the referees meant that there was an average of over three bookings a match, with nearly one dismissal every three games.

Some of the most exciting football was played by Cameroon, the first African nation to reach the World Cup quarter-finals. They approached their games with a refreshing naivety, but their propensity for cynically hacking opponents down in full flight does not bode well for third-world football.

Never has there been a World Cup so devoid of star quality. There were some great names on view, but most of them appeared to have left their skills at home — or rapidly had the stuffing knocked out of them. Diego Maradona, still arguably the world's best player, worked hard to guide what was a shadow of the 1986 champion side to the final, but all too rare were the glimpses of his footballing genius. He was, however, the most fouled player in the tournament. The Dutch stars were equally disappointing, showing none of the commanding style that made Holland such exciting and popular European champions in 1988.

Sensational opening

World Cup '90 opened sensationally, with defending champions Argentina going down to Cameroon. The Africans, despite their unbeaten performance in the 1982 World Cup, were given no hope, but they beat an unrecognizable Argentina side 1–0, despite finishing up with nine men.

Hosts Italy, the favourites, were unrecognizable, too. They actually played creative, attacking football — until they came near goal. It needed a strike from inspirational substitute "Toto" Schillaci in the 78th minute, four minutes after he went on, to beat a thoroughly outplayed Austria in their first match. Vialli was one star who did enhance his reputation as Italy went on to win their three group matches. They were the only side not to concede a goal in the first round, although they struggled to beat the United States.

West Germany qualified with ease, and were top scorers in the first round with 10 goals — three more than the total scored in England's group. England muddled through once more, with Bobby Robson inexplicably imposing on them a sweeper system which they had never practised before. They got through by beating Egypt 1–0 in the only match not drawn. Had the over-cautious North African side equalized, all four teams would have finished with identical records. As it turned out, Holland and the Republic of Ireland joined England in the next round.

David O'Leary's penalty for the Republic of Ireland against Romania.

Scotland, in their seventh World Cup finals, preserved their record of never getting past the first round. They added another inglorious chapter to their history of humiliating defeats when they lost 1–0 to Costa Rica. And although they beat Sweden — everyone did — they were subsequently undone by a late Brazilian goal, and put out of the tournament. Brazil, although they won their three matches, were not even a poor imitation of their exciting sides of yesteryear.

England rely on luck

England's progress to the semi-finals, their best World Cup showing apart from 1966, was down to the creative inspiration of Paul Gascoigne, the opportunism of David Platt and Gary Lineker, and no little luck, although they played some good football. Belgium hardly deserved to be beaten in a splendid, hard-fought second-round match, but Platt scored a spectacular winning goal in the last minute of extra time, getting behind the Belgian defence to hook home a Gascoigne free-kick. Platt also put England ahead against Cameroon, before England found themselves in serious trouble, 2–1 down with eight minutes to go. But Gascoigne drove them forward, and twice Lineker was brought down in the box, each time converting the spot-kick.

Elsewhere there had been some more thrills and even one or two games of good football. Jack Charlton's achievement in getting the Republic of Ireland to the quarter-finals was monumental. They were not pleasing to watch, but they performed heroically. Substitute David O'Leary clinched a penalty shoot-out against Romania, although they then went out gallantly to a single goal against the Italians.

The best match of the tournament was the last-16 clash between old rivals West Germany and Holland, made even more

In soccer's sick showpiece, both semi-finals were decided on penalties, before a sterile final, with two Argentina players sent off, was decided by the only goal, a late West German penalty.

Brehme scores... a fitting way to end the 1990 World Cup.

combative by the fact that three Dutch stars played for AC Milan and three Germans for Inter. Indeed, the Rijkaard-Völler confrontation proved rather too belligerent, and the two sides were left with 10 men after 21 minutes. Nevertheless, the match was a classic, with the much-fouled Matthaus and particularly Klinsmann outstanding for West Germany in their 2–1 win.

The Germans were less convincing against Czechoslovakia, but deserved to go through, while Argentina were positively struggling. Brazil should have thrashed them before a brilliant Maradona pass was expertly converted by Caniggia for the only goal of the game. Then, in the quarter-finals, after Yugoslavia's Sabanadzovic was sent off, they were held for an hour and a half by 10 men before finally winning on penalties.

Now, it was penalties all the way. In the first semi-final, Maradona, playing on his home ground in Napoli, inspired Argentina to a gritty performance against Italy, who had their poorest game of the finals. Halfway through the second half, Caniggia equalized Schillaci's early goal, and Argentina then held out despite losing Giusti, sent off, for the second period of extra time. They went through to the final again after keeper Goycochea made two fine saves in the penalty decider. But they would be without the cautioned Caniggia and Olarticoechea for the final, as well as Giusti.

England played their best football in the semi-final, and neither they nor West Germany deserved to lose. Gascoigne again was the driving force, never afraid to run at the German defence or try something new. Shilton was desperately unlucky when a Brehme shot from a free-kick was deflected over him, but Lineker equalized 10 minutes from the end. Gazza's famous tears flowed after he was booked for a silly foul and he knew he would miss the final. But Pearce and Waddle missed their penalties, and England were not in it — their consolation, the fair play award.

Veteran Roger Milla, a World Cup hit for Cameroon.

A squalid finale

Franz Beckenbauer became the first man to manage and captain World Cup-winning sides when West Germany beat Argentina 1–0 in Rome thanks to a Brehme penalty six minutes from the end. There is very little else to say about the final, except that the team who most consistently played the best football in Italy won it. Like the whole tournament, it was high in drama, low in football. The Germans dominated the match, but could not finish their chances. Monzon became the first player ever sent off in a World Cup final, for a bad foul on Klinsmann after 64 minutes; but the 84th-minute penalty, for a challenge on Völler by Sensini, was less clear-cut. When Dezotti was also expelled two minutes later for forcefully trying to retrieve the ball from a time-wasting opponent, his teammates went mad, and Maradona was booked for dissent. It was a fitting ending to a World Cup most people wanted to forget.

FINAL SCORE

FIRST ROUND

Group A

Italy	1	Austria	0
Czechoslovakia	5	United States	1
Italy	1	United States	0
Czechoslovakia	1	Austria	0
Austria	2	United States	1
Italy	2	Czechoslovakia	0

	P	W	D	L	F	A	P
Italy	3	3	0	0	4	0	6
Czech.	3	2	0	1	6	3	4
Austria	3	1	0	2	2	3	2
U S	3	0	0	3	2	8	0

Group B

Cameroon	1	Argentina	0
Romania	2	USSR	0
Argentina	2	USSR	0
Cameroon	2	Romania	1
USSR	4	Cameroon	0
Romania	1	Argentina	1

	P	W	D	L	F	A	P
Cameroon	3	2	0	1	3	5	4
Romania	3	1	1	1	4	3	3
Argentina	3	1	1	1	3	2	3
USSR	3	1	0	2	4	4	2

Group C

Brazil	2	Sweden	1
Costa Rica	1	Scotland	0
Brazil	1	Costa Rica	0
Scotland	2	Sweden	1
Brazil	1	Scotland	0
Costa Rica	2	Sweden	1

	P	W	D	L	F	A	P
Brazil	3	3	0	0	4	1	6
Costa Riva	3	2	0	1	3	2	4
Scotland	3	1	0	2	2	3	2
Sweden	3	0	0	3	3	6	0

Group D

Colombia	2	UAE	0
West Germany	4	Yugoslavia	1
Yugoslavia	1	Colombia	0
West Germany	5	UAE	1
Yugoslavia	4	UAE	1
West Germany	1	Colombia	1

	P	W	D	L	F	A	P
W. Germany	3	2	1	0	10	3	5
Yugoslavia	3	2	0	1	6	5	4
Colombia	3	1	1	1	3	2	3
UAE	3	0	0	3	2	11	0

Group E

Belgium	2	South Korea	0
Uruguay	0	Spain	0
Spain	3	South Korea	1
Belgium	3	Uruguay	1
Spain	2	Belgium	1
Uruguay	1	South Korea	0

	P	W	D	L	F	A	P
Spain	3	2	1	0	5	2	5
Belgium	3	2	0	1	6	3	4
Uruguay	3	1	1	1	2	3	3
S. Korea	3	0	0	3	1	6	0

Group F

England	1	Rep. of Ireland	1
Holland	1	Egypt	1
England	0	Holland	0
Rep. of Ireland	0	Egypt	0
England	1	Egypt	0
Rep. of Ireland	1	Holland	1

	P	W	D	L	F	A	P
England	3	1	2	0	2	1	4
Rep. Ireland	3	0	3	0	2	2	3
Holland	3	0	3	0	2	2	3
Egypt	3	0	2	1	1	2	2

SECOND ROUND

Cameroon	2	Colombia	1
(after extra time)			
Czechoslovakia	4	Costa Rica	1
Argentina	1	Brazil	0
West Germany	2	Holland	1
Rep. of Ireland	0	Romania	0
(after extra time)			
Rep. of Ireland won 5–4 on penalties			
Italy	2	Uruguay	0
Yugoslavia	2	Spain	1
(after extra time)			
England	1	Belgium	0
(after extra time)			

QUARTER-FINALS

Argentina	0	Yugoslavia	0
(after extra time)			
Argentina won 3–2 on penalties			
Italy	1	Rep. of Ireland	0
West Germany	1	Czechoslovakia	0
England	3	Cameroon	2
(after extra time)			

SEMI-FINALS

Argentina	1	Italy	1
(after extra time)			
Argentina won 4–3 on penalties			
West Germany	1	England	1
(after extra time)			
West Germany won 4–3 on penalties			

THIRD-PLACE MATCH

Italy	2	England	1

FINAL

West Germany	1	Argentina	0

Stadio Olimpico, Rome, 8 July 1990. Attendance 73,603

West Germany: Illgner, Berthold (Reuter), Kohler, Augenthaler, Buchwald, Brehme, Littbarski, Hassler, Matthaus, Völler, Klinsmann (Scorer: Brehme pen.)

Argentina: Goycochea, Lorenzo, Serrizuela, Sensini, Ruggeri (Monzon), Simon, Basualdo, Burruchaga (Calderon), Maradona, Troglio, Dezotti

Leading scorers
6 Schillaci (Italy)
5 Skuhravy (Czechoslovakia)
4 Lineker (England), Matthaus (West Germany), Michel (Spain), Milla (Cameroon)

Arsenal suffer at the Sharpe end

WHEN MANCHESTER United arrived at Highbury for a fourth-round Rumbelows (League) Cup tie on 28 November, Arsenal had conceded only two goals at home all season. The Gunners were unbeaten, and still challenging Liverpool for the First Division leadership. When United left a shell-shocked Arsenal Stadium, Arsenal had conceded a further six goals and were out of the Rumbelows Cup.

Manchester put on a performance that night reminiscent of the Busby Babes of the fifties. And, indeed, it was a relative "babe" who stole the show, 19-year-old Lee Sharpe, recently converted from a full-back to a winger. After Clayton Blackmore had put United ahead in the first minute and Mark Hughes had finished a move started by Sharpe, the youngster scored the goal of the game himself, cutting in from the left and curling a superb 25-yarder over Seaman. It was hard to believe that United were without their captain, Bryan Robson, as they went in 3–0 up at half-time. Arsenal also found it somewhat mind-boggling, because they had shared the play.

After the interval, Arsenal came back at United with two goals from Smith. But in their eagerness to find an equalizer, they left gaps at the back. This was fatal with Sharpe in such dazzling form, and in the last 20 minutes United carved their way through the Arsenal defence in a series of lightning breaks. Sharpe scored two more to complete his hat-trick and Danny Wallace completed the rout at 6–2. This was Arsenal's first defeat of the season and their heaviest home defeat for 70 years, and a warning to the rest that United are getting it together.

Sharpe heads Manchester United into a 4–2 lead.

Gunners find brawl pointless and costly

ARSENAL, UNBEATEN but desperately trying to stay in touch with runaway First Division leaders Liverpool, suffered a major setback on 12 November when an FA disciplinary committee docked them two points for their part in the disgraceful brawl at Old Trafford on 20 October. Manchester United had one point deducted, and both clubs were fined £50,000, as the FA decided to get tough, especially in view of Arsenal's poor recent disciplinary record. They were involved in a similar brawl last season at Highbury with Norwich, for which they were fined £20,000 and the visitors £50,000, and were lucky to get away with another deplorable incident soon afterwards, at Villa Park, with their protests transgressing the limits of reasonable behaviour towards the referee.

Now they find themselves eight points behind a relentless Liverpool side who have dropped only two points in their 12 matches. Arsenal, who beat United 1–0, may find the loss of those two hard-earned points breaking their grip on Liverpool's coat-tails.

Sharpe leaves the Arsenal defence gaping as he completes his hat-trick.

FAR-out herOES

THE FAROES ARE a group of islands in the far North Atlantic, somewhere between the northern tip of Scotland and Iceland. They are part of the Kingdom of Denmark, but are self-governing in most matters, including, it seems, football. On 12 September 1990, they made their debut in the European Championship, in Group 4 of the qualifying competition. It was a home match with Austria, played in Landskrona, Sweden, because UEFA would not permit them to play on any of their own 12 suitable artificial pitches. Only 1,544 people turned up to see the game, but they witnessed a little piece of soccer history, arguably the most incredible result in international soccer: Faroe Islands 1 Austria 0.

How this team of part-timers, all amateurs — electricians, clerks, sheep-farmers, and the like — beat a nation of the standing of Austria, no longer a major European power but still good enough to reach the 1990 World Cup finals, is a mystery. Certainly the Austrian team manager Josef Hickersberger could not explain it, as he returned to Vienna to hand in his resignation. But a goal after 61 minutes from Torkil Nielsen, who works in a timber shop, won the Faroes the game, and made him into a folk hero back home, where the 47,000 islanders turned their bleak, remote habitat into one big celebration party.

After all, they were the only country in the world with a 100 percent record in major international competition.

Dalglish walks alone: Anfield stunned

KENNY DALGLISH suddenly resigned his Anfield job on Friday, 22 February, after nearly 14 years of unrivalled success as player and manager of Liverpool. With Liverpool leading the League and having just drawn an epic fifth-round FA Cup replay with neighbours Everton 4–4, the outside world had no inkling of what was going on in Mr Dalglish's mind, and nor did the Anfield board until the day before.

At a routine meeting on Thursday morning, Mr Dalglish, 40 next month, told his colleagues that he could go on no longer, the stress had become too much. For the next 10 hours, the board did everything within their power to persuade him to stay, perhaps to wait until the end of the season, or even take a sabbatical. But Mr Dalglish would not change his mind. At a Press conference the following morning, he struggled to explain why he was leaving the most successful club in Britain. It was not a sudden decision, but he had to make it because the pressure he was putting himself under — through his desire to be successful — had become too much to bear.

The immediate reaction at Liverpool — from the players, the Anfield staff and the fans — was utter disbelief. An idol of the Kop since he joined Liverpool in 1977 and achieved the seemingly impossible by replacing Kevin Keegan, Dalglish enjoyed remarkable success as a player. He won three European Cup medals and seven Championship medals (the last two as player-manager) to add to the four won with Celtic in Scotland. He scored over 100 goals in both Scotland and England, won a record 102 Scottish caps and equalled Denis Law's record of 30 goals for Scotland. Taking over as Liverpool manager at a very difficult time, straight after the Heysel disaster, he kept them at the top of English football, continuing the unprecedented run of success established by Shankly, Paisley and Fagan, and achieving something even his illustrious predecessors failed to manage — the League and Cup double in 1986. He retired from the playing side in 1989, and guided Liverpool to another League title last season.

This marks the end of an era at Anfield. As coach Ronnie Moran takes over as caretaker-manager, the question on everyone's lips must be: Are we seeing the beginning of the end of Liverpool's supremacy in English football?

Goodbye to Anfield: Dalglish announces his decision to resign the Liverpool job.

SOCCER SOUNDBITES

"Watching Kenny Dalglish walk out of Anfield was the saddest moment of my life."

PETER ROBINSON,
Liverpool chief executive.

Arsenal win battle of the giants

ONLY FOUR DAYS after their sensational home defeat by Manchester United in the Rumbelows Cup, Arsenal took on and comprehensively beat League leaders Liverpool 3–0 at Highbury. It was truly a battle of the giants, between two sides unbeaten in the League after 14 matches.

It was a vital match for Arsenal, after their midweek humiliation, and defeat would have left them trailing by nine points. Manager George Graham brought in O'Leary for only his second start of the season, and he played a superb game as sweeper, shoring up the shell-shocked Arsenal defence. Liverpool manager Kenny Dalglish, however, made a puzzling selection, aimed, it seems, to protect their six-point lead rather than exploit any Arsenal uncertainty. It failed miserably.

Arsenal took the lead in the 20th minute, when Merson scrambled in a header after Thomas twice had the Liverpool defence in a panic. Then, four minutes after the interval, a delightful Merson pass set left-winger Limpar away. The Swedish international, in his first season in English football, has, rightly or wrongly, earned a reputation for diving. So when he burst between Gillespie and Ablett and went crashing to the turf, Liverpool were most unhappy to see the referee pointing to the spot. Those who have been defeated by such decisions at Anfield over the years, however, will have little sympathy for Dalglish's men.

Dixon converted the penalty, and Smith rounded off Arsenal's victory near the end after the ubiquitous Merson had opened up the Liverpool defence with a slick back-heel. Now Arsenal had moved up within striking distance of the champions and the title race was really on.

Merson heads Arsenal into the lead with the Liverpool defence in disarray, as they were to be so often.

Gascoigne the Spur: Arsenal semi-detached at Wembley

PAUL GASCOIGNE, back after a stomach operation only 34 days earlier, made a hero's appearance in the first FA Cup semi-final ever held at Wembley, and scored what his manager described as "one of the best goals ever seen there" to inspire Spurs to a famous 3–1 triumph over North London rivals Arsenal.

After a midweek run-out in the League, Gascoigne was surely not even half fit, and he played for just 61 minutes, but this will always be known as "Gazza's match". It took him only 10 minutes to respond to manager Venables's challenge to prove he is the most talented footballer of his generation. First he scored his goal, an audacious, sensational 35-yard free-kick that flashed past the ruin of Arsenal's defensive wall and the groping fingers of Seaman into the top corner of the net. With the adrenalin pumping, Gascoigne was everywhere, collecting every ball from his keeper, running at defenders, wanting to take every free-kick. In the 10th minute, an exhilarating exchange of passes with Paul Allen stretched the Arsenal defence to breaking point, Smith could not provide a defender's clearance and Lineker pounced on the error to put Spurs two up. With Stewart and Samways working feverishly in midfield, Spurs retained the initiative until just before half-time, when Smith rose to a Dixon cross from the right and powered a header past Thorstvedt. The League leaders, beaten only twice all season, came out in the second half determined to continue their comeback. And with Gascoigne soon going off, it was left to the brave Thorstvedt and his crossbar to keep Spurs ahead.

Then came the killer blow, from Lineker who, along with Gascoigne, has so often seemed little more than collateral in Tottenham's financial confusion this season. Picking the ball up in the centre-circle, he took it forward unchallenged before hitting a speculative shot, the sort Seaman has been saving with ease all season. But the keeper, still perhaps unnerved by Gazza's early thunderbolt, merely helped it into the net. Spurs were in their ninth FA Cup final, and Arsenal's dreams of the double were in tatters.

Gascoigne elated after his fifth-minute wonder goal.

Blackmore and Bruce revive Busby years

MANCHESTER UNITED added another memorable chapter to their proud European history when they overcame Montpellier 2–0 in France on 19 March to reach the last four of the Cup-Winners' Cup 3–1 on aggregate. Their triumph over the highly rated French side, who had already eliminated former European champions PSV Eindhoven and Steaua Bucharest from this season's competition, will stand alongside any of those in recent years.

United had seemed doomed to failure in this quarter-final, after conceding a precious away goal to the well-organized Frenchmen at Old Trafford a fortnight earlier. But Montpellier, with a formidable home record, could not make up their minds whether to protect their advantage or go for a straight victory. United took the decision out of their hands with goals either side of the interval, the first from a free-kick by the unsung Clayton Blackmore, which squirmed out of Barrabe's hands, the second after Blackmore was fouled, Steve Bruce converting the penalty.

To win now, Montpellier needed three goals, and they never looked like getting one of them.

Robson (7) bursts through the Montpellier defence.

Crisis at Spurs: world record bid for Gazza

ITALIAN CLUB LAZIO confirmed on 15 March that they had made a world record bid of £8.5 million for Tottenham's England star Paul Gascoigne, and claimed they had been given an option to buy. As Gascoigne left hospital after a stomach muscle operation, he was briefed on the position with the Roman club. His chief concern, now, is to get fit in time for the FA Cup semi-final with Arsenal in a month's time at Wembley.

Gascoigne, born in May 1967, developed at Newcastle and is now one of the few British players with a genuine chance of being rated world-class. His departure for Italy seems a foregone conclusion.

With Spurs in deep financial crisis, it looks like they will have to sell their most valuable asset if they are not to go under. Manager Terry Venables was meanwhile desperately trying to put together the necessary finance to complete the £20 million takeover of the club, but there was little evidence that his group had the money in place.

Tenth title for Arsenal: Liverpool capitulate

ARSENAL CELEBRATED their 10th League title at Highbury on the evening of 6 May — clinched when Liverpool lost 2–1 at Nottingham Forest in the afternoon — with a 3–1 win over Manchester United. That was appropriate, for United had been their opponents in two traumatic matches earlier in the season, when Arsenal had been docked two points for their part in the brawl at Old Trafford and then suffered that humiliating 2–6 Rumbelows Cup exit at Highbury. All this was forgotten, however, when Alan Smith put his hat-trick past United, with the Arsenal crowd celebrating a record-breaking season. And five days later, again at Highbury, when George Graham collected his Barclays Manager of the Season award, the Gunners gave an exhibition, in their 6–1 demolition of Coventry, full of imagination and flair that had often been missing during their season-long battle with Liverpool for the title.

Anders Limpar: provided Arsenal with flair... and goals.

Arsenal lost only one of their 38 League games — the fewest in the history of the League except for Preston's unbeaten season 102 years ago, when they played only 22 matches in the League's first season. They went a club record 24 matches unbeaten, before losing that game, 2–1 at Stamford Bridge to Chelsea on 2 February. David Seaman, their close-season £1.3 million signing from QPR, was ever-present, conceding only 18 League goals. Also ever-present in their back four were Dixon, Winterburn and Bould, and skipper Tony Adams returned with great courage after the shame of his mid-season "rest" (a spell in prison for a drink-drive offence) to lead them immediately to a crucial victory at Anfield in early March. Alan Smith led their scorers, and the League's with 23 goals, and the inspirational Merson chipped in with 13. Kevin Campbell scored eight of his nine goals in a vital 10 matches when he came into the side late in the season. But perhaps the most popular character with the fans was Anders Limpar, the impish Swedish international, who treated them to three of his always spectacular 11 goals in that last "exhibition" match against Coventry.

Souness takes over at Anfield

FORMER LIVERPOOL star and Glasgow Rangers manager Graeme Souness was confirmed as Liverpool's new manager on 16 April in succession to Kenny Dalglish. Caretaker manager Ronnie Moran had made it clear that he did not want to be considered for the job on a permanent basis. Mr Souness, 37, spent seven seasons at Anfield under Bob Paisley, during which Liverpool won three European Cups, five Championships and four League Cups. After two years in Italy with Sampdoria, he went to Rangers as player-manager, was sent off after 37 minutes of his debut match against Hibs in August 1986 and, despite frequently falling foul with the Scottish FA, has guided the Glasgow club to three Championships and four League Cups. He leaves Rangers on top of the League again, but very unhappy at losing him. He joins Liverpool, possibly at a watershed in their fortunes, second in the table, but trailing Arsenal now by five points. He has signed a five-year contract at Anfield worth around £350,000 a year, said to be £100,000 more than he was earning in Scotland.

Mr Souness's first job will be to prepare Liverpool for their next match, at home to Norwich, and in the longer term to produce a side capable of cashing in on the club's imminent return to Europe after their six-year ban following the Heysel disaster.

Souness comes out for his first match in charge of Liverpool.

SOCCER SOUNDBITES

"I believe he is making the biggest mistake of his life. Time will tell."

DAVID MURRAY,
Rangers chairman, on Souness's move.

Wednesday's Wembley win

SHEFFIELD WEDNESDAY surprised Manchester United 1–0 in the Rumbelows (League) Cup final, but, satisfying as this must have been for manager Ron Atkinson, sacked by United four years ago, he gained more pleasure 17 days later when Wednesday clinched their return to Division One at the first time of asking.

At Wembley, it was Irish international John Sheridan who won the match for Wednesday after 37 minutes, with a volleyed goal of such quality that it was out of place in a lack-lustre League Cup final newly sponsored by Rumbelows. Nevertheless, it gave Sheffield their first major domestic trophy for 56 years.

Manchester manager Alex Ferguson was left to lament that his side could beat Liverpool and Arsenal — inflicting their first defeats of the season — and win at Elland Road ("perhaps the most intimidating venue in Europe") on the way to the final, and then go out to a Second Division side.

Maxwell the hero in Scottish Cup thriller

MOTHERWELL AND Dundee United, two lesser lights on the Scottish scene, produced a fitting climax to the Scottish season — a seven-goal thriller, in which the heroics of Motherwell's injured keeper Ally Maxwell and a goal from their "super sub" Steve Kirk tipped the balance.

This was the sixth Scottish FA Cup final for both clubs, but only Motherwell had won the Cup before, in 1952. Poor Jim McLean, Dundee United's long-serving — and long-suffering — manager, had seen them lose five finals during his 20 years in charge, and now it was his younger brother Tommy who became the latest manager to upstage him.

There is no denying Motherwell deserved to win, and would probably have had a smoother passage but for Maxwell's injury, sustained in a collision soon after the interval, which left him with bruised ribs, double vision and nausea. They had taken a first-half lead, and an undamaged Maxwell would surely have saved United's equalizer, which passed under his body in the 55th minute.

Motherwell came storming back with two quick goals, but United soon pulled one back, and a last-minute equalizer by Jackson, who just beat the struggling Maxwell to a huge punt from his own keeper, took the match into extra time. Substitute Steve Kirk, who had moved off the bench to score three times before in Motherwell's Cup run, kept up his record with a header after five minutes. After that it was up to Maxwell, and although he could see two balls, he always stopped the right one.

Super sub Kirk (extreme left) heads the extra-time winner for Motherwell.

FOOTBALL FOCUS

- Wayward 30-year-old fading star Diego Maradona, who brought Napoli unprecedented success and wealth since his record transfer in 1984, tested positive for cocaine in a random dope test following an Italian Serie A game on 17 March, and was banned from professional soccer for 15 months.
- Torquay became the first club to win promotion on penalties, beating Blackpool 5–4 after their play-off final was drawn 2–2, to earn a place in Division Three.
- Two international "giants" were slain on 5 June in European Championship qualifiers, world champions West Germany losing to an Ian Rush goal for Wales at Cardiff Arms Park and Italy going down 2–1 in Norway.

Barcelona reject Hughes gives them the old one-two

MARK HUGHES, rescued from a nightmare with Barcelona by Alex Ferguson three years ago, rewarded Manchester United by scoring the goals that won them the European Cup-Winners' Cup in Rotterdam, when they beat his old Spanish club 2–1 on a memorable night for English football. Maybe it was not a great game. But United won it well, and in so doing they have restored English football, at the first opportunity, to its pre-Heysel standing. And their fans, some two-thirds of the 45,000 crowd in the bleak, concrete bowl of the De Kuip Stadium, played their part to perfection, deliriously happy but, as they rightly declared themselves, "the best behaved supporters in the land". It was indeed fitting, and a great relief, that this was the night United's "Red Army", responsible for some notorious incidents in the past, had signed a disarmament treaty.

On the field, Bryan Robson was immense. He may no longer be needed by England manager Graham Taylor, but he typified everything that is good about the English game. Ably assisted by the bullish Hughes, he drove United forward in wave after wave of attacks that shook Barcelona out of their stride and finally broke them. The first goal came after 68 minutes, when Bruce headed a Robson free-kick into goal. Hughes ran on to give it a nudge, but generously insisted after that Bruce's effort had crossed the line. There was no doubt who scored the second, as Hughes, confirming his reputation as a scorer of "great goals", raced free, took the ball wide of the keeper and spectacularly belted the ball into the net from the narrowest of angles.

A typical Ronald Koeman free-kick ignored the defensive wall and beat the brave Sealey, playing despite a knee injury, to give United an anxious last 10 minutes, not least Ferguson, who emulates Mr Cruyff by winning this competition with different sides.

Brian McLair (left) and Bryan Robson with the Cup-Winners' Cup.

Spurs shatter Clough's dream despite Gazza's shattered knee

"GAZZAMANIA" TOOK on a new meaning at Wembley, when Spurs met Nottingham Forest in the FA Cup final. Not the hype and the spin-off industry surrounding England World Cup star Paul Gascoigne since his famous tearful exit in Italy, but the mental aberration that sent him rampaging around the pitch like a whirling dervish in the first 15 minutes, almost handing the Cup to Forest and finishing up with a self-inflicted injury that could seriously damage his career.

If this really was Gascoigne's last game for Spurs — although his serious knee-ligament injury might yet prejudice his pending transfer to Lazio — it was a singularly inglorious one. In a misguided attempt to live up to his media image as the "cheeky chappie superman" who would win this game on his own and maybe deliver Spurs from the hands of the receivers into the bargain, Gascoigne's first contribution was to catch Forest's Garry Parker on the chest with a follow-through straight out of the manual of kick-boxing. Escaping a yellow card for this was his first miracle of the afternoon, and an indictment of the kind of misguidedly lenient refereeing so often seen in Cup finals. A caution at this stage might have prevented the excesses that followed, but the overactive Gascoigne continued to hog centre stage, arms flailing about, until he once more overstepped the mark with an appalling scything tackle — rather a kick — on Gary Charles just outside the Spurs box. Although the Forest right-back soon recovered from the foul, it left the perpetrator writhing, seemingly in an attempt to avoid punishment. He did so, from an extraordinarily tolerant referee, whose main concern appeared to be to avoid controversy at all costs. As it turned out, Gascoigne was badly hurt, and, to add insult to injury, Stuart Pearce scored from the free-kick.

So Gazza the superman was carried off, which, paradoxically, turned out well for Spurs, because not only could they replace him, with Nayim, but they were now able to get down to playing football. This they did, to excellent effect. Paul Stewart was outstanding in midfield and scored a fine equalizer, too, but not before Lineker had a goal disallowed and a penalty saved, by Mark Crossley, who had brought him down and was another player lucky to escape a card of some colour. Stewart's goal came in the 55th minute, a right-foot cross-shot after being set free by the tireless Paul Allen.

Spurs were very much on top, with Forest tactically bereft of ideas, so it came as a shock at the end of 90 minutes when Brian Clough took his eccentricity too far and a leaf out of Paul Gascoigne's book of crass stupidity by exchanging pleasantries with a young policeman when his young team were crying out for his managerial advice. It was Terry Venables who won the tactical battle hands down, and no surprise when Spurs scored the winning goal in extra time, courtesy of the unfortunate defender Des Walker, who headed a corner into his own net. But this was in keeping with the madness of the day.

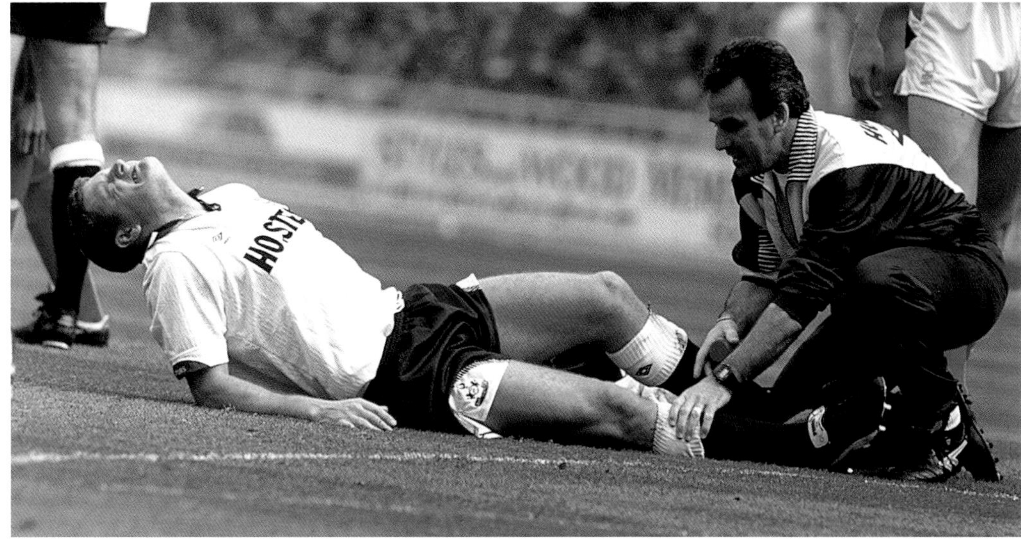

Paul Gascoigne is put on a stretcher and carried off after 15 minutes of lunacy.

Des Walker (4) heads into his own net for Spurs' winner.

FINAL SCORE

Football League
Division 1: Arsenal
Top scorer: Alan Smith (Arsenal) 23
Division 2: Oldham Athletic
Division 3: Cambridge United
Division 4: Darlington
Footballer of the Year: Gordon Strachan (Leeds United)

FA Cup Final
Tottenham Hotspur 2 Nottingham Forest 1
(after extra time)

League Cup Final
Sheffield Wed 1 Manchester United 0

Scottish League
Premier Division: Rangers
Top scorer: Tommy Coyne (Celtic) 18
Division 1: Falkirk
Division 2: Stirling Albion
Footballer of the Year: Maurice Malpas (Dundee United)

Scottish FA Cup Final
Motherwell 4 Dundee United 3
(after extra time)

Scottish League Cup Final
Rangers 2 Celtic 1
(after extra time)

European Cup Final
Red Star Belgrade 0 Marseille 0
(aet) Red Star won 5–3 on penalties

Cup-Winners' Cup Final
Manchester United 2 Barcelona 1

UEFA Cup Final
Inter Milan beat Roma 2–0, 0–1

European Footballer of the Year 1990
Lothar Matthaus (Inter Milan & West Germany)

Leading European Scorer (Golden Boot)
Darko Pancev (Red Star Belgrade) 34

World Club Championship
Red Star Belgrade (Yugoslavia) 3 Colo Colo (Chile) 0

Triumph for Venables as Sugar saves Spurs

AFTER A LONG-drawn-out saga, manager Terry Venables has finally won his battle to take over ailing Spurs, teetering on the brink of oblivion with debts of some £20 million. Backed by multi-millionaire businessman Alan Sugar, chief of the Amstrad computer giant, Venables fought off a last-minute bid by Derby chairman Robert Maxwell, who would have had to sell his shares in that club had he been successful. The £7.25 million deal was formally signed on 22 June to end almost a year of uncertainty. As the football world takes in the magnitude of what Mr Venables has done — while guiding Spurs to their Cup final triumph at the same time — they learnt that he had, according to Mr Sugar, put in a "gi-normous" amount of his own money, thought to be about £3.6 million.

Mr Sugar will become non-executive chairman and Venables non-executive MD, working in tandem at the club with a first-team coach, probably his assistant Doug Livermore. The first priority of the new consortium will be to put Spurs on a more solid financial footing, and Mr Sugar warned fans not to expect the club to be involved in the transfer market for some time. The on-off move of Paul Gascoigne to Lazio will be sorted out one way or another, but it will be surprising if they can afford not to sell him. And to add a twist to a day of high financial dealing, Blackburn confirmed that they have made a bid of £2 million for Spurs and England striker Gary Lineker.

Happy days at Spurs: Sugar (left), Gascoigne and Venables.

SOCCER SOUNDBITES

"You'd have to be mad not to want to keep Gascoigne, but if there has to be life after Gazza, so be it."

TERRY VENABLES.

Souness spends £5m for starters

LIVERPOOL MANAGER Graeme Souness forked out £5.1 million on two players in mid-July in the space of two days: England centre-back Mark Wright and Wales striker Dean Saunders, both from Derby County. In doing so, the tough-talking Scot confirmed his promise, made when he took over the Anfield hot seat last April, that he was prepared to axe old favourites and introduce new faces to keep Liverpool at the top of British soccer.

Wright's fee was £2.2 million, while Saunders cost £2.9 million, a new record for a British club. Wright faces the difficult task of stepping into the shoes of Alan Hansen, who retired last season after recurring problems with knee injuries. Mr Souness, who stole Saunders — the son of a former Liverpool player — from under the noses of Everton and Forest, expects him to link up well with John Barnes and Ian Rush.

Bari bust record for £5.5m Platt

DAVID PLATT BECAME the most expensive player in British football history when Italian club Bari paid Aston Villa £5.5 million for him on 20 July. Platt, the versatile, goalscoring England midfielder, was given a free transfer by Manchester United seven years ago. And although Crewe made a tidy £200,000 profit when they sold him to Villa three years later, manager Dario Gradi ruefully points out that he accepted the deal from Graham Taylor, then Villa manager, rather than an alternative £150,000 plus a percentage of a future transfer. By joining unfashionable Bari, Platt has gambled that a bigger Italian club will later step in and acquire his services.

SOCCER SOUNDBITES

"David can go on to become a truly great player."

DARIO GRADI,
Platt's manager at Crewe.

No Turkish delight for England

ENGLAND'S unsatisfactory 1–0 victory at Wembley over Turkey — a team they twice demolished 8–0 in the 1980s — leaves them needing a draw in Poland to go through to the finals of the European Championship, when a more convincing win would have put them virtually out of reach of their rivals. As the crowd chanted "What a load of rubbish" at the end, it was Graham Taylor's first experience of this familiar Wembley anthem of disappointment. And had it not been for Alan Smith's 22nd-minute goal, and then the agility and outstretched fingertips of Chris Woods, who denied Unal the honour of scoring what would have been Turkey's first ever goal against England, the evening would have been even more embarrassing for Mr Taylor. Woods, indeed, found himself the busier of the two keepers, as Mr Taylor's pre-match instructions to shoot on sight seemed to have reached the wrong dressing-room. Now we must wait until next month, when the last matches in the group are played, to know the outcome.

Alan Smith (left) heads England's winner.

SOCCER SOUNDBITES

"... a team that could not possibly play together... a selection mistake by the manager..."

SIR ALF RAMSEY'S
unusually harsh criticism of England and Graham Taylor.

Lineker rescue act clinches England's place in Sweden

GARY LINEKER, not for the first time, came to the rescue of England in Poznan on 13 November to book them a place in Sweden for next summer's European Championship finals. With England only 13 minutes away from defeat — and elimination — he scored an equalizer that, though well deserved, had begun to look increasingly unlikely the more frustrated they became.

Panic had set in after 31 minutes, when sweeper Szewczyk gave Poland the lead with a 40-yard shot that took a deflection off Mabbutt's heel. Only five minutes earlier, Andy Gray of Crystal Palace, thrown into this crucial match for his international debut, had missed a golden opportunity. At half-time, Graham Taylor replaced Gray with Alan Smith, to give Lineker some company up front, but England made and missed several chances.

They also survived a strong penalty appeal after Woods spilled a shot and, Poland claimed, impeded Furtok as he went for the ball. Almost immediately, Lineker, England's captain, made a powerful run on the right and won the latest in a stream of corners. Mabbutt headed Rocastle's kick to the far post, where Lineker improvised an acrobatic volley to beat the stunned Polish keeper. Had he not done so, it would have meant Jack Charlton's Republic of Ireland going through, not Poland, as their 3–1 win in Turkey gave them by far the best goal difference.

Lineker celebrates the goal that puts England into the European Championship finals.

Soccer crisis: League clubs £130m in debt

ACCORDING TO AN independent survey, Football League clubs are collectively up to £130 million in debt and are "not capable of either managerially or financially facing that challenge". The report, "The Bankrupting of English Football", privately produced by sports consultant Dr Simon Pitt, also warns that more than a dozen of the 93 League clubs face extinction. Dr Pitt's findings were drawn from a voluntary and confidential response to his questionnaire, which produced replies from 61 clubs.

The report blames the crisis in football on the spiralling cost of players' wages, signing-on fees and transfers, allied to a drop in spectator interest and revenue in the last decade, which has left more than 75 per cent of the clubs in the red. Another increasingly heavy burden is the cost of policing matches, which has almost doubled to £6.1 million in the last year. The biggest problem most leading clubs face is the implementation of the Taylor Report, where the revenue needed to build all-seater stadiums by the 1994 deadline has outstripped ability to raise it.

Dr Pitt says the game is "undercapitalized and over-borrowed", and in any other business circumstances small companies such as these, with high fixed overheads and declining marginal revenues, would have gone bankrupt long ago.

United out of Cup on penalties

MANCHESTER UNITED earned the dubious distinction in the fourth round of the FA Cup of becoming the first Division One side in the history of this illustrious competition to be knocked out by the gimmicky method of a penalty shoot-out.

Following their goalless draw at the Dell, United were the firm favourites to beat lowly Southampton at Old Trafford. But after going two goals down inside 21 minutes, to goals by Stuart Gray and Alan Shearer, they were grateful to be given the opportunity of taking part in the ritual lottery. For that they have to thank their Ukrainian winger Andrei Kanchelskis, who scored just before the interval, and the ever-persistent Scot, Brian McClair, who equalized a minute into injury time.

United appeared to have won it in extra time, when Bryan Robson's header looked to have crossed the line; but the referee did not have the benefit of a television replay, which would have confirmed the score, so the penalty decider came into play. The two United players who will be haunted by their misses were England's Neil Webb and teenage Welsh international Ryan Giggs. The Saints put all four of theirs away, without recourse to their regular penalty-taker Matthew Le Tissier, and when Tim Flowers saved the last shot, United had only the dismal consolation of a place in the record books.

Robson's header: surely over the line.

Keegan returns to Newcastle: Ardiles sacked

KEVIN KEEGAN bustled back into the life of Newcastle United on 5 February as the struggling Second Division side sacked Ossie Ardiles and took the astonishing gamble of appointing the glamorous, but untried, former England star as their 15th manager since the war. Presented with the formidable challenge of saving the north-eastern giants from the indignity of relegation to the Third Division for the first time, Mr Keegan struck a positive attitude that will be familiar to those who saw him play in a career that took in successful spells at Liverpool, Hamburg, Southampton and finally Newcastle, where he enjoyed an Indian summer and a love affair with the Geordie fans. And it is because of those supporters that Keegan — who, as the first English footballing millionaire, doesn't need the money — allowed himself to be lured out of retirement. While listening to Mr Keegan's rallying cry, the media were still trying to work out exactly how it was that Mr Ardiles, in the job for only 11 months, had been sacked only three days after director Douglas Hall and his father, the chairman Sir John Hall, had taken the trouble to deny rumours of such an event. Mr Keegan, nearly 41, has not yet signed a contract, and he and his No. 2, Terry McDermott, have 16 games left to save second-from-bottom Newcastle from the drop.

Ossie Ardiles — sacked.

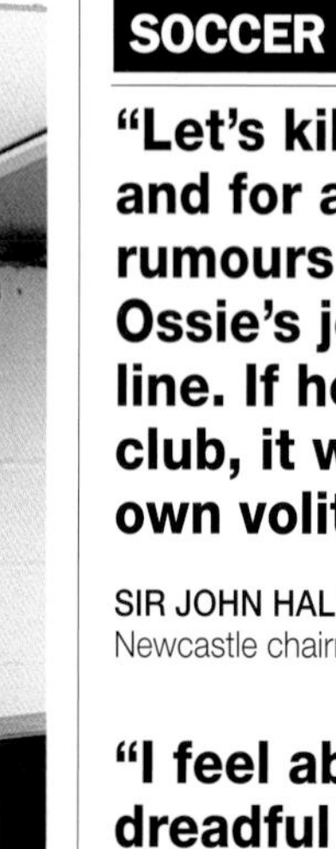

Kevin Keegan back at Newcastle: a tough task.

SOCCER SOUNDBITES

"Let's kill off once and for all the rumours that Ossie's job is on the line. If he leaves the club, it will be of his own volition."

SIR JOHN HALL,
Newcastle chairman, 2 February.

"I feel absolutely dreadful about what has happened... when I said those words, I meant each and every one of them."

SIR JOHN HALL,
5 February.

New Premier League confirmed

THE BREAK-UP OF the 104-year-old Football League was given official confirmation at Lancaster Gate on 20 February when the FA Council approved the formation of the new FA Premier League, to start in August. The unpaid, non-executive chairman, appointed in December, is Sir John Quinton, former chairman of Barclays Bank, and the chief executive is accountant Rick Parry. They have still to make their peace with the PFA's Gordon Taylor, who is demanding a say in the new League's decision-making process.

The Premier League will have 22 clubs, to be reduced to 20 by the end of the 1994–95 season, a compromise forced upon the FA by the clubs' chairmen despite the original idea having been to cut down on the amount of football played. It will be linked by three-up/three-down promotion and relegation to what will be the First Division of the old Football League, merely the Second Division under a new name. Referees in Premier League matches will wear a green uniform (first change, black); there will be a 15-minute half-time interval; and three substitutes (including a goalkeeper) will be permitted on the bench, any two of whom may be used.

The confirmation must have been particularly satisfying for FA chief executive Graham Kelly, after all the fuss since it was first proposed 10 months ago in the FA's "Blueprint for the Future of Football". But he must be disappointed with the rejection of the original 18-club concept, and has found it hard to explain how it will differ from the current First Division — apart, that is, from the few cosmetic changes detailed above and the higher prices that its member clubs will no doubt feel entitled to charge.

First riot for two years

IN THE FIRST SERIOUS case of hooliganism inside an English football ground for two years, rioters at St Andrews caused the Third Division match between Birmingham City and Stoke City to be held up for half an hour. It was announced that the game was abandoned but, after the ground was cleared, the managers agreed to play out the last 35 seconds, and the two sides just kicked the ball to each other until the referee blew for time.

The trouble began within seconds of Stoke's equalizer in injury time. About 400 angry Birmingham supporters swarmed on to the playing area and made towards the Stoke end. One of them, who was later identified and arrested, hit the referee, Roger Wiseman.

After being involved in several notorious crowd incidents in recent years, Birmingham have worked hard on rebuilding their image. But in the light of this latest incident, Birmingham manager Terry Cooper has said he is seriously considering leaving the club, and chairman Samesh Kumar admitted that he was in despair for the club's future.

However, Mr Kumar's remarks alleging "some scandalous decisions by the referee" are at best counter-productive. At Anfield, Liverpool manager Graeme Souness similarly described the referee after his team's match with Southampton as "a disgrace". It is comments such as these, rather than controversial decisions by match officials, that are more likely to cause crowd trouble, and it is about time that the FA took stronger measures to put a stop to irresponsible public condemnation of those officials by people within the game.

'Always look on the bright side...'

AS MANCHESTER UNITED suffered the final blow to what were only a short while ago heavily odds-on chances of winning their first Championship for 25 years — going down 2–0 to Liverpool at Anfield on 26 April — it did not help manager Alex Ferguson and his men much when the Kop choir burst out into a chorus of "Always look on the bright side of life". With Leeds being crowned champions after their same-day victory at Bramall Lane, there is only bitter disappointment for Manchester, who a week ago were two points ahead with a game in hand over their rivals. But three defeats in that time — their first home reversal of the season, by Forest, and losses to bottom club West Ham and now Liverpool — have seen them snatch failure out of the very jaws of triumph.

This should not be allowed to detract from Leeds's fine achievement, however. They have battled with Manchester for the leadership all season. They are unbeaten at home, and have lost only four League matches altogether. All credit to manager Howard Wilkinson, who in less than four years has transformed Leeds from a side fighting to stay in the Second Division into the champions of England. In doing so, he has banished from Elland Road the ghosts of the Revie era for good.

Leeds have been strong in all departments, but their midfield has been outstanding: the evergreen Gordon Strachan, Wilkinson's most inspirational signing, the combative David Batty and the elusive Gary McAllister, and Gary Speed playing wide. It is ironic that newly elected Footballer of the Year Strachan, the key man in the Leeds revival, should have been put out to grass by Alex Ferguson three years ago, with doubts surrounding his ability to keep up with the pace of top-level football. In goal, John Lukic won his second Championship medal, while other ex-Arsenal men shone in the centre: Chris Whyte in defence and Lee Chapman up front. Wilkinson added an extra touch of flair and finesse with the introduction of French international striker Eric Cantona for the last third of the season, usually as substitute, and the popular chant of "Ooh, ah, Cant-o-nah" became a familiar sound on the terraces as Leeds fought their way to the title.

Cantona, who came out of self-imposed retirement to inspire Leeds.

Leeds captain Gordon Strachan, still full of running at 35.

Strike threat averted

THE THREAT OF A strike by England's leading footballers was averted, following a meeting between the Professional Footballers' Association and the newly formed Premier League on 27 April, when PFA chief executive Gordon Taylor agreed to accept a minimum £1.5 million of television revenue next season. This represents a remarkable 50 per cent increase on the original offer. After that had been made, the PFA had circularized First Division players and received an overwhelming mandate to strike.

The deal means that, in addition to receiving 10 per cent of the first £10 million of TV income, the PFA will collect five per cent of the balance. This money is to be used for benevolent, educational and insurance purposes.

FINAL SCORE

Football League
Division 1: Leeds United
Top scorer: Ian Wright (Arsenal 24, Crystal Palace 5) 29
Division 2: Ipswich Town
Division 3: Brentford
Division 4: Burnley
Footballer of the Year: Gary Lineker (Tottenham Hotspur)

FA Cup Final

Liverpool	2	Sunderland	0

League Cup Final

Manchester United	1	Nottingham Forest	0

Scottish League
Premier Division: Rangers
Top scorer: Ally McCoist (Rangers) 34
Division 1: Dundee
Division 2: Dumbarton
Footballer of the Year: Ally McCoist (Rangers)

Scottish FA Cup Final

Rangers	2	Airdrieonians	1

Scottish League Cup Final

Hibernian	2	Dunfermline A	0

European Cup Final

Barcelona	1	Sampdoria	0

(after extra time)

Cup-Winners' Cup Final

Werder Bremen	2	Monaco	0

UEFA Cup Final
Ajax Amsterdam beat Torino 2–2, 0–0 (on away goals)

European Footballer of the Year 1991
Jean-Pierre Papin (Marseille & France)

Leading European Scorer (Golden Boot)
Ally McCoist (Rangers) 34

World Club Championship

São Paulo (Brazil)	2	Barcelona (Spain)	1

Non-qualifiers Denmark are European champions

A POPULAR QUIZ question of the future may be: who won the European Football Championship after failing to qualify for the finals? The answer is Denmark, who came into the 1992 finals in Sweden after UEFA decided that Yugoslavia, torn by civil war, could not take part. Denmark, who had finished second to Yugoslavia in their qualifying group, were invited to step in at only 11 days' notice.

With their squad hastily assembled, Denmark kicked off with a match against England, joint favourites along with France to qualify from their group. The Danes were the tournament outsiders, and played like it in the first half. But after the interval they got on top, and in the 61st minute went closest to a goal when a shot from John Jensen hit the inside of a post. A 0–0 draw was a satisfactory start.

In their second match, in Stockholm, the Danes were the better side in the first half against Sweden, but went down to Swedish enthusiasm and industry when Brolin scored in the 58th minute. With one match to come, Denmark were bottom of the group. France had been playing well within themselves, with the "easy" match against Denmark to come, but their aristocratic air was disturbed when Henrik Larsen put the Danes ahead after eight minutes. Jean-Pierre Papin equalized on the hour, and Denmark remained as good as out until 12 minutes from time. Then Lars Elstrup, who had gone on as a substitute 11 minutes earlier, scored the winner. And Sweden's defeat of England meant that Denmark had squeezed into the semi-finals, along with the host nation.

John Jensen scores Denmark's first goal in the final.

In the semis, the Danes took on the powerful favourites Holland, who had clinched their group with a superb 3–1 defeat of Germany. Denmark shocked the confident Dutch after only five minutes, when Larsen again headed them into the lead. Holland, tackling strongly, then forced themselves back into the game and Bergkamp equalized in the 23rd minute. But Larsen struck for a second time nine minutes later to restore Denmark's lead. Holland pressed throughout the second half, and the Milan connection finally produced the equalizer five minutes from time when Gullit and Van Basten combined for Rijkaard to score brilliantly.

Now, with Brian Laudrup and Henrik Andersen off injured and defender John Sivebaek limping at centre-forward, the Danes once more had their backs to the wall. But they somehow survived extra time, and in the penalty shoot-out Peter Schmeichel saved Holland's second kick, from Van Basten. No one else failed, and Kim Christofte accepted the honour of putting Denmark into the final.

Germany had played in fits and starts during the tournament, and had edged out Sweden 3–2 in the other semi. But any relief they felt at not having to face Holland again soon vanished when Denmark went ahead after 18 minutes with a goal by Jensen, set up by Vilfort and the impressive Povlsen. The Germans came strongly, but Denmark remained cool and in control. They had chances in breakaways and, in the 78th minute, Christiansen headed the ball down for Kim Vilfort to control it and slip it in off a post. The latecomers, the rank outsiders, had beaten the world champions and won the European title.

SOCCER SOUNDBITES

"We still don't understand what we have done."

PETER SCHMEICHEL,
Manchester United and Denmark goalkeeper, after his team won the European Championship.

"They came at us playing direct football. They were more English than the English."

GRAHAM TAYLOR,
explaining England's defeat by Sweden.

Taylor's trusty combinations come badly unstitched

ENGLAND, WITH HIGH expectations, flopped badly in the European Championship, coming last in their group. They looked good for a while in their first match, against substitutes Denmark, whom they confidently expected to beat. But all they scored were two yellow cards, for Martin Keown and Keith Curle in the first 10 minutes, and they were lucky not to concede a goal in the second half.

The match against France was disappointing, with the French playing for a draw and getting it. Stuart Pearce, badly butted in the face by Boli in a nasty off-the-ball incident, returned straight from treatment to shiver the cross-bar with a free-kick, but the match ended goalless.

England needed to beat Sweden to be sure of a semi-final place. They made a promising start, Platt scoring in three minutes with a volley after a fine move on the right involving Batty and Lineker. But they still lacked imagination. Eriksson equalized after 51 minutes, and Brolin scored a fine winner with eight minutes left.

Graham Taylor inevitably came in for considerable criticism over his team selection. Injuries before the finals had robbed him of three right-backs, Gary Stevens, Rob Jones and Lee Dixon, and three other players occupied this spot in England's games — Keith Curle, Andy Sinton and David Batty — none of whom was a natural in the position. John Barnes and Mark Wright were also late withdrawals.

Lineker is taken off, and denied the chance of a record.

Taylor shuffled his team around trying to find a winning combination, even switching from a back four to a sweeper and back again in the three matches. Skipper Gary Lineker had three partners up front: Smith, Shearer and Platt. Taylor failed to instil any flair into the play, however, and was criticized for not including Nigel Clough, who might have brought a touch of subtlety into the build-ups.

But Taylor's main crime in the eyes of the Press and the fans was his decision, in the game against Sweden, to take off Lineker half an hour from the end of what turned out to be his last match for England, thus depriving him of the chance of overtaking Bobby Charlton's record goal total, and appearing to cast the blame on his skipper for England's failure.

Premier League reaches for Sky

WATCHING LIVE Premier League soccer on television will cost viewers a fee in its first season. The BBC and BSkyB signed a £304 million deal that gives them both Premier League action for five seasons. Sky will transmit matches live — on Sunday afternoons and Monday evenings — while the BBC will revive the Saturday evening "Match of the Day" highlights programme. But the three million owners of Sky satellite dishes will have to take out a subscription to watch their 60 live matches a season.

FOOTBALL FOCUS

- FIFA rule that all international referees must be able to speak English.
- Everton's Northern Ireland international Norman Whiteside, 26, is forced to retire in June 1991 after an unsuccessful struggle against a knee injury.
- The convictions of UEFA (ordered to compensate Heysel disaster victims and their families) and secretary-general Hans Bangerter (three-month suspended sentence for gross negligence) were confirmed in Belgium's highest court in the third and final hearing of the case in October.
- Cup-final tradition was reversed, with the losers going up first to receive their medals, but the FA boobed, Sunderland getting the winners' medals, Liverpool the losers'.
- Gary Lineker went to Sweden with 48 international goals to his name, one behind Bobby Charlton's England record, and was odds-on to equal and beat it — but he failed to score.
- The Paul Gascoigne transfer saga was finally completed at the end of the season, after the knee injuries and the operations, and he joined Lazio to a hero's welcome after a year in limbo.
- Scotland enjoyed a more successful European Championship than England, despite also failing to reach the semi-finals. They were unlucky to lose to Germany after matching them for much of the game; they held Holland for 76 minutes, and they outplayed the CIS. And their fans behaved impeccably, unlike the English with their drunken revelling and the Germans, who rioted in Gothenburg after their defeat by Holland.

Souness takes heart from final

HAVING TWICE survived elimination from the FA Cup by the width of the cross-bar against Second Division clubs — Ipswich in the fifth round and Portsmouth in the semi-finals — Liverpool faced yet another Division Two club in the final. Their opponents, Sunderland, had already put out three First Division sides in West Ham, Chelsea and Norwich.

Manager Graeme Souness, recovering from heart surgery, was on the Liverpool bench against doctor's advice, and could not bear to watch at times. In the event, Liverpool's class asserted itself, and his team won comfortably enough, thus earning themselves a place in Europe for 1992–93. Steve McManaman was the man of the match, and Michael Thomas and Ian Rush — with a record fifth goal in FA Cup finals — scored.

Sunderland's run to the final at least ensured that the job of manager went to Malcolm Crosby, who was for weeks only the caretaker as Sunderland's successes went on and on.

Little stress for Souness at the Cup final.

FINAL SCORE

EUROPEAN CHAMPIONSHIP 1992

Group 1

Sweden	1	France	1
England	0	Denmark	0
England	0	France	0
Sweden	1	Denmark	0
Sweden	2	England	1
Denmark	2	France	1

	P	W	D	L	F	A	P
Sweden	3	2	1	0	4	2	5
Denmark	3	1	1	1	2	2	3
France	3	0	2	1	2	3	2
England	3	0	2	1	1	2	2

Group 2

Holland	1	Scotland	0
CIS	1	Germany	1
Germany	2	Scotland	0
Holland	0	CIS	0
Holland	3	Germany	1
Scotland	3	CIS	0

	P	W	D	L	F	A	P
Holland	3	2	1	0	4	1	5
Germany	3	1	1	1	4	4	3
Scotland	3	1	0	2	3	3	2
CIS	3	0	2	1	1	4	2

SEMI-FINALS

Germany	3	Sweden	2
Denmark	2	Holland	2

(aet) Denmark won 5–4 on penalties

FINAL

Denmark	2	Germany	0

Gothenburg, 26 June 1992. Attendance 37,800

Denmark: Schmeichel, Sivebaek (Christiansen), Nielsen K, Olsen L, Christofte, Jensen, Povlsen, Laudrup B., Piechnik, Larsen, Vilfort (Scorers: Jensen, Vilfort)
Germany: Illgner, Reuter, Brehme, Kohler, Buchwald, Hassler, Riedle, Helmer, Sammer (Doll), Effenberg (Thon), Klinsmann

Blackburn Rovers back in top flight

BLACKBURN ROVERS chose the right season to win promotion from the Second Division. They went straight into the new Premier Division after winning a Wembley play-off final against Leicester City.

The last Premier spot was not decided until 25 May, more than two weeks after the Cup final. Rovers' David Speedie was brought down in the penalty area, and Mike Newell scored from the spot for the only goal of the game. Blackburn's appearance in the top flight will be their first since 1966.

There were two ironies in their achievement. Their late chairman, Bill Fox, as president of the Football League, had fought tooth and nail against the new Premier League, which his club were now joining. And Kenny Dalglish, their manager, who had been lured to Blackburn by retired steel magnate Jack Walker, with the help of £5.5 million to spend in the transfer market, found himself returning to the pressures of the top division, which had forced him to give up the Liverpool managership only 15 months earlier.

Dalglish: feeling the pressure at Blackburn?

Vinny pays for video nasty

THE FA CAME DOWN hard on Vinny Jones for his part in the now notorious video "Soccer's Hard Men". At a disciplinary hearing on 17 November, they handed the Wimbledon midfielder a record £20,000 fine and a six-month suspension, itself suspended for three years. The fine is the heaviest imposed on a footballer in England, dwarfing the £8,500 Aston Villa's Paul McGrath was fined for newspaper comments about his previous club, Manchester United.

Vinny Jones (left): no stranger to trouble.

Wimbledon chairman Sam Hammam, whose initial reaction when he first heard about the offending video was to describe his wayward player as a "mosquito brain", felt the punishment was unduly harsh. He accused the FA of having double standards, citing some of the recent indiscretions of Paul Gascoigne, for example, which, he suggested, had been treated as innocent pranks.

The FA, however, felt otherwise about a video that attempts to portray the unsavoury aspects of the game, and which has been described as a manual on how to commit fouls. Jones, who pleaded guilty to bringing the game into disrepute, had offered an apology as soon as the furore erupted, and announced that he would be handing his fee — said to be £1,300 — to a charity. He'll need it now, however, to help pay his fine — unless the video's producers pay it for him.

The end of Magpies' overture

NEWCASTLE'S barnstorming start to the season finally came to an end on 24 October, when it was least expected, at home to Grimsby Town. So after 11 straight wins — only two away from equalling Reading's record start — Kevin Keegan's men have at last given some hope to the chasing pack, now "only" nine points or more behind.

Without the injured Kevin Sheedy and David Kelly, the Magpies appeared subdued, and lowly Grimsby won a thoroughly well-deserved victory with a 25-yard drive from Clive Mendonca, who had twice earlier hit the woodwork. If the Mariners continue to play like this, they will have no trouble staying in the First Division, while Newcastle's momentum towards the Premier League is unlikely to be affected by this first setback.

The tremendous interest generated by this remarkable run has paid off at the gate and helped to defray Keegan's salary.

Brave new world, familiar feeling

THE ENGLISH FOOTBALL season began on 15 August to a metaphorical fanfare of trumpets ushering in the new FA Premier League. At first glance, the nine-match programme appeared to suggest that they had reverted to the original idea of an 18-club "Super League". But that was forgetting the needs of BSkyB and its satellite dishes, which look like becoming a major influence on the scheduling of fixtures, with their live telecasts of regular Sunday afternoon and Monday evening fixtures. On Sundays, they would be competing with a regional First Division (old Second Division) match on ITV and a plum from the Italian Serie A on Channel Four.

With stadiums in the process of being converted to all-seaters, building work took the gloss off the historic opening. Arsenal's bright idea of covering their North Bank eyesore with a huge mural of spectators — already criticized for being ethnically unrepresentative — backfired on their team, who could not score at their hitherto favoured end, and the Premier League favourites were beaten 4–2 by Norwich after leading 2–0 at half-time.

Anyone looking for evidence of a brave new world on this first day would have noticed a difference in the play. But this was not due to the much-heralded Premier League, but to a fundamental change in the laws that came into practice this season, known familiarly as the "back-pass law". Framed to cut down on time-wasting, this revolutionary legislation made it an offence for a goalkeeper to handle the ball, on pain of an indirect free-kick, when it was deliberately passed to him by a team-mate, unless the ball was headed or chested. Some keepers soon showed a flair for this additional "sweeper" role with hefty kicks upfield, while others demonstrated how easy it was to get in a tangle when under pressure from an onrushing striker.

A "subdued" North Bank for Arsenal's 1992–93 opener, as the mural screening development work gets its first airing.

FOOTBALL FOCUS

- Norwich, who disputed the Premier League title for most of the season and led the table on several occasions, finished third despite conceding more goals than they scored (61–65). On 16 January, having played 24 matches, they found themselves in the unusual situation of being the leaders with a negative goal difference (35–36).
- AC Milan paid Torino a world record £13m for 23-year-old Italian international winger Gianluigi Lentini in July 1992.
- Leeds United enjoyed an incredible reprieve against Stuttgart in the first round of the European Cup, after fighting back from 3–0 down in the first leg to win 4–1 at Elland Road and going out — so they thought — on goal difference. Then it was found that the German champions had played four, instead of the permitted three, foreign-born players, and Leeds won a hastily arranged decider 2–1 in Barcelona. But they went out to Glasgow Rangers in the second round after two 2–1 defeats.
- Albion Rovers, bottom of Dvision Two in Scotland, used 44 players in their 39 league games.

Fergie woos Frenchman for scoring power

ALEX FERGUSON ended his long search for a new striker when he persuaded the popular French star Eric Cantona to join Manchester United from Leeds on 26 November. This sensational coup has not pleased Elland Road fans, who took the much-travelled Cantona, 26, to their hearts last season as he helped them win the title.

Leeds manager Howard Wilkinson felt the move was in the interests of all concerned, and that Cantona would stand a better chance of a regular first-team place with Manchester. The fee, believed to be in the region of £1.5 million, takes Ferguson's spending to over £18 million. Since pulling out of a close-season duel with Blackburn for Alan Shearer, who went to Ewood Park for £3.6 million, he paid Cambridge £1 million for Dion Dublin, who promptly broke a leg, and had a £3.5 million bid for Sheffield Wednesday's David Hirst turned down.

Manchester's lack of goals lately has been worrying, and it will be interesting to see how Cantona's flair and touch combines with the more explosive skills of Mark Hughes up front. There is another intriguing aspect of the move: how will the fiery Cantona settle at such a big club?

Gascoigne's ill wind blows nobody any good

PAUL GASCOIGNE'S tendency to play the fool in front of the television cameras has landed him in more trouble. The England midfielder incurred the wrath of an Italian member of parliament, who has called for him to be fined for belching into a microphone. Gascoigne was asked to comment on his exclusion from the Lazio team on 24 January, and his undignified response was broadcast on national television. Although the enraged MP, Giulio Maceratini, has a point when he says that a top sportsman who earns millions has a duty to set a better example to young people, it is difficult to take seriously any politician who complains about wind.

Paul Gascoigne (blue shirt, middle) still finds something to smile about at a Lazio training session.

Peter Shilton sent off for first time

PETER SHILTON was sent off for the first time in his career, in his 971st League game, after conceding a penalty with a "professional foul" in Plymouth's 2–0 Second Division defeat at Hull on 28 August. The Plymouth goalkeeper-manager, who is in his 42nd year, brought down Hull's Graeme Atkinson after 26 minutes, and received his marching orders from referee Paul Harrison.

Stand-in keeper Nicky Marker, a defender, saved the penalty, but Hull scored two late goals against Plymouth's 10 men to go top of the table.

Why do FIFA need a kick-in?

A MEETING OF the International Board, the game's law-making body, in February, gave FIFA permission to experiment with substituting a "kick-in" for the throw-in. The trials will take place in UEFA and FIFA junior tournaments later in the year. The idea — the brainchild of FIFA general secretary Sepp Blatter — is so flawed that it could only come from the muddle-headed confines of Zurich.

The hitherto ultra-conservative guardians of the game's laws have panicked since the welter of adverse criticism hit them following the 1990 World Cup, and have in recent years come up with all kinds of gimmicks to "improve" the game as a spectacle.

It is one thing to cut down on unnecessary time-wasting, but speeding the game up, which is one reason given for the kick-in, will not necessarily make for more entertaining football. There are many who believe that the game has become too fast as it is. And, anyway, why they think that a kick-in will be taken any quicker than a throw-in is a mystery. Swindon player-manager Glenn Hoddle, when he heard of the experiment, described it as a farce, and said he might as well pack the game in, and leave it to the 6ft 4in strikers and long-kicking merchants. If this hare-brained idea had come from anywhere but FIFA, it would surely have been kicked into touch by the International Board. The actual experiments will be unrepresentative, scheduled as they are for youth football. And, of course, there is the usual piece of nonsense written into the experimental law — as with the throw-in, a player can not be ruled offside from a kick-in. In other words, if the ball is near the touchline, it will be cheaper to foul an opponent than kick the ball into touch. Let's see how long it takes FIFA to spot that one.

Bobby Moore dies: a true hero of football

Bobby Moore: universally mourned.

WHEN BOBBY MOORE died on 24 February, just nine days after announcing to the world that he had cancer, not only the footballing world mourned, but all those whose hearts had been filled with pride when he held the World Cup aloft at Wembley in 1966, as captain of England, felt a great sense of loss. For Bobby Moore was more than a gifted footballer and an inspirational captain. He came to represent the ideals of a long ago age, when sportsmanship still had a place in the game.

It would be naive to think that these ideals were not crumbling long before Moore finished playing. But he was the epitome of the footballing hero, blessed with a wonderful temperament and an unquenchable will to win — but not if it meant compromising his principles of fair play. Three years running, he climbed the Wembley stairs as captain to receive a valued trophy — the FA Cup and European Cup-Winners' Cup with West Ham, then followed by the crowning glory of the World Cup.

Not for Moore the crunching tackle made with no respect for life and limb. He was unsurpassed as a reader of the game, and as No.6 to a stopper centre-half, he won the ball by anticipation. His distribution, especially his long passing, was the envy even of the midfield generals. Moore won more friends and admirers in the 1970 World Cup, and his duel with Brazil's Pele was as memorable as any goal. After he retired, he was never really a success as a manager or as a businessman. But he made an indelible impression on the game, as one of its true heroes. His death, at 51, leves the world a poorer place.

City beaten by Nayim hat-trick and shamed by crowd

THE FACT THAT Manchester City's Terry Phelan scored arguably the best goal of the season, albeit in a lost cause, when he ran through the entire Tottenham team, was lost in the havoc that ensued at Maine Road in the FA Cup quarter-final on 7 March. Ostensibly to celebrate this gem of a goal, which pulled City back to 2–4 down with three minutes left, the home fans poured from the new £6 million all-seater Umbro Stand onto the pitch in the forlorn hope of having the tie abandoned. Although there was no violence, it required 13 mounted police to clear the pitch so the game could be finished.

City fans were understandably disappointed that Spurs had overwhelmed them after Sheron had given them an early lead, and, thanks largely to a Nayim hat-trick, had put the result beyond doubt before full-back Phelan's piece of bravado. But there is no possible excuse for the sort of behaviour that has almost been eradicated inside grounds over the last few years, and City might well find themselves in trouble with the authorities.

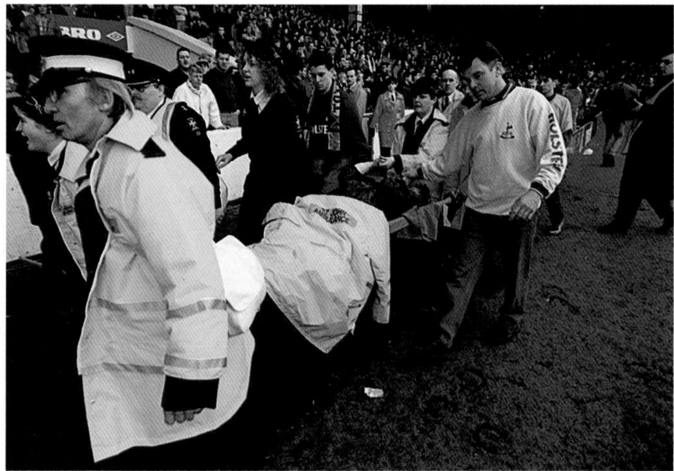

Stretcher bearers walk over the hoof prints on the Maine Road pitch.

Adams banishes those 'donkey' jibes

TONY ADAMS, 26, whose England career seemed to have taken a nose-dive since those early days of much promise and potential as a future captain of his country, established himself as a defensive rock in England's heartening triumph over Turkey on 31 March. In a sinister atmosphere of violence and intimidation from the 50,000 crowd in Izmir, he stood firm at the back while goals from Platt and Gascoigne ensured England stayed on course for World Cup 94. Then, just four days later, he led Arsenal to victory over Spurs in the second FA Cup semi-final between the North London rivals held at Wembley in three years. And it must have given him immense satisfaction to avenge that bitter defeat in 1991, by heading the only goal of the game 11 minutes from time.

Arsenal fans have never lost faith in Adams, despite his off-field transgressions, and he has repaid them by leading the club to two Championships. Those unwarranted "donkey" jibes he has stoically suffered at grounds around the country appear pretty asinine themselves now.

The life of Brian

BRIAN CLOUGH, 58, said farewell to his adoring Nottingham Forest fans at the City Ground on 1 May. It was Forest's last home match, and it mattered little that Sheffield United beat them 2–0 and consigned them to relegation, after the most unsuccessful season of Mr Clough's long, colourful and hugely controversial career. And, true to form, it ended in controversy, too, as he announced his retirement amid persistent rumours, and issued libel writs against a Sunday newspaper and a club director over allegations of excessive drinking.

Despite Forest's lack-lustre performance, their biggest crowd of the season, 26,752, preferred to remember the many major honours this gifted eccentric had brought them. He arrived 18 years ago, after triumphs at Derby and tribulations with Leeds and Brighton, and put the name of Nottingham Forest on the football map again, not only in England but all over Europe. When his teams won, they did so with style, a brand of passing, on-the-floor football that became the hallmark of the teams he built and coached along with his partner, the late Peter Taylor. A showman, a maverick and an individualist, he was always at the centre of the great debate, the rallying cry when things went wrong on the international scene — "Clough for England!". Whether he would have been a success is another matter, and it is highly unlikely that the FA would have put up with his arrogance for long.

So the fans paid a last tribute to their hero. He'd taken them from the Second Division to the First, to League Cups, to the Championship and to double glory in Europe, and now he'd taken them down again. But what a trip it had been!

Brian Clough: the one and only.

Steve Morrow celebrates his Cup-winning goal.

Morrow sorrow — dropped after scoring winner

STEVE MORROW scored Arsenal's winning goal in their 2–1 victory over Sheffield Wednesday in the Coca-Cola (League) Cup at Wembley and then broke an arm in a freak accident during the celebrations at the end of the game. Morrow, 22, an Irish international full-back, but unable to establish a place in the Arsenal first team, came into the midfield because of injuries, and did an excellent marking job on Sheridan in the final. The goal, his first for the club, came after 68 minutes, when Carlton Palmer failed to clear a Merson cross and Morrow appeared out of nowhere to crash the ball past Woods.

Wednesday had made an encouraging start when John Harkes, who two years ago became the first American to play at Wembley, became the first American to score there, after only nine minutes, slamming the ball home after a cross from King was not properly cleared. Waddle failed to justify the media and public protest mounted when he was excluded from the England squad during the week, and it was Arsenal's Merson who played the star role. Always a danger when he ran at the Wednesday defence, he equalized with a swerving volley from outside the box that had Woods stretching in vain.

At the final whistle, Tony Adams hoisted Morrow onto his shoulders. He fell awkwardly as his skipper let him down, and was in obvious agony. He was given oxygen and a pain-killing injection before being carried off, while his subdued team-mates collected their medals and the sorrowful Adams hoisted the Cup. Sheffield will have their chance of revenge when the two sides meet again in the FA Cup final in May, but Morrow will not be facing them.

Zambian team killed in air crash

ALL BUT FOUR members of the Zambian football squad were killed on 28 April, when the aircraft taking them to a World Cup qualifying match against Senegal crashed into the sea after taking off from Libreville, Gabon, following a refuelling stop. The 30 people on board all died. Four squad members who play for European clubs escaped — they were to join the party in Dakar. Early signs are that Zambia are determined to carry on and try to qualify for the World Cup finals for the first time.

'Excuse me, Mr Ferguson, you are champions'

ALEX FERGUSON had taken nearly seven years to put Manchester United back on top of English football, to guide them to their first League Championship since 1967. And when the great moment arrived, on 2 May, he was not in the dugout urging his men on and leaping up at the final whistle. He was on the golf course, oblivious to the progress of Aston Villa, who had fought for the title tooth and nail with United over the last few weeks and were the only side now that could prevent a Manchester triumph. He was putting on the last green when a fellow member approached, with the words: "Excuse me, Mr Ferguson, you are the champions. Oldham have won at Aston Villa."

The following evening saw the biggest party in the history of modern British soccer, as United's team captain Steve Bruce and club captain Bryan Robson collected the new Premier League trophy in front off 40,000 delirious fans at Old Trafford and then celebrated by beating Blackburn 3–1. It was a night of high emotion, and Sir Matt Busby, the last manager to taste such success, was there to share the glory. In between, five managers — Wilf McGuinness, Frank O'Farrell, Tommy Docherty, Dave Sexton and Ron Atkinson — have tried and failed to fill the shoes of Sir Matt, who built three great United sides. Mr Atkinson, now in charge of Villa, did his best to spoil Alex Ferguson's season. And at one stage, it looked as if United might repeat last year's attack of spring nerves, when they blew their chances in one fateful week, and Mr Ferguson was desolate. But he kept faith with his team — and his own belief in them — added a touch of French spice during the season to pep them up, and won the title with style and panache commensurate with the club's best traditions.

Steve Bruce crowns Bryan Robson Premiership king.

It was entirely appropriate that Bryan Robson, again plagued with injury, played enough matches to earn a Championship medal. He has been a wonderful servant to the club. For once he did not play a leading role, but this season Paul Ince has filled his shoes admirably, for England as well as United. The side, which gave a joyous demonstration of their individual and collective skills against Blackburn for their celebrating faithful fans, was: Schmeichel, Parker, Irwin, Bruce, Sharpe (Robson), Pallister, Cantona, Ince, McClair (Kanchelskis), Hughes, Giggs — the "class of 93".

United's fourth great side since the war contains names that can be mentioned in the same breath as such mighty icons of the past as Best, Charlton, Law and Edwards. Eric Cantona — Ferguson's master-stroke, when he signed him from Leeds in November — became the first player to win Championship medals with different clubs in successive seasons. And Mr Ferguson, having had considerable success with Aberdeen, became the first manager to win League titles north and south of the border. With the precocious young talents of Lee Sharpe and Welsh genius Ryan Giggs flowering into maturity, Mr Ferguson can look forward to further triumphs in seasons to come.

Champion style: Ryan Giggs scoring for United against Southampton in February.

Linighan leaves it late

Ian Wright (left) puts Arsenal ahead in the replay.

ANDY LINIGHAN, Arsenal's stopper, broke the hearts of Sheffield Wednesday fans at Wembley on Thursday, 20 May, when he headed Arsenal's winner a minute before the end of extra time in their FA Cup final replay. But he won the undying gratitude of the majority of neutral fans who detest the penalty shoot-out, which would have been the method used to decide the winners for the first time ever in an FA Cup final.

It was not a classic final, only marginally better than Saturday's grinding bore when Wednesday's Hirst equalized a first-half goal by Wright. Linighan had made that Arsenal goal, heading a Davis free-kick back across goal for Wright, nursing a broken toe, to head in. And it was the quicksilver Wright who gave Arsenal a 35th-minute lead in the replay, running on to an Alan Smith flick to beat Woods and score his 10th goal of Arsenal's Cup campaign — before having to be substituted again.

In the second half, however, as Wednesday wrested control from Arsenal, Waddle equalized in the 68th minute and Bright missed a great chance to put them in front three minutes later. He did not, however, miss Linighan's face with his elbow in what was one of many unsavoury clashes that soured the game.

Linighan, for two years a £1.3 million misfit at Highbury, jeered by the fans, had forced his way into the side earlier in the season when Bould was injured. His last-minute, point-blank header from Merson's corner not only won Arsenal a place in next season's Cup-Winners' Cup, but it put his former club Norwich in the UEFA Cup.

Historically, Arsenal, playing in their record 12th FA Cup final, recorded their sixth win and became the first club to pull off the FA Cup/League Cup double in one season. George Graham completed a unique feat of winning the three major English domestic honours as both player and manager. In seven years at Highbury, he has built a formidable, winning team. His next ambition must be to produce a team that everyone can love.

The battered Linighan (far left) becomes Arsenal's hero with a towering last-minute header.

Souness stays on at Anfield

LIVERPOOL CREATED a sensation at the end of the season by not sacking their manager, Graeme Souness. Director Tony Ensor, presumably the only member of the Anfield board not to go along with what was a startling and mysterious U-turn, resigned when the decision to keep their controversial manager was announced. The team, which was never in the running for the League title, finished sixth in the table and did not qualify for Europe — failure for a club that has dominated English football for so long. A subdued Souness put the rumours of his imminent dismissal down to Press speculation, and insisted that the team he took over was never going to win anything. He was not dissatisfied with the way rebuilding was proceeding. Of more concern to the directors, however, must be Liverpool's disciplinary record, as six players were sent off during the season. They must surely fear that Souness is hardly the man to reverse this disturbing trend.

Venables gets the sack as Sugar turns sour

WHILE ARSENAL were winning the FA Cup at Wembley, another soccer drama was unfolding on the other side of North London, at White Hart Lane, where Spurs chief Terry Venables was once more desperately trying to get backing to buy out the current major shareholder, Alan Sugar. Two years ago, it was electronics tycoon Sugar who came to Venables's aid when the club looked like going under or being taken over by Robert Maxwell. Now Sugar was himself cast in the role of villain, having sensationally, and completely out of the blue, sacked Mr Venables as chief executive of Spurs on 14 May. The following day, Mr Venables was temporarily reinstated by a High Court order, and battle commenced.

As a player, Venables helped Spurs to win the FA Cup in 1967, then completed a double by managing the club to a repeat performance in 1991. The immediate reaction of players and fans to the dismissal of such a popular figure was one of complete shock. Venables, hailed as the club's saviour, is regarded as "Mr Tottenham", and it was hard to find an ally for Mr Sugar inside the club — apart, that is, from the three directors who voted Mr Venables off the board.

Mr Sugar has been slow to assert that he had no quarrels with the chief executive's handling of the footballing side, and that the dispute was about the interference of Mr Venables and his advisers in financial matters. But the fans, the players and the club's administrative staff have made it only too clear that the removal of a man who exerts such a profound influence at every level of Tottenham's operations could well bring the whole edifice crashing down.

FINAL SCORE

Football League
Premier Division: Manchester United
Top scorer: Teddy Sheringham (Nottingham Forest 1, Tottenham Hotspur 21) 22
Division 1: Newcastle United
Division 2: Stoke City
Division 3: Cardiff City
Footballer of the Year: Chris Waddle (Sheffield Wednesday)

FA Cup Final

Arsenal	1	Sheffield Wed	1
(after extra time)			
Replay: Arsenal	2	Sheffield Wed	1
(after extra time)			

League Cup Final

Arsenal	2	Sheffield Wed	1

Scottish League
Premier Division: Rangers
Top scorer: Ally McCoist (Rangers) 34
Division 1: Raith Rovers
Division 2: Clyde
Footballer of the Year: Andy Goram (Rangers)

Scottish FA Cup Final

Rangers	2	Aberdeen	1

Scottish League Cup Final

Rangers	2	Aberdeen	1
(after extra time)			

European Cup Final

Olympique Marseille	1	AC Milan	0

Cup-Winners' Cup Final

Parma	3	Royal Antwerp	1

UEFA Cup Final
Juventus beat Borussia Dortmund 3–1, 3–0

European Footballer of the Year 1992
Marco van Basten (MAC Milan & Holland)

Leading European Scorer (Golden Boot)
Award discontinued

England humbled by USA in another Taylor shambles

IT COULDN'T HAPPEN again - but it did. The nightmare of England's humiliating World Cup defeat in Belo Horizonte in 1950 at the hands or the United States was relived in Foxboro, Massachusetts, where Graham Taylor's "team", still smarting from their disastrous display in Oslo, succumbed 2-0 to the unrated 1994 World Cup hosts in the US '95 Cup.

The beleaguered England manager, lifted earlier by the news of Norway's draw in Rotterdam, fielded a weakened side against the Americans, with Nigel Clough replacing the absent Paul Gascoigne. He saw his new central-defence partnership of Gary Pallister and Carlton Palmer embarrassed by the skill and vision of Coventry's Roy Wegerle, but it still came as a shock when England went a goal down two minutes before half-time. It was scored with a header by Thomas Dooley, the German-born Kaiserslautern striker who had not visited the USA until last year. England's humiliation was completed midway through the second half when the gangling, red-bearded Alexi Lalas, on as substitute for the injured Dooley, headed home a corner. US keeper Tony Meola made two brilliant saves when Ian Wright broke through to deny England even a consolation goal. The defeat has left England in utter disarray, with public and press baying for Taylor's resignation.

SOCCER SOUNDBITES

"I don't think there is a need for a new manager."

PETER SWALES,
chairman of the FA's international committee.

Wegerle (17) and Harkes celebrate USA's victory over England.

Sugar-Venables saga unearths sensational allegations

THE RUNNING BATTLE between Spurs chairman Alan Sugar and former chief executive Terry Venables for control of the club reached the High Court on 10 June with 2,500 pages of sworn statements. Among these were the sensational allegations by Mr Sugar of corrupt practices he found at the club and in football, Including under-the-counter payments to managers of other clubs to ease through big transfer deals.

One incident, in particular, was highlighted, namely a "bung", as it is called, to Nottingham Forest manager Brian Clough when his striker Teddy Sheringham moved to Spurs for £2.1 million. This allegation - quickly denied by Mr Clough - was in the form of a sworn affidavit by Mr Sugar, and mentioned a considerable cash payment said to have been handed over at a secret meeting in a motorway service station.

Mr Sugar, who also heads the computer and electronics company Amstrad, is contesting an injunction to prevent him removing Mr Venables from the Tottenham board. He received a hostile reception from Spurs fans outside and inside the court. Mr Venables, although enjoying the support of a section of the club's fans, is opposed by the majority of directors.

Superficially, it is a case of two powerful personalities competing for control of a club. But as allegations unfold of the seamier side of football, it is the game that is really on trial.

Tottenham supporters show their support for Venables.

Double-Dutch misery for England

ENGLAND'S American dream was dashed at Rotterdam on 13 October when Holland beat them 2-0 and left them requiring a minor miracle next month to qualify - a seven-goal win in Bologna over San Marino plus a Dutch defeat in Poland, where Norway have just clinched their World Cup place with a 3-0 win.

This crucial match hinged on a controversial decision of the German referee Karl Josef Assenmacher in the 60th minute. With the score 0-0, David Platt ran on to an Andy Sinton through pass, leaving Koeman in his wake and with only the keeper to beat. But Koeman desperately pulled him back on the edge of the box. It was a blatant red-card offence, as Koeman later himself admitted, but the referee gave only a free-kick. Tony Dorigo, who had hit a post with a free-kick In the first half, took it, but had his shot charged down. This was particularly galling for England and her supporters when exactly the same thing happened at the other end, but the referee ordered the kick to be retaken, booked Paul Ince for arguing and - irony of ironies - Koeman chipped the wall to beat David Seaman and put Holland ahead.

For all Graham Taylor's bleating afterwards, it must be said that Frank Rijkaard had a perfectly good goal for Holland disallowed in the first half for offside. Taylor, whose job was well and truly on the line, had to be cautioned by a FIFA official for encroaching too near the pitch. Dennis Bergkamp clinched it for Holland with a low shot after 70 minutes, and when Paul Merson hit a post with another free-kick, it was typical of England's luck on the night.

To add to England's woe, some 1,400 football fans were arrested before the game, most of them reported to be English, although it appeared that the Dutch police overreacted, detaining 600 of them for not having tickets.

Platt is fouled by Koeman.

Ooh ah, off you go - Eric Cantona sent off as United go out of Europe

GALATASARAY, thanks to their remarkable 3-3 draw at Old Trafford a fortnight ago, eliminated Manchester United from European Cup when they held the English Champions to a goalless draw in Istanbul. And to complete United's night of misery, French star Eric Cantona was sent off in the mayhem that followed the final whistle. It was an expensive defeat for the English champions, who looked to have booked their place in the lucrative league phase of the competition when they took that 2-0 lead against the unfancied Turks after only 13 minutes of their home leg. In a night of frustration, Cantona complained throughout about Galatasaray's time-wasting tactics, at one stage causing an ugly scene on the running track when he went to retrieve the ball from the home bench. At the final whistle, after shaking match referee Kurt Rothlisberger by the hand, he gestured and said something to the Swiss French-teacher that had him reaching for the red card.

United were lucky to go in level at half-time, and after the interval their play became more ragged as desperation set in. Cantona's reactions and his inability to control his temper incited an already hostile and hysterical crowd, and at the end both he and Bryan Robson were struck by police in the players' tunnel. The banners proclaiming "Welcome to Hell" on United's arrival were indeed prophetic.

Eric Cantona is escorted away following his red card after the game.

England out - misery against San Marino

ENGLAND'S elimination from the 1994 World Cup was confirmed on a dismal night in Bologna in front of the smallest crowd ever to watch an England match - the 2,378 who turned up to see them face the part-timers of San Marino in a last, desperate attempt to score the seven goals that might have saved them. They scored the seven all right, but only after San Marino had scored what is believed to be the fastest ever goal in a competitive international.

Less than 10 seconds had elapsed when computer clerk Davide Gualtieri latched on to a pathetic Stuart Pearce back-pass to give the tournament's minnows a sensational lead. It took England 22 minutes to recover their composure and equalize through Paul Ince, and, with Ian Wright hitting four, they went on to rack up seven. It was not quite the seven-goal victory they needed if Holland were to lose by a goal in Poland. But in the event it was academic, because the Dutch side won 3-1 and took the second qualifying place in the group, Norway having already gone through.

This was only San Marino's second goal in the tournament, their other coming against Turkey last October, and in the end they conceded 46 in their 10 matches. England have reached their lowest ebb since 1977, when they last failed to qualify for the World Cup finals. The thousand England fans in Bologna were predictably chanting for Graham Taylor's head, and San Marino almost embarrassed England further before Wright scored the seventh goal, when Bacciocchi hit an upright.

SOCCER SOUNDBITES

"My foul was outside the area, but I expected to see the red card"

RONALD KOEMAN,
the Dutch captain, who scored Holland's opener a few minutes after the referee failed to send him off for bringing down David Platt in a clear goalscoring position

Hounded Taylor steps down at last

ENGLAND MANAGER Graham Taylor finally resigned from the job a week after England's failure to qualify for the 1994 World Cup. It was perhaps one of the more predictable acts of a man who has baffled the press, the public and even his own players with his team selection and tactics.

It was evident after his handling of England in Sweden last year that Taylor was not the man for the job. But no one should have had to endure the vilification Taylor has suffered from sections of the popular press in a puerile campaign that breached all principles of reputable journalism. It was a campaign that possibly backfired, because it precluded sensible debate and made it almost impossible for the FA to remove him without seemingly capitulating to the rabble.

Like his predecessor Bobby Robson, Taylor was allowed to go on too long. Also like Robson, Taylor was an outstanding club manager who failed to reproduce his success at the highest level. This in part was due to lack of vision, but most England managers have been hamstrung by a governing body still run by club chairmen who sometimes do not appear to regard the interests of the national side as paramount, and who must take their share of the blame for England's fate.

Creator of the Busby Babes dies, aged 84

SIR MATT BUSBY, one of the out-standing figures in post-war British football, died in hospital at Cheadle on 20 January after a long illness. He was a gentle Scot who became the father figure of English football and one of the greatest managers in its history.

During an illustrious career, Sir Matt achieved success first as a player, a wing-half with Manchester City and Liverpool, winning a single cup for Scotland in 1956, and after the war as a manager, the far-seeing architect of three outstanding Manchester United sides. Under Busby, United, without a major trophy since before the First World War, soon became one of England's leading clubs.

As his ageing side broke up, he replaced them with the "Busby Babes", potentially the greatest club side of all time before they were decimated in the Munich Air Disaster of 1958. Busby was haunted regularly by memories of this tragedy, in which he came so close to death himself. But he not only recovered his health, he was able to draw on infinite resources of courage and determination to build yet another great team, one that was to become, in 1968, the first English side to win the European Cup. He was knighted shortly after this, became a director of United in 1971, and had been president of the club since 1980.

But Busby's influence in football was not just as the creator of a great club. He led English club football into Europe when the rest were prevaricating, and he captured the imagination of soccer fans all over the world with the style of his teams.

Busby was a family man, and he was a paternalist, too, in the tough world of football. He always cared, he always forgave. He earned loyalty and love from all who worked with and for him. And he won the respect and admiration from everyone he came in contact with. Above all, he was a humble man, a symbol of sport on its highest plane.

As tearful fans, some of them children, laid flowers outside Old Trafford and stood silently in the Manchester drizzle, tributes to Sir Matt poured in. Bobby Charlton, however, himself a Munich survivor and one of the most famous of the Babes, was too distraught to say anything at this time.

SOCCER SOUNDBITES

"Winning isn't the test of real achievement. There should be no conceit in victory and no despair in defeat"

SIR MATT BUSBY

Sir Matt's hearse stops outside Old Trafford for two minutes' silence.

Venables in, Souness out

Terry Venables appointed as England's new Coach.

AS ENGLAND announced their new supremo, or "coach" as Terry Venables will be called, another controversial character, Graeme Souness, stepped down from what has become the hottest seat in English club football, manager of the declining Liverpool side. While Venables has been charged, at least until the 1996 European Championships, with restoring the national side to its former glory (a heady triumph some 30 years earlier), Souness departed because he failed to restore Liverpool to the high plane they occupied until relatively recently.

Venables was not only the people's choice, but the professional's choice, and he owes his selection largely to the fact that the FA employed the ex-pro Jimmy Armfield to make soundings with the game. Venables, despite his extra-curricular activities, emerged as the outstanding candidate. It was clear at the press conference on the Wembley pitch, however, that both sides have negotiated a get-out clause in the event of unforeseen consequences.

The new coach knows that he will inherit many of the frustrations that have plagued his predecessors, not east the fact that international football comes second to the domestic game. It will be fascinating to see not only how he goes about rebuilding the England side, but how he faces up to the enigma of the FA, who give the impression to be 100 percent in favor of progress yet at the same time are reluctant to change their system.

The formal announcement of Souness' departure from Anfield was made by Liverpool chairman David Moores, who last May saved him form dismissal when there was widespread expectancy that a change of management was imminent. While Souness could be forgiven his occasional lapses, in the end it was his lack of success that brought his downfall. He has reached an agreement with the club over the unexpired 27 months portion of his £1.25 million five-year contract.

Roy Evans, promoted to assistant manager at the end of lastseason, will take charge until a successor is appointed.

SOCCER SOUNDBITES

"I want to play good football but not fantasy football (playing well and losing). We must have a system that the players understand. It's up to me to make it as simple as possible."

TERRY VENABLES

SOCCER SOUNDBITES

"Liverpool football club is all about winning things and being a source of pride to our fans. It has no other purpose."

DAVIS MOORES,
Liverpool chairman.

Villa put paid to United's dream of treble

ASTON VILLA destroyed Manchester United's dream of the domestic treble at Wembley on Sunday 27 March when they beat the League leaders and FA Cup semi-finalists 3-1 in the Coca-Cola Cup final. It was a thoroughly deserved victory in which Villa out-thought and outplayed United to clinch a place in next season's UEFA Cup. To add to United's troubles, Andrei Kanchelskis became their fourth player to be sent off in five games and will miss the FA Cup semi-final.

Dalian Atkinson scored Villa's first goal of the Final.

The win was particularly sweet for Villa manager Ron Atkinson, sacked by United in 1986, who enjoyed a repeat of his triumph three years ago when he led Sheffield Wednesday to victory over his former club in a League Cup final. His tactics worked to perfection. With Dean Saunders as a lone striker, his five-man midfield swamped United. The masterstroke was using striker Dalian Atkinson in an unfamiliar position on the right of midfield, and he and Tony Daley on the other side gave full-backs Earl Barrett and Steve Staunton superb protection against deadly wingers Ryan Giggs, who was substituted, and Kanchelskis.

Villa took the lead in the 25th minute through Atkinson, who beat Les Sealey, deputizing for the suspended Peter Schmeichel, from 10 yards alter good work by Townsend and Saunders. The game turned on a 70th-minute tackle by man-of-the-match Kevin Richardson, Villa's captain, which robbed Lee Sharpe of an almost certain goal. Five minutes later Saunders touched in a Richardson free-kick at the near post to put Villa two up.

Mark Hughes brought United back into the match with a goal seven minutes from time. But Kanchelskis handled a goal-bound Atkinson effort on the line. The referee had no choice but to send the Russian off, and Saunders converted the penalty to clinch the trophy for Villa.

United are now only three points ahead of Blackburn in the Premiership and face Oldham in the FA Cup semi-final In a fortnight without three key players - Andrel Kanchelskis, Eric Cantona and Roy Keane.

Arsenal's triumph a boost for English pride

A FLASH OF brilliance by veteran striker Alan Smith in the 20th minute was enough to give underdogs Arsenal victory over holders Parma in the Cup-Winners' Cup final in Copenhagen on 4 May. Without four key players, including the suspended Ian Wright, they showed that the traditional virtues of the English domestic game are still good enough to beat Europe's elite. And, as well as increasing the quota for English clubs in European competition next season, their victory gives England a much needed boost after the disappointment of elimination from the World Cup.

This is not the first time they have triumphed without the inspirational Wright, their leading scorer. In the second round, back in November, they went to Belgium, albeit with a 3-0 lead, and sensationally beat Standard Liege 7-0 at a time when they had only three goals in six Premiership away games to their credit.

Without the injured John Jensen and David Hillier, George Graham had no qualms about playing the young Ian Selley and Steve Morrow in central midfield, and they were both outstanding. Morrow, the Irish international full-back who seems to have been around for ages yet is still only 25, is best remembered for breaking his arm celebrating Arsenal's Coca-Cola Cup win last year (more so than scoring the winner). In Copenhagen he played a key role in subduing the small Gianfranco Zola, a pivotal figure in Parma's success, and typified Arsenal's expertise in nullifying the opposition's strengths.

Smith, as always relentlessly competitive but scrupulously fair, led his line in his usual unselfish way, winning particular praise from his manager for his overall performance - and his goal was a bit special, too. Lorenzo Minotti, the Parma captain, attempted to bicycle-kick the ball clear, but it fell to Smith, who chested it down and, with two opponents converging on him, hit a sweet left-foot volley in-off the near post from the edge of the box.

Parma had no one to compare with Arsenal captain Tony Adams, who has matured into one of the most effective and inspirational defenders in Europe, while his partner Steve Bould was as valuable on the night. Apart from a couple of early efforts, one of which hit a post, Tomas Brolin - the Swede who made Graham Taylor a turnip in 1992 - was ineffective. And the dangerous Colombian Faustino Asprilla was given little chance to shine.

Arsenal, although having less of the play, made the more clear-cut chances. David Seaman, in Arsenal's goal, needed pain-killing injections before the start, but was never really tested - a tribute to Graham's tactics and to his team's ability to carry them out. With six major trophies in his eight seasons at Highbury, Graham has established himself as one of the finest managers in the history of English football.

SOCCER SOUNDBITES

"Arsenal were the better side. They showed how to control our system of play, and to me they are the least typical English team I have seen."

NEVIO SCALA,
Parma coach

Steve Morrow is safely at the back as Arsenal celebrate.

Manchester United secure double: Chelsea capitulate after disputed penalty

Manchester United players celebrate with the FA Cup.

MANCHESTER UNITED, who retained their Premiership title 12 days earlier when Blackburn finally cracked, beat Chelsea 4-0 at Wembley on 14 May to win the FA Cup and become only the fourth. club this century to complete the double - after Spurs (1981), Arsenal (1971) and Liverpool (1988).

It wasn't the classic Cup final everyone hoped for, nor was it by any means as one-sided as the score suggests, United's first two goals coming from penalties. Chelsea, who had inflicted United's only League defeat at Old Trafford as well as one of their three away defeats during their Premiership campaign, both by 1-0 with the goal scored each time by Gavin Peacock, were desperately unlucky to go in at the interval without at least a goal lead. They had the only real goal attempts of the half - four of them - the last of which came after 25 minutes when, Peacock picked up a poor Pallister clearance and hit a dipping 20-yard volley over Schmeichel's head but on to the cross-bar and back into play.

United began to press more at the start of the second half, although still without looking dangerous. Suddenly, on the hour, it all changed, and within nine minutes they were three up and the game was over. But it was Chelsea who handed the match to the champions rather than United taking charge.

First, Eddie Newton made an unnecessary late tackle on Dennis Irwin in the box - a clear penalty, and Cantona stroked the ball low to the right, sending Kharine the wrong way.

Five minutes later came the controversial second penalty. David Elleray, whose firm refereeing - he had booked Chelsea defender Erland Johnsen in the second minute, United's Captain Steve Bruce in the 18th - could not be, faulted up to this point, had a difficult decision to make. Sinclair misjudged a diagonal through-ball from Hughes and had to bring down Kancheiskis. Elleray was in a good position to judge that deliberate unfair contact had been made, but should have consulted his linesman, for TV replays showed it occurred outside the box. In any event, he should have sent Sinclair off, as the Russian winger was clear with only the. keeper to beat. Perhaps he felt that by awarding a penalty he would get himself off this undesirable hook. Anyway, Cantona produced a carbon copy spot-kick and justice was done.

Chelsea player-manager Glenn Hoddle brought himself on to calm things down, but it was too late. His young, inexperienced side had started chasing the game after the first penalty and were playing right into United's hands. A slip by Sinclair gave Hughes the ball and the Welsh striker clinically moved into the box and placed the ball past Khharine.

The rest of the play was academic. Cantona missed a sitter immediately after the third goal, and in injury time Paul Ince took the ball round the Chelsea keeper and unselfishly put a fourth goal on a plate for substitute McClair.

Manchester United have proved themselves outstandingly the best team in the country, not only by their magnificent double, which was so nearly an unprecedented treble, but also with the heights their football has reached so many times during the season. But at Wembley Chelsea exposed tactical shortcomings that will have to be corrected if United are to conquer Europe.

Derby players attacked as fans invade pitch

DISGRACEFUL SCENES of crowd violence at the New Den, in which visiting Derby players were assaulted, may lead to Millwall haying their ground closed again. The second leg of the First Division play-off was halted twice because of invading spectators, in the first half (for 19 minutes) because of an apparent problem with tickets, but in the second (15 minutes) as a result of a concerted effort to cause trouble. Millwall, who had their old ground closed four times in the past, must now fear receiving similar punishment

Derby scored their second goal to go 4-0 up on aggregate, after 22 minutes, but this prompted fighting in the east stand, and some 10 minutes later some fans moved on to the pitch as they fought with police. A few people from the west stand then ran on, and referee Brian Hill took the players off. Derby scored again on the resumption.

The crowd trouble persisted after the regular interval, and the referee had to take the players off again 15 minutes from the end. About 50 people ran on to the field and Derby keeper Martin Taylor was knocked to the ground. Their defender Paul Williams had to body-swerve attempts' to obstruct him. He had received racist taunts throughout the game, and he and their other black player Gary Charles were substituted three minutes before the end - for their own safety - a sad reminder of the hooliganism that once dogged English football.

FOOTBALL FOCUS

- On 16 October, in a Division Three match at Hereford, Colchester became the first League club to have both keepers sent off - John Keeley and Nathan Munson - for "professional fouls". They lost 5-0.

- In July, Rangers broke the British transfer record with £4m for Duncan Ferguson from Dundee United, and Manchester United paid Forest an English record £3.75m for Roy Keane. Blackburn Rovers signed Tim Flowers from Southampton in early November. for £2m, a world record for a keeper.

- Non-League Kidderminster Harriers won 2-1 at Birmingham (Division One) in the third round of the FA Cup, then beat Preston (Division Three) 1-0 in the fourth round, before losing 1-0 to Premier side West Ham in the fifth round. They finished top of the GM Vauxhall Conference but, because they had not brought their ground up to the required standards by the deadline of 31 December, they were denied entry to the League, and Division Three bottom club Northamptom were reprieved.

- Barry Town beat 22-times winners Cardiff 2-1 In the final of the Welsh Cup to qualify for the European Cup-winners' Cup

- Last year's European Cup winners Olympic de Marseille were rocked by a bribery scandal involving an end-of-season (1992-1993) league fixture with Valenciennes. Repercussions were still being felt at the end of this season, by which time Marseille had been stripped of the French title, expelled from this season's European Cup and lost the right to contest the Super Cup and Toyota Cup, relegated to the 2nd Division for 1994-95 and banned from signing new players. Their chairman Bernard Tapie, business tycoon and former government minister, was bailed on charge of corruption and interference with witnesses and ordered to give up ownership of the club. General manager Jean-Pierre Berries was banned from football for life, and players Eydelie (Marseille) and Robert and Burruchaga (Valenciennes) were banned until 1996.

- Tottenham Hotspur were hit by punishments unprecedented in English football for breaking League rules in the 1980s with illegal loans to players. The north London club were barred from the 1994-95 FA Cup, given a 6-point penalty in the 1994-95 Premiership and fined a record £1.5 million.

Milan masters win European Cup

AC MILAN gave notice to European Champions Cup aspirants such as Manchester United that it will take something special to prise their hands from a trophy they have won in devastating. fashion with a 4-0 victory over Barcelona in Athens. Italian champions this season for the third time in succession, they were, however, underdogs as they took on Barcelona without their suspended key defenders Barest and Costacurta.

Yet instead of sitting back and trying to catch the Spanish champions on the break, as might have been expected, Milan proceeded. to take them apart with a magnificent display of positive, attacking football that was a delight to watch. And at the same time, they defended so well that their keeper was hardly tested by the much-vaunted Barcelona strikers, the Bulgarian Hristo Stoichkov and the Brazilian Romario, or anyone else for that matter.

Daniele Massaro opened the scoring midway through the first half after the elusive Dejan Savicevic had broken clear on the right and closed in on goal. The former Yugoslav star popped the ball across for the unmarked Massaro to squeeze in at the far post. The second goal, in first half stoppage time, came as the climax to a 14-pass movement, including the throw-out by Rossi, which finished with Donadoni breaking down the left and cutting the ball back from the bye-line for Massaro to drive in from 15 yards.

If Barcelona coach Johan Cruyff harboured any thoughts of a comeback, they were killed off two minutes after the break, when Savicevic dispossessed Nadal near the touchline on the right and struck an exquisite volley with the inside of his left foot from the edge of the box, over Zubizarreta into the far corner of the net. Ten minutes later man-of-the-match Savicevic hit a post after a quickly taken free-kick, but the influential midfielder Marcel Desailly, on the winning side also last year with Marseille, then powered his way through and curled the ball past the hapless Barcelona keeper.

Milan played out the last half-hour without extending themselves, and indeed Savicevic missed a fine chance to make it 5-0 near the end after a cross from the bye-line by Donadoni.

It was Milan's third European Cup in six years, their fifth in all, and with Ruud Gullit returning next year, they will certainly take some stopping.

Marcel Desailly holds up the Cup.

FINAL SCORE

Football League
Premier Division: Manchester United
Top scorer: Andy Cole (Newcastle United) 34
Division 1: Crystal Palace.
Division 2: Reading
Division 3: Shrewsbury Town.
Footballer ot the Year Alan Shearer (Blackburn Rovers)

FA Cup Final

Manchester Utd	4	Chelsea	0

League Cup Final

Aston Villa	3	Manchester Utd	1

Scottish League
Premiere Division: Rangers
Top scorer: Mark Hateley (Rangers) 24
Division 1: Falkirk
Division 2: Stranraer
Footballer of the Year Mark Hateley (Rangers)

Scottish FA Cup Final

Dundea Utd	1	Rangers	0

Scottish League Cup Final

Rangers	2	Hibernian	1

European Cup Final

AC Milan	4	Barcelona	0

Cup-Winners' Cup Final

Arsenal	1	Parma	0

UEFA Cup Final
Inter-Milan beat Salzburg 1-0, 1-0

European Footballer of the Year 1993
Roberto Baggio (Juventus & Italy)

Dundee United beat 'jinx' to win Scottish Cup

DUNDEE UNITED defied bookmakers' odds of 92 against them as well as their 20-year-old jinx - they had been losing finalists six times since 1974 - to beat Rangers 1-0 at Hampden and win the Scottish FA Cup for the first time in their history. The goal was scored by Craig Brewster two minutes after the interval and was the result of a terrible defensive blunder. But against a Rangers side attempting to achieve an unprecedented back-to-back domestic treble, they were worthy winners.

Great credit must go to Ivan Golac, in his first season as manager, whose bold policy of playing three in attack paid off. The endless harassing of this trio - Brewster, Christian Dailly and Andy McLaren - never allowed Rangers to settle and was, Indeed, responsible for the goal. Dave McPherson fatally played the ball back to Ally Maxwell, whose attempted clearance was blocked by Dailly and cannoned back off the keeper again Dailly then took the ball round him and, from the narrowest of angles, rolled it against the far post for the alert Brewster to tap in.

The United fans were thrilled by the pace and adventure of their side, but Rangers were always in the game. Their greatest effort came late on, when Stuart McCall made a magnificent run down the left, beating man after man with his power and skill before pulling the ball back, only for Van de Kamp to make an astonishing save from Mikhailichenko's six-yard shot on the turn. It was clear, then, that Dundee United's name was on the Cup at last.

Christian Dailly (left) looks on during Dundee's first ever Scottish Cup win.

The best team won

Despite a goalless final, this was a successful World Cup, well organized by the Americans, who justified FIFA's faith in them. It was blessed with record crowds (average 68,592), impeccably behaved, and played for the most part in the best of spirits. Television schedules meant that many matches were played in conditions of intense heat and humidity, however, but FIFA's new law interpretations had the desired effect of producing open, attacking play and allowing skill to flourish.

Brazil's captain Dunga celebrates victory in time-honoured fashion.

THE FORMAT for the finals was retained with the exception that, in the first-round groups, a win would be worth three points instead of two. FIFA, still not recovered from the panic that beset them after the much-criticized 1990 finals in Italy, introduced a number of late instructions to referees for interpreting the laws. They were brought in with good intentions, to make the game more attractive and increase goal-scoring. For the most part they worked well, although there was some confusion and a few referees were over-zealous with their red and yellow cards.

The two most contentious rulings on interpretation involved making the "tackle from behind" a red-card offence and giving attacking players more advantage in offside situations. Both new interpretations needed more clarification and testing before being put into practice, fairly, and Brazil's first two goals against the Netherlands in the quarter-finals should probably not have been allowed.

The mandatory stretchering-off of injured players worked very well and prevented the feigning of injury, although "diving" for free-kicks remained a problem. Using true linesmen rather than referees to run the lines was a welcome return to sanity, although FIFA's continued insistence on spreading appointments around their membership deprived the tournament of some of the world's best officials.

A capacity crowd of 94,000 packs the Rose Bowl in Pasadena, California, for the climax of World Cup USA '94.

Disappointment

Cameroon were a disappointment after their brilliant showing in 1990, but Nigeria confirmed Africa's wealth of talent by finishing top of their group with a goal difference bettered only by Brazil. Perhaps the biggest disappointment was the much-vaunted Colombian side, who came bottom of their group and were beaten 2-1 by the United States in a match that confirmed the hosts as a team to be taken seriously. The captain of the vanquished, defender Andres Escobar, who put through his own goal, was murdered in a Medellin car park on his return home to Colombia, a tragedy that puts into perspective the ups and downs of success and failure on the football field.

This followed close after the disgrace of Diego Maradona, who failed a random drugs test after Argentina's second match and was soon expelled from the tournament.

With no sides in the finals, British allegiance was switched to the Irish team, coached by Jack Charlton, and made up entirely of players from the English and Scottish leagues. They brought off the first sensation of the finals when Ray Houghton's spectacular goal gave them a 1-0 victory over Italy. All four teams in the group finished level on both points (four) and goal difference (zero), with Norway, scorers of only one goal, the team to miss out.

Among the personalities, to

The World Cup was decided on penalties for the first time, and Roberto Baggio's miss that gave Brazil victory was a sad climax to what ahd been a thrilling tournament deservedly won by the best team.

Romario, under pressure from Paolo Maldini, won the Golden Ball as the best player of the Tournament.

make their mark in the first round was Saudi striker Saeed Owairan, who scored the finest individual goal of the finals, against Belgium. But the individual performance of the tournament was supplied by Valencia's Russian star Oleg Salenko. Without an international goal to his name before the finals, he scored five - a World Cup record - as Russia beat Cameroon 6-1 in a vain effort to quality for the next round of the competition.

Knock-out stages

In the last sixteen, Ireland again found themselves in the heat of Orlando, where they could not recover from defensive lapses by Phelan and keeper Bonner against Holland. An error of another kind marked Belgium's exit, when Swiss referee Kurt Rotlisberger refused them a penalty against Germany. He admitted his mistake after seeing a video, and FIFA decided not to use him again in the tournament.

Brazil, despite having Leonardo sent off for elbowing American Tab Ramos, went through, thanks to Bebeto, while Nigeria were on the verge of taking a mighty scalp, after Italy's Zola had been sent off. They led until the 88th minute, when Roberto Baggio finally came alive, equalized, and scored the winner from the spot in extra time. Argentina succumbed 3-2 to the Romanians and the genius of Hagi in one of the most memorable matches of the tournament, and Eastern Europe made it two in the last eight with Bulgaria's victory over Mexico on penalties.

In the quarter-finals Bulgaria chalked up a famous triumph over holders Germany. Romania, however, suffered the mortification of going out on penalties for the second successive World Cup, beaten by Sweden after a dramatic see-saw game. Meanwhile, Italy had beaten Spain 2-1, and Holland lost a five-goal thriller to Brazil after clawing back a two-goal deficit.

In the first semi-final, the Italians at last put on the style, with Roberto Baggio scoring two magical goals to defeat Bulgaria. But he injured a hamstring to threaten his appearance in the Rose Bowl.

Brazil made heavy weather of beating Sweden in the second semi-final despite controlling much of the game. Romario clinched a final place with an 81st minute header from Jorginho's cross.

Stalemate

In the final, the defensive qualities of both sides triumphed. Italy brought back Baresi, three weeks after keyhole surgery to his knee, for the banned Costacurta, and the AC Milan veteran was magnificent. So, too, was Paolo Maldini, who started in the middle of defence before reverting to his natural left-back position when Mussi went off in the first half. Brazil's central defensive pair, Aldair and Marcio Santos, were outstanding, but they lost their influential right-back Jorginho after 20 minutes. The latter's replacement Cafu, however, provided some of the best chances, which Romario and Bebeto uncharacteristically squandered. A cameo performance from young substitute Viola in the second period of extra time injected some spice into the game.

But the match finished goalless, and for the first, and hopefully the last, time a World Cup final had to be decided on penalties. The battling Baresi ballooned the first kick over the bar. Pagliuca saved Brazil's first, from Marcio Santos, but Taffarel saved Italy's fourth, from Massero. Brazil's captain Dunga shot his team into the lead, before finally Roberto Baggio lifted his kick over the goal to give Brazil victory.

In the end, the best side won. Despite the 120-minute deadlock, Brazil were a joy to watch, and they thoroughly deserve to be the first country to win the World Cup for a fourth time.

FINAL SCORE

Group A

United States	1	Switzerland	1
Colombia	1	Romania	3
United State	2	Colombia	1
Romania	1	Switzerland	4
United States	0	Romania	1
Switzerland	0	Colombia	2

	P	W	D	L	F	A	P
Romania	3	2	0	1	5	5	6
Switzerland	3	1	1	1	5	4	4
US	3	1	1	1	3	3	4
Colombia	3	1	0	2	4	5	3

Group B

Cameroon	2	Sweden	2
Brazil	2	Russia	0
Brazil	3	Cameroon	0
Sweden	3	Russia	1
Russia	6	Cameroon	1
Brazil	1	Sweden	1

	P	W	D	L	F	A	P
Brazil	3	2	1	0	6	1	7
Sweden	3	1	2	0	6	4	5
Russia	3	1	0	2	7	6	3
Cameroon	3	0	1	2	3	1	1

Group C

Germany	1	Bolivia	0
Spain	2	South Korea	2
Germany	1	Spain	1
South Korea	0	Bolivia	0
Bolivia	1	Spain	3
Germany	3	South Korea	2

	P	W	D	L	F	A	P
Germany	3	2	1	0	5	3	7
Spain	3	1	2	0	6	4	5
S Korea	3	0	2	1	4	5	2
Bolivia	3	0	1	2	1	4	1

Group D

Argentina	4	Greece	0
Nigeria	3	Bulgaria	0
Argentina	2	Nigeria	1
Bulgaria	4	Greece	0
Greece	0	Nigeria	2
Argentina	0	Bulgaria	2

	P	W	D	L	F	A	P
Nigeria	3	2	0	1	6	2	6
Bulgaria	3	2	0	1	6	3	6
Argentina	3	2	0	1	6	3	6
Greece	3	0	0	3	0	1	0

Group E

Italy	0	Ireland	1
Norway	1	Mexico	0
Italy	1	Norway	0
Mexico	2	Ireland	1
Ireland	0	Norway	0
Italy	1	Mexico	1

	P	W	D	L	F	A	P
Mexico	3	1	1	1	3	3	4
Ireland	3	1	1	1	2	2	4
Italy	3	1	1	1	2	2	4
Norway	3	1	1	1	1	1	4

Group F

Belgium	1	Morocco	0
Holland	2	Saudi Arabia	1
Saudi Arabia	2	Morocco	1
Belgium	1	Holland	0
Morocco	1	Holland	2
Belgium	0	Saudi Arabia	1

	P	W	D	L	F	A	P
Holland	3	2	0	1	4	3	6
S Arabia	3	2	0	1	4	3	6
Belgium	3	2	0	1	2	1	6
Morocco	3	0	0	3	2	5	0

SECOND PHASE

Germany	3	Belgium	2
Spain	3	Switzerland	0
Saudi Arabia	1	Sweden	3
Romania	3	Argentina	2
Holland	2	Ireland	0
Brazil	1	United States	0
Nigeria	1	Italy	2
(after extra time)			
Mexico	1	Bulgaria	1
Bulgaria won 3-1 on penalties			

QUARTER FINALS

Italy	2	Spain	1
Holland	2	Brazil	3
Bulgaria	2	Germany	1
Romania	2	Sweden	2
Sweden won 5-4 on penalties			

SEMI-FINALS

Bulgaria	1	Italy	2
Sweden	0	Brazil	1

THIRD-PLACE MATCH

Sweden	4	Bulgaria	0

FINAL

Brazil	0	Italy	0
Brazil won 3-2 on penalties			

Pasadena Rose Bowl, Loas Angeles 17 July 1994, Attendance 94,194.

Brazil: Taffarel, Jorginho (Caffu), Aldair, Marcio Santos, Branco, Mauro Silva, Dunga, Mizinho, Zinho (Viola), Babeto, Romario.

Italy: Pagliuca, Mussi (Apolloni) , Baresi, maldini, benarrivo, Berti, Albertini, D Baggio (Evani), Donadoni, R Baggio, Massaro.

Leading scorers:
6 Salenko (Russia), Stoichkov (Bulgaria).
5 K Anderson (Sweden), R Baggio (Italy), Klinsmann (Germany), Romario (Brazil).

Sugar captures German in second foreign raid

TOTTENHAM have signed Jürgen Klinsmann, the German World Cup striker and one of the most accomplished players in world football, for a relatively modest £2 million. Spurs chairman Alan Sugar continued his crusade to bring world-class footballers to White Hart Lane with the surprise acquisition of Monaco's former European Player of the Year while holidaying off his luxury yacht in the south of France.

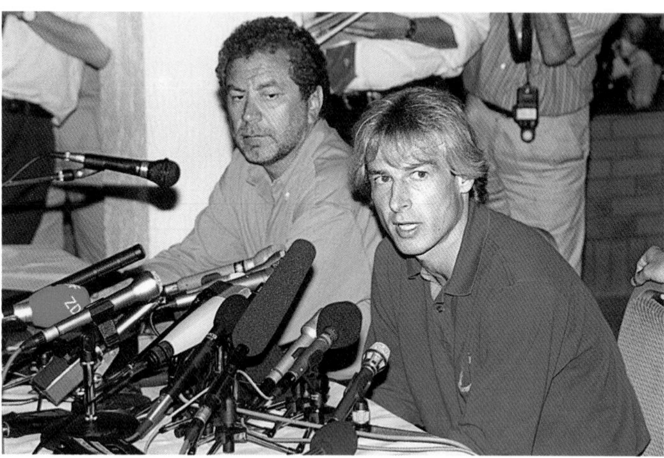

Klinsmann speaks to the Press watched by his new chairman.

News of the remarkable capture of Klinsmann was leaked two hours before another World Cup player, Romanian forward Ilie Dumitrescu, was introduced to the waiting media at White Hart Lane after joining the club for £2.6 million from Steaua Bucharest.

Tottenham, who are confident they will not encounter any work-permit barriers, insist they have not finished adding to their squad, and the signing of the enigmatic Klinsmann, now 30 and scorer of five goals in America, will not harm their selling power.

Klinsmann, formerly with Stuttgart and Inter, arrives with a reputation for feigning injury, although he was perfectly behaved in the World Cup.

SOCCER SOUNDBITES

"I don't remember him from the World Cup, but I'm sure he impressed me and will do a great job at Spurs."

ALAN SUGAR,
Spurs chairman, after arranging the transfer of Dumitrescu while manager Ossie Ardiles was away.

"Is there a diving school in London?"

JURGEN KLINSMANN,
pre-empting his reputation at his first Press conference on arrival at Tottenham.

Magpies steal a march on Antwerp

THE REMARKABLE Newcastle United success story moved into a glorious new chapter last night as Kevin Keegan's exciting team celebrated the ending of a 17-year European exile by tearing apart Belgian opposition.

A two-legged UEFA Cup first-round tie was under control almost from the first minute, Robert Lee, new to the England ranks, proving the chief executioner of an outclassed Antwerp by scoring his first goal in a sparkling hat-trick.

With Scott Sellars joining him on the scoresheet for the first time this season and substitute Steve Watson adding an individualistic fifth goal near the end, the second leg at St James's Park will assume carnival proportions for the team who sit on top of the Premiership with maximum points.

Newcastle had indicated on their journey to this Belgian port that they would not alter their flowing style to suit European demands and were confident of gaining some reward for an attacking policy. But even their most partisan fans were pinching themselves as the sheer magnitude of the victory sank in.

Billy Wright – A golden figure of the English game

BILLY WRIGHT, former England and Wolverhampton Wanderers captain, has died at the age 70.

Wright was the first golden boy of English football in the post-war era. As such, he set standards of excellence on and off the field that were aspired to subsequently, and upheld, by equally godlike successors such as Bobby Charlton and Bobby Moore.

Blessed with blond good looks, boundless enthusiasm, utter reliability and a sunny disposition, Wright was a natural target for hero-worship even in the days before the influence of the media became all-powerful. Today, he would never have been off the front and back pages of the tabloids.

The glittering statistics of his 18-year playing career tell much of the story: three League Championship medals (1954, 1958 and 1959) and an FA Cup winners medal (1949) with his club, Wolves; Footballer of the Year in 1952; the first player from any country to win 100 caps; captain of England 90 times, a record he shares with Moore.

What that catalogue of success does not reveal is all the hard work and determination that went into it. Wright made the grade by refusing to take no for an answer. For one thing, he had to get over the disappointment of being rejected by the martinet of Molineux, Major Frank Buckley, because he was considered too small.

Buckley eventually relented, and Wright, a Shropshire lad born at Ironbridge in 1924, joined the Wolves groundstaff at 14 on a wage of £2 per week. That was not long before the outbreak of the Second World War; so this budding professional was 21 by the time the hostilities ceased and he could get on properly with his career.

Billy Wright was a great captain who led by example.

Wright did not hang about in the next 14 years. By 1959, when he retired, he had made 541 peacetime appearances for Wolves, his only club, including 490 in the League. He missed only 3 of England's first 108 matches after the war. To mark his 100th cap in April 1959, the Football Association made him an honorary life member. And he was awarded the CBE.

Not much more than 5ft 9in tall, Wright had been a free-scoring centre-forward as a boy. When he turned professional, however, he began as an inside-forward before switching to wing-half and then centre-half, the position in which he really made his name and enjoyed most of his success.

Again, that was something of a triumph against the odds. Although short for a centre-half, he made up for his lack of inches with the remarkable spring in his heels. A fine reader of the game, Wright could also time a tackle with the best of them. As a captain, he led by example. And there could be no finer one.

Wright managed Arsenal from 1962 to 1966, and later became head of sport for ATV. He was made a director of his beloved Wolves in 1990.

Tottenham axe falls on Ossie

SPURS MANAGER Ossie Ardiles has lost his job after 16 months at White Hart Lane. The man who paid the price for failure complained of outside influences, of being used as a "pawn in a battle", referring to the ongoing conflict between Alan Sugar, the Spurs chairman, and former manager and chief executive Terry Venables, now coach of England.

Ardiles, whose fate was effectively sealed by last Wednesday's 3–0 Coca-Cola Cup defeat at Notts County, also revealed that he rejected the opportunity to work with a head coach. It is believed Sugar was keen to bring in former England coach Don Howe or Dutchman Leo Beenhakker.

The fact that Ardiles' return, in terms of League victories, is worse than any of his predecessors in modern times goes some way to explaining why he was sacked. He had three years of a lucrative contract to run, and is likely to receive in excess of £500,000 compensation.

Steve Perryman, another former Tottenham player and assistant to Ardiles, has been made caretaker manager.

Grobbelaar in bribes inquiry

Bruce Grobbelaar leaves court at the end of the saga.

ALLEGATIONS that Bruce Grobbelaar, the Southampton FC and Zimbabwe soccer player, took bribes from a betting syndicate to fix Premier League match results are to be investigated. Officials from the Football Association and the FA Carling Premier League will hold an urgent meeting following claims in *The Sun* newspaper that Grobbelaar was paid thousands of pounds by a Far East syndicate.

The article alleges that the arrangement goes back to 1992 and involves several matches with his present club and Liverpool, his former team. The newspaper claims the player accepted £40,000 to determine the score of a match staged last November and was promised a further £175,000 to fix scores in other contests.

It is alleged that, while being secretly filmed by the newspaper, the player openly discussed his involvement in the "fixing" of several games over the past 12 months — among them a Premier League game played last weekend — as well as international fixtures with Zimbabwe.

Paul Merson admits cocaine abuse

THE FOOTBALL Association and Arsenal FC indicated yesterday that Paul Merson, the England player, would not face serious disciplinary action following an admission that he had spent up to £150 a day on cocaine. Merson, 26, said in a newspaper interview, for which he is believed to have been paid £100,000, that he had spent more than £2,000 on the drug over the past year and been given even more.

Although the FA has recently begun random testing of players and threatens players with suspension or disbarment if they are caught with traces of cocaine, its chief executive said Merson was unlikely to be punished. Mr Graham Kelly said there would be an immediate investigation of the case, but the emphasis would be upon treatment and rehabilitation, the question of disciplinary action being secondary.

Paul Merson at the highly-emotional press conference.

SOCCER SOUNDBITES

"Our concern is for the player and his family and for the interests of the club and the game."

GRAHAM KELLY,
explaining the FA's soft line on Paul Merson's revelation.

Spanish inquisition for United: Ferguson's men outpassed, outclassed and overwhelmed

OUTPASSED, outclassed and eventually utterly overwhelmed, Manchester United last night received a brutal reminder of the dangers that proliferate in Europe's higher echelons. On a deceptively gentle Mediterranean evening, Barcelona, defending in depth and attacking from every angle, simply overran the erstwhile Champions League Group A leaders. No one expected such an inquisition.

This humbling reverse, which equalled their worst result in Europe, dragged United down from first to third in the toughest section of the four. As United sloped off a dream-wrecking field called the Nou Camp, they were assailed with calamitous news: Gothenburg, whom Alex Ferguson's men visit on November 23, had prevailed at Galatasaray. The Swedes, against all expectations, were leaders.

The only consolation of a Nou Camp nadir confirmed by goals from Hristo Stoichkov, with two, Romario and Albert Ferrer, was that it heralded the end of Eric Cantona's suspension following his red card in Turkey last season. The Frenchman's intelligence and passing will be much needed in Sweden and for the subsequent, potentially fraught visit of Galatasaray, last season's nemesis.

The suddenness of Barcelona's attacks was a new experience for some of the United players. It was a lesson that began within eight minutes, when Stoichkov thundered home his first, and continued to the final whistle.

Nothing went United's way. Ince had a legitimate penalty claim refused after 75 minutes.

Rarely can foreigner permutations have caused Ferguson and United so many problems. The inclusion of the attacking Welshman, Ryan Giggs, ensured the omission of another foreigner. No one expected the unfortunate casualty to be Peter Schmeichel, United's imposing goalkeeper, a decision Ferguson defended vigorously.

Gary Walsh, an inexperienced 26-year-old whose early years were partly endured on the surgeon's slab, stepped up into the most intimidating arena of them all. The drums, the whistles, the noise presented an unforgiving, unforgettable sight and sound.

Romario's performance confirmed him as one of the most gifted, awe-inducing players on the world stage. One could only wonder how Schmeichel would have fared against him and Stoichkov, though Walsh was hardly to blame. Barcelona were that good.

Jensen goal no consolation for wretched Arsenal

Jensen (third left) watches as his shot curls in.

BOOS AND JEERS from disenchanted fans echoed around Highbury as Arsenal said farewell to a wretched year of cocaine abuse, nightclub brawls, "bung" allegations and often sub-standard play. They were emphatically outplayed by QPR, their west London rivals, who thoroughly deserved their 3–1 victory.

Even Arsenal's equaliser in the 65th minute was no consolation for the club, although it provided the fans with a moment to savour. It was scored by Danish international John Jensen, who has become a cult figure with the fans by his failure to score a goal in two-and-a-half years and 98 games.

When he did break his duck it was a beauty, a fierce, curling shot from the edge of the penalty area that gave Tony Roberts no chance in goal.

But with nine minutes left and Arsenal 3–1 down, the Highbury scoreboard went blank, as if in shame. Stop the clocks, cancel the New Year. Only the makers of "I was there when Jensen scored" T-shirts will have felt like celebrating after another Saturday of self-loathing at Highbury. No home win in the League since Oct 23, only two Premiership victories in 11 games. Boring football plus success is fine. But not this.

Geordies furious as Cole moves to rivals for record £7million

FOUR DAYS of secret negotiations ended with the surprise announcement that Manchester United had signed Andy Cole, Newcastle United's prolific goalscorer, for a record £6 million plus the £1m-rated Keith Gillespie. The extent of the delight at Old Trafford and dismay on Tyneside was matched by general disbelief across football.

The game's capacity to shock is endless, but few people would have believed that Newcastle would off-load their prize asset to such great rivals. Even Cole was shocked.

In terms of fee and drama, Alex Ferguson's remarkable coup surpassed his swoop for Eric Cantona from Leeds United two years ago. Now, as fans of Leeds and Newcastle watch bitterly from afar, Cole and Cantona link up to take on the Premiership.

The £7 million deal for Cole provoked angry scenes outside St James'. While Cole, who set a Newcastle scoring record of 41 goals in winning last season's PFA Young Player of the Year Award, was completing negotiations, Newcastle supporters jammed the switchboards of the club and local media in protest.

SOCCER SOUNDBITES

"I'm in charge – not you. It is a good deal, too good to turn down."

KEVIN KEEGAN,
Newcastle manager, to the shocked fans after selling Andy Cole to Manchester United.

Cantona – off, over the top and out

THERE WERE extraordinary scenes at Crystal Palace in an evening Premiership match when Manchester United's wayward French star Eric Cantona finally exceeded the bounds of acceptable behaviour in a sensational and shameful incident.

It was bad enough being sent off for kicking an opponent. But on his way to the dressing-room Cantona reacted violently to the barracking from home fans. He suddenly leapt up and lunged with both feet, in kung-fu fashion, at a spectator standing behind the touchline barrier, before wading in with both fists.

The fracas was broken up by police and stewards before Cantona was led away by his team-mate Peter Schmeichel and United's kit-man Norman Davies. Fans jeered and threw tea at the Frenchman while other United players remonstrated with the crowd.

Police said that there had been allegations of assault against both Cantona and another United player, Paul Ince, from two spectators. The players were allowed to go home with the rest of the team, but police planned to interview them further.

The FA have promised rapid action against Cantona, who has already been booked five times this season. His sending-off at Palace was his fifth in just over a year. His 'roll of shame' in France includes fines and suspensions for punching his own goalkeeper, calling a former national coach a "shitbag", throwing his shirt at a referee before storming off the pitch, and calling members of a disciplinary board collectively "idiots" and doing the same individually when asked to repeat himself. He has already been suspended three times since coming to England in 1992, yet he has inspired his clubs (Leeds and Manchester United) to three Championships and is idolized at Old Trafford.

He has gone too far this time, however, and is sure to receive at the very least a lengthy suspension.

Eric Cantona really goes over the top this time.

Memory of Raith will haunt Celtic

CELTIC'S term in purgatory was extended by Raith Rovers at Ibrox when the Scottish First Division side won a penalty-kick decider after 90 minutes and extra-time had left the teams deadlocked at 2–2.

The Glasgow giants' failure to win honours for five years had seemed to be on the brink of reversal when, after conceding the opening goal to Stephen Crawford, they equalized through Andy Walker and then went ahead through Charlie Nicholas with only five minutes left to play. Yet, unbelievably, Raith retorted by drawing level within two minutes through Gordon Dalziel to take the tie to extra-time.

Just as they had done against Airdrie in the semi-finals, Raith scored from all their regulation five kicks as well as the first of the sudden-death attempts. The 12th kick was taken by the Celtic captain, Paul McStay, who watched in anguish as goalkeeper Scott Thomson dived low to his right to beat the ball away.

Rioting fans stop match

Chanting England followers, intent only on making trouble.

SHAMEFUL. Simply shameful. Last night's sickening actions by England's violent camp followers not only forced the abandonment of an international billed as a "friendly". As missiles cascaded down from the visitors' section of Lansdowne Road's West Stand, as frightened photographers and substitutes ran for cover, the brutal evidence that hooliganism still stains the national game was there for all to witness.

England's ability to play host to a safe European Championships next year must be severely in doubt after last night's ugliness.

England have always been followed by a mindless minority. The chants of "No surrender to the IRA" were predictable, but the intensity of the subsequent violence towards Irish fans was completely unexpected.

Police said that 40 English supporters and three Irish people had been arrested. At least 20 people were treated in hospital.

The unfortunate catalyst was David Kelly's 22nd-minute goal for Ireland against an England team looking bereft of ideas. Within seconds the first ripped-out seat was flung into the cold Dublin night air. Other objects swiftly followed, one which almost his England's Graham Le Saux. The metal rods which held the seats in place were then torn out and chucked forward.

The game was officially abandoned by the Dutch referee, Denis Jol, at 28 minutes. It was the first time an England international had ended prematurely in such disgrace

It was the fourth Wednesday night when trouble scarred English football. First Eric Cantona's assault at Crystal Palace, then the attack on referee Rodger Gifford at Blackburn Rovers, then the fighting of Chelsea fans after penalty defeat to Millwall, and now this.

SOCCER SOUNDBITES

"We are appalled. It is a terrible situation and there are no words strong enough to say how ashamed we are."

TERRY VENABLES,
England coach, after the mayhem at Lansdowne Road.

Arsenal sack Graham over 'bung' scandal

GEORGE Graham was sacked as manager of Arsenal yesterday for failing to "act in the best interests of the club".

Graham, 50, has been the subject of a Premier League inquiry into allegations that he accepted a cash "bung" as part of the transfers of foreign players to the club. Arsenal's board of directors, having received the details of the League's findings, decided that it could not stand by one of the most successful managers in the club's history, the man who brought them six major honours in eight years.

The club pre-empted the interim report of the Premier League's inquiry, which will be released tomorrow, sacking Graham seven hours before last night's Premiership game against Nottingham Forest, which Arsenal won 1–0.

Graham wasted little time in responding to his dismissal and said that he would be seeking legal assistance to "vigorously contest" his sacking. On a reported £300,000 a year, he will not receive compensation for the remainder of his contract, which was due to run until May 1997.

There has been speculation about his position since the first allegations in November that he accepted a £285,000 payment from the £1.1 million transfer deal that brought Danish international John Jensen to Arsenal in 1992. Graham claimed the money was a gift from the Norwegian agent Rune Hauge and said that he returned the money to Arsenal. "I have made no money from transfers," he insisted.

George Graham – shamed.

Rosenthal routs Saints at Dell – Cup joy for Spurs

TRAILING 2–0 to Southampton in an exhilarating FA Cup fifth-round replay at The Dell, Spurs suddenly found their balance and belief to force extra-time and then win a remarkable match 6–2.

Ronny Rosenthal, the former Anfield striker introduced by Gerry Francis late in the first half to enliven Spurs' hitherto tepid attack, proved the catalyst for this spectacular comeback. Two goals swiftly followed in normal time, Rosenthal completing his hat-trick midway through the first period of the extra half-hour. The rest was exhibition stuff, with goals flowing from Teddy Sheringham, Nick Barmby and Darren Anderton.

Rosenthal, who had scored only once this season, revealed afterwards that Francis had ordered him "to take the initiative" when he came on after 44 minutes. He accomplished his mission with a display of left-footed shooting that eclipsed every other contribution to this minor epic.

Francis must now work out how to accommodate the Israeli international as Spurs seek a place in Europe.

It is a sweet dilemma for Spurs' inspirational manager. Tottenham's chances of prospering in either of England's premier tournaments appeared slim until Alan Sugar's lawyers overturned an FA punishment of a six-point deduction and banishment from the FA Cup. Since then, Tottenham have marched up the table and now face Liverpool in the last eight of the Cup.

Police swoop on footballers in bribe enquiry – Fashanu and Grobbelaar arrested

THREE LEADING footballers – Bruce Grobbelaar, Hans Segers and John Fashanu – were arrested yesterday by detectives investigating allegations of match fixing.

John Fashanu, one of the three footballers arrested.

A London-based Malaysian businessman, Heng Suan Lim, and Fashanu's girlfriend, Melissa Kassa-Mapsi, were also held over claims that a Far East betting syndicate bribed players.

All five were being kept overnight at separate police stations in Hampshire. Det. Chief Insp. Rod Davis, leading the investigation, said the 20 officers involved in the operation had seized all manner of property and documents during the co-ordinated raids.

All those arrested were linked to the same alleged conspiracy, he said. "It is a unique inquiry in that it involves football. But, apart from that, it is like many other inquiries which the police undertake."

It is the latest in a series of blows to the reputation of the Premier League. The Arsenal manager George Graham was sacked following allegations of financial irregularities, the Chelsea captain Dennis Wise was convicted of assault and charges are pending against Manchester United's Eric Cantona and Paul Ince.

Grobbelaar, 37, is the Southampton, Zimbabwe and former Liverpool goalkeeper, Hans Segers, 33, Wimbledon's Dutch goalkeeper, and Fashanu, 31, the Aston Villa and former Wimbledon striker who also presents the ITV programme Gladiators and is a Unicef ambassador.

So overwhelming were the clichés as English football was confronted by this doomsday scenario that they lost the power to shock. The FA were unable to air their initial reactions owing to "legal restraints", but stressed that the players' clubs retained the right to select their suspect stars once they were released by the police.

Elsewhere, rumours were amplified and tales of Malaysian informers, known only by their first names, abounded.

Brilliant McManaman steers Liverpool to Coca-Cola Cup glory

THE FA CUP remains the real thing, but yesterday's Coca-Cola Cup final proved an increasingly absorbing spectacle. Amid lengthening shadows, two famous old clubs competed with characteristic grace, Liverpool emerging winners through the zestful brilliance of Steve McManaman.

Much had been made of the Merseysiders in Bolton's camp, McAteer, Stubbs and Seagraves, but it was McManaman, one of Liverpool's own locals, who stole the show in this, the "Friendly Final". The 23-year-old, almost speechless when Sir Stanley Matthews handed him his medal, was also a deserved recipient of the first Alan Hardaker man-of-the-match trophy.

One of England's few successes here in midweek, McManaman, the new wizard of the dribble, again confirmed his prodigious talent, continually taking on and beating Bolton shirts. Wanderers simply had no answer to the wanderer in red.

Twice, either side of half-time, McManaman skipped through, his positive intent bringing him fine goals. If his first was assisted by lower-division defending, his second was truly magnificent, a mazy dribble crowned with the most confident of finishes.

The final seemed over, the underdogs' passion spent. Then, with one of those strikes that lifts whole throngs from their seats in delight or despair, Alan Thompson, another emerging young English winger, scored a splendid goal to force the tensest of climaxes. Up in the Royal Box, Matthews's bright eyes shone with pleasure. As in 1953, wingers had orchestrated mayhem.

Here was fulsome evidence that football, for all its myriad off-field problems, remains a healthy beast. Rumours of the national sport's death are clearly premature. Both sets of supporters applauded each other, the mutual respect reflected by the warm post-match embraces of the rival players. A feeling of togetherness suffused all in attendance: football's family was one.

McManaman beats the Bolton defence to score his first goal.

FOOTBALL FOCUS

● The British transfer record was broken three times during the season, each time for a striker, Blackburn's £5m for Norwich's Chris Sutton in July 1994 being smashed by Manchester United's £7m acquisition of Andy Cole from Newcastle in January 1995, before Liverpool paid Forest £8.5m for Stan Collymore in June.

● Everton's sacking of manager Mike Walker in November after only 10 months was a shock, despite only 6 victories in 35 matches. New manager Joe Royle made the perfect start at Goodison with a 2–0 victory over Liverpool to take Everton off the bottom of the table.

● A Scottish League record of 4 Stranraer players were sent off in their 8–1 defeat at Airdrie – this after they went 1–0 up in the first minute.

● Discharged from an addiction clinic in mid-January, Paul Merson (Arsenal) admitted at a Press conference to being an alcoholic in addition to being addicted to gambling, although the FA confirmed that his cocaine abuse was a minimal problem.

● Manchester United's 9–0 defeat of Ipswich at Old Trafford on 4 March set a new Premiership record.

● New Law changes to take effect next season provided for 3 subs whether or not the keeper is included, and the offside law was reworded to avoid penalizing a player not interfering with play.

● Premier club Sheffield Wednesday suffered their worst ever home defeat, 7–1 against Forest on 1 April.

● Wembley history was made on 23 April with the first sudden-death decider – sub Paul Tate scored in the 103rd minute to give Birmingham a 1–0 victory over Carlisle in the Auto Windscreen Shield fina.

● The troubled English season closed with a classic play-off at Wembley, Bolton returning to the top echelon after 15 years by coming back from 2–0 down to beat Reading after extra time.

● Chelsea manager Glenn Hoddle pulled of the coup of the season at the end of May, signing 32-year-old Dutch star Ruud Gullit from Sampdoria on a free transfer, and new Arsenal manager Bruce Rioch made his first signing in June, another Dutch star, Dennis Bergkamp, from Inter for £7.5m.

Seaman left high and dry by Nayim

DOWN AND OUT for London in Paris. How cruel this game can be. Arsenal were within 20 seconds of a penalty shoot-out when David Seaman, the man whose goalkeeping has so often rescued an ageing side, was beaten from fully 50 yards. Reluctantly, disbelievingly, Highbury handed their European Cup-Winners' Cup to Real Zaragoza.

Insult was added to iniquity when the red-shirted legions realized which Spaniard had so humiliated their beloved keeper. It was Nayim, formerly of Tottenham Hotspur. They will be chanting his name at White Hart Lane on Sunday.

Nayim's opportunist strike was particularly unjust on Seaman, whose penalty saves had carried Arsenal to the final, where his athleticism again served the holders well on an evening of increasing drama. The devastating denouement was also the roughest of justice on Tony Adams, the Gunners' inspirational captain.

Esnaider put Zaragoza ahead after 69 minutes, but Arsenal replied within 6 minutes through John Hartson.

David Seaman lies devastated with the ball in the net.

Everton plunge United into double despair

MANCHESTER UNITED'S worst fears were realized yesterday, when they were left empty-handed at the end of a season to which they have contributed so much. Desperately missing the guile of the suspended Eric Cantona, the deposed English champions had no answer to Paul Rideout's first-half goal for Everton or the tenacity with which the Merseysiders clung to the FA Cup: their first trophy in eight years.

United certainly worked hard enough to break down Everton, especially in the second half. But on the few occasions they did pierce a defence that has let in only one goal throughout the Cup run, they found Neville Southall in no mood to let his 650th appearance for the Goodison Park club be spoiled by having to pick the ball out of his net.

Southall, 36, was outstanding, as was man of the match Dave Watson in central defence and Anders Limpar in attack. Limpar's speed of thought and movement was the key to the counterattacks with which Everton won this absorbing, though unremarkable final.

FINAL SCORE

Football League
Premier Division: Blackburn Rovers
Top scorer: Alan Shearer (Blackburn) 34
Division 1: Middlesbrough
Division 2: Birmingham City
Division 3: Carlisle United
Footballer of the Year: Jurgen Klinsmann (Tottenham Hotspur)

FA Cup Final
Everton 1 Manchester Utd 0

League Cup Final
Liverpool 2 Bolton Wanderers 1

Scottish League
Premier Division: Rangers
Top scorer: Tommy Coyne (Motherwell) 16
Division 1: Raith Rovers
Division 2: Greenock Morton
Division 3: Forfar Athletic
Footballer of the Year: Brian Laudrup (Rangers)

Scottish FA Cup Final
Celtic 1 Airdrieonians 0

Scottish League Cup Final
Raith Rovers 2 Celtic 2
(aet) Raith won 6–5 on penalties

European Cup Final
Ajax 1 AC Milan 0

Cup-Winners Cup Final
Real Zaragoza 2 Arsenal 1

UEFA Cup Final
Parma beat Juventus 1–0, 1–1

European Footballer of the Year 1993
Hristo Stoichkov (Bulgaria & Barcelona)

World Club Championship
Velez Sarsfield 2 AC Milan 0

Blackburn lose at Anfield but win crown for Dalglish

AT THE cacophonous conclusion of this truly tense piece of sporting theatre, both sets of supporters joined in a delirious, hugely cheeky rendition of "Always Look on the Bright Side of Life", the song seemingly under copyright to the dethroned champions Manchester United.

All corners of Anfield were united. This was a day for "You'll Never Walk Alone" and "You'll never beat Jack Walker", everyone present revelling in the perfect result for Anfield: a deserved triumph for Liverpool and a deserved title for Blackburn Rovers, who secured their first championship in 81 years by a point from United.

What a finale to the season. How refreshing after a year of negatives that England's premier trophy should go to a friendly, family-orientated club. What a finale to the match. Blackburn's emotional rollercoaster ride of recent weeks was encapsulated by last-minute see-sawing.

When Jamie Redknapp curled in a wonderful winner for Liverpool, suddenly, cruelly, Rovers looked in danger of losing the race they had largely dominated since late November. To be sure of the title, they had needed to win, and that was now impossible. Then, seconds later, came news of the final whistle at West Ham, where United had failed to achieve the victory they required. Cue euphoria.

All Anfield danced with joy. It could have been Kenny Dalglish's testimonial. Rovers' Scottish manager, his face unlined by the passing years, remains revered at this famous old ground.

The Kop certainly welcomed King Kenny back in style, successfully willing him to join Herbert Chapman and Brian Clough as the only managers to win titles with two clubs.

It could have been Ewood. Blue-and-white scarves proclaiming allegiance to Dalglish's present employers were held aloft by the host hordes; Rovers' 3,000 fans, touched by the reception, repaid the compliment by waving a large Liverpool flag.

Bonhomie pervaded. All combined in chanting "Dalglish", their voices savouring the second syllable, as if scared of parting.

Over at Upton Park, Alex Ferguson's decision to leave Mark Hughes on the bench for the first half and play Andy Cole, who missed two late chances, alone in attack will provide one final debating point in a season of trouble and tumult.

Alan Shearer (left) and Chris Sutton with the Premiership trophy.

The Impact of Foreign Players

By Henry Winter

From Ardiles to Zola, Zondervan to Asprilla, countless foreigners have clambered ashore in England, but the most influential overseas player of all never set boot here. Jean-Marc Bosman, whose landmark legal case precipitated freedom of contract and movement within EC countries, was the man who ripped open the doors to English dressing-rooms, allowing in everyone from enlightened missionary to simple mercenary.

The explosion in numbers of foreign footballers was primed by Bosman. Some, like Eric Cantona, were already in residence, but Bosman, the little-known Belgian, accelerated the Continental drift of English football. Domestic clubs could now recruit out-of-contract foreign stars without paying a fee; those still in contract saw their transfer values decrease but salaries rise. The free-transfer market went into overdrive.

Cantona

Bosman opened up the floodgates, but it was Cantona who had given notice of the quality that could be found abroad. There had been high-profile foreigners before the Frenchman, such as Ossie Ardiles and Ricky Villa who arrived at Tottenham Hotspur after Argentina's World Cup success of 1978, but it was Cantona who embodied the English obsession with foreigners in the Nineties.

A moody but brilliant presence for Leeds United briefly, and then Manchester United gloriously, Cantona encouraged club chairmen and managers to buy foreign. Under his talismanic influence, United became serial winners of silverware.

Arguably Cantona's most important legacy has been the lessons and feelings he inspired in a whole generation of United players. "We learnt from Eric's actions, the way he played and trained," said Ryan Giggs, United's Welsh winger. "Gary and Philip Neville, Nicky Butt, Paul Scholes, David Beckham and myself stay behind after training now and just practise free-kicks and shooting. These are things we've always done because that was what Eric always used to do."

A winning formula

Peter Schmeichel, the loud and intelligent Dane who kept goal so commandingly for United, ranks only just behind Cantona in importance to the Nineties success story at Old Trafford. Other clubs sought to emulate United. Chelsea, seeking to rejoin the game's super-elite, invested fistfuls of francs and lorryloads of lire in foreigners, primarily to good effect.

Eric Cantona makes a forcible point to Steve Hodge of Leeds.

Gianfranco Zola helped to restore Chelsea's former glories.

Gianfranco Zola, the magical little Italian, followed Cantona as Footballer of the Year. Albert Ferrer, the experienced Spanish international, won many friends with his feisty style of play. Ruud Gullit, initially a player in the Premiership before his defensive vulnerability saw him move into management, similarly delighted many.

It has been little surprise to find London clubs like Chelsea and Arsenal attracting some of the leading foreigners. Zola and his successor as Footballer of the Year, Arsenal's Dutch inside-forward Dennis Bergkamp, have both settled in London's centre (Zola) and classier suburbs (Bergkamp).

Peace off the pitch

Both famous footballers appreciate being left in peace. Bergkamp can head down the garden centre and not face any hassle. Zola relishes being able to walk with his family in Hyde Park without being pursued by vast numbers of gawpers as would happen in Italy.

"London is very welcoming for everybody," said Graeme Le Saux, Zola's team-mate at

Peter Schmeichel was the world's No. 1 goalkeeper.

Stamford Bridge. "All the foreigners at Chelsea love London. It has a real cutting edge to it. That's an important factor for any player, as Middlesbrough found to their cost. They are probably the biggest example of foreign players coming over and seeing the contract before they've seen the city. If you or your family are not happy in a place, what hope has your career got?"

Middlesbrough saw plenty of quicksilver service from Brazil's Juninho, but other foreigners appeared to treat the Riverside as some giant piggy-bank to be plundered. Fabrizio Ravanelli, of Italy and the Planet Moody, hardly endeared himself to the Northeast public with his moaning and griping about poor standards. The dressing-room spirit suffered and few lamented Ravanelli's departure.

Yet London has also experienced some dreadful foreigners, most notably the Dutchman Jeroen Boere and Romania's Florin Raduciou at West Ham United. Some of them appeared to prefer shopping at Harvey Nichols to playing at Coventry, Derby or Everton.

Man management

But the trend has generally been positive in London. Astute managers, like the Frenchman Arsene Wenger at Arsenal, ensure they do their homework into a transfer target's character. Highbury has been particularly well-served by foreigners in the late 1990s.

The French pair, Emmanuel Petit and Patrick Vieira, built the midfield platform for the assault on the 1997–98 Double. Bergkamp, drafted in pre-Wenger, and his Dutch compatriot Marc Overmars have proved attacking catalysts on any number of occasions. The 1998 FA Cup final was won largely thanks to Overmars's pace.

Overmars, as fast on his feet as he is fluent in English, was well-equipped to deal with life in England. Yet the Premiership's high-speed nature can be a shock to incomers from more tactically obsessed leagues where the game is more chess-like than rollerball.

Tough but fair

"The biggest difference is the pace of the game here," said Dietmar Hamann, the German international who joined Newcastle United from Bayern Munich. Players like Hamann induced a tactical awareness, a sense of responsibility towards team shape. "The foreigners have brought into English football a sense that the most important thing is that you are well-organized," said Hamann.

The talented German midfielder relishes the general sporting nature of the Premiership. "It's very honest because no one wants you to get booked," he said. "If you foul them they get up immediately. When I watch German matches on television, I say 'get up' because it is not as honest as here."

The foreign invasion has broadened the horizons of local players. Hassan Kachloul became the first Moroccan in English football when he moved to Southampton. Not many English players know about Ramadan, the Muslim holy period of daylight fasting so Kachloul explained it to them, though he has given up fasting because of the toll it takes on his career.

Fasting is certainly a new concept to a world once inhabited by steak-eaters, chip-lovers and pie merchants. Diet has been another area where many foreigners have influenced the native professional. Ray Parlour at Arsenal had a relatively bad diet until Wenger arrived to change the canteen menu. Soon, everyone was eating broccoli. Encouraged by Wenger, Parlour toned down on the booze and became an England international. "There are so many foreign coaches coming here who are bringing in different diets and things like not drinking," said Giggs.

The foreign invasion extends beyond players. Wenger has won the Double at Arsenal, Gianluca Vialli and Gullit have enjoyed success at Chelsea. Gerard Houllier was charged with the difficult duty of reviving Liverpool. Yet Wenger himself has warned of the dangers to the national team of clubs buying foreign. But as long as foreigners like Cantona, Bergkamp and Zola continue to deliver silverware, then chairmen and managers will continue to look overseas.

Dutchman Dennis Bergkamp settled in England better than Italy.

Arsenal move into new era with Platt deal

WHILE ALLEGATIONS of past misdemeanours by George Graham, Arsenal's former manager, were being discussed by an army of legal representatives, the club signalled their intent to move into a new era at Highbury by signing David Platt, the England captain, from Sampdoria for £4.75 million.

Arsenal may have enjoyed success under Graham, but it came with a reputation for dull football. That image may change under new manager Bruce Rioch, who has yet to take charge of his team for a match, but has already spent £12.25 million on two players from Italy's Serie A – Platt and Dutch star Dennis Bergkamp.

After four years in Italy, Platt decided to return to England and take his total transfer fees to a world record £22.15 million – a long way on from being given a free transfer to Crewe after a "failed" apprenticeship at Manchester United. He spent four years with Crewe before Graham Taylor took him to Aston Villa for £200,000, starting his extraordinary transfer trail. Bari signed him for £5.5m in 1991, Juventus for £6.5m in 1992, and Sampdoria for £5.2m in 1993.

In order to attract two of the highest profile players in Europe, Arsenal's wage structure has been altered radically, with Bergkamp earning a reported £25,000 a week and Platt likely to be on a similar amount.

Platt's decision to leave Italy was prompted by Sampdoria's clear-out of stars after they failed to qualify for Europe and when, without the suspended Platt, they were knocked out by Arsenal.

David Platt (left) with manager Bruce Rioch and Dennis Bergkamp.

Match-fixing charges

THE LONG-DRAWN-OUT "match-fixing" affair took another step with the charging of players Bruce Grobbelaar, John Fashanu and Hans Segers, accused of taking money to fix matches. The alleged offences were said to have been committed between February 1, 1991, and March 15, 1995.

The three, together with Fashanu's wife and a Malaysian businessman, will have to answer to counts of corruption as well as conspiracy. All were bailed to appear at Southampton magistrates' court at a later date.

Grobbelaar is due to play for Zimbabwe on Sunday, and the police have returned his passport.

Save of the century

GOAL-LESS but not soul-less was perhaps the best way to describe England's 0–0 draw with Colombia in their Wembley friendly.

The new order hardly set England's world in motion again but, in the wake of earlier disappointments, Terry Venables will have derived much pleasure from a thoroughly deserved draw, particularly from the dynamic display between midfield and attack of Nick Barmby, who took to the international stage as if all his career had been building toward this moment.

But the highlight of the night, replays of which should enliven many a dull evening, was a thrillingly unorthodox save from Rene Higuita, the Colombian keeper. What he calls his "scorpion kick", having its first showing in Britain, eschews the simple catch on the line and involves throwing himself forward and kicking up his heels behind him to clear the ball. Had this been a gymnastics competition, he surely would have been awarded a maximum ten.

Higuita illuminated a dull game.

Guilty Graham stands to lose £1m after one-year ban

GEORGE GRAHAM, the former Arsenal manager, was banned from football for a year after being found guilty of misconduct by a Football Association commission of inquiry.

But while he contemplates his absence from the game and an ultimate loss of around £1 million, he may consider that the stigma attached to the FA's verdict and punishment could outweigh any material penalties. For the first time since Don Revie was banned for 10 years, a punishment later overturned in the High Court on a technicality, a manager in English football has been barred from working.

Graham has been disgraced by accepting payments totalling £425,500 from Norwegian agent Rune Hauge,who spoke in his defence. Graham returned the payments, which he had considered an "unsolicited gift", to Arsenal with interest.

Those payments formed part of the transfers which took Pal Lyderson from Norwegian club IK Start to Highbury, and John Jensen from Brondby, of Copenhagen.

Graham must wait until June 30, 1996, before he can be re-employed. The FA will notify FIFA of the ban and, as in the Eric Cantona case, they will expect them to endorse it worldwide.

The ban is defined as "all-over involvement in football administration, management or coaching, including the signing and transfer of players".

The committee accepted that Graham had not signed the players to "obtain any personal gain", and took account of his exemplary football and disciplinary record in considering punishments. Though the FA did not fine Graham, his personal losses have mounted up.

When dismissed from Arsenal, he had two years of a £250,000 contract remaining, plus the promise of a testimonial that would have netted about £200,000. His personal legal costs are estimated at £200,000, and his bill for the inquiry £100,000.

SOCCER SOUNDBITES

"It [the commission] was satisfied that when he received the money, he must have known it was connected with the transfers."

FOOTBALL ASSOCIATION SPOKESMAN,
on the findings of the commission looking into the George Graham affair.

Brazilian star for Boro: Robson's great coup

LIGHT THE BEACONS on the hills, let the bells ring out, tell every child to wear a smile. The despatches from São Paulo carry almost unbelievable tidings. Brazil's No 10 is coming to England.

An intense feeling of excitement, almost privilege, is permissible. Little Juninho, 22, whom nature has blessed with a precocious talent as if in apology for his frail frame, entranced England during this summer's Umbro Cup. São Paulo's sorcerer, who captivated Villa Park, Goodison Park and Wembley, returns to take up permanent residence at Middlesbrough.

After medical and work permit formalities are completed, he is expected to make his debut against Manchester United at Old Trafford on October 28.

Those who have yet to witness Juninho's artistry, his appetite for the ball, however fierce the fray, will soon understand why Bryan Robson pursued him with a tenacity that echoed the Middlesbrough manager's playing days.

Once more England stands indebted to Robson, who is revered in Brazil. "All along Juninho has expressed a preference to play for him," said Keith Lamb, Middlesbrough's chief executive. "The difficult part was persuading São Paulo to sell."

When people around the globe think of England, they will say that is where Juninho chose to play, where he could find greater riches even than in Italy.

His arrival for £4.75 million gives the hosts of Euro 96, and bidders for a future World Cup, increased credibility. The Premiership, financially strong and teeming with talent, both domestic and imported, has moved within sight of Italy's Serie A. Who next? Baggio for Bolton?

Bryan Robson (left) parades Juninho to the Middlesbrough fans.

Transfer system kicked out of court

Jean Marc Bosman (middle) at a press conference.

PROFESSIONAL SOCCER is facing a period of turmoil after a European court proposed that clubs should not be able to charge a transfer fee for players whose contracts have expired.

The case at the European Court of Justice in Luxembourg was brought by Jean-Marc Bosman, a Belgian player who claimed that the transfer system restrained him as a trader in his skills. He took the Belgian FA, UEFA and RC Liege to court after the club blocked his transfer to a French club when his contract had ended.

Carl Otto Lenz, an advocate-general of the court, is recommending that a full tribunal should rule the current system unlawful. It is considered unlikely that the court would throw out the advice. The findings also mean that the ban on more than three foreign players in a team would also be lifted.

Football's governing bodies and clubs in Britain believe that few major clubs would be unscathed, and the vast majority of smaller ones would lose a valuable source of income from selling promising players.

Under the current system, players who fall out of contract can be sold to other clubs for a fee over and above terms agreed with the player. The Bosman case, if ratified, means that players would become free agents at the end of their terms and could sell themselves to any interested club. They would find themselves in a huge international market.

If the court's decision is ratified, it is binding on all member states. But the sport will probably be given up to five years to find a workable system.

SOCCER SOUNDBITES

"We believe that three-quarters of full-time footballers would lose their jobs under the proposed arrangements."

CHRIS HULL,
Football League spokesman.

Blackburn's European Cup knock-out misery

BLACKBURN VOWED not to go out of the Champions' League without a fight and, sadly, they were as good as their word when Graeme Le Saux, David Batty and Tim Sherwood were involved in an extraordinary exchange of blows after only five minutes of Rovers' latest European defeat by Spartak Moscow.

Twenty minutes later Sherwood and Colin Hendry had to be pacified after exchanging harsh words. And just when it seemed things could not get worse, Hendry was sent off in the 75th minute for a foul on Andrei Tikhonov.

Blackburn's European knockout – a wholly appropriate word after what happened in Moscow – meant they lost their discipline and another Group B tie. Playing poorly is one thing, but there can be no excuses for the complete lack of professionalism shown by the English champions.

The first incident started when Le Saux took the ball off Batty and conceded a throw-in. Le Saux appeared to throw a punch at Batty, and Sherwood, the captain, moved in angrily with an arm raised – he did not seem to fit the role of a peacemaker. It happened in front of the Blackburn dug-out, and Rovers manager Ray Harford was on his feet yelling at his players.

Then Sherwood lost the ball and conceded a foul when attempting to win it back. Hendry offered his view of this, which did not please Sherwood, and teammates moved in to silence the war of words.

Spartak, who maintained their 100% record, scored three superb goals. Their victory confirmed them as group winners, with a place in the European Cup quarter-finals.

Ireland beaten but unbowed

Kluivert (right) scores his second to clinch the match.

IRISH SONGS filled Anfield, but they were sounds emitted bravely, sportingly in defeat. How Euro 96 will miss the good humour of the green choirs, their ability to bring smiles to passers-by, their wonderful singing to soften any cynic's heart.

Here, in a passionate play-off for a place at next summer's European Championship finals, was fulsome testimony to the presence of purity within a game so often associated with greed, selfishness and other inelegant, unsporting virtues. How fitting that such a thrilling contest should be decided by Patrick Kluivert, a talented teenager who represents everything positive about the Ajax way.

Here was confirmation of the Amsterdam club's importance in showing the world, and particularly Britain, how to play the game. Blessed with a body that can twist athletically while withstanding any challenge, capable of complete mastery of the ball, Kluivert dominated the night, scoring once in each half to quell the spirited resistance of the depleted Irish.

So, the Euro 96 hosts gain Kluivert and his sophisticated Dutch colleagues, but glaringly in the debit corner will be the absence of Jack Charlton and his magnificent travelling support. It is hard to imagine the followers of England, some of whom had defiled Dublin earlier this year, dancing away into the cold night, expressing their disappointment simply through relentless renditions of "Always Look on the Bright Side of Life".

Despite the unique tension of this night of drama, both sets of supporters proved admirable models of togetherness. The orange third joined the green party in a raucous version of "You'll Never Walk Alone".

If Anfield rang to Irish sounds, the match was predominantly in Dutch hands. It was Ajax versus the Premiership, total football versus total commitment. It was a game of contrasting styles, but complete respect between the two sides.

When the game was over, every ounce of energy spent by two sets of committed opponents, the night's sporting nature continued to the very end, when the Dutch hordes stood to applaud Charlton. If only every match could be like this.

SOCCER SOUNDBITES

"Housewives used to have pictures of the Pope or John F. Kennedy on the walls. Now they have replaced them with pictures of Jack."

NIALL QUINN,
Republic of Ireland striker.

Manager in a million Charlton quits Irish

IN 93 INTERNATIONAL matches spanning nearly 10 years, Jack Charlton rewrote Irish football history. A statement shortly before Christmas confirmed what many Irishman had feared, that Charlton's remarkable relationship with the Republic of Ireland had come to an end.

As Charlton had stood on the Anfield pitch after the 2–0 defeat by Holland in last week's European Championship play-off, with a green scarf in one hand and a cigar in the other, it was clear he had managed Ireland for the last time. He had planned a holiday in Spain before announcing his retirement, but the Football Association of Ireland wanted an early decision, and forced him into a premature announcement.

Charlton transformed a team who were going nowhere into one who reached two World Cup finals, making it to the last eight in 1990. As on the occasion when Charlton returned from the finals in Italy, the traffic in Dublin was brought to a standstill. The man who could do no wrong in Irish eyes was begged to stay, but as supporters toasted his remarkable spell late into the night, the Football Association of Ireland began the process of finding a successor.

Little's big day as Villa crush Leeds: Serb's strike points way

Dwight Yorke, on the ball, a major player for Aston Villa this season.

RARELY have Wembley winners deserved victory more than Aston Villa in the Coca-Cola Cup final. Brian Little's disciplined adventurers, their youthful exuberance directed by the canny minds of Andy Townsend and Paul McGrath, were, to a man, superior to Leeds United.

Leeds' inexplicable inability to rise to their first cup final appearance in 23 years completely frustrated their legion of long-suffering loyalists.

Villa played with passion, and all in accord with Little's masterplan of mixing attacks with pace and patience. Little had had an inkling that the hitherto erratic Savo Milosevic would score a really important goal for Villa this season. And so it proved, the tall striker putting Villa into a lead that was embellished by Ian Taylor and the splendidly consistent Dwight Yorke.

Milosevic's strike after 21 dull and uninspired minutes set up Villa's victory. The Serb, racing through, poured the full momentum of that erratic left boot into it, which arched up and over John Lukic, a quite wonderful goal. After that, there was never any doubt that Villa were off to Europe.

Collymore steals Magpies' thunder

Stan Collymore, right, broke Newcastle's hearts.

LIVERPOOL 4 NEWCASTLE 3. Football does not come much better than this. Even the moon was eclipsed by a match of quite monumental brilliance at awestruck Anfield, as Stan Collymore's injury-time winner sent both the Kop and the championship race into orbit.

The result brings the resurgent Reds within two points of Newcastle and five of Manchester United, who will have enjoyed the result as much as Liverpool.

Newcastle had played so well, so spiritedly, and yet have still only acquired four points from a possible 18. Their football is such a joy to behold, so full of pace and verve. But too often it is a joy to play against.

Liverpool went ahead, within two minutes, from a move begun and finished in irresistible fashion by Robbie Fowler.

Newcastle could have been overwhelmed. Instead, searching and finding the heroes Keegan told them they had within them, they rose magnificently to the challenge. Buoyed by the Blaydon Races crashing against their backs, Newcastle simply charged at Liverpool. Robert Lee was outstanding, tackling back with the tigerish diligence so urgently needed.

Peter Beardsley and Les Ferdinand chased everywhere. At one point Ferdinand followed Collymore almost into town. Such work deserved reward. It duly came, thanks to Faustino Asprilla's penetration and Ferdinand's sharp shooting.

The poacher turned goalmaker moments later, controlling Watson's clever clearance in the centre circle, Ferdinand sensed David Ginola's forward dart, and the Frenchman sprinted 40 yards towards the Kop before lifting the ball in past James.

Within 10 minutes of the restart Liverpool had levelled, when Steve McManaman drilled in a low ball which arrowed past everyone except Fowler, whose left foot did the rest.

Back came Newcastle, regaining the lead almost with their next surge. Lee's through ball sprung Liverpool's offside trap, allowing Asprilla to run in and slip the ball past James before celebrating with a cartwheel.

Game over? Not a chance. McAteer and Batty shared a silly spat before Liverpool hit back in compelling fashion, McAteer bending in a wonderful pass for Collymore to steer a close range equaliser under Srnicek.

Worse was to befall Newcastle. James saved magnificently from Ferdinand before their night collapsed. Barnes, hitherto quiet, combined with Ian Rush before sliding a pass out to Collymore on the left. Taming the ball with his right foot, he curled it with his left between Srnicek and his right-hand upright. The title race had taken yet another turn.

Venables to quit

TERRY VENABLES is standing down as England's soccer coach to concentrate on a series of legal battles over his business affairs and the long-running dispute with the Tottenham Hotspur chairman Alan Sugar, as well as libel actions against the BBC and the *Daily Mirror*.

Venables, 53, who became coach in January 1994, told the Football Association in early January that he was quitting after this summer's European Championships because he believed his court commitments would hamper England's 1998 World Cup campaign.

The FA said it was deeply disappointed but understood Venables' "absolute determination to clear his name".

Gazza King of the Scots

PAUL GASCOIGNE scored a hattrick against Aberdeen at Ibrox to secure the eighth consecutive Scottish League title for Rangers only hours after being named Footballer of the Year by his fellow players.

When the players reappeared from their dressing room after this dramatic victory to be presented with the Scottish championship trophy, they had exchanged their light blue jerseys for T-shirts, each bearing the number eight – coincidentally the number of the shirt worn by the flamboyant England star.

Aberdeen took the lead after 20 minutes, but within two minutes Gascoigne, boring past defenders like a high-powered drill, surfaced at a tight angle a few yards from Michael Watt's left-hand post. Others would have checked and looked for a supporting player. Gascoigne simply swept the ball over the head of the astounded Watt before his No 8 jersey disappeared from sight beneath his celebrating teammates.

Rangers would have to endure a fraught hour before the title came within reach, and again, inevitably, it was Gascoigne who administered the decisive stroke. Gathering the ball in his own half, he scampered off across the centre circle, brushed Paul Bernard aside and strode on to finish with a lofted drive beyond the exposed Watt.

With four minutes remaining, Gascoigne coolly deposited a spot-kick in Aberdeen's net and the contest was over.

Thus was Walter Smith's gamble of £4 million – the stake he placed on an overweight, controversial figure who had not played at the height of his form for three years – totally justified.

A celebrating Gascoigne is hugged by team-mate David Robertson.

Hoddle for England

AFTER MONTHS of speculation, the FA finally introduced the new England supremo to press and public on May 2, Chelsea manager Glenn Hoddle having agreed to their offer of a four-year contract. The one consolation for bereft Chelsea fans was Ruud Gullit's assertion that he would not leave the Bridge.

Hoddle's contract begins on June 1, and, although he will not take up the reins until Terry Venables' Euro 96 adventure reaches a conclusion, he will meet the England players at the Bisham Abbey training ground. The thought of Hoddle, capped 53 times, being "introduced" to the elite of this generation is an interesting one: the majority of England's tyros list Hoddle as their boyhood hero in those programme profiles.

Although not the FA's first choice, Hoddle clearly has many admirers within Lancaster Gate. His unblemished image helps explain the length of his FA contract, twice that of Venables.

Hoddle, at 38 England's youngest manager, promises an age of enlightenment driven by the many young talents now blossoming onto the international scene.

Venables (right) and Hoddle, his successor as England boss.

SOCCER SOUNDBITES

"If Terry had been manager when I was playing, I think I would have won a lot more caps."

GLENN HODDLE,
on being appointed Venables' successor as England coach.

United's young guns clinch title

BUOYED BY KIDS and kidology, Alex Ferguson secured his third Premiership title in four years at Middlesbrough on the last Sunday of the season, a performance of gathering confidence perfectly reflecting Manchester United's triumphant campaign.A possible "double" awaits.

Ferguson's fledglings deserve their praise. As United's gleeful hordes chanted "You'll never win the League with the kids", a mocking reference to Alan Hansen's early-season verdict, the charge of the slight brigade was enacted again, with David Beckham, Paul Scholes, Philip Neville and Nicky Butt to the fore.

Ferguson's commitment to youth makes United worthy winners – by four points after Newcastle were held at home by Spurs – of such a stirring championship. Yet, when the haze of hangovers drifts away, United will acknowledge fully that the glue that held the red dream together, the common bond, was a more senior member of the dressing room: Eric Cantona.

United finished comfortable 3–0 winners. But, sadly, if inevitably, their supporters used the occasion to taunt Kevin Keegan, Newcastle's manager who had reacted so testily to Ferguson's earlier mind games. Their banners and chants were in poor taste. Keegan and his team have contributed fully to a magnificent championship race, the most open and exciting in years. Newcastle's season-long threat makes Manchester United's achievement even greater.

Manchester United celebrate their Premiership triumph.

FOOTBALL FOCUS

- Everton and Scotland striker Duncan Ferguson was jailed for three months in October for head-butting an opponent while a Rangers player.

- Blackburn's Alan Shearer (3) and Lars Bohinen (2) destroyed Nottingham Forest's 25-game unbeaten run in the League, shattering England's sole survivors in Europe on the eve of their UEFA Cup tie against Lyon, with a sensational 7–0 victory at Ewood Park to celebrate as Jack Walker officially opened his newly built ground – this after Forest fans had poured scorn on their former hero, the Norwegian Bohinen.

- Siberian temperatures producing snow and ice restricted the first-class programme on Jan 27 to 3 FA Cup 4th-round ties, 1 Endsleigh League game, 5 Tennents Scottish Cup matches and a solitary Scottish League match. A total of 55 games in England and Scotland were called off – only 2 short of the all-time record set on Feb 9, 1963, when just 7 Football League fixtures survived and none at all in Scotland of the 64 arranged.

- The night before going into hospital for an operation to a groin injury (with two games of the season remaining, in order to be recovered in time for England's Euro 96 campaign), Alan Shearer scored twice in Blackburn's 3–2 victory over Wimbledon to reach 31 goals in the Premiership and create a piece of history as the first man since the 1930s to score 30 or more goals in the top flight in three successive seasons, something Jimmy Greaves fell one short of achieving in 1964–65.

- Eric Cantona's choice as Footballer of the Year provoked a certain amount of controversy, for while everyone admired his magnificent comeback, there were those who felt it made a mockery of an award intended for a player who must "by precept and example" be the best, on and off the field.

- Needing a win on the last day of the season to clinch the last UEFA Cup place, Arsenal were a goal down to bottom club Bolton at Highbury before goals by pre-season signings David Platt and Dennis Bergkamp in the last 10 minutes saw them through.

- Man-of-the-Match Brian Laudrup made a hat-trick for Gordon Durie and scored twice himself as Rangers beat Hearts 5–1 in the Scottish Cup final to register their 13th "double".

Cantona crowns United's second "double"

HISTORY WAS MADE at Wembley by the Frenchman who seems to do nothing else. Eric Cantona, newly crowned as Footballer of the Year, scored the goal that won this severely disappointing FA Cup final for Manchester United and conferred upon them the unique honour of becoming the first club to complete the coveted League and Cup "double" twice.

Cantona also made a handsome contribution to United's winning of the Premiership title, of course. His return last October, after serving an eight-month suspension for attacking an abusive Crystal Palace fan, was rightly seen as the catalyst that enabled the Old Trafford club to overhaul Newcastle after being 12 points behind.

The very fact that United's clinching goal was Cantona's 19th of the season indicates as clearly as possible his determination to make up for an avoidable absence that probably cost United the "double" last season. Little wonder he ran like a man demented to celebrate his winner with the United fans and bench.

Eric Cantona displays his Footballer of the Year trophy.

United deserved their victory because they were always the better side in a match that failed miserably to live up to its billing as a celebration of two of the youngest and most talented sides in the land.

It was, essentially, a triumph based on hard work and sound tactical planning. Although there were very few flashes of the inspired football everyone had expected from such a plethora of talent, one could not help but admire the unflagging industry and concentration of men like Roy Keane and Ryan Giggs in United's midfield.

Together with Nicky Butt and David Beckham, Keane and Giggs prevented John Barnes, Jamie Redknapp and Steve McManaman from establishing any kind of hold over the area of the field where most of the Merseysiders' damaging moves begin. McManaman, harried at every turn, never looked like getting the time and space to be Liverpool's match-winner, as he has so many times before.

Stan Collymore and Robbie Fowler were no more impressive up front. Fowler, the scourge of United until now, was not allowed even the slightest sniff of a chance.

Nor was Andy Cole any better for United. Preferred to Paul Scholes because manager Alex Ferguson thought his pace might unhinge the Liverpool defence, the £7 million striker failed three times in the first 16 minutes with good chances. Despite his failings, United might have taken an early lead but for an exceptional save by David James from a snap Beckham volley.

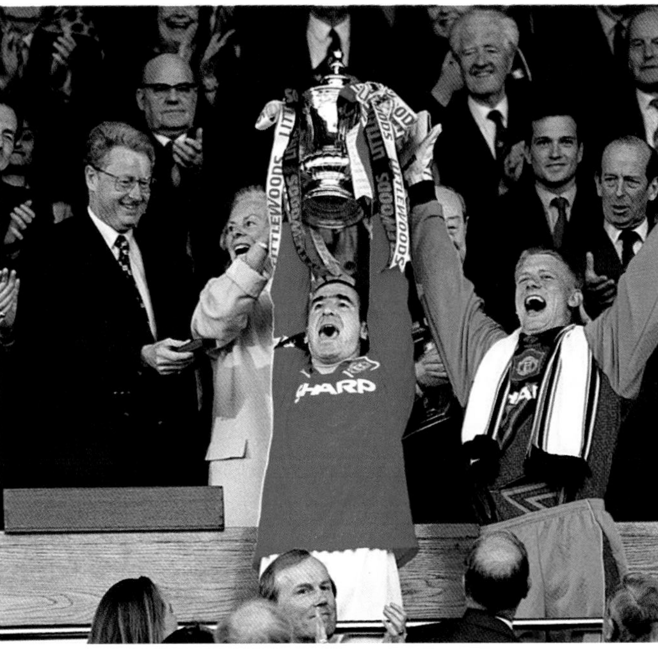

Manchester United captain Cantona hoists the FA Cup at Wembley.

In contrast, only twice in the whole game did Liverpool really look like scoring. Once James had saved from Cantona soon after the restart, the match seemed to be drifting inexorably towards extra time with only the substitutions of Scholes for Cole and Rush for Collymore and the bookings of Phil Babb and Neville to relieve the tedium.

Then, five minutes from the end, James came majestically off his line to claim Beckham's corner from the right, but misjudged things slightly and could only punch away weakly towards the edge of the penalty area, where Cantona was waiting.

A crisp, right footed volley flew into the net through a crowd of players and the rest, quite literally, is history.

Juventus champions of Europe: Ajax pay the penalty

THIS was such a beguiling encounter that Radio Vatican sent two reporters – the first time the Catholic Church has applied for accreditation for a football game. They saw a classic that went all the way and established Juventus as the champions of Europe after they won a penalty shoot-out 4–2.

The Old Lady of Juventus versus the young bucks of Ajax. The Amsterdam contingent thronging Rome during the day wore T-shirts airing the claim "Ajax equals Art" and lay in the parks like so many jam sandwiches toasting under the sun.

At the end of regular time the question of European hegemony was still in the balance as the Dutch and Italian champions from last year staggered beyond a 1–1 draw created by goals from Fabrizio Ravanelli for Juventus and Jari Litmanen for the reigning European champions.

Vladimir Jugovic's acrobatic flip when he scored the decisive penalty was a suitably exuberant celebration and Gianluca Vialli lifted the trophy in possibly his last match as captain of Juventus.

Juventus's triumph represents a record ninth European Cup victory for Italian clubs – one more than England. The game itself demonstrated to the nations of Europe how this summer's championship in England should be played, with 19 shots on goal and no end of adventurous, attacking football.

FINAL SCORE

Football League
Premier Division: Manchester United
Top scorer: Alan Shearer (Blackburn) 31
Division 1: Sunderland
Division 2: Swindon
Division 3: Preston North End
Footballer of the Year: Eric Cantona (Manchester United)

FA Cup Final
Manchester United 1 Liverpool 0

League Cup Final
Aston Villa 3 Leeds 0

Scottish League
Premier Division: Rangers
Top scorer: Pierre Van Hooijdonk (Celtic) 26
Division 1: Dunfermline Athletic
Division 2: Stirling Albion
Division 3: Livingston
Footballer of the Year: Paul Gascoigne (Rangers)

Scottish FA Cup Final
Rangers 5 Hearts 1

Scottish League Cup Final
Aberdeen 2 Dundee 0

European Cup Final
Juventus 1 Ajax 1
Juventus won 4–2 on penalties

Cup-Winners Cup Final
Paris St-Germain 1 Rapid Vienna 0

UEFA Cup Final
Bayern Munich beat Bordeaux 2–0, 3–1

European Footballer of the Year 1995
George Weah (AC Milan & Liberia)

World Club Championship
Ajax 0 Gremio 0
Ajax won 4–3 on penalties

Germany's Golden Goal

With 16 teams in the finals for the first time, the European Championship of 1996 in England was billed as a major sporting event – perhaps not on a par with a World Cup or an Olympic Games, but three weeks of intense competition between most of the world's best international sides, with blanket TV and Press coverage and the promise of a feast of football. It did not disappoint. Although it was plagued by a rash of red and yellow cards, and littered with penalties, it produced high drama. And the "Golden Goal", which failed to materialize in four matches when it was up for grabs, finally appeared to crown the tournament.

The format for Euro 96 was straightforward – four round-robin groups of four teams, the top two in each group going through to the knock-out stage. But there were significant differences in each stage that had not been seen in such a major tournament before – the tie-breaking regulations for placing teams with the same number of points, and the sudden-death extra time from the quarter-finals onwards.

Teams level on points after the three group matches had been played would be separated by first (out of eight criteria!) the points gained in matches between the teams in question, then by goal difference between the teams, then by most goals between the teams, down to Fair Play conduct (7th) and drawing lots (8th). In the knock-out stage, if the teams were level after 90 minutes, extra time would be played until a deciding goal – the "Golden Goal" – was scored, and, if there was no goal scored in the two 15-minute periods, a penalty decider, or "shoot-out", would take place.

The group regulations, which lessened the chance of teams progressing on the strength of goals scored against a weak side, were not as complicated as they appeared at first glance. There was certainly no excuse for the inability of TV producers and commentators to keep viewers apprised of the situation and possibilities when the last, vital matches of a group were being played simultaneously.

As far as the Golden Goal is concerned, the jury is still out. With extra time in two quarter-finals and both semi-finals unproductive of goals or, apart from the England–Germany semi-final, any real excitement, it brought very little that was positive to the tournament. The problem of penalty shoot-outs still remains. Most true fans would prefer to see real football decide such important contests. Penalties is like having a one-over slog decide the result of a cricket Test match.

Bright start

The tournament got off to a bright start, with a well-organized but unpretentious

David Seaman saves Spain's fourth spot-kick, taken by Miguel Angel Nadal, to clinch a semi-final place for England.

Germany were favourites because they were Germany, not because they were anywhere near as good as their great sides of the past. But they had the same team spirit and the utter self-belief that in the end won the day.

Czech star Karel Poborsky squirms through the French defence in the semi-finals.

opening ceremony at Wembley before the first match, between England and Switzerland, that accorded sufficient dignity to the proceedings without forgetting that the fans had come to see the football. And, with the whole nation holding their breath, there was no crowd trouble. All the doubts about holding such a competition in England were soon to be allayed, as match after match passed with little sign of the hooliganism that once made English fans the pariahs of European football.

England, too, made a bright start. Ince to Gascoigne, through to Shearer, and wham, the ball was in the back of the Swiss net after 23 minutes. Shearer's international goal drought was over – when it mattered most. But England lost the initiative in the second half, and Swiss pressure brought a deserved equalizer seven minutes from time, even if it did come from a dubious penalty, scored by the dangerous Turkyilmaz, given when the ball hit Pearce's hands from a point-blank shot. England looked tired: the fans could not be blamed for wondering if those lurid tabloid tales of drunken orgies in Hong Kong and on the flight home were not exaggerated after all.

Dress rehearsal

It took a while for the tournament to warm up. The three matches the following day produced only one win, ominously by Germany, by 2–0 over the Czech Republic. There was surely no one at Old Trafford, apart from perhaps a few Czech optimists, who could have dreamt this was a rehearsal for the final, especially as the Czechs had waiting for them in the so-called "Group of Death" Italy and Russia. But it was not all joy for the Germans, with stand-in captain Jürgen Kohler injured and out of the tournament and six others yellow-carded by English referee David Elleray. Bookings were already beginning to look like a lottery, so inconsistent was the standard of refereeing, and with two bookings automatically suspending a player for one match, coaches were looking ahead with concern to the knock-out stage.

Scotland, coming into the competition as joint 80–1 outsiders with Turkey, rode the insult and weathered the Dutch storm to throw Group A wide open. Admittedly they were lucky when John Collins's blatant handball on the goal-line went unseen by the referee, but the goalless result against the third favourites gave their confidence a tremendous boost. It also put pressure on England, and the whole country was alive in anticipation of Saturday's meeting at Wembley.

Before then, though, Euro 96 got well into its stride. Italy beat Russia 2–1 at Anfield, with Casiraghi scoring both goals in an impressive team performance. Italy and Germany would surely now qualify from Group C. The second round of matches then saw Holland beat Switzerland 2–0 at Villa Park to add an extra edge to the forthcoming Auld Enemy match. And no major tournament would be complete without a "ball-over-the-line" controversy. The incident occurred in the Group B match at St James' Park in which Bulgaria beat Romania 1–0. The game began sensationally when World Cup star Stoichkov brilliantly burst through a hesitant Romanian defence to put Bulgaria 1–0 up after three minutes. But after half an hour, Munteanu, running on to a lay-back, hit a thunderous drive from outside the box crashing on to the crossbar. As TV replays showed, the ball bounced down a foot over the line, but neither the referee nor the linesman saw it and Romania were denied a perfectly good equalizer.

Pundits were quick to blame the officials, and of course there were cries for action replays. But firstly there is no reason for either official to be on the line (the only position for judging such incidents) for a shot from outside the box, and secondly all the objections levelled at use of the electronic eye would not apply if an extra official – a goal judge as in ice hockey – were positioned at each end. Poor Romania, they were out of the running before they played their last match.

The plot thickens

The following day came the first real shock. Italy's coach, the controversial Arrigo Sacchi, changed his winning formula, drafting in five new players, and the Czechs beat them 2–1. Now they had a mountain to climb. Sacchi was not the only coach with a headache, however. The usual behind-the-scenes ructions were taking place in the Dutch camp, and Guss Hiddink sent the influential Ajax midfielder Edgar Davids home.

The England–Scotland clash at Wembley drew the biggest gate of the tournament, 76,864, and lived up to expectations. After a tight first half with Scotland territorially superior but with barely a chance at either end, England came out after the interval like a new team. Redknapp, on for Pearce, began to direct the midfield, and his Liverpool colleague McManaman, switched from left to right, began to run at defenders. Soon he

SOCCER SOUNDBITES

"There was no gloating afterwards. He came up and shook each Scottish player by the hand. He's a bigger man than people would think."

ALLY McCOIST,
Scotland striker, after his Rangers team-mate Paul Gascoigne had helped England beat Scotland.

SOCCER SOUNDBITES

"There is nothing to be downhearted about, apart from the result. ... I am very proud of my team."

TERRY VENABLES,
departing England coach.

Stefan Kuntz celebrates Germany's Golden Goal, although he very nearly invalidated it.

released Gary Neville on an overlapping run on the right. Over came the perfect cross, and Shearer came in at the far post to head it home.

England failed narrowly several times to increase their lead before Seaman brilliantly clawed out a Durie header to prevent a Scottish equaliser. The real drama was to come, though. Scotland broke away 13 minutes from time and Adams was adjudged to have brought down Durie with a sliding tackle in the box – penalty. Was this Switzerland all over again? No. Seaman somehow managed to deflect McAllister's kick over the bar with his left elbow as he dived to his right. Then, collecting the ball from the resultant corner, Seaman, threw it out to the left, a couple of passes and Gascoigne was running on to a bouncing ball at the other end, flicking it over Hendry with his left foot and hitting a glorious low volley with his right past the helpless Goram.

Scotland were never going to recover from such a double blow. And, what's more, England's confidence was sky high. The whole country was behind the team, and the words ringing down from the stands, "Football's coming home", were now perhaps not just a dream.

The next day, Klinsmann made his first appearance, having been suspended from Germany's first game, and scored twice in their 3–0 victory over Russia, the first a goal of sheer class. This virtually assured the Germans – but not certainly – of a place in the last eight. The other match produced a virtuoso performance from Croat striker Davor Suker at Hillsborough in Group D. With Denmark 2–0 down and only minutes to go, it was no surprise to see the blond head of keeper Schmeichel popping up at the other end for a corner. Suddenly, however, he was hurtling back to his own goal as Croatia gained possession. Over came a massive 50-yard pass from right to left, Suker taking it in his stride and accelerating away from his marker. Schmeichel got back just in time, but Suker calmly took the ball on and chipped it with the outside of his left foot over the blushing keeper and into the far corner of the net. Suker turned to take a bow, the holders were out of the tournament, and Manchester United's double-winning guardian sat open-mouthed on the ground wondering if this had affected his reputation as the world's best goalkeeper.

So near, yet so far

The third round of group games produced the best team performance of the tournament and very nearly the sensational elimination of Holland. Some might have expected England to shut up shop with a 1–0 half-time lead, courtesy a Shearer penalty won when Ince was tripped after tricking his way past Danny Blind into the box. But soon after the interval, in 12 rampant minutes, they put another three past the Dutch keeper, set off by a Sheringham header from a corner. Then came a wonderful team goal as England tore the Dutch defence to shreds – McManaman to Gascoigne, a powerful, incisive run into the box, a perfectly timed sideways touch to Sheringham, a dummy to shoot but another flick on to Shearer and the ball was swept into the net with a flourish. There was more to come, Sheringham first to the ball as Van der Sar could only parry Anderton's deflected shot.

All this while Scotland were peppering the Swiss goal up at Villa Park with only a super strike from McCoist (he missed two or three easier chances) to show for their superiority. It would have been enough to see them through, but Holland managed to score at Wembley with 12 minutes to go, a goal from the not fully fit striker Kluivert, just on as a sub and put clear by a clever flick from Bergkamp. Beaten – humiliated, according to their own Press – by 4–1, the Dutch were through, nevertheless, to the quarter-finals. It would be difficult for them to recover their composure. But for England, the whole country was gripped in football fever. Bring on the Spaniards.

There was great theatre, too, the next day in Group C, as Italy desperately needed to beat Germany at Old Trafford to stand a chance of survival. But luck was against them. German keeper Andreas Köpke should have been sent off for bringing down Casiraghi in the seventh minute, but was left to save the

FOOTBALL FOCUS

● The "home" side for each match was determined by the Euro 96 draw. So it was Scotland vs England at Wembley on 15 June, a unique event in the oldest international fixture in world football.

● Perhaps the strangest and most unprecedented occurrence in Euro 96 was the sight and sound of thousands of Scots cheering England goals. It happened at Villa Park, where Scotland were struggling to extend their lead over Switzerland, but commentary from Wembley on transistors in the crowd gave the Scottish fans hope that England would whip the Dutch by a margin sufficient to put Scotland through. In the end, they were thwarted by a late Dutch goal.

● The officials, as usual in a big tournament, came in for severe criticism, much of it justified. Right at the death, the Czechs claimed there was a player in an offside position when Bierhoff scored his Golden Goal. The referee, Pierluigi Pairetto of Italy, overruled his linesman presumably because he did not think Kuntz was interfering with play, a view vindicated when the Czech keeper Petr Kouba admitted afterwards that he was "watching the ball only," and could not say if there was an opponent in an offside position.

SOCCER SOUNDBITES

"It's great when you get so much praise for just doing your job well. I will take it all because you know it can go the other way."

DAVID SEAMAN,
England keeper, after his second man-of-the-match award.

resultant penalty, a weak effort from Zola, and went on to win the man-of-the-match award as Germany battled the last half-hour with 10 men after Strunz's dismissal. The Italians would still have made it had not Smicer grabbed a last-ditch equalizer for the Czechs at Anfield in a roller-coaster 3–3 draw with Russia. The Russians clawed back a 2–0 half-time deficit, and took the lead with five minutes to go before the final drama.

It's a knock-out

England, as in the '66 World Cup, were still at Wembley, and they rode their luck in a tough semi-final against Spain. The match was pretty even, and Spain's veteran keeper Zubizarreta was kept busy. But England survived a 34th-minute scare when Salinas swept the ball in only to be judged offside: the action replay demonstrated he wasn't. Just before half-time, England's new hero, the giant Seaman, had to sprint out of his area to frighten the runaway Manjarin into parting with the ball, and soon after the interval the referee booked Alfonso for "diving" when he might easily have punished Gascoigne's rash tackle with a penalty. There were no golden goals, and the match went to a penalty decider highlighted by the courage of Stuart Pearce, after his experience in the 1990 World Cup, for taking, and scoring, a spot-kick, and for the Seaman save that clinched England's place in the semi-finals.

Later, at Anfield, France needed penalties to beat Holland in a disappointing match, Lama's save from Seedorf's spot-kick winning the day. On the Sunday, Germany beat Croatia but lost Klinsmann with a bad injury, and Poborsky scored the cheekiest goal of the tournament with an outrageous chip to put the rapidly improving Czechs, reduced to 10 men after 82 minutes, through at the expense of a classy Portugal side.

A spot of déjà vu

With due respect to the brave Czech Republic side, who, despite missing four players suspended, ground France down to win on penalties at Old Trafford, the real final came a few days early, the clash of the Titans at Wembley between England and Germany.

Despite a despicable attempt by one national newspaper to stir up old grievances and transform the England–Germany match into a replay of the Second World War, even the most aggressive England fans appreciated the attraction of being civilized hosts inside Wembley, and the match was viewed for the most part in the friendliest of spirits. Without the inspirational Klinsmann and against an England side brimming with confidence, the Germans never wilted. Not even when Shearer gave England a dream start, heading in an Adams flick-on from Gascoigne's corner after only 2 minutes 15 seconds. Back came the Germans, and they were level on the quarter-hour. They struck through England's perceived weak point, the lack of a regular right-back with the suspension of Gary Neville. The cross came in from the left and Kuntz converted with ease.

England regained the initiative, but could not find the finish to break the Germans down as they dominated the second half. Extra time, for the first time in the tournament, was sensational, played at an extraordinary pace with both teams going for the throat, all out for that Golden Goal. After just two minutes McManaman was through to the right bye-line and Anderton just reached his cross at the near post before the keeper, only to see his effort rebound from the post into Köpke's arms.

Four minutes later and Kuntz headed in from a corner, but the whistle had gone for a foul, and England breathed again. Another two minutes and every English fan in the country was out of his seat as Shearer crossed superbly from the right, only for Gascoigne to shuffle his feet fatally and he failed to make clean contact in front of an open goal. Gascoigne was everywhere, but he failed to reach a similar, more difficult chance soon after. It was end to end stuff, but the match went to a shoot-out.

In this dramatic restaging of the 1990 World Cup semi-final, Germany were once again the winners on penalties. There were 12 kicks from the mark, and 11 of them gave the keepers little or no chance. The 11th kick, taken by England defender Gareth Southgate who had a wonderful tournament, was less than perfect and Köpke saved. For the record, stand-in captain Andreas Möller slammed in the winner. Win or lose, this is no way to decide a football match.

The golden shot

The final had to be an anti-climax, at least for the England fans. Beset by injuries, Bertie Vogts had little option but to field the brave Klinsmann, by no means fully recovered, nor was defender Thomas Helmer. The Czechs went ahead from a penalty by Berger after 58 minutes, given for a foul on Poborsky. The culprit Matthias Sammer, brilliant as an attacking sweeper, made too many defensive errors to warrant his rave ratings, but the offence was clearly outside the box, and the system is at fault when communication between linesman and referee cannot get such incidents right.

Anyone who bet against the Germans, though, had ignored 30 years of football history. On came Olivier Bierhoff for Scholl, and after 72 minutes the substitute equalized, heading in a Ziege free-kick from close in at the far post. Where was the keeper?

Extra time was needed yet again. But this time there was a Golden Goal – or should it be Platinum in a major final? After five minutes, Klinsmann found Bierhoff on the edge of the box. He swivelled and fired a shot, slightly deflected, that the hapless keeper could only touch before it spun into the net. There was a moment, shades of '66, when the referee consulted the linesmen about a possible offside. But the goal stood, and Germany had won the Henri Delaunay Trophy for the third time. No other country has won it more than once.

FINAL SCORE

FIRST ROUND

Group A

England	1	Switzerland	1
Holland	0	Scotland	0
Switzerland	0	Holland	2
Scotland	0	England	2
Scotland	1	Switzerland	0
Holland	1	England	4

	P	W	D	L	F	A	P
England	3	2	1	0	7	2	7
Holland	3	1	1	1	3	4	4
Scotland	3	1	1	1	1	2	4
Switzerland	3	0	1	2	1	4	1

Group B

Spain	1	Bulgaria	1
Romania	0	France	1
Bulgaria	1	Romania	0
France	1	Spain	1
France	3	Bulgaria	1
Romania	1	Spain	2

	P	W	D	L	F	A	P
France	3	2	1	0	5	2	7
Spain	3	1	2	0	4	3	5
Bulgaria	3	1	1	1	3	4	4
Romania	3	0	0	3	1	4	0

Group C

Germany	2	Czech Republic	0
Italy	2	Russia	1
Czech Republic	2	Italy	1
Russia	0	Germany	3
Russia	3	Czech Republic	3
Italy	0	Germany	0

	P	W	D	L	F	A	P
Germany	3	2	1	0	5	0	7
Czech Rep	3	1	1	1	5	6	4
Italy	3	1	1	1	3	3	4
Russia	3	0	1	2	4	8	1

Group D

Denmark	1	Portugal	1
Turkey	0	Croatia	1
Portugal	1	Turkey	0
Croatia	3	Denmark	0
Croatia	0	Portugal	3
Turkey	0	Denmark	3

	P	W	D	L	F	A	P
Portugal	3	2	1	0	5	1	7
Croatia	3	2	0	1	4	3	6
Denmark	3	1	1	1	4	4	4
Turkey	3	0	0	3	0	5	0

QUARTER-FINALS

Spain 0 England 0
(aet. England won 4–2 on penalties)
France 0 Holland 0
(aet. France won 5–4 on penalties)
Germany 2 Croatia 1
Czech Republic 1 Portugal 0

SEMI-FINALS

France 0 Czech Republic 0
(aet. Czech Republic won 6–5 on penalties)
England 1 Germany 1
(aet. Germany won 6-5 on penalties)

FINAL

Germany 2 Czech Republic 1
1–1 90 min.; Germany scored Golden Goal

Wembley, 30 June 1996. Attendance 73,611

Germany: Köpke; Sammer, Helmer, Babbel, Strunz, Scholl (Bierhoff), Eilts (Bode), Hässler, Ziege, Kuntz, Klinsmann.
Czech Republic: Kouba; Rada, Kadlec, Suchoparek, Hornak, Nedved, Bejbl, Nemec, Poborsky (Smicer), Berger, Kuka.

Leading scorers
5 Shearer (England)
3 Klinsmann (Germany), Laudrup B (Denmark), Stoichkov (Bulgaria), Suker (Croatia)

Shearer joins Newcastle for world record £15 million

NEWCASTLE manager Kevin Keegan stole a march on Premiership champions Manchester United with the sensational signing of England striker Alan Shearer from Blackburn Rovers for £15 million. This eclipses the previous world record of £13 million Milan paid Turin in 1992 for Gianluigi Lentini.

While Alex Ferguson scoured foreign fields for Manchester United's reinforcements, Keegan simply sought the largest domestic name of all. As Shearer packed his boots and headed back to his roots, the people of Newcastle celebrated. One of their own was coming home.

As a Geordie boy, Shearer once queued for four hours to witness Keegan's debut at St James' Park. That was a pull Manchester United could never offer a proud product of Wallsend Boys Club. Add to this the reality that Blackburn chairman Jack Walker would never sell the symbol of Rovers' renaissance to Old Trafford.

Blackburn were unwilling sellers, but, thanks to an escape clause in Shearer's contract, the board had no choice. The Ewood Park terraces should desist from dissent. The club were obliged to accede to the wishes of a popular player, who brought them their first title in 81 years and a profit of £11.4 million.

Although Manchester United remain the bookmaker's favourites to retain their title, the "last piece in the jigsaw", as chairman Sir John Hall put it, gives Newcastle a potentially awesome attacking unit. Shearer, Les Ferdinand and Faustino Asprilla are enough spearheads for three clubs, let alone one, a situation that will surely not last long. Ferdinand will doubtlessly be chased by clubs in his native south.

Kenny Dalglish's decision to relinquish managerial responsibilities at Blackburn may partly have influenced the thinking of Shearer, who deeply admires Dalglish, with whom he shares such characteristics as self-discipline and selfless commitment. But, while Rovers are in danger of remaining a middle-ranking Premiership club with happy memories of promotion and championship seasons, the big guns grow even bigger.

Newcastle and Manchester United have joined Liverpool in creating an elite within the elite, with the possibility of the Premiership beginning every season as a three-horse race.

SOCCER SOUNDBITES

"This is the big one we wanted. This is a signing for the people of Newcastle."

KEVIN KEEGAN
Newcastle Manager

Alan Shearer carries the tag of world's most expensive player.

Hoddle is up and running

ENGLAND made a flying start to their World Cup qualifying campaign, and Glenn Hoddle to his reign as England coach, with a comfortable 3–0 victory over Moldova in Kishinev, in this first meeting between the two countries.

Even allowing for injuries — Tony Adams, Darren Anderton, Steve McManaman and Teddy Sheringham were absent — Hoddle made significant changes to the team employed by Terry Venables in Euro 96, advertising his affection for the 21-year-old Manchester United midfielder David Beckham by drafting him straight into the starting line-up.

Hoddle's 3-5-2 formation will need more work, but he must have been surprised by predecessor Terry Venables' claims that his use of full-backs in the wide midfield roles was overly defensive. This view was placed in its context when both of Hoddle's attacking full-backs, Gary Neville and Andy Hinchcliffe, played their part in England's opener, scored by Nick Barmby in the 24th minute.

A minute later England were two up. Paul Ince lifted the ball across to Paul Gascoigne, who headed over the Moldovan keeper. The previous day the two England midfielders had made the headlines at practice, when Ince found himself "mooning" the camera as Gascoigne pulled down his trousers — a prank that caused inordinate fuss in the media. New captain Shearer rounded off the victory on the hour when he clipped the ball over the keeper after good work by Gareth Southgate and Neville. Moldova missed a penalty and probably deserved a goal, but it was England's day. Hoddle is up and running.

England's bench looks on in Moldova.

Matthew Harding killed in air crash

Harding's floral tribute.

CHELSEA vice-chairman Matthew Harding died in a helicopter crash on 22 October after watching the club he loved lose 2–1 at Bolton in a third-round Coca-Cola Cup tie. The helicopter came down in a field near Middlewich, Cheshire, killing all five aboard.

The self-made multi-millionaire was a great friend of the ordinary fan, and was mourned universally. He received tributes from leading political figures as well as the football world.

Harding, 42, a staunch supporter of "New Labour", recently made a highly publicized pledge of £1 million towards Mr Blair's general election campaign. His resources, crucial to Chelsea's ground development and the recruitment of expensive foreign stars, have helped revive Chelsea as a force in English football. His death leaves a question mark over the financing of the club.

SOCCER SOUNDBITES

"Chelsea was his passion and he did a huge amount to help the club he loved."

PRIME MINISTER JOHN MAJOR

United slammed for second time in a week

SOUTHAMPTON 6 Manchester Utd 3. Manchester United suffered a second humiliating defeat in six days, exacerbated by another red card for Roy Keane. Compounding their 5–0 humiliation at Newcastle last Sunday, the champions succumbed to the sorcery of diminutive Israeli Eyal Berkovic, the tormenting of Matthew Le Tissier and the accomplished finishing of Norway's Egil Ostenstad, who hit a hat-trick.

This was as comprehensive a defeat as United have suffered since Bobby Robson's Ipswich beat them 6–0 in 1980. Southampton scored goals of sophistication and played with enormous self-belief generated principally by the playmaking of the brilliant Berkovic, who chipped in with two goals himself.

United might have expected a less traumatic afternoon had Keane, returning from injury, not been sent off. His first booking, for dissent, was entirely unnecessary. Eric Cantona was booked for the same reaseon, and was lucky not to join Keane after a lunge at a Southampton defender.

With Newcastle also beaten, 2–0 at Leicester, United remain five points off the pace, behind the Magpies and new leaders Arsenal, who welcomed back their former manager George Graham with a 3–0 defeat of Leeds. But it is early days yet.

Egil Ostendstad celebrates as Southampton hit United for six.

Beckham scores 'goal of the season' on opening day

SUFFICE to say that Pele would have been proud of it, not to mention the watching Johan Cruyff. The excellent David Beckham may have a way to go before he warrants being spoken of in the same breath as those two, but his injury-time strike from just inside his own half was the exception to the rule.

His outrageous lob completely hoodwinked stranded Wimbledon keeper Neil Sullivan, and it clinched Manchester United's 3–0 win at Selhurst Park. Manager Alex Ferguson described it as "the goal of the season already". The 26,000 crowd stood almost as one to applaud Manchester United's 300th goal in the Premiership, which for sheer impudence and accuracy will take some beating.

Beckham's performance, never mind the goal, was most timely, with the England squad for the World Cup qualifier against Moldova due to be announced in a few days.

Arsenal wait for Wenger

FRENCHMAN Arsène Wenger will be the new Arsenal manager, replacing Bruce Rioch, who was sacked last week after barely a year at the helm. It's not official, but it's the worst-kept secret in football.

Yesterday Arsenal signed two Frenchmen in time to register for the UEFA Cup. Patrick Vieira, Senegal-born France Under-21 midfielder, comes from AC Milan for a reported £3.5 million, while another midfielder, Rémi Garde, 30, arrives from Strasbourg on a free transfer.

Arsenal remained silent, but Garde inadvertently let the cat out of the bag when he said: "I'm glad to be joining Arsenal and delighted to have the opportunity to work with Arsène Wenger".

The reason for Arsenal's reticence is the difficulty they are having in securing Wenger's release from Japanese club Nagoya Grampus Eight. Stewart Houston has been asked to take over at Highbury as caretaker, probably until the end of September.

A close friend of David Dein, the driving force behind Arsenal, Wenger, 47, has always taken a keen interest in Arsenal and has expressed a great admiration for the side under George Graham. He seems an excellent choice.

Perhaps we should call Wenger Arsenal's new coach, and not their new manager. It would be surprising if his mastery of the Continental system of specialized management was not as attractive to the Highbury hierarchy as his record of success at Strasbourg, Nancy, Monaco and now Grampus Eight.

Worth the wait: Arsène Wenger.

Gascoigne genius denies Hearts

RANGERS 4 HEARTS 3. Paul Gascoigne, despite another of the intermittent performances that have characterized his play lately, abruptly imposed himself on the Scottish Coca-Cola Cup final in spectacular style.

Hearts had clawed their way back into the game after going 2–0 down to goals from Ally McCoist in the first half hour, and were on level terms just before the hour mark thanks to an opportunist goal by Steve Fulton just before the interval and then a John Robertson strike.

Enter Gascoigne, fastening on to loose possession 35 yards from goal and striding forward down the inside-right channel to whip a superbly controlled drive between Gilles Rousset and his left-hand post. Then he worked a delicately measured one-two with Charlie Miller inside the box before placing a precise shot over the diving keeper.

However, Hearts were in better shape to handle Rangers than they were five months ago, when they were on the rough end of a 5–1 hiding by the champions in the Scottish Cup final. They came back fighting again, and had not Andy Goram made an inspirational save to deny Neil Pointon, the outcome might have been different. But their reply came too late to divert the silverware to the capital, David Weir's header beating Goram in the final minute.

Despite the goals of genius from veterans McCoist and Gascoigne, the man of the match was Hearts winger Neil McCann.

SOCCER SOUNDBITES

"Although Gascoigne did very little, what he did was genius."

HEARTS MANAGER JIM JEFFERIES

Gascoigne (left) and McCoist celebrate with the Scottish Cup.

Shut-out and champagne for Shilton on 1,000th League appearance

THERE WERE trumpets blaring and a red carpet laid out for Leyton Orient's goalkeeper as he took the field for a Third Division game against Brighton on Sunday, 22 December. It was a historic occasion in Football League history, for Peter Shilton was making his 1,000th League appearance.

It was one of the easiest games for the 47-year-old former England keeper, who won a record 125 caps for England, and it was not surprising he kept a clean sheet against a club desperately struggling to stay in the League. This 2–0 win was the third shut-out in Shilton's four-match Orient career so far.

Shilton made his first League appearance back in 1966, for Leicester, starting on £8 a week. He made 286 appearances for them before moving to Stoke, where he made another 110. Then came Nottingham Forest (202), Southampton (188) and Derby (175). He chalked up another 34 in his spell as player-manager with Plymouth, to reach a total of 995 League games. Since then it has taken him five clubs and two years to reach the magic number, for at Wimbledon, Bolton, Coventry and West Ham, only Bolton gave him a game — just one.

A crowd of 7,944 turned out at Brisbane Road to witness the historic event, and the two teams formed a guard of honour when Shilton came out onto the pitch. The ceremony was more arduous than the match, for Shilton had no more to do than take a few goal-kicks, clutch a couple of corners and bend low to catch a curling cross. After that he went home for a bottle of champagne with his mum and dad.

Peter Shilton (right) makes his 1,000th League appearance.

McGinlay hits hat-trick in demolition of Spurs

BOLTON 6 Tottenham 1. Premiership opposition, which proved an insurmountable obstacle last season, continue to tumble out of the Coca-Cola Cup at the hands of Bolton, although the First Division leaders' humbling of Tottenham exceeded all expectations.

Quite why a Bolton side that managed only five home wins during last season's harrowing stay in the top flight should pulverize such top-class opposition after disposing of Chelsea in the third round is perplexing. But buoyant confidence and the form of John McGinlay would appear to represent the bulk of the answer.

The irrepressible Scot, one of six survivors of the team beaten 2–1 by Liverpool in the final of this competition 19 months ago, scored a hat-trick. Central defender Gerry Taggart and fellow striker Nathan Blake also chipped in, and when substitute Scott Taylor scored within a minute of joining the fray, Bolton were in the realms of fantasy.

As if that were not enough, a corner from Scott Sellars in injury time appeared to cross the line too, but manager Colin Todd was happy to settle for just the six. For Gerry Francis, who has rightly acquired a reputation for producing teams of defensive rigour, this represented comfortably the worst defeat of his reign at Tottenham.

Abdication of "King" Keegan

KEVIN KEEGAN resigned as manager of Newcastle United on 8 January, shocking a city that draws such comfort and joy from the club. The moment the whispers were confirmed, supporters converged in their hundreds on St James' Park, the club's stadium, many of them in tears.

A banner was raised, exhorting "Please stay Kevin, we all believe in you", but the fans' hopes were dashed when a club official read out a statement from Keegan:

"It was my decision and my decision alone to resign. I offered my resignation at the end of last season, but was persuaded by the board to stay. I feel that I have taken the club as far as I can, and that it would be in the best interests of all concerned if I resigned now. I wish the club and everyone concerned with it the very best for the future."

While the timing was surprising, with the team well placed in three major competitions, there is little doubt that Keegan, 45, has been ill at ease recently.

Like Newcastle's colours, his hair has become a mixture of black and white, a reflection of the unremitting pressure that comes with managing a club as big as Newcastle. Anyone who has attended a match at St James' Park will appreciate the burden Keegan lived with. Anyone who has watched Newcastle train before 1,000 autograph-seeking fans will understand that this pressure is relentless.

Part of Keegan's problem is that he cares; he cares for the people of Tyneside. Although he was born near Doncaster, his father and grandfather were miners in the Newcastle area and, of course, the last club he played for was Newcastle. So he was considered a true Geordie.

The adulation has been little short of phenomenal. On each match day, as a crescendo of noise signalled the imminent kick-off, the final song is always the same, the theme tune of the film *Local Hero*. It was for Keegan. After all, when he was appointed manager in 1992, he saved them from relegation to the old Third Division and then took them up to the Premier League.

Keegan's name is tattooed on forearms across the region, baby boys are named "Kevin", and a night out in Newcastle invariably ends with chants of: "We are Geordies, super-Geordies, Keegan is our King."

Sadly for Geordies everywhere, the "King" has abdicated.

SOCCER SOUNDBITES

"How can he leave us? He is god around here — he is even bigger than God. He is the life of Newcastle."

TEARFUL YOUNG NEWCASTLE GIRL FAN

Chelsea oust Liverpool in second-half comeback

CHELSEA looked dead and buried when Liverpool smoothly took a two-goal lead after 20 minutes of their fourth-round FA Cup tie at Stamford Bridge. Goals by Robbie Fowler and Stan Collymore had underlined the superiority John Barnes and Steve McManaman had gained in midfield.

The second half was a different story, as Ruud Gullit put on Mark Hughes as a substitute to spark off a sensational comeback and one of the most thrilling 45 minutes seen at Stamford Bridge for many a day.

Hughes came out of the tunnel like a lion seeking a kill. He scored within five minutes to put Chelsea back in the game, and his feisty, distracting presence also liberated the two Italian strikers who provided the rest of the goals, Gianfranco Zola (1) and Gianluca Vialli (2). Just as important, according to Gullit, was the third Italian, Roberto Di Matteo, whom he pushed forward to stifle Barnes.

Zola was terrific, making runs, making plans and making dashes back to thwart Liverpool incursions. He scored the equalizer with a screamer from 20 yards after 58 minutes. Vialli climaxed the comeback with classic finishing, a haughty flick with the outside of his right boot and a deft header from a Zola free-kick. It was a triumph for teamwork from exceptional individuals. The Chelsea fans, not long ago in despair, danced with delight.

Tempers fray as Chelsea turn Liverpool's advantage on its head.

Disconsolate David Batty (left) and Ian Walker walk off the pitch.

World Cup setback for England

ENGLAND suffered their first World Cup reverse on home soil when Gianfranco Zola scored the only goal of the game after 18 minutes at Wembley to give Italy the initiative in Group 2.

The Chelsea striker created a half-chance for himself and drilled the ball past Ian Walker, deputizing for the injured David Seaman in goal. No blame should be attached to the keeper, as a slight deflection by Spurs team-mate Sol Campbell gave him no chance.

England missed Tony Adams and Teddy Sheringham. But they also lacked inspiration. England did most of the attacking, but Italy are not known for squandering the lead. In the end quality triumphed over quantity.

England remain on top of the group on goal difference, but Italy, with three wins out of three, have a game in hand.

United clinch title without kicking a ball

MANCHESTER United won the Premier League for the fourth time in five seasons, clinching the title with two games to go thanks to Wimbledon's 2–1 victory at Selhurst Park over Liverpool and Newcastle's failure to win at West Ham.

They have retained the Championship without what could be termed a big-name signing. Manager Alex Ferguson has had to make do with modest recruits from Norway in Ole Gunnar Solskjaer and Ronny Johnsen, unknowns at the time but household names a year on.

Instead, Ferguson has relied on the boys he has turned into men over the last few years, moulding an outstanding crop of Youth Cup-winning talent around the pivots of the four title campaigns — Eric Cantona, Peter Schmeichel, Gary Pallister, Denis Irwin and Ryan Giggs — and Roy Keane, the uncompromising Irish stalwart of three Championships.

Cantona, who arrived at Old Trafford as a brilliant but controversial talent, has proved to be the cornerstone on which Ferguson has built. No player in modern times has had a bigger say in the destiny of the major domestic honour. The Frenchman's inspiring performances enabled Ferguson to end the taunts of 26 barren years, and his continued brilliance has been largely responsible for their dominance of the Premiership.

Manchester United celebrate their fourth Premiership title.

FOOTBALL FOCUS

● Nigeria were sensational gold medal winners at the Atlanta Olympic Games, pulling off a breathtaking 3–2 victory over Argentina in the final. This came after their thrilling comeback from 3–1 down in the semi-finals to beat Brazil 4–3.

● George Graham, the disgraced former Arsenal manager who was banned by the FA for a year for accepting an agent's "bung", returned to football after a 19-month sabbatical. He was appointed manager of Leeds in September when they dismissed Howard Wilkinson after 8 years. Four months later, the FA appointed Wilkinson as their first technical director

● Still awaiting the arrival of their new manager Arsène Wenger from Japan, Arsenal were left in disarray in mid-September when caretaker manager Stewart Houston left to take over at QPR and on the same day their captain Tony Adams admitted to being an alcoholic.

● On 14 September, Hearts had four players sent off in losing their Premier League match 3–0 to Rangers at Ibrox, equalling the Scottish record of Stranraer two seasons ago.

● After a dispute about floodlights, Estonia failed to turn up for their rescheduled afternoon kick-off against Scotland for their World Cup qualifier in Tallinn's Kadriorg Stadium. The Scots kicked off, and the referee promptly abandoned the match. At first Scotland were awarded the match 3-0, but after an appeal it was eventually played in Monaco in February and resulted in a goalless draw.

● In one of football's worst ever disasters, more than 80 spectators died and some 200 were injured in Guatemala City at a World Cup qualifier between Guatemala and Costa Rica. Many of the victims were children, crushed and smothered as they tried to escape from overcrowded stands.

● Duane Darby scored six as Third Division Hull survived a scare against Northern League minnows Whitby in a first-round replay of the FA Cup. The former Torquay striker netted his fourth a minute from the end of normal time to bring Hull back to 4–4, and hit another two in extra time as they ran out 8–4 winners.

● In January, bottom Premiership club Middlesbrough were docked 3 points for illegally and unilaterally calling off their game with Blackburn in December because sickness, injury and suspension had left them with no alternative. At the end of the season they were relegated by just 2 points — and they were beaten in the two cup finals, a unique "treble".

● Rangers did the first Old Firm "quadruple" over Celtic on their way to the Championship. They won 2–0 and 3–1 at home and 1–0 twice away, Celtic's only home defeats. Celtic beat Rangers 2–0 in the quarter-finals of the Scottish Cup, but were knocked out in the semis by First Division Falkirk, who won their replay 1–0 to reach their first final for 40 years.

● A 1–0 win at Dundee United on 7 May clinched the Scottish Premier League for Rangers with one game to play. This was their ninth title on the trot, equalling Celtic's record (1966–74).

● Iran beat the Maldives 17–0 in an Asian Zone match to set a World Cup scoring record.

Chesterfield denied historic win by referee in classic semi

CHESTERFIELD 3 Middlesbrough 3. In a breath-taking classic of an FA Cup semi-final, Chesterfield equalized with a minute left of extra time. It was a fitting climax to one of the finest Cup-ties in the competition's 125-year history.

The story runs like this. In the first half Middlesbrough squander chance after chance and have Vladimir Kinder sent off. Chesterfield go 2–0 up after an hour, Middlesbrough pull one back, Chesterfield have a perfectly good goal disallowed, Boro equalize and then take the lead 11 minutes into extra time. But Jamie Hewitt brings the Second Division side back with 61 seconds left of an impossibly dramatic match.

For Boro now there is a massive fixture pile-up: a Coca-Cola Cup final replay, this replay, and a desperate struggle against relegation. Chesterfield, rooted in anonymity at 13th place in Division Two, will feel no semblance of fatigue.

Watching the game was like seeing 11 millionaires dragged up a rather dark alley. Yet it was Chesterfield, not Middlesbrough, who finished up robbed. David Elleray, the referee, admitted as much after the game. With the score at 2–1 to the tiddlers, Chesterfield's Jonathan Howard hit a fierce shot that rebounded from the crossbar and over the Middlesbrough goal-line. Elleray originally suggested that he had blown for a foul by Andy Morris after the ball hit the bar. But, after watching the video replay, he clearly changed his mind, accepting the ball had crossed the line. At 3–1 it would surely have been lights out for Middlesbrough.

Chesterfield are the fourth-oldest club in the League, and a noted goalkeepers' academy, but they will not be offended by the observation that they have one of those names soon forgotten when Final Score comes on. But no one will patronize them now. To get to Old Trafford's "drama festival", they had to overcome Bolton (away), Nottingham Forest and Wrexham.

Only the dead of spirit and the cold of heart could want Middlesbrough to fail. In a dry age, their daring has been a source of wonder. But Chesterfield have already turned their town blue. And they might still do the same to Boro.

Victory in Katowice lifts England's World Cup hopes

ALAN SHEARER'S reputation as a striker of world renown was further enhanced in Katowice against Poland as he masterminded England's passage towards a World Cup qualifying denouement in Italy in October. And even if England lose that match it is likely they will head for France as the best-finishing runner-up, thus eliminating the need for a play-off.

A fifth-minute goal, taken with Shearer's customary coolness, followed by one in injury-time from Teddy Sheringham, gave England a 2–0 victory and provided them with the three points that brings a place in the finals that much closer.

It was a satisfying night for manager Glenn Hoddle. But even before the game, the FA had made it clear that his position was safe whether or not England qualified for France 1998.

England hero Alan Shearer (9).

Di Matteo's bolt from the blue is final blow to Boro

CHELSEA won the FA Cup for the second time with two excellent goals, but not much else. The London team were so superior on the day, they ought to have won a disappointing final with far more style and authority. Middlesbrough, perhaps exhausted at the end of their long and trying season, offered little resistance on a hot and humid afternoon.

The game was over almost as soon as it had started, Chelsea's Roberto Di Matteo striking a potential knock-out blow with a stunning goal in record time — 43 seconds to be precise.

Middlesbrough never really recovered from this setback and, despite Chelsea's growing caution, rarely looked like threatening Ruud Gullit's achievement of becoming the first foreigner to manage an FA Cup-winning team.

The game's most disappointing feature was the failure of the two little geniuses, Chelsea's Gianfranco Zola and Boro's Juninho, to vie with each other as creative forces. Juninho struggled throughout to escape the midfield attentions of Di Matteo, rightly voted man of the match, Eddie Newton and Dennis Wise. But Zola, while not at his best, did make his side's second goal quite superbly.

Chelsea might not have made this a final to remember, but there can be no questioning their right to parade the most famous domestic cup in the world for the first time since 1970. Their victories over Liverpool, Leicester and Wimbledon, conquerors of Manchester United, on the way to Wembley are testament enough.

Bryan Robson's gamble on the fitness of Fabrizio Ravanelli failed heartbreakingly when the Italian striker pulled up after only 21 minutes with a recurrence of the sciatic nerve problem he had developed in that thrilling 3–3 draw against Manchester United at Old Trafford less than a fortnight earlier.

If Middlesbrough, beaten in the Coca-Cola Cup final and relegated from the Premiership, had any hopes of salvaging something from their season, Di Matteo's early strike must have filled them with foreboding. Running unchallenged from inside his own half to a shooting position some 25 yards out, the Italian unleashed a searing shot that dipped sharply over Boro's young keeper Ben Roberts.

Chelsea's strange unwillingness for a long time to go in search of a second, clinching goal encouraged Middlesbrough to go forward, but there were few chances made at either end. But Boro's final, desperate attempt to draw level cost them dear as Chelsea hit them on the break eight minutes from time. The ball shuttled neatly between Eddie Newton and Dan Petrescu before the Romanian chipped a pass to Zola, running in at the far post. It looked to be going behind him, but the diminutive Italian improvised brilliantly by flicking the ball back with the outside of his right foot to Newton, who steered it into the net.

That was the signal for Gullit to take pity on his erstwhile friend, the cold-shouldered Gianluca Vialli, and let him have, as substitute for Zola, the couple of minutes in the sun for which the distinguished Italian striker had prayed.

SOCCER SOUNDBITES

"I'm pleased for Mr Ken Bates, our chairman, who has done a great deal. And I'm thinking of Matthew Harding. This is also for him."

CHELSEA MANAGER RUUD GULLIT

FINAL SCORE

Football League
Premier Division: Manchester United
Top scorer: Alan Shearer (Newcastle) 25
Division 1: Bolton Wanderers
Division 2: Bury
Division 3: Wigan Athletic
Footballer of the Year: Gianfranco Zola (Chelsea)

FA Cup Final

Chelsea	2	Middlesbrough	0

League Cup Final

Leicester City (after extra time)	1	Middlesbrough	1
Replay: Leicester (after extra time)	1	Middlesbrough	0

Scottish League
Premier Division: Rangers
Top scorer: Jorge Cadete (Celtic) 25
Division 1: St Johnstone
Division 2: Ayr United
Division 3: Inverness Caledonian Thistle
Footballer of the Year: Brian Laudrup (Rangers)

Scottish FA Cup Final

Kilmarnock	1	Falkirk	0

Scottish League Cup Final

Rangers	4	Hearts	3

European Cup Final

Borussia Dortmund	3	Juventus	1

Cup-Winners' Cup Final

Barcelona	1	Paris St Germain	0

UEFA Cup Final
Schalke beat Inter-Milan 1–0,0–1
(4–1 on penalties aet)

European Footballer of the Year 1996
Matthias Sammer
(Borussia Dortmund & Germany)

FIFA World Player of the Year 1996
Ronaldo (Barcelona & Brazil)

World Club Championship 1996

Juventus	1	River Plate	0

Roberto Di Matteo blasts Chelsea ahead in the first minute.

The Cult of the Manager

By Byron Butler

Ron Atkinson, celebrated and itinerant football club manager of the last quarter of the 20th Century, once disclosed with sublime humility that "it's bloody tough being a legend." His right to a pedestal in his profession's Hall of Fame is debatable; but he was undoubtedly very good at being famous.

He managed two triumphs in the FA Cup, two in the League Cup and two or three promotions — an above average but hardly outstanding record for a man hired by some of the biggest clubs in the country, including Manchester United, Aston Villa and Sheffield Wednesday, during his 25 years as a builder of teams. He was never quite a champion.

Charlton and Busby, flanked by Murphy (left) and Cavanagh.

Mr Bojangles

Atkinson's renown, however, was greater than his achievements. He did as much as anyone to make the modern football manager a cult figure, the image, voice and spirit of his club, and also a sort of tribal leader whose views on football and life are deemed worthy of public notice.

This celebrity was largely media-created and evolved slowly until television's coverage of the game began to blossom in the 1960s. Managers are still famously insecure — around a third of them are fired every season — but at least they burn brightly until they lose one game too many.

Atkinson succeeded because he was shrewd and experienced and also because he smiled a lot, had an engaging sense of humour, sported a tan, sunglasses and a jangle of gold jewellery and appeared on television a lot. His playboy image wasn't always true to the inner man, but it didn't really matter. His public character, his choice, was the one which counted. And "Big Ron" was always in demand. For every club chairman who sacked him there was always another ready to employ him.

Ron Atkinson (left) discusses tactics with Steve Coppell in their Manchester United days.

That's entertainment

If Atkinson had been born a few generations earlier his sense of fun and style might have directed him towards the music halls. The early football manager was a largely anonymous figure, an administrator who did most of his work in an office. The tracksuit manager (even the tracksuit itself) belonged to the distant future. Chairmen and directors often picked sides, captains ruled on format and tactics, and trainers brought up the rear as players prepared for action with brisk walks along local streets.

Some of the old pioneers were ahead of their time, including William Sudell who fashioned the Invincibles of Preston; Tom Watson who guided Sunderland and then Liverpool to their first great days; and John Cameron who as player-manager-secretary inspired Tottenham to win the FA Cup in 1901 when they were in the Southern League. All were strong, charismatic men, but who is aware of them a hundred years on? The newspapers of their day confined themselves to the ebb and flow of the game itself.

The Chapman era

Later on, during the middle age of English professional football, Herbert Chapman created two sides good enough to win the League championship in three successive seasons — Huddersfield (1924–26) and Arsenal (1933–35) — but, more than that, his lordly personality and innovative ideas redefined the job of the manager. He created and thrived on news.

Chapman was one of a kind, however, until Matt Busby, of Manchester United, and Stanley Cullis, of Wolverhampton Wanderers, surfaced after World War Two. Each led their club to

Brian Clough (left) and Terry Venables at the 1991 FA Cup final.

three titles in the 1950s, both men of national fame, great dignity and iron resolve yet different in so many other ways. Busby was a flexible idealist with a burning faith in natural talent. Cullis was a martinet committed to pace, strength and directness. Their legacy endures.

Other men made indelible marks, including the refined Arthur Rowe of Tottenham, but it wasn't until just before England won the World Cup that managers began to become cult figures — and then it was like a star burst.

In the picture

It wasn't a coincidence, of course, that the game's media was now changing and expanding. BBC's *Match of the Day* began in 1964, and quickly became required viewing, and Sunday afternoon highlights shown by commercial television stations attracted healthy audiences. Newsagents' shelves sagged under the weight of football magazines and the newspapers weighed in with more column inches.

There was now a requirement to get "inside" the game, to anticipate news, provide colour and background and explore (and, if necessary, create) personalities. Thus managers — first dignified by a Manager of the Year award in 1966 — were quickly seen in a new light. They were mostly articulate, opinionated, occasionally controversial and available — an ideal first point of inquiry and reference. And managers, on the whole, were happy to oblige. The platform made them public figures and many milked the opportunity for all it was worth.

The main men

Busby himself was still the high priest of his profession, Munich behind him, triumph in the European Cup ahead of him, but managers across the board were identified as characters in their own right.

There was Bill Nicholson's Yorkshire clout and savvy at Tottenham, Don Revie's divine authority at Leeds, Joe Mercer's famous smile at Aston Villa and then Manchester City, the self-effacing expertise of Bertie Mee at Arsenal, Jimmy Hill's beard at Coventry, Ron Greenwood's scholarly vision of the game at West Ham, the bounce and humour of Tommy Docherty at Chelsea, Harry Catterick's astuteness at Everton, Alec Stock's bright sagacity at Queens Park Rangers and Dave Bowen's Welsh charm at Northampton.

Some, of course, would have become national figures even if there'd been no television, radio or newspapers. Bill Shankly, for example, "Shanks", with his Cagney-strut, cropped hair and gravel voice, was a natural showman, a spinner of dreams, a man of simplicity, but never a simple man. "He'd have been great in war, another Winston Churchill," said one of his players. All this hugely loved man did, as it happens, was create the modern Liverpool.

Then there was Brian Clough, of Derby County and Nottingham Forest, a brilliant and stimulating autocrat who defied analysis. A self-confessed "big 'ead", perhaps, but a man who was the darling of the media for 20 years. He was sometimes too good, and often too impossible, to be true.

Silverware

But even men like Shankly and Clough don't go on for ever. They are irreplaceable but, somehow, they have to be replaced. Shankly was followed by Bob Paisley, dear homespun Uncle Bob, who in 10 years proceeded to win more silver pots than any manager of an English club before or since.

Managers were thus confirmed as stars in their own right and, by the time the 1990s arrived and the Premiership was born, the men who shaped the nation's top football teams were household figures.

Alex Ferguson, of Manchester United, led the way but, all about him, were men like George Graham, Terry Venables, Kenny Dalglish, Kevin Keegan, Martin O'Neill, Joe Kinnear, Jim Smith and Arsène Wenger, who was one of a new wave of perceptive foreign coaches. Some of them changed clubs regularly; but their names always carried weight and raised expectations.

The game, in truth, may belong to the players and fans, but the manager is always centre-stage.

Alex Ferguson (left) with his assistant Brian Kidd, who became Blackburn manager in 1998.

Ian Wright beats Cliff Bastin's Arsenal scoring record

Ian Wright celebrates his record-setting goal.

IAN WRIGHT hit a hat-trick for Arsenal at Highbury on 13 September to beat the long-standing club scoring record. Having gone a month without scoring a Premiership goal, Wright, 33, was feeling the tension. But scoring twice in England's 4–0 World Cup qualifying victory over Moldova at Wembley in midweek eased the pressure that was building up.

Bolton scored first on a sunny afternoon to cast some gloom over an expectant crowd after just 13 minutes. But eight minutes later Wright scored his first with a rasping right-foot cross-shot from an astute Dennis Bergkamp pass. This goal equalled Bastin's record of 178 League and Cup goals and launched Wright into a wild celebration that was somewhat premature. Whipping off his shirt, he ran down the touchline in front of the West Stand proudly revealing a white vest displaying the magic number 179.

The flamboyant striker sheepishly admitted afterwards to messing up his celebration, but it took him only another four minutes to break the record that had stood for 58 years. Bolton's keeper could not hold a Bergkamp shot and Patrick Vieira set Wright up with a tap-in from six yards.

Ray Parlour made it 3–0 just before the interval, and Wright completed his hat-trick and Arsenal's 4–1 victory 10 minutes from time, volleying home a David Platt pass — an appropriate stage for Arsène Wenger to put on a substitute and allow the record-breaker to take a standing ovation.

SOCCER SOUNDBITES

"It was such an easy chance that I was actually happy before I put the ball in the net."

IAN WRIGHT, of his record-breaking goal.

McManaman solo tips tie Liverpool's way

STEVE McMANAMAN snatched a priceless stoppage-time equalizer for Liverpool to cap a remarkable UEFA Cup first round, first leg confrontation at Celtic Park. The Bhoys almost wilted under the pressure of Liverpool's dominance in the first half, but came back to take the lead, only to lose it in the dying minutes.

A crowd of 48,526 generated a great atmosphere, but it went silent after six minutes when Owen, sent scampering clear by a clever flick by Karlheinz Riedle, left Celtic defenders trailing, drew keeper Jonathan Gould and chipped confidently into the net.

Celtic responded to fanatical support after the break, and drew inspiration from a brilliant save by Gould to deny Riedle. A second goal then might have clinched the tie. Instead, Celtic swept upfield to equalize. McNamara played a neat one-two with Craig Burley and hit the ball past David James. James then pulled down Henrik Larsson for the penalty that put Celtic ahead and sent the pulsating stadium into delirium

But McManaman had the last word. Picking the ball up near his own penalty area, he went on a run, cutting a swathe through Celtic's defence until he got within shooting range. Then he let fly, lashing the ball past Gould and silencing the crowd again.

Asprilla's hat-trick gives Newcastle fine start in Champions League

NEWCASTLE'S first Champions' League tie produced one of the best performances their fans have ever seen. Taking on mighty Barcelona, Newcastle took a 3–0 lead, with a hat-trick from Colombian Faustino Asprilla, before the Spanish giants made it 3–2 late in the game.

Faustino Asprilla (left) scores from the penalty spot against Barcelona.

Asprilla, who scored from a penalty and two fine headers, may have grabbed the spotlight, but the performance of Keith Gillespie on the right flank was a throw-back to the days when wingers ruled supreme. It was his crosses that Asprilla converted for his last two goals.

In the first half, Newcastle touched heights few believed achievable against such illustrious opponents. Their lead would have been more than two, but for the uncertainty of Danish striker Jon Dahl Tomasson in front of goal.

Asprilla's third excuse for his trademark somersault came after 49 minutes. Luis Enrique pulled a goal back in the 73rd minute, and Luis Figo shot through a ruck of players in the 88th, giving Newcastle a few anxious moments before the final whistle.

Hungary humiliated 7–1 in Budapest in World Cup play-off

HOW ARE the mighty fallen! Hungary, proud victors over England 43 years ago in Budapest by seven goals to one, suffered defeat by the same score at the hands of Yugoslavia in the same city.

The return half of this World Cup play-off is purely academic. Yugoslavia's motley crew, inspired by Real Madrid striker Predrag Mijatovic, who scored a hat-trick, humiliated the Hungarians, who were but a pale shadow of the Magic Magyars of Ferenc Puskas and co.

Hungary were outclassed, one down after a minute, four down after 26. They crumbled completely under the stunning assault with which Yugoslavia, the Serbia/Montenegro remnant of the former Republic, immediately hit them. This collection of mercenaries from Spain (5), Italy (4), Japan (1) and a lone home player, Ivica Kralj, in goal, produced textbook teamwork.

Their fourth goal, Mijatovic's first, nonchalantly set up by Tenerife midfielder Szavisa Jokanovic with a lazy sidestep and rolled slide-rule pass, produced a burst of appreciative applause from the despondent home fans. The finish was a rocket into the net from 14 yards of which Puskas would have been proud, and the crowd spontaneously recognized the quality of their executioners.

Coach Slobodan Santrac took Mijatovic off after 54 minutes, but if Hungary thought the pressure would ease, the substitute, Aston Villa's Savo Milosevic, strolled through for the seventh goal nine minutes later. Bela Illis drew mocking cheers from the shell-shocked fans when he scored for Hungary five minutes from time.

Keegan takes charge at Fulham

THE STORIES Fulham insisted were "pure speculation" the day before were confirmed on 24 September in a blaze of publicity at Craven Cottage. Kevin Keegan has agreed to take charge at Fulham as "chief operating officer". It is quite a public-relations coup for Mohamed Fayed, the owner of Harrods, who paid an estimated £30 million to take control of Fulham last season.

Keegan dramatically left Newcastle last season, saying he had no interest in returning to football. But after being a guest in the Harrods executive box at Craven Cottage last week, when Fulham played Wolves in the Coca-Cola Cup, he had a change of heart.

Just as Keegan enjoyed the financial backing of Sir John Hall at Newcastle, Fayed's millions could enable him to bankroll the rise of another former force in English football.

Fulham manager Keegan.

The surreal atmosphere down by the river in London SW6 had a bemusing effect on the 23 Fulham fans who took the trouble to witness the second coming of the former England captain. Outnumbered seven to one by the press, they watched almost in awe as the Harrods "Dream Team" took the pitch to meet the media.

Coming out of retirement for the second time, Keegan attempted to be as serious as he could about taking overall football command of the team standing 11th in Division Two. With him comes team manager Ray Wilkins, a relative failure as QPR manager, and Arthur Cox, Keegan's mentor and now Fulham's chief scout. The chairman, Fayed, who arrived flanked by a posse of burly security men, preferred to stay silent.

Keegan has been given a "clean slate", and so previous manager Micky Adams, who brought Fulham back from the Third Division last season, has been paid off. Estimates of the pay-off for the remaining four years plus of his contract range from £300,000 to half a million, so it is not surprising that he should immediately take a two-week holiday.

England's draw in Rome is passport to World Cup finals

Paul Gascoigne (left) and Paul Ince celebrate in Rome.

In a match marred by violence in the stands, England took everything the Italians could throw at them to emerge with a goalless draw, which ensured automatic qualification for the World Cup finals next year in France. Italy will have to win a two-legged play-off to join them.

It was a night to remember. On the field, the blood-stained captain, Paul Ince, badly cut after a first-half collision, reflected the spirit of the triumphant England team. The resilience, organization, skill and sheer team spirit of the side Glenn Hoddle has built out of the progress made in Euro 96 was enough to resist one of the toughest opponents in world football and earn the point needed to the top of Group 2. In doing so, they wrecked Italy's proud record of previously having won all 15 World Cup games staged in their capital city.

Tony Adams made light of his recent injury problems and suspect form to organize England's defensive resistance with the determination and character of a real leader, while Ince, David Batty and Paul Gascoigne ran themselves into the ground in central midfield.

England also survived the test of temperament better, having three players booked (Sol Campbell, Gareth Southgate and Gascoigne) to the six of the Italians, who also had Angelo Di Livio sent off for a second caution 14 minutes from time.

Off the field, Italian riot police and English fans fought a running battle in the stands throughout the first half. Sports Minister Tony Banks was at the match and immediately announced that the FA would be holding an inquiry.

SOCCER SOUNDBITES

"Glenn Hoddle pitched his team selection exactly right. "

ROY HODGSON,
Blackburn and former Switzerland manager

Spurs offer Gross some home truths

CHRISTIAN GROSS, the new Spurs manager, witnessed one of the most extraordinary capitulations by a team one is ever likely to see. Hard as it may be to credit from this humiliating scoreline, Spurs were actually more than a match for their high-flying London rivals for half this game.

After their big-hearted win at Goodison last week — Gross's first selection in charge — and the first 45 minutes here, the Swiss coach might have been tempted to believe he had it cracked. How wrong could one be. The only cracks were those that existed below the surface of this new-found bravado, ones that once located by Chelsea were soon turned into gaping chasms.

Spurs had equalized a 40th-minute strike by Tore Andre Flo with a goal from Ramon Vega three minutes later. But a second-half blitz of five goals saw Spurs suffer their worst home defeat since losing another London derby 6–0 to Arsenal in 1935, when they finished up getting relegated.

Flo went on to complete his hat-trick, and the other goals came from Roberto Di Matteo, Dan Petrescu, a sublime volleyed chip, and Mark Nicholls. Frank Leboeuf and Gianfranco Zola also made important contributions to Chelsea's fireworks display.

It was the second time this season that Chelsea have hit someone for six away from home. It is doubtful whether Spurs will enjoy being in the same company as Barnsley, but they remain only two places above the bottom club. Chelsea continue to chase leaders Manchester United, whose 3–1 win at Anfield maintained their three-point advantage.

Two embarrassing months on Tyneside

After four weeks in an FA Cup wonderland, Stevenage Borough finally surrendered to Newcastle at St James' Park in a fourth-round replay. But the Vauxhall Conference team, 97 places below their Premiership opponents in football's pyramid, did not allow the Magpies an easy passage into the next round.

Alan Shearer, starting a game at St James' for the first time in eight months, scored in each half to add to the goal he claimed in the initial tie, which ended 1-1. By the time Gary Crawshaw reduced the arrears for Stevenage, the breath, if not the spirit, had been sucked out of the plucky semi-professionals.

Ill feeling had been generated between the clubs – in a dispute over the suitability and safety of Stevenage's Broadhall Way ground – largely owing to the mismanagement of Newcastle's PR. But Stevenage would never forget the day their heroes held the team who had humbled Barcelona earlier in the season. And now, at St James' Park, they had even less to lose.

At the final whistle, the jeers that had rung out around the stadium for the seeming impudence shown by the upstarts from the south turned into generous applause. The Stevenage players stayed on the pitch and milked the occasion to the full.

All in all it was a bad two months for Newcastle. Freddy Shepherd and Douglas Hall, respectively chairman and vice-chairman, resigned in disgrace on 23 March. They were driven out of office following relentless criticism in the light of an story in the *News of the World* that they had ridiculed fans and players, and insulted Tyneside women, while being secretly filmed in a Spanish brothel. Sir John Hall – father of Douglas – will be caretaker chairman until May.

The remarks of the pair – branded "loud-mouthed, philandering drunkards" – made fun of manager Kenny Dalglish and striker Alan Shearer. But perhaps most damaging was the way they sneered and mocked some of football's most loyal fans for buying overpriced club merchandise.

Chelsea crumble in face of inspired United onslaught

CHELSEA 3 Manchester Utd 5. It was heralded as the tie of the round: and it was. It was expected to be a close-fought battle, Cup-holders and third in the Premiership versus champions and leaders: but it wasn't. Before Chelsea scored three late goals to inject some sort of respectability into the scoreline, Manchester United destroyed the men in blue, counter-attacking with brutal effectiveness and running up five goals. Only then did Chelsea find any semblance of team cohesion or pride — but it was far too late.

The game was a collection of duels, match-ups across the pitch, dominated by the men in red. Nicky Butt, again outstanding, and Paul Scholes were masters of midfield, dealing almost dismissively with Roberto Di Matteo and acting captain Mark Hughes, patently out of position, deputizing for the suspended Dennis Wise.

Chelsea looked toothless in attack without Hughes, Tore Andre Flo resembling a sapling among giant redwoods. They did not trouble United until Flo departed, allowing Gianluca Vialli to bring his pace and trickery into play. The Italian scored twice in the last eight minutes to make it 3–5.

Where United really hurt other teams is the relentless way they hound opponents into conceding possession. Ferguson's players hunt in pairs or threes, one making the initial challenge while the others lurk like practised pickpockets. United's speed in possession makes such a capacity even more potent.

Butt characterizes this tackling brio. Unfussy in collection and careful in distribution, he surely is displaying the form that warrants England inolvement against Chile next month.

David Beckham and Andy Cole can also expect Wembley summonses such was their sustained excellence. Beckham scored the first two, Cole the third and fourth, either side of the interval. Sheringham hit United's fifth in the 74th minute, and Chelsea did not even start until the reds dropped their concentration and Graham Le Saux chipped Peter Schmeichel four minutes later.

So Chelsea salvaged some late pride, but their three goals may have more of an effect on United. Such aberrations will doubtless be used by Ferguson and Brian Kidd to maintain the desire that sets this team apart from the rest.

SOCCER SOUNDBITES

"I didn't have to be here to see this, because I was ill in bed all Saturday. But if I had not been here, perhaps there would have been nobody to make the changes and we would have lost 5–0."

CHELSEA MANAGER **RUUD GULLIT**

Disgraced directors, Freddie Shepherd (right) and Douglas Hall.

Out of the blue – a Ruud shock for Chelsea fans and City

New Chelsea boss, Gianluca Vialli.

RUUD GULLIT has been sacked as manager of Chelsea, allegedly after he and the club had fallen out in an acrimonious row over his reported demand for a salary of £3.5 million a year.

In a development that startled both the sporting world and the City, Gullit, 35, was asked to leave before the expiry of his contract, which was due to end in the summer. The former Dutch international, one of football's greats, whose few games this season have been mostly as a substitute, was immediately replaced as player-manager by another of the club's foreign imports, the Italian striker Gianluca Vialli.

The sacking comes as a bolt from the blue, as Gullit has been credited with transforming the fortunes of a club that had underachieved in recent years. They heralded their return to the soccer elite last May by winning the FA Cup. This season they stand second in the Premiership and have reached the semi-finals of the Coca-Cola Cup and the quarter-finals of the European Cup-Winners' Cup.

Now, on the eve of their biggest games of the season — against Arsenal, Manchester United and Real Betis — they have replaced the eloquent, dread-locked Gullit with the softly spoken, shaven-headed Vialli. A tremendous task lies ahead for the Italian, but he will allow himself a private smile, as Gullit had left him out of the side so many times.

SOCCER SOUNDBITES

"I was astounded to find out from the media that I have been replaced as Chelsea coach by Gianluca Vialli. I was only asked to attend one meeting in the last six months to discuss the future... At no time during my discussion [five weeks ago with MD Colin Hutchinson] was there any doubt in my mind that I would re-sign."

RUUD GULLIT

Arsenal clinch Premiership with panache

IT WAS THE stuff of fantasy. Arsenal clinched the Premiership title with a sequence of 10 wins climaxed by this 4–0 defeat of Everton at Highbury. In December, after a home defeat by Blackburn, they were languishing in sixth place, 13 points behind the leaders Manchester United with only one game in hand. Since then they have recorded 15 wins and three draws in 18 games to build up an unassailable lead over the previous champions with two matches to go.

As the songs of praise cascaded from the terraces, Arsène Wenger, smiling like a new father, at last cradled the Carling chalice, the English championship trophy that had never before been in the cultured clasp of a foreign manager.

Arsenal are not supposed to settle championships with flamboyant 4–0 victories, but this triumph encapsulated Wenger's effect on this most English of clubs. A minute before the final whistle, they produced a magnificent cameo that embodied the Frenchman's influence.

Suddenly Steve Bould was Dennis Bergkamp, metamorphosing from stopper to playmaker with a delicate lofted pass from midfield over the Everton defence and perfectly into the path of fellow central defender and captain Tony Adams. What was he doing there? Answer, a passable impersonation of Ian Wright, as he latched onto the ball and lashed an unstoppable left-foot volley past the Everton keeper.

Here was thrilling testament to Wenger's impact, the liberating of centre-halves to create as playmakers and finish as strikers. It was sheer theatre. Adams just stood there, captain supreme, relishing the moment. No histrionics, no wild cavorting with shirt pulled up over face. His expression said it all..

Tony Adams celebrates after scoring Arsenal's title-winning goal.

Arsenal leave United reeling

MANCHESTER UNITED 0 Arsenal 1. This was the day and the game that confounded all who were foolish enough to believe the Premiership title race was over as early as Christmas. The only consolation for the pundits who crowned United as champions so prematurely is that, unlike a generous Manchester bookmaker who has already paid out on United winning the title, they do not have to count their mistake in hard cash.

United still enjoy a six-point lead over Arsenal and a vastly superior goal difference, yet only the very committed or the very brave would bet against the London club catching them now. The late goal by Marc Overmars that brought the Gunners a richly deserved victory at Old Trafford means, with 10 games to play, the outcome is in their own hands. And their current form is such that there is every chance they will exploit their games in hand to the full.

United's defeat was underlined by the menace given to Arsenal's attacks by the pace and trickery of Overmars on the left. The Dutch international might easily have had a hat-trick in the first half. Turning the inexperienced John Curtis inside-out, he not only came close with three dangerous efforts, but should have had a penalty when Curtis brought him down in desperation.

The winning goal 11 minutes from the end started with a flighted pass from Martin Keown inside his own half. Dennis Bergkamp and Nicolas Anelka both headed the ball on and Overmars headed it forward himself before accelerating away smoothly and calmly steering it past Peter Schmeichel. Game on, as they say.

FOOTBALL FOCUS

- Ronaldo was playing in the Copa America when his transfer to Inter-Milan from Barcelona was revealed, at a reported world record of £17 million.
- Jason Crowe, a 90th minute substitute for Arsenal against Birmingham City, was sent off after just 33 seconds on the pitch, a record for the Coca-Cola Cup (League Cup). The 19-year-old, making his first-class debut, had replaced Lee Dixon, the only Arsenal regular in a "reserve eleven" that still won the tie 4–1 after extra time.
- Ian Rush equalled Geoff Hurst's record of 49 goals in the League Cup when he scored in Newcastle's 2–0 3rd-round victory over Hull.
- Rangers' Italian striker Marco Negri set a new Scottish League record by scoring in 10 consecutive matches, scoring 23 goals in the process. He dried up after that, but still finished with 32 goals from 29 appearances, enough to be the League's top scorer.
- Floodlight failures in three Premiership matches prompted a Premier League inquiry and allegations of sabotage by Far East betting syndicates.
- Preston idol Tom Finney, in his 76th year, was knighted in the New Year honours. England's 1966 World Cup goalscoring hero Geoff Hurst received a knighthood in the Queen's Birthday honours.
- The United States reached the final of the Concacaf Gold Cup by beating world champions Brazil for the first time. Preki Radosavijevic, once of Everton, scored the only goal. But their hero was Leicester City's goalkeeper Kasey Keller, who kept the rampant Brazilians at bay.
- At 18 years and 51 days, Liverpool striker Michael Owen became the youngest player to represent England this century — 124 days younger than Duncan Edwards — when he made his debut in a 2–0 defeat by Chile at Wembley in February. Wolves defender Ryan Green, a reserve yet to make his senior debut, became the youngest player to win a full Wales cap when he played in a friendly against Malta in June at the age of 17 years and 226 days, beating Ryan Giggs's record by 96 days.
- Just before the start of the World Cup, the Swiss former FIFA secretary Sepp Blatter was elected president of FIFA. He beat the favourite, Sweden's Lennart Johansson, the current UEFA president, by 111 votes to 80.

Cheerio ten-in-a-row: Celtic triumph at last

IT WENT RIGHT down to the last Premier League matches of the season. But it wasn't just about Celtic winning their first League title since 1988. It was also about retaining their record of nine championships in a row which Rangers had equalled last season.

It was, seemingly, their title a week earlier, but Dunfermline had sneaked a late equalizer. Celtic had one more chance. A defeat of St Johnstone at Parkhead would be enough. Leading scorer, Swedish international Henrik Larsson, settled the nerves in the third minute, with a curling shot high into the net. The towering stands emitted an incredible wall of sound, full of force and passion.

Craig Burley, the Scottish Player of the Year, Paul Lambert and Larsson all failed to convert chances, and Simon Donnelly was foiled by the keeper. On the hour Wim Jansen brought on Harald Brattbakk, and the Norwegian obliged 12 minutes later, slotting home a Jackie McNamara cross from the right. It was the goal that sealed victory and the title.

Dutch coach Jansen had emulated Arsène Wenger's triumph south of the border, by becoming the first foreign coach to win a championship in Scotland, although it didn't change his mind about leaving Celtic Park.

But the crowd, able to relax at last and bask in the glory of their side's triumph, had only one thought in their collective mind. Parkhead reverberated to the anthem, "Cheerio, ten-in-a-row". A little petty, perhaps, but now the celebrations could begin.

Celtic are champions at last.

Scottish Cup returns to Edinburgh after 42 years

NOBODY except their own gave Hearts a chance of taking the Scottish Cup back to Edinburgh for the first time in 42 years. Rangers might have surrendered their League title to Celtic after nine years, but surely they would not finish the season without a major trophy? They did, but not before a pulsating last 10 minutes when they pulled back to 2–1 and threw everything at Hearts in an effort to equalize.

Hearts made a sensational start when, with barely half a minute gone, their captain Steve Fulton was toppled by Ian Ferguson on the edge of the Rangers box. Colin Cameron, who had not yet touched the ball, stepped up and thrashed the spot-kick past Andy Goram.

Rangers, several of whose players were completing their careers with the club as well as their manager Walter Smith, gradually took control of the game. But Hearts managed to survive, and then surprisingly scored again in the 53rd minute when Stephane Adam took advantage of a slip by Lorenzo Amoruso to make it 2–0.

Ally McCoist, brought on after the interval, scored for Rangers to set up a breathtaking climax — "the longest 10 minutes of my life," according to Hearts manager Jim Jefferies, Scotland's Manager of the Year. For Rangers, it was the end of an era, the first time without a trophy for 12 years.

Zola's touch of genius a rhapsody in blue

FROM STAMFORD BRIDGE to Stockholm, the blue flag is flying over Europe. Gianfranco Zola's wonderful goal, a masterpiece of anticipation and execution, swept Chelsea to the Cup-Winners' Cup, so echoing the feats of Osgood and Co. 27 years ago. The final's technical flaws were forgotten amid the majesty of substitute Zola's 71st-minute strike and the celebrations it precipitated.

Zola (left) and Vialli show off the Cup-Winners' Cup.

Since being appointed Ruud Gullit's successor in February, Vialli has won both the Coca-Cola and Cup-Winners' Cups. Zola had been injured at the end of the season, so Vialli did not risk him from the start. Chances fell Chelsea's way, but without Zola's subtlety they lacked that finishing touch.

The fans had been calling for Mark Hughes. Instead Vialli sent Zola scurrying into the fray to replace Flo. How inspired this proved. Zola immediately raced on to Wise's superbly chipped pass through the middle, one touch nudging the ball forward into the box. And, as the keeper advanced, the Italian thumped a rising drive into the net. He had been on the pitch for 22 seconds.

Zola was named Man of the Match, yet that recognition could well have gone to Wise, a captain who kept his team resolutely positive during spells when the Germans threatened most.

Wenger's new Arsenal complete the double

ARSENAL won the FA Cup to complete the fabled League and Cup double as easily as everyone had expected. Newcastle did not stop trying but could never find the creative sparkle to trouble a formidable side.

There may have been only two goals in it, but the shots planted in the back of Newcastle's net by Dutch winger Marc Overmars and French striker Nicolas Anelka were scarcely an accurate reflection of the Gunners' overall superiority as they became only the second club, after Manchester United, to win the double twice.

Newcastle must have known there was to be no escape from a thoroughly miserable season when, in the second half, Nicolaos Dabizas and Alan Shearer hit the woodwork with the score at 1–0.

Arsenal, without their double Player of the Year, the injured Dennis Bergkamp, rarely played with the fluency and intensity that had brought them 10 consecutive Premiership victories and the title. But they did not need to. All that was required of them was the defensive solidity for which they are renowned and a shrewd exploitation of the Newcastle rearguard's chronic lack of pace.

Both goals came from balls hit over the top for the speedy Overmars, first, and then Anelka to outstrip the Magpies' defence. The providers were Emmanuel Petit and Ray Parlour respectively, the latter named Man of the Match. Parlour, indeed, did some clever and useful things and never stopped running, but he was no more influential than either of Arsenal's midfield powerhouses, the French pair Petit and Patrick Vieira.

Overmars goes past Pistone and is about put Arsenal ahead.

As the 1–4 booking count indicates, Newcastle clearly felt that their best chance of victory lay in trying to muscle Arsenal out of their usual rhythm. Shearer's was the first name to go in the referee's book, for a reckless late tackle on Tony Adams at the end of the first half, a wild lunge obviously the product of the mounting frustration he felt at being unable to make any impression on Arsenal's cast-iron back four.

Indeed, the first real chance Shearer had was the result of a stumble by Martin Keown after 64 minutes that allowed him to dart through and shoot past David Seaman, but onto the base of the far post. He had one more real chance, late on when Newcastle, 2–0 down, were making a last effort to salvage something from the game. But Nigel Winterburn, one of Arsenal's unsung heroes, did what he does regularly, suddenly coming from nowhere to nick the ball away.

What a triumph this season has been for Arsène Wenger, only 19 months at Highbury and now the double under his managerial belt. If Manchester United are still likely to be fixed in the memory as the club of the nineties, it could be that Arsenal are the club for the new millennium.

FINAL SCORE

Football League
Premier Division: Arsenal
Top scorer: Dion Dublin (Coventry), Michael Owen (Liverpool), Chris Sutton (Blackburn) 18
Division 1: Nottingham Forest
Division 2: Watford
Division 3: Notts County
Footballer of the Year: Dennis Bergkamp (Arsenal)

FA Cup Final

Arsenal	2	Newcastle United	0

League Cup Final

Chelsea	2	Middlesbrough	0
(after extra time)			

Scottish League
Premier Division: Celtic
Top scorer: Marco Negri (Rangers) 32
Division 1: Dundee
Division 2: Stranraer
Division 3: Alloa Athletic
Footballer of the Year: Craig Burley (Celtic)

Scottish FA Cup Final

Hearts	2	Rangers	1

Scottish League Cup Final

Celtic	3	Dundee United	0

European Cup Final

Real Madrid	1	Juventus	0

Cup-Winners' Cup Final

Chelsea	1	Stuttgart	0

UEFA Cup Final

Inter Milan	3	Lazio	0

European Footballer of the Year 1997
Ronaldo (Inter Milan)

FIFA World Player of the Year 1997
Ronaldo (Inter Milan & Brazil)

World Club Championship 1997

Borussia Dortmund	2	Cruzeiro	0

Hoddle axes Gascoigne from World Cup squad

PAUL GASCOIGNE found himself out of England's World Cup squad as manager Glenn Hoddle pruned it down from 28 to 22 at their training camp in La Manga, Spain. The omission of the midfield maestro caused a sensation, as it had appeared that his off-field transgressions had been forgiven.

The errant genius was given the two games in Casablanca, against Morocco and Belgium, to prove his fitness. There were moments of magic, but Hoddle clearly did not feel he had done enough to warrant inclusion for the tournament.

SOCCER SOUNDBITES

"He [Paul Gascoigne] is yesterday's man, whose only contribution to the future of the game is as an example of the dangers of drinking on an empty head."

MICHAEL PARKINSON, *Daily Telegraph* columnist

SOCCER SOUNDBITES

"Newcastle's wonderful supporters applauding Tony Adams and his men up the steps. The game for a few moments is wrested from its tightening corporate grip and is handed back to the people."

ITV's **BRIAN MOORE,** working his last FA Cup Final, with his abiding memory

The World Cup comes home

It was French lawyer Jules Rimet who pioneered football's first World Cup tournament in 1930, and it has taken 68 years for France to win the trophy. In doing so, they scored the first "golden goal" of the World Cup and survived a penalty decider, but they comprehensively beat holders and favourites Brazil in the final. The number of finalists was increased to 32, but there were no easy matches. Nor were there any major surprises. But there was a great deal of excitement and drama — not least, the mystery surrounding Ronaldo's appearance in the final — and there were some outstanding goals.

For club and for country: France's Petit (left) and Vieira.

These finals were the biggest yet. The number of countries taking part was increased from 24 in the last finals to 32 — whittled down from the 170 who played in continental qualifying competitions over nearly two years. The 64 matches were scheduled over a period of nearly five weeks. They were played at 10 venues across France, from 10 June to 12 July, when an estimated 1.7 billion viewers watched the final live on television.

With thousands of supporters pouring into France from many countries, security was a major feature of the organization of the tournament. There were some serious incidents outside the stadiums, but the offenders were kept mostly under control and for the most part opposing fans enjoyed mixing together in good spirit.

This was the first World Cup to employ the "golden goal" tiebreaker, or "sudden death" in extra time, a rule used previously in other tournaments, including Euro 96. Also new to the World Cup was the board displayed by the fourth official at the end of each half to show how much stoppage time the referee was adding on.

For the first round, the teams were divided into eight groups of four, in the usual round-robin format. Only the first two teams from each group would go through to the second round, from which stage the tournament continued on a knock-out basis

Scotland jinxed again

As adept as Scotland have been at qualifying for World Cup finals, once there, they had never managed to progress further than the first round. Sadly for all the Scots who followed their team around France in the best of spirits, these finals were to prove no exception.

Scotland had the honour of playing in the opening match of the tournament, a dubious honour in that they were pitted against the holders and favourites, Brazil. However, they acquitted themselves extremely well, but were hit by an early goal and conceded an own goal. The first goal of the World Cup was a near-post header by Cesar Sampaio after just four minutes. Where were the Scottish defence? John Collins replied from the spot 25 minutes later, but then came the killer goal. With 16 minutes to go, a blocked shot bounced off Tommy Boyd over the Scottish line. At the end their fans cheered them on as though they had won.

Cesar Sampaio (yellow, middle) scores the first goal of France 98.

In their second match, a Craig Burley equalizer against Norway midway through the second half kept Scotland in with a chance. But the Celtic midfielder, Scotland's Footballer of the Year, went from hero to villain when he was sent off in their next match, a 3–0 thrashing by Morocco. The African side themselves were desperately unlucky not to go through, pipped for second place in Group A by Norway, who came from behind to beat Brazil 2–1 with an 89th-minute penalty.

As for Brazil, there were signs of their "beautiful game" in the first-round matches, but fans and admirers were waiting still for them to really turn it on.

England scrape in

England scraped through to the second stage, as they have done before, with less than convincing performances in a group they should have dominated. They made a reasonable start with a 2–0 win over Tunisia, but that was no better than it should be.

Defeat in their next match by Romania left England struggling to qualify in second place. Coventry's Viorel Moldovan put the Romanians ahead soon after

It was evident from the first round that France lacked a world-class striker. But they made up for this with a midfield oozing power and flair and an outstanding pair of attacking full-backs. They conceded only two goals in the whole tournament.

half-time. Dan Petrescu beat his Chelsea team-mate Graeme Le Saux to score their 90th-minute winner after young Michael Owen had given England hope with an opportunist goal a few minutes earlier. In stoppage time, Owen very nearly put them level, but his shot crashed against a post. The Liverpool striker had certainly made an impression in the 20 minutes or so he was on the field.

For the vital game with Colombia, England manager Glenn Hoddle appeared to bow to public opinion by starting with Owen and Manchester United midfielder David Beckham. Owen had finished the first two games and Beckham had played an hour against Romania after Paul Ince was injured. England killed off the game in half an hour, going two up through a spectacular Darren Anderton volley and a typical Beckham free-kick. They dominated the match and 2–0 was scant reward for their superiority. Romania drew with Tunisia, so England qualified in second place to set up a second-round clash with old enemy Argentina.

Argentina untroubled

Argentina finished with maximum points in the first round and were the only team not to concede a goal in the group matches. However, they had a nervous start against Japan, their prolific striker Gabriel Batistuta scoring the only goal. But they pulverized Jamaica, Batistuta hitting a hat-trick, with the other two coming from Ariel Ortega the skilful playmaker whose burden is living up to the "New Maradona" tag.

Argentina made sure of first place with a 1–0 win over Croatia. The surprise of the group was the "wooden-spoon" match in which Jamaica beat the more fancied Japan 2–1. In an entertaining game played for pride by two countries making their Cup debuts, goals by Theodore Whitmore either side of the interval flattered Jamaica. When Japan pulled one back 15 minutes from time, their fans went wild, but at the end it was the Jamaican players celebrating their victory while their supporters danced in the stands. It was hard to believe that both teams were out of the competition.

Laurent Blanc: golden goal man.

France advance

It was obvious from the start that France's most lethal strikers were their rebellious lorry drivers. They scored nine goals in their three first-round matches, more than any other country, but only two of these were from strikers. And although they won all their matches, victories over South Africa and Saudi Arabia were nothing to get excited about.

Their second win, 4-0 over Saudi Arabia, was gained at the expense of losing their playmaker and most influential player Zinedine Zidane for two matches after he was red-carded in the 70th minute. The Saudis had already been reduced to 10 men 50 minutes earlier, and they never looked like challenging the host country.

Another blow for the French was the loss with a torn hamstring of their ungainly striker Christophe Dugarry, who had scored their first goal against South Africa. He missed more than he put away, but France were going to be hard put to find a replacement.

France's coach Aimé Jacquet played a much-changed side in their last match, by the end of which all his squad apart from the two reserve keepers had enjoyed a taste of the World Cup. They beat Denmark, for whom Peter Schmeichel was making his 103rd international appearance, 2–1 to top the group.

The early verdict on France was that they were going to be formidable opponents whoever they met in the knock-out stage. Even without Zidane, they could choose a powerful midfield, with Didier Deschamps, Petit, Alain Boghossian, Patrick Vieira, Christian Karembeu, Thierry Henri and others, all available, allowing Djorkaeff to drop off a lone striker. Wing-backs Bixente Lizarazu and Lilian Thuram gave France width and added firepower. But could they really win the World Cup without a sharp-shooter up front?

Nigeria impress

Arguably the most entertaining match of the first round was Nigeria's 3–2 defeat of Spain. The Africans, impressive Olympic champions, twice came back from a goal down before Oliseh Sunday, the Ajax libero but midfielder for his country, returned a clearance with a thunderous half-volley from outside the box to score the winner. Spain, one of the favourites for the tournament despite their disappointing World Cup history, were then held to a goalless draw by Paraguay, who proceeded to qualify in second place by beating a much-changed Nigeria 3–1. Spain's 6–1 drubbing of Bulgaria, perhaps the most impressive first-round performance of all, was thus in vain.

Other favoured sides who were not entirely convincing in the qualifying were Holland and Germany. Holland did thrash the minnows of the group, South Korea, 5–0, but carelessly threw away a 2–0 lead against Mexico in their last match. The Mexicans had pulled back from two down against Belgium, too, and this cost the Belgians dearly when they were also held by South Korea.

Germany were always going to qualify from a group containing the United States and Iran, but 2–0 wins against each of these sides is not the stuff of champions. They drew 2–2 with Yugoslavia, who also qualified with even-less convincing 1–0 victories over the minnows. The United States were hugely disappointing in their emotive clash with Iran, deservedly losing 2–1.

Italy and Chile qualified from Group B, in which Cameroon disappointed. Chile drew all three of their matches. They almost beat Italy in the opening game. Goals either side of the interval by the impressive Marcelo Salas, scourge of England at Wembley, put them 2–1 up. But Roberto Baggio, whose penalty miss cost Italy the 1994 World Cup, bravely scored a late equalizer from the spot.

Brazil, Danes coast

The only comprehensive victors in the last 16 were Brazil and Denmark, both by 4–1. Brazil, without playing particularly well, coasted through their match with Chile, thanks to two goals apiece from Cesar Sampaio and Ronaldo.

Denmark suddenly found their form and dazzlingly brushed Nigeria aside. The pride of Africa were made to look like novices. Goals from Peter Moller and Brian Laudrup left them 2–0 down in 12 minutes, and second-half strikes from Ebbe Sand and Thomas Helveg sealed the issue.

Okocha is consoled by Jørgensen as Denmark end Nigeria's run.

Blanc means gold

In other matches, France edged through to the quarter-finals with the first golden goal in World Cup history, defender Laurent Blanc shooting past Paraguay's keeper Jose Luis Chilavert, one of the stars of the tournament, in the 23rd minute of extra time, while Holland and Germany left it very late in normal time to beat Yugoslavia and Mexico, respectively.

The last match of the round, England's clash with Argentina, was the most dramatic, possibly the most exciting of the championship. There was a penalty after five minutes when England keeper David Seaman was adjudged to have brought down Diego Simeone and Batistuta scored from the spot. The referee evened matters up five minutes later when Owen went down in the box, allowing Shearer to put England level. Another five minutes and England were in the lead with one of the goals of the tournament, as Owen darted and swerved his way through the Argentina defence before slamming the ball home. But Javier Zanetti equalized following a clever free-kick just before the interval to set up a mouth-watering second half.

Beckham got himself sent off immediately after half-time for a kick at Simeone, right in front of the referee. Ten-man England had an uphill fight for 75 minutes. At one stage Sol Campbell headed the ball in, but it was disallowed for a foul by Shearer. No blame could be attached to Paul Ince and David Batty for missing their penalties. But England were out.

Italy lose shoot-out

One penalty shoot-out followed another, as France knocked Italy out after a goalless draw. It was no more than they deserved, having completely outplayed the lacklustre Italians. This time it was Luigi Di Biagio who was the fall guy, slamming their fifth spot-kick against the bar.

That evening in Nantes, Brazil beat Denmark 3–2 in a thriller, a see-saw match climaxed by Rivaldo's winner on the hour. Barcelona's attacking midfielder, appropriately in Pele's No.10 shirt, produced a performance that encapsulated every intoxicating quality of Brazilian football, including two superb strikes past Schmeichel.

The following afternoon, Dennis Bergkamp provided the stamp of greatness with a late winner against Argentina, avenging Holland's defeat by the South Americans in the 1978 final. It was acclaimed the goal of the tournament, yet it was typical Bergkamp, poetry in motion as he controlled a 50-yard floated pass from Frank De Boer, sidestepped his marker Roberto Ayala and volleyed the bouncing ball past the keeper, all in one flowing, seamless movement.

The last quarter-final was an unprecedented rout of Germany by Croatia, a 3–0 defeat crowned by an impudent goal from Davor Suker. All the goals came after the 40th-minute dismissal of Christian Worns, whose loss left an ageing team without enough staying power. It marked the end of an era.

Dennis Bergkamp (8) scored the goal of the finals and it allowed Holland to snatch a second-round win.

Beckham's World Cup went sour.

Brazil are spot-on

Holland had the better of the first half in their semi-final with Brazil. Edgar Davids ran the midfield, but Holland failed to convert any of the chances they created.

Straight after the interval, however, Ronaldo put Brazil ahead with the first chance he had. It looked like being the winner, until Kluivert nodded in an equalizer from Ronald De Boer's cross three minutes from time.

Frank De Boer was outstanding in keeping Brazil at bay during extra time, so it went to penalties. The first four Brazilians scored with seeming ease. Claudio Taffarel saved the last two Dutch efforts and Brazil were in the final again.

SOCCER SOUNDBITES

"David Beckham's sending off cost us dearly. It was a mistake, but these things happen in football. I am not denying it cost us the game."

GLENN HODDLE,
England coach

FOOTBALL FOCUS

● One new "technique" was introduced in France 98. Mexican winger Cuauhtemoc Blanco twice split the South Korea defence by wedging the ball between his feet and jumping between two defenders — a ruse promptly dubbed the "Blanco bounce" by commentators.

● A star of the group matches was Nigerian midfielder Augustine "Jay Jay" Okocha, whose repertoire of tricks and ball skills became as familiar to the spectators as his bleached ginger hair. The Romanian players turned out for their last group match with their hair dyed yellow. It must have affected their play because they very nearly lost to Tunisia.

● Cameroon defender Rigobert Song became the first player to be sent off in two World Cups when he received his marching orders against Chile. In USA 94 against Brazil he was, at 17, the youngest player ever to be sent off in the World Cup finals.

● Former winning World Cup captain Lothar Matthäus came on as sub for Germany in the game against Yugoslavia to equal the record of playing in five World Cups and set a new record by playing his 22nd match in a finals tournament. He increased this by three before Germany were eliminated.

Thuram is the hero

France had the fright of their lives in the other semi-final. They dominated the first half, but had Blanc sent off following a clash with Slaven Bilic, who made the most of minimal contact. Croatia struck with a sucker-punch moments after the restart. A wonderful reverse pass by Aljosa Asanovic

Kluivert scores in the semi-final.

split France's defence and fell to Suker. He killed it with a touch and then flicked a powerful left-footer past Fabien Barthez.

Croatia's jubilation was short-lived. Thuram, responsible for giving Suker the space to score, charged upfield, forced Zvonimir Boban to lose possession, then took a pass from Djorkaeff to coolly place the ball into the net for his first international goal. His second followed 20 minutes later, when he again won the ball after pressuring the opposing defence, and again slotted it home like the striker France were missing.

Vive la France

There was high drama even before the start of this first-ever hosts v holders World Cup final. Ronaldo's name was missing from the team sheet handed in by the Brazilians. Rumours were that he was in hospital. Then a new team sheet appeared, by permission of FIFA, and Ronaldo was back in the starting line-up. In the event, he made a poor showing, as did the team as a whole.

Blaming Ronaldo's indisposition — according to some sources, he had a fit during the previous night — is an oversimplification of Brazil's problems. They were completely overrun and overpowered in midfield. France's first World Cup triumph was founded on the goals of Zidane and Petit and the way they shook Brazil out of their measured stride.

Djorkaeff, playing just behind the lone striker, was superb, swerving past yellow shirts like a breeze through daffodils. Petit pursued every ball with relentless intent. Then there was Zidane, the ball his willing accomplice as he pushed France forward. It was Zidane who put France into a 2–0 half-time lead, scoring his first goals of the tournament in the 27th and 45th minutes, uncharacteristically, from headers from inswinging corners.

After half time, Ronaldo's only attempt was blocked by Barthez and then substitute Denilson hit the bar. France soon regained control and threatened to increase their lead but, after 68 minutes, Desailly was sent off for two yellow cards. Petit dropped back to partner Blanc's replacement, Frank Leboeuf of Chelsea. In the last minute, with the game safe, Petit moved forward, took a pass from Arsenal colleague Vieira and glided the ball past Taffarel to make it 3–0.

The French public, largely aloof at first to the privilege of hosting the World Cup, had warmed to their team as the tournament progressed, and now their joy knew no bounds.

Zinedine Zidane is unmarked as he scores with a header in the final.

FINAL SCORE

FIRST ROUND

Group A

Brazil	2	Scotland	1
Morocco	2	Norway	2
Scotland	1	Norway	1
Brazil	3	Morocco	0
Brazil	1	Norway	2
Scotland	0	Morocco	3

	P	W	D	L	F	A	P
Brazil	3	2	0	1	6	3	6
Norway	3	1	2	0	5	4	5
Morocco	3	1	1	1	5	5	4
Scotland	3	0	1	2	2	6	1

Group B

Italy	2	Chile	2
Cameroon	1	Austria	1
Chile	1	Austria	1
Italy	3	Cameroon	0
Italy	2	Austria	1
Chile	1	Cameroon	1

	P	W	D	L	F	A	P
Italy	3	2	1	0	7	3	7
Chile	3	0	3	0	4	4	3
Austria	3	0	2	1	3	4	2
Cameroon	3	0	2	1	2	5	2

Group C

France	3	South Africa	0
Saudi Arabia	0	Denmark	1
South Africa	1	Denmark	1
France	4	Saudi Arabia	0
South Africa	2	Saudi Arabia	2
France	2	Denmark	1

	P	W	D	L	F	A	P
France	3	3	0	0	9	1	9
Denmark	3	1	1	1	3	3	4
South Africa	3	0	2	1	3	6	2
Saudi Arabia	3	0	1	2	2	7	1

Group D

Paraguay	0	Bulgaria	0
Spain	2	Nigeria	3
Nigeria	1	Bulgaria	0
Spain	0	Paraguay	0
Nigeria	1	Paraguay	3
Spain	6	Bulgaria	1

	P	W	D	L	F	A	P
Nigeria	3	2	0	1	5	5	6
Paraguay	3	1	2	0	3	1	5
Spain	3	1	1	1	8	4	4
Bulgaria	3	0	1	2	1	7	1

Group E

Holland	0	Belgium	0
South Korea	1	Mexico	3
Belgium	2	Mexico	2
Holland	5	South Korea	0
Holland	2	Mexico	2
Belgium	1	South Korea	1

	P	W	D	L	F	A	P
Holland	3	1	2	0	7	2	5
Mexico	3	1	2	0	7	5	5
Belgium	3	0	3	0	3	3	3
South Korea	3	0	1	2	2	9	1

Group F

Yugoslavia	1	Iran	0
Germany	2	United States	0
Germany	2	Yugoslavia	2
United States	1	Iran	2
Germany	2	Iran	0
United States	0	Yugoslavia	2

	P	W	D	L	F	A	P
Germany	3	2	1	0	6	2	7
Yugoslavia	3	2	1	0	4	2	7
Iran	3	1	0	2	2	4	3
United States	3	0	0	3	1	5	0

Group G

England	2	Tunisia	0
Romania	1	Colombia	0
Colombia	1	Tunisia	0
Romania	2	England	1
Colombia	0	England	2
Romania	1	Tunisia	1

	P	W	D	L	F	A	P
Romania	3	2	1	0	4	2	7
England	3	2	0	1	5	2	6
Colombia	3	1	0	2	1	3	3
Tunisia	3	0	1	2	1	4	1

Group H

Argentina	1	Japan	0
Jamaica	1	Croatia	3
Japan	0	Croatia	1
Argentina	5	Jamaica	0
Argentina	1	Croatia	0
Japan	1	Jamaica	2

	P	W	D	L	F	A	P
Argentina	3	3	0	0	7	0	9
Croatia	3	2	0	1	4	2	6
Jamaica	3	1	0	2	3	9	3
Japan	3	0	0	3	1	4	0

SECOND ROUND

Italy	1	Norway	0
Brazil	4	Chile	1
France	1	Paraguay	0
France won on "golden goal" rule			
Nigeria	1	Denmark	4
Germany	2	Mexico	1
Holland	2	Yugoslavia	1
Romania	0	Croatia	1
Argentina	2	England	2
Argentina won 4–3 on penalties			

QUARTER FINALS

Italy	0	France	0
France won 4–3 on penalties			
Brazil	3	Denmark	2
Holland	2	Argentina	1
Germany	0	Croatia	3

SEMI FINALS

Brazil	1	Holland	1
Brazil won 4–2 on penalties			
France	2	Croatia	1

THIRD PLACE MATCH

Holland	1	Croatia	2

FINAL

France	3	Brazil	0

Stade de France, Saint-Denis, Paris, 12 July 1998. Attendance 80,000

Brazil: Taffarel, Cafu, Aldair, Junior Baiano, Cesar Sampaio (Edmundo), Roberto Carlos, Dunga, Ronaldo, Rivaldo, Leonardo (Denilson), Bebeto

France: Barthez, Thuram, Leboeuf, Desailly, Lizarazu, Karembeu (Boghossian), Deschamps, Zidane, Petit, Djorkaeff (Vieira), Guivarc'h (Dugarry)
(Scorers: Zidane 2, Petit)

Leading scorers
6 Suker (Croatia)
5 Batistuta (Argentina), Vieri (Italy)
4 Salas (Chile), Hernandez (Mexico), Ronaldo (Brazil)

The day football saw red

A TOTAL OF 21 dismissals in England and Scotland made Saturday 26 September one of the worst days on record for discipline. The 14 red cards flourished south of the border included three Southend players during their side's 2–1 defeat at Swansea.

The man who hit the headlines, however, was Sheffield Wednesday striker Paolo Di Canio, who was immediately suspended by his club for pushing referee Paul Alcock to the ground at Hillsborough in the Premiership match against Arsenal.

Di Canio had just been sent off after an ugly mêlée developed involving 16 players. His response, violently shoving the Kent official in the chest with both hands, was inexcusable and will no doubt earn the temperamental Italian a long suspension. But Alcock's staggering descent to the turf appeared highly theatrical and, had he been a player, might have earned him a yellow card for "diving".

At any rate, he quickly recovered and produced his red card again to dismiss Arsenal's Martin Keown for his perceived part in the fracas. A late goal by Wednesday's Lee Briscoe inflicted the champions' first Premiership defeat of the season.

Hoddle sacked at last for "error"

Glenn Hoddle at the press conference announcing his departure.

GLENN HODDLE was sacked as England coach on 2 February, after he and the FA finally bowed to the wave of public and press anger over his remarks implying that the disabled were responsible for their own suffering. His dismissal, after 30 months in the job, was inevitable when it became clear that he had lost the confidence of the fans, the public and, as it emerged the previous day, prime minister Tony Blair.

Looking composed at the press conference, 41-year-old Hoddle read a brief statement in which he accepted that he had made an error of judgement in a newspaper interview and stated that it was never his intention to cause any hurt by his remarks.

However, it has to be said that Hoddle had become an embarrassment to England long before his interview in *The Times*. His spiritual beliefs became less of an asset once they manifested themselves in his unfailing trust in the powers of his mentor, faith healer Eileen Drury. And his stature was further diminished by his indiscreet ghost-written diary of England's World Cup campaign.

Hoddle, who was on a salary of £350,000, had a record as England coach of 17 wins, six draws and five defeats. His departure followed a prolonged meeting of the FA's 16-strong international committee. Howard Wilkinson, the FA's Technical Director, will replace him, at least for the upcoming friendly against the current world champions France.

SOCCER SOUNDBITES

"You and I have been physically given two hands and two legs and half-decent brains. Some people have not been born like that for a reason; karma is working from another lifetime."

ENGLAND COACH GLENN HODDLE

United run riot: 4 for super-sub Solskjaer

OLE GUNNAR SOLSKJAER upstaged Andy Cole and Dwight Yorke in remarkable fashion as leaders Manchester United beat Nottingham Forest 8–1 at the City Ground, a score that must have sent a shiver of apprehension round the rest of the Premiership. Just when Cole and Yorke had confirmed their right to be regarded as United's first-choice strikers with two goals apiece, Solskjaer came on as substitute for Yorke and scored four times in the last 13 minutes.

It was a devastating spell by the Norwegian, who helped create a record away win for the Premiership. It leaves Forest firmly planted at the bottom of the table with just over a third of the season remaining, while United maintain their four-point lead at the top. Chelsea were unconvincing 1–0 home winners over strugglers Southampton to stay second, while Arsenal had an impressive 4–0 win away to West Ham at Upton Park to remain a further point behind.

FA chief Kelly quits in row over £3 million loan

THE FOOTBALL ASSOCIATION was thrown into chaos on 15 December when Graham Kelly resigned as chief executive but the chairman, Keith Wiseman, refused to quit after a vote of no confidence. This followed allegations that the FA of Wales had been promised a £3.2 million loan from the English FA in return for helping Mr Wiseman to become a vice-president of FIFA. The loan, which was to be spread over eight years, was allegedly promised without other senior FA officials being consulted.

However much the FA spin doctors may dress up these events, the extraordinary developments at Lancaster Gate bear all the hallmarks of a putsch. A modern movement exists within the FA, men and women who are determined to turn it into a sporting body fit for the millennium, able to live on level terms with the powerful players, avaricious chairmen and TV moguls who now dominate the game. They seek to change an organization that is still Victorian in essence — the deep carpets, framed images of former worthies and a sense of atrophy that frustrates many within. Some of the FA's most positive, thrusting employees were thinking of leaving, such was their irritation at the organization's behemoth nature. This revolution was triggered from within, when an opportunity was seen to launch it.

The complaint against Wiseman and Kelly was that they acted without authority, when the football world was distracted by the World Cup. There was never any hint of impropriety.

But what of Kelly? If the hand of sympathy is to be extended to anyone it is to this loyal servant of the FA. His period at Lancaster Gate was not one of ego-stretching, but of service to the sport.

SOCCER SOUNDBITES

"I believe that everything that we did was in the best interests of the FA and of English football."

GRAHAM KELLY, FA CHIEF EXECUTIVE

Kanu causes Cup chaos, but FA agree to unprecedented rematch

NWANKWO KANU, the Nigerian international striker, made his debut for Arsenal at Highbury on 13 February when he came on as a substitute in the 64th minute of their 5th-round FA Cup tie against Sheffield United, Twelve minutes later his action caused complete consternation and resulted in a decision unique in the 118 years of the competition and some 50,000 ties.

With the score at 1–1 — headed goals from Patrick Vieira and Sheffield's Brazilian striker Marcelo, respectively — the Sheffield keeper Alan Kelly booted the ball out of play so that team-mate Lee Morris could receive attention. Arsenal's Ray Parlour threw the ball back in Kelly's direction after the injured player had been replaced. So far, so good. Footballing etiquette had been observed.

But then the gangling Kanu, a £4.5 million signing from Inter, loped after the ball and crossed it for Marc Overmars to nip in almost unchallenged and put the ball in the net. The Sheffield team, momentarily stunned, stared in disbelief for a second before all hell broke loose.

Angry Sheffield United players confront Kanu (left) and Overmars after the controversial second goal.

Joined by manager Steve Bruce, they demonstrated and protested all over the pitch while he jostled and gesticulated, ranted and raved — at referee Peter Jones, a linesman, the Arsenal players, security officers and anyone who would listen. Bruce at one stage tried to take his men off, but they failed to respond.

Pandemonium reigned for many minutes before the referee could restart the game. He had to award a goal. The actions of Kanu and Overmars might have been morally wrong, but they were legally right. For unknown reasons they had disregarded an unwritten law of sportsmanship. Indeed, Arsenal had suffered a similar injustice at Highbury two seasons ago when Blackburn striker Chris Sutton's flouting of tradition cost them a European Cup place.

This time, however, the offending club were quick to try to redress matters. The bemused Kanu was sincerely apologetic and, in an unprecedented move, Arsenal manager Arsène Wenger, having consulted vice-chairman David Dein, offered to have the result, a 2–1 win for Arsenal, annulled and the tie played again. It was a sporting gesture, applauded at home and abroad, but even more remarkable was the FA's speedy agreement to allow the re-run — a decision taken in minutes.

Ten days later the tie was played again, and the Gunners won fair and square, by the same score. Overmars scored Arsenal's first and was instrumental in Dennis Bergkamp's second. Kanu, on as a sub again for little over 10 minutes, kept a low profile.

George Graham back on the trophy trail with Spurs

EVEN IN THE full flush of victory, Tottenham Hotspur's supporters still refused to sing the name of their manager, George Graham, a man so deeply associated with Arsenal. Yet this trophy, the Worthington League Cup, Spurs' first for eight years, was rooted in the principle that drove Graham to such success at Highbury: unstinting determination, witnessed most stirringly in their refusal to accept the adversity of losing a team-mate.

Graham's first silverware at Highbury was also a League Cup, and his phenomenal impact since joining Spurs deserved reward this season. He has organised and inspired, drilled and driven Tottenham's previously underachieving players into Europe.

Allan Nielsen's stoppage-time header, which gave Spurs their 1–0 victory over Leicester at Wembley, intoxicated Tottenham's entourage but served only to relieve the few neutrals present of further purgatory, such was the dire nature of a so-called showpiece occasion.

With Spurs' David Ginola, one of the few players present worthy of such an illustrious stage, double-marked out of the game, neither side offered much creativity. Only in the last half-hour did this encounter begin to impersonate a final, but it required a red card to stir the players into action. Justin Edinburgh retaliated after a fierce tackle from Rob Savage, who made a meal of the incident. Nevertheless, the Spurs full-back had raised his hands and had to go.

Savage's behaviour incensed Spurs' players and fans alike, and he was constantly booed until Leicester manager Martin O'Neill took him off in the last minute. This seemed to liberate Spurs from their vendetta against the Leicester midfielder. Steffen Iversen went charging down the inside-right channel and crossed low into the six-yard box. Kasey Keller could only parry the ball, and as it bounced up Nielsen dived low to head Spurs into Europe.

One-nil was a familiar score to Graham. He had not only brought a trophy to his new club in his first season — as he had at Arsenal — but he had dragged Spurs up from the depths.

Scholes hat-trick lights up England's brave new world

KEVIN KEEGAN'S magic touch remains intact. It survived the transition from Newcastle and Fulham to the notoriously difficult England scene, and inspired a notable match-winning hat-trick by Paul Scholes against Poland at Wembley on 27 March. The Manchester United midfielder's tour de force gave England the qualifying victory for Euro 2000 they needed so desperately after their poor start under Glenn Hoddle.

There was some concern in English minds when Polish captain Jerzy Brzeczek cancelled out one of Scholes's first two goals before the interval, but there was never much doubt about the outcome once he had completed his hat-trick 20 minutes from the end.

Keegan should be congratulated on patching the England team together from the remnants of a squad reduced to the bare bones by injury and suspension. He had the courage to prefer Scholes to Ray Parlour, the man in form and the hot tip for selection in midfield. Together with Tim Sherwood, another of Keegan's inspired selections, Scholes gave England solidity as well as penetration in the middle.

The gamble on Steve McManaman was less successful, however. Short of match practice, the Liverpool player proved peripheral in more ways than one on the left flank.

Perhaps the significance of England's victory is best measured in terms of the opposition. Poland have been transformed in just over a year by new coach Janusz Wojcik. They came into the game unbeaten in eight matches and leading the group with maximum points from two matches. England are now a point in front of them, but Poland have a game in hand, as do new two-point leaders Sweden.

Scholes and Keegan are all smiles after the former's hat-trick.

SOCCER SOUNDBITES

"Do one thing for me — please respect both national anthems."

KEVIN KEEGAN'S message to the crowd before the start of his first match as England's caretaker-coach.

Sky's £623m bid for Man United falls at the final hurdle

THE CONTROVERSIAL £623 million bid by Richard Murdoch's TV giant BSkyB for Manchester United plc, launched in September 1998, was finally blocked on 9 April 1999 by the government. It was defeated because Trade and Industry secretary Stephen Byers endorsed the Mergers and Monopolies Commission recommendations.

This was a big blow for club chairman Martin Edwards and his fellow directors, who had been quick to accept the takeover bid. They felt it would herald a new era for United in which the club would be financially stronger and able to compete on level terms with the foreign clubs already in multinational company ownership. And had the bid been successful, Edwards' 14 per cent stake was estimated to be worth as much as £80 million.

The decision, on the other hand, was a triumph for the "little man" — the ordinary fans as well as the minor shareholders, who banded together when all seemed lost. It did not help that the vast majority of United supporters at first seemed not to care much and thought the takeover was good news. The campaigns of IMUSA (the Independent Manchester United Supporters' Association) and SUAM (Shareholders United Against Murdoch) quickly gained momentum — and eventually David slew Goliath.

Champagne night for Nationwide leaders

LONG-TERM LEADERS of Nationwide Divisions 1 and 2, Sunderland and Fulham, both clinched promotion on the same night, Tuesday, 13 April.

Sunderland won their Premiership place in tremendous style, a 5–2 victory at relegation-threatened Bury, featuring a 23-minute hat-trick for Kevin Phillips, who added a last-minute fourth for good measure, and a 20th goal of the season for striking partner Niall Quinn.

With a 15-point lead over both Bradford and Ipswich, only the latter, with a game in hand and five matches to play, could theoretically catch them now. The celebrations began in earnest.

Fulham, too, enjoyed a three-goal win, beating promotion hopefuls Gillingham 3–0 at Craven Cottage. Walsall, 16 points behind in second place with six games to play, could still catch them for the Division 2 championship, but they are now out of reach of Preston and the other chasing teams.

It was not until the last 10 minutes of the game, however, that Fulham could be sure of ending their 13 years in the wilderness of the lower orders. That is when Chris Coleman and Geoff Horsfield added to the lead given them by Barry Hayles in the 22nd minute. And as Craven Cottage rocked in jubilation, the players celebrated in grand prix style, showering manager Kevin Keegan with champagne.

Bank-rolled by Harrods owner Mohamed Fayed, who bought the run-down club for £20 million two years ago, and energised by the inspiration of Keegan, Fulham have not only been the Second Division's class act, but are manifestly equipped for another promotion drive next season. Keegan has spent £12 million in recruiting more than 20 players since being appointed 19 months ago, and will have a further £11 million to strengthen the squad during the summer as Fulham aim to reclaim top-flight status last held in 1968.

Kevin Keegan: going up.

Schmeichel and Giggs take United to Wembley

Lee Dixon cannot stop Ryan Giggs mesmeric run to semi-final glory.

IF THIS WAS not the finest semi-final in the history of the FA Cup, there can have been mighty few better. No exercise in tension and attrition this, but a compelling epic of flowing football, a classic between the two English giants, Manchester United and Arsenal. And it was crowned by Ryan Giggs's glorious winner deep into extra time.

Stung by Dennis Bergkamp's equaliser to David Beckham's magnificent opener, reduced to 10 men following Roy Keane's deserved dismissal, and needing all the reflexes of Peter Schmeichel to keep out a Bergkamp penalty, United showed their resilience and then their brilliance in the extra period.

Under siege, they broke out through the surging figure of Giggs, whose mazy run from inside his own half carried him past tiring Arsenal legs and breath-takingly into the box before his rising drive from an acute angle beat David Seaman. It was a sensational goal, a fitting climax to a match that offered everything.

United had begun well. When Schmeichel launched the ball long and high downfield after 17 minutes, Teddy Sheringham turned it inside to Beckham, whose instant response from 25 yards the ball swerving across the diving Seaman into the net.

Fired up, United played with precision and confidence, the ball rarely wasted. Yet Arsenal are never more dangerous than when wounded, and as the half drew to a close Schmeichel was forced to make saves in quick succession from Patrick Vieira and Emmanuel Petit.

If the first half was exciting, the second was compelling. United should have extended their lead, but first Ole Gunnar Solskjaer dragged his shot wide when well placed and then Seaman made a superb save from Jesper Blomqvist.

Arsenal had to make their move, and just after the hour Marc Overmars exploded into the game, giving Arsenal width and menace.

Robbed of a goal by an off-side flag on Sunday, United were relieved moments later when Nicolas Anelka's close-range strike was rightly ruled out after Schmeichel failed to hold Bergkamp's stinging shot. The force remained with Arsenal, particularly when Keane departed in the 74th minute for felling Overmars, compounding his earlier foul on Bergkamp.

Bergkamp should have settled it in the second minute of stoppage time following Phil Neville's trip on Ray Parlour, but Schmeichel went the right way and made a magnificent save to send the game into extra time.

With the prospect of penalties looming, Arsenal were pressing for a winner. Then Vieira placed a square ball straight into the path of Giggs on the United left, 10 yards inside his own half.

Over 13 touches and 70 yards later the ball ended up in the back of the net leaving the England keeper helpless. It provided a fitting climax to an epic battle.

SOCCER SOUNDBITES

"I can't remember much about it. I just got the ball and set off."

RYAN GIGGS,
on his sensational semi-final winner.

United's glorious comeback in Turin

WITH BARELY time to draw breath after last week's epic FA Cup semi-final victory over Arsenal and then a 3–0 win over Sheffield Wednesday on Saturday to stay top of the Premiership, Manchester United took another giant step on their way to what would be a remarkable treble. On an enchanting evening at the Stadio Delle Alpi, they showed all their mental character and counter-attacking class to reach the European Cup final with a thrilling victory over Juventus.

Alex Ferguson's team arrived in Turin on level terms (1–1) thanks to a last-minute equaliser from Ryan Giggs a fortnight ago at Old Trafford when they had been outclassed by Juventus. But within 10 minutes they were 2–0 down, to goals from striker Filippo Inzaghi.

Many teams might have melted before the heat of the Italians' early onslaught. But by the 34th minute they had completely turned the match around with headers from Roy Keane and Dwight Yorke.

Now they had the advantage. And they kept the Italians at bay before Andy Cole scored a few minutes from the end to clinch the tie 4–3 on aggregate and set up a Nou Camp meeting with Bayern Munich.

Beckham and Schmeichel celebrate.

United win back title — first leg of "treble"?

THE LAST DAY of the Premiership season, and the equation was simple for Manchester United. All they had to do at Old Trafford was beat Tottenham and the title was theirs. If they slipped up, an Arsenal victory over Aston Villa at Highbury would snatch it from their grasp for the second year running.

Chelsea had dropped out of the race, but Arsenal were looming large, even taking the lead, as the last fixture-packed couple of weeks unfolded. But defeat at Elland Road on Tuesday, Arsenal's first since December, had placed the ball firmly back in United's court, only for them to leave the Highbury side a chink of light when Blackburn held them to a draw at Ewood Park — confirming Rovers' relegation — on Wednesday.

Alex Ferguson won his fifth Premiership Trophy in seven seasons.

The stage was set for the final Sunday and an unlikely scenario at Highbury, with Arsenal fans chanting "Come on you Spurs," when news of Les Ferdinand's goal at Old Trafford blasted through on their transistors midway through the first half.

Up at Old Trafford, with many players below par and a makeshift central defence, the magnificent Roy Keane was holding his side together. Then David Beckham calmed the nerves, finishing off a great breakaway with an unstoppable drive in the 42nd minute. Alex Ferguson put Andy Cole on for Teddy Sheringham at half-time, and the substitute took less than two minutes to put United 2–1 ahead.

It did not matter that midway through the half another substitute put Arsenal in front at Highbury. Kanu, scorer of so many vital and exquisite goals on the run-in to the Premiership denouement, gave Arsenal victory 1–0.

United held firm against Spurs, and the Premiership trophy was back at Old Trafford, for the fifth time in seven seasons. One down and two to go.

Keeper's goal keeps Carlisle from Conference

THEY COULD not have been nearer the abyss. Carlisle were done for, their 71-year history of League football apparently over. Then came a breathtaking finish they will never forget.

Stoppage time was ticking away, and Carlisle needed another goal. Their players edged forward for a corner, nervous, desperate. And up, too, came their keeper Jimmy Glass. The corner came over, striker Scott Dobie got his head to it, the Plymouth keeper parried the ball and it fell to Glass, just outside the box. He thumped it straight back and it flew into the net.

In a moment, this unlikely hero, on loan from Swindon for the last few weeks of the season, was buried under a pile of delirious team-mates and fans. The referee cleared the pitch, insisted on a restart and blew for time as soon as the ball was in play.

For Carlisle, it was a stunning escape. They were safe for another season. Disbelief was all around, but nowhere more than in Scarborough, where, their match with Peterborough having finished in a draw eight minutes earlier, they were still milling around listening to transistors. They were devastated. With Third Division safety only seconds away, it was snatched from them. The communal slump was staggering as they heard that a goalkeeper in distant Cumbria had condemned them to a return to the Conference just 12 years after they had arrived in the Football League.

Back at Carlisle, the celebrations were beginning. There were still a few chants and banners saying "Knighton Out", a reference to their vilified chairman Michael Knighton, blamed for their desperate situation — the same Michael Knighton who had once tried to buy Manchester United.

SOCCER SOUNDBITES

"You never know what's going to happen in football. For Christ's sake, I've just scored the winner."

JIMMY GLASS, ON-LOAN KEEPER ON BEING ASKED IF HE WOULD BE STAYING AT CARLISLE.

FOOTBALL FOCUS

- Manchester United finally extracted striker Dwight Yorke from Aston Villa for a club record £12.6m on 20 August.
- A fortnight into the season, Newcastle brought in Ruud Gullit to replace unsuccessful manager Kenny Dalglish.
- England made a disastrous start to their Euro 2000 campaign, losing 2–1 in Sweden and having Paul Ince sent off.
- Barry Fry took Peterborough down to his old home Underhill for a Division 3 match and they won 9–1, Barnet being reduced to 9 men. Guiliano Grazioli, having returned from Stevenage, scored 5.
- Arsenal's experiment of playing their home European Cup ties at Wembley misfired; they won only one out of three.
- Sheffield Wednesday's Paolo Di Canio was banned for 11 matches for his assault on referee Paul Alcock in their League match against Arsenal, a punishment slammed by referees as being too lenient.
- Sir Alf Ramsey, who gave English football its greatest triumph when he managed the World Cup winning team in 1966, died on 30 April at the age of 79.
- Kevin Keegan changed his mind about the England job in mid-May and severed his Fulham ties to sign a £1m-a-year contract as England's full-time senior coach to the end of the 2002 World Cup finals. Draws with Sweden and Bulgaria, however, left England with a lot to do to qualify for Euro 2000 next season.
- Teddy Sheringham scored the opening goal for Manchester United in the FA Cup final just 90 seconds after replacing the injured Roy Keane.
- Inter Milan, who did not qualify for Europe next season, smashed the world transfer record when they paid Lazio a reported £28m in June for striker Christian Vieri.
- Celtic announced their first technical director, their old star Kenny Dalglish, who will have his former Liverpool team-mate John Barnes as chief coach.

Man United win Holy Grail with a minute of magic

WHAT A cliffhanger! This magnificent Manchester United side simply refuse to give up. When all seemed lost, when the German jinx again appeared to hold sway over an English side, United drew on their reserves of stamina and playing staff in sensational fashion.

Teddy Sheringham and Ole Gunnar Solskjaer emerged from the dug-out to dig United out of trouble. Both struck in stoppage time to snatch a 2–1 victory and give United a record treble and the European Cup for the first time in 31 years — all on the anniversary of what would have been Sir Matt Busby's 90th birthday. It was brilliant and breathtaking, a finish that defied belief.

It had seemed all over. Familiar stories of German tactical discipline eclipsing English enthusiasm had been filed down countless telephone wires. But the nation's presses were stopped mid-turn, because United have ingrained within them a never-say-die spirit. They had been down for most of the match, since Mario Basler's fifth-minute free-kick. And Bayern had twice hit the woodwork late in the second half. Alex Ferguson's men had been out-thought by the Germans but never out-fought. They rode their luck, and when they hit back, it was like a thunderbolt.

Ole Gunnar Solskjaer celebrates his European Cup-winning goal.

The catalyst was David Beckham's corner-taking. His first flag kick swung over, and there was Peter Schmeichel, up from his goal, pressuring Bayern's proud defence. The ball flashed in a blur around the box, headed by Dwight Yorke back to Ryan Giggs, whose scuffed shot was hooked firmly in by Sheringham. United had done it again, and no one gave Bayern much chance in extra time now.

Extra time? Who needed it? The jubilant United fans had barely sat back in their seats when Gary Neville appeared on the left wing to force a corner. Beckham lifted in another gem, Sheringham glanced it on and Solskjaer, close in, pounced to volley it home. The meticulous Germans had been beaten by two set-pieces. Amazing.

It would be some time before United's accomplishment would sink in. And they had achieved it without the suspended Paul Scholes and Roy Keane's midfield drive and leadership. Schmeichel was captain in his last match for United, and, their saviour on so many occasions over the years, it was fitting that he lifted the coveted trophy.

FINAL SCORE

FOOTBALL LEAGUE
Premier Division: Manchester United
Top scorers: Jimmy Floyd Hasselbaink (Leeds), Michael Owen (Liverpool), Dwight Yorke (Manchester United) 18
Division 1: Sunderland
Division 2: Fulham
Division 3: Brentford
Footballer of the Year: David Ginola (Tottenham Hotspur)

FA Cup Final
Manchester United 2 Newcastle United 0

League Cup Final
Tottenham Hotspur 1 Leicester City 0

Scottish League
Premier Division: Rangers
Top scorer: Henrik Larsson (Celtic) 29
Division 1: Hibernian
Division 2: Livingston
Division 3: Ross County
Footballer of the Year: Henrik Larsson (Celtic)

Scottish FA Cup Final
Rangers 1 Celtic 0

Scottish League Cup Final
Rangers 2 St Johnstone 1

European Cup Final
Manchester United 2 Bayern Munich 1

Cup-Winners' Cup Final
Lazio 2 Real Mallorca 1

UEFA Cup Final
Parma 3 Marseille 0

European Footballer of the Year 1998
Zinedine Zidane (Juventus)

FIFA World Player of the Year 1998
Zinedine Zidane (Juventus & France)

World Club Campionship 1998
Real Madrid 2 Vasco Da Gama 1

Rangers' treble

NO CLASSIC — few Old Firm finals are — but Rangers completed a sixth domestic treble with a 1–0 defeat of Celtic at the rebuilt Hampden Park. A goal from Rod Wallace ensured that Dick Advocaat became the first foreign manager to supervise a clean sweep of domestic honours.

There was no hint of the nastiness that brought the Scottish game into disrepute when the teams met three weeks ago in the Scottish Premier League decider. Referee Hugh Dallas, the victim of a hooligan's coin that day, incurred the wrath of Celtic fans when correctly refusing them a penalty for handball in the dying minutes as a Paul Lambert shot cannoned off 'Gers captain Lorenzo Amoruso's arm.

But there was no violence this time. Celtic fans streamed out of Hampden as Rangers players tossed Advocaat into the air. When, eventually, he came down to earth, he revealed that he had accepted a new two-year contract.

Manchester City emulate United

IT MUST have been difficult for Manchester City supporters, living in the shadow of United's successes in the Nineties. While their team floundered around in the lower divisions, seeing one new dawn after another proving to be false, United piled triumph upon triumph.

The low point was reached in 1998, when the club was not only relegated to the Second Division, but also struggled to make an impression on runaway leaders Fulham and the chasing pack. A fine late season run ensured City's place in the play-offs, if not automatic promotion.

City defeated Wigan Athletic over two leags to reach the play-off final at Wembley. Gillingham were their opponents. Surely they would brush those soft southerners aside and begin their climb back to the top echelons of English football.

But City squandered their chances in the first half and nerves began to show. It took until the 81st minute to break the deadlock, and it was Gillingham who did it thanks to their record signing, at £500,000, Carl Asaba.

The sky-blue side of Wembley sat stunned and when, in the 86th minute, Asaba's confident back-heel allowed Robert Taylor to claim his 21st goal of the season with a thundering half-volley, thousands of City fans took to the exits.

But with six seconds of normal time left, Kevin Horlock pulled one back. City fans began to believe in the improbable. Then Dickov pounced on a deflected clearance and, in the fourth minute of added time, sent half of Wembley into delirium.

Police and stewards, to their credit, allowed City's departing fans back in to witness extra time and then penalties. City's 20-year-old keeper Nick Weaver made two saves and they won the shoot-out 3–1. It rounded off a wonderful week for the city of Manchester.

Heroes of the Nineties

By Henry Winter

Like little children locked in a sweet-shop, or gamblers blinking at three cherries with the "hold' button flashing, professional footballers have never had it so good as they did in the 1990s. A young man with a nice smile and an eye for goal can make his weight in gold. Ask Michael Owen, a millionaire while still a teenager. The beautiful game has become the bountiful one.

Agents clamour around the best footballers. Business covets them. They are offered lucrative boot contracts, sponsorships and modelling assignments. All the while, cash-registers ring merrily in the background, providing a fitting sound-track to the story of the heroes of the 1990s. Another day, another deal.

Money talks

Some time back, a Liverpool player asked his manager how much the fine would be if he missed a day's training. Told £10,000, he whipped out his chequebook, squiggled in the figure, handed it over and headed off on a day's modelling assignment, for which he was handsomely rewarded.

United by their magnetic attraction for the money men, the heroes of the Nineties are actually a diverse breed, from Bryan Robson to Ian Wright, Roy Keane to Alan Shearer. Some possess a dark side, a wilful streak of indiscipline while others make cub scouts look like Black Sabbath roadies.

Midfield magic

Any list of Nineties heroes is bound to be subjective, but two talented midfielders, Gary McAllister and Bryan Robson, deserve to be considered among the 10 most influential British footballers of the decade. McAllister earned championship success at Leeds United in 1992, but almost did not go to Elland Road, having held talks with Nottingham Forest on deciding to leave Leicester City.

Liverpool and England striker Michael Owen is a star of the future.

Paul Gascoigne enjoyed the highest of highs and lowest of lows.

Brian Clough, Forest's manager, asked the cowboy-boot-wearing Scot if he was related to John Wayne. McAllister rode off quickly up the M1 to Leeds, where his passing and leadership qualities brought swift success. His determination in the face of debilitating injury, his ready humour, intelligence and sense of responsibility makes the Scot one of the model professionals of the Nineties.

Robson was another who captained club and country with real pride. Manchester United's Englishman was a star who spanned the Eighties and Nineties, winning praise and prizes with his unmatched dynamism, his unquenched hunger and his ability to arrive in the box to score. Bobby Robson, his England manager, encapsulated his namesake's influence when he opined that England were "a taller, prouder team" when Bryan played.

Keane, a successor to Robson as United's driving force and leader, shared Robson's capacity to ensnare the headlines away from match-day, but few could live with the Irishman when the whistle went. Box to box, tackle to tackle, Keane was a coach's dream, particularly when he stopped becoming a referee's nightmare.

Sins and sinners

For a period, his United team-mates nicknamed the wild-eyed Irishman "Damien" after the crazed character in *The Omen*. Alex Ferguson described Keane as "the most victimized player in football". He was not. Keane sinned and was sinned against,

Roy Keane — the heart of soul of Manchester United's midfield.

but all his actions carried one trademark, that of a winner. The onset of maturity has simply made Keane a more popular one.

Far more controversial than Keane, Paul Gascoigne was the hero and tragic figure of the Nineties. His Italia 90 performances, and raging free-kick past Arsenal's David Seaman in the 1991 FA Cup semi-final, are the very stuff of sporting legend. Unfortunately, where Gascoigne the footballer was blessed with greatness, Gazza the tabloid fodder was touched by madness.

Like Gascoigne, Tony Adams found himself in the whirlwind, senses-shredding grip of an alcohol problem. A drink-driving offence brought incarceration for Adams, but he took his punishment like a man, just as he has done all the slings and arrows of his life. Through all the problems, the drinking, the marital tensions, Adams kept winning for Arsenal because that is the nature of the man. His sobering up, his shying away from the lads' night out stands as a symbol for the sea-change in English football.

Striking strikers

Many would question the right of Adams and, his old team-mate, Ian Wright, to be perceived as role models. But they are, having shown a willingness to address inner flaws. Wright, once a study in rage, made mistakes, such as his awful follow-through on Peter Schmeichel, the Manchester United goalkeeper. But Wright earned widespread respect and admiration because of his acquiring of self-control, his enthusiasm and ability to conjure goals from thin air.

Ebullience characterized him. Wright bounced out of a building site and into his first day's training at Crystal Palace with the declaration that we would play for England. He did and with real distinction at times. Some managers would have Wright in their squad simply for his uplifting personality.

Notwithstanding Wright's prolific career, Shearer has to be ranked the English striker of the Nineties, a championship-winner at Blackburn Rovers and serial scorer for his country. The Geordie's qualities, his indefatigability and desire to score, was acknowledged when Kenny Dalglish made Shearer Britain's most expensive player. Dalglish had no qualms, saying that Shearer "turns draws into victories".

Kevin Keegan then made Shearer the world's most expensive player for a time. His determination, in the face of injury or criticism, is awesome. If Stan Collymore possessed one-tenth of Shearer's mental strength, he would be a prodigious forward.

Alan Shearer was England's top scorer at Euro 96 and France 98.

Arsenal linchpin Tony Adams.

England's Alan

England's captain, who famously remarked that one of his hobbies was creosoting the fence, is often described as bland and boring in public. While at Blackburn, Graeme Le Saux observed that Shearer was "23 going on 50". But Shearer's job is not to entertain the nation with wisecracks and telling comments but to score goals which he does again and again and again.

If he had listened to Ferguson's sweet words of praise, Shearer could have been Manchester United's striker-in-chief, revelling in the crosses supplied by two photogenic but industrious wide men, Ryan Giggs and David Beckham. Both possess the skills to play the show-man but neither is showy. Giggs is remarkably sane given the flashbulb-popping attention he receives. Beckham enjoys the limelight and regular poses for fashion shoots. "But he isn't a superstar among the England lads," said Keegan. "He mixes fantastically."

So, too, does Owen, who became known across the globe the moment that fabulous strike crashed into Argentina's net at the World Cup. Owen's life has changed and so have people's reaction to him, but he himself hasn't, continuing to tease team-mates, see old friends and live close to his parents. Where the form of many international players dipped, life for Owen has never tasted sweeter.

Arise, Sir Alex

THE QUEEN ventured into football punditry, telling Sir Alex Ferguson that his achievement in winning a domestic and European treble was unlikely to be emulated. She made her prediction as she bestowed a knighthood on Sir Alex, the Manchester United manager, at Buckingham Palace. Sir Alex wore a kilt in the Ferguson tartan.

He said he had discussed horse racing with the Queen – a sport in which both are interested. "Her Majesty said she hoped I would have time for my horses – I own two and have shares in four. Football management is such a pressurised thing – horse racing is a release." Sir Alex also received the Freedom of the City of Manchester.

Sir Alex Ferguson wore the Ferguson tartan at his investiture.

Robson back where he belongs

BOBBY ROBSON returned to English football, at the age of 66, when he was named as successor to Ruud Gullit as manager of Newcastle United. The appointment was the fulfilment of a lifetime's ambition for Robson, who was returning to his native North East to become the club's sixth manager of the 1990s.

It was 17 years since he last managed a club side in England, taking Ipswich Town to unexpected success in the FA Cup and UEFA Cup. He later led England to a World Cup semi-final before working abroad. In nine seasons away from England, Robson was involved with five championship-winning teams: at PSV Eindhoven, Porto (twice each), and Barcelona (as director of football).

"My feeling is that my health is good, my motivation is very high and I've still got terrific ambition," he said. "My job is not to be in the office doing other things. My job is with the players. That's how I see myself."

Two years earlier, Newcastle had failed to recruit Robson because Barcelona refused to release him. When Robson arrived, on 3 September, Newcastle were 19th in the table after Gullit's disappointing spell. His first home game was against Sheffield Wednesday and the crowd watched in wonderment as Newcastle won 8–1, thanks mainly to five goals from Alan Shearer. Newcastle went on to reach an FA Cup semi-final and finished 11th in the Premiership.

Red shame gets worse

Dennis Wise was sent off for punching Liverpool's Vladimir Smicer.

IF THE AUTHORITIES thought the 21 dismissals on one day last season were bad, they were horrified to see no fewer than 26 players sent off in England and Scotland on 16 October – a record number of sending offs in one day. Of the total, 14 players saw red in England and a further 12 were given early baths north of the border.

In the Premiership, Warren Barton (Newcastle), Kevin Davies (Southampton) and Watford's Mark Williams all departed early, along with Chelsea's Dennis Wise – for the ninth time in his career – and team-mate Marcel Desailly. Wise was dismissed for striking Liverpool's Vladimir Smicer in a 1-0 defeat at Anfield.

In Division One, Nottingham Forest's player-manager David Platt, Manchester City's Kevin Horlock and Jim Magilton of Ipswich also were sent off. In Scotland, three players were shown red cards in the goalless draw between Airdrie and Dunfermline.

Hoddle returns a saint

ALMOST A YEAR after Glenn Hoddle relinquished his post as England coach, he returned to the Premiership as manager of Southampton, on 28 January. Hoddle's appointment, on an initial 12-month contract, came about when Southampton decided to allow Dave Jones leave of absence to concentrate on his impending trial, on charges of child abuse.

On the south coast, the scene was predictably chaotic as Hoddle returned. There was an air of a man on trial, but Hoddle wasted little time in responding with conviction to questions over the manner of his departure from the international scene and his relationship with faith healer Eileen Drewery. When asked if he regretted his comments, Hoddle said: "I'm glad you asked me that question, because I never said those things. They were not portrayed anywhere near what I was talking about. I know what I said, and those are not my beliefs – I never believed that's the punishment for disabled people. They were untruths and it's been unfortunate for anyone that it is the disabled who got upset about it. But that's life."

Hoddle, 42, joined a club with two Premiership wins from their last nine and in a relegation battle. Jones issued only a short statement, through his solicitors, which said he would not comment until he had continued talks with his lawyers. Southampton were 19th when Hoddle arrived, but he succeeded in keeping them in the Premiership, the club finishing in 17th place.

Glenn Hoddle returned to football management at Southampton.

United spurn FA Cup for Brazil

MANCHESTER UNITED, the holders, took the unprecedented step of withdrawing from the FA Cup after accepting an invitation from FIFA to take part in the World Club Championship in Brazil between 5 and 14 January.

The tournament coincided with the fourth round of the FA Cup and the participation of United, whose FA Cup success of 1999 formed part of their unique treble, was seen as important for a successful England bid to stage the 2006 World Cup.

Before the Football Association had suggested that United withdraw, they considered several alternatives, such as giving United a bye until the fifth round. That was considered impossible because to "parachute" a team into the fifth round would cause an enormous ripple-back effect on the tournament, and could mean 40 smaller clubs having to play another round of the FA Cup, or 20 Conference clubs coming into the competition two rounds earlier.

As a result, the FA had to have a "wild card" draw for the lucky loser, meaning that one of the 20 clubs to lose in the second round would get a second chance, to keep the numbers correct. The fortunate team, Darlington, having lost 3–1 at Gillingham in round two, were drawn to play at Aston Villa – where they lost 2–1.

United were keen not to play a considerably weakened side in the Cup, so took the reluctant step of withdrawing and flew to South America, where their participation in the World Club event was less than successful. They drew 1–1 with Necaxa, of Mexico, in Rio and, also in Rio, lost 3–1 to Vasca da Gama. They finished with a 2–0 win over the Australians of South Melbourne but failed to qualify for the final or third place play-off. Corinthians were the eventual winners, beating Vasco da Gama 3–1 on penalties after a 0–0 draw.

Manchester United failed to win the inaugural World Club Cup in Brazil, but they did spend three weeks in South American sunshine.

United hit for five on day of indiscipline

CHELSEA produced one of the the shocks of the Premiership season, on 3 October, when Manchester United were beaten 5–0 and lost their place at the top of the table. United arrived at Stamford Bridge after a nine-game unbeaten start to the season but Chelsea, whose only defeat so far had come at Watford, delivered a stunning challenge to Sir Alex Ferguson's championship contenders.

Chelsea opened the scoring after only 27 seconds, Gustavo Poyet beating Massimo Taibi, who had briefly unseated Mark Bosnich as United's first choice goalkeeper. Poyet added another, Chris Sutton – newly recalled to the England squad – supplied his first Premiership goal since arriving for £10 million from Blackburn, Henning Berg scored an own goal and Jody Morris completed the rout.

United had Nicky Butt sent off after 22 minutes for kicking Denis Wise, as they headed towards their first domestic defeat of 1999, let alone the season, their heaviest loss since the 5–0 reverse at Newcastle in October 1996 and their biggest defeat by Chelsea.

On the same day, Patrick Vieira, Arsenal's French international, spat at Neil Ruddock following his sending off in a 2–1 defeat at West Ham, who had Marc Vivien Foe dismissed. Vieira was later involved in an incident in the tunnel after being verbally abused by a West Ham fan. Gary Lewin, the Arsenal physiotherapist, and a police officer intervened before Vieira reached the changing rooms.

Vieira apologised for the incident, admitting his behaviour was "inexcusable" but he was heavily punished, receiving a six-game ban and a record £45,000 fine by the Football Association after being found guilty of two misconduct charges, relating to the spitting incident, swearing at a police officer and damaging the electronic board used by the fourth official in the tunnel.

SOCCER SOUNDBITES

"Can we play you every week?"

CHELSEA FANS taunt Manchester United fans during the 5-0 thrashing at Stamford Bridge.

"My behaviour after being sent off was inexcusable. Although I was subjected to provocation, I am ashamed of my action."

PATRICK VIEIRA, who was sent off against West Ham, then spat at Neil Ruddock. The Football Association imposed a record fine and long suspension on the Arsenal midfielder.

Wizard of the dribble dies, aged 85

The funeral cortege for Sir Stanley Matthews passes through the streets of Stoke-on-Trent.

SIR STANLEY MATTHEWS, one of England's greatest footballers, died in a Newcastle-under-Lyme hospital on 23 February after a short illness at the age of 85. The Wizard of the dribble, Sir Stanley, had had a fall while on holiday in Tenerife a week earlier and also had suffered heart problems.

It seemed somewhat fitting that the former Stoke City and Blackpool winger, who was capped 54 times for his country and twice became European Footballer of the Year, had died just two hours before England's friendly against Argentina at Wembley. The England players donned black armbands and there was a minute's silence at a stadium he graced so many times.

Born in Hanley, Staffordshire, on 1 February 1915, Sir Stanley joined Stoke at the age of 14 and turned professional at 17. He made 710 League appearances for Stoke and Blackpool. His career ran to the record-breaking age of 50 years and five days and was recognised with a knighthood shortly before he retired in 1965. Despite his stature as one of the game's greats he never earned more than £50 a week, plus £25 a game bonus.

"The ball ran for me today," Matthews would tell dazed opponents after a game, as though he genuinely did not understand what all the fuss was about. His mere presence on the right wing was enough to add 10,000 to the gate. While he was at Stoke in the Thirties, the average home crowd was 66,000.

The son of a featherweight boxer, Sir Stanley will be best remembered for his role in the 1953 FA Cup Final. With 20 minutes to go, Blackpool were 1–3 down to Bolton. Up to this point, Matthews had had a quiet game. Now, as the defence tired, he became irresistible. Stan Mortensen scored one from a Matthews cross and then scored again from a free kick. In injury time, Matthews ghosted past two defenders before cutting the ball back for Bill Perry, who hammered home the winner to beat Bolton 4–3. Outside Bolton, the entire country rejoiced.

For the funeral, police estimated more than 250,000 lined the streets of Stoke-on-Trent, believed to be the country's third largest funeral gathering outside the Royal Family. Sir Stanley had always said that he preferred the pitch when it was heavy and preferably raining. It magnified the trance in which he held defenders. As the hearse passed Stoke's old Victoria Ground, where he first played as an apprentice in the Thirties, the rain fell briefly, and there was bright sunshine.

Football lost another famous name on 14 April, when former Middlesbrough and England forward Wilf Mannion, known as the "Golden Boy", died aged 81.

SOCCER SOUNDBITES

"My abiding memory is of the sight of his disappearing No 7 on an orange shirt, and the relief that he was running the other way. The back of Stan is how most defenders remember him."

JIMMY ARMFIELD, former Blackpool and England fullback.

Elliott double sinks Tranmere

LEICESTER City claimed the Worthington Cup, on 27 February, securing their place in Europe with a 2–1 win in an intoxicating final against First Division Tranmere Rovers, thanks to two goals from Matt Elliott. The game also included two referees and one red card. Tranmere's Clint Hill was sent off – for the 10th time – for a professional foul on Emile Heskey, taking the legs and a handful of the shirt of the England striker who was through on goal.

Elliott's first goal put Leicester on track for a victory. But David Kelly equalised, and extra time looked likely until Elliott struck again nine minutes from the end. Referee Alan Wilkie lasted only 57 minutes. He injured a calf, left on a stretcher and was replaced by Phil Richards. Possibly the happiest man on the pitch was Leicester's veteran striker Tony Cottee, who finally won a winner's medal.

The earlier stages were highlighted by a remarkable administrative error by West Ham. In a fifth round tie at Upton Park, Hammers drew 2–2 with Aston Villa and went on to win 5–4 on penalties. But it was later noted that West Ham included Manny Omoyimni for the final six minutes of extra time – even though he had appeared for Gillingham in the competition in the second round, while on loan.

West Ham hoped merely to be fined for what manager, Harry Redknapp, called a "genuine mistake" in playing Omoyimni, but risked expulsion. The 21-year-old forgot he had been involved with Gillingham but the Football League decided, instead, to replay the game and, again, it went into extra time after finishing 1–1 in 90 minutes. This time Villa won 3–1, and later, two West Ham office staff resigned.

Manny Omoyimni played for West Ham and Gillingham in the 1999–2000 League Cup.

Tragedy mars European adventure

A Galatasaray shirt lies on top of a Manchester United scarf and floral tributes as football mourned.

ENGLISH clubs' European campaigns were tarnished by the deaths of two Leeds fans, in Istanbul, on 5 April. Manchester United relinquished their Champions' League crown at the quarter final stage while Arsenal went on to reach the UEFA Cup final, losing to Galatasary. But it was the deaths of Christopher Loftus and Kevin Speight the night before Leeds's UEFA Cup semi-final, first leg, that overshadowed the rest of the competition.

The tragedy put the tie into perspective. Leeds lost 2–0 in the Ali Sami Yen stadium where Leeds' fans were upset by the fact that there was no minute's silence and the home side did not wear black armbands.

Leeds insisted the second leg be played at Elland Road, warning they would consider withdrawing if the match were switched to a neutral venue. The game went ahead at Elland Road, with Galatasaray sending 11 members of an anti-terrorist group to protect their players.

For the second leg, Peter Ridsdale, the Leeds chairman who had helped identify one of the victims in Turkey, appealed for calm with a newspaper advert. The depression caused by the tragedy did not help Leeds's players; they lost 4–0 at home to Arsenal before the return leg.

Even with a ban enforced by UEFA, Turkish businesses in Leeds were offered protection. All police leave was cancelled and reinforcements summoned from neighbouring counties, while an extra 200 stewards, all wearing black armbands, were drafted into the stadium.

At 7.20pm Galatasaray ran on to the pitch, wearing black for the warm-up as a mark of respect to the dead fans, and bearing flowers which they laid on the soaked Yorkshire soil to some applause. Claudio Taffarel, their Brazilian goalkeeper, broke ranks and handed his bouquet to a Leeds fan.

The emotion of the evening was too much for Leeds. Galatasaray were 2–0 up by half time and though Eirik Bakke scored twice for Leeds, they had Harry Kewell sent off and hopes of an all-English final evaporated.

In the other semi-final, Arsenal, who having been knocked out of the Champions' League, had overcome Nantes, Deportivo La Coruña and Werder Bremen, beat Lens 1–0 at home in the first leg and, in the second leg in France won 2–1 thanks to an 86th minute winner from Kanu.

Security ahead of the final, in Copenhagen, between Arsenal and Galatasaray, was of paramount concern and, perhaps predictably, there were further scenes of violence. At least five fans were seriously injured as hundreds of Galatasaray and Arsenal supporters fought a 45-minute running battle before the start.

The game itself was a disappointment; after a goalless draw, Galatasaray, the first Turkish team to reach a major final, won 4–1 on penalties in Copenhagen's Parken Stadium after both Davor Suker and Patrick Vieira missed from the spot. Galatasary also had Gheorghe Hagi sent off for striking Arsenal's Tony Adams.

In the Champions' League, both Manchester United and Chelsea reached the quarter-finals. Chelsea enjoyed a remarkable campaign including a 5–0 win against Galatasaray in Istanbul and, having beaten Barcelona 3–1 at Stamford Bridge in the first leg of their quarter final, forced the tie into extra time in the Nou Camp. Rivaldo gave Barcelona the lead and Luis Figo added a second. Tore Andre Flo replied for Chelsea but another Barcelona goal, by Dani, took the tie into overtime.

Rivaldo, who had missed a penalty in the 86th minute, made no mistake the second time in the 98th minute after Celestine Babayaro had been sent off for bringing down Patrick Kluivert, who completed a remarkable 6–4 win for Barcelona. United, meanwhile, held Real Madrid to a goalless draw in the Bernabeu thanks to a fantastic display by Mark Bosnich but, at Old Trafford, Roy Keane put through his own goal and then Raul struck twice after the break. David Beckham reduced the arrears with a sensational reply and Paul Scholes struck a penalty late on but United had paid for their early mistake.

Real beat Bayern Munich in the semi-final before overcoming Valencia 3–0 in impressive fashion in Paris, with Steve McManaman scoring the second goal.

Ruud awakening for United signing

Ruud van Nistelrooy (right) greets United fans when his transfer was announced, but it all went wrong.

ON 20 APRIL, Manchester United announced the £18.5 million signing of PSV Eindhoven striker Ruud van Nistelrooy, breaking the British transfer record. The Dutchman watched United beat Chelsea prior to a taking a medical but he failed the tests, returned to Holland – and, while attempting to prove his fitness, broke down in agony while training with PSV. He let out a yell after falling awkwardly and hobbled off the pitch.

He was taken to hospital where an exploratory operation revealed that van Nistelrooy, 23, who was already known to be suffering from a medial ligament injury, had damaged anterior cruciate ligaments in his right knee. Ironically, he had earlier refused United's requests to undergo keyhole surgery to discover the extent of the problem. United insist they will remain interested in signing him.

Play-off joy for Keegan

ALAN SHEARER scored his first hat-trick for England in a 6–0 Euro 2000 qualifying rout of Luxembourg, at Wembley, on 4 September. It was a perfect response from Shearer, whose performances had been attracting mounting criticism.

Kieron Dyer made an impressive debut, while two goals from Steve McManaman and another, by Michael Owen, put Kevin Keegan's team in second place in Group Five, level on points with chief rivals Poland but with a better goal difference. It was the first of the two wins they needed to be sure of qualifying for the play-offs.

But a goalless draw in Warsaw four days later against a backdrop of sporadic but nasty crowd violence, meant that England's hopes had dwindled. David Batty was sent off and the Poles needed only to avoid defeat in Stockholm, on 9 October, to progress to November's play-offs at England's expense, Sweden already were guaranteed a place in Euro 2000 as group winners.

England attacked gallantly but relied on the determined defending of Tony Adams and, two minutes from time a superb save from Nigel Martyn to deny Andrzej Juskowiak, to retain some semblance of interest in Euro 2000.

However, Sweden were determined to do their best and, on a dank, cold Stockholm afternoon, Poland lost 2–0, and so England made it into the play-offs. Kennet Andersen and Henrik Larsson scored to help Sweden end their programme with seven wins in eight games.

The draw for the play-offs was made in Aachen and England got what they had feared – a tie against Scotland. It did mean, however, that they avoided trips to Ukraine, Turkey or Slovenia. The Republic of Ireland, meanwhile, were drawn against Turkey.

In the first leg, at Hampden Park, on November 13. England won 2–0, thanks to two goals from Paul Scholes. Ireland, meanwhile, drew 1–1 with Turkey in Dublin. In the return, at Wembley, four days later, England survived most of a Tartan onslaught. Scotland were the better team and won 1–0 with a goal from Don Hutchison, but it was not enough to take Craig Brown's team through. The Republic of Ireland's campaign also came to an end when they drew 0–0 in Bursa and went out on away goals. In the other play-offs, Denmark overcame Israel and Slovenia beat Ukraine.

SOCCER SOUNDBITES

"Tusen tack"

KEVIN KEEGAN saying a "thousand thanks" to the Swedes in their native language.

FOOTBALL FOCUS

- Sammy McIlroy left Macclesfield to become manager of Northern Ireland while Mark Hughes was given control of Wales.
- Arsenal sold Nicolas Anelka to Real Madrid for £22.9 million after lodging official protests to FIFA and the FA about an illegal approach.
- The final of the Women's World Cup in the Rose Bowl, Pasadena, was watched by 90,185, the largest crowd to attend a women's sporting event. The US beat China 5–4 on penalties.
- The Football Association named Geoff Thompson as chairman and Adam Crozier as chief executive.
- Torquay's Worthington Cup tie against Portsmouth was postponed because it clashed with the solar eclipse and the pressure of visitors to the town was too much for police.
- Robbie Keane, a 19-year-old Irishman, became the most expensive teenager in British football history when he joined Coventry from Wolves for £6 million.
- UEFA award Euro 2004 to Portugal, who beat favourites Spain and a joint bid by Austria and Hungary.
- On 26 December, Chelsea made history when they played against Southampton at The Dell without a single British player in their starting line-up.
- The five "forgotten" members of England's 1966 World Cup winning team received MBEs: Alan Ball, Nobby Stiles, George Cohen, Ray Wilson and Roger Hunt.
- The Scottish League Cup first round tie between Clydebank and East Stirling, on 31 July, had a paid attendance of only 29, the lowest crowd for a competitive Scottish fixture. Clydebank were homeless and played at Greenock Morton's Cappielow Park ground.
- Owen Price, 14, scored what is believed to be the fastest ever goal, timed at 4.07 seconds, for Ernest Bevan College against Barking Abbey in the Heinz Keutchup Cup Final at Highbury in May.
- Premiership action entered the electronic age when referees were linked to their assistants by two-way radios.

Super Cally

CELTIC suffered arguably the most humiliating result in their 112-year history when they went out of the Tennent's Scottish Cup in the third round against First Division Inverness Caledonian Thistle on 8 February.

John Barnes and his assembly of expensive international stars were eclipsed by a spirited and inventive side, who were accorded generous salutes by the home supporters as they left the field. Barry Wilson gave Inverness the lead, Mark Burchill responded for Celtic but an own goal by Lubomir Moravcik followed by a penalty from Paul Sheerin gave the Highlanders an unforgettable 3–1 victory.

Inverness fell to Aberdeen in a fourth round replay. They went on to reach the final, only to lose 4-0 to Rangers, completing their latest double, having won the Premier League by 18 points ahead of Celtic, who were able to claim CIS Scottish league Cup as consolation, with Aberdeen again the beaten finalists. Changes to the SPL meant that two new clubs were voted into the SFL – Elgin City and Peterhead, both from the Highland League.

SOCCER SOUNDBITES

"Super Cally go ballistic, Celtic are atrocious."

HEADLINE proclaiming Inverness Caledonian Thistle's win over Celtic.

Inverness Caledonian Thistle players celebrate at Celtic Park.

Easy does it for United

MANCHESTER UNITED claimed their sixth title in eight years on 22 April, with four games to spare, when they won 3–1 at Southampton with goals from David Beckham, Ole Gunnar Solsjkaer and a Francis Benali own goal. United had started the season by losing the Charity Shield but the success at The Dell was their seventh successive victory and they went on to win the remaining four to finish the season with records galore.

Teddy Sheringham's 65th-minute goal in an inconsequential game at Aston Villa on the season's final day, couple with Arsenal's 4–2 defeat at Newcastle allowed United to win the title by 18 points, an all-time top division record which eclipsed Everton's 13-point margin in 1985. In addition, they claimed more victories, 28, than any other team in this or any of the previous seven Premiership seasons. Their 11th successive League win was another first in the Premiership.

The 97 goals United scored beat the 82-goal Premiership record set by Newcastle in 1994 while their average attendance at Old Trafford – 58,017 – was also a Premiership record. Top scorer was Dwight Yorke, with 20 while, interestingly, 14 of Andy Cole's 19 League goals were scored at Old Trafford. United lost only three games – equalling their record fewest defeats, set in the previous season. United also failed to score in only two games, at Chelsea and Newcastle, equalling the club record set in the 1967–68 season.

Dwight Yorke (left) and Andy Cole celebrate another league title.

FINAL SCORE

FOOTBALL LEAGUE
Premier Division: Manchester United
Top scorer: Kevin Phillips (Sunderland) 30
Division 1: Charlton Athletic
Division 2: Preston North End
Division 3: Swansea City
Footballer of the Year: Roy Keane (Manchester United)

FA Cup Final
Chelsea 1 Aston Villa 0

League Cup Final
Leicester City 2 Tranmere Rovers 1

Scottish League
Premier Division: Rangers
Top scorer: Mark Viduka (Celtic) 25
Division 1: St Mirren
Division 2: Clyde
Division 3: Queens Park
Footballer of the Year: Barry Ferguson (Rangers)

Scottish FA Cup Final
Rangers 4 Aberdeen 0

Scottish League Cup Final
Celtic 2 Aberdeen 1

European Cup Final
Real Madrid 3 Valencia 0

UEFA Cup Final
Arsenal 0 Galatasaray 0
(aet. Galatasaray win 4–1 on penalties)

European Footballer of the Year 1999
Rivaldo (Barcelona)

FIFA World Player of the Year 1999
Rivaldo (Barcelona and Brazil)

World Club Cup
Corinthians 0 Vasco Da Gama 0
(aet. Corinthians win 3–1 on penalties)

FIFA Intercontinental Cup 1999
Manchester United 1 Palmeiras 0

France's Dutch delight

For the first time, the finals of a major tournament were held jointly by two countries, with the games shared by Belgium and Holland. Sceptics were soon silenced as Euro 2000 turned into a colourful festival of football. France became the first World Cup holders to then claim the European crown. The Final, like so many of the enthralling games before it, had a dramatic conclusion.

THE LOGISTICS OF staging a tournament in two nations were always going to be tough, but Belgian-Dutch co-operation meant that the competition went off generally smoothly. It started in Belgium, on June 10, and finished in Holland on July 2; in between there were very few poor games. A feast of entertainment and a spirit of adventure produced a record 85 goals in 31 matches.

The format for the 16-team tournament was the same as in Euro 96, with the top two from each of four groups of four going to the quarter-finals, from where the tournament became a knockout competition with the "Golden Goal" rule enforced in extra-time. Eight stadiums were used, four each in Holland – at Amsterdam, Eindhoven, Rotterdam and Arnhem – and Belgium – at Liege, Bruges, Brussels and Charleroi.

Referees were determined to clamp down on foul play. Worried that violence on the field of play might ignite hooliganism off it, UEFA reminded the referees that all dangerous tackles should be punished automatically with a red card. They heeded the warning, showing 10 red cards.

Phil Neville is consoled by David Beckham (7) after he gave away the late penalty.

Standard set

The opening game, in Brussels, between Belgium and Sweden started slowly, but turned into a thriller. Little happened for the opening 42 minutes, but Bart Goor's goal for Belgium changed all that. When, 30 seconds after the resumption, Emile Mpenza almost lifted the roof off the stadium with a spectacular second, the scene was set for frantic action. Sweden attacked and got a lifeline when Belgian goalkeeper Filip de Wilde slipped, allowing Johan Mjallby to score, but Belgium held on.

France, Italy and Holland, the three main favourites, all won their opening games. In Arnhem, Italy needed a penalty to finally overcome Turkey 2–1 and Holland's 1–0 win over Euro 96 finalists the Czech Republic also came from the penalty spot. In Bruges, France enjoyed a 3–0 win over Denmark.

England opened against Portugal, in Eindhoven, and when they led 2–0 after 18 minutes, through Paul Scholes and Steve McManaman, they began to believe they could make up for 34 years of hurt. How wrong they were. Luis Figo replied for Portugal four minutes later and Joao Pinto headed Portugal level in the 37th minute. Portugal claimed the winning goal through Nuno Gomes. Reigning champions Germany were held 1–1 by Romania in Liege, while Norway stole a 1–0 victory over Spain in Rotterdam.

Early promise

If Euro 2000 had shown early promise, the tournament took off in Charleroi when Yugoslavia met the unknown Slovenians, who had gained independence from Yugoslavia in 1991. Slovenia led 3–0 after an hour, courtesy of two goals and an assist from Zlatko Zahovic. But substitute Ljubinko Drulovic and Savo Milosevic, twice, replied for Yugoslavia.

Italy, France, Holland and Portugal claimed quarter-finals places by winning their second games. In Charleroi, England met Germany with both countries desperate for a win after bad results. Not since the 1966 World Cup final had England beaten the Germans in a competitive game. The game, and some old scores, were settled when Alan Shearer directed a clever header into the German net. In Amsterdam, Slovenia went down 2–1 to Spain, while Yugoslavia defeated Norway.

Co-hosts Belgium exited Euro 2000 disappointingly with a 2–0 defeat by Turkey, courtesy of more aberrations from de Wilde who, after errors of judgement had given Davor Suker two goals, completed a miserable personal tournament with a red card.

England faced Romania in Charleroi needing just a point for qualification. David Seaman was injured in the warm-up and was replaced by Nigel Martyn. Romania took the lead through Cristian Chivu – at 19, the tournament's youngest player – but Shearer scored with a penalty and Michael Owen put England ahead in the last minute of the first half. However, it all went wrong in the second half. Dorinel Munteanu equalised following a weak punch by Martyn and after strong Romanian pressure, Phil Neville fouled Viorel Moldovan and Ioan Ganea converted a last-minute penalty. England were out, as were Germany, after Portugal won 3–0, Sergio Conceicao scoring all three.

Still vibrant

Despite the exits of Belgium, England and Germany, the tournament still had much to offer. In Bruges, Spain squeezed victory from a seven-goal thriller against Yugoslavia. If Yugoslavia's comeback against Slovenia had been spectacular, Spain's response to being a goal down in added time was nothing short of spectacular. Yugoslavia led 3–2, three minutes into the seven of added time, but

FOOTBALL FOCUS

- After every match fans were invited to submit their individual player ratings on UEFA's official Euro 2000 website. No fewer than 358,940 votes were cast, determining the supporters' Team of the Tournament. The Team was: Toldo (Italy), Thuram (France), Maldini (Italy), Davids (Holland), Cannavaro (Italy), Nesta (Italy), Figo (Portugal), Totti (Italy), Kluivert (Holland), Zidane (France), Zenden (Holland).

- Roger Lemerre had a short spell of compassionate leave after the game against the Czech Republic in order to be with his dying father. Sadly, Maurice Lemerre, 86, died before his son could get to his side.

- Four pairs of brothers played for their countries: Belgium's Emile and Mbo Mpenza, England's Gary and Phil Neville, Sweden's Patrik and Daniel Andersson and Holland's Frank and Ronald de Boer.

- No fewer than 10 red cards were shown. Yugoslavia collected one in each of their first three matches, with Sinisa Mihajlovic, Jovan Stankovic and Mateja Kezman all sent off. Others to be dismissed included Patrik Andersson, Filip de Wilde, Gheorghe Hagi and Alpay Özalan. Nuno Gomes received his red card after the final whistle of Portugal's semi-final against France, but the strangest sending was that of Czech midfielder Radoslav Látal who was dismissed from the dug-out, having already been substituted against Holland.

Gaizka Mendieta then converted a penalty; in the sixth, Alfonso poached a winner. Not only did the win take Spain through with Yugoslavia, it meant Norway, who played out a tedious 0–0 draw with Slovenia, were out.

The final group games saw the Czech Republic beat Denmark 2–0, leaving the Danes goalless and pointless, while France met Holland in Amsterdam. France – group leaders on goal difference – rested nine players but still led twice. Holland, desperate to stay at home during the knock-out stages, equalised twice and won 3–2 to achieve their aim.

If the group games had offered a fascinating start to the tournament, the second phase did not disappoint. Hosts in 2004, Portugal had shown, that they were emerging as potential winners, and they overcame Turkey 2–0. Italy beat Romania by the same score. Sadly, Gheorghe Hagi's final competitive international in a career spanning three World Cups, two European Championships and 125 internationals ended with a red card.

If Holland had been confident before they met Yugoslavia in Rotterdam, they were totally exuberant after winning 6–1. The Yugoslavs were mainly undone by a Patrick Kluivert hat-trick. Milosevic's late strike was barely a consolation, but it did win him the Golden Boot with six goals.

Fascinating contest

France met Spain in a controversial and dramatic tie in Bruges. Zinedine Zidane gave France a lead, but Mendieta equalised with a penalty. France regained the lead, Youri Djorkaeff scoring with a blistering shot. In the dying minutes, Fabien Barthez pulled down Abelardo but with Mendieta taken off, Raul took the kick – and missed.

So Portugal met France in the Brussels semi-final and with Rui Costa and Luis Figo so influential in earlier games, the Portuguese had real hopes of reaching the Final. They took the lead through Nuno Gomes and dominated the first half. Five minutes after half-time France equalised through Thierry Henry. Now the French were on top, claiming a succession of corners and creating chance after chance.

The game went into extra time and was heading for penalties until, in the 117th minute, Zidane converted a penalty after Abel Xavier had handled Sylvain Wiltord's cross. The Portuguese protested bitterly, believing the handball was accidental and rushed to assistant referee Igor Sramka, whose raised flag had alerted referee Gunter Benko to the incident. Portugal's excessive protests led to long suspensions for Xavier (nine months), Nuno Gomes (eight months) and Paulo Bento (six months) from all UEFA competitions.

Dutch spot of bother

The other semi-final was every bit as dramatic, with Italy taking their place in the Final after winning a fascinating contest against the Dutch on penalties in Amsterdam. Francesco Toldo only played because of a pre-tournament injury to first choice Gianluigi Buffon, but he inspired the Italians. He saved a first-half spot-kick from Frank de Boer and when Kluivert hit a post with a second-half penalty, Italy began to believe. In extra time Marco Delvecchio squandered two chances for Italy and the game ended goalless. When Paul Bosvelt saw his shoot-out effort saved by Toldo, Italy were victorious.

Three weeks of marvellous entertainment, excitement, drama and controversy culminated in a Final with all of the those features. France claimed another trophy thanks to another Golden Goal. A succession of chances were created in a tight opening, the best falling to Didier Deschamps who shot over. With Thierry Henry proving a handful, France held the upper hand though Francesco Totti threatened to score for Italy.

Italy replaced Stefano Fiore with Alessandro Del Piero, in the 53rd minute, and he made an early impression, helping Italy claim the game's first goal, two minutes after his introduction. Totti fed Pessotto and his centre was volleyed home by Delvecchio. Italy were in charge, but Delvecchio and Del Piero missed great opportunities. Time was running out for France, who brought on Wiltord, David Trezeguet and Robert Pires. In added time, Wiltord cut in from the left to beat Toldo and extra time was needed.

In the 103rd minute, Fabio Cannavaro, normally so assured in his clearances, played Demetrio Albertini into trouble, Pires created more space, allowing Trezeguet, due to join new club Juventus after the tournament, to claim a breath-taking strike and win the Final.

Euro 2000 was considered the finest European Championship to be staged so far. As the golden petals rained down on Deschamps and his conquering French team while they paraded the Henri Delaunay trophy, few could think of a more fitting ending to the first senior final of the 21st century.

Referee Gunter Benko flourishes the red card as Portugal's players argue against his penalty decision to France in the semi-final.

FINAL SCORE

FIRST ROUND

Group A

Romania	1	Germany	1
Portugal	3	England	2
Portugal	1	Romania	0
England	1	Germany	0
Portugal	3	Germany	0
Romania	3	England	2

	P	W	D	L	F	A	P
Portugal	3	3	0	0	7	2	9
Romania	3	1	1	1	4	4	4
England	3	1	0	2	5	6	3
Germany	3	0	1	2	1	5	1

Group B

Belgium	2	Sweden	1
Italy	2	Turkey	1
Italy	2	Belgium	0
Sweden	0	Turkey	0
Turkey	2	Belgium	0
Italy	2	Sweden	1

	P	W	D	L	F	A	P
Italy	3	3	0	0	6	2	7
Turkey	3	1	1	1	3	2	4
Belgium	3	1	0	2	3	5	3
Sweden	3	0	1	2	1	4	1

Group C

Norway	1	Spain	0
Slovenia	3	Yugoslavia	3
Spain	2	Slovenia	1
Yugoslavia	1	Norway	0
Norway	0	Slovenia	0
Spain	4	Yugoslavia	3

	P	W	D	L	F	A	P
Spain	3	2	0	1	6	5	6
Yugoslavia	3	1	1	1	7	7	4
Norway	3	1	1	1	1	1	4
Slovenia	3	0	2	1	4	5	2

Group D

France	3	Denmark	0
Holland	1	Czech Republic	0
France	2	Czech Republic	1
Holland	3	Denmark	0
Holland	3	France	2
Czech Republic	2	Denmark	0

	P	W	D	L	F	A	P
Holland	3	3	0	0	7	2	9
France	3	2	0	1	7	4	6
Czech Rep	3	1	0	2	3	3	4
Denmark	3	0	0	3	0	6	0

QUARTER-FINALS

Portugal	2	Turkey	0
Italy	2	Romania	0
Holland	6	Yugoslavia	1
France	2	Spain	1

SEMI-FINALS

France	2	Portugal	1

1–1 90 min.; France scored Golden Goal

Italy	0	Holland	0

(aet. Italy won 3–1 on penalties)

FINAL

France	2	Italy	1

1–1 90 min.; France scored Golden Goal

Rotterdam, 2 July 2000. Attendance 50,000

France: Barthez; Thuram, Lizarazu (Pires), Vieira, Blanc, Desailly, Deschamps, Dugarry (Wiltord), Henry, Zidane, Djorkaeff (Trezeguet).
Italy: Toldo; Cannovaro, Maldini, Pessotto, Nesta, Iuliano, Delvecchio (Montella), Albertini, Totti, Di Biagio (Ambrosini), Fiore (Del Piero).

Leading scorers
5 Kluivert (Holland), Milosevic (Yugoslavia)
4 Nuno Gomes (Portugal),
3 Henry (France), Conceicao (Portugal), Zahovic (Slovenia)

Rio moves as records tumble

RIO FERDINAND became the world's most expensive defender as transfer records tumbled both at home and abroad. The West Ham player also became the most expensive footballer in Britain after his £18-million move to Leeds United in November. The fee eclipsed both the £15 million Newcastle paid Blackburn for Alan Shearer and the £10.75 million Manchester United paid PSV Eindhoven for central defender Jaap Stam in 1998.

United, though, later set the record for the highest transfer fee paid when Ruud van Nistelrooy, whose dream move had broken down a year earlier, finally agreed to a £19-million switch to Old Trafford from PSV in time for next season.

Fees were tumbling elsewhere; Luis Figo, later to be named European Football of the Year, joined Real Madrid from Barcelona for £37.4 million, only weeks after Parma's Hernan Crespo had joined Lazio for £36 million.

However, fears that the transfer system could crumble were voiced throughout the season as the European Commission sought to outlaw the existing FIFA international transfer regulations, claiming they violated the Treaty of Rome.

After months of negotiations a new system was agreed, to come into force next season. The new agreement means that, in future, players can only be transferred during one transfer window in the close season, with a limited window available during the winter break enjoyed by most other European countries.

Deft defending: Rio Ferdinand.

FA sows new seeds

THE FOOTBALL ASSOCIATION announced, in February, that it was to build England's new National Football Centre – "the biggest and best of its kind in the world" – for a completion date of 2003. The £30-million, state-of-the-art base is to be built on a 350-acre site near Burton-on-Trent, in Derbyshire, and is partly modelled on France's successful academy at Clairefontaine, near Paris, which produced the golden generation that captured the 1998 World Cup and 2000 European Championship. Accommodation will be of a "high to excellent" standard and the prime function will be as a preparatory centre for the national team before games.

Taylor goes in a series of surprises

New broom: Gianluca Vialli is unveiled as Watford's new manager.

AFTER 29 years in football management, Graham Taylor announced he was to retire. The former England manager, at the age of 56, decided to finish his days at Watford, where he enjoyed his greatest success over two spells.

Taylor took Watford to an FA Cup final and runners-up place in the old First Division and later won promotion to the Premiership, after winning the play-off final. He will be replaced by former Chelsea manager Gianluca Vialli.

Vialli was one of several high-profile Premiership victims during the season. The Italian lasted five Premiership games at Chelsea before being sacked, and was later replaced by Claudio Ranieri, the Italian formerly at Valencia.

Gerry Francis, the former Spurs manager, left Queens Park Rangers in February, and in March the shock news came that George Graham was leaving Spurs, ousted by ENIC, the new owners of Tottenham.

Sir Alan Sugar had relinquished ownership of Spurs to ENIC and Graham was the first victim, sacked by David Buchler, the club's new vice-chairman.

Spurs immediately moved for former favourite Glenn Hoddle, who had returned to management at Southampton after his fateful time as England coach.

But perhaps the biggest surprise was the announcement that Harry Redknapp was leaving West Ham, 37 years after first joining the club. Redknapp saw the Hammers secure their place in the Premiership for another season: then the club claimed he had "agreed to part company". Redknapp had been in charge for seven years and was only the eighth manager in West Ham's history.

At the end of the season another Premiership manager departed, with Joe Royle being sacked by Manchester City following the club's relegation to the First Division. In his place came Kevin Keegan, the former England coach, making a shock return to club management seven months after quitting his national role.

One man who made a surprise reappearance in management was Terry Venables. The former England coach rejected an earlier offer from Middlesbrough chairman Steve Gibson to aid Bryan Robson's flagging outfit, citing commitments in the coming season to ITV's new football coverage.

He was persuaded to take over as head coach in the short term and the response to his arrival was nothing short of a miracle as Boro' rallied to safety.

SOCCER SOUNDBITES

"Anyone who cares for Spurs will see this is a bizarre and inexplicable decision."

GEORGE GRAHAM, Tottenham manager after his sacking

African tragedies threaten World Cup

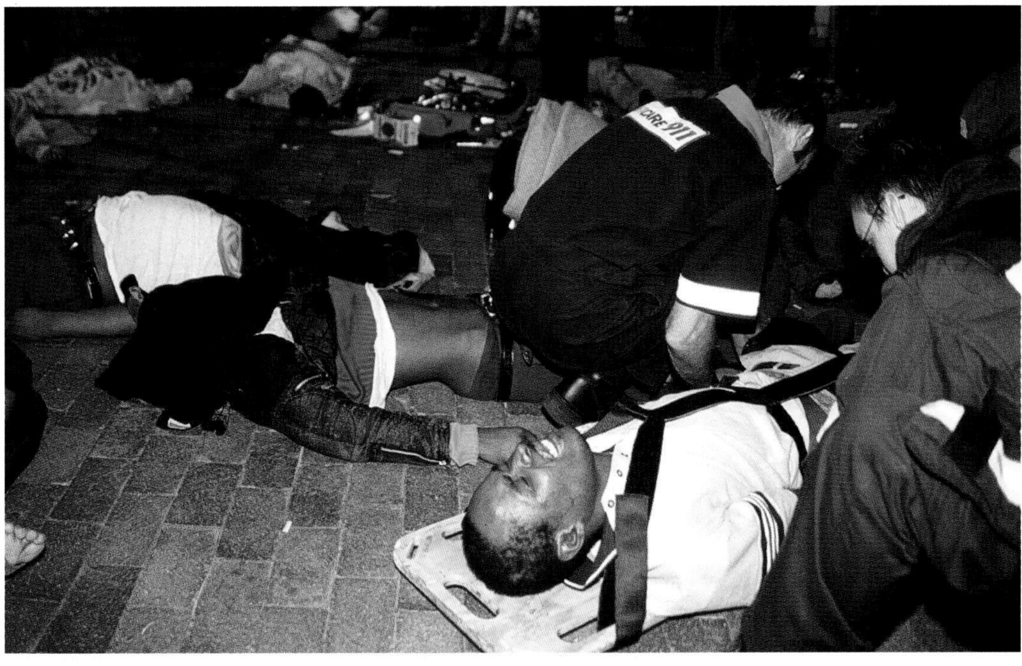

Ellis Park victims: 43 people were crushed to death in Johannesburg.

THERE WAS a succession of tragedies at football stadiums in Africa, which opened an argument as to whether the continent was fit to stage the World Cup finals in 2010. The first took place in Harare in July, when 13 supporters were crushed to death after police fired tear-gas into a 50,000 crowd to quell growing unruliness.

In April, 43 people died and 155 were injured at Ellis Park, Johannesburg, during the game between Orlando Pirates and Kaizer Chiefs when thousands of fans surged into a ground already full. FIFA, which had promised South Africa the World Cup, responded by insisting the disaster would not affect their chances.

But there was a worse disaster the following month when 126 fans died at the 45,000-capacity Accra Stadium in Ghana's capital. Hearts of Oak were leading 2–1 against Asante Kotoko of Kumasi with five minutes left in the match when Asante supporters began throwing bottles and chairs on to the field.

Police responded by firing tear-gas, creating panic in the stands as spectators rushed to escape but, according to witnesses, the main gate was locked.

Germany wins World Cup

DESPITE interventions by Nelson Mandela and the King of Belgium and even talk of death threats to one member of the FIFA executive, South Africa failed to take the 2006 World Cup to Africa.

They lost by just one vote – 12–11 – to Germany, with Charles Dempsey, from New Zealand, abstaining.

England's hopes of staging the event had been thwarted earlier. After a three-and-a-half year campaign costing £10 million, England secured five votes in the first ballot, but were eliminated after securing only two in the second.

Alec McGivan, who headed the campaign, claimed that hooliganism during Euro 2000 had undermined any chance of success.

An extraordinary day began for Dempsey at 6.30am when he was phoned by Nelson Mandela.

The former South African president pleaded with Dempsey – who was known to be backing England – to switch to South Africa once England were eliminated.

But before the vote began the 78-year-old Dempsey read out a letter, drafted by a lawyer in Auckland, saying that as he had been falsely accused of taking bribes and had received death-threats, he would withdraw from the voting process once England were out. South Africa considered making a legal challenge to the decision but were later assured that they would be awarded the 2010 World Cup finals.

United again

MANCHESTER UNITED won the title again, securing the Premiership earlier than at any time during their previous six successful campaigns. United romped to their seventh Premiership win in nine seasons.

Their highlight was the remarkable 6–1 win over closest challengers Arsenal in February, United's best win over the Gunners for 44 years, taking them 16 points clear.

The world's richest club declared its intentions off the pitch; in February they announced a multi-billion-dollar sporting franchise link-up with the New York Yankees, the world's biggest baseball team.

On the pitch, United continued to dominate and won the title on 14 April. Manchester having beaten Coventry 4–2 in the morning, it was down to Arsenal to beat Middlesbrough at Highbury. Yet, remarkably, Boro' found themselves two goals up at half-time despite having failed to put a shot on target, thanks to own-goals by Edu and Silvinho. Boro' took charge and Hamilton Ricard's third goal handed United the title – with five games and 35 days of the season remaining.

Perhaps understandably, United finished poorly; they lost their last three games, the first time they had suffered three successive defeats since the 1996–97 season.

Arsenal finished second for the third successive season, while Liverpool secured the third Champions' League spot by stealing third place on the last day of the season with a 4–0 win at Charlton, and just three days after winning the UEFA Cup.

At the other end, Bradford's two-year stay came to an end while Manchester City lasted just one season; and Coventry's stay in the top division, which had began in 1967, finally came to an end when they lost 3–2 at Aston Villa, after leading 2–0.

Title success: Manchester United still on top.

Leeds so close

MANCHESTER UNITED, Arsenal and Leeds carried the torch for English football in the Champions' League – and all three enjoyed memorable campaigns, though it was Leeds who came closest to a remarkable place in the Champions' League final.

They had to qualify for the right to participate but overcame TSV Munich, winning 2–1 at home – despite having Olivier Dacourt and Eirik Bakke sent off – and 1–0 away. That took Leeds into the first group – and a 4–0 thrashing by Barcelona. Yet a Lee Bowyer goal earned Leeds a memorable win over AC Milan and, following a 6–0 home win and 0–0 away draw with Besiktas, they held Barcelona 1–1 at Elland Road, where only an equaliser in the fourth minute of added time from Rivaldo denied Leeds a famous win.

Leeds went into their final game needing a point against Milan and got it, Dominic Matteo's effort cancelling Serginho's goal – after Andriy Shevchenko's penalty had hit a Leeds post.

In the second group stage, with Barcelona and Juventus knocked out, Leeds were drawn against Real Madrid, Lazio and Anderlecht. A 2–0 defeat at home to Madrid suggested Leeds had achieved too much, too quickly, but a remarkable 1–0 win in Rome against Sven-Göran Eriksson's Lazio, thanks to Alan Smith's late goal, offered Leeds' campaign hope and two wins over Anderlecht, the second a remarkable 4–1 victory in Belgium, confirmed Leeds' place in the final eight.

After a 3–2 defeat in Madrid and a 3–3 draw at home to Lazio – with Sinisa Mihajlovic stealing a last-minute equaliser – Leeds went into the knock-out stages and earned another remarkable result, a 3–0 win over Deportivo La Coruna. A goalless draw in Spain confirmed Leeds' place in the semi-final – against Valencia, last season's beaten finalists.

It was one tie too many for Leeds. They managed only a goalless draw at Elland Road and, the day before the return leg, learned that Bowyer was banned as a result of his foul on Valencia's Juan Sanchez in the first leg. Without arguably their most influential player Leeds were undone, losing 3–0, but it had been an incredible adventure.

Manchester United had felt this could be their season in Europe; they had a reasonably comfortable passage to the quarter-finals, holding Valencia to two draws on the way, but faced the old foe in Bayern Munich and, after losing 1–0 at Old Trafford, were beaten 2–1 in Munich.

Similarly, Arsenal had started strongly, beating Lazio and drawing against Bayern Munich. An impressive 2–1 win over Valencia, thanks to a rare goal from Ray Parlour, set them up for the return, but the away goal was to prove costly; Valencia won 1–0 in Spain and qualified to meet Leeds.

The Champions' League final was a disappointing affair, with Bayern Munich beating Valencia 5–4 on penalties in Milan after the teams had drawn 1–1 over 120 minutes. It was Munich's first European Cup success for 25 years.

Keegan out, Eriksson in

KEVIN KEEGAN'S 20-month reign as England coach came to an unexpected end when, having seen his country lose 1–0 to Germany in a World Cup qualifier, the final game to be played at Wembley Stadium, he resigned.

Keegan had been heavily criticised for his tactical naivety during the previous summer's European Championship finals, and the defeat by Germany left England with an uphill struggle.

Keegan said: "I know it is not good timing. I came in under difficult circumstances... Absolutely no one is to blame but myself. I did the job to the best of my ability. I am not the man to take it that stage further. I have to be true to myself. Kevin Keegan has given it his best shot."

Dejected: Kevin Keegan after England's defeat at Wembley.

Four days later England travelled to Finland for another World Cup qualifier. Howard Wilkinson was in temporary charge and England drew 0–0, leaving them with one point at the bottom of Group Nine.

Now the hunt was on for a successor, and it was never going to be an easy task to find a replacement at such a stage of the season. Adam Crozier, the Football Association's chief executive, formed a six-man think tank.

Former England manager Terry Venables was the people's choice, but after a four-hour meeting the FA dismissed the chance of him returning.

Aimé Jacquet, the former coach of France, and former Germany coach Berti Vogts were also linked, but privately, the man the FA wanted was Sven-Göran Eriksson, the Swede in charge of Lazio.

The Italian side were struggling and Lazio president Sergio Cragnotti agreed to release his coach ahead of the expiry of his contract in June.

On 30 October Eriksson agreed to take over with effect from 1 July. However, a month later the FA secured Eriksson's services ahead of schedule, with the Swede installed in time for the March qualifiers against Finland and Albania.

For the friendly in Italy, Leicester's Peter Taylor took charge. England lost 1–0 in Turin, but Taylor's experiment with youngsters Rio Ferdinand, Kieron Dyer, Gareth Barry, Seth Johnson, Jamie Carragher and Emile Heskey was seen as a success.

Eriksson secured his release even earlier, taking charge for the 28 February friendly against Spain, at Villa Park. Eriksson had watched every Premiership team and rapidly formed an opinion of the players at his disposal.

His first squad included surprises, the biggest being Charlton defender Chris Powell. Three Coles were included, Arsenal's Ashley, West Ham's Joe and Manchester United's Andy, while there was also a recall for Teddy Sheringham.

The start was perfect – England won 3–0, with goals from Nick Barmby, Heskey and Ugo Ehiogu – but it got even better when England took maximum points from their next two qualifiers.

Against Finland, Eriksson made David Beckham captain and the Manchester United midfielder took his responsibilities seriously, leading England to a 2–1 win and received a standing ovation from the Kop, after Michael Owen had equalised Gary Neville's own goal and Beckham had scored the winner.

Next stop was Albania, and Andy Cole finally scored for his country, at the 13th attempt, after Owen and Paul Scholes had put Eriksson's men in charge, finishing with a 3–1 win and second place in their qualifying group. It could not have been a better start for Eriksson.

New face: Sven-Göran Eriksson.

SOCCER SOUNDBITES

"I have just not been quite good enough."

KEVIN KEEGAN, England coach after announcing his resignation

Football mourns the passing of greats

IT WAS A SAD SEASON which saw the passing of several influential figures in the game. In November, Len Shackleton died at the age of 78. Originally with Bradford Park Avenue and Newcastle, he spent most of his career at Sunderland and won five caps for England.

In March, Stan Cullis passed away at the age of 85. He was very much a man of Wolves, with whom he was player, coach and manager, winning three League titles in the '50s. Another former manager, Alec Stock, also died at the age of 84. He led Yeovil to one of the most famous FA Cup shocks of all time, against Sunderland, and was manager when Fulham got to the FA Cup final in 1975.

In April referee Mike North died after he collapsed while taking charge of the Third Division game between Southend and Mansfield.

Scotland lost two of its most famous sons. In April Jim Baxter, the former Rangers and Scotland player, died of liver cancer aged 61. Arguably Scottish football's finest player, Baxter won three League championships, three Scottish cups, four League Cups and 34 caps. In May, the game mourned the death of Bobby Murdoch, aged 56, a key member of the Lisbon Lions, the Celtic team which won the 1967 European Cup.

Famous son: Former Rangers and Scotland player Jim Baxter.

FA get tough

THE FOOTBALL ASSOCIATION announced a disciplinary crackdown on players and managers with the threat of 12-match suspensions, points deductions and fine of up to £250,000 for clubs or individuals who misbehaved. It also introduced a video advisory panel to judge on incidents missed by referees, but both came into question early in the season.

Arsenal manager Arsène Wenger was given a 12-match touchline ban and fined four weeks' wages after being found guilty of threatening physical behaviour towards a fourth official, Paul Taylor, when his team played Sunderland on the season's opening day. Wenger appealed and, as late as February, he avoided a ban but was fined £10,000.

The FA's three-man video advisory panel were called upon after a call for the red card shown to Liverpool's Gary McAllister for his challenge on Arsenal's Patrick Vieira by referee Graham Poll to be reduced to a caution.

This was what the advisory panel recommended, but they were overruled by an FA disciplinary commission and so McAllister served a three-match ban.

End of the line for Wembley

THE GREAT WEMBLEY SAGA reached an impasse when in May the Football Association admitted it could not afford to finance the rebuilding of the national stadium.

The FA had asked the Government for £150 million to continue with the project.

When it was not forthcoming, the future of Wembley as the national stadium was put into serious doubt.

Earlier, in December, the FA decided to remove Ken Bates as chairman of Wembley, replacing him with Sir Rodney Walker.

But with the project costs rising to a remarkable £660 million, the FA started to look at alternatives, such as building a national stadium in the Midlands.

FOOTBALL FOCUS

- Sheffield Wednesday goalkeeper Kevin Pressman made history on the opening day of the season when he was sent off after 13 seconds at Wolves.
- Stan Collymore announced his retirement at the age of 30. The England striker joined Bradford from Leicester and five weeks later moved to Real Oviedo, where he lasted another five weeks before ending his career.
- Referees were told they no longer had to caution players who took off their shirts to celebrate goals.
- Barclaycard were named the new sponsors of the Premier League, paying £48 million to replace former backers Carling.
- Colin Hendry received a six-match international ban from FIFA after the Scotland captain elbowed San Marino's Nicolo Albani. The ban was later reduced to three games.
- Iran set a World Cup record, beating Guam 19–0, but Australia bettered that in April, beating American Samoa 31–0 in Coffs Harbour, New South Wales – three days after beating Tonga 22–0. Archie Thompson scored 13 in the record rout.
- The trial of Leeds players Lee Bowyer and Jonathan Woodgate, accused of attacking an Asian student, collapsed after the judge ruled that a tabloid newspaper article had "derailed" proceedings.
- A survey revealed that the average Premiership footballer now earns £400,000 a year.
- Ledley King's goal for Tottenham at Bradford, scored after just 10 seconds, was the fastest-ever goal in the Premiership.
- The BBC was outbid by ITV for Premiership highlights. ITV's £183 million deal brings an end to BBC's Match Of The Day Saturday night show.
- Ipswich Town manager George Burley won the Carling Manager of the Year, the first time a newly-promoted manager had won this accolade.

Spot-kicks foil Blues

THE FIRST major cup final to take place at the Millennium Stadium, Cardiff, saw Liverpool win the Worthington Cup after overcoming dogged resistance from First Division Birmingham City, who were bidding to qualify for European competition for the first time since 1962. They produced a fine performance, taking Liverpool to extra time and penalties, where they suffered the agony of defeat to hand Liverpool their first trophy for five years.

In the final Robbie Fowler scored a wonderful first-half goal to give Liverpool the lead but Birmingham rallied and levelled with a penalty deep into added time when Stephane Henchoz fouled Martin O'Connor and Darren Purse converted the kick. After five spot-kicks each in the penalty shoot-out, the game was still level and went to sudden-death. Jamie Carragher scored for Liverpool, but City teenager Andy Johnson, in front of the Liverpool fans, saw his kick saved by Sander Westerveld and Liverpool won their first trophy of the campaign.

To add insult to Birmingham's season, they went out of the play-offs on penalty kicks, losing 4–2 to Preston at Deepdale in May.

SOCCER SOUNDBITES

"What's happened tonight hasn't sunk in yet. I'm still a bit numb."

GARY MCALLISTER, Liverpool midfielder after helping his club win three trophies

SOCCER SOUNDBITES

"The lads are in tears in the dressing room but this is the beginning of Wycombe, not the end."

LAWRIE SANCHEZ, Wycombe manager after the FA Cup semi-final defeat by Liverpool

Dortmund delight for hat-trick heroes

A NAME once synonymous with European success was once again at the top; Liverpool, for too long out of the European limelight, claimed their first European trophy for 17 years with a victory in a game to rank alongside some of the great finals in history.

On their way to the UEFA Cup final, Liverpool had narrowly beaten Rapid Bucharest, eased passed Slovan Liberec 4–2 on aggregate and then overcome Olympiakos with a 2–0 home success. Their next test was against Serie A leaders Roma and they sealed their passage with a magnificent 2–0 win in the Olympic Stadium, thanks to two goals from Michael Owen.

In the quarter-finals, Liverpool beat Porto, again with Owen scoring, after Danny Murphy had given them the lead.

Having held Barcelona to a 0–0 draw in the Nou Camp, they stole a winning goal in the semi-finals through a Gary McAllister penalty.

Now to Germany where they met Deportivo Alaves, who included former Manchester United striker Jordi Cruyff but were considered as very much the underdogs.

Riding high: Liverpool show off their haul of trophies.

It proved to be the final that had everything: eight goals in normal time, two dismissals and, to crown an extraordinary evening, a golden goal to hand Liverpool the trophy.

Within two minutes Liverpool were ahead through Markus Babbel: then Steven Gerrard extended their advantage. Alaves responded through Ivan Alonso but before half-time Liverpool were 3–1 up, when McAllister converted a penalty after Owen had been grounded.

Alaves responded again, Javi Moreno scoring, and then Moreno added a second to make it 3–3. Robbie Fowler was introduced and within seven minutes had regained the lead for Liverpool, but Jordi levelled again – and so to extra time.

With the first goal the one to count the pressure was on, and Alaves lost both Magno and Karmona to red cards. When McAllister sent a 117th-minute free kick into the Spanish box it found the net off the head of defender Delfi Geli. Not surprisingly McAllister, at the ripe age of 36, was named Man of the Match.

The celebrations were put on hold, because Liverpool then faced a trip to Charlton, where they earned a Champions' League place. That achieved, 400,000 took to the streets of Liverpool to herald a new era.

FA Cup still brimming with romance

THE FA CUP proved that tradition remains an important part of the game's history; though the venue for the final was different – Cardiff's Millennium Stadium replacing Wembley for at least three seasons – the romance was still there.

Kingstonian got further than Manchester United, the Nationwide Conference club beating second-division Brentford and Conference rivals Southport before drawing at another Division Two side, Bristol City. Sadly for Geoff Chapple's side, they lost the replay.

Tranmere staged a remarkable comeback against Southampton in a fifth-round replay. Southampton were leading 3–0 at half time but the struggling First Division outfit responded with a 21-minute Paul Rideout hat-trick and a late winner from Stuart Barlow.

But there were more surprises to come in the FA Cup, with Wycombe Wanderers winning the hearts of a nation with the manner in which they came so close to reaching the final.

Wycombe went all the way to Villa Park and a semi-final tie against Liverpool. For long spells Wycombe were the equal of Gerard Houllier's team and not until the 78th minute, when Emile Heskey scored, did Liverpool looked like winning. Robbie Fowler's 83rd-minute free kick extended their advantage, though Keith Ryan responded late on to give 20,000 Wycombe fans something to remember.

In the other semi-final Arsenal beat Spurs 2-1 at Old Trafford with goals from Patrick Vieira and Robert Pires.

The Gunners dominated for long spells against Liverpool in the final and finally scored through Freddie Ljungberg.

But Michael Owen responded for Liverpool with a 83rd-minute equaliser and then the winner with just two minutes left.

O'Neill inspires new Celtic era

MARTIN O'NEILL left Leicester to take over at Celtic in the summer of 2000 – and led the club into a new era, stealing the Premier League from Rangers and winning the League Cup.

They completed the treble at the end of May when they beat Hibs 3–0 in the Scottish Cup final.

O'Neill's revolution saw Celtic win their first eight games, drop only four points from the opening 16 fixtures and claim the title with five games to spare, after a 1–0 home win over St Mirren.

Celtic's runaway success threw into disarray the plans of the Scottish Premier League, who had concocted an idea to split the League into two sections of six for the final five games. The idea was to increase the intensity at the end of the season but Celtic, who won the title by 15 points, put paid to that.

Highlight of the season was the remarkable 6–2 win over Rangers, in which Chris Sutton scored inside a minute. Architect of their success on the field was Henrik Larsson, the Swedish international signed for just £650,000 and who scored 53 goals, including 35 in the SPL. He also netted a hat-trick to win the League Cup, in the 3–0 win over Kilmarnock.

Celtic revolution: Martin O'Neill led his side to a treble in Scotland.

Cascarino comes clean

TONY CASCARINO faced the threat of having his record wiped from international football history after revealing he had never been eligible to play for the Republic of Ireland, despite scoring 19 goals in a record 88 appearances

London-born Cascarino, then playing for Gillingham, applied for an Irish passport in 1985 after being told he qualified for the Republic through his grandparents. His mother, Teresa, was adopted by a family named O'Malley, from Westport, and definitely qualified for Irish citizenship – but, crucially, she never took up this option.

In 1996, when FIFA's new rules demanded players must be citizens of the country they represented, Cascarino – who by then had won 64 caps – needed an Irish passport. His mother told him she had been adopted, a fact she had been unaware of until 1982. A passport was still granted, possibly because of Cascarino's services to the state.

FINAL SCORE

Football League
Premiership: Manchester United
Top scorer: Jimmy Floyd Hasselbaink (Chelsea) 23
Division 1: Fulham
Division 2: Millwall
Division 3: Brighton & Hove Albion
Footballer of the Year: Teddy Sheringham (Manchester United)

FA Cup Final
Liverpool 2 Arsenal 1

League Cup Final
Liverpool 1, Birmingham City 1 (After extra time, Liverpool win 5–4 on penalties)

Scottish League
Division 1: Livingston
Top scorer: Alan Gilzean (Dundee) 32
Division 2: Partick Thistle
Division 3: Hamilton Academicals
Footballer of the Year: Henrik Larsson (Celtic)

Scottish FA Cup Final
Celtic 3 Hibernian 0

Scottish League Cup Final
Celtic 3 Kilmarnock 0

European Cup Final
Bayern Munich 1 Valencia 1
(Bayern Munich win 5-4 on penalties)

UEFA Cup Final
Liverpool 5 Deportivo Alaves 4
(Liverpool win with extra-time golden goal)

European Footballer of the Year 2000
Zinedine Zidane (Juventus & France)

World Club Championship 2000
Boca Juniors 2 Real Madrid 1

Ipswich Europe-bound

IPSWICH TOWN qualified for the UEFA Cup after a season of completely unexpected success, just a year after winning promotion to the Premiership via the play-offs. Manager George Burley saw his side threaten to qualify for the Champions' League at one stage, but eventually they finished fifth, getting into Europe for the first time since 1983.

Architect of their success was former Huddersfield striker Marcus Stewart, whose 19 goals left him as the second-highest scorer in the Premiership. Included in his haul was a hat-trick at Southampton, the first by an Ipswich player since Kevin Wilson scored three against Stoke in 1985.

Not only did Ipswich finish fifth but they also became only the third team to win the play off final (they beat Barnsley) and thus avoid automatic relegation back to Division One.

FOOTBALL FOCUS

- Queens Park Rangers rejected a deal to merge with Wimbledon after the Football League had backed the proposed amalgamation.

- West Ham striker Paolo Di Canio received a letter of congratulation from FIFA President Sepp Blatter after his actions in the 1–1 draw at Everton when, in a goal-scoring position, he saw Everton's Paul Gerrard lying on the floor and caught the ball rather than trying to score.

The impact of foreign coaches

WHEN Ipswich Town's Scotsman, George Burley, was voted the 2000–01 Manager of the Year for guiding a newly-promoted club into Europe, Gèrard Houllier let rip. Fresh from winning the Worthington, FA and UEFA cups, the Liverpool coach was incensed that he had been overlooked. The reason, the Frenchman mused darkly, was that he was "foreign".

HOULLIER POSSESSES a good sense of humour but even my attempts to tease him about Burley's award, telling him how huge the Manager of the Year trophy was, that all three of Houllier's cups could fit inside it, failed to draw even an ironic smile from the usually cheery Frenchman.

Continental drift

Whatever his understandable frustration, Houllier's argument was flawed. After initial misgivings forged by the hapless Aston Villa tenure of the Czech Jozef Venglos, the English game has welcomed and benefited from an influx of foreign coaches. Take England, who looked to the respected Swede, Sven-Göran Eriksson. Look at Arsenal, as deeply indebted to Arsène Wenger as Liverpool to Houllier. A third Frenchman, Jean Tigana, vivified Fulham.

Already appreciative of foreign influences with the arrival of countless Continental players, such as Peter Schmeichel, Dennis Bergkamp, Eric Cantona and Gianfranco Zola, English football was receptive to the thoughts of managers from abroad. Fans and players like winners, whether they are from Marlow, Marseille or Mars. Eriksson lifted the gloom after Kevin Keegan. Wenger did the Double. Houllier did a Treble. Tigana won the First Division Championship. Silverware is always a short-cut to supporters' hearts.

New brooms

Hailing from different footballing cultures, coaches like Eriksson, Wenger, Houllier and Tigana brought in new ideas, which were accepted by native players because they patently improved them. Initially, Arsenal's English contingent were shocked at Wenger's impact on the training-ground menu. Steak-and-chips were out; broccoli and steamed fish were in. Though not the first Frenchman to question English cuisine, Wenger argued cogently that fry-ups, biscuit binges and the habit of putting milk and sugar in tea were not conducive to a healthy lifestyle.

Alcohol should be taken only in moderation and preferably wine, not beer. All Arsenal players responded to Wenger's advice: Nigel Winterburn and Lee Dixon freely admit the scientific Frenchman extended their careers. Tony Adams became teetotal, while Ray Parlour, after some long chats with Wenger, cleaned up his act, lost weight and looked an athlete.

Houllier, too, challenged the drinkers at Liverpool and altered the culinary intake. Entering the Melwood canteen now is like walking into a health farm. Yet taste has not been sacrificed at the altar of steamed vegetables. The food is excellent. The players tuck in with relish (cholesterol-free relish, of course).

A little nous

Yet foreigners like Houllier do not see their methods as particularly innovatory, simply the application of common sense to a profession which demands optimum fitness.

A coach whose high standing in the game is such that managers like David O'Leary call for advice, Houllier has always resented the perception of him as a "French revolutionary who came in to Liverpool with a guillotine".

He preferred to see his impact as more evolution than revolution, but what Houllier did was create an environment in which players could prosper. Melwood's training facilities have been upgraded, the food improved, the coaching strength-

Treble winner: Gérard Houllier with the UEFA Cup.

ened. It is the philosophy which underpins life at Clairefontaine, the almost mystical French centre of excellence which groomed players like Thierry Henry, and was overseen by Houllier in his former role as France's technical director.

A tactical tale

At Fulham, Tigana was another who espoused the Clairefontaine creed of accentuating technical ability while making footballers alive to a game's tactical rhythms. Under Tigana, Fulham players like Sean Davis, an Englishman inspired by his French manager, were allowed to express themselves within a framework of organised excellence. Clairefontaine is held up as a footballing Camelot by the authorities in England, and it was no surprise that the FA decided to build their own version in the Midlands.

At the tail-end of his playing days, Tigana used to drive from matches all over France to attend coaching sessions at Clairefontaine. Houllier recalled how Tigana once drove through the night to make a 9.00 am lesson at the centre in the woods near Paris.

French fancy: Jean Tigana celebrates Fulham's First Division tite with owner Mohammed Fayed.

Separating the men from the boys

Like Eriksson, Houllier and Wenger, Tigana studied the art of management and particularly man-management. These foreign coaches are not the type of tub-thumpers or teacup-throwers who used to stalk English dug-outs like Tyrannosaurus Rexes. It is hard to imagine any of this erudite foursome reacting like Sir Alex Ferguson in administering paint-peeling blasts. The thought of Wenger flinging a plate of butties at someone, as Ferguson once did in his Aberdeen days, defies belief. Besides, if the health-conscious Wenger ever dreamt of throwing sandwiches at a player, he would cut the crusts off first.

Wenger coaxes and cajoles, not screams or shouts. He treats players like adults not children. Ditto Tigana. Just listen to the testimony of his players. "He's a very good manager at psychology," said Louis Saha, the Fulham forward. "He makes players very confident very quickly." But there was a tough streak as goalkeeper Maik Taylor acknowledged: "Jean Tigana's very laid-back but if you cross him you soon know about it. We have felt the full force of his unhappiness." Beneath the cerebral exterior lurks a tough streak. England's players knew they let Eriksson down at their peril.

Eriksson could spend too little time with England players to work on their technique, but at club level, the players of Fulham, Liverpool and Arsenal developed under the thoughtful tuition of their foreign coaches. When Mohammed Fayed was considering employing Tigana, Michel Platini congratulated the Fulham chairman on his choice because players knew Tigana would improve them. Davis, for one, responded hungrily to Tigana's advice. "He makes good players great," reflected Fayed.

The same sentiments could be heard at Arsenal, where Parlour came on immeasurably, and Liverpool, where Michael Owen's left foot became more of a weapon after Houllier encouraged him to work on all aspects of his game. Robbie Fowler, hitherto famed for his work inside the penalty area, developed into an all-round force with his movement and link-play outside the box.

Man-management: Arsene Wenger treats his players like adults.

The flip side

Not all foreign coaches impress. Venglos is one of the most respected technical coaches in the world, and a valued contributor to UEFA's technical department, but he flopped badly at Villa. The early impression of Claudio Ranieri at Chelsea was that the side did not seem to be developing under him. And as for Christian Gross at Spurs, the less said the better. But for all Houllier's fear of an anti-foreign streak at work, the majority of English fans and players have welcomed intelligent, inventive coaches like Eriksson, Wenger, Tigana and Houllier himself. Success knows no boundaries.

Zidane in £48m Real deal

MANCHESTER UNITED's standing in world football was put into context on 9 July when Real Madrid broke the world record transfer fee by signing France captain and FIFA World Footballer of the Year Zinedine Zidane from Juventus for nearly £48 million. The French midfield magician has agreed a four-year contract worth around £3.8 million a year after tax.

While United were putting the finishing touches to a British record £23.5 million deal for Lazio's Juan Sebastian Veron, Madrid doubled that amount to break the previous record by £11 million – set when Luis Figo arrived in Madrid from Barcelona a year ago.

Zidane was introduced to the press by Real legend Alfredo di Stefano, a gesture – pairing Zidane with Figo – recalling the combination of Di Stefano with Hungary's Ferenc Puskas in 1959–60, a duo that terrified defences across Europe.

Whether the fee will ever be surpassed is unlikely. FIFA's new guidelines on transfers are expected to have an impact on the domestic game as players see out their contracts in order to benefit from substantial signing-on fees.

If the shirt fits, wear it: Zinedine Zidane prepares to don all-white.

Germany 1 England 5

Owen sparks England to historic triumph

With three goals, Michael Owen was England's chief executioner.

ALL ENGLISH EYES were transfixed by the scoreboard for the last 15 minutes of this match, a vital World Cup qualifier in Munich at the beginning of September. No, the scoreboard didn't lie. After all the years of heartache and torment since the last great triumph over the Germans in the 1966 World Cup final, England fans could hold their heads high again.

At last the catalogue of defeats at the hands of their great rivals in the major championships could be forgotten – 3–2 at Leon in the 1970 World Cup, 3–1 at Wembley in the 1972 European Championships, later semi-final defeats on penalties in both competitions, a 1–0 reversal at Wembley in this qualifying group... all now could be consigned to the scrapheap of football history.

And yet England had made an inauspicious start, going a goal down to Carsten Jancker's sixth-minute strike. But they took this setback in their stride, putting into practice Sven-Göran Eriksson's simple tactics: the quick counter-attack whenever England had possession. The midfield architects were the inspirational David Beckham, Paul Scholes, and Steven Gerrard, the chief executioner Michael Owen.

It was Owen who put England level from close range seven minutes later. Then England survived a horrible miss by Deisler and a snap shot from Bohme that was heading for the bottom corner before David Seaman made a crucial save at full length.

This seemed to take the fight out of the Germans, and Gerrard demoralized them further with a wonderful long-range drive that put England in front just before the interval.

In the second half, Beckham and Emil Heskey manufactured Owen's high-speed second, and his hat-trick arrived when Gerrard dispossessed Ballack and ushered Owen through to humiliate Kahn again. The speed and sharpness of Owen had left the German defence in tatters, and with 16 minutes remaining Scholes and Beckham combined to put Heskey through to make it 5–1.

The myth of German supremacy has been exploded, but England still have to qualify for the 2002 World Cup.

[A sad epilogue to England's night of triumph was the passing of much-loved broadcaster Brian Moore, who died a few hours before the game.]

SOCCER SOUNDBITES

"We all know we've made history tonight. We all know we are part of something special."

STEVEN GERRARD,
One of England's heroes against Germany

Ten-man Ireland have World Cup finals in sight

THE REPUBLIC of Ireland, down to 10 men after the 58th-minute dismissal of Gary Kelly for a second bookable offence, rallied to beat Holland 1–0 in Dublin and stay top of their qualifying group. Jason McAteer, who scored in the 2–2 draw in Amsterdam, collected a pass from Steve Finnan and hit the winning goal from seven yards.

Ireland had been on the ropes, surviving because of Holland's profligacy in front of goal and the referee's decision not to award the visitors a penalty when Shay Given upended Ruud van Nistelrooy after a laughable mix-up with Steve Staunton.

Defeat virtually condemns Holland to sitting out the 2002 World Cup. Unbeaten Ireland, with just their home game with Cyprus to come, are unlikely to qualify directly, however. Portugal, 7–1 victors in Andorra, have both Cyprus and Estonia to play and look certain to head the group on goal difference, while Ireland will face a play-off with Asian opponents.

Ireland manager Mick McCarthy recalled the time Ireland were 12 seconds away from qualifying for Euro 2000, when Macedonia's equalizer condemned them to a play-off with Turkey, which they lost on away goals. He has been criticized ever since, but he has rebuilt the ageing side he inherited from Jack Charlton in 1996 and, despite not having the quality his predecessor could call upon, he has taken Ireland to their third consecutive play-offs.

Jason McAteer celebrates after the goal that finishes Holland.

Tottenham (3) 3 Manchester United (0) 5

AT THE half-time interval in this extraordinary match, Premiership champions Manchester United found themselves three goals down to a Spurs side who were maybe as surprised as they were. Obviously, they had an urgent problem: how to discover, in the time it took to drain a cup of tea, a palliative for a defensive malaise that had seen them concede 10 goals in three-and-a-half away matches. Spurred on by the exhortations of Sir Alex Ferguson, they came up with one: outscore the opposition.

A hat-trick of headers in 25 minutes cancelled out the advantage Tottenham had established in a pinch-yourself first half, and the conclusive act of a mind-boggling second was the low drive from Sebastian Veron that had all but assured United of three points before David Beckham shot past Neil Sullivan to clinch it.

It was no consolation for Tottenham to reflect that they had taken part in a match that, whatever happens in the rest of the season, will be recalled as one of the best. Their legs seemed to drain as the tide of events turned, and Glenn Hoddle now has a repair job on his hands.

The most shocked member of Hoddle's team was perhaps Dean Richards. When you are an £8 million centre-back, to concede five goals on your debut must be at least perturbing, even when you have scored one at the other end.

Richards owed his goal, after 15 minutes, to Christian Ziege's superb low-trajectory corner, escaping the supposed marking of Ruud van Nistelrooy and glancing a header past Fabien Barthez. White Hart Lane shuddered in ecstasy.

Ziege then fed Gustavo Poyet, whose clever through ball left the United rearguard looking ragged, with Gary Neville continuing his habit of playing opponents onside. Les Ferdinand strode on to beat Barthez with a crisp, low drive. Ziege scored the third goal himself, just before the interval, heading in a Poyet cross.

What a difference it was in the second half, when United, bolstered by the presence of Ole Gunnar Solskjaer, on for the injured Butt (himself deputising for the suspended Roy Keane), and Mikael Silvestre for Denis Irwin, made Ziege and company look pedestrian. In less than a minute, Andy Cole had reduced the arrears, heading in a Gary Neville cross. Next, from Beckham's corner, Laurent Blanc rose to head his first goal for United. And United were level when, in the 72nd minute, Van Nistelrooy appeared on the end of a Silvestre cross to send yet another header beyond Sullivan.

Veron's goal came four minutes later, Beckham's three minutes from time to seal an extraordinary win.

It's level pegging as Van Nistelrooy scores United's third against Spurs.

SOCCER SOUNDBITES

"God help the rest of us when United start getting clean sheets."

GLENN HODDLE,
after watching his team blow a 3–0 half-time lead over Manchester United

Déjà vu as Gascoigne limps out

PAUL GASCOIGNE's self-inflicted injury at Goodison Park took one back to the Cup final of 1991, when, playing for Spurs, he made a crazy tackle on Forest's Gary Charles that shattered his own knee and arguably his career. This time the tackle, a wild lunge at Frederic Kanoute, was for Everton against West Ham, and it left him with strained knee ligaments – not such a serious injury but, in view of the delicate state of the 34-year-old's career, one that might spell the beginning of the end.

Gascoigne has become so peripheral a figure at Everton that they have learned to live without him, as they proved by winning 5–0 with embarrassing ease after he left the field. He lasted only three minutes, and bizarrely – or perhaps not, considering this is Paul Gascoigne – he refused to leave the field, the Everton physio Rob Ryles having practically to wrestle him to the touchline and walk him back to the dressing room under close arrest.

Gascoigne has been facing up to the demons in his life by admitting that he is an alcoholic. But after this injury, one wonders whether he might soon need to summon even greater inner strength to face up to losing something he will miss even more than drink – his status as a professional footballer.

England's great escape

ENGLAND have qualified for the 2002 World Cup finals in Korea and Japan thanks to their captain David Beckham, who scored a stoppage-time equalizer against Greece at Old Trafford, to Greece's inability to finish and to Germany, who spurned the chance to qualify directly by failing to beat Finland at home.

With his side 2–1 behind and facing a play-off tie to qualify for the finals next year, Beckham bent a 30-yard free-kick into the top-left corner of the net to give England the draw and the point that luckily saw them through. His goal, 1 minute 25 seconds before the final whistle, came at the end of a disappointing display by England, who twice fell behind against their poorly rated opponents.

England, needing to beat Greece to ensure qualification, went 1–0 down nine minutes before half-time, when Charisteas penetrated the flimsy barrier represented by Rio Ferdinand and Martin Keown.

Tottenham Hotspur's Teddy Sheringham came on for Robbie Fowler after 67 minutes and equalized with his first touch, but Nikolaidis restored Greece's lead just two minutes later.

England failed to perform, and were certainly nowhere near the form they had shown against Germany in Munich. Most of the players were stricken by nerves and underperformed, with the exception of keeper Nigel Martyn, who made two vital saves, Sheringham and, of course, Beckham.

Not only did he score the goal that put England through, but he put on a captain's performance with a work-rate that earned praise from a relieved Sven-Göran Eriksson. All this would have been in vain, however, had not Finland held Germany to a goalless draw in Gelsenkirchen and condemned them to a play-off with Ukraine.

Beckham is not the only one punching the air after his equalizer.

SOCCER SOUNDBITES

"One had to go in. I had quite a few free-kicks and was disappointed with most of them. When I got my last chance, Teddy Sheringham said he would have it, but I decided I'd take it."

DAVID BECKHAM,
England captain, on his crucial free-kick

Cardiff un-Cork Crazy Gang Spirit

AS CARDIFF staged one of the greatest upsets in FA Cup history, there were echoes for manager Alan Cork of Wimbledon's Crazy Gang defeating Liverpool's Culture Club in the 1988 final. Before his side ran out at Ninian Park to face Leeds, Cork told them: "If you want to be a hero, today's the day for it."

How well they responded to his words, turning fantasy into reality in thrilling, deserved fashion in this Welsh bear-pit. Assembled at a cost of scarcely £2 million, these unheralded Second Division journeymen conjured up the game of their lives to defeat the team currently leading the Premiership and book a fourth-round trip to either Southend or Tranmere.

Cork's men tore into Leeds, playing with intelligence and even a touch of swagger at times, making a mockery of their ranking 54 rungs down the professional ladder. Leeds combusted, Alan Smith departing just before the interval for flinging an arm at Andy Legg with the score at 1–1, Mark Viduka and Graham Kavanagh having traded fine goals. When Scott Young swept in the winner with four minutes left, Cardiff were in dreamland. For David O'Leary, the defeat of his Leeds team evoked painful memories of the famous reverse he suffered in Wales with Arsenal against Wrexham 10 years ago.

Unfortunately, the behaviour of the Cardiff fans did not match that of their players. Bottles and coins were thrown during the match, and a touchline walk by Cardiff chairman Sam Hammam served only to inflame the Leeds fans. The situation worsened at the final whistle. About 2,000 Cardiff supporters ran onto the pitch and taunted their Leeds counterparts. Referee Andy D'Urso was struck by a missile, Leeds players were hit by bottles and some players threatened, and the visitors' coach was attacked as it tried to leave. Order wasn't restored until riot police with dogs arrived to drive the fans back.

Sam Hammam savours victory.

Spurs end drought against Chelsea to reach final

SPURS CHALKED up their first victory over Chelsea for nearly 12 years to reach the Worthington Cup final. Down 2–1 from the first leg of the semi at Stamford Bridge, they walloped their nemesis 5–1 at White Hart Lane – the 27th attempt since the last time they beat them in February, 1990.

Referee Mark Halsey will have reason to remember this match, as he sent a fuming Jimmy Floyd Hasselbaink off in error, Mario Melchiot being the culprit who lashed out at Spurs captain Teddy Sheringham. This was in the 55th minute, by which time Spurs were three up, with goals from Steffen Iversen, who wiped out Chelsea's overall lead after less than two minutes, Tim Sherwood (his first of the season), and Sheringham, who struck a magnificent drive from the edge of the 18-yard box. Spurs put the issue beyond doubt in the last 15 minutes with further goals from Simon Davies and Sergei Rebrov, before Mikael Forssell hit a late consolation for Chelsea.

Sergei Rebrov scores number five against Chelsea.

Vogts confirmed as Scotland's first foreign manager

THE SCOTTISH FA confirmed Bertie Vogts as Scotland's new coach on 13 February. David Taylor, the SFA chief executive, who was in Kuwait where Vogts is currently national coach, finally announced that the former Germany coach will succeed Craig Brown.

The Kuwait FA have agreed to terminate Vogts's contract to allow him to take over Scotland duties on 1 March, giving him time to prepare fully for Scotland's match against France on 27 March. Vogts, formerly Germany's national coach, will be Scotland's first foreign manager

Celtic clinch title

CELTIC WON their first back-to-back league titles for 20 years when they thrashed Livingston 5–1 at Parkhead on 6 April. Rangers, with five games to play, are 16 points adrift and cannot now catch the leaders.

Henrik Larsson hit a hat-trick and John Hartson scored two, as Celtic piled on five goals in an hour.

Wilson replied for Livingston, who are currently in fourth place. Sweden international Larsson, who scored his 100th League goal, took his Premier League tally for the season to 29. He modestly gave the credit for Celtic's success to the defence, citing the performances of players such as Robert Douglas, Bobo Balde, Joos Valgaeren, Johan Mjallby and Stephen Crainey.

Larsson also praised midfielder Paul Lambert for setting up two of his goals. Club captain Lambert won the man-of-the-match award.

Celtic (103 points) went on to win the League by 18 points from Rangers, three more than last season. Livingston finished third, a massive 45 points behind Celtic. The champions sustained only one Premier League loss all season, a 2–0 reversal at Aberdeen just before Christmas. And they won 18 of their 19 home games, dropping points only to Rangers with a 1–1 draw after the title was sewn up.

SOCCER SOUNDBITES

"If you don't have a tight defence, then you don't have anything. If those guys behind me hadn't been playing so well, I wouldn't be sitting here talking about the title."

HENRIK LARSSON,
Celtic's prolific goalscorer

Heartbreaking exit from Europe as United fail to solve Veron conundrum

TO THE cacophonous crowing of 30,000 Germans, Manchester United went out of the Champions League on the away-goals rule at Leverkusen. United fought like lions against the fading of their season's light, but to no avail. There will be no romantic return to Glasgow for Sir Alex Ferguson, probably no trophies at all for the champions of England.

United's season has been destroyed in consecutive nights. Arsenal's 2–0 victory at Bolton puts them in complete control of the Premiership. Now United have fallen from Europe, let down by defensive mistakes in the home leg and the utter inability of Juan Sebastian Veron to fit into United's system.

Roy Keane had given United hope with a superb strike, but Oliver Neuville's equalizer seconds before half-time carried this exciting Bayer Leverkusen side into the 15 May final at Hampden Park.

As the Germans celebrated their unexpected journey to the final, United's players filed away, disconsolate. When the post-mortems begin, focus will turn on the defence, which needs strengthening, on the injuries to Beckham and Neville and, above all, the Veron conundrum.

Apart from Nicky Butt's caution, the first half had appeared to be heading for the break in a highly satisfying manner for United. Keane's goal, fabulously conceived and gloriously executed, had come slightly against the run of play.

But just as thoughts were turning towards the interval, Neuville struck. It was little more than Bayer deserved for their commendable commitment to attack. Sometimes they resemble more a Spanish than a German side.

United were deeply troubled, struggling to accommodate Veron into their 4-4-1-1 system. But where there is Keane there is hope. Echoing his bravura display at Juventus three years ago, United's captain and catalyst dragged his side into the game, willing them on and driving them forward. For a while United played like seasoned European campaigners. But then their lead disappeared, as Laurent Blanc and Ronny Johnsen looked on while Michael Ballack slid the ball in for Neuville to lift over Barthez.

In the second half United knew the odds and the away goals were against them. They had to take risks. In the last half hour first Ole Gunnar Solskjaer and then Diego Forlan came on. Keane – who else? – brought a fine save from Jorg Butt, and both subs went close. Even Barthez went up for a corner. But Leverkusen held firm and now head for Glasgow.

Arsenal steal the glory

NOW CHELSEA know how Arsenal must have felt last year when Liverpool's Michael Owen pinched the FA Cup from under their noses.

Having largely outplayed their fellow Londoners for most of this poor final, Chelsea were beaten by two late goals so superb they belonged to another, better match. Arsenal will hardly worry about the justice of the result though, not when it gives them the first leg of the FA Cup and League double.

Now, thanks to that brace of wonderful strikes by Ray Parlour, otherwise anonymous, and the remarkable Freddie Ljungberg, scorer of seven goals in his last six games, the Gunners will go marching up to Old Trafford on Wednesday brimming with confidence and believing themselves more than capable of clinching the Premiership on the ground of their greatest rivals for honours, Manchester United.

But for nearly 70 minutes at the Millennium Stadium in Cardiff, it all looked like going horribly wrong for Arsène Wenger and his team. With Frank Lampard and Emmanuel Petit winning the critical midfield battle against Patrick Vieira and Parlour, Chelsea were having the better of the contest.

They went close several times, but were hampered by the palpable lack of fitness of their leading striker Jimmy Floyd Hasselbaink, who had been fighting to recover all week from a calf injury. He stayed on to the 68th minute, when he was replaced by Gianfranco Zola. Ironically, this was a signal for Arsenal to score the first of their two wonderful goals.

In the 69th minute, Parlour joined a swift Arsenal attack down the middle, took a few steps and then let fly into the top corner from about 25 yards, giving Carlo Cudicini no chance. Ljungberg's clinching goal 10 minutes later was a brilliant solo effort demonstrating both his tenacity and his skills, as he stole the ball on the left, muscled past John Terry, and curled a beauty round Cudicini and inside the far post.

It was enough to earn him the man-of-the-match award. Manchester United and England beware.

Freddie Ljungberg's strike takes the FA Cup back to north London.

Lovenkrands double sinks Celtic

Peter Lovenkrands heads a last-gasp winner for Rangers.

THE OLD FIRM may be headed in the long run for one or other of the English leagues, but while Celtic and Rangers remain north of the border Scottish football will never be short of explosive drama.

As a spellbinding Cup final unfolded, the season's most significant figures seemed destined for disappointment.

Lorenzo Amoruso, the Scottish players' choice as player of the year, playing with pain-killing injections, gifted Celtic their two goals. Then Paul Lambert, the Scottish football writers' choice as player of the year, threw his captain's arm-band away in disgust just before the interval, as his gamble on playing with an ankle injury shuddered to a halt,

By contrast to Lambert, Barry Ferguson, the Rangers captain, emerged as the undisputed man of the match, leading from mid-field in emphatic fashion. His exquisite second-half strike – a curling 25-yard drive that rebounded from the post while his side trailed 2–1 – was worth the admission money alone. And the delectable free-kick for the Gers' second equalizer, bent like Beckham, was a joy.

Bobo Balde outjumped Amoruso to set up John Hartson for the Celtic opener after 19 minutes, but two minutes later Peter Lovenkrands latched onto a loose ball to square the match. Balde restored Celtic's lead after the break, eluding Amoruso again to head home.

Lovenkrands, summoned from the Ibrox shadows when Alex McLeish took over in December, has repaid the manager in spades whenever Rangers have met Celtic since then. Having hauled them back into contention in the first half, now, with only 10 seconds of stoppage time remaining, he strained to reach Neil McCann's swirling cross and bounced the match-winning header past Rab Douglas.

McLeish's unbeaten run against Old Firm rivals Celtic now extends to four games, and Lovenkrands has scored five times this season against Rangers' bitterest rivals.

FOOTBALL FOCUS

● While Zinedine Zidane was moving across Europe in the summer of 2001 for a world record fee, another signing caused as much of a stir in England, when Sol Campbell moved across north London on a free transfer from Spurs to Arsenal, where he soon picked up League and Cup medals. Decried as a "Judas", Campbell received death threats from irate Tottenham fans who had previously worshipped him. Brought up through Spurs youth ranks, he had played 315 games for the club.

● Scottish 2nd Division side Berwick Rangers went close to repeating their giant-killing act of 1966–67 in the Scottish FA Cup when they beat Rangers 1–0, but this time, in the third round, the result was 0–0, and Rangers won the replay at home 3–0.

● Boston United were promoted to the Football League after edging Dagenham and Redbridge with a vastly superior goal difference at the top of the Nationwide Football Conference.

● England Under-21s substitute Jermain Defoe (West Ham) scored against Holland in 3.6 seconds with his first touch.

● Doncaster Belles were runners-up in both women's league and cup competitions. They finished eight points behind champions Arsenal LFC in the National Division and were beaten 2–1 by Fulham at Selhurst Park in the FA Women's Cup final.

● Airdrie were runners-up to promotion winners Partick in the Scottish 1st Division despite being on the verge of financial collapse, but the club had to fold. This saved Falkirk from relegation to the 2nd Division and Stenhousemuir to the 3rd. The vacancy in the 3rd Division was filled by Gretna and, when later Clydebank also folded, their place in the 2nd Division was taken by the newly formed Airdrie United!

● The Premiership attracted a total of 13,043,118 paying customers during the season, a new attendance record. The Football League aggregate for the three divisions was 14,716,162, also a record since the formation of the Premiership.

● Newcastle and former England manager Bobby Robson was knighted in the Queen's Jubilee Honours for his services to football. As a player, he won 20 caps for England, first at inside-right and then at wing-half. At club level, he was a prolific scorer for Fulham and West Brom.

Arsenal clinch the Premiership at Old Trafford

LIFE DOES not get much sweeter than this for Arsenal. Playing with all the steel and swagger of champions, the high-class, high-speed raiders from Highbury deservedly secured the Double in their rivals' backyard via the 1–0 scoreline so famously associated with Arsenal.

"Hand it over Ferguson," chanted the ecstatic visiting fans of Manchester United's loosened hold on the Premiership trophy. Sir Alex cannot argue: his side managed only one shot on target all game and were overwhelmed by Arsenal's fluid passing in the second half.

Arsenal have been undeniably the superior side all season, and this game showed them at their best, exuding determined organization in defence, composure and movement in midfield and confidence in attack.

They produced a commanding performance, with Patrick Vieira driving them forward from midfield, Ray Parlour running everywhere, fetching and carrying, harrying and passing. Freddie Ljungberg was similarly diligent.

As the second period unfolded, Arsenal sought to impose their fast-moving style on proceedings. Back came United, a football match now breaking out from the scuffling prevalent in the first half. It was a Silvestre howler that led to Arsenal's winning goal.

He conceded possession to Parlour, who sent Sylvain Wiltord and then Ljungberg down the inside-right channel. The Swede ran at Laurent Blanc and sent in a fizzing shot that startled Fabien Barthez. The French keeper managed to parry the ball out, but only to Wiltord, who deftly slotted it past him. As Wiltord stood with one arm aloft à la Denis Law, the celebrations raged around him.

Arsenal continued to cruise to their 12th League win on the spin, and finished the season unbeaten away from home, the first time this has been achieved in the top flight since Preston in 1888–89, the inaugural season of the Football League.

SOCCER SOUNDBITES

"Securing the Double had a dreamlike quality about it. I don't believe in gloating, but it meant so much to take the title away from one of the best teams in Europe on their home soil."

LEE DIXON,
Arsenal right-back

Sylvain Wiltord slots home past Barthez at Old Trafford.

Zidane hits goal fit for a king

ONCE AGAIN, Glasgow belonged to the white-liveried magicians from Real Madrid. An exquisite left-foot volley from Zinedine Zidane, a goal that would comfortably have graced that fabled 1960 final, proved the worthiest of winners at Hampden Park.

Real had taken the lead on nine minutes through Raul. But within five minutes Bayer Leverkusen were level. Bernd Schneider drove in a free-kick from the touchline for Lucio to make amends for an earlier error and head in. The second half, though goalless, was full of fast, exciting football, and with Bayer straining every muscle to get back into the game, the hero was Real's young keeper Casillas, who made a string of breathtaking saves. His opposite number Butt went up for corners towards the end, but Real held out, and Zidane's volley turned out to be the winner, one of the finest goals ever seen in a final.

FINAL SCORE

Football League
Premiership: Arsenal
Top scorer: Thierry Henry (Arsenal) 24
Division 1: Manchester City
Division 2: Brighton & Hove Albion
Division 3: Plymouth Argyle
Footballer of the Year: Robert Pires (Arsenal)

FA Cup Final

Arsenal	2	Chelsea	0

League Cup Final

Blackburn Rovers	2	Tottenham Hotspur	1

Scottish League
Premier League: Celtic
Top scorer: Henrik Larsson (Celtic) 29
Division 1: Partick Thistle
Division 2: Queen of the South
Division 3: Brechin City
Footballer of the Year: Paul Lambert

Scottish FA Cup Final

Rangers	3	Celtic	2

Scottish League Cup Final

Rangers	4	Ayr United	0

European Cup Final

Real Madrid	2	Bayer Leverkusen	1

UEFA Cup Final

Feyenoord	3	Borussia Dortmund	2

European Footballer of the Year 2001
Michael Owen

FIFA World Player of the Year 2001
Luis Figo (Real Madrid and Portugal)

World Club Championship 2001

Bayern Munich	1	Boca Juniors	0

Back to Brazil

For the first time, the World Cup was staged jointly by two countries, Japan and South Korea. The organization of the first World Cup to be held in Asia was outstanding, and the Koreans in particular proved splendid hosts. With champions France shooting themselves in the foot in the First Round, Brazil breezed to their fifth World Cup triumph, and striker Ronaldo erased the bitter memory of 1998 to beome the leading scorer. South Korea played some stirring football to light up the tournament and reach the semi-finals.

THE 2002 WORLD CUP kicked off on 31 May in Seoul, with holders and favourites France expected to make short work of Senegal, who were playing in their first World Cup. Instead, France went down to a shock 1–0 defeat. Without their two great playmakers, Robert Pires and the inspirational Zinedine Zidane, who tore a muscle in France's last warm-up match, France were disappointing. And they showed no improvement in their next group match, drawing 0-0 with Uruguay and losing star striker Thierry Henry, who contrived to get himself red-carded. A not fully fit Zidane returned for the third game, but France lost 2–0 to Denmark when they needed a reversal of that score to survive. So the holders were out – without scoring a goal!

Spain won their three matches in Group B as expected, and Paraguay edged out South Africa by virtue of their "goals for" column. Brazil also chalked up three wins, in Group C, but not before they were made to work hard by Turkey in their opening game, which they won 2–1 thanks to a late penalty for a foul arguably outside the box. China's first venture in the World Cup finals finished with no points, no goals and nine in the "against" column.

In Group D Poland went down 2–0 to South Korea, who chalked up their first-ever victory in their sixth finals tournament. Then Portugal, one of the tournament favourites, found themselves three down to the United States inside 36 minutes. They did eventually pull two goals back, but that was not enough. After beating Poland 4–0, however, Portugal needed to beat South Korea to progress. The Portuguese lost their nerve, lost two players with red cards and finally lost the match 1–0. The US, despite losing 3–1 to Poland, also made the last 16.

For once Germany were not considered among the favourites, but they came out in Group E with all guns blazing, and pulverized Saudi Arabia 8–0, their striker Miroslav Klose notching a hat-trick of headers. The Republic of Ireland drew 1–1 with African champions Cameroon, Matt Holland providing the second-half equalizer. Against Germany, they were a goal down to a Klose strike until Robbie Keane levelled the scores in stoppage time. They then beat Saudi Arabia 3–0 to go through – a commendable performance considering the loss of captain Roy Keane, who was sent home in disgrace on the eve of the finals by the FA of Ireland after a row with manager Mick McCarthy.

Group of Death

Dubbed the "Group of Death", Group F consisted of England, Sweden, Argentina and Nigeria. After being out for seven weeks with a much-publicized broken bone in his left foot, captain David Beckham led England out for their first game, against Sweden, and soon placed a corner onto the head of Sol Campbell for the centre-back to score his first international goal. But Beckham tired in the second half and was withdrawn. Sweden took over the midfield and equalized, and by the finish England manager Sven-Göran Eriksson was thankful to take a draw against his native country. Their next game, against Argentina, who had scraped a win over Nigeria, was regarded as a "grudge match" after Beckham's sending-off in 1998 and England's defeat on penalties. This time it was a Beckham penalty that won the match. Now Argentina had virtually to beat Sweden to stay in the tournament, but a draw saw them eliminated as England also drew with Nigeria to go through behind Sweden on goal difference.

Seaman can only look on as Ronaldinho's free-kick smacks the net.

Italy were favourites to win Group G, but they found themselves needing to beat Mexico in their last game to be sure of staying in the tournament. They could only draw, thanks to a late Del Piero equalizer. But the disappointing Croatians lost to Ecuador to allow Italy a reprieve.

Expectations were high for co-hosts Japan in Group H, even though they had never won a match in a World Cup finals tournament. They drew with Belgium and then beat Russia and Tunisia to top the group. Their unlikely hero was non-stop midfielder Junichi Inamoto, who scored against both European countries, after a season with Arsenal without playing in the Premiership.

The last eight

Germany beat Paraguay 1–0 with a goal from Oliver Neuville a couple of minutes from the end. England brushed Denmark aside at Niigata (Japan), with first-half goals from Rio Ferdinand, Michael Owen and Emil Heskey, to stroll into the last eight 3–0.

Sweden lost to Senegal after Henri Camera scored the winner, a "golden goal" in extra time with the score at 1–1. Ireland excelled themselves against Spain despite going down early on to a header from Fernando Morientes. They earned two second-half penalties, Iker Casillas saving the first from Ian Harte but having no chance with Robbie Keane's spot-kick in stoppage time. The young Real Madrid keeper was the hero when the match went to penalties, saving another two to send Ireland out of the finals.

The United States powered their way into the quarter-finals with a 2–0 win over Mexico, and Brazil beat Belgium by the same score: Rivaldo and Ronaldo scored their goals.

Japan subsided to a 12th-minute header from Turkey's Umit Davala. South Korea looked like going the same way when Christian Vieri headed Italy in front in the 18th minute. But they never gave up, and equalized three minutes from full time. With three minutes of extra time left, Ahn headed the golden goal.

Brazil k.o. England

Although England went ahead in the first half of their quarter-final against Brazil through Owen, they looked tired and never seemed to have sufficient belief in themselves. Brazil equalized on the stroke of half-time with a goal from Rivaldo, and five minutes after the interval Ronaldinho hit a spectacular (or speculative, depending on his intentions) free-kick from 30 or more yards that dipped over David Seaman's head and into the England goal. Ronaldinho was red-carded for a high tackle on Danny Mills. But despite their numerical advantage, England failed to mount one decent assault on the Brazilian goal for the rest of the game.

Outplayed by a US side full of running, Germany nevertheless reached the semi-finals thanks to Michael Ballack's first-half header, a match-saving goalkeeping display by Oliver Kahn and the failure of referee Hugh Dallas to award the Americans a penalty for a blatant handball on the line by Torsten Frings. The other two quarter-finals went to extra time. Spain were held 0–0 by South Korea, who then won on penalties. Turkey needed a golden goal to beat Senegal.

The semi-finals

Germany crept into the final with a 1–0 win to put paid to South Korea's inspired run. Michael Ballack scored the goal in the 75th minute.

In the other semi, Ronaldo will be remembered not only for the 49th-minute goal that gave Brazil victory over Turkey, but also for the extraordinary haircut he sported. Here was a man not yet back to his best, but showing many signs of his former greatness.

Brazil regain crown

At the final hurdle, the German machine failed, as Brazilian flair threw a spanner into the works. It took the superfit South Americans 67 minutes to break down the German defence, which had conceded only one goal thus far in the finals. Keeper Khan made perhaps his first serious mistake in the tournament – he failed to hold a low 20-yarder from Rivaldo, and Ronaldo pounced to put Brazil one up.

Twelve minutes later Ronaldo put the result beyond doubt to give Brazil their fifth World Cup triumph. It was Germany's fourth defeat in seven finals. Despite all the earlier upsets, the old order had been restored and the two traditional giants of world football – meeting, strangely enough, for the first time in a World Cup – brought the curtain down on a memorable tournament.

Ronaldo plants the ball beyond Oliver Kahn's despairing reach.

FINAL SCORE

FIRST ROUND

Group A

Senegal	1	France	0
Denmark	2	Uruguay	1
Senegal	1	Denmark	1
France	0	Uruguay	0
Denmark	2	France	0
Senegal	3	Uruguay	3

	P	W	D	L	F	A	P
Denmark	3	2	1	0	5	2	7
Senegal	3	1	2	0	5	4	5
Uruguay	3	0	2	1	4	5	2
France	3	0	1	2	0	3	1

Group B

Paraguay	2	South Africa	2
Spain	3	Slovenia	1
Spain	3	Paraguay	1
South Africa	1	Slovenia	0
Spain	3	South Africa	2
Paraguay	3	Slovenia	1

	P	W	D	L	F	A	P
Spain	3	3	0	0	9	4	9
Paraguay	3	1	1	1	6	6	4
South Africa	3	1	1	1	5	5	4
Slovenia	3	0	0	3	2	7	0

Group C

Brazil	2	Turkey	1
Costa Rica	2	China	0
Brazil	4	China	0
Turkey	1	Costa Rica	1
Brazil	5	Costa Rica	2
Turkey	3	China	0

	P	W	D	L	F	A	P
Brazil	3	3	0	0	11	3	9
Turkey	3	1	1	1	5	3	4
Costa Rica	3	1	1	1	5	6	4
China	3	0	0	3	0	9	0

Group D

South Korea	2	Poland	0
United States	3	Portugal	2
South Korea	1	United States	1
Portugal	4	Poland	0
Poland	3	United States	1
South Korea	1	Portugal	0

	P	W	D	L	F	A	P
South Korea	3	2	1	0	4	1	7
United States	3	1	1	1	5	6	4
Portugal	3	1	0	2	6	4	3
Poland	3	1	0	2	3	7	3

Group E

Ireland	1	Cameroon	1
Germany	8	Saudi Arabia	0
Germany	1	Ireland	1
Cameroon	1	Saudi Arabia	0
Germany	2	Cameroon	0
Ireland	3	Saudi Arabia	0

	P	W	D	L	F	A	P
Germany	3	2	1	0	11	1	7
Ireland	3	1	2	0	5	2	5
Cameroon	3	1	1	1	2	3	4
Saudi Arabia	3	0	0	3	0	12	0

Group F

Argentina	1	Nigeria	0
Sweden	1	England	1
Sweden	2	Nigeria	1
England	1	Argentina	0
Sweden	1	Argentina	1
England	0	Nigeria	0

	P	W	D	L	F	A	P
Sweden	3	1	2	0	4	3	5
England	3	1	2	0	2	1	5
Argentina	3	1	1	1	2	2	4
Nigeria	3	0	1	2	1	3	1

Group G

Mexico	1	Croatia	0
Italy	2	Ecuador	0
Croatia	2	Italy	1
Mexico	2	Ecuador	1
Mexico	1	Italy	1
Ecuador	1	Croatia	0

	P	W	D	L	F	A	P
Mexico	3	2	1	0	4	2	7
Italy	3	1	1	1	4	3	4
Croatia	3	1	0	2	2	3	3
Ecuador	3	1	0	2	2	4	3

Group H

Japan	2	Belgium	2
Russia	2	Tunisia	0
Japan	1	Russia	0
Belgium	1	Tunisia	1
Japan	2	Tunisia	0
Belgium	3	Russia	2

	P	W	D	L	F	A	P
Japan	3	2	1	0	5	2	7
Belgium	3	1	2	0	6	5	5
Russia	3	1	0	2	4	4	3
Tunisia	3	0	1	2	1	5	1

SECOND ROUND

Germany 1 Paraguay 0
England 3 Denmark 0
Senegal 2 Sweden 1
Senegal won on "golden goal" rule
Spain 1 Ireland 1
Spain won 3–2 on penalties
United States 2 Mexico 0
Brazil 2 Belgium 0
Turkey 1 Japan 0
South Korea 2 Italy 1
South Korea won on "golden goal" rule

QUARTER-FINALS

Brazil 2 England 1
Germany 1 United States 0
South Korea 0 Spain 0
South Korea won 5-3 on penalties
Turkey 1 Senegal 0
Turkey won on "golden goal" rule

SEMI-FINALS

Germany 1 South Korea 0
Brazil 1 Turkey 0

THIRD-PLACE MATCH

Turkey 3 South Korea 2

FINAL

Brazil 2 Germany 0

Yokohama, Japan, 30 June 2002.
Attendance 69,029

Brazil: Marcos, Lucio, Roque Junior, Edmilson, Cafu, Kleberson, Gilberto Silva, Roberto Carlos, Ronaldinho (Juninho Paulista), Rivaldo, Ronaldo (Denilson)

Germany: Khan, Frings, Linke, Ramelow, Metzelder, Hamann, Jeremies (Asamoah), Schneider, Bode (Ziege), Neuville, Klose (Bierhoff)

Leading scorers
8 Ronaldo (Brazil)
5 Miroslav Klose (Germany)
5 Rivaldo (Brazil)

United sign Ferdinand for £30m plus

LIKE ALL the internationals who have gone before him, Rio Ferdinand followed Sir Alex Ferguson obediently into Old Trafford on 22 July. The latest high-profile signing to succumb to the lure of the nation's biggest club, he is – according to Manchester United's manager – at 23, potentially the best centre-half in the world.

Ferdinand's family took pride of place in the front row of Old Trafford's Salford Suite to listen to the United chief executive, Peter Kenyon, read out the eye-watering mathematics of British football's biggest transfer. Ferdinand's former club, Leeds United, will receive £15 million immediately, another £14.3 million in July 2003, and the final £4 million over Ferdinand's five-year contract.

This was a bitter blow for Leeds manager Terry Venables, who has accused Manchester United of believing they are "entitled to everything". And there are many others who resent the financial power Ferguson wields in a hard-up Premiership.

Ferdinand would have arrived a lot earlier had it not been for West Ham's reluctance to sell the defender to Manchester United six years ago when he was spotted by Ferguson's scouts while on loan to Bournemouth. Some £50 million and two British record transfer fees later, Ferdinand's arrival at United comes just weeks after Laurent Blanc's decision to stay at the club for one more year. Although Wes Brown, Ferdinand's companion on a recent holiday in Las Vegas, will also challenge for a place in the heart of United's defence, it is likely to be the 36-year-old Frenchman that the England centre-half lines up alongside.

SOCCER SOUNDBITES

"We have every right to try to improve ourselves, despite what some people think."

SIR ALEX FERGUSON,
Manchester United manager, on his acquisition of Rio Ferdinand

Clubs facing closure after court verdict

MANY FOOTBALL CLUBS face the threat of extinction after the Football League yesterday lost their £131.9 million claim against Carlton and Granada, parent companies of the now defunct ITV Digital. A High Court judge ruled that the League failed to extract sufficient written guarantees in ITV Digital's original contract with them, and that Carlton and Granada were therefore not liable.

First Division chairmen had been fearing this outcome and blamed the way the League officers had handled the affair. Millwall chairman Theo Paphitis said they were not fit to run a kebab house. The loss of television income has already had an affect, with managers sacked and a record number of players released as clubs try to find ways of offsetting the losses incurred.

Justice Langley made it clear that he thought the central plank of the League's case was totally without merit. The league had done the deal with Ondigital (ITV Digital's previous incarnation) and relied on a document which said: "Ondigital and its shareholders will guarantee all funding to the Football League."

But this statement was subject to contract, never ratified in a final contract, and was more a gentleman's agreement, which did not stand up in court. Mr Justice Langley concluded that there was no guarantee by either company of ITV Digital's obligations under that contract.

Then, in a truly damning conclusion, he opined that the League had started "unpromisingly" and finished as badly as it had begun. It is extremely unlikely that the League will appeal. Clubs already smarting at the legal bills the League have run up will not take kindly to further feathering of lawyers' nests.

SOCCER SOUNDBITES

"We're a billion-pound industry and it can't be run like a kebab house. And if this is a kebab house, then these are not the people I would put in charge."

THEO PAPHITIS,
Millwall chairman, on the Football League officials

Scotland's darkest hour

FROM THE HEIGHTS of the clifftop Toftir pitch, Scotland stared into the abyss as schoolteacher John Petersen struck twice in the opening 12 minutes to put the Faroe Islands 2–0 up in this opening qualifier for Euro 2004. In the end, though, Scotland clung on to the barest respectability by their fingertips.

Bertie Vogts had already made the worst start of any Scotland manager, having previously witnessed defeats against France, Nigeria, South Korea, and South Africa. But this draw in his first competitive fixture must rank as his worst result yet.

Against the Premiership partnership of Christian Dailly and David Weir, Petersen was twice aided and abetted by Jakup Borg, who passes the time between international appearances by working as a clerk in a sports shop.

Both of them play for Bolteflagid B36, in the Faroese capital, Torshavn, which might explain their telepathic understanding. But nothing can account for the utter inertness at the heart of the Scottish back four. Indeed, the striker should have had a hat-trick and secured an incredible win for his country, but the ball took an unlikely bobble and he blazed over the bar of an open goal early in the second half.

It was always likely that Scotland would be able to run the legs off their opponents over the 90 minutes. In the end, they salvaged a point and saved a little face with goals from Paul Lambert and Barry Ferguson after 61 and 83 minutes. But the Scottish FA and the team's fervent supporters will not be impressed with a share of the spoils against a country that boasts a population that would easily fit inside Hampden Park.

John Petersen (10) celebrates the Faroe Islands' second goal.

Henry shears sheepish Leeds

THE LEEDS UNITED programme had made much of a recent history of ferocious competition. But for Arsenal, this was like being savaged by a flock of dead sheep. They would happily trade another 30 bouts of the petulant resistance put up by a humiliated Leeds for the retention of their Premiership title, which Arsène Wenger's men will probably achieve anyway: a verdict no doubt shared by the many sportsmanlike Leeds fans who stayed to applaud them from the field.

Along with Terry Venables' team, a few records fell to the champions. No longer, for instance, can Chesterfield claim a unique distinction in the English game, not now that Arsenal have eclipsed their 1929–30 team by scoring in 47 consecutive League matches. No longer can Nottingham Forest supporters dine out on tales of how Brian Clough's side went 22 top-division matches unbeaten away from home in 1977–78. This was Arsenal's 23rd bountiful journey.

Maybe Wenger, when he said they could go all season without losing, was simply stating the obvious. While they still, of course, have a great deal to prove in Europe, Arsenal's domestic supremacy might well become even more emphatic.

Venables drooled over Arsenal's performance after the match. He mentioned Thierry Henry, whose speed, movement, touch and perception bewildered Leeds like PSV in midweek before them. But Wenger had excellence all over the pitch.

Appearing half a yard slower to every ball, Leeds were immediately subjugated by Vieira and tortured by the trickery of Henry, Kanu, Sylvain Wiltord, and – by no means least – Kolo Toure, whose name will surely rate airing in the same breath as his more renowned colleagues before long. The goals came from Kanu (2), Toure, and Henry, with Kewell sneaking one in for Leeds. Only one Leeds player did his standing no harm – and that was Paul Robinson, in goal. Otherwise the defeat would have been worse.

SOCCER SOUNDBITES

"Manchester United have been exceptional for 10 years – but I've not seen anything as good as that."

LEEDS MANAGER TERRY VENABLES
after Arsenal's performance at Elland Road

The Gunners rout Roma

MEMORIES OF a sorrow-laden stay in Serie A while an unvalued Juventus employee were spectacularly banished by Thierry Henry in Rome's Olympic Stadium. In recording Arsenal's first Champions League hat-trick, a wondrous affair comprising vibrant shooting and dead-ball expertise, Henry launched his team's second-phase Group B campaign in style.

Rome may not have been built in a day, but Henry demolished it in 90 minutes. Equalizing Antonio Cassano's early strike with a firm right-footed shot of his own, Henry then secured the points for Arsenal in a purple patch midway through the second half. Displaying the range of his armoury, Henry put Arsenal ahead with his left foot and then scored a superb free-kick to make it 3–1.

Roma were stunned, their fans heading for the exits while the players looked at each other in disbelief. They had paid for failing to concentrate like hawks when Henry was around. But this wasn't a one-man show. The Italians had also been punished by an Arsenal side blending discipline and dynamism, with Patrick Vieira and Gilberto in particular terrific in central midfield.

Hat-trick hero Henry returns to haunt Italian football.

Rooney, 16, guns down the champions

THE LONG unbeaten run is over, left in tatters by a precocious 16-year-old with dynamite in his boots and a dazzling future ahead of him. Wayne Rooney thundered a 30-yard drive beyond David Seaman with just a minute of normal time remaining. This was Arsenal's first away defeat in the Premiership since May 2001.

Arsène Wenger, the Arsenal manager, proclaimed Rooney as the greatest prospect in English football after his stunning goal gave Everton a 2–1 win over Arsenal. Rooney also made history for himself as the Premiership's youngest-ever scorer.

So Wenger's perceived (but misquoted) "boast" that his superlative team could defend their title by remaining unbeaten all season long has come to grief, ending a sequence of 30 unbeaten Premiership games which began a mile away from this ground, at Anfield, on 23 December last year. However, there was a bittersweet moment for Everton supporters as they saw their local rivals Liverpool leapfrog Arsenal into first place after their 1–0 win at Leeds earlier in the day.

Rooney, a Merseysider who is set to sign a £10,000-a-week contract with the club when be turns 17 in a few days, arrived on the field as a substitute with 10 minutes left. Replacing Tomasz Radzinski who had earlier equalized a Freddie Ljungberg goal, the teenager's impact was immediate.

The Everton manager David Moyes, who has already gone on record saying he believes Rooney could be the greatest player in Everton's history, afterwards paid tribute to a "wonder goal". But he tempered his praise by adding that the youngster sometimes frustrated the coaching staff with his persistence in attempting long-range shots, conceding however that on this occasion he had a serious chance and took it pretty well!

Roo-mania is born as the boy wonder scores the winner versus Arsenal.

Eriksson's experiment blows up

ENGLAND SENT out two teams against Australia at Upton Park and still lost, humiliatingly and deservedly so. Losing to Australia in the Ashes and Davis Cup is expected, but this first-ever footballing defeat to the men from Down Under was deeply embarrassing.

As well as Wayne Rooney, Jermaine Jenas and Francis Jeffers performed after the break, they were let down by a remarkably inept first-half display by Sven-Göran Eriksson's senior XI, who were fortunate not to concede more than the goals from Tony Popovic and the outstanding Harry Kewell.

When the dishevelled seniors departed at the break, England looked far more secure defensively, where Ledley King and Wes Brown worked well in tandem, far more assertive in midfield, where Jenas and Owen Hargreaves excelled, and, particularly, far more adventurous in attack, where Jeffers scored and Rooney threatened throughout.

But the damage had been done. The seniors should be sent videos of the second 45 minutes that captured the hunger characterizing the Rooney generation. Only Michael Owen and David Beckham had looked interested. The kids were more than all right in the second period, but they were still punished late on by Brett Emerton's strike.

This is what you get when you treat international footballers like precious works of art, borrowed from their owners on the understanding that they are not exposed to harsh light. It was quite right that Australia had a player called Chipperfield, because this was a circus – of the absurd. And now England go to Liechtenstein for their next qualifying match pursued by anger and ridicule.

Eriksson's team go down under.

Fergie's antics leave Beckham in stitches

DAVID BECKHAM sought to maximize the embarrassment for Sir Alex Ferguson after receiving just a mumbled apology in the dressing-room on Saturday when the Manchester United manager kicked a football boot into his player's face.

The England captain, emboldened by Ferguson's refusal to make a full apology for the extraordinary incident that left him with two stitches in his head, left his home in Cheshire for training with his long hair swept back off his forehead and the wound in full view of the waiting photographers. There was no attempt to disguise the fact that Beckham had been hurt by the boot that Ferguson – albeit unintentionally – kicked at him, but this was also an opportunity for the player to outmanoeuvre a manager who has disciplined him publicly in the past.

Although Ferguson's infamously short temper has caused him to throw teacups at his players at Aberdeen and smash a glass bottle of soft drink at St Mirren, he has never before injured a player during one of his rages.

So just what was it that made the boss so mad? Watching his side get knocked out of the FA Cup in the fifth round by their heirs apparent Arsenal – their first defeat at Old Trafford in 21 matches – must have hurt. Rubbing salt in the wound was the fact that the double champions won without being at their strongest. Thierry Henry and Dennis Bergkamp were rested in preparation for Tuesday's Champions League fixture against Ajax at Highbury – a daring, almost arrogant, coup by Arsène Wenger, Sir Alex's great rival.

Indeed, Arsenal did not just knock United out, they knocked the stuffing out of them psychologically. Sir Alex had predicted that the result could prove a pivotal moment of the season for the two clubs. So it could, but matters have now swung appreciably, perhaps decisively, in Arsenal's favour. This might have been on his mind when he lashed out in the dressing-room.

SOCCER SOUNDBITES

"If I did it a hundred times, a million times, it could not happen again. If it did I'd have carried on playing."

SIR ALEX FERGUSON,
on the boot incident

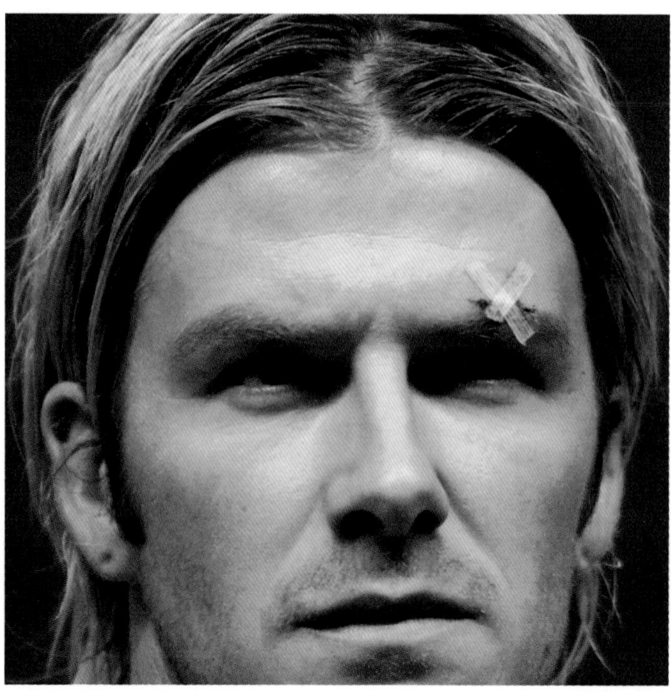

Working those angles – Beckham did not seek to hide his wound.

Gerrard steals the Keane copyright

IT'S STRANGE to think of Liverpool as underdogs, but that is what they were going into this Worthington (League) Cup final, uncharacteristically floundering seventh in the Premiership, 12 points behind their opponents Manchester United in second place and 20 points behind leaders Arsenal. United, however, an organization notoriously sensitive about infringement of their copyright, were distraught to watch Liverpool's Steven Gerrard deliver the type of dynamic, box-to-box display that once was the trademark of Roy Keane.

Keane strove hard to inspire his disappointing team-mates, but with his edge tempered by that debilitating hip problem, Keane was blunted brutally by the brilliant Gerrard. Gerard Houllier decided to give his midfield ace the freedom of Cardiff, encouraging him to raid forward as Dietmar Hamann shielded the back four with his customary expertise.

A few minutes before the interval, Gerrard struck Liverpool's first, a fine 25-yarder that took a deflection off David Beckham. He hounded Keane and Juan Sebastian Veron when United, thrillingly, attempted to claw their way back into this unbelievably tense final. And when Michael Owen raced away to slot in a second five minutes from time, Gerrard could begin preparing to spray the champagne over his comrades, and they got a real soaking as the party began.

Celtic castaways sink Liverpool

TWO PLAYERS cast aside by the Premiership, Alan Thompson and John Hartson, returned to English soil for this second-leg UEFA Cup quarter-final to deliver spectacular reminders of what had been so dismissively shipped off to Scotland. If Thompson's free-kick strike on the cusp of half-time was good, it still failed to touch the grandeur of Hartson's second-half gem that drove Celtic into a first European semi-final since 1974 – 2–0 on the night and 3–1 on aggregate.

Liverpool, whose season now rests on somehow qualifying for the Champions League, were stunned. But for all their possession, the pride of Anfield were deservedly defeated by Martin O'Neill's well-organized, well-motivated men. Bobo Balde was excellent in defence, Neil Lennon anchored ably, while their attacking moves were often a joy to behold on an epic occasion.

Thompson's free-kick sets Celtic on their way against Liverpool.

United out as Ferguson blunders

ON AN EVENING of enchanting football at Old Trafford, David Beckham reminded Sir Alex Ferguson, Real Madrid, and the watching world of his exceptional qualities, making a complete mockery of Ferguson's horrendous mistake in leaving him on the bench until midway through the second half, when he charged on and struck twice.

For all Beckham's efforts and the tireless contribution of Ruud van Nistelrooy, the damage had already been done, inflicted by Ronaldo's hat-trick as Real deservedly progressed to a Champions League semi-final against Juventus. At the final whistle, Beckham swapped shirts with Zinedine Zidane, who had again so damaged United's equilibrium. Beckham may be acquiring a Real top of his own soon. Old Trafford know class when they see it, and they applauded Real off the pitch as well as cheering Beckham, who returned their salute in the manner of a man saying his farewell.

So United, 3–1 down from the first leg, won on the night, Real on aggregate, but football overall. A fitting feast for the watching Alfredo Di Stefano and Sir Bobby Charlton, this was a joyous roller-coaster ride of a tie, utterly compelling to watch as attacks flowed from end to end. It was, though, a dispiriting night for Rio Ferdinand, humiliated by Ronaldo, for Fabien Barthez, alarmingly out of position for Ronaldo's first, and for Roy Keane, whose sluggish contribution confirmed the waning of the captain's once dominant powers.

Yet in-between keeping check on the breathless football on view, the eye kept being drawn back to the extraordinary sight of Beckham sitting on the bench. Juan Sebastian Veron was clearly not fit enough, while Ole Gunnar Solskjaer hardly justified Ferguson's decision to dispense with Beckham's dead-ball expertise and work ethic. Ferguson has never shied away from controversial selections, but this Beckham gamble was ridiculous.

Van Nistelrooy hit United's first equalizer, the second came from an own goal and the third from a Beckham trademark free-kick. Beckham, sensationally, still was not done. He finished off a lightning break at the far post: 4–3 to United, but they still needed two. Beckham came raiding again but Real held firm, losing on the night but winners overall, and winning countless new friends for their free-flowing, imaginative football. No wonder Beckham fancies a spell at the Bernabeu.

Leeds sack wrong man as farce continues to run

LEEDS UNITED should relocate to London's West End after this long-running farce. But it isn't funny. Terry Venables is only one of around 20 employees to lose their jobs at Elland Road this week.

The first intimation that there was something amiss came 14 days after the chairman, Peter Ridsdale, hired him to be the Messiah. Venables signed a two-year deal on 8 July, some eight months ago. Rio Ferdinand was sold to Manchester United on 22 July. Though his sacking was announced only yesterday, Venables left Leeds in stages, as bits of his spirit departed the club with each bank-appeasing sale.

There was damage to Venables' pride with Peter Reid's temporary appointment yesterday, but (protected by his contract) not to his wallet.

Really, though, Leeds got rid of the wrong man. Look at the record. Fourteen months after guiding them to a Champions League semi-final against Valencia, David O'Leary is sacked. The board then snatch Venables from his ITV studio, but begin a desperate rolling fire sale. Finally, Venables is sent back to London with his severance pay and Ridsdale hires someone who was sacked by Sunderland.

How Ridsdale has managed to survive these multiple calamities is beyond comprehension. He has subscribed heavily to the fantasy in English football that you could use tomorrow's earnings to buy paradise today. In Yorkshire, this conceit disintegrated the moment Leeds failed to re-qualify for the Champions League. When the economy dipped and depressed television and transfer revenues, "for sale" boards went up all over the squad. Out went Ferdinand, Robbie Keane, Olivier Dacourt, Lee Bowyer, Robbie Fowler, and Jonathan Woodgate, whose departure to Newcastle on 30 January finally turned the manager into Terry Untenable. He stayed, of course, but probably only out of loyalty to his remaining players and to avoid having to depart on Ridsdale's terms.

Terry Venables was forced to preside over a rolling fire sale.

United regain title as Arsenal falter

ON 5 APRIL, Manchester United reduced Arsenal's Premiership lead to goal difference, beating Liverpool 4–0 at Old Trafford while the defending champions were held 1–1 at Villa Park. After a midweek defeat at Real Madrid in the Champions League, United went up to Newcastle, six points behind them in third place. It looked like a tricky fixture, but so poor and compliant were the home side that United could afford to give them a goal start before following that with a spectacular 6–2 thrashing, Paul Scholes scoring three and creating havoc with his passing.

So, with Arsenal involved in an FA Cup semi-final the next day, United would stay three points clear at least until the Wednesday, when they would face a title showdown at Highbury.

Billed as the match of the season, this fixture lived up to its name. It wasn't decisive, but here was English football at its intoxicating best, full of nip and tuck, end-to-end moves, wonderful waves flowing between a transfixed Clock End and North Bank. It encapsulated all the rivalry between the Premiership's finest sides, well-matched thoroughbreds contesting a compelling race. And, as is customary when these two giants meet, there was a great deal of controversy too.

United went ahead in the middle of the first half with a beautifully taken goal by Ruud van Nistelrooy, after a defence-splitting pass from Ryan Giggs.

A second-half revival saw Thierry Henry break clear from his shackles – every time he gathered the ball, two, sometimes three, of Ferguson's men had formed a quick-reacting ambush unit – for long enough to deflect an Ashley Cole shot into the United goal. And then the Frenchman put Arsenal ahead, albeit with an offside goal that was allowed to stand. But a minute later United swept upfield and Giggs equalized with a header to set up the most breathless of finales, a fitting advertisement for Premiership fare beamed around the world.

All shared points are equal, but some are more equal than others. A triumphant Sir Alex Ferguson revelled in the draw, gained at the home of his biggest rivals. Not only did it keep United three points clear, but the champions finished with some notable absentees: with eight minutes left Sol Campbell was dismissed for flicking an elbow into Ole Gunnar Solskjaer's face right in front of a linesman, and Patrick Vieira, Arsenal's captain, had been forced to hobble off after barely half an hour when his heavily bandaged knee could take no more.

In the final title run-in, both teams won their next match, but then Arsenal, 2–0 up at Bolton with 16 minutes to go, let two of the points slip away. United won their next two matches, at Spurs 2–0 and home to Charlton 4–1. The next day Arsenal went down 3–2 at home to relegation-threatened Leeds to present the title to Manchester United. They enjoyed some consolation in Cardiff when they beat Southampton 1–0 in the FA Cup final.

Quick on the draw – United take a point at Highbury.

The men from Ibrox take their place as champions.

Old Firm in shoot-out for title

THE LAST DAY of the Scottish Premier League season, and the scene was set for the closest finish in the long history of Celtic-Rangers rivalry.

With completely identical win-draw-loss figures, the two sides also had the same goal difference, but Rangers were in front by virtue of having scored one more goal.

Consequently, with Rangers expected to beat fifth-placed Dunfermline at Ibrox and Celtic to win at fourth-placed Kilmarnock, it was about goals. The odds favoured Rangers slightly: they had the advantage of a home fixture, while defending champions Celtic had an awkward trip to Rugby Park, just four days after their mentally and physically draining UEFA Cup final defeat by Porto, 3–2 with the winner coming in extra time.

In a thrilling finale that will go down in Old Firm legend, Rangers pipped Celtic to the title, but the issue remained on a knife-edge until almost the final kick.

In the end, the title went to Rangers, for a world record 50th time, after a 6–1 win. But Celtic fought until the last in their 4–0 victory, even leapfrogging Rangers at the top of the table for 10 minutes before their rivals stepped up a gear and settled the issue with Mikel Arteta's last-minute penalty.

Six days later at Hampden Park, Rangers beat Dundee in the Scottish Cup final to complete the domestic treble.

Real clinch Beckham deal at last

AFTER MONTHS of speculation and cloak-and-dagger wheeler-dealing, David Beckham has at last become a Real Madrid player. Manchester United have agreed a deal for an initial fee of £18 million for the England captain to move from Old Trafford to the Bernabeu. The agreement also includes clauses which could enable United to get another £7 million should Real achieve certain targets, such as winning the Spanish League and the Champions League in the coming seasons.

Beckham, who was due to return for pre-season training on 9 July, will now come back from a personal promotional tour of the Far East for a medical in Madrid on 1 July, prior to being unveiled by the club the next day. Beckham had barely touched down in Tokyo on the latest of his lucrative personal tours before his new employers, Real Madrid, revealed moves to clip the wings of their new signing.

Relentless self-promotion and a willingness to jet across the globe at seemingly a moment's notice ultimately played a key role in Beckham's departure from Manchester United to the Spanish capital. Although Real have accepted that the England captain's celebrity will be a useful tool in the club's drive to exploit the Far East market, where Beckham's star shines even brighter than that of American basketball legend Michael Jordan, the nine-time European champions have no intention of allowing Beckham's off-field interests to detract from business on the pitch.

As part of his £4 million-a-year deal at the Bernabeu Stadium, Real will claim 50 per cent of the midfielder's image rights. Monies earned from Beckham's deals with the likes of Pepsi, adidas, Castrol and Marks & Spencer will remain in the 28-year-old's pocket. But club policy dictates that any endorsements struck while a Madrid player will see half of the fees handed over to the club's players' pool.

Beckham, likely to make his debut against a Chinese XI in Beijing on 2 August, is clearly going to have to earn the right among his team-mates to claim the status he enjoyed at Old Trafford. And with Brazilian specialist Roberto Carlos in the side, he may even have to accept a diminished responsibility on free-kicks.

Peter Kenyon, Manchester United's chief executive, has shed more light on the Beckham sale by revealing that a combination of Sir Alex Ferguson's wish to freshen up his squad and the player's failure to react positively to the offer of new contract talks left the club with no option but to sell.

Real Man: David Beckham.

SOCCER SOUNDBITES

"This is an amazing opportunity for me at this stage in my career and a unique and exciting experience for my family. I know that I would always regret it later in life if I had turned down the chance to play at another great club like Real Madrid."

DAVID BECKHAM

Cameroon do Foe proud

FRANCE AND Cameroon struggled to throw off the tragedy of Marc-Vivien Foe's death as a golden goal in the 97th minute from Thierry Henry settled this subdued Confederations Cup final. Despite appeals to cancel the final as a mark of respect to Foe, Sepp Blatter, the FIFA president, had insisted that it go ahead.

The night at the Stade de France was thick with emotion, with Cameroon, led by Foe's lifelong friend Rigobert Song, discarding their traditional green and yellow colours for plain white with black armbands.

The former Manchester City and West Ham player's widow, Marie-Louise, was joined by her late husband's brother at the match which Cameroon decided to play as a poignant tribute to their fallen "Indomitable Lion". After an emotional minute's silence for the midfielder, who died on Thursday after collapsing during his team's semi-final win over Colombia, the two sides struggled to find a real cutting edge.

France had the better chances to start with, but the African side were well in the game by the break. The best chance of the first half fell to Djibril Cisse, who headed just past Cameroon's post after brilliant work by Henry down the left culminated in a cross. After limited chances in the second half, Henry poached the winner in extra time when he ran onto a pass from Lilian Thuram to nudge the ball past the advancing goalkeeper with his knee.

Foe had been expected to return to Manchester City, where he had been on loan, for the start of next season after negotiating a free transfer from Lyons earlier in the week. The defensive midfielder was a key figure in City's impressive return to the Premiership following promotion from the First Division 12 months ago, and had been regarded by manager Kevin Keegan as one of the success stories of the club's season.

[An autopsy later revealed that Foe died of natural causes, probably from an almost undetectable congenital heart condition.]

FOOTBALL FOCUS

- Arsenal's record run of scoring in 55 consecutive League matches came to an end on 7 Dec with their 2–0 defeat at Old Trafford.
- Wayne Rooney's record as the youngest Premiership scorer lasted less than 10 weeks, as James Milner, 16 years 357 days, scored in Leeds' 2–1 win at Sunderland on Boxing Day to beat it by 3 days.
- Sunderland finished their season on their third manager (Mick McCarthy, after Peter Reid and Howard Wilkinson) and with 15 defeats in a row. This left them rock bottom with 19 points, the lowest-ever Premiership tally.
- Chelsea beat Liverpool 2–1 at Stamford Bridge to snatch fourth place in the Premiership on the last day – and a place in the Champions League.
- The Premiership's two French managers, Arsène Wenger (Arsenal) and Gerard Houllier (Liverpool) were recognized in the Queen's Birthday Honours with honorary OBEs for their contributions to English football and Franco-British relations.

FINAL SCORE

Football League
Premiership: Manchester United
Top scorer: Ruud van Nistelrooy (Man United) 25
Division 1: Portsmouth
Division 2: Wigan Athletic
Division 3: Rushden and Diamonds
Footballer of the Year: Thierry Henry (Arsenal)

FA Cup Final
Arsenal 1 Southampton 0

League Cup Final
Liverpool 2 Manchester United 0

Scottish League
Premier League: Rangers
Top scorer: Henrik Larsson (Celtic) 28
Division 1: Falkirk
Division 2: Raith Rovers
Division 3: Morton
Footballer of the Year: Barry Ferguson (Rangers)

Scottish FA Cup Final
Rangers 1 Dundee 0

Scottish League Cup Final
Rangers 2 Celtic 1

European Cup Final
AC Milan 0 Juventus 0
(Milan won 3-2 on penalties)

UEFA Cup Final
Porto 3 Celtic 2
(after extra time with silver goal)

European Footballer of the Year 2002
Ronaldo (Real Madrid)

World Club Championship 2002
Real Madrid 2 Olimpia Asuncion 0

The Russians are coming as Chelsea FC goes for £150m

ROMAN ABRAMOVICH, the 36-year-old billionaire buying Chelsea Football Club for £150m, is one of the new breed of Russian businessmen suddenly flavour of the month in the City, despite their unusual and colourful backgrounds.

Even by the standards of the Square Mile, which has seen its fair share of exotic characters, the Russian billionaires are exceptional. Often under 40, they amassed huge wealth in the privatizations of the early 1990s. Russian capitalism then had all the features of the Wild West, and workers were given shares in their companies by President Yeltsin.

As most workers were poor and ignorant of the ways of capitalism, young entrepreneurs were able to snap up the shares for almost nothing.

Mr Abramovich was close to Boris Berezovsky, a media magnate and car-maker, and soon prospered under his umbrella. He was elected governor of Russia's Chukotka province in 2000 with over 90 per cent of the vote.

Mr Abramovich now owns a big shareholding in Sibneft, the oil giant. Thought to be worth from $3 to $6 billion, he can easily afford to pay £150m in cash for Chelsea Village, the holding company, including about £90m of debt.

According to a spokesman, he is a sports nut and has been looking for a while for a football club to buy. He wanted one that had real potential and which also needed some investment.

SOCCER SOUNDBITES

"Just who have we invited to the table?"

TONY BANKS MP,
Chelsea fan and former Sports Minister, on Roman Abramovich's takeover at Chelsea

Roman Revolution – Chelsea have gone from paupers to princes.

Young gun Rooney

WAYNE ROONEY slapped a down payment on his birthright by becoming the youngest scorer in England's history. At 17 years and 317 days, Rooney succeeded Michael Owen, the man playing alongside him in England's 2–1 win in Macedonia.

If the precocious talent of Rooney helped England back into this European Championships qualifying game, it was the maturity of Beckham that allowed England to recover from a first half that, at times, was truly dreadful. Beckham once again demonstrated his talismanic qualities in an England shirt. His single-mindedness, even bloody-mindedness, in pursuit of victory, inspired his team to rediscover some sort of cohesion in the second half.

England's unconvincing defending undid them in the 27th minute, allowing Gorgi Hristov to shoot home in off David James's legs. They laboured to produce a response and Beckham showed his frustration with a foul on Hristov that brought a yellow card.

But minutes into the second half Beckham launched the ball into the Macedonia box and substitute Emil Heskey, a replacement for Frank Lampard, headed down for Rooney to claim his place in history with a crisp right-foot shot into the corner.

Beckham had suddenly taken it upon himself to be England's driving force in midfield, and the sight of the willing Heskey offered him a convenient target. The latter distracted the defence when Beckham chipped into the box in the 62nd minute, and John Terry was bowled over. Beckham – who else? – took the penalty himself, driving it firmly into the corner.

Rooney writes himself into history.

Humiliated Arsenal in the dock

THE SHAMEFUL serial offending of Arsenal under Arsène Wenger will today bring this proudest of clubs the humiliating charge of "failing to control their players" following an unsavoury skirmish at Old Trafford. The face of the beautiful game was ravaged with scars and tears; 52 Arsenal expulsions under Wenger in seven years borders on a crime wave.

A manager notoriously blind to his player's transgressions, Wenger may not have seen the incidents at the end when Martin Keown, Ray Parlour, and Lauren confronted Ruud van Nistelrooy, Manchester United's striker whose thespian tendencies had contributed to Patrick Vieira's 81st-minute dismissal. Keown leapt up and brought a forearm down to Van Nistelrooy's head, while Parlour and Lauren steamed in like playground bullies.

But significant others did. The Football Association are to launch an investigation into both clubs' behaviour at the final whistle, for Cristiano Ronaldo, United's winger, and Gary Neville also got themselves involved.

Arsenal had been incensed by the manner of Vieira's departure and particularly Van Nistelrooy's part in their captain's downfall. Vieira had just been booked by Steve Bennett for a seemingly legitimate challenge on Quinton Fortune. The mercury rose as if someone was holding a blow torch against it. Moments later, Vieira leapt above Van Nistelrooy to head clear and was caught by the Dutchman as they fell to earth. Vieira, lying two yards from Van Nistelrooy, kicked out innocuously but the United striker jumped back like a matador evading a fiery bull. From Bennett's angle, it looked like Vieira had made contact, particularly given Van Nistelrooy's exaggerated reaction. In truth, it was an air shot by Vieira, but the fact that Vieira made no contact was irrelevant: he kicked out and had to walk.

With the match heading for goalless stalemate, United now sensed their chance: when Keown nudged Diego Forlan over in the box, Van Nistelrooy was presented with a penalty. But he thundered the ball into the crossbar, his third successive penalty miss.

The final whistle sounded like a call to arms to certain Arsenal players. There was no serious contact, but the repercussions will run and run.

Panic sacking by Spurs gave Hoddle no chance

UNTIL LAST NIGHT, Glenn Hoddle had the hardest job in the Premiership, because managing Tottenham has long meant juggling the club's rich sense of history with the relative poverty of their current status. But last night we also learned that Tottenham are a club in complete panic.

No matter how badly the start of the season has gone, Hoddle's treatment has been disgraceful. He deserved to be given more than just six games to try to turn around a struggling side.

Having sanctioned about £12 million-worth of summer transfers, the board were looking for a significant improvement quickly, and that has not happened. The damning statistic is that, in 2003, Spurs have won 22 points from 23 games, the worst record in the Premiership.

Marrying the supporters' expectations with the team's performance has always been White Hart Lane's biggest problem. But it is a malaise that goes right to the heart of the club. At Tottenham, they want pretty-pretty football. George Graham tried to tell them that their passion for flair was costing the club dear and he was vilified for it. Now, Tottenham find themselves at crisis point once again. Against Southampton, Tottenham were awful. The White Hart Lane faithful, perhaps respectful to a man who was one of the truly great players of Spurs' under-achieving history, booed the team rather than the manager.

But it has been obvious that the lack of respect by too many of the team has affected performances. Now the players, their jobs secure, will train today under caretaker manager David Pleat, the club's director of football.

SOCCER SOUNDBITES

"I'm going to go home to look at Teletext. A bag of crisps, a can of Coke and three hours of Teletext, that'll do me."

GORDON STRACHAN,
as his team Southampton beat Spurs 3–1 to move into fourth place

White Hart Lane's prodigal son is to move on once more.

England hold Turkey to qualify for Portugal

ENGLAND'S FOOTBALLERS have issued some momentous statements in recent days, but none of such stirring significance as the one delivered here in the heaving, seething Sukru Saracoglu stadium in Istanbul.

Commitment etched in every challenge, every run, this performance was a statement of intent by David Beckham and his white-shirted collective. Not only did England parade their patriotism to the people back home, but they reminded the rest of Europe that they must be taken seriously at Euro 2004.

Desire and tactical discipline characterized the movements of all of Sven-Göran Eriksson's 11 hungry men. If they will excuse the analogy in the wake of Rio Ferdinand's delayed drugs sample, they showed a lot of bottle. Everything Turkey threw at them, fair and foul, England withstood. When Beckham was being elbowed and insulted, the captain simply redoubled his efforts to get England the point they needed.

Chances came, moments of real adventure in the attacking third. And when the outstanding Steven Gerrard charged in from the left, winning a penalty off Tugay, England had their opportunity.

Beckham had already broken one deadlock last week, the impasse between players and FA over Ferdinand's treatment. Here, surely, was his moment to end another stalemate. Up he strode. Suddenly, his left foot slipped on the uneven ground, bringing his head back, scrambling the sights and sending the penalty into orbit.

As the crowd crowed, so did some Turks on the pitch. Alpay, who switches between charm and odiousness effortlessly, stood over Beckham and gloried in the England captain's misfortune. Beckham bit, pushing his face towards Alpay, and the fuse was well and truly lit, finally launching the half-time brawl in the tunnel.

As the players headed towards the dressing room, Alpay ran past Beckham and shouted "Go **** your mother". The "Villan", by club affiliation and nature, pushed his finger into Beckham's cheek and then up his nose.

Beckham chased him down the tunnel, and everyone joined in for what Gerrard described as "a lot of argy-bargy". It was, as Eriksson would say, like a scene from the Wild West. Fortunately, the sheriff was in town, a tall, bald authority figure called Pierluigi Collina, who promptly summoned Beckham and Alpay to his quarters to calm them down.

In the second half, the Turks became increasingly desperate, throwing on attacking subs and throwing themselves to the floor, notably Sukur. The clock ticked down unbearably slowly. Eriksson, such a canny coach, rang the changes well, bringing in the pace of Kieron Dyer from deep and Darius Vassell up front to stretch Turkey. More twists and turns were negotiated, and then Collina blew the final whistle and the whole of England could exhale in relief.

Elation set in. England were at Euro 2004. Once reviled, Beckham is now his country's guiding light. And England's performance was also a vindication of the pro-player stance taken by Eriksson over the Rio Ferdinand issue and the threat of strike action by the squad. What those who criticized the England coach for backing his players overlooked is the fact that he had to get a performance out of them against Turkey. He couldn't go and slam his players and then expect them to perform for him. And tactically, once again, he got it absolutely spot on. His record in matches of significance is excellent, having lost only that game to the Brazilians. Now he can prove himself in Portugal.

SOCCER SOUNDBITES

"I am not going to let silly things go on and ruin this game because this is such a big game. Go into the changing rooms now and calm things down."

REFEREE PIERLUIGI COLLINA,
taking a firm half-time hand with Beckham and Alpay

Scotland, Wales out – and Turkey!

THE SECOND LEG of the play-offs for the last Euro 2004 places saw Scotland torn to shreds by the Dutch and the Welsh dream shattered by Russia. But the biggest shock was the elimination of Turkey, third in the last World Cup, by little Latvia.

Scotland, one up from the first leg, were no match for Holland in Amsterdam. Technically and tactically superior, Holland turned on the style to reach Euro 2004 with a comprehensive men-against-boys 6–0 whipping of Scotland, who were too quick to concede free-kicks and too slow to defend them. Ruud Van Nistelrooy scored a fine hat-trick, but the Dutch forward was assisted by hugely generous defending, an initially over-aggressive Scotland giving away far too many fouls. James McFadden's winner at Hampden Park was cancelled out after only 13 minutes, after which Scotland collapsed.

On a night of tension and anxiety, Wales were ultimately unable to rise to the task of beating Russia, having done so well to have earned a goalless draw in Moscow four days earlier. Predictably, the atmosphere inside the Millennium Stadium, Cardiff, was stunning, with 70,000 Welshmen singing 'Land of My Fathers'. But, cruelly, Mark Hughes's valiant men were beaten by an early first-half goal, and were in the end outclassed.

Latvia, who achieved independence from the old Soviet Union in 1991, reached their first major finals. This had looked unlikely when Turkey overturned their 1-0 deficit to lead 2-1 on aggregate after 64 minutes. But two minutes later the Latvians scored a crucial away goal and then another to take the tie 3–2.

Holland drub Scotland.

Henry re-ignites Arsenal's campaign

IN RIPPING UP the record books as well as Inter Milan's defence in sensational fashion at the San Siro, Arsenal brilliantly regained control of their Champions League destiny. Here were Arsène Wenger's men finally delivering in Europe, imposing their domestic dynamism on a foreign field to scintillating effect.

Lombardy skies wept incessantly and they wept for Inter. Never before had a side representing Serie A, Europe's acknowledged citadel of expert defending, conceded five goals at home in the Champions League. Rarely had defenders of the calibre of Fabio Cannavaro, Ivan Cordoba, Marco Materazzi and Javier Zanetti, opponents who will fight forwards for gulps of air let alone glimpses of the ball, had their senses so scrambled by such fast-moving zephyrs as Arsenal's.

In 90 glorious minutes, particularly in a pulsating finale, Arsenal kept racing through Inter's midfield and back-line, kept raiding to bring goal after goal from the magnificent Thierry Henry, who struck twice, Freddie Ljungberg, Edu and Robert Pires.

What a turnaround: Arsenal landed in Lombardy bottom of Group B and departed in second place behind Lokomotiv Moscow, who had defeated Dynamo Kiev earlier in the day. The qualification equation now is far more attractive: victory over Lokomotiv at Highbury in a fortnight will guarantee Wenger's side safe passage through to the last 16.

If Arsenal's goalscorers inevitably took the limelight, the rearguard more than contributed. Jens Lehmann was outstanding in goal, while his back four coped well with Inter's surges. But Henry was the star of the show, putting on an individual performance of quite breathtaking brilliance. The Footballer of the Year repeatedly glided in and out of opponents down the left, utterly bemusing the Inter defence. This was the team who had shaken Arsenal to the core with that 3–0 defeat in the opening game of the group at Highbury 10 weeks ago. And Henry missed a penalty that night. Sweet revenge.

SOCCER SOUNDBITES

"The only performance I can compare this with was England's 5–1 in Munich, but this was even better."

ASHLEY COLE,
after Arsenal's 5–1 demolition of Inter

Thierry Henry put on a display of breathtaking brilliance in Milan.

10-man City bring off comeback of the century

UNBELIEVABLE. One of the greatest comebacks in the history of the FA Cup carried Manchester City, depleted but never dispirited, from the edge of oblivion to a fifth-round date with Manchester United. Sensational.

Spurs seemed to be strolling it at half-time in this fourth-round tie at White Hart Lane, 3–0 up with goals from Ledley King, Robbie Keane and Christian Ziege. City had been outfought completely; second to the ball time after time, so often it was almost embarrassing. And just before the interval they went down to 10 men when Joey Barton was dismissed, stupidly getting a second yellow for dissent. The City faithful stood there, stunned by the apparent nightmare unfolding in front of them, as all around cockerels crowed.

But talk about a game of two halves. City responded in magnificent style in the second half, shrugging off their numerical disadvantage with an effervescent display that had Spurs rocking on their heels. The exceptional Sylvain Distin headed in a Tarnat free-kick in the 48th minute. As City raced forward at every opportunity, nerves seeped into Spurs' play. Paul Bosvelt scored just after the hour, Shaun Wright-Phillips levelled with a fine strike after 80 minutes, and Jon Macken's famous, last-minute header sealed the fairytale. Unbelievable.

SOCCER SOUNDBITES

"Where's the nearest JobCentre?"

CITY MANAGER KEVIN KEEGAN,
to his No. 2 Derek Fazackerley as they walked down the tunnel at half-time

Football mourns a Gentle Giant

John Charles – never booked.

BRITISH AND ITALIAN football were united in mourning on 21 February following the death at 72 of John Charles, the man who rose from humble South Wales stock to become the greatest player of his generation and arguably one of the most gifted footballers of all time.

Nicknamed "The Gentle Giant", he was never sent off or even booked in his entire career. A minute's silence was observed at Old Trafford before Manchester United's draw with Leeds, the club where he became a legend after making his first-team debut at the age of 17.

Tributes also poured in from Juventus, the Turin club for which Charles scored 93 goals in 155 matches and where, 41 years after he last pulled on the No. 9 shirt, he is still revered as the most talented player ever to wear the famous black-and-white stripes.

Charles's career began on the ground staff of his local side, Swansea, before, in 1947, he was snapped up as a junior by Leeds. At 6ft 2in, he was equally at home in defence and attack, and many of his 316 appearances for Leeds were at centre-half.

But it was his success as a striker for which he will be best remembered, combining power, strength, speed and an awesome ability in the air. In the 1953–54 season, he scored 42 goals in 39 league matches – still a club record. In 1956 he helped Leeds gain promotion into the old First Division, and the following year, in his first season in the top flight, he found the net 38 times.

After moving to Juventus in 1957 for a record fee of £65,000, he scored 29 goals in his first season, an achievement that helped secure both the title and the Italian Footballer of the Year award. It was the first of three championships for Juventus during Charles's time there. He also won 38 caps for Wales following his debut as an 18-year-old, scoring 15 goals and playing in the last Wales team to take part in a World Cup finals, in Sweden in 1958.

SOCCER SOUNDBITES

"We mourn a great champion and a great man. He is a person who represented the sport in the best and purest manner."

ROBERTO BETTEGA,
Juventus vice-president and former Italy international

Eriksson loses subs battle

THE INTERNATIONAL FA Board, which comprises four members of FIFA and one each from the four home nations, met at the end of February.

They accepted FIFA's proposal to cut the substitutes allowed in friendly internationals to six, despite England's efforts to retain Sven-Göran Eriksson's total freedom to experiment in non-competitive matches. Eriksson's policy of substituting large numbers of players has been criticized by fans for making games they have paid to see uncompetitive.

The FA also failed in their attempt to persuade FIFA to turn the experimental rugby-style 10-yard rule into law. The IFAB insisted that it continue as an experiment for one more year.

The IFAB also confirmed they were abandoning silver and golden goals, so after Euro 2004 tie-breakers will revert to 30 minutes extra time and then penalties. Also returning is the rule earning an automatic caution for players who celebrate goals by peeling off their shirts.

Middlesbrough's time to party

ONE SHORT BLAST of the referee's whistle shortly before 4 pm on 29 February signalled sweet release from the longest of heartaches for Middlesbrough, blowing away the bitter memories of failed finals, liquidation, relegation, and decade after decade of frustration. This 2–1 Carling Cup defeat of Bolton Wanderers was not simply about vanquishing respected opponents over 90 pulsating minutes. This classic of a cup tie was about ending 128 years of hurt for these proud Teessiders. A club conceived in the Victorian era at last tasted real victory.

That one short blast had Juninho dancing in front of fans who have endured so much, whose dreams of a trophy and entry to Europe were realized by this wonderful little Brazilian, by the peerless Gareth Southgate, Bolo Zenden, Gaizka Mendieta, Franck Queudrue and all of their comrades in red.

And so, as Southgate stepped up to become the first Middlesbrough captain to receive a major honour, the legions from the Riverside roared their delight. A party so long in the planning got under way in earnest.

Triumph also brought deserved reward for their chairman, Steve Gibson, who has invested so much money and emotion in his childhood love. Gibson's manager, Steve McClaren, also gained a significant, silvery return on his team-building and on his ability to coax committed displays from top-class talents discarded by bigger clubs.

Spare a thought, too, for poor Bolton. Their fans sang relentlessly. Their players worked diligently. It was not enough. Already stunned by Joseph-Desire Job's second-minute opener, Bolton railed against Mike Riley four minutes later, upset by the referee's decision to punish the hapless Emerson Thome for knocking over Job in the box. The feeling of injustice seizing Bolton minds intensified when Zenden accidentally touched his successful penalty kick twice.

But Bolton were ultimately not quite strong enough in defence or attack to outmanoeuvre Boro. The industrious Kevin Davies did score, striking after 20 minutes and raising hopes of a revival.

Boro's resistance movement was superb. George Boateng worked overtime in midfield. Juninho kept racing through only for Bolton's defenders to turn avenues of opportunity into culs-de-sac for the busy Brazilian. But Juninho had the last dance.

Juninho ends 128 years of hurt.

Eriksson jilts Chelsea to sign up for England

ENGLAND COACH Sven-Göran Eriksson, who freely admits flirting with covetous clubs, yesterday (28 March) agreed a two-year contract extension to 2008. After demeaning his England job by discussing employment prospects with Chelsea last week, Eriksson received a £1 million-a-year wage rise. A talented coach is in charge of England, but his recent conduct is unbecoming indeed.

Thursday's visit to Chelsea's chief executive Peter Kenyon and past discussions with Roman Abramovich, their billionaire benefactor, were not just tea on the table, but the chance to replace the doomed Claudio Ranieri as Chelsea coach.

Eriksson explained without a hint of embarrassment that he had met Kenyon and Abramovich, discussed "possibilities" regarding the Chelsea job, but insisted he had done nothing wrong.

Either shamelessly brazen or spectacularly naive, Eriksson clearly does not appreciate that selecting 11 men to realize a nation's sporting dream is a handsomely paid honour requiring unequivocal commitment. But no words of contrition could be prised from the tightest of lips for the dalliance with Chelsea that ran alongside his negotiations with the FA's top brass.

Sven – settled in the job?

A Bridge too far for Arsenal

IT WAS always going to be a difficult fortnight for Arsenal, four games in 14 days in three competitions, against their two great rivals, Manchester United and Chelsea. And now their dreams of the treble are shattered, knocked out of the Cup by United and the European Champions League by Chelsea. They still lead the Premiership, unbeaten after 30 games. But Chelsea, having played a game more, are only four points behind, and Arsenal's thoughts must go back to last season when they blew the title from a much better position.

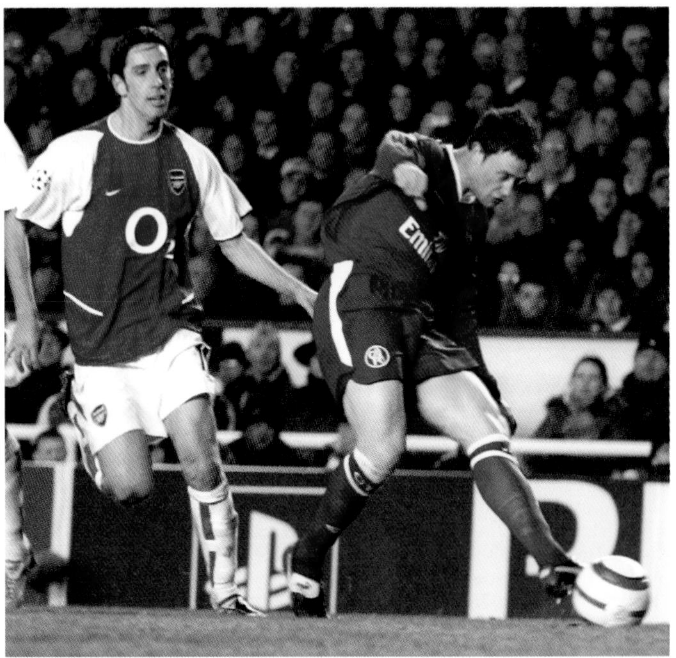

Wayne Bridge scores to send Arsenal out of the Champions League.

Fourteen days ago, Arsenal came away from the Bridge with a 1–1 draw in the first leg of the Champions quarter-final. At this time, they led the Premiership by nine points from Chelsea, 12 from United. But Chelsea beat Wolves on the Saturday, and Arsenal let two points slip at Highbury after outplaying United.

Arsenal arrived at Villa Park to defend their twice-won FA Cup in the semi-finals – their opponents, Manchester United. This time Arsenal, going for a record fourth consecutive final, were outplayed, and went down 1–0. Meanwhile, Chelsea's win at Tottenham cut Arsenal's Premiership lead to four points.

Undeterred by the fact that they had not beaten Arsenal in 17 previous meetings, Chelsea travelled the few miles to Highbury on the Tuesday night for the second leg of the Champions League quarter-final full of confidence. Inspired by the dynamic Frank Lampard and the rocklike John Terry, they refused to yield despite going behind to a Jose Antonio Reyes strike on the stroke of half-time. It was Lampard who pounced on Jens Lehmann's parried save six minutes after the interval to level the scores.

This was a classic Cup contest, a feast for the watching millions around the globe marvelling at a real ding-dong London derby played with European touch and technique.

With three minutes remaining, Chelsea surged forward. Left-back Wayne Bridge played a one-two with Eidur Gudjohnsen and stroked the ball past Lehmann for the all-important away goal. Chelsea were in the semis. And Claudio Ranieri, under intolerable pressure all season from Chelsea's powerbrokers, unashamedly wept tears of joy.

Gunners clinch title at White Hart Lane – again

ONCE AGAIN, Arsenal borrowed their neighbours' house for a party, yet this time Tottenham seemed not to mind. The sun shone on everyone at White Hart Lane. The indomitable showmen of Arsenal basked in the glow of a 13th title in the ground where they were crowned champions in 1971. Spurs fans were warmed by their team's resilience in fighting back to secure pride and virtual safety at the other end of the table.

Arsenal needed only a point to clinch the title, having reasserted themselves 16 days earlier on Good Friday, when they twice came back from behind to beat Liverpool 4–2 at Highbury. That result and the manner in which it was achieved was a message to Chelsea and Manchester United that there would be no slips like last season. And as those two challenges faded away, Arsenal continued to play exhilarating football, led by Thierry Henry, who scored a hat-trick against Liverpool and another four in their next home game, against poor Leeds.

At White Hart Lane, Arsenal started in the same vein. When Henry seized on a loose ball just outside his own penalty area after two minutes, his colleagues were off and running, haring towards Kasey Keller's goal, Spurs players choking on Arsenal's vapour trails. Bergkamp peeled away to the left, knowing the pass would come. Henry found him effortlessly, Bergkamp transferred it across the middle and there was Patrick Vieira sliding in to score from 10 yards, having made an astonishing break from the back

The champions-elect added a glorious second in the 34th minute through Pires, but in the second half Jamie Redknapp put Spurs back in the game, and a mad moment by keeper Jens Lehmann at the end gave them a penalty, converted by Robbie Keane, and a point.

Arsène Wenger refused the offer of champagne, asking for "only water" because "we have four games to go". The Frenchman might have become the first Arsenal manager to lift three championships, moving ahead of Herbert Chapman and George Graham, but he clearly had eyes on another prize – going through the season unbeaten.

Arsenal join the Invincibles

RELEGATED LEICESTER at home seemed an easy last hurdle in Arsenal's quest to go through a league season unbeaten, but at half-time they trailed to a goal from Highbury old boy Paul Dickov and were playing so lethargically that few were willing to predict the recovery needed for them to equal the 115-year-old unbeaten record of the inaugural champions from Preston. But Professor Wenger must have delivered a history lesson during the interval, for his men stirred themselves enough for Thierry Henry, with a penalty, and Patrick Vieira to earn the club their 26th victory of an immortal season.

The players had been back on the field only a couple of minutes when Frank Sinclair brought down Ashley Cole, destroying Paul Durkin's hopes of a card-free swansong – out came yellow – and Henry stroked his 30th league goal of the campaign, becoming the first Arsenal player to reach that figure since Ronnie Rooke 56 years ago. Vieira's winner was beautifully made by Dennis Bergkamp and majestically taken by the captain.

Arsenal seized the Premiership high ground on 10 January with a 4–1 demolition of Middlesbrough and never looked back. Thierry Henry has been little short of sensational bearing down on goal, Dennis Bergkamp has defied age and markers, Robert Pires has continued to conjure up endless creativity, while Patrick Vieira has been immense as a king among ball-winners. Class acts in a class of their own.

The complacency and defensive uncertainty that contributed to last season's collapse have been dispelled. Sol Campbell has found a pacey, mobile central-defensive partner in Ivory Coast international Kolo Toure, the revelation of the season in London N5.

Guided by the best manager in the land, Arsenal's players have been models of consistency. They have become even more formidable on learning to lengthen their fuses after the disciplinary nadir of Old Trafford. From hot-heads to ice-cool champions, Arsène Wenger's men have matured into deservedly the best team in the land as well as the most beautiful.

The beautiful and the damned good!

Different class

THE TWO CUP finals produced predictable results, with the underdogs completely outclassed, although it took the favourites, Manchester United and Celtic, a while to impose themselves. At Cardiff, Millwall demonstrated why they were still in the First Division. They had only two attempts at goal all afternoon, both blocked.

At Hampden Park, Dunfermline, albeit fourth-place finishers in the Scottish Premier League, but a massive 45 points and (with a negative goal difference) 87 goals behind champions Celtic, acquitted themselves better and actually led at half-time through Andrius Skerla's 40th-minute looping header.

But if you're talking about class, Henrik Larsson has it in spades, and the Swedish striker scored twice in the second half before Stilian Petrov netted a late third to clinch the Cup and League double, for the second time in Martin O'Neill's four years in charge. It was a fitting farewell for Larsson, leaving Celtic now after scoring a total of 242 goals in his wonderful seven years at the club.

The Manchester United fans were also treated to a virtuoso performance – from Cristiano Ronaldo. He dribbled and dummied with studs, ankles, soles, toes, and heels. Nothing below the knees was unused. Yet he cut the frills to place a perfect header into the net to put United into a 44th-minute lead.

This was a record fifth FA Cup triumph for United manager Sir Alex Ferguson, but little consolation for what for United was a disappointing season.

Ruud Van Nistelrooy scored a penalty in the 65th minute after Ryan Giggs was fouled and made it 3–0 with a late tap-in from a Giggs cross. Inexplicably, England manager Sven-Göran Eriksson gave him the man-of-the-match award when even Van Nistelrooy's mum would probably have given it to Ronaldo.

Henrik Larsson bows out of the Scottish Cup with a flourish.

FOOTBALL FOCUS

● With their two Euro 2004 qualifying games safely negotiated, England retained their record of never conceding a goal to Turkey, all in qualifying matches for either the World Cup or the European Championships. Their record: P 10, W 8, D 2, L 0, F 31, A 0.

● Livingston beat Hibs 2–0 in the final of the CIS Insurance (League) Cup to win their first-ever major trophy. At the time, they were one of three Scottish top-flight teams in administration.

● Leeds, contesting a European Cup semi-final only three years ago but whose financial state has led to the sale of many of their best players, were relegated from the Premiership.

● Crystal Palace's 1–0 victory over West Ham United in the First Division play-off final earned them an estimated £25 million jackpot, the reward for playing in the Premiership next season. The match, at Cardiff's Millennium Stadium, drew a crowd of 72,523 – 1,173 more than the FA Cup Final.

● Liverpool replaced Houllier with Valencia's Rafael Benitez, which left the Valencia job open for Ranieri.

FINAL SCORE

Football League
Premiership: Arsenal
Top scorer: Thierry Henry (Arsenal) 30
Division 1: Norwich
Division 2: Plymouth
Division 3: Doncaster
Footballer of the Year: Thierry Henry (Arsenal)

FA Cup Final
Manchester United 3 Millwall 0

League Cup Final
Middlesbrough 2 Bolton 1

Scottish League
Premier League: Celtic
Top scorer: Henrik Larsson (Celtic) 30
Division 1: Inverness CT
Division 2: Airdrie United
Division 3: Stranraer
Footballer of the Year: Jackie McNamara

Scottish FA Cup Final
Celtic 3 Dunfermline 1

Scottish League Cup Final
Livingston 2 Hibernian 0

European Cup Final
Porto 3 Monaco 0

UEFA Cup Final
Valencia 2 Marseille 0

European Footballer of the Year 2003
Pavel Nedved (Juventus and Czech Republic)

World Club Championship 2003
Boca Juniors 1 AC Milan 1
Boca won 3–1 on penalties

Heroes of the New Millennium

By Henry Winter

THEY ARE THE heroes of our footballing times, the stars who attract the headlines, the money and the idolatry. Shimmering with silver-screen allure, they dominate the small screen in the corners of a nation's living-rooms, bringing a touch of Hollywood glamour into millions of lives. They are the heroes who offer a glimpse of dreams fulfilled, of magic made real and a personal guarantee of gripping instalments of drama.

The English Premiership is a playhouse, overflowing with scene-stealers and scene-shifters, and audiences have been flocking to Highbury to watch the Three Musketeers.

France's finest, Thierry Henry, Patrick Vieira and Robert Pires, made Arsenal the best show in town, providing a rival attraction to the Theatre of Dreams at Manchester United. Suddenly all the rave reviews were being pinned up outside Highbury rather than Old Trafford.

Leading man Thierry Henry enjoys top billing on the star-filled stage at Highbury.

Swashbuckling stars

Some of the drama produced by Arsenal's swashbuckling heroes could have been transferred across town to London's West End. Henry, a one-man blockbuster act, goes through defences like jagged lightning bursts, switching this way and that, using his electric pace, natural athleticism and velvet touch to usher the ball into the net. Footballer of the Year Oscars kept coming his way. Charming and modest off the field, Henry is an idol blessed with grace as well as myriad footballing gifts.

If Henry enjoys top billing at Highbury, Vieira is not far behind. To describe Vieira as a ball-winner is akin to calling Michelangelo a painter and decorator. Vieira has turned repossessing the ball into an art form. Arsenal's tall, sinewy captain could relieve opponents of the ball with his stare let alone one of those famous tackles which range from pickpocket to bulldozer. Vieira uses those impossibly long legs to nick the ball, often flicking it up and over his foe's head, and sprints forward, his mastery confirmed.

Patrick Vieira takes on Paul Scholes and Roy Keane.

Vieira then often seeks out Henry or Pires, the Musketeer with the D'Artagnan whiskers. Pires is hardly an elegant mover, scuttling upfield like a Coldstream Guardsmen running for a bus, but his touch and vision make him special. With a drop of a shoulder, a sudden change of direction and flick of a pass, Pires creates havoc and chances in equal measure.

Drama and dynamos

The Three Musketeers have gone down a storm at the English box office, even leading to standing ovations at supposedly intimidating venues like Fratton Park and Elland Road. United, though, refuse to be completely upstaged. The sold-out sign hangs outside Old Trafford for every performance, particularly when stars like Ruud van Nistelrooy and Paul Scholes have received rapturous applause for their displays.

Van Nistelrooy is a great scorer of goals rather than a scorer of great goals. The Dutchman is the master of the well-timed run and nudge over the line, the close-range poaching, the turn and shot past a startled keeper. Cold and clinical, Van Nistelrooy operates like an assassin, picking off chances. Yet he works hard for the team, tracking back to hound opposing defenders who have the temerity to steer the ball upfield.

Scholes, too, sweats overtime for the cause. The England midfielder loathes the limelight, would rather look at old programmes of his beloved Oldham Athletic than attend premieres, and does all his talking on the pitch. With spectacular eloquence! "Paul Scholes, he scores goals," sing the fans and what a repertoire! Ghosting through unnoticed to apply the finishing touch or

In Wayne Rooney, Everton have unearthherd a gem that also glitters for England.

thundering one in from 25 yards, Scholes is a constant threat.

Danger lurks all over Premiership arenas, not least when Wayne Rooney, the young gunslinger, swaggers into town. It is not just the venomous shot with little back-lift that so terrifies defenders. It is Rooney's clever link-play between midfield and attack, his perceptive first touch and awareness of team-mates' positioning, that set him apart as a hero. Everton have unearthed a gem that also glitters for England.

Scarcely a mile down the road from Everton's Bellefield training ground lies Melwood, where two more local heroes have been raised. Steven Gerrard is that rare breed, an Englishman who can turn adversity into victory through strength of personality, accuracy of pass, driving runs from midfield or explosive shots. Another established England international, Michael Owen, thrives on quick service from midfield, racing forward to beat a keeper through speed and control and sheer determination.

Sadly, Owen's England partnership with Alan Shearer never really gelled. Shearer retired from the international scene and intensified his plundering of Premiership defences. This tough Geordie keeps muscling markers out of the way, keeps drilling shots in and keeps defying those who dared suggest his battle-scarred legs were about to yield for good. In good time, Shearer will decide when it is pipe-and-slippers time.

If Shearer represents England's past, Frank Lampard and David Beckham form its vibrant present. Lampard has come of age at Chelsea, maturing so impressively as man and midfielder that English pulses instinctively quicken when he picks up possession, looking to release team-mates or send a pile-driver raging through the air until its passage is stopped by the net.

Grace and greatness

Beckham has become a 21st-century phenomenon, generating vast riches for himself through his relentless self-expression on the pitch and self-promotion off it. Strip away all the hype about the Beckham brand and what remains is a likeable lad with an outstanding knack of moving a ball unerringly around a patch of grass.

Trusting people can be difficult for the rich and famous but Beckham has forged a close alliance with Sven-Göran Eriksson, the man charged with reviving England's fortunes. Beckham and his fellow-internationals all took to the quiet Swede because he treated them like adults, proving that motivation can be provided through quiet words not teacups around the ears.

Eriksson's reputation ensured covetous glances from newly wealthy clubs like Chelsea, which was bought by the Russian billionaire, Roman Abramovich after he flew over London in his helicopter and noticed the pitch. Within days, fans were sporting Cossack hats, dancing to Kalinka music and revelling in the sight of so many stars alighting at Stamford Bridge.

Problems persist. Diving is a boil disfiguring the face of the Beautiful Game. Chelsea fielded a team lacking any Englishmen, although have since reversed such a dangerous trend for club and country. Crazy player wages carried some clubs to the brink of oblivion. The wonderful Champions League has lessened the elite's interest in the FA Cup. But the Premiership show goes on. To rapturous acclaim.

Liverpool's driving force, homegrown talent Steven Gerrard.

Modern Greek odyssey

Greece had never won a match at a major tournament before and started as 100–1 outsiders, yet they beat host country Portugal twice and also accounted for favourites and holders France on their remarkable journey to become champions of Europe – truly a modern Greek odyssey.

PORTUGAL STAGED a thrilling and successful European Championship finals tournament, proving excellent hosts. Their team, inspired by fervent support from the people, reached the final. But their party was spoiled by the unfancied Greek side, who confounded all predictions by taking the final 1–0.

Greece began the tournament by beating Portugal in the first match of Group A. That 2–1 defeat was put down to a nervous performance by the hosts in front of their own expectant crowd. Portugal showed their true form when they beat Russia 2–0, but they still had to defeat Spain to go through. They had never beaten their larger neighbour in a competitive international before, but half-time substitute Nuno Gomes scored the only goal, turning to sweep in a 22-yarder in the 57th minute.

After a goalless draw between Switzerland and Croatia, Group B caught fire with a sensational clash between tournament favourites France and an England side of which much was expected. Despite having most of the play, France found themselves 1–0 down to a 38th-minute Frank Lampard header from a David Beckham free-kick. Indeed, the England captain could have clinched the match late in the second half, when Wayne Rooney broke away and was fouled by Mikael Silvestre in the French box. Maybe Silvestre should have been sent off, but Beckham failed to punish his former Old Trafford colleague with a weak penalty saved by Barthez. Still, it looked like a hard-fought, backs-to-the-wall victory for England but substitute Emil Heskey, on for Rooney, needlessly gave away a free-kick outside England's box, and Zidane swept the ball past David James. England were totally shattered, three minutes later when Thierry latched on to a careless Steven Gerrard back-pass and was brought down by James, another culprit perhaps lucky to stay on the pitch. However, James failed to stop Zidane's spot-kick and the holders started the defence of their trophy with a remarkable 2–1 win.

Wayne Rooney, seen here scoring against Croatia, was perhaps the outstanding talent of Euro 2004.

France then stumbled to a 2–2 draw with Croatia and England beat Switzerland 3–0. Rooney scored twice for England. The Evertonian gathered more rave notices after another stunning performance – and two more goals – in England's 4–2 defeat of Croatia. But two late goals by Henry gave France a 3–1 victory over Switzerland and a seemingly easier quarter-final against Greece, while England had to play Portugal.

The demise of Italy

Group C saw the demise of one of the tournament favourites, Italy. All the teams beat Bulgaria – Sweden by 5–0, with two in two second-half minutes by Henrik Larsson on his international comeback. Italy were held to draws, 0–0 by Denmark and then 1–1 by Sweden. This left the two Scandinavian countries requiring a draw – 2–2 or more – from their last match for them both to go through whatever Italy's result against Bulgaria. There were whispers in the Italian camp of an "agreement" between Sweden and Denmark before the match, which were reinforced after the two sides did indeed draw 2–2. But the desperate 89th-minute equalizer from Sweden's Mattias Jonson – hardly a put-up job – left Italy, last-minute victors themselves over Bulgaria, with no more than a discredited conspiracy theory to show for what by their standards was a set of poor performances.

The Czech Republic were the only country to win all three of their opening matches. Liverpool striker Milan Baros starred for the Czechs, scoring in all three of their Group D matches. In their last game they made nine changes from the side that had defeated Holland 3–2, yet still beat an admittedly lacklustre German team 2–1 to knock the three-times champions out. Holland beat Latvia 3–0, with a brace from Ruud van Nistelrooy, to join the Czechs in the quarter-finals. But 500–1 outsiders Latvia had been a revelation, leading the Czechs at half-time before succumbing to two late goals and then drawing 0–0 with Germany.

Out go the favourites

England and France, pre-tournament fancies perhaps to meet in the final, were both shown the door in the quarters. England's age-old vulnerabilty in penalty shoot-outs was again exposed, this time by Portugal. England could not have wished for a better start, Michael Owen putting them ahead in the third minute. But after 27 minutes England suffered a mighty setback when talisman Rooney broke a bone in his foot that finished his tournament. England courageously took everything Portugal could throw at them and kept Portugal at bay for 80 minutes after Owen's opener, until Spurs' forgotten man Helder Postiga, who had come on for Figo, equalized with a header. Even so, England could have won it in the last minutes of normal time, when Campbell nodded the ball over the line – only for referee Urs Meier controversially to judge that Terry had fouled keeper Ricardo. The excitement didn't let up in extra time and, when Rui Costa scored a brilliant goal after five minutes of the second period, Portugal celebrated as if they had won. But England came back five minutes later, Lampard turning in Terry's header from a corner. England made a disastrous start to the penalty competition, when Beckham slipped (as in Turkey) and lofted the ball high over the bar. But Rui Costa later missed and, with the tally 5–5, Darius Vassell struck a poor penalty that was saved by Ricardo. The home keeper then became a national hero as he strode up to smash the decisive kick past James.

The second quarter-final was tame by comparison, as Greece deservedly eliminated reigning champions France, who succumbed to a towering header from the unmarked Angelos Charisteas in the 69th minute. Then Holland beat Sweden on penalties following a goalless 120 minutes. After one miss from each side, keeper Edwin Van der Sar, a tower of strength for Holland, guessed correctly to save from gallant Sweden captain Olof Mellberg, leaving winger Arjen Robben, Chelsea's latest acquisition, to slot home the decider. In the last quarter-final, the Czechs went marching on, hitting three second-half goals against Denmark. Milan Baros, who spent most of last season either injured or on Liverpool's bench, took his tally to five with two of them.

Portugal continued to enjoy their party in the semi-finals with a 2–1 win over Holland and their fans celebrated reaching a major final for the first time. Their stars were Ronaldo, who opened the scoring with a fine header, Figo, who produced another terrific display and midfielder Maniche, who scored a superb second goal, bending a tremendous drive round Van der Sar at the far post. But when Jorge Andrade looped an attempted clearance over his own keeper, they had to defend well for half an hour to clinch their place in the final.

In the other semi, the Greeks caused another upset, against probably the most fluid and attractive team in the competition, the Czech Republic. But after losing their most influential player, Pavel Nedved, to a first-half knee injury, the Czechs were not the same team. However, as the match entered extra time, it was difficult to see where a Greek goal was coming from. Then, just as the turn-around was looming, the centre-back Traianos Dellas stole up for a corner and headed home, giving the Greeks a "silver goal".

Whatever the result of the final, the winners would be the first champions managed by a foreign coach. It was the organization and tactics of German coach Otto Rehhagel against the flair of Brazilian Luis Felipe Scolari. The German won the battle, again adjusting his tactics to produce a team effort. The Greeks shackled the individual brilliance of Portugal's stars. And in one of their surprise attacks they broke away to force a corner. Angelis Basinas' kick was met by a powerful header from Werder Bremen striker Charisteas in the 57th minute to give Greece the winning goal. But it was the Greece defenders who won the plaudits, in particular Roma centre-back Dellas, who had another storming match. Above all, though, it was their teamwork that enabled Greece to pull off the biggest shock in the history of the European Championship.

One for all and all for one – Charisteas rounds off all Greece's teamwork with the winner in the final.

SOCCER SOUNDBITES

"Eriksson does this all the time, substituting offensive players with defensive ones. His tactics cost England a chance of success."

TERRY PAINE,
former England international, speaking on South African TV after England's defeat by Portugal

FINAL SCORE

FIRST ROUND

Group A

Portugal	1	Greece	2
Spain	1	Russia	0
Greece	1	Spain	1
Russia	0	Portugal	2
Spain	0	Portugal	1
Russia	2	Greece	1

	P	W	D	L	F	A	P
Portugal	3	2	0	1	4	2	6
Greece	3	1	1	1	4	4	4
Spain	3	1	1	1	2	2	4
Russia	3	1	0	2	2	4	3

Group B

Switzerland	0	Croatia	0
France	2	England	1
England	3	Switzerland	0
Croatia	2	France	2
Croatia	2	England	4
Switzerland	1	France	3

	P	W	D	L	F	A	P
France	3	2	1	0	7	4	7
England	3	2	0	1	8	4	6
Croatia	3	0	2	1	4	6	2
Switzerland	3	0	1	2	1	6	1

Group C

Denmark	0	Italy	0
Sweden	5	Bulgaria	0
Bulgaria	0	Denmark	2
Italy	1	Sweden	1
Italy	2	Bulgaria	1
Denmark	2	Sweden	2

	P	W	D	L	F	A	P
Sweden	3	1	2	0	8	3	5
Denmark	3	1	2	0	4	2	5
Italy	3	1	2	0	3	2	5
Bulgaria	3	0	0	3	1	9	0

Group D

Germany	1	Holland	1
Czech Rep	2	Latvia	1
Latvia	0	Germany	0
Holland	2	Czech Rep	3
Holland	3	Latvia	0
Germany	1	Czech Rep	2

	P	W	D	L	F	A	P
Czech Rep	3	3	0	0	7	4	9
Holland	3	1	1	1	6	4	4
Germany	3	0	2	1	2	3	2
Latvia	3	0	1	2	1	5	1

QUARTER-FINALS

Portugal	2	England	2
Portugal won 6-5 on penalties			
France	0	Greece	1
Sweden	0	Holland	0
Holland won 5-4 on penalties			
Czech Rep	3	Denmark	0

SEMI-FINALS

Portugal	2	Holland	1
Greece	1	Czech Rep	0
(Greece won on "silver goal" rule)			

FINAL

Greece	1	Portugal	0

Estadio da Luz, Lisbon, 4 July 2004.
Attendance 62,865

Greece: Nikopolidis; Seitaridis, Dellas, Kapsis, Fyssas, Zagorakis, Katsouranis, Bassinas, Giannakopoulos (Venetidis 76), Charisteas, Vryzas (Papadopoulos 80)

Portugal: Ricardo; Miguel (Ferreira 43), Andrade, Carvalho, Nuno Valente, Costinha (Rui Costa 60), Maniche, Figo, Deco, Ronaldo, Pauleta (Gomes (73)

Leading scorers
5 Baros (Czech Republic)
4 Rooney (England), Van Nistelrooy (Holland)
3 Zidane (France), Larsson (Sweden), Tomasson (Denmark), Lampard (England)

Brian Clough dies

Flowers placed by the bust of Brian Clough at Nottingham Forest's City Ground the day after he died.

BRIAN CLOUGH, one of football's most charismatic proponents, and arguably the best manager England never had, died as a result of stomach cancer, aged 69. In statistical terms he won two European Cups, back-to-back, two League titles, and four League Cups; Brian Clough's success in his chosen field, though, was more than just facts and figures.

The man who gave himself the nickname 'Ol' Big 'Ead' when he received the OBE in 1991, was the most outspoken and controversial of figures throughout his career, yet he became one of the game's most respected managers. When he died, in September, fans, many in tears, laid flowers outside the gates of the two Midlands clubs he transformed out of all recognition, Derby County and Nottingham Forest.

Garry Birtles, who played under Clough at Forest, said: "We thought he was indestructible. It's like a member of your own family dying." Martin O'Neill, the Celtic manager, another of Clough's signings for Forest, added: "He was like Britain's Mohammed Ali. He was just so charismatic."

Clough, never one for false modesty, once gave a self-assessment, declaring himself if not the best manager in the country, certainly "in the top one".

There were many who did not disagree; however, among those who did were the Football Association, who famously overlooked him as a replacement for Don Revie as England manager in 1977 because, he claimed with typical bluster, they were frightened of him.

After a serious leg injury ended his career prematurely – he scored 204 goals for Middlesbrough in 222 games, and a further 63 in two years at Sunderland – he cut his managerial teeth at Hartlepool before joining Derby in 1967. He took them to the League title in 1972 before walking out, along with his assistant Peter Taylor, after a series of acrimonious disputes with the board.

He had spells with Brighton and Leeds, where he lasted 44 days, before moving to Forest, and taking them to the most successful period in their history: he won the League in 1978, only the second man to guide two different clubs to the title, and followed that with the European Cup in 1979 and 1980. However, his last season as a manager, in 1993, was marred by his first relegation.

Ten years later, he underwent a liver transplant, the culmination of years of heavy drinking. Soon after, he was diagnosed with cancer.

Chelsea's illegal approach for Ashley Cole

CHELSEA were fined a record £300,000 by the Premier League, and received a suspended three-point deduction, after being found guilty of making an illegal approach to Ashley Cole, Arsenal's England left-back.

An independent commission concluded that Cole had met at the Royal Park Hotel in London with Chelsea officials, including manager Jose Mourinho and chief executive Peter Kenyon, to discuss a potential transfer to Stamford Bridge, without the prior permission of his employers.

Cole was fined £100,000 – later reduced to £75,000 on appeal – and Mourinho was fined £200,000, also later reduced to £75,000. The commission decided that Cole had been "manipulated to a large extend by his agent [Jonathan Barnett]", who had his licence suspended for 18 months on top of a £100,000 fine.

The financial penalty imposed on the player was intended to make it "unlikely that Ashley Cole would ever be tempted in this way again". It was more than a year before Cole would finally move across London in a deal that cost Chelsea £5 million as well as defender William Gallas switching to Arsenal.

In his subsequent autobiography, Cole would claim that the Arsenal board had treated him as a "scapegoat" and that they had "fed him to the sharks" over the affair. Arsenal fans were not so forgiving, suggesting he had only left the club for more money, nicknaming him thereafter 'Cashley Cole'.

A year on and Ashley Cole would finally move across London to join Chelsea and Jose Mourinho.

SOCCER SOUNDBITES

"If people come to your window and talk to your wife every night, you can't accept it without asking what is happening."

ARSENE WENGER, justifies Arsenal's displeasure over Chelsea's illegal approach for Ashley Cole.

"I ended up drinking more than I could have justified if I'd won every trophy available in every season of my career."

BRIAN CLOUGH, talking about his battle with alcoholism.

Glazer takes over United

THE takeover of Manchester United by the American tycoon Malcolm Glazer caused much consternation among supporters, many of whom believed it signalled the death of the club.

Fans feared that the way the takeover was to be financed, taking on a debt of £660 million, some of it based on United's assets, for which the annual interest was around £60 million, would damage the club. In addition, they objected to the fact that it would lead to escalating ticket prices at a time when the club were earning more and more money through television and sponsorship deals.

For some it was too much, and their protest led them to form a breakaway team, FC United, known as the Red Rebels, who would compete in the North West Counties League.

The takeover was a long drawn-out saga that lasted more than half the season, starting in November when Glazer, owner of the Tampa Bay Buccaneers NFL team, used his £205 million stake in the club to force out three directors. He was given a May deadline to decide whether to pursue a takeover, and then bought up the shares of JP McManus and John Magnier, the Irish racing millionaires, to give him a majority holding.

Glazer finally gained full control in June through Red Football Ltd, and converted the plc into a private company.

Mourinho's 'hush' gesture at Carling Cup final

JOSE MOURINHO claimed his first trophy as Chelsea manager, though he was not present to see the denouement of a storming comeback to beat Liverpool and win the Carling Cup in extra time. Mourinho had been banished from the touchline and watched for nearly three-quarters of an hour on a television monitor in an interview room at the Millennium Stadium.

Mourinho's 'crime' was to put his finger over his mouth as if to hush nearby Liverpool fans after Steven Gerrard had diverted Paulo Ferreira's free-kick past his own goalkeeper for Chelsea's equaliser 11 minutes from time. Initially it was thought a police officer had instructed fourth official Phil Crossley to dismiss Mourinho for "public order purposes"; it later transpired Crossley had made the decision.

Mourinho's gesture led to him being banished from the pitch.

Mourinho, however, said that his gesture was made not against rival fans, but towards the press box to advise the media to "cool down" in their criticism of his team. "They talk too much after we lost two games and tried to do everything to take confidence from us," he said.

"I have to adapt to you," he told the press afterwards, "but you have to adapt to me. I want to win trophies; I don't want to love you."

The FA, who could have taken sanctions against the Chelsea manager, decided not to charge him, and he escaped with a warning. "For a gesture, it was fairly low down the scale of provocation," Frank Clark, of the League Managers' Association, said. "He didn't swear at anyone and it wasn't obscene."

The incident overshadowed a tumultuous finale. Gerrard's inadvertent deflection equalised John Arne Riise's opener, and forced an extra half-hour during which Didier Drogba and Mateja Kezman continued the Chelsea fightback. Antonio Nunez's late goal reduced the final score to 3–2.

Celtic lose Scottish title on last day

Celtic's Craig Bellamy sits on the pitch dejected after Motherwell scored two goals in the dying minutes to deny his team the title.

CELTIC suffered a last day of the Scottish Premier League season they would rather forget. Not only did it become clear that Martin O'Neill was about to stand down as manager, the reigning champions conceded two late goals to relinquish the title to the other side of Glasgow.

Celtic were ahead with only two minutes of normal time left at Motherwell when everything turned on its head. In that brief time, O'Neill saw an almost immaculate record sullied. Had Celtic held on, or taken any of the multitude of chances they contrived to miss in the second half, they would have been champions by a clear margin.

Then, O'Neill could have stood down having won the title for the fourth time in five years, with the other lost only on goal difference to Rangers two years before. However, he departed with a less resounding three from five, and the knowledge that Celtic had held their destiny in their own hands.

"So now, after 38 games, we have nothing to show, and we are devastated," O'Neill said. "It hurts more than losing the UEFA Cup final in Seville [in 2003]."

Terry Butcher, the Motherwell manager and a former Rangers captain, threw on forwards in the closing minutes as Celtic suddenly looked a spent force. Coincidentally, Scott McDonald, who scored the two goals, and Gerry Britton, sent on to play alongside him, were both self-confessed Celtic fans.

"They were very special goals, the most significant of my career," McDonald said. "I'm a Celtic man and so are most of my friends, so I don't think they'll be talking to me for a long time."

At the height of Celtic's earlier bombardment came news that Rangers had gone ahead at Hibernian. "The thought [that it could go wrong] must have been crossing the minds of many people when we didn't score during that spell," O'Neill said. "On any normal day we would have taken our chances and we shouldn't have lost the game."

O'Neill confirmed a few days later that he was leaving the club to care for his wife Geraldine, and would be replaced by Gordon Strachan. His parting gift was victory, a week later, in the Scottish Cup final, when Celtic beat Dundee United.

Liverpool win Champions League from 3–0 down

LIVERPOOL, down and out at half-time, came back to win the European Cup for the fifth time in their history after a penalty shoot-out in one of the most extraordinary evenings of football. Inspired by a stupendous performance from captain Steven Gerrard, Liverpool picked themselves up from the depths of despair to win 3–2 on penalties after 120 minutes of excitement.

"At 3–0 down at half-time I thought I was going to be in tears after the final whistle," Gerrard said. "But the manager said keep our chins up and try and score early – and we did."

Jerzy Dudek celebrates after saving the penaly that gave Liverpool victory over AC Milan in the 2005 Champions League Final.

Gerrard tore into Milan from the first whistle of the second half, scoring the first goal himself, creating the space for Vladimir Smicer to add a second, and then winning the penalty for Xabi Alonso to drive Liverpool level – all inside the first 15 minutes. "When the captain scores all the team play the same," manager Rafa Benitez said in praise of Gerrard.

Benitez's decision at half-time to introduce Dietmar Hamann, stiffening Liverpool's midfield, released Gerrard to play further forward to match-winning effect.

Liverpool's other hero on a memorable night in Istanbul was goalkeeper Jerzy Dudek, who not only made a sensational double save to prevent Andrei Shevchenko winning the game for Milan in open play, but saved penalties from Andrea Pirlo and, finally, Shevchenko in a shoot-out during which the Italians failed to convert three of their five kicks.

Dudek revealed that the wobbly-legged antics of Bruce Grobbelaar during a similar penalty finale 21 years earlier, when Liverpool beat Roma, had stuck in his mind. "Of course I watched it [in 1984]," he said. "That was my inspiration. You wouldn't have given a lot for our chances at half-time, but the boys were absolutely magnificent."

However, for the first 45 minutes Liverpool could not handle Milan's midfield of Pirlo, Gennaro Gattuso, Clarence Seedorf and the outstanding Kaka. Indeed, Liverpool had not settled down when Pirlo bent in a free-kick in the first minute for veteran defender Paolo Maldini to open the scoring.

Kaka played a prominent part in Hernan Crespo's two goals which seemed to put Milan out of reach: his through ball gave Shevchenko the space to cross for the first, and his dash through the middle set Crespo free just before half-time to score with a clinical, dinked finish.

The Liverpool fans chanted throughout the interval: "We're gonna win 4–3." The players responded with a never-to-be-forgotten second-half display.

Sven and the FA secretary

SVEN-GORAN ERIKSSON managed to remain in his job as England manager after details were made public of an affair with Faria Alam, a secretary at the Football Association. However, the fall-out had a drastic effect on the FA, and while Eriksson escaped unscathed, apart from damage to his reputation, some high-placed members of the executive did not.

Mark Palios, the FA chief executive, who also had an affair with Alam, would eventually resign, and director of communications Colin Gibson also left after details were revealed of an attempted deal to disentangle Palios, at the expense of Eriksson, with the *News of the World*.

The FA had responded to initial allegations about Eriksson's dalliances with an official denial, only to be forced to admit that both relationships were true.

Alam, 39, a former Bangladeshi model, had joined the FA in 2003 as PA to executive director David Davies, against whom she would later make allegations of sexual harassment. She soon began the affair with Palios, and when he finished with her, she became involved with Eriksson.

Eriksson persuaded her to deny they had embarked on a relationship when it became public knowledge. Indeed the FA issued a statement from Alam's lawyers saying: "There is no truth whatsoever in the suggestion that our client and Mr Eriksson were having, or have had, a sexual relationship".

However, when further details emerged, the FA had to backtrack, and launched an inquiry into the way the claims were handled. Eriksson, though, said: "I wish to state unequivocally that I have at no time either categorically confirmed or denied any relationship with Faria Alam."

Soon after, the *News of the World* revealed that Gibson had tried to broker a deal with the paper whereby he would give "chapter and verse" on Eriksson's affair with Alam in return for keeping Palios out of the picture.

Alam resigned at the height of the scandal, and her claims against the FA for unfair dismissal and breach of contract were rejected by an industrial tribunal. Indeed, they branded her claim of sexual harassment against Davies as "a figment of her fertile imagination".

In a damning 16-page indictment of Alam's behaviour, the tribunal ruled that her evidence was "contradictory", and that she made "unfounded" allegations against Davies and "the threat of further disclosures" to pressure the FA into paying her off.

FOOTBALL FOCUS

- Arsenal's 5–1 win over Crystal Palace in February was notable not only for its size, but also for the fact that, for the first time, they fielded a team without an English player in their ranks. Earlier, in late autumn, a 2–0 defeat by Manchester United ended a 49-game unbeaten run in the Premier League that earned them the epithet 'The Invincibles'.

- David Prutton, the Southampton midfielder, was handed a 10-match suspension, and a £6,000 fine, after admitting two charges of improper conduct: apart from failing to leave the field promptly following a second yellow card against Arsenal, he also pushed referee Alan Wiley several times as he continued to argue.

- Jacques Santini's reign at White Hart Lane lasted just 13 games before the former France national team manager left Tottenham Hotspur under a cloud, to be replaced by Martin Jol.

- The Wembley authorities decided to dedicate a bridge after Billy, the horse ridden by PC George Scorey, who helped control the crowd at the first FA Cup final there in 1923. The name 'White Horse' was chosen by the public ahead of Live Aid, Sir Alf Ramsey, Sir Geoff Hurst, Sir Bobby Charlton and a mass vote from north of the border for Jim Baxter.

Chelsea's first title for 50 years

Captain John Terry celebrates Chelsea's first league title for 50 years.

WHEN Chelsea received the Premiership trophy eight days before the end of the season, 13 white-haired old men walked on to the pitch to join in the celebrations. They were the surviving members of the team who had won the First Division title in 1955, and who had never had the trophy formally presented to them.

"We're sorry it's taken 50 years," the stadium announcer said as Roy Bentley, the Chelsea pensioners' captain, was handed the trophy by John Terry and Frank Lampard, his modern-day successors.

Chelsea had wrapped up their first league success in half-a-century a week earlier, with three games still to play, with victory over Bolton at the Reebok Stadium. They would overhaul Manchester United's record 92 points in a season with a sensational win at Old Trafford in their penultimate game, and eventually finish with 95 points.

Jose Mourinho, whose first trophy as Chelsea manager was in the Carling Cup final in February, said: "My nature is not to be happy, but to want more. This is the beginning of a process; this is not the end.

"This is my first season, and I have five more years on my contract," he warned the rest of the Premiership. "I am already thinking about next season."

In finishing a dozen points ahead of deposed champions Arsenal, Chelsea had raised the bar in terms of points. But for a bad day at Manchester City in October, their only league defeat of the season, they might even have stolen Arsenal's 'Invincibles' tag.

Their football might not have been the most exhilarating, and they did not show the breathtaking qualities of Arsenal in full flight, but their counter-attacking style was reminiscent of their closest rivals.

Lampard, the Footballer of the Year, reacted to Chelsea's detractors: "There have been some harsh words spoken about us not being attractive and that the best two teams in the Premiership are in the final of the FA Cup [Arsenal and United]. But the best team wins the league and we have done that."

Terry, a home-grown player, summed up what it meant to end the 50-year drought. "It feels very emotional," he said. "I just want to break down and I probably will when I get back to my hotel room on my own, [and] I sit back and watch it on TV. We've made a lot of sacrifices this year, trained hard and worked hard, and it's paid off."

Fergie's 1,000th game in charge of United

SIR ALEX FERGUSON became only the second man to preside over 1,000 matches with one club; the other was one of his predecessors at Manchester United, Sir Matt Busby, who finally retired after reaching 1,080.

The build-up to match No 1,000 – a routine Champions League win against Lyon – gave Ferguson, 62, the opportunity to look back over his 18-year reign at Old Trafford. He approved of some of the innovations that had happened during his time, including the introduction of the Premier League, and the way the arrival of Sky television had taken the game to heightened levels of interest.

However, he said: "With that you bring a certain penalty, and the penalty is how the profile of footballers has changed. You have to think that maybe the part that agents play in projecting that image now has become too much."

The years – during which he had won eight Premiership titles, five FA Cups, and two European trophies – have mellowed Ferguson. "Nothing will affect me in the same way it would, maybe 18 years ago," he said. "If I lost then, I took it very badly. Now there's a maturity about me. I've seen it all before. I'm not getting my knickers in a twist about it. If I'm not happy about something I make sure it doesn't happen again. If I can."

FINAL SCORE

Football League
Premiership – Chelsea
Top scorer – Thierry Henry (Arsenal) 25
Championship – Sunderland
League 1 – Luton Town
League 2 – Yeovil Town
Footballer of the Year – Frank Lampard (Chelsea)

FA Cup final
Arsenal 0 Manchester United 0
(aet; Arsenal won 5–4 on pens)

League Cup final
Liverpool 2 Chelsea 3
(aet)

Scottish League
Premier League – Rangers
Top scorer – John Hartson (Celtic) 25
Div 1 – Falkirk
Div 2 – Brechin City
Div 3 – Gretna
Footballer of the Year – John Hartson (Celtic)

Scottish FA Cup final
Celtic 1 Dundee United 0

Scottish League Cup final
Motherwell 1 Rangers 5

European Cup final
Liverpool 3 AC Milan 3
(aet; Liverpool won 3–2 on pens)

UEFA Cup final
Sporting Lisbon 1 CSKA Moscow 3

European Footballer of the Year 2004
Kaka (AC Milan & Brazil)

World Club Championship 2004
Porto 0 Once Caldas 0
(Porto won 8–7 on pens)

Liverpool win sensational FA Cup final

THE last FA Cup final to be played at Cardiff's Millennium Stadium, its temporary home for fully six seasons while Wembley was rebuilt, was arguably one of the best in the competition's long history. Liverpool won it comfortably enough on penalties against West Ham, but only after they equalised for the second time just as it was announced there would be an additional four minutes at the end of normal time.

Veteran cup final watchers were struggling to find comparisons: at one stage the 1979 Arsenal-Manchester United classic had become the yardstick, after the Matthews final of 1953, and Manchester United's success in 1948. The 125th final itself felt like a throwback, where the referee had little to do, and both sides were committed to attack.

Liverpool's Jose Reina makes a crucial save. The Reds would eventually defeat West Ham on penalties.

West Ham, who had led 2–0 and 3–2, lost the shootout 3–1. But it was in keeping with the marvellous spirit of the day that Peter Crouch was quick to lope across the pitch and console the tearful Anton Ferdinand after he missed the decisive kick. In return the West Ham fans stayed on at the end to applaud Liverpool's lap of honour.

That had not looked likely as West Ham raced into a two-goal lead within half-an-hour through Jamie Carragher's own goal and a second by Dean Ashton. Djibril Cisse pulled one back before half-time, and Steven Gerrard levelled the scores for the first time nine minutes into the second half. When Paul Konchesky lofted a cross over Pepe Reina's head, and inside the far post, it looked as if West Ham would hold on.

It was then, though, that Gerrard popped up with what was fast becoming a trademark equaliser in the 90th minute, driving home a devastating shot of power and precision from outside the penalty area. In the penalty shootout, Reina restored his reputation with saves from Yossi Benayoun, Konchesky and Ferdinand to complete the afternoon's turnaround.

England lose to Northern Ireland

ENGLAND'S passage to the finals of the 2006 World Cup was not without incident. Though they only lost one game along the road to qualification, that defeat was significant for the humiliation felt one September night in Belfast.

There had not been a night like it for Northern Ireland, 1–0 winners thanks to David Healy's goal, since they knocked out the hosts Spain in the 1982 World Cup finals.

For England it was a defeat that ranked with the one by Norway in 1981. After all, they had not lost to Northern Ireland in Belfast since 1927, nor been beaten by them anywhere since 1972.

In qualification terms, it meant England needed to beat both Austria and Poland in their final matches to top their group, and avoid the necessity of trying to progress through the play-offs. In the end they beat Poland 2–1 at Old Trafford in the final match to finish one point ahead of the Poles.

The lacklustre performance against the Irish, though, put serious question marks over Sven-Goran Eriksson's tactics. It put an indelible blot on his record as England manager; he could not dissociate himself from the meekness of his team's surrender.

England never looked like responding to the winner scored by Healy, who was plying his trade with Leeds United in the Championship. Steven Davis put him through and Paul Robinson was not able to prevent his drive finding the far corner of the net.

To make matters worse for England, Wayne Rooney was finally punished for a sustained period of petulance with a yellow card for raising an arm at Ireland's Keith Gillespie that earned him a suspension for the next match against Austria.

Middlesbrough lose UEFA Cup final

STEVE McCLAREN'S reign as manager of Middlesbrough ended the way it started five years earlier – with a 4–0 defeat. They had been thrashed by Arsenal upon his arrival, and were similarly despatched on his departure by Sevilla in the final of the UEFA Cup.

It was not the farewell present that McClaren would have wanted, nor the one his new masters at the FA would have liked after appointing him as England manager less than a week earlier.

Sevilla, with right-back Daniel Alves outstanding in defence and attack, were comfortable winners in Eindhoven, though there were moments when it seemed Middlesbrough might stage the sort of second-half comeback that had accounted for Basle and Steaua Bucharest in earlier rounds.

McClaren's response was to be bold, throwing on strikers Maccarone and Yakubu, but it just weakened the team at the back.

"It is the finale of my Middlesbrough career," McClaren said afterwards, "one which I have thoroughly enjoyed. It has ended on a bad note, but that's football. I will reflect on what I have done for the football club over five years in the next few days. I have left it in a very good condition to go on.

"There are a lot of good young players, good senior players, a good chairman and resources and staff. It is a fantastic club to work for and I have enjoyed the five years. I am sad to go but people move on in football and I move on. I start a new chapter tomorrow."

Pondering his own rapid rise, McClaren said: "The last few weeks have been a roller-coaster with many highs and many lows, and this is one of the lows."

Chelsea's second Premier League title

Chelsea celebrate winning the Premiership title following their home match against Manchester United.

YOU wait 50 years for a League title, and suddenly two come along together. It's a lot like London buses. Chelsea followed up their 2005 Premiership win in Jose Mourinho's first season by winning it again in his second, 12 months later. Of the 76 league matches in those two seasons, they won 58 and lost only six, two of them after they had secured the title. They out-scored the opposition by an average of four goals to one, and few champions, in any era, have got close to that ratio.

What made the second one even sweeter was that it was achieved in their ante-penultimate game of the season, in front of their own fans at Stamford Bridge, and with a thumping 3–0 victory over Manchester United, their closest rivals.

Apart from losing to Barcelona in the Champions League, and Mourinho getting his tactics wrong in the FA Cup semi-final against Liverpool, Chelsea barely put a foot wrong all season.

Chelsea dropped a mere two points at home in the League, and Mourinho acknowledged the fact by throwing first his jacket, then his winner's medal, into the fans in the Matthew Harding Stand. "One of the reasons we are champions is that we have a very good record at home, and the fans are a part of that, so I wanted to share the moment with them," he explained.

Though Chelsea's football was not of the sexy variety, they were efficient, their style epitomised by Frank Lampard's indefatigable influence in midfield, and John Terry's indomitable spirit in defence.

The goal that completed the rout of United at the end of April was one for team-play and the never-say-die attitude of Ricardo Carvalho. From his own penalty area, he played the ball to Lampard, and never stopped running as the ball passed to Joe Cole, and then back to Carvalho, who cut in and sent a smooth right-footer into the far corner.

Spurs final-game sickness bug

TOTTENHAM HOTSPUR'S final game of the season turned into a mystery worthy of Agatha Christie. Spurs travelled to Upton Park to play West Ham knowing that a victory would assure them of fourth place and qualification for the Champions League ahead of rivals Arsenal; instead they arrived in East London with 10 first-team players violently sick, and doubting whether they would be able to field a full complement.

Spurs officials tried desperately, but vainly, to have the match postponed. It went ahead and Spurs lost 2–1 to West Ham, while Arsenal, beating Wigan in their farewell game at Highbury, charged past to snatch fourth place.

Initially it was thought that the players were suffering from food poisoning, and suspicion centred on a batch of lasagne served up the night before the game at the team's hotel, the five-star Marriott at Canary Wharf.

However, further investigation by the Health Protection Agency and Tower Hamlets environmental health department found that the Tottenham party had been exposed to a sickness virus before they arrived at the hotel. A request to have the game replayed was turned down by the Premier League.

Sven and the 'Fake Sheikh'

THE Football Association announced in January that Sven-Goran Eriksson would be released, two years early, from his contract as England manager after the summer's World Cup Finals. It followed injudicious comments Eriksson had made to an undercover Sunday newspaper journalist, known as the 'Fake Sheikh', during a visit to Dubai.

In the revelations, spread over several weekends, Eriksson expressed interest in walking out on the England job to become Aston Villa manager, suggested there was corruption within the game, and made personal comments about David Beckham, Wayne Rooney, Rio Ferdinand, Michael Owen and Sir Alex Ferguson.

In describing the newspaper story as a "scandal", Eriksson added: "I think it could only happen in this country, that's for sure. It's better to have a job with a lot of pressure than one without pressure, but I did get fed up with reading about my private life and I think people got fed up with reading about my private life.

SOCCER SOUNDBITES

"It is his temper... he's come from a poor family. His father was a boxer... he could have been a boxer as well."

SVEN-GORAN ERIKSSON, gives an insight on Wayne Rooney to the 'Fake Sheikh'.

"We should talk about football but, unfortunately, it's difficult in this country."

When he left he still had two years left on a £5 million-a-year contract. However, he reached a settlement with the FA whereby he would receive £13,000 a week for the first six months after his departure, ending in February 2007, and half that for another six months, or until he found a job.

Eriksson dismissed the notion that the controversy surrounding the ending of his five and a half years with England would be detrimental to the World Cup campaign. "The players couldn't care less about it," he said.

Arsenal lose Champions League final

Lehman's foul and sending off made Arsenal's task of overcoming Bacelona and winning the Champions League all the more difficult.

ARSENAL'S first appearance in a Champions League final ended not only in defeat, beaten 2–1 by Barcelona, but in bitter recriminations, most of them aimed at Terje Hauge, the Norwegian referee. The immediate post-match comments of both Thierry Henry and Arsene Wenger smacked of sour grapes after a controversial evening in Paris.

Henry, the Arsenal captain, was particularly scathing. "I don't know if the referee had a Barcelona shirt on because they kicked me all over the place. Maybe next time I'll learn how to dive. I expect the referee to do his job, but I don't think he did.

"I've been told that the first goal [by Samuel Eto'o] was offside. They are already a good team, so if you help them, it is going to be very difficult to beat them."

Arsenal had already lost Jens Lehmann to a straight red card, and Wenger, their manager, said: "When you play 11 players against 10 and you are still on top, to concede an offside goal and then nothing happens is difficult to accept. It's difficult to accept to lose the game on the wrong decisions. Their goal was offside and it was proven on television. It's part of the game but it's not right. I am angry and frustrated. I don't see much more that my players could do."

Hauge was certainly quick on the draw in the incident in which Lehmann became the first player to be sent off in a Champions League final. The goalkeeper clearly caught Eto'o with his right glove, sending him sprawling. However, Barcelona played on and Ludovic Giuly put the loose ball into the empty net. Annoyingly for Barcelona, the referee refused to allow advantage, and worse for Lehmann he produced the red card. Had he waited to see what happened next, Barcelona would have gone ahead, and Lehmann would not have denied a goal-scoring opportunity.

Instead Sol Campbell headed the 10 men of Arsenal ahead, only for Eto'o to equalise 16 minutes from time, and Juliano Belletti to score the winner with a shot through the legs of Manuel Almunia, Lehmann's replacement in goal.

Accrington's return

ACCRINGTON STANLEY, one of the dozen founder members of the Football League, had declined to such an extent that a century later they had become a byword for footballing failure as epitomised in an advertisement for the Milk Marketing Board.

In the commercial, broadcast on national television in the eighties, a young admirer of Liverpool's Ian Rush was told by his friend that if he did not drink lots of milk he would only be good enough to play for Accrington Stanley. "Who are they?" he asked. "Exactly!" came the blunt reply.

It was a fair point. They had dropped out of the League in the middle of the 1961–62 season, their record expunged, with debts approaching £60,000. In 1968 they were almost wound up completely before Jack Barrett, a postman, leapt to his feet at a meeting to decide the club's future and persuaded the town's mayor, James Madden, to help the club to re-launch.

"I told him I was not prepared to see it go," said Barrett, now 82, who had taken up the position of secretary. "I pointed out that the club were at rock bottom and that they had to start afresh. We had to be prepared to crawl before we could start moving at a decent pace. I told everyone that we should at least give it a try and form a steering committee."

It was a long climb back, through the lower leagues, but at Easter 2006 they were able to celebrate their position as Conference champions and the reclamation of their place in the 92 Club. They won the title by an emphatic 11 points, and coincidentally replaced Oxford United, who had taken their place in 1962.

"Our job is to get people talking about us for being a good football side," John Coleman, their manager, said, "and not being the butt of a milk joke or being founder members of the League. We want to be known for winning games."

SOCCER SOUNDBITES

"What we have achieved will go down in history, but I wouldn't like to think that's where my role ends."

Manager **JOHN COLEMAN**, after Accrington Stanley's return to the Football League.

Hearts usurp Rangers in Scotland

FOR the first time since 1986, Rangers failed to finish even as runners-up in a single competition in Scotland. They ended up third in the Scottish Premier League, split by Hearts from their almost perennial title tussle with Celtic. Hibernian beat Rangers in the Scottish Cup and Celtic in the League Cup.

To rub salt into their wound, Mark Wilson, the Celtic full-back, noted the sea change at the top of the table. "At the moment I have to say that Hearts are our biggest rivals because they've just finished second," he said.

Rangers were only fifth at Christmas, but they were unbeaten in their last dozen matches, winning nine of them, and almost overturned a 20-point deficit. In the end they finished a point adrift of Hearts. Celtic, meanwhile, won the title by 17 points.

Death of George Best

THE end had been coming for a long time; even so, when the death of George Best, at the comparatively young age of 59, was announced in November 2005, it was still a major shock to the world at large. It was assumed that football's Peter Pan would live forever.

In reality it couldn't last. Best could dribble through an entire team, throw a whole defence off-balance with a shake of his hips, bypass a midfield with a delicious through-ball, and score goals with exquisite panache. Yet the one opponent he couldn't beat was the demon drink.

Best hit the self-destruct button at about the time he should have been hitting his peak as a player, going AWOL from Manchester United, making several misguided attempts at comebacks, and finally finding solace in the bottom of a glass. He had already ruined his own liver; then he ruined someone else's, donated as a replacement.

Manchester United fans hold up posters honouring George Best during a tribute to the former player.

Put simply, alcohol robbed George Best of his career, his looks and, ultimately, his life.

Yet no dark detail from his extraordinary odyssey into decay should be allowed to mask the brilliance he had shown on a football pitch in the shirt of Manchester United or Northern Ireland.

He was hailed as a prodigy when he made his debut in September 1963 against West Bromwich Albion, and was given the epithet of 'El Beatle' when he destroyed Benfica in the Stadium of Light one memorable night in 1966. The greatest tangible match of a career that took in 466 games for United, and 178 goals, was the European Cup final of 1968, Benfica again the opponents, when he scored a goal that summed up his impudence and exuberance.

The Belfast Boy won two League Championship medals, was named Footballer of the Year, and European Footballer of the Year, in 1968, and in 1970 came back from a suspension to score six goals in an FA Cup tie against Northampton Town.

His off-field life was just as colourful: he owned boutiques, nightclubs and the girl on his arm was invariably the latest Miss World. It came at a shattering price.

SOCCER SOUNDBITES

"I just thought he was a lovely man. That's why I think he got so many second chances in life. A lot of fans will wax lyrical about his footballing ability, but I remember the other side of him, the human side."

GORDON McQUEEN,
on George Best

Michael Owen joins Newcastle

THEY love a striker at St James' Park and around 15,000 Geordies turned out to mark Michael Owen's arrival at Newcastle United, following in the footsteps of Jackie Milburn, Malcolm Macdonald and Alan Shearer.

It was originally thought that Owen would only sign for Newcastle on a temporary loan from Real Madrid in the hope that Liverpool would invite him to rejoin the club where he started his career. Instead, Liverpool's interest proved lukewarm and Owen put pen to a four-year contract in the North-East.

"I spoke to Liverpool and unfortunately that deal could not come off," Owen said. "That's life. Deals sometimes happen, sometimes don't. All I can do is look to the future with Newcastle and hope to do well in this black and white shirt."

After a troubled season in Spain, Owen said: "I am back where I belong. I love the Premiership and I've missed it while I've been away. The Spanish League is fantastic but doesn't have the passion of the Premiership."

Of the aspirations of a club starved of success for so long, he said: "It would be like winning the World Cup if we won something here."

Oxford bow out of League

LITTLE more than 20 years after they lifted the League Cup at Wembley – and exactly two decades after they were beating Arsenal 3–0 at the old Manor Ground, and not much after they were thrashing Chelsea 4–1 at Stamford Bridge – Oxford United disappeared whence they had come in 1962, and returned to the obscurity of non-League football.

They had dropped out of the top division just before it was re-branded as the Premiership in the early Nineties, and had continued to plummet ever since. A 3–2 home defeat in the final game of the season against Leyton Orient – the injury-time winner scored cruelly by their former striker Lee Steele – confirmed that the decline would result in a spell in the Conference.

Jim Smith, who steered them into the old First Division in 1985, was back as manager for the denouement, though he had only taken over a few weeks earlier from Brian Talbot when the die was already cast.

"This club has been run like a business," Smith said. "Asking players to bring their own sandwiches on the bus and brew their own tea, that's not proper."

Redknapp returns to save Portsmouth

IF it wasn't unlikely enough that Harry Redknapp should return to Portsmouth, a year after his defection to arch-rivals Southampton, he somehow managed to engineer one of the greatest escapes from relegation of all time.

SOCCER SOUNDBITES

"I am bringing back the man who left us a year ago, to his home – our home."

Chairman **MILAN MANDARIC**, welcomes back Harry Redknapp to Portsmouth.

Portsmouth already looked dead and buried when Redknapp answered the call of his "spiritual home" in December. They were 18th at the time, and it got worse before it got better: they collected just eight points from his first 13 games, and only had Sunderland below them as they entered March.

However, two goals from Pedro Mendes in a 2–1 home win over Manchester City set them on a nine-match sequence in which they more than doubled their points total for the season. They won six of those games, collecting 20 precious points, and secured their place in the Premiership in their penultimate fixture, a 2–1 win at Wigan.

Milan Mandaric, the chairman Redknapp had initially fallen out with when he left in 2004, said: "There is no reason why Harry shouldn't be in charge for a long time now. I don't think any other manager could have got us out of this."

When he came back, Redknapp had to make peace with the Portsmouth fans who had chanted "Judas" the last time he had set foot at Fratton Park, flanked by four bodyguards, as manager of Southampton. "I should never have gone," he said. "It was a mistake.

"No disrespect to Southampton, but I should not have done that to the Portsmouth fans. I did not realise what it meant to them. I have got to make it up to them and put right what I did wrong." He certainly did that within five months of taking over from Alan Perrin, a man out of his depth.

Reading's promotion

Reading captain Graeme Murty with the Championship trophy.

ELEVEN years after they had finished runners-up in the equivalent of the old Second Division, in the only season when the second-placed club did not go up automatically, Reading were finally promoted to the Premiership. In 1995 they had to settle for the play-offs, and were 2–0 up in the final against Bolton when they missed a penalty that would have made them unassailable, and eventually lost 4–3.

This time they confirmed their place at the top table at the end of March, with six matches still to play, the earliest-known promotion in history, when they drew 1–1 at Leicester City. They would finish the season with just two defeats in 46 League games, and a 16-point advantage over second-placed Sheffield United.

Recalling the earlier disappointment, chairman John Madejski said: "It was cruelly taken away from us in 1995. But we weren't ready for it then.

"But we're in the Premiership next season, so we can talk openly now about it whereas before it was all ifs, buts and maybes. The trouble with the Premiership, though, is that the whole dynamic changes. Everything starts getting more noughts on the end.

"That is the sadness really – the fact it becomes a much bigger business. It's bad enough in the Championship; it gets even more hairy in the Premiership."

The main concern among the players was who would remain for Reading's first shot at the Premiership. "I hope Steve Coppell gives the lads who've got us there a chance," Graeme Murty, the captain, said. "I'm sure he will, but at the same time he's a ruthless guy and if you don't cut the mustard you won't be in the team. I'm sure pre-season he'll sit us down and say, 'I expect more.' Whether we can deliver is down to us."

The players certainly delivered the week after their travelling fans had sung "The Royals are going up" at the Walkers Stadium: in front of a Madejski Stadium crowd in the mood for celebration, they thrashed Derby County 5–0, and the words of the song changed to: "We are the champions."

Gretna reach the Scottish Cup final

AS recently as the nineties, Gretna were playing in the English FA Cup, the first Scottish club to do so since Rangers more than a century earlier; in 2006, they were playing in the final of the Scottish FA Cup and winning all the plaudits despite losing on penalties to Hearts.

Gretna had gone from playing non-League football in the first division of the Northern Premier League in England to being elected to the Scottish Football League in 2002. Their progress had not exactly been slow there, either: they were promoted after three seasons in Division Three, and went into the cup final at Hampden Park as Division Two champions.

Gretna left the Glasgow stage with most of those watching, both in the stadium and worldwide on television, sharing the overpowering impression that though the trophy went to Hearts, the team from the border area had secured a prize almost as tangible.

"I am emotionally drained but so, so proud of them," said Brooks Mileson, Gretna's owner whose millions had turned them into a credible club in such a short space of time. "And I have such unbelievable memories. I'm a Hearts fan for life now. I've got T-shirts and scarves the Hearts fans threw us as we walked round the pitch at the end. The Hearts supporters applauded us so generously and our fans reacted in the same spirit – it was the best advert for Scottish football."

The begrudgers would say that Mileson's money had bought the Second Division title, and that they had ridden their luck in avoiding Premier League opposition until the final. However, the way they fought back from going behind to Rudi Skacel's goal, equalising through Ryan McGuffie's penalty and forcing the game not only into extra time but to a penalty shootout, could not be denied. It was then, though, that their luck ran out as Hearts triumphed 4–2.

FOOTBALL FOCUS

- Alan Shearer's phenomenal goalscoring career comes to an end. Little more than two months after breaking Jackie Milburn's Newcastle record with his 201st goal for the club, Shearer limped off with a knee injury against Sunderland, in what would prove to be his last appearance. However, not before he had netted his 409th career goal, from the penalty spot.

- Setanta, the Irish pay-TV broadcaster, broke Sky's monopoly on live Premier League games. They won the rights to two of the six available packages, starting in the 2007-08 season. Under the deal, the Premier League will receive £1.7 billion, with BSkyB paying £1.3 billion, and Setanta £392 million.

- Johnny Haynes, the former England captain, died in a car accident the day after his 71st birthday. One of the most accurate passers in the game's history, Haynes won 56 caps, and set appearance (658) and goals (158) records for Fulham, his only club. He was reportedly the first player to earn £100 a week when the maximum wage was lifted in 1961.

- Wigan Athletic, a non-League club as recently as 1978, marked their first season in the Premier League by reaching the final of the Carling Cup. Once there, though, they were soundly beaten, 4–0 by Manchester United.

- Sunderland finished the season with just 15 points – three wins, six draws – the lowest total in the history of the Premier League.

McClaren is England manager

FA Chief Brian Barwick returned from a bout of globe-trotting to appoint Steve McClaren, Sven-Goran Eriksson's No2, as the next England manager. The fact that Portugal's Luiz Felipe Scolari had publicly turned down the job a few days before did little to lift the suspicion that McClaren was the FA's second choice.

The timing of the announcement was strange, coming while he was assisting Eriksson in the preparations for the World Cup finals, and less than a week before Middlesbrough were due to play Sevilla in the UEFA Cup final.

McClaren looked like the cat who had got the cream at the unveiling of his £10 million, four-year contract. "The FA had to pick the best man for the job," he said, "and I believe they have. I have the knowledge, the experience. I have taken part in big games, won big games, and been successful with whichever club I have been to."

Having begun coaching at Oxford United, McClaren's education intensified under Jim Smith at Derby, and then as assistant manager to Sir Alex Ferguson at Manchester United. He won the Carling Cup during his five years as manager at Middlesbrough.

"I've worked with the top players and that is essential for this job," he added. "I have that confidence of working with the top players, in top games, and top tournaments. I believe I have developed, so I sit here with the right credentials to take this job and be successful."

Fleet Street, though not unhappy with the appointment of a home-grown manager, delayed giving its collective blessing to Eriksson's replacement. A true verdict, it was felt, could only be delivered at the end of the qualifying campaign for Euro 2008, McClaren's first objective.

McClaren's appointment followed calls for a homegrown coach.

FINAL SCORE

Football League
Premiership – Chelsea
Top scorer – Thierry Henry (Arsenal) 27
Championship – Reading
League 1 – Southend United
League 2 – Carlisle United
Footballer of the Year – Thierry Henry (Arsenal)

FA Cup final
Liverpool 3 West Ham United 3
(aet; Liverpool won 3–1 on penalties)

League Cup final
Manchester United 4 Wigan Athletic 0

Scottish League
Premier League – Celtic
Top scorer – Kris Boyd (Kilmarnock & Rangers) 32
Div 1 – St Mirren
Div 2 – Gretna
Div 3 – Cowdenbeath
Footballer of the Year – Craig Gordon (Hearts)

Scottish FA Cup final
Heart of Midlothian 1 Gretna 1
(aet; Hearts won 4–2 on penalties)

Scottish League Cup final
Celtic 3 Dunfermline Athletic 0

European Cup final
Barcelona 2 Arsenal 1

UEFA Cup final
Sevilla 4 Middlesbrough 0

European Footballer of the Year 2005
Ronaldinho (Barcelona & Brazil)

World Club Championship 2005
São Paulo 1 Liverpool 0

Roy Keane moves to Celtic, then retires

ROY KEANE saw out the remaining months of his career at Celtic, the club he had supported from a distance as a boy growing up in Ireland. When he was released by Manchester United, he had the choice of Real Madrid and a smattering of Premiership clubs; when he made the debut he dreamt about as a youngster, it turned into a nightmare.

Those of a certain age compared Celtic's Scottish Cup humiliation at the hands of lowly Clyde to Berwick's legendary victory over Rangers in 1967. That result had Bill Shankly spluttering: "It's not true, and even if it is I still don't believe it."

Clyde were fourth in the division below Celtic, and only attracted 901 fans to their previous match at the Broadwood Stadium in Cumbernauld. By beating Celtic 2–1 – and having another two goals disallowed – they completed one of the bigger surprises in a country not used to footballing upsets.

Nor was it what Keane had become accustomed to during a 12-year stay at United where he won seven Premier League titles, four FA Cups and, famously, the Champions League. He added Scottish Premier League and Scottish League Cup medals at Celtic before he retired from football at the end of the season on medical advice.

SOCCER SOUNDBITES

"Over the years, when they start picking the best teams of all time, he will be in there."

SIR ALEX FERGUSON, pays tribute upon Roy Keane's retirement from active service.

Zidane's final act

The 18th edition of the World Cup will be remembered chiefly for two of the unprecedented 28 red cards handed out over the course of the month-long festival of football. The most extraordinary was that shown to the mercurial Frenchman Zinedine Zidane, already voted player of the tournament by FIFA, on his swansong, for butting Marco Materazzi in the final, an incident that largely overshadowed Italy's fourth world championship. The other notable dismissal was that of Wayne Rooney as England departed, as so often, in a quarter-final penalty shootout.

GERMANY may not have won the World Cup, as they did the last time they hosted the tournament as West Germany in 1974, but the experience had a liberating effect on the whole country. There was a sudden upsurge of patriotic spirit and fervour not seen since the Second World War; Germans, who would previously prefer to sit on their hands, embarrassed to show any outward emotion, were waving flags and generally getting in the mood. There were street parties, fireworks exploding into the night sky to mark goals, and outbursts of the song appropriated from England's Euro 96 campaign, 'Football's Coming Home.' The Germans made many friends, wowed by their friendliness, enthusiasm and a transport system that worked; moreover, the stadiums were state-of-the-art, and more importantly, comfortable and accessible.

German fans wave flags as they watch the host's opening match.

They even managed to stage arguably the best opening game of any tournament, even if there was nothing of the previous surprises of Cameroon beating Argentina, or Senegal squeezing past France. With typical Teutonic efficiency they outlasted Costa Rica 4–2, even if they had a scare or two along the way. Paolo Wanchope equalised Philipp Lahm's early goal, and gave the Germans a nervy finale at 3–2 before Torsten Frings hit a late fourth. In between, Miroslav Klose, who would end the tournament as leading scorer with five, the lowest total since 1962, scored twice to restore Germany's lead.

Main challenge

It was next-door neighbours Poland who were expected to provide the main challenge to the hosts in Group A. However, their performance in their first game against Ecuador set the scene for a dreary tournament. They lost 2–0, followed that by going down to Oliver Neuville's last-minute goal against Germany, and picked up their only points from the dead-rubber match against Costa Rica, and even then only after falling a goal behind.

Ecuador confirmed their place in the next round by beating Costa Rica in their second game before finding Germany too powerful in the match to decide who went through top of the group, Klose taking his personal goals tally to four for the tournament.

England kicked off Group B with a disappointing 1–0 win over Paraguay in the heat of Frankfurt, the game decided by Carlos Gamarra's own goal after three minutes when he got his head in the way of David Beckham's free-kick. Paraguay's problems mounted soon afterwards when goalkeeper Justo Villar injured himself making a clearance and his replacement, Aldo Bobadilla, showed a shakiness that England could not capitalise upon.

Sweden got off to a poor start, held 0–0 by Trinidad and Tobago, who England struggled past in their second match thanks largely to the second-half introduction of Wayne Rooney, and late goals from Peter Crouch and Steven Gerrard. With Freddie Ljungberg also striking late in Sweden's 1–0 win over Paraguay, England knew they required only a draw to qualify as group leaders, and avoid Germany in the second round. They duly drew 2–2, though at a price, and only after they had looked set to win until Henrik Larsson's last-minute equaliser. Michael Owen's tournament was cut short when he fell awkwardly after four minutes and damaged his knee, ending his tournament and precipitating a personal injury saga which would continue on and off for the next

"When I was flat on my back with ice-packs around my knee, it wasn't self-pity I was feeling but guilt. I was sending text messages apologising to all sorts of people for letting them down."

England's MICHAEL OWEN, explains how he felt after his injury against Sweden.

Togo's Mamam and Switzerland's Cabanas battle for the ball.

two years. England's best moment of a disappointing campaign came when Joe Cole put them ahead with a dipping volley over keeper Andreas Isaksson. However, Marcus Allback's header at the start of the second half eluded Paul Robinson and Ashley Cole, though when Gerrard, on as a substitute, headed England's second five minutes from time, it seemed the storm had been ridden out. Then, in the dying seconds, England failed to clear a throw-in, and Larsson glanced in the second equaliser.

With two heavyweights paired together in Group C, and Argentina and Holland going through the motions in a 0–0 draw in the final group match, the order at the top of the group was decided by who scored the most goals against soon-to-be-separated Serbia & Montenegro. Holland could only manage one, through Arjen Robben, and Argentina ensured their position as group leaders by hammering six past the hapless Serbs. In a stunning display under the closed roof in Gelsenkirchen, Argentina were three up by half-time, two of them scored by Maxi Rodriguez. However, it was the sending off of Mateja Kezman midway through the second half that sparked the conclusive blitz.

Attacking flair

The Ivory Coast, playing in their first tournament, gained many admirers for their attacking flair, but few for their defensive frailties. They lost 2–1 to both Argentina and Holland, on both occasions paying for their collective naivety. It looked as if they had learnt nothing when they conceded two goals in the first 20 minutes against Serbia in the monsoon that enveloped Munich, but aided by Milan Dudic's handball – the penalty despatched by Aruna Dindane – and the dismissal on half-time of Albert Nadj, they fought back to win 3–2.

Portugal and Mexico duly progressed from Group D, but not without a degree of resistance from the minnows of Angola and Iran. Indeed, after Angola, making their debut on the world stage, had conceded an early, decisive goal to Portugal's Pedro Pauleta in their opening match, they were never headed again. They held Mexico to a goalless draw, and led against Iran through Flavio's goal until a

FINAL SCORE

FIRST ROUND

Group A

Germany	4	Costa Rica	2
Poland	0	Ecuador	2
Germany	1	Poland	0
Ecuador	3	Costa Rica	0
Ecuador	0	Germany	3
Costa Rica	1	Poland	2

	P	W	D	L	F	A	P
Germany	3	3	0	0	8	2	9
Ecuador	3	2	0	1	5	3	6
Poland	3	1	0	2	2	4	3
Costa Rica	3	0	0	3	3	9	0

Group B

England	1	Paraguay	0
Trinidad & Tobago	0	Sweden	0
England	2	Trinidad & Tobago	0
Sweden	1	Paraguay	0
Sweden	2	England	2
Paraguay	2	Trinidad & Tobago	0

	P	W	D	L	F	A	P
England	3	2	1	0	5	2	7
Sweden	3	1	2	0	3	2	5
Paraguay	3	1	0	2	2	2	3
Trinidad & Tobago	3	0	1	2	0	4	1

Group C

Argentina	2	Ivory Coast	1
Serbia & Montenegro	0	Holland	1
Argentina	6	Serbia & Montenegro	0
Holland	2	Ivory Coast	1
Holland	0	Argentina	0
Ivory Coast	3	Serbia & Montenegro	2

	P	W	D	L	F	A	P
Argentina	3	2	1	0	8	1	7
Holland	3	2	1	0	3	1	7
Ivory Coast	3	1	0	2	5	6	3
Serbia & M	3	0	0	3	2	10	0

Group D

Mexico	3	Iran	1
Angola	0	Portugal	1
Mexico	0	Angola	0
Portugal	2	Iran	0
Portugal	2	Mexico	1
Iran	1	Angola	1

	P	W	D	L	F	A	P
Portugal	3	3	0	0	5	1	9
Mexico	3	1	1	1	4	3	4
Angola	3	0	2	1	1	2	2
Iran	3	0	1	2	2	6	1

Group E

United States	0	Czech Republic	3
Italy	2	Ghana	0
Czech Republic	0	Ghana	2
Italy	1	United States	1
Czech Republic	0	Italy	2
Ghana	2	United States	1

	P	W	D	L	F	A	P
Italy	3	2	1	0	5	1	7
Ghana	3	2	0	1	4	3	6
Czech Rep	3	1	0	2	3	4	3
United States	3	0	1	2	2	6	1

Group F

Australia	3	Japan	1
Brazil	1	Croatia	0
Japan	0	Croatia	0
Brazil	2	Australia	0
Japan	1	Brazil	4
Croatia	2	Australia	2

	P	W	D	L	F	A	P
Brazil	3	3	0	0	7	1	9
Australia	3	1	1	1	5	5	4
Croatia	3	0	2	1	2	3	2
Japan	3	0	1	2	2	7	1

Group G

South Korea	2	Togo	1
France	0	Switzerland	0
France	1	South Korea	1
Togo	0	Switzerland	2
Togo	0	France	2
Switzerland	2	South Korea	0

	P	W	D	L	F	A	P
Switzerland	3	2	1	0	4	0	7
France	3	1	2	0	3	1	5
S Korea	3	1	1	1	3	4	4
Togo	3	0	0	3	1	6	0

Group H

Spain	4	Ukraine	0
Tunisia	2	Saudi Arabia	2
Saudi Arabia	0	Ukraine	4
Spain	3	Tunisia	1
Saudi Arabia	0	Spain	1
Ukraine	1	Tunisia	0

	P	W	D	L	F	A	P
Spain	3	3	0	0	8	1	9
Ukraine	3	2	0	1	5	4	6
Tunisia	3	0	1	2	3	6	1
Saudi Arabia	3	0	1	2	2	7	1

SECOND ROUND

Germany	2	Sweden	0
Argentina (aet)	2	Mexico	1
England	1	Ecuador	0
Portugal	1	Holland	0
Italy	1	Australia	0
Switzerland	0	Ukraine	0
(aet; Ukraine won 3–0 on pens)			
Brazil	3	Ghana	0
Spain	1	France	3

QUARTER-FINALS

Germany	1	Argentina	1
(aet; Germany won 4–2 on pens)			
Italy	3	Ukraine	0
England	0	Portugal	0
(aet; Portugal won 3–1 on pens)			
Brazil	0	France	1

SEMI-FINALS

Germany (aet)	0	Italy	2
Portugal	0	France	1

THIRD-PLACE MATCH

Germany	3	Portugal	1

FINAL

Italy	1	France	1
(aet; Italy won 5–3 on pens)			

Berlin, Germany, 9 July 2006
Attendance: 69,000

Italy: Buffon; Zambretta, Cannavaro, Materazzi, Grosso; Camoranesi (Del Piero 86), Gattuso, Pirlo, Perrotta (Iaquinta 61); Totti (De Rossi 61); Toni.

France: Barthez; Sagnol, Thuram, Gallas, Abidal; Vieira (Diarra 56), Makelele; Ribery (Trezeguet 100), Zidane, Malouda; Henry (Wiltord 107).

Leading scorers

Miroslav Klose (Germany) 5
Hernan Crespo (Argentina) 3
Maxi Rodriguez (Argentina) 3
Ronaldo (Brazil) 3
Thierry Henry (France) 3
Zinedine Zidane (France) 3
Lukas Podolski (Germany) 3
Fernando Torres (Spain) 3
David Villa (Spain) 3

Captain Fabio Cannavaro lifts the World Cup for Italy for the fourth time after overcoming France in a final of high drama.

late equaliser gave them their second point of the competition. Portugal won all three matches with Luis Figo orchestrating in his last major tournament, and though Luiz Felipe Scolari rested five players on yellow cards for their final game, they still cruised past Mexico with two goals in the opening 24 minutes.

Keeping their heads

Italy's World Cup campaign was played out against the background of an investigation into match-fixing and bribery in Serie A – nicknamed Calciopoli – which would have serious consequences, principally for Juventus, who would be relegated to Serie B, but also for AC Milan, Fiorentina and Lazio, who would start the season with points deficits. It was almost as if the Italian team wanted to stay away from home as long as possible. However, they managed to keep their heads in Group E while those around them lost theirs. The Czech Republic, who started brightly with a 3–0 victory against the United States, paid the price for red cards in their matches against Ghana and Italy, and went home prematurely after losing both games 2–0. The United States, quarter-finalists four years earlier, fared even worse, collecting just one point from a 1–1 draw with Italy. Ghana took advantage of the carnage around them, and rose from the ashes of defeat in their opening match against Italy to breathe life back into the challenge of the African nations by reaching the last 16 in their first appearance in the tournament.

The plan of Carlos Alberto Parreira, the coach of the defending champions, Brazil, was to build up slowly and reach a peak around the time of the final. Consequently, their opening two matches in Group F, victories over Croatia and Australia, were far from the samba football everyone hopes for from Brazil. However, five changes in the final game against Japan helped them produce glimpses of Brazil at their best with a 4–1 win, most notable for the two goals by Ronaldo, which took him to 14 goals in World Cup finals, and past the record held by Pele. He would add No 15 later in the tournament.

Australia joined Brazil in the second round, thanks to a 3–1 victory over Japan in their opening group game, and a draw in their final one against Croatia. The game, though, will be remembered primarily for a controversial refereeing performance by England's Graham Poll, who finally sent off Croatia's Josip Simunic after showing him a third yellow card, three minutes and another appalling challenge after holding up the second. Poll was lampooned mercilessly ever after. Dario Simic and Brett Emerton were sent off as the game disintegrated into anarchy. Poll also blew the final whistle just as Tim Cahill was about to score Australia's third goal.

That France would progress so far in the competition was not evident from their performances in Group G. They had gone out, as holders, in the first round in 2002, and a repeat for their ageing squad looked possible when they could only draw their first two games against Switzerland and South Korea. It was only when Zinedine Zidane, who turned 34 during the tournament, was suspended for the Togo game that coach Raymond Domenech was forced to play a second striker in a significant reshuffle and they achieved the 2–0 win that carried them through as runners-up.

Switzerland, having drawn with France, made light work of Togo and South Korea, while Togo's first appearance in the finals was riven with discontent within their camp over bonus payments. They even threatened not to play their second match against the Swiss unless they received unpaid bonuses amounting to £100,000 each.

WORLD CUP SOUNDBITES

"If the scandal hadn't happened, I think we wouldn't have won the World Cup. It has given us more strength."

GENNARO GATTUSO,
the Italian midfielder, explains the galvanising effect of the match-fixing investigations back home.

Spain trailed Tunisia for more than an hour of their second Group H match, before the dependable Raul, and the up-and-coming Fernando Torres, scored to help them maintain a 100 per cent record. They had already thrashed Ukraine, who would finish as runners-up, and were able to rest all their first-choice players for the final match against Saudi Arabia, which they won 1–0. Ukraine responded to the Spanish defeat with a 4–0 win over the Saudis, and went through after an ugly win against 10-man Tunisia thanks to a controversial penalty won and converted by Andrei Shevchenko.

While there were goals aplenty in the group matches, there was a comparative dearth in the knockout stages. Germany, though, were an exception all the way through the tournament and ended as top scorers with 14 from their seven matches. They scored two in the first dozen minutes, both by Lukas Podolski, to overpower Sweden in the second round. Sweden were not helped by having central defender Teddy Lucic sent off before half-time, though by then the damage had been done. Argentina required an extra-time winner from Maxi Rodriguez before taming a Mexican side who had taken an early lead. England, meanwhile, progressed against Ecuador with a trademark free-kick from David Beckham in an otherwise dour encounter.

On paper, Portugal against Holland looked like a game for the purists; it did not turn out that way. That Portugal should reach the last eight through Maniche's goal midway through the first half was almost incidental. The match degenerated from a competitive contest into a kicking match, both sides finishing with nine players and a total of 16 yellow cards being shown. Both teams tried to blame Valentin Ivanov, the Russian referee, rather than looking at their own shortcomings.

Italy only got past Australia with a controversial last-minute penalty, converted by Francesco Totti, and that after Marco Materazzi – of whom more, memorably, later – was shown a straight red for bringing down Marco Bresciano, even though he was not the last defender. Switzerland went out despite not conceding a goal during the tournament, beaten on penalties by Ukraine after missing all three of their attempts.

Ghana were the more attractive team against Brazil, but still went out 3–0, while Spain's promise in the group stages evaporated as Zidane showed that age would not wither him with an outstanding performance in France's 3–1 win, capped by his last-minute goal.

The rule of thumb that the Germans can take penalties and England can't, again proved unerringly reliable in the quarter-finals. Germany converted all four of their kicks to beat Argentina after Miroslav Klose had equalised 10 minutes before the end of normal time. The conclusion of the match, though, was marred by an unsightly brawl, with punches thrown, resulting in Germany's Torsten Frings being suspended from the semi-final, and Argentine reserve Leandro Cufre being shown the red card. England, meanwhile, had Wayne Rooney sent off for stamping on Ricardo Carvalho's groin area, though they held on to force a penalty shootout against Portugal for the second tournament running. However, just as at the same stage of Euro 2004, the Portuguese prevailed, England converting just one of their four kicks.

Strangely Cautious

The other quarter-finals finished in normal time, Italy finding no problems in despatching Ukraine 3–0, Luca Toni scoring two of the goals, while France repeated their 1998 World Cup Final win over a strangely cautious Brazil thanks to Thierry Henry's far-post volley.

Though they would beat Portugal for third place, the German dream died in the final moments of extra time in the semi-final against Italy. Just when it looked as if they were heading for penalties again, they conceded goals to Fabio Grosso and Alessandro Del Piero in the 119th and 120th minutes. France defended resolutely against a disappointing Portugal and reached their second final in three competitions courtesy of Zidane's unequivocal penalty after Carvalho touched Henry's trailing leg in a clumsy challenge. The defeat was the first in 13 World Cup finals matches for Luiz Felipe Scolari, the Portuguese coach, who had masterminded Brazil's triumph in 2002.

The bare facts of the final show that Italy were successful with all five of their kicks in the penalty shootout to beat France 5–3 after the match in Berlin's Olympic Stadium had ended 1–1. There was a certain irony in the fact that the only missed penalty should be by David Trezeguet, who had scored the Golden Goal winner when the two countries met in the final of Euro 2000. It was also mere coincidence, but a similarly delicious one at that, that Zidane should put the French ahead from the spot early on, after Materazzi tripped Florent Malouda, and that Materazzi should equalise with a header from a corner shortly afterwards. Coincidental because Zidane and Materazzi would clash five minutes into the second half of extra time. The Italian defender has since admitted making unflattering comments about Zidane's family that so incensed the veteran Frenchman that he turned, off the ball, and butted Materazzi in the chest. The incident was missed by Horacio Elizondo, the Argentine referee, and the worldwide audience of an estimated 715 million watching on television. But it was not missed by the fourth official, Luis Medina Cantalejo, who brought it to the referee's attention, and Zidane became the competition's 28th red card, and the fourth in a World Cup final. The sight of Zidane walking, head bowed, past the trophy, and ultimately out of football, will remain a lasting image of the 2006 tournament.

After an extensive post-tournament investigation by FIFA, Materazzi was fined and handed a two-match ban for his part in the incident, while Zidane was fined and given a three-match suspension, which was largely irrelevant as he had already announced his retirement. Instead he voluntarily served three days' community service. And so ended a great career, if not a great tournament.

WORLD CUP SOUNDBITES

"I do apologise but I don't regret my behaviour because regretting it would mean he was right to say what he said. I heard the words once, then twice, and the third time I couldn't control myself."

ZINEDINE ZIDANE,
gives his side of the butting incident.

France's Zinedine Zidane walks off after receiving a red card.

McClaren and Robinson blunder in Zagreb

LESS than two months into Steve McClaren's reign as manager, England suffered a 2–0 defeat in Zagreb that was not only potentially harmful to their Euro 2008 qualifying hopes, but also put into question the tactical nous of the new man.

McClaren decided to switch from the usual 4–4–2 formation into a 3–5–2 that didn't suit the players selected and played right into Croatia's hands. Slaven Bilic, the Croatian manager who played for West Ham and Everton, was surprised at the change. "I really wanted England to play 3–5–2. We outnumbered them on each side. When they play 4–4–2 they are more solid. They are more comfortable that way because they always play 4–4–2.

"I love England in every way, not only football. I like that they are positive and they say, 'Here we come, we're going to beat you up', but they have to realise that we have a good team. They can't expect to just turn up and beat us."

McClaren was unapologetic. "I know I will get criticised," he said. "I pick the team tactics and if we win I accept the plaudits. If we lose, I accept the criticism. But I don't regret the tactics."

The game will be remembered chiefly, though, for an error by goalkeeper Paul Robinson. It did not help that photographs of an air-shot he played to Gary Neville's back pass, which resulted in Croatia's second goal, had advertisements in the background for Borat, a comedy movie of buffoonery that seemed to sum up England's travails.

Robinson was left out of the next international, a friendly against Spain, and was deeply hurt by the extent of the criticism he suffered. "You look at it," he said, "what could I have done? It was a ridiculous bobble. For people to say it was an error, for people to say it was my fault, that's ridiculous. To get tarred with that brush of 'error-prone' was ridiculous. It wasn't a mistake: I went to kick the ball and the ball wasn't there."

A dejected English defence following Croatia's freak goal.

The Tevez-Mascherano affair

WHEN West Ham announced the transfer coup of the summer with the double signing of the Argentine pair Carlos Tevez and Javier Mascherano, both fresh from the World Cup finals, little did they know how it would all end: Mascherano would be a Liverpool player by the end of January, and play in the Champions League final; Tevez would become West Ham's guiding light as they fought a rearguard action to avoid relegation.

More pertinently, while they escaped a points deduction which would have condemned them to relegation to the Championship, West Ham were fined a staggering £5.5 million for breaking Premier League rules over the signing of the two players.

The judgment sent a strong message to the English game that ownership of players by agents and mysterious offshore companies would not be tolerated. West Ham had belatedly admitted breaking League regulations relating to third-party influence over the policies of a team and another which required all member clubs to act in good faith. Pleading guilty saved them from a far more damaging punishment.

The nub of the problem was that Tevez and Mascherano, who both played for the Brazilian club Corinthians, were owned by Iranian-born businessman Kia Joorabchian through his company Media Sports Investments. He used them as a sweetener in his negotiations with the then West Ham board in his ultimately unsuccessful takeover bid for the club.

West Ham were allowed to rip up Tevez's registration by the League, and continue to play him for the rest of the season after his contract was rewritten. The season ended with a group of Premier League clubs, headed by relegated Sheffield United, threatening legal action over a possible compensation claim. The League agreed to set up an arbitration panel to look into Tevez's registration.

Mascherano played just eight times in West Ham's midfield, and it was not until the final two months of the season that Tevez started to contribute tangibly. He scored seven goals in the final 10 games, including the winner at Manchester United on the last day, to help West Ham complete one of the greatest acts of escapology and remain in the top division.

The start of the affair: Alan Pardew and the Argentines.

Leeds relegated from Championship

SIX years after playing in the semi-finals of the Champions League, and 12 months after reaching the playoff final, Leeds United were relegated to what used to be the Third Division for the first time in their history.

Relegation for the three-time League champions was confirmed on the penultimate weekend of the season when they could only draw 1–1 at home with Ipswich Town. The visitors' 88th-minute equaliser was greeted by a pitch invasion from Leeds fans, and the match was delayed for half-an-hour before the final moments could be completed.

With the club around £35 million in debt, chairman Ken Bates acted swiftly to put the club into administration in the hope that Leeds would suffer the automatic penalty of 10 points that season, when it was effectively meaningless, and start the campaign in League One with a clean slate.

In a further twist, the administrators immediately agreed to sell the club back to a newly formed company headed by Bates.

The Football League did not appreciate the move, and deducted 15 points from Leeds' total for the following season.

Chelsea win FA Cup final

A triumphant Chelsea team celebrate winning the FA Cup final on its return to Wembley.

THE FA Cup's triumphant return to Wembley after six finals in Cardiff was not matched by the football. Chelsea and Manchester United put on a dreary show that was only brightened by the one coherent piece of football in 120 minutes when Didier Drogba scored the only goal.

It arrived four minutes from the end of extra time and not only gave Jose Mourinho the full set of English domestic honours, with Chelsea becoming only the second team after Arsenal in 1993 to win both domestic cups in a season, it also prevented United completing a record fourth League and Cup double.

The showpiece game between the two main protagonists for the Premier League title was not helped by a slow, draining pitch. In the end it was a match too far for many of the participants, and in particular Cristiano Ronaldo, who was stifled by Mourinho's game-plan of doubling-up on him whenever he received the ball.

Paulo Ferreira performed a perfect man-marking job on Ronaldo, though Mourinho insisted: "The plans were not for Ronaldo. The plans were for United because they are a team that kills opponents on the counter-attack. So, first of all, [ensure] no counter-attack."

Sir Alex Ferguson was left to complain about a penalty he believed United should have been awarded when Ryan Giggs was, he claimed, prevented from shooting cleanly by a nudge from Michael Essien.

Ferguson insinuated that referee Steve Bennett had been influenced by Mourinho in the build-up. "That's the way Mourinho is," he said. "He puts referees under pressure every game. There are 22 great players out there, but he talks about the referee all week. Maybe it worked for him in the final."

When John Obi Mikel found Drogba on the edge of the area, the game finally came alive; Drogba played a quick one-two with Frank Lampard before lifting the ball over Edwin van der Sar to seal the game, just as he had in the Carling Cup final.

Bung inquiry reports

EIGHTEEN months after Mike Newell and Sven-Goran Eriksson had suggested in different contexts that a 'bung' culture still existed in football, Lord Stevens finally presented the findings of the inquiry set up by the Football Association in the wake of the allegations.

Newell, then manager of Luton Town, had said he had become frustrated by the constant financial inducements he was offered by agents to buy their players. Eriksson, during the 'Fake Sheikh' interview, had suggested there were two Premiership managers he thought were corrupt.

In the end Lord Stevens, the former Commissioner of the Metropolitan Police, did not find proof of what most people would understand as the classic football 'bung'.

In investigating 326 transfers made between January 2004 and January 2006, he found that just 17 remained questionable. Indeed, in delivering the names of his chief suspects – five clubs, three managers and 15 agents – the Stevens Report posed more questions than it answered.

However, Stevens did make it clear that he had found no evidence of any wrongdoing involving any Premiership club or club official. That was greeted with an enormous sigh of relief from the clubs, many of whom had been waiting anxiously for the shadow of suspicion to be lifted from them.

It was a similar story with a parallel investigation carried out by the BBC's Panorama team, and broadcast in a programme entitled Football's Dirty Secrets. They pointed fingers at several key figures, but failed to make any of the allegations stick.

Beckham moves to the United States

AFTER months of speculation, David Beckham finally announced that he would be concluding his playing career in the United States and signing a £128 million, five-year deal to join Major League Soccer club Los Angeles Galaxy.

The announcement brought an initial outcry from Real Madrid, his then employers, who accused him of stalling over signing a contract extension, and coach Fabio Capello said he would not select him during the remaining six months he was tied to the club. Their attitude softened as Beckham helped Real to their first trophy during his four seasons at the club.

Beckham made a series of key assists during the run-in to La Liga, and Capello admitted: "We made a mistake with David when we decided that he shouldn't play again. Bringing him back was one of the most important factors in us winning the league title."

Beckham said his last season in Spain had been the hardest of his career, but that it had been worth it in the end. "I couldn't have dreamt it any better," he said. "It's been about winning the title for the last six months and it has been an incredible experience."

Of the move across the Atlantic, Beckham said: "I look forward to the new challenge of growing the world's most popular game in a country that is as passionate about its sport as my own."

Timothy J Leiweke, president of AEG, who own LA Galaxy, said: "David is truly the only individual who can build the 'bridge' between soccer in America and the rest of the world."

SOCCER SOUNDBITES

"David Beckham is the great paradox of world football. He was the most galactic of the galacticos off the pitch, but the greatest of earthlings when he walked on to the field."

SPAIN'S *EL PAIS*,
on Beckham time at Real Madrid.

Brawl at the Carling Cup final

CHELSEA and Arsenal were fined £100,000 each and reprimanded for their part in the worst scenes of indiscipline seen at a major cup final when a 20-man brawl broke out towards the end of the Carling Cup final. Three players were sent off as tempers boiled over at the climax of an exciting game won 2–1 by Chelsea.

The Football Association condemned the events at Cardiff's Millennium Stadium as "serious, unacceptable and damaging to the image of the game".

The fuse was lit when John Obi Mikel tugged at Kolo Toure's shirt. The two players were shown red cards, along with Emmanuel Adebayor, who protested his innocence so vehemently that he needed restraining by Gary Lewin, Arsenal's physiotherapist. Emmanuel Eboue would have joined them had referee Howard Webb spotted him punch Wayne Bridge at the height of the fracas. Eboue was later charged on video evidence and banned for three games.

Frank Lampard and Cesc Fabregas were both booked for their parts in the affray, during which Jose Mourinho and Arsene Wenger went on to the pitch to try to calm things down.

Almost lost amid the mayhem was the stirring fightback by Chelsea after Theo Walcott had put Arsenal ahead with a fine curling shot. Didier Drogba, who equalised soon after, scored the winner six minutes from time with a thumping header. Earlier John Terry, the Chelsea captain, had suffered a nasty-looking injury when he was accidentally kicked in the jaw by Abou Diaby and knocked unconscious. He was later discharged from hospital and returned to the stadium to celebrate with his team-mates.

SOCCER SOUNDBITES

"I asked the referee why I'd been sent off and he said I hit someone, but I don't remember hitting anyone."

EMMANUEL ADEBAYOR, protests his innocence after the Carling Cup fracas.

Before the infamous brawl, a brave John Terry was stretchered off following this impact.

Platini elected UEFA president

FOR a player who always made the difficult look so easy on the pitch, Michel Platini will have enjoyed more comfortable victories than the one which elevated him to the king of European football. Platini, 51, was elected president of UEFA, ousting Lennart Johansson after a 17-year reign, by just four votes.

However, Platini's rise from political obscurity gave concern in many corners of Europe. Part of his manifesto was to limit the number of clubs in the Champions League to three from any one country and to cap the amount of money a club could spend on wages and transfers.

Platini's long-term aim, though, was to make the Champions League a credible continent-wide competition again, back to its previous guise as the European Cup, where clubs had to win their national championship to qualify, rather than the privileged rich man's club it had become. Platini said: "We must always see to it that the strong help the weak. Let's defend the national associations against the interests which are threatening them. It is a game before a product, a sport before a market, a show before a business."

Graham Poll quits

GRAHAM POLL, England's most high-profile referee, retired from the game citing the Football Association's refusal to back him in a dispute with Chelsea after he sent off John Terry.

Chelsea players had alleged that during a bad-tempered match at Tottenham in November, Poll had told two of them that their discipline was "out of order" and that they "needed to be taught a lesson." Terry had also claimed that Poll had changed his mind about the reason for dismissing him.

Terry was fined £10,000 after admitting improper conduct, but Poll said he was shocked when the FA would not charge Chelsea after he had reported the club for intimidation.

Poll, who refereed in two World Cups and Euro 2000, as well as the finals of the FA Cup, League Cup and UEFA Cup, will be best remembered for his blunder during the 2006 World Cup finals when he showed the yellow card three times to Croatia's Josip Simunic.

Poll, 43, blew the final whistle of his first-class career in the Championship playoff final between Derby County and West Bromwich Albion at Wembley.

Cech suffers serious injury

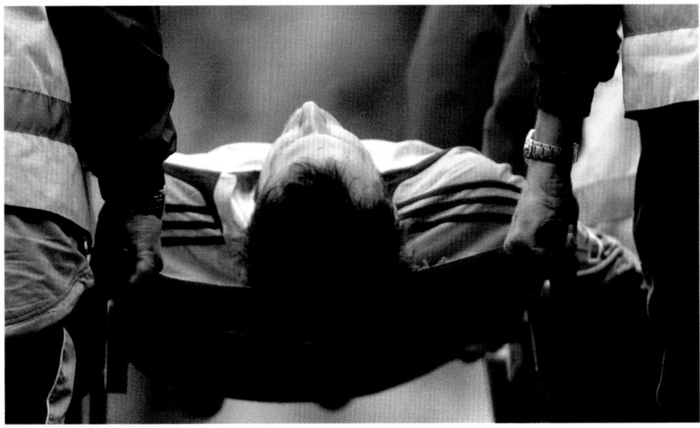

Petr Cech is carried off after a collision with Reading's Stephen Hunt.

WHEN Petr Cech returned to the Chelsea team after missing nearly half the season, the black skull cap he wore became a permanent reminder of the horrific injury he suffered at Reading. Cech required emergency surgery to have two metal plates inserted after Stephen Hunt's knee connected with his head in the opening minute of the match at the Madejski Stadium, leaving the goalkeeper with a depressed skull fracture.

Jose Mourinho, the Chelsea manager, said Cech, 24, was "lucky to be alive" during an emotional post-match discourse during which he suggested Hunt should be charged with violent conduct, and raged – inaccurately as it turned out – against the local ambulance service for being tardy in their response to the incident.

"Hunt clearly flexed his leg to catch Petr," Mourinho said. "He dropped his knee. When the keeper has the ball in his hands, what are you going to do? You are only going in there to hurt him."

Hunt, who was making his full Premiership debut, maintained his innocence. Cech, the injured party, was not a reliable witness for either side, and admitted later that he struggled to recall the moment of impact.

"The last thing I remember is the shaking hands before the game started," he said. "I remember the warm-up; I remember all the way from the hotel to the stadium because I always take the programme and I read a little bit."

Cech described how he watched the incident replayed on television. "I have seen it once and I was surprised," he said. "I thought it happened on the other side of the head. So that just proves that I can't remember anything."

Coincidentally, Chelsea finished a match they won 1–0 with John Terry in goal: substitute goalkeeper Carlo Cudicini was also taken to hospital after a collision with Reading's Ibrahim Sonko in which he swallowed his tongue. Third-choice Henrique Hilario became Chelsea's No1 for a time.

Wembley Stadium completed

AFTER six and a half years of wrangling, recriminations and delays, Wembley Stadium finally opened its doors to the paying public for an Under-21 friendly international against Italy.

Multiplex, the construction company, handed over the keys to the £800 million, 90,000-capacity stadium to the Football Association in mid-March to mark the end of the troubled history of the rebuilding project that had started when the old Wembley hosted its last match back in October 2000.

Multiplex and Wembley National Stadium Ltd had been at each other's throats for years, each blaming the other for the continuing delays in completing the project that had prevented the 2006 FA Cup final being staged there as originally planned.

However, at the hand-over, Ross McDiven, joint managing director of Multiplex, said: "The fact that the stadium is now complete and is a world-class facility is testament to the hard work and perseverance of the Multiplex staff who worked on the project and the contractors who worked alongside us. Multiplex is very proud of what is unquestionably a spectacular building."

Inside, the stadium had the feel of its predecessor, but with improved sight-lines, leg room and proximity to the pitch.

The punters had their opportunity to pass their verdict at the first major trial event, used to test safety and security measures and iron out teething problems. However, the spectators in a 55,000 crowd were barely in their seats when Gianpaulo Pazzini scored the first goal at the new stadium inside 30 seconds. The Italian striker went on to score a hat-trick in a 3–3 draw.

Despite the delays, the new Wembley was hailed a success.

Scotland beat World Cup finalists

THE pre-match build-up had suggested a contest that would resemble Napoleon's Grandee Army against some bedraggled Highland clan; instead, Scotland pulled off one of the most memorable victories in their history by beating France, three months earlier World Cup finalists, in a Euro 2008 qualifier.

For a few dizzying months, with a quarter of the campaign played, the Scots sat on top of Group B, which included the World Cup winners (Italy), runners-up (France) and quarter-finalists (Ukraine), and a nation dared to dream.

The only goal of the match came from Gary Caldwell, the Celtic defender, who prodded home Paul Hartley's beautifully weighted corner. Coincidentally, Caldwell had made his international debut four years earlier in a 5–0 thrashing by the same opponents in the Stade de France.

That night, when David Trezeguet scored the fourth goal for the reigning European champions, he emphasised the point by making a four-fingered gesture towards Caldwell. Five minutes before Caldwell's goal at Hampden Park, Trezeguet had trudged unhappily from the pitch; Caldwell declined the opportunity to respond in kind.

"They are world-class players and have done everything in the game and played for some of the biggest clubs in the world," Caldwell said. "There was no satisfaction in seeing Trezeguet going off. It would be disrespectful to say anything other than that. It would be wrong to gloat. You have to win with humility and enjoy the win.

"We also know that when it comes to playing them in Paris, they will be right up for it. You always get the chance to put one over on people and come the return game they'll be fired up, trying to make amends."

French disappointment was tinged with disdain for the smothering tactics adopted by Walter Smith's Scots. "We face that sort of game every time Arsenal play away," Thierry Henry said. "If we played Scotland 10 times, we would win nine times out of 10. That was the one in 10."

Man United win Premier League

ONLY once, in the Treble-winning season of 1999, have Manchester United won the Premier League title at Old Trafford. They did effectively win it in Manchester, after beating Manchester City at Eastlands with a Cristano Ronaldo penalty, though it was not confirmed until the next evening when Chelsea failed to beat Arsenal at the Emirates.

For several months, it had been widely anticipated that the title would be decided in a one-match shootout between Chelsea and United. However, when that match was played in the following midweek, it was contested between two shadow teams, and Chelsea had to acknowledge publicly, with a guard of honour, that the championship had already been wrested back by Sir Alex Ferguson.

It was somehow fitting and deserving that the goal which sealed Ferguson's ninth league success, and decided his 30th Manchester derby, should be scored by Ronaldo, the Premiership's outstanding performer, and a worthy winner of the writers' Football of the Year award. He scored 17 League goals during the season, a record for a midfield player, and added another six in cup competitions.

However, a close study of the final third of United's season would make anyone wonder how they managed to land the title with two games still to play. By any normal reckoning they ought really to have lost at Anfield, Goodison and Craven Cottage, while Blackburn had outplayed them in the first half at Old Trafford, before succumbing 4–1.

By the end of a season in which they had been beaten just five times domestically, twice each by Arsenal and West Ham, once by Portsmouth, they were a desperately tired team. "What you saw there was human courage," Ferguson said before leaving the City of Manchester Stadium, the title all but achieved.

They had only just returned home after going out of the Champions League in the semi-final to eventual winners Milan, and Ferguson admitted: "You haven't seen the real Manchester United today because there was a tiredness there. You couldn't see our usual sharpness."

Manchester United's Wayne Rooney lifting the Premiership trophy.

Newell fined for sexist outburst

MIKE NEWELL, the Luton Town manager, was fined £6,500 by the Football Association for making derogatory comments about a female linesman. Newell was upset when referee Andy D'Urso and his assistant Amy Raynor failed to award a penalty during a match against Queens Park Rangers.

"She shouldn't be here," he said after the match. "I know that sounds sexist, but I am sexist, so I am not going to be anything other than that. This is Championship football. This is not park football. What are women doing here? It is tokenism – for the politically correct idiots.

"We have a problem in this country with political correctness, and bringing women into the game is not the way to improve refereeing and officialdom."

Andy Williamson, the Football League's chief operating officer, said: "Female officials are an accepted part of the game and these comments are wholly inappropriate. They continue to make a growing impact on the game and Mike Newell needs to get used to the idea."

Later in the season, Jacqui Oatley, 32, became Match of the Day's first female commentator. Dave Bassett took over Newell's misogynistic role, and said: "It undermines the credibility of the programme."

Milan's revenge in Champions League

MILAN gained revenge for defeat by Liverpool in Istanbul two years earlier by beating them in the Champions League final in Athens. Liverpool paid for a lack of adventure from manager Rafa Benitez and their failure to capitalise on positive approach work.

Filippo Inzaghi scored twice, the first just before half-time deflected home off his upper arm, the second an example of his predatory art, while Dirk Kuyt's last-minute consolation was too little and too late. In the final analysis, an unspectacular team won an unspectacular final.

Benitez's culpability centres on his refusal, at 1–0 down, to send on Peter Crouch to supplement the lonely Kuyt in attack until 12 minutes from time. Then, after Inzaghi rolled in his second, Benitez responded by making a like-for-like substitution, replacing full-back Steve Finnan with Alvaro Arbeloa, instead of sending on another forward in the shape of Craig Bellamy.

Benitez's strange lack of adventure meant Paolo Maldini was able to get his hands on the European Cup for the fifth time, as many times as Liverpool have won it in their illustrious history. Somehow Maldini, 39, had managed to force his aching knees and remaining cartilage to one final effort. Only Francisco Gento, the great Real Madrid attacker, has prevailed in more finals (six).

Liverpool had enjoyed better days along the road to Athens. "We've got to another Champions League final and had some great scalps, like Chelsea," Jamie Carragher said, "but no one will remember that. It's about winning and that is what everyone at this club wants to do.

"Beating the likes of Barcelona and Chelsea gives you great confidence, and we have to remember that and take it into next season. We will go again. We have got to do a lot better in the Premiership. We've got to transplant that ruthless efficiency we have in Europe into the League."

Death of Alan Ball

IT didn't seem possible that Alan Ball's heart should pack up at the young age of 61. It was his tireless running and phenomenal stamina upon which England's victory in the World Cup final had been built 41 summers earlier.

Yet, on a warm, sunny spring day in May, a veritable who's who of British football congregated at Winchester Cathedral to mark the passing of the youngest of England's boys of 66: all the surviving members of the team that day were there – with the exception of the excused Martin Peters – so were Kevin Keegan, Trevor Brooking and Sir Alex Ferguson.

"We feel appalled that he isn't going to be around," George Cohen said. "Forget the football, he was a great guy."

In the mind's eye Ball will be forever young, and the moment that summed up his spirit came 10 minutes into extra time at Wembley: Nobby Stiles hit a long pass for Ball to chase along the wing. Ball's first reaction was that he lacked the energy to gather it, but the sight of the West German Karl-Heinz Schnellinger running after it revived his competitive edge. He reached the ball first, and sent over a low cross which Geoff Hurst, on the turn, hammered against the underside of the crossbar. It bounced down on the line, but was given as a goal, and England were ahead 3–2 and the Germans were effectively beaten,

Ball won 72 caps in total: not bad for someone who was told as a youngster that at 5ft 6in he was too small to be a footballer.

Ball was one of the members of the 1966 team who enjoyed a lengthy career as a manager. However, it was a less than successful period of his life, and he eventually retired in 1999.

Everton fans pay tribute to Alan Ball in the stands of Goodison Park.

SOCCER SOUNDBITES

"I've never heard clapping in a church before, but it was a lovely moment."

GORDON BANKS,
after Alan Ball's funeral in Winchester Cathedral.

FOOTBALL FOCUS

- Leroy Rosenior became the new manager of Torquay United – for the record shortest amount of time: a mere 10 minutes. Torquay, relegated from the Football League, reappointed their former manager just before the club was sold to a new consortium, leaving Rosenior out of work, albeit with some compensation.
- Gary Speed became the first player to make 500 appearances in the Premier League in Bolton's home game against West Ham in December. Speed, 37, who played previously for Leeds, Everton and Newcastle, made his 600th top-flight appearance in the final game of the season against Aston Villa.
- Ferenc Puskas, the 'Galloping Major', died at the age of 79. Best remembered for his phenomenal left foot, and his slightly portly appearance, Puskas won three European Cup winners' medals with Real Madrid. Before that, he was the central figure in the 'Magnificent Magyars' Hungarian team who dominated world football in the mid-fifties, and inflicted a 6-3 defeat on England at Wembley in 1953.
- In October, Rafa Benitez caused something of a surprise by naming an unchanged Liverpool team for the first time in 100 games. The starting line-up for the Champions League match against Bordeaux was exactly the same one who had just beaten Aston Villa. It worked, too: Liverpool beat the Frenchmen 3–0.
- Romario, 41, star of Brazil's 1994 World Cup win, scored his 1,000th goal and the celebrations delayed the restart of the game between Vasco da Gama and Sport Recife for 16 minutes. However, the total includes goals at youth level, in friendlies, testimonials, and probably in the garden, too.

More penalty woe for England

ENGLAND'S perennial failure in penalty shootouts at major tournaments filtered down to the Under-21s team, who lost an astonishing conclusion to their semi-final against Holland in the European Championship, 13–12.

"We were ready," said Stuart Pearce, the England manager, who famously missed one for the seniors in the semi-finals of the 1990 World Cup before finding redemption against Spain at the 1996 European Championships. "For weeks we had been practising," he added. Indeed Pearce even staged a competitive practice in front of a packed Carrow Road after a pre-tournament friendly against Slovakia.

"We put a presentation on for the players," he continued, "showing them their best penalties, which way the keeper goes. In the shootouts I've been involved in there have only been three or four successful kicks, so we've taken a step in the right direction."

The two teams had drawn 1–1 during normal play, coincidentally after Leroy Lita and Maceo Rigters had both scored with penalties. Holland, the hosts, went on to beat Serbia 4–1 in the final.

FINAL SCORE

Football League
Premiership – Manchester United
Top scorer – Didier Drogba (Chelsea) 20
Championship – Sunderland
League 1 – Scunthorpe United
League 2 – Walsall
Footballer of the Year – Cristiano Ronaldo (Manchester United)

FA Cup final
Chelsea 1 Manchester United 0

League Cup final
Chelsea 2 Arsenal 1

Scottish League
Premier League – Celtic
Top scorer – Kris Boyd (Rangers) 20
Div 1 – Gretna
Div 2 – Morton
Div 3 – Berwick Rangers
Footballer of the Year – Shunsuke Nakamura (Celtic)

Scottish FA Cup final
Celtic 1 Dunfermline Athletic 0

Scottish League Cup final
Hibernian 5 Kilmarnock 1

European Cup final
AC Milan 2 Liverpool 1

UEFA Cup final
Sevilla 2 Espanyol 2
(aet; Sevilla won 3–1 on penalties)

European Footballer of the Year 2006
Fabio Cannavaro (Juventus, Real Madrid & Italy)

World Club Championship 2006
Internacional (Brazil) 1 Barcelona 0

England fail to qualify

ENGLAND only required a point from their final match, at home against Croatia, to qualify for the finals of Euro 2008. Though they fought back from a two-goal deficit at half-time, they went down in the rain at Wembley. One of the enduring images was of manager Steve McClaren shielding himself under an umbrella; it was not enough to save him from the scorn of a nation thwarted.

The other image that lingered long after the Group E match was of Niko Kranjcar's speculative shot from outside the area which bounced just in front of Scott Carson and squirmed out of his grasp when he bent down to collect it.

That gave Croatia an early lead which they doubled through Ivica Olic, who rounded the goalkeeper to score. However, when England fought back through Frank Lampard's penalty, and a header from substitute Peter Crouch, it still looked as if England would qualify. That was until Mladen Petric drove home the winner.

"We're disappointed as a team," David Beckham said, "and obviously the nation will be disappointed about not qualifying. If you don't win games you don't qualify. We just didn't perform and that's the end of it."

Steven Gerrard, the England captain, said: "The first 15 minutes killed us. We wanted to start quickly, but we found ourselves with a mountain to climb. There was a big improvement in the second half and we should have shut up shop, but we've let it slip."

Defeat by Croatia ended McClaren's Euro 2008 dream.

Crouch's thoughts were with Carson. "Scott's a fantastic young keeper," he said. "He'll be disappointed, but he's still a fantastic prospect." It meant little: it would be Croatia and Russia heading for the finals in Austria and Switzerland in the summer.

Mourinho quits Chelsea

JOSE MOURINHO'S three-year roller-coaster ride with Chelsea came to a typically controversial end less than six weeks into the season. The manager decided to jump ship before he was pushed.

Mourinho had had spats before with Roman Abramovich, Chelsea's billionaire Russian owner, but even he could see the writing on the wall, bowing to the inevitable, after a sluggish start to the season.

Chelsea had ended a 50-year wait for the League title in Mourinho's first season, and won it again in his second, and finished runners-up to Manchester United in his final full season. They also won the FA Cup once, the League Cup twice, and reached the semi-finals of the Champions League on two occasions after Mourinho arrived in June 2004 fresh from winning the European title with Porto.

"Please don't call me arrogant," he said in his first press conference, "but I'm European champion and I think I'm a Special One." The nickname stuck.

However, Abramovich had shown his displeasure publicly by leaving the directors' box at Aston Villa before the end of the 2–0 defeat two weeks earlier, and was unhappy with successive home draws with Blackburn and the semi-professionals of Rosenberg in the days leading up to Mourinho's departure.

The end coincided with the premiere of the Blue Revolution, a behind-the-scenes documentary of Abramovich's reign at Chelsea, in which chief executive Peter Kenyon expounded upon his master's views on football. They included a desire to see "stylish" football and the need to win two Champions League titles every decade.

Mourinho, in turn, had used every opportunity to snipe at the owner's unwillingness to loosen the purse strings to his vast wealth and alleviate a growing injury list. By the end of the third week in September the relationship between the pair, already patched up unconvincingly during the previous season, could take the strain no more.

Martin Jol sacked by Spurs

ON an incredible night at White Hart Lane, Martin Jol was informed officially that he had been sacked as Tottenham manager immediately after losing a Uefa Cup match against the Spanish side Getafe. However, news of Jol's dismissal had leaked shortly before kick-off and it was soon known in the stands where he was accorded a hero's farewell.

It appeared that Jol was also aware that his time was up after apparently receiving a text message from a friend during the match telling him he was about to be fired. The blow was softened by a compensation package worth £4 million for the two years outstanding on his contract.

Despite two successful seasons, during which they had narrowly missed qualifying for the Champions League, Spurs had begun the new campaign with one win in 10 League games, their worst start for 19 years. A 3–1 defeat at Newcastle three days before, which had left them in the bottom three, had been the final straw for chairman Daniel Levy.

In a statement issued late into the night, Jol said: "I can understand the position of the club in light of the results. I have thoroughly enjoyed my time here. Tottenham Hotspur is a special club and I want to thank the terrific staff and players."

In another statement, Levy said: "Our greatest wish was to see results turn in our favour, and for there to be no need for change. We feel honoured that Martin has been manager of our club. There will always be a warm welcome for him at the Lane."

Jol's days were numbered from the moment Paul Kemsley, the club's vice chairman, and club secretary John Alexander were spotted several months earlier holding talks in a Spanish hotel with Juande Ramos, the Sevilla coach, who was ultimately brought in as replacement.

SOCCER SOUNDBITES

"Martin, Martin Jol, he's got no hair, but we don't care, Martin, Martin Jol."

TOTTENHAM FANS, give their departing manager an affectionate farewell.

Scottish player dies mid-match

SCOTTISH football was shocked on the Saturday after Christmas by the mid-match collapse and subsequent fatal heart failure suffered by Phil O'Donnell, the former Scotland international who was playing for Motherwell.

More than 500 mourners attended the Requiem Mass held for the 35-year-old left-sided midfield player who made his debut aged 17, cost Celtic £1.75 million in the mid-nineties, and spent four years at Sheffield Wednesday, which injury reduced to only 20 appearances.

Injuries were a constant problem. Indeed, had he been blessed with consistent fitness, O'Donnell, who made only a single appearance for his country, and that as a substitute, would have surely won at least 40 caps.

In a moving address to a player he had known since they came through the ranks at Motherwell from the age of 16, Chris McCart said: "Phil O'Donnell, family man, wonderful footballer, inspirational captain, role model, a great human being, and of course 'Uncle Phil'. Those are just a few of the tributes paid to Phil. His passing has left a great void in all our lives." He left a wife, Eileen, and four pre-teen children.

Eduardo's horrific injury

IN a season besmirched by wild and reckless two-footed challenges, the most horrific injury was suffered by Eduardo, Arsenal's Croatian striker, in a late tackle by Birmingham's Martin Taylor at St Andrew's in February. It was an incident that shocked the game to the extent that even the toughest tacklers showed restraint and control for the rest of the season.

In the immediate aftermath of the double compound fracture to Eduardo's left leg, reaction was extreme. Arsene Wenger, the Arsenal manager, said Taylor should never play again, a view taken up by Eduardo's international team-mates, and Taylor received death threats during the following week. Wenger, however, retracted the more excessive of his comments, though not before they had been widely reported.

The injury, initially thought to be career-threatening, ruled Eduardo out of the summer's European Championship, as well as the rest of the domestic season, and seemed to affect Arsenal's form as they fell away in the Premier League, and went out of the Champions League against Liverpool.

Eduardo was more sanguine and forgiving than many of the people around him. "I don't remember the incident very well," he said, "and it is not something that I want to see again. All I remember is that when I fell, I looked down at my foot and it had turned the other way. The rest is just a blank – it is an unfortunate situation that these things can happen in football."

Slaven Bilic, the Croatian manager, also did not join in the finger-pointing. "The fact Eduardo won't play at the Euros is less important," he said. "Most important is that he recovers as soon as possible."

Taylor was sent off for the incident in which he was beaten by Eduardo's sudden burst of pace. Full of remorse, the centre-half known throughout his career as 'Tiny' visited Eduardo in hospital to apologise and express his own horror. He struggled to reclaim a place in the Birmingham team thereafter.

SOCCER SOUNDBITES

"The tackle was horrendous and unforgivable. When these tackles happen, they always say that he is not that sort of player. But you only have to kill someone once and you have a dead person."

ARSENE WENGER, the Arsenal manager, in the immediate aftermath of Martin Taylor's tackle which broke Eduardo's leg.

Eduardo lies in pain following the challenge by Martin Taylor.

Steve McClaren sacked by England

IT took the members of the Football Association's executive board just 10 minutes to decide that Steve McClaren would pay with his job for England's failure to qualify for their first major tournament since 1994.

Rumblings had started among members during half-time of England's Euro 2008 qualifying defeat at Wembley by Croatia, when they trailed 2–0. Though England equalised in the second half, they went on to lose 3–2, and ultimately finished behind Russia and Croatia in Group E.

The fateful decision was taken at a breakfast meeting the following morning. According to those present, there was no show of hands to end McClaren's disappointing 16-month reign, but it was obvious that the meeting was in complete agreement.

With the main item on the agenda out of the way, discussions then turned to how the next manager would be recruited, and after the shambles of McClaren's appointment, the board decided against forming an unwieldy sub-committee and gave chief executive Brian Barwick their blessing to lead the search. He would be able to call on expert help in the process, though his recommendation would be vetted by the board.

Of wider importance, the board gave Barwick the job of conducting what chairman Geoff Thompson described as a "root and branch" review of the national team. "We need to look at all aspects of the senior team's operation," Thompson said. "Players are getting to a certain level, but then not getting in the first team at their clubs."

Gordon Taylor, chief executive of the PFA, said: "We have got to create a Team England concept that has the same priority as clubs like Chelsea and Arsenal. If we don't, it will be just like shuffling the chairs on the Titanic."

McClaren's tenure was the shortest of any England manager to date. He was in charge for just 18 matches, of which half were won, and five lost. His assistant, Terry Venables, was also dismissed.

Fabio Capello appointed by England

ENGLAND'S search for the "world-class coach" who would wipe away the memories of the Steve McClaren era, lasted just 26 days. In that time Brian Barwick, the Football Association's chief executive, canvassed far and wide for opinion, and came up with the Italian Fabio Capello, who had managed heavyweight clubs like Real Madrid, Milan and Juventus.

It came at a price. Capello's salary started at £4.8 million a year, and would rise sharply, so that if he stayed until Euro 2012 it would average annually around £6 million. The deal also has a 10-day cooling-off period after the 2010 World Cup when either employer or employee can walk away. In other words, if Capello proved to be a failure on the road to Johannesburg, the FA could cut their losses easily.

No one was considering that possibility when Capello, 61, was formally introduced. "Fabio is a winner," Brian Barwick said.

However, Sir Alex Ferguson, an adversary in countless Champions League confrontations, said: "Hopefully, he gets the support he needs. It is not going to be an easy job. There is a tremendous pressure on the England coach which Fabio will understand when he is two minutes into the job.

"The national team manager should be experienced, have a good CV, a presence, and be the right age. Fabio Capello has all those things. He will command the respect of the players."

Capello said: "I believe that English footballers are born with the will to win inside them as well as the ability to win, and I hope to be the man to get that out of them. I am confident that I will."

First, though, Capello admitted he would have to get to know the strengths and weaknesses of his new charges. "I have to watch all of the England games in the last campaign [Euro 2008]. The style that England adopt will depend on the players available to me. There should be a style of play, but it is equally important to be flexible."

The King returns to Newcastle

THEY say you should never go back. But that did not stop Kevin Keegan accepting Mike Ashley's offer to return as Newcastle United manager more than 11 years after he left.

In taking over from Sam Allardyce, who lasted less than eight months in the job, Keegan, 56, became Newcastle's fifth manager in three and a half years. Keegan himself had not been in football management since leaving Manchester City three years before.

Yet Keegan's return to the club he also graced as a player was seen as messianic rather than prodigal; Newcastle were struggling near the foot of the Premier League, having collected just one point from their previous five games, and needed an injection of Keegan magic.

Indeed, just hours after he had agreed to return to the North-East, his arrival at St James' Park, mid-way through an FA Cup replay against Stoke, resulted in such tumult on the terraces that it inspired the players to a 4–1 win.

Keegan said: "I know the club as a player and manager, and know what it's like. I know what the fans want. Some of the previous managers who haven't had that experience would have had to come and find out. This is a very special club. It is not a normal football club and people outside the area will never understand.

"I think I'm the best qualified person to come here and turn it around. I've got the chance to come here and show people and, more importantly, the fans that I can. I've got a head start on this. The job doesn't scare me. When I've gone into other jobs, there have been a lot of questions to be answered. I know those questions and answers here."

However, Newcastle failed to win any of their first nine games under the new man, and it was only a late-season flurry that pulled them away from the relegation zone.

SOCCER SOUNDBITES

"He's the people's choice. The supporters want him there and it's great to see him back"

LES FERDINAND
on Kevin Keegan's return to Newcastle.

MK Dons win at Wembley, 20 years after Wimbledon

TWENTY years after Wimbledon's Crazy Gang beat Liverpool to win the FA Cup, their successors, relocated acrimoniously and renamed Milton Keynes Dons, returned to Wembley to land the Johnstone's Paint (JP) Trophy. By also being crowned as champions of League Two, the Dons had set about trying to emulate their predecessors who spent 14 successive seasons in the top flight.

The MK Dons had been criticised for gaining back-door entry to the League by moving Wimbledon from south London to north Buckinghamshire. They were often taunted by opposition fans with "You've got no history", and described as "Franchise FC."

Paul Ince, their manager, was able to respond at the end of a successful season: "This will be the start of our history."

They beat Grimsby 2–0 in the final of the JP Trophy (a competition for League 1 and 2 clubs), and Pete Winkelman, the man who masterminded the reincarnation, said: "It doesn't get much better than this." He may have revised his opinion when the Dons finished the League season top, five points clear of Peterborough United.

In an intriguing twist, AFC Wimbledon, the team formed by disenfranchised fans, gained promotion from the Rymans Premier League, to take them within two further promotions of the Football League.

Spurs win Carling Cup

Robbie Keane celebrates with his Spurs team-mates after beating Chelsea in the Carling Cup final.

TOTTENHAM HOTSPUR ended a nine-year barren spell without a trophy when they landed the Carling Cup in extra time against Chelsea. Head coach Juande Ramos had been in charge for just four months when Spurs beat their bitter London rivals for only the third time in 43 meetings dating back to the start of the nineties.

"This one perhaps has a special flavour to it because it was against a team who were supposedly superior to us," Ramos said, comparing it to the occasions when his previous club, Sevilla, beat the likes of Barcelona and Real Madrid.

"It's been a long time since Tottenham have achieved success like this," he said. "The team have been improving little by little in terms of security and confidence."

Spurs had come from behind to win the trophy for the fourth time in their history. Didier Drogba, scoring for the third domestic final in succession, caught Paul Robinson flat-footed with a free-kick that curled into the opposite side of the goal.

However, Spurs equalised when linesman Martin Yerby spotted Wayne Bridge handle in the box as Aaron Lennon lifted the ball through to Tom Huddlestone, and referee Mark Halsey confirmed the decision. Dimitar Berbatov waited for Petr Cech to commit himself before sweeping the ball into the other side. Spurs' winner came four minutes into extra time, Jermaine Jenas whipping in a free-kick that Jonathan Woodgate headed beyond the goalkeeper.

"We were the best team," said Woodgate, who had joined from Middlesbrough during the previous month's transfer window, "and hopefully we can push on from this next year. Everybody dreams of scoring the winning goal at Wembley in a Cup final."

The match was a tactical nightmare for Avram Grant, who had taken over from Jose Mourinho five months earlier, and he had to endure a series of brickbats in the aftermath.

SOCCER SOUNDBITES

"This can be the start of something special. I dreamt of this moment as a kid."

ROBBIE KEANE,
after Tottenham's success in the Carling Cup.

Portsmouth win FA Cup

The Portsmouth players celebrate after beating Cardiff City 1–0 to win the FA Cup for the first time since 1939.

WHILE there were three Premier League representatives in the semi-finals of the Champions League, there was only one in the last four of the FA Cup; however, Portsmouth prevailed in the end, beating the eventual Championship winners West Bromwich Albion in the semi-finals, and Cardiff in the final. Barnsley made up the quartet.

Portsmouth's success at Wembley was the first major honour for Harry Redknapp in a managerial career that started a quarter of a century earlier; it also ended a season in which he had been touted as a potential replacement for Steve McClaren as England manager, and in which he had been arrested by Metropolitan Police investigatng corruption in football. He was released on bail.

Redknapp is a football-obsessive. "I watch every game," he said. "If there's a game on over in the park, I'll go and watch the kids play. If I didn't love football, I probably would turn it in, but I wouldn't know what to do with my time. There's no way I'm going to pack up. I love the job. I don't know what I'd do without football. It's the only thing that interests me in life."

Kanu, who had scored in the semi-final, struck the only goal in the final to take the Cup to Portsmouth for the first time since 1939. His close-range nudge over the goal-line was a calamity for Peter Enckelman, Cardiff's on-loan goalkeeper, who fumbled John Utaka's cross.

Though Cardiff finished in the middle of the Championship, their manager Dave Jones was still disappointed. "You've got to let us wallow in our self-pity," he said. "I've just lost a Cup final. Being a Championship club doesn't soften the blow. I wanted to win."

Meanwhile, over in the Portsmouth camp they were making plans for the future. "We're not going to stand still now," chief executive Peter Storrie said. "We need to build on this. We want to retain the FA Cup for a start, and do better than we did this year in the League. We had a great season, finishing eighth, but maybe we can go up a couple more places next year."

Aldershot return

ON the day, 16 years earlier, that Aldershot Town had begun their phoenix-like rise from the ashes of liquidation, and expulsion from the Football League, they were presented with a bottle of rum by their first opponents. It had remained untouched in the boardroom until it was opened when a draw at Exeter City in mid-April signalled their return as Conference champions.

Aldershot's rise from the fourth tier of non-League football to the League in just 16 years is unprecedented in modern times, and unlikely to be repeated. "We had to start from the very beginning when we reformed," John McGinty, Aldershot's chairman since 1992, said. "We were eventually let back in at Rymans Three level, down with the village teams, no disrespect to them.

"Our first game was against Clapton, and their chairman, who was in the trade, gave us a canister of rum. It has sat in the directors' display cabinet for 16 years and now we can crack it open. Our rum day isn't a bad day, though!"

Aldershot finished the season with 101 points from their 46-game programme, 15 points better off than second-placed Cambridge United.

Teddy Sheringham retires

MORE than 24 years after he made his first appearance, aged 17, for Millwall, Teddy Sheringham finally made his last one, aged 42, for Colchester United. In between he scored 350 goals in more than 900 senior games, plus 11 in 51 internationals for England.

The highlights of a career that also stopped off at Aldershot, Nottingham Forest, Tottenham, Portsmouth and West Ham, included two goals in the unforgettable 4–1 win over Holland during Euro 96, and the equaliser for Manchester United in the 1999 Champions League final against Bayern Munich.

His longevity was an astonishing achievement, but it was Sheringham's speed of thought, and intelligence, that belied the slowing of pace wrought by the ageing process.

His final appearance was a cameo during Colchester's final match at Layer Road, a 1–0 defeat by Stoke City. He missed the last game of the season because of a toe injury that troubled him for much of his farewell campaign.

"It's been disappointing for the last two or three months with us being relegated," Sheringham said. "It's been a sad season. But I've had a lot of good ones over the years and I suppose it just tells me it's the right time to retire."

Man United retain Premier League title

MANCHESTER UNITED left it until the last afternoon of the season to retain their Premier League title, winning away at Wigan Athletic while Chelsea could only draw at home with Bolton Wanderers. United finished with a two-point cushion.

It was with gloriously appropriate football theatre that their two match-winners at the JJB Stadium should be Cristiano Ronaldo, Footballer of the Year and the Premier League's top goalscorer, and Ryan Giggs, now a veteran at Old Trafford. Indeed, Giggs's goal, coming off the bench, was the perfect celebration on the day he equalled Sir Bobby Charlton's record of 758 appearances for United.

Sir Alex Ferguson, winning the Premier League title for the 10th time in 15 years, said: "As soon as it started raining, I was thinking, 'How am I going to get Giggs into this game?' because he is fantastic on soft ground. His balance, his ability to beat a man, are supreme. Maybe it was fate that he scored."

United had eaten into Arsenal's early lead, and then held Chelsea at arm's length in the final few months. "This team is a young one and has plenty of years left," Ferguson said. "It has a lot of experience in Edwin van der Sar, Ryan Giggs and Paul Scholes. That kind of experience allows young players to develop."

For that reason, Ferguson, 66, had no intention of giving up the job he had done for nearly 22 years. "Retire?" he said. "That wife of mine just bullies me, so she'd throw me out of the doors at seven o'clock in the morning! So that's a definite no. Oh no, I dare not risk the wrath of that lass from the Gorbels. She's quite a formidable person! I am proud to have survived for so long [at United], but it is easier for me than the rest because I am at such a great club."

A few weeks earlier, Kevin Keegan had suggested that the Premier League was "boring" because the same sides kept winning it. The final-day excitement made his comments seem hollow.

SOCCER SOUNDBITES

"I sent a message to Alex Ferguson congratulating him. He is a great manager and a great person. I congratulated him for a great season and for the title."

AVRAM GRANT,
after Chelsea were beaten into second place in the Premier League by Manchester United.

Rangers lose UEFA Cup final

RANGERS' 64th match of a season that refused to end – they still had four more to play – resulted in a 2–0 defeat by Zenit St Petersburg in the final of the UEFA Cup. It was no surprise that the Rangers players slumped to the ground on the final whistle.

"That is the way football is in Britain," manager Walter Smith said. "If you want success you have to accept this number of games. We have no winter breaks, but I cannot claim it affected the result. We would have liked time to clear our heads, but we had four or five days to prepare."

However, Smith added: "I cannot speak highly enough of this group of players. I don't think anyone thought this season would lead to a European final."

Indeed, few along the road to the final at the City of Manchester Stadium would have anticipated them getting that far. Indeed, the final was Rangers' 19th European game of a season stretching back to July, and included four goalless draws, an away-goals win and a penalty shoot-out.

"We have a team who fight extremely hard and whose work ethic has taken us a long way," Smith said. "What we have lacked in the last few games has been someone with creativity."

That was not something missing for the Russians, coincidentally managed by Dick Advocaat, Smith's predecessor at Ibrox. In Andrei Arshavin, they had the game's outstanding player, and he played his part in the opening goal scored by Igor Denisov. Konstantin Zyryanov slid in the second just before the end.

Barry Ferguson waves to the fans following Rangers' UEFA Cup defeat.

It was estimated that around 175,000 supporters had followed Rangers from north of the border, less than one in 10 in possession of a ticket. Unfortunately, the casualty rate in the city afterwards was one Russian fan stabbed, 42 arrests, and 15 police officers injured.

FOOTBALL FOCUS

- Joey Barton, Newcastle's England international midfielder, was jailed for six months for assault and affray after admitting his part in a street attack in Liverpool city centre at Christmas. "It's a crying shame for a player who clearly is very talented," Gordon Taylor, chief executive of the PFA, said. "He's come from a difficult background and he's had a history of troubles. We will continue to try and help."
- Tommy Burns, the former Celtic player and manager, died after a two-year fight against skin cancer, aged 51.
- David Beckham became only the fifth player to win 100 caps for England when selected to play in a friendly against France in Paris. He follows Billy Wright, Bobby Charlton, Bobby Moore and Peter Shilton to the landmark.
- Cristiano Ronaldo's mightily impressive performances for Manchester United were acknowledged when he was named both Footballer of the Year by the writers, and Player of the Year by his peers, for the second season running.
- The Republic of Ireland followed England's lead by appointing an Italian, Giovanni Trapattoni, as successor to Steve Staunton as manager. Scotland, meanwhile, went for one of their own by naming George Burley, the Southampton manager, to take over from Alex McLeish, who moved to Birmingham City.

Man United win all-English Champions League final

The Manchester United team celebrate winning the Champions League after overcoming Chelsea.

AFTER the dull spectacle of the FA Cup final 12 months earlier, Manchester United and Chelsea produced a memorable Champions League final which resulted in United being crowned European champions for the third time, albeit after an epic penalty shootout.

After 120 pulsating minutes in Moscow, the 14th kick of the shoot-out, taken by Chelsea substitute Nicolas Anelka, was saved by Edwin van der Sar to give United a 6–5 victory. Earlier, Cristiano Ronaldo, the undoubted star of a season in which United also won the Premier League title, had missed his kick, while Chelsea's talismanic captain John Terry had slipped at the crucial moment and put his kick wide when a successful attempt would have won the match.

Ronaldo, with his 42nd goal of the season, had put United in front with a well-directed header, only for Frank Lampard to equalise just before half-time. As tempers threatened to boil over towards the end of extra time, Chelsea's Didier Drogba was sent off for slapping Nemanja Vidic during a fracas.

For Sir Alex Ferguson, it was his second European title with United. "In 1999 the victory was sudden and unexpected," he said. "Here, I told myself that if we take all our penalties correctly then we win it. But once Cristiano missed it became nail-biting, and once it was all over we all felt incredibly tired."

The triumph came during the 50th anniversary year of the Munich air disaster. Sir Bobby Charlton, a survivor of the 1958 crash, and now a director at Old Trafford, led the team up to receive the trophy. Coincidentally, his record appearances for the club was broken when Ryan Giggs went on as a late substitute. "I think the Munich anniversary gave us a cause," Ferguson said. "Once you have a cause you become very difficult to battle against."

Ferguson added: "For me, the moment of euphoria was when Edwin saved that penalty. I feel very proud and sometimes you have to pinch yourself that it has happened to you. But the feelings drained away quite quickly. I will soon start thinking about next season and defending the European Cup."

For Avram Grant, his opposite number, the defeat signalled the end of an eight-month spell in charge during which Chelsea had finished runner-up in the Premier League, Carling Cup and, finally, the Champions League. He was sacked three days after the final.

Derby suffer earliest relegation

DERBY COUNTY broke a succession of unwanted records during a woeful season, including the earliest relegation from the Premier League in history. That was confirmed at the end of March after their 32nd fixture, one less than Sunderland's previous worst, set in 2003 and 2006.

In addition, Derby finished with the lowest number of points (11), the least number of wins (one), the fewest number of goals (20), and the largest goal difference (minus 69). They conceded six goals in a game four times, five goals twice, and four goals on three occasions.

Paul Jewell, who had taken over when Billy Davies departed 14 games into the season, said: "We had six points when I came, so I was left a tough hand. I haven't been able to bluff my way to a winning hand with a bad one.

"I'd never had a relegation as a manager before, and it ain't pleasant. But I've had two promotions from the Championship [with Bradford and Wigan] and I know what it takes. I've never been more determined in my life to see a job through than this one."

FINAL SCORE

Football League
Premiership – Manchester United
Top scorer – Cristiano Ronaldo (Man United) 31
Championship – West Bromwich Albion
League 1 – Swansea City
League 2 – MK Dons
Footballer of the Year – Cristiano Ronaldo

FA Cup final

Portsmouth	1	Cardiff City	0

League Cup final

Tottenham Hotspur	2	Chelsea	1

Scottish League
Premier League – Celtic
Top scorer – Scott McDonald (Celtic) 25
Div 1 – Hamilton Academical
Div 2 – Ross County
Div 3 – East Fife
Footballer of the Year – Carlos Cuellar (Rangers)

Scottish FA Cup final

Rangers	3	Queen of the South	2

Scottish League Cup final

Rangers	2	Dundee United	2

[aet; Rangers won 3-2 on pens]

European Cup final

Manchester United	1	Chelsea	1

[aet; Manchester United won 6-5 on pens]

UEFA Cup final

Zenit St Petersburg	2	Rangers	0

European Footballer of the Year 2007
Kaka (AC Milan & Brazil)

World Club Championship 2007

AC Milan	4	Boca Juniors	2

Spain end 44-year wait

Despite being the best side on view, Spain never quite stamped their authority on Euro 2008, while runners-up Germany failed to take any significant scalps en route to the final. Surprise of the tournament was Turkey, who came back from a goal down three times in the semis before Germany finally beat them.

Sixteen countries contested the finals of this 13th European Football Championship, which started life as the European Nations' Cup in 1959–60. Split into four round-robin groups for the first round, with the top two qualifying, it moved into a knock-out contest from the quarter-finals.

Sparks from Ronaldo

Earlier, Portugal had beaten Turkey and the Czech Republic. Although quiet in the first of these matches, Manchester United's Cristiano Ronaldo came into his own against the Czechs, scoring one and making the other two in their 3–1 victory. Deco, pulling the strings in midfield, opened the scoring after eight minutes, mopping up when Petr Cech could only parry Ronaldo's shot. But the Czechs drew level nine minutes later when Libor Sionko headed in from a corner. Deco, however, continued to probe, and after 63 minutes found Ronaldo who put Portugal ahead again. In stoppage time, they sealed victory when the pair combined to lay on an easy goal for substitute Quaresma.

Turkey's vital match with the Czech Republic turned out to be a cliffhanger. The two countries had identical records, so a draw would mean a shoot-out. With 15 minutes to go the Czechs were cruising, having scored in each half, but a goal from Arda Turan put Turkey in with a chance. This grew fainter as the minutes ticked by, but the turning point came in the 87th minute when the Czech keeper, Chelsea's Petr Cech, made one of his rare, but monumental, blunders, dropping a cross at the feet of a grateful Nihat Kahveci, Turkey's captain, who had no trouble equalizing. And it was Nihat who scored the winner a couple of minutes later, this time with a spectacular curler worthy of winning any match.

The six matches in Group B produced only 10 goals, but there was never any doubt that Germany, the tournament favourites, and Croatia would go through. When they clashed, after both winning their first matches, it was the latter who emerged 2–1 victors, after making the Germans look very ordinary. To add to Germany's grief, substitute Bastian Schweinsteiger, arguably their best player, got himself sent off in the 90th minute, receiving the first red card of the tournament.

Andrei Arshavin inspired Russia to a 3–1 victory over Holland in the quarter-finals.

Holland wiped the floor with their opponents in Group C, hammering both Italy and France, both previous champions, by three clear goals, before sending out their reserves to see off Romania 2–0. Their nine goals were shared among seven players. Italy beat France far more easily than the 2–0 scoreline suggests, sending Les Bleus home with their tails between their legs and not for the first time mismanaged by the hapless Raymond Domenech. Romania could only draw with France so went out with them.

The scoring star of Group D was undoubtedly David Villa, who was helped immensely by his striking partner Fernando Torres. Villa hit a hat-trick in Spain's first match, against Russia, and although Roman Pavlyuchenko pulled one back four minutes from time substitute Cesc Fabrigas restored the three-goal margin in the 90th minute with his first international goal. It says much for Russia's coach Guus Hidink that he restored confidence in his squad after this beating and, with Andrei Arshevin back after suspension, they proceeded to beat Greece, the holders, and Sweden and follow Spain into the quarter-finals. Without the element of surprise that helped them in 2004, Greece were unable to put up much of a defence of their title. However, they were not disgraced, and indeed held the lead against an albeit much-depleted Spain, but they lost all three games and went out quietly.

Fabregas lifts Spain's "curse'

"Once" is unfortunate, "twice" an unlucky coincidence, but "three times" becomes a "curse". Call it superstition if you like, but a lot of people take these things seriously. The curse in question was a date – the 22nd of June. For the first bit of bad news, you have to go back to the 1986 World Cup in Mexico, when Spain drew 1–1 with Belgium in the quarter-finals and lost 5–4 on penalties – on the 22nd of June. Ten years later, in the 1996 European Championships in England, again in the last eight, Spain drew 0–0 with England at Wembley and then lost 4–2 on penalties – again on the 22nd of June. And yet again it happened, on that same accursed date, the 22nd of June, in the 2002 World Cup quarter-finals, when joint hosts South Korea held Spain to a goalless draw before beating them 5–3 in the shoot-out.

Now the year is 2008, the venue Vienna, and Spain and Italy are goalless after extra time in the quarter-finals of the European Football Championships. The date is the 22nd of June, and the players are aware of its significance. In nine competitive meetings Spain had not beaten Italy since winning their first clash in 1920. Now it's down to penalties, and the goalkeepers are among the best in the world, Iker Casillas for Spain, Gianluigi Buffon for Italy, both captain of their team. After four spot-kicks each, Spain lead 3–2, thanks to two saves by Casillas to the one by Buffon. Fabregas steps up, possibly the coolest person in the hushed stadium. And he proceeds to send Buffon the wrong way. No problem. No more curse.

Meanwhile, Russia were causing a stir thanks to a couple of dazzling performances from playmaker Andrei Arshavin. He inspired his team to beat Sweden and second place in Group D and then in the quarter finals shatter the much -fancied Dutch with his pace and movement. But Russia and Arshavin were overwhelmed by Spain in the semis.

Bursting bubbles

The semi-finals saw the bursting of a couple of bubbles. The underdogs were defeated. Russia and Turkey, who had provided so many thrills and heart-stopping moments to the tournament, were seen off by the two favourites.

Turkey put up more of a fight, but they were up against an obdurate side in Germany. Nevertheless, they had the Germans really rattled when Kazim Kazim, raiding down the right, hit the bar twice in 10 minutes. The second of these assaults led to a lucky goal, it dropping to Ugur Boral who somehow contrived to nudge the ball through Jan Lehmann's legs and over the line. Their lead lasted all of four minutes before, in Germany's first attack, Schweinsteiger converted a Podolski cross from the left. Germany continued to press, and left-back Philipp Lahm was as usual in the thick of it. It was his cross that Kloser headed in after 79 minutes to put the Germans ahead. It was time now for Turkey to do their Houdini act, and sure enough they did so in the 86th minute when right-back Sabri left Lahm standing and crossed for Semih to equalize. This conversely galvanized Lahm into spectacular action as he tore into the box, played a one-two with Hitzlsperger, and slammed the ball into the net – in the 90th minute. Get out of that one Turkey – even Houdini couldn't do that. But they left Basle with their heads held high and their reputation enhanced.

Putting Cesc Fabrigas on in the 34th minute for the injured Villa was a masterstroke of the wily Luis Aragones, enabling him to push Xavi up, and the Barcelona maestro surged through a spread-eagled Russia defence five minutes after the interval to convert a cross from club-mate Andres Iniesta. Xabi Alonso came on for Xavi after 68 minutes and at the same time Daniel Guiza replaced the profligate Fernando Torres. Five minutes later Guiza converted a perfect chip over the Russian defence by Fabrigas, who was now running the show. Finally David Silva availed himself of a Fabrigas cross to make it 3–0 and clinch a place in the final against Germany.

Torres' scoring return

Subbed after 68 minutes of the semi-final, Fernando Torres returned straight to the starting line-up for the final to score the winner against Germany and win the Henri Delauney Cup for Spain.

Spain dominated the game and the 1–0 scoreline did not do them justice. Keeper Casillas did not have a save to make, such was their superiority.

However, they nearly came a cropper in the opening minutes when a nervous Sergio Ramos misjudged a pass and let Klose in, only for the German striker to be foiled by Puyol. Spain did not mount a fluent attack until the 15th minute, when Lehmann had to fingertip a deflected cross away for a corner. Encouraged by this, Spain – and Torres in particular – cranked up the pressure. Torres hit the post with a header, and then in the 33rd minute put Spain ahead with a beautifully taken goal. He touched on a through pass from Xavi, raced round the stationary Lahm, and, as Lehmann came out, lifted the ball over him into the net.

Germany coach Joachim Low found himself in a desperate situation as his team were being seriously outplayed. He took Lahm off at the break, replacing him with Marcell Jansen. His captain, Ballack, was struggling not only with cuts and bruises from a collision with Spain's Marcos Senna that had needed extensive treatment in the first half, but also a muscle strain that had needed a pre-match test. He stayed on while Low made some desperate substitutions, bringing on strikers Kevin Kuranyi and Mario Gomez, but it was Ballack who came closest to scoring when he slammed a volley just wide and then brought a diving save from Casillas with a cross. Meanwhile Spain were searching for a clinching goal, with a header from Sergio Ramos that tested Lehmann and a shot from Iniesta kicked off the line by Torsten Frings. It didn't come, but the final whistle did, and Casillas went up to collect the trophy. Torres earned the man-of-the-match award, capping a wonderful season with both Liverpool and Spain. And for Spain, it was a thoroughly deserved triumph after years of underperforming in major finals tournaments.

Torres beats the challenge of goalkeeper Jens Lehmann to score Spain's Euro 2008 winning goal.

FINAL SCORE

FIRST ROUND

Group A

Czech Republic	1	Switzerland	0
Portugal	2	Turkey	0
Portugal	3	Czech Republic	1
Turkey	2	Switzerland	1
Switzerland	2	Portugal	0
Turkey	3	Czech Republic	2

	P	W	D	L	F	A	P
Portugal	3	2	0	1	5	3	6
Turkey	3	2	0	1	5	5	6
Czech Republic	3	1	0	2	4	6	3
Switzerland	3	1	0	2	3	3	3

Group B

Croatia	1	Austria	0
Germany	2	Poland	0
Croatia	2	Germany	1
Austria	1	Poland	1
Croatia	1	Poland	0
Germany	1	Austria	0

	P	W	D	L	F	A	P
Croatia	3	3	0	0	4	1	9
Germany	3	2	0	1	4	2	6
Austria	3	0	1	2	1	3	1
Poland	3	0	1	2	1	4	1

Group C

France	0	Romania	0
Holland	3	Italy	0
Romania	1	Italy	1
Holland	4	France	1
Italy	2	France	0
Holland	2	Romania	0

	P	W	D	L	F	A	P
Holland	3	3	0	0	9	1	9
Italy	3	1	1	1	3	4	4
Romania	3	0	2	1	1	3	2
France	3	0	1	2	1	6	1

Group D

Spain	4	Russia	1
Sweden	2	Greece	0
Spain	2	Sweden	1
Russia	1	Greece	0
Spain	2	Greece	1
Russia	2	Sweden	0

	P	W	D	L	F	A	P
Spain	3	3	0	0	8	3	9
Russia	3	2	0	1	4	4	6
Sweden	3	1	0	2	3	4	3
Greece	3	0	0	3	1	5	0

QUARTER-FINALS

Germany	3	Portugal	2
Turkey	1	Croatia	1

Turkey won 3–1 on penalties

Russia	3	Holland	1
Spain	0	Italy	0

Spain won 4–2 on penalties

SEMI-FINALS

Germany	3	Turkey	2
Spain	3	Russia	0

FINAL

Spain	1	Germany	0

Ernst Happel stadium, Vienna, 29 June 2008
Attendance 51,428

Spain: Casillas; Sergio Ramos, Puyol, Marchena, Capdevila, Senna, Iniesta, Xavi, Fabregas (Xabi Alonso 63), Silva (Cazoria 66), Torres (Guiza 78)

Germany: Lehmann; A Friedrich, Mertesacker, Metzelder, Lahm (Jansen 46), Frings, Hitzlsperger (Kuranyi 58), Schweinsteiger, Ballack, Podolski, Klose (Gomez 79)

Leading scorers

4 Pavlyuchenko (Russia), Villa (Spain)
3 Podolski (Germany), Senturk (Turkey), Yakin (Switzerland)

Luton Town in freefall

LUTON TOWN face relegation for the third time in a row after being hit by a record points deduction, to take effect next season. Already deducted 10 points by the FA for misconduct – paying agents via a third party – they have now been penalized a further 20 points in order to be allowed to remain in the Football League, in the Blue Square Premier Division. This was because they failed to satisfy the League's insolvency rules. The combined 30-point penalty is the biggest such penalty in the Football League's history. The League also stipulated that the new holding company, Luton Town 2020, must pay any unsecured creditors 16 pence in the pound and forego the right of appeal.

The 20-point deduction related to Luton's inability to agree upon a Company Voluntary Agreement (CVA), the League pointing out that this was the third time in 10 years that the Bedfordshire club had found themselves in such a position. Director of the newly formed club Stephen Browne said: "We have tried to do everything openly and honestly and we placed our faith in the footballing authorities. Obviously the very clear message from both the FA and the Football League is that doing such a thing is a total waste of time. Once again the faithful supporters are left high and dry and once again a policy of honesty is not recognized at all by the footballing authorities."

League chairman Brian Mawhinney, however, stated that "the board's primary responsibility is to protect the integrity of their competitions," often meaning "making difficult decisions which require balancing the interests of fans, the club's creditors and the other teams in the League".

Marta, "Pele with skirts"

MARTA VIEIRA da Silva, widely regarded as the best female footballer in the world, was born on 19 February 1986 in Dois Riachos, Alagoas. She grew up in poverty after her father left her mother when she was a baby. Her footballing skills were evident from an early age and bear comparison with those of Pele, earning her the nickname from the man himself "Pele with skirts". A striker for Brazil, Marta plays in midfield for Swedish club Umeå Idrottsklubb and lives in the city of Umeå.

She starred for Brazil when they won silver at the 2004 Olympic Games, and again in the FIFA Under-19 Women's World Championship that same year, when they finished fourth, but Marta, with six goals, won the Golden Ball award as the player of the tournament. Among her finest accomplishments are winning the FIFA Women's World Player of the Year award in both 2006 and 2007.

Playing for Brazil in the 2007 FIFA Women's World Cup, Marta was joint leading scorer with Norway's Ragnhild Guldbrandsen with 5 goals. Brazil beat the USA 4-0 in the semi-finals. They lost to Germany in the final, but Marta was still player of the tournament.

Marta scored two brilliant goals for Brazil in their 4–0 thrashing of China at the 2008 Beijing Olympics. But, despite her impressive performance in the final against the United States, Brazil lost 1–0 to an extra-time goal.

In the 2007 domestic season, Marta scored 20 goals in 18 matches for Umeå IK. She also won a Swedish Cup medal when Umeå beat AIK Stockholm 4–3, rounding off a hat-trick three minutes from time. She was the league's top scorer in 2004, 2005, and 2006.

After Brazil's win over the USA Under-20s in the Pan American Games, Marta's boot-print was recorded in cement at the Maracana stadium, the first woman to be so honoured.

Redknapp appointed manager by Spurs

AFTER Tottenham's worst ever start to a season – six defeats and two draws in their first eight matches – they have sacked manager Juande Ramos and appointed Harry Redknapp in his place. Portsmouth admitted that they have "reluctantly agreed" to let Redknapp go after being offered £5 million in compensation by Spurs. Redknapp will take charge for the game against Bolton later today at White Hart Lane. Also fired by Spurs are sporting director Damien Comolli and Ramos's two first-team coaches, Gus Poyet and Marcos Alvarez, in a clear-out that will enable Redknapp to appoint his own team.

"It's going to be done tonight, so I'll be in place by tomorrow," Redknapp said. "I will go in the dressing-room before the game and at half-time. Hopefully we can get a result tomorrow. Tottenham offered crazy money and if we're honest it was too good for Portsmouth to turn down. I love Portsmouth and I loved my time there. We had some fantastic success and I'd never been happier. But it's a great deal for Portsmouth, £5 million for me, and it's a chance for me to see what I can do."

Ramos will be entitled to considerable compensation as his £4 million a year contract was due to run until 2011. He was appointed as manager almost exactly a year ago, and after a bright start led the team to success in the Carling Cup. But after that Spurs' form declined rapidly, and, despite recruitment in the summer, they fell apart before this season had barely begun.

Their UEFA Cup group campaign also got off to a poor start when they went down 2–0 at Udinese. And after two of their players, David Bentley and Jonathan Woodgate, went public in criticism of the team's displays, Levy finally lost patience with Ramos's faltering regime.

Tony Adams and Joe Jordan will take over as interim managers at Portsmouth. And despite the despair felt by Pompey fans at his departure, Redknapp insists it was best for all parties. "It's difficult, the funds are tight. We were talking about selling players in January," he said.

SOCCER SOUNDBITES

"Tottenham have come in and offered £5 million, which is good for the club, and if we're all being honest it was a deal which is good for the club and a chance for me to manage a big club before I retire. It worked out okay for everybody."

Portsmouth manager **HARRY REDKNAPP** on his "transfer" to Tottenham

Harry Redknapp contemplates hitting the big time with Spurs.

Theo Walcott hits England hat-trick

ENGLAND were a delight against Croatia, delivering the most expansive football since the thrashing of Germany in 2001, the highlight of which was Theo Walcott's hat-trick.

The Arsenal attacker was at his irresistible best, tormenting Croatia with his pace and eye for goal. If Walcott's hat-trick takes the headlines, praise should be showered on England manager Fabio Capello for getting his tactics spot-on.

England were denied a clear penalty after 20 minutes. Rooney drilled a magnificent cross to the right which Walcott transferred first time into the middle. As Heskey attacked the ball, he was dragged down by Simunic.

The injustice stirred England. Driving forward again, they enjoyed luck when Pranjic's attempted clearance rebounded off Robert Kovac and fell to Walcott, who drilled the ball hard past goalkeeper Stipe Pletikosa.

Simunic then felled Walcott as he raced at the Croatian defence, leaving England's bench outraged. Carted away on a stretcher, Walcott was patched up before resuming. Simunic received a yellow card, a laughably lenient punishment.

Later, Simunic blocked off Rooney, an offence that drew only a free-kick. Slovakian referee Lubos Michel finally brandished a red when Robert Kovac incapacitated Joe Cole with an elbow to the head.

The assault on Cole put England's players on even more of a mission. With Jermaine Jenas stiffening central midfield, England exploited their numerical advantage. Rooney cut in from the left, passed to Lampard, who found Heskey. The Wigan striker laid the ball off to Rooney, whose pass to Walcott was perfectly weighted and the Arsenal man capped off one of the best England goals for years.

Now in complete control, England added a third through Rooney, who side-footed England into the driving seat of Group Six.

Even Mario Mandzukic's riposte could not stop the carnival on the away terrace, which intensified when Walcott scampered through to seal his hat-trick.

The pace and finishing of 19-year-old Theo Walcott prove too much for Croatia.

Little support for London 2012 GB Olympic team

THE ANNOUNCEMENT made by Lord Moynihan, the chairman of the British Olympic Association, that plans for a Great Britain football team at the London Games in 2012 will go ahead has infuriated the football associations of Scotland, Wales, and Northern Ireland, who all remain firmly opposed to the concept of a united team.

The Scottish FA, the Football Association of Wales, and the Irish FA have been incensed by Moynihan's statement that Great Britain "must and will have a team" to compete in the 2012 Olympics. They argue that there has been no agreement with FIFA to ensure that the Home Nations' rights as individual members of sport's governing body will be upheld. FAW and IFA share the fears of Gordon Smith, the chief executive of the SFA, who said: "We are opposed to the concept of a British football team. As we have said many times before, we feel that such a move would threaten the independent status of the Home Nations. We will always do what is best for the sport in Scotland." They remain unconvinced by the assurances of FIFA president Sepp Blatter that the one-off would have no consequences on the way the world governing body recognizes the independence of the football associations of England, Scotland, Wales, and Northern Ireland.

"We always said that we would keep an open mind," Howard Wells, chief executive of the IFA, told *The Daily Telegraph* yesterday. "But FIFA have failed to make their position clear. It looks like we need to reopen the dialogue."

But despite their rigid stance on the concept as a whole, the SFA have retracted statements made last October that vowed to take measures to prohibit players registered in Scotland from taking part in a GB team. "It would be very difficult to stop a player taking part in the team if they wanted to do so," a spokesman said. "But the SFA would be strongly opposed to it, and would tell the players of that."

So it is clear that, without the support of the three Celtic associations, the BOA will look to press on, and field a side consisting exclusively of English players, although Wells believes that the chances of that going ahead are slim.

SOCCER SOUNDBITES

"Great Britain must and will have a [football] team to compete in 2012."

LORD MOYNIHAN,
British Olympic Athletics chairman

Man City strike oil and sign Robinho

MANCHESTER CITY had for long suffered under the shadow of their glamorous neighbours, United, so when they suddenly found themselves negotiating a British transfer record deal with Spanish giants Real Madrid for a top Brazil striker their fans greeted the move with unbridled delight. So how could City suddenly leap into the picture? The answer to this conundrum arrived in the shape of the Abu Dhabi United Group, an Arab investment company, who took the club over. Suddenly City had become one of the richest football clubs in the world. No time was lost as the final day of the window had arrived, and, given the speed with which the transaction was carried out, there must have been very little or no haggling.

So what did City, and manager Mark Hughes, get for their money, a cool £32.5 million (€42.5 million) with wages of around £160,000 (€210,000) a week?

They got a 24-year-old striker, whose CV boasted a fine record of achievement for club and country. He was born Robson de Souza on 25 January 1984, later taking the footballing name of Robhino. He had the good fortune to be personally chosen by Brazil legend Pele as his "heir apparent" at only 15 years of age, and at the age of 18 signed his first professional contract with Pele's old club Santos. He led his new club to their first Brazilian Championship title since Pele himself played for the club. After three successful seasons with Santos, European clubs had begun to show an interest in him, and Santos began to realize it would become increasingly difficult to hold on to their star player, who had scored 46 goals in 111 league games in three seasons and a bit. Eventually, in July 2005, Spanish giants Real Madrid signed Robinho by agreeing to pay a fee determined by the buyout clause in his Santos contract – €24 million (£18.5m).

Robinho's scoring rate went down in Spain, but his close control at speed and running at opponents' defences and his forays onto the wings produced countless opportunities for his team-mates.

Robinho was Real's third-highest scorer during his Madrid years, behind outright strikers Raul and Ruud Van Nistelrooy, and only Guti achieved more assists. But only time will tell whether the huge outlay the "oil-rich" Manchester City have made is justified.

Robinho celebrates before the Eastlands faithful.

Spurs and Arsenal in eight-goal thriller

WITH ONE MINUTE of normal time remaining, Arsenal were 4–2 up and seemingly coasting to a fluent, well-deserved victory over their great rivals Tottenham Hotspur. But Harry Redknapp had taken charge of the Premiership's bottom club just five days earlier, and had already instilled in them a fighting spirit and a belief in themselves that were missing.

What an amazing match this was, fast and furious with for the most part football of the highest order. And there were eight goals and a 94th-minute equalizer that stunned Arsenal manager Arsene Wenger and his team and reduced their fans to silence.

Spurs' recovery started when Gael Clichy slipped over and lost the ball to Jermaine Jenas, who then surged towards goal before lashing in a terrific, swerving left-footer.

Then, with only seconds remaining, Luka Modric burst through and smashed the ball on to a post. As it came back out, the lightning-fast Aaron Lennon was first to react and slotted the ball home.

Tottenham had shown good form in the first half, emulating their hosts with some fine passing, but when this talented Arsenal side settled down they proved too good for their rivals. But great as this match was, it has to be said that the plethora of goals was down largely to the wretched performances of the two goalkeepers.

It might perhaps be unfair though to blame Arsenal's Almunia for the opening goal, after 13 minutes, a quite stunning blast from some 40 yards out by ex-Arsenal winger David Bentley, who spotted the keeper off his line.

Fortunately for Arsenal, Gomes was soon to show what an encumbrance he can be to his own side. Jenas could testify to this when he rose in an attempt to beat Mikael Silvestre to a Robin van Persie corner, only to find his keeper punching him in the side of the head when trying to punch the ball clear. The result of this was to allow Silvestre to grab a 37th-minute equalizer, his first goal since arriving from Manchester United in August.

Arsenal continued to turn the heat on, and with Van Persie to the fore they took complete control of the game. First he swung in a free-kick from which a half-decent keeper might have prevented centre-back and captain William Gallas putting Arsenal in front with a header: 2-1.

Three goals in four second-half minutes ensued. First Arsenal scored, extending their lead to 3–1, when Samir Nasri raced on to a beautiful pass from Van Persie, lifted the ball over the advancing Gomes and then watched as Emmanuel Adebayor beat Alan Hutton to the final touch. Spurs bravely fought back and made it 3–2 in the 67th minute when Almunia failed to hold a powerful strike from Huddlestone and presented Darren Bent with an easy chance to score. But no sooner had Spurs reduced the deficit than Hutton conceded possession cheaply to Adebayor, who slipped the outstanding Van Persie in for Arsenal's fourth goal: 4–2.

What came after that was fantasy football.

SOCCER SOUNDBITES

"Amazing!"

The usually loquacious Spurs manager **HARRY REDKNAPP'S** only rational utterance at the end of the game.

Wilshere becomes a young gunner

JACK WILSHERE made his Premier League debut for Arsenal against Blackburn Rovers at Ewood Park on 13 September 2008, coming on as an 84th-minute substitute. In doing so he became Arsenal's youngest ever League player, at 16 years and 256 days old. The previous record had belonged to Gerry Ward (now deceased), who was 16 years and 321 days when he made his League debut in 1953. But Wilshere is not the youngest player to have represented the Gunners first team in any competition. That honour still belongs to Cesc Fabregas, who was 16 years and 177 days when he played in the Carling Cup in 2003.

Displaying a toughness and resolve that belie his frail-looking stature, Wilshire possesses tenacity, wonderful control, sharp dribbling skills, and above all the ability to see and pick out a pass with speed and accuracy with his deadly left foot.

When Wilshere replaced Robin van Persie at Ewood Park that afternoon, he simultaneously broke two records. Not only did he become the youngest player to have represented the club in the Premier League, but he also broke a much more long-standing record as the youngest Arsenal player to have played in the Football League since the club's formation in 1886.

Chelsea win FA Cup

Chelsea players lift the FA Cup after beating Everton 2–1 in the final.

EVERTON DISPELLED any doubts their faithful followers might have had that they could not overcome favourites Chelsea after just 25 seconds, the time it took for Louis Saha to score. This was a new record for an FA Cup final, surpassing the 43 seconds it took Chelsea's Roberto di Matteo to strike against Middlesborough in 1997. John Obi Mikel was at fault when he only partially headed a cross from the left. Marouane Fellaini got his head to the ball and Saha saw his chance and whipped a left-foot volley in at the near post. Petr Cech, unsighted by his defenders, had no chance. Saha had earned himself a place in FA Cup history.

But it wasn't enough. The consistently brilliant Frank Lampard was to be the star of this show. Didier Drogba scored his customary Wembley goal to equalize. But it was Lampard who scored the superb winner, the 21st of another prolific campaign – not bad for a midfielder! Lampard was outstanding throughout the season, bringing consistency as well as flair to a side that often threatened to lose their way.

The Chelsea equalizer came when Nicolas Anelka drifted in from the right, leaving the ball for Lampard, who chipped it delicately to Malouda out wide. He had ample time to look up and produce the perfect cross. And there was Drogba to power in an unstoppable header.

Chelsea were in command, mounting attack after attack, with Lampard at the heart of everything. With 18 minutes to go, Anelka fed the ball into Lampard's feet and the England midfielder shimmied right to try to make space for a shot. Phil Neville, ever alert, swept across to try to block the ball, but overran it as Lampard cut back. For a moment Lampard lost his footing, but he recovered and hit a fading shot with his left foot that Howard got gloves to but couldn't keep out.

Everton rallied to make one last assault on the Chelsea goal. Moyes sent on James Vaughan for the tiring Saha, and the substitute was soon sprinting down the left and floating a cross to the far post, where Cech did well to push the ball away from Tim Cahill.

In triumph, Guus Hiddink was modest and dignified. Having climbed the 107 steps, he seemed almost reluctant to lift the trophy, but encouraged by Ray Wilkins he accepted the adulation of the Chelsea fans, a flourish that brought to a glorious end a whirlwind affair between the Dutchman and this club.

Rangers clinch SPL title on last day

IT WAS AS USUAL a two-horse race. But familiarity does not breed contempt, nor even boredom, in these annual struggles for bragging rights in the coming-togethers of the two dominant Glasgow sides. And with all due respect to the various cup tournaments, it is the league, the Scottish Premier League (SPL), that takes pride of place.

The head-to-head clashes between the two protagonists almost invariably determine the champions. This season the duel went to the wire. The destination of the SPL trophy was in the balance until the last day – in fact, it was literally in the air, with a helicopter carrying the precious cup, ready to land it for presentation at either Tannadice Park, where Rangers were playing Dundee United, or Celtic Park, where the home side were entertaining Hearts. Any win would have given Rangers the title, and in the event they emerged 3–0 victors.

Celtic had virtually thrown in the towel the previous week with a goalless draw at Hibs, the title, in their minds, having been lost when they were defeated 1–0 eight days earlier at Ibrox, where Celtic had more of the play without ever being able to translate it into goals. Two Jan Vennegoor of Hesselink headers, one smuggled off the line by goalscorer Steve Davis, and a shot wide from substitute Aiden McGeady were the total outcome of the visitors' possession.

The all-important goal was scored by Northern Ireland midfielder Davis in the first half thanks to some clever play by Kenny Miller. Thereafter the threat from Rangers was limited to a cross from Steven Whittaker that hit a post, and Kris Boyd's miss when one-on-one with keeper Artur Boruc, again after fine work by Miller.

There were three games left and a draw and two wins clinched it for Rangers.

Kris Boyd was Rangers' leading scorer with 27, including seven penalties – top SPL scorer by a mile – while Kenny Miller notched up 10.

Chelsea suffer Barca heartbreak

YOU MIGHT SAY that Andres Iniesta's spectacular strike deep into stoppage time was worthy of winning any game, but it wrecked Chelsea's dreams of a second successive Champions League final appearance against Manchester United amid chaotic scenes at Stamford Bridge.

Chelsea looked to have kept Barcelona at bay on a night of nerve-jangling tension after Michael Essien's 20-yard blockbuster in the ninth minute. But with Guus Hiddink's side hanging on – and fuelled by a sense of injustice after Norwegian referee Tom Ovrebo had rejected a string of penalty appeals – Iniesta beat Petr Cech from the edge of the box to send Barcelona into the final on away goals.

It was a heartbreaking conclusion to a dramatic encounter in which Chelsea had four strong appeals for penalties ignored, the clearest being a blatant handball by Gerard Pique after the break.

Chelsea looked to be on their way to a European final as well after a superb defensive display that restricted the visitors all night until Iniesta's deadly strike.

The Catalan giants posed the first threat when Xavi's effort took two deflections before Jose Bosingwa cleared from almost on the goal-line. And Chelsea took advantage of that escape to make a breakthrough after only nine minutes. Frank Lampard's pass was half-cleared but there seemed little danger until Essien met the loose ball with a thunderous left-foot volley that left Valdes stranded as it ripped past him high into the net off the bar.

Barcelona's response was predictably measured as they refused to stray from their trademark passing approach, but it failed to reap any rewards. Indeed, it was Chelsea who had the better chances despite having less of the possession.

Chelsea made the first of a series of penalty appeals when Malouda appeared to be hauled down by Alves inside the box, only for the referee to signal a free-kick just outside the area. Drogba was the next to appeal when he was tugged back by Abidal, but referee Ovrebo ignored his claims.

Drogba was again left appealing in vain for a penalty after colliding with Yaya Toure, but Barcelona's giant midfield man looked to have just got a touch on the ball.

And Ovrebo was involved again 10 minutes from time when Pique handled under pressure from Nicolas Anelka, but once again he was in no mood to point to the spot.

As the game entered the final minutes of stoppage time, the one moment of magic Chelsea feared from this gifted Barcelona side arrived to steal their dreams of a second successive final away from them at the last gasp.

United's hat-trick of titles equals English league record

MANCHESTER UNITED completed a hat-trick of Premier League titles when they finished the season with 90 points, four ahead of Liverpool with Chelsea a further three points behind. It was 17 January before they went in front, with a 1–0 win at Bolton, and after that they were never headed. Eighteen of their 68 goals were scored by Cristiano Ronaldo, including four penalties, Wayne Rooney notched 12 goals and Dimitar Berbatov nine. Only Liverpool outscored them, with 77 goals, and both Chelsea and Arsenal equalled their 68. The only other clubs to achieve a hat-trick of titles have been Huddersfield (1923–24 to 1925–26), Arsenal (1932–33 to 1934–35), Liverpool (1981–82 to 1983–84), and United themselves (1998–99 to 2000–01).

This was United's 18th title in the top flight, equalling Liverpool's record. They have dominated the Premier League since its inception in 1992–93, winning a remarkable 11 out of the 17 titles on offer. Masterminding this feat throughout has been manager Sir Alex Ferguson, blending experience with youth and cleverly buying in new talent as and when he felt it necessary, and he usually kept one step ahead of United's closest rivals, Arsenal and Chelsea. During this period, United never finished out of the top three.

United celebrate a third consecutive Premiership title.

United consistently played exciting, attacking football, particularly dangerous on the break, backed up by a solid, mean defence – only Chelsea matched their 24 "goals against" – with keeper Edwin Van de Sar and the centre-back pairing of captain Rio Ferdinand and Nemanja Vidic outstanding. So too were midfielders Darren Fletcher and Park Ji-Sung, and the evergreen Ryan Giggs, whose skill and experience were used wisely by the gaffer.

FOOTBALL FOCUS

- At 15 years and 45 days, striker Reuben Noble-Lazarus became the youngest ever Football League player when he came off the bench for Barnsley in their 3–0 defeat at the hands of Ipswich at Portman Road on 30 September. He surpassed the record of 15 years and 158 days set by Albert Geldard (Bradford PA) in 1914 and equalled by Ken Roberts (Wrexham) in 1951.
- Edwin Van der Sar (Manchester United) set a new Premier League record by going 1,311 minutes without conceding a goal, equivalent to more than 14 matches. After United's 2–1 defeat at Arsenal on 8 November he was not beaten until 21 February when Blackburn lost 2–1 at Old Trafford.
- Ashley Cole (Chelsea) won a record 5th FA Cup winner's medal, including the first three with Arsenal.
- Spain took their run of unbeaten internationals to 35 (including 32 wins), equalling the record held by Brazil.
- Reading boss Steve Coppell celebrated his 1,000th match in management with a 1-0 win at Doncaster. He also managed Manchester City and Crystal Palace.
- Manchester United's Nemanja Vidic was sent off after 49 minutes of the Club World Championship against Quito (Ecuador), but a Wayne Rooney goal on 73 minutes won the match for United.

Treble for Barca as Messi mauls Manchester United

Lionel Messi guides a looping header beyond Edwin Van der Sar to put the Champions League final result beyond doubt and secure for Barca a unique treble.

IN ROME nothing could console Manchester United's magnificent supporters, who gave their team all-out vocal backing yet were rewarded with a disappointing performance. Uncertain defensively, United were careless in possession and lacking focus in attack.

Ferguson's decision to start Ryan Giggs in the hole in a 4-2-3-1 formation backfired badly, leaving Ronaldo isolated and Michael Carrick and Anderson badly exposed. Given the stage, Andres Iniesta, Xavi, and Lionel Messi ran the show. Like Ronaldo, the left-sided Wayne Rooney cut an increasingly frustrated figure, waiting for a ball that rarely came such was Barcelona's dominance of possession.

Chasing the game after Samuel Eto'o's 10th-minute strike, Ferguson naturally had to introduce more attackers, first Carlos Tevez, then Dimitar Berbatov, but he upset the balance of the team. First it was 4-2-4, then effectively 4-1-5. This gave Iniesta and Xavi acres of midfield to themselves, and Barcelona just kept battering away at United's defence. They soon added a second, this time headed in by Messi.

Ferguson was gracious in defeat, saluting the fabulous individual talents that make Barcelona so special, yet this was also a victory founded in hard work. Xavi and Iniesta did to Premier League opponents what the English often do to Continental foe: hound them out of possession. Messi, so small of stature yet so immense of talent, industrious as well as inventive, ended the debate over who was the best player on the planet. Ronaldo, after a bright opening during which he seemed to adopt a shoot-on-sight policy, was too subdued.

Deceptively, as it transpired, United had been the first to show, flying from the traps. Ronaldo tested Victor Valdes with a first-minute free-kick and Ji-sung Park almost reached the rebound. Still United menaced, Ronaldo firing two shots wide. But Barcelona's canny young coach, Pep Guardiola, was tweaking his front-line, switching Messi and Eto'o.

Suddenly, the little Argentinian magician was through the middle, and United seemed distracted. Iniesta darted into a pocket of space, releasing the ball down the inside-right channel. Eto'o was off and running, cutting in towards goal, embarrassing Nemanja Vidic with the speed and angle of his attack. As Carrick slid in, and Edwin van der Sar threw himself across, Eto'o flicked the ball with his right foot between the keeper and the post.

Barcelona were ahead and were not in the mood to surrender the ball, let alone the lead.

Rio Ferdinand sought to lift United's spirits. Their fans responded, even as the pride of Old Trafford were given a lesson in possession by Barcelona. The eye kept being drawn to the darting box of tricks that was Messi, who dribbled past Carrick and Vidic, was knocked over, jumped up and kept going. Messi's blue boots were everywhere, striking dread into United hearts, one minute skipping away from Ferdinand, the next playing one-twos with Iniesta.

When United did get hold of the ball, Barcelona's pressing was relentless. The Spanish side swept into untended space, and Thierry Henry would have scored but for Van der Sar's reflexes. Xavi struck a free-kick onto the post. A deserved second goal soon arrived, however, when Xavi, enjoying the freedom of Rome, crossed for Messi, the shortest player on the pitch, to loop a header back over Van der Sar and ensure Barca were the first Spanish club to complete the treble.

Ronaldo's Real deal

CRISTIANO RONALDO has informed Manchester United of his desire to leave Old Trafford for the Bernabeu, and the Premier League champions have now granted his wish by allowing him to speak to Real over a possible transfer.

Having failed to prise the Portugal international away from Old Trafford last summer, Real have now stunned United with the size of their £80 million offer for the 24-year-old, who cost the Premier League champions £12.2m as a 17-year-old from Sporting Lisbon in 2003.

In his four seasons with United Ronaldo amassed 75 goals in 119 Premier League matches. He was voted the Football Writers' Association Footballer of the Year in 2006–07 and 2007–08, and both European Footballer of the Year and World Player of the Year in 2008. He has been accused of being arrogant, but some would say he is entitled to be. However, in going to Spain he will almost certainly have to be at his best to match Barcelona's mesmerizing Leonel Messi.

FINAL SCORE

Football League
Premiership – Manchester United
Top scorer – Nicolas Anelka (Chelsea) 19
Championship – Wolverhampton Wanderers
League 1 – Leicester City
League 2 – Brentford
Footballer of the Year – Ryan Giggs (Man United)

FA Cup final
Chelsea 2 Everton 1

League Cup final
Manchester United 0 Tottenham Hotspur 0
(Manchester United won 4–1 on penalties)

Scottish League
Premier League – Rangers
Top scorer – Kris Boyd (Rangers) 27
Div 1 – St Johnstone
Div 2 – Raith Rovers
Div 3 – Dumbarton
Footballer of the Year – Gary Caldwell (Celtic)

Scottish FA Cup final
Rangers 1 Falkirk 0

Scottish League Cup final
Celtic 2 Rangers 0 (aet)

European Cup final
Barcelona 2 Manchester United 0

UEFA Cup final
Shakhtar Donetsk 2 Werder Bremen 1 (aet)

European Footballer of the Year 2008
Cristiano Ronaldo (Manchester United & Portugal)

World Club Championship 2008
Manchester United 1 LDU Quito 0

The football world mourns Sir Bobby

SIR BOBBY ROBSON, one of the most revered and respected personalities in world football, has died at the age of 76 after a long battle with cancer. He was England's manager from 1982 until 1990, the year that he took the side to within a penalty-kick of the World Cup final.

Robson was appointed to the England job on the strength of his successes over a decade with unfashionable Ipswich Town, which he had transformed into a club capable of challenging for European trophies.

As England coach Robson had taken the national side to the 1986 World Cup quarter-finals, where they came up against Argentina, and were knocked out by Diego Maradona's controversial "Hand of God" goal.

Four years later in Italy and the side came through to a semi-final meeting with Germany. Yet again luck went against Robson. The Germans scored with a freak deflection off Paul Parker, and though Lineker equalized, the match went to penalties. Waddle ballooned his attempt over the bar, and England were out.

Robert William Robson was born at Sacriston, County Durham, on 18 February 1933. He played professional football for both Fulham and West Bromwich Albion and was picked for England 20 times, scoring four goals.

After brief management roles in Canada with Vancouver Whitecaps and Fulham in the UK, he became manager of Ipswich Town in 1969. Working mostly with young players and almost no funds, he turned Ipswich into one of the best sides in Europe.

Between 1973 and 1982 the club qualified for European competition every year, and in 1982 narrowly finished second in the League. In 1978 Ipswich beat Arsenal in the FA Cup final, and three years later, even more impressively, won the UEFA Cup by defeating the AZ 67 Alkmaar 5–4 in a two-legged final.

Robson enjoyed his palmiest days as a club manager when he took a series of ever more prestigious jobs with European sides after leaving England behind in 1990. In 1991 and 1992 he guided PSV Eindhoven to the Dutch title. The next year he was appointed coach at Sporting Lisbon, but was sacked after a season. He was quickly snapped up by their rivals Porto, an ailing club that Robson soon turned around, steering them to the Portuguese championship in 1994 and the league and cup double the next season.

The following year, Robson contracted a potentially fatal cancer of the mouth. He endured two operations to remove the tumour and successfully overcame his illness. He returned to coaching, and in 1997 reached perhaps the pinnacle of his club career when he was appointed manager of Barcelona.

Having persuaded the Catalan giants to sign the almost unknown Ronaldo from PSV, he won the Spanish cup and the European Cup-Winners Cup that season, and finished second in the league. As so often at Barca, this last achievement was not considered good enough, and he was moved upstairs as chief scout. Six months later he returned to PSV for a brief second spell before being offered – at the age of 66 – the coach's job at the club he had supported as a boy, Newcastle United.

The side were then struggling but within two years Robson had them back in the Champions League and at home snapping at the heels of the two dominant teams of the time, Arsenal and Manchester United.

In 2002 his services to football were recognized with a knighthood and he retired, aged 71, at the end of the 2004 season.

Robson's long battle with cancer was well-documented, and he established the Sir Bobby Robson Foundation to set up a centre in Newcastle to fight the disease.

Sir Bobby was one of football's most respected managers.

Beckham's 6–0 England swansong

THEY ARE A TINY COUNTRY, a minnow in football terms, but they still have to be beaten and beaten well. And this is just what Fabio Capello's men did. There have been slip-ups before but there was never any danger of one here at Wembley against Andorra in a World Cup qualifying match. The flying right-back Glen Johnson was the star of the England show, creating opportunities for England's attackers with almost every forward sally.

England went one up in four minutes, Wayne Rooney heading in Johnson's pinpoint cross. Poor Andorra, England's right-winger was Theo Walcott, even faster than Johnson, who put him clear to cut the ball back for Frank Lampard to make it 2–0. Rooney was in his element, buzzing around up front intent on capitalizing on Johnson's crosses. Sure enough, over came another juicy opportunity and the striker put it away to give England a three-goal lead going into the break.

David Beckham, making his record (for an outfield player) 112th and last appearance for England, came more into the frame in the second half. One of the best passers of the ball the game has known, he put one on a plate for Peter Crouch, which the lanky striker eschewed. With the game well beyond Andorra's reach, Capello took the opportunity to bring on some fresh faces. Jermain Defoe was quick to stake his claim for a starting role with a couple of goals, Beckham chalking up two assists. The first was a header from a low corner-kick via Johnson, the second a trademark free-kick which keeper Koldo couldn't hold. Defoe penetrated the Andorran defence once more, the ball ran loose, and Crouch didn't miss this time – 6–0.

Beachball beats Liverpool

THREE STRAIGHT DEFEATS and another title challenge in tatters. It did not help the despondent mood in the Liverpool camp that this loss came down to an incident tinged with comedy.

Darren Bent's winner deflected off a beachball on its way into the net, leaving Liverpool keeper Pepe Reina stranded, baffled, and then furious. The truth is that the referee should have followed the rulebook and stopped play when a foreign object appeared on the pitch – that is, if he saw it – and restarted with a dropped ball.

Liverpool's players protested, but, while they could consider themselves unfortunate in that instance, there was little doubt that Sunderland deserved to win the game.

Having taken that – admittedly fortunate – lead in the fifth minute, Steve Bruce's team never looked back.

The in-form Bent had four good chances to kill the game, two in each half, but couldn't quite capitalize on any of them. It was down mainly to Reina and the woodwork that he did not. Steed Malbranque missed a wonderful chance, too. In contrast, Liverpool offered little as an attacking force until deep into seven minutes of added time, when Craig Gordon had to make an excellent double save from Dirk Kuyt and substitute David Ngog. Had he not, it would have been a miscarriage of justice. As the game drew to a close, Sunderland grew nervous. They need not have done, because, beachball or not, this was soon a victory to savour.

Chelsea thrash Wigan 8–0 to clinch title

Chelsea celebrate winning the Premiership title following their home match against Wigan.

A POINT AHEAD of Manchester United after a see-saw season for the two clubs, Chelsea just needed to win to clinch the Premiership title, but they did it in style.

Chelsea's triumph was totally deserved. They saw off their rivals, winning all the head-to-heads with Manchester United, Arsenal, and Liverpool, and played with panache, even weighing in with 103 goals.

Didier Drogba claimed the Golden Boot with 29 goals, and Frank Lampard, magnificent again today, contributed a highly praiseworthy 22 from midfield.

The early goal that Chelsea craved arrived after six minutes. A Drogba free-kick crashed into Wigan's wall, and Chelsea's Ballack reacting quickest headed it back into the box. Malouda, off-side but unflagged, chested the ball down and Nicolas Anelka applied the finishing touch: 1–0.

Finding themselves with plenty of space, Kalou and Drogba combined and Lampard burst through, only to be hauled down by Gary Caldwell, who was dismissed by Martin Atkinson – against 10 men, a beating was turning into a potential massacre.

Drogba now revealed his selfish streak, dissolving in a strop when Lampard, Chelsea's designated penalty-taker, quite rightly assumed responsibility for the kick. "It's 1–0" he mouthed at Drogba before making it 2–0, driving in a low shot. Chelsea tore into Wigan in the second half. They were utterly imperious. Kalou played a one-two with Lampard and made it 3–0. Then Lampard, really hitting the heights, crossed for Anelka to finish brilliantly: 4–0. Drogba's desperation for the Golden Boot was soon sated. Lampard set him up for a simple, far-post finish: 5–0. Then Mario Melchiot brought down the irrepressible Ashley Cole and Lampard, almost smiling, threw the ball to Drogba, who drilled the penalty in off the post: 6–0. Following good work from Joe Cole, Drogba pounced again: 7–0. And then came Ashley Cole making it 8–0.

Among the records set by this victory were the 103 goals that Chelsea scored in a season. And for Chelsea it was the first time they had scored eight goals in their top-flight history.

But there would be no rest for these record-breakers. Six days later they had a date with relegated Portsmouth at Wembley, aiming to complete their first ever League and Cup double.

Happy Premier League returns

BOTH Newcastle United and West Bromwich Albion returned to the Premier League at the first attempt after last season's relegation to the Championship. It was glory all the way for Newcastle from the very beginning as they leapt into the lead from their starting-blocks and were never headed, in fact never really challenged. They went unbeaten for a club-record 15 games, they ensured promotion with a month of the season remaining, and they were unbeaten at home for the first time in over 100 years, swatting away a West Brom attempt to catch them by running up seven wins on the trot. They lost only four league matches, amassed 102 points, boasted a goal difference of 55, and regularly drew home crowds of over 50,000. Captain Kevin Nolan was also the Championship's Player of the Year and Chris Hughton the Manager of the Year.

Meanwhile West Brom's season, while not as spectacular as Newcastle's, was hugely successful in that they won promotion.

In the last nine seasons the Baggies have been promoted or relegated seven times. It surely is about time they introduced some stability at the club.

Portsmouth go bust

PORTSMOUTH FC, with debts of about £60m, have become the first ever Premier League club to go into administration. Already eight points adrift at the bottom of the table, they will be docked nine points as a result of this action. With 12 matches left this season, barring a miracle, they will be playing Championship football next season.

Pompey, who have had four owners this season, were due to face a winding-up order on 1 March, but decided to go into administration in a bid to survive.

As well as struggling at the bottom of the Premier League, Portsmouth have suffered a catalogue of ongoing financial problems. Players have been paid late on four occasions this season, while the club is also involved in a separate dispute with former owner Sacha Gaydamak over whether they have missed a deadline in paying a £9m chunk of the £28m they owe him.

SOCCER SOUNDBITES

"That club will never die. That club has a lion's heart. The fans love their club, they will always be there."

MILAN MANDARIC,
Chairman of Portsmouth from 1998 to 2006 and now Leicester chief

It has been a tumultuous two years at Fratton Park since manager Harry Redknapp, who moved to Tottenham last season, steered them to FA Cup glory in 2008 – their first significant silverware for 58 years. As a result of having to sell their best players, Portsmouth lost the first seven matches of this season. England striker Jermain Defoe and Lasanna Diarra were sold in January 2009, and Defoe's England team-mates Peter Crouch and Glen Johnson followed at the end of last season. Despite the threat of the club being forced into offloading its only assets like this, many fans will be relieved they still have a club to support with fixtures remaining unaffected. Pompey travel to Burnley on Saturday before the FA Cup quarter-final clash with Birmingham the following weekend – yes, they're still in the Cup!

Fulham reach the Europa League final

Fulham's Simon Davies celebrates his equalizing goal against Atletico Madrid in the 2010 Europa League final.

IN THE PREMIER LEAGUE, Fulham have been happy with a mid-table position for years. To come seventh, as they did last season, was a major accomplishment, and it earned them entry into the Europa League. Few observers of the game gave them the slightest of chances to progress more than a round or two, let alone reach the final. Yet this is what they did.

The adventure began in the group stages, their first match a creditable 1-1 draw away to CSKA Sofia. Fulham qualified for the 32-club knock-out stage by finishing runners-up to Roma. They had needed to win their last game away to Basle, and this they did 3–2 thanks to two goals from striker Bobby Zamora and one from midfielder Zoltan Gera.

Gera was soon influential in the knock-out stage, giving Fulham the lead in the third minute of their home leg against Shakhtar Donetsk. Adriano equalized after 32 minutes, but Zamora scored in the second half to boost Fulham's confidence ahead of their next meeting. In the Ukraine, Brede Hangeland scored in the first half to put Fulham 3–1 up on aggregate. Shakhtar pulled one back after 69 minutes, but to no avail.

Few gave Fulham a chance when they were drawn in the next round against the mighty Juventus. And when the Italians won their home leg 3–1, and led after just two minutes at Craven Cottage, it was no exaggeration to say that the tie seemed all but over. But nothing seemed to faze Fulham. In went the goals, Zamora after 9 minutes, Gera after 39 and a 49th-minute penalty, and the American Clint Dempsey in the 82nd minute to seal the comeback.

Fulham swept past German club Wolfsburg in the quarter-finals, winning 3–1 on aggregate, and in the semis they faced Hamburg. After a goalless first leg away, they came from behind with late goals from Simon Davies and Gera sending them to the final.

Fulham met Atletico Madrid in the final and were outplayed early on. Atletico took the lead after 32 minutes through Diego Forlan, only for Simon Davies to equalize five minutes later.

The game went to extra time, and Fulham were four minutes away from a penalty shoot-out when Forlan struck again. Now there was too little time for another comeback and the adventure was over.

Rangers win cup with nine men

RANGERS won the Scottish League Cup (Co-op Cup) at Hampden Park thanks to an 84th-minute Kenny Miller goal in the final against St Mirren, despite the extraordinary handicap of being reduced to nine men for the last 20 minutes or so. They went down to 10 men in the 53rd minute when Kevin Thomson was sent off for a dangerous tackle on his namesake Steven, and in the 71st minute Danny Wilson saw red for a "professional foul" on Craig Dargo.

With 11 v 11, Saints – strong underdogs – nevertheless dominated the first half. They made a positive start when Billy Mehmet robbed David Weir and crossed towards the back post and a deflection forced Sasa Papac to head out of play. In a couple of rare Rangers attacks, Steven Whittaker sent in a low drive which St Mirren keeper held, and then set up Miller for a run and shot but the striker could not keep his effort down.

The Rangers' keeper Neil Alexander wanted too much time with a backpass and was almost caught out by Jack Ross, but the ball rebounded for a goal-kick. The keeper looked more assured moments later when he made a goal-line clearance from Steven Thomson, who had latched on to Michael Higdon's cut-back.

From the resulting corner, the ball broke out to defender David Barron, and he clipped the top of the crossbar with a long-range pile-driver. Saints continued to pressure the Rangers defence, and Higdon fired into the side netting after latching on to Mehmet's flick-on.

Saints missed an opportunity when Ross headed a long ball down to Mehmet, who turned Weir before sending a tame shot into Alexander's arms.

It was "all the Thomsons" eight minutes after the interval when referee Craig Thomson sent off Kevin Thomson for a late lunge on Steven Thomson during another St Mirren attack. The flashpoint brought an unpleasant edge to the game, and the referee called for calm.

Rangers sought to take advantage of a growing number of set plays, but neither Kris Boyd nor Edu could find the target with headers. A Nacho Novo free-kick created chaos in the St Mirren box before Higdon made a crucial block to divert Miller's shot wide. Higdon then featured at the other end when he just failed to make good contact with a Thomson cross.

Dargo then came on for Mehmet and made an immediate impact as he chased a long ball. He was blatantly pulled back by Danny Wilson, who was promptly sent off for denying St Mirren a clear goal-scoring opportunity.

But the Buddies struggled to make their numerical advantage count and they were punished on a breakaway, when substitute Steven Naismith crossed for Miller to head beyond Gallacher.

The shell-shocked Saints pushed for an equalizer but could not find a way through a resolute Rangers defence.

For St Mirren it was heartbreak as they failed to secure their first League Cup triumph. Meanwhile Rangers celebrated their 26th.

Gerrard made England captain

FABIO CAPELLO has confirmed that Liverpool's powerhouse midfielder Steven Gerrard will be England's captain for the friendly international against Egypt at Wembley on Wednesday. Gerrard leads the side in place of the injured Rio Ferdinand, who was promoted to skipper after John Terry's demotion. Ahead of the World Cup, the England boss said he was keen to move on from the reports of Terry's alleged affair with Wayne Bridge's former partner. "The important thing is how the players perform on the pitch and not what happens outside," stated Capello. The Italian is expecting an "interesting" match on Wednesday and hopes the fans will not boo Terry.

"I am delighted that I will be leading the boys out," said Gerrard. "The players have a responsibility to forget about what's being written off the field and focus on what we can do on the pitch."

Blues win their first Double

David couldn't quite slay Goliath at Wembley: Chelsea players celebrate beating relegated Pompey.

IT SHOULD HAVE BEEN easy for Premiership champions Chelsea. On paper, Portsmouth – they had lost their first seven games and were relegated, rock bottom of the Premiership, and with debts of £138 million, a ban on new signings, followed by administration and a nine-point penalty – could have expected a similar fate to Wigan's 8–0 humiliation in the league five days earlier. Pompey, though, had shown commendable spirit in the closing weeks of the season despite their plight, most notably when they beat Tottenham 2–0 in their FA Cup semi-final.

Remarkably, with great effort and fortitude, and a massive amount of luck, the underdogs held firm for almost an hour before Didier Drogba recorded his customary Wembley goal minutes after Pompey had missed a penalty. It was a trademark Drogba effort, a 20-yard free-kick which he curled round the defensive wall and into the far corner of the net, well worthy of winning an FA Cup final – which it did.

It was no more than the 10–1 on favourites deserved, for they had struck the woodwork five times before the interval. Frank Lampard, after shooting narrowly wide, scraped the outside of a post with a long-range effort. Then Salomon Kalou contrived to miss an open goal from five yards out, lifting a cross from Ashley Cole on to the bar. Three minutes later skipper John Terry headed Florent Malouda's free-kick against the bar, and soon after that David James diverted a rasping shot from Drogba against a post. The England keeper was the busiest man on the pitch, while his teammates were floundering under this constant assault. But when Drogba hit the post just before half-time Chelsea fans could have been forgiven for thinking this might just not be their day.

Meanwhile Chelsea midfielder Michael Ballack had been forced off the field with an injury that threatened to keep him out of the forthcoming World Cup, the result of a brutal challenge from Kevin-Prince Boateng.

Portsmouth were largely bystanders as Chelsea settled in their opponents' half and the only way they appeared likely to unsettle Ancelotti's team was by a series of bone-shaking challenges, particularly from Michael Brown on Lampard. More acceptable was Pompey's determined defending, which was typified by Aaron Mokoena's double block to deny Drogba. But although Portsmouth's threat was minimal, they would have taken the lead in the 22nd minute in their first serious attack but for a brilliant save from Chelsea keeper Petr Cech. Aruna Dindane had broken free on the right, got to the Chelsea by-line, and crossed for Boateng, whose close-in volley was diverted goalwards by Frederic Piquionne. However, Cech, virtually unemployed until now, reacted instinctively to swat the ball away one-handed and prevent the favourites suffering an early blow.

Portsmouth's confidence had clearly been boosted by their first half survival efforts and they started the second period much more positively. Boateng volleyed narrowly over in the 51st minute, then had an even better chance to score four minutes later when Juliano Belletti – on for Ballack – brought down Dindane to concede a penalty. Once again, though, Cech came to Chelsea's rescue, saving the Portsmouth midfielder's attempt with his legs. The effect of the miss appeared to puncture Portsmouth's self-belief. Portsmouth's spirit weakened and Lampard blew the chance to wrap up the win with two minutes left when he missed from the spot after being brought down by Brown.

Even their defeat and looming relegation could not subdue the Pompey fans, arguably the most loyal and vociferous in the country, and they kept up their singing and foot-stomping long after the final whistle. Manager Avram Grant, appointed in late November, summed up his feelings at the end of a traumatic season when he said, with a tear in his eye, simply "the supporters are the best".

Notts County's new money recruits Sven and Sol

THERE WAS NO WARNING, not a whisper. The news broke suddenly. Sven Goran-Eriksson, one-time manager of the England team, has taken over as director of football at Notts County, the oldest professional football club in the world but now languishing in the lowest division of the Football League. They might call it League 2, but that fools nobody – at least it shouldn't – it's what used to be known as the Fourth Division.

The club was bought a week earlier by Munto Finance, a Middle East consortium. Formed in 1862 and among the founders of the Football League in 1888, County have been in the doldrums in recent years. The last time they were in the top flight was in the early 1990s.

The move was announced at an official Press conference on 21 July with the mandate of seeing the side become an established Championship club within five years.

Rather than assuming managerial duties – Ian McParland will continue as first-team manager – the 61-year-old Swede will take on a more executive role, most importantly handling all transfer negotiations (he signed Sol Campbell, who made one appearance for the club). He will also oversee such areas as the club's training facilities, player development, youth academy, and scouting network. He will be joined by his assistant, Tord Grip, who assumes the role of general advisor. Eriksson's remuneration will be linked with Notts County's progress through the leagues.

It is a remarkable appointment. Eriksson has been out of work since April after his dismissal as Mexico's manager. He has been linked with a number of roles, but he has chosen to join a club who finished 19th in the fourth tier of English football last season and whose attendances hover around the 5,000 mark. He has never been one to shirk a challenge.

Benitez calls it a day at Anfield

IT CAME AS NO SURPRISE when the announcement was made on 3 June that Liverpool manager Rafael Benitez was leaving Anfield. The club's managing director, Christian Purslow, and "ambassador" Kenny Dalglish will now lead the search for a new manager, but the club has set no timescale for a replacement to be found. It is believed Benitez will receive a severance package worth around £6 million.

Benitez's departure comes after the Anfield Board and chairman Martin Broughton lost faith in his ability to deliver Champions League football, and they decided to act before the start of the new season.

Broughton said: "Rafa will forever be part of Liverpool folklore after bringing home the Champions League following the epic final in Istanbul, but after a disappointing season both parties felt a fresh start would be best for all concerned."

Benitez said: "It is very sad for me to announce that I will no longer be manager of Liverpool FC... I'll always keep in my heart the good times I've had here, the strong and loyal support of the fans in the tough times, and the love from Liverpool. I have no words to thank you enough for all these years and I am very proud to say that I was your manager.

"Thank you so much once more and always remember: You'll never walk alone."

Liverpool's declining performance, combined with Benitez's unwillingness to acknowledge failings on his part, was at the heart of the Board's loss of faith. When he guided the club to second in the Premiership in 2008–09, expectations grew that Benitez could end a 20-year wait for the title in 2010, but those hopes faded after a poor start. In fact the club regressed, and his exit will end a volatile six-year tenure notable for European success and political intrigue, but not the title the Kop craved.

SOCCER SOUNDBITES

"I'll always keep in my heart the good times I've had here... I am very proud to say that I was your manager."

RAFA BENITEZ

Four-goal Messi destroys Arsenal

Lionel Messi single-handedly puts Arsenal to the sword with four sublime goals at the Nou Camp.

IT WAS THE FIRST TIME Lionel Messi had scored four goals in a match. The unlucky victims were Arsenal, and there was absolutely nothing they could do to dim the Argentinian's brilliance. Two late goals at the Emirates in the first leg of this Champions League quarter-final had enabled Arsenal to come to the Nou Camp on level terms. And when they unexpectedly went ahead with a goal in the 18th minute in Barcelona, their supporters allowed themselves to dream. But three minutes later Messi equalized, and when he completed his hat-trick before half-time the dream had turned into a nightmare.

Nevertheless, who is to say Messi would have enjoyed so much possession had the visitors been able to field the likes of Alex Song, Robin van Persie, William Gallas, Andrei Arshavin, and above all Cesc Fabregas.

The Gunners weathered the inevitable Barcelona storm for a while, and indeed took the lead when Nicklas Bendtner converted a square pass from Theo Walcott at the second attempt.

Messi, however, soon curbed Arsenal's enthusiasm. Lacking Gallas, Arsenal's defence looked shaky, particularly the part covered by Silvestre, whose poor control gifted the ball to Messi. The response was instant, Messi shimmying past Clichy before ramming the ball home.

Walcott sought to rally Arsenal, racing down the right, before being crudely stopped by Busquets. Barcelona showed they could mix it.

Messi began and finished the move that put Barca in front, Pedro eventually laying the ball off for the little genius, who ghosted past the hapless Silvestre and hammered in his second.

Then the Malian Seydou Keita gained possession in midfield, and quickly sent Messi scampering down the inside-left channel to lift the ball beautifully over Almunia.

Messi produced another masterpiece in the second half. The little maestro glided past Emmanuel Eboue and then outpaced Vermaelen. Manuel Almunia saved his first effort, but Messi then impudently rolled the ball through the keeper's legs for his fourth. Magic.

FOOTBALL FOCUS

- Kris Boyd was again leading scorer in the Clydesdale Bank Premier League with 23 goals, a tally that included a five-goal haul in the 7–1 win over Dundee United at the end of December – a night when he surpassed Henrik Larsson's 158 as all-time top scorer in the SPL.
- When Arsenal visited Fratton Park on New Year's Eve, neither they nor Portsmouth started with an English player. Only in the last few minutes did any Englishmen come on, Craig Eastmond for Arsenal and Michael Brown for Portsmouth. Arsenal won the game 4–1.
- David Will, former president of the Scottish FA, died at he age of 72. A solicitor by profession, he became involved in football through his local club Brechin City. He also served as a vice-president of FIFA for over 15 years, in which capacity he was not averse to standing up to president Sepp Blatter and even attacking him over finances.
- Wayne Rooney became the third Manchester United recipient of the FWA Footballer of the Year award in four years after Cristiano Ronaldo won it twice, a run interrupted only by Liverpool's Steven Gerrard.
- Lowly Portsmouth took Premier League champions Manchester United to penalties after a goalless draw in the 2008 FA Community Shield but lost the shoot-out 3–1.
- In a change to law 14, feinting when taking a penalty kick is now permitted in the run-up, but is treated as a cautionable infringment once the run-up is completed.

Mourinho masterminds Inter win

THE GOALS were scored by Diego Milito, but the Argentinian striker was the first to concede that the credit for Inter Milan's 2–0 win over Bayern Munich in the final of the Champions League belonged to coach Jose Mourinho who masterminded the triumph. His well-drilled side kept Bayern at bay, and when Inter broke away Milito was there to clinch victory.

Bayern, however, would not have been underestimated. They had their own "special" coach in Louis van Gaal. They also had more recent pedigree in this competition, contesting as they were their third final in 11 years. Inter last made the final in 1972, and won their two titles in '64 and '65.

To reach the final, which was held at Real Madrid's Bernabeu stadium, Inter had needed to overcome Chelsea and then Barcelona, while Bayern's victims included Manchester United.

It has to be said, this Bayern side were poor in defence, while Inter were virtually unshakable throughout. That was to be the deciding factor. Mourinho builds his team and tactics on defence and organization, but it should not be forgotten that his sides have also included first-class attackers. This one boasted the wily Dutchman Wesley Sneijder in midfield, and Milito was partnered up front by the pacy Samuel Eto'o. Bayern's dangerman was the former flying Chelsea and Real Madrid winger Arjen Robben, a great dribbler who loves to come inside and shoot.

Robben showed the first willingness to attack after only three minutes of the match, but he was crudely hacked down by Walter Samuel. For the next half-hour very little of note happened on the pitch. Inter sat there waiting for Bayern to do something they could snuff out, while the German side deployed Robben to look for attacking possibilities.

The game badly needed a goal. And it came in the 34th minute by leave of route one. Inter keeper Julio Cesar took possession and punted the ball upfield, down the middle, looking for one of his front men. He found Milito, who just used his strength to win a header and power straight for goal. The Argentinian then played a one-two with Sneijder before lifting an unstoppable drive over the advancing Hans-Jorg Butt in Bayern's goal to put Inter one up.

In the second half Bayern upped the offensive but it was to no avail though, because Inter shortly after went into a two-goal lead.

Eto'o was the provider, putting Milito into the heart of the Bayern defence, but with still a lot to do. First there was Van Buyten to get past, which he did with a drop of the shoulder, and then he skilfully steered the ball past the goalkeeper with ease.

Just before the 90 minutes was up, Mourinho substituted Milito, who left the field to a standing ovation from the 80,000 crowd. Inter might have won the Cup without him, but they would not have done it with such panache. One wonders whether Mourhino cared.

Inter celebrate ending a 45-year wait for European football's top prize.

Well and Hibs share a dozen

MOTHERWELL striker Lukas Jutkiewicz scored with a spectacular stoppage-time volley from a near impossible angle to complete a remarkable comeback from 6–2 down against Hibs at Fir Park. This brought the home side level in a match that set a new record aggregate for the SPL – and kept the Steelmen in pole position, a point ahead of their rivals, in the race for Europa League football with just one round of fixtures left.

Hibs were coasting midway through the second half after Anthony Stokes netted twice to add to Colin Nish's first-half treble and Derek Riordan's effort. But Giles Coke and John Sutton both hit their second goals of the game which, along with Tom Hateley's free-kick, allowed Motherwell the chance to level. And Jutkiewicz did so in style just moments after his team's hopes had appeared to vanish, when Ross Forbes missed a penalty.

Motherwell remain a point ahead of Hibernian going into the final game of the season as they chase the fourth-place finish that would guarantee a place in the Europa League.

Rangers scrap to SPL win

IT WAS THE USUAL two-horse race for the SPL title, at least for the latter part of the season. It looked like being a thriller from the start. Celtic won five and drew one of their first six matches, with a 14–5 goal tally. Meanwhile it was a roller-coaster ride for Rangers with three wins (goals 10–3) followed by three goalless draws. This left Celtic top of the table with 16 points to Rangers' 12.

However, Dundee United gave them a run for their money. The Terrors went 14 games with only one defeat, drawing with and beating Celtic in this sequence, before they came up against Rangers, who beat them 3–0 at Tannadice. Thereafter their challenge evaporated.

Celtic led the table on and off until mid-December, when they lost 2–1 at Hearts. This was the signal for Rangers to take over. The Gers enjoyed a purple patch in December, reeling off six straight wins – 3–1, 3–0, 3–0, 6–1, 4–1, 7–1 – in the last of which, against Dundee United, Kris Boyd helped himself to five goals. The run was finally halted at Celtic Park with a 1–1 draw, but they remained undefeated in the SPL for the rest of the season apart from an extraordinary 4–1 defeat at the end of March by St Johnstone after being eliminated from the Scottish FA Cup by Dundee United earlier in the same week. But they were still 10 points ahead of Celtic in the league with a game in hand, and although Celtic won their last eight matches under new caretaker-manager Neil Lennon, Rangers ran out worthy SPL champions by six points.

FINAL SCORE

Football League
Premiership – Chelsea
Top scorer – Didier Drogba (Chelsea) 29
Championship – Newcastle United
League 1 – Norwich City
League 2 – Notts County
Footballer of the Year – Steven Gerrard (Liverpool)

FA Cup final
Chelsea 1 Portsmouth 0

League Cup final
Manchester United 2 Aston Villa 1

Scottish League
Premier League – Rangers
Top scorer – Kris Boyd (Rangers) 23
Div 1 – Inverness CT
Div 2 – Stirling Albion
Div 3 – Livingston
Footballer of the Year – David Weir (Rangers)

Scottish FA Cup final
Dundee United 3 Ross County 0

Scottish League Cup final
Rangers 1 St Mirren 0

European Cup final
Inter Milan 2 Bayern Munich 0

UEFA Cup final
Atletico Madrid 2 Fulham 1

European Footballer of the Year 2009
Lionel Messi (Barcelona and Argentina)

World Club Championship 2009
Barcelona 2 Estudantes 1
(aet)

Spain reign

No more the bridesmaids, as they stylishly showed in the 2008 European Championships, Spain came out of the 2010 World Cup as rightful champions. Apart from one or two wobbles on the way, this Spanish side thoroughly deserved their World Cup triumph. They were the best team in the finals, and they played the best football. The South African hosts put on a splendid show, although Nelson Mandela, the 91-year-old "father" of the nation, was prevented from appearing at the opening ceremony by a personal tragedy. However, although very frail, he attended the final at Soccer City.

After what was the first World Cup played on African soil, FIFA Secretary General Jerome Valcke asserted that: "The resounding success of the 2010 FIFA World Cup has set a new benchmark against which future global showpieces will be judged." Be that as it may, also highlighted during the tournament was a flaw in the law that should have been rectified long ago with a simple solution, namely that if a defender on the goal line stops a "certain goal" by handling the ball on the goal line, the referee should be empowered to award a goal – like the penalty try in rugby. Such a situation occurred in the Ghana-Uruguay quarter-final, in which Ghana were deprived of an extra-time last-minute winner by Luis Suarez, who sacrificed himself in this way, and in so doing prevented Ghana becoming the first African country to reach the semi-finals of the World Cup. Asamoah Gyan missed the resultant penalty, the game went to penalties, and, in front of over 84,000 spectators – some bemused, some exultant – Uruguay won the shoot-out 4–2.

The sound of the tournament – the ear-splitting African vuvuzela.

Shaky starts

Spain made a shaky start to their campaign, losing 1–0 to Switzerland in what looked an easy group. The European champions were hot favourites to continue their run of success, coming to the match with 12 wins on the trot and only one defeat in their last 49 internationals. They played their usual passing game but it continued to be broken up by Switzerland's mass defence and they created few opportunities. They fell behind in the 52nd minute on the counter to a scrambled goal by Gelson Fernandes, and although both sides hit the woodwork there was no further scoring. However, Spain eased their way through their next match 2–0 over Honduras, with David Villa scoring both goals as well as missing a penalty. Over-elaboration probably cost them a more convincing victory. Switzerland gained only one more point, leaving Spain to top the group on goal difference from Chile. But four goals in three games was a poor return for such a talented side.

England, too, made a shaky start in their group, failing to beat the USA. They couldn't have wished for a better start to the game, though, Steven Gerrard racing through to find the net after only five minutes. But Fabio Capello's men allowed the USA to gain the upper hand, and then keeper Robert Green allowed a speculative shot along the ground by Fulham's Clint Dempsey to slip through his hands for a 40th-minute equalizer. Even so, they had more than half a game to capitalize on their supposed superiority, but with the much-vaunted Wayne Rooney largely anonymous they failed to make any further dents in the USA defence or in their indomitable spirit.

WORLD CUP SOUNDBITES

"It is African culture, we are in Africa and we have to allow them to practise their culture as much as they want to."

FIFA president **SEPP BLATTER** on vuvuzelas

Matters went from bad to worse when England were held to a goalless draw in their next match, by Algeria, and only a 1–0 must-win victory over Slovenia kept them in the competition. The newly drafted-in Spurs striker Jermain Defoe volleyed the goal in the 23rd minute. One more goal and they would have topped the group instead of qualifying behind the USA, and this would have repercussions later because it meant they had to face Germany in the second round. Meanwhile it was a goal from Landon Donovan in the dying seconds that gave the USA a 1–0 victory over Algeria that left them not only on top of

A distraught Rob Green after his howler against the USA.

their group but also still in the tournament.

As it happens, Germany, fielding a young side orchestrated by midfielder Mezut Ozil, did not have it all their own way in Group D despite opening up with a 4–0 thrashing of Australia. Then Serbia beat them 1–0. This setback was largely the result of the referee's harsh decision to send off striker Miroslav Klose in the 37th minute after two borderline yellow cards. Germany went behind almost immediately to a goal from close in by Milan Jovanovich, but spurned the chance of an equalizer when Lukas Podolski produced a tame penalty, a very rare miss by the Germans. But then Serbia twice hit the woodwork before the end.

Out go the hosts

The hosts South Africa were drawn in the very difficult Group A. And although they were eliminated only on goal difference they finished above France, who suffered a World Cup to forget. In the match that opened the tournament on 11 June, South Africa earned a creditable draw with Mexico, veterans of many World Cups. But they were outclassed 3–0 by group winners Uruguay, Diego Forlan scoring twice. The capitulation of France marked a sad chapter in the history of the 2006 runners-up. They imploded as a mixture of infighting and player revolt against coach Raymond Domenech and his questionable selections and tactics culminated in the sending home of striker Nicolas Anelka for verbal abuse during the interval in the Mexico game, which France lost 2–0. Sadly, Domenech had lost control – and the respect – of his players, who refused to train before their last match, which they lost 2–1 to South Africa. This was a consolation farewell victory for the hosts, despite its being the first time the home country had been eliminated in the first round.

Argentina and Holland reigned supreme in their respective groups, both winning the maximum nine points. Coached by Diego Maradona, Argentina had their troubles qualifying for the tournament, but the brilliance of Lionel Messi dominated their group matches and although not scoring himself, he played a big part in Gonzalo Higuane's hat-trick against South Korea. While not quite hitting the heights, Holland got stuck in as coach Bert Van Marwijk proved he was fully prepared to "win ugly" – an omen of things to come.

FINAL SCORE

FIRST ROUND

Group A

South Africa	1	Mexico	1
France	0	Uruguay	0
Uruguay	3	South Africa	0
Mexico	2	France	0
Uruguay	1	Mexico	0
South Africa	2	France	1

	P	W	D	L	F	A	P
Uruguay	3	2	1	0	4	0	7
Mexico	3	1	1	1	3	2	4
South Africa	3	1	1	1	3	5	4
France	3	0	1	2	1	4	1

Group B

South Korea	2	Greece	0
Argentina	1	Nigeria	0
Argentina	4	South Korea	1
Greece	2	Nigeria	1
Nigeria	2	South Korea	2
Argentina	2	Greece	0

	P	W	D	L	F	A	P
Argentina	3	3	0	0	7	1	9
South Korea	3	1	1	1	5	6	4
Greece	3	1	0	2	2	5	3
Nigeria	3	0	1	2	3	5	1

Group C

England	1	USA	1
Slovenia	1	Algeria	0
USA	2	Slovenia	2
England	0	Algeria	0
USA	1	Algeria	0
England	1	Slovenia	0

	P	W	D	L	F	A	P
USA	3	1	2	0	4	3	5
England	3	1	2	0	2	1	5
Slovenia	3	1	1	1	3	3	4
Algeria	3	0	1	2	0	2	1

Group D

Ghana	1	Serbia	0
Germany	4	Australia	0
Serbia	1	Germany	0
Australia	1	Ghana	1
Germany	1	Ghana	0
Australia	2	Serbia	1

	P	W	D	L	F	A	P
Germany	3	2	0	1	5	1	6
Ghana	3	1	1	1	2	2	4
Australia	3	1	1	1	3	6	4
Serbia	3	1	0	2	2	3	3

Group E

Holland	2	Denmark	0
Japan	1	Cameroon	0
Holland	1	Japan	0
Denmark	2	Cameroon	1
Japan	3	Denmark	1
Holland	2	Cameroon	1

	P	W	D	L	F	A	P
Holland	3	3	0	0	5	1	9
Japan	3	2	0	1	4	2	6
Denmark	3	1	0	2	3	6	3
Cameroon	3	0	0	3	2	5	0

Group F

Paraguay	1	Italy	1
New Zealand	1	Slovakia	1
Paraguay	2	Slovakia	0
Italy	1	New Zealand	1
Slovakia	3	Italy	2
New Zealand	0	Paraguay	0

	P	W	D	L	F	A	P
Paraguay	3	1	2	0	3	1	5
Slovakia	3	1	1	1	4	5	4
New Zealand	3	0	3	0	2	2	3
Italy	3	0	2	1	4	5	2

Group G

Portugal	0	Ivory Coast	0
Brazil	2	North Korea	1
Brazil	3	Ivory Coast	1
Portugal	7	North Korea	0
Brazil	0	Portugal	0
Ivory Coast	3	North Korea	0

	P	W	D	L	F	A	P
Brazil	3	2	1	0	5	2	7
Portugal	3	1	2	0	7	0	5
Ivory Coast	3	1	1	1	4	3	4
North Korea	3	0	0	3	1	12	0

Group H

Chile	1	Honduras	0
Switzerland	1	Spain	0
Chile	1	Switzerland	0
Spain	2	Honduras	0
Spain	2	Chile	1
Switzerland	0	Honduras	0

	P	W	D	L	F	A	P
Spain	3	2	0	1	4	2	6
Chile	3	2	0	1	3	2	6
Switzerland	3	1	1	1	1	1	4
Honduras	3	0	1	2	0	3	1

SECOND ROUND

Uruguay	2	South Korea	1
Ghana	2	USA	1
(aet)			
Germany	4	England	1
Argentina	3	Mexico	1
Holland	2	Slovakia	1
Brazil	3	Chile	0
Paraguay	0	Japan	0
(aet; Paraguay won 5–3 on penalties)			
Spain	1	Portugal	0

QUARTER-FINALS

Holland	2	Brazil	1
Uruguay	1	Ghana	1
(aet; Uruguay won 4–2 on penalties)			
Germany	4	Argentina	0
Spain	1	Paraguay	0

SEMI-FINALS

Holland	3	Uruguay	2
Spain	1	Germany	0

THIRD-PLACE MATCH

Germany	3	Uruguay	2

FINAL

Spain	1	Holland	0
(aet)			

Soccer City, Johannesburg, South Africa, 11 July 2010
Attendance 84,490

Spain: Casillas, Sergio Ramos, Pique, Puyol, Capdevila, Busquets, Xabi Alonso (Fabregas 87), Iniesta, Xavi, Pedro (Navas 60), Villa (Torres 105)

Holland: Stekelenburg, Van de Wiel, Heitinga, Mathijsen, Van Bronckhorst (Braafheid 105), Van Bommel, De Jong (Van der Vaart 99), Robben, Sneijder, Kuyt (Elia 70), Van Persie

Leading scorers

5: Diego Forlan (Uruguay)
Thomas Muller (Germany)
Wesley Sneijder (Holland)
David Villa (Spain)

Uruguay's Luis Suarez keeps his side in the tournament with a blatant hand-ball to deny a Ghana goal.

New Zealand unbeaten

The only team to remain unbeaten in the 2010 World Cup was New Zealand, who drew their three group matches. It was not enough to keep them in the competition, but they did finish above the holders Italy, who failed to win a match.

Brazil tore up no trees in Group G, but were relieved to get through the so-called "group of death". Portugal joined them in the second round thanks to their 7–0 annihilation of North Korea followed by two goalless draws, leaving the Ivory Coast as the odd one out, with Didier Drogba nursing a broken elbow.

Knock-out stage

Now the tournament had been trimmed down to the last 16, the knock-out stage; defeat equalled elimination. Among those to go out at the first hurdle were England, USA, and Portugal. The England-Germany game threw up another highly controversial incident, when a long-range drive from Frank Lampard hit the underside of the crossbar and clearly bounced down well over the line – clearly, that is, to everyone but the match officials, who failed to award a goal, a coherent case for those in favour of goal-line technology. It would have completed England's comeback from 2–0 down and perhaps given them some impetus going into the second half, but it should not be allowed to hide the truly inept performance by England's central defence, namely John Terry and Matthew Upson. How they missed the injured Rio Ferdinand. Manager Fabio Capello tried to hide behind this misfortune, but he fooled no-one. Both his team selection and his tactics were highly suspect. In any case, Germany were worthy winners, completing England's 4–1 drubbing – their biggest defeat ever in a World Cup – with two second-half strikes from the young Thomas Muller.

For the USA it was perhaps a bridge too far, although they took the improving Ghana to extra time before Asamoah Gyan took advantage of a defensive lapse and volleyed in the winner.

Portugal had the misfortune to draw Iberian neighbours Spain. With Ronaldo ineffective, Portugal still managed to stay in the game until the 63rd minute, when Villa collected a brilliant backheel from Xavi and scored at the second attempt. Spain remained in control without increasing their lead and their possession football prevailed.

Brazil were far too good for Chile in the last 16, while the other three South American countries all got through to the quarter-finals, albeit Paraguay needing penalties to oust Japan. Chile could look back with pride, having entertained with an attacking game throughout their tournament. Carlos Tevez shone for Argentina against Mexico, allowed one goal, a header from Messi's cross that was patently offside, and scoring with a magnificent curling strike from the edge of the box. Uruguay edged past South Korea 2–1, both goals coming from Suarez, one of them also curled in from the edge of the area. Holland calmly and efficiently beat Slovakia by the same score.

The quarter-finals were all very tight bar one, the 4–0 demolition of Argentina by Germany. In the battle of tactics, Joachim Low won hands down, even to the extent of nullifying the Messi threat for most of the game thanks to a fine performance by Bastian Schweinsteiger. Maradona did not appear to have any tactics. He certainly had no answer to Germany's counter-attacking strategy. Miroslav Klose scored two goals on what was his 100th international appearance. A disciplined Holland beat Brazil 2–1 with second-half goals from Wesley Sneijder after Robinho had put the South Americans ahead in the 10th minute. With star playmaker Kaka strangely ineffective, Brazil could not come back. Coach Dunga resigned, but to make sure two days later the Brazilian Federation sacked him.

Uruguay beat Ghana thanks to the infamous hand of Suarez, and Spain edged Paraguay 1–0, needing more than a slice of luck to get away with it. First, Paraguay had a "goal" denied for a dubious offside decision as replays appeared to confirm, and then the result hinged on penalties in regular time. Iker Casillas made one brilliant save from Oscar Cardozo before Xabi Alonso converted one at the other end only to have it ruled out for encroachment. Justo Villar saved the retake. The referee then denied Spain another, cast-iron penalty as Villar flattened Fabregas, who had come on after 56 minutes for the out-of-touch Fernando Torres. Finally Spain scored, seven minutes from time, Villa notching his fifth of the tournament, latching on to the ball when sub Pedro's attempt came back off the post.

Holland took an 18th-minute lead over Uruguay in the first semi-final when Giovanni Van Bronckhorst fired in one of his specials, a piledriver from outside the box which gave keeper Fernando Muslera no chance. Forlan then produced one of his specials in the 41st minute, imparting such a swerve on the controversial Jabulani ball that keeper Maarten Stekelenburg could only flap at it as it flew into the net. Holland brought on Rafael Van de Vaart for the second half and he livened things up. With 20 minutes to go, Holland scored two goals in four minutes thanks to Sneijder and Arjen Robben. Uruguay never gave up, and Maxi Pereira snatched a stoppage-time goal – too little, too late.

Spain notched up their third consecutive 1–0 victory when they overcame Germany in the second semi-final. It was an unusual goal for the Spaniards, coming from a Xavi corner which was headed home in the 73rd minute by their captain and centre-back Carles Puyol, arriving late and unmarked in the goalmouth. Their win was due largely to their ruthless and ceaseless pressing of the Germans over all parts of the field. They had a bit of luck, though, when Sergio Ramos pressed a little too much, clipping Ozil's leg just outside the box, a foul that the Hungarian referee chose to ignore but which many a referee would have punished with a card, even a red one. So Spain joined Holland in the final, ensuring that there would be a new name on the FIFA trophy.

In the match that few people care about, the play-off for third place, Germany beat Uruguay 3–2 at Port Elizabeth in an entertaining see-saw game. Germany took the lead when Muslera could only parry Schweinsteiger's

WORLD CUP SOUNDBITES

"Mine is the real 'Hand Of God'. I made the save of the tournament."

An unrepentant **LUIS SUAREZ** after his handball on the line led to Uruguay's survival in the 2010 World Cup at the expense of Ghana

Holland's tough tackles were not enough to down Spain.

swerving shot and Muller tapped the ball in. Uruguay soon equalized when the unpopular Suarez put Edison Cavani through. After the interval Forlan gave Uruguay the lead with a spectacular volley, but five minutes later Marcell Jansen headed Germany level, and eight minutes from time the young midfielder Sami Khedira forced home a corner. Forlan, voted the player of the tournament, almost had the last word, but his stoppage-time free-kick came back off the bar.

What a shame that Holland decided to play it rough in the final. They turned it into a running brawl, with eight bookings for themselves (including two for Everton's John Heitinger, who was sent off) and five for Spain. Unlike in the 1970s, when they were twice runners-up playing their "total football" and admired throughout the footballing world, now they were being almost universally regarded with disdain.

Strangely, though, it was Holland who manufactured the best chances, and Casillas was called into action more than once to prevent the speedy Robben breaking through. Spain meanwhile persevered with their attractive passing game, although it was deep into extra time before it paid dividends. Cesc Fabregas, who had come on as an 87th-minute substitute, broke through almost immediately, one on one with the keeper, but had his shot saved. However, he made amends in the 26th minute of extra time with a perfectly weighted, defence-splitting pass to Iniesta, who slid the ball in for the winner. Spain were worthy winners, becoming world champions for the first time.

WORLD CUP SOUNDBITES

"I've made a small contribution in a very tough game, a very rough game. There were all sorts of things happening on the pitch but Spain deserved to win."

Modest match-winner **ANDRES INIESTA** after scoring Spain's winner in the 2010 World Cup final against Holland

Captain Iker Casillas leads the celebrations for Spain.

Arsenal mix-up hands Birmingham Carling Cup

BIRMINGHAM shocked hot favourites Arsenal at a packed Wembley in the final of the Carling Cup as striker Obafemi Martins, who is on loan from Russian side Rubin Kazan, scored in the last minute of normal time to take advantage of a defensive mix-up. The Gunners failed to clear a Nikola Zigic flick-on, leaving Martins a simple tap-in to snatch a 2-1 victory and win the Midlands side their first major trophy since taking this prize in 1963.

Zigic,whose selection owed much to his potential aerial threat to Arsenal, was a thorn in their side throughout. McLeish's decision to include him was vindicated as the giant striker, who, remarkably, had scored only seven goals before this occasion, put Birmingham into the lead after 28 minutes, heading home after Johnson's power in the air exposed Arsenal's uncertainty at set-pieces.

Arsenal, after six years without a trophy, and without their injured captain Cesc Fabrigas and speed merchant Theo Walcott, had appeared somewhat nervous as their normally penetrative passing game failed to reap reward in the first half. Arsenal's Andrei Arshavin forced Foster into a fine save on the turn as the favourites attempted to exert early authority. Foster was tested again, when he had to block a swerving drive from Nasri as a thrilling first 45 minutes drew to a close. But they produced a moment of genuine class to draw level six minutes before half-time. Jack Wilshere rattled Ben Foster's woodwork from the edge of the area and, when Birmingham failed to clear, Arshavin crossed for an airborne Van Persie to volley brilliantly beyond the reach of the keeper.

Birmingham were a model of grit and fight in the second half, and their success was a tribute to the outstanding work of manager Alex McLeish, who masterminded the triumph. Defender Roger Johnson was a commanding figure, and all the bravery displayed by him and his team-mates in the face of a late Arsenal onslaught was rewarded in sensational circumstances in the dying moments.

Martins scores to avert extra time and win the cup for Birmingham.

Rooney's wonder goal thwarts Man City

IT WAS A GOAL that will be replayed on the small screen and talked about for the rest of the season, and longer if Manchester United win the Premier League.

So much in sport is decided by fine margins, from a tight offside call here to a match-winning penalty there. The thin line between acclaim and blame was seen in Rooney's performance. The United striker, by his own admission, had not played well, largely shackled by City centre-back Vincent Kompany. The headlines would not have been favourable had he not produced a moment of magic.

Suddenly, all that recent criticism was forgotten. United's woe at suffering their first reverse of the campaign by lowly Wolves at Molineux was blown away by one touch. Media barbs at Rooney this season have been bizarre. He was poor at the World Cup, clearly distracted by off-field problems and still shaking off his ankle trouble. But class will out. And class is something Rooney has in abundance, at least on the football field. Goals from overhead kicks are far from unusual, but to pull one off in a crucial, top-of-the-table local derby, in which United were being comfortably held – and against the England goalkeeper, Joe Hart – is, well, class.

Both managers had fielded conservative line-ups. However, City started with more purpose and, after just four minutes, some clever play between Silva, Micah Richards, and Carlos Tévez presented Silva, being played onside by Nemanja Vidic, with a close-range chance that he poked wide.

As the game wore on, United began to settle. Much of their threat was coming from Nani, who delivered an array of crosses and speculative shots. The City defence have been good this season, but were caught out for United's first goal, allowing Ryan Giggs to release Nani with a brilliant first-time pass. Nani's touch and finish were similarly exceptional, on any other day a goal to remember.

Mancini's side deservedly equalized, albeit with a flukey goal, Edin Dzeko's shot diverting in off Silva's back. Mancini, naturally cautious, really needs to find a solution up front and maybe give his No 10 Dzeko a run of starts to build up his partnership with Tevez. Manchester's other No 10 certainly found a solution to settle a game and possibly the title race.

Rooney's overhead kick lifts his – and United's – season.

Real win first Copa del Rey for 18 years

REAL MADRID notched up their first trophy under Jose Mourinho when Cristiano Ronaldo's extra-time winner secured a 1–0 Copa del Rey final victory over arch-rivals Barcelona. With penalties looming in an occasionally violent clash at Valencia's Mestalla stadium, the Portuguese star leapt high to head home the 103rd-minute winner from Angel Di Maria's inch-perfect cross.

Remarkably, this was Real's first Copa success for 18 years, and it was gained in Mourinho's first season since joining from Inter Milan. Second in La Liga, eight points behind Barcelona, Real had been in danger of suffering a third barren season on the trot. Moreover, this gives Real a much-needed boost ahead of their upcoming European Champions League semi-final clashes with Barca.

Mourinho previously enjoyed Copa del Rey successes in 1997 and 1998, oddly enough as assistant to Barcelona coaches Bobby Robson and Louis Van Gaal. He has now won cups in four different countries, following triumphs in Portugal with Porto, England with Chelsea, and Italy with Inter.

England's World Cup Woe

A despondent England 2018 bid team looks on as Russia trump them to host football's biggest contest.

DESPITE the combined forces of prime minister David Cameron, Prince William, and David Beckham, England's bid to host the 2018 World Cup failed miserably. It collapsed at the first hurdle, gaining only two votes. The question is "Why"?

The prize went to Russia – not to Spain-Portugal nor to Belgium-Holland. But if that was a surprise, what about Qatar's winning the right to stage the 2022 tournament? And why was this even considered at this stage of the proceedings? Indeed, why on earth were Qatar even in the running when there were countries like Australia and the United States around? Not a footballing nation and with a population of about 700,000 – not to mention Celsius temperatures in the fifties – Qatar was an inexplicable choice.

Notwithstanding these anomalies, England were in large part responsible for their own downfall. After a string of major own goals during the campaign to stage the tournament, the final attempt to persuade football's world governing body was too little too late. Maybe the airing of Panorama's exposure of corruption in FIFA could have been delayed, but this would knowingly have allowed the congress to take place without a challenge. Andy Anson, bid chief executive, blamed the failure on tactical voting and said England did not land votes it was promised: "There were other votes we thought we were going to get that would have taken us way into the second round and beyond. Some of those didn't materialize. I don't know which ones."

The bid looked to have suffered from a backlash against corruption investigations into FIFA members by BBC's Panorama and the *Sunday Times* over the last two months. Six FIFA officials were suspended last month following a *Sunday Times* investigation, and Panorama claimed three other FIFA members had taken bribes in the 1990s.

The bid also generated confusion as its board constantly changed, and was engulfed in a scandal in May when Lord Triesman was forced to quit after making pie-in-the-sky allegations of collusion between two countries in the competition.

Newcastle's great comeback

AT HALF-TIME Newcastle United were on their knees, battered, bewildered and waiting to be beaten by a rampant Arsenal side that had been running rings round them for 45 minutes. Having lost in the FA Cup to Stevenage and tamely to Fulham the previous week, Newcastle were already on the slide, but with the sale of talismanic striker Andy Carroll the fear was of free-fall.

It was not just that their local hero and best player had been sold, it was that nothing had been done to replace him. Alan Pardew entered the dressing room at half-time 4–0 down with credibility at stake and a crowd turning on him.

What happened next was astonishing. The comeback had its seed in Arsenal folly, with the needless sending-off of Diaby. From that point on Arsenal's afternoon fell apart. Walcott had just gone close to a fifth goal when Dowd awarded the home side a penalty, which Barton converted with ease. Score 1–4, but at best a consolation goal, surely? With 15 minutes to go, the ball dropped kindly in front of Best, and he smashed it past Wojciech Szczesny. It was 2–4 and game on.

With seven minutes left Arsenal conceded a soft penalty, which Barton impishly chipped straight down the middle. With three minutes left and the crowd on their toes, Newcastle conjured up an equalizer: an unstoppable left-foot volley from Cheik Tiote that levelled the scores at 4–4.

At the final whistle St James' Park erupted. At half-time Arsenal had looked like champions, while Newcastle were heading for the Championship. An inspired 45 minutes of football changed all that. It was the biggest ever comeback in the Premier League.

Stoke City storm to FA Cup final

AFTER MORE THAN 127 YEARS of trying, Stoke City finally made it to an FA Cup final thanks largely to a wonderful first-half semi-final display at Wembley together with some woeful defending by their opponents, Bolton Wanderers. They were three up after half an hour through goals from Matthew Etherington, Robert Huth, and Kenwyne Jones, and two more in the second half from Jonathan Walters affirmed their superiority. Not since Chelsea beat Watford 5–1 in 1970 has a team scored five goals in an FA Cup semi-final, and this is the biggest winning margin since 1939, when Wolves beat Grimsby also by 5–0.

In addition to winning a place in the FA Cup final, where Manchester City lie in wait, they have almost certainly qualified for next season's Europa League.

Four minutes after surviving a penalty appeal, Stoke opened the scoring. Bolton defender Paul Robinson's sloppy cross-field pass fell invitingly to Etherington and the Stoke winger responded with a low left-footed drive beyond Jussi Jaaskelainen.

Another six minutes and Stoke had added a second goal, and again it was the failure of the Bolton defence to clear that led to Huth's ninth goal of the season, a first-time right-foot volley into the bottom corner.

A third goal, on the half-hour, put Stoke in total command. Jermaine Pennant, a problem for Martin Petrov for most the afternoon, dispossessed the Bulgarian inside his own half, drove across field and then found Jones with a perfect pass. The tall striker carried the ball forward before finishing superbly.

Having been thwarted in quick succession by a couple of saves from Jaaskelainen, Stoke added a fourth in the 68th minute with the best goal of the day, the outstanding Walters collecting the ball just inside the Bolton half and running through three opponents before dispatching an unstoppable low drive beyond the despairing Jaaskelainen.

And, in the 81st minute, Walters added insult to injury with a fortuitous goal, scoring his second and Stoke's fifth when he controlled Wilkinson's mis-hit effort on the far edge of the six-yard box and his flighted shot got a deflection to beat Jaaskelainen.

United make it 19 League titles

IN WHAT EFFECTIVELY was the showdown for the Premiership title, Arsenal having dropped away, Manchester United slaughtered Chelsea 2–1 at Old Trafford. And if that seems a contradiction in terms, it only goes to emphasize the margin by which United dominated this game from the moment that Javier Hernandez – Chicarito – scored the fastest goal of the season, in 36 seconds. Giggs eased the ball to the outstanding Park, who swept it forward, and a slight feint of the Mexican's shoulders wrong-footed Petr Cech as he stroked the ball into the net.

To stand a realistic chance of retaining their title, Chelsea had to win this one. Otherwise, a point for United at Ewood Park or later against Blackpool at Old Trafford would be enough for United to clinch the title. But they rarely got a chance even to equalize as United continued to press, forcing them to yield possession. The deciding second goal arrived as early as the 23rd minute when Giggs and Park created another magical moment from a corner, and the Welshman tricked his way past Salomon Kalou before lifting the ball across for Vidic to head in.

The Red Devils savour the moment of knocking Liverpool off the perch of most top-flight titles.

Occasionally the champions stirred. Edwin van der Sar saved well from Kalou and then pushed away a Didier Drogba free-kick. Just after the hour, Ancelotti played his last card, the spectacularly off-form £50million striker Fernando Torres. The Spaniard ran hard enough but there was no cohesion in the Blues' attack. Nevertheless, with 20 minutes remaining, Ivanovic headed down a deflected cross for Lampard to neatly turn in. But they never looked like scoring another. Howard Webb blew the final whistle and the United players gathered in a jubilant huddle. One more point, against Blackburn Rovers at Ewood Park or Blackpool at Old Trafford and they would have their historic 19th title to move ahead of Liverpool. Ferguson was ecstatic.

SOCCER SOUNDBITES

"I never thought we'd win 19 titles when I was appointed manager almost 25 years ago."

SIR ALEX FERGUSON,
Manchester United manager

Dons make League return

AFTER 120 MINUTES of goalless endeavour, AFC Wimbledon beat Luton Town 4–3 on penalties in the Blue Square Premier League play-off final to enter the Football League for the first time. The club were only formed as a non-league outfit in the Combined Counties League nine years earlier in protest over the FA's decision to dissolve the original Wimbledon and replace them with MK Dons 80 miles up the M1.

There was little to choose between the sides in a game that was frenetic from start to finish, with both sides hitting the woodwork late in normal time. In extra time the Dons missed several good chances to finish the game off.

AFC Wimbledon Keeper Seb Brown was the shoot-out hero, saving two spot-kicks and leaving top scorer Danny Kedwell to convert the winning penalty and ignite the blue and yellow celebrations. It was a deserved result, for the Dons had finished second in the Blue Square table, six points ahead of the Hatters.

QPR reprieved and promoted

WHAT AN ACHIEVEMENT. In just 13 months, QPR manager Neil Warnock has led the club from being under a serious threat of relegation to promotion to the Premier League as the Championship winners.

Warnock's team enjoyed a little celebration at Loftus Road after the Football Association's announcement – just before kick-off – that it would not be docked points over the Alejandro Faurlin affair. After last weekend's win at Watford clinched the title and a return to the top flight after a 15-year-long absence, it was feared the club might have been hit with a points deduction that would force them to engage in the precarious end-of-season play-offs. However, the club were found guilty of only two of the seven charges concerning the alleged third-party ownership of Faurlin and fined £875,000 instead, a drop in the ocean compared with the £60million said to be the reward for entry into the Premiership, made up of extra revenue and then parachute payments if the club is subsequently relegated.

Once fears of being docked as much as 15 points were allayed, a belated promotion party began and could not be marred by a 2–1 defeat to Leeds United. Rangers took the lead through Iceland striker Heidar Helguson after just 27 seconds, but Max Gradel levelled it for Leeds when he lobbed keeper Radek Cerny, and Ross McCormack was helped by a deflection when scoring the winner in the second half. This is the seventh promotion Warnock has accomplished, with a number of clubs, equalling the record held jointly by Graham Taylor and Dave Bassett.

And Rangers have done it in style, surpassing their rivals with the best football by far in the division. Their shining star has been the Moroccan Adel Taarabt, Football League Player of the Year, a footballer of extraordinary talents who somehow slipped under the Tottenham net. Next season he will be able to display those talents for Rangers in the Premier League – that is if he doesn't get snapped up by one of the big boys. He has without doubt been the onfield inspiration for QPR in their campaign, an attacking, goalscoring midfielder, always looking to do something different. At 21, he has the world at his feet. One flaw, however, is his temperament, which leads to the occasional show of petulance, something that is said to have led Manchester United to cool their interest in him.

Among Rangers' most reliable defenders have been keeper Radek Cerny and central defenders Fitz Hall and Clint Hill. A few teams outscored QPR over the campaign, but look at the goals against column and you will see a different story, only 32 conceded, including 25 clean sheets.

Taarabt led the club goalscorers in the Championship with 19, followed by Heider Helguson (13), Jamie Mackie (9), Tommy Smith (6), and Wayne Routledge (5), so expect a striker or two to be on Warnock's shopping list.

Bale hat-trick in vain

Tottenham's Gareth Bale shines against Inter.

TOTTENHAM'S AMAZING resurgence against European champions Inter Milan was due almost entirely to the efforts of a 21-year-old phenomenon called Gareth Bale. The young Welshman hit a remarkable hat-trick from left-back against one of the most impenetrable defences in the world.

Bale had sprinted nearly 70 yards with the ball at his feet for his first goal. His last two goals were scored in stoppage time. And all this was with 10 men, after goalkeeper Heurelho Gomes's dismissal.

Until then, Spurs were severely outplayed, with Samuel Eto'o – two goals, two assists – the main executioner. It took just 68 seconds to carve Spurs' deplorable defence open and for Javier Zanetti to score. Soon after, Jonathan Biabiany sprinted on to a through ball, but Gomes raced from goal and upended him. A clear penalty – and Gomes had to go. Replacement keeper Carlo Cudicini's first job was to pick the ball out of the net from Eto'o penalty. More disastrous defending, together with more Eto'o brilliance, and Spurs soon found themselves 4–0 down.

Suddenly, Bale revived Spurs with a run down the left flank of the pitch that boasted immense power and unstoppable determination, before he beat Julio Cesar with a low drive. Now in stoppage time, the indomitable Bale set off on another extraordinary run to beat Cesar again with a low left-foot cross-shot, a virtual carbon-copy of his first goal.

Finally, Aaron Lennon set up Bale, who drilled the ball in for a magical hat-trick. What a performance – one that will be remembered for a long, long time. A night of hovering humiliation turned, by one man, into a night of glorious failure.

All change at Anfield as "King Kenny" comes back

THINGS DIDN'T WORK OUT for Roy Hodgson at Anfield, and Liverpool's new owners, US company New England Sports Ventures (NESV) – owners of the Boston Red Sox – appointed former 'Pool player, captain, and player-manager Kenny Dalglish in his place. Dalglish's success – 10 wins, three draws, and just three defeats in his five months since then – has served to make his permanent appointment a formality.

The move comes after former owners Tom Hicks and George Gillett removed the temporary restraining order blocking the £300m sale. Meanwhile, Hicks and Gillett may now take legal action in England to secure damages after dropping a claim lodged in Texas. The claim in the Dallas court was for £1billion in damages, with the American pair claiming the deal was "illegal" and an "extraordinary swindle".

Still, there was an air of relief as NESV's purchase was confirmed, a move that will allow major creditors Royal Bank of Scotland to be paid the £237m it is owed. A club statement revealed: "The transaction values the club at £300m and eliminates all of the acquisition debt placed on LFC by its previous owners, reducing the club's debt-servicing obligations from £25m–£30m a year to £2m–£3m."

Dalglish has made plain his delight at having the chance to return to a post he vacated in 1991, while NESV have been impressed by the stunning reversal in form overseen by the Scot in his four months in charge. Dalglish has been widely acclaimed as the reason behind the club's turnaround in fortune – it has been calculated that Liverpool would be second in the Premier League standings had the season started when the former manager reclaimed the reins.

Dalglish stopped the rot at Anfield with a dose of true Red grit.

Walter Smith retires with 10th SPL title

WALTER SMITH brought down the curtain on his highly successful managerial career in spectacular fashion by overseeing Rangers' 5–1 demolition of Kilmarnock at Rugby Park. In this, his second spell as Rangers boss, he completed a hat-trick of titles while notching up his 10th SPL triumph overall.

Rangers came out of their blocks like greyhounds, and the match was over as a contest almost before it had begun. It took them just seven minutes to race into a three-goal lead, with Kyle Lafferty – a controversial £3.8million signing from Burnley in 2008 – scoring two of them before going on to complete his hat-trick in the second half. Sandwiched in between those was one from Steven Naismith, and Croatian striker Nikica Jelavic scored the other soon after the interval.

The win took the total of victories under Smith's management to a round 400. Rangers' feat in winning the championship and League Cup as well as making the last 16 of the Europa League more than justified Smith's choice of summer pre-season spending – the whole pot of £4million on Jelavic rather than add squad players.

In the event, the gamble on Jelavic, allied to Smith's vast experience and motivational powers, paid handsomely. However, Rangers lost control of the title race when they were beaten at home by Dundee United at the start of April, but they doggedly clung to Celtic's coat-tails until their rivals also stumbled, at Inverness, two weeks ago.

That turned out to be the decisive twist of an always compelling campaign. Rangers, with their noses in front and the tape in sight, were remorseless, sweeping aside Motherwell, Hearts, Dundee United, and now Kilmarnock to keep Celtic at bay.

The win means the veteran boss Smith signs off with 10 championships, and a total of 21 trophies, over his two spells at Ibrox, as he now makes way for Ally McCoist.

SOCCER SOUNDBITES

"I'll have a wee drink just now, I think."

WALTER SMITH,
after the game

Light Blues come out of the wilderness

THIS WAS A DISAPPOINTING Cup final for all but Manchester City fans, whose joy at capturing silverware after 35 years in the wilderness was understandable. Stoke City could not reproduce anything like the form they showed when annihilating Bolton 5–0 in the semi-finals, but Manchester City took 74 minutes to transfer their dominance to that one-goal winner. This was due largely to the brilliance of Tomas Sorensen in the Stoke goal and partly to David Silva's uncharacteristic profligacy in front of goal.

It was the first significant return for the millions poured into City since they were transformed into the world's richest club by the Abu Dhabi United Group in September 2008. Manager Mark Hughes failed to capitalize on this tremendous opportunity, and it was not until he was replaced by ex-Inter boss Roberto Mancini in December of 2009 that City began to look like a side seriously capable of challenging the established Premiership elite.

City captain Carlos Tévez was back after a month out, and Mancini chose to play him with Mario Balotelli – reputedly on £220,000 a week – and Silva on either side, and Yaya Touré free to roam behind. Touré scored the winner with 16 minutes to go. Finding himself 15 yards out with the ball dropping in front of him, he drilled in a left-foot half-volley.

Sorensen's heroics were jeopardized by the inexplicable behaviour of Robert Huth, the German centre-back, who chose to elbow Balotelli in the face as early as the 13th minute, a clear red-card offence that referee Martin Atkinson apparently missed. Five minutes before the interval Huth did get booked for a challenge with both feet off the ground on Micah Richards, but further misdemeanours went unpunished.

Only once did Stoke come close to scoring, when, just after the hour, Kenwyne Jones burst through, but England keeper Joe Hart came out and blocked his effort. City had relatively little trouble seeing out the game.

Carlos Tevez lifts Manchester City's first silverware since 1976.

Going down or staying up

WEST HAM UNITED were the first Premier League club to be relegated in 2011, and the first thing they did was to sack their manager, Avram Grant.

The Hammers' demise left a further five clubs in danger of relegation to the Championship with one round of matches remaining, and as many as five managers fearing the chop as well as the drop. Dropping into the Championship is a disaster for any club largely because of the massive loss of income, especially from television revenues, although there are the so-called "parachute" payments from the Premier League to provide financial assistance for relegated clubs. Two of the clubs would end the day desperately needing it.

The five Premiership clubs on the brink were bottom club Wigan on 39 points (managed by Roberto Martinez), Blackpool (Ian Holloway) and Birmingham (Alex McCleish) on 39, and Wolves (Mick McCarthy) and Blackburn (Steve Kean) on 40. In this situation, factors such as the opposition in the last match and whether home or away might be important, as well as number of points and goal difference.

There was to be no argument about Blackpool's plight – away to already-crowned champions Manchester United, who would be formidable even if they put out a reserve side. Two of the teams were playing each other: Wolves entertaining Blackburn; Birmingham were at Spurs, and Wigan travelled to Stoke. So Wolves were the only side playing at home.

It was a roller-coaster ride for all of them, with fortunes see-sawing this way and that. Blackpool miraculously went 2–1 up at Old Trafford, but United as ever came back to win 4–2 to shoot the Seasiders back down to the Championship. They were followed down by Carling Cup winners Birmingham, beaten 2–1 at White Hart Lane. These two defeats meant Wolves stayed up despite losing, so a relieved manager Mick McCarthy finished with a smile on his face.

Semi-pro women's league launched

WITH THE launch of the Semi-pro Women's Football League, for the first time in this country all the players will be paid for their club endeavours. This is a giant step forward for women's football. Selected from a shortlist of 16 applicants, the league consists of eight teams: Arsenal, Chelsea, Doncaster Rovers Belles, Birmingham City, Liverpool, Everton, Bristol Academy, and Lincoln Ladies.

This competition will replace the traditional winter Women's Premier League. The clubs will play each other twice, home and away, in a season running from April through to October. Each club will have to operate within strict financial guidelines. One of these calls for a wage cap, which stipulates that out of a club's 20-woman squad only four players may be paid more than £20,000 a year.

"Obviously, it's not the millions the men earn," said England manager Hope Powell, speaking at the League's launch at Wembley this week. "But, for the top players, coupled with the central contracts from the England set-up, it means they will be able to earn a living from the game."

Five of the current England Ladies squad play in America, in the Women's Professional Soccer League. Powell hopes that the new league will help arrest the talent drain.

She pointed to the fact that football is the top female participation sport in this country, with 1.3 million registered players. But she stressed the need for young girls to get involved and stay in the game: "If there are good opportunities to play, if the environment is right, conducive and professional, if they see role models on the TV every week, they'll be more likely to."

SOCCER SOUNDBITES

"When I played it was pay-to-play ... Now they are getting paid to play."

HOPE POWELL,
England coach

United no match for Barca

FOOTBALL FOCUS

● Chelsea sacked their 2010 double-winning manager Carlo Ancelotti in a corridor at Goodison Park minutes after the club's 1–0 defeat to Everton on the last day of the season. This was not unexpected because of his failure to maintain a sustained challenge to Manchester United domestically or in Europe.

● Manchester United midfield star Paul Scholes, 36, retired at the end of the season and will join United's coaching staff. He made his debut in the 1994-95 season and chalked up 676 appearances for his one club, scoring 150 goals. He retired from international football in 2004, having scored 14 goals in 66 appearances for England.

● In the Championship play-off final, annually billed as the world's most valuable match to win – with its lucrative entry to the Premier League – Swansea beat Reading 4–2 at Wembley before a crowd of 86,000 spectators. The Swans were cruising at 3–0 up, but the Royals pulled it back to 3–2 and hit a post before Scott Sinclair completed his hat-trick, which included two penalties, to clinch it for Swansea.

● Scott Parker of relegated West Ham was voted FWA Footballer of the Year, ahead of Gareth Bale (Spurs), who won the PFA award. Jack Wilshere (Arsenal) won the Young Player award. Emilio Izaguirre (Celtic) won the Scottish award.

● A 1–0 victory at Stoke on the last day of the season enabled Wigan to stay in the Premier League, a great achievement for manager Roberto Martinez and chairman Dave Whelan, after spending several weeks in the shadow of relegation at the bottom of the table. Martinez showed his loyalty by refusing offers to leave the club.

THE PLAUDITS rained down on Barcelona at Wembley, where they won the European Cup with a slick 3–1 defeat of Premier League champions Manchester United, which was much more convincing than the scoreline suggests. Even when Wayne Rooney equalized Pedro's 27th-minute goal within seven minutes, it encouraged only the most hopeful of optimists among United fans to believe they could upset the odds. Worthy as Sir Alex Ferguson's side were to carry the flag for England, Barcelona's football gave the appearance of coming from another planet.

Ferguson opted to keep faith with the attacking partnership of Rooney and Javier Hernandez – but Michael Owen surprisingly replaced leading scorer Dimitar Berbatov on the substitutes bench. Barca's injured captain Carlos Puyol was on the bench. At left back, incredibly, was Eric Abidal, some 10 weeks after having surgery to remove a malignant liver tumour.

The key factor in Barcelona's victory was their passing. With Lionel Messi, Andres Iniesta, and Xavi running rings round the United midfield and defence, the Spanish champions dominated possession. And Rooney's goal was United's only shot on target, compared with a stunning 13 attempts from Barca.

United made the brighter start, pressing well and not allowing Barca to settle in the opening stages. But it didn't last long. Pedro's opening goal was all about movement, as Xavi put him in with a defence-splitting pass and he hammered a low shot inside Edwin Van der Sar's left-hand post. Their second goal was all about Lionel Messi, who somehow nullifed the presence of the four defenders in front of him by taking a snap shot from 25 yards which swerved low past Van der Sar's dive and inside the same post – Messi's 53rd goal of the season.

Barcelona wrapped it up in the 69th minute with a goal just as special, this time from David Villa with a 22-yard curler.

Pep Guadiola, the man who masterminded Barca's triumph, brought captain Puyol on for the last few minutes, although it was Abidal who was given the honour of hoisting the cup aloft.

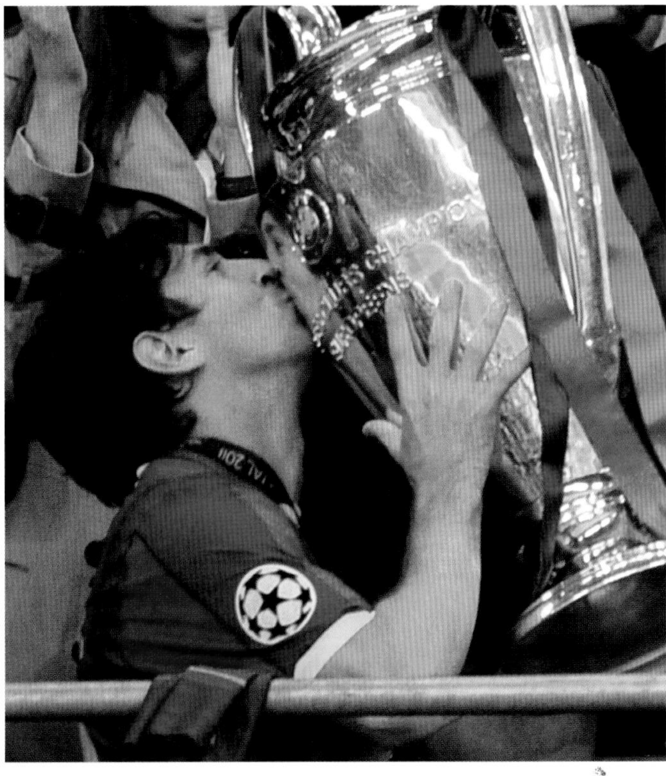

Messi was star of the show in a masterful performance for Barca.

FINAL SCORE

Football League
Premiership – Manchester United
Top scorer – Dimitar Berbatov (Man United), Carlos Tevez (Man City) 20
Championship – Queens Park Rangers
League 1 – Brighton & Hove Albion
League 2 – Chesterfield
Footballer of the Year – Scott Parker (West Ham)

FA Cup final
Manchester City 1 Stoke City 0

League Cup final
Birmingham City 2 Arsenal 1

Scottish League
Premier League – Rangers
Top scorer – Kenny Miller (Rangers) 21
Div 1 – Dunfermline Athletic
Div 2 – Livingston
Div 3 – Arbroath
Footballer of the Year – Emilio Izaguirre (Celtic)

Scottish FA Cup final
Celtic 3 Motherwell 0

Scottish League Cup final
Rangers 2 Celtic 1

European Cup final
Barcelona 3 Manchester United 1

UEFA Cup final
FC Porto 1 SC Braga 0

World Footballer of the Year 2010
Lionel Messi (Barcelona and Argentina)

World Club Championship 2010
Inter Milan 3 TP Mazembe 0

Celtic nations contest new championship

TAKING THE place of the Home International Championship, the Carling Nations Cup was a round robin tournament contested by the British Isles nations minus England – that is, Northern Ireland, the Republic of Ireland, Scotland, and Wales. The first running of this tournament took place in Dublin in February and May of 2011.

Scotland and Ireland emerged from the first round of matches as the two contenders for the crown, leaving Wales and Northern Ireland to fight over the wooden spoon (Wales won 2–0). Ireland and Scotland both won 3–0, against Northern Ireland and Wales, respectively, back in February. Then in May Ireland thrashed their northern neighbours by a record 5–0, Tottenham's Robbie Keane, their captain, scoring two. His second was a from a penalty that saw Adam Thompson red-carded and Keane sportingly remonstrating – in vain – to keep his opponent on the pitch. Meanwhile Scotland came from a goal down to beat Wales 3–1.

With a superior goal difference, Ireland, managed by Giovanni Trapattoni, needed only to draw the decider with Scotland. In the event, they beat them 1–0 with a 23rd-minute goal scored by Keane, his 49th for his country, to be crowned winners, their first silverware for 25 years.

City are champions at last

IN THE MOST exciting climax to a Premier League season, Manchester City scored twice in injury time of their final game to overhaul neighbours United and become champions for the first time in 44 years. The denouement of their match against Queens Park Rangers was all the more breathtaking because City knew only all three points would do because United were heading for victory at Sunderland. As the clock ticked beyond 90 minutes, City trailed 2–1.

Then, as long-suffering City fans made for the exits, Edin Dzeko headed the equaliser. The clock showed 91 minutes 51 seconds. Suddenly there was a glimmer of hope. News filtered through that United had indeed won, so City needed to score again. Furthermore, at Stoke, Bolton had failed to secure the win they required to overtake QPR at the other end of the table. City's opponents were safe and appeared to relax.

Suddenly, Sergio Aguero powered through the middle, exchanged passes with Mario Balotelli, before shooting powerfully past Paddy Kenny. If anyone inside the Etihad Stadium had glanced at the clock they would have noted that 93 minutes 20 seconds had elapsed. Cue pandemonium. Aguero wheeled away, twirling his shirt above his head. According to the City captain, Vincent Kompany, there were tears rolling down the Argentine's face when his team-mates caught up with him.

Roberto Mancini, City's relieved manager, said: "It's been a crazy season and a crazy last minute. Five minutes from the end, I didn't think we'd win the game. But we deserved to win this and deserved to win the title. We were on top for 20 games."

QPR had contributed to the tension. They fought back after Pablo Zabaleta had put City ahead, and led through goals by Djibril Cisse and Jamie Mackie.

However, the fact that the match finished after those at Sunderland and Stoke was largely due to time lost during disgraceful scenes that resulted in QPR being reduced to ten men. Joey Barton claimed Carlos Tevez started the contretemps, and retaliated with an elbow that sent Tevez tumbling. Barton's response to the red card that followed was splenetic: he kicked Aguero in the back of the knee, attempted to butt Kompany and tried to get at Balotelli before being restrained.

Barton was left facing a lengthy suspension for his outburst. City, by contrast, kept their heads and gained their reward.

Sergio Aguero is buried beneath an avalanche of euphoria after his late, late goal seals City's title.

The fall and rise of Carlos Tevez

IN A REMARKABLE stand-off spanning six months between manager and player, Carlos Tevez was cast into the equivalent of football's wilderness after he walked out on Manchester City. The dispute spiralled from a confrontation with manager Roberto Mancini in the dugout during a Champions League defeat at Bayern Munich in September when it was reported Tevez refused to go on as a substitute.

Mancini said the Argentine would never play for City again, but he was unable to offload him during the January transfer window at the club's £28 million valuation. Tevez responded by suggesting he had been treated "like a dog" during the incident in Munich, but later claimed it had been the result of a misunderstanding. During the storm that followed, and while the case was being investigated internally by City, Tevez took an unauthorised flight to Buenos Aires, and spent three months in Argentina before returning to Manchester.

The pair finally kissed and made up in February, once Tevez had apologised and withdrawn an appeal to the Premier League against club fines totalling more than £1.5 million, the sum payable after being found guilty on multiple charges of misconduct. In all, the episode cost the player around £9.3 million in fines and lost earnings.

Tevez returned to first-team action, as a substitute, in a 2–1 win against Chelsea in March; the following month his rehabilitation was complete with a hat-trick in a 6–1 thrashing away at Norwich City on the way to the Premier League title.

SOCCER SOUNDBITES

"You want to say it's the best moment of your life but, if I'm honest, please never again this way."

VINCENT KOMPANY after Manchester City's nerve-jangling, title-deciding victory over Queens Park Rangers

Goals galore

IF GOALS EQUAL entertainment then the Premier League was a veritable theatre of screams as a record 1,066 goals were scored at an average of 2.81 a game.

Predictably, where there were bulging nets the two Manchester clubs weren't far away: City managed 93 in the League to United's 89, and the goal difference with which City prevailed in the title race may have rested significantly on their barely believable 6–1 win at Old Trafford.

There were a number of high-scoring games, and not all of them involved top against bottom. On several memorable occasions teams from the top six seemed to take great delight in battering each other into submission. Indeed, on one memorable day at the end of August, City found their 5–1 away win at Tottenham trumped by United's 8–2 demolition of Arsenal. Two months later Arsenal crossed London and beat Chelsea 5–3.

Abramovich scoops the ultimate prize

Didier Drogba powers home Chelsea's equaliser to force extra time.

CHELSEA FINALLY ACHIEVED the Champions League success demanded by owner Roman Abramovich to justify the millions of pounds lavished in its pursuit over the previous decade.

However, the premier European trophy was secured without the brand of swaggering, sexy football the Russian billionaire had hoped for; on several notable occasions during the campaign Chelsea found themselves with their backs against the wall, but fought their way out with grit and determination.

They had been written off for the first time when they returned from Naples, and the first leg of the knockout round, 3–1 in arrears; they responded by taking the second leg to extra time before beating Napoli 5–4 on aggregate.

In the semi-final they could only eke out a 1–0 advantage to take to Spain against holders Barcelona. Things looked grave when captain John Terry was sent off for an unnecessary foul in the Nou Camp, but the ten men played with such fortitude they held on for a 2–2 draw. It was a portent of what was required in the final against Bayern Munich.

The squad seemed to thrive on adversity and united beneath the flag when former player Roberto di Matteo took over from Andre Villas-Boas, who was sacked less than nine months into the job at the end of March.

Against Munich they had to contend with the match being played in their opponents' backyard, going behind to Thomas Muller's goal eight minutes from time, and finally taking part in a penalty shoot-out at the end housing the Germans' supporters.

Chelsea were comprehensively outplayed on the night and had to withstand a long and considerable German bombardment. Statistically, Chelsea had one corner (from which they scored) to Bayern's 20, and nine shots in 120 minutes to Munich's 34. But cometh the hour, cometh the man. The talismanic Didier Drogba not only headed home Chelsea's equaliser in the 89th minute, he also stepped up to side-foot the winning penalty to complete a 4–3 shoot-out win.

In a moment of dignified sportsmanship, amid the wild celebrations that followed, Drogba sought out vanquished rivals Arjen Robben and Bastian Schweinsteiger. The pair had been superb all night. But Robben missed a penalty during extra time and Schweinsteiger missed the decisive kick in the shoot-out.

SOCCER SOUNDBITES

"I believe a lot in destiny. It was written a long time ago that we would win but we did not know it and we had to believe. This team is amazing. I want to dedicate this to the managers and players we had before."

Chelsea match-winner **DIDIER DROGBA** pays his tributes in Munich

Gary Speed dies

The football world woke in shock and disbelief on Sunday 27 November to learn of the death of Gary Speed, the incumbent Wales manager.

Speed was found hanging at his home in Cheshire, and though suicide was suspected, coroner Nicholas Rheinberg recorded a narrative verdict. He said it was impossible to determine whether the 44-year-old father-of-two had intended to end his life; his death may have been the result of an unfortunate accident. Friends said he had seemed his usual self in the BBC studio after an appearance on *Football Focus* on Saturday lunchtime.

The disbelief came because Speed seemed the most grounded of individuals. Indeed, Howard Wilkinson, his manager when Leeds won the First Division in 1992, spoke for everyone who encountered Speed when he said: "He was ordinary as a bloke, very nice, very genuine, very honest, very hardworking. He was a joy to manage. I think I played Gary in every position apart from goalkeeper, and never did his face change or did he seem annoyed when I told him."

Speed was the first player to reach 500 appearances in the Premier League during a career that took in Leeds, Everton, Newcastle, Bolton and Sheffield United; at the latter he was briefly manager before succeeding John Toshack in the Wales job. Speed played 85 times for his country, and under his stewardship Wales climbed FIFA's world rankings from their lowest position of 117th to 45th. His future, like his past, looked bright.

Chelsea land cup double

THE FA CUP broke with tradition and staged the final with a 5.15 p.m. kick-off rather than the usual three o'clock. Not only that, it was played on the same day as Premier League, League 1 and 2 fixtures, thus denying a significant portion of the football-watching community the opportunity of catching the game live on television.

The official reason given was the need to provide a four-week gap between the end of the domestic season and the start of the European Championship, as well as avoiding a clash with that day's League programme; cynics might suggest that television executives prefer tea-time kick-offs to boost ratings and had been handed the perfect excuse.

Chelsea won the 131st edition of the competition, and in the process of beating Liverpool 2–1 established a number of records. Principal among them was Didier Drogba's achievement in becoming the first player to score in four different FA Cup finals; his 52nd-minute goal was the eighth he had scored at Wembley in eight competitive appearances. Among other records toppled, Ashley Cole collected his seventh winner's medal, and John Terry became the first captain to lift the trophy four times with the same club.

Ramires gave Chelsea the lead, which Drogba's goal doubled. Until then it had been a comfortable early evening for the west Londoners. But after Andy Carroll thumped the ball past Petr Cech midway through the second half, Chelsea found themselves staging the type of rearguard action with which they were becoming familiar.

It looked for a moment as if Liverpool had brought the game level when Cech pushed Carroll's header on to the underside of the crossbar. Carroll wheeled away in celebration before quickly realising that Phil Dowd had not awarded the goal. Subsequent replays indicated that the ball had indeed not crossed the goal-line.

John Terry in racist abuse slur

AFTER MORE than 11 months of wrangling, a resolution was reached in the infamous John Terry-Anton Ferdinand racism case. Terry's offensive three-word, four-syllable retort to Ferdinand had ramifications for the game beyond the boundaries of a routine Premier League fixture between Queens Park Rangers and Chelsea.

The aftermath of the altercation at Loftus Road on 23 October cost the England team a captain, a centre-half and a manager. It enriched the legal profession as the case dragged on, the results of which did little to appease the anti-racism lobby.

The furore revolved around an incident five minutes from the end of the west London derby. Terry and Ferdinand exchanged words after the Chelsea player had been penalised for a foul, and the disagreement continued as they resumed positions for the free-kick.

In the subsequent court case it was said that Ferdinand had goaded Terry about an alleged extra-marital affair; Terry's response, couched in industrial language, included a reference to Ferdinand's colour. Ferdinand was initially unaware of the racist content until shown video footage.

When the Metropolitan police received an anonymous complaint the day after the match they were duty-bound to launch an investigation. The FA became involved when QPR complained to them. During the months that followed, the FA would strip Terry of the England captaincy, which led in turn to the resignation of manager Fabio Capello, who felt the decision should have been his alone. Then, in September 2012, just before the start of his personal hearing at the FA, Terry announced his immediate retirement from international football.

In the meantime, days after returning from England's unsuccessful Euro 2012 campaign, and at the end of a four-day hearing, Terry was cleared at Westminster Magistrates Court of making a racist insult to Ferdinand. Shortly afterwards the FA charged him with using abusive and/or insulting words and/or behaviour towards Ferdinand, as well as having made reference to the player's ethnic origin.

Terry had always maintained he was only repeating in the form of a question whether that was what Ferdinand thought he had said to him. But the FA report stated they considered that defence to be "improbable, implausible and contrived", and they were "satisfied" that his comments were used as an insult. They suspended Terry for four matches and fined him £220,000, but added that they felt he was "not a racist".

In a statement apologising for his comments, Terry said: "Although I am disappointed with the FA judgment, I accept that the language I used, regardless of context, is not acceptable on the football field or indeed in any walk of life."

John Terry makes his point to referee Chris Foy during Chelsea's controversial match against Queens Park Rangers at Loftus Road.

SOCCER SOUNDBITES

"It's wholly acceptable in parts of the Middle East to chop off the hands of thieves, but we wouldn't tolerate it here, and it's the same when it comes to racism."

PFA chairman **CLARKE CARLISLE** explains graphically why the word with which Luis Suarez abused Patrice Evra is unacceptable in Britain

Suarez pays the penalty

LUIS SUAREZ discovered to his cost the size of the cultural differences between Britain and his homeland of Uruguay, after admitting using racist language during an altercation with Manchester United's Patrice Evra at Anfield on 15 October. He was hit with an eight-match suspension and a £40,000 fine.

The Liverpool striker, who said he used the N-word once, claimed it did not necessarily have the same racist connotations back in South America. Evra claimed Suarez used the term at least ten times.

The FA's independent regulatory commission recognised that they were dealing with one of the most inflammatory cases in English football history and spent five days deliberating.

Suarez tweeted immediately: "Today is a very difficult and painful day for me and my family." Lord Ouseley, chairman of the anti-racism group Kick It Out, said: "This charge is not saying Luis Suarez is a racist. It's saying, on this occasion, he used racist language. It doesn't make him a bad guy – he needs to learn what is acceptable." Clarke Carlisle, chairman of the PFA, said: "There are definitely cultural differences for a lot of players coming from South America and from the Continent into England. But even though those differences do exist, we still expect people who come and work here to adhere to the standards and the laws of this land."

Liverpool did not come out of a saga that dragged on for two months particularly well: they maintained football's tribal mentality beyond the boundaries of common sense. They were still bristling with indignation when the two teams met again in February and Suarez refused to shake the Frenchman's hand in the pre-match ritual, a snub that had United manager Sir Alex Ferguson fuming: "He is a disgrace to Liverpool Football Club." Both Suarez and his manager Kenny Dalglish later apologised.

History repeats itself

ENGLAND'S CUSTOMARY elimination from major football tournaments on penalties was replicated again by the Great Britain men's team at the 2012 Olympic Games. After two wins and a draw in their group matches, GB were beaten 5–4 in the quarter-final shoot-out by South Korea after a 1–1 draw.

It was the first Games to which GB had sent a team since 1960. The team largely comprised under-23 players and caught the public's imagination, attracting crowds totalling nearly 300,000 to their four games.

GB women competed for the first time and won all three of their group games before succumbing in the quarter-finals, beaten 2–0 by Canada. Their 1–0 win over Brazil at Wembley was watched by more than 70,000.

Craig Bellamy celebrates scoring GB's opening goal against Senegal.

Capello out, Hodgson in

FABIO CAPELLO'S four-year tenure as England coach ended abruptly and controversially with his resignation over a matter of principle in the long-running John Terry racism saga.

The FA had unilaterally stripped Terry of the national team captaincy a week before because of his impending court appearance on charges of racial abuse, having initially indicated he could keep the armband. The timing of Terry's trial, now scheduled for immediately after the European Championship, had influenced the FA's U-turn. They had expected the case to be concluded during the spring, and FA chairman David Bernstein said: "Going into a major tournament with this overhanging was not the thing that we wanted."

Capello felt the decision undermined his position. He said: "I acted the way I always have in football. I cannot permit interference from the FA in my work. I have always been clear who should manage the team and the dressing room, and who has to take decisions."

The 65-year-old gave his views to Italian broadcaster RAI the previous weekend, and Bernstein admitted: "[His] backing of John Terry clearly wasn't helpful the way it came across. It did give the impression of a conflict."

The matter came to a head when Capello met Bernstein and FA general secretary Alex Horne to discuss his misgivings. When Bernstein saw him again an hour later the Italian had already decided to resign; the FA did not attempt to talk him round.

During his time in office Capello led England through successful qualification campaigns for the 2010 World Cup and Euro 2012. But England's performances in South Africa, where they scraped through the group stage before crashing 4–1 to Germany, did little to justify Capello's £6 million-a-year salary.

It would be another three months, and less than six weeks from England's first game at the Euros, before Roy Hodgson was named as successor. The much-travelled Hodgson had been manager at West Bromwich Albion for the previous 15 months and still had two fixtures in the Premier League to fulfil before he could concentrate on his new role.

The 64-year-old came with a distinguished CV: at club level it included Inter Milan, Blackburn, Grasshoppers, Copenhagen, Fulham and Liverpool; on the international scene he had been in charge of Switzerland, Finland and the United Arab Emirates.

Capello, meanwhile, moved on to become coach of the Russian national team.

Roy Hodgson starts his reign as England manager in defiant pose at his unveiling.

England beat the World and European champions

THE PENULTIMATE GAME of Fabio Capello's 42-game reign as England coach not only produced the most startling result, it also pointed to a more promising future.

England marked Remembrance weekend with an unexpected 1–0 victory in a friendly at Wembley against the reigning world and European champions, Spain. It was not a particularly pretty display, but England stuck firmly to their disciplined defensive orders and smothered everything the Spaniards threw at them. A well-nigh full-strength Spain utterly dominated possession, hit the post through David Villa and wasted several late opportunities for an equaliser.

Frank Lampard, captaining his country for the first time, scored the only goal on 49 minutes, nodding home after Darren Bent had hit a post. "It's a day to remember," said Lampard, "and I'll never forget it. It might be the last time I captain England but I don't really care, not now I have worn that armband once at Wembley."

The performance in midfield of Scott Parker, running himself into the turf, was a metaphor for England on this evening: he may not have the talent of his adversaries, but he compensated with sheer sweat and courage.

England were without Wayne Rooney and Steven Gerrard, with John Terry left on the bench, but their comparatively young team boded well for tasks ahead. Indeed, Capello said: "These players will be really important for the next Euros because they played without fear. They played with personality. I could see that physically and technically they were good enough."

Redknapp cleared of all charges

THE CLOUD THAT hung over Harry Redknapp for five years was finally lifted when a jury unanimously acquitted him on charges relating to tax evasion during his time at Portsmouth. Redknapp and co-defendant Milan Mandaric, now the Sheffield Wednesday chairman, who was also found not guilty, both maintained that the case should never have reached Southwark Crown Court.

Redknapp was accused on two counts of concealing £187,000 of transfer bonuses in a Monaco bank account set up in the name of his dog, Rosie. Mandaric was also charged with cheating the public purse, but the 73-year-old's claim that he was providing a tax-free loan to his then Portsmouth manager was accepted by the court. The case stemmed from a police inquiry into alleged football corruption.

"My family have really pulled through it these last five years that this has been hanging over us," said 64-year-old Redknapp. "I'm just looking forward to getting home to my wife Sandra. It has been a nightmare."

The verdict, after two days of deliberation at the end of a two-week trial, came just hours before Fabio Capello resigned as England coach. Redknapp was immediately installed as favourite to succeed him. But not only did Redknapp not replace the Italian, he was sacked by Tottenham despite leading them to fourth place in the Premier League. "I had four great years at Spurs," he said. "All you can do is leave the club in a better state than you found it. And I did that, for sure."

SOCCER SOUNDBITES

"I always believed in the truth, and always believed in the British justice system."

Former Portsmouth chairman **MILAN MANDARIC** after being found not guilty of tax evasion along with manager Harry Redknapp

Muamba cheats death

WHEN FABRICE MUAMBA collapsed, and remained motionless on the White Hart Lane pitch in front of 35,000 spectators, and millions watching live on television, it was one of the most harrowing scenes witnessed at a football ground. That Muamba survived a massive cardiac arrest, after being clinically dead for 76 minutes, is a modern-day miracle.

Muamba later recalled he was back-pedalling to fulfil his defensive duties when he was gripped by an inexplicably severe headache, and found he couldn't run another step. He felt confused, his head spinning, his vision scrambled: he saw two Scott Parkers ahead of him. And then he went down. He remembers nothing of what happened next.

Technically, by the time his head hit the turf, he was dead. As Bolton and Tottenham's medical teams, augmented by leading heart specialist Dr Andrew Deaner (a spectator sitting close to the White Hart Lane pitch who came out to help), attempted to resuscitate him, his heart did not respond.

Nothing sparked it back into action: adrenalin injections, massage, the vigorous application of a defibrillator, nothing. It was only in the hospital operating theatre fully 76 minutes later that doctors tried their last resort: electrical stimulus. Suddenly, Muamba's heartbeat returned.

Throughout the ordeal, everyone at the FA Cup quarter-final watched in anguish, both sets of fans united in chanting his name in the hope it would pull him through. When the match was abandoned, they trooped out in stunned silence.

During the weeks that followed, his progress was punctuated with regular bulletins. His plight touched the whole football family: Lionel Messi wore a T-shirt before a Barcelona game: "Fabrice!!!! We are behind you".

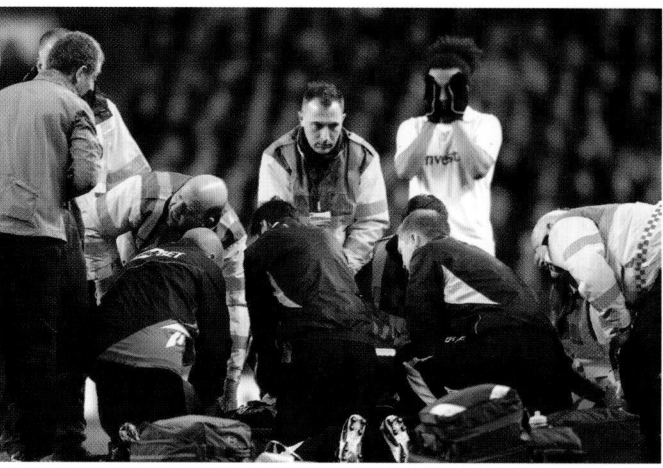

Medical staff fight to save Fabrice Muamba's life at White Hart Lane.

Paradoxically, a Premier League football ground was probably the best place for the Congo-born, former England Under-21 midfielder to collapse. There was an ambulance, a team of doctors and the right equipment on hand. "If it happened to me in my house I don't think I would be here," Muamba said much later.

Muamba was subsequently fitted with a pacemaker that kicks in whenever his heart suffers an irregular beat. However, he is unlikely to play football professionally again.

SOCCER SOUNDBITES

"When it happened, the right people were there for me. They did an unbelievable miracle on me."

FABRICE MUAMBA pays tribute to the medical specialists who brought him back to life

King Kenny captures silverware...but loses his job

SERIAL WINNERS in the past, Liverpool had never set foot on "new" Wembley's hallowed turf, nor won a trophy since 2006. Then, in the space of three months, the returned Messiah, Kenny Dalglish, led them to the north London promised land on three occasions: for the Carling Cup final and the semi-final and final of the FA Cup; importantly, the old trophy-lust was sated in the Carling Cup.

Not that Liverpool had it all their own way in the final against Cardiff. On a rollercoaster afternoon they fought back to lead 2–1 with three minutes of extra time remaining, only for Ben Turner to take the game to penalties. Even in a nervy shoot-out they trailed their Championship opponents until, eventually, Anthony Gerrard, scion of the Merseyside dynasty, missed the decisive kick. In a memorable cameo, Liverpool's captain Steven put aside his own unbounded joy after the unfortunate denouement to run across and console his crestfallen cousin. "I love him, he's family," said Steven in explanation.

Before that, Liverpool had gone behind to Joe Mason's early goal before Martin Skrtel and, in extra time, Dirk Kuyt struck to turn the tables.

Dalglish took Liverpool back to Wembley twice more in the spring, beating Everton in the FA Cup semi-final and then losing to Chelsea in the final. However, in these days when qualifying for the Champions League is paramount, three appearances at Wembley were not enough to keep Dalglish in the manager's chair and he was sacked 11 days after the FA Cup final. Liverpool's energies had been spent on their cup exploits and they only finished eighth in the Premier League, their lowest position for 18 years.

Eighteen months after he was recalled to stabilise Anfield, the 61-year-old Dalglish was dismissed by the club's American owner, John W. Henry. Dalglish admitted: "Of course I'm disappointed with results in the League, but I would not have swapped the Carling Cup win for anything as I know how much it meant to our fans to be back winning trophies."

Liverpool players swamp Pepe Reina after their shoot-out win.

Hearts beat Hibs

THE FINAL ACT in a dreadful season for Hibernian was played out in the Scottish Cup final where they were thrashed 5–1 at Hampden Park by their arch-rivals Hearts.

So bad an afternoon was it that their anguished supporters were already leaving with half an hour still to play. By that stage they were already 4–1 down and had just seen defender Pa Kujabo sent off for a second yellow card.

In losing the first all-Edinburgh final since 1896, Hibs were also finishing as runners-up for the ninth time. For Hearts, by contrast, it was their eighth success in the competition.

Tactically, Hibs knew they had to defend resolutely but conceded a first goal to Darren Barr after 15 minutes and a second to Rudi Skacel before the half-hour mark.

Though James McPeake pulled one back before half-time, the damage was done in the five minutes after the break. Kujabo pulled back Suso Santana and Hibs were reduced the ten men. Danny Grainger converted the penalty and Ryan McGowan added an immediate fourth. Fifteen minutes from time, with the stadium half-empty, Skacel scored his second.

FOOTBALL FOCUS

- Paul Scholes's retirement lasted just seven months before he responded to an injury crisis at Manchester United and donned his boots for an FA Cup tie against Manchester City. The former England international played regularly again in the United midfield and signed a one-year extension to his contract at the end of the season.

- Stiliyan Petrov, Aston Villa's captain, was diagnosed with acute leukaemia after he developed a fever in a match against Arsenal. During his treatment Villa fans marked the 19th minute of games with a round of applause in honour of the popular Bulgarian's shirt number.

- Leyton Orient and Dagenham & Redbridge slogged out what is believed to be the longest penalty shoot-out of consecutive successful kicks in English football and maybe the world. Their Football League Trophy tie was only decided on the 28th spot kick, at 14–13, when Orient's Ben Chorley missed.

- Forty-eight years after Jimmy Hill led Coventry City out of the old Third Division, the club dropped back into the third tier of the English game. During that time, Coventry spent 33 consecutive seasons in the top flight and won the FA Cup for the only time in their history in 1987.

- Kevin Poole, the oldest player still active in the League, aged nearly 49, finally hung up his goalkeeping gloves after a 31-year professional career that began at Aston Villa in 1981. Poole enjoyed League Cup and play-off success at Leicester during the Nineties, and finished his career at Burton Albion where he became goalkeeping coach.

Celtic are champions for the 43rd time

Celtic's success in landing the Scottish Premier League is tinged with relief.

CELTIC WRAPPED UP their first Scottish Premier League title in four years in impressive style by beating Hearts 5–0 at Parkhead in their final match. However, the destination of the trophy with which they were presented that afternoon had been clear ever since the only other contenders, Rangers, had been deducted ten points for going into administration.

In the end, Celtic finished 20 points ahead of their imploding rivals, and a devastating spell of 17 consecutive victories to the end of February, the centrepiece of a 21-game unbeaten run, emphasised their superiority. The overwhelming margin of their 43rd League success was particularly sweet because they had finished runners-up to Rangers in each of the three preceding seasons.

Celtic owed significant gratitude to the goals of Gary Hooper, who was the League's top scorer with 24, which increased to 29 in all competitions. Hooper took his record in two seasons since joining the club from Scunthorpe to a round 50 with all five in the demolition of Hearts on the last day.

The 24-year Essex-born striker completed his season's work with the minimum of effort: three of the quintet required little more than the nudge of his boot to find the net. He completed his hat-trick inside the first 40 minutes after grabbing the ball when Joe Ledley was toppled by Arvydas Novikovas and taking the penalty himself.

Midway through the second half Hooper did break sweat when he latched on to Kris Commons's pass and waltzed round goalkeeper Jamie MacDonald to roll the ball into the unguarded net. His fifth in the dying seconds required only the deftest of touches. It gained Celtic a degree of revenge because it was Hearts who ended their hopes of a double when they beat them in the semi-final of the Scottish Cup.

Rangers go into liquidation

GLASGOW RANGERS, the most successful club in the history of Scottish football, went into liquidation in June 2012 after a painful season of financial disintegration.

The club which had won the League title a record 54 times in their 139-year history, the Scottish Cup on 33 occasions, the League Cup 27 times, and the European Cup-Winners' Cup in 1972, went into administration in February over money owed to the taxman. The subsequent ten-point deduction effectively ended hopes of a fourth successive League success, handing the title to cross-city rivals Celtic.

However, Rangers' failure four months later to reach agreement with unsecured creditors owed a total of £134 million, including HMRC, spelt the end for the famous old club. The business, assets and history were sold to a new company and a phoenix club emerged from the ashes.

Though the new owners applied successfully to become members of the Scottish FA, accepting a one-year transfer embargo in the process, they were not so fortunate in their application to join the Scottish Premier League. Instead they were elected into the Scottish Football League, and they were placed in Division Three for the start of the 2012–13 season after 25 of the 30 member clubs voted in favour of their demotion to the lowest tier.

If there was any consolation amid the financial meltdown, it was that Rangers won the Old Firm derby at Ibrox in March, thereby preventing Celtic the unmitigated joy of winning the title in their enemies' backyard.

FINAL SCORE

Football League
Premier League – Manchester City
Top scorer – Robin Van Persie (Arsenal) 30
Championship – Reading
League 1 – Charlton Athletic
League 2 – Swindon Town
Footballer of the Year – Robin Van Persie

FA Cup final
Chelsea 2 Liverpool 1

League Cup final
Cardiff City 2 Liverpool 2
(aet; Liverpool won 3–2 on pens)

Scottish League
Premier League – Celtic
Top scorer – Gary Hooper (Celtic) 24
Div 1 – Ross County
Div 2 – Cowdenbeath
Div 3 – Alloa Athletic
Footballer of the Year – Charlie Mulgrew (Celtic)

Scottish FA Cup final
Hibernian 1 Hearts 5

Scottish League Cup final
Kilmarnock 1 Celtic 0

European Cup final
Bayern Munich 1 Chelsea 1
(aet; Chelsea won 4–3 on pens)

UEFA Europa League final
Atletico Madrid 3 Athletic Bilbao 0

World Footballer of the Year 2011
Lionel Messi (Barcelona and Argentina)

World Club Championship 2011
Santos 0 Barcelona 4

Spain retain their title

Spain continued to gorge themselves at football's top tables, becoming the first nation to win three major tournaments in a row and the first to successfully defend the European title. They drew comparisons with the great teams of the past – the 1970 Brazilians in particular – yet while their stylish play often delighted, the occasional selections without a recognised striker drew sighs of disapproval. England, under new management, went out again in a quarter-final penalty shoot-out, though few would argue that the superior Italians did not deserve to progress.

Fears about the joint capabilities of Poland and Ukraine to stage the 14th European Championship had been circulating since UEFA awarded the hosting rights in late 2007. Indeed, UEFA expressed repeated concerns themselves about the level of preparation right up until the draw for the tournament in December 2011; they even had a Plan B in place to move the games elsewhere if Ukraine, in particular, did not meet their agreed schedule for building venues and improving infrastructure.

There was plenty of scare-mongering in the media during the lead-up to the tournament, about violence and racism, apparently endemic in both countries and awaiting the chance to raise their ugly heads. There were also concerns about big increases in hotel prices, the difficulty for fans in moving around the vast distances, and whether the rail and air transport systems could cope.

True, some foreign fans were discouraged from travelling, but, as usual, the pre-tournament horror stories proved to be hot air. The 31 games attracted attendances totalling 1.4 million, the highest aggregate in European Championship history, and those returning from the 24-day orgy of football reported that the locals were friendly and accommodating.

On the pitch, Euro 2012 was considered to be one of the best European Championships seen with none of the dead-rubber matches that have blighted recent World Cups. Unhappily, 2012 marked a watershed in its history: it was the last Euro with 16 entrants; from Euro 2016, 24 countries will compete in the finals with a consequent lowering of the overall standard widely anticipated.

Hosts' poor showing

The only tangible downside of awarding the role of hosts to Poland and Ukraine was that neither nation progressed to the knockout stages. That Poland should leave their own party was no real surprise: they were the lowest ranked of the competitors; Ukraine, though, were thought capable of riding the tide of home euphoria beyond the opening exchanges.

Mario Balotelli heads home for Italy against Germany.

Poland finished bottom of a topsy-turvy Group A in which every team lost one game; the Poles, though, were the only side not to win. The finishing order could not have been predicted after the first round of matches. Certainly at half-time in the opening game against Greece, a Robert Lewandowski goal up and the Greeks reduced to ten men when Sokratis Papastathopoulos was shown a harsh second yellow card, Poland's party looked to have started with a bang. But Dimitris Salpingidis equalised early in the second half before Polish keeper Wojciech Szczesny was sent off for bringing down the goalscorer. Incredibly there were only three red cards in the entire tournament and two had come inside the first 70 minutes. However, replacement goalkeeper Przemyslaw Tyton kept out Giorgos Karagounis's penalty with his first touch and the hosts breathed a sigh of relief.

In the other match, Russia suggested they might make a significant impact on the tournament. With Alan Dzagoev scoring twice, the Russians crushed the Czech Republic 4–1. That, though, was as good as it got for Russia; their early exit following a draw with Poland and defeat by Greece was not mourned after their fans misbehaved atrociously inside and outside stadiums.

The Czechs bounced back against the understrength Greeks, scoring twice in the opening six minutes through Petr Jiracek and Vaclav Pilar in a 2–1 win. Jiracek also scored the only goal against Poland in the closing game to turn the Czech Republic from apparent no-hopers to group winners.

Karagounis, meanwhile, had been one of the Greek heroes in their unlikely success at Euro 2004, and eight years on he was the central figure in their equally unexpected 1–0 win over Russia. Karagounis celebrated his record-equalling 120th cap by scoring right on half-time. But he was denied a clear penalty in the second half, and to add insult was booked for diving, thereby rendering him unavailable for the quarter-final.

Ukraine may not have reached the last eight, but unlike their co-hosts they did manage a victory in Group D. They trailed on their opening night to Zlatan Ibrahimovic's 52nd-minute goal for Sweden. But they quickly turned things around and had the game wrapped up within the next ten minutes. Veteran striker Andriy Shevchenko headed home twice to earn the man-of-the-match award, a bearhug from coach Oleg Blokhin and an ovation from a grateful nation.

However, the heavens opened, both metaphorically and meteorologically, in their next game against France. A ferocious thunderstorm in Donetsk forced referee Bjorn Kuipers to take the drenched players off after just four minutes; incredibly the match restarted an hour later and Jeremy Menez and Yohan Cabaye scored in quick succession to grab a 2–0 win for France.

England's campaign

The French had started with a 1–1 draw against England thanks to Samir Nasri's equaliser before half-time. Joleon Lescott's header from a Steven Gerrard free-kick was England's only shot on target during the game, and they had to stage a rearguard action to hang on to their point.

England were similarly fortunate in their remaining group matches. Though they beat Sweden 3–2, it was an error-strewn

Ashley Young smashes England's third kick against the crossbar during the quarter-final penalty shoot-out defeat by Italy.

performance. Gerrard was again the provider for Andy Carroll to put England ahead, but Glen Johnson turned Olof Mellberg's header into his own net before Mellberg put the Swedes in front. The subsequent introduction of Theo Walcott swung the game again as the winger hit the equaliser and then set up Danny Welbeck to score the winner courtesy of a clever flick with his back to goal.

England had Wayne Rooney restored after suspension against Ukraine, and though decidedly rusty the striker headed the only goal. However, Ukraine should have been back in the game when Marko Devych's shot was knocked into the air by Joe Hart; as the ball looped under the crossbar it was hooked clear by John Terry. There was no signal from any of the officials, including goal-line assistant Istvan Vad, though subsequent replays showed the ball to have gone well over the line. The Hungarian team of officials were sent home in disgrace. England survived to top the group after France were surprisingly beaten 2–0 by a Swedish team already eliminated.

The group of death

Group B was labelled "the Group of Death" when it was drawn, and it proved to be the most open with all four countries going into the final games with varying degrees of hope. The biggest surprise was the implosion of Holland, finalists in the World Cup just two summers before. They were beaten in all

SOCCER SOUNDBITES

"There are five referees on the pitch and the ball is 50 centimetres behind the goal-line. Write what you want. You've seen it."

Ukraine manager OLEG BLOKHIN on the "goal" that was not given against England

John Terry hooks away Marko Devych's shot from behind the goal-line.

Striker Andriy Shevchenko places the second of his two goals past Sweden's goalkeeper Andreas Isaksson to give hosts Ukraine their only success.

SOCCER SOUNDBITES

"Spain are like an orchestra. They involve everyone. They very rarely misplace passes."

Manager GIOVANNI TRAPATTONI after the Republic of Ireland were thrashed 4–0 by the world champions

three games as Robin Van Persie, Wesley Sneijder and Arjen Robben failed to rise to the occasion.

The warning signs were there in the first game when they dominated Denmark but still lost to Michael Krohn-Dehli's goal midway through the first half. Van Persie, top scorer in the English Premier League, was finally on the scoresheet in the second round of matches, but his unstoppable shot 17 minutes from time was mere consolation as Mario Gomez had already netted twice in Germany's 2–1 win. Gomez had also scored the only goal in the Germans' 1–0 victory over Portugal.

The Portuguese then raced into a two-goal lead against Denmark through Pepe and Helder Postiga, but were indebted to substitute Silvestre Varela's goal three minutes from time for a 3–2 win. In between the Danes responded with two from Nicklas Bendtner.

So the two quarter-final places were still available ahead of the third games. Germany completed their 100 per cent record by beating Denmark 2–1 despite Krohn-Dehli equalising Lukas Podolski's opener. Lars Bender side-footed home the winner ten minutes from time. In the other game, Rafael Van der Vaart gave the Dutch brief hope against Portugal. Thereafter it was the Cristiano Ronaldo show. Kept quiet in the previous two games, Ronaldo twice hit the post and could have doubled the two goals he did score as Portugal claimed second spot.

Irish despair

In comparison, Group C went more or less as expected. The Irish were beaten by the three other teams, and Spain's late defeat of Croatia ensured that Italy joined them in the quarter-finals.

Spain began the defence of their title with a 1–1 draw against the Italians. Coach Vicente Del Bosque showed his intent by selecting a team without a recognised forward with Cesc Fabregas employed in the "withdrawn striker" role. The decision was vindicated when Fabregas finished off one of Spain's few trademark passing moves for the equaliser. Substitute Antonio Di Natale had given Italy the lead; it was the only time Spain were behind in the tournament, and even then only for four minutes.

The Republic of Ireland's best hopes for advancement rested on claiming something from their opening game against Croatia. But they conceded after three minutes to Mario Mandzukic's header, and though they equalised through Sean St Ledger, they were undone either side of half-time by Nikica Jelavic and Mandzukic's second. Spain reinstated Fernando Torres up front against the Irish and he scored twice, the first coming after just four minutes, in a resounding 4–0 victory.

Italy, notoriously slow starters in major finals, could only draw with the resilient Croatians, their goal coming direct from Andrea Pirlo's outstanding free-kick, later equalised by Mandzukic. The Irish put up more fight against Italy and were not beaten until the last minute when Mario Balotelli added to Antonio Cassano's 35th-minute goal to complete a 2–0 win. The Republic had Keith Andrews sent off for a second yellow card, this one for dissent. Spain, meanwhile, gave a less-than-convincing display in pushing Croatia out of the competition with an 88th-minute winner from Jesus Navas.

Knockout phase

The Czechs' improvement in the 13 days since they were downtrodden by the Russians came to an end in the quarter-finals at the hands of Portugal, or more precisely the feet of Ronaldo. The Czechs packed their defence, and despite Ronaldo hitting the crossbar twice, once from a long-distance free-kick, it looked as though they might hang on. But

Referee Bjorn Kuipers suspends Ukraine's watery game against France.

with 11 minutes left Ronaldo stooped at the far post to head in Joao Moutinho's cross.

Germany had reached the last eight with three group victories, but that did not deter coach Joachim Low from breaking the age-old convention concerning changing a winning side. In an attempt to freshen up his team, Low replaced his entire forward line, including dropping Gomez to the bench despite three tournament goals already. He was rewarded with a 4–2 defeat of Greece. Even so, it took Germany 39 minutes to break through, Philipp Lahm powering home. Though Giorgos Samaras equalised, the Greeks were overwhelmed during a 13-minute blitz in which Sami Khedira, Miroslav Klose and Marco Reus all scored to take Germany to their fourth successive semi-final. Salpingidis converted a last-minute penalty for Greece.

France set out to try and contain Spain. But their plans were disrupted when Xabi Alonso headed home after just 19 minutes. The goal forced France out of their defensive shell and they had Spain on the back foot until Alonso added the second from the penalty spot in time added on.

England were emphatically outplayed by Italy in the fourth quarter-final, yet held on for 120 goalless minutes. When Riccardo Montolivo hit the crossbar with Italy's second kick in the penalty shootout, and Rooney converted his, England finally had their noses in front. But Pirlo, so imperious during the game, changed the dynamics of the contest when he chipped his kick down the middle, in the style of Antonin Panenka's famous penalty in the Euro 1976 final. The pressure proved too much for the two Ashleys, Young and Cole, who both missed, as Italy deservedly swept through 4–2.

The last four

Spain's semi-final against Portugal was also goalless after 120 minutes of cat-and-mouse with few chances. The Portuguese harried and chased Spain out of their usual elegant style, reducing them to uncharacteristic long balls. Strangely, Portugal held back Ronaldo to take their fifth penalty, but the shootout did not go that far. Instead, Fabregas sealed it with the ninth kick to take Spain through 4–2.

Germany had never beaten Italy in a competitive international, and that record extended to eight games. Balotelli, Italy's mercurial striker, scored both goals in a 2–1 victory, the first a towering header, the second a thumping shot as he unlocked Germany's offside trap. Low had reverted to his original strike force after the changes of the quarter-final, but the Germans were outplayed. Mesut Ozil's 92nd-minute penalty was far too late.

Spanish showpiece

Spain may have been decried at times during the tournament for a reluctance to turn their abundant possession into tangible reward; in the final they married their pretty passing with a ruthlessness that utterly demolished Italy.

Spain had already signalled their intentions before David Silva headed home Fabregas's centre after 14 minutes. Defender Jordi Alba scored the second four minutes before half-time, set up by man-of-the-match Xavi's perfectly-weighted ball. Any hope the Italians may have had of a second-half revival evaporated when their third substitute, Thiago Motta, collapsed with an injury just three minutes after coming on, and they had to play the last half-an-hour reduced to ten men. However, it was not until Torres was introduced late on that Spain really went for the jugular. Torres scored the third, again set up by the outstanding Xavi, and then laid the ball back for fellow substitute Juan Mata to roll in the fourth.

SOCCER SOUNDBITES

"I'm not strong, nor fast, nor skilful. I'm a player from the street. Without my team-mates, without space, I am nothing."

Midfielder XAVI, man of the match in the Euro 2012 final, plays down his individual importance to the team

Goalkeeper Iker Casillas raises the spoils of Spain's latest triumph.

FINAL SCORE

FIRST ROUND

Group A

Poland	1	Greece	1
Russia	4	Czech Republic	1
Greece	1	Czech Republic	2
Poland	1	Russia	1
Greece	1	Russia	0
Poland	0	Czech Republic	1

	P	W	D	L	F	A	P
Czech Republic	3	2	0	1	4	5	6
Greece	3	1	1	1	3	3	4
Russia	3	1	1	1	5	3	4
Poland	3	0	2	1	2	3	2

Group B

Holland	0	Denmark	1
Germany	1	Portugal	0
Holland	1	Germany	2
Denmark	2	Portugal	3
Portugal	2	Holland	1
Denmark	1	Germany	2

	P	W	D	L	F	A	P
Germany	3	3	0	0	5	2	9
Portugal	3	2	0	2	5	4	6
Denmark	3	1	0	2	4	5	3
Holland	3	0	0	3	2	5	0

Group C

Spain	1	Italy	1
Rep of Ireland	1	Croatia	3
Italy	1	Croatia	1
Spain	4	Rep of Ireland	0
Croatia	0	Spain	1
Italy	2	Rep of Ireland	0

	P	W	D	L	F	A	P
Spain	3	2	1	0	6	1	7
Italy	3	1	2	0	4	2	5
Croatia	3	1	1	1	4	3	4
Rep of Ireland	3	0	0	3	1	9	0

Group D

France	1	England	1
Ukraine	2	Sweden	1
Ukraine	0	France	2
Sweden	2	England	3
Sweden	2	France	0
England	1	Ukraine	0

	P	W	D	L	F	A	P
England	3	2	1	0	5	3	7
France	3	1	1	1	3	3	4
Ukraine	3	1	0	2	2	4	3
Sweden	3	1	0	2	5	5	3

QUARTER-FINALS

Czech Republic	0	Portugal	1
Germany	4	Greece	2
Spain	2	France	0
England	0	Italy	0

(aet; Italy won 4–2 on pens)

SEMI-FINALS

Portugal	0	Spain	0
(aet; Spain won 4–2 on pens)			
Germany	1	Italy	2

FINAL

Spain	4	Italy	0

Olympic Stadium, Kiev; 1 July 2012
Attendance: 63,170

Spain: Casillas, Arbeloa, Pique, Ramos, Alba, Busquets, Xavi, Alonso, Silva (Pedro 59), Fabregas (Torres 75), Iniesta (Mata 87).

Italy: Buffon, Abate, Barzagli, Bonucci, Chiellini (Balzaretti 21), Pirlo, Marchisio, Montolivo (Motta 57), De Rossi, Balotelli, Cassano (Di Natale h-t).

Leading scorers
3 Mario Balotelli (Italy), Alan Dzagoev (Russia), Mario Gomez (Germany), Mario Mandzukic (Croatia), Cristiano Ronaldo (Portugal), Fernando Torres (Spain).

Ferguson retires on a high

THE MOST SUCCESSFUL MANAGER in English football history announced his retirement two weeks after the club he painstakingly built in his image won the Premier League for the thirteenth time under his command. Sir Alex Ferguson stepped down from Manchester United to smell the roses after more than 26 years at the helm.

His record of achievement is unlikely to be beaten; if it is, whoever does so will, in the words of Fred Trueman in another sport, "be bloody tired". Aside from dominating the first 21 years of the Premier League's existence, Ferguson oversaw five FA Cup triumphs and four League Cups; in Europe, he won the Champions League twice – once, in 1999, as part of a League, FA Cup and European Treble – and the Cup-Winners' Cup, his first silverware, in 1991. There were sundry others, too numerous to list, but which kept the Old Trafford trophy-polisher in continuous employment.

His final success – winning the domestic league with four games to go – summed up his *modus operandi*. Within minutes of the disappointment of losing the title to neighbours Manchester City the previous season, the now 71-year-old Scot's mind was already focused on regaining it.

Striker Danny Welbeck recalled: "We were travelling home from Sunderland on the coach and the manager went round all the young players and said to them, 'Never forget this, because this will win you titles. This will make some of you into men and be the best you can be'. When the manager says things like that to you, you really want to take note of it."

The summer signing from Arsenal of Robin van Persie, the League's top scorer in 2011–12, underlined his intent. It was therefore somehow appropriate that Van Persie should score the first-half hat-trick against Aston Villa that sealed the championship. The Dutchman was the latest marquee recruit in a catalogue of great players to grace Old Trafford under Ferguson: from Paul Ince and Roy Keane to Eric Cantona and Wayne Rooney, not forgetting Paul Scholes, Ryan Giggs and David Beckham who came through the club's youth system.

A man who mixed the charming with the charmless, who invented the so-called 'hair-dryer treatment', and who was grudgingly respected worldwide, Ferguson was always on a one-eyed mission to keep United at the very top. There can be little doubt that he succeeded. His anointed successor, David Moyes, the Everton manager, had some footsteps to follow.

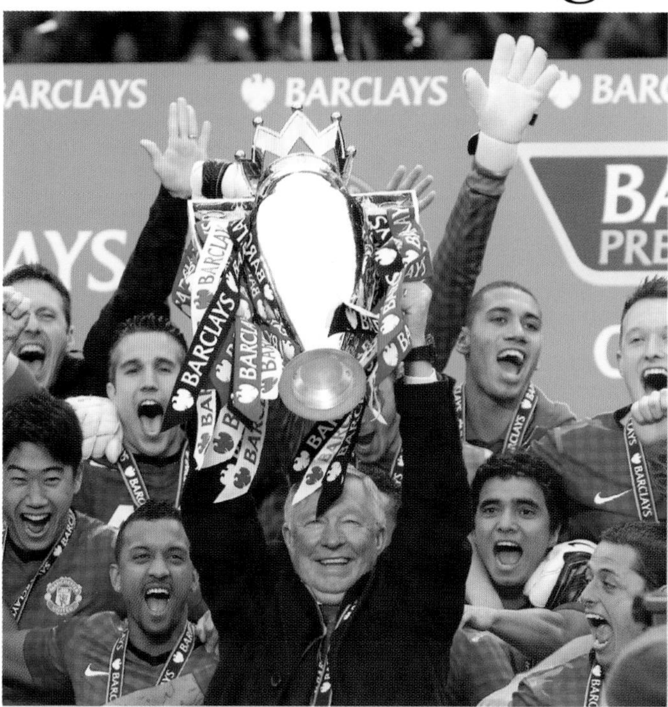

Sir Alex Ferguson marks the end of his incredibly successful 27 years at Manchester United by regaining the Premier League trophy.

SOCCER SOUNDBITES

"It was important for me to leave an organisation in the strongest possible shape and I believe I have done so."

Retiring Manchester United manager **SIR ALEX FERGUSON** writes his own epitaph

Hillsborough verdicts overturned

THE UNSTINTING DETERMINATION of the Hillsborough Families Support Group finally paid off after more than 23 years' campaigning to bring justice for the 96 supporters who died in 1989. In December 2012, the High Court quashed the original inquest verdicts of accidental death and Home Secretary Theresa May announced a criminal investigation in the light of fresh evidence.

Overturning the inquest verdicts had been a priority for the families since the publication in September of the Hillsborough Independent Panel report. This had provided evidence to suggest that the cut-off time of 3.15 p.m., by which the original inquest said all 96 were dead, was seriously flawed. Dr Bill Kirkup, the medical expert on the Hillsborough panel, found that 41 of those who died could have survived past that time.

Lord Chief Justice Lord Judge said that evidence alone was enough to quash the original verdicts. He also cited evidence of "deliberate misinformation surrounding the disaster", including proof that 116 police statements provided in the aftermath had been amended to improve the police position.

"The Lord Chief Justice used the word 'vindication'," said Trevor Hicks, whose two daughters died at the FA Cup semi-final in April 1989. "This is a giant leap for the families. It's clear now justice is on its way."

Jon Stoddart, the former chief constable of Durham, was appointed by the Home Secretary to head a criminal investigation, which would run alongside an existing investigation by the Independent Police Complaints Commission.

Stoddart would look into the alleged cover-up that followed the disaster. The fatal events at Sheffield Wednesday had started when police opened an exit gate on the Leppings Lane terrace to relieve congestion outside the ground, allowing fans to flood into an already overcrowded pen. However, senior police officers had subsequently claimed drunken fans forced the gate open, and allegations of theft and sexual assault were spread by police spokesmen to the media and investigating authorities.

Stoddart said: "My role is to ensure that we determine exactly what happened in the lead-up to and on the day of the disaster and establish where any culpability lies."

Pan-European Euro 2020

THE FINALS of the 2020 European Championship will be played across the Continent with 13 cities staging the matches instead of one or two host countries. UEFA said there would be no more than one venue per country, but that the semi-finals and final would be held in the same stadium. The venues would be announced in September 2013.

Michel Platini, UEFA president and architect of the pan-European plan, said the move would allow smaller countries a slice of the action because a 24-team tournament would be financially and logistically impossible for them to stage.

Platini claimed to have talked round sceptical supporters'groups, who he said would benefit from the change. "Poland and Ukraine was a great Euro," he said, "but it was very expensive, almost as expensive as the Olympic Games." He admitted: "It is perhaps a bit of a zany idea, but it is a good idea."

Little Wigan stun City to win Cup

Roberto Martinez and Dave Whelan share Wigan's first silverware.

THE FA CUP'S FAIRYTALES have usually been told before the world's oldest knockout tournament reaches Wembley; for once a notable giant-slaying was reserved for the final itself. Little Wigan, from the foothills of the Premier League, pulled off one of the biggest surprises in recent history by beating Abu Dhabi-rich Manchester City, Premier League champions less than a year before.

It was somehow fitting that the only goal should fall to Ben Watson, the Wigan substitute who had just returned to action after suffering a broken leg.

The significance would not have been lost on anyone with a historical perspective, because Wigan's owner Dave Whelan had broken his leg playing in the 1960 Cup final for Blackburn Rovers. The FA gave Whelan special dispensation to lead out his side, and he ended the day drenched in champagne, courtesy of a mischievous employee. It did nothing to dampen his enthusiasm.

Whelan eschewed City's chequebook-waving antics. His shrewd accounting ensured that Wigan had shown a profit the previous season for the first time in six years: a £4.3 million surplus on a turnover of £52.6 million. Someone worked out that the average cost of a City player was £16.4 million, while Wigan's entire team was assembled for £12.8 million. A gulf in class was not evident on the pitch where Wigan dismissed bookmakers' odds of 9–1 against their success.

If the carrot-topped Watson, rising at the near post to catapult home Shaun Maloney's 91st-minute corner, stole the headlines, the undoubted star of the show was the young winger Callum McManaman, cousin of Steve. The latest wizard of Wembley had City panicking every time he received the ball. He drew two reckless, yellow-card challenges from Pablo Zabaleta, who became only the third player to be sent off in an FA Cup final, the first at the new Wembley.

The victory was a triumph for manager Roberto Martinez, the Spaniard who had first joined Wigan as a player in the club's Third Division days of the mid-1990s. He stuck with his philosophy of football *sin miedo* (without fear) at Wembley and it paid off handsomely.

However, just three days after winning their first trophy, Wigan entered the history books as the first FA Cup winners to be relegated in the same season, ending their eight-year Premier League stay. And, a few days after the season, Martinez resigned.

SOCCER SOUNDBITES

"To be able to win the FA Cup against a powerhouse of European football, in the manner that we've done, is an incredible chapter of this competition."

Wigan manager **ROBERTO MARTINEZ** tries to put the victory over Manchester City in its historical context

Luton invoke the glory days

LUTON TOWN, giants before being brought to their knees in recent years by administration and points deductions, became slayers of former equals during a rollicking FA Cup run. In beating Norwich City, the team from the Blue Square Premier became the first non-League club since Sutton United in 1989 to knock out opposition from the top-flight. What was more, they performed their giant-killing in Norwich's backyard.

Less than a decade earlier, Luton had been hovering around the Championship play-off places, but in the intervening period had suffered three successive relegations and a 30-point deduction for irregular payments to agents. At last the Bedfordshire club, stuck in the wilderness outside the Football League for a fourth season, were making headlines for positive reasons.

Luton had already beaten Championship side Wolves 1–0 in the third round thanks to Alex Lawless's goal at Kenilworth Road. In the next round, Stuart Fleetwood and JJ O'Donnell combined to set up fellow substitute Scott Rendell for the 80th-minute winner at Carrow Road.

Rendell, the epitome of a journeyman striker, claimed not to have seen his goal. He recounted: "There was a roar and I turned to see the ball nestling in the net behind the goalkeeper. It was incredible."

As in all the best Cup stories, there were any number of archetypal romantic subplots. The best belonged to 35-year-old goalkeeper Mark Tyler, whose heroics kept out Norwich: it transpired he had been released, aged 14, by none other than the team he had just helped eliminate. "I used to perch in the stands here on a crate because I was so little," he recalled. "To come back to the place where it all started is magnificent." However, the fairytale did not last much longer: Luton were flattened 3–0 at home in the fifth round by Millwall.

Millwall shame

HOOLIGANISM REARED ITS HEAD during the FA Cup semi-final between Millwall and Wigan at Wembley. The trouble was confined to the end reserved for Millwall supporters, where a group of around 20 fought among themselves and then with police officers who tried to intervene.

Images of bloodied men and crying children were broadcast to a television audience of millions around the world in the first serious outbreak of violence inside a ground since all-seat stadiums were introduced more than 20 years ago.

Alex Horne, the FA's general secretary, said they "deplored" the scenes, which were "unacceptable". Danny Shittu, the Millwall captain, said: "It's a small minority but things like that should not be happening. It should have been a great day for both sides." Roberto Martinez, manager of Wigan, whose 2–0 win was overshadowed, added: "It's a shame. A minority leave a nasty taste for the majority."

Millwall had worked tirelessly to rid the club of a malevolent reputation stretching back more than a century. A spokesman said: "We are devastated by the scenes we saw, which are in danger of undoing much of the good work we have done to try and change the perception of the club."

Police move in to try and break up fighting in the Millwall section at Wembley during the FA Cup semi-final against Wigan.

Clattenburg cleared in Chelsea race row

LEADING PREMIER LEAGUE REFEREE Mark Clattenburg was accused by Chelsea of using racist language towards one of their players during an explosive League match against Manchester United at Stamford Bridge. Following lengthy FA and police investigations, and after being relieved of his refereeing duties for four weeks, Clattenburg was cleared of the allegations. Chelsea midfielder John Obi Mikel, however, was punished for his post-match altercation with the official.

Clattenburg had sent off two Chelsea players, including Fernando Torres for diving, and allowed United's winning goal to stand despite strong evidence that scorer Javier Hernandez was offside. Towards the end of an acrimonious afternoon other Chelsea players alleged that they heard Clattenburg say to Mikel while showing him a yellow card for dissent: "Shut up, you monkey." The Nigerian did not hear the exchange himself, but was sufficiently incensed when told that he later confronted Clattenburg in the referee's dressing room.

Chelsea made a formal complaint to the FA soon after the game, though the FA cleared Clattenburg of any wrongdoing a month later. A police investigation, launched after the incident was reported by a representative of the Society of Black Lawyers, was dropped on the grounds that "no victim had come forward" and there was "no evidence any offence had been committed".

Mikel was found guilty of misconduct by an independent FA regulating commission, and suspended for three games, and fined £60,000. However, the FA revealed the sanction would have been "significantly longer" had the player not genuinely thought he had been racially abused by Clattenburg.

The punishment was described as lenient by Prospect, the referees' trade union, and their national secretary Alan Leighton said: "For entering the referee's dressing room and threatening and intimidating the referee to the extent that he feared for his safety, the penalty was no longer than had the player been sent off for serious foul play."

An exonerated Clattenburg said: "To know you were innocent of something but that there was the opportunity for it to wreck your career was truly frightening. I hope no referee has to go through this in the future."

Referee Mark Clattenburg brushes aside John Obi Mikel's protests during Chelsea's controversial League clash with Manchester United.

Suarez takes a bite

LUIS SUAREZ, THE LIVERPOOL STRIKER who is no stranger to controversy, was suspended for ten matches for biting Chelsea defender Branislav Ivanovic during a League game at Anfield in April. Television cameras showed Suarez take a bite of the Serbian's arm, even though referee Kevin Friend did not see the incident.

Suarez, who had scored his 30th goal of the season in the 2–2 draw, apologised to Ivanovic post-match for his "inexcusable" behaviour, but still thought seriously about appealing the ban before accepting he would miss the last four domestic fixtures of the season, and the first six of the next.

An Independent Regulatory Commission upheld the FA's claim that the standard three-game suspension for violent conduct was insufficient, and added a further seven. It was, after all, not an isolated case: Suarez, then with Ajax, was banned for seven matches in 2010 after admitting biting the PSV Eindhoven midfielder Otman Bakkal. He was dubbed 'the cannibal' by the Dutch media and quickly sold to Liverpool.

There were calls from inside and outside the game for Liverpool to rid themselves of a player who continued to sully their image. The 26-year-old Uruguayan had been among the front-runners for both the PFA and football writers' annual awards, but lost support in the aftermath of the incident. Manager Brendan Rodgers initially appeared to be washing his hands of the wayward player, but later said that when Suarez was available again, "we will have the opportunity to welcome a better person and player".

Branislav Ivanovic tries to fend off the attentions of Luis Suarez.

Hazard tackles ball-boy... and loses

EDEN HAZARD, Chelsea's Belgian forward, was sent off in the closing stages of the League Cup semi-final against Swansea City for kicking a ball-boy. Hazard was trying to retrieve the ball from 17-year-old Charlie Morgan, who refused to hand it back when the ball went out for a goal-kick; Morgan fell to the ground and Hazard attempted to free the ball from beneath him with his foot. The boy reacted as if he had been caught in the ribs.

Chelsea were trailing 2–0 on aggregate with time running out at the Liberty Stadium. Hazard, 22, was shown a straight red card by referee Chris Foy, but the FA decided not to increase the statutory three-match suspension for violent conduct, deeming it sufficient punishment. Both Hazard and Chelsea apologised straight after the match to Morgan, who said he would not be pressing charges.

It later transpired the ball-boy was the son of Swansea multi-millionaire director Martin Morgan, and had claimed on his Twitter page before the game that he had been drafted in to time-waste should the need arise.

Reaction to the incident was mixed. Harry Redknapp, the Queens Park Rangers manager, called Morgan's actions "disgusting", and added: "You can imagine the frustration – you're a player trying to reach a cup final, but there's this kid behaving like an idiot who won't give the ball back. I can think of a lot of players who would have kicked a bit harder than Hazard did. He just toe-poked the ball away." Liverpool's former Swansea manager, Brendan Rodgers, said he knew Morgan well. "There was maybe a wee bit of gamesmanship by Charlie but certainly nothing sinister," he said.

In the aftermath, the FA reminded clubs that ball-boys and other personnel at pitch-side should act in the appropriate manner at all times.

SOCCER SOUNDBITES

"The king of all ball boys is back making his final appearance #needed #for #timewasting."

Swansea ball-boy **CHARLIE MORGAN**'S tweet before the League Cup semi-final against Chelsea

Swansea take League Cup glory

Swansea City celebrate the end of their 100-year wait to win a trophy by landing the League Cup at Wembley.

IN BEATING BRADFORD CITY 5–0 to win their first trophy, and in the club's centenary season, Swansea City became the first side to take the League Cup outside England. Their Wembley success would have been unthinkable a decade earlier when the Welsh club recorded a last-day victory against Hull to avoid dropping into the Football Conference.

Vanquished Bradford, members of the Premier League as recently as 2001, had plummeted in the opposite direction, passing upwardly-mobile Swansea on the way. But in a momentous giant-killing run they had become the first team from the fourth tier to reach a major final for more than half a century. Their fans sang throughout the demolition job on the pitch, and unfurled a huge commemorative flag to remember the 56 fans who died in the 1985 fire at Valley Parade.

Bradford, though, were dissected with a ruthless precision, and it was not until three minutes from time that they mustered a shot, otherwise Swansea goalkeeper Gerhard Tremmel would have been utterly redundant.

The League One side held out for sixteen minutes before Nathan Dyer slid home Swansea's first. Dyer curled home his second, two minutes into the second half, by which time the Spaniard Michu had put the game beyond reach with his nineteenth goal of a season nowhere near finished.

On the hour Bradford lost goalkeeper Matt Duke, hero of a series of penalty shootouts en route to Wembley, sent off for bringing down Jonathan de Guzman. There followed an unseemly squabble between Swansea players over who should take the kick – Dyer insisted, rather petulantly, that he be allowed to complete his hat-trick – but de Guzman prevailed and duly beat Duke's replacement, Jon McLaughlan. De Guzman added Swansea's last-minute fifth to round off the largest winning margin in a League Cup final.

Swansea manager Michael Laudrup insisted the victory still paled in comparison to the club's escape in 2003 and promotion to the Premier League in 2011. "Maybe those two moments were more important," he said, "but I think the first major trophy ranks very highly in the history of a club."

SOCCER SOUNDBITES

"It's one thing to win a cup with Barcelona, Madrid or Juventus. But to win it with a smaller team like Swansea is absolutely fantastic."

Swansea manager **MICHAEL LAUDRUP** quantifies success in the League Cup

Bradford's giantkillers

BRADFORD CITY COLLECTED a hat-trick of Premier League scalps on the way to becoming the first club from the fourth tier to reach a major cup final since Rochdale back in 1962. Wigan and Arsenal were knocked out in penalty shootouts during Bradford's remarkable League Cup campaign, but Aston Villa were humiliated 4–3 over the course of two legs in the semi-final.

Bradford had beaten the side 62 places above them in football's pyramid, 3–1 in the first leg at Valley Parade with goals from Nahki Wells, Rory McArdle and Carl McHugh. But few outside Yorkshire seriously thought that they would hold on to that advantage at Villa Park, especially since Villa returned home with the benefit of an away goal by Andreas Weimann. Indeed, when Christian Benteke reduced Bradford's cushion in the first half of the second game, it looked as though the long run that started in mid-August at Notts County would come to an end.

However, James Hanson's equaliser soon after the break not only unravelled Villa's brittle belief, it spurred on the League One team to new heights of persistence and obduracy. Weimann's 89th-minute goal merely flattered Villa in the final analysis.

Phil Parkinson, the Bradford manager, said: "Over the last ten years there hasn't been a great deal to cheer about being a Bradford City supporter. I'm so pleased we've given them a reason to go into work and be able to hold their heads up high and be proud of the club."

Managerial slaughter

IN A SAVAGE CULLING SEASON for the managerial profession, more than half of the 92 League clubs changed their coach. Among the most high-profile departures, Roberto di Matteo was sacked just six months after leading Chelsea to the FA Cup and Champions League 'double', while Roberto Mancini was dismissed a year to the day after Manchester City won the Premier League.

In total, 47 clubs finished the season with a different manager to the one who started in August; some clubs chopped and changed to an alarming degree, notably Blackburn and Nottingham Forest, who had nine managers between them.

The majority of the 57 who had left their posts by the end of the League season, were sacked; many were the victims of unreasonable expectations in the board rooms, though there was a small proportion of resignations by managers head-hunted to fill the new vacancies.

Richard Bevan, chief executive of the League Managers' Association, described the statistics as "embarrassing". He said, "I'm not sure where the arrogance of football comes from that we don't have to behave as any other industry. It's embarrassing for the game that all of those sackings are unfair dismissals. The volatility is undermining the profession. We need to work as a group – the Premier League, the Football League, the PFA, the LMA – to ensure that we have better training not only for managers, but also an understanding of how you run a football club."

British clubs fail in Champions League

BRITAIN'S ONLY REPRESENTATION in the Champions League beyond the first knockout round was to host the final at Wembley Stadium for the seventh time. The Premier League had supplied contestants in seven of the previous eight finals, with three clubs (Liverpool, Manchester United and Chelsea) winning the trophy during that period; this time, for the first year since 1996, not one English or Scottish side reached the quarter-final stage.

Arsene Wenger, manager of Arsenal, said: "It's a massive disappointment for English football because for many years we are not used to that. It's a massive wake-up call for us. That means the rest of European football has caught up with us and we have to take that into consideration about the future."

Arsenal at least made a fight of it. After losing the first leg of their round-of-16 tie 3–1 at the Emirates against Bayern Munich, they managed to level the aggregate score in Germany before going out on the away-goals rule.

Manchester United departed at the same stage, despite drawing in Madrid against Real. However, they lost the home leg 2–1 when Nani's contentious dismissal proved to be the turning point. Celtic, who had finished runners-up in their group ahead of Benfica, found Juventus too powerful, bowing out 5–0 on aggregate.

Chelsea, the European champions, and Manchester City, the Premier League champions, failed to qualify from their groups. Chelsea finished third behind Juventus and Shakhtar Donetsk and were parachuted into the Europa League. David Luiz, Chelsea's Brazilian defender, admitted: "There was embarrassment in the dressing room. We won the Champions League last season and to get knocked now is a great disappointment. This is a big club and big clubs deserve to play in big games; the best games in the world are in the Champions League."

City did not even have the consolation of dropping into the Europa League. They were unable to win any of their six group fixtures, drawing all their home ties against Borussia Dortmund, Real Madrid and Ajax, and losing the away legs. Roberto Mancini, the City manager, said: "I think that the season is long – you have Champions League, FA Cup, Premier League – but there are a lot of teams better than us in the Champions League. Everything can change if you can play in the Champions League in February [in the knockout rounds], but we can't do anything now."

Nani's red card earns him some consolation from Jose Mourinho.

Consolation prize for Chelsea

CHELSEA BECAME THE FIRST English club to complete the grand slam of European trophies when they beat Benfica 2–1 to add the Europa League (formerly the Fairs and UEFA Cup) to the Champions League and Cup-Winners' Cup.

The European champions were only playing in the lesser regarded competition because of their dismal performance in the Champions League, which precipitated the departure of Roberto di Matteo as manager. But they made the most of their second chance and in the final at the Amsterdam Arena were rewarded with Branislav Ivanovic's 93rd-minute headed winner.

Fernando Torres cast aside a long spell of indifferent form to score Chelsea's first, holding off defender Luisao and going around goalkeeper Artur. Benfica equalised soon after with Oscar Cardozo's penalty, awarded against Cesar Azpilicueta for handball, before Ivanovic found redemption for missing last season's Champions League final through suspension.

It was a personal triumph for 'interim' manager Rafa Benitez, who had struggled to win over the Chelsea support because of his previous affiliation with Liverpool, and who left the post four days later. He said: "When you have a manager who is leaving and yet you see them still fighting hard right to the end, you have to be pleased."

Branislav Ivanovic rises above the Benfica defence to plant Chelsea's second goal, which won them the Europa League final.

Celtic claim Barca's scalp

ON THE NIGHT Celtic celebrated the 125th anniversary of their formation, the latest group to wear the green and white hoops claimed one of the biggest scalps in world football, beating Barcelona 2–1 in the Champions League. "I think it was one of the greatest nights in the club's recent history," said manager Neil Lennon.

Celtic had served notice in the reverse fixture in Group D when they were only beaten in the Nou Camp by Jordi Alba's winner in the fourth minute of injury time after Georgios Samaras had put the Scottish champions ahead early on.

For the return at Parkhead, Celtic's severely-depleted squad had the fortitude and occasional good fortune to overcome a side who had won two of the previous four Champions League titles. In the final analysis, Lionel Messi's injury-time strike proved to be that extreme rarity: a consolation goal for Barcelona.

The Spaniards were relentless, but not wholly convincing. Messi hit the crossbar before Victor Wanyama headed past Victor Valdes to put Celtic ahead. Tony Watt, an 18 year old making only his eleventh first-team appearance, added the second when he drove home a low shot. Rod Stewart, a renowned Celtic supporter, was among the 60,000 crowd and was spotted wiping away tears at the final whistle.

Tito Vilanova, the Barcelona coach, was gracious in defeat.

SOCCER SOUNDBITES

"The players are heroes; they are heroes to me. I can't speak highly enough of their performance. They will go down in the history books of the club as the team who beat probably the best team in the world."

Manager **NEIL LENNON** after Celtic's remarkable victory over Barcelona

Celtic stroll to the double

FOOTBALL FOCUS

● Frank Lampard became Chelsea's record goalscorer when he equalled, then beat Bobby Tambling's 203 with both goals in a 2–1 win at Aston Villa. It was a remarkable feat for a midfield player and Lampard admitted: "I never dreamed I would get near 200 goals, even 50 or 100."

● The flamboyant Swede Zlatan Ibrahimovic destroyed England when he claimed all four goals in the 4–2 friendly win to mark the opening of Stockholm's Friends Arena. The fourth, an outrageous overhead kick from close to the touchline, was put forward as being one of the best goals ever scored.

● Dave Sexton, widely revered as one of the best coaches this country has produced, died aged 82. A one-time Manchester United manager, Sexton led Chelsea to success in the FA and European Cup-Winners' Cups as well as taking unfashionable Queens Park Rangers to runners-up spot in the old First Division.

● Former England captain David Beckham retired from football at the end of the season, aged 38. One of the best dead-ball specialists the game has known, Beckham won 115 international caps during a career in which he played for Manchester United, Real Madrid, Los Angeles Galaxy, Milan and Paris Saint-Germain.

● The Premier League voted to introduce goal-line technology from the 2013–14 season, awarding the contract to British firm Hawk-Eye. The system uses seven cameras per goal to detect whether the ball crossed the line and the manufacturers claim it is "millimetre accurate, ensuring no broadcast replays could disprove the decision".

THE ABSENCE OF RANGERS from the upper echelons of Scottish football turned the annual two-horse race into the equivalent of a one-horse walkover: Celtic duly cantered to the double of Premier League and FA Cup, though they missed the treble when they lost to St Mirren in the semi-finals of the League Cup.

In so doing, Neil Lennon became the third Celt to win the double as both a player and a manager, equalling the accomplishments of Jock Stein and Billy McNeill.

With their Glasgow rivals confined to the fourth tier, Celtic could only play what was put in front of them. The comparative lack of competition did not dilute the pleasure of Lennon, his players and supporters; the manager admitted after winning the League for a second season that his overwhelming emotion was "one of immense pride in the players". He added: "When they really put their minds to it they show what a great team they are."

Celtic finished 16 points clear of Motherwell and had the title wrapped up by the third week in April when they beat Inverness Caledonian Thistle 4–1. The Scottish Cup was added five weeks later when they beat Hibernian 3–0 at Hampden Park to win the competition for the 36th time in their 125-year existence.

Celtic already had the first final to be staged on a Sunday sewn up inside half an hour. By then Gary Hooper had taken his season's tally to 31 with two far-post goals from crosses by Anthony Stokes. Hooper might have had a hat-trick, but Mikael Lustig's second-half cutback eluded him and Joe Ledley angled home Celtic's third on the turn.

Hibs prevented a similar humiliation to the one they suffered a year earlier at the hands of Edinburgh rivals Hearts. However, they were unable to break their unenviable record of losing 10 Scottish Cup finals since they last won the trophy in 1902. Lennon said: "I knew what it would have meant to Hibs to win the Cup and I didn't want us to go down in history and have that thrown at us."

Celtic's Gary Hooper (right) wheels away after scoring the opening goal of the Scottish Cup Final against Hibernian.

SOCCER SOUNDBITES

"We are disappointed, but we lost to the better side and there is no shame in losing to Celtic."

Hibernian manager **PAT FENLON** is philosophical after defeat in the Scottish Cup final

Rangers start all over again

RANGERS CAME WITHIN A WHISKER of beginning life at the bottom end of Scottish football with an ignominious defeat. Their face-saving equaliser at Peterhead arrived with only 20 seconds of normal time remaining, bundled over the line off Andrew Little's thigh after a header by Kevin Kyle had hit the crossbar.

Rangers had been demoted to Division Three after the club's former incarnation had gone into liquidation during the summer. But the notion that their first season outside Scotland's elite would be an unbroken procession looked to be misplaced when Rory McAllister and Scott McLaughlin overturned the lead given Rangers by Barrie McKay and put Peterhead in front.

Ally McCoist, the Rangers manager, admitted he was relieved to gain a point from the 2–2 draw. "If the boys at any time thought this was going to be a cake-walk, they know where they are now," he said. "It's the first game and we're not going to start panicking." Carlos Bocanegra, the Rangers defender, said: "They fought and kicked until the end and that's something we can expect all season."

First-game nerves over, Rangers lived up to expectations and went on to win the division by the end of March.

FINAL SCORE

Football League
Premiership – Manchester United
Top scorer – Robin van Persie (Manchester United) 26
Championship – Cardiff City
League 1 – Doncaster Rovers
League 2 – Gillingham
Footballer of the Year – Gareth Bale (Tottenham Hotspur & Wales)

FA Cup final
Manchester City 0 Wigan Athletic 1

League Cup final
Bradford City 0 Swansea City 5

Scottish League
Premier League – Celtic
Top scorer – Michael Higdon (Motherwell) 26
Div 1 – Partick Thistle
Div 2 – Queen of the South
Div 3 – Rangers
Footballer of the Year – Leigh Griffiths (Hibernian & Scotland)

Scottish FA Cup final
Hibernian 0 Celtic 3

Scottish League Cup final
St Mirren 3 Hearts 2

European Cup final
Borussia Dortmund 1 Bayern Munich 2

UEFA Europa League final
Benfica 1 Chelsea 2

World Footballer of the Year 2012
Lionel Messi (Barcelona & Argentina)

FIFA Club World Cup 2012
Corinthians 1 Chelsea 0

INDEX

Page numbers in italics refer to captions to illustrations

Aberdeen 44, 66, 83, 133, 172, 180, 190, 196, 197, 200, 205, *205*, 214, 228, 249, 281, 333
Aberdeen Rovers 11
Abramovich, Roman 344, *344*, 374
AC Milan *149*, 149, 182, 234, *234*, 256, 267, 356, 372
Accrington Stanley 107, 360
Adams, A. 31
Adams, Micky 297
Adams, Tony 225, *225*, 234, 247, 258, 259, 265, 273, 286, 287, 292, 299, *299*, 313, *313*
Adamson, Jimmy 103
Adcock, Tony 228
Adebayor, Emmanuel 370
Ademir 76, 77
Advocaat, Dick 311, 378
Africa, stadium tragedies 323
Aguas, José 106, 107
Aguero, Sergio 404, *404*
Airdrieonians 40, 41, 45, 335
Airdrie United 335
Aitken, Andy 21, 22
Aitken, Roy 179
Ajax Amsterdam 148, 283
Alberto, Carlos 131, 137
Albertosi, Enrico 137
Albion Rovers 36, 72
Albiston, Arthur 178, 198
Alcock, C.W. 8, 14, *15*
Alcock, Paul 306, 310
Aldair 269
Aldershot 60, 66, *66*, 182, 240, 377
Aldridge, John 213, 227, *227*, 233, 234, 236, *236*
Alfonso 287
Alkmaar 186
Alladyce, Sam 376
Allback, Marcus 365
Allchurch, Ivor 88, 97, 122
Allchurch, Len 88
Allen, Clive 184, 222
Allen, Jack 53, 55
Allen, Les 105
Allen, Paul 246, 249
Allison, George 55, 58, 64
Allison, Malcolm 125, *125*, 180
Alloa Athletic 38
Alonso, Xabi 356
Alsop, Gilbert 54
Altobelli, Alessandro 193
Amancio 126
Amarildo 108, 109
"Amateur era" 14-15
Ambler, Roy 107
Amoros, Manuel 193
Amoruso, Lorenzo 334
Anastasi, Pietro 125, 141
Anderlecht 92, 133, 162, *162*, 200
Andersen, Henrik 254
Anderson, Joe 37
Anderson, Viv 70, 176, 178, 181, 204
Anderton, Darren 273, 286, 287
Andorra 331
Andrade, Jorge 353
Andrade, José 51
Anelka, Nicolas 301, 318, 379
Anfield 41
Angola 365
Antic, Raddy 197
Appleyard, Bill 21
Arbroath 11, 186
Archibald, Steve 189, 215
Arconada, Luis 201, 206
Ardiles, Osvaldo 175, 176, *176*, 186, 189, 200, 252, *252*, 271
Arentoft, Ben 131
Argentina 22, 49, 51, *51*, 79, 174, 175, 303, 304, 336
Armfield, Jimmy 140, 264
Armstrong, George 140, 165
Armstrong, Gerry 192
Armstrong, Ken 89
Arsenal 20, 21, 23, *23*, 36, 41, 44, 45, 46, 47, 49, 52, 53, 54, 55, *55*, 58, 59, 61, 64, 65, 66, 67, 70, 74, 75, 80, 82, 85, 91, 93, 94, 129, *129*, 133, 138, 139, 140, 143, 144, 172, *172*, 178, 181, 182, *182*, 184, 198, 221, *221*, 227, 234, 235, 244, 245, 247, 256, 259, 261, 265, *265*, 271, 272, 273, 275,289, 296, 299, 301, 307, 309, 310, 323, 324, 328–9, 332, 333, 334, 335, 339, 342, 344, 346, 348, 349, 360, 374, 418
Arsenal LFC 342
Arshavin, Andrei 378
Artemio Franchi Trophy 210
Asaba, Carl 311
Ashley, Mike 376
Ashton, Dean 358
Ashman, Ron 98
Asprilla, Faustino 265, 281, 296, *296*
Assenmacher, Karl-Josef 262
Astle, Jeff 126, *126*, 139
Aston Villa 10, *10*, 12, 16, 19, 21, 29, 31, 36, 37, 38, 52, 59, 70, 74, 93, 97, 133, 166, 185, 191, 250, 265, 280, *280*, 417
Aston, John 127
Aston, Ken 108, *108*
Athersmith, Charlie 16, 26, 27
Athletic Bilbao 92
Atkinson, Dalian 265
Atkinson, Graeme 257
Atkinson, Ron 190, 220, *220*, 247, 260, 265, 294, 294
Atyeo, John 91
Auld, Bertie 123, 124, 132, *132*, 133
Australia 340
Austria 24, 52, 54, *54*, 56-7, 62, 79, 81
Ayr United 34, 46
Ayresome Park 33
AZ 67
Babb, Phil 283
Bache, Joe 27
Baggio, Roberto 269
Bailey, Gary 178, 195, *195*, 197, 198
Baily, Eddie 76, 78
Baker, Alf 45
Baker, Gerry 102, 110
Baker, Joe 104, 111
Bako, Jaroslav 235
Balde, Bobo 334
Ball, Alan 118, 119, 121, 126, 143, 144, 147, 158, 177, 373
Ballack, Michael 333, 337
Balmer, Jack 69
Balotelli, Mario 404, *410*, 412
Bambrick, Joe 49, *49*, 65
Bangerter, Hans 255
Banks, Gordon 105, *112*, 118, *124*, 131, 136, *137*, 138, 140, *140*, 142, 143, 146, 373
Banks, Ralph 82
Banks, Tony 344
Barber, Keith 160
Barber, Tom 31
Barbosa 77
Barcelona 215, 218, 233, 248, 267, 271, 322
Barclays Bank 224
Barclays Manager of the Season: 1991 247
Baresi, Franco 268, 269
Bari 250
Barlow, Bert 64
Barmby, Nick 273, 278, 288
Barnes, John 201, *201*, 204, 224, 225, 233, 235, 236, 239, 250, 254, 281, 283, 319
Barnes, Peter 160
Barnes, Ron 107
Barnes, Walley 80, 88
Barnet 140, 310
Barnett, Geoff 143
Barnsley 28, 30
Barnwell, John 180
Baros, Milan 352, 353
Barrett, Earl 265
Barron, Paul 184
Barry Town 266
Barthez, Fabien 331, 333, 335, 352
Barton, Joey 378, 404
Barton, Brian 363, 375
Bartram, Sam 67, 83
Basinas, Angelis 353
Bassett, Dave 157
Bassett, William (Billy) 12, 26, *26*
Bastin, Cliff 49, 52, *52*, 58, 59, 61
Bates, Ken 204, 228, 323, 368
Bates, Mick *141*, 149
Batista, João 192
Battiston, Patrick 193, *193*
Batty, David 253, 254, *262*, 279, 281, *291*
Bauld, Willie 74
Bauwens, Dr 64
Baxter, Jim 104, 112, 122-3, 124, 325
Bayer Leverkusen 333, 335
Bayern Munich 159, 162, *162*, 191, 223, 311, 324, 418
Baynham, Ron 99
Beardsley, Peter 216, 224, 225, 226, *226*, 227, 230, 233, 234, 236, 281
Bearzot, Enzo 193
Beasant, Dave 227, *227*
Beasley, Pat 59
Beattie, Andy 86
Beattie, Dick 114
Beattie, Kevin 159
Bebeto 269
Beckenbauer, Franz 126, 137, 143, 155, 159, 160, 174, 201, 243
Beckham, David 282, 283, 289, 303, 304, *304*, *309*, 313, 330, 331, 332, *332*, 333, 336, 340, 341, 343, 344, 345, 350, 352, 353, 364, 367, 369, 374, 378,419
Bedford Town 93, 113
Belfast Celtic 36
Belgium 45, 50, 51, 54, 56, 62, 71, 183
Bell, Alec 24, 29
Bell, Colin 123, 125, 131, 136, 143, 147, 150, 151, 158
Bell, Eric 82
Bell, Harold 91
Bell, Robert "Bunny" 59
Bellone, Bruno 201
Bellamy, Craig *406*
Bene, Ferenc 131
Benfica 107, *107*, 116, 127, 418, *418*
Benitez, Rafa 356, 372, 373, 418
Bennett, Alec 20
Bent, Geoff 95
Bentley, Roy 68, 74, *74*
Berger, Patrik 287
Bergkamp, Dennis 254, 262, 274, 276, 277, *277*, 278, 282, 287, 304, *304*, 309
Berkovic, Eyal 289
Bernabeu, Santiago 102
Bernard, Mike 142, *142*
Bernard, Paul 281
Bernes, Jean-Pierre 266
Berry, Johnny 92, 92, 93, 94
Bertoni, Daniel 175, *175*
Berwick Rangers 120, 335
Best, George 4, 116, *116*, 123, 123, 126, *126*, 127, *127*, 128, *128*, 132, *132*, 140, *140*, 143, 147, *164*, 169, 220, 361
Bett, Jim *190*
Bettega, Roberto *166*
Betts, M.P. 8
Bevan, Richard 417
Biavati, Amedeo 63, 64
Bierhoff, Olivier 286, 286, 287
"Big freeze" 110, *110*
Bingham, Billy 96, 98, *98*, 198
Birmingham 42, 52, 61, 74, 88, 90, 207, 252, 266, 274, 326
Birtles, Garry 176, 177, *177*, 183, 354
Bishop Auckland 78
Black, Eric 196, 197, *197*
Black, Tommy 54
"Black Diamond" see Leonidas
Blackburn Olympic 10
Blackburn Rovers 11, *11*, 12, 30, 40, 41, 59, 66, 102, 113, 140, 235, 255, 265, 266, 275, 279, 322
Blackburn, Fred 17
Blackmore, Clayton 244, 246
"Black Panther" *see* Eusebio
Blackpool 66, 70, 79, 83, 85, 91, 121, 316
Blair, Jimmy 44
Blairgowrie 59
Blanc, Laurent *303*, 304, 331, 333, 335
Blanchflower, Danny 8, 92, 92, 96, 101, *101*, 107, 111, 112, 114, 121, *122*, 123
Blanchflower, Jackie 93, 94
Blanco, Cuauhtemoc 304
Blatter, Sepp 257, 300
Blenkinsop, Ernie 65
Blind, Danny 286
Bliss, Bert 39
Blissett, Luther 194, *194*
Blokhin, Oleg 411
Bloomer, Steve 13, 26, 34, *35*, 60, 65
Bloor, Alan 143
"Blueprint for the future" 184
Bly, Terry 104, 105
Blyth Spartans 172
Boersma, Phil 156
Bohinen, Lars 282
Boli, Basile 254
Bolton Wanderers 13, 20, 31, 39, *43*, 44, 47, 61, 66, 82, 94,140, 274, 290, 333, 342, 347, 408
Bon Accord 11
Bonds, Billy 142, 184, 185, *185*
Bone, Jimmy 142
Bonetti, Peter 121, 134, *134*, 136, 141, 143
Bonhof, Rainer 155, 182
Boniek, Zbigniew 193
Boninsegna, Roberto 137
Boniperti, Giampiero 84
Bonner, Pat 228, 268
Book, Tony 125, 129, *131*, 132
Booth, Tommy 160
Borussia Moenchengladbach 103, 149, 168
Bosman, Jean-Marc 276, 279
Bossis, Maxime 193
Boston United 91, 335
Botasso, Juan *53*
Bottom, Arthur 89, *89*
Bould, Steve 234, 247
Bournemouth 93, 198
Bowden, Ray 59
Bowen, Dave 94, 97
Bowles, Stan 159, 166
Bowyer, Ian 176, 179, 183
Bowyer, Lee 324, 325
Boyce, Ron 113
Boyes, Walter 58
Boyle, Tommy 32, *32*, 37
Bozsik, Joszef 84, 86, 97, 101
Brabrook, Peter 113
Bracewell, Paul 206, 213
Bradford City 29, 33, 37, 45, 47, 207, 323, 417
Bradford Park Avenue 66, 133
Bradford, Joe 52
Bradley, Gordon 73
Bradley, Keith 125
Brady, Liam 173, 178, 179, *179*, 182, 224
Bramall Lane 9, *9*
Brand, Ralph 112
Brazil 62, 63, 76, 77, 91, 96, *96*, 97, 99, 131, 136, 137, 189, *189*, 201, 223, 302, 303, 304, 305, 336, 337
Brazil, Alan 191
Brehme, Andreas 243, *243*
Breitner, Paul 191, 193
Bremner, Billy 115, 123, 130, *130*, 132, 133, 139, *139*, 141, 143, 144, 148, 149, 150, 151, 154, 156, *156*, 159, 160, 165, 170, 181
Bremner, Des 183
Brennan, Bobby 85
Brentford 207
Brewster, Craig 267, 267
Bridge, Wayne 348, *348*
Briegel, Hans-Peter 183
Briggs, Tommy 88
Bright, Mark 239
Brighton 66, 207
Bristol City 22, 23, 151
Bristol Rovers 59, 207
British Empire Exhibition authorities 39
British Ladies Football Club 12, *12*
Britton, Cliff 66, *66*
Broadbent, Peter 122
Broadcast matches 45, 212, 230
Broadis, Ivor 81
Brockbank, J. 9
Brolin, Tomas 254, 265
Brook, Eric 58, 60
Brooke, Garry 186
Brooking, Trevor 142, 162, 182, *182*, 185, 187, *187*, 188, 189
Brotherton, Noel 183
Brown, Alex "Sandy" 17, *17*
Brown, Allan 98
Brown, Ally 198
Brown, Bob 47
Brown, Craig 333
Brown, George 44, 65
Brown, José Luis 217
Brown, Laurie 170
Brown, Tony 139
Bruce, Steve 246, 248, 260, *260*, *266*, 307
Brown, Wes 338
Bruges 163, 173
Bryant, Eric 72
BSkyB 308
Buchan, Charlie 31, 33, *33*, 44, *44*, 45, 47, 48
Buchan, Martin 161, 178
Buchanan, Jock 47
Buckley, Alan 198
Bulgaria 352
Burbanks, Eddie 60
Burgess, Ron 78
Burkinshaw, Keith 176, 186, 200
Burley, Craig 302
Burley, George 173, 378
Burnley 32, 37, 38, 44, 47, 68, 82, 103
Burns, Kenny 172, 176, 179, 181, 183
Burns, Tommy 378
Burruchaga, Jorge 216, 217, 266
Bury 16, 18, 39, 72
Busby Advisory Committee 191, 194, 208
"Busby Babes" see Manchester United
Busby, Sir Matt 94, 95, *95*, 99, 116, 126, 127, *127*, 128, *128*, 220, 235, 260, 264, *264*, *294*, 294-5, 357
Busby, Viv 172
Butcher, Terry 226, 230, 233
Butler, Joe 31, *31*, 45
Butt, Jorg 333
Butt, Nicky 282, 283, 331, 333
Byrne, Roger 91, 92, *92*, 95, 96, 113, 113
Cabrini, Antonio 193
Caesar, Gus 227
Cafu 269
Calcio 42
Callaghan, Ian 113, 116, 118, 152, 156, 168
Callaghan, Nigel 194
Camara, Henri 336
Cambridge Rules 42
Cambridge United 133
Cameroon 242, 336, 343
Campbell, John 27
Campbell, Kevin 247
Camsell, George 45, *45*, 46, 47, 48, 65, 98
Campbell, Sol 333, 342, 352, 360
Canario 103
Caniggia, Claudio 243
Canon Football League 196
Cantona, Eric 253, *253*, 257, 263, *263*, 266, 272, *272*, 274, 275, 276, *276*, 282, 283, *283*, 289, 292
Capello, Fabio 369, 371, 375, 406, 407
Capital One Cup 417, *417*
Cardiff City 37, 39, 41, 45, 47, 67, 72, 94, 125, 266, 332, 408
Cardozo, Oscar 418
Carey, Johnny 69, 70, 74, 80, 128
Carling Cup 347, 408
Carlisle, Clarke 406
Carlisle United 58, 91, 310
Carol of Romania, King 54
Carr brothers 235
Carroll, Andy 405
Carter, Philip 221
Carter, Raich 60, *60*, 65, 66, 67, 101
Cascarino, Tony 237, 327
Case, Jimmy 160, 161, 168, *168*, 173, 176, 178, 183, 197
Casillas, Iker 337, *413*
Casiraghi, Pierluigi 283, 287
Cassano, Antonio 339
Castilla 184, *184*
Castro, Hector 51
Catenaccio 123
Caton, Tommy 186
Catterick, Harry 110, *110*
Cavem, Domiciano 106
Cea, Pedro 51
Cech, Peter 371, 376, 405
Celtic 16, 17, 19, *19*, 23, 24, 25, 29, 32, 34, 35, 36, 37, 38, 40, 41, 45, 46, 47, 52, 53, 54, 58, 64, 72, 79, 83, 93, 121, 124, 125, 129, 132, 133, 133, *133*, 139, 140, 142, 144, 146, 148, 153, 167, 179, 204, 205, 219, 233, 237, 272, 292, 296, 300, 300, 310, 311, 327, 333, 334, 335, 341, 342, 349, 353, 363, 409, *409*, 418, 419, *419*
Central League 41
Ceresoli, Carlo *58*
Cerezo 192
Chalmers, Len 103
Chalmers, Steve 121, *129*
Champions League *see* European Cup
Channon, Mick 147, 150, 161, 169, 189, 205
Chapman, F.W. 25
Chapman, Herbert 36, 38, 40, 44, 47, 49, 54, 55, *55*, 59, 64, 65, 80, 85, 170, 273, 294
Chapman, Lee 253
Charity Cup 24
Charity Shield 25, 124, 156
Charles, Gary 213, 249, 266, 332
Charles, John 8, 73, 88, 94, 96, 97, 100, *100*, 101, 107, 122, 347, *347*
Charles, Mel 88
Charlton Athletic 67, 68, 93, 111, 342
Charlton, Bobby 92, *92*, 94, *94*, 95, 96, 98, 102, 109, 112, 113, 116, 118, *118*, 123, 125, 127, 128, 133, 136, 147, *147*, 162, 191, 220, 254, 255, 264, 270
Charlton, Jack 113, 117, 118, 119, 124, 130, 132, 134, *138*, 143, 147, 151, 153,167, *167*, 184, *184*, 228, 229, 237, 243, 251, 268, 280, 331
Chelsea 23, 33, 36, 47, 53, 57, 60, 67, 74, 75, 88, 89, 90, 94,111, *111*, 117, 121, 134, *134*, 141, 143, 144, 160, 204, 222, 228, 266, 291, *291*, 293, 298, 299, 300, 313, 333, 334, 344, 348, 354, 355, 357, 359, 369, 370, 405, *405*, 406, 416, *416*, 418
Cherry, Trevor 148, *148*, 151, 156
Chester Report 195
Chesterfield 228, 292
Cheyne, Alex 47
Chiarugi, Luciano *149*
Chile 51, 303
Chilton, Allenby 70, 80
China 208, 336
Chisholm, Gordon 205, *205*
Chisholm, Ken 73
Chislenko, Igor 118, 119
Chivers, Martin 123, 143, 147, 153
Chorley 220, *220*
Christofte, Kim 254
Clairefontaine 322
Clapton Orient 66
Clark, Clive 120
Clarke, Allan 123, 131, 132, 140, 141, 143, 144, 149, 150, 159, *163*, 226
Clarke, Roy 90
Clarke, Vic 180
Clarke, Wayne 226, *226*
Clattenburg, Mark 416, *416*
Clay, Ernie 188, 221
Clayton, Ron 91, 98, 102
Clegg, J.C. 9
Clegg, Sir Charles 47
Clegg, W.E. 9
Clemence, Ray 147, 163, 166, 168, 172, *172*, 173, 176, 190, 222
Clodoaldo 137
Clough, Brian 98, 102, *102*, 107, 129, 144, 146, *146*, 157, 158, 167, 171, 172, 177, 179, 183, 172, 219, *219*, 231, *231*, 249, 259, *259*, *262*, 275, 295, *295*, 354
Clough, Nigel 231, 254, 262
Clyde 28, 72, 363
Clydebank 335
Coca-Cola Cup 259, 271, 274, 280
Cockburn, Henry 80
Cohen, Avi 181
Cohen, George 118, 124
Colaussi, Gino 63
Colchester 138, 266
Cole, Andy 272, 274, 275, 283, 324, 331
Cole, Ashley 342, 346, 354, 365, 405
Coleman, Neville 93
Collar, Enrique 111
Collins, Bobby 98, 117, 130
Collins, John 283
Collymore, Stan 274, 281, 281, 283, 324
Colman, Eddie 92, *92*, 94, 95
Colombo, Felici 182
Coluna, Mario 106, 116
Combi, Giampiero 57, *57*
Common, Alf 21, *21*
Compton, Denis 66, 74, 75
Compton, Leslie 66, 74, *74*, 75, 79
Comunale Stadium 71
Conen, Edmund 56
Conn, Alfie 148, *148*, 167, *167*
Connelly, George 133, 148
Connelly, John 102, 103, 116, 118
Connolly, Paddy 41
Conroy, Terry 142, 143
Conti, Bruno 200
Cook, Billy 33
Cook, Laurence 38
Cooke, Charlie 121, 123, 124, 134, 141
Cooper, Davie 211, *211*, 219, 220
Cooper, Paul 181, 190
Cooper, Terry 130, 133, 136, 151, 252
Cooper, Tom 65
Coppell, Steve 171, 178, 187, 235, 240, 362
Copping, Wilf 58, *58*
Corinthians 15
Cork, Alan 332
Cormack, Peter 146, 147, 150
Corrigan, Joe 186
Costa Pereira, Alberto da 107, 116, 118
Costa, Flavio 77
Costa, Rui 352
Cottee, Tony 230
Coulston, Frank 142
Courtney, George 195
Coventry City 222, *222*, 323, 409
Cowan, Jimmy 16, 26, 73, 78
Cowans, Gordon 185, 191
Cowdenbeath 33
Cox, Arthur 297
Cox, Freddie 74, 93
Cox, Jack 22
Cox, Sammy 101
Crabtree, Jimmy 27
Craig, Jim 121, 142
Crawford, Ray 103, 138, *138*
Crawford, Stephen 272
Crawshaw, Tom 21
Crayston, Jack 58

Crerand, Pat 113, 116
Crespo, Hernan 322, 336
Cresswell, Lieutenant 8
Crickmer, Walter 95
Cripps, George 36
Croatia 286, 287
Croatia 303, 304, 305, 352
Croker, Ted 180
Crompton, Bob 27, 70, 81
Crooks, Garth 172, 186
Crooks, Sam 49, 65
Cross, David 184
Crossley, Mark 249
Crouch, Peter 358, 364, 372, 374
Crowe, Jason 300
Crozier, Alan 324
Cruyff, Johan 4, 153, *153*, 155, 166, 175, 181, 233, 248, 267
Cruz, Fernando 107
Crystal Palace (ground) 18
Crystal Palace 23, 37, 153, 184, 233, 239, 240
Cuba 62
Cudicini, Carlo 334, 371
Cuggy, Frank 31
Cullis, Stan 8, 66, *66*, 88, 220, 294-5, 325
Cummings, George 59
Cunningham, Andy 48
Cunningham, Laurie 187
Cunningham, Willie *89*
Cup Winners' Cup *see* European Cup Winners' Cup
Curie, Kurt 254
Curle, Keith 254
Curran, Terry 184
Currie, Tony 150, *190*
Curry, Tom 95
Curtis, George 222
Curtis, Norman 83
Cush, Wilbur 96
Cussins, Manny 157
Cutler, Reg 93
Cyprus 331
Czech Republic 285, 286, 287, 332, 333, 410
Czechoslovakia 57, 63, 163
Czerniatinski, Alex 200
Czibor, Zoltan 87, *87*, 104

Da Rui 69
Da Silva see Leonidas
Da Silva, Eduardo 373
Dagenham & Redbridge 335, 409
Dailly, Christian 267
Daines, Barry 176
Daley, Steve 180
Daley, Tony 265
Dalglish, Kenny 142, 146, 148, 150, 154, 167, 169, *169*, 170, *170*, 171, 172, 173, *173*, 176, 178, *178*, 181, 185, *185*, 187, 189, *189*, 195, 199, 200, 203, 214, *214*, 215, 221, 226, 233, 236, 245, 247, 255, *255*, 275, 310, 406, 408
Dallas, Hugh 311
Daly, Gerry 161, 181
Daniel, Peter 158, 181
Daniel, Ray 80
Darby, Duane 292
Darlington 41, 91, 315
Darwen 12, 14
Davala, Umit 337
David, Ben 75
David, Mario 108
Davies, Len 40, 45
Davies, Roger 158, 162, 189
Davies, Simon 333
Davies, Willie 41
Davies, Wyn 107
Davis, Paul 221
D'Avray, Mich 189
Dawson, Alex 113
Dawson, Ally 220
Dawson, Jerry 37
Day, Mervyn 162
Dean, Billy "Dixie" 45, 46, *46*, 48, *48*, 52, *52*, 53, 60, 65, 100
Dean, Norman 125
Deans, Dixie 144, *144*, 148
Dear, Brian 115
Deeley, Norman 102
Defoe, Jermain 335
Del Sol, Luis 109
Delaney, Jimmy 70, 83
Dellas, Traianos 333
Dempsey, Charles 323
Dempsey, John 141
Denmark 25, 30, *30*, 198, 254, 303, 304, 336, 352, 412
Deportivo La Coruña 324
Derby County 13, 19, 36, 52, 60, 67, 72, 91, 144, 146, 158, *158*, 162, 181, 266, 379, 379
Derby, Lord 33
Derwall, Jupp 201
Desailly, Marcel 267, 267
Devey, John 16, *16*, 26, 27
Devonshire, Alan 182, 185
Devych, Marko 411, *411*
Di Canio, Paolo 306, 310, 327
Di Matteo, Roberto 293, *293*, 417
Di Stefano, Alfredo 90, *90*, 92, 101, *101*, 103, *103*, 106,108, 109, 112, 114
Dibble, Andy 227, *227*, 231
Dickinson, Jimmy 83, 113, 186
Dickson, Bill 70
Didi 91, 96, 97, 101, 109
Diet 277
Dimmock, Jimmy 37, *37*
Disasters: Accra Stadium 323; Bradford City 207, *207;* Burnden Park 66, *66*, Ellis Park 323; Harare 323; fires 207, *207;* Heysel Stadium 209, 221, 222, 223; Hillsborough 232, *232*, *233*, 238, *238*, 414; Ibrox Park 18, *18*, 139; Lima riot 113, *113;* Munich plane crash 9, 94, *94*, *264;* Superga plane crash 73; Zambian plane crash 259
Dismissals 306
Ditchburn, Ted *92*
Dittborn, Carlos 108
Dixon, Johnny 93
Dixon, Kerry 194, 212
Dixon, Lee 243, 246, 247, 254, *309*, 333
Dobing, Peter 142
Docherty, Tommy 130, 147, 154, 161, 168, 170, 260
Dodgin, Bill *83*
Doherty, Peter 60, 65, 67, 96
Doig, Ted 18, 19, *19*, 22
Domarski, Jan 150, *150*
Domenech, Raymond 366
Donadoni, Roberto 267
Donagy, Mal 192
Doncaster Belles 335
Doncaster Rovers 68
Donington School 8
Dooley, Derek 81, 83, *83*
Dooley, Thomas 262
Dorado, Pablo 51
Dorigo, Tony 262
Dougan, Derek 102, 140, 144, 220
Douglas, Bryan 104
Douglas, Rab 334
Downs, Dicky 30
Downsborough, Peter 129
Doyle, Mike 160
Drake, Ted 8, 55, 58, *58*, 59, *59*, 60, 65, 66, 100, 128
Drogba, Didier 355, 369, 370, 376, 379, 405, *405*
Drury, Eileen 306
Drury, George 67
Dublin, Dion 257
Ducadam, Helmut 215, *215*
Ducat, Andy *36*
Duckworth, Dick 24, 27
Dudek, Jerzy 356
Duffy, Chris 68, *68*
Duke, Matt 417
Dulwich Hamlet 39
Dumbarton 13, 38
Duncan, Dally 65
Dundee 28, 41, 72, 83, 112, 342
Dundee Harp 11
Dundee United 180, 196, *196*, 223, 248, 267, *267*
Dunfermline 46, 130, 211, 342, 349
Dunga 268, 269
Dunlop, Albert 98
Dunlop, Billy 22
Dunmore, David 89
Dunne, Tony 116, 147
Duquemin, Len 78
Durie, Gordon 282, 286
Durnberger 191
Durrant, Iain 219, 230
Dutch East Indies 62
Duxbury, Mike 197
Dwight, Roy 99, *99*
Dyet, Jim 49
Dyke, Dickie 72, *72*
Dynamo, Moscow 145
Dyson, Jack 90
Dyson, Terry 105, 111, *111*
Dzajic, Dragan 127
Dziekanowski, Dariusz 237, *237*

East Fife 61, 75
Eastham, George *103*, 104, *104*, 111, 143, *143*
Edwards, Duncan 89, 90, *90*, 91, 92, *92*, 94, 95, 96, 101, 128
Edwards, George 70
Edwards, Louis 170
Edwards, Martin 308
Eduardo 373, 373
Egypt 56
Eintracht Frankfurt 103, 107
Elland Road 38
Elleray, David 266, 292
Ellis, Sam 117
Elstrup, Lars 254
England (women) 148
England *8*, 9, *9*, 10, 16, 18, 19, 24, 30, *30*, 31, 34, 36, 40, 45, 47, 48, 49, 53, 54, *54*, 58, 60, 61, *61*, 62, 64, 66, *66*, 69, 71, 73, 74, 75, 78, 79, 81, 84, 85, 86, 88, 89, 90, 91, 98, 99, 102, 104, 107, 112, 113, 118, 119, 121, 124,131, 135, 140, 143, 147, 166, 169, 187, 188, 198, 201, 204, 208, 212, 221, 224, 225, 233, 242-3, 250, 254, 262, 263, 264, *264*, 273, *273*, 284, 285, 286, 287, 288, *288*, 291, 293, 297, 302-3, 304, 308, 310, 324, 330, 332, 336, 337, 340, 344, 345, 347, 348, 352–3, 407, *407*, 410, 411, *411*, 412, 419
England see also Great Britain
English clubs ban 209
English clubs ban: lifted 210
English, Sam 53
ENIC 322
Ensor, Tony 261
Eriksson, Lars 254
Eriksson, Sven-Göran 324, 328, 336, 369
Escobar, Andres 268
Estonia 292, 331
Estudiantes 128
Europa League 418, *418*
European Championship 127, 160, 163, 183, 201, 225, 229, 244, 248, 250, 251, 254, 255, 279, 284-7, 320-1, 331, 338, 345, 346, 352–3, 410–13, 414
European Commission 322
European Cup (Champions League) 90, 92, 103, 104, 107, 121, 126, 127, 133, 135, 148, 159, 162, *162*, 168, 173, 176, 179, 183, 187, *187*, 191, 209, 215, 223, 234, 236, 267, 283, 317, 324, 405, *405*, 415
European Cup-Winners' Cup 105, 111, 115, 121, 125, 130, 134, 141, *141*, 144, 145, 149, *149*, 162, 182, 184, *184*, 196, 200, 204, 207, 237, 246, 248, *248*, 261, 265, 275, 300
European Nations Cup 103, 110
Eusebio 106, 107, 112, 116, 118, 127
Evans, Bobby 95
Evans, David 191, 213
Evans, Dennie 91
Evans, Jimmy 38
Evans, Roy 264
Everton 21, 22, 33, 35, 40, 46, 52, 53, 54, *54*, 60, 64, 66, 75, 83, 110, *110*, 117, 130, 166, 199, 206, 207, 208, 210, 213, 225, 233, 275, 332, 339
Evra, Patrice 406
Exeter 153, 186
Eydelie, Jean-Jacques 266

FA, The 42-3, 407
FA Amateur Cup final 20; 1951 – 78, *78*
FA Cup 8, 9, 10, 11, 12, 13, 14, 16, 17, 18, 19, 20, 21, 22, 24, 28, 29, 30, 32, *32*, 33, 34, 35, 37, 39, *39*, 40, 45, 49, *49*, 52, 53, *53*, 54, *54*, 55, 58, 60, 61, 64, 67, 68, 70, 75, 79, 82, 83, 88, 89, 90, 91, 93, 98, 102, 113, 115, 117, 121, 126, 133, 138, 143, 148, 160, 161, 168, 173, 181, 182, *182*, 197, 199, 200, 208, 213, 221, *222*, 223, 227, 233, 239, 240, 246, 249, 251, 255, 266, 273, 275, *281*, 281, 293, 301, 313, 332, 334, 342, 346, 349, 405, 415, *415;* extra time 30; replays 134, 142, 190, 249, 261
FA Premier League 252, 253, 255, 256, 260, *260*, 266, 404, 414, 419
FA *see* Football Association
FA Youth Challenge Cup 94
Fabregas, Cesc 412, 413
Faeroes 244
Fagan, Joe 199, 214, 245
failures 300
Fairclough, David 160, 176, 181
Fairfoul, Tom 34
Fairs Cup 117, 131, 133, 141 *see also* UEFA Cup, Europa League
Falcao 192
Falkirk 24, 31, 83
Falkirk 292, 333
Farm, George 79, *79*
Faroe Islands 338
Farrell, Peter 74
Fashanu, John 274, 274, 278
Fashanu, Justin 190
Fayed, Mohamed 297, 308
Fear, Keith 151
Fédération Internationale de Football Association *see* FIFA
Felix 137
Fenlon, Pat 419
Fenwick, Terry 230
Ferdinand, Anton 406
Ferdinand, Les 281, 331
Ferdinand, Rio 322, 332, 336, 338, 406
Ferguson, Alex 190, 196, 203, 214, 220, 226, 247, 248, 253, 257, 260, 271, 272, 275, 282, *293*, *310*, 314, 333, 335, 338, 340, 341, 337, 406, 414, *414*
Ferguson, Barry 334
Ferguson, Billy 121
Ferguson, Bobby 142
Ferguson, Duncan 266, 282
Ferguson, Hughie 49
Fernandez, Lorenzo 51
Fernie, Willie 95
Ferrari, Giovani 63
Ferrer, Albert 271
Ferreyra, Bernabe *50*
Ferrini, Giorgio 108, *108*
Festival of Britain 79
Feurer, Herbert 204, *204*
Feyenoord 160
FIFA 20, 22, 50, 62, 74, 268, 300, 322
Figo, Luis 322, 330, 352
Finland 332
Finnan, Steve 331
Finney, Tom 68, 69, *69*, 71, 74, 75, 76, 78, 79,81, 96, 99, 100, 300
Fiorentina 104
Fischer, Klaus 193 "Fixed" matches 112, 114, 115, 170
Fleitas Solich 141
Fleming, Jim 55
Flewin, Reg 72, *72*
Floodlighting 9, *9*, 80, *80*, 91, 113
Flowers, Ron 109
Flowers, Tim 266
Foe, Marc-Vivien 343
Foggon, Alan 131
Fontaine, Just 96, 97
Football Association 8, 14, 90, 112, 209, 229, 306, 322
Football Association of Ireland 280
Football League 11, 15; break-up 252; centenary 224; club debts 251; soccer violence plans 210; sponsorship 196, 224
Football League Cup *see* League Cup
Football Spectators Bill 231
Footballer of the Year 70, 73, 129, 131, *131*, 140, 168
Forbes, Alex 75, 82
Ford, Dave 117
Ford, Trevor 100
Forfar 49
Forlan, Diego 333, 344
Forrest, James 11, 112, 133
Forssell, Mikael 333
Foster, Steve 197
Foulke, Billy "Fatty" 17, 27, *27*, 92, 94, 126
Fowler, Robbie 281, 283, 332
Fox, Bill 255
Fox, Peter 194
France 47, 50, 51, 62, 201, 210, 287, 303, 304, 305, 322, 336, 343, 352, 353
Francis, Gerry 273, 322
Francis, Trevor 166, 169, 177, *177*, 179, *179*, 190, 228
Friaca 77
Frizzell, Jimmy 183
Frontzeck, Michael 220
Fry, C.B. 161
Fryatt, Jim 113
Fulham 60, 113, 130, 158, 221, 297, 308, 323, 328-9

Gaetjens, Larry 76, *76*
Galatasaray 317
Gallacher, Hughie 40, 45, *45*, 46, *46*, 47, 48, *48*
Gallagher, Patsy 32, 41, 41, 48
"Galloping Major" *see* Puskas, Ferenc
Gannon, Eddie 83
Garde, Rémi *289*
Gardner, Alex 21
Garrincha 96, 97, 109
Garwood, Colin 182
Gascoigne, Paul 230, *230*, 242, *242*, 243, 246, *246*, 249, 249, 250, *250*, 255, 256, 257, 258, 262, 281, *281*, 285, 286, 287, 288, 290, *290*, *297*, 301, *312*, 313, 332
Gaskell, Dave 113
Gateshead 60
Gauld, Jimmy 114
Geddis, David 173
Gemmell, Tommy 121, 129, 132, 133
Gemmill, Archie 124, 144, 156, 174, *174*, 176, 177, 179
Gennoe, Terry 177
"Gentle Giant" see Charles, John
Gentile, Claudio 192
Gento, Francisco 103, 112, 126
George V, King 32, *32*
George, Charlie 133, 138, 139, 140, *140*, 143, 162, 164, *164*, 221
George, Jacques 218
George, Ricky 142, *142*
Germano 107, 116
Germany 56, 61, 62, 284, 285, 286, *286*, 287, 303, 304, 323, 330, 332, 337, 352, 412; *see also* West Germany
Gerrard, Anthony 408
Gerrard, Steven 330, 340, 350, *351*, 352, 408
Gerson 137
Gestido, Alvaro 51
Ghiggia, Alcide "Chico" 77
Gibson, Colin 226
Gibson, Jimmy 46
Gibson, Steve 322
Gidman, John 190
Giggs, Ryan 251, 260, *260*, 271, 283, 309, *309*, 313, 342
Giles, Johnny 130, *130*, 132, 133, 138, 144, 148, 149, 159, 167, 169
Gillespie, Billy 31, 32, 48
Gillespie, Gary 221, 226, 236, 239, 243
Gillespie, Keith 272, 296
Gillies, Don 151
Gillingham 228, 311
Gilzean, Alan 121, 146
Ginola, David 281
Giresse, Alain 193, 210
Given, Shay 331
Gladwin, Charlie 31
Glasgow Celtic *see* Celtic
Glasgow Rangers *see* Rangers
Glass, Jimmy 310
Glazer, Malcolm355
Glazzard, Jimmy 83
Glentoran 36
Goal-line technology 419
Goddard, Paul 184, 183
Godwin, Tommy 74
Golac, Ivan 267
Golden Boot 203
Golden Goal 284, 285, 287, 302, 304
"Golden Head" see Kocsis, Sandor
Gomes, Nuno 352
Goodall, John 11, 26, *26*
Goodall, Roy 65
Goodison Park 34, 46, 332
Goram, Andy 286
Goring, Peter 75
Gornik Zabrze 134
Gothenburg 223
Gough, Tony 180, 211
Goulden, Len 61
Gow, Gerry 151
Gowling, Alan 160
Goycochea, Sergio 243
Grabowski, Jurgen 137
Graca, Jaime 127
Gradi, Dario 250
Graf Zeppelin *49*
Graham, Arthur 160
Graham, Dick 138, 140
Graham, George 234, 243, 247, 261, 273, *273*, 278, 292, 307, 322
Graham, John 11
Graham, Milton 198
Grainger, Colin 90, 91, *91*
Gray, Andy (Crystal Palace) 239, *239*, 251
Gray, Andy (Wolves/Everton) 180, 181, *181*, 199, 206, 207, *207*, 208
Gray, Eddie 130, 134, 141, 144, 149
Gray, Stuart 251
Grazioli, Giuliano 310
Grealish, Tony 197
Great Britain 69, 406, *406*
Greaves, Jimmy 99, 102, 104, 106, 107, *108*, 109, 111, 112, *112*, 113, 118, 121, 123, 125, 133, 140, 282
Greece 62, 332, 352, 353, 410, 412
Green, Ryan 300
Greenhoff, Brian 161, 166, 169
Greenhoff, Jimmy 143, 168, *168*
Greenwood, Ron 113, 115, 171, *171*, 183, 187, 188, 193, 194
Gregg, Harry 94, 96, 97
Greig, John 143, 148, 172
Gretna 335, 362
Griffiths, Mal 73
Griffiths, Tommy 59
Grimes, Ashley 227
Grimsby Town 37, 61
Grimsdell, Arthur 37
Grobbelaar, Bruce *189*, 190, 193, 213, 221, 234, 271, *271*, 274, 278
Grosics, Gyula 97
Gross, Christian 298
Groves, Perry 221, 227
Groves, Vic 94
Guaita, Enrico 57
Gualtieri, Davide 263
Guatemala City 292
Guigue, Marcel 91
Gullit, Ruud 229, *229*, 234, *234*, 254, 267, 274, 282, 293, 299, 310
Gunn, Alan 204
Gurney, Bobby 60
Guttmann, Bela 106
Guy, Dickie 157, *157*
Gylmar 91, 109

Haan, Arie 162
Haffey, Frank 104, *104*
Hagan, Jimmy 66
Hall, Douglas 252, 298, *298*
Hall, Sir John 252
Hall, Willie 64, *64*, 146, 158, 160
Haller, Helmut 119
Hamann, Dietmar 277
Hammam, Sam 332, *332*
Hamburg 183
Hamilton, Tom 38, 46
Hammam, Sam 256
Hampden Park 34, 41, 45, 46, 60, 70, 333, 338
Hampson, Jimmy 54, *54*
Hampson, Walter 40
Hampton, Harry 21, *21*, 27, 31
Hamrin, Kurt 97
Hancocks, Johnny 73, 88, 101
Hannah, George 88
Hansen, Alan 173, 183, 189, 199, 233, 250, 282
Hanson, Stan 82
Hapgood, Eddie 54, 58, 65
Hapoel Club of Tel Aviv 80
Hardaker, Alan 120, 170
Harding, Matthew 289, *289*
Hardy, Billy 45
Hardy, Sam 22, 27, 31, 34, *34*, 35
Harford, Mick 231
Harford, Ray 279
Harkes, John 259
Harlow 180, 182
Harmer, Tommy 98, 101
Harper, Joe 133, 160
Harris, Gordon 118
Harris, Jimmy 98
Harris, Peter 74
Harris, Ron 134, *163*
Harrop, Jim 31
Harston, Ted 60
Harte, Ian 337
Hartford, Asa 144, 169, 203
Hartson, John 273, 333, 334, 341
Harvey, David 126, 133, 144, 149, 151, 156
Haslam, Harry 176
Hassall, Harold 78
Hasselbaink, Jimmy F 333, 334
Hateley, Mark 216, 228
Hauge, Rune 273, 278
Havelange, Joao 153, 154
Hay, David 150
Hayes, Joe 90
Hayes, Martin 227
Haynes, Johnny 90, 91, 96, 101, 104, 109, 111, 123, 363
Hazard, Edin 416
Hazledine, Geoff 91
Headington United see Oxford United
Hearts 34, 94, 161, 213, 214, 282, 290, 292, 300, 360, 374, 408
Heath, Adrian 206, 223
Hebberd, Trevor 213, *213*
Hector, Kevin 144, 158
Hedley, George 24
Heighway, Steve 140, 160, *160*, 161, 168, 173
Helmer, Thomas 287
Henderson, Willie 112, 123
Hendon 153
Hendry, Colin 233, 279, 286
Henry, Ron 111
Henry, Thierry 336, 339, *339*, 342, 346, *346*, 348, 349, 350, *350*, 352
Herberger, Sepp 62, 86
Herd, Alex 79
Herd, David 79, 113
Hereford United 94, 142, 144
Herrera, Helenio 109
Herriot, Jim *144*
Hesford, Robert 61
Heskey, Emile 330, 336

INDEX

Hewitt, Joe 22
Hewitt, John 196, 214
Hibbitt, Ken 151
Hibbs, Harry 52, 65
Hibernian 40, 70, 79, 83, 90, 146, 218, 408, 419, *419*
Hickersberger, Josef 244
Hidalgo, Michel 201
Hiddink, Guus 286
Hidegkuti, Nandor 84, 86, 87
Higgins, Alex 28
Highbury 41, 67, 256, *256*
Higuita, Rene 278, 278
Hill, Brian 266
Hill, Gordon 161
Hill, Jimmy 104, 162, 191
Hill, Ricky 227
Hillsborough 36, 47, 414
Hilsdon, George 23
Hinton, Alan 118, 144
Hirst, David 257, 261
Hitchens, Gerry 104, 107, 109
Hockey, Trevor 153
Hoddle, Glenn 186, 189, 222, 257, 266, 274, 282, *282*, 288, 293, 297, 301, 306, *306*, 313, 322, 331, 343, *343*
Hodge, Steve 216, 231, *276*
Hodgson, Roy 407, *407*
Hoeness, Uli 143, 159, 163, 191
Hogan, Jimmy 54
Hogg, Billy 25
Hohberg, Juan 87
Holland 50, 153, 166, 200, 254, 262, 263, 285, 286, 287, 303, 304, 331, 335, 346, 352, 353
Holland, Pat 162, *162*
Holley, George 23, *23*
Holliday, Eddie 102
Hollins, John 134, 141, 143
Holmes, Nick 177
Holton, Cliff 102
Holton, Jim 150
Holzenbein, Bernd 163
Home International Championship *see* International Championship
Home Park 49
Hong Kong 208
Honved 88
Hooliganism/riots 160, 167, *167*, 169, *169*, 266, 273, *273*, 415; Anfield 212; Birmingham death 207; Celtic fans 204, *204;* Continental 222, 255; Cup-Winners' Cup final 145; Dusseldorf 229; Euro 2000 322; Elland Road 139,140; Geoffroy-Guichard Stadium 171; Hampden Park 27; Istanbul 317; Kenilworth Road 183, 205; Luton away fans ban 213, 219; Maine Road 258, *258;* Milk Cup 204; Moenchengladbach 220; Old Trafford 152, 244; Oldham 184; Paris 159, *159;* Peking 208; police veto 240; Rotterdam 153, *153;* St Andrews 252; St James's Park 152; Stamford Bridge 184, 228, *228;* Valley Parade 210, *210*, 219; Wembley 415; *see also* Disasters: Heysel Stadium
Hooper, Gary 419, *419*
Hooper, Mark 58
Hope, Robert 126
Hopkinson, Eddie 102
Houchen, Keith 222, *222*
Houghton, Bob 179
Houghton, Ray 213, 228, *228*, 233, 237, 268
Houllier, Gérard 328–9, 340
Houseman, Peter 134
Houston, Stewart 292
Howard, Pat 153
Howe, Don 98, 140, 271
Howie, Jim 22, 24
Hrubesch, Horst 183, 193
Huddersfield 36, 37, 38, 40, *40*, 41, 44, 45, 49, 52, 59, 61, 83, 95, 148, 228
Hudson, Alan 143, 158, 173
Hufton, Ted 39, 46
Hughes, Emlyn 147, 163, 168, *169*, 176
Hughes, John 124, 124, 133
Hughes, Mark 206, *206*, 208, 211, 231, 240, 244, 248, 257, 266, 273, 291
Hull City 37, 257, 292
Hulme, Joe 52, 54
Hungary *8*, 50, 56, 62, 63, 84, 85, 86, 87, 297
Hunt, Rev. Kenneth 24, 25, *25*
Hunt, Roger 115, 116, *116*
Hunt, Ron 120
Hunter, Archie 10, 26
Hunter, Jack 10
Hunter, John 28
Hunter, Norman 115, 127, 130, 132, 136, 139, 143, 149, 150, 151
Hurst, Geoff 113, *113*, 118, 123, *123*, 128, *128*, 136, 142, 143, 300
Husband, Jim 126, 132
Hutchins, Don 160
Hutchinson, Ian 134
Hutchison, Tommy 150, 154, 186
Hyde 11
Hysen, Glenn 236

Ibrahimovic, Zlatan 412, 419
Ibrox Park 18, 18, 139
Inamoto, Junichi 336
Ince, Paul 240, 260, 263, 266, 271, 272, 274, 283, 288, 297, *297*
Intercontinental Cup 210
Inter-Milan 121, 346
International Board 41, 42, 43, 194, 257, 347
International Championship 10, 11, 19, 23, 31, 32, 49, 60, 73, 183, 200, 201;
International Football Association Board *see* International Board
Inverness Caledonian Thistle 319
Ipswich 106, *106*, 113, 173, 181, 186, 189, 194, 327
Iran 292
Ireland 11, 18, 31, 32, 40, 47, 48; *see also* Northern Ireland, Republic of Ireland
Iremonger, Albert 27
Iriarte, Santos 51
Irish Cup 36
Irvine, Brian 249
Irwin, Denis 266, 266, 331
Isaaksen, Andreas *412*
Israël, Rinus 133, *133*
Italian FA 117
Italy 50, 52, 58, 63, 64, 71, 94, 166, 283, 286, 287, 291, 297, 303, 304, 336, *410*, 412, 413
Ivanovic, Branislav 416, *416*, 418, *418*
Iversen, Steffen 333

Jack, David 39, *39*, 47, *47*, 48, 49, 52, 56, 64, 65
Jackson, Alex 44, *44*, 46, *46*, 48, *48*
Jackson, Darren 248
Jacquet, Aimé 324
Jair 77
Jairzinho 131, 136, *136*, 137
Jamaica 303
James, Alex 46, 49, 52, 53, 54, 59, 64, 65, *65*
James, David 283
Jancker, Carsten 330
Jansen, Wim 300
Japan 62, 303, 332, 336, 337
Jefferies, Jim 161, 300
Jenkins, Ross 194
Jennings, Pat 124, 143, 146, *146*, 153, 158, 173, 178, 184, 198, 206, *206*, 212, *212*, 214, 217
Jensen, John 254, *254*, 272, 273, 278
Jeunesse Hautcharage 144
Jewell, Jimmy 61
John, Bob 43, 53, 54
Johnsen, Erland 266
Johnsen, Ronny 333
Johnson, David 159
Johnson, Terry 172
Johnson, Willie 174, 176, 178, 181, *189*
Johnston, Craig 190, 199, 200, 213
Johnston, Harry 79
Johnston, Maurice ("Mo") 219, 227, 236, *236*, 238
Johnston, Tom 70, 83, *83*
Johnston, Willie 145
Johnstone, Bobby 78, 88, 90
Johnstone, Derek 140, 148, 161, *161*, 167, 172
Johnstone, Jimmy 121, 123, 123, 124, 133, 135, 142
Jol, Martin 374
Jones, Barry 123
Jones, Bryn 64, *64*
Jones, Cliff 111
Jones, Dave 313
Jones, Mark *92*, 93, 95
Jones, Mick 130, 134, *134*, 143, 149, 151
Jones, Peter 307
Jones, Rob 254
Jones, Tom 49
Jones, Vinny 227, 256, *256*
Jonquet, Robert 97
Jordan, Clarrie 68
Jordan, Joe 149, 150, *150*, 154, *154*, 159, 174, 178
Jorginho 269
Josimar 217
Juanito, Juan 196
Jugovic, Vladimir 283
Jules Rimet Trophy 77, 117, *119*
Juninho 279, *279*, 347, *347*
Juskowiak, Erich 97
Juventus 28, 141, 209, 222, 283, 309, 330, 339, 347, 415

Kachloul, Hassan 277
Kahn, Oliver 337
Kamara, Chris 226
Kanchelskis, Andrei 251, 263, 266
Kanoute, Frederic 332
Kanu, Nwankwo 307, *307*
Kavanagh, Graham 332
Kay, Tony 110, 112, 114
Keane, Robbie 318
Keane, Roy 265, 266, 282, 289, 312-13, *313*, 331, 333, 336, 337, 340, 346, 363
Keeble, Vic 89
Keegan, Kevin 9, 144, 146, 147, *147*, 149, 152, *152*, 156, *156*, 158, 159, 160, 161, *161*, 163, *163*, 166, 168, 169, 170, 172, 180, *180*, 183, 187, 188, *189*, 193, 245, 252, *252*, 256, 279, 281, 282, 291, 297, *297*, 308, *308*, 310, 322, 343, 376
Keeley, John 266
Keenor, Fred 40, 43, 48, 49
Kellow, Tony 186
Kelly, Bob 36, 37, 46
Kelly, David 256, 273
Kelly, Eddie 133, 140
Kelly, Graham 232, 249, 252, 271, 306
Kelsey, Jack 83, *83*, 96, 97, 101
Kempes, Mario 175, 182
Kendall, Howard 113, 126, 206, 207, 220
Kennedy, Alan 183, 187, *189*, 190, 193, 200, *200*
Kennedy, Ray 133, 139, 140, 151, 160, 161, 168, 173, 176, *176*, 181, 183, 189, 199
Kenny, Vince 83
Kenyon, Peter 338, 343
Keown, Martin 254, 332, 344
Ker, R.W. 9
Kevan, Derek 96
Kharine, Dimitri 266
Khomich, "Tiger" 67
Kick-offs 43
Kidd, Albert 213, *213*
Kidd, Brian 127, *127*, 132, *293*
Kidd, Walter 214, *214*
Kidderminster Harriers 266
Kilcline, Brian 222
Kilmarnock 34, 36, 47, 113
Kindvall, Ove 133
King, Ian 103
King, Phil 239
Kingis Park 49
Kinnaird, Hon. A.F. (Lord) 12,*12*, 26, *26*, 29
Kinsey, Noel 90
Kirk, Steve 248, *248*
Kirke-Smith, A.S. 9
Kirton, Bill 36
Klinsmann, Jürgen 243, 270, *270*, 286, 287
Klose, Miroslav 336
Kluivert, Patrick 280, *280*, 287, 305
Knighton, Michael 237, *237*, 310
Kocsis, Sandor 84, *85*, 86, 87, 88, 100, 104
Koeman, Ronald 248, 262, *262*
Köhler, Jürgen 283
Kohlmeyer, Werner 87
Kompany, Vincent 404
Kopa, Raymond 97, 103, 112
Köpke, Andreas 287
Korea 332, 336
Kouba, Petr 286
Krankl, Hans 207
Kress, Richard 103
Krisp, Thomas 220
Krol, Ruud 175
Kubala, Ladislao 84
Kuipers, Bjorn *410*, 412
Kumar, Samesh 252
Kuntz, Stefan 286, 287
Kyle, Bob 44

La Ronde, Everald 198
Labone, Brian 110, 126
Lacy, John 176
Lahm, Philipp 413
Lalas, Alexi 262
Lama, Bernard 287
Lambert, Jack 49, 52, 54
Lambert, Raoul 163
Lambert, Paul 333, 334
Lampard, Frank Sr 162
Lampard, Frank 334, 352, 353, 407, 419
Lancashire Region 35
Langenus, John 51
Langland, Johnny 28
Langley, Jim 120
Langton, Bobby 69
Large, Frank 132
Larsen, Henrik 254
Larsson, Henrik 333, 349, *349*, 352
Latchford, Bob 166
Latvia 62, 346, 352
Laudrup, Brian 254, 282, 417
"Laughing Cavalier" *see* Jackson, Alex
Law, Denis 98, 104, 107, 111, 112, *112*, 116, 124, 128, 132, 147, 150, 151, 152, *154*, 160, 220, 245
Lawler, Chris 149
Lawless, Scott 415
Lawrenson, Mark *189*, 190, 199, 214
Lawrie, Bobby 142
Lawton, Tommy 64, 65, 66, *66*, 69, 70, *70*, 71, 100
Layne, David "Bronco" 112, 114
Lazarus, Mark 120
Lazio 246, 253, 322, 330
Le Saux, Graham 273, 279
Le Tissier, Matthew 251, 289
Leadbetter, Jimmy 106
League Championship 29, *29*, 31, 33, 139, 144, 147, 151, 158, *158*, 160, 172, 185, 190, 214, 333, 342, 349
League Cup 104, 120, 129, *129*, 134, 142, 143, 151, 160, 177 first winners 11; replay 166, 172, 185 *see also* Capital One Cup; Coca- Cola Cup; Littlewoods Cup; Milk Cup; Rumbelows Cup; Worthington Cup
Lee, Colin 172
Lee, Francis 123, 134, 136, 143, 158
Lee, Robert 270, 281
Lee, Sammy 183, *189*, 199
Leeds City 33, 36, 37, 38, 53
Leeds United 37, 44, 94, 113, 117, 130, 132, 133, 134, *134*, 138, 139, 140, 141, 143, 144, 148, 149, 151, 156, 157, 159, 170, 178, 207, 219, 226, 253, 256, 280, 332, 338, 339, 341, 342, 368
Legg, Andy 332
Leicester City 37, 39, 41, 47, 49, 53, 61, 72, 73, 130, 180, 186, 307, 315, 349
Leicester Fosse 25
Leighton, Jim 196, 238, 240, *240*
Leith 33
Lennon, Neil 418, 419
Lennox, Bobby 132, 133
Lentini, Gianluigi 256
Leonardo 269
Leonidas da Silva 62, 63
Lewis, Dan 43, *43*
Lewis, Reg 75, *75*
Leyton Orient 83, 290, 409
Liddell, Billy 75, 78, 100
Liedholm, Nils 97
Lievesley, Leslie 73
Limpar, Anders 245, 247, *247*, 275
Lincoln City 37, 93
Lincoln, Dean of 34
Lindsay, Alex 147
Lineker, Gary 203, *203*, 213, 216, *217*, 218, *218*, 224, *224*, 228, 233, 235, 242, 243, 246, 249, 250, 251, *251*, 254, *254*, 255
Linesmen 43, 411
Linighan, Andy 261, 261
"Lion of Vienna" *see* Lofthouse, Nat
Lipton Cup 22
Lishman, Doug 80, *80*, 82
Lister, Bert 128
Littbarski, Pierre 193
Little, Brian 166, *166*, 280
Littlewoods Cup 221, 227, 231, 239
Livermore, Doug 250
Liverpool 17, 20, 22, *22*, 23, *23*, 32, 34, 38, 39, 68, 69, 73, 113, 116, *116*, 140, 147, 149, 152, 156, 160, 161, 163, 168, 170, 172, 173, 176, 178, 181, 183, 186, 187, 189, *189*, 190, 193, 197, 198, 209, 210, 212, 214, 215, 221, 226, 227, 232, 233, 234, 236, 239, 243, 247, 253, 255, 261, 264, 274, 280, 291, *291*, 296, 323, 326, 328–9, 339, 340, 341, 342, 356, 358, 359, 405, 406, 408, *408*, 416
Lloyd, Larry 147, 149, *149*, 176, 183
Ljungberg, Freddie 334, *334*, 335
Lofthouse, Nat 81, *81*, 83, 89, 94, *94*, 100
Loftus, Christopher 317
Logan, Jimmy 13, *13*, 73, 80, 82, *82*, 83, 101
Long Eaton 177
Longson, Sam 146
Lorimer, Peter 130, 144, 147, 148, *148*, 149, 157, 159
Loughborough Town 16
Love, James 14
Lovenkrands, Peter, 334, *334*
Lukic, John 221, 233, 280
Luton Town 59, 60, 99, 111, 160, 183, 197, 203, 213, 219, 227, 231, 413
Luxembourg 43
Lyall, John 171, 182
Lyderson, Pal 278
Lynch, Andy 167
Lyons, Mick 166

Mabbutt, Gary 222, 251
Macari, Lou 144, 161, 168, *168*, 169
Macauley, Archie 99
MacDonald, Alex 161, 172
MacDonald, John 190
Macdonald, Malcolm 142, 148, 158, *158*, 188, *188*, 228
MacDougall, Ted 144
Macedonia 331
Machado 63
Mackay, Dave 107, 111, 113, 114, 121, *121*, 123, 129, 131, 158
Mackenzie, John 180
MacKenzie, Steve 186
MacLeod, Ally 174
Madeley, Paul 130, 141, 149, 166
Madjer, Rabah 223
"Magic Magyars" *see* Hungary
Mahoney, John 138, 138
Maier, Sepp 159, 163, 163
Maine Road 37
Maldini, Paolo 269
Maldives 292
Male, George 63
Maley, Tom 20
Maley, Willie 20
Malmö 179
Malone, Dick *163*
Malpas, Maurice 238
Malta 200
Managers 294-5, 417
Manchester City 20, 29, *29*, 33, 37, 43, 44, 45, 54, *54*, 55, 60, 61, 63, 66, 88, 90, 96, 98, 104, 125, 134, 151, 152, 186, 197, 228, 258, *258*, 311, 322, 323, 343, 346, 404, *404*, 405, 413, 418
Manchester United 9, 24, 25, 29, *29*, 34, 36, 40, 70, *70*, 72, 78, 80, 83, 89, 91, 92, *92*, 93, 94, 95, 99, 111, 113, 116, 125, 126, 127, 128, 132, 147, 152, 161, 168, 171, 172, 178, 193, 198, 200, 208, 210, 212, 218, 220, 226, 237, 240, 244, 245, 246, 247, 248, 251, 253, 260, 263, 264, 265, 266, 271, 274, 275, 282, *282*, 289, 292, *292*, 298, 299, 306, 308, 309, 310, 311, 313, 319, 322, 323, 324, 330, 331, 333, 333, 338, 339, 340, 341, 342, 343, 344, 349, 355, 372, 378, 380, 380, 404, 406, 414, *414*, 416, 418, *418*
Mancini, Roberto 404, 417
Mandaric, Milan 407
Mangnall, Dave 60
Manjarin, Javier 287
Mann, Micky 180
Mannion, Wilf 69, *69*, 71, 73, 76, 78, *78*, 101, 313
Maradona incident 218; referee ruling 255
Maradona, Diego 192, 216, 217, 218, *218*, 224, *224*, 242, 43, 248, 268
Marcio Santos 269
Marindin, Captain 28
Mariner, Paul 173, 186, 188, 189
Marsh, Rodney 120, *120*, 151
Martin, Alvin 188
Martin, Con 74
Martin, Lee *240*
Martin, Norrie 120
Martinez, Roberto 413, *413*
Martyn, Nigel 239, 240, 332
Maschio, Humberto 108
Mason, Jim 73
Masopust, Josef 109, 114
Maspoli, Roque 77, *77*
Massaro, Daniele 267, 269
Massie, Alex 63
Masson, Don 169, 171, *171*, 174
Match fixing 34
Matthaus, Lothar 198, 216, 243, 304
Matthews, Sir Stanley 8, 58, 60, 61, 64, 65, *65*, 66, 67, 69, 70, 71, 74, 76, 78, 79, 82, *82*, 84, *85*, *86*, 89, 91, 94, 100, *101*, 107, *107*, 111, *111*, 114, *114*, 122, *122*, 274, 313
Maxwell, Ally 248, 267
Maxwell, Robert 200, 203, 250, 261
Mazurkiewicz, Ladislao 137
Mazzola, Valentino 71, 73
McAllister, Gary 253, 286, 312, 323, 326
McAteer, Jason 274, 281, 331, *331*
McAvennie, Frank 226
McCall, Stuart 233, 267
McCalliog, Jim 117, 143, 161
McCann, Neil 290, 334
McCarthy 331, 336
McClair, Brian 219, 251, 266
McClaren, Steve 363, 368, 373
McLeish, Alex 334
McCloy, Peter 143
McCluskey, George 218
McCluskey, Pat 160, 179
McCoist, Ally 238, *238*, 283, 287, 290, *290*, 419
McColl, R.S. (Bob) 14, 16, 21
McCombie, Andrew 19
McCormick, Jimmy 89
McCracken, Bill 60
McCreadie, Eddie *111*, 117
McDermott, Terry 168, 172, 173, 176, 183, 187, 189, 190
McDonald, Colin 96
McDougall, Frank 203
McDowell, John 162
McDowell, Les 90
McFadyen, Bill 53
McFarland, Roy 144, 158
McFaul, Iam 142, *142*, 150
McGhee, Mark 190, 196, 203
McGiven, Alec 323
McGinlay, John 290
McGinley, Billy 160
McGovern, John 157, 172, 176, 177, 179, 193
McGrain, Danny 150, 169, 179
McGrath, Mick 102, *102*
McGrath, Paul 208, 222, *226*, 256, 280
McGrory, Jimmy 41, 43, 46, 48, 52, 63
McGuinness, Wilf 170, 260
McIlroy, Jimmy 96, 103, 122
McIlroy, Sammy 178
McIlvenny, Eddie 76
McKay, Derek 133
McKenzie, Duncan 162
McLaren, Andy 267
McLaughlin, J.H. 15
McLean, Jim 180, 196, 196, 248
McLean, Tommy 161, 248
McLeish, Alex 190, *196*, 211
McLeod, Murdo 179
McLintock, Frank 138, 139, 140, 144
McMahon, Steve 221, 226, 227, 236, 239
McManaman, Callum 413
McManaman, Steve 253, *274*, 283, 287, 296
McMenemy, Jimmy 29
McMenemy, Lawrie 161, 171, 180, *180*, 222, *222*
McMullan, Jimmy 46, *46*
McNab, Bob 133, 140, 143
McNaught, Ken 191
McNeill, Billy 133, 142, 144, 237
McParland, Peter 93, *93*, 96, 97, *97*
McPhail, Billy 95
McPhail, Bob 46, 60, 63
McPherson, Dave 267, 267
McQuade, Denis 142
McQueen, Gordon 151, 169, 172, 178, 193
McQueen, Tommy 203
McStay, Paul 272
McStay, Willie 46
McWilliam, Peter 21, 22, 37
Meadows, Jimmy 89
Mears, Brian 167
Meazza, Guiseppe 57, 58, 63
Medwin, Terry 97, 98, 103, 107
Mee, Bertie 140
Meiklejohn, David 46, 48
Meisl, Hugo 54
Melchior, Ernst 79, 81
Melchiot, Mario 333
Mellor, Peter 158
Melrose, James 226
Mendonca, Clive 256
Meola, Tony 262
Mercer, Joe 64, 66, *66*, 74, 75, *75*, 80, 82, 101, 123, 123, 152
Meredith, Billy 20, 20, 23, 24, 26, 29
Merrick, Gil 81, 84, 85, 86, 90
Merson, Paul 243, *243*, 259, 261, 262, 271, *271*, 274
Merthyr Town 37
Metcalfe, Vic 83
Mexico 50, 51, 62, 131
Michels, Rinus 229
Middleboe, Nils 30
Middlesbrough 33, 43, 153, 167, 279, *279*, 292, 293, 347, 358
Middleton, Ray 91
Midland Region 35
"Mighty Atom" see Gallagher, Patsy
Mijatovic, Predrag 297
Mikel, John Obi 416, *416*
Milburn, Jackie 68, 73, 76, 79, *79*, 80, 88, *88*, 100
Milk Cup 189, *189*, 199, 203, 213
Milla, Roger 192, 229, 243
Millar, James 112
Millar, Jimmy 18, 27
Miller, Joe 233
Miller, Tommy 34
Miller, Willie 196, *200*, *203*, 211
Millennium Stadium 326
Millichip, Bert 203, 207, 219, 221, 249
Mills, Danny 337
Mills, David 177, 183

Millwall 37, 46, 60, 205, 266, 338, 349, 415, *415*
Milosevic, Savo 280
Milton, Arthur 81
Milton Keynes Dons 376
Mimms, Bobby 230
Minotte, Lorenzo 265
Minter, Billy 39
Mitchell, Bobby 79, 80, 88
Mitchell, J.F. 39
Mitic, Rajko 76
Mitten, Charlie 70
Mobley, Vic 117
Mochan, Neil 95
Molby, Jan 214, 215, *215*, 221, 227
Moldova 288
Möller, Andreas 287
Moncur, Bobby 131, *131*
Montgomery, Jim 128, *128*, 148, *148*
Monti, Luisito 51, 56, 58
Montpellier 246
Moore, Bobby 115, 118, 119, *119*, 123, *123*, 135, 136, *137*, 142, *142*, 147, 158, *158*, 167, 258, *258*, 270
Moore, Brian 330
Moores, David 264
Moran, Doug "Dixie" 106
Moran, Kevin 195, 208, *208*
Moran, Ronnie 245, 247
Mordue, Jackie 31
Morgan, Charlie 416
Morgan, Richie 125, 128
Morgan, Roger 120, *120*
Morgan, Trevor 198
Morgan, Willie 150
Morgans, Ken 94
Morientes, Fernando 337
Morley, Haydn 12
Morley, Tony 185, 191
Morlock, Max 87
Morris, Fred 36
Morris, Johnny 70, 72
Morrissey, John 126, 132
Morrow, Steve 259, *259*, 265, *265*
Mortensen, Stan 66, 67, 69, 70, 71, *71*, 74, 75, 78, 79, *79*, 82, 84, 100
Mortimer, Dennis 185, 191
Morton 31, 70, 72
Morton, Alan 46, 48, 65
Morton, Harry 59
Moscow Dynamo 67, *67*
Moscow Spartak 88
Moscow Torpedo 125
Moseley, Graham 197
Moses, Remi 190
Moss, Frank 58, *58*
Motherwell 34, 52, 53, 54, 79, 248
Mountfield, Derek 206
Mourinho, Jose 354, 354, 355, 355, 374
Moyes, David 339
Mozley, Bert 74
Muamba, Fabrice 408, *408*
Mudie, Jackie 82
Muhren, Arnold 197, 229
Mullen, Jimmy 76, 84, 101
Muller, Dieter 163
Muller, Gerd 136, 143, 153, *153*, 159
Mullery, Alan 112, 121, 127, 136, 143, 158
Munich 1860 113
Munro, Francis 144, *144*, 151, 220
Munson, Nathan 266
Munteanu, Dorinel 285
Murdoch, Bobby 121, 133, *133*, 135, 323
Murdoch, Rupert 308
Murphy, Jimmy 94
Murphy, Peter 90
Mussi, Roberto 269
Mutch, George 61, *61*

NAC Breda 125
Nanninga, Dirk 175
Nani 418, *418*
Napoli 222
Narey, David 192
Nasazzi, José *50*, 51
National Football Centre 322
National Footballers' War Fund 35
National Membership Scheme 238
Nations Cup see European Football Championships
Nayim 258, 275
Neal, Phil 163, 168, *169*, 187, *189*, 198, 199, 200
Nedved, Pavel 353
Needham, David 181, *181*
Needham, Ernest "Nudger" 13, 26-7
Neeskens, Johan *154*, 155, 166
Negri, Marco 300
Neighbour, Jimmy 185
Neill, Terry 178, 198
Nejedly, Oldrich 57, 63
Nelson, Sammy 177, *177*
Nethercott, Ken 99
Netherlands *see* Holland
Netzer, Günter 143, 149
Neville, Gary 286, 287, 331, 333
Neville, Philip 282
Neuville, Oliver 333, 336
Newcastle United 19, 21, 23, 25, 28, 29, 37, 39, 41, 44, 45, 53, 68, 70, 72, 79, 80, 88, 91, 94,113, 121, 131, 142, 153, 252, 256, 270, 272, 280, 291, 296, 298, 301, 314, 322, 342
Newell, Mike 255, 372
Newport County 68, 140
Newton, Eddie 266, 266
Newton, Keith 136
Nicholas, Charlie 198, 211, 219, 221, *221*, 272
Nicholl, Chris 162, 166, 171, 177
Nicholson, Bill 78, 98, 105, 106, 112, 121, 153, 157, *157*
Nicol, Steve 200, 236
Nielsen, Allan 307
Nielson, Sophus 27
Nielson, Torkil 244
Nigeria 292, 303, 336
NiKono, Thomas 192
Ninian Park 332
Nilsson, Lennard 223
Nish, David 148
Nistelrooy, Ruud van 318, 322, 331, *331*, 341, 342, 344, 346, 349, 350
Niven, George 83
Norris, Sir Henry 36, 46
North, Mike 325
Northampton 55, 130, 132, 266
Northern Ireland 49, 75, 94, 113, 140, 183, 188, 198, 202, 237, 358 *see also* Great Britain
Norway 62, 238, 302
Norwich City 33, 66, 85, 99, 160, 205, 207, 208, 210, 236, 413
Nottingham Forest *34*, 35, 40, 72, 98, 130, 172, 177, 178, 181, 183, 231, 232, 249, 259, 262, 306
Notts County 13, 39, 44, 70, *70*, 153, 199, 271
Numbered shirts 47, 54, *54*
Nyberg, Arne 63

Ocwirk, Ernst 81
O'Connell, Seamus 89
O'Donnell, Frank 60
O'Donnell, Phil 374
O'Farrell, Frank 147, 170, 260
O'Grady, Mike 130
O'Hare, John 144, 157, 172
O'Leary, David 178, 234, *242*, 243, 245, 332, 341
O'Neill, Martin 179, 183, 327
O'Reilly, Gary 239, 240
O'Rourke, Jim 146
Okocha, Augustine "Jay Jay" *303*, 304
Olarticoechea, Julio 243
Old Etonians 9, 10, 14
Old Trafford 29, 37, 332
Oldham Athletic 33, 37, 38, 40, 59, 239, 240, 263
Olsen, Morten 198, 200
Olympic Games football 25, 30, 50, 406, *406*
Olympic Stadium, Berlin 61, *61*
Olympique Marseille 236, 266
"Operation Own Goal" *222*
Ormond, Willie 147, 154
Orsi, Raimondo 57
Osborne, Roger 173
Osgood, Peter 134, 141, 143, 144, 161
Ostenstad, Egil 289, *289*
Ottaway, C.J. 9
Overmars, Marc 277, 299, 301, *301*, 307, *307*, 309
Owairan, Saeed 269
Owen, Michael 300, 303, 304, *312*, 313, 330, *330*, 334, 336, 337, 340, 344, 352, 361, 364
Owen, Syd 98
Oxford United 113, 198, 205, 213, 361

Paddon, Graham 158
Pagliuca, Gianluca 269
Paine, Terry 112, 118, 169, *169*, 353
Paisley, Bob 160, 168, 170, 173, 176, 181, 188, 190, 195, 199, 214, 245, 247, 295
Pak Doo Ik 118
Palethorpe, Jack 58, 59
Pallister, Gary 262, 266
Palmer, Carlton 259, 262
Palmer, Geoff 151
Panenka, Antonin *163*
Paphitis, Theo 338
Papin, Jean-Pierre 254
Paraguay 216, 217, 336
Pardew, Alan 235, 239
Parker, Garry 249
Parkes, Phil 144
Parkes, Phil B. 185
Parkinson, Jack 22, *22*
Parkinson, Phil 417
Parks, Tony 200, *200*
Parlane, Derek 148, 167
Parlour, Ray 277, 301, 334, 335
Parma 265
Parry, Rick 252
Partick Thistle 37, 142, 335
Partizan Belgrade 208, 237
Paulinho 91
Payne, Joe 59, *59*, 60, 63
Peacock, Alan 109
Peacock, Gavin 266
Peacock, Keith 117
Pearce, Stuart 243, 249, 254, 263, 285, 286, 287
Pearson, Stan 70, 80
Pearson, Stuart 168, 182
Pegasus 78, *78*
Pegg, David 92, 92, 94, 95
Pele 96, *96*, 97, 99, 108, 118, 131, 133, *133*, 136, *136*, 137, *137*, 154, 155, 171, 185, 201, 224
penalty-kicks 43
Pennington, Jesse 27, 29
Pentland, Fred 47
Perry, Bill 82
Perryman, Steve 145, 271
Peru 51
Peterborough United 104, 310
Peterhead 419
Peters, Jan 166
Peters, Martin *115*, 118, 119, 123, *123*, 124, 135, 136, 143, 145, 147, 150, 160
Petersen, John 338, *338*
Petit, Emmanuel *302*, 334
Petrie, John 11
Petrov, Stilyan 409
Pettigrew, Willie 180
Peucelle, Carlos 51
Pfaff, Alfred 103, *223*
Phelan, Terry 240, 258, 269
Phillips, Ted 106, *206*, 211, 213
Pickering, Fred 117
Pickles (the dog) 117, *117*
Pierce, Gary 151
Pike, Geoff 182, *183*
Pimenta, Ademar 63
Piola, Silvio 62, 63, 64
Pires, Robert 336, 350
Pirlo, Andrea 413
Pitch invasions *see* Hooliganism/riots
Planicka, Frantisek 57, 63
Platini, Michel 193, *193*, 201, 210, *210*, 217, 224, 370
Platt, David 242, 250, 254, 258, 262, *262*, 278, *278*, 282
Players' strike 253
Players' Union 27
Pleat, David 223
Plymouth 49, 153, 167, 200, 257
Poborsky, Karel 283, 287
Pointer, Ray 103
Poland 62, 150, 233, 262, 263, 293, 308, 336, 410
Poll, Graham 370
Poole, Kevin 409
Port Vale 36, 83, *83*, 225, *225*
Porterfield, Ian 148
Porto 171, 223, *223*, 342
Portsmouth 37, 43, 47, 53, 61, 64, 72, *72*, 74, 91, 182, 186, 362, 377
Portugal 47, 69, 331, 336, 352–3
Potter, Fred 142
Potts, Harry 68, 103
Powell, Barry 181
Powell, Ivor 66
Poyet, Gus 331
Pozzo, Vittorio 57, *57*, 58, 63
Preedy, Charlie 49
Premier League 253, 255, 256, 333
Pressman, Kevin 323
Preston 11, *13*, 32, 36, 38, 43, 60, 61, 113, 133, 266
Price, David 178
Price, Owen 318
Priest, Fred 13
Professional Footballers Association (PFA) 104
Professionalism 14-15
Prosser, Neil 180
PSV Eindhoven 249, 322
Puc, Antonin 57, *57*, 63
Purcell, Bob 34
Purnell, C.H. 25
Puskas, Ferenc 84, *84*, 85, 87, 88, 100, *100*, 103, 106, 109, 112, 114, *114*, 330
Pye, Jesse 73, *73*, 74, 91
Pym, Dick 47

Queen of the South 83
Queen's Park 8, 15, 41
Queen's Park Rangers 25, 37, 38, 94, 120, 125, 206, 208, 213, 221, 272, 322, 404, 406
Quigley, Eddie 167
Quinn, Jimmy 20, 23, 27, 52
Quinn, Niall 221
Quinton, Sir John 252
Quixall, Albert 99

Racing Club (Argentina) 124
Radford, John 133, *133*, 139, 140, 143
Radford, Ron 142
Rae, Alex 142
Rahn, Helmut 87, *87*
Raisbeck, Alec 17, *17*, 22, 28
Raith 34, 61, 72, *272*
Ramires 405
Ramsey, Chris 197
Ramsey, Sir Alf 73, 76, 78, 79, 81, *81*, 84, 106, 107, 110, 118, 121, 131, 136, 143, 146, 147, 150, 152, *152*, 156, 310
Rangers 13, 16, 17, 20, *20*, 21, 23, 31, 34, 35, 36, 37, 38, 40, 41, 43, 46, 47, 53, 54, 55, 58, 64, 66, 67, 70, 72, 75, 79, 83, 95, 103, 107, 112, 120, 121, 123, 139, 140, 144, 145, 148, 161, 167, 172, 179, 190, 197, 212, 218, 219, 220, 228, 233, 236, 266, 267, *267*, 281, 282, 290, 292, 300, 311, 333, 334, 335, 342, *342*, 360, 378, 409, 419
Ranieri, Claudio 322
Rapid Vienna 204, 207
Ratcliffe, Kevin 206, 208
Rattin, Antonio 118, 208
Ravanelli, Fabrizio 277, 283
Raybould, Alec 22
Raynor, George 77, 97
Reader, George *77*
Reading 214, 362
Real Madrid 90, 92, 102, 104, 126, 141, 162, 187, 196, 322, 330, 335, 341, 343
Real Sociedad 236
Real Zaragoza 275
Reaney, Paul 130, 132, *138*, 143, *144*, 148
Rebrov, Sergei 333, *333*
Red cards 306
Redknapp, Harry 322, 362, 377, 407
Redknapp, Jamie 275, 286
Rees, Mark 198
Referees 43
Rehhagel, Otto 353
Reid, Peter 199, 206, 208, 213, 216
Reid, Sammy 120
Reilly, Lawrie 73, 78, 100
Reims 90
Rendell, Scott 413
Rensenbrink, Robert 162, 175
Renton 11
Rep, Johnny 175, 186
Republic of Ireland 62, 74, 225, 228, *228*, 237, 251, 331, 336–7, 412
Rest of Europe 84
Rest of the UK 81
Rest of the World XI 112
Revie, Don 73, 89, 113, 130, 139, 147, 151, 156, 157, 158, 159, 166, 170, *170*, 174, 178, 180, *180*, 233
Rice, Pat 140, 144
Richards, Dean 331
Richards, John 151, *151*, 181
Richardson, Billy "G." 54
Richardson, Jimmy G. 55
Richardson, Kevin 199, 263
Rideout, Paul 273
Rijkaard, Frank 234, 243, 254, 262
Rimet, Jules 50, 51 *see also* Jules Rimet Trophy
Rimmer, Ellis 49, 58
Rimmer, Jimmy 191
Rioch, Bruce 158, 274, 278, *278*
Ritchie, Andy 239, *239*
Ritchie, John 138, 143, 172
Riva, Luigi 136
Rivaldo 304, 305
Rivelino 137
Rivera, Gianni 136, 137
Rix, Graham 173, 178, 181, *182*
Robb, George 98
Robben, Arjen 405
Robert, Christophe 266
Roberto 63
Roberts, Charlie 24, *24*, 27, 29
Roberts, Graham 189, *189*, 190, 200, 226
Roberts, Tony 272
Robertson, David 281
Robertson, Jimmy 121
Robertson, John 172, *172*, 179, 183, *183*
Robertson, Sandy 11
Robinson, Bill 68, 72
Robinson, Paul 339
Robledo, George 79, 80
Robson, "Pop" 162
Robson, Bobby 104, 171, 194, *194*, 201, 204, *204*, 210, 216, *216*, 219, 225, 229, 249, *249*, 263, 314, 333
Robson, Bryan 188, 190, 192, *192*, 197, 198, 202, 204, 216, 219, 224, *224*, 225, 226, 240, 244, 246, 248, *248*, *251*, 251, *260*, 260, 263, 278, 279, *279*, *312*, *322*
Robson, Jim 103
Rocastle, David 221, 227, 251
Rocheteau, Dominique 193, 210
Rogan, Anton 249
Rogers, Don 129
Roma 117
Romania 50, 51, 283, 302-3, 304
Romario 267, 268, 269, 271
Rome 297, 339
Ronaldo 300, 303, 337, *337*, 341, 353
Ronaldo, Cristiano 412
Rooke, Ronnie 67, 71
Rooney, Wayne 339, *339*, 344, *344*, 351, *351*, 352, *352*
Roper, Don 80
Rose Bowl, Pasadena 268
Rosebery, Lord 16
Rosenthal, Ronnie 273
Ross, James 59
Ross, Jimmy 11
Rossi, Paolo 182, 192, *192*
Rossi, Sebastiano 267
Rotherham 49
Rothlisberger, Kurt 263
Rough, Allan 174
Rougvie, Doug 205
Rous Cup 208, 223
Rous, Sir Stanley 55, 153, 154
Rowe, Arthur 78
Rowley, Arthur 83, 113
Rowley, Jack 70, 70, 72, 80
Royal Engineers 8, *8*, 9
Royle, Joe 132, 274, 322
Ruddock, Neil 225
Ruffell, Jimmy 39
Rules: away goals 220 card system: abolished 169, 186; corner-kicks 41, *41* end-of-season play-offs; 235; experimental 194; goal average/difference 140, 162; goalkeeping 125; goalline technology 419; handball controversy 195; kick-in 257; offside 41, *41*, 44, 48, 130, 178, 274; pitch laws 19; points system 184; "professional foul" 191; promotion/relegation system 153, 248; referee/ball contact 190; substitutes 223
Rumbelows Cup 244, 245, 247
Rummenigge, Karl-Heinz 191, 192, 193, 198, 217
Rush, Ian 183, 189, *189*, 190, 199, 203, *203*, 206, 211, 215, 221, 230, *230*, 233, *233*, 234, 236, 239, 248, 250, 255, 281, 300
Russell, David 11
Russell, Moses 40
Russell, Robert 172, 179
Russia 346, 352, 410
Rutherford, Jack 21, 53
Ryan, Gerry 197
Ryan, Johnny 95
Ryden, John 98
Ryles, Rob 332

Sabanadzovic, Refik 243
Sacchi, Arrigo 286
Sadler, David 126, *126*
Sagar, Ted 83, *83*
St Albans City 39
St Andrews, Birmingham 110, *110*
St Etienne 162, 171
St James's Park 43
St John, Ian 102, 113, *113*, 116, 143, 188
St Johnstone 132
Salako, John 240
Salas, Marcelo 303
Salenko, Oleg 269
Salinas, Julio 287
Samaras, Giorgos 413
Sammels, John 133
Sammer, Matthias 287
Sampaio, Cesar *302*
Sampdoria 222
Samways, Vinny 246
San Marino 262, 263
Sanchez, Lawrie 227
Sanchez, Leonel 108
Sandford, Ted 58
Sansom, Kenny 184
Santamaria, Jose 103
Santos, Djalma 109, 112
Sarosi, Gyorgy 63
Sarti, Giuliano 121
Saudi Arabia 162, 336
Saul, Frank 117
Saunders, Dean 250, 263
Saunders, Ron *183*, 191
Savicevic, Dejan 267
Scanlon, Albert 94
Scarborough 223, 310
Schaefer, Hans 87
Schalke 04 134
Schiaffino, Juan 77, 87
Schiavio, Angelo 56, *56*, 57
Schillaci, "Toto" 242, 243
Schlosa, Claudio 257
Schmeichel, Peter 254, 263, 266, 271, 272, *277*, 286, 309, *309*, 311
Schneider, Bernd 333
Schnellinger, Karl-Heinz 137
Schoen, Helmut 155
Scholar, Irving 223
Scholes, Paul 282, 283, 308, *308*, 330–1, 409
Scholl, Mehmet 287
Schroif, Wilheim 109
Schumacher, Harald 193, 217
Schuster, Bernd 183
Schweinsteiger, Bastian 405
Scolari, Phil 353
Scorey, Constable 39, *39*
Scotland *8*, 9, *9*, 10, 11, 16, 17, 18, 19, 34, 36, 40, 43, 46, *46*, 47, 48, 49, 52, 53, 54, 60, 66, *66*, 73, 74, 75, 78, 79, 88, 89, 98, 104, 107, 121, 124, 133, 147, 150, 169, 171, 202, 208, 238, 255, 283, 286, 292, 302, 333, 338, 346
Scott, Alex 110
Scott, Elisha 38, *38*, 71
Scottish "treble" 72, 112, 129, 161
Scottish Coca-Cola Cup 290
Scottish FA Cup 11, 16, 17, 20, *20*, 23, 24, 28, 31, 36, 41, 54, 60, 61, 72, 79, 83, 120, 129, 133, 148, 161, 167, 172, 190, 197, 200, 211, 214, 300, 311, 333, 342, 349, 408, 419, *419* *see also* Tennents Cup
Scottish Football Association 9
Scottish League 36; founded 17; founding clubs 13
Scottish League 40, 44, 342, 419
Scottish League Championship 16
Scottish League Cup 95, 131, 142, 146, 161 replay 180 *see also* Skol Cup
Scottish Premier League: 161, 408, 419
Scoular, Jimmy 88, 123
Scunthorpe 94, 133
Sealey, Alan 113, *113*
Sealey, Les 231, *231*, 248, 263
Seaman, David 244, 246, 247, 262, 273, *273*, 286, *286*, 287, 330, 336, 339
Seed, Jimmy 37, 47, *47*
Seedorf, Clarence 287
Seeldrayer, Rudolphe 50
Seeler, Uwe 136
Segers, Hans 274, 278
Sellars, Scott 270
Selley, Ian 263
Sendings off 306, 314
Senegal 336
Sewell, John 81, 84, 85
Sexton, Dave 220, 260, 419
Shackleton, Len 68, 68, 70, 72,101, 323
Shankly, Bill 116, 147, 152, 156, *156*, 188, *188*, 199, 245, 295
Sharp, Graeme 199, 206, 207, 208, 215, 225
Sharpe, Lee 244, *244*, 260, 263
Shaw, Frank 13
Shaw, Graham 161, 183
Shearer, Alan 228, 251, 254, 257, *273*, 282, 283, 286, 288, *288*, 293, *293*, 301, 313, *313*, 318, 322, 351
Sheedy, Kevin 206, 207, 236
Sheffield Association 43
Sheffield FC 20
Sheffield United 13, 17, *17*, 18, 33, 37, 43, 47, 59, 68, 307, *307*
Sheffield Wednesday 12, 39, 47, 53, 55, 58, 78, 83, 104, 117, 133, 240, 247, 259, 261, 274
Shelbourne 36
Sheldon, Jackie 34
Shepherd, Albert 28, *28*
Shepherd, Freddy 298, *298*
Shepperd, Bill 54
Sheridan, John 247, 259
Sheringham, Teddy 262, 273, 286, 293, 311, 332, 333, 377
Sheron, Mike 258
Sherwood, Steve 199, *199*

INDEX

Sherwood, Tim 333
Shevchenko, Andriy 410, *412*
Shilton, Peter 150, 172, 176, 181, *181*, 183, 202, 203, 216, 233, 235, 243, 257, 290, *290*
Shimwell, Eddie 70
Shreeves, Peter 225
Shrewsbury 205
Sillett, John 222
Silva, David 413
Silvestre, Mikael 331, 335, 352
Simeone, Diego 304
Simmons, Dave 138
Simonsen, Allan 198, *198*
Simpson, Jimmy 65
Simpson, Neal 196, 230
Simpson, Ronnie 124
Sinclair, Frank 266
Sindelar, Matthias 54
Sinton, Andy 254, 262
Sissons, John 113
Sivebaek, John 254
Skinner, Bobby 48
Skol Cup 208, 219, 228
"Slavery" contract 104
Smart, Roger 129
Smicer, Vladimir 287
Smith, Alan (Arsenal) 234, 244, 245, 246, 247, 250, *250*, 251, 254, 261, 265
Smith, Alan (Leeds) 332
Smith, Alec 26
Smith, Billy 38, 41, 49
Smith, Bobby 98, 104, 105, *105*, 110, 113
Smith, Denis 138
Smith, G.O. *13*, 26
Smith, Gordon 197
Smith, Graham 138
Smith, Jack 39
Smith, Jim 46
Smith, Joe 48
Smith, Leslie 88
Smith, Mr H. 33
Smith, Tommy 115, 116, 146, *146*, 152, 168, *168*
Smith, Walter 281
Smyth, Sammy 73
Snelders, Theo 249, *249*
"Soccer – The Fight for Survival" 184
Socrates 192, 217
Solskjaer, Ole Gunnar 306, 311, *311*, 333
Somers, Peter 27
Song, Rigobert 304
Souness, Graeme 173, 174, *189*, 199, 202, 203, 206, 212, 212, 218, 219, 220, 224, 233, 236, 239, 247, *247*, 250, 252, 255, *255*, 261, 264
South Africa 323, 336
South Korea 336
South, Sir Arthur 210
Southall, Neville 199, 203. 206, 207, 208, 214, 275
Southampton 16, *16*, 18, 161, 177, 189, 210, 289, 315, 322, 345
Southend 34, 306
Southgate, Gareth 287, 347
Southport 52
Spackman, Nigel 227
Spain 47, 50, 53, 54, 56, 62, 75, 76, 200, 201, 206, *284*, 287, 336, 352, 407, 410, 412, 413, *413*
Speed, Gary 253, 405, *405*
Speedie, David 204, 255
Speight, Kevin 317
Speirs, Jimmy 29, *29*
Spink, Nigel 191, *191*
Sporting Lisbon 125
Sprake, Gary 115, 130, 133, 138, *138*, 151
Springett, Ron 110, 117, *117*
Sproson, Phil 225
Spurdle, Bill 88
Spurs *see* Tottenham Hotspur
Srnicek, Pavel 281
Stabile, Guillermo 51, *51*
Stainrod, Simon 184
Stam, Jaap 322
Stamford Bridge *36*, 37, 67, *67*, 167, 333
Stamps, Jack 67
Standard Liege 265
Stanton, Pat 146
Stapleton, Frank 178, 181, 190, 197, 208, 240
Stapley, Harry 25
Stark, John 214, 214
Staunton, Steve 239, 265, *265*, 331
Steaua Bucharest 215, 234
Steel, Billy 73, *73*, 79
Steel, Tommy 69
Steele, Freddie 60, *60*, 65, 85
Stein, Brian 205, 227
Stein, Colin 139, 145
Stein, Jock 121, 129, 130, 132, 144, 211, *211*
Stenhousemuir 335
Stephens, Kirk 185
Stephenson, Clem 38, *38*, 40
Stepney, Alec 124, 127, 161, *161*
Steven, Trevor 206, 207
Stevenage Borough 298
Stevens, Gary (Brighton) 197, *197*
Stevens, Gary (Everton/Rangers) 206, 233, 254
Stevenson, Willie 115
Stewart, Alan 89
Stewart, Paul 228, 230, 246, 249
Stewart, Ray 185
Stielike, Ulrich 183
Stiles, Nobby 116, 118, 124, 128
Stock, Alec 72, 120, 158, 325
Stockport 37, 38, 167
Stoichkov, Hristo 267, 271, 285
Stoke City 35, 59, 61, 66, 68, 93, 111, 138, 142, 143, 172, 252, 316
Stokes, Alf 98
Stokes, Bobby 161, *161*
Stokoe, Bob 88, 148
stoppage time 302
Storey, Peter 138, *138*, 140, 144
Strachan, Gordon 190, *190*, 196, 205, 226, 253, *253*
Strange, Alf 65
Stranraer 274
Strunz, Thomas 287
Struth, Willie 83
Stubbins, Albert 69
Sturrock, Paul 180
Suarez, Luis (Spain) 109
Suarez, Luis (Uruguay) 406, 416. *416*
Substitutes, first 117
Sudell, Major William 15
Sugar, Alan 250, *250*, 261, 262, *270*, 273, 281, 322
Suggett, Colin 139
Suker, Davor 286
Summerbee, Mike 125
Summers, Johnny 95
Sunday matches 153
Sunday soccer 153
Sunderland 18, 19, 25, 31, 44, 45, 58, 60, 61, 66, 72, 74, 94, 111, 128, 133, 148, 194, 204, 208, 222, 249, 255, 308
Sunderland, Alan 173, 178
Sutcliffe, John 13
Suter, Fergus 14
Sutton, Chris 274, 275
Swan, Peter 112, 114, *114*
Swansea 41, 47, 347, 416, 417, *417*
Sweden 50, 57, 62, 63, 76, 336, 352, 353, 411, *412*, 419
Swift, Frank 55, *55*, 71, 73, 95, 101
Swinbourne, Roy 88, *88*
Swindin, George 107
Swindon Town 39, 129, *129*, 130, 186, 249
Switzerland 52, 62, 69, 285, 286, 352
Symon, Scot 125

Taffarel 269
Talbot, Brian 173, *181*
Tambling, Bobby 110, 118, 121, 419
Tapscott, Derek 94
Tardelli, Marco 183, 193
Tate, Paul 274
Taylor Report 238, 251
Taylor, Alan 158
Taylor, David 333
Taylor, Ernie 79
Taylor, Gordon 230, 252, 253
Taylor, Graham 246, 250, 251, 254, 262, 263, 278, 322
Taylor, Ian 280
Taylor, Jack 155
Taylor, Martin 266
Taylor, Peter 150, 172, 179, 183
Taylor, Tommy 91, 92, *92*, 93, 94, 95, 96
Temple, Derek 117, *117*
Tennents Cup 241
Terry, John 334, 405, 406, *406*, 411, *411*
Tevez, Carlos 368, 404
Thickett, Harry 13
Thijssen, Frans 186
Third Division 35
Third Division North 38
Third Lanark 20, 53
Thomas, Clive 174
Thomas, Danny 200
Thomas, Michael 234, *234*, 255
Thompson, Alan 274, 341, *341*
Thompson, Harold 180
Thompson, Ian 198
Thompson, Peter 116, 118
Thompson, Phil 169, 172, 173, *187*, 188, *189*
Thomson, Charlie 31
Thomson, J.J. 9
Thomson, John 53, *53*
Thomson, Scott 272
Thorn, Andy 239
Thornton, Willie 72
Thorstvedt, Erik 238, 246
Tichy, Lajos 97
Tigana, Jean 193, 328
Tilkowski, Hans 119
Tilson, Freddy 55, 65
Tinkler, Ray 139
Tinn, Jack 64
Titkos, Pal 63
Todd, Colin 144, 146, 158, 166
Tomaszewski, Jan 150, 155, 235
Torino 73, 256
Torocsik, Andres 174
Torquay 248
Torres, Fernando 413, 418
Toshack, John 125, 144, 152, 160
Tostao 136, *136*
Toth 86, 87
Tottenham Hotspur 17, *17*, 33, 36, 37, 38, *43*, 44, 55, 60, 78, 92, 93, 98, 102, 104, 105, 107, *107*, 111, 113, 121, 145, *145*, 146, 153, 157, 176, 186, 189, 200, 210, 222, 225, 249, 250, 261, 262, 262, 266, 270, 298, 307, 322, 331, 332, 333, 335, 345, 346, 348, 359, 376, 376, 408
Townley, William 12, *12*
Trainer, Jimmy 11
Tranmere 59
Transfer fees 21, 47; record spent 130, 230, 250, 322
Trapattoni, Giovanni 412
Trautmann, Bert 88, *88*, 90, *90*, 101
Treaty of Rome 322
Trebilcock, Mike 117
Tresor, Marius 193
"Triple Crown" 40, *40*, 60
Trollope, John 186
Troup, Alec 46
Tueart, Dennis 160, *166*
Tufnell, Harry 30, *30*
Tully, Charlie 83
Tunstall, Fred 41
Turek, Toni 87
Turkey 204, 224, 250, 263, 285, 331, 336, 337, 345, 346
Turnbull, Alec "Sandy" 29, 34
Turner, Bert 67
Turner, Charlie 68
Turner, Chris 194
Turner, Graham 205, 220
Turner, Hugh 49
Tyler, Mark 415

UEFA: English clubs ban 210, 218, 221, 231 Heysel Compensation 255 player nationality ruling 240 UEFA Cup 141, 145, *145*, 149, 153, 161, 163, 186, 200, 223, 261, 270, 282, 341, 342
Ujpest Dozsa 131
Ukraine 332. 410, 411, *411*, *412*
United Arab Emirates 170
United Kingdom 25, *25*
United States 300, 336, 337
United States 50, 51, 56, 62, 76, 113, 262
Uprichard, Norman 97
Upton Park 340
Ure, Ian 129
Uruguay 22, 49, 50, 51, *51*, 56, 62, 76, 77, 131, 210, 336
USSR 103
Utley, George 33

Valdano, Jorge 217
Valencia 182, 322, 324
Valenciennes 266
Valley Parade 207, *207*, 219
Van Basten, Marco 229, *229*, 234, 254
Van Breukelen, Hans 229
Van Den Hauwe, Pat 206, 208
Van der Elst, François 162, 183
Vandereycken, Rene 183
Van der Kerkhof, Rene 175
Van der Sar, Edwin 286
Van Persie, Robin 414
Van Wyk, Dennis 205
Varela, Obdulio 77
Vava 109
Veitch, Colin 28
Venables, Terry 215, 218, 224, 225, 230, 236, 246, 249, 250, *250*, 261, 262, *262*, 264, *264*, 273, 281, 282, *282*, 285, *295*, 322, 324, 338, 341, *341*
Veron, Juan Sebastian 330, 333
Vernon, Roy 110
Vialli, Gianluca 242, 283, 291, 299, 300, *300*, 322
"Victory" internationals 36
video evidence 325
Viduka, Mark 332
Vieira, Patrick 289, *302*, 315, 325, 334, 335, 342, 350, *350*
Vieri, Christian 310, 337
Vilfort, Kim 254
Villa, Ricardo 176, *176*, 186, 186
Viollet, Dennis 92, *92*, 94, 103
Vogts, Berti 287, 324, 333, 338
Völler, Rudi 217, 243
Vukas, Bernard 84

Waddell, Willie 83, 100
Waddle, Chris 216, 222, 225, 236, *236*, 243, 259, 261
Wages, maximum 18, 39, 104
Waiters, Tony 167
Wake, Harry 39
Walden, H. 28
Wale, Sidney 153, 157
Wales 9, 21, 23, 36, 39, 40, *40*, 48, 49, 54, 60, 75, 81, 169, 171, 183, 201, 206, 225, 248, 346, 405; *see also* Great Britain
Walford, Steve 178, *178*
Walker, Andy 237, 272
Walker, Billy 48, 65
Walker, Clive 204, 205
Walker, Des 249, *249*
Walker, Ian 291, *291*
Walker, Jack 255, 275, 282
Walker, Mike 274
Walker, Ray 225, *225*, 237
Walker, Sir Rodney 323
Walker, Tommy 60, *60*, 65, 79
Wall, George 24
Wallace brothers 235
Wallace, Charlie 31
Wallace, Danny 240, 244
Wallace, Ian 184
Wallace, Jock 120, 212
Wallace, Willie 132, 133
Walsall 54, 198, 200
Walsh, Charlie 58
Walsh, Gary 271
Walsh, Paul 194, 230
Walter, Fritz 63, 87, 90, 97
Walthamstow Avenue 83
Wanderers FC 8
Ward, Peter 172
Waring, Pongo *52*, 65
Wark, John 173, 186, *186*, 199
Warnes, Billy 54
Watford 30, 182, 194, 199, 200, 322
Watson, Ben 415
Watson, Dave 275
Watson, Steve 270
Watson, Vic 19, 39, 128
Watt, Michael 281
Wayman, Charlie 68
Weaver, Sam 51, 51
Webb, David 134, *134*, 164
Webb, Neil 224, 231, *231*, 235, *235*, 240, 251
Wedlock, Billy 23, 23
"Wee Blue Devil" *see* Morton, Alan
Wegerle, Roy 231, 262, *262*
Weir, Peter 196
Welsh FA 306
Welsh FA centenary 81
Welsh, Don 68
Wembley Stadium 39, *39*, 40, 41, 45, 46, 46, 49, 169, *169*, 324, 325, 371
"Wembley Wizards" *see* Scotland
Wenger, Arsène 277, 289, *289*, 299, 301, 307, 328–9, 334, 344, 348
West Bromwich Albion 10, *10*, 11, 12, 33, 36, 52, 58, 61, 83, 85, 120, 126, 130, 139, 167
West Germany 87, 119, 143, 155, 163, 174-5, 183, 198, 248
West Ham 39, 113, 115, 128, 142, 158, 162, *162*, 182, *182*, 184, 185, 218, 239, 266, 322, 332, 338
West, Colin 225
West, Enoch "Knocker" 29, 34, *35*
West, Gordon 117
Wetterstroem, Gustav 62
Whalley, Arthur 32
Whalley, Bert 95
Whelan, Dave 102, 414, *415*
Whelan, Liam "Billy" 92, *92*, 93, 95
Whelan, Ron 189, *189*, 190, 195, *195*, 199, 215, 221, 236, 237
Whitby 292
White Hart Lane 67
White, David 228
White, John 88, 89, 107, 111, 114, 121
Whiteside, Norman 195, 197, 198, 208, *208*, 224, 255
Whittaker, Tom *58*, 80
Whyte, Chris 198, 253
Wigan Athletic 58, 414, *415*
Wigan Borough 49
Wilkins, Ray (1980s/'90s) 197, 204, 216, 297
Wilkins, Ray 91
Wilkinson, Howard 253, 257, 292, 306, 324, 405
Williams, Bert 73, 74, 75, *76*, 76, 78
Williams, Evan 135, 177, 204, 221
Williams, Paul 266
Williamson, James 38
Willimowski, Ernst 62
Wills, Len 85
Wilshaw, Dennis 88, 89, *89*
Wilson, Andy 19
Wilson, Bob 129, 139, *139*, 140
Wilson, Danny 231
Wilson, Hugh 27, *27*
Wilson, Ray 118
Wilson, Terry 231
Wilson, Tom 98
Wiltord. Sylvain 335, *335*
Wimbledon 157, 169, 227
Wimmer, Herbert 143, 149
Winterbottom, Walter 69, 104, 110
Winterburn, Nigel 227, *227*, 234, 247
Wise, Dennis 227, 274, 300, 314
Wiseman, Keith 306
Withe, Peter 172, 185, 191, *191*, 204
Wolverhampton Wanderers 24, *24*, 30, 37, 60, 61, 64, 69, 73, 74, 88, 91, 93, 94, 102, 145, *145*, 151, 170, 220, *220*, 415
Women's international, first 148
Wood, Norman 32
Wood, Ray *92*, 93, *93*
Woodburn, Willie 101
Woodcock, Tony 172, 177, 200, *200*, 204, *204*
Woodroofe, Tom 61
Woods, Chris 172, 173, 226, 233, 250, 251, 259, 261
Woodward, Vivian 14, 25, *25*, 26, 37
Woolfall, Daniel Burley 22
Woolwich Arsenal *see* Arsenal
Workington 169
World Club Championship 102, 124, 128, 315
World Cup 49, 50-1, 56-7, 62-3, 74, 76-7, 86-7, 96-7, 108-9, 118-19, 136-7, 150, 154-5, 166, 174-5, *175*, 187, 192-3, 204, 206, 208, 216-17, 235, 238, 242-3, 268-9, 302-5, 323, 331, 332, 336–7; seating rule 240
World War I 34-5
World War II 66-7
Worrall, Freddie 64
Worthington Cup 307, 325, 333, 340
Wrexham 332
Wright, Billy 71, 73, 74, 75, 76, 81, 84, *84*, 85, 88, 91, 93, 96, 98, *98*, 99, 101, 102, 107, 117, 135, 270, *270*
Wright, Ian 204, 235, *235*, 239, 240, *240*, 261, *261*, *262*, *263*, *265*, 296, *296*, 313
Wright, Mark 250, 254
"Wunderteam" *see* Austria
Wylde, Rodger 185
Wycombe Wanderers 326
Wynne, Sam 44

Xavi 413

Yashin, Lev 109, 112, 114, *114*
Yeats, Ron 116, 188
Yeovil 72, *72*, 325
Yorath, Terry 144, 159
York City 89, 172
Yorke, Dwight 280, 280, 310
Young, Alec 123
Young, Alex 110
Young, Alf 61
Young Ashley *411*, 412
Young, George 74, 83
Young, Gerry 117
Young, Neil 125, 134, *134*
Young, Scott 332
Young, Willie 160, 182
Yugoslavia 50, 51, 225, 297

Zabaleta, Pablo 415
Zagalo, Mario 97, 108, 109
Zambia 259
Zamora, Ricardo 56
Zapata, Ramirez 192
Zeljeznicar 146
Zeze 63
Zico 192, 217
Zidane, Zinedine 303, 305, 305, 330, *330*, 335, 336, 341, 364, 367, 367
Ziege, Christian 287, 331, 346
Zito 109, 109
Zizinho 77
Zoco, Ignacio 126, 141
Zola, Gianfranco 265, 269, 276, 276, 287, 291, 300, 300, 334
Zozimo 91
Zsengeller, Gyula 63
Zubizarreta, Andoni 267, 287

The publishers would like to thank the following sources for their kind permission to reproduce the pictures in this book:

Action Images: 332t, /Alex Morton: 333, 339t; /Tony O'Brien: 331t, 334t; /John Sibley: 352, 353; /Lee Smith: 349b; /Darren Walsh: 331b, 335, 340b; Associated Press; **Associated Sports Photography; Norman Barrett; Colorsport; Getty Images:** 407, 415br; /Lars Baron: 412br; /Shaun Botterill: 328, 329bl, 337; /Clive Brunskill: 150, 318, 351b; /Simon Bruty; /David Cannon: 336; /Graham Chadwick: 320, 388; /Chris Cole; /Phil Cole: 384; /Adrian Dennis/AFP: 344t, 391, 392, 398t, 416c; /Hoang Dinh Nam/AFP: 395; /Paul Ellis/AFP: 404; /Stu Forster: 323br, 327, 332b; /Christopher Furlong: 355t; /Lluis Gene/AFP: 403; /Paul Gilham: 408bl; /Laurence Griffiths: 344b, 348b, 351t, 363, 387, 402, 405tl, 411br; /Scott Heavey: 417; /Julian Herbert: 315bl; /Mike Hewitt: 359, 415tl; /Clint Hughes: 405br; /Hulton Archive: 347t; /Jasper Juinen: 418l; /Ross Kinnaird: 316b; /Glyn Kirk/AFP: 376; /Christof Koepsel: 418b; /Christopher Lee: 368b; /Alex Livesey: 341t, 346t, 380, 386, 401r, 414; /Ian MacNicol: 419; /Pierre-Philippe Marcou/AFP: 397t; /Clive Mason: 349t, 350t, 389; /Jamie McDonald: 381; /Jeff J Mitchell: 409; /Filippo Monteforte/AFP: 411t; /Steve Morton; /Dean Mouhtaropoulos: 406t; /Pascal Pavani/AFP: 360; /John Peters/Manchester United: 361; /Matthew Peters/Manchester Utd: 350b; /Gary M. Prior: 334b; /Tom Purslow/Manchester United: 3, 400; /Ben Radford: 358; /Chris Ratcliffe/AFP: 382; /Michael Regan: 399, 410; /Clive Rose: 401tl, 408c; /Martin Rose: 412t; /Roberto Schmidt/AFP: 396, 397b; /Paballo Thekiso/AFP: 394; /Bob Thomas/Popperfoto: 393; /Mark Thompson; /Nigel Treblin/AFP: 390; /UEFA: 413; /VI Images: 6-7; /Darren Walsh/Chelsea FC: 385; /Ian Walton: 345; /Andrew Yates/AFP: 398b, 406b, 416br; **Herald and Evening Times; Liverpool Daily Post & Echo; Mirrorpix; Popperfoto/Monte Fresco; Press Association Images:** 314l, 315m, 371; /Matthew Ashton: 324br, 326, 330r; /Fabian Bimmer/AP: 364; /Barry Bland: 325; /Jon Buckle: 329tr, 325; /Adam Butler; /Peter Byrne: 373; /Lynne Cameron/Rangers FC: 378; /Danie Coetzer: 323tl; /David Davies: 338; /Mike Egerton: 324bl, 339b, 340t, 346b, 347b, 366, 383; /Empics Sport: 330l; /Nigel French: 348t; /John Giles; /Maggie Haroun: 314r; /Owen Humphreys: 368t; /Ross Kinnaird; /Tony Marshall: 365; /Paul Marriott: 322tr; /Andrew Medichini/AP: 367; /Steve Mitchell: 317; /Steve Morton: 322bl; /Rebecca Naden: 370; /Lefteris Pitarakis/AP: 357; /Nick Potts: 319bl, 321; 362, 375; /Martin Rickett: 372, 374, 379; /Peter Robinson; /Murad Sezer/AP: 356; /Neal Simpson: 316tl, 341b, 342t; /Sang Tan/AP: 355b, 371t; /Rui Vieira: 354t; /Darren Walsh/Chelsea FC: 354b, 369; /John Walton: 342b, 343; /Lewis Whyld: 377; **Reuters; Sporting Pictures; SNS Group:** /Alan Harvey: 319tr; **Topfoto.co.uk**

Every effort has been made to acknowledge correctly and contact the source and/copyright holder of each picture, and Carlton Books Limited apologises for any unintentional errors or omissions which will be corrected in future editions of this book.